T3-BNJ-293

THE YEAR'S WORK IN MODERN LANGUAGE STUDIES

THE YEAR'S WORK IN MODERN LANGUAGE STUDIES

GENERAL EDITOR
STEPHEN PARKINSON

ASSISTANT EDITOR
LISA BARBER

SECTION EDITORS

LATIN, FRENCH, OCCITAN
LISA BARBER, M.A., D.PHIL

ITALIAN, ROMANIAN, RHETO-ROMANCE
JOHN M. A. LINDON, M.A.
Professor of Italian Studies, University College London

ROMANCE LINGUISTICS, SPANISH, CATALAN, PORTUGUESE, GALICIAN, LATIN AMERICAN, SLAVONIC
STEPHEN PARKINSON, M.A., PH.D.
Lecturer in Portuguese Language and Linguistics, University of Oxford

CELTIC
DAVID A. THORNE, M.A., PH.D.
Professor of Welsh, University of Wales, Lampeter

GERMANIC
DAVID A. WELLS, M.A., PH.D.
Professor of German, Birkbeck College, University of London

VOLUME 65
2003

MANEY PUBLISHING
for the
MODERN HUMANITIES RESEARCH ASSOCIATION
2005

The Year's Work in Modern Language Studies may be ordered from the Subscriptions Department, Maney Publishing, Hudson Road, Leeds LS9 7DL, UK.

ISBN 1 904350 48 8

ISSN 0084-4152

Produced in Great Britain by
MANEY PUBLISHING
HUDSON ROAD LEEDS LS9 7DL UK

CONTENTS

ABBREVIATIONS

PREFACE

This volume surveys work, published in 2003, unless otherwise stated, in the fields of Romance, Celtic, Germanic, and Slavonic languages and literatures. An asterisk before the title of a book or article indicates that the item in question has not been seen by the contributor.

The attention of users is drawn to the lists of abbreviations at the end of the volume, which are also available on-line via the MHRA's WWW site (http://www.mhra.org.uk/Publications/Journals/ywmls.html).

The Editors have heard with great sorrow of the deaths of Brian Levy, editor of the Latin, Romance Linguistics, French and Occitan Studies sections from 1992 to 1998, and contributor of the Early Medieval French Literature from 1981 until 1988, and of Øysten Rottem, contributor on Norwegian Literature from 1988 to 2002.

This volume also marks the last contributions of two long-serving editors and contributors: David Wells, former General Editor and contributor of articles on Medieval German Literature for over 30 years, will now relinquish the editorship of the Germanic Languages section, and David Thorne will give up the editorship of the Celtic Studies section, having already passed on the responsibility for Welsh Language Studies. We owe both a great debt of gratitude, and wish their successors well.

Many authors, editors and publishers supply review copies and offprints of their publications. To these we and our contributors are grateful, and we would invite others to follow their example, especially in the case of work issuing from unusual, unexpected, or inaccessible sources of publication. We would ask that, whenever possible, items for review be sent directly to the appropriate contributor; where no obvious recipient can be identified, as in the case of books or journal issues relating to a number of fields, the item should be sent to one of the editors, who will distribute the contents accordingly.

The compilation of a contribution to the volume, especially in the field of the major languages and periods of literature, is a substantial research task requiring wide-ranging and specialized knowledge of the subject besides a huge reading effort accompanied by the constant exercise of critical judgement. We are deeply grateful to the authors who have devoted significant amounts of increasingly precious research time to this enterprise. The measure of their task is indicated by the number of sections for which the editors have failed to find contributors; we encourage approaches from potential contributors or groups of contributors for future volumes.

The completion of this volume would not have been possible without the ever-increasing contribution of Lisa Barber, Assistant Editor and compiler of the Index. Thanks are also due to the other institutions and individuals who have contributed in one way or another to the making of the volume, in particular Paolo Rambelli, Outi Jokiharju, David Gillespie, the secretarial and administrative staff of the Faculty of Modern Languages of Oxford University, and our printers, Maney Publishing, particularly Liz Rosindale and Anna Thrush, who have helped guide this complex operation to its annual conclusion.

January 2005 S.R.P., L.B., J.M.A.L., D.A.T., D.A.W.

1

LATIN

I. MEDIEVAL LATIN

By Christopher J. McDonough, *Professor of Classics, University of Toronto*

1. General

R. J. Hexter, 'Ovid in the Middle Ages: exile, mythographer, lover', pp. 413–42 of *Brill's Companion to Ovid*, ed. Barbara W. Boyd, Leiden, Brill, 2002, xiii + 533 pp., organizes the medieval responses around three aspects of Ovid's poetic persona that had the greatest appeal to the experiences of Latin writers, including Modoin, Walahfrid Strabo, Baudri of Bourgueil, as well as the authors of the *Ecloga Theoduli* and the *Carmina Burana*. J. Dimmick, 'Ovid in the Middle Ages: authority and poetry', pp. 264–87 of *The Cambridge Companion to Ovid*, ed. Philip Hardie, CUP, 2002, xvi + 408 pp., explores the responses of William of St Thierry, Andreas Capellanus, the *De vetula*, the anonymous *Antiovidianus*, John Gower's *Vox clamantis*, and Chaucer, as he reconstructs the personal and institutional agendas produced by their readings of Ovid's works. F. T. Coulson, 'Addenda and corrigenda to *Incipitarium Ovidianum*', *JMLat*, 12, 2002: 154–80, catalogues new MSS and the incipits of newly discovered texts. E. Haberkern, 'Die lateinischen Handschriften des Augustiner-Chorherrenstifts Indersdorf. Ein Gang durch eine mittelalterliche Klosterbibliothek', *MJ*, 38: 51–88, traces the history of the Bavarian monastery from the 13th c., lists benefactors and their gifts, and reconstructs the intellectual currents based on a collection which covers theology, medicine, law, and the liberal arts.

É. Delbey, 'La poétique de la *copia* chez Venance Fortunat: le livre IV des épitaphes dans les *carmina*', *REL*, 80, 2002: 206–22, studies the epitaphs of the laity, bishops, and ecclesiastics to show how Venantius transformed the pathos of classical elegy to serve an aesthetic that glorified God. J.-F. Cottier, 'La paraphrase latine, de Quintilien à Érasme', *ib.*, 237–52, constructs a taxonomy of paraphrase based on the conceptual distinction between imitative and explanatory reformulation. B. Bakhouche, 'L'allégorie des arts libéraux dans les *Noces de Philologie et Mercure* de Martianus Capella (II)', *Latomus*, 62: 387–96, notes deviations from Capella's text in descriptions of the personified Arts in the *Carmen de septem artibus liberalibus* of Theodulf of Orleans. M. Ferré, 'La genèse du second livre des

Institutiones de Cassiodore', *ib.*, 61, 2002: 152–62, reconstructs the origin of the work based on irregularities in the arrangement of chapters. J. V. Fleming, 'Muses of the monastery', *Speculum*, 78: 1071–106, explains how the transmission of the Latin language through the study of poetry contributed to a culture in which medieval monks became the patrons as well as the producers of imaginative literature. J. Leclercq-Marx, 'Du monstre androcéphale au monstre humanisé. À propos des sirènes et des centaures, et de leur famille, dans le haut Moyen Âge et à l'époque romane', *CCMe*, 45, 2002: 55–67, views the progressive humanization of mermaids and sirens in hagiography, didactic works, epics, and sculpture, as the result of merging an oral culture, full of 'nordic' elements, with a Mediterranean written culture. F. Dolbeau, 'Un domaine négligé de la littérature médiolatine: les textes hagiographiques en vers', *ib.*, 129–39, identifies the classroom practice of poetic paraphrase as an important factor in spreading metrical and rhythmical texts of hagiography, before he argues that versified lives, cast in an epic register, were limited to the private domain of meditation and individual devotion. M. J. Curley, 'Five *Lecciones* for the feast of St Nonita: a text and its context', *CMCS*, 43, 2002: 59–75, edits the sole extant liturgical text for the mother of St David and examines the reasons for its survival among the papers of William Worcester (1415–1485). M. Cavagna, 'La *Navigatio sancti Brendani* et ses liens avec la tradition visionnaire', *MedRom*, 26, 2002: 30–48, finds common elements between descriptions of the infernal isles and earthly paradise and the eschatological tradition, especially the division of Hell into upper and lower parts. P. Stotz, 'Pegasus mit Fuss-Fesseln. Von der Behinderung des Dichterns durch das Versmass am Beispiel der Eigennamen in der lateinischen Dichtung des Mittelalters', *MJ*, 37, 2002: 1–32, examines poetological statements by a wide range of writers from Prudentius to Walter of Wimborne regarding the metrical difficulties caused by proper names for writers of Latin quantitative poetry. J. Szövérffy, 'Beiträge zur Typengeschichte der lateinischen Hymnen. Grundlage einer umfassenden Hymnengeschichte', *ib.*, 38: 39–49, identifies structural peculiarities in the liturgical hymns and sequences of Ambrose, Sedulius, Caesarius of Arles, and Abelard. J. Ziolkowski, 'Old wives' tales: classicism and anti-classicism from Apuleius to Chaucer', *JMLat*, 12, 2002: 90–113, examines the negative stereotypes conveyed in the images of old women and discusses why Christian writings continued to view their speech and behaviour as contemptible and a source of fear. J. Reid, 'The Lorica of Laidcenn: the biblical connections', *ib.*, 141–53, analyses the biblical components of a phrase that recurs in several variations in many lorical texts, Latin and vernacular. S. Tuzzo, 'La

Vita sancti Gregorii Papae contenuta nel cod. Montepessulanus *H. 48*', *BSL*, 32, 2002: 128–37, establishes that the codex is an anomaly in the MS tradition of Paul the Deacon's biography, because of numerous interpolations inserted from John the Deacon's hagiography of St Gregory. D. Frye, 'From *locus publicus* to *locus sanctus*: justice and sacred space in Merovingian Gaul', *NMS*, 47: 1–20, includes the hagiographical tales of Gregory of Tours as one of many agents that changed the definition of sacred and public space. G. Folliet, 'La fortune du dit de Virgile "Aurum colligere de stercore" dans la littérature chrétienne', *Sac*, 41, 2002: 31–53, documents the reception of this adage in 36 authors extending from Alcuin and Sedulius Scottus to Thomas Chobham and beyond, noting that it was especially deployed to justify the appropriation of pagan material by Christian writers. U. Kindermann, 'König Chilperich als lateinischer Dichter', *ib.*, 247–72, re-edits and re-arranges a corrupt praise poem into the form of rhythmic trochaic septenarii, before he discusses its fusion of pagan and Christian concepts. K. D. Fischer, 'Neues zur Überlieferung der lateinischen *Aphorismen* im Frühmittelalter', *Latomus*, 62: 156–64, analyses previously unrecognized excerpts from a translation of the Hippocratic work preserved in Paris, BnF, lat. 11218. L. Castaldi, 'Per un'edizione critica dei *Dialogi* di Gregorio Magno: ricognizioni preliminari', *FilM*, 10: 1–39, exhaustively reviews previous editions and the manuscripts on which they depend in order to underline the need for a critical text. R. Guglielmetti, '"Super Cantica canticorum." Nota sulla tradizione dei commenti di Ruperto di Deutz, Bernardo di Clairvaux, Guglielmo di Saint-Thierry, Beda e Alcuino', *SM*, 43, 2002: 277–86, reports findings concerning MSS that preserve the commentary, some containing only anonymous fragments. C. Torre, 'Da Seneca a Martino di Braga (*De Ira* I 1, 4)', *Maia*, 54, 2002: 81–85, studies Martin's appropriation of Seneca's treatise and discovers evidence to support the case for retaining a manuscript reading in Martin's work.

2. Anglo-Saxon England

L. Lazzari, 'I *colloquia* nelle scuole monastiche anglosassoni tra la fine del X e la prima metà del' XI secolo', *SM*, 44: 147–77, investigates the colloquies of Aelfric and Aelfric Bata to assess levels of Latin competence and for their documentary value as sources of information regarding daily activities in the schools. D. W. Chapman, 'Germanic tradition and Latin learning in Wulfstan's echoic compounds', *JEGP*, 101, 2002: 1–18, identifies the grammatical notion of compounding and rhetorical tropes and figures as possible influences on the vernacular device of echoic compound pairs.

D. Bitterli, 'Exeter Book riddle 15: some points for the porcupine', *Anglia*, 120, 2002: 461–87, adduces the Latin tradition of zoological writings to support the century-old argument that favours the porcupine as the solution to the longest OE riddle in the collection. M. R. Godden, 'King Alfred's preface and the teaching of Latin in Anglo-Saxon England', *EHR*, 117, 2002: 596–604, argues that the possible meanings and the vague phrasing of the words 'hieran hade' weigh against the likelihood that it refers to a programme designed to ensure a Latinate clergy. R. Sharpe, 'The naming of Bishop Ithamar', *ib.*, 889–94, underlines the appropriateness of Ithamar's unusual name, which derived from an Old Testament figure associated with the temple priesthood. A. Sheppard, 'The King's family: securing the kingdom in Asser's *Vita Alfredi*', *PQ*, 80, 2001[2002]: 409–39, discusses the implications of Asser's transition from chronicle to biography, as he makes Alfred's performance of lordship and the *familia* central to his *Life*. T. D. Hill, 'A riddle on the Three Orders in the *Collectanea Pseudo-Bede*', *ib.*, 205–12, offers a solution that takes *bipes* as a reference to the king and *tripodem* as the throne, which is supported by the three orders that comprise the Christian nation. R. L. McDaniel, 'An unidentified passage from Jerome in Bede', *NQ*, 248: 375, notes that a passage in Bede, *In Epistolas VII Catholicas*, is a quotation from Jerome, *Adversus Jovinianum* 1.7. A. J. Kleist, 'The division of the ten commandments in Anglo-Saxon England', *NMi*, 103, 2002: 227–37, attributes the uniform treatment of the Decalogue in five texts, including Wulfstan's *De cristianitate*, to the influential exegesis of Aelfric of Eynsham. A. Bisanti, 'Un carme mediolatino sulla battaglia di Brunanburh', *MJ*, 37, 2002: 195–207, contends that the poem has important documentary value, and associates it with panegyrics that were written to celebrate battles and victories between the 8th and 10th cs. M. R. Godden, 'The Anglo-Saxons and the Goths: rewriting the sack of Rome', *Anglo-Saxon England*, 31, 2002: 47–68, suggests that Bede's association of the end of Roman Britain with the sack of Rome in 410 may be his version of the *translatio imperii* theme, which is one of many readings regarding the significance of Rome's fall for British history.

3. The Carolingian and Ottonian Period

J. Black, 'Psalm uses in Carolingian prayerbooks: Alcuin and the preface to *De psalmorum usu*', *MedS*, 64, 2002: 1–60, evaluates Alcuin's contribution to private devotion and the evolution of the prayerbook tradition to the mid-9th c., before he presents a critical edition of the preface. S. Passi, 'Il commentario inedito ai Vangeli attribuito a "Wigbodus"', *SM*, 43, 2002: 59–156, argues on the basis of contents and sources that the *Quaestiones in Evangelia*, anonymously transmitted in four MSS, belong to Wigbod. L. Bernays, 'Versstrukturen in Walahfrid Strabos Gedicht "De carnis petulantia"', *MJ*, 37, 2002: 189–94, explains that the varied verse structure not only prevents monotony, but also provides a key for articulating the poem into two asymmetrical parts. F. Brunhölzl, '*O cara anima.* Ein frühkarolingischer Rhythmus', *ib.*, 38: 19–28, discovers an acrostich that intertwines the names of the addressee, Irmingard, with that of the poet, a certain Ingilpreht. B. Solinski, 'Le *De uita et fine sancti Mammae monachi* de Walahfrid Strabon: texte, traduction et notes', *JMLat*, 12, 2002: 1–77, reconstructs the origins of this neglected hagiography at Langres between 838 and 841, before he offers the first translation, based on the edition of E. Dümmler. P. Meyvaert, 'Medieval notions of publication: the "unpublished" *Opus Caroli regis contra synodum* and the Council of Frankfurt (794)', *ib.*, 78–89, adduces evidence from the physical condition of Vatican City, Biblioteca Vaticana Apostolica, lat. 7207, the original working MS, to prove that Charlemagne never gave permission for the treatise to be copied and released to the public. T. Gärtner, 'Zum spätantiken und mittelalterlichen Nachwirken der Dichtungen des Alcimus Avitus', *FilM*, 9, 2002: 109–221, documents the reception of Avitus's poetry by 55 writers, including Arator, Aethicus Ister, Alcuin, Petrus Riga, and Walter of Châtillon. D. Bachrach, 'Confession in the *Regnum Francorum* (742–900): the sources revisited', *JEH*, 54: 3–22, discusses an episode from the *Waltharius* that sets Walther's realistic religious behaviour against the background of historical confessions made by soldiers to priests. S. Coupland, 'The Vikings on the Continent in myth and history', *History*, 88: 186–203, uses several accounts of the sack of Nantes in 843 to illustrate their progressive elaboration of an image of the Vikings as typically cruel, cunning, and superhuman in size. L. L. Coon, 'Historical fact and exegetical fiction in the Carolingian *Vita S. Sualonis*', *Church History*, 72: 1–24, investigates Ermenrich of Ellwangen's biography to explore contemporary views on historical writing, the invention of a monastic foundation narrative for Fulda, and the role of exegesis in writing hagiography. K. M. Delen et al., 'The *Paenitentiale Cantabrigiense.* A witness of the Carolingian contribution to the tenth-century reforms in England', *Sac*, 41, 2002: 341–73, offer a new edition based on Cambridge, Corpus Christi College 320, before they locate its origin in 10th-c. England, possibly in Canterbury, and document its debt to Bede, Egbert, and Halitgar of Cambrai. J. Whitta, '*Ille ego Naso*: Moduin of Autun's Eclogues and the *renouatio* of Ovid', *Latomus*, 61, 2002: 703–31, suggests that Moduin's assumption of Ovid's persona and the appropriation of Ovidian language served to reinstate Ovid from readerly and literary exile. M. Cupiccia, 'Anastasio Bibliotecario traduttore delle omelie di Reichenau (Aug. LXXX)?', *FilM*, 10:41–102, answers the question affirmatively, based on the convergence of several characteristics in the translation with Anastasian usage. P. C. Jacobsen, 'Gesta Berengarii und Waltharius-Epos', *DAEM*, 58, 2002:205–11, posits a direct relationship between *Gesta* 1.202–04 and *Waltharius* 1401–04, with priority given to the latter. M. Giovini, '"*Ut Flaccus dicit.*" L'*Antapodosis* di Liutprando e Orazio: forme dell' intertestualità', *Maia*, 54, 2002:87–111, documents the reception of Horace's *Odes* in Liudprand's writings; Id. 'Eufonia asinina: il carme *De asino ad episcopum ducto*', *ib.*, 373–85, detects in this irreverent poem a forerunner of the satiric tone that evolved in animal fables; Id., 'Come trasformare un bordello in una casa di preghiere. Il motivo della verginità redentrice nell'*Agnes* di Rosvita di Gandersheim', *ib.*, 589–617, examines a central episode in which a chaste prisoner transforms a brothel, and notes the lyrical way in which Hrotsvitha appropriates her source, a 6th-c. pseudo-Ambrosian *epistula*, while S. Fonte, 'Il funzionamento verbale di *despero*: un caso di analogia nella sintassi di Rosvita di Gandersheim', *FilM*, 10:103–09, documents Hrotsvitha's tendency to expand the use of the classical accusative and infinitive construction in her dramatic and hagiographical writings. A. Breeze, 'A Welsh crux in an Aethelwoldian poem', *NQ*, 248:262–63, emends a pun on the word *iornum* in the *Altercatio magistri et discipuli* to *diornum*, meaning 'blameless'. D. Chapman, '*Anima quae pars*: a tenth-century parsing grammar', *JMLat*, 12, 2002:181–204, analyses the text's structure and sources, which include Murethach's grammar, before he offers an edition based on Worcester, Cathedral Library, MS Q.5, an English MS probably produced at Christchurch, Canterbury. D. Heller-Roazen, 'Des altérités de la langue. Plurilinguismes poétiques au Moyen Âge', *Littérature*, 130:75–96, includes in his analysis of the dialectics of bilingualism the so-called *aube* of Fleury, which begins: *Phebi claro nondum orto iubare.* P. Cavill, 'Analogy and genre in the legend of St Edmund', *NMS*, 47:21–45, studies the transformation of Edmund's death into a martyrdom story in Abbo of Fleury's *Passio sancti Eadmundi* and Aelfric's shortened version of it in the *Lives of the Saints.* P. W. Tax, 'Die lateinischen Schriften Notkers des Deutschen. Altes und Neues', *BGDSL*, 124, 2002:411–41, sets out positive and concrete arguments that establish Notker as the author of three works transmitted in Zurich, Zentralbibliothek, C 98. C. Jeudy, 'Remi d'Auxerre et le livre II de l'*Ars maior* de Donat', *Holtz Vol.*, 131–41, tracks the evolution of Remigius's teaching by examining the two versions of his commentary.

4. The Eleventh Century

A. Somfai, 'The eleventh-century shift in the reception of Plato's *Timaeus* and Calcidius's *Commentary*', *JWCI*, 65, 2002: 1–21, analyses glosses, diagrams, and MS production to document the transition of interest from the Commentary to the *Timaeus* itself, a move that generated new interpretations and a wider readership. T. J. H. McCarthy, 'Literary practice in eleventh-century music theory: the *colores rhetorici* and Aribo's *De musica*', *MAe*, 71, 2002: 191–208, places Aribo's treatise in the context of a renewed interest in rhetoric and notes the imprint of the *ars dictandi* upon it. S. Lazard, 'La structuration du lexique dans le *Vocabularium* de Papias', *RLiR*, 66, 2002: 221–43, examines the letter B and identifies three approaches that were used to establish relationships between words: the etymological, derivational, and the polysemous. T. Gärtner, 'Zu den dichterischen Quellen und zum Text der allegorischen Bibeldichtung des Eupolemius', *DAEM*, 58, 2002: 549–62, surveys the editions and translations of the poem, before he suggests emendations based on the poet's use of classical intertexts. H. Hoffmann, 'Irische Schreiber in Deutschland im 11. Jahrhundert', *ib.*, 59: 97–120, tabulates a list of MSS that illuminate the scribal activities of Irish scholars, including Marianus (Muiredâc) in Regensburg and in Würzburg, before printing excerpts from Ovid's *Heroides* 6 and 7, which have been ignored by modern editors. R. Veit, 'Quellenkundliches zu Leben und Werk von Constantinus Africanus', *ib.*, 121–52, reassesses the three sources for Constantine's life as a prologue to establishing the canon of his translations and their Arabic sources. C. Munier, 'Pour l'origine trévire de l'"Ecbasis cuiusdam captivi"', *MJ*, 37, 2002: 209–26, reviews the internal and external evidence that points to a monastic school in Trier, either Saint-Maximin or Saint-Euchaire, as the point of origin for the poem around 1100. M. Schilling, 'Narrative Struktur und Sinnkonstituierung in der "Ecbasis captivi"', *ib.*, 227–45, examines the poem for insight into the history of the origin of medieval fictional narrative before Chrétien de Troyes emerged, and argues that its structural devices have their roots in ancient literature. H.-H. Kortüm, 'Der Pilgerzug von 1064/65 ins Heilige Land. Eine Studie über Orientalismuskonstruktionen im 11. Jahrhundert', *HZ*, 277: 561–92, studies the historical sources that represent Arabs, who allegedly attacked a group of German pilgrims, as cruel and cannibalistic, and finds therein an early attempt to construct an exotic world that contrasted strongly with the Christian ideal. M. Frassetto, 'Heretics and Jews in the writings of Ademar of Chabannes and the origins of medieval anti-Semitism', *Church History*, 71, 2002: 1–15, points to the influence of apocalyptic anxiety for Ademar's belief that

Jews were allied with Muslims and Saracens as enemies of the faith. J. A. Bowman, 'The bishop builds a bridge: sanctity and power in the medieval Pyrenees', *CHR*, 88, 2002: 1–16, reconstructs from diplomatic and hagiographical records a portrait of Bishop Ermengol of Urgell, who reputedly died while trying to build a bridge for his community. P. Chiesa, 'Le *Vitae* romane di Giovanni Calabita', *AB*, 121: 45–102, presents critical editions of two lives, the second of which, probably from the circle of Bruno of Segni and Peter of Porto, freely reworks the 9th-c. *Vita* of Anastasius Bibliothecarius. E. Nemerkényi, 'Latin classics in medieval libraries: Hungary in the eleventh century', *Acta antiqua Academiae Hungaricae*, 43: 243–56, examines various sources, including a letter by Fulbert of Chartres to bishop Bonipert of Pécs and the inventory of the abbey of Pannonhalma, to reconstruct the classical holdings of several libraries. O. Diard, 'Histoire et chant liturgique en Normandie au XIe siècle: les offices propres particuliers des diocèses d'Évreux et de Rouen', *AnN*, 53: 195–223, discusses the original synthesis that was achieved in the literary, hagiographical, and musical production of two houses, the result of the rivalry between William of Volpiano and Isembert, monk of Saint-Ouen.

5. The Twelfth Century

J. Martínez Gázquez, 'Trois traductions médiévales latines du Coran: Pierre le Vénérable–Robert de Ketton, Marc de Tolède et Jean de Segobia', *REL*, 80, 2002: 223–36, reconstructs the historical circumstances that produced cooperative translations, each one a reaction and valuable witness to contact with Muslims in Spain over three centuries. L. Georgianna, 'Periodization and politics: the case of the missing twelfth century in English literary history', *MLQ*, 64: 153–68, illustrates the silence surrounding 'English' writing after 1066 by analysing William of Malmesbury's *Gesta regum Anglorum* as an example of England's signal contribution to historiography, a work that revised Bede's Anglo-Saxon myth in order to accommodate the new arrivals in England. C. Sanok, 'Almoravides at Thebes: Islam and European identity in the *Roman de Thèbes*', *ib.*, 277–98, notes the significance of the romance's transformation of its classical model, Statius's *Thebaid*, which introduced contemporary Muslim communities as allies of both the Theban and Argive armies, thereby offering a definition of cultural identity based on interaction rather than inheritance. C. S. Jaeger, 'Pessimism in the twelfth-century "Renaissance"', *Speculum*, 78: 1151–83, examines the terms, concepts, and metaphors used in the self-conception of the age as expressed in historiography, the schools, poetry, and the culture of love, and discovers a consistent view that was marked by thoughts of decline and nostalgia. E. M. Treharne, 'The form and function of the twelfth-century Old English *Dicts of Cato*', *JEGP*, 102:465–85, examines the contexts in which three independent OE versions of the *Disticha Catonis* appear and argues from the codicological evidence that they were intended for devotional reading by individual monks or by a religious instructor. E. Baumgartner, 'Les Danois dans l'*Histoire des ducs de Normandie* de Benoît de Sainte-Maure', *MA*, 108, 2002:481–95, documents how and why Benoît came to posit a much more direct link between Trojans, Danes, and Normans than had Dudo of St Quentin and William of Jumièges, his principal sources. B. Librová, 'Le renard dans le *cubiculum taxi*: les avatars d'un *exemplum* et le symbolisme du blaireau', *MA*, 109:79–111, analyses the ambiguous symbolic status of the badger as a literary figure, and finds that the Latin and French tradition of the fox's usurpation of the badger's lair appears to be a medieval invention. A. Bisanti, 'Il *Novus Avianus* di Alessandro Neckam nel quadro delle riscritture mediolatine di Aviano', *Maia*, 54, 2002:295–350, surveys the various adaptations into prose and verse that the fables of Avianus underwent in the service of the medieval curriculum. C. J. McDonough, 'Horace, Hugh Primas and whores', *Maia*, 55:549–54, documents the role of Horace, *Sat.* 1.2 in the genesis of a medieval satire. F. J. Griffiths, 'Brides and *dominae*: Abelard's *Cura monialium* at the Augustinian monastery of Marbach', *Viator*, 34:57–88, discusses the creation of Strasbourg, Bibliothèque du Grand Séminaire, MS 37, an important document on the pastoral care of religious, and analyses parallels between the text *Beati pauperes* and the monastic philosophy of Abelard, as expressed in sermon 30 and Letters 7 and 8 of his correspondence with Heloise. B. Vinken, 'Die Autorität der Form in Abaelard und Heloise', *DVLG*, 76, 2002:181–94, reads the correspondence as a story of *conversio*, the metamorphosis of a carnal love into a new definition of spiritual relationship, in which the changed nature of their love achieves fulfilment in the form of their lives. P. von Moos, 'Die *Epistolae duorum amantium* und die säkulare Religion der Liebe. Methodenkritische Vorüberlegungen zu einem einmaligen Werk mittellateinischer Briefliteratur', *SM*, 44:1–115, rejects the attribution of the letters to Abelard and Heloise as highly improbable and argues that they originated in France or Italy as highly revised stylistic exercises, not model letters, the product of a school of the late *ars dictaminis*, or they represent a brilliant achievement of early humanistic epistolary art. R. Jakobi, 'Leithandschrift oder Stemma? Ein Musterfall', *ib.*, 361–65, adduces evidence that the 1977 edition of the Vergil commentary fathered on Bernard Silvestris and edited by J. W. and E. F. Jones is not the original text, but represents a secondary redaction. S. I. Sobecki, 'From the *Désert liquide* to the sea of romance: Benedeit's *Le Voyage de Saint Brendan* and the Irish *Immrama*', *Neophilologus*, 87:193–207, challenges the relationship between the Anglo-Norman poem and the *Navigatio sancti Brendani*, arguing that it lies much closer to the Irish *immrama*. S. Daub, 'Vergil und die Bibel als verschränkte Prätexte — ein poetisches Experiment', *Rheinisches Museum für Philologie*, 146:85–102, identifies classical and late antique intertexts that Laurence of Durham, *Hypognosticon* 8.1–36, incorporated into his life of Christ. E. J. Mickel, 'Mercury's Philologia and Erec's Enide', *RPh*, 56, 2002:1–22, argues that the description of Enide's dress and her intellectual qualities are modelled on the portrait of Philology by Martianus Capella. T. M. Buck, 'Von der Kreuzzugsgeschichte zum Reisebuch. Zur *Historia Hierosolymitana* des Robertus Monachus', *DVLG*, 76, 2002:321–55, identifies Robert's novelistic conception of history, manifest in his account of the First Crusade, as an important element in its popularity, which resulted in its inclusion in a 16th-c. book of travellers' tales. A. Classen, 'Epistemology at the courts: the discussion of love by Andreas Capellanus and Juan Ruiz', *NMi*, 103, 2002:341–62, views both works as communicative enterprises that make instrumental use of courtly love and language to analyse the multiple functions of discourse and to investigate human existence, while B. Löfstedt, 'Andreas Capellanus aus sprachlicher Sicht', *Latomus*, 61, 2002:438–42, tabulates several of the work's linguistic oddities. K. Krönert, 'Rezeption klassischer Dichtung in der Weltchronik Ottos von Freising', *MJ*, 37, 2002:33–73, reviews Otto's presuppositions and historiographical principles, before he demonstrates that Otto knew Vergil and Lucan directly and modelled his history on their epics. E. Mégier, 'Fabulae ou histoire? Mythologie grecque et exégèse typologique dans la chronique d'Otton de Freising', *Mediaevistik*, 15, 2002:15–30, discusses the extent to which the spiritual interpretation of Greek mythology in Otto's chronicle can be read as evidence of an openness to mythology in understanding the Bible. R. Jakobi, 'Indien in der Solin-Paraphrase des Theodericus', *MJ*, 37, 2002:247–55, demonstrates that the didactic poem 'De monstris Indie' represents an excerpt from Theodericus's versification of Solinus's *Collectanea*, before he edits the work based on two MSS. W. Blümer, 'Arnulf von Lisieux und der lateinische Prosarhythmus im Hochmittelalter', *ib.*, 257–75, analyses three passages in order to demonstrate the importance of quantity in the rhyming technique of Arnulf's prose. D. A. Traill, 'Carmen Buranum 59: a plea for chastity — or free love?', *ib.*, 38:189–98, uncovers a subtext that undercuts the serious surface message and concludes that its parody of Gratian's legal language places the poem after 1150.

C. Weinberg, 'The giant of Mont Saint-Michel: an Arthurian villain', *BJR*, 84, 2002:9–23, suggests that the episode of Arthur the giant-killer in Geoffrey of Monmouth's *Historia regum Britanniae* prefigures his victory over the Romans and serves to symbolize the greatness of kingship. M. Sinex, 'Echoic irony in Walter Map's satire against the Cistercians', *CL*, 54, 2002:275–90, discusses the intratextual clues that Map used to direct the reader's response towards an ironic interpretation of echoic utterances, in which the speaker dissociates himself from the opinions he is replicating. G. Scannerini, O.S.B., 'Mistica o misticismo? Un approccio patristico ad Aelredo di Rievaulx, *De oneribus* S. 2 (3)', *AC*, 54, 2002:134–85, examines the doctrinal, Augustinian, frame in which Aelred sets his sermon's account of visions experienced in a female monastery, before he provides a text and translation of the sermon. P. Gatti, 'Note su alcune citazioni presenti nelle *Derivationes* di Osberno', *Maia*, 54, 2002:619–22, identifies among Osbern's sources misattributed quotations from Lucan, Prudentius, Priscian, Macrobius, and Marbod of Rennes. T. Gärtner, 'Der Übertritt der Seele beim Kuss. Nachtrag zu den literarischen Quellen des Alanus ab Insulis im Einleitungsgedicht zu *De planctu naturae*', *FilM*, 10:123–26, points out two intertexts that connect Alain's preface with an anonymous love poem. A. Bisanti, 'L'*interpretatio nominis* nella tradizione classico-medievale e nel *Babio*', *ib.*, 127–218, surveys the antonomastic use of proper names in Latin and vernacular sources from Paul the Deacon to Alexander Neckam, before he discusses the comedy's verbal play on the names of Viola, Babio, Petula, Fodius, and Croceus. R. J. Karris, 'St Bonaventure's use of *distinctiones*: his independence of and dependence on Hugh of St Cher', *FranS*, 60, 2002:209–50, notes Bonaventure's skill in rhyming word-play in creating his own distinctions and in those he adapted from Hugh. U. Mölk, 'Gelehrtes Wissen für Gesellschaft und Vaterland. Philologische Bermerkungen zu den *Variae historiae* des Guido Pisanus', *CN*, 62, 2002:109–35, describes the contents of Brussels, Bibliothèque Royale, 3897–3919, and identifes an excursus on Italy and Pisa attached to the *Excidium Troiae* as a prose version of Vergil, *Aeneid* 10.166–200. P. Stirnemann, 'Un manuscrit de Claudien fabriqué à la cour de Champagne dans les années 1160', *Holtz Vol.*, 53–57, concludes from examining London, BL, Egerton 2627, a MS produced at Troyes for Henry the Liberal, that Claudian was read in court circles as well as in the schools. L. Jocqué and D. Poirel, 'De Donat à Saint-Victor: un *De accentibus* inédit', *ib.*, 161–92, edit from Erlangen, Universitätsbibliothek 186 (*olim* 357) a prologue by Gilduin, first abbot of Saint-Victor, followed by lists of accentuated words that ensured the correct pronunciation of Latin during communal prayers. A. G. Rigg, 'Henry of Huntingdon's herbal', *MedS*, 65:213–92, describes the structure, contents, and treatment of Henry's verse herbal, which recasts much of Macer Floridus, before he edits selected texts based on Prague, Knihovna metropolitni kapituly M. VI (1359).

6. The Thirteenth Century

A. Neff, '"Palma dabit palmam": Franciscan themes in a devotional manuscript', *JWCI*, 65, 2002:22–66, reveals the programmatic unity of Florence, Biblioteca Medicea Laurenziana, Plut. 25.3, a MS assembled to promote the spiritual life of the reader; it begins with a didactic poem that incorporates verses from the *Carmina Burana*. V. Greene, 'Qui croit au retour d'Arthur?', *CCMe*, 45, 2002:321–40, finds that texts proclaiming the return of Arthur from a terrestrial paradise are motivated to portray an idealized image of Bretons as heroic warriors ready to protect the independence of their nation. L. Minervini, 'Modelli culturali e attività letteraria nell'Oriente latino', *SM*, 43, 2002:337–48, documents the various types of Latin and vernacular texts, liturgical, historical, rhetorical, and legal, that were copied in the Eastern empire and which mediated an intercultural dialogue with the West. M. Giovini, 'L'*Equus* di Paolino, I *Calcaria* di Polla et la notte di tregenda dell'avvocato Fulcone: I "Promessi sposi decrepiti" di Riccardo da Venosa', *Maia*, 54, 2002:351–71, examines the theme of old age debated in the elegiac comedy *De Paulino et Polla*, and recovers the classical sources, especially Cicero and Ovid, on which the arguments of each side rest. J. L. Peterson, 'The transmission and reception of Alberic of Montecassino's *Breviarium de dictamine*', *Scriptorium*, 57:27–50, interprets the codicological arrangements of five MSS to reveal how, when, and why the text was used for prose composition, grammatical study, and epistolary art. R. McNabb, 'Innovations and compilations: Juan Gil de Zamora's *Dictaminis epithalamium*', *Rhetorica*, 21:225–54, notes Juan's appropriation of ideas from Italian and French schools, before he discusses how distinctively he treats the *salutatio*, *exordium*, and *narratio*. I. Draelants, 'Le *Liber paradoxi*: un pseudo-Cicéron du XIIe siècle?', *RBPH*, 80, 2002:401–11, edits extracts from the *De moralibus* of Arnald of Saxe's encyclopedia, which are falsely attributed to Cicero's *Paradoxa*. E. Feistner, 'Vom Kampf gegen das "Andere". Pruzzen, Litauer und Mongolen in lateinischen und deutschen Texten des Mittelalters', *ZDA*, 132:281–94, investigates the interaction between the discourses of identity and alterity by examining accounts of contacts with non-Christian cultures in such works as Peter of Duisburg's *Chronicon Terrae Prussiae* and William of Rubrouck's *Historia Mongalorum*. M. Tarayre, 'L'image de Mahomet et de l'Islam dans une grande encyclopédie du moyen âge, le *Speculum historiale* de Vincent de Beauvais', *MA*, 109: 313–43, reveals the strategies Vincent used to construct a negative portrait of the Prophet and explains it as a reflex to the menace Islam was perceived to represent. H. O. Bizzarri, 'Algunos aspectos de la difusión de los *Disticha Catonis* en Castilla durante la Edad Media (1)', *MedRom*, 26, 2002: 127–48, documents the *Distichs* in vernacular proverbial literature, before tracking its reception up to the mid-15th c.; Id., *ib.*, 270–95, discusses the translation of the *Distichs* by Martín García and the version of Gonzalo García de Santa María. I. Bejczy, 'A medieval treatise on the cardinal virtues (Cambridge, St John's College, ms. E. 8 [111], fol. 62v-64r)', *MJ*, 38: 239–47, edits a work consisting mainly of quotations from Halitgar's *De vitiis et virtutibus* and Cicero's *De inventione* 2.53–55. C. Giordano, 'Die "Elucidarium" — Rezeption in den germanischen Literaturen des Mittelalters. Ein Überblick', *ib.*, 171–87, establishes that the vernacular tradition invariably combines translation with adaptation, and demonstrates that the third book of the theological *summa*, *De futura vita*, was a favourite of preachers and those who described the after life, while book 2, *De rebus ecclesiasticis*, was less popular. M. Schürer, 'Das Beispiel im Begriff. Aspekte einer begriffsgeschichtlichen Erschliessung exemplarischen Erzählens im Mittelalter', *ib.*, 199–237, traces the continuity of the *exemplum* in Aristotle, the *Rhetorica ad Herennium*, and Quintilian, before he examines texts which theorize the device, especially that of Humbert of Romans, who discussed the traits, use, and functionality of exemplary narratives. F. delle Donne, 'Le formule di saluto nella pratica epistolare medievale. La *Summa salutationum* di Milano e Parigi', *FilM*, 9, 2002: 251–79, discusses the similarities and differences in a compilation of model salutations, before he presents parallel editions of the work. J. Goering and R. Rosenfeld, 'The tongue is a pen: Robert Grosseteste's *Dictum 54* and scribal technology', *JMLat*, 12, 2002: 114–40, edit and translate a text, based on Oxford, Bodleian Library, MS Bodley 798, dealing with a mystical interpretation of the process by which a medieval scribe prepared a pen for writing, which was one of the scholastic lectures Robert delivered to Oxford Franciscans from 1229–1235. J. Kerr, 'The open door: hospitality and honour in twelfth/early thirteenth-century England', *History*, 87, 2002: 322–35, includes evidence from Walter Map and William of Malmesbury in a review of secular and monastic perceptions regarding the reception of guests. G. A. Loud, 'The kingdom of Sicily and the kingdom of England, 1066–1266', *ib.*, 88: 540–67, interprets the general ignorance of affairs in Norman Italy among English writers, including William of Malmesbury and Henry of Huntingdon, as reflecting a diminished sense of *Normanitas* in England and the growth of an English identity. E. Könsgen, 'Opusculum domni Yteri de Wascheio. Zisterziensergedichte aus der Handschrift Troyes BM 215', *AC*, 54, 2002: 120–33, edits a poem in elegiac distichs, in which Itier presents an ascetic interpretation of his life as a monk. G. Dinkova-Bruun, 'Medieval Latin poetic anthologies (VII): the biblical anthology from York Minster Library (MS. XVI Q 14)', *MedS*, 64, 2002: 61–109, describes the contents and analyses the unity of design and thematic organization of the 103 poems she edits. C. J. McDonough, 'Paris, Bibliothèque nationale de France, lat. 16483: contents, audience, and the matter of Old French', *ib.*, 131–216, investigates the authorship and audience of the sermons to articulate a context for assessing the sociolinguistic significance of the numerous OF words. D. A. Traill, 'Philip the Chancellor and F10: expanding the canon', *FilM*, 10: 219–48, argues on lexical and metrical grounds for attributing to Philip more of the poems contained in the tenth fascicle of Florence, Laurentian, Plut. 38, including some previously assigned to Peter of Blois. B. Grévin, 'Jérémie et Sapho. Analyses métriques du livre des Lamentations en milieu franciscain au XIIIe siècle', *ib.*, 249–71, presents the opposing perspectives of Pierre de Jean Olivi and Roger Bacon regarding the poetical structure of *Lamentations*, the former based on an analysis of classical metres, including Sapphics, the latter on the view that the book possessed its own rules that were lost in translation. H. Zimmermann, 'Die *Otia imperialia* des Gervasius von Tilbury. Prefatio und decisio 1, cap. 1–9. Einleitung, Text, Übersetzung und Kommentar', *Mediaevistik*, 15, 2002: 51–183, edits the beginning of the history, presenting the text in a form that displays the ubiquity of rhyming prose, a marked feature of the preface.

7. The Fourteenth and Fifteenth Centuries

M. Caesar, 'De la France à l'Italie: Nicole Oresme et la prédication de Nicoluccio da Ascoli OP', *AFP*, 72, 2002: 161–85, investigates the authorship of a collection of model sermons that are attributed to Oresme in Paris, BnF, MS lat. 16893, the majority of which J. B. Schneyer assigned to Nicoluccio. M. L. Lord, 'Benvenuto da Imola's literary approach to Virgil's *Eclogues*', *MedS*, 64, 2002: 287–362, examines the *accessus* and selected eclogues to find that Benvenuto's increased knowledge of the classics and his critical judgement in literary matters evince a humanist stance. G. Morgan, 'Medieval misogyny and Gawain's outburst against women in *Sir Gawain and the Green Knight*', *MLR*, 97, 2002: 265–78, invokes scholastic Aristotelian thought on the question of sexual differentiation as part of an argument challenging the view that Gawain despised womankind, one that he finds at odds with the poem as a whole, while R. J. Moll, 'Frustrated readers and conventional decapitation in *Sir Gawain and the Green Knight*', *ib.*, 793–802, studies historical texts, including Geoffrey of Monmouth's *Historia regum Britannie* and the *De ortu Waluuanii nepotis Arturi*, for clues to the character of Arthur's nephew in English romances, and concludes that they support the case for Gawain's multivalent nature. E. Campbell, 'Sexual poetics and the politics of translation in the Tale of Griselda', *CL*, 55:191–216, emphasizes Petrarch's focus on Griselda's moral value in his Latin translation of Boccaccio's vernacular story, in a study that explores the relationships medieval authors created between readers and texts. J. Usher, 'A quotation from the *Culex* in Boccaccio's *De casibus*', *MLR*, 97, 2002:312–23, discovers that similar geographical references used to describe the wreck of the Greek fleet returning from Troy directly connect Boccaccio's work with the pseudo-Virgilian *Culex*, a copy of which he personally transcribed. M. Donnini, 'Sopra alcune presenze dell'*Epitoma rei militaris* di Vegezio nel *Liber secretorum fidelium crucis* di Marino Sanudo il Vecchio', *SM*, 44:347–59, documents the presence of Vegetius's treatise in a work that exhorts Christians to study military discipline as a means to maintain control of the Holy Land. G. Braccini and S. Marchesi, 'Livio xxv, 26 e l'"Introduzione" alla *Prima giornata*. Di una possibile tessera classica per il "cominciamento" del *Decameron*', *Italica*, 80:139–46, find that Boccaccio enlists details from Livy's description of a plague in several places where his principal model, Paul the Deacon, is deficient or divergent. A. Heil, 'Dantes "Thessalien": Pharsalus oder Philippi? Eine Bemerkung zu Dante Alighieri, Epist. 5, 7–10', *MJ*, 37, 2002:75–81, contends that the allusion to Thessaly is not to the events of 48 BCE, when Caesar granted amnesty to Brutus, but to 42 BCE, when the later Augustus brought Julius Caesar's assassins to justice. H. Halmari and R. Adams, 'On the grammar and rhetoric of language mixing in *Piers Plowman*', *NMi*, 103, 2002:33–50, argue that the poet mingles brief Latin phrases with ME to communicate his knowledge of religious literature to a devout, bilingual audience. J. A. Mitchell, 'Boethius and Pandarus: a source in Maximian's *Elegies*', *NQ*, 248:377–80, claim that Boethius's role as a pander in Chaucer's *Troilus and Criseyde* derives from *Elegy* 3, in which he figures both as a *praeceptor amoris* and as a go-between for the love-sick youth and his girl. C. F. Heffernan, 'Three unnoticed links between Matthew of Vendôme's *Comedia Lidie* and Chaucer's *Merchant's Tale*', *ib.*, 158–62, points to shared mythological associations, imitation by opposition in January's encomium on marriage and wives, and the replication of the polyptoton in *Lidia* 454, as grounds enough to conclude that Chaucer had direct knowledge of the comedy. D. T. Benediktson, 'Cambridge University

Library Ll l 14, F. 46r–v: a late medieval natural scientist at work', *Neophilologus*, 86, 2002:171–77, identifies Aldhelm as the source of a taxonomical lexicon of animal sounds. R. D. Schiewer, 'Eine deutschsprachige Überlieferung des "Miraculum I" Wichmanns von Arnstein', *ZDA*, 131, 2002:436–53, discusses the unique vernacular version of the Latin text preserved in Munich, Staatsbibliothek, Cgm 531, and argues that the alterations are modelled on the texts of German "Mystikerinnen". M. Hagby, '*Parturiunt montes, et exit ridiculus mus*? Beobachtungen zur Entstehung der Strickerschen Kurzerzählungen', *ZDA*, 132:35–61, reports that the search for models for the German narratives leads into four broad areas of the medieval *exemplum*, important sources of which include the *Vitae patrum*, *Physiologus*, and the *Disciplina clericalis*. D. R. Carlson, 'Whethamstede on Lollardy: Latin styles and the vernacular cultures of early fifteenth-century England', *JEGP*, 102:21–41, edits and translates a polemical poem, using it to explore the conflict within Latin between the scholastic tradition and emergent humanism, which was itself informed by tensions within English. Id., 'The "Opicius" poems (British Library, Cotton Vespasian B. iv) and the humanist anti-literature in early Tudor England', *RQ*, 55, 2002:869–903, analyses the design and contents of a MS presented to the English king, Henry VII, *c.*1492, containing five classicizing poems that were written not for circulation, but solely to celebrate the king's military and political magnificence. A. F. D'Elia, 'Marriage, sexual pleasure, and learned brides in the wedding orations of fifteenth-century Italy', *ib.*, 379–423, surveys the revival of the *epithalamium* by 11 humanists at the courts of Ferrara, Milan, and Naples and reveals their use of classical literature, philosophy, and contemporary history to praise the learning and rhetorical skill of brides. G. Ianziti, 'Leonardi Bruni and biography: the *Vita Aristotelis*', *ib.*, 805–32, views the innovative work as a partisan attempt to counter the negative aspects of the portrait of Aristotle publicized in Ambrogio Traversari's translation of Diogenes Laertius's *Lives of Eminent Philosophers*. V. Cox, 'Rhetoric and humanism in quattrocento Venice', *RQ*, 56:652–94, uses a letter of 1489 by Ermalao Barbaro praising the civic eloquence of Bernardo Giustinian to underline the importance of deliberative debate in Republican Venice and its influence in developing rhetorical culture in Italy. P. Laurens, 'Trois lectures du vers virgilien. Coluccio Salutati, Giovanni Gioviano Pontano, Jules-César Scaliger', *REL*, 79, 2001[2002]:215–35, discusses Salutati's conception of poetry, which held that the structure of verse contained the equivalent of the harmony of the spheres, with reference to his allegorical poem, *De laboribus Herculis*. J. M. Luxford, 'A previously unlisted manuscript of the Latin *Brut* chronicle with Sherborne continuation', *MAe*, 71,

2002:286–93, identifies Geoffrey of Monmouth's *Historia regum Britanniae* and Ranulf Higden, *Polychronicon*, among the sources used to compile the contents of Cambridge, Trinity College, MS R. 7.13, a copy of London, BL, Harley MS 3906, two MSS which situate the Benedictine abbey of Sherborne in the context of British and English history from the earliest times. T. Haye, 'Der Satiriker Francesco Filelfo — ein Lucilius der Renaissance', *Philologus*, 147:129–50, argues that the voluminous satire Filelfo directed against the corrupt Signoria of Florence was not a purely literary genre, but an instrument of political and personal struggle, in which he criticized influential contemporary figures by name. D. Marsh, 'Aesop and the Humanist apologue', *RenS*, 17:9–26, provides a typology of characters contained in the Renaissance apologue, a sub-species of the *exemplum*, with particular attention to the model provided by Leon Battista Alberti's *Centum apologi*. R. Chavasse, 'The *studia humanitatis* and the making of the humanist career: Marcantonio Sabellico's exploitation of the literary genres', *ib.*, 27–38, views Sabellico's literary achievement as historian, commentator, and editor of classical texts as the means that ensured his status in contemporary intellectual life. A. Fowler, 'The formation of genres in the Renaissance and after', *NLH*, 34:185–200, surveys the new genres and the importance of the metaphors associated with them, before he discusses how the three major medieval modes were expanded in the so-called *rota Vergiliana*, which was popularized by John of Garland. D. Rundle, 'Carneades' legacy: the morality of eloquence in the Humanist and papalist writings of Pietro del Monte', *EHR*, 117, 2002:284–305, focuses attention on Pietro's reworking of Poggio's *De avaritia*, to which he brought stylistic improvement and increased clarity of purpose, before he concludes that humanist orators could ill afford to indulge in insincerity. F. N. M. Diekstra, 'The indebtedness of XII *Frutes of the Holy Goost* to Richard Rolle's *The Form of Living* and to David of Augsburg's *De exterioris et interioris hominis compositione*, Part I', *ESt*, 83, 2002:207–38, 'Part II', *ib.*, 311–37, attributes the uneven stylistic quality of XII *Frutes* to the compiler's lack of skill in integrating various sources, which included Guillaume Peyraut's *Summa de vitiis* and *Summa de virtutibus*. W. Freytag, 'Petrarchas ciceronianische Inventionskunst in Fam. IV 1, besonders in der Hirtenepisode seiner Wanderung auf den Ventoux', *ib.*, 89–126, examines how topical invention is presented in sections 7–8 of the work, before summarizing the present state of research on the theme. W. Strobl, '"Imitatus Ciceronem ac Hieronymum meum": zur Theorie des Übersetzens bei Hilarion aus Verona', *BHR*, 65:571–87, edits the preface to Hilarion's translation of a work by Dorotheos of Gaza in order to assess his importance as a translator. A. Iacono, 'Un ignoto codice del *Parthenopeus* di Giovanni Gioviano Pontano', *BSL*, 33:128–39, discovers a codex copied from an exemplar that preserves an older redaction of the poem. D. Hobbins, 'The schoolman as public intellectual: Jean Gerson and the late medieval tract', *AHR*, 108:1308–37, focuses on the emergence of a new literary form which enabled authors to broadcast their views on current topics, such as usury and magic, to non-academic audiences, a shift that altered the nature of scholarly discourse. B. Hall and M. J. Edwards, 'The commentary on Claudian *De Raptu Proserpinae* by Pierfrancesco Giustolo', *SM*, 44:367–459, present a first edition based on the unique codex, Naples, Biblioteca Nazionale V. D. 24. R. A. Powell, 'Margery Kempe: an exemplar of late medieval piety', *CHR*, 89:1–23, examines the *Meditaciones vite Christi* of Johannes de Caulibus and Richard Rolle's *Incendium amoris* in order to set the English mystic in the context of contemporary religious life. J. Robert, '*Carmina Pieridum nulli celebrata priorum.* Zur Inszenierung von Epochenwende im Werk des Conrad Celtis', *BGDSL*, 124, 2002:92–121, examines how Celtis deploys astrological knowledge to describe himself as a threshold figure, who inauguarated a new epoch of poetry in Germany, before he provides a text and translation of the *Poema ad Fridericum.* F. Fürbeth, 'Die "Epitoma rei militaris" des Vegetius zwischen ritterlicher Ausbildung und gelehrt-humanistischer Lektüre. Zu einer weiteren unbekannten deutschen Übersetzung aus der Wiener Artistenfakultät', *ib.*, 302–38, notes the many reasons other than military praxis for the popularity of the treatise and illustrates this by reconstructing its reception in the ducal court of Vienna in the form of the first German translation, which is preserved in Seitenstetten, Stiftsbibliothek, cod. LXV. M. Donnini, 'Un inedito di Antonio da Rho: la *Metrica commendatio summi pontificis Martini V*', *Franciscana*, 4, 2002:149–68, illuminates the humanist culture of a Franciscan by analysing the style and contents of a classicizing poem, which he edits from a unique MS, Milan, Biblioteca Ambrosiana, B 116 *sup.* G.; and P. Contamine, 'Noblesse, vertu, lignage et "anciennes richesses". Jalons pour l'histoire médiévale de deux citations: Juvénal, *Satires* 8,20 et Aristote, *Politique* 5,1', *Holtz Vol.*, 321–34, notes the engagement of Latin and French texts, from Heriger of Lobbes to Christine de Pizan, with two quotations dealing with the idea of nobility and their ideological deployment in debates regarding its definition. S. Pittaluga, 'Lettori umanistici di Ovidio', *ib.*, 335–47, concentrates on the reception of the *Metamorphoses* in Latin and vernacular writings.

NEO-LATIN

POSTPONED

2
ROMANCE LANGUAGES
I. ROMANCE LINGUISTICS

By John N. Green, *University of Bradford*

1. Acta, Festschriften

It has been a good year for conference proceedings, even without the five volumes of Acts of the Salamanca Congress (*CILPR 23*), which I plan to review together next year. The American Linguistic Symposium on Romance Languages is well represented. *LSRL 31* assembles 21 papers on phonology, morphology, syntax, and — a welcome innovation — on pragmatics and sociolinguistics; though of a good standard, they are mostly monolingual in focus. *LSRL 32* brings together 21 contributions distributed between 'theory' (phonological and syntactic, mainly applied to French and Spanish) and, less usually, language acquisition; the comparative items are further discussed below. The 15th annual meeting of European Romanists but only the third to be published as a collected volume, *Going Romance 2001*, presents 19 papers concentrating on syntax drawing data from a good range of varieties. The German annual colloquia are represented by *RK 13*, dealing with literacy in a non-native Romance language, from Late Latin and the Middle Ages to the present day; and by *RK 14*, devoted to the creation of canons in Romance linguistics.

A handsome 70th birthday tribute, *Ex traditione innovatio. Miscellanea in honorem Max Pfister septuagenarii oblata*, Darmstadt, WBG, 2002, pairs a volume of 19 revised reprinted essays giving a judicious overview of the master's preoccupations and scholarly methods across three decades, *1: Max Pfister, scripta minora selecta, de rebus Galloromanicis et Italicis*, ed. Martin-D. Glessgen and Wolfgang Schweickard, xxxviii + 503 pp., with a more conventional set of offerings centred on the *LEI*, and problems of etymology and textual scholarship in Italian and Rhaeto-Romance, *2: Miscellanea sociorum operis in honorem magistri conscripta*, ed. Günter Holtus and Johannes Kramer, xii + 434 pp. *Fest. Paufler* is a treasure trove of information on the distribution and interaction of Romance varieties in the Americas. Two other substantial dedication volumes, *Fest. Ernst* and *Messner Vol.*, offer interesting fare from individual languages but little of comparative scope; both include full bibliographies of their dedicatees (respectively 3–14 and 351–61).

ASR, 116, ed. Claudia Foppa and Esther Krättli, is dedicated to Alexi Decurtins on his 80th birthday. *Lengas*, 53, appears as a memorial to Charles Camproux, with a tribute by R. Lafont to this multifaceted scholar, writer, and activist (7–9) and a re-evaluation by J.-P. Chambon (11–31) of C.'s contribution to dialectology — innovative and willing to break free of the shackles of neo-Gilliéronian method.

2. General Romance and Latin

Under the foreboding title, 'Historical Romance linguistics: the death of a discipline?', *La corónica*, 31.2, ed. S. N. Dworkin, assembles 14 reactions from distinguished practitioners, most of whom are studiously upbeat in the face of current recruitment problems and the scaling-back of graduate training programmes. S. N. Dworkin, 'Thoughts on the future of a venerable and vital discipline' (9–17), sees much excellent work done on individual languages but worries about who will train the next generation of comparativists; J. R. Craddock, 'Reflections on a premature intimation of impending doom' (19–23), is optimistic about historical research despite the closure of the Berkeley comparative PhD programme; M. T. Echenique-Elizondo, 'Perspectivas de la lingüística diacrónica' (25–33), rejoices in solid, if theoretically non-pyrotechnic, progress in the history of Spanish; J. Kabatek, 'La lingüística románica histórica' (35–40), advocates the historical revitalization of Romance texts; P. Koch, 'Historical Romance linguistics and the cognitive turn' (41–55), underscores the richness of Romance data, especially for onomasiology; M. Loporcaro, 'Muhammad, Charlemagne and apocope', (57–65), points out the impoverishment of European cultural history that would follow the demise of Romance linguistics; J. Lüdtke, 'Para la historia de la lengua' (67–72), sees the re-establishment of history of language courses as the route to revival; R. Pellen, 'Diacronía y descripción del cambio lingüístico' (73–82), sets an ambitious research agenda in graphology, syntax, and discourse, emphasizing the connections that are easily overlooked and require multi-dimensional expertise in research; R. Penny, 'A sociolinguistic perspective' (83–88), sees the paradox of a discipline flourishing at research level but withering beneath; J. Rini, 'Romance linguistics: an evolving discipline' (89–95), avers that new directions in research can still excite students; J. C. Smith, 'Future perfect or future in the past?' (97–102), points to signs of a quiet revival of comparativism if judged on a world scale; D. Wanner, 'Romance linguistics is alive and well' (103–13), acknowledges the loss of the 19th-c. 'all-encompassing' edifice but is enthused by the potential of new interpretive frameworks; K. J. Wireback, 'From Romance to linguistics' (115–25), sees a long-term cycle of disciplinary cross-fertilization in which Romance could easily recapture the momentum; and R. Wright, 'The renaissance of a discipline' (127–34), urges more imaginative definitions to celebrate revival, growth, and new branches of research, particularly in Late Latin and sociolinguistics.

Adams, *Bilingualism*, assembles 14 papers from a 1998 symposium, together with a long introduction stressing the pervasive nature of bilingualism and contact in the ancient world, notably between Latin and Greek but by no means confined to them. The themes are further developed in James N. Adams, *Bilingualism and the Latin Language*, CUP, xxviii + 836 pp., vast, learned, full of new research, and with a nice balance between discussion of general themes and specific case studies, including Claudius Terentianus and bilingualism in Egypt, where by far the richest evidence survives. If bilingualism is defined liberally, most emperors and the upper echelons of Roman society were bilingual or multilingual for centuries, with consequences in diglossia, code-switching, Hellenization, and language attitudes and policies. Latin emerges as a major cause of language death in the west of the Empire, but not in the east, where Greek remained prestigious and offered shelter to other minority languages.

Roger Wright, *A Sociophilological Study of Late Latin* (Utrecht Studies in Medieval Literacy, 10), Turnhout, Brepols, viii + 389 pp., reprints, with revisions, 25 papers covering linguistic and textual interpretation from the 9th to the 13th cs, many of which have featured in these pages; the collection is coherent and persuasive, but the conclusion that it would have been better if the 'Carolingian linguistic reforms had not happened at all' (359) could have robbed us of sociophilology itself and the stimulus for many other valuable contributions to historical linguistics. The current level of interest in what used to be a tiny research field, can be gauged from the two substantial volumes of *CHLM 3*, the acts of the 2001 León conference, in which 22 papers directly address linguistic aspects of medieval Latin and the emergence of the Romance languages, aside from many others with tangential relevance.

A further onslaught by W. Mańczak, 'Discussion sur l'origine des langues romanes', *Allières Vol.*, 453–61, reviews recent compendious works in which, he claims, Romance origins are either cloaked in silence, brushed aside as questions of dubious definition, or tacitly admitted to have followed the evolutionary path via Classical Latin that he has steadfastly championed. M. also contributes 'The method of comparing the vocabulary in parallel texts', *Journal of Quantitative Linguistics*, 10:93–103, a clear summary of what he claims to have achieved in Romance linguistics and elsewhere by the application of his controversial taxonomic method since the late 1970s. Continuing earlier work on correspondences of discourse features in literary translations (see *YWMLS*, 64:6), M. Gawełko, 'Essai de classification fonctionnelle des langues romanes', *RPh*, 55, 2001–02[2003]:21–40, offers a summary table and location of Romance varieties on a spectrum from synthesis to analysis, with the rank order Romanian > Spanish > Italian > Portuguese > French; it has a number of surprises, not least the separation of Spanish and Portuguese.

3. History of Romance Linguistics

Important research on the crystallization of canons, in both literary and linguistic scholarship, is reported in *RK 14*, whose 18 papers span precursors of Romance linguistics to present-day trends, with further sections on neighbouring disciplines and the position and prospects of *Romanistik* in German-speaking universities, witness: P. Braselmann, 'Antonio de Nebrija: grammaticus canonicus' (37–64), M. Pfister, 'Kanonbildung im Bereich der romanischen Etymologie' (261–68), C. Duttlinger, 'Kanon und Kanonbildung in der Höflichkeits- und Komplimentforschung' (363–83), C. Seidl, 'Kanonbildung in der lateinischen Sprachwissenschaft' (441–70), A. Schönberger, 'Zur normativen Wirkung der "communis opinio" in der deutschen Romanistik' (387–416), and J. Kramer, 'Zum romanistischen Fächerkanon' (417–26), with a riposte by A. Schönberger, 'Concedo multa, sed nego consequentia' (427–38). A valuable comparative analysis by M.-D. Glessgen of 'Les manuels de linguistique romane, source pour l'histoire d'un canon disciplinaire', *ib.*, 189–259, spanning the entire period from Diefenbach to Posner, tackles the neglected issue of the influence exerted on conceptualization by early treatises and compendious reference works — one might, for instance, be forgiven for thinking that Bourciez and Elcock were presenting different disciplines.

RLaR, 106.1, 2002, ed. Teddy Arnavielle and Liliane Dulac, carries nine essays celebrating the multi-faceted œuvre of 'Gaston Paris (1839–1903), philologue, médiéviste, grammairien', including: T. Arnavielle, 'Sur quelques idées-force de Gaston Paris' (3–16), largely on P.'s willingness to accept metaphor as a vehicle for scientific understanding but disapproval of the specific one chosen by his pupil Darmesteter in *La Vie des mots*; G. Bergounioux and J.-C. Chevalier,

'Gaston Paris et la phonétique' (17–40), reminding us that P. contributed several major items on phonetics, including his thesis on the role of Latin stress in the history of French, and later used his expertise to good effect as a reviewer, notably of Bourciez and Grammont; A.-M. Frýba-Reber, 'Gaston Paris et la Suisse' (81–107), concentrating on his relations with Tobler, Morel, and Schuchardt; and P. Swiggers, 'Gaston Paris et les débuts de la philologie romane en Belgique' (109–22), tracing the support given by P. to M. Wilmotte and the first generation of Belgian Romanists at the École Normale de Liège. Swiggers also contributes 'La canonisation d'un franc-tireur: Hugo Schuchardt et la romanistique', *RK 14*, 269–304, painting a very human portrait of a questing polymath, impatient of rigid models, attracted by intellectual affinity, repelled by 'schools', and not easily accommodated within any conventional canon.

In view of the fraught political relations between France and Germany in the 19th c., K. Bochmann, 'La *Revue des langues romanes* et la romanistique allemande du XIXe siècle', *RLaR*, 106, 2002: 173–83, is surprised to find universal cordiality, respect, and even veneration between scholars of the two nations; *RLaR* was widely available in Germany and cited in the *Zeitschrift für romanische Philologie* almost as often as *Romania*. Yet there were ripples: U. Bähler, 'Correspondance de Karl Bartsch et Gaston Paris de 1865 à 1885', *Romania*, 121: 1–42, supplements the three tranches published in the 1920s and 1930s by Mario Roques; the letters are indeed cordial, though Bartsch was by far the better correspondent, and there are evident barbs about Meyer, which may account for the truncated publication, since Roques owed much to Meyer and had inherited directly from him the editorship of *Romania*.

4. Phonology

In a long and thoughtful review, D. Recasens, 'Weakening and strengthening in Romance revisited', *RivL*, 14: 327–73, questions the attribution of numerous Romance changes, from lenition to rhotacism and vocalization, to a decrease in the degree of articulatory constriction; such 'weakening' could not account for alveolar contact retraction, aspiration of front fricatives, or metatheses, among others, for which gestural decomposition and acoustic and perceptual factors should all be considered. In 'Due note sul raddoppiamento fonosintattico', *RPh*, 56: 307–18, M. Loporcaro seems keen to shed the burden of uniqueness: the syntactic contexts that regularly led to doubling in northern Italian (ET VIDES > /vː/, DAT PANE > /pː/) may have produced similar outcomes in Mozarabic xarjas, though the modern Florentine pronunciation of *tu* as /tːu/ is less easily explicable. Very well exemplified from Old Spanish and French, F. Martínez-Gil, 'Consonant intrusion in heterosyllabic consonant-liquid clusters', *LSRL 31*, 39–58, argues that an Optimality account of rising sonority in what used to be called 'buffer consonant epenthesis' is both simpler and more insightful. Further work on the proposed Advanced Tongue Root feature (see *YWMLS*, 62:20) is reported by A. Calabrese, 'On the evolution of the short high vowels of Latin into Romance', *LSRL 32*, 63–94, which claims support from extra-Romance data for his hypothesis that late Latin vowel mergers were due to a repair strategy resolving the anomalous combination of [+high, -ATR].

P. Hirschbühler and M. Labelle, 'Residual Tobler-Mussafia in French dialects', *LSRL 32*, 149–64, claim that comparative dialectology (including a judicious admixture of Piedmontese) will solve some synchronic problems. Nonetheless, on the basis of a large corpus of Old Catalan, S. Fischer, 'Rethinking the Tobler-Mussafia Law', *Diachronica*, 20:259–88, is convinced that phonology has nothing to do with clitic placement; it is rather due to a change in the parameter governing Verb movement to Σ^0, which ceased to be categorical and allowed competing clitic orders (the point is more fully developed in Susann Fischer, *The Catalan Clitic System*, Berlin, Mouton de Gruyter, 2002, xiv + 252 pp., a revision of her Potsdam PhD thesis).

5. Inflectional Morphology

In 'Latin static morphology and paradigm families', *Winter Vol.*, 87–99, W. U. Dressler distinguishes dynamic from static forms (those learned whole, unanalysed, and not necessarily in active use), claiming that very little Latin static morphology survived into Romance and moreover that most dynamic forms became static. Drawing on an unusual range of Indo-European data, B. Drinka, 'The formation of periphrastic perfects and passives', *ICHL 15*, 105–28, explains similarities by proposing that Latin calqued the HAVE perfect on the Greek model, crucially bleaching the original passive participle, so that it would serve as non-passive in the perfect and non-perfect in the passive. P. de Carvalho's neo-Guillaumean discussion, ' "Gérondif", "participe présent" et "adjectif déverbal" ', *Langages*, 149:100–26, challenges the view that there was confusion between these forms in late Latin: Gallo-Romance privileged subjects and their continuity in the discourse and so needed participles, whereas Ibero-Romance focused on event structure and needed gerundives. Meanwhile, D. G. Miller asks 'Where do conjugated infinitives come from?', *Diachronica*, 20:45–81, drawing on Romance and wider data, and replying that this 'unnatural' development arises from purposive subjunctives and personal pronouns re-analysed as AGR markers.

L. Tasmowski and S. Reinheimer, 'Existe-t-il un paradigme du pronom personnel dans les langues romanes?', *RF*, 115:149–70, concede that competing developments in determiners and weak pronoun sets undermined cross-linguistic coherence, but defend the paradigm for individual languages, as the locus of grammaticalization in progress. Very well documented, as ever, R. de Dardel, 'Le syncrétisme du datif et de l'accusatif dans le pronom *ille*', *RLiR*, 67:405–30, identifies five main types in Proto-Romance, all jostling to merge third-person datives and accusatives (as had happened with first and second persons) but in apparent disarray over number and gender marking; the complexity of D.'s tables apparently still does not allow for mutual influence in ILLI + ILLU sequences, from which the notorious *gelo*, *glielo* derived. Applying a pan-Romance perspective to 'Il pronome *loro* nell'Italia centro-meridionale', *VR*, 61:48–116, M. Loporcaro concludes that the ILLORUM type (with local phonological variants) was the standard late Latin expression for non-reflexive third-person possession across the entire empire, and therefore indigenous in Tuscan and not borrowed from Gaul.

An unusual slant on borrowing is offered by M. Polinsky and E. van Everbroeck, whose 'Development of gender classifications', *Language*, 73:356–90, uses connectionist simulation to model gender changes between Latin and French following the realignment of paradigms; formal cues, analogy, and frequency give reasonable results, but accuracy is vastly improved by supplementary information on gender assignment in Celtic.

6. Morphosyntax and Typology

Eduardo D. Faingold, *The Development of Grammar in Spanish and the Romance Languages*, Basingstoke, Palgrave–Macmillan, xiv + 149 pp., is an extraordinarily ambitious attempt to link first and second language acquisition, creole genesis, and historical linguistics; his case studies focus on articles and demonstratives, prepositions and adverbs, the learning of modality and the loss of the future subjunctive (for which he can demonstrate a catastrophic decline in Argentinian legal registers in the 1880s). M. Sabanéeva, 'Aux sources latines des articles français', *FM*, 71:167–78, challenges the received wisdom that definite articles emerged before indefinite; the gradual slippage in meaning as unity markers turn into indefinites is hard to identify and the typological commonness of the process can lead to its being overlooked. J. Kabatek, 'Gibt es einen Grammatikalisierungszyklus des Artikels in der Romania?', *RJ*, 53:56–80, finds a cline of usage,

French > Spanish > European Portuguese > Brazilian, matching Greenberg's types O, I and II, but with enough differences in Brazilian to question the linearity of the developments; macro-typology, he concludes, can always be tempered by local factors.

Fiorentino, *Romance Objects*, represents the proceedings of a symposium held in Rome in 2000, with ten papers on object marking as a general phenomenon and seven case studies on transitivity effects in Romance, including C. Company Company, 'Transitivity and grammaticalization of object' (217–60), on the unequal struggle in Spanish between the multifunctional dative and the accusative patient to achieve object status; and G. Fiorentino, 'Prepositional objects in Neapolitan' (117–51), a corpus-based comparison with Spanish and Romanian, revealing uniformity only in the marking of tonic personal pronouns, and strongly suggesting independent and parallel historical evolutions. A contrasting Optimality account by J. Aissen, 'Differential object marking', *NLLT*, 21:435–83, wishes to escape from hierarchies of animacy, pointing instead to compromises between the conflicting principles of iconicity and least effort.

E. Blasco Ferrer, 'Tipologia delle presentative romanze e morfosintassi storica', *ZRP*, 119:51–90, demonstrates that Romance presentatives almost all require a support clitic pronoun or adverbial (*c'est*, *c'è*, *hay* < *ha* + *i(bi)*, etc) and draws on typological theory to validate his plausible reconstruction of their evolutionary trajectory. More general than its title, A. Vañó-Cerdá, '*Esser* y *star* con predicados nominales en retorrománico', *RLiR*, 67:463–97, deals with the lateral spread of *star* from locative adverbials, to attributive complements (which has wide resonance in Ibero-Romance and elsewhere), but then — it seems, uniquely — on to the mere affirmation of a state or quality. K. Schulte, 'Pragmatic relevance as a cause for syntactic change', *ICHL 15*, 377–89, explores the development of prepositional complementizers in Romance as a gelling of co-occurrence patterns of matrix verbs with particular types of adjunct. Finally on conditionals, a startling answer to the question why *que* can be used to introduce a protasis even though it invites ambiguity in this role is proffered by E. Sánchez Salor, 'El *quod* latino y el *que* español introductores de condicionales', *RELing*, 32, 2002:413–40; early Latin conditionals used a correlative structure QUOD . . . SIC, with QUOD posing the hypothesis and SIC the outcome, but the increasing polyvalency of QUOD left it unsuitable for this function and it was often omitted, leaving unmarked the very clause that most needed marking, so SIC passed across to do the job, thereby leaving the apodosis unmarked; vestiges of the older structure can, however, still be found in modern Romance.

7. Generative Syntax

In her important pan-Romance research on *Clitics Between Syntax and the Lexicon*, Amsterdam, Benjamins, xii + 279 pp., Birgit Gerlach convincingly argues that clitics have inflection-like properties, such as clustering in fixed orders, but are not yet affixal inflections, since they bind to words not stems; the choice of individual clitics is determined by the interaction of violable constraints of markedness and faithfulness (this latter pressing for the explicit morphological marking of sentential arguments).

I. De Crousaz and U. Shlonsky, 'The distribution of a subject clitic pronoun in a Franco-Provençal dialect and the licensing of Pro', *LI*, 34:413–42, identify three factors that influence the emergence of subject marking in what was a Pro-drop language: rich verbal inflection, government by a complementizer and doubling by a clitic. M. Suñer worries whether 'The lexical preverbal subject in a Romance null-subject language', *LSRL 31*, 341–57, is necessarily in the A-bar position and decides that it is, despite some contrary appearances. S. Béjar and M. Rezac, 'Person licensing and the derivation of PCC effects', *LSRL 32*, 49–62, examine pronoun compatibility and crossover phenomena (e.g. *le lui* but not **vous lui*). A. M. Martins, 'Deficient pronouns and linguistic change in Portuguese and Spanish', *Going Romance 2001*, 213–30, seems perplexed to find that *se* and the defective accusative and dative pronoun series remain as X^0 elements throughout the history of the respective languages with no attempt to change category or make good. In 'Weak forms as X^0', *LSRL 32*, 95–110, A. Castro and J. Costa take up a proposal originally made by A. Cardinaletti for Italian prenominal possessives and preverbal adverbs, concluding that European Portuguese broadly matches, with the addition of one sub-type.

Observing that Latin vocatives were not uniformly or unambiguously marked, A. Moro, 'Notes on vocative case', *Going Romance 2001*, 247–61, concludes that they are noun phrases outside the thematic grid of the predicate, though they can be co-referential with items inside the grid. V. Déprez, 'Constraints on the meaning of bare nouns', *LSRL 31*, 291–310, unusually combines conventional Romance data with Creole to bolster her hypothesis of 'plural-parameter' languages. D. also contributes 'Determiner architecture and phrasal movement in French lexifier creoles', *Going Romance 2001*, 49–74, exploring the considerable syntactic variation disguised by the apparent morphological uniformity of {-la}. In 'Past participle agreement with pronominal clitics and the auxiliary verbs', *ib.*, 193–212, P. Law seeks to explain why French and Italian, uniquely among the Romance standards, have both concord and auxiliary selection, proposing a structural condition that the argument must be outside the syntactic projection of the predicate with which it agrees. According to M. C. Cuervo, 'A control-vs-raising theory of dative experiencers', *LSRL 32*, 111–30, an explanation for the fact that Spanish and Italian *seem* verbs do not accept reflexive clitics can be found by comparing *seem* structures with other unaccusative and epistemic predicates. Bringing to light 'An exceptional exclamative sentence type in Romance', *Lingua*, 113:713–45, X. Villalba contrasts the common patterns introduced by *que* and *come* with *que* + *de* + adjective, which does not involve right-dislocation but does require a 'null exclamative degree operator'.

Three items represent the burgeoning sub-field of language acquisition in a generative perspective. L. Davidson and G. Legendre, 'Defaults and competition in the acquisition of functional categories in Catalan and French', *LSRL 31*, 273–90, find that French children relying on the infinitive as their initial default form acquire TNS before AGR, whereas Catalans, relying on the third person singular as their default, acquire AGR first. A. Bel, 'The syntax of subjects in the acquisition of Spanish and Catalan', *Probus*, 15:1–26, finds, not very surprisingly, that there is early convergence of children's and adults' grammars; her early versions of Spanish and Catalan clearly have Tense, except in non-finite structures which can be treated as truncated (and, one might add, match those of adult grammars). Finally, in 'Relative clause formation in Romance child's production [*sic*]', *Probus*, 15:47–89, M. T. Guasti and A. Cardinaletti seek to exonerate French and Italian children from the charge that their failure to pied-pipe prepositions must mean that they have not learned to form relative clauses by WH-movement; no, say the intrepid authors, it is because pied-piping belongs to higher registers and is learned later at school.

8. Discourse and Pragmatics

Béatrice Coffen, *Histoire culturelle des pronoms d'adresse. Vers une typologie des systèmes allocutoires dans les langues romanes*, Paris, Champion, 2002, 319 pp., comprehensively describing Romance address patterns from the Roman Empire to modern creole, notes that a *tu*: *vous* distinction is almost universal, and wonders whether this obligatory signalling of interpersonal relations is a sufficient justification for the linguistic cost. It certainly used to be, according to Eleanor Dickey, *Latin Forms of Address. From Plautus to Apuleius*, OUP, xii + 414 pp., who studies attestations of all forms of address, from honorary titles to insults, and the implications for social interaction, observing that the niceties mattered in ancient Rome and that infringements could be punished.

A long and well informed discussion of the troublesome pairs theme/rheme, given/new, known/unknown, exemplified from Romance, leads M. Arcangeli, 'Schegge di sintassi della communicazione', *ZRP*, 119:1–50, to a neo-Hallidayan solution, in which the pairs relate, respectively, to dynamic discoursal axes of thematization (or individuation), information, and identification. E. Lavric contrasts 'Español *tal*, italiano *tale*', *RLiR*, 67:179–206, with the history of *tel* in French, where the now obligatory determiner has limited the sense to qualitative anaphora, while Spanish and Italian have a second, referential reading probably inherited from Latin. According to L. S. Florea, 'La concession comme hypothèse infirmée', *RLiR*, 67:137–58, the argumentative purpose of a concessive is not to oppose or restrict, but to invalidate a hypothesis; in this, Romanian and French agree, though they mark concession in divergent ways. A thoughtful comparison by M. Iliescu, 'Die logisch-semantische Präposition "mit"', *Fest. Ernst*, 169–82, finds that French and Romanian match in the expression of comitative meaning, but diverge in sociative, mainly because French can make a distinction between neutral and deliberate senses (*un café au lait* vs. *aujourd'hui je prends mon café avec du lait*). On a lighter note, comparing 'Énoncés portant sur les échanges de nature rituelle (salutations et souhaits)', *RRL*, 44, 1999[2003]:13–19, G. Scurtu and A. Rădulescu find that Rom. *noroc* and *la mulţi ani* do the work of at least five expressions in French.

9. Lexis

Blank, *Kognitive Onomasiologie*, brings together eleven contributions from a recent symposium, with an overview by A. Blank and P. Koch, 'Kognitive romanische Onomasiologie und Semasiologie' (1–15), several papers dealing with the conceptual semantics of individual languages (with aspect and possession as recurrent themes), and a section experimenting more openly with cognitive grammar, including K. Störl, 'Perspektiven einer onomasiologisch orientierten Grammatik' (153–72), and R. Kailuwait, 'Zur einzelsprachlichen Realisierung universeller semantischer Rollen' (131–51), musing on whether the linking algorithm of Role- and Reference-Grammar would be useful in modelling interlanguage. Another onomasiological project, the *Dictionnaire étymologique et cognitif des langues romanes*, is somewhat disingenuously advertised by P. Gévaudan, P. Koch, and A. Neu, 'Hundert Jahre nach Zauner', *RF*, 115:1–27, who claim that Z.'s pioneering pan-Romance study of the names of body parts remains valid but needs updating within a historico-cognitive framework. A. Thibault and M.-D. Glessgen, 'El tratamiento lexicográfico de los galicismos del español', *RLiR*, 67:1–53, complaining that there is no comprehensive account or even agreed set of criteria for identifying loans or their degree of integration, announce the solution: their own *Diccionario de Galicismos*!

Onomastic typology can solve difficult etymologies, claims W. B. Lockwood, 'On the origin of Lat. *hirundo* and Gr. *χελιδών*', *Glotta*, 77, 2001[2003]: 217–18; across many cultures, swallows are named after their swift flight or their forked tails, and the close parallel between the two morphologically odd forms HIRUNDO and HARUNDO, 'reed, cleft stick' cannot be coincidental, though both may originate from a common shape *HERUNDO. M. Alinei, 'Streghe come animali, animali como streghe', *Allières Vol.*, 327–35, proposes a new etymology for *brujo / bruja* 'witch' and its Ibero-Romance congeners based on *bruco* 'caterpillar, grub' < Med. Lat. BRŪC(H)US / BRŪC(H)ULUS < Italo-Gk. βροῦκος, since larvae were widely reputed to have medicinal or toxic properties. J. Grzega, 'Quelques remarques sur le vieux problème des noms du coq en Gascogne', *RLiR*, 67: 223–30, essentially backs Gilliéron against Wartburg's mild reservations and H. Polge's strong objections: GATTU is pan-Romance, has a large derivational family and is much more likely to survive in a scrap with GALLU, which has rivals in Gascony and lacks family support; PHASĀNU and VICĀRIU do have plausible semantic motivation to take over, but Gilliéron fails to prove the inevitability of replacement after homonymic clash — a case of the chickens coming home to roost.

Also according to J. Grzega, 'Zur Geschichte von fr. *trouver* und seinen Verwandten', *ZRP*, 119: 222–31, TŬRBĀRE is the right etymon, as Baist and Schuchardt proposed a century ago; its metathesis is no problem, nor the intervocalic devoicing in Provençal, but G.'s attractive solution to the previously intractable semantics lies in hunting terminology, with VL **torbár* 'confuse' also meaning 'start, startle (of game)', thence Gallo-Rom. **trǫβár* 'ferret out, sniff out', and later 'find', in a near parallel to Ibero-Rom. *aflar* > *hallar*. Drawing on the European linguistic atlas, W. Viereck and M. Goldammer, '*Ouvrier*, *Arbeiter*, *workman*, *rabočij*, *obrero*, *operaio*', *Winter Vol.*, 405–17, trace a number of etyma including OPERĀRIU, which specialized as a 'church worker, parish clerk' before widening out again, but by far the commonest semantic association linked 'work' with 'pain, labour, torture'; like Rom./Mold. *muncitor*, related to the Slavic *мука* 'torture', *travailleur* < *travailler* < *TRIPALIĀRE (< TREPĀLIUM 'instrument of torture') kept its association with torture until the 17th c., the improved social status of work being really quite recent.

Seeking to explain a realignment in -I- stems that started in archaic Latin but seemed to stall, J.-P. Brachet, 'Normalisations morphophonologiques dans la flexion des adjectifs latins et dans leurs dérivés', *Latomus*, 62:261–74, proposes that the new nominal suffix -ITIA was favoured by the analogical pattern -INTER/-NTIA : -ITER/-ITIA. A. Harrison and W. J. Ashby, 'Remodelling the house', *FMLS*, 39:386–99, draw on grammaticalization theory to trace the unidirectional development of CASĀ into Fr. *chez*. J. Timmermann, 'La verbalisation des adjectifs de couleur en français, espagnol et italien', *VR*, 61:1–31, offers grids that reveal numerous derivational possibilities but highly erratic uptake; the only generalization seems to be that natural colour processes can be verbalized (*elle a blanchi*, *rougi*) but 'unnatural' or induced colours remain unpredictable (*il a blanchi la maison*, **rougi la paroi*). The third volume of *Gender Across Languages*, ed. Marlis Hellinger and Hadumod Bussmann, Amsterdam, Benjamins, xiv + 390 pp. (see *YWMLS*, 64:13–14) completes coverage of the Romance standards with E. Schafroth, 'Gender in French' (87–117), on structures and derivational patterns, and E. Burr, 'Gender and language politics in France' (119–39), amply demonstrating that intervention is no more systematic than native intuition.

10. Sociolinguistics and Dialectology

The second instalment of *Atlas linguistique roman*, ed. Michel Contini and 15 named collaborators, Grenoble, Centre de Dialectologie — Rome, Istituto Poligrafo e Zecca dello Stato, 2002, has appeared as a folio of 20 maps, accompanied by extensive commentaries (as in vol. 1, which appeared in 1996). All of vol. 2 is devoted to names of insects and small animals; while the maps are beautifully clear, using symbols to indicate the distribution of cognates and partial cognates, readings are not available for every census point, and one must wonder who will use this elegant lexical and derivational data, when so far only one map in vol. 1 (the outcomes of L + yod, attributed to M. Contini) allows phonological isoglosses to be drawn.

Lengas, 54, is devoted to linguistic conflict in Romance, with special attention to Occitanie, Corsica, and Romania, and prefaced by a helpful overview, 'Le concept du "conflit linguistique" aujourd'hui. Essai d'une mise à jour' (7–22), by G. Kremnitz, who also contributes a 30-year perspective on his doctoral work, 'Martinique: dreißig Jahre soziolinguistischer Entwicklung', *Fest. Paufler*, 339–45, noting that political changes and improved schooling have raised community competence in French without as yet undermining Creole, but that public debate is now urgently needed on its future status as a potential regional lingua franca. Taking Catalonia as a case study, E. Querol, 'A new model for the evaluation of language planning', *Sociolinguistica*, 16, 2002:129–42, shows how the combination of three variables usually treated separately, attitude, motivation, and identity, together predict language choice to a high level of accuracy. A project to foster multilingual reading competence in Romance through interlingual transfer has begun publishing its theoretical bases and practical learning materials: **EuroComRom. Historische Grundlagen der romanischen Interkomprehension*, ed. Horst G. Klein and Christina Reissner, Aachen, Shaker, 2002, 206 pp., and related works are extensively and quite sympathetically evaluated by A. Gather, *RF*, 115:498–507.

American Romance contacts through bilingualism and language intertwining are well documented throughout *Fest. Paufler*, including: B. Bagola, 'Deux réalités linguistiques: le français et l'italien à Montréal' (61–72), K. Störl, 'Die Sprachkontakte des Französischen in der Sprachgeschichte Louisianas' (145–65), I. Martínez Gordo, 'Rebeldía lingüística ante la marginalidad. El criollo haitiano en Cuba' (333–37), C. Prieto, 'Le français et le créole en Guadeloupe' (347–63), C. Pérez-Gauli, 'El lunfardo' (555–70), A. Dieckmann, 'Le fragnol. Französisch-spanischer Sprachkontakt in Argentinien' (571–78), and E. Giacomazzi, 'Il "cocoliche": un'espressione del contatto tra l'italiano et lo spagnolo in Argentina' (579–91). Numerous subtle convergences in morphosyntax are documented (and others in phonology suspected) by S. Barme, 'Galicisch-brasilianisch-lateinamerikanisches spanisch', *ZRP*, 119:578–96, whose companion piece, 'Zum (ibero-) romanischen Ursprung einiger (morpho-) syntaktischer Strukturen des Papiamentu und des español caribeño', *ib.*, 232–55, seeks to rehabilitate superstrate explanations for creolization, but this time his detailed list of features is less compelling since many of them represent quasi universals that can certainly be found in non-Romance creoles. In a sober assessment of 'Stratum and shadow', Andersen, *Language Contacts*, 11–44, B. Mees examines the rather ineffectual use made of sprachbunds and adstrate theories in western Indo-European, taking alleged Gaulish influence on Gallo-Romance as a case study; perhaps, he concludes, they should be the explanations of last resort. Similarly, comparing the posited influence on the elaboration of Romance of 'Das langobardische und das fränkische Superstat', *FLinHist*, 24:71–92, F. Jodl remains unconvinced that Langobardish could have had any appreciable effect on north Italian Latin.

II. FRENCH STUDIES*

LANGUAGE

By Glanville Price,
University of Wales Aberystwyth

1. General and Bibliographical

We open this survey with an important new volume, *Le Grand Livre de la langue française*, ed. Marina Yaguello, Seuil, 499 pp., which is aimed at 'un large public à travers l'espace francophone' but which is none the less scholarly for that, being as it is the work of a team of renowned specialists: C. Marchello-Nizia, 'Le français et l'histoire' (11–90), covers external history (accompanied by *textes commentés*), a (necessarily selective) treatment of historical grammar, and pronunciation; had F. Gadet, 'La variation: le français dans l'espace social, régional et international' (91–152), devoted rather less space to such topics as creoles and areas of *la francophonie* where French is a second language, she could have expanded to advantage her coverage (good, so far as it goes) of social and regional variation (which, even better, could have been accorded separate chapters) in the main French-speaking areas of Europe and North America; M. Yaguello, 'La grammaire' (153–258), achieves a considerable *tour de force* 'en s'appuyant sur l'interface entre syntaxe, sémantique et pragmatique'; B. Tranel, 'Les sons du français' (259–315), is comprehensive but not always as well planned or as illuminating as one would wish; C. Blanche-Benveniste, 'La langue parlée' (317–44) and 'L'orthographe' (345–89), can both be recommended but one regrets that the former does not offer a fuller treatment; J.-P. Colin, 'Le lexique' (391–456), covers a good deal of ground interestingly but lacks the space to delve deeply enough into some aspects; J. Pruvost, 'Les dictionnaires: histoire et méthode' (456–89), is, as one would expect, authoritative; it is not the author's fault that É. Genouvrier, 'Enseigner la langue française maternelle' (491–541), strikes this reviewer at least as being somewhat out of place in this volume — the 50 pages allocated to it might better have been distributed among other chapters.

Structures linguistiques et interactionnelles dans le français parlé, ed. Anita Berit Hansen and Maj-Britt Mosegaard Hansen (*Etudes Romanes*, 54), Copenhagen, Museum Tusculanum, 200 pp., publishes papers given at an international colloquium at the University of Copenhagen in

* The place of publication of books is Paris unless otherwise stated.

June 2001, the aim of which was to 'discuter dans quelle mesure il serait possible d'intégrer différentes approches théoriques et méthodologiques afin d'aboutir à une description plus riche de la langue parlée'; the contributions include (in addition to two dealing with the French of non-native speakers): V. Traverso, 'Aspects de la négociation dans un polylogue' (11–30); L. Mondada, 'La construction du savoir dans les pratiques scientifiques d'équipes de recherche: analyse de trajectoires d'objets de discours et de savoir' (31–67); P. Touati, 'Approche à une modélisation de la prosodie transphrastique du français parlé' (69–88); A. B. Hansen and M.-B. Mosegaard Hansen, 'Le [ə] prépausal et l'interaction' (89–109), on a recent innovation in Parisian French, as in *Bonjour-ə! Ce soir-ə?*, and including useful bibliographical references to discussion elsewhere, from 1987 onwards, of the phenomenon; and A. Coveney, 'Le redoublement du sujet en français parlé: une approche variationniste' (111–43), on another feature that has attracted increasing interest in the last 30 years or so. Yves Cortez, **Le Français qu'on parle: son vocabulaire, sa grammaire, ses origines*, L'Harmattan, 2002, 209 pp. Volker Fuchs and Serge Melenc, **Linguistique française: français langue étrangère: la communication en français*, Frankfurt, Lang, 220 pp.

CILPR 23 includes a number of items that fall under different headings of this survey but which, for convenience, are grouped together here: Y. C. Morin, 'Syncope, apocope, diphtongaison et palatalisation en galloroman: prolèmes de chronologie relative' (I, 113–691); L. Hétu, 'L'évolution du *ó* accentué dans les dialectes du Nord de la France' (I, 209–19); R. Sampson, 'L'*i* nasal: une voyelle éphémère en français' (I, 295–300); P. de Carvalho, 'Héritage et innovation: de la double morphologie du verbe "d'existence" en ancien français au passé ("imparfait") et au futur' (I, 329–42); J. R. Klein, 'Troncation et structures morphosémantiques "aléatoires"' (I, 371–76); D. Apothéloz and F. Zay, 'Syllepses syntagmatiques dans l'improvisation orale' (II.1, 47–59); T. Arnavielle, 'La forme en *-ant* et les limites de la prédication' (II.1, 61–67); C. Buridant, 'L'interjection en français: esquisse d'une étude diachronique. Le cas de *hélas*' (II.1, 169–84); B. Combettes, 'Grammaticalisation et marqueurs de topicalisation en français' (II.1, 249–55); G. Dostie and R. Landheer, 'Quelques observations sur trois classifieurs français: *espèce*, *genre* et *sorte*' (II.1, 291–301); I. Evrard, 'La diathèse en français: un essai de synthèse' (II.1, 303–16); D. Gaatone, 'Syntaxe, lexique et sémantique: le cas des prépositions "vides"' (II.1, 359–65); A. M. Knutsen, 'La série verbale en français populaire d'Abidjan' (II.1, 485–90); J.-M. Messiaen, 'Naissance du participe présent (1500–1670): incidences et description' (II.2, 65–88); M. Nowakowska, 'L'adjectif de relation en contexte contrastif' (II.2, 133–45); M. Pierrard, 'Les emplois prépositionnels de *comme*: de la prédication à la quantification' (II.2, 187–88); K. Ploog, 'La restructuration de la diathèse en français abidjanais: l'exemple des auxiliaires verbaux' (II.2, 199–208); L. Pop, '*Eh bien* c'est la fin d'un parcours' (II.2, 217–31); M. E. Roitman, 'Configuration polyphonique et stratégie rhétorique. Étude sur l'emploi de la négation *ne* . . . *pas* dans des éditoriaux du *Figaro*, de *Libération* et du *Monde*' (II.2, 271–83); C. Schapira, 'Qui est *on*?' (II.2, 363–71); A. Sierra Soriano, 'Emploi et traduction de "tiens"' (II.2, 387–402); M. Ţenchea, 'Prépositions de temps et négation' (II.2, 451–63); D. Van Raemdonck, 'COI: Complément Objectivement Inutile' (II.2, 473–86); H. Abé, 'A propos de la polysémie de la locution *plus ou moins*' (III, 3–10); O. Bertrand, 'Les néologismes religieux dans la traduction de *La Cité de Dieu* par Raoul de Presles ou comment christianiser le lexique latin' (III, 43–47); R. Hänchen, 'L'évolution du langage du marketing en France' (III, 217–25); P. Kunstmann, 'Base lemmatisée d'ancien français: étapes et produits dérivés' (III, 267–70); O. Ozolina, 'Corrélation sémantique des doublets étymologiques dans la langue française du XIVe au XXe siècle' (III, 37–66); J. Schön, 'Le "parler familier", un modèle français' (III, 437–40); G. Sokolova, 'Aspect sémantique d'helvétismes phraséologiques de la langue française' (III, 469–72); M. Tabatchnik, 'Racines psychomécaniques de la polysémie lexicale: recherches d'une méthode' (III, 473–78); M.-G. Boutier, 'Verbes centraux du dispositif des chartes médiévales: essai d'analyse' (IV, 39–51); L. Löfstedt, 'La grammaire de la traduction en afr. du Décret de Gratien' (IV, 161–69); F. Skutta, 'Une grammaire de la discontinuité' (IV, 387–95); M. Willems, 'Les binômes synonymiques au XIVe et au XVIe s.' (IV, 415–29); A. Boone and P. Hadermann, 'La subordination dans les grammaires françaises d'aujourd'hui' (V, 135–43); L. Dagenais, 'La prolifération de la marque d'usage FAMILIER au XVIIIe siècle (Académie 1718, 1740, 1762 et 1798)' (V, 163–68); and R. Martin, 'L'historiographie du français' (V, 375–82).

2. History of Grammar and of Linguistic Theory

John Palsgrave, *L'Éclaircissement de la langue française (1530)*, ed. and trans. Susan Baddeley (Textes de la Renaissance, 69), Champion, 775 pp., consists of a photographic reproduction of the original edition with an introduction, bibliography, an annotated French translation, and a 60-page 'Index des formes graphiques françaises', listing all the forms quoted by Palsgrave. **Lyon et l'illustration de la langue française à la Renaissance*, ed. Gérard Defaux, Lyons, ENS, 541 pp.

CLF, 22 (2000[2001]), which has the subtitle 'Inférences directionelles, représentations mentales et subjectivité', includes A. Reboul, 'La représentation des éventualités dans la Théorie des Représentations Mentales' (13–55), J. Moeschler, 'Le Modèle des Inférences Directionelles' (57–100), C. Berthouzouz, 'Le Modèle Directionnel d'Interprétation du Discours' (101–46), L. de Saussure, 'Les "règles conceptuelles" en question' (147–64), B. Sthioul, 'Aspect et inférences' (165–87), I. Tahara, 'Le passé simple et la subjectivité' (189–218), N. Dobinda-Dejean, 'Référents évolutifs et représentations mentales: vers une ontologie des référents évolutifs' (210–39), A. Rocci, 'L'interprétation épistémique du futur en italien et en français: une analyse procédurale' (241–74), and one article each on Serb and Swahili. Under the umbrella title, 'La diachronie entre théoricité et empiricité', and the editorship of O. Soutet, *FM*, 71.2, associates somewhat uneasily a heterogeneous collection of articles, each of interest in its own right: S. Prévost, 'La grammaticalisation: unidirectionnalité et statut' (144–66), M. Sabanééva, 'Aux sources latines des articles français' (167–78), V. Montagne, 'L'expression hypotaxique et paratactique de la concession dans l'*Heptaméron* (1550) de Marguerite de Navarre' (179–210), C. Badiou-Monferran, 'Quelques aspects de la concurrence des graphies *ore*, *ores* et *or* au début du XVIIe siecle: distribution sémiologique et recomposition du système des connecteurs' (211–47), and F. Torterat, 'La *coordination* correspond-elle à une *jonction explicite*? Pour une relecture de la contribution de Gérald Antoine' (248–63).

A substantial part of *CFS*, 55, is devoted to a Round Table, 'La phonologie dans l'œuf', held in Geneva on 16 June 2001; of the eight papers included, only the following have some relevance to French: G. Iannàccaro, '"La rectification des données sensorielles": deux itinéraires phonologiques dans l'Italie entre les deux guerres' (35–48), which brings in the *Atlas linguistique de la France*; M. Mahmoudian, 'Apports de la phonologie; limites et perspectives' (49–62); and I. Vilkou-Pustovaïa, 'De quoi la *linguistique de la parole* traite-t-elle chez Saussure? Éléments pour une relecture du *C.L.G.* à partir des phonologie[s]' (115–36); other contributions to the volume of at least marginal (and sometimes greater) relevance to French are: C. Bota, 'La question de l'ordre dans les cours et les écrits saussuriens de linguistique générale. Essai de refonte géométrique' (139–67); I. Callus, '*Jalonnante* and *parathlipse*: encountering new terminology in Ferdinand de Saussure's researches into anagrams' (169–202); M.-C. Capt-Artaud, 'Phonologie et pertinence: les aléas de constant' (203–14); R. de Dardel, '*Quare* causal en protoroman' (215–27), mainly on Gallo-Romance; C. Marrone, '"Naturel" versus "historique" dans le *Cours de linguistique générale* de Saussure' (229–39); and

I. Callus, 'A chronological and annotated bibliography of works referring to Ferdinand de Saussure's anagram notebooks' (269–95).

K. Hunnius, 'Vulgärlatein und gesprochenes Französisch. Zur Entstehung des Konzepts des *français avancé*', *ZRP*, 119:510–19, is a discussion paper. P. Lauwers, 'Peut-on parler d'une conception "verbo-centrale" dans la grammaire française "traditionnelle"?', *ZFSL*, 113:113–30: yes.

3. History of the Language

Jean Forest, **L'Incroyable Aventure de la langue française: racontée depuis sa naissance à Rome jusqu'à sa greffe réussie en Amérique*, Montreal, Triptyque, 258 pp. *FMLS*, 39.4, is a special issue, 'Aspects of linguistic change', ed. R. Anthony Lodge, which publishes papers given at an AFLS conference at St Andrews in August 2002: C. Marchello-Nizia, 'Changes in the structure of grammatical systems: the evolution of French' (371–85), deals at some length with the 'upheaval' of the demonstrative system, the replacement of *moult* by *beaucoup* and *très*, and very briefly with a new distinction between indefinite pronouns and determiners (*chacun/chaque*, etc.) and with the separation between adverbs and prepositions; A. Harrison and W. J. Ashby discuss the development of *chez* from *casa* (386–99); L. Schøsler, 'Grammaticalisation of valency patterns? An investigation into valency patterns and support verb constructions, based on diachronic corpora' (400–13), is characteristically well documented and argued; S. Marnette, 'Indirect discourse in a diachronic and pangeneric corpus of French: forms and strategies' (414–26), has interesting insights, but her subject (covering as it does the whole of French from the 11th c. to newspapers and magazines of the year 2002, widely varying genres, and, for the modern period, both the written and the spoken language), is too vast to be tackled adequately within the scope of one short article; D. Trotter, 'Not as eccentric as it looks: Anglo-French and French French' (427–38), argues forcefully and persuasively for the incorporation of Anglo-Norman into the mainstream history of French (see also p. 48 below); R. Sampson, 'The loss of French prosthesis and the problem of Italianisms' (439–49), identifies factors that need to be taken into account in order to explain the presence or absence of prosthesis in late Middle and early Modern French; two other contributions are not French-based.

Maria Polinsky and Ezra Van Everbroeck, 'Development of gender classifications: modeling the historical change from Latin to French', *Language*, 79:356–91, attempt to explain the restriction of gender systems 'using the type of morphophonemic and frequency information that is accessible in acquisition and language contact' — thereby leaving out of account both the data provided by other Romance languages and other relevant factors.

The interest and significance of Harald Völker's thoroughly researched volume, *Skripta und Variation. Untersuchungen zur Negation und zur Substantivflexion in altfranzösischen Urkunden der Grafschaft Luxemburg (1237–1281)* (*ZRP*, Beiheft 305), xvi + 309 pp., extend far beyond the scope of the somewhat narrow geographical and chronological field suggested by the title; more's the pity that so many *romanistes* now read German only with difficulty, if at all. P. Brosman, Jr, discusses 'Intervocalic West Germanic *h* in Old French', *Romania*, 120, 2002: 483–504.

4. Texts

MoyFr, 51–53, 'Traduction, dérimation, compilation, la phraséologie', ed. Giuseppe Di Stefano and Rose M. Bidler, is a special issue publishing the proceedings of an October 2000 conference in Montreal. The majority of the contributions are chiefly of literary interest, but the following, though mainly dealing with specific texts, are at least *en marge de la linguistique*: M. Barsi, 'Quelques phrasèmes d'un "texte inédit" de la *Chronique de Pierre Belon du Mans, médecin*' (19–39); F. Duval, 'La connexion interphrastique dans deux traductions du *Romuleon* (XVe s.)' (211–47); A. M. Finoli, 'Locutions dans *Jehan d'Avennes*' (279–90); P. Kunstmann, 'Les formules de salutation dans les *Miracles de Notre Dame par personnages*: inventaire, analyse, valeur pragmatique' (373–86); A. Malmborg, 'Les mots savants dans deux textes de Jean de Meun' (459–67); M. Thiry-Stassin, 'Le vocabulaire en action: problèmes de vocabulaire dans les vies des prophètes Helyas, Helisee et Jonas (Namur, XVe siècle)' (559–69); C. Thiry, 'Néologismes et créations verbales dans la traduction par Jean Wauquelin des *Chroniques de Hainaut* de Jacques de Guise' (571–91); D. A. Trotter, 'Traduction ou texte authentique? Le problème des chartes' (593–611); and M. T. Zanola, 'Phrasèmes sémantiques et pragmatiques dans le lexique des sciences du XVe siècle: pour une typologie de la formation phraséologique' (641–50). A. Hanham, 'The copycat scriveners of Bruges', *NZJFS*, 24: 5–18, discusses four 14th-15th-c. conversation manuals.

The series 'Textes de la Renaissance' has recently included editions of four texts of considerable linguistic interest: Joachim Périon, **Dialogues: de l'origine du français et de sa parenté avec le grec*, ed. Geneviève Demerson and Alberte Jacquetin, Champion, 832 pp. (the text is in Latin); Joachim du Bellay, **La Deffence et illustration de la langue françoyse*, ed. Oliver Millet, Champion, 464 pp.; Robert Estienne, **Traicté de la grammaire françoise*, ed. Colette Demaizière, Champion, 202 pp.; and

Jean Pillot, **Institution de la langue française — Gallicae linguae institutio, 1561*, ed. Bernard Colombat, Champion, 768 pp.

V. Mecking, 'A propos du vocabulaire du *Livre de raison* (1664–1684) de Jean-Gaspard de Grasse, chanoine de Cavaillon', *RLiR*, 67:231–60, identifies some 30 *premières attestations* and numbers of Italianisms, regionalisms, neologisms, legal technical terms, etc.

5. Phonetics, Phonology, Prosody

H. Walter, 'La dynamique phonologique peut-elle dépendre de la dynamique lexicale?', *Linguistique*, 38.2, 2002:133–37, notices a decline in the use of anglicisms in *-ing* and wonders whether this could lead to the eventual disappearance of the nasal velar phoneme, a status that she had been prepared to confer on it 20 years ago (see *YWMLS*, 45:23). L. Condrea, 'Parlons encore de ce *e* caduc qui ne veut pas tomber', *ib.*, 39.1:157–59, is a follow-up to a 1990 article by H. Walter (see *YWMLS*, 52:33). C. L. Smith, 'Vowel devoicing in contemporary French', *JFLS*, 13:177–94, concludes, from a study based on only six speakers, that 'devoicing only occurs in sentence-final vowels, but in more contexts than expected'. C. Féry discusses 'Markedness, faithfulness, vowel quality and syllable structure in French', *ib.*, 247–80.

CLF, 23, 2001, subtitled 'Prosodie: carrefour entre syntaxe, analyse du discours, psychologie des émotions et interprétation simultanée' ('prosodie' being defined 'au sens le plus large d'ensemble des variations de hauteur, d'intensité, de durée, de timbre affectant la parole'), includes T. Bänziger et al., 'Prosodie de l'émotion: étude de l'encodage et du décodage' (11–37), O. Bagou, 'Validation perceptive et réalisations acoustiques de l'implication emphatique dans la narration orale spontanée' (39–59), A. C. Simon, 'Le rôle de la prosodie dans le repérage des unités textuelles minimales' (99–125), A. Grobet, 'Note sur le marquage prosodique de l'organisation informationnelle et topicale' (127–42), A. Grobet and A. C. Simon, 'Différents critères de définition des unités prosodiques maximales' (143–63), A. Grobet and A. Auchlin, '*A l'attaque!* vers une typologie des prises d'élan dans le discours' (165–87), and three papers falling outside the scope of *YWMLS*. Anne Lacheret-Dujour, **La Prosodie des circonstants en français parlé*, Leuven–Paris, Peeters, xii + 210 pp.

6. Orthography

S. Baddeley and L. Biedermann-Pasques, 'Histoire des systèmes graphiques du français (IXe–XVe siècle): des traditions graphiques aux innovations du vernaculaire', *Linguistique*, 39.1:3–34, is an original piece of work, based on the *Eulalie*, the *Passion du Christ*, the *Alexis*, and five later texts.

7. Grammar

Old and Middle French

L. Löfstedt, 'A propos de la traduction en ancien français du participe et du gerundium latins', *NMit*, 104: 211–35, based on her edition of the Old French translation of Gratian's *Decretum*, is presented as an 'étude préliminaire'. *Évolution et variation en français préclassique: études de syntaxe*, ed. Bernard Combettes, Champion, 324 pp., includes G. Siouffi, 'Le regard des grammairiens' (19–67), commenting on a score of 16th-c. and 17th-c. grammarians, and five studies (based, in the interests of homogeneity, on a corpus of eight *récits de voyage* dating from 1558 to 1636) on clearly defined, but not overly restricted, features: J.-P. Seguin, 'Enchaînement et usage du point' (69–137); J. Baudry, 'Les syntagmes nominaux coordonnés par "et"' (139–69); B. Combettes, 'Variation dans la structure du syntagme verbal' (171–210); M. Glatigny, 'Les relatifs' (211–70); and I. Landy-Houillon, 'Les constructions détachées' (271–313). N. Sarre, 'Diachronie des pronoms indéfinis à base nominale du moyen français au français classique', *RLiR*, 67: 117–36, deals with *âme*, *homme*, *personne*, *chose*, and *rien*. A. Rodríguez Somolinos discusses '*Ainz* et *mais* en ancien français', *Romania*, 120, 2002: 505–41.

Modern French

Apart from a bibliography of the dedicatee's publications and four brief articles on her life and work, the great majority of the contributions to *La Syntaxe raisonnée. Mélanges de linguistique générale et française offerts à Annie Boone à l'occasion de son 60e anniversaire*, ed. Pascale Hadermann, Ann Van Slijcke, and Michel Berré (Champs linguistiques), Brussels, de Boeck Duculot, 378 pp., have to do with modern French syntax: C. Blanche-Benveniste, 'Le double jeu du pronom *on*' (43–56); D. Gaatone, 'La nature plurielle du subjonctif français' (57–78); P. Vachon-L'Heureux, 'Le mot fait sur mesure ou les ressources étonnantes de la mécanique mentale seconde' (79–92), on 'mots de discours' either well-established, e.g. *un je-ne-sais-quoi*, or invented ad hoc, e.g. *l'école chaise-pupitre-papier-crayons*; D. Willems, 'Polyvalance syntaxique et ambiguïté discursive' (93–101), prompted by what W. considers an 'emploi insolite' of the verb *se rendre* in 'elle s'est rendue volontairement à la justice internationale'; M. Herslund, 'Article et pronom. Réflexions sur le syntagme nominal' (105–16); G. Kleiber and M. Riegel, 'Les pronoms évoluent-ils avec les référents?' (117–49) — apparently they do; D. Leeman, '*Me* et *moi* dans la complémentation verbale' (151–66); R. Van Deyck, 'Le "pronom personnel" dans la tradition grammaticale' (167–81); S. Feigenbaum, 'L'antonyme en extension: le cas de *sans*' (185–94); J. Garrido, 'La pertinence à l'inverse: connexion et discours' (195–202); J.-M. Léard and M. Pierrard, 'L'analyse de *comme*: le centre et la périphérie' (203–34); L. Melis, 'Le groupe prépositif comme déterminant du nom' (235–50); S. Rémi-Giraud, 'A propos du circonstant de phrase: le cas exemplaire du complément de lieu' (251–65); O. Halmøy, 'Le gérondif: une originalité du français?' (269–79); and D. O'Kelly and A. Joly, 'Du genre à l'individu dans la détermination du nom (étude comparée de l'anglais, de l'irlandais et du français)' (281–96); the remaining few contributions fall outside the scope of *YWMLS*.

O. Anokhina, 'Différences observées pour les définitions des noms concrets et les noms abstraits, ou pourquoi "de l'amour à la haine il n'y a qu'un pas"', *IG*, 97:41–45, derives from her Paris doctoral thesis, 'Étude semantique du nom abstrait en français', 2000.

A. Coveney (who has a gift for witty titles), '"Anything *you* can do, *tu* can do better": *tu* and *vous* as substitutes for *on* in French', *JSoc*, 7:164–91, concludes that, as in Quebec, there is a preference in European French (or at least in his corpus of material from the *département* of the Somme) for *tu* (more so than *vous*) rather than *on* as an indefinite pronoun, a point he also picks up in '"All for *on* and *on* for all": *on* and its competitors in spoken French', *Francophonie*, 27:8–12. M. Silberztein, 'Finite-State description of the French determiner system', *JFLS*, 13:221–46, is for those who understand the statement in the abstract that the proposed grammar 'is available in the form of a library of 150 Finite-State graphs and is compiled into a Minimal Deterministic Finite-State Transducer of over 5,000 states and 113,000 transitions'.

Three well thought out articles highlight the interest of different aspects of anaphora: A. Theissen, 'Article partitif et lecture associative: une association difficile', *TrL*, 46:7–25, which recognizes that 'l'anaphore associative est une problématique particulièrement riche et complexe', and S. Whittaker's two articles, 'Essai de description de l'expression anaphorique: *le N en question*', *ib.*, 27–48, and 'Étude contrastive des expressions *Ledit N* et *Le N en question*', *RLiR*, 67:445–62.

C. Rouget, 'Impersonnel, quasi-impersonnel et pseudo-impersonnel en français parlé', *RevR*, 38:151–62, proposes a new classification of *il est* and *c'est* + complement + *que*-clause or *de* + infinitive. L. Palm, 'La querelle de *ces bijoux* de Georges Marchais. Sur la fonction cataphorique du déterminant en français', *RevR*, 38:3–28, deals principally with the construction in which 'l'expression indexicale *Ce N* forme avec une proposition relative subséquente un SN générique'.

As the title of the volume suggests, the contributions to *Temps et aspect: de la grammaire au lexique*, ed. Véronique Lagae, Anne Carlier, and Céline Benninger (*Cahiers Chronos*, 10), Amsterdam–NY, Rodopi, 2002, vii + 215 pp., deal with a variety of parts of speech, but for convenience they are itemized here; with some exceptions, they relate specifically, and in most cases solely, to French: D. Amiot, '*Re-*, préfixe aspectuel?' (1–20), D. Battistelli and J.-P. Desclés, 'Modalités d'action et inférences' (21–40), A. Carlier, 'Les propriétés aspectuelles du passif' (41–63), N. Flaux, 'Les noms d'idéalités concrètes et le temps' (65–78), L. José, 'Les compléments de localisation temporelle sans préposition: le cas des noms d'unités' (119–31), V. Lagae, 'Le passif pronominal: une forme complémentaire du passif périphrastique?' (133–49), K. Paykin, 'Événements, états et substances: un essai météorologique' (183–99, contrasting French with English and Russian), and H. de Penanros, '*Lors de, au moment de* ou *à l'occasion de*?' (201–15). *Modes de repérages temporels*, ed. Sylvie Mellet and Marcel Vuillaume (*Cahiers Chronos*, 11), Amsterdam–NY, Rodopi, ii + 249 pp., includes (in addition to four papers falling outside the scope of *YWMLS*) A.-M. Bertonneau and G. Kleiber, 'Un imparfait de plus . . . et le train déraillait' (1–24), Co Vet, 'Aspect et décomposition lexicale' (25–36), M. Bras, A. Le Draoulec, and L. Vieu, 'Connecteurs et temps verbaux dans l'interprétation du discours' (71–97), J. Bres, 'Non, le passé simple ne contient pas l'instruction [+ progression]' (99–112), C. Vetters, 'L'aspect global: un effet secondaire d'un contenu procédural?' (113–31), P. Laurendeau, 'Concomitance temporelle, quantification des procès et causalité inférée en co-énonciation parlée' (133–49), P. Meyer, 'Le temps dessiné', on the representation of time in *bandes dessinées* (151–72), D. Amiot, 'De l'antériorité à la postériorité: mode de repérage temporal et type de préfixes' (173–89), L. José, 'Noms temporels et adjectifs déictiques. Le problème de l'opposition *l'an dernier* vs **l'instant dernier*' (211–22), and H. Kronning, 'Auxiliarité, énonciation et rhématicité' (231–40).

R. Ogden and J. Kelly, '[J. C.] Carnochan, [N. C.] Scott and [E. M.] Whitley's "Prosodic analysis of French irregular verbs"', *TPS*, 101–57–80, describe the history of an unpublished paper, dating from 1954, by three of J. R. Firth's co-workers, and explain the Firthian phonological analysis it contains. K. Taji, 'A propos du futur antérieur', *IG*, 97:37–41, distinguishes between temporal and non-temporal uses. M. Labelle discusses 'The selectional restrictions of Fr. tenses', *CanJL*, 47, 2002:47–66. A. Rabatel, 'Les verbes de perception en contexte d'effacement énonciatif: du point de vue *représenté* aux discours *représentés*', *TrL*, 46:49–88, seeks to open a new chapter 'dans l'histoire déjà fort riche des rapports entre le discours rapporté et les théories de l'énonciation'. C. Leclère, 'Organization of the lexicon-grammar of Fr. verbs', *LInv*, 25:29–48, is based on the lexicon-grammar developed at the Laboratoire d'Automatique Documentaire et Linguistique.

N. Schapansky, 'The speakers of negation in French: contrariety versus contradiction', *Lingua*, 112, 2002:793–826, claims that we must recognize 'two levels, parataxis and hypotaxis' and 'two types of negation at the syntactic level, contrary negation realized by *ne* and contradictory negation realized by *ne pas*'. In a well-documented article that includes a survey of earlier research into the topic, F. Martineau and R. Mougeon, 'A sociolinguistic study of the origins of *ne* deletion in European and Quebec French', *Language*, 79:118–52, argue that *ne* deletion was infrequent before the 19th c., that it spread more rapidly in Quebec French than in European French, and that the transformation of subject pronouns into affixes may have been a contributory factor in the rise of *ne* deletion, at least in some varieties of French.

S. Jollin-Bertocchi, 'La polyvalence de l'adverbe *maintenant*', *IG*, 97:26–30, is illustrated only from the works of Le Clézio.

Ludo Melis, **La Préposition en français*, Gap, Ophrys, 150 pp. M. Aurnagne and D. Stosic, 'La préposition *par* et l'expression du déplacement', *CLe*, 81:113–39, leads to 'une caractérisation sémantique et cognitive de la notion de "trajet"'. L. José, '*Marcher trois heures* et *marcher pendant trois heures*: peut-on marcher sans ellipse?', *BSLP*, 96, 2001:207–26, seeks to define the semantic and syntactic difference between the two constructions.

CPr, 37, 2001, 'Topicalisation et partition', includes: A. Theissen, 'Petite incursion dans la jungle topicale' (27–44); P. Cappeau and J. Deulofeu, 'Partition et topicalisation; *il y en a* "stabilisateur" de sujets et de topiques indéfinis' (45–82); D. Crevenat-Werner, '*Cinq Belges dont un Wallon*: un *dont* déviant ou non?' (83–102); B. Combettes and S. Prévost, 'Évolution des marqueurs de topicalisation' (103–24); and J.-M. Debaisieux, 'Contraintes syntaxiques et discursives des emplois de *quant à* et *en ce qui concerne*' (125–46). M. Rouquier discusses 'Les constructions liées: *c'est une saine préoccupation que l'horticulture*', *BSLP*, 97, 2002:153–86.

Y. Grinshpun discusses 'Interjections, genres de discours et régime rhétorique', *IG*, 97:31–36, with particular (indeed, sole) reference to *quoi!* K. Rys, 'L'exclamation de degré et l'absence d'ancrage', *TrL*, 46:89–115, concentrates on 'les exclamatives de degré qui sont formellement proches des assertives'.

IG, 98, devoted to the topic 'Phrase et énoncé' and covering both structural analysis and terminology, includes: J. Léon, 'Proposition, phrase, énoncé dans la grammaire: parcours historique' (5–16); G. Kleiber, 'Faut-il dire *adieu* à la phrase?' (17–22); J. Gardes Tamine, 'Phrase, proposition, énoncé, etc. Pour une nouvelle terminologie' (23–27); B. Bosredon and I. Tamba, 'Aux marges de la phrase écrite: analyse d'unités typographiques autonomes' (28–38); and M.-D. Gineste, 'De la phrase à la proposition sémantique. Un point de vue de la psychologie cognitive du langage' (48–51).

8. Lexicography

The reissue of Fréderic Godefroy, *Lexique de l'ancien français*, ed. J. Bonnard and A. Salmon, with a preface by Jean Dufournet, Champion, 636 pp., is to be welcomed. Kurt Baldinger, *Etymologien*, vol. 3 (*ZRP*, 315), covers the *FEW*, vols 21–23, and includes a full 'Register' (divided into 'Wortregister', 'Etymaregister', and 'Autorenregister') to all three volumes (pp. 499–771). A. Francoeur, 'Les discours de présentation du *Dictionnaire de l'Académie française*', *CLe*, 83:57–84, covers all editions from 1694 onwards. Antoine Furetière, **Les Couleurs*, ed. Cécile Wajsbrot, Caheilhan, Zulma, 139 pp., is a selection of articles from F.'s *Dictionnaire universel* (1690). Philibert Joseph Le Roux, **Dictionnaire comique, satyrique, critique, burlesque, libre et proverbial, 1718–1786*, ed. Monica Barsi, Champion, 912 pp. F. Gaudin, 'Le monde perdu des dictionnaires de Maurice Lachâtre (1): le *Dictionnaire universel* (1852–1856)', *CLe*, 83:85–104, is to be followed by studies of M. L.'s later dictionaries.

K. Van den Eynde and P. Mertens, 'La valence: l'approche pronominale et son application au lexique verbal', *JFLS*, 13:63–104, describe the methodological framework of an on-going lexical database, PROTON, which is described as 'un dictionnaire de valence verbale'; judging by the specimen entry provided (that for the verb *dégager*), this will not be user-friendly. M. Mathieu-Colas, 'La représentation des verbes dans un dictionnaire électronique', *CLe*, 81:51–67, deals with general problems not with a specific dictionary.

Henri Bertaud du Chazaud, **Dictionnaire des synonymes et mots de sens voisin, édition 2003–2004*, Gallimard, 1853 pp. Marc Baratin and Mariane Baratin-Lorenzi, **Dictionnaire des synonymes*, Hachette, 631 pp. Michel Parmentier, **Dictionnaire français/anglais des comparaisons. English/French Dictionary of Similes*, Stanké, 2002, 213 pp. M.-C. L'Homme, 'Acquisition de liens conceptuels entre termes à partir de leur définition', *CLe*, 83:25–48, studies how hyperonymy, hyponymy, meronymy, and holonymy are expressed in some 2000 definitions in four French dictionaries of computing. M. Glatigny, 'L'article *Arabe* dans un certain nombre de dictionnaires français', *ib.*, 105–30, looks at 90 monolingual dictionaries from Nicot (1606) to the *Grand Robert.* M. E. Scullin, 'Les dictionnaires français: un lieu privilégié du sexisme?', *ib.*, 131–51, concludes that they are. B. Lamiroy et al., 'Les expressions verbales figées dans quatre variétés de français', *ib.*, 153–72, discusses a project designed to provide a dictionary of *expressions figées* in the French of Belgium, Quebec, France, and Switzerland.

W. Sarcher reviews 'Le vocabulaire français d'origine allemande dans les dictionnaires existants', *Linguistique*, 39.1 : 169–72.

9. Lexicology

U. Malizia, 'Un fichier de lexicographie musicale du Moyen Âge: essai de la lettre *A*', *QFLR*, 17, 2002[2003]: 95–116, illustrates, with lengthy (sometimes unnecessarily lengthy) examples from texts, a *fichier* he has prepared of medieval musical terms and that one would hope to see published (with briefer quotations) in its entirety. C. Féron, 'Polysémie et évolution sémantico-syntaxique: l'exemple des adverbes *sans faille* et *sans faute* (français médiéval et langue du XVIe siècle)', *Romania*, 121 : 461–500, shows that Nicot and Furetière wrongly equate the two idioms.

Gilbert Millet and Denis Labbé, *Les Mots du fantastique et du merveilleux*, Belin, 495 pp., is an impressive addition to the series 'Le français retrouvé' (see *YWMLS*, 64: 23–24 and 28); it is not so much a dictionary as an encyclopaedia of topics and concepts, ranging widely from the relatively general (e.g. *âge d'or*, *bande dessinée*, *érotisme*, *lévitation*, *magie*, *monstre*, *réincarnation*, *vengeance*) to the more specific (*arc-en-ciel*, *combustion spontanée*, *diable*, *lycanthrope*, *messe noire*, *pentacle*, *vaudou*) and the highly specialized (*Frankenstein*, *leprechaun*, *tarasque*, *triangle des Bermudes*); thematically and chronologically, it ranges from the Classical, the biblical, and the mythological to the medieval (e.g. *Graal*, *Nostradamus*, *Templiers*) to the modern and the ultra-modern (*détective*, *mesmérisme*, *télékinésie*, even *Harry Potter*), with a marked cinematographic interest; all in all, a book to be consulted and enjoyed. Marie Treps, *Les Mots voyageurs: petite histoire du français venu d'ailleurs*, Seuil, 368 pp., is both an enjoyable and an informative survey, geographical and historical, of some 2000 loan-words in French; six chapters or '*voyages*' take us successively to the Orient (here including also Greece and the Maghreb), the northern seas (i.e. the Netherlands and Scandinavia), northern and central Europe (German, Slavonic, and Hungarian words), '*au delà des Pyrénées et aux confins des cartes*' (an unsatisfactory umbrella term for Spanish,

Portuguese, Amerindian, African, and Asian words), Italy, and '*outre-Manche et outre-Atlantique*'; chapters are subdivided thematically; the narrative structure permits the bringing-in of semantically related words, many of them with dated first appearance and comments on the reasons for their adoption into French. Sophie Fournier, **Badaboum et autres onomatopées*, Bonneton, 160 pp. H. Walter, 'Les noms des mammifères: motivation et arbitraire', *Linguistique*, 39.2 : 47–60, deals with scientific names and their French equivalents. Agnès Pierron, **Dictionnaire de la langue du théâtre; mots et mœurs du théâtre*, Robert, 2002, xi + 608 pp. Albert Doillon, **Le Dico de l'argent*, Fayard, 425 pp. O. Anokhina, 'Sur le mécanisme de référence des noms abstraits', *CLe*, 81 : 39–49, is illustrated by French examples.

Apart from an introduction dealing in general terms with the history of 'language planning' (*en anglais dans le texte*) and a chapter of 'Réflexions préliminaires sur le purisme et l'interventionnisme', Michel Chansou, *L'Aménagement lexical en France pendant la période contemporaine (1950–1994): étude de sociolexicologie*, Champion, 213 pp., consists of an informative and indeed welcome chronological survey, beginning with 'Les initiations privées de 1950 à 1972' (in which Alain Guillermou, the *Comité d'étude des termes techniques français*, and Aurélien Sauvageot figure prominently); there follow chapters on 'La mise en place d'une politique de la langue (1966–1973)', the law of 31 December 1975, the periods 1981–1988 and 1988–1993, and the *loi Toubon* of 1994; a final chapter on 'Les conditions d'implantation dans l'usage de créations néologiques' takes as test cases the words *gazole* and *ingénierie*.

Pierre J.-L. Arnaud, **Les Composés timbre-poste*, Lyons U.P., 168 pp. C. Schnedecker, 'La question du nom propre répété dans la théorie dite du centrage et ses problèmes', *JFLS*, 13 : 105–34, may well have much of value to offer to those who have the interest and the doggedness to work their way through it, but it is unlikely to appeal to a wide readership.

F. Gobert, 'La denomination *étymologie populaire* ou l'utopie d'une terminologie non ambigüe', *CLe*, 81 : 5–37, is illustrated almost exclusively by French examples. J. Grzega, 'Zur Geschichte von fr. *trouver* und seinen Verwandten: Anmerkungen zu einem alten Problem', *ZRP*, 119 : 222–31, seeks to combine two previously proposed etymologies for *trouver*, arguing highly speculatively that the original etymon was TURBARE but that, in the course of its history, reflexes of the word were influenced by reflexes of *TROPARE. M. Kramer, '*Jarnac* et *bilboquet*. Deux curiosités lexicographiques vues à travers des attestations textuelles', *CLe*, 81 : 69–82, draws attention to dangers of misrepresentation. **L'Invention verbale en français contemporain*, ed. Jean Rousseau, Didier, 95 pp.

10. Onomastics

J.-P. Chambon, 'Sur une issue toponymique de AMNIS en Gaule chevelue et sa date (le premier nom de Martres-de-Veyre, Puy-de-Dôme)', ZRP, 119:571–77, argues that a form *AMNÓIALU bears witness to 'le latin apporté en Arverne durant la toute première phase de la romanisation'.

11. Dialects and Regional French

Michel de Certeau, Dominique Julia, and Jacques Revel, **Une politique de la langue: la Révolution française et les patois, l'enquête de Grégoire*, Gallimard, 2002, 472 pp.

The latest addition to Bonneton's 'Dictionnaires du français régional' (see *YWMLS* 62:47 and references thereat, and 63:42 and 43), Fernand Carton and Denise Poulet, *Le Parler du Nord Pas-de-Calais*, Bonneton, 125 pp., is a glossary (of upwards of 1000 entries) by two authoritative scholars, with definitions and, in most cases, examples and/or localization (the area is divided into nine sub-areas), and in some cases etymologies. The European Bureau for Lesser Used Languages is bringing out a series of informative and attractively produced booklets on languages within its remit, two of which fall within the scope of this survey: Michel Francard, *Langues d'oïl en Wallonie*, Brussels, EBLUL, 2001, 48 pp., defines 'wallon' and 'Wallonie' in both historical and linguistic terms (covering not merely Walloon in the strictest sense but also the Picard, Champenois, and Gaumois areas of Belgium); with the aid of a number of particularly useful maps, F. surveys linguistic research and Walloon literature (with extracts), and reviews the *vitalité actuelle* of the regional languages in question (their demography and their role in such fields as cultural life, education, the media, religion, and legislation, and, while acknowledging the threats they face, concludes that their decline is perhaps not as inevitable as is sometimes supposed; Jean-Jacques Chevrier and Michel Gautier, *Le Poitevin-saintongeais: langue d'oïl méridionale*, Brussels, EBLUL, 2002, 48 pp., includes an outline history of the region, a brief linguistic description (the principal phonetic and morphological features) using a *graphie normalisée*, surveys of the written and oral literary traditions, accounts of linguistic research and of movements seeking to defend the local language and culture, and two specimen texts (one prose, one verse, with translations); both volumes are also available in English. The new series 'Bibliothèque de linguistique romane' (see *YWMLS*, 64:31), continues with Yan Greub, **Les Mots régionaux dans les farces françaises*, Strasbourg, SLR, 416 pp. and a CD of maps.

J. Auger, 'Les pronoms clitiques sujets en picard: une analyse au confluent de la phonologie, de la morphologie et de la syntaxe', *JFLS*, 13:1–22, has both historical and descriptive dimensions and is to be followed up by further articles.

J.-P. Chambon, 'A propos du *Trésor étymologique* comtois de Colette Dondaine', *RLiR*, 67:499–532, annotates 348 entries in C.D.'s *Trésor étymologique des mots de la Franche-Comté* (see *YWMLS*, 64:31). Simone Fauvet, **Glossaire des patois de la Beauce et du Gâtinais*, Royer, 222 pp. Catherine Bougy, Stéphane Laîné, and Pierre Boissel, **A l'ouest d'oïl, des mots et des choses*, Caen U.P., 286 pp. Jean Lanher and Alain Litaize, **Le Parler de Lorraine: dictionnaire du français régional*, Bonneton, 2002, 159 pp. Jean Le Dû, **Du café vous aurez?: petits mots du français de Basse-Bretagne*, Crozon, Armeline, 240 pp. Charles Mourain de Sourdevalle, **Premier dictionnaire patois de la Vendée*, ed. Pierre Rézeau, La Roche-sur-Yon, Centre vendéen de recherches historiques, 352 pp.

12. Channel Islands French

Mari C. Jones, *Jèrriais: Jersey's Native Tongue*, Jersey, Le Don Balleine, 59 pp., seeks to provide an account of the Jèrriais dialect that will be accessible to the general reader. It both complements her earlier book, *Jersey Norman French* (see *YWMLS*, 63:44) (in particular, in including a survey of Jèrriais writers), and updates it in some respects. N. Spence, 'Parlers jersiais et parlers bas-normands', *RLiR*, 67:159–77, provides an informative survey of inherited common features and parallel developments, particularly in phonology but with reference also to morphology, syntax, and vocabulary.

13. Anglo-Norman

D. Trotter, 'L'anglo-normand: variété insulaire ou variété isolée?', *Médiévales*, 45:43–54, concludes that 'l'anglo-normand avait beau être insulaire, il n'était pas pour autant isolé' (see also p. 37 above).

14. French in North America

P. Martin, 'Le système vocalique du français du Québec. De l'acoustique à la phonologie', *Linguistique*, 38.2, 2002:71–88, has both descriptive and theoretical goals. J. Brown, 'Code-convergent borrowing in Louisiana French', *JSoc*, 7:3–23, argues that 'a richer understanding of lexical borrowing is revealed once the focus of analysis extends from the word to the contact of morphological systems'.

15. French in Africa

Edmond Biloa, **La Langue française au Cameroun: analyse linguistique et didactique*, Berne, Lang, xi + 342 pp. F. Ngom discusses 'The social status of Arabic, French, and English in the Senegalese speech community', *LVC*, 15:351–68. A. Stein discusses 'Lexikalische Kombinatorik im afrikanischen Französisch', *ZFSL*, 113:1–17.

16. Sociolinguistics

Françoise Gadet, **La Variation sociale en français contemporain*, Gap, Ophrys, 135 pp.

17. Discourse Analysis and Textual Analysis

CLF, 24, 2002, subtitled 'Nouveaux regards sur les mots du discours', includes C. Rossari, 'Les adverbes connecteurs: vers une identification de la classe et des sous-classes' (11–43), A. Beaulieu-Masson, 'Quels marqueurs pour parasiter le discours?' (45–71), L. Choueiri, 'Des limites d'une représentation reichenbachienne de la temporalité' (73–107), O. Inkova-Manzotti, 'Les connecteurs accommodants: le cas de *autrement*' (109–41), A. Razgouliaeva, 'Combinaison des connecteurs *mais enfin*' (143–68), M. Carel, ' "Occupe-toi d'Amélie": emploi contrastif de *mais* et illustration' (169–205), O. Ducrot, 'Quand *peu* et *un peu* semblent coorientés: *peu après* et *un peu après*' (207–29), J. Moeschler, 'Connecteurs, encodage conceptuel et encodage procédural' (265–92), and L. de Saussure and B. Sthioul, 'Interprétations cumulative et distributive du connecteur *et*: temps, argumentation, séquencement' (293–314), together with one paper each on German and Spanish.

S. Whittaker, 'Pour une description textuelle et discursive de l'expression anaphorique *ledit N*', *JFLS*, 13:159–76, contrasts the practice in legislative, journalistic, and literary texts.

18. Contrastive Studies

Essais sur la grammaire comparée du français et de l'anglais, ed. Philip Miller and Anne Zribi-Hertz, Vincennes U.P., 265 pp., includes the following essays: L. Haegeman, 'La distribution du verbe et du nom en français et en anglais' (15–51), D. Bouchard, 'Les SN sans déterminant en français et en anglais' (55–95), M.-T. Vinet, 'Quantification et structures nominales évaluatives en français et en anglais' (97–128), P. Miller and B. Lowrey, 'La complémentation des verbes de perception en français et en anglais' (131–88), and A. Zribi-Hertz,

'Réflexivité et disjonction référentielle en français et en anglais' (189–227); though the editors tell us that each author 's'est efforcé à ce que sa méthode, ses catégories, son formalisme et ses hypothèses soient transparents pour tout lecteur linguiste', the underlying generativist approach (more marked in some of the essays than in others) is likely to reduce the appeal and the utility of the volume for many of its putative readers.

M. Ditchéva-Nikolova and J.-Y. Dommergues discuss 'Un modèle bipolaire du groupe nominal complexe. La place de l'adjectif épithète en français et en bulgare', *IG*, 99:3–7. L. M. Tovena and M. Van Peteghem, '*Différent* vs *autre* et l'opposition réciproque et comparatif', *LInv*, 25:149–70, contrast French with German and English. G. Rebuschi, 'Coordination et subordination', *BSLP*, 96, 2001:23–60, and *ib.*, 97, 2002:37–94, contrasts French with a number of other languages, both Indo-European (Hittite, Gothic, Russian) and non-Indo-European.

EARLY MEDIEVAL LITERATURE

By Sara I. James, *Honorary Research Fellow, University of Hull*

1. General

Catherine Hanley, *War and Combat, 1150–1270: The Evidence from Old French Literature*, Cambridge, Brewer, ix + 261 pp., is an ambitious project that should attract the attention of a wide range of specialists. Divided into two separate parts, this study first analyses what H. refers to as 'The reality and ideals of war' before progressing to its literary representation. In this first section, H. briefly but thoroughly sets the stage by reviewing the context in which medieval people viewed war: the background and ideologies of combatants, their weapons, armour, and tactics all contribute to the background in which tales of conflict flourished. The second part, 'War and combat in literature', divides the texts studied into chronicle, epic, and romance. As H. judiciously states, it is not always easy to define works as belonging to one genre or the other; still less is it valid to accept chroniclers' accounts as 'true', while dismissing epic poetry as pure fiction. In analysing this particularly rich and complex period of history and literature, H. has avoided the pitfalls of many interdisciplinary works and produced a volume of sound scholarship.

Sylvia Huot, *Madness in Medieval French Literature: Identities Found and Lost*, OUP, 224 pp., studies the ways in which characters who go mad through 'a dangerous excess of individuality', become bereft of both personal and collective identity in the process. Drawing on an eclectic range of recent critics (Foucault, Butler, and Žižec's interpretations of Lacan), H. examines how medieval writers, in common with modern theorists, define identity, social belonging, and exclusion. H. divides the chapters into different representations of madness, with appropriate literary examples of each type. Ch. 1 discusses the 'two poles of objection and sublimity', known by other theorists as liminality, defining people who are excluded and revered on account of their difference. Ch. 2 studies the communal function performed by characters such as court fools and village idiots, while ch. 3 looks at violent manifestations of madness. Ch. 4 is concerned with the construction of heterosexual and heterosocial identity for men, and the behaviour that may subsequently be classified as deviant. Ch. 5 studies that great mainstay of romance, 'lovesickness', while ch. 6 looks at physical conditions such as lycanthropy and sleepwalking. J. Maurice, 'Réécritures narratives et discours médical sur la folie aux XIIe et XIIIe siècles', *Romania*, 120:432–48, studies recent critical analyses and trends, both anachronistic and text-based, used to interpret medieval representations of madness (or what passes for such) in the *Folies Tristan*. However, M. extends his study to include Rainouart in *Aliscans* and Lancelot in the *Chevalier de la charrette*.

P. Ménard, 'Le sentiment de la décadence dans la littérature médiévale', Baumgartner, *Progrès*, 137–53, draws on Guillaume de Lorris's *Roman de la rose*, Wace's *Roman de Rou*, *La Vie de saint Alexis*, Marie de France, and other sources, including Occitan and later medieval texts, to contrast modern optimism with what he sees as a medieval nostalgia for an often-idealized past. What medieval authors perceived as decadence is expressed through apocalyptic visions, the end of the Arthurian world, an obsession with death, and laments for past heroes ('*Ubi sunt . . .*?'), along with frequent ruminations on age and ageing.

2. Epic

W. van Emden, 'Le chef-d'œuvre épique', Bianciotto, *L'Épopée romane*, 395–412, offers a brief but invaluable overview of critical views of the *Roland*, tracing polarized schools of thought on the poem and their eventual ramifications for the definition of 'chef-d'œuvre' (if indeed such a thing exists). P. Ménard, 'Humour, ironie, dérision dans les chansons de geste', *ib.*, 203–26, proposes a typology in which certain types of humour are linked with women or men, friend or foe. He concludes in echoing the traditional view that burlesque humour cheapens the poems and disrupts their unity of tone. C. M. Jones, 'Les chansons de geste et l'Orient', *ib.*, 629–45, touches very briefly (as J. regretfully admits) on the different 'Oriental' themes evoked in *chansons de geste*: geography, ideology, the Holy Land (which is equally a cursed land), exoticism, and eroticism. The reader is left wanting more from this survey which, for reasons of space, is necessarily brief. J. E. Merceron, '*Par desoz terre une volte soltive*: étude du cliché narratif du souterrain sarrasin utilisé lors d'un siège ou d'une invasion épique', *ib.*, 937–47, observes that such tactics elicit admiration, unease, and contempt at the duplicity from Christian characters (and, presumably, for medieval audiences). C. F. Clamote Carreto, 'Dérision, division, déviation. Incidences poétiques de l'imaginaire marchand sur quelques chansons de geste des XIIe et XIIIe siècles', *ib.*, 265–80, looks at the 'mercantile' themes of purchase, exchange, and acquisition, as seen in the *Chanson de Roland*, the *Charroi de Nîmes*, *Hervis de Metz*, the *Enfances Vivien*, and other texts. These themes not only emphasize class differences, but also show tensions within the aristocratic class at the centre of the epic. However, these tensions contribute to an eventual renewal of the genre, rather than weakening it.

P. E. Bennett, 'Le norman, le picard et les koïnés littéraires de l'épopée au XIIe et XIIIe siècles', *BDBA*, 21:43–56, studies the linguistic clues and comments on dialect available in excerpts from Conon de Béthune, *La Chanson de Roland*, *La Chanson de Guillaume*, *Aspremont*, and *Le Couronnement Louis*. P. Kunstmann, 'Le lexique de la chanson de geste: étude du vocabulaire de trois chansons (*Roland*, *Couronnement Louis*, *Prise d'Orange*) en contraste avec des œuvres historiques de Wace et des romans de Chrétien de Troyes', Bianciotto, *L'Épopée romane*, 909–15, is an ambitious project for six pages. K. concludes that his linguistic analyses of vocabulary indicate a generic gap smaller than previously thought; however, he does concede that this may well be due to differences in style, rhetoric, and content. S. Marnette, 'Nord et sud: chansons de geste d'oc et d'oïl', *ib.*, 927–35, explores the possibility that a comparative study of narrative voice and positioning can help define both genre and dating. A. Moisan, '"Dieu qui maint en trinité." Présence du divin dans l'action épique', *ib.*, 959–67, surveys and lists the formulae invoking God, the Trinity, and other sacred beings, in what may be considered preliminary notes for a concordance. Y. Otaka's 'La valeur monétaire exprimée dans les œuvres épiques', *ib.*, 969–78, fulfils a similar function, although with almost no commentary. G. Buti, 'Christian anagoge and the Germanic worldcentric attitude in the romance epic and its reception', *ib.*, 749–57, believes that *chansons de geste* provide proof that Germanic folklore, surviving the spread of Christianity, permeated epic. There are few texts cited in support (primarily the *Roland*) and the excerpts chosen are not wholly convincing.

ROLAND AND CHARLEMAGNE. Cesare Segre's classic 1971 edition of *La Chanson de Roland* has been re-published in a revised edition (TLF, 968), 389 pp., with critical apparatus translated by Madeleine Tyssens and the glossary established by Bernard Guidot. It is a timely project that should be welcomed by *Roland* scholars.

Fierabras, chanson de geste du XIIe siècle, ed. Marc Le Person (CFMA, 142), Champion, 694 pp., is based on the MS Escorial M.III–21 (MS E), narrating Charlemagne's adventures in Spain and the aid given by the convert giant Fierabras. The tale is recounted in 13 versions (including one short) in *langue d'oïl* and one in *langue d'oc*.

Robert Morrissey, *Charlemagne and France: A Thousand Years of Mythology*, Notre Dame U.P., xv + 391 pp., is Catherine Tihanyi's translation of M.'s original *L'Empereur à la barbe fleurie: Charlemagne dans la mythologie et l'histoire de France* (Gallimard, 1997). Chs 2 and 3 will interest literary scholars the most as ch. 2, 'Poetic space, political reflection' (43–84), analyses the emperor's role in establishing and maintaining religious, feudal, and national order in the *Chanson de*

Roland, the *Pseudo-Turpin*, *Galien*, *Fierabras*, *Aspremont*, and the rebel barons cycle, while ch. 3, 'Rewriting history' (85–111), examines the construction of Charlemagne's *persona* in Mousket's chronicles and in Aubert's *Grandes Chroniques de France*.

J. V. Ganzarolli de Oliveira, '*Chanson de Roland*: a beleza como paradigma da moralidade na idade média', Bianciotto, *L'Épopée romane*, 527–40, sees the poem as the central work on war and morality in the Middle Ages. M. J. Schenck, 'If there wasn't a *Song of Roland*, was there a "trial" of Ganelon?', *Olifant*, 22: 143–57, combines close reading of the Ganelon episode with reference to early medieval legal practices, including Anglo-Norman law, Danelaw, Frankish law, and 'folklaw'. H. D. Engelhart, 'Motivations religieuses dans la *Chanson de Roland*: Ganelon comme anti-saint', Bianciotto, *L'Épopée romane*, 493–97, sees the moral and didactic value of the *chansons de geste* as a compelling reason for their probable recording by clerics. A. Fassò, 'Roland est sage et Charlemagne injuste', *ib.*, 499–507, considers Charles a perfect example of the king who, while venerated for being royal, is nevertheless inadequate; it is Roland whose judgments prove most accurate and wise. D. Kullmann, 'Le début de l'épisode de Baligant', *ib.*, 577–87, draws attention to aspects of the episode that she feels have been neglected in the debate over its place in the *Roland*. L. Duprez, '*La Chanson de Roland*. Qu'est-ce qu'un *osberc*?', *ib.*, 813–23, bases his work on the study of 32 translations of the poem, to amend what he perceives to be a loose translation of *osberc* (usually rendered in English as 'hauberk'). J. L. R. Bélanger, 'Women's equal rights in the twelfth century church in France, as seen in the old French epics, especially *the Chanson de Roland*', *ib.*, 423–30, sees in the phrases 'Or seit fait par marrenes' (*Roland*, v. 3982, à propos of Bramimonde's baptism) and the formulaic 'a moillier et a per' clear evidence of gender equality that later critics have overlooked or failed to attribute to the period.

H. Tétrel, 'Le *Pseudo-Turpin* et l'*Aspremont* norrois: la branche IV de la Karlamagnússaga est-elle une composition mécanique?', *Romania*, 120: 326–52, studies the Agolant saga that comprises the fourth branch in the light of various theories as to why this particular branch deviates from the supposed model. It is not clear whether this is due to incomplete MSS serving as models, or to the compiler's innovating initiative. S. López Martínez Morás, 'La prise de Nobles dans le *Pseudo-Turpin*', Bianciotto, *L'Épopée romane*, 175–91, queries the identity of the city, named as an object of siege and conquest in texts such as the *Chanson de Roland*, David Aubert's *Grandes Chroniques*, the *Karlamagnússaga*, the *Chronique saintongeaise*, and others. A. Corbellari, 'Parcours du désir et de la cruauté dans *La Chanson d'Aspremont*', *ib.*,

465–73, continues the 'rehabilitation' (begun by W. Calin), of this text.

M. Bonafin, 'Il *Voyage de Charlemagne* e il riso', Mühlethaler, *Parodie*, 17–26, sees in this epic a demonstration of the anthropologist Fabio Ceccarelli's theory of laughter as mechanism of expressing domination and submission.

GUILLAUME D'ORANGE AND THE GARIN CYCLE. *Le Moniage Guillaume*, ed. Nelly Andrieux-Reix (CFMA, 145), Champion, 358 pp., is based on the long version using as base MSS Paris, BnF, fr. 774 (A1) and the Milan Trivulziana (A4), to recount Guillaume's final (monastic) adventures, which close the cycle. N. Bard, 'Les fonctions génériques du comique dans les *Moniages*', Bianciotto, *L'Épopée romane*, 245–51, sees the critical role of humour as defining these texts within the Orange–Monglane cycle, bringing it to an end and providing a point of departure for a new generation of *chansons de geste*. P. Rossi, 'Il cavaliere-eremita o il guerriero-asceta: epopea medievale francese e epopea indiana a confronto', *ib.*, 714–24, sees the two seemingly opposite types brought together via a cross-cultural trifunctional dynamic (echoing the research of G. Dumézil and J.-H. Grisward), culminating in the *Moniage Guillaume*. P. E. Bennett, 'Carnaval héroïque et écriture cyclique dans la geste de Guillaume', *ib.*, 253–63, offers a brief overview of his current research into the rich interpretive possibilities in applying aspects of Bakhtinian theory to *chansons de geste*. Through the notions of carnival and dialogism, both the dominant group and those reacting against it are defined, and the official ideology better understood, ultimately reinforced. B. notes that all the major characters, not only the obviously 'carnavalesque' ones, such as Rainouart and Guielin, reinforce this dynamic. The article is dense and leaves the reader eager for further developments of this thesis. H. Gallé, 'Optimisme ou pessimisme épique? L'éternel retour dans *Aymeri de Narbonne*', *ib.*, 509–25, sees in this poem, apparently so buoyant and positive, a beginning of the prolonged cyclical struggles to save king, kingdom, and Christianity. Like Charlemagne, the Narbonnais are fated to have no peace. M. Ott, 'La *Mort Aymeri de Narbonne*: paradoxe de la tradition', *ib.*, 617–52, includes *Guibert d'Andrenas* in her study, which sees the two poems as a mini-cycle within themselves, each meaningless without the other.

E. A. Heinemann, 'Patterns in the presentation of discourse in the *Charroi de Nîmes*', *Olifant*, 22:72–87, details the computer programme he has developed to trace patterns of introductory speech in this particular epic. C. Almeida Ribeiro, 'Renouart au tinel: endroit et envers de la dérision', Bianciotto, *L'Épopée romane*, 237–44, sees the creation of a cycle-within-a-cycle, starring Rainouart, as a poetic means of framing and containing a character whose intervention, though necessary to save a paralysed 'ideal', seems absurd, almost accidental. S. Dieckmann, 'Le style épique et les fonctions narratives dans *Girart de Vienne*', *ib.*, 481–91, sees the judicial conflict between Girart and the queen as an example of how epic construction, while formulaic, allows for highly individualized poetic variation. **Le Siège de Barbastre*, ed. Bernard Guidot, Champion, 2002.

OTHER EPICS. S. Kay, 'Singularity and specularity: desire and death in *Girart de Roussillon*', *Olifant*, 22:11–38, posits the *chanson de geste* as a genre of individualism, realized best through the acts of killing and dying. Here, Charles's and Girart's attempts to assert each one's will and individuality over the other, even at the expense of their given word, reinforce their mutual dependence as victor and vanquished. Each attempt to better their standing only succeeds in levelling, and the narrator makes it clear that his characters' excessive singularity is not a model to follow. D. Maddox, 'Du déclin au renouveau: Vézelay, *Girart de Roussillon*, et l'*inventio* des reliques de la Madeleine', Baumgartner, *Progrès*, 95–109, suggests that the history of the abbey at Vézelay, and the creation of legends associated with it, mirrors a pattern of decadence, reaction, and progress. The epic poem, with its references to the origins of Vézelay, is thus part of this 'rehabilitation' campaign, according to M.

A. Labbé, 'Sous le signe de saint Jacques: chemins et routes dans la représentation épique de l'espace', Bianciotto, *L'Épopée romane*, 99–116, evokes *Raoul de Cambrai*, *Gerbert de Metz*, and *Renaut de Montauban* to demonstrate the importance of Compostella on the collective medieval imagination. M. Botero García, 'Les deux images du roi Louis dans *Raoul de Cambrai*', *ib.*, 431–39, sees the traditionally weak Louis as far more complex a character than previously thought. D. Boutet, 'Fonction et signification du personnage de Gautier dans *Raoul de Cambrai*', *ib.*, 441–48, argues that Gautier, far from being a simple narrative tool, adds further dimensions to the cast of masculine characters, notions of good and evil, and the definition of knighthood. M. Madureira, 'Les enjeux du monde féodal: l'ordre impossible dans *Raoul de Cambrai*', *ib.*, 601–09, examines the complex role of law in the poem, and the distinctions between right and wrong, between upholding feudal order and establishing practical solutions in the face of flouted 'ideals'. S. Kinoshita, 'Fraternizing with the enemy: Christian-Saracen relations in *Raoul de Cambrai*', *ib.*, 695–703, sees Bernier's penitential travels in Saracen Spain as conducive to his redemption. However, in making the point about the mutual respect shown between opponents in *Raoul*, K. over-emphasizes the negative portraits of some Saracens in the *Chanson de Roland*. F. E. Sinclair, 'Loss, re-figuration and death in *Raoul de Cambrai*', *FS*, 57:297–310, boldly claims that the poem's inherent lack (of father, of patriarchal authority, of cogent feudal order) characterizes all *chansons de geste*. J. Chaurand, 'L'onomastique de Raoul de Cambrai. Les noms de personne', *BDBA*, 21:145–56, considers the names of characters directly linked to the action, with family and geographical provenance playing a determining role.

S. C. O. Malicote, '"Cil novel jougleor": parody, illumination and genre renewal in *Aiol*', *Romania*, 120:353–405, gives a lengthy introduction about the court of Flanders and its role in the patronage and production of both re-workings and original pieces. The court of Jeanne, countess of Flanders, is given especial attention in this study, which is thorough and flows well, covering much of the circumstances of a literary work's creation, all of which are key to interpreting what might have been deliberate allusions to contemporary figures. M. considers *Aiol*'s reference to its *jongleur*, its relationship to the work *Audigier* and the parodic *Prise de Neuville*, concluding that the traditional view of shifting tastes from epic to romance is far too simplistic. Works from differing genres borrowed from, commented upon, and parodied themselves and others. F. Denis, 'Ironie et humour dans *Gui de Bourgogne*', Bianciotto, *L'Épopée romane*, 281–89, sees the poem as typifying the dynamic by which epic uses humour and laughter to relieve the tension of conflict. J.-H. Grisward, 'La cuisine et la guerre: aspects de la fonction guerrière dans la Geste des Lorrains', *ib.*, 549–65, demonstrates that Begon's presence is not for purely humorous effect, but in fact necessary to the bipartite structure embodied in Garin and Begon. One is neither less nor more than the other: they complement and complete each other. D. Ion, 'La parenté comme outil narratif dans *Garin le Lorrain*', *ib.*, 567–75, shows how family defines groups, values, and loyalties, and provides a rich source of both alliances and conflicts, all of which are exploited in epic. N. Lenoir, 'L'eau et la mer dans la *Chanson d'Aiquin* (*ca* 1190–1200)', *ib.*, 917–25, admires the poet's great skill in weaving into his work the theme, rare for the epic genre, of water. The poet thereby acknowledges both the local geography (Brittany) and exploits water's symbolic significance.

3. Romance

Derek Pearsall, *Arthurian Romance: A Short Introduction*, Oxford, Blackwell, viii + 182 pp., is an accessible, broad survey of much of European Arthurian lore, as well as commentary on later, modern reworkings (Twain, White, and others) and film. Ch. 2, 'The romancing of the Arthurian story: Chrétien de Troyes' (20–39), and ch. 3, 'The European flourishing of Arthurian romance: Lancelot, Parzival, Tristan' (40–59), are appropriate for undergraduates or non-specialists embarking on a study of early medieval French literature; notes, index, and bibliography are accordingly brief.

C. Ferlampin-Acher, 'Merveilleux et comique dans les romans arthuriens français (XIIe–Xve siècles)', *ArLit*, 19:17–47, sees the two *topoï* come together in their common attributes — both depend on perception and play with it — and their common effect, to throw hero and audience off-guard. Paradox, exaggeration, and elliptical moments leading to bafflement occur throughout works such as *Le Chevalier au lion*, *Les Continuations Perceval*, *Les Merveilles de Rigomer*, *Le Bel Inconnu*, *Eneas*, *Le Livre d'Artus*, and many later texts.

N. Ciccone, 'To love or not to love', *ICLS 9*, 231–37, traces the development of self-conflict in romance and its philosophical emphasis on reasoning and willpower. M. Lignereux, 'Approche de la notion de contexte en ancien français', *ib.*, 189–97, studies the performative verbs linked to oaths, vows, and promises, quoting from Chrétien's and Béroul's texts. B. Ramm, ' "Por coi la pucele pleure": the feminine enigma of the Grail Quest', *Neophilologus*, 87:517–27, analyses the emerging feminine role in the Grail narratives, from *Perceval* through the *Tristan en prose* to the *Queste*. Although initially an openly misogynistic tale, from which women are banned, the Quest develops into one in which women, according to R., play roles crucial in underpinning the essentially male venture. N. J. Lacy, 'Naming and the construction of identity in *Li Chevaliers as deus espees*', *RPh*, 56:203–16, studies not so much naming conventions in this neglected text as the unusual character development of the heroine.

V. Gontero, 'L'*Anel faé*. Analyse d'un motif merveilleux dans la littérature arthurienne en vers des XIIe et XIIIe siècles', *LR*, 57:3–18, analyses the development of the ring as symbol of affection, loyalty, and (through lapidary associations) various virtues. The narratives cited include *Amadas et Ydoine*, *Floire et Blancheflor*, the lais *Désiré*, *Mélion* and *Yonec*, the *Chevalier de la charrette*, the *Continuations Perceval*, the *Chevalier au lion*, and the *Merveilles de Rigomer*. The supernatural aspect and powers of gems give rings their own narrative within the tales, according to G.

CHRÉTIEN DE TROYES. Dana E. Stewart, *The Arrow of Love: Optics, Gender and Subjectivity in Medieval Love Poetry*, Lewisburg, Bucknell U.P. — London, Assoc. Univ. Press, 186 pp., interests us here because of the first chapter, 'Through a glass brightly: vision and the arrow of love in Chrétien de Troyes' *Cligès*' (33–48). Examining Alexander's and Soredamors's respective monologues analysing the link between sight and love, S. debates whether the metaphor relates more to Aristotelian optical theory than to Marian imagery. S. Bianchini, '*Interpretatio nominis* e *pronominatio* nel *Cligès* di Chrétien de

Troyes', *VR*, 61 : 180–221, compares the Celtic and Christian significance of names.

K. Casebier, 'Ovid's medieval metamorphosis: techniques of persuasion in Chrétien de Troyes' *Philomena*', *PQ*, 80, 2001 : 441–62, compares rhetorical and narrative strategies used by both authors to provoke moral reaction and to enhance authorial commentary. E. J. Mickel, 'Mercury's Philologia and Erec's Enide', *RPh*, 56 : 1–22, uses close textual analysis to support K. Uitti's view that Enide is influenced by Martianus Capella's work.

A. Rieger, 'La bande dessinée virtuelle du lion d'Yvain: sur le sens d'humour de Chrétien de Troyes', *ArLit*, 19:49–64, contains an anachronistic insistence on Chrétien's provision of a 'virtual' comic strip. The idea of re-reading the text as a series of vignettes that illuminate the lion's 'personality' and give it another, comic dimension, is appealing. However, the continual reference to 'bande dessinée', combined with the lack of any reference to illustrations in the MS tradition, weakens the article. M. M. Pelen, 'Madness in *Yvain* reconsidered', *Neophilologus*, 87 : 361–69, sees the vocabulary and theme of madness as not limited to the 'wild man' episode, but integral to the entire story.

C. Luttrell, '*Le Conte del Graal* et d'autres sources françaises de l'*Histoire Peredur*', *Neophilologus*, 87 : 11–28, views the 13th-c. Welsh poem *Historia Peredur ab Efrawg* as definitely influenced by Chrétien's *Conte del Graal*, as well as by *Le Bliocadran*, the *Second Continuation*, and the prose *Lancelot*. M. T. Bruckner, 'L'imaginaire du progrès dans les cycles romanesques du Graal', Baumgartner, *Progrès*, 111–21, sees Chrétien's work evoke the Biblical wastelands of the prophet Isaiah and offer its continuators an ambiguous and ambivalent moral vision. R. Deist, 'Perceval's inner wanderings: growing out of childhood in Chrétien de Troyes's *Conte du Graal*', *ICLS* 9, 223–29, observes parallels between the forest episodes, the female characters of Perceval's mother and Blanchefleur, and the relationship between Perceval and his mother, all of which contribute to his coherent development as a knight. L. Gowans, 'The *Eachtra an Amadáin Mhóir* as a response to the *Perceval* of Chrétien de Troyes', *ArLit*, 19 : 199–230, argues for the close relationship between the two texts and for a greater appreciation of the former. C. Guardado da Silva, 'A floresta e o medos na "épica" de Chrétien de Troyes', Bianciotto, *L'Épopée romane*, 859–66, sees both the *Chevalier de la charrette* and *Perceval* as epics. For the Chrétien specialist in search of (very) light relief, there is H. Arden and K. Lorenz, 'The Harry Potter stories and French Arthurian romance', *Arthuriana*, 13.2 : 54–68.

OTHER ARTHURIAN. C. Gîrbea, 'Royauté et chevalerie célestielle à travers les romans arthuriens (XIIe–XIIIe s.)', *CCMe*, 46: 109–34, observes parallel systems of regal (Arthurian) authority and of that which governs the 'celestial' knight, who must sometimes bypass the earthly representatives of divine order and justice. G. draws on examples from the *Queste del Saint Graal*, *Perlesvaus*, the *Didot Perceval*, *Partonopeus de Blois*, *Le Chevalier de la charrette*, *Merlin* (and *Suites*), *La Mort Artu*, *Erec et Enide*, *Jaufré*, *Rigomer*.

R. Barber, 'Chivalry, cistercianism and the Grail', Dover, *Companion*, 3–12, demonstrates how the *Queste* combines reflections on the secular institution of chivalry, the status of knighthood, and Cistercian theological underpinnings. E. Baumgartner, 'The *Queste del saint Graal*: from *semblance* to *veraie semblance*', trans. C. Dover, *ib.*, 107–14, demonstrates how the author takes pre-existing Arthurian themes, episodes, and characters and imbues them with his broader eschatological message.

E. Kennedy, 'The making of the *Lancelot-Grail Cycle*', Dover, *Companion*, 13–23, gives a brief yet thorough and compelling overview of the main points of debate about the unity of the cycle. Given the overarching themes of the Grail quest and the MSS developing them, K. concludes, rightly, that it is too much to expect 'unity' (especially in the modern sense) from such a work. F. Bogdanow, 'The *Vulgate Cycle* and the *Post-Vulgate Roman du Graal*', *ib.*, 33–51, discusses the intertextual clues in various Arthurian texts and MSS that have allowed reconstruction of the *Cycle*. B. sees the *Post-Vulgate* as an underappreciated work, one that has done much to knit together apparently heterogeneous incidents of the Arthurian tradition. D. Kelly, 'Interlace and the cyclic imagination', *ib.*, 55–64, wonders if Horace's condemnation of cyclical poems and their authors is just. He concludes that, in the case of the Grail narrative, the work is both coherent and deliberate. C. J. Chase, 'The gateway to the *Lancelot-Grail Cycle*: *L'Estoire del saint Graal*', *ib.*, 65–74, analyses the manner in which the *Estoire* sets itself up as an introduction to the cycle. She points to the elaboration of genealogies and geographies that establish the context in which 'later' events in earlier texts unfold, creating both parallel and flashback effects. P. Tylus, 'Fragment de Cracovie de l'*Estoire del saint Graal*', *CL*, 63:73–81, provides an edition and textual analysis, with full codicological details, of this MS. R. Trachsler, 'A question of time: romance and history', Dover, *Companion*, 24–32, continues the debate about medieval perceptions of the relative veracity of epic and chronicle by turning our attention to romance as historiography. As he justly points out, collections show romance interpolated with 'historical' accounts in such a way as to make clear that medieval audiences did not distinguish between the two in the way that later readers have done. The *Lancelot-Grail*

Cycle in particular falls between historiography and romance, according to T., drawing as it does upon both Wace and Chrétien. A. Combes, 'The *Merlin* and its *Suite*', trans. C. Dover, *ib.*, 75–85, likens the *corpus* to a polychrome print, each text and successive inking leading to a richly-coloured whole. C. Dover, 'The book of Lancelot', *ib.*, 87–93, compares the representation of Lancelot in verse and prose, noting the differences in historical and spatial context. She also discusses at some length the necessary link between rhetorical devices and the audience's subsequent enjoyment of such a lengthy work. M. T. Bruckner, 'Redefining the center: verse and prose *Charrette*', *ib.*, 96–105, examines the prose romance's canny amplification of certain aspects of Chrétien's tale, which is subsumed into the *Lancelot.* Other aspects are severely abbreviated. The effect is to develop the individual character as well as key themes such as the definition of heroism, through the cart and tomb episodes. N. J. Lacy, 'The sense of an ending: *La Mort le Roi Artu*', *ib.*, 115–23, acknowledges that, following the *Queste*, *La Mort le Roi Artu* can be seen as something of an anti-climax. However, its foreshadowing, use of portents, and emphasis on the destructive nature of Lancelot and Guinevere's affair, add to the interpretation that the ends of Lancelot, Arthur, the Round Table, and Camelot have indeed been long foreordained. Codicologists, art historians, and generalists will all enjoy A. Stones, ' "Mise en page" in the French *Lancelot-Grail*: the first 150 years of the illustrative tradition', *ib.*, 125–44.

B. Milland-Bove, 'La pratique de la "disconvenance" comique dans le *Lancelot en prose*: les mésaventures amoureuses de Guerrehet', *ArLit*, 19: 105–15, sees the episodes she cites as not simply nods to the *fabliau* and *farce* traditions, but as serving a more serious function of questioning the courtly model. This function is of a piece with the entire work, enhancing its complexity. F. Brandsma, '*Lancelot* Part 3', *ib.*, 117–33, reflects on the making of the prose work, looking at issues of MS tradition and compositional unity. F. Zambon, 'Dinadan en Italie', *ib.*, 153–63, examines how this particular character from the *Lancelot en prose* not only flourishes in Italian literature, but crosses genres.

TRISTAN AND ISEUT. Thomas, *Le Roman de Tristan, suivi de la Folie Tristan de Berne et la Folie Tristan d'Oxford*, ed. Felix Lecoy, trans. Emmanuèle Baumgartner and Ian Short (CCMA, 1), Champion, 445 pp., gives a facing-page translation in prose. The introduction's focus is on certain key words and phrases and their role in unveiling the text's major themes. Critical apparatus is limited: information on the base MS covers just over three pages, and rejected readings, bibliography, glossary, and index are all brief, indicating perhaps a student audience for this work.

ROMANS D'ANTIQUITÉ. Thomas de Kent, *Le Roman d'Alexandre ou Le Roman de toute chevalerie*, ed. Brian Foster and Ian Short, trans. Catherine Gaullier-Bougassas and Laurence Harf-Lancner (CCMA, 5), Champion, lxxxii + 741 pp., provides a serious introduction, including study of the plot, author, source documents, historical *remaniements*, and the influence of epic and romance. The translation is in prose, given on the facing page to the original, with variants, bibliography, glossary, and index at the end. P. Kunstmann, 'Les campagnes d'Alexandre: de l'histoire à l'épopée', *Olifant*, 22:131–42, compares classical accounts with the *Roman d'Alexandre* to confirm that he is portrayed as a medieval paragon of knighthood and a crusader. P. Ménard, 'Les illustrations marginales du *Roman d'Alexandre* (Oxford, Bodleian Library, MS Bodley 264)', Braet, *Laughter*, 75–118, strongly rejects the interpretations of S. Huot, M. Camille, and S. K. Davenport, all of whom, in his view, over-interpret illustrations that often bear no relation to the text at hand, much less seek to subvert it. Their intention, M. contends, was primarily to amuse.

C. Sanok, 'Almoravides at Thebes: Islam and European identity in the *Roman de Thèbes*', *MLQ*, 64:277–98. The *Roman de Thèbes* differs from other contemporary *romans antiques*; whereas they use the myths of Troy to establish parallels with the Anglo-Norman court and culture in a linear fashion, the *Roman de Thèbes* emphasizes a cyclical view of history. However, it *does* propose a newer and broader view of the world through its inclusion and depiction of various other warrior races, e.g., the Almoravides. *IL*, 55.2, is a special dossier entitled 'Autour du *Roman de Thèbes*': S. Franchet-d'Espèrey, 'La *Thébaïde* de Stace et ses rapports avec le *Roman de Thèbes* (prologue, épilogue et causalité)' (4–10), studies the technical and narrative commonplaces within the two works, but in the context of the epic tradition. F.-d'E. concludes that the older work is darker in tone, more tragic, less attentive to the 'plaisir de la narration' — but is this a change of philosophy, style, or both? M.-M. Castellani, 'Généalogies thébaines et passé mythologique dans le *Roman de Thèbes*' (15–22), contends that these passages reveal the mythology that underpins the entire poem: humans and gods interact far more than elsewhere in the work, and the importance of these passages is, according to C., disproportionate to the space assigned to them. A. Petit, 'Capanée dans le *Roman de Thèbes*' (23–29), analyses this character's singularity; given an importance in the French work that he lacks in the Latin original, Capanée possesses what P. calls 'desmesure'. His gigantism, his rage, his 'desmesure', all mark him as an epic hero of the French tradition.

M.-M. Castellani, 'Le programme iconographique du manuscrit de Saint-Pétersbourg *d'Athis et Prophilas*', *Ateliers*, 30:27–37, studies both the artistic and codicological aspects of the illuminations, analysing the careful and detailed link between text and image.

OTHER ROMANCES. Robert d'Origny, *Le conte de Floire et de Blancheflor*, ed. Jean-Luc Leclanche (CCMA, 2), Champion, xxviii + 222 pp., discusses the phonology of four MSS (three complete plus one fragment) in some detail in the introduction, which also analyses themes of *conjointure*, space, and time. The translation provided is a facing-page prose version of MS A.

Renaut de Beaujeu, *Le Bel Inconnu*, ed. Michèle Perret, trans. Michèle Perret and Isabelle Weill (CCMA, 4), Champion, xix + 415 pp., gives a facing-page prose translation. The introduction is thematic, with especial attention to the notion of courtliness subverted, but there is no information on the MS used for the edition.

Le Roman de Gliglois, ed. Marie-Luce Chênerie (CFMA, 143), Champion, 208 pp., shows a knight torn between duty to serve and his love for a disloyal lady. Loyal to friends and lord, he is finally rewarded. The tale is contained in one (burned) MS.

Nancy B. Black, *Medieval Narratives of Accused Queens*, Gainesville, Florida U.P., xviii + 261 pp., studies the *topos* of noblewomen unjustly accused, sorely tested, then restored to former status. Given the prevalence of the narrative in various cultures and ages, it is a folkloric theme that has been little studied in medieval literary criticism. B. furthers her scope by analysing the texts in manuscripts within the pictorial and textual context that gives them meaning. Of particular relevance here is ch. 2, 'The handless queen', in which B. studies the heroine of *La Manekine*, a powerless victim who falls prey to the sins of others. (Unlike some critics, B. rejects outright the notion of the heroine's self-mutilation as 'justified' self-punishment.) Although B. does not make this explicit, the heroine, who spends most of the story a cipher, yet recovers name, status, and identity at the end, is the opposite of the Empress of Rome in Gautier de Coinci's tale (see below, p. 000), whose name, status, and identity are strongly reiterated throughout her tale, and all of which she gives up. C. J. Harvey, 'Incest, identity and uncourtly conduct in *La Manekine*', *ICLS 9*, 161–68, sees the work as questioning identity, especially socially constructed identity, which is undermined by the unworthy behaviour displayed by some of the highest-born protagonists. Philippe de Remi, says H., thereby distorts an ideal vision of love and gender. B. N. Sargent-Baur, '*Prologus/epilogus est, non legitur*', *RoQ*, 50:2–11, is an introduction and general reflection on trends in scholarship over the past generation, veering (in S.-B.'s view) from simplistic to cynical ('ironic'). She then examines Philippe de Remi's *Manekine* and *Jehan et Blonde* and the relationship between the main texts and their prologues and epilogues. These are deliberate guidelines for reading and S.-B. explicitly warns readers against the anachronism and arrogance of medievalist critics who all too often presume to know the author's meaning better than he did. C. Harvey, 'The discourse of characterization in *Jehan et Blonde*', Godsall-Myers, *Speaking*, 145–66, is interested in how Philippe de Remi, unlike many medieval authors, notes differences in languages and customs. H. studies the use of language in particular to denote foreignness, courtliness, and individuality.

H. Braet, 'Entre folie et raison: les drôleries du MS B.N., fr. 25526', Braet, *Laughter*, 43–74, observes that, like much illumination, that which 'illustrates' the *Roman de la rose* in this MS is ambiguous and resists both interpretation and over-interpretation.

P. Eley et al., '*Cristal et Clarie* and a lost manuscript of *Partonopeus de Blois*', *Romania*, 120:329–47, studies the use of *Cristal et Clarie* in establishing other texts, as it borrows from a variety of sources, including *Athis et Prophilias*, Wace's *Brut*, *Erec et Enide*, *Yvain*, *Le Conte du Graal*, *Partonopeus de Blois*, and *Narcisus*. The authors further provide extracts from both *Cristal et Clarie* and MS V of *Partonopeus de Blois* in order to compare them.

P. S. Noble, 'Le comique dans *Les Merveilles de Rigomer* et *Hunbaut*', *ArLit*, 19:77–86, shows how the authors of both texts draw heavily upon Chrétien's work, but differ greatly in their approach to the use of humour. Whereas the author of *Rigomer* mocks and satirizes his characters and, by extension, the Arthurian courtly world, the author of *Hunbaut* is far more sober. K. Pratt, 'Humour in the *Roman de Silence*', *ib.*, 87–103, questions the conclusions drawn by many modern critics. Fascinated by the complex play on gender in *Silence*, and thereby inferring a proto-feminist agenda, have they perhaps ignored the misogyny implied in intertextual references to the *fabliaux* and other genres?

4. Lais

R. L. Krueger's chapter on Marie de France in Dinshaw, *Companion*, 172–83, surveys all too briefly Marie's work in its historical and literary context. It is not clear for whom the article is written, however, as the complete lack of any meaningful excerpts from the works themselves, even in translation, seems to be at odds with the volume's prefatory statement that its purpose is to study texts and 'writings of remarkable women'. J. Brumlik, 'Incest and death in Marie de France's *Deus Amanz*', *ICLS 9*, 169–77, considers Marie's possible allusions to the themes of father/daughter incest and the folkloric motif of the tested suitor. E. Datta, 'Variations sur l'espace dans le lai du *Chaitivel*', *ib.*, 215–21, muses on the different types of space characters inhabit (towers, towns, etc.) as well as the larger framework of the '*espace courtois*'. A. Hopkins, '*Bisclavret* to *Bisclarel* via *Melion* and *Bisclaret*: the development of a misogynous *lai*', *ib.*, 317–23, looks at the differing presentations of the wife, her actions and guilt, in each version.

R. Brusegan, 'La plaisanterie dans le *Lai de Nabaret*', Braet, *Laughter*, 129–41, analyses at length the simple joke of a brief *lai*: scolded by her husband for vanity, a women suggests he become equally vain by growing his beard and sideburns, thereby turning the joke against him. F. Le Saux, 'The theology of love in the *Lai de l'Oiselet*', *ICLS 9*, 91–97, determines that the *lai* is far more morally ambivalent than it may appear at first. The bird, who sets itself up as a teacher, pronouncing on love spiritual and secular, is no less flawed than the *vilain* of the piece.

5. Religious Writings

Guillaume de Berneville's *La Vie de saint Gilles*, ed. and trans. François Laurent, Champion, lxiv + 308 pp., is based on the Biblioteca Laurentiana MS and provides a facing-page translation. The introduction is considerable, treating not only the plot, but also the Latin source, *Vita sancti Aegidii*, published with a translation at the end of the volume. L. further analyses the saint as literary character and the work's style. The critical apparatus includes a discussion of the MS tradition, principles of edition, rejected and amended readings, and brief index, glossary, and bibliography. In addition to the Latin source, L. also provides an edition and translation of various fragments in French verse.

S. I. Sobecki, 'From the *désert liquide* to the Sea of Romance: Benedeit's *Voyage de saint Brendan* and the Irish *immrama*', *Neophilologus*, 87:193–207, challenges the view that Benedeit's source was the *Navigatio*; rather, he was more influenced by the *immrama*, which S. defines as 'maritime voyage-tales'.

O. Collet, 'Gautier de Coinci: les œuvres d'attribution incertaine', *Romania*, 121:43–98, provides an edition of the *Nativité Nostre Dame* as well as an analysis. M. Okubo, 'Autour de la *Nativité Nostre Dame* et de son attribution à Gautier de Coinci', *Romania*, 121:348–81, uses O. Collet's article in the previous issue of *Romania* as a point of departure to re-open the question, seemingly closed by the research of P. Långfors and F. V. Koenig. The first chapter of Black, *Accused Queens* (see above, p. 63), 'The Empress of Rome' (20–36), emphasizes the textual prominence given to this tale by Gautier de Coinci, as it is placed at the mid-point of the later, two-volume MS, a stark contrast to tales of repentant sinners. The empress is a person characterized by virtue and strength, unlike so many of Gautier's protagonists. Offered riches and glory by her repentant husband, the emperor who has unjustly banished her, the empress underlines both her secular power and her sanctity by choosing instead the cloistered life. B. notes that, although the empress warns against the lusts and evils of men, her final choice is to submit to male authority (as B. interprets it).

E. Campbell, 'Separating the saints from the boys: sainthood and masculinity in the old French *Vie de saint Alexis*', *FS*, 57:447–62, analyses gender identity in the context of exchange, both worldly and spiritual. The saint's role as giver and given affects his status as, respectively, subject and object and, by extension, his masculinity and femininity.

C. R. Sneddon, 'On the creation of the *Old French Bible*', *NMS*, 46:25–44, dates the work no earlier than 1230 and speculates on its composition (inspired by the *Bible moralisée*) and intended recipients. D. Robertson, '*Or escoutez, signor . . . si com lisant trovon*: la chanson biblique d'Herman de Valenciennes', Bianciotto, *L'Épopée romane*, 1001–08, provides a useful introduction to the *Roman de Dieu et sa Mère*, a late 12th-c. version of selections of the Bible in, according to R., epic form.

A. P. Tudor, 'Past and present: the voice of an anonymous medieval author', *Mediaevalia*, 24:19–44, explores to what extent the character and opinions of a nameless author can become known to us. Using the *Vie des Pères* as a case study, T. considers the text in relation to how it echoes the past (sources and analogues) and reflects the present (the society for and within which it was produced). T. concludes that a sensitive examination of textual evidence does indeed allow us to know quite intimately an anonymous medieval author. C. Galderisi, 'Le "crâne qui parle": du motif aux récits. Vertu chrétienne et vertu poétique', *CCMe*, 46:213–31, studies the ways in which this *topos* occurs in literature, folklore and, in particular, in *Crâne* and *Païen* from the *Vie des pères*. M. G. Dawson, 'Reading conversion in French medieval saints' lives', *ib.*, 325–50, considers two influential saints' lives, Guernes de Pont-Sainte-Maxence's *Vie de saint Thomas Becket* and Rutebeuf's 'Vie de sainte Marie l'Egyptienne'. D. concludes that although — or because — there is a huge gap between the saint's heroic life and the audience's more prosaic existence, stories of saintly conversion do not need to be imitated in order to be transforming.

J. Batany, 'Quelques effets burlesques dans le *Livre des manières*', Braet, *Laughter*, 119–28, sees in Etienne de Fougères's didactic work a humorous criticism of the pretensions of burghers and women, whose lofty social aspirations contrast amusingly with the reality of their respective estates.

6. Lyric

Les Dits d'Henri d'Andeli, ed. Alain Corbellari (CFMA, 146), Champion, 227 pp., provides a brief but thorough introduction and critical apparatus for 'La bataille des vins', 'La bataille des sept arts', 'Le lai d'Aristote', and 'Le dit du chancelier Philippe', accompanied by a diplomatic edition of six extant MSS. C. has also published 'Aristote le bestourné: Henri d'Andeli et la "révolution cléricale" du XIIIe siècle', Mühlethaler, *Parodie*, 161–85, according to which the *Lai d'Aristote* is both a subject for generic debate and an important stage in the development of the cleric as interventionist author. C. views this *lai* is the last instance of a subtle and optimistic view that prevailed before the appearance of such 'misogynistic' authors as Rutebeuf, Jean de Meun, and Richard de Fournival. M. L. Meneghetti, 'Parodia et auto-parodia. Il caso Conon de Béthune (R 1325)', *ib.*, 69–85, compares the apparent inherent structural contradictions in 'Bele doce dame chiere' with Raimbaut de Vaqueiras's 'Eras quan vey verdeyer', proposing that the work resulted from a set poetic competition.

J. T. Grimbert, 'Songs by women and women's songs: how useful is the concept of register?', *ICLS 9*, 117–24, uses the *chansons de femmes* to suggest that, with such borrowing from and interplay between registers (the *registres aristocratisant* and *popularisant*, in P. Bec's terms, *requête d'amour* and *la bonne vie* in P. Zumthor's), it is well to review the number, classification, and inherent justification of such typologies. W. Pfeffer, meanwhile, revisits the question of textual clues to an author's gender in 'Complaints of women, complaints by women: can one tell them apart?', *ib.*, 125–31.

7. Roman de Renart

K. Sullivan, '"Filz a putein, puant heirites": the heterodoxy of Renart', *Reinardus*, 16:183–94, studies the seeming contradiction in Renart's being appreciated for the same trickery and deviousness associated with heretics. J. R. Simpson, 'The fox and the lion's share. Tyranny, textuality and *jouissance* in the *Roman de Renart* (*Le partage des proies*)', Horn, *Possessions*, 21–36, firstly establishes the theoretical (Lacanian) underpinning to his study, that of the father/ruler's being required to sacrifice enjoyment in himself and repress it in others (and Others) in order to maintain the *status quo*. S. re-reads Noble's insistence on sharing caught prey as a witting, but not explicit, acknowledgement that he must renounce *jouissance* to retain the illusion of his legitimacy as king. Moreover, in duping the duper, Noble dispossesses Renart of his own tale.

8. Fabliaux

Chevalerie et grivoiserie: fabliaux de chevalerie, ed. Jean-Luc Leclanche (CCMA, 3), Champion, xxii + 281 pp., places all the critical apparatus at the beginning of the volume. The texts included are *Le Prêtre et le chevalier*, *Beranger au long cul*, *La Mégère émasculée*, *Guillaume au faucon*, and *Le Fouteur*, with facing-page prose translations. *Le Jongleur par lui-même: choix de dits et de fabliaux*, ed. Willem Noomen, Louvain–Paris, Peeters, vi + 365 pp., offers 16 texts with facing-page translation into modern French. There is a brief introduction on the provenance and history of *jongleurs*, *dits*, and *fabliaux* and a page on editorial decisions taken with the versions N. has chosen from the *Nouvel recueil complet des fabliaux* or the most recent edition of the relevant *dits*. Each text is preceded by a brief introduction, discussing the MS and edition, dating, and literary aspects of the work in question.

J. Merceron, 'Des souris et des hommes: pérégrination d'un motif narratif et d'un *exemplum* d'Islam en chrétienté. A propos de la fable de "L'Hermite" de Marie de France et du fabliau de *La Sorisete des Estopes*', *CCMe*, 46:53–69, places these works in the context of an existing tradition, which includes Arabic versions of the fable. C. A. Adkins, 'Beastly mothers — beastly sons: *Richeut*', *Reinardus*, 16:3–17, analyses the effects of Richeut's immoral, often animalistic behaviour on her son, Samson. Not only is the tale a cautionary one about the importance of upbringing, but it parallels human and animal activity, referring not only to examples from the animal world, but also to *Renart*. T. Hunt, 'Les *us* des femmes et la *clergie* dans *Richeut*', Braet, *Laughter*, 155–72, finds this somewhat sinister tale, often classed as a *fabliau*, better defined not as a parody of the courtly novel, but as a *travesti* of the genre, with the women on top. C. Bégin, 'Le fabliau, genre didactique (étude sur *La Damoisele qui ne pooit oïr parler de foutre*)', *Reinardus*, 16:19–29, believes the work is an object lesson through humour, reflecting on the nature of chastity, ignorance, and meaning.

9. Drama

L. T. Ramey, 'Jean Bodel's *Jeu de saint Nicolas*: a call for non-violent crusade', *FrF*, 27.3:1–14, argues that a close reading of the text reveals Bodel to have been a prophetic pacifist. N. Pasero, 'Satira, parodia e autoparodia: elementi per une discussione (in particolare di Guido Cavalcanti e Adam de la Halle)', Mühlethaler, *Parodie*,

27–44, sees in the *Jeu de la feuillée* a parodic interplay between the idealized courtly lady and the disillusioned author.

10. Historiography and Chronicle

The History of the Holy War: Ambroise's 'Estoire de la Guerre Sainte', ed. Marianne Ailes and Malcolm Barber, 2 vols, Woodbridge, Boydell, xv + 211, xix + 214 pp., is a valuable and accessible edition and translation. Vol. I (Text), includes a relatively brief introduction covering the MSS and previous editions, language, and principles of edition, with an index following the original text. Vol. II (Translation) offers a chronology and maps, a comprehensive introduction about the author, dating, historical setting and importance, literary value, and notes on translation. A further index follows the modern English prose translation.

W. Sayers, 'Ships and sailors in Geiffrei Gaimar's "Estoire des Engleis"', *MLR*, 98:299–310, studies the sea-faring vocabulary of the work, adding to A. Bell's previous lexical notes.

E. Mullally, 'Did John of Earley write the *Histoire de Guillaume le Maréchal*?', *ICLS* 9, 255–64, is strongly in favour of the attribution on stylistic and practical grounds and vigorously refutes P. Meyer's view that John of Earley only commissioned the work, another John being the actual author.

LATE MEDIEVAL LITERATURE

By Nicole Lassahn, *University of Chicago*

1. Romance

J. Cerquiglini-Toulet, 'Écho et Sibylle, la voix féminine au moyen âge', *Equinoxe*, 23, 2002:81–91, explores theories of the gendered voice in medieval accounts, arguing that the feminine voice is incarnated in figures like Echo. In her, 'Altérités dans le langage: émotions, gestes, codes', *Littérature*, 130:68–74, C.-T. meditates on otherness in 14th-c. literature and in Villon, using animal speech and feminine speech as *foci*. A. Ballor, 'Il mito di Giasone e Medea nel quattrocento francese', *SFr*, 47:3–22, examines the myth as history, moral, and *exemplum* of unhappy love in a wide range of 14th-c. works inspired by the *Roman de Troie*. C. Ferlampin-Acher, 'La nuit des temps dans *Perceforest*: de la nuit de Walpurgis à la nuit transfigurée', *RLaR*, 106, 2002:415–35, studies the relationship between night and the genre of the *roman*. E. Gaucher, 'Les nuits diaboliques de Richard sans Peur (1496)', *ib.*, 437–53, argues that Richard's diabolical lineage relates to his inability to feel fear, and treats both the *Roman de Richart* and the *mise-en-prose* of the *Vie du terrible Robert le Dyable*. C. Cooper-Deniau, 'Le diable au Moyen Âge, entre peur et angoisse. Le motif de "l'enfant voué au diable"et la légende de Robert le diable', *TLit*, 16:27–45, traces the legend from the 12th c. to the 15th c., focusing on the coexistence of a frightening devil with a ridiculous one. A. Corbellari, 'Le château illuminé et les pièges de l'amour: l'éclat ambigu des pierres taillées', *MoyFr*, 50, 2002:61–69, argues for a change in the symbolic value of the castle in the late middle ages; examples include Martin le Franc, René d'Anjou, and Machaut. A. M. Babbi, 'Le "Guerrin meschino"d'Andrea da Barberino et le remaniement de Jean de Rochemeure', *ib.*, 51–53:9–18, details the reception of the matter of France, from both epic and romance traditions, in northern Italy. Nancy B. Black, *Medieval Narratives of Accused Queens*, Gainesville, Florida U.P., xviii + 261 pp., examines multiple instances of two stories, the Constance story and the story of the Empress of Rome, popular for over two centuries. French works covered are Gautier de Coinci (the earliest example), *La Manekine* (Philippe de Rémi), the *Roman du Comte d'Anjou* (Jehan Maillart), parts of the *Miracles de Nostre Dame par personnages*, and *La Belle Hélène de Constantinople* (Jehan Wauquelin).

Patricia Victorin, '*Ysaïe le Triste*': *une esthétique de la confluence: tours, tombeaux, vergers et fontaines*, Champion, 2002, 501 pp., explores issues of lineage both in terms of the Arthurian characters within the text and in terms of literary history, as later forms, such as the *mise-en-prose*, refer to previous genres and practices. Parts of the book focus on place and time, lineage, reception, and rewriting, and the *roman* as memory or reliquary. David A. Fein, *Displacements of Power: Readings of the 'Cent nouvelles nouvelles'*, Lanham, U.P. of America, vii + 111 pp., presents political readings of each of seven of the tales; Fein is especially concerned with the notion of marriage as alliance. The book contains chapters on tales 1, 28, 33, 38, 43, 55, and 99. C. Galderisi, 'Du langage érotique au langage amoureux: représentations du *créaturel* dans le *Petit Jehan de Saintré* et dans la nouvelle XCIX des *Cent nouvelles nouvelles*', *MoyFr*, 50, 2002: 13–29, explores how erotic language is linked to bodily love and the body in these two works. M. C. Timelli, '*Erec* and *Cligés* en prose: quelques repères pour une comparaison', *ib.*, 51–53: 159–75, searches for common traits shared by these *mises-en-prose* other than Chrétien de Troyes as source. A. M. Finoli, 'Locutions dans *Jehan d'Avennes*', *ib.*, 279–90, provides an account of the idioms used in this *roman*, including how and when he employs thematic patterns. L. Evdokimova, 'Natura, ars, imitatio: l'image du "poète parfait" dans les "Douze Dames de Rhétorique" ', *ib.*, 263–77, explores the way that the poem uses these terms and how they relate to each other as a kind of rhetorical theory of the perfect poet. J. Koopmans, '*Courtois d'Arras* (vers 1250) par Courtois d'Arras', *LR*, 56, 2002: 3–25, proposes a new date, new author, and hence a new cultural context (the *Pui d'Arras*) for the *Courtois d'Arras*. N. Cartlidge, 'Aubrey de Bassingbourn, Ida de Beauchamp, and the context of the "Estrif de deus dames" in Oxford, Bodleian Library MS Digby 86', *NQ*, 47, 2000: 411–14, places this short debate poem in the context of others found in the manuscript; he also discusses evidence found in the colophon which relates to provenance and readership.

B. Sargent-Baur, 'Prologus/epilogus est, non legitur', *RoQ*, 50: 2–11, focusing on the *Manekine* and *Jehan et Blonde*, re-examines the relationships between prologues and whole works, arguing that the author's explicit statements about meaning are often (wrongly) disregarded in contemporary criticism. F. Clier-Colombani, 'Des fenêtres ouvertes sur l'imaginaire', *Senefiance*, 49: 67–83, ties the window to other motifs: death, mirrors, and water; the essay is general, but covers *Mélusine* perhaps more than the other (multiple) examples. F. Wolfzettel, 'La "découverte" du folklore et du merveilleux folklorique au Moyen Age tardif', *MoyFr*, 51–53: 627–40, examines La Sale's conception of the marvellous, folkloric, and mythic in his writings. V. Dang, 'Vers une revalorisation d'Énée en France: le *Séjour d'honneur* d'Octavien de Saint-Gelais', *CRM*, 10: 121–29, argues that Octavien uses the *Ovide moralisé* to rehabilitate Aeneas and emphasizes his overseas journey rather than his betrayal of Dido in order to present him as an ideal prince. F. Duval, 'Les sources du *Séjour d'honneur* d'Octavien de Saint-Gelais', *Romania*, 121:164–91, studying those texts used directly by Octavien, argues for an emphasis on more diverse 15th-c. texts rather than earlier texts which are important because of their place in the 20th-c. canon. G. Polizzi, '*Par les fenestres qui lors estoient ouvertes*: le motif de la fenêtre merveilleuse dans les romans de la fin du Moyen Age', *Senefiance*, 49:357–72, traces the window on to another world in some late medieval works, including *Perceforest*, the *Séjour d'honneur*, and the *Livre du cuer d'amour espris* of René d'Anjou.

2. Epic

F. Sberlati, 'Eroi verso Oriente: l'esotismo nella letteratura medievale', *AnI*, 21:427–46, explores depictions of the Orient in French and Italian travel narratives, contrasting these to crusading and other chivalric narratives; the major French example is the *Entrée d'Espagne*. C. Harvey, '*La Manekine* et ses avatars: *Lion de Bourges*', *MoyFr*, 51–53:339–48, examines both the source relationship between these two texts and the transformation of the *roman* into epic. C. Gaullier-Bougassas, 'Alexandre, héros païen ou héros pré-chrétien? Deux stratégies opposées de réécriture à la fin du Moyen Âge', *ib.*, 305–26, compares attitudes towards Alexander's religious beliefs and his divine election in two late versions of the story: *Renart le Contrefait* and Jean Wauquelin's *Histoire du bon roi Alexandre*. M. Raby, 'L'argent: cette nouvelle merveille des merveilles dans la version en prose de la *Chanson d'Esclarmonde*', *FCS*, 28:212–23, argues that the rewriting of an epic in the form of a romance affects the epic feature of the marvellous; specifically, he argues that in this work money becomes a kind of saviour, solving the evils of society, and in this sense is miraculous.

3. Drama

Les Mystères de la Procession de Lille, ed. Alan E. Knight, vol. II, *De Josué à David*, Geneva, Droz, 668 pp., continues K.'s edition of these mystery plays which were performed for the procession at Lille beginning about 1270. P. Kunstmann, 'Les formules de salutation dans les *Miracles de Nostre Dame par personnages*: inventaire, analyse, valeur pragmatique', *MoyFr*, 51–53:373–86, explores the idioms used by those who are saying farewell, using the *Miracles* as a corpus. L. Pierdominici, 'Conter et juger dans les *Arrêts d'Amour* de Martial d'Auvergne', *FCS*, 28:199–211, investigates the tension between the text as juridical — a series of discrete trials — and narrative — this series is narrated to us.

4. Fabliaux

Chapter 5 of Lisa Renée Perfetti, *Women and Laughter in Medieval Comic Literature*, Ann Arbor, Michigan U.P., ix + 286 pp., argues that the wives in two 15th-c. and 16th-c. French farces undermine clichés about feminine loquacity and reinforce the value of women's work. A. Conte, '*Du Vilain Mire*: origine e struttura di un *fabliau*', *MedRom*, 26, 2002 : 366–83, studies the sources for this anonymous fabliau from the second half of the 13th c.; these sources include Jacques de Vitry and Nicole de Bozon. T. van Hemelryck, 'Classé x en moyen français [. . .]: des saints facétieux', *MoyFr*, 50, 2002 : 93–114, catalogues comic uses of saints in the late middle ages. C. Deschepper-Archer, 'Traduire, vous voulez rire? Le fabliau des *Braies au Cordelier* et la farce de *Frère Guillebert* en français moderne', *ib.*, 71–91, considers the role of humour in the modern translation of this medieval work as it moves from fabliau to farce.

5. Lyric

Gert Pinkernell, *François Villon: biographie critique et autres études*, Heidelberg, Winter, 2002, 176 pp., contains seven essays on late-medieval literature, mostly on Villon. The first is an updated biography of the poet; it is followed by three essays on individual poems, and two on Villon's reception. The final piece is a study of two ballads written by Marie de Clèves. E. Cayley, 'Drawing conclusions: the poetics of closure in Alain Chartier's verse', *FCS*, 28 : 51–64, examines Chartier's own vocabulary of closure, arguing that his works contain a deliberate tension between closure and open-endedness. G. Angelo, 'A most uncourtly lady: the testimony of the *Belle dame sans mercy*', *Exemplaria*, 15 : 133–57, considers courtliness as both erotic and judicial in both the Chartier poem and the ensuing *querelle* in order to examine how 'parameters of language [are] enforced within the debate.' D. Hult, 'La courtoisie en décadence: l'exemple de *La Belle Dame sans merci* d'Alain Chartier', Baumgartner, *Progrès*, 251–60, reading the poem in the context of the *querelle* over it, locates the decadence of courtly love not inside its own system but within the malaise of aristocratic society itself. P. Noble, 'Les deux traductions anglaises du *Quadrilogue invectif* d'Alain Chartier', *MoyFr*, 51–53 : 469–77, argues, on the basis of changes made to them, that the two translations were made for two very different groups of readers. S. Bliggenstorfer, 'Phraséologie et satire: le cas d'Eustache

Deschamps', *ib.*, 79–90, explores the relationships between satiric content and the genres of the *formes fixes*. G. Roccati, 'Analyse thématique et ordinateur: quelques réflexions à propos d'Eustache Deschamps', *SLF*, 27, 2002: 11–26, concerns methodology, using Deschamps as a test case for a thematic analysis of an entire corpus of texts. E. Roesner, 'Labouring in the midst of wolves: reading a group of *Fauvel* motets', *EMH*, 22: 169–245, argues that the different texts from BNF, MS ff. 146 together 'yield a collective commentary on the state of the monarchy and the realm'. R. Crespo, 'Richard de Fournival, *Lonc Tans me sui escondis* (R. 1541)', *Romania*, 121: 382–414, provides a new edition of this text with extensive line-by-line notes. F. Wolfzettel, 'Y a-t-il une conscience historique dans la lyrique courtoise du Moyen Âge?', Baumgartner, *Progrès*, 215–29, explores the medieval historical consciousness by examining how the concept of novelty was employed over the course of two centuries of lyric production.

MUSIC AND TEXT. A. Stone, 'Self-reflexive songs and their readers in the late fourteenth century', *EMus*, 31: 181–94, considers the phenomenon of first-person lyric practice from a reader's point of view, examining those cases where this technique is transmitted in writing rather than oral performance. A. Butterfield, '*Enté*: a survey and reassessment of the term in thirteenth- and fourteenth-century music and poetry', *EMH*, 22: 67–101, reconsiders the varied meanings of the term (traditionally thought to mean 'grafted') in both musical and poetic contexts, especially the motet. Y. Plumley, 'An "episode in the south"? *Ars subtilior* and the patronage of French princes', *ib.*, 103–68, is an account of MS distribution for late French song repertory (*c.*1380 to 1420): most chansons survive in southern and Italian witnesses, while most northern sources preserve *ars nova* works; her 'Intertextuality in the fourteenth-century *chanson*', *MusL*, 84: 355–77, is a survey of late-14th-c. citation and allusion, arguing that these practices were more common and more mainstream than is sometimes thought; and in 'Playing the citation game in the late fourteenth-century *chanson*', *EMus*, 31: 20–39, she examines the use of citation — musical and textual, especially refrains — in later medieval music, including Machaut's adaptation of this practice to polyphony. D. Leech-Wilkinson, 'Articulating *ars subtilior* song', *ib.*, 7–18, examines minim rests as evidence for phrasing in late medieval songs, especially in Machaut. O. Ellsworth, 'Musical representations of the ass', pp. 93–96 of *Tales within Tales: Apuleius through Time*, ed. Constance S. Wright and Julia Bolton Holloway, NY, AMS, 2000, xv + 198 pp., gives quite a short account of musical representations of the ass in medieval culture, including a brief reference to the *Roman de Fauvel*.

6. Historical Texts

B. Ribémont, 'Dire le vrai et chanter des louanges: *La Prise d'Alexandrie* de Guillaume de Machaut', *CRM*, 10:155–72, 173–90, connects the problem of how to laud the hero (Pierre de Lusignan) and tell the historical truth to the intersection of genres: *dit* and history. C. Gaullier-Bougassas, 'Images littéraires de Chypre et évolution de l'esprit de croisade au XIVe siècle', Baumgartner, *Progrès*, 123–35, argues that Machaut's *Prise d'Alexandrie* and Mézières's *Songe du Vieil Pèlerin* both present a renewed crusading ideal as a kind of spiritual progress, one that responds to the loss of the Holy Land by placing more emphasis on Cyprus as a site of Roman Christianity in the East and on Peter I as the last great crusading hero. S. Huot, 'Dangerous embodiments: Froissart's Harton and Jean d'Arras's *Mélusine*', *Speculum*, 78:400–20, compares these two instances where a supernatural or magical being takes human form in order to explore the role of the body in the construction of identity. M.-T. de Medeiros, 'Dans le sillage de Jean le Bel: la chute d'Edouard II chez Jean d'Outremeuse et chez Froissart', *CRM*, 10:131–42, considers both accounts in relation to Jean le Bel as a source text.

M. Rus, 'L'espace du temps à la fin du moyen âge', *RZLG*, 27:3–13, explores the 15th-c.'s idea of the present and the end of time using universal histories, chronicles, biography, and histories of particular groups. C. Croizy-Naquet, 'Insertion et réécriture: l'exemple du *Roman de Troie* dans la deuxième rédaction de *l'Histoire ancienne jusqu'à César*', *MoyFr*, 51–53:177–91, focuses on Helen's *enlèvement* as a site where this historian uses a literary source. E. Langille, 'Traduire *La Chronique* de Guillaume de Tyr', *ib.*, 387–94, considers the translation and the changes made to its account of crusading in terms of different kinds of history (and fiction): literary history, myth, and history of the orient. C. Thiry, 'Néologismes et créations verbales dans la traduction par Jean Wauquelin des *Chroniques de Hainaut* de Jacques de Guise', *ib.*, 571–91, catalogues neologisms and words not in the dictionary found in this translation. S. Marnette, 'Sources du récit et discours rapportés: l'art de la représentation dans les chroniques et les romans français des 14e et 15e siècles', *ib.*, 435–57, considers narrative strategies for constructing historical truth, especially direct discourse, in both *romans* and chronicles. T. van Hemelryck, 'La ou les traductions françaises des *Annales historie illustrium principum Hanonie* de Jacques de Guise? L'éclairage de la tradition manuscrite', *ib.*, 613–25, considers whether or not there are two translations of this text, using the evidence of the MS tradition as well as the history of philological activity on it. E. Inglis, 'Image and illustration in Jean Fouquet's *Grandes Chroniques de France*', *FHS*, 26:185–224, examines the relationships between these miniatures and the political contexts of the events depicted in the text and the manuscript and its circulation. J. Dufournet, 'Grandeur et modernité de Philippe de Commynes (1447–1511)', *FCS*, 28:111–23, overviews Commynes's life and works; this is a printed version of Dufournet's plenary address at the fourth Congress on Fifteenth-Century Studies, July 2000. K. Casebier, 'History or fiction? The role of doubt in Antoine de La Sale's *Le Paradis de la royne Sibille*', *ib.*, 37–50, argues that the narrative asides cause the reader to doubt the truthfulness of the tales, which purport to be accurate historical accounts, even though these asides ostensibly contain 'facts'. C. Emerson, 'Who witnessed and narrated the *Banquet of the Pheasant* (1454)? A codicological examination of the account's five versions', *ib.*, 124–137, uses both codicological evidence and internal contradictions within the accounts themselves to evaluate the reliability (and possible historical identity) of the narrator/witness to the events. G. Palumbo, 'Un nuovo manoscritto de *Les Trois Fils de Rois* e alcune riflessione su David Aubert copista', *MedRom*, 26, 2002:161–217, is a description of London, BL, MS Harley 4408 and its connections to other MSS and extant editions; P. also makes a case based on this codicological evidence for David Aubert as an early editor.

7. Religious and Philosophical Works

S. Mueller-Loewald and J. Dufournet, 'Quatre figures féminines apocryphes dans certains *Mystères de la Passion* en France', *FCS*, 28:173–83, examine the addition of apocryphal female characters as a strategy for adding emotional content to the passion narrative: a story difficult to alter in other ways. C. Buchanan, 'The Campsay collection of Old French saints' lives: a re-examination of its structure and provenance', *Scriptorium*, 57:51–83, re-examines the relationship of the late 13th-c. or early 14th-c. MS (London, BL Addit. 70513) to its provenance; in particular he reconsiders the idea that it was read aloud at mealtimes at a convent in Campsay, in Suffolk, and the possibility that it had a lay patron. M. Longtin, 'Maçons, trois fenêtres s'il vous plaît! *Le Mystère de sainte Barbe en 5 journées*: un décor qui se construit?', *Senefiance*, 49:307–18, considers dramatic treatments of the windows in the tower in this version of the Barbara story, windows from which one sees nothing. A. Gross, 'Vision et regard: la métaphore de la fenêtre dans une enluminure du Livre d'Heures de Marie de Bourgogne, *cod. vind.* 1857', *ib.*, 193–208, considers the roles of the miniatures within a historical and codicological context. D. Hüe, 'Psaumes et prières, paraphrases et réécritures', *MoyFr*, 51–53:349–72, explores paraphrase as a form of literary adaptation distinct from other kinds of adaptation such as commentary. M. Thiry-Stassin, 'Le vocabulaire en action: problèmes de vocabulaire dans les *Vies* des prophètes Helyas, Helisee et Jonas (Namur, XVe siècle)', *ib.*, 559–69, treats the use of Latin and latinate vocabulary in Frère Thomas de Lemborc's translation of three saints' lives.

Jeanette Beer, *Beasts of Love: Richard de Fournival's 'Bestiaire d'amour' and a Woman's 'Response'*, Toronto U.P., x + 214 pp., treats not only the *Bestiaire d'amour* but also an anonymous *Response* found in four of the MSS. Beer argues that this *response* undermines Richard's structure, which she examines in chs 1–4, while ch. 5 treats the *Response*, and a final chapter considers further reception. P. Squillacioti, 'Appunti sul testo del "Tesoro"in Toscana: il bestiario nel MS Laurenziano Plut. XLII.22', *SMV*, 48, 2002:157–69, discusses this mid-14th-c. reception and translation of the bestiary portion of Latini in Tuscan dialect. M. T. Zanola, 'Le langage des pierres précieuses et l'expression des sentiments', *MoyFr*, 50, 2002:47–60, traces the symbolic value of gems in the middle ages.

WOMEN'S SPIRITUAL WRITING. Maud Burnett McInerney, *Eloquent Virgins from Thecla to Joan of Arc*, NY, Palgrave, 250 pp., explores the narrative of the virgin martyr as a literary genre, one which is in many cases purely literary. Ch. 6 concerns several early French vernacular examples, and an epilogue treats Joan of Arc. M. Jeay and K. Garay, 'Douceline de Digne: de l'usage politique de l'extase mystique', *RLaR*, 106, 2002:475–92, consider the episodes of ravishment and levitation in Douceline's life as both a demonstration of her sanctity and a public demonstration of her powers which has a political dimension in the context of images of sacred kingship in France. M.-R. Bonnet, 'Douceline et le Crist, ou la fenêtre ouverte', *Senefiance*, 49:43–55, also considers Douceline's visions, which B. characterizes as Franciscan, arguing that these fantastic events place the narrative between human and divine, between earthly and heavenly. N. Margolis, 'Joan of Arc', Dinshaw, *Companion*, 256–66, examines writings about Joan and her influence on constructions of female authority. J. Summit, 'Women and authorship', *ib.*, 91–108, examines women in relation to medieval theories of authorship and *auctoritas*, with special reference to Christine de Pizan and Marguerite Porete. J.-C. Mühlethaler, 'Quand Fortune, ce sont les hommes. Aspects de la demythification de la déesse, d'Adam de la Halle à Alain Chartier', Foehr-Janssens, *Fortune*, 177–206, claims that in three late-medieval treatments of Fortune her power or traditional presentation is subverted.

8. Instruction Manuals and Conduct Books

G. Nachtwey, 'Geoffroi de Charny's *Book of Chivalry* and violence in *The Man of Law's Tale* and *The Franklin's Tale*', *EMS*, 20: 107–20, uses Charny's work as a source for a historical account of chivalry during the 14th c., and to explore attitudes toward legitimate violence in the middle ages. M. Johnston, 'Gender as conduct in the courtesy guides for aristocratic boys and girls of Amanieu de Sescás', *ib.*, 75–84, concerns two paired texts of advice for each sex addressed specifically to aristocratic readers, arguing that aristocratic status may be more important than gender in determining behaviour in these texts. G. Dumas, 'La fenêtre dans les traités de peste de la région de Montpellier aux XIVe et XVe siècles', *Senefiance*, 49: 157–66, compares house and human body within these texts about the plague, which she considers part of a didactic genre written for a lay or general audience and responding to a particular audience-need in a particular time period. A. M. De Gandt, 'Autobiography as a rhetorical strategy in the *Livre du Chevalier de la Tour Landry pour l'enseignement de ses filles*', *Mediaevalia*, 23, 2002: 61–74, considers the persuasive value of those passages from the text which meet modern standards of autobiography. V. Sekules, 'Spinning yarns: clean linens and domestic values in late medieval French culture', pp. 79–91 of *The Material Culture of Sex, Procreation and Marriage in Premodern Europe*, ed. Anne L. McClanan and Karen Rosoff Encarnacíon, NY, Palgrave, 2002, xiv + 285 pp., rather than assuming that household cleanliness is imposed on women by men, explores the ways that women use ideals of clean linen in household culture; the essay treats Christine de Pizan's *Treasure of the City of Ladies* and her *Book of Three Virtues*, and *Le Menagier de Paris*. M. T. Zanola, 'Phrasèmes sémantiques et pragmatiques dans le lexique des sciences du XVe siècle: pour une typologie de la formation phraséologique', *MoyFr*, 51–53: 641–50, details the beginnings of mathematical terminology in French.

9. Translation

Guillaume Tardif, *Les Facecies de Poge: traduction du Liber facetiarum de Poggio Bracciolini*, ed. Frédéric Duval and Sandrine Hériché-Pradeau, Geneva, Droz, 314 pp., is an edition of Tardif's translation from Latin to French of these moral tales, popular in the very late 15th century. L. Evdokimova, 'La traduction en vers et la traduction en prose à la fin du XIIIe et au début du XIVe siècles: quelques lectures de la *Consolation* de Boèce', *MA*, 109: 237–60, argues that verse and prose translations of Boethius in the late middle ages differed in function and audience, namely that those in verse were more philosophical and historical while the prose translations united didactic and creative functions. M. Boulton, 'Jean Galopes, traducteur des *Meditationes Vitae Christi*', *MoyFr*, 51–53:91–102, argues that this translation may be for a lay audience since it combines political and religious goals for a faithful king and his country. L. Brook, 'Jean le Bègue, interprète iconographique de Salluste', *ib.*, 103–12, examines Oxford, Bodleian Library, MS Orville 141, which dates from the beginning of the 15th c. and contains a French translation of the text with Latin gloss, attributed to Jean le Bègue. O. A. Duhl, 'La *Nef des folles* selon les cinq sens de nature, "translaté"du latin en français par Jehan Drouyn (1498): traduction, compilation, innovation', *ib.*, 193–210, considers this version, a synthesis of the multiple Latin and French versions of the *Nef des fous*, as translation, as adaptation, and as a mode of transmission between cultures. A. Bengtsson, 'Le dérimage et la traduction de la *Vie de Sainte Geneviève*', *ib.*, 63–77, studies the relationships between the 14th-c. translation, the Latin source, and the 14th-c. *mise-en-prose.* C. Buridant, 'La "traduction intralinguale" en moyen français à travers la modernisation et le rajeunissement des textes manuscrits et imprimés: quelques pistes et perspectives', *ib.*, 113–57, argues for translation within a language (as opposed to translation from one language to another) as a sort of interpretive or rewriting activity. E. Suomela-Härmä, 'Stratégies de traduction dans la première version française des "Triomphes" de Pétrarque', *ib.*, 547–58, compares this 15th-c. prose French translation to the Italian original, with an emphasis on where it has gone wrong.

10. Bi- and Tri-Lingualism, including French in England

A. Taylor, 'Manual to miscellany: stages in the commercial copying of vernacular literature in England', *YES*, 33:1–17, considers early (mid-13th-c.) professional production of instructional manuals (e.g. William of Waddington's *Manuel de péchés)* and Anglo-Norman romances (e.g. Grosseteste's *Chasteau d'amour*) as precursors to miscellanies. A. Butterfield, 'Articulating the author: Gower and the French vernacular codex', *ib.*, 80–96, uses constructions of authorship from the *Rose*, *Fauvel*, and the works of Machaut and Froissart to assess Gower's use of Latin in the *Confessio Amantis*. J. Scahill, 'Trilingualism in Early Middle English miscellanies: languages and literature', *ib.*, 18–32, considers literary aspects of tri-lingual miscellanies. Three of the essays in *New Readings of Chaucer's Poetry*, ed. Robert G. Benson and Susan J. Ridyard, Cambridge, Brewer, 200 pp., treat some aspect of a French source in Chaucer. H. Cooper, '11: Chaucerian poetics'

(31–50), mentions the *Rose*, Froissart's *Meliador*, and Edward the Black Prince's *Livre de seynt medicines*; J. Fleming, 'The best line in Ovid and the worst' (51–74), the *Rose*, mostly as a source for Ovid; and R. B. Palmer, 'Chaucer's *Legend of Good Women*: the narrator's tale' (183–94), more extensively, Machaut's two *Jugement* poems, the *Voir dit*, and Froissart's *Prison amoureuse*. C. McDonough, 'Paris, Bibliothèque nationale de France, lat. 16483: contents, audience, and the matter of Old French', *MedS*, 64, 2002: 131–216, studies in detail this particular sermon collection, focusing on bilingualism and audience in preaching; he includes a detailed codicological description and a separate list of all the French words included in the manuscript. B. Merrilees, 'Renvois et réseaux sémantiques dans un dictionnaire bilingue du 15e siècle', *MoyFr*, 51–53:459–67, treats a two-volume, indexed, Latin-French dictionary whose structure differs from that of other medieval lexicographical tools, partly because of its referential system. D. Trotter, 'Traduction ou texte authentique? Le problème des chartes', *ib.*, 593–611, examines the influence of Latin and Latin forms on documents in the French vernacular.

II. Individual Writers

CHRISTINE DE PIZAN. *Christine de Pizan: A Casebook*, ed. Barbara K. Altmann and Deborah K. McGrady, NY, Routledge, xiii + 296 pp., includes a preface (xi-xiii) by Charity Cannon Willard about early Christine studies, and an introduction (1–5) by the editors, which explains that, unlike other Routledge casebooks, this contains new, invited work and no reprinted articles. R. Blumenfeld-Kosinski, 'Christine de Pizan and the political life in late medieval France' (9–24), argues that Christine's change from observer of political events in France to a stance as the 'voice of France' also changed the form and genre of her literary production. L. Walters, 'Christine de Pizan as translator and the voice of the body politic' (25–41), explores Christine's changing use of translation as part of a programme to legitimize the French royal family as well as the French language. E. J. Richards, 'Somewhere between destructive glosses and chaos: Christine de Pizan and medieval theology' (43–55), asks how much Christine knew, as a woman, about the (largely male) field of theology, arguing that she defined herself as a poet-theologian, following the example of Thomas Aquinas. M. Zimmerman (trans. G. Stedman), 'Christine de Pizan: memory's architect' (57–77), argues that Christine adopted textual strategies designed to preserve her memory through posterity, since she was particularly at risk of being forgotten as a female intellectual. R. Brown-Grant, 'Christine de Pizan as a defender of women' (81–100), re-examines Christine's defence of women in the context of other medieval pro-feminist writers, arguing on this basis against the notion — gleaned by evaluating her in the context of modern feminism — that she was conservative. R. L. Krueger, 'Christine's treasure: women's honor and household economies in the *Livre des trois vertus*' (101–14), argues that, unlike male-authored conduct books for women, Christine emphasizes women's economic roles, appealing to their reason (through political theory) rather than to fear (through *exempla*). T. Fenster, 'Who's a heroine?: the example of Christine de Pizan' (115–28), argues for the Sibylle, and for Christine herself, as female exemplar, in the absence of other heroines. J. L. Kellogg, '*Le Livre de la Cité des Dames*: reconfiguring knowledge and reimagining gendered space' (129–46), describes the relationship between the material world and the medieval female subject position by examining the shifting conceptions of space in the *Cité des Dames*. T. Adams, 'Love as metaphor in Christine de Pizan's *ballade* cycles' (149–65), reads Christine's lyric poetry in the context both of her three lyric cycles and of her work as a whole, especially the relationship between her lyric love poems and her narrative feminist works. M. Desmond, 'The *Querelle de la Rose* and the ethics of reading' (167–80), examines how Christine adapts the semi-public rhetoric of letter-writing into the vernacular tradition and for a female voice. A. Tarnowski, 'The lessons of experience and the *Chemin de long estude*' (181–97), links the poem's three 'beginnings', to her authority as a female writer and her participation in political questions of her day. L. Dulac and C. Reno, 'The *Livre de l'advision Cristine*' (199–214), working from recent criticism, link autobiographical and political readings of the *Advision*. M. Boulton, ' "Nous deffens de feu, [. . .] de pestilence, de guerres": Christine de Pizan's religious works' (215–28), sets Christine's religious works in the context of vernacular devotional practice and religious writing, arguing that her practice was innovative. J. Laidlaw, 'Christine and the manuscript tradition' (231–49), treats Christine's autograph and presentation MSS, linking them to Christine's 'publishing' career. N. Margolis, 'Modern editions: makers of the Christinian corpus' (251–70), examines Christine's place in a nationalistic scholarly programme through a survey of critical editions from the 17th c. onwards.

B. McCormick, 'Building the ideal city: female memorial praxis in Christine de Pizan's *Cité des Dames*', *StLM*, 36: 149–71, examines Christine's use of architecture and other memory devices as part of an ethical (i.e. pro-feminist) history. S. Dudash, 'Christine de Pizan and the "menu peuple" ', *Speculum*, 78: 788–831, is an examination of Christine's later prose works as a politically engaged intercession between noble and non-noble (*menu*) persons. D. Hult, 'The *Roman de la Rose*, Christine de Pizan, and the *querelle des femmes*', Dinshaw, *Companion*, 184–94, places the *querelle* in an accessible chronological narrative of Christine's literary career. B. Ribémont, 'L'"automne"de Christine de Pizan', Baumgartner, *Progrès*, 79–91, analyses several elements of decadence in Christine de Pizan as decline, that is, a sense of lateness or *fin de siècle*. J. Holderness, 'Compilation, commentary, and conversation in Christine de Pizan', *EMS*, 20:47–55, reads the opening of part one of the *Advision Cristine* as a form of commentary on its sources: texts by Dante, Boethius, Alain de Lille, and Christine herself; she claims that the passage 'deheroicizes human life, but at the same time invests it with the possibility for seeking and finding knowledge'. The first part of Margaret W. Ferguson, *Dido's Daughters: Literacy, Gender, and Empire in Early Modern England and France*, Chicago U.P., xiv + 506 pp., traces the ways that gender, literacy, and the growth of nationalism are related; the last four chapters are case studies of reading practices, and ch. 4, 'An empire of her own: literacy as appropriation in Christine de Pizan's *Cité des Dames*', uses Christine as an example of a French female reader. E. Allen, 'Incest in the story of Tancredi: Christine de Pizan's poetics of euphemism', pp. 191–223 of *Incest and the Literary Imagination*, ed. Elizabeth Barnes, Gainesville, Florida U.P., 2002, 382 pp., argues that Christine, in reframing this story as a defence of women, departs from Boccaccio, by removing the incest from the story, but that this also removes his attendant critique of feudal organization and renders Christine complicit in systems of courtly patronage. D. M. González Doreste and F. D. M. Plaza Picón, 'A propos de la compilation: du *De claris mulieribus* de Boccace à *Le Livre de la Cité des Dames* de Christine de Pisan', *MoyFr*, 51–53:327–37, argue that Christine's use of her source is a kind of game, a sort of compilation which makes simple comparison with her sources inadequate. A. Schoysman, 'Les deux manuscrits du remaniement de l'*Epitre Othéa* de Christine de Pizan par Jean Miélot', *ib.*, 505–28, describes the features, relationship, *mise-en-page*, gloss, and prologues of these two MSS. G. Angeli, 'Encore sur Boccace et Christine de Pizan: remarques sur le *De mulieribus claris* et le *Livre de la cité des dames* ("Plourer, parler, filer mist Dieu en femmes"I. 10)', *ib.*, 50, 2002: 115–25, explores Christine's complicated use of Boccaccio's own rhetorical strategies in order to make fundamentally different claims.

GUILLAUME DE DIGULLEVILLE. P. Maupeu, 'La tentation autobiographique dans le songe allégorique édifiant de Guillaume de Digulleville: *Le Pèlerinage de vie humaine*', pp. 49–67 of *Songes et songeurs (XIIIe–XVIIIe siècle)*, ed. Nathalie Dauvois and Jean-Philippe Grosperrin, Quebec, Univ. Laval, 253 pp., comparing the first and second versions, explores the tensions between allegory and autobiography.

F. Pomel, 'Enjeux d'un travail de réécriture: les *incipits* du *Pèlerinage de vie humaine* de Digulleville et leurs remaniements ultérieurs', *MA*, 109:457–71, compares Digulleville's 1355 revision, as well as two later versions by other authors (1465 and 1500), with the earlier (and currently edited) version of 1330, using changes in the *incipits* to gauge reception and rewriting.

GERSON. B. McGuire, 'Patterns of male affectivity in the Late Middle Ages: the case of Jean Gerson', pp. 163–78 of *Varieties of Devotion in the Middle Ages and Renaissance*, ed. Susan C. Karant-Nunn, Turnhout, Brepols, xv + 213 pp., reads sources (especially familial letters) concerning Gerson's inner, affective life, in relation to his political and theological goals, e.g. his response to papal schism.

JEAN DE MEUN. Daniel Heller-Roazen, *Fortune's Face: The Roman de la Rose and the Poetics of Contingency*, Baltimore, Johns Hopkins U.P., xiii + 206 pp., considers various aspects of contingency within both halves of the poem together. Beginning with a theoretical account of medieval theories of Fortune, the book moves through the ambiguities inherent in the first-person narration, the figure of *Fortuna* herself, and the problems of free will and foreknowledge. L. Rossi, 'De nouveau sur Jean de Meun', *Romania*, 121:430–60, connects 18 documents in the State Archives of Bologna concerning debts contracted by a figure who is probably Jean de Meun to him and to his part of the *Rose*. A. Malmborg, 'Les mots savants dans deux textes de Jean de Meun', *MoyFr*, 51–53:421–33, compares Jean's use of latinate words in his French compositions and in texts he translated into French from Latin. P.-Y. Badel, 'Alexandre dans le *Roman de la Rose* et le *Songe du vieil pèlerin*', *Romania*, 121:415–429, compares the last of four mentions of Alexander in the *Rose* (in Nature's confession, ll. 18732–56) to Mézières's use of the same figure, arguing that Jean de Meun uses him to talk about inherited nobility, while Mézières is concered with Alexander as conqueror. C. Lucken, 'Les Muses de Fortune. *Boèce*, le *Roman de la Rose* et Charles d'Orléans', Foehr-Janssens, *Fortune*, 145–76, analyses the parallels between Boethius's *Consolatio*, the *Roman de la Rose*, and Charles d'Orléans's *Retenue d'amours*, with Philosophy, Reason, and Fortune herself respectively counselling the poets on the vicissitudes of life and love. B. Newman, 'Did goddesses empower women? The case of Dame Nature', Edler, *Gendering*, 135–55, examines the personified Nature as a gendered figure in Jean de Meun's *Rose*, Heldris of Cornwall's *Roman de Silence*, and Christine's *Livre de la mutacion de Fortune*. M. Osborn, 'Transgressive word and image in Chaucer's enshrined *coillons* passage', *ChRev*, 37:365–84, in exploring the *Rose* as source for Chaucer, includes a lengthy account of Reason's discourse about *coillons*.

MACHAUT. E. E. Leach, 'Love, hope, and the nature of *merci* in Machaut's musical *balades Esperance* (B13) and *Je ne cuit pas* (B14)', *FrF*, 28: 1–27, contrasts the role of *merci* in these paired ballads and places them within the sequence of the *Louange des Dames*. A. Butterfield, 'The art of repetition: Machaut's *balade* 33, *Nes qu'on porroit*', *EMus*, 31: 347–60, uses this Machaut lyric as an example of a more general critical dilemma: a close reading of a medieval text. M. Bent, 'Words and music in Machaut's motet 9', *ib.*, 363–88, reads the text of this motet with a focus on its musical and sound qualities, for example, rhyme, hocket, repetition, polyphony, and rhythmic structure. S. Huot, 'Reading across genres: Froissart's *Joli Buisson de Jonece* and Machaut's motets', *FS*, 57: 1–10, argues that Froissart alludes to three of Machaut's motets, 10, 12, and 15, in order to examine the relationship between erotic and spiritual love.

Alexandre Leupin, *Fiction and Incarnation: Rhetoric, Theology, and Literature in the Middle Ages*, Minneapolis, Minnesota U.P., xxiv + 259 pp., writes generally about epistemology and the book; ch. 9, 'Disincarnation: Guillaume de Machaut', concerns issues of *ordenance* and truth in Machaut's *Voir Dit*. C. Galderisi, ' "Ce dient nobles et bourjois": la destinée poétique de Canens/Caneüs dans *Le Livre du Voir Dit*', *MoyFr*, 51–53: 291–303, links the meaning of *éthimologique* with the concepts of truth and verisimilitude using this episode from Machaut's *Voir Dit* as example. F. Ferrand, 'Au-delà de l'idée de progrès: la pensée musicale de Guillaume de Machaut et le renouvellement de l'écriture littéraire dans le *Voir Dit*', Baumgartner, *Progrès*, 231–49, explores the relationship between poet and composer in a time when music was presenting itself as new and poetry as melancholic, or backward-looking. J. Drobinsky, 'La fenêtre comme mise en scène du regard dans les manuscrits enluminés de Guillaume de Machaut', *Senefiance*, 49: 143–56, argues that the miniatures that depict Guillaume at a window are ways of describing author and authorship, especially the author's relationship to the world and his audience. S. Bazin-Tacchella, 'La floraison des textes sur la peste aux XIVe et XVe siècles: les pièces en vers', *TLit*, 16: 167–86, treats Machaut's *Jugement Navarre*, as well as a lesser known 16th-c. text, and the 15th-c. *Poème de la peste* by Olivier de la Haye, exploring differences between these literary texts and contemporary non-literary accounts.

THE SIXTEENTH CENTURY

By Gilles Banderier, *Basle*

1. General

The outstanding work for the year is undoubtedly *The Oxford Dictionary of the Renaissance*, ed. Gordon Campbell, OUP, xlviii + 864 pp. This is a research tool of the highest importance, which should always stay at hand, and is imposing, admirably documented, and intensely detailed. The most important contribution to humanist studies is Joscelyn Godwin, *The Pagan Dream of the Renaissance*, London, Thames and Hudson, 2002, 292 pp., which deals with the irruption of Greek and Roman deities into 16th-c. court culture. A beautiful book, and also a discerning analysis by a distinguished scholar of outstanding range, revealing a rare sympathy and understanding on the author's part. Giuseppe Mazzotta, *Cosmopoiesis. The Renaissance Experiment*, Toronto U.P., 2001, xvi + 106 pp. To say that 16th-c. men discovered a new world beyond the Atlantic ocean and created a new world inside their own minds is an old commonplace, but this little yet rich book shows also how Renaissance minds did not have our concepts of specialization: science, philosophy, literature, and arts were all, for better or worse, seen as a unison. The discussion is wide and general, but of import to any study of 'civilisation'. *A Companion to the Worlds of the Renaissance*, ed. Guido Ruggiero, Oxford, Blackwell, 2002, xii + 562 pp., is an elegant and informative introduction.

William N. West, *Theatres and Encyclopedias in Early Modern Europe*, CUP, 2002, xvi + 296 pp., is a valuable study of high scholarship, describing the real meaning of the word *theatre* during the Renaissance, and provides a fascinating look inside 16th-c. mentality. L. Van Delft carries on a parallel inquiry with three important articles: 'Fertilité d'une forme polygraphique: le genre du *theatrum* savant', *LitC*, 49:113–30; '*Theatrum Mundi*: l'encyclopédisme des moralistes', Büttner, *Sammeln*, 245–67; and '*Theatrum Mundi* revisité', *Tobin Vol.*, 35–44. *Textures of Renaissance Knowledge*, ed. Philippa Berry and Margaret Tudeau-Clayton, MUP, 228 pp., is a collection of essays which 'recurrently illustrate how the constitution of subjects and objects of knowledge entailed denial or negation of a disturbing epistemic difference or alterity'. Of special interest are S. Clucas, 'Magic, science and religion in the Renaissance' (35–57), and E. Guild, 'Montaigne's *commerce* with women' (98–116).

Kessler, *Res*, is the product of an interdisciplinary colloquium held at Wolfenbüttel in October 1998. This volume of *acta* is imposing and admirably documented. Of particular note are: H. Mikkeli, 'Art and

Nature in the Renaissance commentaries and textbooks on Aristotle's *Physics*' (117–30), M.-L. Demonet, 'Les êtres de raison, ou les modes d'être de la littérature' (177–95), and N. G. Siraisi, 'Disease and symptom as problematic concepts in Renaissance medicine' (217–40).

Michel Jeanneret, *Eros rebelle. Littérature et dissidence à l'âge classique*, Seuil, 332 pp., shows brilliantly how the rise of the Counter-Reformation produced a rather unexpected consequence: a sudden explosion of pornographic literature, in which the Renaissance's soft and cheerful eroticism turned to sordid blasphemy. Enlightening pages are devoted to Ronsard, Montaigne, and Béroalde de Verville. See also Joan DeJean, *The Reinvention of Obscenity. Sex, Lies and Tabloids in Early Modern France*, Chicago U.P., 2002, xii + 204 pp., which explores this little-known avenue and the effects of the Counter-Reformation.

Michel Jeanneret, *Perpetual Motion. Transforming Shapes in the Renaissance from da Vinci to Montaigne*, trans. Nidra Pollet, Baltimore–London, Johns Hopkins U.P., 2001, xiv + 320 pp., is a fine and precise translation of this already classic book on the complex and ever-changing Renaissance world. The chapter on Du Bartas deserves special mention. *Espaces de l'image*, ed. Richard Crescenzo, Nancy U.P., 2002, iv + 274 pp., gathers essays from more or less young scholars, studying the role of visual perception in 16th-c. and 17th-c. French culture. It is an interesting volume, though the poor quality of the illustrations has to be deplored. Of especial note are the articles by M. Pintarič, 'Ironie et image de soi dans les *Regrets* de Du Bellay' (3–11), C. Simonin, 'Les portraits de femmes auteurs ou l'impossible représentation' (35–53), C. Bouzy, 'Emblèmes et entrée: Boissard ou l'image emblématique entre tradition et historiographie' (57–75).

François Deserps, *Recueil de la diversité des habits*, printed in Paris in 1562, has been translated as *The Various Styles of Clothing*, transl. Sara Shannon, ed. Carol Urness, Minneapolis, Minnesota U.P., 2001, 186 pp. The 1562 edition was luxuriously illustrated with 121 woodcut illustrations, lavishly reproduced here, and the whole will be of interest not only to historians of fashion, for it is also a profession of relativistic faith: ever since the gates of Eden clanged shut with such depressing finality, mankind has been engaged in a ceaseless struggle for food, shelter — and clothing.

Court Festivals of the European Renaissance. Art, Politics and Performance, ed. J. R. Mulryne and Elizabeth Goldring, Aldershot, Ashgate, 2002, xxiv + 402 pp., contains papers by M. M. McGowan, 'The Renaissance triumph and its classical heritage' (26–47); R. Cooper, 'Court festival and triumphal entries under Henri II' (51–75); M. Chatenet, 'Etiquette and architecture at the court of the last Valois' (76–100);

and N. Le Roux, 'The politics of festivals at the court of the last Valois' (101–17). Natalie Zemon Davis, *Essai sur le don dans la France du XVIe siècle*, trans. D. Trierweiler, Seuil, 272 pp., was originally published in 2000 and appears in French with unusual rapidity. It is a brilliant reflection upon the notion of the gift, taking in views from sociology, religious history, and anthropology according to Marcel Mauss's theories. The author uses emblem books, diaries, memoirs, and other sources.

Louis XII en Milanais, ed. Philippe Contamine and Jean Guillaume, Champion, 394 pp., notably contains P. Contamine, 'Jean d'Auton, historien de Louis XII' (11–29), G. Le Thiec, 'De Milan à Constantinople: Louis XII et la croisade dans la culture politique du temps' (67–107); B. Chevalier, 'Le cardinal Guillaume Briçonnet et le parti du concile à Milan' (129–47); and P. L. Mulas, 'Les manuscrits lombards enluminés offerts aux Français' (305–22). *L'Italia letteraria e l'Europa*, ed. Nino Borsellino and Bruno Germano, Rome, Salerno, 2001, 280 pp., contains two articles of interest for French studies: J. Balsamo, ' "Du Florentin les lamentables voix": mythe pétrarquien et modèle pétrarquiste en France au XVIe siècle' (109–26), which shows that Renaissance writers considered Petrarch as one of their contemporaries. His works were widely printed and disseminated, not condemned to a manuscript twilight, like so many other medieval poets, in Italy and elsewhere. J. Risset, 'Dante en France. Histoire d'une absence' (59–71), provides some notes on D.'s reception.

Doris R. Creegan, *Echos de la Réforme dans la littérature de langue française de 1520 à 1620*, Lewiston, Mellen, 2001, x + 486 pp., is a perplexing book, dealing with an (?over-)vast field of knowledge and studying Rabelais, Marot, the French translations of the Psalms, as well as Ronsard, Du Bartas, and d'Aubigné. C. gives very lengthy quotations, unusually short analysis, and uses some out of date critical references.

Marie-Claude Malenfant, *Argumentaires de l'une et l'autre espèce de femme. Le statut de l'"exemplum' dans les discours littéraires sur la femme (1500–1550)*, Montreal, Laval U.P., xviii + 548 pp., is an eminently readable book and offers important insights into the male view of 'hysteria', and men's misogyny. See also R. A. Carr, 'The resolution of a paradox: Alexandre de Pontaymeri's response to the *Querelle des femmes*', *RenS*, 17:246–56. Mentioned by d'Aubigné in his list of notable poets active during the reign of Henri IV, Pontaymeri gave a late response to an old debate. Rainier Leushuis, *Le Mariage et l'"amitié courtoise' dans le dialogue et le récit bref de la Renaissance*, Florence, Olschki, xiv + 286 pp., minutely examines the notion of marriage during the Counter-Reformation and especially in the works of Erasmus, Castiglione, Rabelais, and Marguerite de Navarre: weddings and marriage may provide writers with either comical or tragical situations. See also C. M. Bauschatz, 'Rabelais and M. de Navarre on 16th-c. views of clandestine marriage', *SCJ*, 34:395–408. *Le Mariage dans l'Europe des XVIe et XVIIe siècles: réalités et représentations*, ed. Richard Crescenzo, Marie Roig-Miranda, and Véronique Zaercher, 2 vols, Nancy U.P., iv + 376, 280 pp., is an interesting collection of various essays. *Veufs, veuves et veuvage dans la France d'Ancien Régime*, ed. Nicole Pellegrin and Colette H. Winn, Champion, 348 pp., contains the proceedings of a symposium held in Poitiers (June 1998) and contains several papers of interest for Renaissance scholars: B. H. Beech, 'Madeleine Boursette, femme d'imprimeur et veuve' (147–57), K. M. Llewellyn, 'Les veuves dans l'*Heptaméron* de M. de Navarre' (159–68), E. Viennot, 'Veuves de mère en fille au XVIe siècle: le cas du clan Guise' (187–98), T. Lüttenberg, 'L'habit des veuves et la construction de l'état moderne au XVIe siècle' (247–57), and C. H. Winn, 'Ecriture, veuvage et deuil. Témoignages féminins du XVIe siècle' (275–98).

Registres du Conseil de Genève à l'époque de Calvin, ed. Paule Hochuli Dubuis (THR, 372), xxviii + 466 pp., minutely publishes documents from 1 May to 31 December 1536, and will be an invaluable resource for historians interested in the study of the rise of the Genevan theocratic republic. This volume is a genuine masterwork of paleographical scrutiny and historical scholarship. Jean-François Maillard, Judith Kecskeméti, and Monique Portalier, *L'Europe des humanistes (XIVe–XVIIe siècles)*, CNRS, 544 pp., is the second and revised edition of this repertory, originally published in 1995. It contains 2350 entries for writers and scholars, giving biographical data and a list of classical and also some medieval authors they helped to save for future readers. *Diffusion des Humanismus. Studien zur nationalen Geschichtsschreibung europäischer Humanisten*, ed. Johannes Helrath, Ulrich Muhlack, and Gerrit Walther, Göttingen, Wallstein, 2002, 464 pp., is an important volume consisting of a number of valuable essays by various authorities, among whom F. Collard, 'Paulus Aemilius' *De rebus gestis Francorum*. Diffusion und Rezeption eines humanistischen Geschichtswerks in Frankreich' (377–97).

George Hugo Tucker, *'Homo Viator'. Itineraries of Exile, Displacement and Writing in Renaissance Europe* (THR, 376), xx + 396 pp., is a wide-ranging synthesis, including careful and considered studies on the *Tabula Cebetis* and the works of Du Bellay. This impressive book is also a cautious reappraisal of a problem only partially tackled before: why did Renaissance men travel? One important reason was for the necessities of learning, moving from one university to another in a time when books were still expensive. *Les Échanges entre les universités européennes à la Renaissance*, ed. Michel Bideaux and Marie-Madeleine

Fragonard (THR, 384), 404 pp., with contributions from many of the most established scholars in the field of the history of universities, is a composite volume devoted to the *peregrinatio academica*. The essays of most concern to French scholars are N. Bingen, 'Les étudiants de langue française dans les universités italiennes' (25–43), J. K. Farge, 'Was Paris a regional or an international university?' (61–66), J.-M. Le Gall, 'Les moines et les universités' (69–92), M. Huchon, 'Rabelais, les universités et la mobilité' (143–58), L. Felici, 'Liberté des savoirs et mobilité: circulation des hommes et des idées à l'université de Bâle au XVIe siècle' (187–98), M.-C. Tucker, 'Maîtres et étudiants écossais à la faculté de droit de l'université de Bourges' (301–09), J. Balsamo, 'L'université de Reims, la famille de Guise et les étudiants anglais' (311–27), and I. Maclean, 'Trois facultés de médecine au XVIe siècle: Padoue, Bâle, Montpellier' (349–358).

Henri II et les arts, ed. Hervé Oursel and Julia Fritsch, Ecole du Louvre, 460 pp., is the outcome of a conference held in 1997. Before his tragic death in a tournament, Henri II had been genuinely responsive to æsthetic beauty, this being celebrated by several contemporary writers. This collection of articles of a high standard includes T. Crépin-Leblond, 'Sens et contresens de l'emblématique de Henri II' (77–92), M.-P. Laffitte, 'Les reliures exécutées pour Henri II, conservées à la BnF' (221–30), the late M. D. Orth, 'L'enluminure au temps de Henri II' (249–60), E. A. Brown, 'Les *Heures dites de Henri II* et les *Heures de Dinteville*' (261–92), J. Balsamo, 'Les poètes d'Anet' (417–25), C.-G. Dubois, 'Henri II et les arts' (427–36). On Ronsard's commendatory verses for Henri II's entry into Paris, see also A.-P. Pouey-Mounou, 'Ronsard et le roi de gloire', *Ménager Vol.*, 233–43.

Renaissance Reflections. Essays in Memory of C. A. Mayer, ed. Pauline M. Smith and Trevor Peach, Champion, 2002, 280 pp., a tribute to a great scholar, contains in particular D. Bentley-Cranch, 'Marot's *Etrennes aux dames de la court*' (57–83); C. Reuben, 'Marot's translation of the Psalms in the service of Reformation' (107–27); J. H. Williams, 'Writing and publishing in 16th-c. Scotland: some French connections' (129–44); T. Peach, 'La théâtralité du *Cymbalum mundi*' (145–59); S. Anglo, 'The popularity of Machiavelli in 16th-c. France' (195–212); M. M. McGowan, 'Montaigne and involuntary memory: ways of recollecting Rome' (213–26), and P. M. Smith, 'Goulart et la *Satyre Menipée*' (227–46).

'Écrire et conter'. Mélanges de rhétorique et d'histoire littéraire du XVIe siècle offerts à Jean-Claude Moisan, ed. Marie-Claude Malenfant and Sabrina Vervaecke, Quebec, Laval U.P., xiv + 236 pp., is a valuable Festschrift including J.-P. Beaulieu, 'La *dispositio* du recueil épistolaire: unité et variété dans les *Epistres* d'Hélisenne de Crenne' (37–52),

Y. Bellenger, 'La répétition dans la poésie du XVIe siècle' (53–67), A. L. Gordon, 'La rhétorique défensive de Ronsard dans *La Responce aux injures et calomnies*' (69–82), N. Bochenek, 'Les exordes des quatre discours politiques de Ronsard' (83–96), F. Paré, 'Formes du récit dans les *Nouvelles histoires tragiques* de Bénigne Poissenot' (97–109), B. Dunn-Lardeau, 'Le merveilleux dans l'œuvre de Marguerite de Navarre: critique et réminiscences' (161–77), D. Desrosiers-Bonin, 'L'*Epistre* de Marie d'Ennetières et les écrits du groupe de Neuchâtel' (179–91). *Strategic Rewriting*, ed. David Lee Rubin, Charlottesville, Rookwood, 2002, xii + 288 p., contains two articles of special interest: G. H. Tucker, 'Déchets, déchéance et recyclage: corps, corps du monde et corps-texte chez Du Bellay et Montaigne' (1–24), and I. A. R. De Smet, 'Going public: rewriting and self-fashioning in the early poetry of J.-A. de Thou' (25–42). Timothy Hampton, *Literature and Nation in the Sixteenth Century: Inventing Renaissance France*, Ithaca–London, Cornell U.P., 2001, xviii + 290 pp., contains chapters on Rabelais, Marguerite de Navarre, Du Bellay, and Montaigne. On the evolution of national sentiment, see the interesting article by W. Kemp, 'L'introduction et la diffusion de "patrie" en français au XVIe siècle', *Rickard Vol.*, 213–42.

Among major influences on French 16th-c. literature, those of Ariosto and Tasso have long been noted. *L'Arioste et Le Tasse en France au XVIe siècle*, PENS, 292 pp., is an important book covering a vast field and with very detailed analyses, with contributions including J. Balsamo, 'L'Arioste et Le Tasse. Des poètes italiens, leurs libraires et leurs lecteurs français' (11–26); B. Périgot, 'L'Arioste et Rabelais face au roman' (39–52); K. W. Hemper, 'Traditions discursives et réception partielle. Le *Roland furieux* de l'Arioste dans *L'Olive* de Du Bellay' (53–74); J. Vignes, 'Traductions et imitations françaises de l'*Orlando furioso* (1544–1580)' (75–98); M. Miotti, 'Le théâtre de l'Arioste en France' (99–118); C. Lastraioli, 'Les *Satires* de l'Arioste et leur diffusion confidentielle en France' (119–40); D. Boccassini, 'Présences du Tasse et de l'Arioste dans le tracé de l'écriture montaignienne' (141–58); C. Cavallini, 'L'Arioste, le Tasse, Montaigne. Carrefours historiques et littéraires' (159–69); D. Bjaï, 'De l'Arioste au Tasse. Les muses italiennes de Jean de Boyssières' (171–85); B. Méniel, 'Le projet épique de Nicolas de Montreux' (187–202); D. Mauri, 'Les traductions françaises de l'*Aminta* au XVIe siècle' (217–31).

The decline of classical and biblical culture among present students (i.e. among future teachers), the permanent and fashionable change in critical methods, the emphasis given to gender, colonial, and *banlieue* studies in university courses may be the first tolling of the funeral bell for Renaissance scholarship. *L'Étude de la Renaissance 'nunc et cras'* (THR, 381), 396 pp., is a useful *mise au point* by some of the greatest authorities in the field.

2. Book History

Bibliography and book history have made wonderful progress over the last few decades, but hitherto there has been lacking a good handbook in French, worthy of comparison with Philip Gaskell's *New Introduction to Bibliography* (1972). It is of course very difficult to reduce such a vexed subject to a few pages. François Roudaut, *Le Livre au XVIe siècle. Eléments de bibliologie matérielle et d'histoire*, Champion, 206 pp., brings together much that until now could only be found scattered in various places. No aspect of the question seems to have been left unconsidered. Jean-François Gilmont, *Le Livre et ses secrets*, Leuven U.P. — Geneva, Droz, 442 pp., is a treasure gathering up 30 years of minute yet lively scholarship. A lecture given by G., *La Fabrication du livre au XVIe siècle*, is now printed in a handsome booklet, Brussels, Musée de la Maison d'Érasme, 16 pp.

We currently complain about information overload, brought on by newspapers, television, and the World Wide Web, and can offer little consolation other than suggesting that strangely, as history shows, our species survived an earlier deluge of information, and, some say, even advanced because of it. A. Blair's informative study on 'Reading strategies for coping with information overload, ca. 1550–1700', *JHI*, 64: 11–28, reminds us that, as early as 1545, Conrad Gesner was already complaining about the 'confusing and harmful abundance of books'. Renaissance readers developed an impressive range of methods to face this. Some of them are still in use or have been slightly adapted: the private commonplace book, for instance, was a kind of stock-material for would-be writers, as discussed by A. Grafton, 'Les lieux communs chez les humanistes', Décultot, *Lire*, 31–42. On the same topic, see Earle Havens, *Commonplace Books: A History of Manuscripts and Printed Books from Antiquity to the 20th century*, New Hampshire, New England U.P., 2002, 100 pp., and B. W. Ogilvie, 'Renaissance naturalists and information overload', *JHI*, 64: 29–40.

Humanists of the past, as indeed scholars of the present day, were poor men without their private libraries (in so far as public or university libraries were almost everywhere a luxury). *Les Humanistes et leur bibliothèque*, ed. Rudolf De Smet, Leuven, Peeters, 2002, 286 pp., is a work of highly-recommended serious scholarship, covering a rich range of sources. Two contributions deal with French writers: R. De Smet, 'La bibliothèque de Marnix à travers sa correspondance' (211–30); and T. Berns, 'Philosophie de la bibliothèque de Montaigne: le difficile trajet des mots aux choses' (193–209), who seems not to know that a catalogue of what remained of Montaigne's library was compiled in 1997 (overlooked also in *YWMLS*: G. de Botton and F. Pottiée-Sperry, 'A la recherche de la "librairie" de Montaigne', *BBib*, 2, 1997:254–98). Françoise Waquet, *Parler comme un livre. L'oralité et le savoir (XVIe–XXe siècle)*, Albin-Michel, 432 pp., studies the role of oral communication among scholars.

Martine Furno, *Une 'fantaisie sur l'antique'. Le goût pour l'épigraphie funéraire dans l''Hypnerotomachia Poliphili' de Franceso Colonna* (THR, 377), 336 pp., is worth reviewing here, for this novel, published anonymously in 1499, was (not undeservedly) called 'the most beautiful book in the world' and it has fascinated generations of French readers. This study brings together much useful information, has excellent and detailed footnotes, and numerous excellent illustrations.

The history of the Renaissance book usually concerns itself with the description of printed books, yet one must not forget the huge quantity of manuscripts produced during the first decades following the invention of printing. *L'Art du manuscrit de la Renaissance en France*, Paris, Somogy — Chantilly, Musée Condé, 2001, 96 pp., presents the catalogue of an exhibition held at the Musée Condé. The preface reminds us that the advent of printing did not kill the art of illuminated manuscripts, which included books of hours, translations of sometimes printed texts written by Erasmus and Marguerite de Navarre (*La Coche*), and Amyot's version of Euripides's *Troyennes*.

The Sixteenth-Century French Religious Book, ed. Andrew Pettegree, Paul Nelles, and Philip Conner, Aldershot, Ashgate, 2001, xviii + 366 pp., contains the following papers: G. A. Runnalls, 'Religious drama and the printed book during the late 15th and 16th c.' (18–37); A. M. Saunders, 'The 16th-c. French emblem book as a form of religious literature' (38–67); K. Maag, 'Education and works of religious instruction in French' (96–109); J.-F. Gilmont, 'La naissance de l'historiographie protestante' (110–26); D. Hartley, 'Religion and the State: Du Bellay's views on the duties of the most Christian king and his subjects' (127–37); K. Cameron, 'Satire, dramatic stereotyping and the demonizing of Henry III' (157–76); P. Nelles, 'Three audiences for religious books in 16th-c. France' (256–85); and R. Kuin, 'Private library as public danger: the case of Duplessis-Mornay' (319–58). *Nugae Humanisticae*, 2, Brussels, Musée de la Maison d'Erasme, 2001, 160 pp., is devoted to the 'Index à l'époque humaniste' and includes an interesting article by R. Bodenmann and J.-F. Gilmont, 'La fabrication des index de livres au XVIe siècle' (11–18).

Olivier Christin, *Les Yeux pour le croire. Les Dix Commandements en images (XVe–XVIIe siècle)*, Seuil, 160 pp., examines images of wide diffusion produced by printers (in part because the majority of the population, called by Luther *Herr Omnes*, remained illiterate). Engravings were an ideal medium for the diffusion of new ideas. Milan Pelc, '*Illustrium imagines.*' *Das Porträtbuch der Renaissance* (SMRT, 88), 2002, viii + 306 pp., contains an interesting catalogue.

3. Humanism, Theology, and the History of Ideas

Paolo Rossi, *Logic and the Art of Memory. The Quest for a Universal Language*, transl. Stephen Clucas, Chicago U.P., 2000, xxviii + 334 pp., and Lina Bolzoni, *The Gallery of Memory. Literary and Iconographic Models in the Age of the Printing Press*, transl. Jeremy Parzen, Toronto U.P., 2001, xxvi + 332 pp., are useful English translations of already classic books. From Ramon Lull to Leibniz, Rossi brillantly studies the neglected tradition of artificial memory. L. Bolzoni's inquiry, first published in 1995, is as if a summary of the Renaissance mind, describing the codes and illustrations used to strengthen memory. Both books are the most important studies for the early modern period on this topic since Frances Yates's seminal *The Art of Memory* (1966).

Ann Moss, *Renaissance Truth and the Latin Language Turn*, OUP, viii + 306 pp., 'relates the story of the shift from [. . .] the Latin of late medieval intellectuals, to [. . .] the revitalized classical Latin of the humanists'. This exciting and clear-sighted study on the European diffusion of knowledge, commonplaces books, and Neo-Latin novels, covers a wide range of sources, such as Perotti's *Cornucopiae* and Calepino's dictionary. The Renaissance was the golden age of philologists and translators, and Pascale Hummel, '*Philologus auctor*'. *Le philologue et son œuvre*, Berne, Lang, xii + 426 pp., is an exigent book on an exigent subject, tracing the development of philological and scientific method. A typical example of humanistic exchange is given by Gian Vincenzo Pinelli and Claude Dupuy, *Une correspondance entre deux humanistes*, ed. Anna Maria Raugei, 2 vols, Florence, Olschki, 2001, cxxviii + 770 pp. Although these letters exchanged between two scholars are not devoid of literary interest, their documentary value predominates. *The Politics of Translation in the Middle Ages and the Renaissance*, ed. Renate Blumenfeld-Kosinski, Luise von Flotow, and Daniel S. Russell, Ottawa U.P., 2001, 222 pp., contains the proceedings of a conference held at the University of Pittsburgh in April 1997. A concise introduction by D. Russell (29–35) is followed, among other papers, by K. Lloyd-Jones, 'Erasmus, Dolet and the politics of translation' (37–56); P. Hendrick, 'From the certainties of scholasticism to Renaissance relativism: Montaigne, translator of Sebond' (175–90); E. Tilson, 'Montaigne's *traduction* of Sebond: a comparison of the *Prologus* of the *Liber creaturarum* with the *Préface* of the *Théologie naturelle*' (191–202).

Jean Wirth, *Sainte Anne est une sorcière, et autres essais*, Geneva, Droz, 298 pp., owes its puzzling title to its thorough interpretation of a hardly edifying engraving by Hans Baldung Grien (1511). This neat paperback reprints several essays on Renaissance atheism, devotion to holy images, or its counterpart, iconoclasm, and the struggle Protestants faced in purging the cult of the saints from their culture and religion. *The Adventure of Religious Pluralism in Early Modern France*, ed. Keith Cameron, Mark Greengrass, and Penny Roberts, Oxford, Lang, 2000, 322 pp., publishes the papers from a conference held in Exeter. The following contributions are worthy of note: A. Tallon, 'Gallicanism and religious pluralism in France in the 16th century' (15–30); P. Roberts, 'Religious pluralism in practice' (31–43); L. Racaut, 'The cultural obstacles to religious pluralism in the polemic of the French wars of religion' (115–27); L. Petris, 'Faith and religious policy in Michel de L'Hospital's civic evangelism' (129–42); Y. Roberts, 'Baïf and the adventure of pluralism' (143–57); R. Bonney, 'The obstacles to pluralism in early modern France' (209–29). On the Trent Council and its consequences, see Guy Bedouelle's enlightening synthesis, *La Réforme du catholicisme (1480–1620)*, Le Cerf, 2002, 162 pp. Alain Tallon, *Conscience nationale et sentiment religieux en France au XVIe siècle*, PUF, 2002, 316 pp., is concerned with the rise of Gallicanism. *De Michel de L'Hospital à l'Edit de Nantes. Politique et religion face aux Eglises*, ed. Thierry Wanegffelen, Clermont-Ferrand U.P., 2002, 612 pp., is an essay in comparative history (unfortunately without an index), containing L. Petris, 'L'éloquence de L'H. dans ses discours de 1560 à 1562' (259–77); W. J. A. Bots, 'Du Bellay, diplomate irénique' (295–304); J. Miernowski, '"Politique" comme injure dans les pamphlets au temps des guerres de religion' (337–56); G. Schrenck, 'De L'H. à l'Edit de Nantes: le regard d'A. d'Aubigné sur la tolérance des Politiques' (391–403); and A.-M. Cocula, 'L'H., La Boétie et Montaigne' (565–73). Glenn S. Sunshine, *Reforming French Protestantism. The Development of Huguenot Ecclesiastical Institutions, 1557–1572*, Kirksville, Truman State U.P., xiv + 194 pp., is a stimulating and precise *vue d'ensemble* which takes recent research into account. *Society and Culture in the Huguenot World, 1559–1685*, ed. Raymond A. Mentzer and Andrew Spicer, CUP, 2002, xviii + 242 pp., contains some remarkable contributions, such as T. Watson, 'Preaching, printing, psalm-singing: the making and unmaking of the Reformed church in Lyon, 1550–1572' (10–28); L. Racaut, 'Religious polemic and Huguenot self-perception and identity' (29–43, on martyrologues and controversists); P. Roberts,

'Huguenot petitioning during the wars of religion' (62–77); M. Greengrass, 'Informal networks in 16th-c. French Protestantism' (78–97); K. Maag, 'The Huguenot academies: preparing for an uncertain future' (139–56); B. Roussel, 'Funeral corteges and Huguenot culture' (193–208).

Xavier Le Person, *'Practiques' et 'practiqueurs'. La vie politique à la fin du règne de Henri III (1584–1589)* (THR, 370), 2002, 658 pp., is a minutely detailed study on the uses and sometimes abuses of political treachery and dissimulation during the last years of the reign of Henri III, finally murdered by a perfidious monk. This important study is summed up in Id., '"Practiques" et "practiqueurs" au temps d'Henri III', *HES*, 22: 349–65.

Conflits politiques, controverses religieuses. Essais d'histoire européenne aux XVIe–XVIIIe siècles, ed. Ouzi El Yada and Jacques Le Brun, EHESS, 2002, 284 pp., is a collection of various interesting papers, including A. Jouanna, 'Etre "bon Français" au temps des guerres de religion: du citoyen au sujet' (19–32), and D. Crouzet, 'Louis Dorléans ou le massacre de la Saint-Barthélemy comme "coup d'estat"' (77–99), based on an unpublished account of the slaughter (BnF, MS fr. 4922), the *Histoire des origines de la Ligue.* On a Protestant polemical weapon (the 'Taxe des parties casuelles de la boutique du pape', established by the Vatican chancellery in 1471 and detailing the rates of absolution for every offence), read M. Lazard, 'Antoine du Pinet et la taxe de la boutique du Pape', *RHPR*, 83: 157–69. Irena Backus, *Historical Method and Confessional Identity in the Era of the Reformation (1378–1615)* (SMRT, 94), xii + 416 pp., deals with the use of history in 16th-c. religious controversies, continuing the work of Polman's *L'Élément historique dans la controverse religieuse du XVIe siècle* (1932). The author 'draw[s] the reader's attention to the creative role of history in the Reformation era as a decisive factor in the affirmation of confessional identity'. The documentation is most detailed and thorough, the bibliographies and footnotes excellent. Sébastien Castellion, *La Genèse (1555)*, ed. Jacques Chaurand, Nicole Guenier, Carine Skupien Dekens, and Max Engammare (TLF, 553), 324 pp. Professor of Greek in Basle, Castellion published in 1555 his French translation of the Bible with the printer Jehan Hervage. This publication was lampooned by his enemies, Calvin and Bèze. This present and very good edition gives Castellion's commendatory letter to Henri II, his 'Moyen pour entendre la sainte écritture', and his translation of the book of Genesis. See also B. Boudou, 'Henri Estienne et la traduction par Castellion de la Bible en français', *Ménager Vol.*, 522–32.

Littératures, 47, 2002, is devoted to 'Fictions du savoir à la Renaissance' and includes remarkable contributions by H. Cazes,

'Théâtres imaginaires du livre et de l'anatomie: *La Dissection des parties du corps humain*, Charles Estienne' (11–30); M. Marrache-Gouraud, 'Histoires et autres traces de fiction dans le *Traité de la peste* d'A. Paré (1568)' (31–42); S. Arnaud, 'Les fictions astrales de J. Peletier du Mans' (43–53); O. Guerrier, 'Fictions du droit et espace littéraire' (55–65, on Montaigne); E. Mehl, 'Le complexe d'Orphée. Philosophie et mythologie au XVIe siècle' (87–100); M. Bouchard, 'L'invention fabuleuse de l'histoire à la Renaissance (Bodin et La Popelinière)' (101–14).

Magic, Alchemy and Science, 15th-18th centuries. The Influence of Hermes Trismegistus, ed. Carlos Gilly and Cis van Heertum, 2 vols, Florence, Centro Di, 2002, 590, 334 pp., is the lavishly illustrated catalogue of an exhibition held in Venice. Charles Zika, *Exorcising our Demons. Magic, Witchcraft and Visual Culture in Early Modern Europe* (SMRT, 91), xxii + 604 pp., gathers papers and lectures already published, but the whole appears to be one of the major contributions of the year, rich in suggestion and persuasive in argument. *Secrets of Nature. Astrology and Alchemy in Early Modern Europe*, ed. William R. Newman and Anthony Grafton, Cambridge (Mass.), MIT, 2001, 444 pp., is an important book on the occult sciences, errors of taste during the rise of rationalism, but a permanent element of the Renaissance *Weltanschauung*. Among major influences on 16th-c. views is that of the German physician and alchemist Paracelsus: *Paracelsian Moments. Science, Medicine and Astrology in Early Modern Europe*, ed. Gerhild Scholz Williams and Charles D. Gunnoe Jr., Kirksville, Truman State U.P., 2002, xxii + 274 pp., is a collection of essays on P.'s *Nachleben* in Europe, and especially in France, with D. Scoggins's contribution on 'Astrology's degradation in the five books of Rabelais' (163–86). The word 'alchemist' was sometimes an insult, as shown by M. Martin, 'Portrait de l'orateur en alchimiste', *NRSS*, 21.2:71–84. Armando Maggi, *Satan's Rhetoric. A Study of Renaissance Demonology*, Chicago U.P., 2001, x + 260 pp., is a book of the highest importance, showing how magic and alchemy were never far from heresy. The Renaissance was a period of brilliant rationalism, but also one haunted by the devil, when even the future bishop Pierre Bérulle wrote a treatise on demonology. On this kind of literature and on the witch-hunt, see P. G. Maxwell-Stuart, *Witch Hunters. Professional Prickers, Unwitchers and Witch Finders of the Renaissance*, Stroud, Tempus, 158 pp., which contains chapters on Martín Del Rio and Pierre de Lancre, both closely linked to Montaigne; and M. Closson, 'L'invention d'une "littérature de la peur"', *TLL*, 16:47–63.

Ambroise Paré (1510–1590). Pratique et écriture de la science à la Renaissance, ed. Evelyne Berriot-Salvadore and Paul Mironneau, Champion, 472 pp., presents conference papers devoted to Paré, father of modern surgery and surgeon to four kings of France, whose writings were seminal (the other great 16th-c. French physician, Jean Fernel, wrote in Latin). *Les Pithou. Les lettres et la paix du royaume*, ed. Marie-Madeleine Fragonard and Pierre-Eugène Leroy, Champion, 494 pp. Born in Troyes, the Pithou brothers fled to Switzerland and Germany during the civil wars and became respectively a lawyer, a historian, and a theologian. Nicolas compiled the history of his native province during the wars, Pierre became a renowned barrister and one of the authors of the *Satire Ménipée*. These conference papers deal not only with the Pithou family, but also with their links with other writers (De Thou and Etienne Pasquier), and present some unpublished documents. Stéphane Mund, *'Orbis Russiarum'. Genèse et développement de la représentation du monde 'russe' en Occident à la Renaissance* (THR, 382), 600 pp., studies how French, German, and Italian diplomats and businessmen faced the world later referred to by Churchill as 'a riddle, wrapped in a mystery, inside an enigma'. Readers of Herodotus and Pliny, they were unable to recognize in the Russians they actually met either ancient Scyths or any nation described by classical authors; very low temperatures, the roughness and drunkenness of Russian people offended them. Both before and after Herberstein's famous account, the image of Russia was invariably negative. An immensely learned work.

L'Eloge du prince. De l'Antiquité au temps des Lumières, ed. Isabelle Cogitore and Francis Goyet, Grenoble, ELLUG, 388 pp., points to avenues which future research might profitably follow. See especially J. Dervaux, 'Lieux de mémoire, lieux d'éloge: les Grands Rhétoriqueurs et l'histoire' (169–87); B. Périgot, 'L'éloge ambigu du prince dans le *Gargantua*' (189–208); U. Langer, 'La flatterie et l'éloge: Claude Chappuys et François Ier' (209–22); F. Cornillat, 'Eloge et tragédie dans la poétique de Jodelle' (223–50); D. Quint, 'Montaigne et Henri IV' (251–60); P. Debailly, 'L'éloge du prince dans la satire classique en vers' (261–80).

On the background to French humanism, Henri D. Saffrey, *L'Héritage des Anciens au Moyen Âge et à la Renaissance*, Vrin, 2002, 318 pp., is an excellent collection of various scholarly articles on the neoplatonist tradition. Originally published in 1987, it now appears in a second edition, including three new papers. Carl Joachim Classen, *Antike Rhetorik im Zeitalter des Humanismus*, Munich–Leipzig, Saur, x + 374 pp., is a collection of articles written between 1968 and 2002.

4. Poetry

Yves Pauwels, *L'Architecture au temps de la Pléiade*, Monfort, 2002, 176 pp., is a book originally intended for art historians, but well worth studying by literary scholars for its discussion of the fascination of architecture for French poets, whose works often use similes between poetry and the art of building. Cynthia Skenazi, *Le Poète architecte en France. Constructions d'un imaginaire monarchique*, Champion, 344 pp., studies from Lemaire de Belges to Ronsard, via Marot and Du Bellay, the fortunes of a Horatian simile likening poetry to a building. An enlightening study. J. Balsamo, 'Les poètes français et les anthologies lyriques italiennes', *Italiques*, 5, 2002: 9–32, studies the use of Italian collections and their presence in French private libraries. Cathy Yandell, *Carpe Corpus. Time and Gender in Early Modern France*, Newark, Delaware U.P. — London, Associated U.P., 2000, 282 pp., studies the vexed notion of time in Renaissance French poetry, taking in Ronsard and the women poets Pernette du Guillet, Louise Labé, Anne de Marquets, Catherine des Roches, and Nicole Estienne in particular. Alfred Glauser, *Ecriture et désécriture du texte poétique. De Maurice Scève à Saint-John Perse*, Saint-Genouph, Nizet, 2002, 162 pp., contains two chapters on Scève and Ronsard.

5. Theatre and Rhetoric

Le Théâtre français des années 1450–1550. Etat actuel des recherches, ed. Olga Anna Duhl, Dijon U.P., 2002, xviii + 98 pp., contains papers by C. Mazouer, 'La comédie de la Renaissance contre la farce médiévale?' (3–14), which sees a full separation between medieval comedy and its Renaissance counterpart, and by M. Lazard, 'Quelle Renaissance dans la comédie du XVIe siècle?' (73–87), holding exactly the opposite point of view. Note also J. Persels, 'The Sorbonnic trots: staging the intestinal distress of the Roman Catholic Church in French Reform theater', *RQ*, 56: 1089–111, whose title is self-explanatory. Old men and women have been staple characters in literature since Antiquity and they are often encountered in Renaissance comedy. M. Kern's remarkable article on 'La représentation de la vieillesse dans la comédie française de la Renaissance', Müller, *Alterungsprozesse*, 217–33, states that 'la comédie française de la Renaissance constitue en quelque sorte le moment de la naissance du vieillard comme personnage original dans le théâtre français' and studies the representation of old people in love. On young or old women, see M. Lazard, 'Les félicités (très) terrestres des femmes dans quelques comédies de la Renaissance française', *Memini*, 6, 2002: 285–304.

François Calvy de La Fontaine is a little-known translator. His rewriting of Sophocles is examined by M. Mastroianni, 'Traduction des textes anciens et élaboration linguistique à la Renaissance française', *SFr*, 136, 2002: 71–98. J.-C. Ternaux, 'Ovide, Ronsard et

Le Breton: à propos d'*Adonis*', *RAR*, 16: 63–85, studies the influence of Ronsard on Guillaume Le Breton's tragicomedy. Etienne Jodelle, *Didon se sacrifiant*, ed. Jean-Claude Ternaux, Champion, 2002, 160 pp., is on the border between tragedy and epic. Jacopo Sannazaro's pastoral *Arcadia* was widely read and found in France an extraordinarily skilled translator, Jean Martin, whose work was published in 1544 and replaced only in 1737, and is now reissued by Jean-Claude Ternaux, Reims U.P., 200 pp.

6. Emblematica

An Interregnum of the Sign. The Emblematic Age in France. Essays in Honour of Daniel S. Russell, ed. David Graham (Glasgow Emblem Studies), Glasgow Univ., Dept. of French, 2001, xx + 252 pp., is a valuable and elegant *Festschrift* (lacking an index, alas), including contributions on Scève, Georgette de Montenay, Pierre Coustau, French editions of Alciato, the production of emblem books, and the engraver Pierre Woeiriot. Alison Adams, *Webs of Allusion. French Protestant Emblem Books of the 16th century* (THR, 378), 326 pp., lavishly illustrated, is the first monograph to deal with emblem collections issued by Huguenot writers. In the 17th c., French emblem books were a Jesuit speciality but, some decades earlier, the most important emblematists belonged to the opposite party. This beautiful book studies Georgette de Montenay, Bèze, Boissard and, more briefly, Paul Perrot de la Sale. Indexes of names, mottoes, and biblical references complete the whole, but there is no bibliography. See also P. Eichel-Lojkine, 'Boissard et la question du régicide', *Ménager Vol.*, 75–88; A. Adams, 'The transformation of classical motifs in Corrozet's *Hecatongraphie*', *SFr*, 138, 2002: 597–605, on emblems as a memory-tool; and C. Henebry, 'Figures of speech: the *Emblematum liber* as a handbook of rhetorical ornaments', *Neophilologus*, 87: 173–91.

7. Individual Authors

D'AUBIGNÉ. The inclusion of A. in the *agrégation* programme is doubtless responsible for the striking revival of interest in his great epic. An overhaul of the already classical edition has been published: *Les Tragiques*, ed. Jean-Raymond Fanlo, 2 vols, Champion, 1126 pp., a very thorough work, indispensable to all readers. Directly connected with the *agrégation* course, *Agrippa d'Aubigné — 'Les Tragiques' (livres VI et VII)*, ed. M.-M. Fragonard, P. Debailly, and J. Vignes, Univ. Paris-VII, 162 pp., is a useful (though incomplete) overview of the last parts of the epic, divided into three sections ('Intertextualité biblique et dialogisme', 'Tragique et théologie', and 'Prophétisme et eschatologie'). The invasion of Valteline by Spanish soldiers in July 1620 prompted a great number of lampoons, and G. Banderier, 'Quelques vers inédits d'A.', *BHR*, 65: 149–54, focuses on a booklet, using as an epigraph eight lines from the *Tragiques*, interesting in so far as d'Aubigné's poetry is seldom quoted by contemporary writers and as these lines seem to belong to unknown drafts. Neither unknown verses nor first drafts are to be found in V. Ferrer, 'Un manuscrit retrouvé d'A.', *id.*, 125–34. Various texts sent to or related to d'Aubigné are edited by G. Banderier, 'A. et le "grand dessein": un document inédit', *PFSCL*, 30: 197–207; Id., '*Analecta Albineana*. Documents inédits relatifs à A.', *BSHPF*, 149: 669–92. See also Id., 'A. et le thème du désert', Nauroy, *Désert*, 251–66; G. Schrenck, 'Variations sur le psaume 118 dans l'œuvre d'A.', *Ménager Vol.*, 407–17, and J.-C. Ternaux, 'A. et Ovide: la fable de Lycaon', *Néraudeau Vol.*, 287–92.

BÈZE. *Correspondance de B.*, éd. Alain Dufour, Béatrice Nicollier, and Hervé Genton (THR, 380), vol. xxv, xxviii + 408 pp., displays the same high level of scholarship as the former volumes. It contains only a single year of correspondence (1584). One may note the presence of a letter from B. to the poet and alchemist Jean de Sponde. B. Nicollier, 'B. et les Bourbons protestants', *BSHPF*, 149: 9–41, studies the relationship between the religious leader and the Protestant members of the royal family. On his historical works, see A. Dufour, 'B. historien', *Ménager Vol.*, 89–100; and, on his devotional poetry, V. Ferrer, 'Variations autour du psaume 51: les méditations de B., d'Aubigné et de Duplessis-Mornay', *BSHPF*, 149: 705–18.

DU BARTAS. A sparse year for Du B. studies: G. Banderier, 'Notes et documents sur Du B. (II)', *BSAHLSG*, 104: 461–69; Id., 'Un émule de Du B. au siècle des Lumières: Dulard (1696–1760)', *CRAC*, 22: 103–108; Id., 'L'édition nîmoise de la *Sepmaine* (1581)', *BBib*, 1: 127–38; Id., 'Images, *memoria* et encyclopédie dans la *Sepmaine*', *Cahiers Diderot*, 13: 33–48; C. Clark-Evans, 'The brain and nervous system in two French Renaissance "scientific poets": Pernette du Guillet and Du B.', *BHR*, 65: 289–303.

DU BELLAY. A new edition of Du B.'s works, presenting them in chronological order, is in progress under the editorial supervision of Olivier Millet. The first volume, *Deffence, et illustration de la langue françoyse*, ed. Francis Goyet and Olivier Millet, Champion, 462 pp., provides a 300–page long and in-depth commentary. Sabine Forero-Mendoza, *Le Temps des ruines. L'éveil de la conscience historique à la Renaissance*, Seyssel, Champ Vallon, 2002, 222 pp., contains some pages on Du B. (172–87), whose rivalry with Ronsard is studied by G. Defaux, 'Du Bellay, Ronsard et l'Envie', *Ménager Vol.*, 197–205.

On Italian influences, see A. Bettoni, 'Il sonetto di Veronica Gambara sulla predestinazione in B.', *Italiques*, 5, 2002 : 33–52.

MARGUERITE DE NAVARRE. S. de Reyff, 'La fonction d'une image dans la méditation spirituelle de M.', Nauroy, *Désert*, 211–34, treats the topic of the desert in M.'s works. N. Cazauran, 'Sur trois récits de l'*Heptaméron*', *NRSS*, 21.2 : 5–20, studies particularly the 11th and 13th *récits*, whereas the 70th is treated by H. James, 'Royal jokes and sovereign mystery in Castiglione and M.', *MLQ*, 64 : 399–425. On her poetry, see N. Cazauran, 'M.: le deuil en dialogues', *Ménager Vol.*, 343–57, and H. Orii, 'Le cercle sans circonférence dans *Les Prisons* de M.', *NRSS*, 21.2 : 21–34 (a welcome translation of an article originally written in Japanese).

MONTAIGNE. Pride of place goes this year to a volume of miscellaneous studies, both in French and English, *Le Visage changeant de M.*, ed. Keith Cameron and Laura Willett, Champion, 394 pp., divided into six sections: 'Le portrait de M.', 'M. et sa bibliothèque', 'La méthode de M.', 'M. et ses lecteurs', 'M. et Mlle de Gournay', 'M. et les Anglo-Saxons'. The whole volume makes a valuable contribution to M. studies. Bruno Roger-Vasselin, *M. et l'art de sourire à la Renaissance*, Saint-Genouph, Nizet, 416 pp., sees how although M. had all reason to be deeply pessimistic, he yet chose to smile at us across the centuries, and it is impossible not to respond. B. Roger-Vasselin, 'Les trois tendances de l'ironie chez M.', *SFr*, 139 : 84–89. Marie-Luce Demonet, *À plaisir. Sémiotique et scepticisme chez M.*, Orléans, Paradigme, 428 pp., is a complex book, collecting lectures and already published articles scattered among various learned journals and CD-ROMs. The author studies M.'s relations to the scholastic tradition, and Chapter 15 appears also in Kessler, *Res*, 177–95. A philosophical interpretation of M.'s *Essais* is given by Ann Hartle, *M., Accidental Philosopher*, CUP, viii + 304 pp., who tries to evaluate M. not only as an eminent writer, but as an original philosopher. H. investigates M.'s scepticism and the form itself of the 'essay' with an original and refreshing approach. See also Tzvetan Todorov, *M. ou la découverte de l'individu*, Tournai, La Renaissance du Livre, 2001, 48 pp. Sainte-Beuve, *Causeries sur M.*, ed. François Rigolot, Champion, 240 pp., gathers together the articles, papers, and reviews written by the great 19th-c. critic on the author of the *Essais*, and also on Charron and La Boétie, with some notes and discussion of *Port-Royal* and its relevance to Montaigne. *Des signes au sens: lectures du livre* III *des 'Essais'*, ed. Françoise Argod-Dutard, Champion, 264 pp., publishes the papers of a symposium held in Bordeaux (November 2002). A.-M. Cocula analyses the role of the wars of religion in France in the conception of the 3rd book (11–33); D. Bjaï stands 'Au seuil des *Essais* de 1588' (35–52); A. de Souza Filho examines the famous chapter of 'Des Coches' (53–89); C. Magnien focuses on 'Des Boyteux' (91–102); F. Argod-Dutard writes on 'La part du lecteur: écriture et implicite' (103–19); G. Magniont studies M.'s influence on Pascal (121–30). A. Tournon looks at the endings of various chapters ('Des ajustements énigmatiques', 133–50); M.-L. Demonet's and C.-G. Dubois's contributions deal with the role of physiognomony (151–78), and witch-hunting (179–200); Y. Bellenger discusses 'le thème de la vieillesse' (201–15), and J.-Y. Pouilloux the essay on moral virtue (217–34); G. Mathieu-Castellani manages to look at M.'s creative unconciousness (235–53). A stimulating 'philological reading' of M.'s 'Des coches' is given by J. Brody, 'Anatomie d'une lecture philologique', *BSAM*, 31–32:49–75. C. Couturas, 'Repères médiévaux et renaissants vers la prud'hommie selon M.', *RHR*, 56:41–59, considers this important moral idea. André Tournon and Vân Dung le Flanchec, *'Essais' de M., livre III*, Neuilly, Atlande, 2002, 316 pp., and Jean-Yves Pouilloux and Françoise Argod-Dutard, *'Essais', livre III*, Armand Colin, 2002, 152 pp., are two small guides for undergraduates.

Hugh Grady, *Shakespeare, Machiavelli, and M. Power and Subjectivity from 'Richard II' to 'Hamlet'*, OUP, 2002, x + 286 pp., studies, from a modern point of view (Adorno, Lacan) M.'s subjectivity and his political culture. On the everlasting discussion about the base text of the *Essais*, neither party being able to convince the other, read the opposing papers by A. Tournon, 'Du bon usage de l'édition posthume des *Essais*', *BSAM*, 29–30:77–91, and J. Céard, 'M. et ses lecteurs: l'édition de 1595', *ib.*, 93–106. May we suggest that the whole debate be given a decade or two of benign neglect? E. Loughran, 'Tentative beginnings: M. rewrites his early essays', *Neophilologus*, 87:371–83, studies two essays, 'De la tristesse' (I, 2) and 'Comme l'ame . . .' (I, 4). *MonS*, 15, is devoted to his *Journal de voyage*, a minor work, considered here in isolation. Concetta Cavallini, *L'Italianisme de M.*, Fasano, Schena — Univ. Paris-Sorbonne, 368 pp. O. Roth, 'M. und La Rochefoucauld: humanistische Selbsterforschung und moralistische Kritik', *WRM*, 26, 2002:101–14, and *ib.*, 27:19–42, focuses on M.'s influence on the concept of *honnêteté*. On his political thought, see B. Périgot, 'Le politique chez M.', *RAR*, 16:109–28. On M.'s self-perception of his moderately successful public career see C. Jordan, 'M. on property, public service, and political servitude', *RQ*, 56:408–35. S. Miyakawa's study on 'L'empereur Julien et l'apologie de soi dans les *Essais*', *RAR*, 16:41–54, is unfortunately in Japanese, with an alluring French summary.

On La Boétie, see E. Podoksik, 'B. and the politics of obedience', *BHR*, 65:83–95, and M. Magnien, 'Pour une attribution définitive du *Memoire sur l'Edit de janvier* à B.', *Ménager Vol.*, 123–32.

Marie le Jars de Gournay, *Apology for the Woman Writing*, ed. and trans. Richard Hillman and Colette Quesnel, Chicago–London, Chicago U.P., 2002, xxviii + 176 pp. Renaissance scholars will focus on the 'Promenade de Monsieur de Montaigne' (1594), Gournay's only work of fiction, translated here for the first time into English, with a good introduction. Giovanna Devincenzo, *Marie de Gournay. Un cas littéraire*, Fasano, Schena — Univ. Paris-Sorbonne, 2002, 350 pp., is a biographical and almost hagiographic study on the life and works of M.'s 'fille d'alliance'. A. Legros, 'M. et Gournay en marge des *Essais*', *BHR*, 65:613–30, focuses on the collaboration between M. and Marie Le Jars de Gournay.

RABELAIS. Myriam Marrache-Gouraud, *'Hors toute intimidation'. Panurge ou la parole singulière* (THR, 374; *ERab* 41), 428 pp., is a doctoral dissertation devoted to the merry Panurge, the most puzzling and protean character of the Rabelaisian universe, displaying high standards of thoroughness, precision, and attention to detail. Alison Williams, *Tricksters and Pranksters. Roguery in French and German Literature of the Middle Ages and the Renaissance*, Amsterdam–Atlanta, Rodopi, 2000, viii + 236 pp., contains an important chapter on Panurge (177–208). See also V. Zaercher, 'Le banquet du *Tiers-Livre* à l'épreuve des *topoi* symposiaques', *SFr*, 136, 2002:99–108. *ERab*, 42 (THR, 379), 144 pp., is a thin volume of essays, including a useful index of R.'s works as referred to in the first 40 volumes of the series. John Parkin, *Interpretations of R.*, Lampeter, Mellen, 2002, x + 218 pp., contains chapters on R. and Guillaume Coquillard, his youthful and mature years, the influence of epic, a close Bakhtinian analysis and interpretation, and a discussion on the *Cinquième livre*, of much debated authenticity. *De Rabelais à Sade. L'analyse des passions dans le roman de l'âge classique*, ed. Colas Duflo and Luc Ruiz, Saint-Étienne U.P., 132 pp., contains a study by L. Gerbier on 'Maîtrise des passions et genèse du sujet dans le *Tiers-Livre*' (11–20). Peter Gilman, *Le Héros masqué de 'Pantagruel'. Une nouvelle introduction à l'œuvre de R.*, Soirans, p.p., 2001, iv + 196 pp., tries to explain, in a rather unusual style, why R. wrote *Gargantua* after *Pantagruel* and claims that the title-page of *Pantagruel* is an attack against Lemaire de Belges's *Illustrations*. Daniel Martin, *R. Mode d'emploi*, Saint-Genouph, Nizet, 2002, 234 pp., tries to interprete the *Pantagruel* in the light of the art of memory. This approach is only half-convincing. Gerard Sharpling, *The Role of the Image in the Prose Writings of Erasmus, R., Marguerite de Navarre, and Montaigne*, Lampeter, Mellen, iv + 228 pp., deals especially with the *Quart-Livre*.

R. also wrote humanist letters, influenced by Cicero's epistolography. His correspondents were, among others, Budé and Erasmus. Claude La Charité, *La Rhétorique épistolaire de R.*, Québec, Nota Bene,

306 pp., is the first book to study these letters for themselves, comparing them with contemporary correspondence handbooks (which are thoroughly analysed). D. M. Posner studies the use of architectural imagery in his article on 'The temple of reading: architectonic metaphor in R.', *RenS*, 17:257–74. On the storm in R.'s *Quart-Livre*, see a brilliant commentary by O. Pot, 'Prolégomènes pour une étude de la tempête en mer (XVIe–XVIIIe siècles)', *Versants*, 43:71–133.

RONSARD. Véronique Denizot, *'Comme un souci aux rayons du soleil'. R. et l'invention d'une poétique de la merveille (1550–1556)* (THR, 373), 352 pp., studies first the metaphor of the *souci* (the emotion and also the marigold flower), then the first poetical works of R., an enthusiastic young man, whose ambition was to rejuvenate French poetry by his own efforts. D. considers R.'s poetry as a poetry of surprise, and in *R. — 'Les Amours'*, Gallimard, 2002, 232 pp., she provides also a commentary on R.'s *canzoniere*, studying the influence of Petrarch, the composition of the collection, and the links between biography and poetical fiction. Primarily intended for undergraduates, this little book will also be useful to scholars. Jean M. Fallon, *His Story, Her Story. A Literary Mystery of Renaissance France*, NY, Lang, xviii + 200 pp., includes discussion of a poem ascribed to R. and collected in his diaries by Pierre de l'Estoile among a group of poems related to the murder of a woman by her husband. Literary scholarship turns into a detective story! On another unsolved mystery, involving Antoine Caron's *Funérailles de l'Amour* and an anonymous poem entitled *Obsèques d'Amour*, see B. H. Beech and G. T. Beech, 'A painting, a poem, and a controversy about women and love in Paris in the 1530s', *SCJ*,34:635–52. F. Rouget, 'Sur des vers retrouvés de R.', *Ménager Vol.*, 271–80, deals with an unknown piece of poetry, printed posthumously in 1619. R. E. Campo, 'R.'s Eutrapelian *Gaillardise*', *Neophilologus*, 87:529–51, analyses an unnoticed aspect of his poetry. Y. Bellenger, 'Note sur le nom d'Ovide dans la poésie de R.', *Néraudeau Vol.*, 279–86, is a list of quotations.

8. Minor Writers

POETRY. Hélène Casanova-Robin, *Diane et Actéon. Éclats et reflets d'un mythe à la Renaissance et à l'âge baroque*, Champion, 494 pp., is a two-fold book. The first part is concerned with Greek, Latin (especially Ovid), and medieval literature and their reception; the second with 16th-c. poetry, including consideration of artistic representations. A precise and enlightening study. On editions of Ovid during the 16th c., see H. Cazes, 'Les bonnes fortunes d'Ovide au XVIe siècle', *Néraudeau Vol.*, 239–64. On the borderline of mythology and sexuality, see

M. Rothstein, 'Mutations of the androgyne: its functions in early modern French literature', *SCJ*, 34:409–37.

In 1533, the discovery of the so-called grave of Laura, Petrarch's beloved, raised the same enthusiasm among learned people as would do, today, the discovery of Mozart's burial place. A well-documented article of D. Maira, 'La découverte du tombeau de Laure entre mythe littéraire et diplomatie', *RHLF*, 103.1:3–15, reminds us of this cultural event and its impact on contemporary poetry. Among poets of the first half of the Renaissance, Jean Bouchet aroused special interest: *Jean Bouchet, traverseur des voies périlleuses*, ed. Jennifer Britnell and Nathalie Dauvois, Champion, 314 pp., publishes the proceedings of the first symposium ever devoted to him. It will become an indispensable tool of reference. See also N. Dauvois, 'Morale, politique et eschatologie dans *Les Regnars traversans* de J. Bouchet', *Ménager Vol.*, 179–87. Denis Huë, *Petite anthologie palinodique (1486–1550)*, Champion, 2002, 458 pp., is a selected collection of poems written for the *Puys de Palinods*, from MSS kept in Oxford, Paris, and Saint Petersburg.

Mady Dépillier, *Louise Labé. La première féministe*, Nice, Losange, 138 pp., makes no claim to scholarly accuracy. If L. was, according to the sub-title, the first feminist, she was obviously not the last. This strange book is more a eulogy of feminism than a biography of L., and literary analysis is lacking. On Italian influences and their traces in her poetry, see D. Martin, 'Louize Labé Lionnoize et le "vieil rommain": l'Italie et l'italien dans le volume des *Euvres*', *SFr*, 138, 2002:589–96. Mary B. Moore, *Desiring Voices. Women Sonneteers and Petrarchism*, Carbondale–Edwardsville, Southern Illinois U.P., 2000, XVI + 290 pp., contains a chapter on L.

Emblems of Desire. Selections from the 'Délie' of Maurice Scève, ed. and trans. Richard Sieburth, Philadelphia, Pennsylvania U.P., xlviii + 174 pp., is a bilingual anthology which comes with a lengthy introduction, interesting even for those able to read S.'s poetry in the original. The emblems of the 1544 edition are lavishly reproduced. Thomas Hunkeler, *Le Vif du sens. Corps et poésie selon Scève*, Geneva, Droz, 324 pp. S.'s poetry seems to be, on a first reading, completely disembodied, yet the human body is present in his work: the female body, the dying body, and the buried body. See also Id., 'Lire *Délie* à la lumière du *dolce stil nuovo*', *Italiques*, 5, 2002:53–75. On a rhetorical device, see C. Alduy, '*Délie* palimpseste', *SFr*, 139:23–38. M. Clément, 'S. et le *Paradoxe contre les lettres*', *BHR*, 65:97–124, discusses a minor booklet of 1545 ascribed to the poet of *Délie*.

Several studies are devoted to Michel de L'Hospital: P. Galand-Hallyn, 'L'H. à l'école de Jean Salmon Macrin dans les *Carmina*', *BHR*, 65:7–50; M.-D. Legrand, 'La figure du roi dans le *Traité de la réformation de la justice* attribué à L'H.', *Ménager Vol.*, 41–51; L. Petris, 'Hatred in L'H.'s poetry and policy', *RenStud*, 17 : 674–94.

Yvonne Roberts, *Jean-Antoine de Baïf and the Valois Court*, Berne, Lang, 2000, 232 pp., is a full-length and chronological account of B.'s political poetry. A lyrical poet and political propagandist, he was financially supported by Catherine de Medici and Henri III. See also J. Vignes, 'Ovide métamorphosé dans les *Poèmes* de B.', *Néraudeau Vol.*, 265–77. Remy Belleau, *Œuvres poétiques*, vol. v, ed. Guy Demerson, Champion, 480 pp., includes the last works of B. printed during his lifetime: his French translation of Anacreon's odes, his poems on jewels and precious stones, and his paraphrase of the *Song of Songs*. D. also edits vol. VI, Champion, 272 pp., which includes his posthumous publications, essentially a translation of Aratos's poem on constellations. M. F. Verdier, 'Mort et sépulture de René de Lorraine et Louise de Rieux, protecteurs du poète Belleau', *NRSS*, 21.2 : 53–55, examines a biographical point.

Etienne Jodelle, *Les Amours. Contr'Amours*, ed. Emmanuel Buron, Saint-Etienne U.P., 204 pp., is a handsome paperback edition, including a glossary, of this original collection. *Pontus de Tyard, poète, philosophe, théologien*, ed. Sylviane Bokdam and Jean Céard, Champion, 414 pp., is an important collection of articles (with sections such as 'T. en son temps', 'La poésie et les arts', 'Dialogue et encyclopédie', 'La Bible et les noms'), which contains many articles of note, most of them models of precision and elegance, filling a long-felt need. One may add H. Marek, 'Ovide relu par T.', *Néraudeau Vol.*, 293–302.

Catherine d'Amboise, *Poésies*, ed. Catherine M. Müller, Montreal, Ceres, 2002, 112 pp., is a careful edition of a forgotten poet, whose work is preserved in a single illuminated MS written in 1525–1530 (BnF, fr. 2282). Some illustrations are taken from her prose works (Paris, Arsenal, MS 2037). *Jean-Baptiste Chassignet*, ed. Olivier Millet, Champion, 398 pp., is the first collection of essays devoted to this poet. Marc-Claude de Buttet, *L'Amalthée*, ed. Sarah Alyn-Stacey, Champion, 586 pp., is a handy volume, carefully presented, of a work which has long required a modern edition. B. was a Savoyard, a writer of sonnets, a friend of Jean Dorat, the patron saint of the *Pléiade*. See also the same author's, 'B. et la publication du *Premier livre des vers*', *NRSS*, 20.2, 2002 : 25–35.

On more minor poets, see O. Millet, 'Poésie et musique: l'œuvre de Louis des Masures et ses "cantiques" ', *Ménager Vol.*, 371–80, and G. Banderier, 'Notes sur Christofle de Gamon', *BHR*, 65 : 317–29, presenting some unpublished or not readily accesible liminary pieces written by this poet and alchemist. His *Semaine* (in reply to Du Bartas's poem), first published in 1609, was partly translated into Latin, probably before 1623, by a hitherto unknown French woman writer,

Françoise Pautrard. Flaminio de Birague, *Les premières œuvres poétiques (1585)*, ed. Roland Guillot and Michèle Clément (TLF, 557), xcii + 256 pp., is a good edition (but not exempt from misprints). B.'s poetical works can by no means be called a hidden masterpiece, but this edition contains in particular a 570-line poem on a Persian theme. Poetry is said to be 10% inspiration and 90% perspiration. Poets lacking inspiration and not wishing to perspire may have used Maurice de La Porte's dictionary of rhymes, studied by A.-P. Pouey-Mounou, 'Les exercices de style des *Epithetes* de La Porte', *BHR*, 65:51–67.

PROSE. *Voyage au Levant. Les observations de Pierre Belon du Mans, de plusieurs singularités et choses mémorables, trouvées en Grèce, Turquie, Judée, Egypte, Arabie et autres pays étranges*, ed. Alexandra Merle, Chandeigne, 2001, 608 pp. Born in 1517, not far from Le Mans, Pierre Belon was a genuine Renaissance man. He studied in Germany and was a botanist, a physician, and a chronicler. He was finally murdered in 1564. This edition reproduces the first printing of his work (1553). Despite the modernization of the spelling, it is a very good edition, with no less than five indexes (names, geography, botany, zoology, and thematic). Bertrand de La Borderie, *Le Discours du voyage de Constantinople*, ed. Christian Barataud and Danielle Trudeau, Champion, 250 pp. La Borderie travelled through Turkey between 1537 and 1538. He wrote the first French description of Greece and Asia Minor after the fall of Constantinople, a puzzling verse account of his diplomatic mission. Related texts by Jean de Véga, André Thevet, Pierre Belon du Mans, and Nicolas de Nicolay are given in appendices. On the same subject, Alexandra Merle, *Le Miroir ottoman. Une image politique des hommes dans la littérature géographique espagnole et française (XVIe–XVIIe siècles)*, Univ. Paris-Sorbonne, 284 pp., does a great service to scholarship. On a related subject, see M. Yardeni, 'Protestantisme et utopie en France aux XVIe et XVIIe siècles', *Diasporas*, 1, 2002:51–58.

Jean Pillot, *Institution de la langue française (Gallicae linguae institutio)*, ed. Bernard Colombat, Champion, cxx + 272 + 366 pp. Born in Lorraine, P. was a political counsellor, living in a little Alsatian principality. His grammar of the French language, which won great fame, was especially intended for young German noblemen wishing to learn French. This translation comes with a substantial introduction. John Palsgrave, *L'Éclaircissement de la langue française (1530)*, ed. and transl. Susan Baddeley, Champion, 775 pp., is the first French translation of the 'first real grammar of the French vernacular' (G. A. Padley), intended for English readers. Palsgrave taught French to Henry VIII's sister, Mary, who was to be married to Louis XII. This excellent (although incomplete) edition reproduces the 1530 English edition, printed in Gothic type, and gives an accurate translation into modern French. Robert Estienne, *Traicté de la grammaire françoise*, ed. Colette Demaizière, Champion, 202 pp. E. belonged to the great dynasty of printers and stationers, and was also a lexicographer and the author of student manuals, such as the valuable one edited here. See also W. Schleiner, 'Linguistic *xenohomophobia* in 16th-c. France: the case of Henri Estienne', *SCJ*, 34:747–60, and W. Kemp, 'Early Paris editions of Erasmus's *Colloquia* revisited: Robert Estienne's 1529 selection and the Censors', *BBib*, 2:223–37. Joachim Périon, *Dialogues de l'origine du français et de sa parenté avec le grec*, ed. and trans. Geneviève Demerson and Albertine Jacquetin, Champion, 828 pp. P. was a Benedictine, admirer of Budé, in opposition to Ramus; one of the great Greek scholars of his time, he produced four books of dialogues, dedicated to Henri II, in which he tried to prove the relationship between French and Greek, in order to demonstrate that French is as important a language as Greek was. The 1555 Latin edition is reprinted and translated into French with abundant notes.

Another old and baffling riddle (fortunately of little consequence) is the *Cymbalum mundi*. Since its publication in 1537, it has inspired dozens of hypotheses, counter-hypotheses, and has destroyed more than one academic reputation. It is prudently and traditionally ascribed to Bonaventure des Périers. *Le 'Cymbalum Mundi'*, ed. Franco Giacone (THR, 383), xvi + 608 pp., is an attempt, if not to solve the enigma, at least to provide a cautious reappraisal, in a broadly literary-historical perspective.

Gabriel Chappuys, *Les Facétieuses Journées*, ed. Michel Bideaux, Champion, 898 pp. C. was a prolific translator into French of nearly 100 books from Latin, Italian, and Spanish. He also adapted Francesco Sansovino's *Cento novelle scelte*. This little-known collection of short-stories is here carefully edited and presented. Sansovino also wrote a treatise on letter-writing (1564), translated by C. in 1588, and now reissued under the title *La Lettre, le secrétaire, le lettré. De Venise à la cour de Henri III*, ed. Mireille Blanc-Sanchez, 2 vols, Grenoble U.P., 2000–01, 200, 284 pp. These two volumes contain valuable studies by M. Blanc-Sanchez, 'Sansovino et son *Del Secretario*', P. de Capitani, 'Un traducteur français de textes italiens à la fin de la Renaissance. C.', P. Mula, 'De Venise à Paris. *L'art des secrétaires* de C. entre traduction et création', followed by the annotated text of C.'s translation. Luc Vaillancourt, *La Lettre familière au XVIe siècle. Rhétorique humaniste de l'épistolaire*, Champion, 460 pp., studies epistolography from Antiquity to the Renaissance and analyses, from a rhetorical viewpoint, some 16th-c. collections of letters in Latin and French. The author sees in the slow transformation of this genre an influence from the art of worldly conversation.

Nicolas Pasquier, *Le Gentilhomme*, ed. Denise Carabin, Champion, 384 pp. P. was the son of the barrister and writer Estienne Pasquier. He grew up and lived constantly in the shadow of his eminent father and never achieved fame. His *Gentilhomme* is a handbook written for young noblemen, dealing with education, military values, and duels.

Jean Boucher, *La Vie et faits notables de Henry de Valois*, ed. Keith Cameron, Champion, 208 pp., shows how questionable books may shape history. B., unknown to modern lay readers, was one of the most active members of the French Catholic League. Henri III was murdered a few months after the publication of this lampoon disguised as a biography, which was a genuine call to murder. Pierre de l'Estoile, *Registre-journal du règne de Henri III*, ed. Madeleine Lazard and Gilbert Schrenck (TLF, 559), 352 pp., is the sixth and last volume, as carefully annotated and presented as always, of this edition. It covers the period from 1588 to the murder of Henri III.

Jacques Ferrand, *Traité de l'essence et guérison de l'amour ou de la mélancolie érotique*, ed. Gérard Jacquin and Eric Foulon, Anthropos, 2001, xxiv + 244 pp., is a valuable critical edition, reprinting a 1610 copy of this treatise quoted by Burton in his *Anatomy of Melancholy*. Brian Nance, *Turquet de Mayerne as Baroque Physician. The Art of Medical Portraiture*, Amsterdam–NY, Rodopi, 2001, xiv + 238 pp., is a study which, although only marginally within the scope of this section, should be mentioned. M. was a not unimportant physician, knighted by King James I, who served four kings and was a correspondent of d'Aubigné. Joël Coste, *La Littérature des 'erreurs populaires'*, Champion, 2002, 612 pp., studies French popular medicine and its popularization.

Marguerite de Cambis, *Epistre consolatoire de messire Jean Boccace envoyée au Signeur Pino de Rossi (1556)*, ed. Colette H. Winn, Champion, lxx + 90 pp. presents the translation of a letter sent by Boccacio to one of his friends, who fled into exile after a failed plot. This little book is a useful bilingual edition of a barely known text. Pascal Lardellier, *Les Miroirs du paon. Rites et rhétoriques politiques dans la France de l'Ancien Régime*, Champion, 352 pp., studies royal entries from a political point of view, as a 'show' organized by the monarchy.

Christiane Deloince-Louette, *Sponde commentateur d'Homère*, Champion, 2001, 472 pp. Better known as a devotional poet, S. was also an alchemist and a philologist, who published in 1583 an annotated edition of Homer, with a Latin translation. See also a stylistic study of his meditative prose by S. Lardon, 'Rhétorique du sacré et du profane dans les *Meditations* de S.', *SFr*, 136, 2002: 3–23.

Bruno Petey-Girard, *Les Méditations chrétiennes d'un parlementaire. Etude sur les premières œuvres de piété de Guillaume du Vair*, Champion, 442 pp., is a doctoral thesis, of impeccable erudition, setting V.'s first printed works against their historical, religious, philosophical, and rhetorical background. On the Stoic revival, see also A. Tarrête, 'Les héros stoïciens, des martyrs païens ?', *RSH*, 269:87–110. On the pastor Simon Goulart, several studies have appeared: G. Banderier, 'Documents sur G. (II)', *HLov*, 52:159–78; D. Carabin, 'Comment G. indexe-t-il le Plutarque d'Amyot?', *BHR*, 65:331–45; and A. C. Graves, 'G., continuateur du martyrologe de Crespin', *RSH*, 269:53–86. Marie-Claire Bichard-Thomine, *Noël Du Fail conteur*, Champion, 2001, 628 pp., studies the narrative art of this Breton lawyer. On another writer of short-stories, see L. M. Rouillard, 'Raping the rose, 16th-c. style: modernising the medieval in day two of *Le Printemps* d'Yver', *FMLS*, 39:15–26.

On Jean Bodin's historical and juridical theories, see J. Stoll, 'Empirical history and the transformation of policical criticism in France from Bodin to Bayle', *JHI*, 64:297–316, and A. Ribeiro de Barros, 'B. et le projet d'une science du droit. La *Juris Universi Distributio* (1578)', *NRSS*, 21.2:57–70.

M. J. Giordano, 'Reverse transmutations: Béroalde de Verville's parody of Paracelsus in *Le Moyen de parvenir*', *RQ*, 66:88–137, compares V.'s novel to a critical alchemical furnace. V. Luzel, 'Une pièce liminaire de V.', *NRSS*, 21.2:85–93 has unearthed a little-known (and also little-inspired) piece of poetry. Guillaume Postel, *Des admirables secrets des nombres platoniciens*, ed. Jean-Pierre Brach, Vrin, 2001, 288 pp., is a valuable bilingual edition of this Latin treatise, written during Postel's stay in Venice (1549) and preserved in London, BL, MS Sloane 1412.

Claude Haton, *Mémoires*, éd. Laurent Bourquin et al., CTHS, 2001–2003, xxxii + 562, 584 pp. Born in Champagne, this Catholic priest wrote a long series of memoirs, not published until the mid-19th c. and overdue for this new edition, with a transcription of Paris, BnF, MS fr. 11575.

THE SEVENTEENTH CENTURY

By J. Trethewey, *University of Wales, Aberystwyth*

1. General

Jean-Marc Chatelain, *La Bibliothèque de l'honnête homme: livres, lectures et collections en France à l'âge classique*, Bibliothèque nationale de France, 211 pp., presents his subject matter in a volume of an elegance which is a modern tribute to the age he deals with. He tackles every aspect of the relationship between the *honnête homme* and books, starting with a definition of what reading means to such a person whose aim would be to achieve 'un certain rapport au livre établi sur la volonté de ne jamais abstraire la lecture de l'expérience et du commerce du monde'. C. then gives us an account of the origins and evolution of this *rapport*. He indicates the kind of books the *honnête homme* would wish to be acquainted with and own: 'des livres pour la conversation [. . .], des livres comme conversation'. Thence to the library, its ordering, its presentation, the presence in it of old and prestigious original editions, its 'luxe et sobriété'. C. introduces us to a fortunately preserved example: 'le cabinet des livres de Châtre de Cangé', which is described in detail, with many of its splendid bindings illustrated. Finally, descriptions are given of Cangé's collection of the 'poésies de Clément Marot conservées dans des reliures doublées de la fin du XVIIe et du début du XVIIIe siècle' which are the bindings considered 'comme l'achèvement même de ce qu'on a appelé [. . .] "la politesse des livres"'.

Sellier, *Essais*, collects articles and papers previously published between 1972 and 2002, among which five *inédits*, including 'Imaginaire et catégories esthétiques du Grand Siècle' (365–85), which finds S. intrigued by the categories *baroque* and *classicisme*, and by *coincidentia oppositorum* and *clair-obscur*; (the other papers are reviewed under individual authors' names below). Bertrand, *Penser la nuit*, collects colloquium *actes* which attempt various answers to the question: 'Au début des temps modernes, comment était vécue la nuit?' These answers draw material from different periods, different countries and different disciplines, so that it is hardly surprising that astronomy and mechanistic philosophy, travel, and names such as Marguerite de Navarre, Ronsard, Chapman, Shakespeare, and Milton are prominent. See below for reviews of individual papers.

S. van Damme, 'Les martyrs jésuites et la culture imprimée à Lyon au XVIIe siècle' *RSH*, 296: 189–205, examines the 'pratiques culturels des jésuites lyonnais au tournant des XVIIe et XVIIIe siècles' to show 'l'exceptionnelle densité sociale et culturelle de l'objet martyr dans une ville d'Ancien Régime', and to demonstrate the Company's 'stratégie de visibilité'. **Bible et littérature*, ed. Olivier Millet (Travaux et recherches des universités rhénanes, 18), Champion, 240 pp. Claudia Julienne, *Dictionnaire de la Bible dans la littérature française: figures, thèmes, symboles, auteurs*, Vuibert, 489 pp., has taken on a task that is perhaps too much for a lone lexicographer. Her coverage of the 17th c. leaves many gaps.

Joan DeJean, *The Reinvention of Obscenity: Sex, Lies, and Tabloids in Early Modern France*, Chicago–London, Chicago U.P., 2002, xii + 204 pp., sets out to 'recreate the trajectory as a result of which *l'obscène* first assumed the role it may be losing'. That re-creation involves her in scrutinizing three examples: firstly Théophile and his 'sodomite sonnet' from *Le Parnasse des poètes satiriques* (1622); then the anonymous *L'École des filles* (1655); and finally Molière's *L'École des femmes* (1662) together with the works that this play's *Querelle* inspired. M.'s comedy was the chief factor by which '*obscénité* began its active life in a modern language in a precise context, the Paris of the 1660s'. Jean-Christophe Abramovici, *Obscénité et classicisme* (Perspectives littéraires), PUF, 322 pp., follows the same paths as D., but goes as far as the Revolution. He divides his study into three sections, firstly 'la part visible des débats sur l'obscène (ceux qui portèrent sur l'honnêteté langagière, la politesse et les Lettres, la mémoire culturelle)', the different ideologies which confronted one another, attacking or defending the arts and freedom of expression. Secondly, A. defines 'les débats sur l'obscène sous l'angle du savoir et de l'esthétique', the frontiers drawn between what is permitted to specialists in certain fields, and what is permitted to lay people approaching those fields. Finally, 'les rapports de l'obscène à l'esthétique invitent [...] à s'interroger sur les principes au nom desquels on proscrivit des Arts et des Lettres certaines représentations jugées trop *sales* ou *grossières*'. The problem of changes in taste had to be tackled, too: how to deal with works once considered acceptable, now found to be stained with 'parties impures'. Conversely, the problem of dealing with material that was, or became, proscribed by new criteria of decorum, and turned into a new field for exploitation by purveyors of pornography. Finally, A. pays tribute to Pierre Bayle, 'le seul à proposer une vraie réflexion sur l'obscénité'. James Grantham Turner, *Schooling Sex: Libertine Literature and Erotic Education in Italy, France, and England 1534–1685*, OUP, xxviii + 408 pp., sets out to show 'how sexuality comes to be a "discipline" or body of knowledge' in the period he has chosen. The French works whose contribution and 'reception-history' are particularly studied are *L'École des filles* and those by, or attributed to, Nicholas Chorier, including *L'Académie des dames*. Sylvie Steinberg, **La Confusion des sexes:*

le travestissement de la Renaissance à la Révolution, Fayard, 2001, xii + 409 pp. C. Jones, 'Phèdre meets the transvestite heroine: fantastic variations on classical themes', *PFSCL*, 30: 379–96, looks at this sort of heroine, 'the most popular literary *femme forte* in the second half of the 17th century'. Mitchell Greenberg, *Baroque Bodies: Psychoanalysis and the Culture of French Absolutism*, Ithaca–London, Cornell U.P., 2001, xii + 278 pp., provides a Freudian reading. He associates 17th-c. Absolutism (G.'s capital) with 'a hybrid accretion across the centuries of history and fiction, of generalizations and myth', and is concerned at 'the continued seduction of the concept defining an outmoded political structure that itself was a fantasy and that nevertheless endures and informs our desire for the *Grand Siècle*'. He feeds our fascination by surveying Molière and carnival (*L'Avare*, *Le Malade imaginaire*), 'Classicism's pornographic body' (*L'École des filles*, *L'Académie des dames*), 'absolutism and androgyny' (the Abbé de Choisy), Marie de l'Incarnation with her insatiable desire for self-mortification, and Racine's theatre which 'ingeniously reconfigures how his protagonists are to negociate the difference between the generations and between the sexes without referring, except in most oblique terms, to the body'. G.'s attitude throughout seems to be prompted by his reading of Freud, and gives the impression, unfortunately, of a considerable distaste for the French 17th century. Dalia Judovitz, **The Culture of the Body: Genealogies of Modernity*, Ann Arbor, Michigan U.P., 2001, 235 pp., studies French literary and philosophical works from the late 16th to the late 18th cs. **Sodomy in Early Modern Europe*, ed. Thomas Betteridge (Studies in Early Modern Europe), MUP, 2002, 192 pp. Robert Muchembled, **Passions de femmes au temps de la reine Margot (1553–1616)*, Seuil, 277 pp.

LitC, 49, has for title *De la polygraphie au XVIIe siècle*, ed. Patrick Dandrey and Delphine Denis. Its two editors plus J.-M. Chatelain, in their 'Présentation' (5–30), separately introduce various phenomena labelled with the keyword, while their 21 contributors study examples from various parts of Europe (but predominantly French): B. Beugnot, 'Le polygraphe, le savoir et la page' (33–46), deals with layout, with typography, and with 'pratiques scripturales et éditoriales' (where he occasionally strays far from the 17th c.), and provides illustrations of layouts of 16th-c. and 17th-c. printed pages; E. Bury, 'L'univers des polygraphes: du cabinet savant à la République des Lettres' (47–58), defines this republic as 'avant tout "commerce", "diffusion", "croisement" et "multiplication" des textes', which to him seems to be 'le milieu naturel du polygraphe'; S. Mazauric, 'Un cas de polygraphie savante: les Conférences du Bureau d'Adresse' (59–69), points out that the particular form of polygraphy manifested by this institution was an important aspect of the 'révolution scientifique du premier

XVIIe siècle'; F. Wild, 'Les ana et la polygraphie' (71–83), finds that later in the century collections abandon 'formes brèves' for longer notices, and successive editions add new entries, in some cases doubling the size of collections, both changes being, in W.'s view, partly due to 'l'abandon de la source orale'; L. van Delft, 'Fertilité d'une forme polygraphique: le genre du *theatrum* savant' (113–30), notes volumes devoted to 'théâtres proprement dit', 'spiritualité', and 'comédie humaine', and volumes of 'inventaires, encyclopédies, *conspectus*', and reproduces illustrations of frontispieces dating from 1570 to 1708; D. Denis, 'Le roman, genre polygraphique?' (336–66), would answer her question in the affirmative because the genre does not have a fixed form, and therefore 'ouvre aux formes narratives un terrain d'expérimentation infini, suscitant de constantes transformations'; T. Cave, 'Polygraphie et polyphonie. Écritures plurielles, de la Renaissance à l'époque classique' (385–400), begins by reconsidering 'le rôle que joue [. . .] l'ensemble des phénomènes que nous dénommerons "polyphonie"', and then looks at examples, particularly at the case of La Rochefoucauld's *Maximes* 'qui a dans ce contexte le statut d'un cas-limite', and then proceeds to justify introducing the term *polyphonie* into a literary context, ignoring musical or linguistic ones. Philippe-Joseph Salazar, **L'Art de parler. Anthologie de manuels d'éloquence* (Cadratin), Klincksieck, 362 pp.

D. Carabin, 'Deux institutions de gentilshommes sous Louis XIII: *Le Gentilhomme* de Pasquier et *L'Instruction du Roy* de Pluvinel', *DSS*, 55:27–38, studies the 'enjeux culturels et politiques' in these two manuals of the 'art équestre'. Delphine Denis, *Le Parnasse galant: institution d'une catégorie littéraire au XVIIe siècle* (Lumière classique, 32), Champion, 2001, 389 pp., traces the 'naissance d'une catégorie' during the period 1640–60, with its 'cartes allégoriques', its *annuaires*, and other celebratory or satirical forms, as well as its principal representatives, observers, and historians such as Donneau de Visé, Gabriel Guéret, La Fontaine, the Chevalier de Méré, Paul Pellisson, Sarasin, Madeleine de Scudéry, Segrais, Sorel, and Voiture.

Wetsel, *Spiritualité*, contains the following: J. Mesnard, 'Être moderne au XVIIe siècle' (7–20), who seeks out uses of the word *moderne* by successive writers, to which, not unnaturally, he adds the word *ancien*, but finds little of significance until he reaches 1688 and the publications of Fontenelle and Perrault; H. Trépanier, 'Le débat autour du langage mystique: l'enjeu d'une "manière de parler"' (51–60), who looks at the confrontations of Surin and Chéron; G. Ferreyrolles, 'Les jésuites et la poétique de l'histoire' (61–79), who refers to works by two Jesuits, Le Moyne's *De l'histoire* (1670) and Rapin's *Instructions pour l'histoire* (1677), both defending the subject against sceptics like La Mothe Le Vayer in his *Du peu de certitude qu'il y a dans l'histoire*; C. Carlin, 'La métaphore du "Miroir du mariage" dans quelques traités catholiques du XVIIe siècle' (95–109), who chooses eight treatises starting with François de Sales's *Introduction à la vie dévote* and ending with Jean Girard de Villethierry's *La Vie des gens mariez* (1695), which latter advises that a metaphorical mirror must be constantly consulted by 'quiconque se veut rendre agréable à Dieu en estat de mariage, et y acquerir de la perfection'.

Encyclopedia of the Enlightenment, ed. Alan Charles Kors et al., OUP, vol. 1, *Abbadie – Enlightenment Studies*, xxi + 430 pp.; vol. 2, *Enthusiasm – Lyceums and Museums*, 449 pp.; vol. 3, *Mably – Ruysch*, 497 pp.; vol. 4, *Sade – Zoology*, 470 pp., has articles which are supranational in coverage, and also many topics of interest to *dix-septiémistes*: Ancients and Moderns, the Académie Française, Cartesianism, clandestine literature, Jansenism, the Jesuits, the Oratorians, and writers such as Bayle, Bossuet, Challe, Fénelon, Malebranche, and Charles Perrault. **Le XVIIe Siècle encyclopédique*, ed. Claudine Nédélec et al. (*Cahiers Diderot*, 12), Rennes U.P., 2001, 210 pp. J. Soll, 'Empirical history and the transformation of political criticism in France from Bodin to Bayle', *JHI*, 64: 297–316, demonstrates how the control of historical 'truth', imposed first by Richelieu, then even more firmly by Louis XIV and his ministers, was lost, and a return to an older tradition of 'pragmatical political science based on historical analysis' took place after the monarch's death.

F. Lagarde, 'Vertu de la terreur classique', *PFSCL*, 30: 463–74, searches Descartes, dictionaries, and the data bank of *American and French Research on the Treasury of French Language Project (ARTFL)*, University of Chicago, 1981–2002, for definitions of *terreur* and related words, and follows these up in specific authors, among them Chapelain, Coëffeteau, Pierre Corneille, Fénelon, Guez de Balzac, Pascal, and Georges de Scudéry. L. Fraisse, 'La littérature du XVIIe siècle chez les fondateurs de l'histoire littéraire', *DSS*, 55: 3–26, writes an optimistic survey which celebrates progress towards the present day on all fronts. G. Banderier, 'Charles Eusèbe de Liechtenstein (1611–1684) et les écrivains français', *ib.*, 341–51, summarizes the life of this prince, and what is known of his relations with Jean Puget de La Serre and Guillaume Colletet.

Mazouer, *Animal*, offers papers, with illustrations, on the arts in various countries. On French literature: D. Lopez, 'L'animal du XVIIe siècle: fond de tableau théologique, mythologique, philosophique (quelques points d'ancrage)' (11–25), finds in Christendom 'la disqualification de l'animal, l'absence de respect, la méfiance ou l'indifférence à son égard', which is to be found both in religious and philosophical attitudes and in a 'résonance populaire', this tradition being opposed by another one stemming from Montaigne, more favourable to animals, less well supported but ultimately more attractive; N. Grande, 'Une vedette des salons: le caméléon' (89–102), dwells, with quotations, on the surprising number of references to this animal from classical antiquity onwards (and particularly from Mlle de Scudéry), 'en vertu des connotations morales qu'impliquaient les attributs physiques dont la tradition l'avait nanti'. Other papers from this volume are reviewed under named writers below.

Wetsel, *Femmes*, contains the following *actes*: D. Denis, 'Préciosité et galanterie: vers une nouvelle cartographie' (17–39), proposes a 'carte provisoire' without as yet any 'frontières assurées', wishing to 'interroger le couple *préciosité* et *galanterie* précisément sous l'angle de sa mise en relation'; M.-O. Sweetser, 'Voix féminines dans la littérature classique' (41–52), finds examples in drama, fiction, and correspondence of situations where, despite the oppressive ascendancy of men, 'les écrivains ont pu concevoir des personnages de femmes autonomes et leur donner une voix'; D. Bertrand, 'Le rire de Christine de Suède: du dénigrement burlesque à l'assomption héroïque' (77–86), contrasts the mockery expressed by Mlle de Montpensier in her *Mémoires* with the 'défense et illustration du rire' undertaken by the Queen in hers; P. Bousquet, 'L'héroïsme féminin au XVIIe siècle entre admiration païenne et représentations chrétiennes' (93–107), would balance the concentration on the gentler 'vertus féminines traditionnelles' with many references in literature and art to the heroism of Lucretia. D. Conroy, 'In the beginning was the image: feminist iconography and the frontispiece in the 1640s', *SCFS*, 24, 2002: 277–92, traces, with the help of four appended illustrations, the evolution of the latter term derived from architecture, and of its use in books during the first half of the 17th c. when it became 'an independent entity', sometimes serving as a form of preface as in the case of four feminist texts for which illustrations are provided: Jacques du Bosc's *Femme héroïque* (1645), Du Moyne's *Gallerie des femmes fortes* (1647), Puget de La Serre's *Temple de la Gloire* (MS, 1647), and Georges and Madeleine de Scudéry's *Femmes illustres ou les Harangues héroïques* (1642). J. Royé, 'La figure de la "pédante" dans la littérature comique du XVIIe siècle', Lyons, *Savoir*, 215–25, inquires into 'les enjeux qui sont en œuvre dans la critique du pédantisme des femmes, enjeux à la fois proches et éloignés de la dénonciation du pédant qui s'exerce si fréquemment dans les textes comiques'. R. quotes *Les Visionnaires* by Desmarets, *Le Cercle des femmes* and *L'Académie des femmes* by Chappuzeau, and letters by Balzac and Chapelain. Jean Desprat, **Madame de Maintenon (1635–1719) ou le prix de la réputation*, Perrin, 489 pp.

Le Tragique, ed. Marc Escola (GF Corpus, 3062), Flammarion, 2002, 256 pp., is a collection of texts on all aspects and manifestations of its subject, in which the French 17th c. figures prominently, with Rotrou, Corneille, and Racine providing examples of aspects of the genre. Corneille and Racine discourse on theory while, for good measure, a series of letters by Mme de Sévigné is quoted on Mlle de Montpensier's failure to get married to M de Lauzun: 'le juste sujet d'une tragédie dans toutes les règles du théâtre'. A 'vade mecum' discusses at length all the theoretical vocabulary of the subject. *Le Comique*, ed. Véronique Sternberg-Grenier (GF Corpus, 3065), Flammarion, 247 pp., follows the same plan as the above, with Descartes, Pascal, Mlle de Scudéry, Rapin, Pascal, and Boileau figuring among theorists, Sorel among prose writers, Scarron (burlesque), Boileau (parody), and La Fontaine among poets, while Corneille and Molière represent the dramatists.

2. Poetry

Nicholas Cronk, *The Classical Sublime: French Neoclassicism and the Language of Literature*, Charlottesville, VA, Rookwood, 2002, ii + 210 pp. Central to this study are chapters on Bouhours's *Entretiens d'Ariste et d'Eugène* and Boileau's *Traité du sublime*, the latter, in C.'s view, being 'perhaps the most innovative text of French classical poetic theory'. Stemming from, but greatly refining, the Renaissance linguistic concept of nomenclaturism, the influence of Boileau's translation of Longinus is felt far beyond the realms of poetry, and is a prominent subject of arguments in the *Querelle des anciens et des modernes*. The classical ideal is, according to C., 'the perfect mapping of *signifiant* onto referent', an ideal only replaced eventually by the Romantics with their notion of the ineffable. This is a much needed study, clearly and succinctly argued. R. Krüger, 'Merveilleux païen ou merveilleux chrétien? Le débat sur l'épopée française et la sécularisation du merveilleux au XVIIe siècle', Wetsel, *Spiritualité*, 289–302, sees in the epic poems of Desmarets, Le Moyne, Carel de Sainte-Garde, Louis le Laboureur, and Georges de Scudéry a renewed form which he calls 'le second merveilleux chrétien', in which the influence of Tasso's *Gerusalemme Liberata* with its 'vision catholique, et même ultra-catholique' is predominant, at least until undermined by the new conceptions put forward by Boileau and Rapin. Hélène Casanova-Robin, *Diane et Actéon: éclats et reflets d'un mythe à la Renaissance et à l'âge baroque* (Études et essais sur la Renaissance, 46), Champion, 493 pp., confines herself generally, as far as *l'âge baroque* is concerned, to 'l'étude d'œuvres poétiques ou picturales appartenant essentiellement au XVIe siècle', but does refer to poets active in the first half of the 17th c., such as Jean Godard, Pierre Le Moyne, and Georges de Scudéry. C. Bourgeois, '"Par l'obscur de la nuit'': les variations d'une métaphore baroque', Bertrand, *Penser la nuit*, 261–80, compares examples of this 'opposition commune à la poésie religieuse de l'ère baroque entre la clarté divine et l'aveuglement de la condition humaine'. He finds them in Chassignet, Du Bartas, Pierre de Croix, La Ceppède, and above all in Claude Hopil whose poetry is compared to contemporary French translations of John of the Cross.

M.-C. Canova-Green, '*Les Triomphes de Louis le Juste* (1649): une épopée du discontinu', *SCFS*, 24, 2002 : 29–41, recalls this sumptuous collective work, 'hétérogène mais aussi discontinu', composed of the engravings of Jean Valdor (of which two are reproduced here), the poetry of Charles Beys and Pierre Corneille, and, 'pour les devises, traductions et autres discours savants' the learned contributions of Henri Estienne, René Bary, and le père Nicolaï.

Véronique Adam, *Images fanées et matières vives: cinq études sur la poésie Louis XIII*, Grenoble, ELLUG, 350 pp., begins with an account of the historical context in which her five poets matured, and a 'parcours en images de la poésie Louis XIII', and then studies them in chronological order: Abraham de Vermeil, Théophile de Viau, Pierre de Marbeuf, Gabriel du Bois-Hus, and Tristan L'Hermite. A. devotes a chapter to each of them as representatives of 'l'ensemble des courants de l'époque'. Each poet makes use, in A.'s view, of a collection of images characteristic of him, and in order to define their 'univers imaginaire' she attempts in each case to 'prendre en compte l'intégralité de l'œuvre'. D. Lopez, ' "Peut-être d'autres héros/ M'auraient acquis moins de gloire": du statut des animaux dans la poésie du XVIIe siècle', Mazouer, *Animal*, 39–72, follows up his introductory paper (see above pp. 115–16) with 'un aperçu de la manière dont les poètes du XVIIe siècle réagissent vis-à-vis de l'animal', noting 'des variations et des renouvellements' compared with earlier times. A number of poets, from Théophile to La Fontaine, are quoted and commented upon. Tony Gheeraert, *Le Chant de la grâce: Port-Royal et la poésie d'Arnauld d'Andilly à Racine* (Lumière classique, 47), Champion, 622 pp., begins by challenging the received opinion that Port-Royal was the enemy of poetry. He then, firstly, attempts to 'mettre en évidence les traits qui constituent les caractères communs de la poésie de Port-Royal', to describe the *corpus* he is studying, and to suggest reasons why the *Solitaires* had recourse to poetry and what were the 'formes obsédantes' which preoccupied them. Arnauld d'Andilly (as both poet and theorist), Le Maistre de Sacy, La Fontaine, Racine, two 'amis du dehors', Godeau and Boileau, and, for theory, Pierre Nicole and Bernard Lamy, all are accorded special attention. In the second part, G. looks at the 'forces centrifuges' which became evident with the general change in public taste occurring round about 1660 causing the eclipse of baroque forms and their replacement by classicism. A series of *annexes* provide us with some examples of Port-Royal literary criticism, and a 'chronologie des principaux ouvrages imprimés du Corpus'. D. Souiller, 'Le monstrueux et le régulier: une antinomie de la poétique baroque européenne (1600–1650)', *RLC*, 77:437–48, quotes Corneille, Descartes, Félibien, Huet, Ogier, and Jean-Pierre Camus among his European theorists and practitioners. Nearly all of them, while apologising, seem quite favourable to the monstrous.

REMI DE BEAUVAIS. T. M. Carr, 'Remi de Beauvais's *La Magdeleine* (1617) and the *apostolorum apostola* tradition', Lyons, *Savoir*, 139–49, seeks to revive interest in this heroic poem, and in the particular tradition to which it belongs, portraying not the usual sinful woman converted but 'the Mary-Magdalen who was sent by Christ to announce his resurrection to the apostles and who became a preacher herself'.

CHASSIGNET. C. M. Probes, 'La littérature et l'art au service de la théologie: le voyage terrestre et le voyage spirituel, la poésie de Jean-Baptiste Chassignet mise en rapport avec les emblèmes de Pierre de Loysi', Wetsel, *Spiritualité*, 81–93, explores the late and somewhat neglected *Sonnets franc-comtois*, illustrated with L.'s emblematic engravings. She concentrates on the *motif* of the journey, paying special attention to certain elements such as 'l'harmonie entre emblème et sonnet, le rôle crucial des images comme "preuves", l'exhortation au lecteur et un appel constant à travers les cinq sens'. Id., 'Le savoir historique à l'intersection de l'art et de la poésie emblématiques: les gravures de Pierre de Loysi mises en rapport avec *Les Sonnets franc-comtois*', Lyons, *Savoir*, 81–90. V. Ferrer, 'Les métamorphoses du bestiaire biblique dans les *Paraphrases sur les CL Pseaumes de David* de Jean-Baptiste Chassignet', Mazouer, *Animal*, 27–38, evokes a long chain of influences intervening between the Psalms and C.'s work, all helping to 'nourrir l'imaginaire du Bisontin'. **Jean-Baptiste Chassignet*, ed. Olivier Millet (Colloques, congrès et conférences sur la Renaissance, 36), Champion, 399 pp., prints colloquium *actes*.

COTIN. D. Moncond'huy, 'L'abbé Cotin, théoricien mondain et praticien de l'énigme au XVIIe siècle', *La Licorne*, 64:157–71, is concerned with C.'s *Recueil des énigmes de ce temps*, first published in 1646, and in particular with the 'Discours sur les énigmes' which prefaces it, and which, because C. has no rivals, renders him sole authority of his time on the genre.

LA FONTAINE. Ralph Albanese, Jr., *La Fontaine à l'école républicaine: du poète universel au classique scolaire*, Charlottesville, VA, Rookwood, vii + 378 pp., has trawled through innumerable *manuels scolaires* to chart the establishment of an almost tyrannical *normalisation* imposed on French pupils at all levels and in all types of schools from the mid-19th c. until 1968, and to define the dominant role played in this process by a version of 'La Fontaine' conceived and imposed by zealous French educationalists. He then reviews the efforts made by more recent scholars to *déscolariser* the poet, to restore the public's faded interest in him by emphasizing the fascination of his 'ambiguïté poétique', and by redefining his contribution to the notion of *francité.* A.'s study is accompanied by a series of appendices which reproduce (not all clearly printed) extracts from primary school manuals of the period. On the whole this is a thorough and absorbing study.

Jean-Charles Darmon, *Philosophies de la fable: La Fontaine et la crise du lyrisme* (Écritures), PUF, 314 pp., follows up work he has done on the relations between epicurean philosophy and literature in 17th-c. France (see *YWMLS*, 60, 1998: 137) with this study of La F. following the poet, 'en un moment de déchéance pour la poésie en général et d'ennui pour le lyrisme en particulier', as he turns to epicureanism and the fable form to try and revitalize lyric poetry. This new departure for La F. springs, D. asserts, from the crisis occasioned by the arrest of Foucault and the abrupt end to the patronage and encouragement he had hitherto received for his more traditional lyric creations. P. Jousset, '*Varietas varietatis* ... La poétique de La Fontaine, une gaie physique de la morale', *DSS*, 55: 71–94, concentrates on *La Cigale et la fourmi* but also spends some time on *Le Loup et le chien maigre* and *Le Lièvre et les grenouilles*, in order to indicate ways in which La F. can be truly appreciated by modern readers. P. Dandrey, 'La Fontaine: une diversité "polygraphique"?' *LitC*, 49: 319–38, waxes as eloquent as a wine expert: the 'poète polygraphe butine à toutes fleurs pour fluidifier et transposer en images parlantes leur nectar qu'il infuse à la faveur de la délectation qu'elles procurent, dans l'effusion d'une connivence enjouée et d'une grâce lumineuse'.

M. Gutwirth, 'Quand l'Histoire s'acoquine avec la fable: *Le Paysan du Danube*', Lyons, *Savoir*, 91–97, concentrates on La F.'s only fable with a fixed historical setting. M. Escola, 'À plumes et à poil: la fable comme énigme', *La Licorne*, 64: 125–56, reprints 'Le loup et le chasseur', noting the impression that La F. gives that this double fable 'condense toutes les "leçons": elle est toutes les *Fables*'. E. however is worried by and dwells upon various imprecisions or vaguenesses in La F.'s narration which in his view render it too enigmatic. Id., *Lupus in fabula: six façons d'affabuler La Fontaine* (L'Imaginaire du texte), Saint-Denis, Vincennes U.P., 251 pp., claims that 'toute fable est en droit inachevée: produit d'une réécriture, on voit mal qu'elle puisse interdire au lecteur de se livrer à son tour à un exercice de transformation.' E.'s 'six façons' are treated in six chapters, each one devoted to a theme illustrated by reference particularly to 'fables doubles', and his 'exercices' are accompanied by various versions of the warning (or promise) that 'une fable peut toujours en cacher une autre.'

FRANÇOISE PAUTRARD. G. Banderier, 'Françoise Pautrard, femme et poète du premier XVIIe siècle', *DSS*, 55:117–59, introduces and puts into print for the first time with extensive notes the best of the poetry of this newly discovered Franc-Comtoise. The piety expressed in these poems is representative of her, B. claims: it is 'l'essentiel de l'œuvre'.

TRISTAN L'HERMITE. N. Mallet, 'L'aumône à la belle disgraciée', *CTH*, 25:28–45, compares various manifestations of the theme of *La belle gueuse* (T.'s title for his version), and summarizes research devoted to it, before concentrating on a neglected example, *The faire begger* (1649, the poet's spelling) by an English contemporary of T.'s, Richard Lovelace, which she finally reproduces and translates. J. Serroy, 'Tristan/Bernard. Le Tristan L'Hermite de Jean-Marc Bernard', *ib.*, 46–54, points to evidence of the influence of T. on B., a poet killed in the Great War. R. Landy, 'Sur quelques airs de Tristan', *ib.*, 80–86, introduces us to poems by T. which were set to music by the 17th-c. French composers Étienne Moulinié, Antoine Boesset, Nicolas Métru, and Michel Lambert. Landy outlines T.'s relations with the music and musicians of his time. A CD accompanies this issue of *CTH* reproducing some of these settings, the words of which are given on pp. 87–94.

3. Drama

SCFS, 24, 2002, contains the following papers: M. Hawcroft, 'Seventeenth-century French theatre and its illustrations: five types of discontinuity' (87–105), is not happy with the perceived notion that book illustrations are meant to be 'a helpful and straightforward anticipation of the text itself', and prefers a more nuanced approach, taking into account 'some of the ways illustrations of seventeenth-century theatre exploit various types of discontinuity in their mode of operation'; W. Brooks, '*Intervalles*, *entractes*, and *intermèdes* in the Paris theatre' (107–25), discusses dramatic 'temps perdu' between acts, the occasional necessity for real time to pass between acts, and also the vital differences in definition between the above French technical terms; D. Conroy, 'The cultural politics of disguise: female cross-dressing in tragi-comedy (1630–1642)' (135–49), looks at attitudes to the practice in drama, and examines 'the role that drama may have played in the construction of gender identity', referring to the plays of some 15 dramatists; K. Ibbett, 'From martyr to mourner: the politics of the unextraordinary' (165–78), reviews plays and paintings dealing with the deaths of saints: Puget de La Serre's *Thomas Morus* (1642), Mme de Saint-Balmon's *Jumeaux martyrs* (1650), and, among the paintings, Hendrick Terbrugghen's 'St Sebastian attended by Irene' and Georges de La Tour's 'S. Sébastien soigné par sainte Irène', both works which 'focus on what might be termed the politics of the unextraordinary, on the translation of the spectacular into the sphere of the quotidian', the focus in all these examples being not on the martyrs themselves but on the grief of concerned relatives or friends witnessing their final moments; M. Poirson, 'La "comédie macabre" — une dramaturgie en rupture: des usages du corps au corps hors d'usage' (191–208), surveys the post-Molière, pre-Marivaux comedies of 1673–1715 (in particular Regnard's *Légataire universel*), looking for suggestions of political preoccupations at this 'moment de réaction, marqué par la remise en cause radicale des anciens dogmes qui ont assuré le succès de la monarchie absolue et de son ordre politico-religieux'. P. Scott, 'Saint Catherine in seventeenth-century French tragedy', Britnell, *Female Saints*, 39–58, summarizes the legends surrounding this ex-saint (removed from the Roman calendar in 1969), and introduces in chronological order the five plays written about her: by Jean Boisson de Gallardon (1618), Étienne Poytevin (1619), Jean Puget de La Serre (1643, in prose), anonymous (1649, the century's most commercially successful on this subject), and the nun known as La Chapelle (1663, see p. 128 below). J. Clarke, 'Of actresses and acrobats', *ib.*, 267–83, examines 'issues relating to the first French female performers, concentrating primarily on questions of genre and morality', from 1545 to the mid-17th c. Alain Couprie, *Mademoiselle de Champmeslé*, Fayard, 327 pp., is a well-researched biography of the actress who created Racine's leading roles with the Hôtel de Bourgogne.

LitC, 48, prints colloquium *actes* on *Jeux et enjeux des théâtres classiques (XIXe–XXe siècles)*, ed. Mariane Bury and Georges Forestier, the four sections of which are labelled: 'Penser' — on definitions and redefinitions of *classique* and *classicisme*; 'Voir' — on productions of the French classics and other plays in the light of these definitions; 'Écrire' — on varying levels of acceptance of 'classics' (ancient Greek and Roman, Elizabethan and Spanish Golden-Age as well as French) by 19th- and 20th-c. authors; 'Jouer' — on different interpretations from different periods and countries. A. Riffaud, 'Deux aventures éditoriales: *Chryséide et Arimand* de Mairet (1630), *Cléagénor et Doristée* de Rotrou (1634–1635)', *PFSCL*, 30:9–28, follows the ins and outs of the 'pratiques éditoriales' and the 'méthodes d'impression' used for the illicit publication of these two tragi-comedies, and gives the dramatists' reactions. *Tobin Vol.* contains papers mainly on theatre: L. Van Delft, '*Theatrum Mundi* revisité' (35–44), contrasts the frequent use of this striking image in the 16th to 18th cs with its present-day very limited usage among scholars who nevertheless find it 'une voie d'accès royale, non à l'âge classique seulement, mais à l'âge baroque, à celui des Lumières'; J. Emelina, 'L'horreur dans la tragédie' (171–79), points to the significant presence in classical tragedy of this emotion and the vocabulary associated with it, despite the disapproval expressed by Aristotle and the seeming indifference of contemporary critics and theorists; B. Norman, 'Hybrid monsters and rival aesthetics: monsters in seventeenth-century French ballet and opera' (180–88), gives examples of the difference between the baroque and classical periods in their portrayal of the monstrous and chooses as representatives two versions of Tasso's 'Armide and Renaud', the first being the *Ballet de la délivrance de Renaud* (1617), libretto by Estienne Durand, and the second, Lully's opera *Armide* (1686), libretto by Quinault; G. Forestier, 'Poétiques de la passion dans la tragédie française' (188–97), evokes the 'complexité ou diversité du nouveau système' — that adopted by the 17th-c. tragic dramatists, as opposed to that of the 16th c., before 'cette mutation dramaturgique'; G. Declercq, 'L'identification des genres oratoires en tragédie française du 17e siècle (*Iphigénie, Cinna*)' (230–38), is concerned in particular with 'l'éloquence judiciaire'; L. W. Riggs, '*Monstres naissants*: masculine birth and feminine subversion in the *Theatrum Mundi*' (266–74), draws not only on Corneille and Racine but also on Molière's *Dom Juan* and *Le Misanthrope* to support his view of true theatre opposed to *Theatrum Mundi*. P. Gethner, 'Mad about Lully: three scenarios for opera mania', Wetsel, *Femmes*, 223–30, discusses the parodic expression in opera of anti-opera sentiments at three stages in the genre's evolution: in the 1670s, the 1680s, and the 1740s. S. Belanger, 'Le héros guerrier et le martyr chrétien: retour sur le merveilleux au théâtre français du début du XVIIe siècle', Wetsel, *Spiritualité*, 203–14, chooses Hardy's *Coriolan*, Gillet de la Tessonerie's *L'art de régner* and Rotrou's *Véritable Saint Genest*, seeking to show 'quel type d'attitude chez les héros était digne de susciter l'admiration', and what was the nature of the *merveilleux* in these plays. G. Spielmann, 'Poétique(s) du merveilleux dans les arts du spectacle aux XVIIe et XVIIIe siècles', *ib.*, 227–40, shows that 'en dépit du manque de discours théorique, la recherche de l'effet visuel et auditif s'est dotée d'une poétique aussi cohérente et complète que sa contrepartie textuelle'. S. promises a much wider coverage of this topic on his website. M. Closson, 'Scénographies nocturnes du baroque: l'exemple du ballet français (1581–1653)', Bertrand, *Penser la nuit*, 425–48, wishes to throw light on the question: 'Comment représentait-on la nuit sur scène aux XVIe et XVIIe siècles?' She finds answers in ballet, a form in which 'ont lieu la plupart des innovations concourant à l'invention des règles de l'illusion sur la scène moderne'. A. Gaillard, 'Le soleil à son coucher: la nuit réversible de la mythologie solaire sous Louis XIV', *ib.*, 449–64, refers to Benserade, to La Fontaine, to *ballet de cour*, and to the disgrace of Fouquet after a too magnificent firework display at Vaux attended by a jealous king and queen.

J. Clarke, 'Catherine Biancolelli or the wit and wisdom of Colombine', Wetsel, *Femmes*, 203–17, looks at the actress's life and career, her physical features and personal contribution to the role of Colombine, and at the traits the role retains through over 30 plays and sketches — 'particularly a moral pragmatism and what might be described as a kind of proto-feminism'. **Les arts du spectacle au théâtre: 1550–1700*, ed. Marie-France Wagner and Claire Le Brun-Gouanvic (Colloques, congrès et conférences: Renaissance européenne, 24), Champion, 2001, 273 pp.

Baccar Bournaz, *Afrique*, prints the following *actes*: L. Annabi, 'La représentation de l'Égypte dans le théâtre baroque en France sous Louis XIII' (249–60), looks at Hardy's *La belle Égyptienne* and Jean-Baptiste Lefrancq's *Antioche* (1625); P. Gethner, 'Carthage et Rome au théâtre: le conflit entre générosité et machiavélisme' (261–69), studies three tragedies: Antoinette Deshoulières's *Genséric* and Thomas Corneille's *La mort d'Annibal*, comparing them with Marivaux's *Annibal*; H. Hemaidi, 'De *La Mort d'Asdrubal* à *La Mort d'Annibal* ou Z. J. Montfleury et Th. Corneille, lecteurs de l'histoire de Carthage' (271–82), compares the two plays and their authors; R. Goulbourne, 'Comédie et altérité: l'Afrique et les Africains dans le théâtre comique du XVIIe siècle' (293–308), claims that 17th-c. comedies 'offrent [. . .] une perspective sur l'Afrique et l'Africain telle qu'elle s'est construite dans la sensibilité collective de la France', and offers 'une approche tant sociologique que dramaturgique' to a dozen comedies from Scudéry's *Le fils supposé* (1634) to Bel-isle's *Le mariage de la reine de Monomotapa* (1682).

Patrick Dandrey, *Les Tréteaux de Saturne: scènes de la mélancolie à l'époque baroque*, Klincksieck, 308 pp., defines *baroque* to include the whole of the 17th c. He first outlines the history of medical and philosophical perceptions of the humours and the temperaments from ancient Greek to medieval Arabic times and thence via Renaissance scholars to modern times, and manifestations of the effects of disordered humours such as 'les épidémies de sorcellerie et de possession'. Armed with this accumulation of lore, he then embarks on an 'itinéraire cohérent [. . .] passant par autant de haltes qui proposent un aperçu sur quelques-unes des principales illustrations du dialogue entre Mélancolie et Théâtre à l'âge baroque'. The *haltes* include an investigation of references to 'le sang de Don Gormas', the wounds caused by the eyes of Agnès in *L'École des femmes* and by those inflicted by Junie in *Britannicus*, the causes of the attraction felt by Pyrrhus and the repulsion felt by Andromaque, and the uttering of an exclamation inspired by Racine's theatre in general: 'que de regards meurtriers, que de sang échauffé, de corps travaillés par le désir!' There is an exploration of Molière's *médecin* plays, followed by another of a whole series of depictions of madness, real or feigned, from Pichou's *Folies de Cardénio* to Tristan's *Folie du sage*. The book ends with a study of 'Molière et la mélancolie: une anatomie de la folie comique'.

ANON. **Alidor ou l'indifférent. Pastorale*, ed. François Lasserre, Alessandria, Ediz. dell'Orso, 2001, 292 pp. Id., 'Recensement du vocabulaire cornélien dans la pastorale d'*Alidor*', *PFSCL*, 30:475–96, examines in detail the vocabulary of the above play of 1626–27, and compares it with that of other early plays by Corneille and with contemporary plays by Mairet, Rotrou, Du Ryer, and Georges de Scudéry, and concludes that C. is its most likely author.

La Comédie de proverbes, pièce comique, ed. Michael Kramer (TLF, 551), Geneva, Droz, 484 pp., is generally attributed to the Comte de Cramail, but K. is more cautious. He devotes a large part of his 150-p. 'Introduction' to an account of the life of C. and the literary works attributed to him, but finally, and convincingly, finds nothing that attaches the play to him more than to other candidates for its authorship. A 'répertoire phraséologique' follows the text, in which the proverbs used are listed in the order in which they appear.

BARBIER. A. C. Montoya, 'La femme forte et ses avatars dans les tragédies de Marie-Anne Barbier', Wetsel, *Femmes*, 163–73, describes the characteristics of B.'s heroines and their ways of influencing their male partners.

BENSERADE. J. Harris, 'Disruptive desires: lesbian sexuality in Isaac de Benserade's *Iphis et Iante* (1634)', *SCFS*, 24, 2002: 151–63, is interested in this play because of the nature of the heroine Iphis, 'a woman who in loving another woman [...] embodies a form of continuity in her sexual orientation that is uncharacteristic of, and hence discontinuous with, most Early-Modern thought on homosexual desire'. J. Prest, 'The gendering of the ballet audience: cross-casting and the emergence of the female ballet dancer', *ib.*, 127–34, looks at the *livrets* of B.'s *ballets de cour*, composed at a period when for the first time female dancers were beginning to appear, and notes a consequent change as the century advances in audience response, carefully guided by B. Id., 'Cross-casting in French court ballet: monstrous aberration or theatrical convention?', *RoS*, 21:157–68, also uses as her main source the verses in B.'s *livrets* which 'offer comment both on individual courtly performers and on their adopted roles', the former being of greater interest to both poet and audience'.

P. finds monstrosity, not only in the spectacle of men appearing dressed as women, but also in that of women appearing as 'seducible attractive' females: 'surely a more monstrous aberration'. M. Cuénin-Lieber, 'L'Afrique dans les ballets de cour de Benserade', Baccar Bournaz, *Afrique*, 319–32, notes the presence particularly of Moors among the characters danced in B.'s ballets, referring mainly to the *Ballet d'Alcidiane* and the *Ballet de Flore*.

BRUEYS. N. J. Lacy, 'Pathelin en 1706: "De l'or dans le fumier"?', *Tobin Vol.*, 163–68, introduces us to *L'Avocat Pathelin* (1706), a 'fundamentally reinvented' version of the 15th-c. *Farce de Maître Pathelin*, first performed at the Comédie-Française and frequently revived there in the 18th and 19th cs.

CHARPENTIER. M. Martin, 'Devilish utterance through sublime expression: the union of the sacred and the profane in Marc-Antoine Charpentier's *Médée*', Wetsel, *Femmes*, 231–37, takes this opera as an example of the way C. uses for dramatic effect styles normally associated with sacred music.

PIERRE CORNEILLE. Liliane Picciola, *Corneille et la dramaturgie espagnole* (Biblio 17, 128), Tübingen, Narr, 2002, 505 pp., presents us with quite a mixed bag. She divides her study into four parts, the first, devoted to 'Corneille et la comédie espagnole', compares C. with Lope de Vega and surveys what C. has learned or imitated from L. It is followed by close studies of *L'Illusion comique*, *Le Menteur* (with its debt to Alarcón) and its *Suite* (back to L.). The second part is concerned entirely with *Le Cid* and with Guillén de Castro's *Mocedades del Cid*. The third begins with *Don Sanche d'Aragon*, continues with C.'s 'romanité à l'espagnole' taking *Horace* and *Sertorius* as examples, and turns finally to Desmarets's *Scipion* and its debt to Calderón's *El segundo Escipión*. The fourth part is concerned with *La Mort de Pompée*, *Héraclius* (indebted to *La Rueda de La Fortuna* by Mira de Amezcua), *Rodogune* and *Attila*, and with Corneille's two martyr tragedies and their relations with *comedias* on similar subjects.

M. Raja Rahmouni, 'L'Afrique de Pierre Corneille ou le lointain obscur', Baccar Bournaz, *Afrique*, 283–91, proposes to '[s]'interroger sur la manière dont l'Afrique s'inscrit dans les drames politiques du plus romain des écrivains classiques', to which end he concentrates on *La mort de Pompée* and *Sophonisbe*. N. Ekstein, 'Knowing irony: the problem of Corneille', Lyons, *Savoir*, 295–304, discusses examples of the 'ironic gap' involving 'contiguity coupled with incompatibility' like that between *Le Menteur* and its *Suite*, and also the 'significant disjunctures' between *La Toison d'or* and its allegorical prologue.

C. J. Gossip, 'Truth, deception and self-deception in *Le Cid*', *PFSCL*, 30:57–70, undertakes a careful, close reading of the play. L. Petris, 'Du pathétique à l'*ethos* magnanime: l'argumentation dans

Cinna de Corneille', *DSS*, 55:217–32, studies the 'fonctionnement particulier' of rhetoric in this play, first looking at the 'présence du pathétique', and then analysing 'la dialectique entre le général et le particulier', and finally showing how C. 'dépasse, à travers la figure d'Auguste, le *pathos* comme le *logos*'. J.-M. Apostolidès, 'La machine à illusions', *Tobin Vol.*, 82–91, claims that Corneille's *Illusion comique* appeared at a time of 'le déclin de la conception magique de l'univers', and was a manifestation of that decline: 'elle rappelle l'existence des spectres, en même temps qu'elle permet leur mutation en personnages de théâtre.' V. Krause, 'Le sort de la sorcière: *Médée* de Corneille', *PFSCL*, 30:41–56, claims that, unlike the alleged witches hunted down and tortured in Europe in the 16th and 17th cs, M. is a 'sorcière-héroïne' having the eloquence to defend herself and attack her judges that the poor victims of witch hunts lacked. J. D. Lyons, 'Tragedy comes to Arcadia: Corneille's *Médée*', *Tobin Vol.*, 198–205, suggests that *Médée* 'lays out a program for future Cornelian and even Racinian tragedy'. It is 'a kind of intergeneric struggle that anticipates the following year's generic hybrid of *L'Illusion.*' Z. Elmarsafy, 'Real selves and false letters in Corneille's *Mélite*', Wetsel, *Spiritualité*, 169–77, sees the play as a '"mission statement", openly announcing the issues that would concern Corneille and French classical theater during the decades following its composition'. E. argues that C.'s 'turn from letters to masks is actually part of his strategy of authorial self-definition'. *La Place royale*, ed. Anne Duprat (Bibliothèque Gallimard, 124), 227 pp., provides a 'texte et dossier', the 'texte' being the first edition of 1637 with modernized spelling, and the 'dossier' composed of an introduction and a series of five 'arrêts sur lecture', the first one preceding Act I, and the remaining four following and commenting on each subsequent act; and finally 'Bilans' which contain *réception*, including C.'s own in the form of his *Examen*. R. Albanese, 'Polarités métaphoriques et spatio-temporelles dans *Polyeucte*', *Tobin Vol.*, 206–13, picks out 'trois antithèses maîtresses, à savoir, les dialectiques élévation/bassesse', 'mobilité/immobilité et constance/inconstance' in order to bring out 'le rôle des métaphores dans l'économie dramatique de la pièce'. J. Miernowski, 'Le plaisir tragique de la haine: *Rodogune* de Corneille', *RHLF*, 103:789–821, points out that C. was particularly fond of this play, that he readily admitted that Cléopâtre was 'très méchante' but that at the same time, while detesting her actions, 'on admire la source dont elles partent.' M. would help us to understand her *méchanceté*, and at the same time our *admiration*, by analysing her soliloquy of Act II, scene 1. C. Guillot, 'Théâtralisation des passions et catharsis: le personnage de Cléopâtre dans le frontispice, signé Charles Le Brun, pour la *Rodogune* de Corneille (1647)', *PFSCL*, 30:29–40, starts by suggesting that this *théâtralisation* follows 'une esthétique normative empruntée ou influencée par l'art oratoire et l'*actio* rhétorique'. G. is then able to show that both Le B., in his frontispiece depicting a moment in the play's dénouement, and C., putting words into the mouth of a witness to this scene, are in agreement as regards bodily stance, movement, and facial expression, and as regards their cathartic effect. Elena Garofolo, **La Sentence dans le théâtre du XVIIe siècle: les tragédies de P. Corneille (1635–1660)*, Lille, Atelier de reproduction des thèses, 612 pp.

JEAN GILLES. P. M. Ranum, 'The Gilles *Requiem*: rhetoric in the service of liturgy', Wetsel, *Femmes*, 239–51, notes the close links between rhetoric and 'musical devices', not only in profane music, but also in sacred, as in G.'s *Requiem*.

LA CHAPELLE. P. A. Scott, 'Cloisters, teaching and tragedy: a rediscovered lost play of 1663', Wetsel, *Femmes*, 151–61, seeks to revive interest in a play about a virgin-martyr, *L'illustre philosophe ou l'histoire de saincte Catherine d'Alexandrie*, by a nun identified as 'La Chapelle', the only known copy of which is in the Bibliothèque de l'Arsenal.

MOLIÈRE. *The Molière Encyclopedia*, ed. James F. Gaines, Westport, CT–London, Greenwood, 2002, xx + 528 pp., is not well served by G.'s introductory assertion that this work is intended for 'the average American reader'. His team of contributors, however, is composed of highly respected and experienced American academics (like G. himself) whose suggestions for further reading and whose bibliography of editions (no translations) and critical studies are as wide-ranging as any serious student of 17th-c. French drama could wish for, and the entries, arranged alphabetically, starting with 'Abominable Book' and ending with 'Zerbinette', cover every relevant aspect of the times, the plays, their characters, themes, sources, influences, and the man himself portrayed, thankfully, with no accretion of unreliable anecdotage or 'romantic fiction'. Claude Bourqui and Claudio Vinti, *Molière à l'école italienne: le lazzo dans la création moliéresque* (Indagini e prospettive, 8), Paris–Turin, L'Harmattan, 271 pp., have written a book 'qui parle autant de gestes que de mots'. They feel (according to B. in his Introduction) that the printed texts of M.'s plays are 'la trace résiduelle d'une activité théâtrale', they are *vestiges* 'qui laissent le chercheur devant une interrogation proche de celle des archéologues', and which he must build on by means of a 'partition rythmique de support à gestes, à grimaces ou à effets scéniques'. B. and V. therefore offer some of the necessary building material by suggesting *lazzi* appropriate to moments in each play. It is V. who presents them in the central section of the book, dividing them into 'lazzi à prédominance gestuelle', 'lazzi à prédominance verbale' and 'lazzi "isolés" '.

B. concludes with an essay on 'le lazzo dans la création moliéresque: pratiques et principes de la digression comique'.

K. Waterson, 'L'univers féminin des comédies de Molière', Wetsel, *Femmes*, 193–201, divides the female characters into four groups: those belonging to comic tradition, those illustrating the comedy of manners, those pertaining to the comedy of character, and 'rôles peu comiques'. W. notes the importance of this last category, and the 'nombre restreint de cibles comiques féminines'. J. F. Gaines, 'Sagesse avec sobriété: skepticism, belief and the limits of knowledge in Molière', Lyons, *Savoir*, 161–71, applies Gassendi's notion of doubt and St. Paul's concept of faith to Molière's comedies, aware that M. 'knew there were believers in his audience, whose sympathies he yearned to capture.' D. Gambelli, 'Frêles voix et morales en mouvement dans le théâtre de Molière', *Tobin Vol.*, 122–29, looks at six of M.'s female characters, all of whom have benefited, in G.'s view, from contact with borrowings made by the dramatist from other writers and from his own earlier plays. M.-F. Hilgar, 'Molière en l'an 2000 à la Comédie-Française', *ib.*, 258–65, reviews four plays presented at a 'festival Molière': *George Dandin*, *L'École des maris*, *Le Mariage forcé*, and *L'Avare*, to which is added a later production of *Le Bourgeois gentilhomme*. Marie-Noëlle Ciccia, **Le Théâtre de Molière au Portugal au XVIIe siècle à la veille de la révolution libérale*, Fondation Calouste Gulbenkian, 618 pp.

Guy Fessier, *Dom Juan de Molière: leçon littéraire*, PUF, 117 pp., provides useful and readable guidance on the myth and the ideas, but has little to say about theatricality. G. Dotoli, '*Dom Juan* de Molière — comédie burlesque?', *Tobin Vol.*, 130–38, in order to establish 'la nature réelle de cette comédie', returns to the text, 'à une lecture philologique "exacte"', notes the influence of Scarron on various aspects of the play and its burlesque 'structure de la discontinuité'. E. Taylor-Woodrough, '*Dom Juan*: no smoke without fire', *FSB*, 88:2–4, offers some social context to Sganarelle's snuff-taking in the opening scene, suggests a few possible pieces of 'business' that might accompany his speech, and detects a suspicion of symmetry with the play's last scene where Dom Juan is dragged down to hell-fire. O. Bloch, '*Le Festin de pierre*, itinéraire de Paris à Amsterdam: Molière et Abraham Gaultier, fiction ou hypothèse?', *LetC*, 11:15–20, has a more *libertine* explanation of Sganarelle's opening scene, and also presents 'une conjecture, ou fantasme [. . .] d'allure saugrenue', that Molière's MS of *Dom Juan* was taken to Amsterdam by the protestant physician from Niort A. G., where it was published in 1683. **Molière, Dom Juan*, ed. Franck Évrard et al., Ellipses, 220 pp.

L. Riggs, 'Reason's text as palimpsest: sensuality subverts "sense" in Molière's *Les femmes savantes*', *PFSCL*, 30:423–33, argues that this play 'is a work that can be read as comprehensively representing and denouncing the synthesis and imposition of a language as a means of constituting and legitimating hegemony.' K. Waterson, 'Savoir et se connaître dans *Les femmes savantes* de Molière', Lyons, *Savoir*, 185–94, believes that this play is M.'s 'comédie la moins comique et la plus racinienne', and claims that 'plus on examine *Les Femmes savantes*, moins on est sûr de pouvoir identifier les personnages normatifs.' **Le malade imaginaire*, ed. Evelyne Amon (Classiques et contemporains, 52), Mignard, 247 pp. R. W. Tobin, *'Civilité et convivialité dans *Le Misanthrope*', *Le Nouveau Moliériste*, 8, 2001 : 145–68. M. Fabienne Wolf, **Le Misanthrope, Molière* (Connaissance d'une œuvre), Rosny-sous-Bois, Bréal, 128 pp. S. Koppisch, '*Monsieur de Pourceaugnac*: comedy of desire', *Tobin Vol.*, 147–54, points first to Oronte's imperious desire to dominate Julie his daughter, then to Pourceaugnac's similar desire to have his absurd social pretensions recognized as valid. Their desires, K. claims, 'set off the chain of comic events that constitute the theatrical spectacles within the play.' J. F. Gaines, 'The violation of the bumpkin: satire, wealth, and class in *Monsieur de Pourceaugnac*', *ib.*, 155–62, presents this play as an example of 'bumpkin satire', a form which 'emerged simultaneously with criticism of usurpation on the French stage', along with Scarron's *Le Marquis ridicule*, and spread eventually to English Restoration comedy. H. Stone, 'Petitions for justice: Molière's *Tartuffe* viewed in the mirror of Pierre de Lancre's witches', *ib.*, 92–99, asserts that the two writers are diametrically opposed. She sees in an episode in L.'s *Tableau de l'inconstance des mauvais anges et demons* (1612) the mirror image of 'the full drama of *Le Tartuffe* [which] includes both M.'s text and the history of its performance'. K. Wine, '*Le Tartuffe* and *Les Plaisirs de l'île enchantée*: satire or flattery?' *ib.*, 139–46, asserts that M. chose 'to introduce his acrid satire as a specifically kingly pleasure, amidst a setting of courtly enchantment' in order to 'associate his devout targets with critics of courtly hedonism'. N. Peacock, '*Tartuffe* on screen and/or the metaphysics of performance', *ib.*, 250–57, concentrates on *Herr Tartuffe* (1926) by Friedrich Wilhelm Murnau, in which a truncated version of the play appears framed by an outer story, and *Tartuffe* by Gérard Depardieu (1984), a filming of rehearsals for a stage production, and asks: 'to what extent do the various levels of representation in these films mirror our performance on the world's stage?'

PUGET DE LA SERRE. P. Scott, 'Les crucifixions féminines: une iconographie de la Contre-Réforme', *RSH*, 269 : 153–74, covers European martyrologies and works of piety generally, but studies in passing P.'s *Sainte Catherine tragédie*, Paris, 1643.

RACINE. Susanna Phillippo, *Silent witness: Racine's non-verbal annotations of Euripides* (Research Monographs in French studies, 14), Oxford, Legenda, xv + 214 pp., examines the two editions of Euripides owned by R., and seeks to discover his purpose in making these hitherto neglected annotations. She suggests they help to identify the raw material that he proposes to use in his creations, and also 'what type of thing' interests him and what are his 'characteristics and capacities as a reader'. P. also addresses such questions as authenticity and chronology. Her caution is evident (always taking care not to 'strain the evidence') in her exploration for signs of R.'s 'reading practices', 'indirect sources' and 'direct adaptations'. An appendix lists all the verbal as well as non-verbal annotations in the two editions of E., to which the notes by Caspar Stiblinus are added. M. Reilly, 'Infernal visions: death and the afterlife in Racinian tragedy', *NFS*, 42:1–11, finds R.'s treatment of death 'unorthodox', and demonstrates this by concentrating on characters' 'expectations and attitudes towards death and how this compares with the way in which their lives actually end'. R. finds that 'the gap between what one would expect from a Christian playwright and what we actually find in Racine is staggering.' She ranges over all the plays, but returns more frequently to *Mithridate*, *Athalie*, and, finally, *Britannicus*, plays in which the central characters are all confident of being able to avenge themselves after death.

A. Viala, '"L'empire de l'Asie"' Martin, *Racine*, 71–79, takes the title quotation from Agamemnon's relation to Arcas in *Iphigénie*: 'L'empire de l'Asie à la Grèce promis' (l.76), quotes this reference by Agamemnon to a wished-for empire, and finds the same desire explicit in *Alexandre le Grand*, *Bérénice*, and *Mithridate* as well as in *Iphigénie*, and implicit in *Andromaque* and *Bajazet*, the Orient being an 'objet de concupiscence' in 'les mentalités dans la France de l'époque classique'; I Martin, 'La tragédie idéale: l'influence de J. Racine sur Sébastien Nicolas Roch Champfort', *ib.*, 147–56, detects this influence in the latter's tragedy, *Mustapha et Zéangir*; A. Blanc, 'Vision de l'Orient chez Racine et ses illustrateurs', *ib.*, 173–82, asserts defiantly that evocation of the Orient in the tragedies 'n'est pas inexistante', and spends more time on the illustrators, examples of whose work — including modern, non-literal representations — are reproduced as an *annexe*, pp. 209–29; F. Dartois-Lapeyre, 'Racine, L'Orient et les livrets d'opéra au XVIIIe et au XIXe siècles', *ib.*, 183–203.

André Blanc, *Racine: trois siècles de théâtre*, Fayard, 733 pp., is firstly a life of the dramatist, setting the plays and other writings in their historical, social, and biographical contexts; and secondly a history of the plays' successive productions with their reception from R.'s death to the present day (which includes a bare but intriguing reference to a 'spectacle *Hip Hop Phèdre*, tragédie-concert rap', undated but surely timeless).

P. Dandrey, '"Ravi d'une si belle vue": le ravissement amoureux dans le théâtre de Racine', *Tobin Vol.*, 72–81, cites as instances *Andromaque*, *Phèdre*, and above all *Britannicus*, in which R. plays on the 'double acception' of the word *ravi*. A. Compagnon, 'Racine and the Moderns', *ib.*, 241–49, draws our attention to the devotion to R. of the 'High Modernists': Claudel, Gide, Valéry, and Proust. J. Campbell, 'Mythologie et savoir: accouplement contre nature ou croisement heureux? L'exemple de *Phèdre* et d'*Iphigénie*', Lyons, *Savoir*, 363–72, reminds us of R.'s deep knowledge of classical literature and that '*Iphigénie* et *Phèdre* sont des pièces savantes', built on a knowledge not only of ancient tales but also of all the subsequent glosses on them. To this must be added R.'s 'souci de vraisemblance', his refusal to countenance supernatural interventions in the action of his plays, whatever the characters themselves may think or believe. And finally, R. must face up to the *Modernes* and their 'méfiance générale à l'égard des connaissances de l'antiquité', their 'désir de rayer la Fable du rayon du savoir'. This desire, R. resists, his aim being to make us recognize 'les limites de tout savoir, et les failles de la noble prétention humaine de tout savoir sur tout'.

Jean Rohou, *Jean Racine — Athalie* (Études littéraires, 69), PUF, 125 pp, provides a clear, succinct synopsis, briefly relates the biblical, social, and theatrical context, studies the text at length, summarizes 'réception et interprétations', and finishes with an exemplary *explication* of II, 5 ('le songe'). D. Mendelson, 'Quand Chateaubriand lisait *Athalie* à Jérusalem: le modèle de cette pièce à l'époque pré-romantique', Martin, *Racine*, 115–32, reads the views C. expressed in his *Itinéraire*. P. Frantz, '*Athalie* au XVIIIe siècle', *ib.*, 133–46, reads d'Alembert, Bernis, Diderot, Dubos, Houdart de La Motte, La Harpe, Louis Racine, Voltaire, and others, and reviews known productions of the time. A. and V. Dugovsky, 'Racine en Russie: l'exemple d'*Athalie*', *ib.*, 157–69, is interested in the attitude to R. of Decembrist circles in the 1820s, and also in the Russian translation of 1970. A. Soare, '*Bajazet* dans l'imaginaire racinien', *ib.*, 33–51, notes R.'s wish in many of his plays to 'doubler l'imagination dramatique d'imagination matérielle, et de faire parler la même langue aux âmes et aux choses'. In *Bajazet*, walking, moving from place to place, is associated with a labyrinth, and with the need for the central character to be led by servants, a need paralleled by their mental and moral states. A. E. Mazawi and I. Martin, '*Bajazet* en arabe; entre traduction et acculturation', *ib.*, 53–62, review the Arabic version of this play in order to 'étudier les modalités implicites et explicites relatives à sa traduction'. D. Brahimi, 'Bérénice, Reine d'Orient' *ib.*,

107–12, ponders on this description, and particularly on the meaning of the word 'Orient'. G. Molinié, 'Poéticité et négativité: Bérénice ou l'Orient saccagé (à propos de *Bérénice* I,4)', *ib.*, 65–68, marshalls much technical vocabulary on the subject of the 'précise détermination techniquement stylématique: *je t'aime/tu ne m'aimes pas*'. E. McClure, 'Sovereign love and atomism in Racine's *Bérénice*', *PLit*, 27:304–17, notes the growing interest during R.'s time in Gassendi and 'the philosophies articulated in the first half of the century', and sees their influence in *Bérénice*, suggesting that it is 'in part a reflection on the pressing question of what holds the universe together'. Laurent Tiesset, *Racine 'Britannicus'* (Connaissance d'une œuvre, 83), Rosny-sous-Bois, Bréal, 2002, 124 pp., gives a trenchant presentation of the text and all relevant contexts. Only his 'annexes' leave something to be desired: his selection of 'jugements critiques' amounts to only three (Boursault, Voltaire, Hugo), all treated with scorn for representing the attitudes of their times; and the authors listed in his all-too-brief bibliography, are also, with honourable exceptions (Elias, Schérer, Bénichou), dismissively treated. D. Blocker, '*Esther* à la cour du Roi de France: l'Orient biblique christianisé, éloge ou dénonciation?', Martin, *Racine*, 81–103, looks for the 'incongruités, incohérences, ambivalences et contradictions des discours que [...] l'absolutisme de Louis XIV a produit ou plutôt tenté de faire à travers l'*Esther* de Racine'. J. Campbell, 'Racine's *Iphigénie*: a "happy tragedy"?', *Tobin Vol.*, 214–21, begins by asking if this play is 'only masquerading as a tragedy', and answers himself by arguing that it has 'on the contrary, an inalienably tragic dimension', and that the '"happy end" is called into question by major structuring elements that this play holds in common with other great tragedies.' M. Sambanis, 'Mettre en scène Racine: à propos des didascalies', *ZFSL*, 113:27–38, in the absence of explicit stage directions in R.'s plays generally, looks for implicit ones in the dialogue of his *Iphigénie*. H. T. Barnwell, '"Moins roi que pirate": some remarks on Racine's *Mithridate* as a play of ambiguities', *SCFS*, 24, 2002:179–90, concentrates first on Mithridate's view of himself quoted above, and then on 'the nature and significance of the dénouement in the original text and in its revision of 1676'. P. Ronzeaud, 'Entre orient et occident: poétique et politique de la ruse dans *Mithridate*', Martin, *Racine*, 17–32, has decided to 'nouer le débat autour de la création racinienne', that is to say 'ruses dramaturgiques', 'ruses poétiques et langagières', and finally 'une politique de la ruse' showing how R. proposes 'un dénouement à l'ambiguïté particulièrement rusée'. S. Bold, 'The anxiety of Senecan influence in Racine, or Phèdre in the labyrinth', *RR*, 92, 2001:417–32, locates Phèdre's labyrinth in Act II, scene 4, lines 634–62. J. Miernowski, 'Le plaisir de la tragédie et la haine de soi: le cas de *La Thébaïde* de Racine', *Poétique*, 134:207–21, compares R.'s play, first with Corneille's *Œdipe*, then with his *Rodogune*, contrasting the exceptional nature of the mutual hatred shown by C.'s brothers with R.'s depiction of 'une haine aussi fratricide qu'elle se confond avec l'amour fraternel.' Racine, an Augustinian despite himself, is offering his audience 'le plaisir inquiétant de la haine de soi'.

ROTROU. *Théâtre complet, 4: Crisante, Le Véritable Saint Genest, Cosroès*, ed. Alice Duroux, Pierre Pasquier, and Christian Delmas, STFM, 2001, 560 pp. provides reliable introductions, texts, and other apparatus for these three tragedies.

SCARRON. S. Berregard, 'Les animaux dans trois œuvres de Scarron: *Jodelet ou le maître valet*, *Dom Japhet d'Arménie* et le *Roman comique*', *PFSCL*, 30:113–30, highlights S.'s apparent lively interest in animals, but claims that 'la manière dont ils se répartissent en dit long sur les différences qui séparent nos deux pièces du *Roman comique.*' Nevertheless, in both genres, according to B., the presence of animals serves to betray S.'s 'image assez négative de l'humanité'. J. Carson, 'Women in Scarron's theatre: the good, the bad and the independent', Wetsel, *Femmes*, 175–91, seeks out comments in the plays on the female condition. S.'s 'good' or 'bad' female characters are so labelled for their conformity or lack of it to social norms. Their attitude to their condition is examined, as is that of the 'independents' who are so called because they do not have a male guardian, and who take advantage — or fail to do so — accordingly. On the whole S. depicts his female characters with sympathy but without showing any desire to change society on their behalf.

GEORGES DE SCUDÉRY. **La Comédie des comédiens*, ed. Isabella Cedro (Biblioteca della ricerca), Fasano, Schena, 2002, 320 pp.

TRISTAN L'HERMITE. D. Dalla Valle, '*El Hado* et le songe dans *El mayor monstruo del mundo* de Calderón et dans *La Mariane* de Tristan', *CTH*, 25:70–74, points out that Herod's dream in T.'s tragedy does not seem to have 'une fonction prophétique' but that nevertheless 'cette fonction existe et se va précisant tout au cours de l'intrigue.' She contrasts this with the sequence of events in Calderón's play on the same subject (and also in Cicognini's *Il maggior mostre del mondo*, an adaptation of Calderón), where a prophecy made at the outset is openly realized through a series of events controlled by fate, whereas T.'s version is a logical working out of a clash of passions. R. Guichemerre, 'Un lyrisme burlesque: *Le Parasite* de Tristan', *ib.*, 75–79, shows how T. fashions out of hackneyed material and stock characters 'une certaine épaisseur humaine' and employs a form of poetry containing 'des aspects inattendus' not to be found elsewhere in his work.

4. Prose

Brouard-Arends, *Lectrices*, prints colloquium papers: M. Bak, 'Lectrices de Port-Royal' (49–57), underlines the obvious — that the nuns read 'comme religieuses' and that what they read 'passaient au prisme de la pensée [. . .] de saint Augustin', but he also looks at some of the writings, particularly *L'Image d'une religieuse parfaite et d'une imparfaite* by Mère Agnès Arnauld; M.-E. Henneau, 'Un livre sous les yeux, une plume à la main: de l'usage de la lecture et de l'écriture dans les couvents de femmes (17e-18e s.)' (69–80), surveys the reading matter of Cistercian nuns ('soumises ou audacieuses') and their written reactions; S. Aragon, 'Pour une rhétorique de la lecture féminine: évolution des images de lectrices dans les fictions françaises du XVIIe au XIXe siècle (de 1656 à 1856)' (455–67), begins her inquiry with Michel de Pure's *La Prétieuse* and ends it with Flaubert's *Madame Bovary* and, in two centuries of expansion of literacy, finds no evidence of a steady, regular evolution, rather, 'le XVIIIe siècle constitue une période d'accalmie' between 'deux grandes périodes d'alphabétisation féminine'; L. Desjardins, 'Lecture et discours de la morale au féminin au XVIIIe siècle' (473–79), finds women going for lighter reading material 'comme celui de la maxime, de la réflexion, du portrait, de la conversation ou de l'essai de morale et en rejetant la lecture des traités scolastiques, trop pédants et méthodiques, étrangers à l'esthétique mondaine'; S. D. Nell, 'Qu'est-ce qu'une lectrice? Les femmes et la possibilité de lire dans *La Princesse de Clèves* et les *Lettres d'une Péruvienne*' (523–31), finds the definitions of *lecteur* and *lire* in the *Dictionnaire de l'Académie Française* and Furetière's *Dictionnaire universel*, and then studies the depiction of female readers in the two novels 'qu'on associe plus souvent à la production de signifiants qu'à leur interprétation'; H. Porré, 'De la femme savante à l'épouse soumise: les idées de l'abbé du Bosc, de Mademoiselle de Scudéry et de Madame de Maintenon sur la femme comme lectrice' (567–73), looks at Du B.'s *L'Honneste Femme* (1632), at Book 10 of S.'s *Le Grand Cyrus* (1653), at an 'entretien' between M. and the teachers at Saint-Cyr commenting on a sermon condemning 'les livres profanes' (1696), and traces a regression from Du B.'s relative approval of female intellectual aspirations to M.'s instruction to the teachers to 'former les jeunes filles de Saint-Cyr pour les rendre épousables'; I. Havelange, 'Des livres pour les demoiselles, XVIIe siècle — 1ère moitié du XIXe siècle' (575–84), notes the predominance in the 17th and early 18th cs of works of pious and moral instruction for girls, followed after 1750 by an explosion, inspired by Rousseau, of more imaginative literature destined for young people and designed to encourage them to pursue a more general education; F. Ringham, 'Les amantes de la fiction au tournant du Grand Siècle' (677–86), reads *paratextes* (among them those accompanying d'Aulnoy's *Récit du voyage d'Espagne*, 1691, Choisy's *Nouvelle Astrée*, 1713, and Marivaux's *Avantures de* ***, 1713–14), to discover 'qui lit la nouvelle ou le petit roman' which became fashionable towards the end of the 17th c. and ousted the long romances; R. also asks 'Où sont repérables les répercussions du changement de l'écriture romanesque?' Sandrine Aragon, **Des liseuses en péril: les images de lectrices dans les textes de fiction de la 'Prétieuse' de l'abbé de Pure à 'Madame Bovary' de Flaubert (1656–1856)* (Les dix-huitièmes siècles, 71), Champion, 732 pp., consults prose fiction and other works in her search for *images*. G. Ferguson, 'The stakes of sanctity and sinfulness: tales of the Priory of Poissy (fifteenth to seventeenth centuries)', Britnell, *Female Saints*, 59–78, studies successive representations, 'idealised on the one hand, salacious on the other', of this Dominican priory, which serve as examples of the treatment meted out by writers to such establishments. 17th-c. works which refer to the convent include Béroalde de Verville's *Moyen de parvenir*, d'Aubigné's *Baron de Fœneste*, and Tallemant des Réaux's *Historiettes*. V. Worth-Stylianou, '*Les Caquets de l'accouchée*: la représentation de la maternité dans la littérature fictive (c. 1475–1622)', *ib.*, 251–65, is interested in the depiction in French literature of social gatherings, and compares the stereotypes shown when such companies are mixed or solely female. She examines the 15th-c. anonymous *Évangiles des Quenouilles*, Guillaume Bouchet's *Sérées* and the anonymous *Caquets*, all 'rédigés par des hommes', concluding that in such works, whatever the social mix evoked, 'seules les voix masculines ont le droit de se prononcer sur les questions savantes'. P. Sellier, 'Pascal, La Rochefoucauld, La Bruyère', Sellier, *Essais*, 295–311, looks at this 'trio canonique' and asks 'la vocation de "moraliste français" ne naîtrait-elle pas d'un rapport au monde au moins partiellement identique chez tous, quel que soit le chatoiement des différences?'

Raymond Baustert, *La Consolation érudite: huit études sur les sources des lettres de consolation de 1600 à 1650* (Biblio 17, 141), Tübingen, Narr, 387 pp., reprints articles published in various journals and collective volumes between 1990 and 2001 in which he has studied 80 texts by some 40 authors, most of them relatively obscure, though a few well-known names stand out, notably Nervèze, Malherbe, and Cyrano. His aim is not to study the *épistoliers* and their techniques, but rather 'c'est à l'éclairage des *sources* antiques et modernes, païennes et chrétiennes, qu'on a voulu s'attacher'. Consequently B. divides his work into two parts, studying the influence firstly of ancient Greek and Roman literature and history, humanism, and *honnêteté*, and secondly of christianity. A series of 'notices bio-bibliographiques' summarizes what B. has gleaned about the life and works of each author, and a 'corpus des lettres' lists all the texts in chronological order with brief notices about their recipients and their deceased subjects. *RHLF*, 103.2, contains seven articles on *La Littérature des non-écrivains*: J. Garapon, 'Amateurisme littéraire et vérité sur soi, de Marguerite de Valois au Cardinal de Retz' (275–85), links the 'refus de la littérature et du métier d'écrivain' by these two memorialists and others with 'une libération de l'imaginaire' and with a private mythology 'que ne vient contredire aucun rappel indiscret de personne à l'historicité des faits', the Queen and the Cardinal providing him, paradoxically, with examples of writing 'indifférente à la littérature et en définitive très littéraire'; G. Haroche-Bouzinac, 'Les lettres qu'on ne brûle pas' (301–08), concerns herself with letters which have survived the authors' urgent instruction, 'brûlez cette lettre!', taking most of her examples from the 18th c.; S. Marchal, '"Je suis un tailleur à qui il a révélé la taille." La relation écrivain-"non-écrivain" dans la correspondance Ducis-Talma' (309–30). Other articles are reviewed under named authors below. E. Gilby, 'Being discrete: the singularity of judgement in the correspondence of Racine and Boileau', *SCFS*, 24, 2002: 209–15, is struck in these letters by 'their very present awareness of their own epistolarity'. This correspondence gives the two royal historiographers 'a platform for a different and mobile kind of ethical modelling whereby they judge themselves judging others'.

F. Butleu, 'Asianisme ou atticisme? Les *Huit Oraisons* de Cicéron (1638), traduction manifeste des "Belles Infidèles"', *DSS*, 55: 195–216, reviews these translations commissioned by Conrart, four by Perrot d'Ablancourt, two by Pierre Du Ryer, and one each by Olivier Patru and Louis Giry. B. pays particular attention to the rendering of two *oraisons* by d'Ablancourt and the one by Patru, and concludes that 'deux personnalités d'écrivain se dégagent ainsi: l'une plutôt *attique*, d'Ablancourt, l'autre plutôt *asiatique*, Patru', and sees in the former the forerunner of 'la prose nerveuse' of many distinguished 17th-c. and 18th-c. writers.

Alexandra Merle, *Le Miroir ottoman: une image politique des hommes dans la littérature géographique espagnole et française (XVIe–XVIIe siècles)* (Iberica-essais, 4), Univ. Paris-Sorbonne, 283 pp., studies the vast number of works written throughout the two centuries in French and Spanish on the 'Turks' (which word included Moors, Arabs, Egyptians, Tartars, even Orthodox Greeks and other eastern Christians), on their religions and customs, on the various aspects of the geography, history, institutions, military power of the Ottoman Empire, and also travel writings and accounts of pilgrimages to the Holy Land. M. excludes fiction, and religious polemical works, being interested only in 'des ouvrages manifestant une volonté informative'. Despite acknowledging different political attitudes (Spanish disquiet, French desire to be friendly and to trade), M. concludes that from all these works 'se constitue un Orient qui, sans doute, est une invention de l'Occident', that 'l'image du monde ottoman n'est autre qu'un miroir'. Among the numerous 17th-c. French writers quoted, the following stand out: Michel Baudier, Ogier Ghislain Busbecq, Pierre Davity, Jacques Espinchard, Jean-Baptiste Tavernier, and Jean Thévenot. *Literature of Travel and Exploration: An Encyclopedia*, ed. Jennifer Speake, 3 vols, NY–London, Fitzroy Dearborn, xxxi + 1479 pp., is mainly concerned either with individual travellers or 'geographical entities'. French 17th-c. entries include Champlain, Lahontan, La Salle, Lescarbot, and Mabillon, with accounts of their lives, their travels, and their writings. C. Curell, 'Les récits des voyageurs français aux Canaries: entre le mythe et la réalité. I. Les Îles Fortunées', Le Disez, *Seuils*, 67–77, refers to travel accounts about 'topiques à charge mythique', starting with André Thevet (1558), followed by Jean Mocquet (1617), and Jacques-Joseph Le Maire (1695), and finishing with 18th-c. and 19th-c. memoirs. B. Pico, 'Les récits des voyageurs français aux Canaries: entre le mythe et la réalité. II. L'"arbre saint" de l'île de Fer', *ib.*, 79–88, concentrates on the French travellers who saw and commented on this fabulous tree, first the credulous ones: André Thevet (1558), Allain Manesson Mallet (1683), and Jean Godot (1704); and then the sceptics: Louis Feuillée (MS undated, early 18th c.), and other 18th-c. and 19th-c. unbelievers. H. T. Campangne, 'L'imaginaire du voyage et de la découverte dans les histoires tragiques', *RHLF*, 103:771–87, examines the numerous 'points de rencontre entre les textes géographiques et les recueils d'histoires tragiques de l'âge baroque'. C. has read both the stories by writers from Boaistuau to Gournay, and also the travellers' memoirs of the period, and notes that, not only is there plenty of evidence that the story-tellers have read the travellers, there are also hints that the latter have read the former and learned from them. H.-G. Funke, 'Le motif de la controverse religieuse dans le récit de voyage utopique français à la fin du XVIIe siècle', McKenna, *Résurgence*, 321–39, notes the emergence of anti-Christian propaganda in utopias and a growing respect for other forms of religion, even for atheism, from the late 17th c. onwards in the works of Foigny, Veiras, Fontenelle, Claude Gilbert, and Lahontan: 'la religion des récits de voyages utopiques semble naître de l'inversion du christianisme européen, emploi frappant du *topos* du monde renversé'. D. D. Grélé, 'L'identité du héros dans les utopies du règne de Louis XIV', *Neophilologus*, 87:209–22, finds two types of utopia, 'depending on the status given to their narrator' who is either 'fragmentary' and no more than a witness providing evidence in a work of political polemic, or a 'true character', a hero whose adventures are more important than the ideological content of the novel. H.-G. Funke, *'Die semantische Entwicklung des Utopiabegriffs vom XVI. bis zum XX. Jahrhundert', *ZFSL*, 113:131–43.

Baccar Bournaz, *Afrique*, prints colloquium *actes*: S. Gadhoun, 'Présence de l'Afrique réelle et mythique dans le *Dictionnaire universel* d'Antoine Furetière' (23–30); S. Poli, 'Stéréotypes d'Afrique dans la lexicographie du XVIIe siècle, entre tradition et modernité' (31–55); S. Linon-Chipon, 'L'Afrique insulaire, l'Afrique des caps, l'Afrique des marges: textes et images de Jean Mocquet (1617) et de Guy Tachard (1686) sur la route maritime des épices' (59–76), studies travel accounts, and also their illustrations, eight of which are reproduced; A. Niderst, 'Le noir dans l'iconographie religieuse du XVIIe siècle' (77–90), is also illustrated; M.-C. Pioffet, 'Des déserts de l'Afrique à ceux de l'Amérique: exploration d'une même topique spatiale' (113–26), finds that her authors, Gomberville and Vincent Leblanc, link the 'déserts' on either side of the ocean without much differentiation; G. Spielmann, 'L'Afrique mise en scène, de l'absence au phantasme' (309–18), notes the striking absence in French literature of the African interior, even as a vague exotic setting, and wishes to examine 'certaines exceptions pour tenter de comprendre les raisons de ce parti pris', these exceptions being drawn from a variety of other European countries and authors. E. Lesne-Jaffro, 'La nuit des Camisards', Bertrand, *Penser la nuit*, 487–504, looks at accounts of the Wars of the Cévennes by protestants Abraham Mazel, Élie Marion, Jacques Bonbonnoux, and Jean Cavalier, which he contrasts with the mockery of Esprit Fléchier. M.-C. Pioffet, 'Destin de la femme naufragée dans la fiction narrative du Grand Siècle', Wetsel, *Femmes*, 141–49, peruses fiction by Gomberville, Mlle de Scudéry, Mme de Villedieu, and others to see how heroines fare in stormy seas, and, unsurprisingly, finds them to be as much dependents and victims there as on dry land. M. Stefanovska, 'L'anecdote dans les ana et les mémoires du XVIIe siècle', Lyons, *Savoir*, 11–20, wishes to throw light on 'l'anecdote comme forme de savoir historique'. She studies in particular the memoirs of Saint-Simon.

ANON. *La seconde après-dînée du caquet de l'accouchée et autres facéties du temps de Louis XIII*, ed. Alain Mercier (Sources classiques, 48), Champion, 272 pp., contains the longest of the eight chapters of *Les Caquets de l'accouchée* (1622), accompanied by nine similar *facéties*, all but the last dating from 1610–1624, that is to say from the beginning of Marie de Médicis's regency ('cet intérim laxiste') to Richelieu's accession to power.

ANGÉLIQUE ARNAULD. M. Rowan, 'Angélique Arnauld's web of feminine friendships: letters to Jeanne de Chantal and the Queen of

Poland', Wetsel, *Femmes*, 53–59, finds in the correspondence of this formidable woman evidence of 'her tenderness and her political acumen'.

ARVIEUX. F. Assaf, 'De l'observation en tant qu'un des beaux arts: le chevalier d'Arvieux en Afrique du Nord', Baccar Bournaz, *Afrique*, 167–80, finds his subject a 'prodigieux observateur' of Tunis.

AUBIGNAC. A. Wygant, 'D'Aubignac, demonologist, II: St Anthony and the satyr', *SCFS*, 24, 2002:71–85, follows up her 'D'Aubignac demonologist, I: monkeys and monsters', *ib.*, 23, 2001:151–71, with an examination of A.'s forthright assertion in his *Des satyres* that a satyr was an animal and therefore unable to speak to St Anthony. Since it *did* speak, however, 'reste donc à conclure que ce Satyre estoit un Demon'. The work which is the subject of W.'s scrutiny has now been published: *Des satyres brutes, monstres et démons, 1627*, ed. Gilles Banderier (Atopia, 30), Grenoble, Millon, 222 pp., is to B. the work of 'un précurseur de l'histoire comparée des religions', despite a strictly 17th-c. Christian outlook coloured, B. asserts, with a 'rationalisme éclairé — ou limité, comme l'on voudra — par la Révélation'.

AULNOY. M.-A. Thirard, 'La réception des contes de fées de Madame d'Aulnoy ou l'histoire d'un malentendu', *PFSCL*, 30:167–95, surveys various facets of the evolving reception of these *contes* from the end of the 17th c. to the present day. R. Böhm, 'La participation des *fées modernes* à la création d'une mémoire féminine', Wetsel, *Femmes*, 119–31, notes a penchant in A. and other female writers of the end of the 17th c. for celebrating exceptional women of the past and their exploits. G. Summerfield, '*Contes de fées* by women of the seventeenth century: new discourses of sexuality and gender', *ib.*, 133–39, uses A.'s work to illustrate her view that A. and writers like her 'denounced the tensions among competing discourses of sexuality and gender to propose their own versions of equality between the sexes'. C. Carlin, 'La nuit du couple: la dissolution du mariage dans l'imaginaire des XVIe et XVIIe siècles', Bertrand, *Penser la nuit*, 505–23, concludes her survey with a lengthy, concentrated study of A.'s novel, *L'Histoire d'Hypolite, comte de Duglas.*

BÉROALDE DE VERVILLE. **Le moyen de parvenir*, ed. Georges Bourgueil, Passage du Nord-Ouest, 2002, 429 pp. D. Mauri, 'Le temps-espace de la nuit dans les romans de Béroalde de Verville', Bertrand, *Penser la nuit*, 121–38, looks at certain episodes from B.'s considerable output to demonstrate the 'statut double de la nuit, à la fois positif et négatif, créateur et destructeur'.

BOSSUET. P. Bayley, 'Bossuet: knowledge and conversion', Lyons, *Savoir*, 171–80, dwells on instances of B. 'seeing knowledge as the key to interior perfection'. Georges Minois, **Bossuet: entre Dieu et le soleil*, Perrin, 747 pp., is a biography.

BOUHOURS. *Les entretiens d'Ariste et d'Eugène*, ed. Bernard Beugnot and Gilles Declercq (Sources classiques, 47), Champion, 592 pp., is a work which has until recently been neglected and undervalued, but is now once again coming into its own. The editors see it as situated 'au confluent de trois formes-modèles: la tradition des œuvres mêlées, les inclassables *Essais* de Montaigne, et la conversation mondaine qui les fond et les englobe', presenting 'comme un microcosme du classicisme'. B. Beugnot, 'Les *Entretiens d'Ariste et d'Eugène*, un théâtre de la culture mondaine', *Tobin Vol.*, 62–71, describes and defends as a 'livre de plaisir' what he calls B.'s '*paideia* de l'honnête homme'.

CHALLE. C. Martin, 'De la critique théologique au roman "réaliste": l'exemple de Robert Challe', *ECentF*, 15:705–28, sees in C.'s *Difficultés sur la religion proposées au père Malebranche*, an example of a work in which theological discussion begins a train of thought which turns the author in later life to the creation of works of fictional realism. C. Meure, 'L'espace et l'aventure dans le *Journal d'un voyage aux Indes Orientales* de Robert Challe', pp. 31–44 of *L'Aventure maritime*, ed. Jean-Michel Racault, Paris–Montreal, L'Harmattan, 2001, 311 pp., is inspired, by Gérard Genette's views on 'traits de spatialité' in literature, to define C.'s 'poétique de l'espace'.

CHAMPLAIN. Francine Legaré, **Samuel Champlain, père de la Nouvelle France* (Les grandes figures, 36), Montreal, XYZ, 172 pp.

CONRART. Nicolas Schapira, **Un professionnel de lettres au XVIIe siècle: Valentin Conrart* (Époques), Seyssel, Champ Vallon, 512 pp., is a biography.

COURTILZ DE SANDRAS. F. Assaf, 'Écriture ou ré-écriture? *Les Apparences trompeuses*: comment ne pas s'y tromper?' *PFSCL*, 30:397–409, takes a second look at this 'pastiche de *La Princesse de Clèves*' of 1715, thought to be by C., in order to decide whether it 'constitue une parodie, si cette parodie est gratuite ou si elle répond à des intentions plus pointues de l'auteur'.

CYRANO DE BERGERAC. **Les États et Empires du Soleil*, ed. Bérangère Parmentier (GF-Dossier), Flammarion, 273 pp. I. Moreau, 'Sur deux conceptions concurrentes de la matière. Contribution à l'analyse du "matérialisme" cyranien', *LetC*, 11:205–13, seeks to explain C.'s juxtaposition in his two novels of a 'matérialisme radical' and 'une position vitaliste proche des théories chimiques', with the intention of explaining 'la nature physique et les transmutations (=transformations) de la matière'. M. Alcover, 'Glanes biographiques (I. À la recherche des Cyrano de Sens. II. Cyrano et Perrot d'Ablancourt)', *ib.*, 215–18, throws light on some of C.'s ancestors and on his relations

with a distinguished contemporary. A. Mothu, 'Éléments d'anthropologie sélénite', *ib.*, 229–50, offers explanations of C.'s satirical intentions in his evocation of the Sélénites, inhabitants of the moon.

DACIER. M.-P. Pieretti, 'L'*Iliade* d'Anne Dacier: les enjeux d'une lecture érudite', Brouard-Arends, *Lectrices*, 281–90, outlines D.'s purpose in translating Homer's poem as she reveals it in her preface.

DONNEAU DE VISÉ. M. Vincent, 'Jean Donneau de Visé, *Le Mercure galant*, ou les choix d'un polygraphe', *LitC*, 49:223–41, praises the journal for its 'sens de l'événement, sa sensibilité à la mode', and its ambition to inform, to teach, to spread the word about everything worthwhile; and D. the man as an 'amateur éclairé', in other words, an *honnête homme*.

DU NOYER. H. Goldwyn, 'L'inscription d'un lectorat féminin dans une des *Lettres historiques et galantes* de Mme Du Noyer', Brouard-Arends, *Lectrices*, 93–101, looks at Letter 62 from vol. 3 of this work of 1712.

MARC-ANTOINE DE FOIX. M. Bouvier, '*L'Art de prêcher* du Père de Foix', *DSS*, 55:287–308, introduces us to this Jesuit and his manual of 1687, the characteristics of which 'permettent de mieux comprendre certaines évolutions dans l'art de prêcher, ainsi que dans les mentalités qui les expliquent'.

JACQUES FONTAINE. *Persécutés pour leur foi: mémoires d'une famille huguenote*, ed. Bernard Cottret, Les Éditions de Paris, 264 pp., is in fact a reprinting, with a 'Postface' by C., of an edition prepared by the Société des livres religieux de Toulouse in 1887 from the MS *Histoire de la famille des Fontaine recueillie par moi Jacques Fontaine, ministre de l'Évangile*, dated Dublin, 1722.

GOMBERVILLE. B. Teyssandier, 'Gomberville: une version mondaine de la polygraphie', *LitC*, 49:297–318, evokes the variety of G.'s works, and describes him as a 'touche-à-tout impatient de mettre ce qu'il connaît ou découvre à la portée du public large'.

GOURNAY. **Les Advis, ou Les Presens de la Demoiselle de Gournay, 1641*, ed. Jean-Philippe Beaulieu et al., vol. II (Faux titre, 219), Amsterdam–NY, Rodopi, 2002, 327 pp. G. Devincenza, 'La femme de lettres selon Marie de Gournay', Wetsel, *Femmes*, 87–92, brings to our attention G.'s defence of 'femmes studieuses', and the 'parcours de formation' which she recommended to all would-be erudite women, a plan of which D. here traces the development. J.-P. Beaulieu, 'Relecture et réécriture dans les recueils de Marie de Gournay', Brouard-Arends, *Lectrices*, 243–51, looks at *L'ombre de la damoiselle de Gournay* for examples which reveal 'la volonté de l'auteure de réunir ses nombreux écrits en un ouvrage [. . .] et de les faire évoluer par un substantiel travail de remaniement.' A. Aragon, 'L'écart entre auteur et lecteur dans l'œuvre de Marie de Gournay', *ib.*, 253–59, wishes us

to imagine the *être fictif* that G. creates to stand for herself as author, and also the *être* or *êtres fictif(s)*, her reader(s), whom she 'évoque, convoque, réprimande, flatte ou éduque', which will allow us to 'approcher de plus près une œuvre dynamique et complexe dont la richesse est généralement sous estimée'.

GUYON. C. Beaudry, 'L'accès au livre: Jeanne Guyon', Brouard-Arends, *Lectrices*, 59–68, bases her findings on a reading of *La Vie de Madame Guyon par elle-même* which reveals this author to have been almost completely self-taught, and her many works to be a product of her own reading with little outside guidance.

HUET. P.-J. Salazar, 'Pierre-Daniel Huet. Le sel et le thé', *LitC*, 49:201–22, expresses his enthusiasm for this writer by sketching seven 'figures du polygraphe', and concludes by defining him as 'un cryptographe qui laisse aux initiés le soin de traverser une forêt de cent espèces pour trouver la clairière de la *gaya scienza*'.

LA BOULLAYE-LE-GOUZ. F. Boulaire, 'Le séjour de François de la Boullaye-le-Gouz en Irlande au seuil de l'Europe à la croisée de deux époques', Le Disez, *Seuils*, 181–94, summarizes and discusses a section recalling a two-month stay in Ireland in 1643 from *Les Voyages et observations du sieur de la Boullaye-le-Gouz, gentilhomme angevin*.

LA BRUYÈRE. Marc Escola, **La Bruyère* I. *Brèves questions d'herméneutique* (Moralia, 6), Champion, 2001, 448 pp.; **La Bruyère* II. *Rhétorique du discontinu* (Moralia, 7), Champion, 2001, 464 pp. P. Sellier, 'Grisaille de La Bruyère: l'enfer vu d'un coin de ciel', Sellier, *Essais*, 281–94, feels rather disappointed by this writer. Although *Les Caractères* 'empruntent aux comiques latins' and 'fassent souvent songer à Molière, à la *commedia dell'arte*, à la foire, à Chaplin, ou à Ionesco', their author 'ne possède ni la force de Pascal, ni la quête obstinée de pureté de La Rochefoucauld. La sarabande des fantoches humaines l'assaille et le malmène.'

LA FAYETTE. G. Giorgi, 'Forme narrative longue, forme narrative brève: le cas de Madame de La Fayette', *LitC*, 49:371–83, sees La F. creating the last of the *romans héroïques* with *Zaïde*, and with *La Princesse de Clèves* the first *nouvelle historique et galante*. G. takes it upon himself to 'cerner les principaux aspects de cette activité, disons, polygraphique'. A. Wallis, 'Ambiguous figures: interpreting attempts to interpret *Zaïde*'s frontispiece', *PFSCL*, 30:507–16, discusses recent articles on Romeyn de Hooghe's frontispiece to the 1671 Amsterdam edition of *Zaïde* in which the novel is accompanied by Huet's *De l'origine des romans*. P. Sellier, 'À quoi rêve une narratrice: "La Princesse de Clèves"', Sellier, *Essais*, 237–46, pursues an 'enquête' which 'essaie de se placer à la source même de l'invention narrative', and which seeks out all the instances that link this novel to *préciosité*, concluding that in it 'la psychologie précieuse se révèle à la source même de l'invention narrative.'

PHILOBERT DE LA MARE. M. Kramer, 'Un recueil de proverbes inédit du XVIIe s. et Philobert de La Mare: une étude des mss. fr. 1599 et 6170 de la Bibliothèque nationale de France', *DSS*, 55:331–40, describes in detail these two MSS that together form a whole which their anonymous collector entitles *Anthologie des proverbes*. K. hopes eventually to publish it.

LA ROCHEFOUCAULD. Q. M. Hope, 'Social strata and social types in the *Maxims* of La Rochefoucauld', *PFSCL*, 30:497–505, comments on maxims which he groups as 'les grands hommes, les héros, les grands esprits', as 'les philosophes', 'les seigneurs, les vaillants', as 'les rois, les princes, les politiques, les favoris', and finally as 'les bourgeois' and 'les gens du commun'. D. McCallam, ' "Une forme frondeuse": the function of discontinuity in La Rochefoucauld's *Maximes*', *SCFS*, 24, 2002:239–48, contrasts La R.'s collection, the discontinuity of which disconcerts the reader, with the continuity of 'the Cartesian, Freudian and *honnête* modes of (self-)consciousness'. However, M. finally concedes that these 'disjunctive remarks trouble more than they destroy'. M. Chihaia, *'Anatomie einer Maxime. Wissen über den Menschen bei La Rochefoucauld und bei Knigge', *ZFSL*, 111, 2001:165–82.

GUILLAUME CHENU DE LAUJARDIÈRE. D. Lanni, 'Les voyages manuscrits et le loisir lettré: l'exemple des manuscrits de la *Relation d'un voyage à la Côte des Cafres* de Laujardière', *FSB*, 88:4–6, refers to the MS copies of this account of a colourful African adventure experienced by a young Huguenot, the features of which, in L.'s view, point to its being 'un exemple de communication réservée'.

LE NOBLE. P. Hourcade, 'Eustache Le Noble, au(x) hasard(s) de la polygraphie' *LitC*, 49:265–80, introduces us to the breadth of Le N.'s forages into diverse forms of literature, some published, some in MS form, some lost.

MÉNAGE. G. Banderier, 'Une lettre inédite de Gilles Ménage', *FSB*, 87:11–13, introduces, reproduces, and thoroughly annotates a letter to an unknown recipient dated Paris, 15 June 1682. The letter is now in the library of the University of Basle, 'Autograph-Sammlung, Geigy-Hagenbach Nr.1374'.

MONTPENSIER. Jean Garapon, **La Culture d'une princesse: écriture et auto-portrait dans l'œuvre de la Grande Mademoiselle (1627–1693)* (Lumière classique, 49), Champion, 442 pp.

MOTTEVILLE. Mélanie Aron, **Les Mémoires de Madame de Motteville: du dévouement à la dévotion* (Publications du Centre d'étude des milieux littéraires, 3), Nancy U.P., 229 pp.

NASSAU. E. Pascal, 'La lectrice devenue scriptrice: lecture épistolaire dans les réponses d'Elisabeth à Charlotte-Brabantine de Nassau', Brouart-Arends, *Lectrices*, 409–18, questions the view that letters are 'une simple partie d'une conversation en absence, selon la formule consacrée', and explains her reservations, the Nassau sisters providing illustrations.

JACQUELINE PASCAL. M. Le Guern, 'Les lettres de Jacqueline Pascal', *RHLF*, 103:267–73, reviews what is preserved of her life's output, from 1639 to her death in 1661, and finds, especially in the earlier ones, 'un incontestable art du récit'.

NICOLAS PASQUIER. **Le Gentilhomme*, ed. Denise Carabin (Textes de la Renaissance, 70), Champion, 384 pp., prints this work of 1611 by the son of Étienne P.

CHARLES PERRAULT. *Les Hommes illustres qui ont paru en France pendant ce siècle. Avec leurs portraits au naturel*, ed. D. J. Culpin (Biblio 17, 142), Tübingen, Narr, xxxx + 535 pp., reproduces, each with its engraved portrait, the *éloges* of 102 eminent Frenchmen from all walks of life, 50 in each of the two volumes originally published in 1696 and 1700 respectively, and two more which, in the 'deuxième état du vol. 1', replaced those of Arnauld and Pascal whose presence had angered the Jesuits. C.'s *texte de base* is that of the second edition of 1700. His Introduction tells of the role in the compilation of P.'s collaborator Michel Bégon, and also explains the rationale behind the hierarchical ordering of the eulogies. P.'s borrowings from other writers' collections of 'brief lives' — some of them almost textual — are noted, as is his taste for embellishing births and deaths with extraordinary, even supernatural, details to give them a 'valeur exemplaire'. Above all, C. emphasizes the ideological purpose of the collection: to 'illustrer la thèse de la supériorité des Modernes qu'il avait soutenue dans la Querelle des Anciens et des Modernes'. In all, this is a very timely and satisfying edition of a work long unjustifiably neglected. P. Sellier, 'La belle au bois dormant', Sellier, *Essais*, 73–93, studies P.'s *conte* with a view to answering 'deux questions générales: le rapport à la mythologie, conte et initiation'.

PÉTIS DE LA CROIX. Franz Hahn, *François Pétis de La Croix et ses 'Mille et un Jours'* (Faux Titre, 229), Amsterdam–NY, Rodopi, 2002, 189 pp., discusses authorship and praises the quality of the stories which, he claims, are more than a mere imitation of Galland's *Mille et Une Nuits*.

TIMOTHÉE PHILALÈTHE. **De la modestie des femmes et des filles chrétiennes dans leurs habits et dans tout leur extérieur*, ed. François Bouchet (Atopia, 28), Grenoble, Millon, 2002, 203 pp., reproduces the text of 1686 (first edition, Liège, 1675).

PURE. M. Maître, '*La Précieuse* de Michel de Pure: de l'impossible *corps* des femmes à la *personne* de la lectrice', Wetsel, *Femmes*, 61–75, claims that 'l'analyse doit prendre en compte [. . .] l'étonnante énergie du mot lui-même de *précieuse*, point de cristallisation lexicale d'une réalité féminine perçue comme nouvelle et qui s'intègre malaisément dans la cartographie morale héritée.'

REGNARD. P. Grouix, 'Visages du nocturne dans *Voyage en Laponie* de J.-F. Regnard (1681)', Bertrand, *Penser la nuit*, 159–78, praises R. for his curiosity, 'infiniment plus vaste que celle de ses contemporains': his 'évocations nocturnes' are 'cohérentes au point de tisser, comme un ensemble cousu de fil noir, un véritable *texte de la nuit*, où le blanc de la page recueille le noir nocturne, lui donne sens.'

SAINT-ÉVREMOND. *Condé, Turenne et autres figures illustres*, ed. Suzanne Guellouz, Desjonquères, 190 pp., contains 22 texts, the longest of which has 18 pages, most of them much shorter. In her 'Présentation', G. justifies her choice and her ordering of the pieces by reference to their form, whether description, dialogue, or narration. Description predominates — portrayals of famous individuals, group portraits, or autoportraits. In all, this is a beguiling collection by a constantly entertaining author, expertly presented and annotated.

MADELEINE DE SCUDÉRY. **Clélie, histoire romaine: troisième partie 1657*, ed. Chantal Morlet-Chantalat (Sources classiques, 44), Champion, 576 pp. S. Genieys, 'L'androgynéité de la "femme généreuse" dans la *Clélie* de Madeleine de Scudéry', Britnell, *Female Saints*, 233–49, examines, in the light of the words *androgynéité* and *générosité* applied to Clélie, her character, her relations with her father, and the marriage alternatives she faces. A. E. Duggan, '*Clélie, histoire romaine*, or Writing the nation', Lyons, *Savoir*, 71–79, sketches her view of 'the structural elements Scudéry borrows from early modern historiography to write *Clélie*' and considers 'how Scudéry differentiates the historical novel (or *fable* as she refers to it) from conventional historical discourses', and 'how [she] redefines glory'. D. Denis, 'Les *Chroniques du Samedi* de Madeleine de Scudéry: du recueil à l'œuvre collective', *SCFS*, 24, 2002: 1–15, refers to the MS 15156 of the Bibliothèque de l'Arsenal, recently published for the first time by D., A. Niderst, and M. Maître (see *YWMLS*, 64: 131), of which she here wishes to 'mettre en évidence les ambiguïtés et les duplicités du texte' and then to inquire into the 'modes de lecture qu'il impose, et le statut qu'on peut lui reconnaître'. A. R. Larsen, 'Anne Marie de Schurman, Madeleine de Scudéry et les *Lettres sur La Pucelle* (1646)', Brouard-Arends, *Lectrices*, 269–79, introduces us to a series of MS letters Scudéry wrote to Schurman after reading a translation of 14 of the Dutch author's letters on women's education entitled collectively *Un tournoi de trois pucelles en l'honneur de Jeanne d'Arc* (1646).

SÉVIGNÉ. R. Duchêne, 'Un horizon qui se perd dans l'infini. À propos de la traduction récente d'un livre de Fritz Nies, *Les lettres de Madame de Sévigné. Conventions du genre et sociologie des publics*', *PFSCL*, 30:209–30, is a review article of this translation by Michèle Greff, with a preface by Bernard Bray (Champion, 2001), of which the German original dates from 1972. D. disapproves on the whole of N.'s study, and seizes the opportunity in this rather trenchant piece to air at length his own view that S.'s letters were intended for their addressees only, and not (*pace* N.) for circulation to a wider readership. C. Cartmill, 'Madame de Sévigné, lectrice de Pierre Nicole: les lettres à l'épreuve de l'essai', Brouard-Arends, *Lectrices*, 351–59, notes that S. discovers in N. 'une idée [. . .] qui selon certains critiques annonce ou préfigure la pensée économique d'Adam Smith', in that he 'expose le bien général qui est la conséquence des intérêts des individus'. Elsewhere she finds less reassuring lessons in N., but at all events C. finds that S. 'fait un usage tout à fait personnel et pragmatique de la lecture de Nicole'.

SOREL. D. Riou, 'La leçon de lecture: Joconde dans l'*Histoire comique de Francion* de Charles Sorel', Brouard-Arends, *Lectrices*, 665–75, analyses the elaborate seduction in Book 10 by Francion, passing himself off as a shepherd, of Joconde, daughter of a rich merchant, which is conducted behind the smokescreen of a debate on *vraisemblance* and pastoral romances. M. Rosellini, '*La Science universelle* de Charles Sorel, monument polygraphique ou "vraie philosophie"?' *LitC*, 49:157–79, finds S. concocting an 'ouvrage déconcertant' which varies from 'une encyclopédie objective des savoirs du temps' to 'la transmission réservée d'une "nouvelle philosophie" assortie d'une délirante "histoire de mon esprit" '.

TRISTAN L'HERMITE. D. Guillumette, 'Tristan et la fable', *CTH*, 25:64–66, comments on T.'s use of the Aesopian fable *The Wolf and the Lamb* in *Le Page disgracié*. J. Prévot, 'Le *je* de cache-cache', *ib.*, 67–69, notes the unheroic, passive role which T. accords to his *je* in *Le Page disgracié*, evidence, says P., of the author's 'tourment intérieur'. D. Augier, 'Un alchimiste en voie de disparition: le problème du philosophe dans *Le Page disgracié* de Tristan L'Hermite', *SCFS*, 24, 2002:217–27, discerns in this episode 'la lumière de ces "contes qu'on fait" sur l'alchimie et que Tristan L'Hermite semble bien connaître'. The episode, A. feels, should be placed 'dans l'imaginaire alchimique du dix-septième siècle afin de voir quels échos peuvent être évoqués'. N. Maillard, 'Fonction et représentation des animaux dans *Le Page disgracié* de Tristan L'Hermite ou Le conteur bavard et la linotte muette', Mazouer, *Animal*, 73–88, finds in the novel 'un tableau vivant et imagé des rapports des hommes et des animaux dans la vie quotidienne'. Animals appear in 'saynètes comiques', in 'épisodes facétieux' (like that of the linnet), in accounts of hunting, all of which are 'l'occasion pour Tristan d'évoquer indirectement la création poétique et littéraire'.

URFÉ. J.-B. Rolland, 'De la source d'Aréthuse à la rivière de Lignon: transposition du roman pastoral à la Renaissance et imaginaire de l'eau dans *L'Astrée* d'Honoré d'Urfé', *DSS*, 55:659–74, begins a re-examination of 'la topique arcadienne', proposing to continue it elsewhere. Here, he dwells on U.'s exploitation of his memories of the Lignon, which 's'inscrit tour à tour dans un imaginaire potamographique et une rêverie aquatique'. Water, therefore, is R.'s subject, because 'sous la plume d'H. d'Urfé, l'eau devient une métaphore complexe de l'être'. F. Orivat, 'Honoré d'Urfé et le mythe de la fontaine de Sorgue: jeux et enjeux d'une rêverie aquatique', *ib.*, 703–14, notes the links in *L'Astrée* between dreams and water, and with this in mind studies the account of the love affair between Daphnide and Alcidon in Books III and IV, which 'plonge au cœur de l'œuvre dans un mouvement inverse de celui du Démon de Sorgas', the latter being a vision experienced by Alcidon. T. Meding, '"Le temps, les services et la perséverence": time and secrets in *L'Astrée*', Lyons, *Savoir*, 271–83, discusses the relationship in the work between the passing of time and the disclosure of secrets, and applies this in particular to the 'Histoire d'Euric, Daphnide et Alcidon' begun in Book 2 and continued and concluded in Books 3 and 4 of the Third Part of the romance. P. Rossetto, 'La nuit apprivoisée dans *L'Astrée*', Bertrand, *Penser la nuit*, 139–57, quotes images and representations of night from the mythology of classical antiquity, and finds them 'enrichies, revivifiées, multipliées dans *L'Astrée*'.

VILLEDIEU. D. Kuizenga, 'Playing to win: Villedieu's Henriette-Sylvie de Molière as actress', *Tobin Vol.*, 113–21, proposes to look at the *Mémoires de la vie de Henriette-Sylvie de Molière* 'through the lens of theater, specifically understanding the novel's protagonist as an actress, and the relationship Villedieu crafts with her readers by analogy to the way audience is posited in the concept of *theatrum mundi*'. **Mémoires de la vie de Henriette-Silvie de Molière*, ed. René Démoris, Desjonquères, 270 pp.

5. THOUGHT

Lyons, *Savoir*, prints papers on various aspects of *savoir* in seven sections devoted in turn to history, religion, feminism, classicism, secrecy, science, and knowledge. Two papers precede these sections: E. Bury, 'La philologie dans le concert des savoirs: mutations et permanence de l'*ars critica* au XVIIe siècle' (17–33), points out that, from the beginning of the 17th c., 'la promotion de nouveaux savoirs a remis en cause la *vérité* du contenu de textes anciens; cette perte devient un apport, en ce qu'elle fonde et rend nécessaire une compréhension proprement historique de ces textes', whereupon B. passes in review the contributors to this new *ars critica* and the 'nouveaux cadres de pensée' that they propose; M. Maître, 'Les "belles" et les Belles Lettres: femmes, instances du féminin et nouvelles configurations du savoir' (35–64), puts forward for our consideration three very different texts, the *Homélies sur l'Epistre de saint Paul aux Hébreux, par Charlotte des Ursins, vicomtesse d'Ochy* (1634), Mlle de Scudéry's 'Histoire des deux caméléons' from her *Nouvelles conversations de morale* (1688), and Mme Geoffrin's *Mémoires* (1760–70), with a view to making 'une approche résolument historique et anthropologique de la différence des sexes'. Other papers are considered under the names of the authors they deal with, except the following: D. J. Kostroun, 'Historical appeal under absolutism: women and Gallicism at Port-Royal, 1690–1709' (99–110), which seeks to 'explore the enigma of Port-Royal's destruction' by examining two types of 'savoir historique' associated with the convent: firstly 'figurist' history (concerned with biblical tropes and the workings of divine providence in human affairs), and secondly 'Gallican' history ('the maintenance of institutional traditions through the study of historical precedent'); V. Schröder, 'Écrire les Gracques au temps de Louis XIV' (121–32), which looks at some of the versions of, and lessons drawn from, the myths surrounding Tiberius and Caïus Gracchus by French writers such as Du Verdier, Bossuet, Saint-Évremond, Saint-Réal, and, finally, Marie-Anne Barbier in her tragedy, *Cornélie, mère des Gracques* (1703); S. O'Hara, '"Savantes en poison": *Médée* and Madame de Brinvilliers' (195–204), which discusses 'two women wielding dangerous knowledge' to deadly effect, the first in Corneille's tragedy, the second as viewed in particular by Mme de Sévigné; L. W. Riggs, 'Mythic figures in the *Theatrum Mundi*: the limits of self-fashioning' (375–83), which analyses and criticizes Louis XIV's absolutism: 'the attempt to enact an identity purporting to be beyond the performative is nonetheless a performance; thus it denies the transcendence being asserted', and also notes, for the benefit of aspiring absolutists, that 'those who exploit myths for their persuasive potency sometimes miss the fact that the myths may carry precisely the meaning their use is intended to hide'; R. provides illustrations from Racine's *Andromaque* and *Phèdre*, and from Molière's *Amphitryon*; D. Bertrand, 'Entre mythe et analyse: palimpsestes savants du rire de Vigenère à Cramail' (389–401), which looks at C.'s *Discours académique du ris* (which first appeared in print in his *Jeux de l'inconnu* of 1630) and comments on the author's reactions in it to V.'s *Images de platte-peinture* (1597).

McKenna, *Résurgence*, prints the following: J.-M. Gros, 'À l'imitation des Anciens' (7–25), regrets the attitude of the Council of Trent and the failure of the Catholic Church in the 16th c. to achieve some sort of 'syncrétisme' via Erasmus with the ancient Greek philosophies; he sees 17th-c. French *libertinage* as an inevitable reaction to the Counter-Reformation, and to underline his point he compares Erasmus's *Banquet religieux* with the *Banquet sceptique* by the 'ancien et payen' La Mothe Le Vayer; B. Roche, 'La réception du chant IV du *De Rerum Natura* par trois auteurs libertins d'histoires comiques' (249–70), looks at the works of writers influenced by the views of Montaigne on Lucretius: Théophile de Viau's *Première journée*, Sorel's *Histoire comique de Francion*, and Cyrano's *Lettres satiriques* and *L'Autre monde*; J.-P. Cavaillé, 'Les libertins: l'envers du Grand siècle' (291–319), is intrigued by recent historiographers who ask 'comment faire une place aux libertins dans le "Grand siècle" sans que, précisément, la grandeur du siècle n'en soit diminuée et son éclat terni?' C.'s investigations cover the period from the late 1880s to René Pintard (1943).

Louis Châtellier, *Les Espaces infinis et le silence de Dieu: science et religion, XVIe–XIXe siècle*, Aubier-Flammarion, 267 pp., introduces his book as 'un essai sur la nature de la foi au temps où s'édifiait la science moderne.' It seeks to 'suivre l'évolution de la pensée des chrétiens au cours de la période dite "moderne" qui est celle aussi d'une considérable révolution scientifique', and is divided into three sections entitled 'Le temps de Galilée' (covering the first half of the 17th c. and including a chapter on 'le père Mersenne et son groupe'), 'Le temps de Newton et de Leibniz' (taking us to the 20s and 30s of the 18th c.) and 'De l'Encyclopédie au transformisme' (to the mid 19th c.). C.'s heroes in all three periods are those who can reconcile piety with scientific curiosity like Mersenne at the beginning of his survey, and Ampère at the end. Michael Moriarty, *Early Modern French Thought: The Age of Suspicion*, OUP, xii + 271 pp., seeks to defend the foremost thinkers of the French 17th c. from the suspicions and condemnations of their contemporaries and immediate successors, and even from themselves. Most of all, however, he seeks to 're-open up some discourses remote in time, and largely in spirit, from the present [. . .] partly to show why they could have seemed true, and partly to show that they can in some sense concern us still'. He wishes to make the 21st c. understand them and their 'view of the world' in their entirety, and to 'clarify the intellectual arguments by which [that] view is supported, [and even] occasionally make them speak to the reader's sensibility and imagination'. The three philosophers whom M. singles out for special attention are Descartes, Pascal, and Malebranche. John J. Conley, *The Suspicion of Virtue: Women Philosophers in Neoclassical France*, Ithaca, NY–London, Cornell U.P., 2002, xi + 222 pp., studies the writings of five 17th-c. women from 'the aristocratic laity of Paris' who in various ways gave a special slant to their studies of virtue, or *the* virtues, cardinal or theological. The introduction sets these women and their works in their historical and social context, tells us of the various genres adopted by them to express themselves and their reasons for rejecting or neglecting others, and dwells on the possibilities for, and limitations on, the education of women of their class and their period. A chapter on each studies Mme de Sablé and her *Maximes*, Mme Deshoulières and her *Réflexions diverses*, Mme de La Sablière and her *Maximes chrétiennes*, Mademoiselle de La Vallière and her *Réflexions sur la miséricorde de Dieu*, and Mme de Maintenon and her *Sur les vertus cardinales*.

CPR, 52, collects papers on *L'ordre de Saint-Benoît et Port-Royal*: T. Barbeau, 'Port-Royal et le mysticisme: une controverse sur la prière entre Pierre Nicole et Dom Claude Martin' (177–94), studies 'la controverse amicale', also involving Antoine Arnauld and Martin de Barcos, in which N.'s anti-mysticism is expressed in his *Traité de l'oraison* (1679), while M.'s more favourable attitude is to be found in his *Traité de la contemplation* (1696); E. Weaver-Laporte, 'Fidélité à la règle de saint Benoît dans les constitutions de Port-Royal' (195–206), finds the structure of the *constitutions* parallel to that of *la Règle de saint Benoît*; D. Donetzkoff, 'Martin de Barcos et Claude Lancelot, commentateurs de la *Règle* de saint Benoît' (221–39), studies two unpublished MSS from the Bibliothèque de Port-Royal by B., both entitled 'L'explication de la règle de saint Benoît' and both accompanied by commentaries by L.

Michel Le Guern, *Pascal et Arnauld* (Lumière classique, 48), Champion, 239 pp., follows chronologically the relationship of these two, chapter by chapter. Their collaborations are considered, such as those on the *Écrits des curés de Paris* and on the *Logique de Port-Royal*. Le G. sums up their relations with the words: 'Sans doute pourrait-on retenir un grand respect de Pascal pour Arnauld, une admiration réciproque, quelques années d'une collaboration étroite dans un combat commun, mais des positions philosophiques irréductiblement divergentes.' Dinah Ribard, **Raconter vivre penser: histoires de philosophes 1650–1766* (Contextes), Vrin, EHESS, 464 pp.

ANGÉLIQUE ARNAULD. T. M. Carr, '"Avez-vous lu la règle?" *Les instructions sur la règle* de la Mère Angélique', *CPR*, 52:207–20, presents these extracts from the *Collection des religieuses*, and explains their importance as a discipline for A.

BAYLE. A. McKenna, 'La correspondance du jeune Bayle: apprentissage et banc d'essai de son écriture', *RHLF*, 103:287–300, studies the 'réseaux de correspondance' of the young B., and is enabled thereby to 'saisir sur le vif comment l'enfant du Carla devient "citoyen du monde"'. Id. and A. Leroux, 'L'édition électronique de la correspondance de Pierre Bayle', *ib.*, 365–73, introduce us to their edition, for which they are using the database ARCANE, 'spécialement élaborée pour l'édition critique'. J. Charnley, 'Bayle, Dos Santos et Ludolf: l'image de l'Éthiopie au XVIIe siècle', *PFSCL*, 30:157–65, recounts the reactions of B. to two books on Ethiopia, by the Dutchman Job Ludolf and the Portuguese João Dos Santos. She concentrates, as does B. himself, on what he finds of interest on religious matters in the books, particularly in L.'s. J. Soll, 'Empirical history and the transformation of political criticism in France from Bodin to Bayle', *JHI*, 64:297–316, supports the idea that empirical history as practised by the Enlightenment was 'a coming of age of Renaissance scholarly culture and erudition', despite the unfortunate intervening 17th-c. experiences of Dupleix, Amelot, and Bayle. E. James, 'Pierre Bayle, atheist or Christian?', *SCFS*, 24, 2002:249–58, considers and reacts to G. Mori's *Bayle philosophe* (1999), and asks 'whether Bayle's philosophical reflection does in fact end in atheism, and whether, in practice, philosophy and faith are so categorically polarized in Bayle as it seems to Mori'. B. Walters, 'Bayle and Moréri: British geographical entries in two seventeenth-century French dictionaries', *ib.*, 259–69, points to and accounts for the difference between the two dictionaries on this topic, with M.'s wider coverage actually dissuading B. from expanding his own in later editions. G. Mori, 'Scepticisme ancien et moderne chez Bayle', McKenna, *Résurgence*, 271–90, reacts at length to Richard H. Popkin's view of B. as a believer whose thinking had left him with only one resource: 'celle de la foi et de la révélation', a view which M. urgently wishes to modify. A. McKenna, 'Pierre Bayle polygraphe', *LitC*, 49:243–63, defines B. as two sorts of *polygraphe*: 'd'une part il communique une très vaste culture au grand public sous une forme digeste; d'autre part, son écriture codée est réservée à l'élite de la République des Lettres'. His works are 'un jeu d'ombre et lumière, paradoxal et fascinant'.

La Raison corrosive: études sur la pensée critique de Pierre Bayle, ed. Isabelle Delpla and Philippe De Robert (Vie des Huguenots, 30), Champion, 292 pp., collects 14 papers under this title which, the editors claim, 'condense les métaphores par lesquelles Bayle désigne la dualité de la raison, critique des erreurs mais aussi destructrice des vérités.' The collection is divided into four sections: I: 'Évolution, contexte, réception', which includes the late E. Labrousse on 'Bayle, ou l'augustinisme sans la grâce' (19–23), E. James on 'La culture classique de Bayle' (25–30), J.-M. Gros on 'La place de la "République des lettres" dans l'œuvre de Bayle: de la correspondance au *Dictionnaire*' (31–39), and M. Chevallier on 'Pierre Bayle et Pierre Poiret, critiques de Spinoza' (41–50); II: 'Lecture critique de la Bible', with two papers examining B.'s dictionary entries on 'Ève et ses filles' and 'David'; III: 'Raison et argumentation', including J.-L. Solière on 'Bayle et les apories de la raison humaine' (87–137), I. Delpla on 'Les parallèles entre idolâtrie et athéisme: question de méthode' (143–73), and F. Markovitz on 'Bayle sur les traces de Sextus' (175–210); and finally IV: 'Dialogue , ironie, pluralisme', which includes two papers on B.'s influence on Leibniz, also A. McKenna on 'L'ironie de Bayle et son statut dans l'écriture philosophique' (245–66), and O. Abel on 'La diversité de l'éthique de Bayle' (267–82). *Correspondance*, ed. Elisabeth Labrousse et al., Oxford, Voltaire Foundation, vol. II: **Du 12 novembre 1674 au 19 novembre 1677*, 2001, xxii + 529 pp.

MARGUERITE BUFFET. F. E. Beasley, 'Marguerite Buffet and *La Sagesse Mondaine*', Lyons, *Savoir*, 227–35, dwells on the divergences of views on language between B. in her *Nouvelles observations sur la langue française* and the Académie Française. I. Ducharme, 'Une formule discursive au féminin: Marguerite Buffet et la *Querelle des femmes*', *PFSCL*, 30:131–55, names only eight 17th-c. published female defenders of the feminist cause, and concentrates on the last of these: M. B. with her *Éloges des illustres sçavantes anciennes et modernes* of 1668. D.'s study, she claims, does not serve the feminist cause, but is simply 'une analyse rhétorique et discursive d'un texte féminin'. Id., 'Marguerite Buffet, lectrice de la Querelle des femmes', Brouart-Arends, *Lectrices*, 331–40, asserts that B.'s *Éloges* are 'la réflexion d'une lectrice avant même d'être l'œuvre d'une auteure'.

FRANÇOIS DE CALLIÈRES. **De la manière de négocier avec les souverains* (Classiques de la pensée politique, 19), Geneva, Droz, 2002, 247 pp.

CHARRON. C. Nadeau, 'Sagesse "sceptique" de Charron? L'articulation du scepticisme et du stoïcisme dans *La Sagesse* de Pierre Charron', McKenna, *Résurgence*, 85–104, proposes to 'étudier les raisons pour lesquelles l'œuvre de Charron est généralement vue comme l'un des intermédiaires principaux du scepticisme ou du pyrrhonisme pour la France du XVIIe siècle.' He has his doubts, however, about this general view, because it seems to him that 'les historiens de ces questions ont généralement tendance à plaquer ce que l'on sait de la réception de l'œuvre de Charron sur cette œuvre elle-même.' N. feels that another 'modèle philosophique hérité de l'Antiquité', apart from scepticism, can be seen in *La Sagesse*: 'celui du stoïcisme', and he wishes therefore to evaluate the two models together.

CYRANO. A. Torero Ibad, 'Cyrano et Lucrèce', McKenna, *Résurgence*, 221–47, finds in C.'s two novels 'une pluralité de personnages [qui] développe des thèses non synthétisables entre elles' on 'une pluralité de thèses philosophiques'. She has decided therefore, not to try and isolate passages 'à tonalité épicurienne', but to consider the whole of both works 'tout en prenant en compte les philosophies avec lesquelles Cyrano fait dialoguer l'épicurisme', aware that C.'s aim is 'une mise en question de la philosophie aristotélicienne'.

DESCARTES. A. Pessin, 'Descartes's nomic concurrentism: finite causation and divine concurrence', *JHP*, 41:25–49, argues that, as in Malebranche so in D., 'since volitions are paradigm representational states, close attention to the representational content of God's volitions has substantial exegetical rewards.' D. McCallam, 'Encountering and countering the "uncanny" in Descartes's *Méditations*', *FS*, 57:135–47, begins by surveying Freud and Jentsch on 'the uncanny', and then points out D.'s interest in many aspects of the same subject ('madness, evil spirits, ghosts, automata and symbolic castration'), explored to justify his 'hyperbolic doubting', all finally countered by invoking the *cogito* 'which guarantees a certain "immortality" each time it is pronounced'.

Desmond M. Clarke, *Descartes's Theory of Mind*, Oxford, Clarendon, viii + 267 pp., gives a thorough and lucid account of an intractable subject — the relationship between mind and body: 'when we attempt to explain any given phenomenon, sooner or later we encounter the limits of our efforts and it is appropriate at that point to signal having reached those limits by an uninformative appeal to the way things are.' That, C. points out, is what D. did when addressing Mersenne in the Sixth Replies. F. Cossutta, 'La métaphysique cartésienne au risque du dialogue philosophique: schèmes speculatifs, formes d'exposition et genres textuels dans le dialogue inachevé *La recherche de la vérité par la lumière naturelle*', *DSS*, 55:233–57, seeks to throw light on the dating of this dialogue, and proposes reasons for its unfinished state. Daniel Giovannangeli, **Finitude et représentation: six leçons sur l'apparaître, de Descartes à l'ontologie phénoménologique*, Brussels, Ousia, 120 pp. Hélène Bouchilloux, *La Question de la liberté chez Descartes: libre arbitre, liberté et indifférence* (Travaux de philosophie, 1), Champion, 250 pp., tackles what she claims to be a neglected point, 'la question fondamentale de la métaphysique de Descartes, plus fondamentale encore que la question de la science'. Her work is an exploration above all of the *Méditations* and of the *Entretien avec Burman* to discover D.'s views on 'la liberté divine', and above all on the uses to which the will with its 'puissance absolue d'arbitrage' is put: because that is where divine freedom lies.

DUVAL. J. Harris, '"La force du tact": representing the taboo body in Jacques Duval's *Traité des hermaphrodites* (1612)', *FS*, 57:311–22, introduces us to a 17th-c. medical writer who not only discusses medical matters but also examines the taboos and difficulties that even specialists like himself encounter when writing or speaking of sex, the body, and 'natural' behaviour.

CLAUDE FLEURY. **Ecrits de jeunesse: tradition humaniste et liberté de l'esprit*, ed. Noémi Hepp and Volker Kapp (Sources classiques, 45), Champion, 240 pp.

FRANÇOIS DE SALES. H. Michon, 'Pourquoi François de Sales utilise-t-il un langage imagé?' Wetsel, *Spiritualité*, 23–37, considers three points: 'le refus d'un langage particulier, l'utilisation de l'image plutôt que du symbole, et celle de la parabole plutôt que de la figure', and attributes all these choices to F.'s desire to express himself clearly and simply.

FÉNELON. J. Le Brun, *'La correspondance philosophique de Fénelon: les lettres à Dom François Lamy et au duc d'Orléans', *RFN*, 93, 2001:208–20. **Revue philosophique*, 2, contains articles on F., pp. 147–272.

FONTENELLE. J. Dagen, 'Fontenelle et l'épicurisme', *RHLF*, 103:397–414, finds F. afflicted with 'une certaine contagion épicurienne', and 'porté à se donner une conception de l'homme et une éthique d'esprit rationnel et d'essence foncièrement matérialiste'. C. Martin, 'Eclipses du soleil, lumières de la raison: la nuit dans les *Entretiens sur la pluralité des mondes* de Fontenelle', Bertrand, *Penser la nuit*, 89–104, asks: 'Si le spectacle inaugural de la lune et des étoiles est autre chose qu'une stratégie rhétorique, comment expliquer l'omniprésence de la nuit dans une œuvre généralement reconnue comme un texte fondateur pour la pensée des Lumières?'

GASSENDI. S. Taussig, 'Gassendi et l'hypocrite: quel masque pour quelle personne?', *PFSCL*, 30:435–62, wants to rescue G.'s thought from being labelled on the surface conformist and underneath epicurean and atheistic, and claims that 'dans la philosophie pratique comme dans la philosophie contemplative, il est impossible de repérer chez Gassendi un double discours'. Id. 'Gassendi contre la métaphore: la nuit', Bertrand, *Penser la nuit*, 73–87, examines references to the subject, mainly in the Latin letters, for his repeated astronomer's objection to the use of night as a metaphor for ignorance. Id., **Pierre Gassendi (1592–1655): introduction à la vie savante* (Monothéismes et philosophie), Turnhout, Brepols, 454 pp. Id., 'Destin et Providence: Gassendi contre le portique', McKenna, *Résurgence*, 203–19, examines G.'s *Vie d'Épicure* (in translation) to elucidate the question of his opposition to the stoic idea of Providence, 'parce qu'elle permet d'éclairer son adhésion à l'épicurisme'.

GABRIEL GERBERON. M. Le Guern, 'Dom Gabriel Gerberon et *L'Histoire générale du Jansénisme*', *CPR*, 52:11–18, introduces us to the life of this Benedictine, and to his *Histoire* of 1700 which in fact is a summary of theological debate around Jansenius's *Augustinus*, concentrating more on discussion in the Spanish Netherlands than in France. F. Vanhoorne, 'Morale et conscience chez Dom Gerberon', *ib.*, 19–32, studies G.'s *Règles des moeurs* (1688), an attack on casuists and on probabilism.

GRENAILLE. *L'Honnête Fille: où dans le premier livre il est traité de l'esprit des filles*, ed. Alain Vizier (Textes de la Renaissance, 64), Champion, 542 pp., reproduces what was in effect the 'troisième partie' of *L'Honnête Fille*, published for the first time in 1640. The editor, in his 'Présentation', explains the changes of plan made by G. in the course of publication which turn this third part into by far the most significant section of the work as a whole. He also traces its reception, from its first appearance to the present, and underlines its importance in the struggle for the promotion of a 'démocratisation de l'esprit', for a recognition of the intellectual equality of men and women.

MME GUYON. **Correspondance. 1, Directions spirituelles*, ed. Dominique Tronc (Bibliothèque des correspondances, 3), Champion, 928 pp. D. Tronc, 'Une filiation mystique: Chrysostome de Saint-Lô, Jean de Bernières, Jacques Bertot, Jeanne-Marie Guyon', *DSS*, 55:95–116, presents the sources of G.'s 'autorité spirituelle', formed, not only by studying the scriptures, but also by a 'filiation reconnue mais peu étudiée' which offered 'un "christianisme" intérieur d'une grande sobriété'. M. M. Randall, 'Mystic edge or mystic on the edge? Madame de Guyon revisited', Wetsel, *Femmes*, 109–17, reviews the reasons why G. is nowadays portrayed more and more in a positive light. D. Guenin-Lelle, 'Jeanne Guyon's influence on Quaker practice: a guiding voice in silence', Wetsel, *Spiritualité*, 39–49, points to the influence of her *Moyen court et très facile de faire oraison* on the Quaker text, *A guide to true peace*.

HUET. A. G. Shelford, 'Thinking geometrically in Pierre-Daniel Huet's *Demonstratio evangelica* (1697)', *JHI*, 63:599–617, deplores the neglect of an important work, claiming that 'the *Demonstratio* is an intellectual biography, not just of the author but of an era.'

JURIEU. H. Goldwyn, 'Censure, clandestinité et épistolarité: *Les Lettres pastorales* de Pierre Jurieu', Lyons, *Savoir*, 285–94, introduces us to these examples of 'littérature d'action' and to the circumstances which inspired their creation and dissemination.

LA MESNARDIÈRE. A. Wygant, 'La Mesnardière and the Demon', Lyons, *Savoir*, 323–34, reveals that this scholar had given up medicine for 'the science of poetry', and that 'the hinge text in this remarkable chiasmatic movement of knowledge had been the *Traitté de la mélancholie*', an attempted explanation of the Loudun possessions. W. then accounts for La M.'s abandoning medicine for poetics.

LA MOTHE LE VAYER. *De la patrie et des étrangers et autres petits traités sceptiques*, ed. Philippe-Joseph Salazar, Desjonquères, 333 pp., collects in all 14 *petits traités* culled from 28 to be found in four volumes of *Opuscules, ou Petits traictez* published between 1643 and 1647. S.'s *texte de base* is that of Dresden, 1756. *Petit traité sceptique sur cette commune façon de parler: 'N'avoir pas le Sens commun*', ed. Lionel Laforestier, Gallimard, 126 pp., is based on the original 1646 edition. The editor summarizes the views of various scholars, some of whom find the text, 'sous une forme ludique', an expression of La M.'s 'anti-rationalisme', his 'scepticisme extrémiste', while others see it (more mildly) as 'une forme de résistance aux partages normatifs de l'âge classique, la promesse d'une raison élargie'.

'*Explication de l'Antre des Nymphes* (Fonds Dupuy, no. 835)', *LetC*, 183–204, is an *inédit* commentary by La M. on an episode in Homer's *Odyssey*. I. Moreau, 'Polémique libertine et querelle du purisme: La Mothe Le Vayer ou le refus d'un "art de plaire" au service du vulgaire', *RHLF*, 103:377–96, finds in this writer's *Dialogues* and his *Considérations sur l'éloquence française de ce temps* an echo of the mistrust felt within the circle of the Dupuy brothers regarding the notion of 'bon usage' then being elaborated, and later promoted by Vaugelas. McKenna, *Résurgence*, prints the following: J.-M. Gros, 'La place du cynisme dans la philosophie libertine' (121–39), who quotes mainly La M. whose attitude displays 'quelque chose qui déborde largement le simple scepticisme'; N. Gengoux, 'Place et fonction de l'épicurisme dans les *Dialogues faits à l'imitation des Anciens* de La Mothe Le Vayer' (141–87), who begins with an analysis of the structure of the *Dialogues* in order to 'situer les références à Épicure (Démocrite ou Lucrèce) dans cette structure', and then sets out to show how La M.'s scepticism is modified by Epicureanism; S. Gouverneur, 'La Mothe Le Vayer et la politique, ou l'usage libertin du scepticisme antique' (189–201), who studies those texts 'qui ont amené à faire de lui un partisan du machiavélisme via le scepticisme' with a view to understanding 'comment il a utilisé le scepticisme de manière libertine et critique envers le pouvoir d'État'. Scepticism is 'un masque pour le libertinage' from behind which to subvert 'le pouvoir en place et son discours légitimant'.

FRANÇOIS LAMY. D. Reguig-Naya, 'Du corps à l'âme: connaître l'homme par la parole à Port-Royal et chez François Lamy', *CPR*, 52:33–47, concentrates on L.'s *De la connaissance de soi-même* (1694), in particular on its second treatise, *Introduction à l'étude de soi-même, où l'on examine l'homme selon son être naturel*, in order to bring out the differences between him and Arnauld and Nicole, as regards their attitudes towards Cartesianism.

MABILLON. *Érudition et commerce épistolaire: Jean Mabillon et la tradition monastique*, ed. Daniel-Odon Hurel (Textes et traditions, 6), Vrin, 688 pp., divides the articles which constitute this 'programme de recherches' into two sections. The first, concerned with 'l'historiographie de la congrégation de Saint-Maur', puts Jean Mabillon — 'à la fois bénédictin et membre de la République des lettres' — at the centre of contributions which cover different aspects of 'l'érudition mauriste'. The second section 'pose la question de la spécificité de l'échange épistolaire en milieu monastique sur le long terme historique', contributors taking their enquiries as far back as the fourth c. AD and forward to Teresa of Lisieux and the dawn of the 20th c. The whole venture, according to H., will eventually include 'l'élaboration de l'inventaire de la correspondance de Jean Mabillon' which, with that of Edmond Martène and Bernard de Montfaucon, is awaiting his attention at the Bibliothèque de Saint-Germain-des-Prés.

MALEBRANCHE. D. Cunning, *'Systematic divergences in Malebranche and Cudworth', *JHP*, 41 : 343–63.

MÉNAGE. **Histoire des femmes philosophes*, trans. from the Latin by Manuéla Vanay, ed. Claude Tarrène, Arléa, 100 pp.

MERSENNE. *L'Usage de la raison, où tous les mouvemens de la raison sont deduits; et les actions de l'entendement, de la volonté, et du liberal arbitre sont expliquées fort exactement*, ed. Claudio Buccolini (Corpus des œuvres de philosophie en langue française), Fayard, 2002, 122 pp., reproduces the only edition (1623) of this work from the only known copy in the Vatican Library. M.'s 'Avant-propos au lecteur' recommends this work as an aid to 'disposer ton ame pour faire son entrée en la celeste Jerusalem, afin qu'elle loüe eternellement son Createur'. Of the two books into which the work is divided, only the first has its own title 'Des mouvemens de la raison, et de tout l'homme interieur'; the untitled second is devoted mainly to the human will and its workings. **La Vérité des sciences contre les sceptiques ou pyrrhoniens*, ed. Dominique Descotes (Sources classiques, 49), Champion, 1040 pp.

NAUDÉ. F. Gabriel, 'Gabriel Naudé et la réception des Anciens: temps, croyances, figures', McKenna, *Résurgence*, 45–83, reads N.'s *Apologie pour tous les grands personnages qui ont été faussement soupçonnés de magie*, among whom are several 'philosophes anciens', defended by N. with clarity and scepticism towards the accusers.

PASCAL. Elisabeth Marie Loevlie, *Literary Silences in Pascal, Rousseau and Beckett*, Oxford, Clarendon, 252 pp., starts with a quotation from St Augustine's *Confessions* which leads her to seek out texts that 'will always slip away from language'. The first part of her study is 'theoretical and descriptive', and the second discusses P.'s *Pensées*, R.'s *Rêveries*, and Beckett's three novels. The exploration of the *Pensées* starts with a study of fragment 233 (Sellier) which evokes the silence of the Hidden God and the reaction of the fearful 'moi', and, via a sequence of references to other fragments, arrives at the conclusion that they 'enact an endless performance of slips and shifts' which 'move towards saying the unsayable as they become movements — waves, silence.' Jacques Plainemaison, *Blaise Pascal polémiste*, Clermont-Ferrand, Univ. Blaise Pascal, 198 pp, is a collection of previously published articles, most of them commentaries on the *Provinciales*, but with a consideration among the final ones of 'la fonction polémique dans les *Pensées*'. *The Cambridge Companion to Pascal*, ed. Nicholas Hammond, CUP, xvi + 287 pp., is a 'reference work for students and non-specialists' which contains essays by 14 scholars covering briefly all aspects of P.'s life and works. There is a substantial general bibliography. Pierre Bourdieu, *Méditations pascaliennes*, Seuil, 291 pp., presents the second edition, 'revue et corrigée', of a work first published in 1997. It takes P.'s *Pensées* as a point of departure for 'la construction théorique d'une anthropologie réaliste' based on 'des traits de l'existence humaine' which P. himself explored: 'force, coutume, automate, corps, imagination, contingence, probabilité'.

M. Bretz, '"Connaissez-vous M. Pascal? Je lui dis que j'avais eu cet honneur". Témoignage inédit d'une religieuse de Port-Royal', *CPR*, 52:307–14, reproduces an extract concerning P. from the *relation de captivité* by Sister Marguerite de Sainte-Gertrude, 'dite la soeur Dupré'. She claims that P. urged her and her fellow *moniales* to retract their previous acceptance of the *Formulaire* condemning the alleged Five Propositions in Jansenius's *Augustinus*. O. Jouslin, 'Pascal poète en prose', *DSS*, 55:715–47, places P., with his biblical inspiration, at the centre of the history of French prose poetry (as did Claudel). C. Braider, 'Pascal's machine: science and theology in the *Provinciales* and the *Pensées*', Lyons, *Savoir*, 345–55, dwells on the 'discours de la machine' (Sellier 680/Lafuma 418–26), and discusses the 'machine' which is never mentioned in the text and is therefore 'an idea only available at a *metadiscursive* level, operating *par derrière*, as the hidden "reason" behind the rhetorical "effect" it was intended to produce'. B. attempts an explanation of the 'machine' by reference to the 'Pascaline' and also to the parable of the wounded traveller told by 'mon ami Janséniste' in the second *Lettre provinciale*.

C. M. Natoli, 'Révélation/Révolution: une réflexion sur la nouveauté dans les *Provinciales* de Pascal', Lyons, *Savoir*, 243–53, reminds us of the traditional notion of 'la nouveauté maléfique' and shows P. applying it to the 'nouvelles règles de morale' vaunted by the spokesman for the Jesuits in the letters.

Bernard Grasset, *Les Pensées de Pascal, une interprétation de l'Écriture*, Kimé, 354 pp., presents his interpretation of this interpretation in three parts: firstly 'Figure, prophétisme et miracles', secondly 'L'Éclat voilé', and finally 'La Clef de lecture'. Pascal, G. suggests, aims to persuade us to search behind the literal for the figurative or the spiritual, to look constantly behind, beneath, and beyond what is before us for the Truth. G. is very readable, persuasive and enthusiastic, but (thankfully) not entirely uncritical. L. Susini, 'La "vraie éloquence" en question dans les *Pensées* de Pascal', *RHLF*, 103:17–29, is aware of the existence in the 17th c. of 'un très vaste mouvement de mise en accusation et de défense de la rhétorique au sein duquel il conviendra de circonscrire nettement la place occupée par Pascal', and goes on to examine P.'s assertion in Sellier 671 that 'la vraie éloquence se moque de l'éloquence'. H. Michon, 'Réflexions sur le statut de la rhétorique dans l'apologétique pascalienne', *DSS*, 55:271–85, considers two in particular, Sellier 430 and 617, which seem to formulate 'un jugement sinon contradictoire, du moins problématique' on the subject. H. Bjornstad, ' "La continuité dégoûte en tout": some notes on Pascal's apologetics of discontinuity', *SCFS*, 24, 2002:229–38, offers a beguiling meditation on P.'s views about discontinuity, including an analysis of the fragment Lafuma 771/ Sellier 636 which contains the title quotation. M. Bouattour, 'L'image de l'Islam dans les *Pensées* de Pascal', Baccar Bournaz, *Afrique*, 345–56, observes that P. makes use of the Moslem religion and attacks it for his own didactic purposes, but concedes that P.'s aim is 'la recherche de la vérité' and that 'malgré tout Pascal a cherché à instaurer des ponts avec la religion musulmane, alors que d'autres ont refusé toute forme de communication'.

D. Ribard, 'Nom d'auteur et effets de lecture: l'*Entretien de Pascal avec M. de Sacy*, XVIIe–XXe siècle', *DSS*, 55:259–70, studies the 'apparitions et effacements d'un dialogue dans les différents livres qui ont porté jusqu'à nous la réflexion pascalienne sur Épictète et Montaigne à l'époque qui précède la rédaction des *Pensées*'. She has therefore looked at the original edition of Fontaine's *Mémoires*, at the 1736 edition of these published by Michel Tronchai, at the possible *apports* of the Père Desmolets and Pierre Coste, and of later editions. *Entretiens avec Sacy sur la philosophie*, ed. Richard Scholar, Arles, Actes Sud, 92 pp., presents us with this extract from Fontaine's *Mémoires*, with its review by P. (and comments by Sacy) of the philosophies of Montaigne and Epictetus, 'les deux plus illustres défenseurs des deux plus célèbres sectes du monde, et les seules conformes à la raison.'

QUESNEL. J. Lesaulnier, 'Petite vie de l'oratorien Claude Séguenot composée par Pasquier Quesnel', *CPR*, 52:315–23, introduces and reproduces this MS of 1713.

SILHON. *De la certitude des connaissances humaines*, ed. Christian Nadeau (Corpus des œuvres de philosophie en langue française), Fayard, 2002, 366 pp., reproduces the Amsterdam, 1662, edition of this work, originally of Paris, 1661, 'où sont particulièrement expliquez les principes et les fondemens de la Morale & de la Politique'.

SURIN. H. Trepanier, 'Les grâces extraordinaires ou les "surnaturelles connaissances expérimentales" de Jean-Joseph Surin', Lyons, *Savoir*, 151–60, discusses the differences that arose between S. and his *directeur spirituel* over his experiences as exorcist among the diabolically possessed Ursulines of Loudun.

THE EIGHTEENTH CENTURY

POSTPONED

THE ROMANTIC ERA

By John Whittaker, *University of Nottingham*

I. General

P. Laforgue, 'Machinisme et industrialisme, ou romantisme, modernité et mélancolie', *RHLF*, 103:63–92, suggests that the industrial development which brought machinery to the attention of writers such as Balzac, Hugo, and Vigny, produced by its effect on their imagination a new and more complex kind of Romantic melancholy which contrasted with the simple unease which was fashionable in the early years of the Romantic era. The proceedings of the two conferences held by the Société des études romantiques in January 2002 and 2003 are published in the same journal: J.-L. Diaz, 'Quelle histoire littéraire? Perspectives d'un dix-neuviémiste', *ib.*, 515–35, introduces the theme, 'Multiple histoire littéraire', and identifies a number of areas in which there is a good deal of work to be done in order to achieve a better understanding of Romanticism; A. Compagnon, 'Philologie et archéologie', *ib.*, 537–42, gives an overview of the changing approaches to 19th-c. literary history during the last 40 years, representing a renewal of interest and of critical techniques; P. Laforgue, 'Histoire littéraire, histoire de la littérature et sociocritique: quelle historicité pour quelle histoire?', *ib.*, 543–67, considers the different points of contact between literature and history, and concludes in favour of a sociocritical perspective; A. Vaillant, 'Pour une histoire de la communication littéraire', *ib.*, 549–62, calls for a revolution in the procedures involved in literary history, and suggests a move to the study of large corpora, for example the detailed analysis of a year of Girardin's *La Presse*, in order to elaborate a poetic history of the form and genre of literary communication; P. Régnier, 'Littérature, idéologies et idéologie de la littérature: un combat toujours actuel', *ib.*, 563–78, notes that the study of literature was essentially a 19th-c. invention, observing however that a better term is needed for the type of analysis which is now involved, perhaps 'littératurologie'; E. Bordas, 'Stylistique et histoire littéraire', *ib.*, 587–89, shows the 19th-c. origins of the modern concept of stylistics; S. Michaud, 'L'exception allemande, ou quelques questions au naturalisme européen', *ib.*, 591–96, notes that the perspective of both French Romanticism and French Naturalism changes radically when one compares them with their German and British counterparts; J.-Y. Mollier, 'Histoire culturelle et histoire littéraire', *ib.*, 597–612, suggests that the association of literary and cultural history is fertile territory for development, and gives a number of glimpses of potentially fascinating subjects of study in the Romantic era; J. Lyon-Caen, 'Histoire littéraire et histoire de la lecture', *ib.*, 613–23, shows the close relationship between the evolution of the reading public and the development of the novel in the years 1830–40 and beyond; M.-E. Thérenty, 'Pour une histoire littéraire de la presse au XIXe siècle', *ib.*, 625–35, calls for further study of 19th-c. newspaper and periodical production, observing the impact of the press upon literature; J.-P. Bertrand, 'Pour une histoire des poétiques (impromptu)', *ib.*, 637–42, calls for a closer association between the study of the literary history which is external to a text and the study of its inner structure and function, the two being by no means incompatible; V. Laisney, 'Choses dites: petite histoire littéraire de la parole au XIXe siècle', *ib.*, 643–53, shows that, though the 19th c. did not favour the spoken word as a form of literary output, a good number of writers of our period left traces of their conversations in the notes and stenographic records made by others, and that these are worthy of our attention; C. Planté, 'La place des femmes dans l'histoire littéraire: annexe ou point de départ d'une relecture critique?', *ib.*, 655–68, finds that the increasing number of women writers, particularly in the first half of the 19th c., was a reflection of the changing role of women in society, observing however that their work has tended to be given comparatively little attention in literary histories.

S. Moussa, 'Méhémet-Ali au miroir des voyageurs français en Égypte', *Romantisme*, 120:15–25, examines the various portraits of the viceroy by French writers from 1805 to 1848, finding that his image is an interesting combination of civilization and barbarism, the emphasis depending on the individual author. J.-L. Diaz, 'Quand le maître devient chef d'école . . .', *ib.*, 122:7–17, examines a significant 19th-c. phenomenon in the socialization of hierarchic relationships between writers as they grouped themselves into 'schools'.

Napoléon, Stendhal et les romantiques: l'armée, la guerre, la gloire, ed. Michel Arrous, Saint-Pierre-du-Mont, Eurédit, 2002, 465 pp., contains the proceedings of the conference held, with the assistance of the Société internationale d'études stendhaliennes and the *Revue internationale d'études stendhaliennes*, at the Musée de l'Armée in November 2001. It contains: M. Arrous, 'Présentation, "Vive Waterloo!", de quelques enjeux de la gloire au regard de l'histoire et de la littérature' (9–19), explaining the intention of the conference to bring together historians and literary scholars in order to combine their areas of expertise; T. Ozwald, 'Le Napoléon de Balzac: une si ténébreuse affaire' (23–37), suggesting that B.'s interest was in anthropological rather than in military history, and that he was therefore inclined to transpose facts and modify events; V. Laisney,

'*La Napoleone* de Charles Nodier, ou l'exaltation romantique sous le Consulat' (39–53), on the satirical ode directed towards the First Consul, published in 1802 and for which, having denounced himself to the police, Nodier was imprisoned; P.-M. Néaud, 'La figure du demi-solde chez Jean-Roch Coignat et Stendhal-Beyle' (55–60), on the army career of the two writers and their difficulties in obtaining payment for their military service; M. Peyroux, 'Stendhal, Napoléon, la colonne Trajane et la colonne Vendôme' (61–82), on S.'s association of N. with Trajan, perhaps on account of the monuments they left to commemorate their victories; J.-T. Nordmann, 'Le Napoléon de Taine, héros romantique' (83–91), on his *Origines de la France contemporaine* of 1887; J.-P. Lautman, 'Paul-Louis Courier juge l'armée' (93–107), concerned with his descriptions of the brutality of war; C. Réquéna, 'Les personnages militaires dans l'œuvre de Prosper Mérimée' (109–33), a re-evaluation of the importance of the military theme in M.'s work, noting the close association which he made between war and literature; J.-C. Yon, 'Les militaires dans l'œuvre d'Offenbach: conventions et subversions' (135–68), observing that the first and the last time that O.'s music was played in the theatre during his lifetime was in connection with military plays, noting their importance in his musical career, and his ability to subvert conventions in order to discredit the army; N. Boussard, 'L'odieux de la paix, l'apologie de la guerre et la nostalgie de la gloire selon Stendhal' (169–93), identifying what S. disliked about war, namely the periods of inactivity during campaigns and the disorder, though also drawing attention to his nostalgia for military activity once peace had returned; G. Bodinier, 'Le courage, la gloire et l'honneur vus par les officiers et les soldats de l'armée du Premier Empire' (197–219), taking evidence from the official documents dealing with N.'s campaigns; M. Di Maio, '"La plus horrible de toutes les scènes": la Bérésina de Balzac' (221–36), on the scenes of battle in the novella *Adieu*, first published in 1830; M. Guérin, 'L'ambition ou la gloire en deuil' (237–63), showing how the literary æsthetics of military glory underwent a transformation between 1830 and 1848; X. Bourdenet, '"Le Saint-Bernard, n'est-ce que ça?": l'épisode du Saint-Bernard dans *La Vie de Henry Brulard*' (265–90), indicating the connection in Stendhal's mind between the Grand-Saint-Bernard and N., perhaps as a result of David's painting of 1801, yet stressing N.'s absence from this episode; J. Garnier, 'L'historiographie militaire de la bataille de Waterloo et son influence sur Stendhal et Hugo' (291–302), comparing the Waterloo episodes in *La Chartreuse de Parme* and in *Les Misérables* with the historical data available, and showing how S. and H. exploited it. The remaining papers are not relevant to our period.

La Vie romantique. Hommage à Loïc Chotard, ed. André Guyaux and Sophie Marchal, Univ. Paris-Sorbonne, 592 pp., contains the proceedings of a conference held in June 2000 in memory of the young expert on Romanticism who died an untimely death. It includes: S. Basch, 'Le cirque en 1879: les Hanlon-Lees dans la littérature' (7–36), mainly concerned with the later years of the century, but showing how far the development of pantomime and music hall was prepared by innovations before 1850; P. Berthier, 'Henri de Marsay: le Rolla balzacien' (37–47), observing the similarities between the character in *La Fille aux yeux d'or* and the one in Musset's poem, though finding that de Marsay is different on account of the rôle which Balzac intends for him, and the two probably derive from a common Romantic conception; T. Bodin, 'Vigny et les *Affaires de la Chancellerie*' (49–71), presenting a number of documents which Chotard had brought to light concerning Lydia Bunbury's inheritance, and which give a refreshing view of the poet's thinking; F. P. Bowman, 'Les caractères du romantisme français' (73–91), giving an overview of the distinctive features of French Romanticism, by comparison with that in other countries; M. Brix, 'Mal du siècle et bovarysme' (93–106), tracing the origins of Bovarysme back to the beginning of the century, though showing that the phenomenon was current long before Flaubert's novel; C. Bustarret, 'Dix autoportraits pour un anniversaire' (107–41), comparing a drawing by Chotard with a number of drawings by writers of our period; B. Chenique, 'Géricault dandy: stratégies de résistance' (143–68), measuring G. against a set of criteria to determine whether he was a dandy, and thereby giving insights into his personality; A. Compagnon, 'Nerval à la chasse' (169–77), concerned with a hunting metaphor in *Les Filles du feu*; B. Daniels, 'La Venise de Vigny: du *More* au *Marchand*' (179–89), showing how the translations of Shakespeare served to develop V.'s dramatic art and to provide him with useful contacts among actors; H. Dufour, 'Portraits du prochain siècle: un recueil de portraits littéraires en 1894' (191–204), showing that the idea of the collection owed something to Sainte-Beuve, though the procedure involved was somewhat different; C. Gaviglio-Faivre d'Arcier, 'À la recherche d'une collection perdue. La bibliothèque musicale de Lovenjoul' (205–20), reminding us of L.'s other interest and the mention in his will of a music library, which now seems to have been lost, though initial research into its existence produces promising results; S. Guégan, ' "Un nid de vipères": Girodet, Stendhal et Guizot au Salon de 1810' (221–37), on the impact of Girodet's *La Révolte de Caire* on a number of writers and artists; A. Guyaux, 'La "pâleur verte" du lendemain' (239–47), giving a panorama of Romantic images of morning light; J.-M. Hovasse, 'Les poèmes de Victor Hugo dans la

Revue des deux mondes (1831–1865)' (249–75), on the seven poems and two articles published therein and the reasons why they were so published; G. Iotti, 'Les métamorphoses de Triboulet' (277–91), a study of the dramatic function of the central character of *Le Roi s'amuse*; A. Jarry, 'En marge du romantisme: les frères Challamel' (293–308), on the brothers Pierre-Joseph and Augustin C., the one an innovative publisher, the other an innovative historian; H. Lacombe, 'Georges Bizet et Victor Hugo: histoire d'une admiration' (309–19), showing that B. found H. to be an important source of inspiration, and noting his efforts to set the poetry to music; F. Lestringant, 'Manon, Murger, Musset: pour une généalogie de la grisette' (321–35), showing how the treatment of the theme of the lady of easy virtue was passed from the abbé Prévost to Henry Murger by way of Musset; S. Marchal, 'Victor Hugo et Jacques Ancelot, de la scène dramatique à l'Académie' (337–61), an account of the friendship and subsequent antagonism between the two; A. Michel, 'Balzac et la vie de bohème' (363–71), suggesting that B. was more attuned to the dangers of the bohemian lifestyle than to its delights; M.-R. Morin, 'Lamartine à cheval' (373–88), on the horses in L.'s life and what he wrote about them; S. Moussa, 'Julia dans *Le Voyage en Orient* de Lamartine' (389–97), showing that L.'s descriptions of his daughter and the account of her death are used for essentially literary purposes; C. Peltre, 'Théodore Chassériau et "les poètes de ces derniers temps"' (399–408), on the painter's declared interest in poetry; R. Pierrot, 'Autour d'Ève de Balzac et des Rzewuski' (409–18), identifying further links between Balzac's family and that of his wife; N. Preiss, 'Au fond, tout au fond de la *Correspondance* d'Alfred de Vigny' (417–18), on the valuable resources of the Archives Sangnier; L. Sabourin, 'Les illustrateurs d'*Éloa*' (419–36), explaining artists' interest in the poem and the value of their illustrations; E. Sala, 'Romantisme populaire et musique: autour d'une chanson savoyarde' (437–53), on the fashion for Savoyard songs; J. Seebacher, 'Narquoiseries de Gobineau' (455–60), celebrating the contribution to work on G. by Jean Gaulmier and by Chotard; J. Thélot, '"*Le Phénomène futur* est une photographie"' (461–74), on Mallarmé's prose poem; P. Toffano, 'À propos d'un procédé de style commun à Chateaubriand et à Proust' (475–82), showing that the similarities of style go beyond *mémoire involontaire* towards a re-ordering of information to correspond with perceptions; P. Tortonese, 'Baudelaire et la *philosophaillerie moderne*' (483–522), on B.'s reaction to the ideas of Gautier and Victor Cousin; F. Wilhem, 'La Vénus d'Ille: une fantaisie de meurtre' (539–54), on the biographical background to the novel; B. Wright, 'Le héros romantique et la Franche-Comté: Julien Sorel et Gustave

Courbet' (555–63), showing how closely the two correspond to the archetype of the Romantic hero.

Écrire la peinture entre XVIIIe et XIXe siècles, ed. Pascale Auraix-Jonchière, Clermont-Ferrand, Univ. Blaise Pascal, 492 pp., contains the proceedings of a conference held by the Centre de Recherches Révolutionnaires et Romantiques at the Université Blaise Pascal in October 2001. It covers a rather broader field than the French literature of our period, and there are papers relevant to the 18th c., to German Romanticism, to the later 19th c. and to the history of art. The following are included: A. Lascar, 'Eugène Sue romancier: la tentation picturale' (187–202), showing that S.'s realism was clearly inspired, though at a certain distance, by paintings; P. Berthier, 'Balzac portraitiste: position picturale du problème' (231–40), observing that B.'s use of painting is less a matter of ekphrasis than an appeal to the reader's ability to create images; M. Brix, 'Frenhofer et les chefs-d'œuvre qui restent inconnus' (241–52), suggesting that *Le Chef-d'œuvre inconnu* prefigured the æsthetics of Mallarmé, also a major preoccupation of 20th-c. art; L. Giraud, 'Stendhal, biographe de Léonard de Vinci' (253–64), showing that the *Histoire de la peinture en Italie* follows a particular biographical methodology which S. had developed; N. Wanlin, 'Esthétique picturale et nostalgie: la disparition de la peinture dans *Gaspard de la Nuit* d'Aloysius Bertrand' (295–310), exploring the links between visual imagery and an interest in the Middle Ages by means of the painters and paintings mentioned; T. Antolini-Dumas, 'Paradoxes et subjectivité: l'itinéraire pictural de Quinet et Custine en Espagne' (311–22), on the different perspectives of Spanish painting in C.'s *L'Espagne sous Ferdinand VII* and Q.'s *Mes vacances en Espagne*; N. Surlapierre, 'Le système du réel et les stratégies de l'égotisme dans *Du principe de l'art et de sa destination sociale* de Pierre-Joseph Proudhon' (323–40), on a work which is a combination of different genres linking the history of art and the history of ideas; M. Giné-Janer, 'Discours et peinture dans *Les Âmes du Purgatoire* de Mérimée' (341–53), suggesting that the novella is based on an imaginary picture; C. Matossian, 'Michelet et Géricault: l'agencement du monde' (417–31), giving particular attention to M.'s lecture of 12 February 1846 at the Collège de France; P. Auraix-Jonchère, 'Ekphrasis et mythologie dans *La Toison d'or* de Théophile Gautier (1839): la Madeleine prétexte' (451–63), exploring the combination of different approaches to reality found in the work.

2. Consulate Writers

CHATEAUBRIAND. P. Antoine, 'Chateaubriand en Égypte: le voyageur désenchanté', *Romantisme*, 120:27–35, shows that, although

C. visited Egypt, what he wrote about the country was more heavily influenced by his preconceived ideas and his imagination than by the, sometimes conflicting, reality which he encountered there. Jean-Paul Clément, *Chateaubriand, 'Des illusions contre des souvenirs'*, Gallimard, 160 pp., is an attractive, well illustrated, and informative introduction which gives a clear perspective of C.'s literary merits. Pierre H. Dubé, *Nouvelle bibliographie refondue et augmentée de la critique sur François-René de Chateaubriand*, Champion, 2002, 885 pp., is an essential tool for those working on C. and the 6019 entries are admirably indexed. Marc Fumaroli, *Chateaubriand, poésie et terreur*, Fallois, 800 pp., sets out to be rather more than a biography, taking as its main focus the slow development of the *Mémoires d'outre-tombe* over the course of nearly half a century. Chapters are devoted to those who influenced C. and/or with whom he came into personal contact, including Ballanche, Pauline de Beaumont, Byron, Joseph Conrad, Fontanes, Milton, Mirabeau, Napoleon, the abbé Raynal, Mme Récamier, Richelieu, Rousseau, Talleyrand, and Tocqueville. Emmanuelle Tabet, *Chateaubriand et le XVIIe siècle, mémoire et création littéraire*, Champion, 2002, 461 pp., is an analysis of C.'s deep interest in the 17th c., particularly evident at the beginning of *Le Génie du christianisme* though present throughout his work, up to and including *La Vie de Rancé*. Tabet takes us beyond C.'s personal predilections to suggest a re-examination of the influence of 17th-c. literature on that of the 19th c., with a reassessment of certain salient features of Romanticism as part of a surviving Augustinian literary tradition. *Écrits politiques (1814–1816)*, ed. Colin Smethurst, Geneva, Droz, 2002, 586 pp., presents all of C.'s political writing during a period of three years which saw the fall of Napoleon, the first Restoration, the Hundred Days, Waterloo, and the second Restoration. This is a sound critical edition of that part of C.'s work which has tended to be forgotten, including newspaper articles and speeches, and is of considerable value for those who seek to understand both the period and the author's political thinking at that time.

MME DE STAËL. E. Gretchania, 'Madame de Staël. Lettres inédites à Fernand Christian', *RHLF*, 103:933–41, presents the text of four previously unpublished letters, written in 1803 and 1808, and preserved in Moscow. F. Lotterie, 'Une revanche de la "femme-auteur"? Madame de Staël disciple de Rousseau', *Romantisme*, 122:19–31, finds that although S. admired R. and used his manner of writing as a model, she was not a disciple in the conventional sense, concentrating on developing her own originality. Claire Garry-Boussel, *Statut et fonction du personnage masculin chez Madame de Staël*, Champion, 2002, 447 pp., is a thorough analysis of the role of male characters in S.'s work, beginning with a typological classification before moving on to an investigation of the triangular equilibrium between husbands, fathers, and lovers in her writing. Attention is given to what is termed the virtual hero and his eventual fall into disgrace. The conclusion stresses the relative vigour of the men who are portrayed, and the significant importance of Jacques Necker as a model. Brunhilde Wehinger, *Conversation um 1800, Salonkultur und literarische Autorschaft bei Germaine de Staël*, Berlin, Walter Frey, 2002, 259 pp., takes S. as the central figure in a discussion of the political and literary importance of conversation at the end of the 18th and the beginning of the 19th centuries. Particular attention is given to the exchanges which were made possible by her salons, also to the changing role of the author.

3. Poetry

BRIZEUX. H. Williams, 'Writing to Paris: poets, nobles and savages in nineteenth-century Brittany', *FS*, 57:475–90, identifies B.'s *Marie* as an important landmark in the development of Breton writing of French expression, showing the significance of his decision to write in French and the importance of his contribution to the bridging of the cultural gulf between Brittany and Paris.

GAY DE GIRARDIN. Madeleine Lassère, *Delphine de Girardin, journaliste et femme de lettres au temps du romantisme*, Perrin, 345 pp., is a biography which lays due emphasis on G.'s writing, with numerous extracts inviting the reader to give further attention to both her poetry and her prose, yet which also gives a detailed account of her complex network of friendships with the writers of the time.

HUGO. A. Ben-Amos, 'Victor Hugo et les enterrements civils', *Romantisme*, 119:21–33, places the poem written for *La Légende des siècles* in 1875 within the context of the funerals H. attended around that time, including those of his sons, and notes the clear allusion to his own future death. E. Pich, '"Zim-Zizimi": la singularité du progrès hugolien', *SFr*, 47:250–58, is an appreciation of the poem. A. Spiquel, 'Épopée, lyrisme et coup d'état: Hugo en 1877', *ib.*, 259–66, is an evaluation of the works of that year. F. Lestringant, '"L'Archipel de la Manche" ou l'insulaire de Hugo', *ib.*, 267–74, considers H.'s work during exile. C. Rétat, 'Hugo et les pierres vivantes', *ib.*, 275–83, is concerned with H.'s references to *William Shakespeare* in later poetry and prose. R. Vignest, 'L'intertextualité latine dans la première série de *La Légende des siècles*', *ib.*, 284–301, explains a number of references by way of Latin verse. L. Sabourin, 'Victor Hugo et Alfred de Vigny', *ib.*, 302–15, is concerned with their early friendship and its impact upon H.'s later work. J.-P. Pouget, 'L'amitié de deux géants: Victor Hugo et Alexandre Dumas père', *ib.*,

316–29, shows the importance of their friendship and the evidence that may be found of it in H.'s writing. A. Poli, 'Victor Hugo e George Sand', *ib.*, 330–52, examines the evidence relating to S.'s appreciation of H.'s achievements. C. Rizza, 'Théophile Gautier: un vieux d'*Hernani*', *ib.*, 353–59, shows the significance of the relationship between the two. M. Richter, 'Hugo nelle *Fleurs du Mal*', *ib.*, 360–77, measures the influence of H. on Baudelaire. J. Viard, 'Pierre Leroux et Victor Hugo', *ib.*, 378–92, gives an account of the contact between the two at the Assemblée, in London, and on Jersey, finding that whereas Sand and Michelet acknowledged their debt to L., H. was inclined to make use of his ideas and writings without attribution. L. Sozzi, 'Le poesie di Hugo in Italia: opinioni, traduzioni, imitazioni', *ib.* 401–10, considers and compares Italian translations and adaptations of H.'s poems.

Victor Hugo (2003–1802). Images et transfigurations, ed. Maxime Prévost and Yan Hamel, Quebec, Fides, 190 pp., contains the proceedings of the 'Imago Hugolis' conference organized by the Montréal Collège de Sociocritique. As the title suggests, the papers are concerned not so much with H.'s work as with the treatment of it. They include: P. Popovic, 'La médiation des tragédiennes: Marie Dorval' (15–28), a fictional dialogue between H. and Pierre Bourdieu; M. Prévost, 'Les mystères de Jersey. Représentations de Hugo en spirite' (29–41), on the 'tables tournantes'; M. Condé, 'Pour Esmeralda: *Notre-Dame de Paris* au cinéma' (43–60), explaining the success of films of the novel, though noting that some adaptation of the story is necessary; P. Brissette, '*Victus sed Victor*: notes sur les photographies de l'exil' (61–76), suggesting that in these photographs, H. finally managed to achieve the public image he had been seeking; B. Melançon, 'Ceci tuer@ cel@' (77–87), on the presence of H. on the internet; I. Daunais, 'Hugo dirait: "J'étais plus près de Dieu que de l'humanité"' (91–106), on Flaubert's admiration for H. and his meeting with him in 1843; M. Cambron, 'Victor Hugo au Québec' (107–38), on the reception of his work and his influence on Québecois writers; M. Angenot, 'Léon Daudet sur Victor Hugo: chose vue' (139–50), on D.'s connections with H.'s grandchildren, through friendship and also through marriage; E. Méchoulan, 'Café au lait avec vinaigre et moutarde: passages de Victor Hugo chez Walter Benjamin' (151–62), on the importance of the figure of H. in B.'s last work; B. Denis, 'Le cabotin sublime et les pisse-froid: Sartre, Hugo et la modernité' (163–74), comparing the concept of engagement in the life and work of the two writers; G. Marcotte, 'D'un Victor l'autre' (175–85), on Victor-Lévy Beaulieu's admiration for H.'s writing.

LAMARTINE. G. Banderier, 'Sur un poème de Lamartine, "À une jeune voyageuse en Suisse"', *FSB*, 88: 6–9, compares the Saint-Point and the Fatio manuscripts, showing that, though the latter is accompanied by the note "bonne version", it is probably a first draft which was extensively reworked.

MUSSET. G. Castagnès, 'Alfred de Musset, ou l'univers de la discontinuité', *NCFS*, 32:9–22, seeks to explain the fragmented, unfinished, discontinuous aspects of M.'s writing as a representation of his æsthetic principles.

4. The Novel

J. Best, 'Quel horizon l'on voit du haut de la barricade', *NCFS*, 31:237–53, compares the representation of the barricade in novels by Dumas, Flaubert, and Hugo, and in paintings by Delacroix and Manet. R. Little, 'The first novels of Hugo and George Sand: a link', *FSB*, 86:7–8, finds similarities between the openings of *Bug-Jargal* and *Indiana* which appear to imply that S. had read the original version of H.'s novel. A. Lascar, 'Le régicide dans le roman français (1824–1853)', *Romantisme*, 119:21–33, begins with Lamothe-Langon's *Le 21 janvier* of 1825, and finds that the death of Louis XVI became a potent image which was used by novelists with increasing frequency, to serve a variety of different purposes. Linda M. Lewis, *Germaine de Staël, George Sand and the Victorian Woman Artist*, Columbia–London, Missouri U.P., xiii + 278 pp., begins with a comparison of the treatment of the questions of female art and female creativity in Corinne and Consuelo, before demonstrating the very considerable impact of their work and their status on a number of Victorian women writers. Arielle Meyer, *Le Spectacle du secret*, Geneva, Droz, 261 pp., compares and contrasts Gautier's *Mademoiselle de Maupin*, Stendhal's *Armance*, Barbey D'Aurevilly's *Les Diaboliques*, and various novels by Zola. All are shown to display the transposition into the 19th-c. novel of a theatrical motif elaborated by Marivaux.

BALZAC. D. Knight, 'Skeletons in the closet: homosocial secrets in Balzac's *La Comédie humaine*', *FS*, 57:167–80, concentrates on B.'s habit of hiding narrative secrets in literal closets, thereby making them more amenable to discovery by accidental or deliberate acts of spying and eavesdropping, and shows how he makes use of a heterosexual convention of stage farce in *La Cousine Bette* in order to reveal its homosocial basis. Rastignac is then followed through *La Maison Nucingen*, *Le Père Goriot*, and *Splendeurs et misères des courtisanes* in an exploration of the epistemology of the closet. J. W. Mileham, 'Desert, desire, *dezesperance*: space and play in Balzac's *La Duchesse de Langeais*', *NCFS*, 31:210–25, examines the novella's principal metaphor of movement through space. C. Rifeli, 'The language of hair in the nineteenth-century novel', *ib.*, 32:83–96, begins with B.'s *Honorine* and *La Peau de chagrin*, before moving on to Flaubert, Maupassant, and Zola.

ABa, 3.3, contains: C. Gaviglio-Faivre d'Arcier, 'Le vicomte de Lovenjoul de la bibliographie à la génétique' (7–25), on the considerable contribution of L. to B. studies in particular, though he also gave attention to Gautier, Nerval, and Sand, his close attention to bibliographical detail providing a basis for the study of the origins of the novels; S. Vachon, 'Notes sur la constitution des dossiers balzaciens conservés dans le fonds Lovenjoul de la bibliothèque de l'Institut' (27–56), on the organization of the manuscripts in the collection, including a list of those sent for binding by Georges Vicaire in 1910–11; R. Pierrot, 'Les enseignements du "Furne corrigé" revisités' (57–71), returning to the ground covered in the article first published in *ABa* in 1965 and giving further attention to the reshaping of *La Comédie humaine* which B. planned and partially executed during the last seven years of his life; S. Le Men, 'La "littérature panoramique" dans la genèse de *La Comédie humaine*: Balzac et *Les Français peints par eux-mêmes*' (73–100), showing that the concept of the illustrated book or serial, fashionable during the Romantic period, influenced the formulation of the idea of *La Comédie*; M. Lichtlé, 'Balzac et l'affaire Peytel: l'invention d'un plaidoyer' (101–65), an account of B.'s response to the case of a lawyer from Belley who was accused of murdering his wife and his servant; G. Séginger, 'De *La Fleur des pois* au *Contrat de mariage*: poétique et politique d'une dramatisation' (167–80), showing how B. revised the first version of the story, adding to its intensity by dramatically concentrating the events into a shorter period; M. Labouret, '"Fabriquer le temps" à rebours: problèmes romanesques et mécanismes reparaissants dans La Torpille' (181–203), evaluating the story of 1838 as a model for a future work involving Lucien de Rubempré, which became *Un Grand Homme de province à Paris*; M. Andréoli, 'Une mosaïque balzacienne: l'exposé du pasteur Becker' (205–26), on a passage from the third chapter of *Séraphîta* and the evolution of its stylistic construction; M. Tilby, 'Autour du *Dernier Chouan*: Balzac et Latouche lecteurs de *Connal, ou les Milésiens*, de Maturin' (229–68), noting the influence of French translations of works by the Irish novelist; C. Smethurst, 'Je Java à Kiew: le moi du voyageur' (269–78), on the influence of Sterne's *Sentimental Journey* and other travel writings on *Une Heure de ma vie* of 1822, *Le Voyage de Paris à Java* of 1831–32, and the *Lettre sur Kiew* of 1847; A. Vanoncini, 'Le pacte: structures et évolutions d'un motif balzacien' (279–92), approaching the difficulty of reconciling thematic, structural, intertextual, and transtextual interpretations through a reading of *Melmoth reconcilié*; P. Berthier, 'Michel Chrestien et la morale républicaine'

(293–314), on the evolution of the character between *Illusions perdues, Un Grand Homme de province à Paris*, and *Les Secrets de la princesse de Cadignan*; B. Méra, 'À propos d'un éventail' (315–26), on the development of the idea behind the provisional chapter heading of *Le Cousin Pons*, based on the image of a fan painted by Watteau, and its connection with B.'s ideas on the representation of reality; V. Monteilhet, 'Les adaptations balzaciennes sous l'Occupation: un cinéma de collaboration ou de résistance' (327–47), concluding that the political alignment of the films based on B.'s novels which were produced during the Occupation is necessarily ambiguous.

Penser avec Balzac, ed. José-Luis Diaz and Isabelle Tournier, Saint-Cyr-sur-Loire, Pirot, 352 pp., contains the proceedings of the conference of the Groupe international de recherches balzaciennes held at Cérisy-la-Salle in June 2000 to mark the bicentenary of B.'s birth and the 150th anniversary of his death. It includes: J.-L. Diaz, 'Penser avec Balzac' (5–10), introducing the two linked themes, 'Balzac pensant' and 'En pensant Balzac', considering B. both as a thinker and as a provoker of thought; J.-P. Courtois, 'Balzac et les Lumières: une lisibilité réciproque' (19–33), a study of the philosophical writings which B. produced during his youth, the 18th-c. sources of his thought, and the later representation of these ideas in *Louis Lambert*; J.-L. Diaz, 'Penser la pensée' (35–49), on B.'s early development of a poetic epistemology which sought to analyse intellectual procedures, while remaining wary of the potential perversity of thought; N. Mozet, 'Balzac, le XIXe siècle et la religion' (51–58), taking Freud as a starting point and placing B. half way between the dogmas which he no longer supported and the theories which had not yet been formulated; O. Heathcote, '"Les deux sexes at autres . . ."' (59–69), showing how B. uncoupled sexuality from biology and associated it with vulnerability, memory, and traumatism, prefiguring the attitudes of our present time; A.-M. Baron, 'L'homme miroir' (71–81), which finds that B. had foreseen almost all psychoanalytical concepts, and demonstrates a clear resemblance between his ideas and Lacanian principles; J. Guichardet, 'Penser/voir avec Balzac: le Paris d'hier et d'aujourd'hui' (83–94), dealing with B.'s interest in the past, as an observer of society at a time when the capital was undergoing considerable expansion; A. Oliver, 'Penser le roman: *Albert Savarus* ou le roman comme transgression' (95–106), beginning with the observation that the idea that the text reflects the relationship with Mme Hanska in 1842 has prevented critics from appreciating the true value of its complex narrative situation and structure, its portrayal of social history, and its moral vision, which make it worthy of consideration as one of his best novels; A. Vaillant, '"Cet X est la Parole": la littérature, ou la science mathématique de l'homme' (107–21), examining the various theories which have been applied to explaining B.'s work, and concluding that only a recognition of the miraculous power of literary creation within B.'s metaphysical system, in effect an early form of 'l'art pour l'art', is suitable for the task; B. Lyon-Caen, 'Balzac ventriloque: une ontologie à l'épreuve du romanesque' (123–28), finding that the way that B. puts ontology to the test through the intermediary of the novel simultaneously changes and subverts it; J.-D. Ebguy, 'Balzac ou "L'autre modernité": le Balzac des philosophes' (129–41), showing that B.'s new kind of writing was able to respond to previous philosophical discourse, and the response to it by later philosophers such as Deleuze, Rancière, and Serres; S. Pietri, 'Crise de l'expérience et crise du conteur: Balzac, Hofmannsthal, Benjamin' (143–51), comparing B.'s appreciation of cultural change in 1831 with that of H. in 1902 and of Benjamin in 1936; F. Schuerewegen, 'Histoire d'un groupe (ou de l'art de bien vieillir en milieu balzacien' (155–64), tracing the history of the Groupe international de recherches balzaciennes from 1979, observing that the plural nature of B.'s work causes us constantly to revise our assessment of him, yet no doubt this was entirely his intention; F. de Chalonge, 'Repenser la poétique avec Balzac' (165–97), reviewing B. studies from the 1960s onwards in response to structuralism, seeking to discover when and why poetics became a fashionable source of new readings of his work, and including interesting data from the index of *Poétique*; P. Laforgue, 'Balzac sociocritique' (199–209), identifying the origins of this approach in Pierre Barberis's *Balzac et le mal du siècle* and Claude Duchet's article in the first edition of *Littérature*, and tracing its history from 1970 to the present; A. del Lungo, 'Balzac postpostmoderne: l'œuvre-miroir, l'œuvre-réseau, l'hyper-roman' (213–34), describing postmodernist readings of B. and indicating some lines of enquiry which are liable to lead to a dead end, for B. is by no means a precursor of postmodernism, though he demonstrates a certain modernity; E. Cullmann, 'Balzac online' (225–32), reviewing material on the internet; A. Péraud, 'Penser Balzac avec l'hypertexte et/ou penser l'hypertexte avec Balzac' (233–41), on the opportunities for new readings which are offered by information technology, and suggesting that CD-ROM may be a more effective medium than paper; C. Planté, 'Balzac penseur du genre' (245–55), giving particular attention to *Une fille d'Ève*, which reveals B.'s awareness of new developments in the relationships between men and women; C. Nesci, 'Speculum de l'autre siècle: réflexions sur le "genre" chez Balzac' (257–65), considering three American readings of *La Fille aux yeux d'or* before concluding that B.'s concept of gender is based on his appreciation of social change and the new position of women in society; V. Bui, 'De "il" à "elle": Balzac penseur du féminin dans *La Femme de trente ans*' (267–74), a study of the novel's consideration of gender issues; T. Kamada, 'Dynamique du sujet écrivant: enjeux de la génétique balzacienne' (277–83), on the essential paradox of the writer, who is supposed to be in charge of his writing, becoming increasingly governed by it, and how an understanding of this can lead to a better understanding of his work; C. Couleau, 'Balzac au miroir de son œuvre: sur la notion de l'auteur induit' (285–92), showing how far the mirror of B.'s fiction can distort reality; C. Barel-Moisan and Aude Déruelle, 'Balzac et la pragmatique: narration et lois du discours' (293–310), demonstrating the value of applying pragmatics to B.'s work, not least the tools of classical rhetoric, which highlight the dialectical opposition between speech and writing; I.-Y. Kim, 'L'ombre du public' (311–21), examining the reception of B.'s writing in 1829, 1830, 1836, and 1844, giving particular attention to *Le Médecin de campagne*, *La Femme supérieure* which was to become *Les Employés*, and *Les Paysans*; A. Mura, 'Balzac relu, réécrit, repensé dans le roman contemporain' (323–37), showing how the public image of B. has changed to the extent that Patrick Rambaud was able to write *La Bataille*, yet B.'s thinking remains at the core of contemporary fiction; I. Tournier, 'Post-face(s)' (339–48), an epilogue drawing attention to the many facets of B.'s writing and inviting the continuation of further study.

Ironies balzaciennes, ed. Éric Bordas, Saint-Cyr-sur-Loire, Pirot, 283 pp., contains the proceedings of a conference held at the Maison Balzac in June 2002. It includes: M. de Gandt, 'Ironies romantiques dans les années 1830' (17–29), a summary of the different types of irony to be found in the works of those years and the misunderstandings which have become attached to Romantic irony; P. Laforgue, 'Ironie et athéisme, ou matérialisme, esprit et calembours dans *Ursule Mirouet*' (31–40), suggesting a reading of the novel which analyses humorous techniques in the light of the convergence of critical discourse in the literature of 1830–40; A. Déruelle, 'Ironies et réalismes: le cas du récit balzacien' (41–53), examining the interplay between realism and the subversion of irony in B.'s narrative; J. David, 'Le jeu sérieux de l'ironie profonde' (55–73), showing that an ironic perspective can be revelatory, as in *La Maison du chat-qui-pelote*, or analytical, as in *La Physiologie du mariage*; P. Schœntjes, 'Valeurs de l'ironie chez Balzac' (75–101), finding that B. uses deep irony as a moralist's tool; B. Lyon-Caen, 'L'usage de la valeur: critique de la raison "panoramique"' (103–19), a study of *Les Français peints par eux-mêmes* and other texts, showing that B.'s distinctive irony is both a form of defence against the dangers he perceived in the social and political changes of the period, and an innovation; A.-M. Paillet-Gruth, 'Ironie et évaluation chez Balzac' (123–42), examining the evaluative scale of B.'s critical discourse; R. Amossy, 'Fonctions argumentatives de l'ironie balzacienne' (143–54), considering the insertion of ironic analyses into B.'s narrative as a means to pursue an argument with polyphonic effect; J. Dürrenmatt, 'Suspensions ironiques' (155–68), analysing rhythm and changes of tempo in B.'s prose; P. Hamon, 'Balzac, écrivain calembourgeois' (169–94), examining the use of *calembours* and other forms of word play as part of a strategy for the representation of reality; A.-M. Baron, 'L'auto-ironie balzacienne avant *La Comédie humaine*: de la *Correspondance* à la *Physiologie du mariage*' (195–204), showing that B.'s ability to make fun of himself is more evident in his letters and early novels than in *La Comédie*; C. Couleau, 'L'ironie balzacienne ou le roman au second degré' (207–23), stressing the thoughtful nature of B.'s novels and the way that they present an outline of available modes of critical response; G. Bonnet, 'Illusions perdues, ironies romanesques' (225–35), showing the importance of the satirical links between irony and the ridiculous; A. Péraud, 'L'ironie textuelle balzacienne ou l'art de composer avec le réel' (237–58), showing that, conversely, irony is also strongly linked to the sublime, rather than standing in opposition to it; J.-D. Ebguy, 'Un "raisonné dérèglement de tous les sens": ce que l'ironie fait à l'histoire' (260–79), concluding that B.'s irony is an integral part of his critical and moral stance as a novelist.

Régine Borderie, *Balzac peintre de corps*, SEDES, 2002, 243 pp., is a detailed analysis of representations of the body in the numerous portraits of *La Comédie humaine*. It explains B.'s interest in physiognomy and compares his approach with that of his predecessors and with other major 19th-c. writers. His portraits are shown to be a response to the complexity of society and the changes taking place in it at that time, be they social, æsthetic, philosophical, or narratological. Bettina Licht, *Balzac, Leben und Werk des Romanciers*, Mainz, Kostheim, 2002, 116 pp., is a short biography with an overview of his work and a summary of key novels. Michæl Lucey, *The Misfit of the Family: Balzac and the Social Forms of Sexuality*, Durham–London, Duke U.P., 310 pp., acknowledges the influence of Pierre Bourdieu, and begins with forms of misfit that manifest themselves as failures of reproduction, before turning to those which involve specifically same-sex relations of various kinds. Pierre Glaudes, *La Peau de chagrin d'Honoré de Balzac*, Gallimard, 257 pp., is a valuable introduction for those who are reading the text for the first time and a useful guide for those who are familiar with it. The essay and dossier are balanced and informative, leading the reader to a clear critical perspective.

DUMAS. Bernard Blancotte, *Alexandre Dumas . . . Un mousquetaire de l'écriture*, Nîmes, Lacour, 82 pp., is a worthwhile brief introduction to D.'s life and work, marking his bicentenary and his reinterment in the Panthéon. Catherine Tœsca, *Les 7 Monte-Cristo de Alexandre Dumas*, Maisonneuve et Larose, 2002, 311 pp., is a biography which gives some indication of how far the novel tended to take over D.'s life. The structure is given by following the name from the port near to his father's birthplace, and then to the novel, before considering its seven further uses during his lifetime: for the chateau at Port Marly; the play; the periodical; the newspaper; the schooner; the Cuban cigar; the recipe.

HUGO. S. Luzzatto, 'La gaffe di Victor Hugo: il romanzo della Rivoluzione dai *Misérables* a *Quatre-vingt-treize*', *SFr*, 47:236–49, is concerned with reactions later in the century to H.'s work.

SAND. J. T. Booker, '*Indiana* and *Madame Bovary*: intertextual echoes', *NCFS*, 31:226–36, finds that, though there is no evidence that Flaubert had read S.'s novel, the two works seem to 'haunt' each other, and one may achieve a better perspective of both by reading them together. I. Hoog Naginski, 'George Sand: ni maîtres ni disciples', *Romantisme*, 122:43–53, takes S. as a case study in the examination of the master/disciple paradigm, giving attention to the correspondence with Flaubert and the way in which she changed Balzac's character Foedora into her Lélia.

Ville, campagne et nature dans l'œuvre de George Sand, ed. Simone Bernard-Griffiths, Clermont-Ferrand, Univ. Blaise Pascal, 2002, 270 pp., contains the proceeding of the conference held at the Centre de Recherches Révolutionnaires et Romantiques in November 2000. It includes: S. Bernard-Griffiths, 'Ville/campagne/nature: regards sur une dialectique récurrente dans l'œuvre sandienne' (11–15), introducing the topic and noting that S.'s writing is at its best when she not only covers each of the three environments but also elaborates links between them; J. Ehrard, 'La ville en France à la fin du XVIIIe siècle' (19–29), showing that, though the urban area only became an important phenomenon in the 19th c., its status underwent a profound change as the century progressed, and positive attitudes to that change derived mainly from 18th-c. writers; B. Hamon, 'George Sand de réconcilier villes et campagnes (mars-juin 1848)' (31–44), on S.'s contribution to the work of the Provisional Government of 1848, and how this led her to change her thinking, rejecting the cause of the urban worker in favour of that of the rural peasant; M. Vanderkerkhove-Caors, 'De La Châtre aux Couperies, itinéraire romanesque et pèlerinage intime' (45–57), on the representation in a number of works, spanning the whole of S.'s literary career, of the small town nearest to Nohant, and of a particular part of the surrounding countryside; H. Bonnet, 'La mythologie sandienne du village dans les *Promenades*' (59–73), identifying Gargilesse as the village, other than Nohant, which featured in her work; C. Planté, 'Oublier Clarens?

(sur *Monsieur Sylvestre* et *Le Dernier Amour*)' (75–89), identifying a common feature of the two novels in the concept of the countryside as a place where a character may seek to recover after a personal crisis; J. Guichardet, 'La présence de Paris dans *Horace*: George Sand dans le sillage balzacien' (91–104), showing that the only novel which has Paris as its sole setting is not so much a reflection of the influence of Balzac as a manifestation of S.'s childhood memories and her feeling that the capital was a place of freedom; S. Bernard-Griffiths, 'Ville, nature et campagne dans *André* (1835) de George Sand' (107–33), finding that the novel plays on the virtual relationships between the three terms, by means of antithesis, synthesis, and inversion; P. Berthier, '*Lettres d'un voyageur*: le cru et le cuit' (135–47), considering the 12 letters in relation to the distance between nature and culture, and finding that they show S. successfully mediating between the two; G. Chalaye, 'La dialectique ville/nature dans *Consuelo* et *La Comtesse de Rudolstadt* de George Sand' (149–65), examining the relative importance of town and country in the two novels, and concluding that S.'s particular virtue is in going beyond the antagonism between nature and culture, and in developing the idea of cultural freedom; A. M. Rea, 'Babylone et Éden: ville et nature dans *Isidora*' (167–81), showing the novel of 1845–46 to represent a transition between the masculine city of the past and the Utopian city of the future, governed by liberated women; L. Giraud, 'Ville et nature, nature et culture dans Lucrezia Floriani' (183–96), considering S.'s views, as represented in the novel, on the natural environment as the ideal setting for a theatrical performance; D. A. Powell, 'La rapsodie de la nature et de la ville dans *La Filleule*' (197–206), on music and nature in the novel, concluding that perceptions of nature are often illusory; C. Grossir, 'Ville, nature et industrialisation dans *Le Péché de Monsieur Antoine* et *La Ville noire*' (207–20), on the only two of S.'s novels to represent the industrial world, the difference between the two, in their approach to the conflict between workers and peasants, being due, at least in part, to the events of 1848 which fell between them; S. Vierne, 'La nature, un refuge dans la ville' (221–35), showing that, when S. was unable to avoid the urban environment, she established in it points of refuge where she was able to regain contact with nature in order to write; N. Abdelaziz, 'Ville et nature: une morale structurelle du roman sandien?' (253–65), concluding that town and country were, for S., part of a moral framework, and that her novels were essentially concerned with moral development.

STENDHAL. Y. Ansel, 'Stendhal: ni Dieu ni maître', *Romantisme*, 122:33–42, seeks to explain the number of times that education is shown to fail, in *Henry Brulard* and the novels, as a reaction to the dominance which it implies. *AnS*, 2, begins with the proceedings of the conference, 'Paysage de Stendhal', held at the Sorbonne Nouvelle in September 2001: X. Bourdinet, '"Les laideurs de la civilisation"' (9–42), showing that S. was able to describe the ugly features of the 19th-c. world, as well as sublime landscapes, and that he was aware of the economics of tourism; F. Spandri, 'Paysages de l'odieux' (43–55), suggesting that S.'s ugly and unpleasant landscapes may be taken to reflect the imperfections of society, and to warn the reader of the dangers of social conflict; M. Marchetti, 'Paysages du sud' (57–73), on references to Naples in *Rome, Naples et Florence*, in the *Journal* and in the *Correspondance*; J.-J. Hamm, 'La chasse dans l'univers stendhalien' (75–88), a study of the motif of hunting and the light that it sheds on S.'s thought processes; S. Sérodes, 'Le lac de Côme ou l'autre naissance du sublime' (89–104), suggesting that S. invented the concept of lacustrian beauty, and worked to make it fashionable in novels; C. Mariette-Clot, 'Paysages silencieux et sublimes: l'obstacle de la description chez Stendhal' (105–14), on the manner of the description of landscape in S.'s travel writings, and his steadfast avoidance of the extremes of hyperbole and of banal realism; P. Jousset, 'La belle et la vilaine: la prose aux prises avec l'opiné' (115–35), on two passages from the *Mémoires d'un touriste*, which show to what extent S.'s literary sensibilities tended to lead him into a conflict between Beauty and Truth; G. Kliebenstein, 'Dysmimesis stendhalienne' (137–59), showing that S. is capable of transposing the reality of landscapes in two ways, either by simplifying their structure or through elaborating detail, involving change of location or anthropomorphism. The volume continues with articles considering the difficulties which S.'s texts present, and stressing the importance of their style in relation to classical models: F. Vanoosthuyse, 'Stendhal et le classicisme: le cas d'*Armance*'(161–77), exploring the classical influences which are visible in the novel; A. Hage, 'Crime et châtiment dans *Le Rouge et le Noir*' (179–209), examining various readings of the themes of crime and punishment, and suggesting that the story of Adrien Lafargue, as recounted in the *Promenades dans Rome*, is an important influence on the novel; S. Shimokawa, 'Stendhal et son penchant aristocratique: la nostalgie d'un monde à jamais révolu' (211–36), suggesting that S. was nostalgic for the old order of the Ancien Régime, that he considered himself to be an aristocrat, and that he associated the death of his mother with that of Marie Antoinette; B. Didier, 'Stendhal subtil interprète de La Fontaine' (237–43), showing the influence of the author of the *Fables* on S.'s life and work. It also includes: Y. Ansel, 'Météorologie romanesque' (245–68), on the changes which Romanticism brought about in the description of the weather, with analysis of meteorological conditions in *Armance*, *Le Rouge et le Noir*, *Lucien Leuwen*, *La Chartreuse*, and *Lamiel*, showing that though S. made use of the Romantic approach to weather, he avoided the imaginative interpretation, his more realistic approach depending on his theories concerning the climate; H. Mattauch, 'Stendhal et le préfet de la Saale' (271–85), including some unpublished letters; Y. Uchida, 'Un article de Stendhal dans *Le Globe*' (287–303), on the possible authorship of an article of the 27 January 1825; J.-J. Labia, '*Rome, Naples et Florence* (1826): les notes et variantes de l'exemplaire Filippi' (305–54), showing S.'s further thoughts on the text of 1817; J. Houbert, '"Courrier avait bien raison . . .": une citation non élucidée de Stendhal' (355–57), on a pamphlet produced by Paul-Louis Courier; Id., 'Contribution à l'histoire du stendhalisme' (359–67), concerning a work which was never published by Jean Carrère, who considered S. to be 'un mauvais maître'.

Brigitte Diaz, *Stendhal en sa correspondance ou 'L'Histoire d'un esprit'*, Champion, 460 pp., is a careful study of the importance of letter writing in S.'s life and work. The letters served many different purposes, but writing them was crucial to S.'s development as a writer. They give evidence of his inner thoughts and his intellectual development, as well as showing him to be involved in the exchange of ideas and critical debate, and they provide valuable information about the origins of the novels. Above all, it is shown that they helped him to become a great writer by providing him with experience of the production of text. Ann Jefferson, *La Chartreuse de Parme*, London, Grant and Cutler, 87 pp., is a useful and accessible introduction for students. Dorothée Kimmisch, *Wirklichkeit als Konstruktion, Studien zu geschichte und Geschichtlichkeit bei Heine, Büchner, Immermann, Stendhal, Keller und Flaubert*, Munich, Fink, 2002, 345 pp., includes two chapters on S., the first dealing with his ideological and historical construction of a social reality, the second with the poetics of his skill in using details to raise the level of his reader's awareness. *Concordances des Chroniques italiennes*, ed. Gregory Lassard and Jean-Jacques Hamm, 2 vols, Hildesheim–Zurich–NY, Olms-Weidmann, 2002, v + 492, 1042 pp., based on the Pléiade edition, is a valuable tool for the analysis of S.'s style, one of a series intended in due course to cover all of S.'s prose fiction.

SUE. Christopher Prendergast, *For the People by the People? Eugène Sue's Les Mystères de Paris*, Oxford, Legenda, 143 pp., examines the ways in which this novel not only became a major phenomenon of 19th-c. popular culture, but also played a significant role in constructing it. Careful attention is given to the reading public of S.'s time and to the influence of their reading habits and preferences upon the writing of the novel. In the conclusion, we are reminded that there is a difference between the perspective of the novel for S.'s readers and that of succeeding generations, though the merits of different views are effectively summarized.

5. Drama

Olga Płaszczewska, *Błazen i błazeństwo w dramacie romantycznym*, Kraków, Universitas, 2002, 157 pp., compares the portrayal and function of fools and jesters in Hugo's *Le Roi s'amuse*, *Marion de Lorme*, and *Cromwell*, and also in Musset's *Fantasio*, with that in translations and other works by Polish dramatists.

HUGO. F. Bruera, 'Victor Hugo sulla scena italiana del Novecento', *SFr*, 47: 393–400, gives an account of 20th-c. performances of H.'s plays on the Italian stage.

LABICHE. François Cavaignac, *Eugène Labiche ou la gaieté critique*, L'Harmattan, 261 pp., is an account of the life and work of the author of 174 plays, vaudevilles, farcical comedies, and burlesques, produced over the period 1837–78. We are shown the extent of L.'s interaction with, and commentary on, the society and institutions of his time. A significant dramatic innovation is shown in the introduction of sexuality into social interaction. L.'s moral ambiguity is carefully examined, and is judged to be a form of psychological realism.

MUSSET. Y. T. Beus, 'Alfred de Musset's Romantic irony', *NCFS*, 31: 197–209, gives particular attention to *Les Caprices de Marianne*, *On ne badine pas avec l'amour*, *Fantasio*, and *Lorenzaccio*, showing that M. frees the dramatist from the physical restraints of the theatre in order fully to express the self-reflexivity of Romantic irony.

6. Writers in other Genres

M.-L. Aurenche, 'Découvrir l'Égypte sans quitter Paris: l'itinéraire du *Magasin pittoresque à deux sous* (1833–70)', *Romantisme*, 120: 47–55, describes the creation of the illustrated journal by a group of Saint-Simonian republicans in March 1833 and introduces the 130 articles which it published on Egypt. *Voyager en France au temps du romantisme*, ed. Alain Guyot and Chantal Massol, ELLUG, 404 pp., takes Stendhal's *Mémoires d'un touriste* as a starting point for a survey of travel writing. It includes: A. Guyot, 'Présentation' (11–16); R. Le Huenen, 'Le voyage romantique: de la lecture à l'écriture' (19–34), tracing the progress of the genre from Volney to Flaubert; G. Bertrand, 'Aux sources du voyage romantique: le voyage patriotique dans la France des années 1760–1820' (35–53), suggesting that Romantic travel is a continuation of an aristocratic tradition; B. Louichon, 'Les enjeux du voyage en (nouvelle) France (1794–1814)' (55–70), based on articles in *La Décade philosophique* and

Le Mercure de France; M. T. Puleio, 'Voyage réel, voyage rêvé: les voyages "archéologiques" des petits romantiques' (71–90), with reference to Dumas, Gautier, Nerval, and Nodier; F. Wolfzettel, ' "Souvenirs d'un voyage . . .": esquisse d'une théorie du souvenir au temps du romantisme' (91–113), noting the stress laid on personal memory in Romantic travel writing; C. Montalbetti, 'Premières pages ou ces microscopiques *Voyages en France* qui s'écrivent à la condition de voyages plus lointains' (117–30), finding that the opening pages tend to grapple with the essential difficulties of the genre; P. Antoine, 'Une rhétorique de la spontanéité: le cas de la *Promenade*' (131–46), showing that stylistic freedom reflects freedom of movement; B. Monier, 'Voyager: la poétique de l'arabesque dans la littérature de voyage stendhalienne en France' (147–68), finding that the *Mémoires d'un touriste* follow the arabesque tradition; M. Braud, 'Le voyage en France de la comtesse Tarnowska' (169–80), on the travel journal of a Polish countess; O. Gannier, 'Des ruines aux monuments historiques: les notes de voyages de l'inspecteur Mérimée' (181–99), on documents connected with M.'s work as inspector-general of historic monuments; S. Moussa, 'Clichés et intertextualité dans *Un Tour en Belgique et en Hollande* de Gautier' (210–14), concentrating on the journey within French Flanders; G. Rannaud, 'Du pittoresque à l'égotisme: une poétique de l'ironie dans le récit de voyage' (215–40), a textual and intertextual study of Stendhal's *Mémoires d'un touriste*; C. W. Thompson, 'Alexandre Dumas et le paradigme du voyage romantique français (*Nouvelles impressions de voyage. Midi de la France*)' (241–51), comparing D.'s travel writing with that of other Romantics and revealing his significant contribution to the genre; F. Chenet-Faugeras, 'La lettre xx du *Rhin* ou le voyage à contre-pied' (253–66), dealing with the problem that Hugo's *Le Rhin* does not fit into any recognisable genre by suggesting that it is an ironic allusion to the travel genre; C. Meynard, 'Le *Tour de France* de Flora Tristan: aux antipodes du récit de voyage romantique?' (267–88), concluding that the work of 1844 is at the very limit of its genre in its use of a pamphleteering style; W. Guentner, 'Flaubert satiriste dans *Par les champs et par les grèves*' (289–308); M. Brix, 'Le Valois nervalien, ou la tentation orientale' (309–21), showing that Nerval associated the Valois with escapism; A. Déruelle, ' "L'Égypte, c'est tout sables." Balzac et le récit de voyage' (325–41), explaining the lack of travel writing by B. by the fact that it is subsumed in other kinds of text; L. Bonenfant, 'Aloysius Bertrand: la fantaisie de la promenade' (343–58), on *Gaspard de la nuit*; D. Méaux, 'La "Mission héliographique": entre inventaire et archéologie' (359–73), on the photographs of historic monuments taken in 1851; M. Viegnes, 'L'étrangeté dans le récit de voyage et le conte fantastique: l'exemple de Mérimée' (375–88), showing that M.'s association of travel with fantasy followed a long tradition; C. Massol, 'Conclusion' (389–95), explaining the emergence of a new genre of domestic travel writing in the late 18th and early 19th c. as a search for a national identity.

HUGO. *William Shakespeare*, ed. Dominique Peyrache-Leborgne, Flammarion, 600 pp., is a text which merits greater attention, not least as a defence of a relative approach to criticism and for the pages concerned with translation. It is admirably presented here, with informative notes and a dossier which sets the work in its broader context.

JOMARD. P. Bret, 'L'Égypte de Jomard: la construction d'un mythe orientaliste, de Bonaparte à Méhémet-Ali', *Romantisme*, 120:5–14, is concerned with the work of the main author of the *Description de l'Égypte*, who as a young surveyor had accompanied Bonaparte's expedition and who, in combining an utopian view of Ancient Egypt with a vision of its contemporary potential for modernization, is shown to have been partly responsible for the Romantic myth of the Orient.

LAMARTINE. *Autour de Lamartine: Journal de voyage, correspondances, témoignages, iconographie*, ed. Christian Croisille and Marie-Renée Morin, Clermont-Ferrand, Univ. Blaise Pascal, 2002, vii + 251 pp., though not specifically concerned with L.'s poetry, gives valuable insights into the poet's life. It contains five articles by M.-R. Morin: 'Correspondances autour du buste de Lamartine par le comte d'Orsay' (109–24), presenting the letters which were discovered in 1967 connected with the sculptor of L.'s bust, one of them including eight strophes of the resulting poem; 'Deux lettres de Lamartine en 1824' (125–30), concerning a letter to Aymon de Virieu and one which was probably addressed to Achille Prévost, at the time when L. was seeking a posting in Florence; 'Souvenirs lamartiniens du préfet Barthélémy' (185–226), connected with the reminiscences of encounters with L. by Hyacinthe-Claude-Félix B., at the time when the latter was serving as préfet in Macon; 'Lamartine au Salon (1822–1899): essai d'iconographie lamartinienne' (227–46), on 120 paintings, drawings, and statues of L. or inspired by his work; 'Lamartine, notes et dates pour biographie: première(?) autobiographie, vers 1834' (247–49), reproducing the notes written on both sides of a single piece of paper, which was sold in 1997. Other articles in the volume are: N. Courtinat, '*Le Voyage en Orient* de Lamartine, journal de voyage et journal intime' (3–60), showing that the *Journal* is worthy of attention, not only for what it reveals of L.'s personal experience, but also for the evidence which it gives concerning his manner of writing; W. Fortescue, 'Lettres retrouvées de Lamartine

(1815–1868)' (63–107), presenting a number of previously unpublished letters, written by L. and by his wife, which have come to light in the British Library, the Bodleian Library, Parisian libraries, and private collections; C. Croisille, 'Marianne de Lamartine au travail: sa collaboration à *l'Histoire de la Restauration*, au *Civilisateur* et au *Nouveau Voyage en Orient*' (130–81), presenting a considerable number of previously unpublished letters addressed to the publisher Guillaume Lejean in 1852, implying that she acted as L.'s secretary.

NERVAL. M. Brix, 'Nerval et le rêve égyptien', *Romantisme*, 120:37–46, finds that the rather negative portrayal of Egypt in *Le Voyage en Orient* is essentially based on what he had read before he went there, and his failure to find there what literary sources had led him to expect.

NODIER. *Questions de littérature légale, du plagiat, de la supposition d'auteurs, des supercheries qui ont rapport aux livres*, ed. Jean-François Jeandillou, Geneva, Droz, lix + 208 pp., is a scholarly critical edition of the work first published in 1812, with an ample and valuable *apparatus criticus*.

SAINTE-BEUVE. Michel Brix, *Sainte-Beuve ou la liberté critique*, Jaignes, La Chasse au Snark, 2002, 93 pp., both observes and justifies the rehabilitation of S.-B., with reference to his voluminous output, his independence of mind, his treatment by Hugo, and by writers of later generations such as Baudelaire and Proust.

TRISTAN. Porfiro Mamani Macedo, *Flora Tristan: la paria et la femme étrangère dans son œuvre*, L'Harmattan, 77 pp., gives particular attention to *Nécessité de faire bon accueil aux femmes étrangères*, *Pérégrinations d'une paria*, and *L'Émancipation de la femme ou le testament de la paria*. We are shown that T.'s ideas derived largely from her life experience, though emphasis is given to her confidence in the ability of women to play an important role in society. Beginning with an analysis of her concept of woman as a pariah, we are led through her reflections on the experience of being foreign, before we come to a summary of her proposals, not only to improve the position of foreign women in society, but the amelioration of society as a whole.

THE NINETEENTH CENTURY (POST-ROMANTIC)

POSTPONED

THE TWENTIETH CENTURY 1900–1945

POSTPONED

THE TWENTIETH CENTURY SINCE 1945

POSTPONED

FRENCH CANADIAN LITERATURE

By Christopher Rolfe, *Senior Lecturer in French, University of Leicester*

1. General

A little surprisingly, but there again perhaps not at all, World War II has loomed large in the French Canadian literary consciousness. Robert Viau, *Le Mal d'Europe. La littérature québécoise et la Seconde Guerre Mondiale*, Beauport, MNH, 2002, 191 pp., discusses the obvious texts whilst addressing key issues that, in several cases, become chapter headings (e.g. 'Pourquoi combattre?', 'Comment combattre?', 'Comment survivre à la guerre?'). Ch. 6, 'Echos distants', is a compelling analysis of recent fiction that deals with the conflict; it includes some excellent pages on the controversial *La Constellation du Cygne* of Yolande Villemaire. Going back in time, *Portrait des arts, des lettres et de l'éloquence au Québec (1760–1840)*, ed. Bernard Andrès and Marc-André Bernier, Sainte-Foy, Laval U.P., 2002, 509 pp., presents 28 essays that explore the emergence of a distinct new culture between the Conquest and the suppression of the Patriotes. All but three of the essays deal with literary topics. These include literary salons, women's correspondence, and the role of the press. Both Pierre-Jean and Pierre de Sales Laterrière feature, as do Pierre du Calvet, Napoléon Aubin, Pierre Chauveau, Etienne Parent. This volume is required reading for all those interested in this key period of Quebec's cultural history. **Sexuation, espace et écriture. La littérature québécoise en transformation*, ed. Louise Dupré, Jaap Lintvelt, and Janet Paterson, Quebec, Nota bene, 2002, 487 pp. *Traité de la culture*, ed. Denise Lemieux, Sainte-Foy, Laval U.P., 2002, 1089 pp., is a massive, comprehensive overview of Quebec culture. Of particular interest to literature specialists will be: L. Robert, 'L'institution littéraire' (343–59); L. Mailhot, 'Œeuvres et auteurs: la réception littéraire' (361–88); M. Lemire, 'La carrière d'écrivain au Québec' (389–402); R. Dion, 'La critique littéraire' (403–21).

Le Lointain. Ecrire au loin. Ecrire le lointain, ed. Magessa O'Reilly, Neil Bishop, and A. R. Chadwick, Beauport, MNH, 2002, 216 pp., brings together papers given at a conference held in St-John, Newfoundland, in 2000. Of particular note are: I. Oore, 'La poétique du lointain dans l'œuvre romanesque de Sergio Kokis' (23–32); M. MacDonald, '*Le Premier jardin* et *Cantique des plaines*: le lointain comme condition et matière de création' (89–100); K.-A. Maddox, 'Errance temporelle et transgressions identitaires dans *Immobile* de Ying Chen' (101–15); and L. Steele, 'Gaston Miron: le long chemin de la révolution' (153–58). *Le Québec et l'ailleurs*, ed. Robert Dion, Bremen, Palabres,

2002, 164 pp., is a collection of essays on a theme which, partly because of immigration and Canada's policy (ideology?) of multiculturalism, tends to attract attention in Quebec. Five of the essays are of particular significance: F. Fortier, 'La rhétorique de l'ailleurs dans le récit littéraire québécois' (25–41); J. Kwaterko, 'L'imaginaire diasporique chez les romanciers haïtiens du Québec' (43–59); G. Fottinger, 'L'ici et l'ailleurs dans la vie et l'œuvre de Gabrielle Roy' (81–104); E. Haghebaert, 'Géopolitique ducharméenne' (105–23); R. Dion, '*The Dragonfly of Chicoutimi.* Un cas extrême d'hétérolinguisme?', (125–37). *Globe*, 6.1, is devoted to the theme of 'Le Québec au centre et à la périphérie de la francophonie'. The following essays deal with literary topics: L. Gauvin, 'Manifester la différence. Place et fonctions des manifestes dans les littératures francophones' (23–42); N. Redouane, 'Ecrivains haïtiens au Québec. Une écriture du dépassement identitaire' (43–64); Y. Bénayoun-Szmidt, 'Littérature francophone en Ontario. De l'histoire et de l'écriture' (65–84); and R. Chapman, 'L'espace francophone dans l'œuvre de Gabrielle Roy' (85–105).

Italies imaginaires du Québec, ed. Carla Fratta and Elisabeth Nardout-Lafarge, Montreal, Fides, 248 pp., is a collection of essays on the theme of how Italy has been fashioned in Quebec literature. Chapters on specific authors include: N. Deschamps, 'L'Italie d'Alain Grandbois' (89–108); G. Dupuis, 'De l'invention au mensonge: le référent italien chez Hubert Aquin et Normand de Bellefeuille' (109–33); A. de Vaucher Gravili, 'Dante et l'Italie dans le paysage textuel de Marie-Claire Blais' (219–30). The more general essays — e.g. P. Rajotte, 'L'Italie dans les récits de voyages québécois du XIXe siècle: entre le mythe et la réalité' (43–61) — are equally as interesting. Georges Desmeules and Christiane Lahaie, *Dictionnaire des personnages du roman québécois: 200 personnages des origines à 2000*, Quebec, L'Instant même, 327 pp., does for the Quebec novel what D. and L. have previously done for the play. *La Littérature pour la jeunesse 1970–2000*, ed. Françoise Lepage, Montreal, Fides, 350 pp., includes, not altogether surprisingly, much that will be of interest to specialists of 'adult' literature. There is, notably, an essay by L. Guillemette, 'L'œuvre pour la jeunesse de Dominique Demers: quelques points de jonction du postmodernisme et du féminisme' (193–218), which brings a new dimension to key concepts. Equally stimulating is D. Chouinard, 'Les jeux de l'identité dans les romans pour adolescents de Stanley Péan' (239–55), which adds considerably to our understanding and appreciation of the immigrant novelist and essayist.

Reconfigurations. Canadian Literatures and Postcolonial Identities, ed. Marc Maufort and Franca Bellarsi, Berne, Lang, 2002, 234 pp., is a collection of essays that focus on the range of Canadian identities that have emerged in recent Canadian literature. Quebec specialists are well served, by essays by and on Marie-Célie Agnant, for example. A particularly fine piece by M.-L. Lord, 'L'épreuve de la marge face à l'Autre: les Etats-Unis dans les romans d'Antonine Maillet et de David Adams Richards' (61–78), compares to good effect the work of representatives from the two linguistic communities in New Brunswick. *QuS*, 35, has a special dossier on Quebec and postcolonialism. There are a number of excellent articles including A. Chanady, 'Rereading Québécois literature in a postcolonial context' (31–44), and R. Chapman, 'Writing of/from the Fourth World: Gabrielle Roy and Ungava' (45–62), which focuses, from a postcolonial perspective, on R.'s representation of the Inuit of Northern Quebec in 'Voyage en Ungava' and *La Rivière sans repos.* Edward Dickinson Blodgett, *Five-Part Invention. A History of Literary History in Canada*, Toronto U.P., 371 pp., is a sophisticated, scholarly book that examines how the five 'parts' of Canada (English Canada, French Canada, First Nations, Inuits, and immigrant communities) develop unique literary histories in response to their notion of nationhood. As far as French Canada is concerned, B.'s study is immensely sympathetic but it is the wider perspective of his comparative approach that is ultimately the most enriching. *Incontournable.*

Pierre Nepveu, *Les mots à l'écoute. Poésie et silence chez Fernand Ouellet, Gaston Miron et Paul-Marie Lapointe*, Quebec, Nota bene, 2002, 361 pp., is a most welcome re-edition of a classic study. D. Scholl, *'Zwischen Ungewissheit und Leidenschaft: die Identitatsproblematik in der frankophonen Dichtung Québecs', in *L'état de la poésie aujourd'hui. Perspektiven französischsprachiger Gegenwartslyrik*, ed. Gisela Febel and Hans Grote, Berne, Lang, 359 pp. L. Bonenfant, '*Le Nigog*: la pratique polémique du poème en prose', *VI*, 28:125–37, discusses the prose poems published in the avant-garde review and suggests that they tacitly supported the aesthetics of its critical discourse.

Théâtres québécois et canadiens-français au XXe siècle. Trajectoires et territoires, ed. Hélène Beauchamp and Gilbert David, Sainte-Foy, Quebec U.P., 456 pp., is a collection of essays from a conference held in Montreal in 2001. A wide range of topics is addressed in what amounts to an indispensable, albeit uneven, survey of the subject. The following articles are all to be found in the excellent *L'Annuaire théâtral, Revue québécoise d'études théâtrales* (*AT*): S. Suriam, 'Théâtre africain et théâtre québécois: un essai de rapprochement', *AT*, 31, 2002:12–32, detects a move towards politically relevant but at the same time formally innovative theatre in Quebec and Africa. N. Desrochers, 'Avatars dramaturgiques ou idéologiques: confession, contrition et comparution dans le théâtre québécois contemporain', *ib.*, 119–33, explores the use of flashbacks, a key element in much recent Quebec theatre. D. Blonde, 'Entre Oreste et Barbe-Bleue: la violence dans la scène familiale québécoise, 1981–2002', *ib.*, 32:129–49. *AT*, 33, contains an interesting dossier on 'Théâtre/roman: rencontres du livre et de la scène', with pieces by the likes of Y. Jubinville, P. Riendeau, R. Villeneuve, and Etienne Fortin.

Silvie Bernier, *Les Héritiers d'Ulysse*, Outremont, Lanctôt, 2002, 243 pp., is a lucid addition to the growing corpus on immigrant writers. The study includes chapters on the 'obvious' writers such as Dany Laferrière, Ying Chen, Sergio Kokis, but also provides a useful introduction to less familiar authors such as Pan Bouyoucas, Aki Shimazaki, Marie-Célie Agnant, and Mauricio Segura (the last two both had new books published in 2003). Nathalie Prud'Homme, *La Problématique Identité collective et les littératures (im)migrantes au Québec. Mona Latif Ghattas, Antonio D'Alfonso et Marco Micone*, Quebec, Nota bene, 2002, 174 pp., analyses *Le Double Conte de l'exil*, *Avril ou l'anti-passion*, and *Le Figuier enchanté* to demonstrate how the quest for identity works on two levels: the one individual, the other collective. Daniel Chartier, *Dictionnaire des écrivains émigrés au Québec 1800–1999*, Quebec, Nota bene, 369 pp., will undoubtedly prove to be an invaluable research tool. It not only provides succinct biographies and accurate bibliographies of over 600 writers, but also includes a number of informative *annexes* (listing, for example, the publishing houses, periodicals, and organizations founded by immigrant writers). Pierre Ouellet, *Asiles. Langues d'accueil*, Montreal, Fides, 2002, 254 pp., can perhaps best be described as a series of musings on francophone writers, including Quebec authors such as Miron (165–70), Jacques Brault (171–74), and Ducharme (175–82). *Littératures mineures en langue majeure*, ed. Jean-Pierre Bertrand and Lise Gauvin, Berne, Lang, 318 pp., is a collection of essays first presented at a conference held in Liège in 2001 dealing with literature(s) on the periphery of metropolitan French. Quebec writers get the lion's share of attention and include Francine Noël, Ferron, Kokis, Brossard, Marie Le Franc, Yolande Villemaire, Ducharme, Godbout. **The Francophone World. Cultural Issues and Perspectives*, ed. Michelle Beauclair, Berne, Lang, 175 pp., covers a range of French-speaking communities with Quebec this time getting less of a look-in.

Une enfance en noir et blanc, ed. Raymond Plante, Montreal, 400 coups, 2002, 96 pp., celebrates 50 years of TV in Quebec. 20 or so writers, journalists, and artists relate their childhood experience of TV. In addition to providing a (nostalgic) glimpse of the medium in Quebec, the volume casts new light on the formative years of writers such as Chrystine Brouillet, Arlette Cousture, Monique LaRue, and Stanley Péan. *Cinéma et littérature au Québec: rencontres médiatiques*, ed.

Michel Larouche, Montreal, XYZ, 202 pp., is an important collection of essays on the links between literature and cinema. For once, the film script is given its due as a literary genre in its own right. D. Bachand, 'Du roman au cédérom. *Le Désert mauve* de Nicole Brossard' (43–53); P. Véronneau, 'Du scénique au filmique. Adaption et scénarios dans *Being at Home with Claude*' (73–91); L. Carrière, 'Les vues écrites et animées de Michel Tremblay' (93–108), are especially recommended. François Ouellet, *Passer au rang de père. Identité sociohistorique et littéraire au Québec*, Quebec, Nota bene, 2002, 155 pp., sets out to show how Quebec society has long been in thrall to various forms of alienating authority, how it has sought to control its own destiny, and how its literature has voiced this quest for symbolic 'fatherhood'. Jean-François de Raymond, *Descartes et le nouveau monde: le cheminement du cartésianisme au Canada, XVIIe–XXe siècle*, Vrin, xii + 333 pp., is unexpectedly and genuinely revealing.

Anthologie de l'essai au Québec depuis la Révolution tranquille, ed. Jean-François Chassay, Montreal, Boréal, 271 pp., a collection of more than 40 essays by 23 different, mostly well-known writers, reveals that the genre is very much alive and kicking in Quebec. The texts are grouped into seven sections of which 'Langue' and 'Ecrire, lire et peindre' are perhaps of particular relevance in the present context.

2. Individual Authors

AQUIN. Jean-Christian Pleau, *La Révolution québécoise. Hubert Aquin et Gaston Miron au tournant des années soixante*, Montreal, Fides, 2002, 271 pp., reassesses the Quiet Revolution in the light of the role played in it by these two major writers. The book is divided into two parts: 'La fatigue d'Hubert Aquin', which essentially deals with his debate with Trudeau, and 'Miron en état d'émeute', which seeks to give due weight to M.'s poetical/political *engagement*.

AUDET. Noël Audet, *Ce qu'il nous reste de liberté*, Notre-Dame-des-Neiges, Trois-Pistoles, 2002, 101 pp., is one of a series of enterprising 'autobiographies' in which writers reveal their aims, influences, professional secrets, and the like. (See also entries under BLAIS and JACOB.) All are recommended even if the horse's mouth, so to speak, is not necessarily unproblematic.

BACQUEVILLE DE LA POTHERIE. C. Cartmill, 'The "epistolary method" and the rhetoric of assimilation in Bacqueville de la Potherie's *Histoire de l'Amérique septentrionale*', *CanL*, 178:31–47, is a lucid account of how LP.'s use of letters facilitates his descriptions — among the first in French — of the Amerindians.

BLAIS. Marie-Claire Blais, *Des Rencontres humaines*, Notre-Dame-des-Neiges, Trois-Pistoles, 2002, 104 pp.

BUIES. Arthur Buies, *Réminiscences* suivi de *Les Jeunes Barbares*, ed. Mario Brassard and Marilène Gill, Notre-Dame-des-Neiges, Trois-Pistoles, 2002, 159 pp., is a welcome edition of these key texts. The bare bones of a critical apparatus are included.

CHEN, YING. I. Girard, 'Stylistique et esthétique dans trois fragments de *La Mémoire de l'eau* de Ying Chen. (Hypothèses d'analyse sociocritique)', *Tangence*, 68, 2002: 137–53, explores, among other things, by what stylistic means Y.C. conveys her world view. N. Sorin, 'The life story in literature class: glimpses of the Other and views of the self', *ib.*, 71: 93–106, examines Y.C.'s *La Mémoire de l'eau* and Feng Ji Cai's *Que cent fleurs s'épanouissent* to show that the life story revolves around the meeting of two cultures, that of the writer and that of the reader.

CYR. *VI*, 28.3, has a dossier on C. The initial article, J. Paquin, 'Variations sur la pente du langage: le poème comme simulacre du raisonnement scientifique' (31–43), usefully locates C. vis-à-vis the *Hexagone* poets before examining the phenomena of interdiscursivity between science and poetry in his work.

DAIGLE. J. den Toonder, 'Voyage et passage chez France Daigle', *DFS*, 62: 13–24, takes François Paré's *Les Littératures de l'exiguïté* as a starting-point for her discussion of the Acadian writer's *Un fin passage*. C. W. Francis, 'L'autofiction de France Daigle. Identité, perception visuelle et réinvention de soi', *VI*, 28: 114–38, focuses on D.'s *Pas pire* and argues that her experimentation is located within a gendered postmodern aesthetics.

DANTIN. Louis Dantin, *Essais critiques*, ed. Yvette Francoli, 2 vols, Montreal U.P., 2002, 528, 488 pp., is a fine critical edition of the essays on Quebec literature written by D. between 1920 and 1942.

DAOUST. A. Gervais, '*Les Cendres bleues*. Du rapport d'un "poème érotique" et d'un "poème policier"', *Tangence*, 70, 2002: 87–109, is an analysis of the narrative and autobiographical aspects of D.'s powerful, disturbing poem.

DESSAULLES. Louis-Antoine Dessaulles, *Discours sur la tolérance* suivi du *Mémoire de l'éveque Bourget*, ed. Adrien Thério, Montreal, XYZ, 2002, 104 pp., is a most welcome edition of two key texts in the battle between the *Institut canadien* and a virulent ultramontanism.

DUBÉ. *CTJ*, 106, has a valuable dossier on the prolific playwright. Of particular interest perhaps is: J. Przychodzen, 'Marcel Dubé, auteur tragique' (86–90).

DUBOIS. N. Sarrasin, 'Rupture et fragments dans le théâtre de René-Daniel Dubois', *AT*, 33: 159–79, analyses *Adieu, docteur Munch* and *Le Troisième Fils du professeur Yourolov* in order to demonstrate how D.'s plays typify the hybridization of genres, fragmentation, and 'une dynamique chaotique' that are characteristic of contemporary Quebec theatre.

ÉTIENNE. **L'Esthétique du choc. Gérard Etienne ou l'écriture haïtienne au Québec*, ed. Danielle Dumontet, Berne, Lang, 224 pp.

FERRON. Jacques Ferron, *Eminence de la Grande Corne du Parti Rhinocéros*, ed. Martin Jalbert, Outremont, Lanctôt, 190 pp., is a collection of material relating to F.'s satirical brainchild, the Parti Rhinocéros set up in 1963. Fascinating in historical terms and also for the light shed on F.'s political thinking. A. Ruiu, 'La littérature et la construction symbolique de la nation', Sparling, *Identities*, 83–92, examines F.'s *Le Salut de l'Irlande* and Aquin's *Prochain épisode* in the light of Benedict Anderson's concept of the 'imagined community'.

GAUVREAU. Claude Gauvreau, *Lettres à Paul-Emile Borduas*, ed. Gilles Lapointe, Montreal U.P., 2002, 450 pp. These letters, dating from just after the publication of *Refus global* to the year before B.'s death in Paris, shed precious light on the *automatiste* movement and on G.'s personal tragedy.

GRANDBOIS. Alain Grandbois, *Poèmes: Les Îles de la nuit, Rivages de l'homme, L'Étoile pourpre, Poèmes épars*, Montreal, L'Hexagone, 216 pp., is a propitious edition with a preface by Jacques Brault.

GROULX. Gérard Bouchard, *Les Deux Chanoines: contradictions et ambivalence dans la pensée de Lionel Groulx*, Montreal, Boreal, 312 pp. J.-C. Pleau, 'Polémique sur un "mauvais livre": l'*Appel de la race* de Lionel Groulx', *VI*, 28:138–59, delves into the motives that inspired G.'s principle adversaries, and suggests that the polemic actually fits into a pattern of political debate in 20th-c. Quebec.

HÉBERT. M.-H. Lemieux, 'Pour une sociocritique du roman *Kamouraska* d'Anne Hébert', *VI*, 28:95–113.

HÉMON. Geneviève Chovrelat, **Louis Hémon, la vie à écrire*, Louvain, Peeters, 326 pp.

JACOB. Suzanne Jacob, *Comment. Pourquoi*, Notre-Dame-des-Neiges, Trois-Pistoles, 2002, 87 pp.

LAFERRIÈRE. Ursula Mathis-Moser, *Dany Laferrière. La dérive américaine*, Montreal, VLB, 341 pp., explores to good effect the autobiographical in L.'s novels. E. A. Brière, 'Langue d'écriture et transculture: le cas des francophones des Amériques', *QuS*, 33, 2002:135–48, contains some insightful comments on Laferrière. K. Colin-Thébaudeau, 'Dany Laferrière exilé au "Pays sans chapeau"', *Tangence*, 71:63–77, is a thematic and formal analysis of L.'s novel *Pays sans chapeau*. It concludes that the motif of exile is too deeply rooted in the psyche of Haïtians for it to be a viable metaphor. A. Boivin, '*Comment faire l'amour avec un nègre sans se fatiguer* ou une dénonciation du racisme à travers la baise', *QuF*, 131:94–97.

LARUE. *VI*, 28.2, has a dossier on L. with essays by the likes of Robert Dion, François Dumont, Katri Suhonen. Two pieces stand out: Susan Ireland rehearses some familiar but nevertheless valuable ideas in 'La maternité et la modernité dans les romans de Monique LaRue' (46–60); Lucie Joubert, '*La Gloire de Cassiodore*: une affaire de genres' (86–97), discusses issues to do with authorial responsibility, the reader's role, and gender that this satirical novel raises.

LATERRIÈRE. Pierre de Sales Laterrière, *'Les Mémoires' de Pierre de Sales Laterrière suivi de 'Correspondances'*, ed. Bernard Andrès, Montreal, Triptyque, 317 pp.

LE FRANC. *Marie Le Franc. La rencontre de la Bretagne et du Québec*, ed. Aurélien Boivin and Gwénaëlle Lucas, Quebec, Nota bene, 2002, 164 pp., is a collection of articles that will perhaps help to rehabilitate a writer whose 'Canadian' output was greater, quantitively at least, than that of her more famous compatriot, Louis Hémon.

LEMELIN. Julie Royer, *Roger Lemelin. Des bonds vers les étoiles*, Montreal, XYZ, 2002, 185 pp., is another biography in the lively, but problematic, 'Grandes figures' series.

LOZEAU. Albert Lozeau, *Œuvres poétiques complètes*, ed. Michel Lemaire, Montreal U.P., 2002, 711 pp., presents the three-volumed edition established by L. just before his death, plus omitted material and *inédits*.

MAILLET. M. Cardy and D. M. Engel, 'Antonine Maillet's *Pélagie-la-Charette*: an Acadian Mother Courage?', *BJCS*, 15, 2002: 157–69, is a deft appraisal of thematic parallels between M.'s novel and Bertolt Brecht's famous play. *DFS*, 62, a special issue devoted to 'Auteures acadiennes: création et critique', includes four essays on M.: H. Fudge, '*Par derrière chez mon père* d'Antonine Maillet: la valorisation de la parole par l'inversion historique' (111–22); D. Chéramie, 'Antonine Maillet et l'intertextualité rabelaisienne: les paroles dégelées'(123–36); M.-N. Rinne, 'L'Acadie d'Evangéline Deusse et l'Irlande de Maria: femmes et frontières chez Maillet et Joyce'(137–45); M.-L. Lord, 'Représentation féminine et auto-représentation dans l'œuvre romanesque d'Antonine Maillet: une figure d'identité' (147–59).

MARTIN. M. Litherland, 'The œuvre of Claire Martin', Muller, *Passages*, 73–78, is a slight piece that nevertheless manages some interesting comments on the autobiographical in M.'s work and how memory works. R. Bourneuf, 'Claire Martin, la note juste', *Nuit blanche*, 91: 22–27, is a succinct introduction to the author (who has started writing again after a gap of some thirty years).

MIRON. Gaston Miron, *Poèmes épars*, ed. Marie-Andrée Beaudet and Pierre Nepveu, Montreal, L'Hexagone, 124 pp. A. Gaulin, 'Gaston Miron. Poète engagé et dégagé', *QuF*, 131: 79–81.

NARRACHE. Richard Foisy, *Jean Narrache: un poète et son double, Emile Coderre*, Montreal, Varia, 508 pp., is the first of a two-volume biography of this all but forgotten 'troubadour' who enjoyed enormous popularity in the thirties for his celebration — significantly using their own vernacular — of ordinary folk.

NELLIGAN. Emile Nelligan, *Rêve d'artiste et autres poèmes*, ed. Yolande Villemaire, Montreal, Les Herbes rouges, 101 pp., is a selection of N.'s poems with the added distinction of a succinct but compelling commentary 'Piano, animaux, vaisseaux des vingt ans' by the author of *La Constellation du cygne.*

NEVERS. Edmond de Nevers, *Lettres de Berlin et d'autres villes d'Europe*, ed. Hans-Jurgen Lusebrink, Quebec, Nota bene, 2002, 276 pp., brings together for the first time all the letters that N. wrote from Europe between 1888 and 1891 and published in *La Presse.*

PAPINEAU. Amédée Papineau, *Lettres d'un voyageur d'Edimbourg à Naples en 1870–1871*, ed. Georges Aubin, Quebec, Nota bene, 2002, 421 pp. P.'s previously unpublished correspondence to his famous father, Louis-Joseph, will be of particular value to those interested in 19th-c. travel literature.

POULIN. I. Gruber, 'L'autoréférentialité et le postmoderne dans *Les Grandes Marées* et *Le Désert mauve*', Sparling, *Identities*, 63–74, argues that the *autoréférentialité* evident in these novels by P. and Brossard is, in fact, an important characteristic of postmodern novel-writing as a whole in Quebec.

RONFARD. Jean-Pierre Ronfard, *Ecritures pour le théâtre*, 3 vols, Montreal, Dramaturges, 2002, 339, 165, 193 pp., makes available seminal contributions to Quebec theatre which had 'restées longtemps enfouies dans les tiroirs profonds [. . .] du NTE'. Each piece is preceded by a terse description of how it was originally staged. Invaluable.

ROY. Gabrielle Roy, *Ma petite rue qui m'a menée autour du monde*, Saint-Boniface, Editions du Blé, 2002, 74 pp., is a further edition of the second manuscript version of the text that was probably a draft for *La Détresse et l'enchantement.* It includes 12 uninspired illustrations by Réal Bérard. Marie-Pierre Andron, *L'Imaginaire du corps amoureux. Lectures de Gabrielle Roy*, L'Harmattan, 2002, 261 pp., betrays its origins as a thesis, but has much to offer, not least its insights into two *inédits*: *La Première Femme* and *Baldur*. See also her 'Le thème du corps dans les romans de Gabrielle Roy', Muller, *Passages*, 32–42, which discusses, amongst other things, the paradox that the body is omnipresent in R.'s work and yet handled with great discretion. **Gabrielle Roy aujourd'hui*, ed. Paul Socken, Saint-Boniface, Plaines, 212 pp.

THÉRIAULT. G. Mossière, 'Présences de l'Autre dans *Agaguk* d'Yves Thériault', *CanL*, 177:80–95, is, as its title suggests, an Eric Landowski inspired analysis of otherness in T.'s novel.

TREMBLAY, M. Louise Carrière, *Michel Tremblay, du cinéphile au scénariste*, Montreal, Les 400 coups, 248 pp., is a revealing study of a less well-known aspect of T.'s output: his writing for the screen. M. Dargnat, 'La tentation du corpus. Du théâtre au roman, de la parole à l'écriture chez Michel Tremblay', Sparling, *Identities*, 51–61, explores identity in T.'s work via the concept of 'corpus', in its linguistic, material, and organic senses. A.-C. Nash, 'Aspects de la verve rabelaisienne chez Francine Noël et Michel Tremblay', Muller, *Passages*, 20–31, explores how both writers share a style rich in playfulness, subversiveness, and fantasy. F. Fortier and A. Mercier, 'La voix du chef-d'œuvre. Figurations et enjeux de la voix dans le récit contemporain', *EF*, 39:67–80, explores how T.'s 'Un simple soldat' from *Douze coups de théâtre* and Bernard Lévy's 'Le chef-d'œuvre' from the *Un sourire incertain* collection 'use the narrative to illustrate the potentialities of the voice, but also, paradoxically, to bring out the necessity of neutralizing that very voice.'

TREMBLAY, R. Rémi Tremblay, *Un revenant*, ed. Jean Levasseur, Quebec, La Huit, xcv + 459 pp., is a fine critical edition of this important historical novel, serialized in 1884 in *La Patrie*. C. G. Schick, 'A picaresque *revenant*', *FR*, 76, 2002:373–83, examines how the novel — which is about two French Canadian mercenaries fighting for the Union during the American Civil War — subverts the ethos of old New France. J. Levasseur, 'Rémi Tremblay: portrait d'un franco-américain patriote', *QuS*, 33, 2002:73–81, is a solid biographical sketch.

TURCOTTE. *Nuit blanche*, 90, has an interview with T. conducted by Linda Amyot (8–13).

VIATTE. *Regards croisés entre le Jura, la Suisse romande, et le Québec*, ed. Claude Hauser and Yvan Lamonde, Sainte-Foy, Laval U.P., 2002, 344 pp., brings together the papers given at an international conference of the same name held in 2001 to celebrate the centenary of the birth of V., the Swiss-born intellectual. The volume is in two parts. Part 1 is devoted to V. himself; part 2 to 'Aspects des relations culturelles entre le Jura, la Suisse et le Québec'. There is much here of general interest for Quebec specialists but essays by D. Maggetti, 'Littérature romande et littérature canadienne au XIXe siècle: les dessous d'une convergence' (151–63), and Micheline Cambron, 'Littérature suisse romande et littérature québécoise: récits et discours fondateurs'(165–88), deal with some interesting literary issues.

CARIBBEAN LITERATURE

By Maeve McCusker, *Queen's University, Belfast*

1. General

Nick Nesbitt, *Voicing Memory. History and Subjectivity in French Caribbean Literature*, Charlottesville–London, Virginia U.P., xviii + 258 pp., is a rich and lucid contribution dealing in particular with the work of Césaire, Maximin, Glissant, Condé, and, in a welcome inclusion, Danticat. The substantial introduction marshalls a wide range of philosophical work (Heidegger, Hegel, Marx, Lukács, Kojève) to analyse attempts by Césaire, Fanon, and Glissant to critique Antillean alienation, and to construct an autonomous subjectivity. The first chapter examines the legacy of Delgrès in the Antillean imagination, and subsequent chapters offer stimulating readings of the authors mentioned above. In addition to these literary analyses, Nesbitt remains attentive to other forms (e.g. music), and offers particularly compelling interpretations of visual culture (banknotes, posters, statues). Gallagher, *Ici-Là,* is an important collection which covers most major contemporary Antillean writers. In addition to an extremely rich introduction and afterword, the volume includes essays of general interest: C. Forsdick, 'Transatlantic displacement and the problematics of space' (181–209), offers a fascinating reading of the enduring obsession for Caribbean writers of the 'cachot de Joux', where Toussaint L'Ouverture was imprisoned and died; M. Laroche, 'Displacement, repositioning, metamorphosis' (125–41), discusses the importance of the homeland for writers of the Haitian diaspora. Aub-Buscher, *Francophone Caribbean,* gives an excellent overview of contemporary debates in literature and language. It includes several pieces of general interest, and of particular note is that by J. M. Dash, 'Postcolonial paradoxes. Francophone Caribbean literature and the *fin de siècle*' (33–44), tracing the persistence of apocalyptic thought in several generations of Antillean writers. *Théâtres francophones et créolophones de la Caraïbe*, ed. Alvina Ruprecht, L'Harmattan, 253 pp., is a useful collection which deals amply with a neglected genre, focusing not only on Martinique and Guadeloupe, but also on Haiti, Saint-Lucia, and Guyana. While figures such as Césaire and Condé, inevitably, loom large, lesser-known dramatists such as Jan Mapou and Mona Guérin are also discussed. Of particular interest for the researcher is the appendix, providing a full index of theatres, groups, and festivals (245–49). Florence Martin and Isabelle Favre, *De la Guyane à la diaspora africaine. Écrits du silence*, Karthala, 2002, 205 pp., attempts to counter Guyana's exclusion from considerations of both *créolité* and *francophonie*; the authors observe, for example, that the earliest Creole-language novel was Guyanese. The first two chapters contain original and valuable readings of the myth of D'Chimbo, and of Élie Stéphenson's writing. It is regrettable, then, that the second half lapses into a general study of writings from the African diaspora. Ch. 3 deals exclusively with Maximin's *L'Isolé Soleil*, ch. 4 with a number of women writers (Condé, Toni Morrison). Despite the authors' attempts to justify their dual focus, the overall effect is unbalanced and incoherent. *L'Ecriture et le sacré. Senghor, Césaire, Glissant, Chamoiseau*, ed. Jean-François Durand, Montpellier, Univ. Paul-Valéry, Montpellier III, 2002, 268 pp., is an uneven collection in which, despite their prominence in the title, the latter two writers are marginal. Alexandra de Cauna, *L'Image des quartiers populaires dans le roman antillais*, Karthala, 181 pp., focuses on Chamoiseau, Confiant, Julia, and Pineau, and is principally concerned with peripheral spaces and 'les quartiers d'habitat spontané'. As the methodological framework is primarily geographical and sociological, literary analysis is limited. On a similar topic, Lucienne Nicolas, *Espaces urbains dans le roman de la diaspora haïtienne*, L'Harmattan, 2002, 304 pp., devotes a chapter each to Métellus, Depestre, Charles, Étienne, Laferrière, and Ollivier. This is a detailed and theoretically-informed treatment of a central topos. Wendy Goolcharan-Kumeta, *My Mother, My Country. Reconstructing the Female Self in Guadeloupean Women's Writing*, Oxford, Lang, 236 pp., is an occasionally predictable study of women writers, including Condé and Schwarz-Bart. J. Jonassaint, 'Tragic narratives: the novels of Haitian tradition', *Callaloo*, 26:203–18, links the obsessive presence of misfortune in 'authentic national Haitian novels' to structural and thematic qualities in Greek tragedy (fatal loss, warnings, explanations). This is a particularly welcome piece as it examines some of the island's older novels (e.g. Lhérisson's *La Famille des Pitite-Caille* and Hibbert's *Séna*, both 1905). M. McCusker, '"This creole culture, miraculously forged": the contradictions of *créolité*', pp. 112–21 of *Francophone Studies/Postcolonial Theory*, ed. Charles Forsdick and David Murphy, London, Arnold, 305 pp., reads the *créolité* discourse through postcolonial theory, arguing that it is precisely because of the movement's inherent contradictions that it has been such an influential, if controversial, theory of identity.

SPECIAL ISSUES OF JOURNALS. *FR*, 76.6, a special issue on Martinique and Guadeloupe, in addition to three articles on Condé, includes an essay on Françoise Éga, a comparative treatment of Glissant and Chamoiseau, and interviews with Pineau and Dracius. *YFS*, 103, entitled 'French and francophone: the challenge of expanding horizons', is a generally useful 'état présent', and includes two pieces of particular interest in Caribbean terms: J. Jonassaint, 'Literatures in the francophone Caribbean' (55–63), and J. M. Dash, '*Caraïbe fantôme*. The play of difference in the francophone Caribbean' (93–105). *EtLitt*, 34.3, 2002, devotes a timely and useful special issue to the work of the recently-deceased author, Émile Ollivier. *RLC*, 302, 2002, is entitled 'Un espace comparatiste: la Caraïbe', and includes articles on Perse, Capécia, Schwarz-Bart, and Chamoiseau.

2. Individual Authors

ALEXIS. M. Munro, 'Wild things: noble savages, exoticisms and postcolonial space in Jacques-Stephen Alexis's *Les Arbres musiciens*', *FS*, 57:55–67, provides a useful account of exoticism, proceeds to a reading of the 'wild man' in the novel, and concludes with a sophisticated problematization of A.'s apparent reproduction of primitivist myths. M. Heady, 'Le merveilleux et la conscience marxiste dans *Les Arbres musiciens* de Jacques-Stéphen Alexis', *EtF*, 17.2, 2002:113–24, studies the contradictions and tensions in A.'s approach.

CÉSAIRE. M. Munro, 'Something and nothing: place and displacement in Aimé Césaire and René Depestre', Gallagher, *Ici-Là*, 143–56, compares and contrasts both writers' attitudes towards space.

CHAMOISEAU. Gallagher, *Ici-Là*, contains three pieces on Chamoiseau: R. Chandler Caldwell, Jr., 'For a theory of the creole city. *Texaco* and the postcolonial postmodern' (25–39), examines the presentation of urban space, while M. McCusker, 'No place like home? Constructing an identity in Patrick Chamoiseau's *Texaco*' (41–60), explores the poetics of the 'case créole' and the metaphorical resonances of building in the same novel; L. Milne, 'The *marron* and the *marqueur*: physical space and imaginary displacement in Patrick Chamoiseau's *L'Esclave vieil homme et le molosse*' (61–82), identifies an ideological shift in C.'s reworking of the myth of the maroon slave, and this figure's relationship to the *marqueur de paroles*. Id., 'Metaphor and memory in the work of Patrick Chamoiseau', *EsC*, 43.1:90–100, links the prevalence of images of the 'abîme' and the womb to a collective imaginary structured around the plantation and the slave ship. R.-M. Réjouis, 'Caribbean writers and language. The autobiographical poetics of Jamaica Kincaid and Patrick Chamoiseau', *Massachusetts Review*, 44, 1–2:213–32, explores the gendering of Creole through two emblematic autobiographies. R. K. Gosson, 'For what the land tells: an ecocritical approach to Patrick Chamoiseau's *Chronicle of the Seven Sorrows*', *Callaloo*, 26:219–34, is a study of the marketplace which is slightly dependent on existing criticism.

D. Chancé, 'De *Chronique des sept misères* à *Biblique des derniers gestes*, Patrick Chamoiseau est-il baroque?', *MLN*, 118:867–94, refutes an over-hasty reading of C.'s latest novel as baroque, through meticulous textual analysis and reference to the author's work more generally. M. Gallagher, 'Re-membering Caribbean childhoods. Saint-John Perse's *Eloges* and Patrick Chamoiseau's *Antan d'enfance*', Aub-Buscher, *Francophone Caribbean*, 45–59, deftly traces intertextual connections in both authors' concern with memory and nostalgia. R. Watts, '"Toutes ces eaux!": ecology and empire in Patrick Chamoiseau's *Biblique des derniers gestes*', *MLN*, 118:895–910, focuses on the literal and figurative uses of water in C.'s latest novel. Id., 'The "wounds of locality": living and writing the local in Patrick Chamoiseau's *Écrire en pays dominé*', *FrF*, 28.1:111–29, is a refreshingly positive reading of C.'s *créolité* which, while not denying the influence of Glissant, argues that C. is more situated in Martinique, hence less susceptible to the openness of the *tout-monde*.

CONDÉ. C. Sanders, '"*Une si belle enfant ne pouvait pas être maudite*": polyphony in Maryse Condé's novel *La Migration des cœurs*', Aub-Buscher, *Francophone Caribbean*, 151-68, is an incisive reading of C.'s novel in terms of Bakhtin's theories of double-voicing and polyphony. D. B. Gaensbauer, 'Protean truths: history as performance in Maryse Condé's *An Tan Revolisyon*', *FR*, 76:1139–50, is an interesting and original 'reading in pairs' of C.'s play and Ariane Mnouchkine's *1789*, while in 'Le rire de la grand-mère: insolence et sérénité dans *Désirada* de Maryse Condé', *ib.*, 1151–60, L. Moudileno shows how C. subverts readers' expectations in her presentation of the grandmother figure. R. F. Jurney, 'Voix sexualisée dans *Moi, Tituba sorcière* de Maryse Condé', *ib.*, 1161–71, focuses on the transgressive nature of Tituba's sexuality, and locates this quality in the context of other contemporary Antillean women's writing.

GLISSANT. Romuald Fonkoua, *Essai sur une mesure du monde au XX siècle. Édouard Glissant*, Champion, 2002, 326 pp., is a rich and original study, primarily concerned with G.'s fiction but attentive also to his poetry and essays, and organized around the themes of 'voyager, connaître', 'savoir, penser' and 'dire, écrire'. F. begins by situating G. in terms of an 'entre-deux', a term he prefers to 'différence', and traces developments in his work, among which an early, and short-lived, concern with the nation, giving way to his later 'travail plus approfondi sur la fiction'. Dominique Chancé, *Édouard Glissant, un 'traité du déparler'. Essai sur l'œuvre romanesque d'Édouard Glissant*, Karthala, 2002, 277 pp., claims a pivotal place for, and takes its title from, *La Case du commandeur.* The study is centrally concerned with notions of 'délire verbal' and the 'tout-monde', and is structured in an appropriately circular, kaleidoscopic fashion, different combinations of novels being treated in each chapter. A huge corpus (including the recent *Sartorius*, 1999) is thus examined with elegance and clarity. C. Britton, 'Space, textuality and the real in Glissant's *Mahogany*', Gallagher, *Ici-Là*, 83–99, demonstrates, through a close reading of two passages, the complex relationship between textuality and referentiality in the presentation of space. B. Cailler, 'From "gabelles"to "grands chaos". A study of the disode to the homeless', *ib.*, 101–24, is a polemical call to revisit G.'s poetry in the light of what she considers critical over-investment in, and occasional distortion of, his theory. D. Fulton, '*Romans des nous*: the first person plural and collective identity in Martinique', *FR*, 76: 1104–14, offers a rewarding reading of G.'s *La Case du commandeur* and Chamoiseau's *L'Esclave vieil homme et le molosse*, demonstrating how the latter develops and departs from G.'s use of the 'nous' perspective, and thus suggests that 'any given *je* enunciates a multiplicity of possible interpretations.'

LAFFERIÈRE. S. Haigh, 'From exile to *errance*: Dany Lafferière's *Cette grenade dans la main du jeune nègre est-elle une arme ou un fruit?*', Aub-Buscher, *Francophone Caribbean*, 60–81, is a cogently-argued account which deals equally with *Comment faire l'amour avec un nègre sans se fatiguer*. Beginning with an examination of the presentation of sexual relationships between 'La Blanche' and 'Le Nègre', the article opens on to broader issues of race and racism, as well as reflecting generally on contemporary Quebecan literature. J. Evans Braziel, 'From Port-au-Prince to Montréal to Miami: trans-American nomads in Dany Laferrière's migratory texts', *Callaloo*, 26: 235–51, is biographically informative and textually attentive.

PINEAU. S. Phillips Casteel, 'New World pastoral. The Caribbean garden and emplacement in Gisèle Pineau and Shani Mootoo', *Interventions*, 5: 12–28, is a theoretically astute reading, which argues that the 'spatial turn' in critical theory has put 'an exaggerated stress on displacement, dislocation and movement at the expense of place', before offering a sophisticated demonstration of how the Caribbean garden 'becomes a space in which to explore the mutual interdependence of place and displacement, roots and routes'. B. Thomas, 'Gender identity on the move: Gisèle Pineau's *La Grande Drive des Esprits*', *FR*, 76: 1128–38, explores sexual stereotype in P.'s novel. V. Loichot, 'Reconstruire dans l'exil: la nourriture créatrice chez Gisèle Pineau', *EtF*, 17.2, 2002: 25–43, focuses on the importance of food for the Antillean immigrant in France, as represented in two P. texts.

PLACOLY. Daniel Seguin-Cadiche, *Une explosion dans la cathédrale, ou regards sur l'œuvre de Vincent Placoly*, L'Harmattan, 2002, 331 pp., is an authoritative, lively, and convincing account of the work of a writer whose unplaceable status in the contemporary canon has resulted in unjustifiable critical neglect.

AFRICAN / MAGHREB LITERATURE

POSTPONED

III. OCCITAN STUDIES

LANGUAGE

By Kathryn Klingebiel, *Professor of French, University of Hawai'i at Mânoa*

1. Bibliographical and General

C. Bonnet, *'Occitan language', *MLAIntBibl*, 3, 2002[2003]: 198–200 (nos. 8289–8347). K. Klingebiel, 'Bibliography of Occitan linguistics for 2002', *Tenso*, 18:153–87. Georges Bonifassi, **Les Publications périodiques en provençal des origines à 1914*, Paris, Univ. Paris-Sorbonne, 2002, 390 pp. G. Marsan, 'Conservation des fonds en langues régionales des Pyrénées: premiers résultats d'une enquête', Massoure, *Langues*, 443–48, presents a brief description of Occitan holdings in 30 municipal libraries, museums, departmental archives, regional associations. J.-L. Massoure provides a general presentation to 'Langues et parlers pyrénéens', *ib.*, 341–54.

Upon the occasion of his retirement, Jean-Claude Bouvier's full bibliography is printed (399–408) in **Espaces du langage: géolinguistique, toponymie, cultures de l'oral et de l'écrit*, Aix-en-Provence, Univ. de Provence, 412 pp.; individual sections of this volume reproduce B.'s key articles on Occitan and Gallo-Romance dialectology; onomastics; orality, identity, and memory; general and Romance linguistics; Occitan and French literature.

The publications of Frank R. Hamlin (1935–2000), including books and articles devoted to Occitan toponymy, particularly of the Hérault, are listed in *OCan*, 84, 2002:3–12, with discussion of his scholarship and research by J. Gulsoy, *ib.*, 13–25. Charles Camproux and his career are remembered by three colleagues: R. Lafont, *LengM*, 53:7–9; J.-P. Chambon, 'Charles Camproux: un dialectologue rebelle?', *ib.*: 11–31; and P. Martel, 'Charles Camproux, un non-conformiste des années 30 en occitan?', *ib.*:33–56. Ernest Nègre's work, with a selected bibliography, is detailed by J. Thomas in *RLiR*, 66, 2002:623–28. The work of Michel Grosclaude (1926–2002) is described by Louis Laborde-Balen, Massoure, *Langues*, 411–17.

2. Medieval Period (to 1500)

PHONETICS AND PHONOLOGY. J. I. Hualde, 'Remarks on the diachronic reconstruction of intonational patterns in Romance, with special attention to Occitan as a bridge language', *Catalan Journal of Linguistics*, 2:181–206 (see <http://www.bib.uab.es/pub/linguistics/

16956885v2p181.pdf>). Occitan is seen as a key to understanding the prosodic divergence of French (lacking phonemic word stress) from both Italo- and Ibero-Romance intonation systems. J.-P. Chambon, 'Brassac—Brassaget, Aydat—Aydazés: traitements phonétiques différenciés au sandhi interne et histoire du peuplement (nord du domaine occitan)', *RLiR*, 66:67–94, is an analysis of phonetic traits 'différenciés au sandhi interne comme critère linguistique de datation', exemplified with place names in -ĀCU + *-ITTU, and a smaller set in –ENSE > medieval Occ. *–az* + *és*.

LEXIS AND LEXICOLOGY. The fourth fascicle of Wolf-Dieter Stempel's *Dictionnaire de l'occitan médiéval* (*DOM*), *afermat-agreable*, has appeared, 80 pp., with the on-going collaboration of Claudia Kraus, Renate Peter, and Monika Tausend. C. Glanemann and U. Hoinkes, *'Pilgerfahrten und Kreuzzuge als Entlehnungsquelle für Gallizismen (Okzitanismen) im Wortschatz des Italienischen', *ZrP*, 118, 2002: 1–24, presents an inventory of Gallicisms and Occitanisms that entered the language as Italian pilgrims wended their way towards Santiago de Compostela, or as foreigners travelled to Rome and the Holy Land.

PARTICULAR SEMANTIC FIELDS. R. M. Medina Granda, *'Francés antiguo *g(i)ens*, catalán antiguo/moderno *gens* y occitano antiguo/moderno *ge(n)s*: algunas razones semánticas en favor de *genus*, como étimo de estas expresiones', *Verba*, 29, 2002:89–220, presents further arguments in favour of an origin in L. GENUS, rather than GENTIUM (<minime gentium>). P. Sauzet studies '*Cor*: còr, còrn, cuèr?', *Oc*, 341, 2001:42–45, in v. 256 of *Roland à Saragosse*, reviewing possible interpretations as either 'horn' or 'heart' and opting for the latter.

ONOMASTICS. M. Mousnier, *'Dépendants du Languedoc occidental (milieu XIe-fin XIIIe siècle): aspects anthroponymiques', pp. 59–88 of *Genèse médiévale de l'anthroponymie moderne*. v.2 *Intégration et exclusion sociale: lectures anthroponymiques. Serfs et dépendants au Moyen Age (Le 'nouveau servage')*, ed. Monique Bourin and Pascal Chareille, Tours U.P., 2002, 218 pp. P.-H. Billy, *'Nommer à Toulouse aux XI-XIVe siècles', *PatRom* 5, 135–49.

GASCON. M. Marchiori, *'Considerazioni linguistiche su "Ai faux ris" [Raimbaut de Vaqueiras]', *EL*, 27, 2002:77–81. G. Tavani, *'O provenzal dos trobadores galego-portugueses e o problema da heterodoxia expresiva', pp. 61–74 of *Iberia cantat: Estudios sobre poesía hispánica medieval*, ed. Juan Casas Rigall and Eva Díaz Martínez, Santiago de Compostela U.P., 2002, 589 pp.

DIALECTS

GASCON. J. Ducos, *'Le censier du diocèse de Comminges de 1387', *RCo*, 117, 2001:345–90. R. Cierbide Martinena, *'Antropónimos de

la Baja Navarra según el Censo de 1350', *PatRom* 5, 81–93. X. Ravier, in collaboration with Benoît Cursente, *'Sur les registres linguistiques du Cartulaire de Bigorre', Massoure, *Langues*, 399–410, introduces a forthcoming edition of this 12th-c. to 13th-c. cartulary with acts in Latin, Gascon, and a 'lingua mixta'. Part of the same text is studied by Ravier in 'Sur la scripta du deuxième censier des "casaux" de Lourdes dans le cartulaire de Bigorre', *Fossat Vol.*, 297–308; the *casau/casal* of the title is understood as a 'complexe agraire et juridique — maisons d'habitation (*casa*), occupants, travailleurs, terres et droits'. Transcriptions of the three MS versions B, P^1, P^2 are appended. P. Delatour, *'Un acte de mariage à Montréjeau il y a sept cents ans: par le notaire Guillaume du Cuing, légiste, professeur puis évêque', *RCo*,119:63–76. F. Nagore Lain, *Los Pirineos: un nexo de unión entre el occitano y el aragonés', *RFR*, 18, 2001:261–96, presents a corpus of 12th-13th-c. Aragonese documents written in Gascon, plus a study of phonetic correspondences and mutual lexical borrowing.

LANGUEDOCIEN (INCLUDING S. PÉRIG.). **Le Registre des informations des consuls de Foix (1401–1402)*, ed. Gabriel de Llobet and Jacqueline Hoareau-Dodinau, Limoges, PULIM, 2001, 230 pp., offers a rich and hitherto untapped source of Occitan lexicon from the departmental archives of the Ariège. W. D. Paden, *'A notarial roll in Latin and Occitan from Asprières (Aveyron), 1284, in the Newberry Library, Chicago', *CN*, 63:7–55. J. Delmas, *'L'inventaire des biens de la commanderie de Sainte-Eulalie du Larzac en 1308', pp. 319–27 of *La Commanderie, institution des ordres militaires dans l'Occident médiéval*, Paris, CTHS, 2002, 360 pp.

PROVENÇAL. P. Martel, *'L'époque médiévale', pp. 105–37 of *Le Gard, de la Préhistoire à nos jours*, ed. Raymond Huard, Saint-Jean d'Angély, Bordessoules, 364 pp. N. Coulet, *'Les noms de baptême en Provence au bas moyen âge: complément d'enquête', *PrH*, 53:175–92. F. Mazel, *'Noms propres, dévolution du nom et dévolution du pouvoir dans l'aristocratie provençale (milieu Xe-fin XIIe siècle), *ib.*, 131–74. C. Aslanov, 'Judéo-provençal médiéval et chuadit: essai de délimitation', *FL*, 134, 2002:103–22, discusses how the language of the *Roman d'Esther* is less a judeo-language than a medieval Provençal *koiné* written with Hebrew letters; on the other hand, *chuadit*, which began to disappear after the French Revolution, was a true vernacular.

LIMOUSIN (INCL N. PÉRIGORD). J. Ros, 'Perigüers e lo Perigòrd a l'Edat-Mejana entre latin, òc e oïl', *PN*, 94, 2002:19–23, shows how administrative uses of Occitan began as early as literary use by the troubadours; forms examined in 14th-c. and 15th-c. documents differ from the modern language mainly in the preterite and in the use of

pronouns. R.-M. Brun, *'Eléments de cartographie routière en Limousin, du XIIe au XVIIe siècle', *TAL*, 23:55–66.

AUVERGNAT. J.-P. Chambon traces and discusses *'Les limites méridionales de la cité des Arvernes et la toponymie: pérennité du cadre géopolitique, unité et horizons de relations de l'Arvernie aux époques antique et tardo-antique', pp. 77–117 of *Mélanges de dialectologie, toponymie, onomastique offerts à Gérard Taverdet*, ed. Jean Foyard and Philippe Monneret, Dijon, ABELL, Univ. de Bourgogne, Faculté de lettres et philosophie, 2001, vi + 620 pp. Id., *'L'Auvergne linguistique au temps d'Odilon', pp. 279–90 of *Odilon de Mercœur, l'Auvergne et Cluny. La 'Paix de Dieu' et l'Europe de l'an Mil* (Actes du colloque de Lavoute-Chilhac, 10–12 mai 2000), pref. Marcel Pacaut, Nonette, Créer, 2002, 316 pp. Further discussion of the interplay between medieval toponymy and history is found in Chambon's 'Le *ministerium Catlatense* (Rouergue) et la genèse du Carladez: de la philologie à l'histoire', *LengM*, 53:87–125, which concludes that 'La circonscription publique carolingienne de Carlat apparaît comme une pure subdivision du *pagus* arverne'. J. Vezole, *'Censier du XIVe siècle, en langue d'oc des fondations et chapellenies de l'église paroissiale Notre-Dame d'Aurillac', *RevHA*, 64, 2002:77–94. Id., *'Comptes en lenga nòstra (1491)', *Lo Convise*, 42, supp.: 1–4. B. Lesfargas and J. Ros, 'Lo jau rostit', *PN*, 98:20–22, explicates Jalmoutier, a commune of St-Vincent, in the canton of Sainte-Eulalie, as < SANCTUS GALLUS + MONASTERIUM.

3. Post-Medieval Period

GENERAL. P. Martel, *'Histoire externe de l'occitan', Ernst, *RS*, 1:829–39. G. Kremnitz, 'Uberlegungen zu einer Sozialgeschichte des Okzitanischen. Sprach, Kulturkontakt und -konflikt', *Fest. Kirsch*, 111–19, takes a fresh look at the traditional distinction between external and internal language history and argues that external factors do indeed determine internal changes, since the position of Occitan among the languages of Europe is unique both in the early date of its separation from Latin and in its lengthy domination by another Romance language. P. Martel, *'L'occitan aujourd'hui', *MSLP*, 8, 2000:183–94. Id., *'Occitan, français et construction de l'état en France', pp. 87–116 of *La Politique de Babel* (Colloque du Centre d'études des relations internationales), ed. Denis Lacorne and Tony Judt, Paris, Karthala, 2002, 348 pp. R. Bistolfi, *'Décentralisation et identité linguistique. Le cas de l'occitan', *LSPS*, 16; in full at <http://www.sourgentin.org/actu/bistolfidecentr.html>.

J.-F. Courouau, *'Les apologies de la langue française (XVIe) et de la langue occitane (XVIe–XVIIe siècles). Naissance d'une double mythographie (1ère partie)', *NRSS*, 21–22:35–52. Id., 'La *Deffence* de Du Bellay et les apologies de la langue occitane. XVIe–XVIIe siècles', *RHR*, 53, 2001:9–32. The volume *Càtars i trobadors. Occitània i Catalunya: renaixenca i futur*, Barcelona, Generalitat, Dept. de Cultura, 265 pp., contains two chapters of interest here: P. Gardy, 'L'occità entre la "dessocialització" i les vel·leïtats renaixentistes. De l'edicte de Villers-Cotterêts a la Revolució' (156–63); and G. Kremnitz, 'Fabra i Alibert: dues llengües, dos camins'(212–17). J.-M. Guillon, *'L'affirmation régionale en Pays d'Oc des années quarante', *Ethnologie française*, 33:425–33. P. Martel, *'Minority languages of metropolitan France: a long road', pp. 303–08 of *Acts of the VIIIth International Conference on Minority Languages*, Santiago de Compostela, Xunta de Galicia, 668 pp. H. Jeanjean, 'Language diversity in Europe: can the EU prevent the genocide of the French linguistic minorities?', National Europe Center Paper No. 102, 2003, available at <http://www.anu.edu.au/NEC/Jeanjean_paper.pdf>. Id., *'Jack Lang and minority languages: a radical change in French linguistic policies? Or more of the same?', pp. 81–93 of *Perspectives on Europe: Language Issues and Language Planning in Europe*, ed. A. J. Liddicoat and K. Muller, Melbourne, Language Australia, 2002, 141 pp. Id., *'La décolonisation française et le mouvement occitaniste', *Mots Pluriels*, 16, 2000; see <http://www.arts.uwa.edu.au/MotsPluriels/MP1600hjj.html>. K. Salhi and H. Jeanjean, 'France and her linguistic minorities: a case of 'domestic colonialism' in Occitania', pp. 137–66 of the authors' *French In and Out of France. Language Policies, Intercultural Antagonisms and Dialogue*, Oxford, Lang, 487 pp., discuss language policies with regard to Occitan.

Robèrt Lafont, **Petita istoria europèa d'Occitània*, Canet, Trabucaire, 245 pp., traces history and language in the Midi. H. Walter, *'Langue française, langues régionales et francophonie', *LS*, 36, 2001:267–74, uses census data to describe the position of Occitan (and France's other minority languages) vis-à-vis French. M. C. Alén Garabato, in collaboration with C. Valcárcel Riveiro, *'A república francesa e as "linguas rexionais ou locais": a situación do occitano e das linguas oilitanas', *ATO*, 47, 2001:323–47. P. Sauzet, *'Réflexions sur la normalisation linguistique de l'occitan', Caubet, *Codification*, 39–61.

In her introduction (5–28) to *Littératures dialectales de la France: diversité linguistique et convergence des destins*, Paris, Champion — Geneva, Droz, 251 pp., Françoise Vielliard traces the teaching of dialectology at the Ecole des Chartes, with special attention to the links between Paul Meyer and Mistral. S. Ragano, Y. Fijalkow, and J. Kijalkow, 'Vers un didactitiel d'Occitan', *Fossat Vol.*, 275–95, describe efforts to provide computer-aided language-learning programmes for Occitan, culminating in the creation and testing of 'Didac d'Oc' (1998–1999).

ORTHOGRAPHY. J. Sibille, *'Ecrire l'occitan: essai de présentation et de synthèse', Caubet, *Codification*, 17–38. G. Kremnitz, 'Changements linguistiques dus à des phénomènes de contact? Le traitement de l'-e de soutien dans les discussions sur la forme référentielle de l'occitan', *LengM*, 53:161–78, finds no movement toward a mutually-acceptable solution. Annexed, pp. 179–87, is a table by Domergue Sumien comparing four approaches for use of the support vowel (Alibert, Lamuela, Sauzet, Taupiac). For the latter, and for others, this is actually a question of language rather than graphy. J. Taupiac, 'Las entre-senhas', *GS*, 491:453–54, chooses the hyphenated version over 'entresenhas' or 'entressenhas' ('renseignements').

MORPHOSYNTAX. A. Razky, 'Aspects des faits de causativité en occitan dans le cadre de la Grammaire fonctionnelle (GF) de Simon C. Dik (modèle 1978)', *Fossat Vol.*, 309–17, neatly summarizes Occitan causativity into three categories: lexical (e.g., *tuar*), morphological (*abraçar*), and syntactic (*far dintrar*, *far que dintrar*) and finds the second to be productive in the modern language. E. Astie publishes 'Una ficha de grammatica transversala: los demonstratius', *LPO*, 39, 2001:11–21, with a wide selection of examples culled from Occitan authors such as Bladé, Arnaudin, Rapin, as well as Mistral, Palay, and modern grammars of Gascon and Béarnais. E. Blasco Ferrer, *'Tipologia delle presentative romanze e morfosintassi storica. Fr. *c'est* e prov. *-i* (*estai*, *fai*, *plai*)', *ZRP*, 119:51–90, considers that Lat. *habet/stat* 'has/stands' + *ibi/hic* ⟶ Pr. *ai/estai*.

LEXIS AND LEXICOLOGY. Joan de Cantalausa, **Lo Diccionari General Occitan*, Rodez, Le Monastère, Cultura d'òc, 1055 pp., is the fruit of a lifetime of work, with more than 100,000 entries and some 200,000 definitions. Id. presents his work: *'Lo diccionari general occitan', *Camins d'Estiu*, 90:11–14, with its two primary motivations: etymology and the natural language of native speakers, concluding that 'totes lo dialèctes occitans son nòstres, que son totes de bon occitan'. See also Id., *'La lenga parlada dins lo *Diccionari General Occitan*', *Lo Convise*, 45:17. Anselme Castanier, **Les Mots coutumiers du Midi: vocabulaire de la ville et de la campagne*, Nîmes, Lacour, 2002, 121 pp., with a healthy component of Occitan terms. Bernard Vavassori, **'A bisto de nas': dictionnaire des mots et expressions de la langue française parlée dans le Sud-Ouest, et de leurs rapprochements avec l'occitan, le catalan, l'espagnol, l'italien et l'argot méridional*, with drawings by Pertuzé, Portet-sur-Garonne, Loubatières, 2002, 271 pp. P. Sauzet defines as 'L'esquizo-lexicografia' (*Oc*, 346, no. 66:36–40) the quasi-absence of Occitan as a source language in the TLFI. Only six French words are shown as derived from Occitan, while Provençal is attributed as source of 276 words in French: 'se pausa une definicion e es una autra que servís'.

PARTICULAR SEMANTIC FIELDS. J.-P. Dalbera and M.-J. Stefanaggi-Dalbera, 'Onomasiologie, sémasiologie, étymologie. Le cas de baudroie, crapaud et autres enflures', *Ravier Vol.*, 89–100, offers a new take on the vexed etymology of fr. *baudroie* (*FEW* 'de source inconnue'). Drawing on data in the new Monaco-based ALCANOM (Atlas Linguistique des Côtes de l'Arc Nord-Occidental de la Méditerranée), the authors find a veritable tangle of semantic connotations among the various etymological types: 'l'enflure (originaire) du crapaud-*bótrakhos* devenue linguistiquement imperceptible avec le temps, se redéploie dans un bric à brac lexical d'objets renflés, gonflés, ventrus, etc.'. M. Roché, 'La suffixation décalée avec oc. *-ièr(a)*', *Fossat Vol.*, 319–34, offers a close look at 'suffixation double' (as expounded by Alibert in the introduction to his dictionary), finding a continuum of examples running from suffixation in series to interfixation (notably with *-anda/enda-*, *-ada-*, *-at-*, *-ass-*). J. Taupiac, 'Eternal', *GS*, 488: 12, accepts both 'eternal' and 'etèrne', but rejects *eternèl* as a gallicism.

ONOMASTICS. Jacques Astor, *Dictionnaire des noms de familles et noms de lieux du Midi de la France*, pref. Pierre Henri Billy, Millau, Beffroi, 2002, 1293 pp. A.'s monumental work provides more than 17,000 person- and place-names, with presentation (i) in alphabetical order, (ii) by theme, and (iii) in encyclopedic format, ending with an all-inclusive index. J. Peytaví Deixona, 'L'apport occitan à l'anthroponymie catalane: le cas de la population des Comtés du Nord du XVIe au XVIIIe siécle', *LengM*, 52, 2002: 31–52, discusses how Catalan and Occitan populations mixed most notably on the plain of Roussillon, where 17th-18th-c. immigration from the north was heaviest. J. Ladet, *'Enquête sur l'étymologie du Rhône', *Rhodanie*, 85: 42–44.

Two articles of interest for Occitan onomastics are found in *Personal Names Studies of Medieval Europe: Social Identity and Familial Structures*, ed. George T. Beech, Monique Bourin, and Pascal Chareille, Kalamazoo, Medieval Institute, Western Michigan Univ., 2002, xvi + 205 pp.: B. Cursente, *'The French Midi reflected in personal names' (87–95), finds a possible correlation with baptismal names found in charts and troubadour names, e.g., *Guilhem*, *Peire*, *Raimon*, *Bernart*; and P. Beck presents a rapid survey of naming practices: *'Personal naming among the rural populations in France at the end of the Middle Ages' (143–56).

TEXTS. M. C. Alén Garabato, *'L'ús de l'occità en els impresos propagandístics durant la Revolució Francesa', *L'Avenç* (Barcelona), 255, 2001: 16–21. The same author has looked at *'A reivindicación da identidade cultural e lingüística occitana través de creación musical (1965–2000)', *Tato Vol.*, 493–508. M. A. Cipres Palacin, *'Las traducciones catalanas del provenzal en la prensa del siglo XIX', *Thélème* (Madrid), 17, 2002: 179–95.

PAREMIOLOGY. A. Lagarda, *'Provèrbes e dires. *Lo lop*', *Camins d'Estiu*, 90: 30.

4. Gascon and Béarnais

GENERAL. B. Dubarry, 'Une dynamique nouvelle: l'exemple des Hautes-Pyrénées', Massoure, *Langues*, 437–41, reports only small progress on the language preservation front in this one area. D. Philps, *Fossat Vol.*, 219–28, whose work with Gascon in the Central Pyrenees has documented 'une très grande cohérence géolinguistique interne', compares the bi-dimensionality of his dialectometric space to the multi-dimensional spaces of Jean Séguy's *Atlas Linguistique de Gascogne*; map 2525 in vol. 6 of the *ALG* is contrasted with map VL3 from P.'s 'Atlas dialectométrique des Pyrénées Centrales' (1985). Jean Lafitte's continuing efforts to capture Gascon as he sees it include: 'Traduire en gascon "enfler, gonfler"; póble ou póple', *LDGM*, 20, 2002: 11–14; 'Escríver [ks] en gascon', *ib.* , 21–22; 'Punts de grafia', *ib.* , 32–33; and 'Toponimes gascons (5) [notamment Muret, Ortés, Luc-Garièr, etc.]', *ib.* , 34–44.

LEXIS AND LEXICOLOGY. Gilbert Narioo, Michel Grosclaude, and Patric Guilhemjoan, **Dictionnaire français-occitan. Gascon* (A-K), Orthez, Per Noste, 520 pp. Bernard Moreux and Jean-Marie Puyau, **Dictionnaire français-béarnais*, Pau, Princi Neguer–Institut béarnais et gascon, 2002, 203 pp. See also Georges Ensergueix, *Atlas* . . ., below, p. 211.

ONOMASTICS. Robert Aymard, **Un nom, un ostau. Noms des maisons pyrénéennes*, Uzos, p.p., x + 75 pp. André Pées, **Bayonne: noms de famille & familles de noms, d'origine langues basque et gasconne*, Anglet, Atlantica, 129 pp. X. Ravier, *'La Bastide de Marciac et son terroir d'après la toponymie', *BSAHLSG*, 2001: 156–66. This volume, entitled 'Mémoire et actualité des pays de Gascogne. Identités, espaces, cultures, aménagement du territoire', includes the acts of the 53rd Congress of the Fédération historique du Midi-Pyrénées (Auch, 2000). J.-F. Le Nail, *'Note sur la toponymie minière des Hautes-Pyrénées', *RCo*, 119: 343–46.

SUBDIALECTS. **Dictionnaire gascon-français (Landes). Suivi de son lexique français-gascon et d'éléments d'un thesaurus gascon par Vincent Foix (1857–1932)*, ed. Paule Bétérous, Michel Belly, and Jacques Plantey, Bordeaux U.P., 796 pp. Éric Chaplain, **Dictionnaire gascon-béarnais français, ancien et moderne*, Pau, Princi Neguer, 2002, 306 pp., includes 25,000 words. Yolande Vidal, with Hugues Teyssier, **Dictionnaire français-gascon. Le Parler du Pays de Buch. Lo Parlar deu Païs de Buc. D'hier à* *aujourd'hui*, Bordeaux, Les Dossiers d'Aquitaine, 315 pp. Guy Dussaussois, **Flore gasconne et gavache de la Gironde*, Pau, Princi Neguer, 2000, 157 pp.

In a study contrasting the mid-20th-c. *ALG* with an unpublished study from the late 18th c., J. Allières, 'La Chalosse (Landes) linguistique de Grateloup (1794) à *l'ALG*', *Fossat Vol.*, 11–25, finds remarkable stability, particularly in verb morphology. J.-L. Massoure, 'D'Aspe à Aspet', Massoure, *Langues*, 419–36, surveying phonetic and morphological features of the Pyrenean valleys from Aspe to Aspet, outlines in particular seven specific features of the *Pays tòy* (Luz, Barèges, Gavarnie, and other Bigourdan valleys), underlining their originality within the Gascon panoply. J. Prugent, *'Sélection de sources et de références bibliographiques sur Sarrancolin consultables aux Archives Départementales des Hautes-Pyrénées', *RCo*, 119:395–98. J. Suïls Subirà, *'Langue occitane et identité territoriale dans le Val d'Aran', Massoure, *Langues*, 355–60, records cautious optimism among the Aranese regarding the future of their language. J. Castex, 'Val d'Aran, cap de Gasconha', *ib.*, 361–77, is hopeful that Aragonese will be recognized just as Aranese has been.

TEXTS. Félix Arnaudin, *Journal et choses de l'ancienne Lande*, ed. Jean-Yves Boutet, Guy Latry, and Jean-Bernard Marquette, Bordeaux, Confluences — Parc Naturel Régional des Landes de Gascogne, 907 pp. This eighth volume of A.'s complete works contains full texts of his journals (1–315), his 'Histoires naturelles' (317–503), and an important selection of various edited or re-edited documents (505–876), e.g., 'Une branche des Pic de la Mirandole à Labouheyre', the two series of 'Choses de l'ancienne Grande Lande', the 'Histoire de la baronnie de Labouheyre' and various notes (les pays landais, le pays de Born, la Grande Lande, Sabres, le Brassenx, Labrit, les petites landes du Bazadais).

5. Southern Occitan

languedocien (including s. périg.)

GENERAL. Florian Vernet, **Dictionnaire grammatical de l'occitan moderne: selon les parlers languedociens*, Montpellier, Centre d'Estudis Occitans, 400 pp.

LEXIS AND LEXICOLOGY. Mireille Braç, Alan Roch, Robert Martí, and Joan-Claudi Serras, *Tot en òc. Diccionari elementari illustrat (lengadocian)*, Puylaurens, IEO, 2002, 503 pp., contains 20,000 lexical entries. Christian Camps, **Expressions familières du Languedoc et des Cévennes*, Paris, Bonneton, 159 pp. Claude Achard has revised and augmented his 'dictionnaire satirique pour le département de l'Hérault et quelques contrées du Midi' as **Les Uns et les autres: sobriquets collectifs, blasons, proverbes, dictons, contes, réputations*, Pézenas, Domens, 737 pp. Georges Ensergueix, **Atlas linguistique de l'Ariège selon l'enquête Sacaze, 1887*, Pamiers, IEO d'Arièja, 356 pp. Maurice Dage, **Dictionnaire carladézien-occitan-français*, ed. Noël Lafon, Aurillac, Lo Convise, 280 pp.; detailing the *parler* of the region of Aurillac, this work is further introduced by its editor in 'Diccionari carladesenc de Maurici Dèza', *Lo Convise*, 43:5. Zéphyr Bosc, **Flore d'Entraygues et de Mur-de-Barrez. Plantas e èrbas* [...] *d'après les florules de Jean Carbonel. Noms français, occitan, scientifique*, Aurillac, Lo Convise, 32 pp., has been augmented from the 1996 edition.

PARTICULAR SEMANTIC FIELDS. C. Camps, 'Nommer les poissons à Agde en occitan et en français régional', *Ravier Vol.*, 53–62, gives everyday Occitan terms for more than 140 fish; local names in French are frequently influenced by the underlying Occitan.

ONOMASTICS. P. Casado, 'Paulette, Marguerite et les autres [...], ou Les fonctionnements onomastiques dans un procès de sorcellerie en Languedoc à la fin du XVe siècle', *NRO*, 41–42: 177–95, is a study of a 1497 document from Clarensac, near Nîmes, with details of a trial for witchcraft: only judges and (male) witnesses are privileged to be recorded by their surname. Id., 'Aires toponymiques et aires dialectales en Languedoc oriental', *ib.*, 165–76, discusses how in the case of the appellatif 'granja' < **granica* and placenames of the type *Grange* (imported from the franco-provençal zone), dialect zone and onomastics do not always coincide. C. Marichy, 'Des localités non identifiées aux environs de Saint-Clément-de-Rivière et de l'apport des monographies microtoponymiques', *EHér*, 30–32, 2001: 353–56, studies a handful of toponyms from two communes in the Hérault in a short article written before Frank Hamlin's *Toponymie de l'Hérault* (Millau, Beffroi) was published in 2000 (see *YWMLS*, 62: 210). G. Costa, *'Stabilité ou/et instabilité des patronymes des Pyrénées-Orientales entre 1841 et 1896', *PatRom 5*, 129–33.

SUBDIALECTS. Gustave Thérond, *Eléments de grammaire languedocienne (1900). Dialecte languedocien cettois*, Puylaurens, IEO-Languedoc–IEO Hérault, and Ville de Sète, 2002, 255 pp. This work, newly presented by Gaston Bazalgues, was originally sub-titled as 'précédés d'une étude sur les origines, les caractères, la littérature de ce dialecte, et suivis d'une liste des principaux idiotismes et d'une liste des principales comparaisons populaires, par un Félibre cettois. Cette – avril 1900'. Jean Carel, **Notes documentaires pour la connaissance de Saint-Affrique, ville historique du Sud-Aveyron*, pref. Jacques Vaizy, Saint-Affrique, p.p., 2002, 113 pp.

TEXTS. **Recherches sur la langue d'oc: 1627*, [Puylaurens], IEO, 2001, 323 pp., is a study of texts collected by Anne Rulman [Hans

Rulman, 1582–1632], presented by Pierre Trinquier, pref. Jean-Claude Richard. The work of R., born of a German Protestant father and a mother from Languedoc, is further studied by P. Trinquier, 'Anne de Rulman et ses recherches sur la langue du pays', *EHér*, 30–32, 2001:327–330. P. Escudo, *'Stratégies et évolutions linguistiques dans l'imprimé toulousain de 1500 à 1617', *RFHL*, 114–15, 2002:31–51.

Christian-Pierre Bedel continues the series 'Al canton. Opération vilatge, Rodez', published in Rodez by the Mission Départementale de la Culture: **Sent-Amans: Camporiès, Florentinh, Montasic, Sent-Aforiás, Uparlac*, pref. René Delmas, 2000, 310 pp.; **La Guiòla: Cassuèjols, Curièiras, Mont-Peirós, Solatges*, pref. Guy Dumas, 2001, 372 pp.; **Sent-Africa: La Bastida, Caumèls-e-Lo Vialar, Ròcafòrt, Sant-Faliç, Sent-Esèri, Sent-Jan, D'Aucàpias, Sent-Roma de Sarnon, Tornamira, Vabre, Verzòls-e-La Pèira*, pref. Jean-Luc Malet, 2002, 429 pp.; **Vilafranca: Marcièl, Morlhon, La Roqueta, Savinhac, Tolonjac, Valhorlhas*, pref. Claude Penel, 2002, 475 pp.; **Milhau-est: N'Agassac, Compèire, Paulhe, canton de Milhau-est*, pref. Jean-Luc Gayraud, 383 pp.; **Milhau-ouest: Comprenhac, Creissèls, Sent-Jòrdi, canton de Milhau-oest*, pref. Guy Durand, 300 pp.

PAREMIOLOGY. Adelin Moulis, **Les Reproubèrbis de menino-bièlho amassats dins le soul parla del païs de Fouich / Les Proverbes de grand'mère recueillis dans le seul dialecte du pays de Foix*, Nîmes, Lacour, 315 pp., from an unpublished MS dated 1947.

PROVENÇAL

GENERAL. Georges Bonifassi, **La Presse régionale de Provence en langue d'Oc: des origines à 1914*, Paris, Univ. Paris-Sorbonne, 393 pp. Jean-Luc Domenge,**Grammaire du provençal varois: le verbe*, La Farlède, AVEP, 2002, 256 pp.

LEXIS AND LEXICOLOGY. P. Blanchet, 'De quelques emprunts au judéo-provençal dans la langue et la culture provençales', *FL*, 134, 2002:123–29. Included are: *sagata* 'égorger', *batau* 'marché conclu', *félibre* (*emé li sefé*) '[fe]libre de la lei', *Magali* 'Marguerite', *Mirèio* 'Myriam', and *Nerto* 'Esther'. Jean-Louis Ramel, **Nos expressions provençales: rassemblées dans les Baronnies*, ill. Marie-Blanche Sigaud and Muriel Harlaut, [Faucon], p.p., 79 pp.

ONOMASTICS. Bénédicte and Jean-Jacques Fénié, *Toponymie provençale*, Bordeaux, Sud-Ouest, 2002, 124 pp., continue their earlier toponymic studies of Gascon (1992) and Occitan/Languedocien (1997) (see *YWMLS*, 60:198, and see also below in the LIMOUSIN section). Their work, defining 'provençal' as an area wider than the linguistic limits of Provence proper, presents scientifically rigorous interpretations for the general audience. B. Cousin, *'Prénommer en

Provence (XVIe–XIXe siècle)', *PrH*, 53:193–224. C. Borello, *'Pierre, Marie, Jean et les autres: prénommer dans la Provence protestante d'ancien régime', *ib.*, 225–39. D. Maure, *'Propos subversifs: les prénoms révolutionnaires marseillais (1790–1792)', *ib.*, 241–55. E. Nicolas, *'Le choix patronymique, vecteur d'intégration: l'exemple de la Provence au début du XIXe siècle', *ib.*, 257–76.

SUBDIALECTS. J. Chirio, 'Originalité du dialecte nissart comparé au provençal', *LSPS*, 152, 2002:53, *ib.*, 153:52, and *ib.*, 154:52, argues that 'un étroit rameau relie le dialect niçois au provençal'. Among the main points of differentiation are presence of proparoxytones, presence of final –a and -e, preservation of a number of final consonants, and loss of intervocalic -s-; all these traits are found in Nissart. Part 3 ends with a list of 21 lexical differences. On the other hand, P. Blanchet, 'De l'identité socio-linguistique: l'exemple du provençal et du niçois', *FL*, 135, 2002:13–25, argues on socio-linguistic grounds for consideration of Nissart as a language, rather than a dialect of Provençal. The Escola de Bellanda has published **Diciounari nissart-francès-Dictionnaire niçois-français*, pref. Adolphe Viani, Nice, Fédération des assoc. du comté de Nice, 221 pp. Jaume Clapié, **Pichin lèxico ilustrat/Petit lexique illustré français-niçois (Grafia clássica)*, adapted Joan-Pèire Baquié, corr. Jaume Pietri and Andrieu Sàissi, Nice, Serre, 227 pp. R. Nathiez, '*Amenda, amèndoula, abalana, estrachana* [vocabulaire de l'amande]', *LSPS*, 150, 2002:47. M. Pallanca, 'Tanta Zoun, Barba Pin e lou "beu couòr d'aglan"', *ib.*, 151, 2002:53, corrects *aglan*, not to *glau* but to *lou miéu bèu couòr de gauch*. Jean-Louis Caserio, **Lexique français-mentonnais*, Menton, Soc. d'art et d'histoire du Mentonnais, 2001, 239 pp.

6. Northern Occitan

limousin (including n. périg.)

MORPHOSYNTAX. H. Stroh, *L'Accord du participe passé en occitan rouergat et en français*, Rodez, Lo Grelh Roergàs, 2002, 130 pp. In this study, which has been very favourably reviewed, a Munich linguist finds 19 cases of differing rules for agreement.

LEXIS AND LEXICOLOGY. J.-P. Chambon, 'A propos d'une édition récente: notes pour le glossaire de François Rempnoux, de Chabanais (1641)', *RLaR*, 106, 2002:163–72, provides additional vocabulary and notes, in complement to Christian Bonnet's recent edition of *François Rempnoux, les amours de Colin & Alyson: la littérature occitane entre baroque et classique*, Gardonne, Fédérop, 2001, 273 pp. M. Chapduelh, 'Biais de dire', *PN*, 95, 2002:20–21, advises his readers to avoid gallicisms in conversation, e.g., not 'Es tombat de Caribde en Scillà', but 'Daus landiers, suata dins las cendres'. This article, continued in *ib.*, 97:13, 24, follows on earlier segments in *PN*, 74, 1997:21–22, and *ib.*, 75, 1997:22–23.

ONOMASTICS. Bénédicte and Jean-Jacques Fénié, *Toponymie nord-occitane. Périgord, Limousin, Auvergne, Vivarais, Dauphiné*, Bordeaux, Sud-Ouest, 128 pp. J. Surpas, 'Los faus noms, diminutius e chafres', *PN*, 94, 2002:17–18; *ib.*, 95:10–13; *ib.*, 96:19–24, categorizes them by trade and by personality trait.

SUBDIALECTS. N. Quint, *'Le Marchois: problèmes de norme aux confins occitans', Caubet, *Codification*, 63–76.

AUVERGNAT (INCLUDING N. PÉRIG.)

GENERAL. F. Daval, *'L'ensenhament de l'occitan dins lo Cantal', *Lo Convise*, 42:16.

SUBDIALECTS. P. Rimbaud, *'Notre langue régionale: l'Auvergnat du pays d'Ambert', *Chroniques historiques du Livradois-Forez* [Ambert], 25:39–44.

LEXIS AND LEXICOLOGY. Etienne Gamonnet, **Glossaire du parler des Boutières*, p.p., 2001, 191 pp., provides vocabulary from Saint-Julien-du-Gua in the northern Ardèche (Haut Vivarais). R. Teulat, *'Diari per dire (3)', *Lo Convise*, 43: 2–3. J. M. Maurí, *'A l'exemple de las bèstias', *ib.*, 43:4. Id., *'Biais de dire', *ib.*, 44:19.

ONOMASTICS. J.-P. Chambon, 'Une église disparue de la banlieue de Clermont-Ferrand. Notes sur l'histoire du microtoponyme *Lize Faite* et de son référent', *NRO*, 41–42:157–64, sees it as < *Gleiza Fraita (gleiza 'église' + fraita 'brisée'). Id., *'Les toponymes issus de lat. PICARIA "fabrique de poix", et leurs congénères dans la toponymie du Massif Central occitan, particulièrement en Velay', *RLaR*, 106, 2002:511–24. Id., *'Pour la datation des toponymes galloromans: une étude de cas (Ronzières, Puy-de-Dôme)', *ER*, 25:39–58. Henri Garnero, *'Essai d'interprétation de la signification du toponyme *Aurillac*, chef-lieu du Cantal', *RevHA*, 64, 2002:95–98.

TEXTS. J. Vezole, *'Testament en òc al sègle XVI (1561)', *Lo Convise*, 44:17.

PAREMIOLOGY. J. Glayal, *'Les dires de chas nautres', *Lo Convise*, 43:18–20, *ib.*, 44:20. Z. Bòsc and J. Carbonel, *'Provèrbis calhòls, locucions risolièiras [. . .]', *ib.*, 45:13–15.

PROVENÇAL ALPIN

ONOMASTICS. Jean-Claude Bouvier, **Noms de lieux du Dauphiné*, Paris, Bonneton, 2002, 224 pp.

SUBDIALECTS. Alain Bouras, Christian Espinas, Gérard Bayel, and Isabelle Gérard, **Petite grammaire de l'occitan dauphinois*, Montélimar, IEO Daufinat-Provènça–Tèrra d'Òc, 2002, 86 pp. Édouard Antoulin,**Patois de Dieulefit* (Drôme), Aix-en-Provence, Edisud, vols 1 (A-E), 2002, 197 pp.; and 2 (F-O), 2002, 157 pp., includes grammar, glossary, expressions, sayings, proverbs.

The acts of a 2002 colloquium held in Romans include several articles of linguistic interest to the Romanais sub-dialect: 'Calixte Lafosse, journaliste et poète-artisan romanais', ed. Jean-Claude Bouvier, with Jean-Claude and Marie-Christine Rixte, *RD*, no. 507–508. Included are: J.-M. Effantin, *'L'écriture de la langue locale: l'occitan à Romans, du Moyen Age à Calixte Lafosse' (39–46); R. Merle, *'C. Lafosse dans l'écriture en "patois" des confins nord-occitans et francoprovençaux' (47–52); J.-C. Rixte, *'Le glossaire de Calixte Lafosse et la lexicographie du parler de Romans' (53–71); P. Floury, *'Le parler romanais d'aujourd'hui' (78–79); J.-C. Rixte, *'Calixte Lafosse (1842–1904), Essai de bibliographie, avec notes et commentaires' (164–91). P. Martel, *'L'occitan fòra França: los Occitans d'Italia', pp. 115–22 of *O occitano, lingua europea*, ed. María Carmén Alén-Garabato, Santiago de Compostela U.P., 122 pp. N. Duberti, *'Il dialetto di Mondovi nel settecento, il dialetto di Viola oggi. Correnti e contrasti di lingua e cultura fra Liguria, Provenza e Piemonte', *BALI*, 25, 2001: 43–51.

LEXIS AND LEXICOLOGY. Han Schook, **Le Trésor du Diois. Glossaire de l'occitan diois et de la culture dioise*, Diemen, p.p., 2002, 114 pp., with 5500 words, hundreds of proverbs and expressions, as well as items of historical information and toponymy.

LITERATURE

MEDIEVAL PERIOD

By Miriam Cabré, *Universitat de Girona*, and Sadurní Martí, *Universitat de Girona*

1. Research Tools and Reference Works

Bibliografia elettronica dei trovatori, ed. Stefano Asperti, <www.bedt.it> is now available on-line. The extraordinary wealth of information offered by this database ranges from the codicological description of all troubadour *chansonniers*, to author and metrical files, and bibliography. Rialto, <www.rialto.unina.it>, includes new editions (Peire Milo by L. Borghi Cedrini), additions to on-going editions (Milone's Raimbaut d'Aurenga), as well as newly available published editions (e.g. Branciforti's Lanfranc Cigala, Guida's *Trovatori minori*, and Avalle's Peire Vidal with a translation by A. Martorano). W. Pfeffer, 'Bibliography of Occitan literature for 2001', *Tenso*, 18, 122–52, is arranged by subject.

2. Editions and Textual Criticism

Francesca Gambino, *Canzioni anonime di trovatori e trobairitz*, Alessandria, Dell'Orso, 268 pp., offers diplomatic and critical editions of 22 *unica*, describing their MS context and the problem of language in French witnesses. Maria Carla Marinoni, *Il poemetto occitanico sulla 'Vita di Maria Maddalena': edizione critica*, Milan, CUEM, 2002, 98 pp., chooses MS F as base, which she has shown to be a different version from Boysset's MS A, but derived from the same archetype (in *'Il poemetto occitanico sulla *Vita di Santa Maria Maddalena*: tradizione con archetipo', pp. 155–65 of *Territori romanzi: Otto studi per Andrea Pulega*, Viareggio–Lucca, Baroni, 2002, 183 pp). Carol Sweetenham and Linda M. Paterson, *The 'Canso d'Antioca': An Epic Chronicle of the First Crusade*, Aldershot, Ashgate, xi + 363 pp., analyse the Madrid fragment from a literary and historical viewpoint, while highlighting the problem of editing such a defective single witness. Hans Christian Haupt, *Le Roman d'Arles dans la copie de Bertran Boysset*, Tübingen, Francke, 326 pp., accompanies the edition with an extensive glossary, and studies sources, *remaniement*, and linguistic differences between the authors and Boysset. L. Milone, 'Tre canzoni di Raimbaut d'Aurenga (389, 1, 2 e 11)', *CN*, 63: 169–254, edits the texts on the basis of exhaustive ecdotic analysis. C. P. Hershon, 'Pistoleta', *RLaR*, 107: 247–341, provides a new edition of the lyrics and the *vida*. P. T.

Ricketts, 'Trois saluts d'amour dans la littérature de l'occitan médiéval', *ib.*, 106, 2002:493–510, edits three anonymous texts from the *COM* corpus. One of these is also edited in S. Marinetti, 'Il salut d'amor *Hai, dolcha domna valentz*', *Romania*, 121:289–328, where an interesting description of MS L and a discussion on editorial problems are added. Pierre Bec, **Le Comte de Poitiers, premier troubadour: à l'aube d'un verbe et d'une érotique*, Montpellier, Univ. Paul Valery, 290 pp., is an edition with commentary. Joan de Castellnou, *Compendis de la conoxença dels vicis que·s podon esdevenir en los dictats del Gai Saber*, ed. Paolo Maninchedda, Cagliari, CUEC, 269 pp., corrects his 2000 edition; the study focuses on the MS tradition. *Biblioteca medievale*, Roma, Carocci, has issued three volumes based on past editions: Jaufre Rudel, *L'amore di lontano*, ed. Giorgio Chiarini, 167 pp.; the anthology Bernart de Ventadorn, *Canzoni*, ed. Mario Mancini, 161 pp.; and Folquet de Marselha, *Poesie*, ed. Paolo Squillacioti, 243 pp., with some corrections to his 1999 edition.

TEXTUAL CRITICISM AND MANUSCRIPT TRANSMISSION. Several articles comment on the recent edition of Marcabru by Gaunt, Harvey, and Paterson: in *Tenso*, 18, M. N. Taylor adds a list of *errata* to his overall review (3–38); and W. D. Paden discusses emendations based on declension, while reflecting on wider troubadour declension issues (67–115); M. Perugi, 'Per un'analisi stratigrafica delle poesie di Marcabruno: note in margine a una nuova edizione critica', *SM*, 44:532–600, criticizes Bédierism as well as linguistic and metrical aspects of the edition.

S. Conte, '*Soudadier, per cui es jovens* (BdT 293,44): richiami esegetico-biblici nella representazione della chimera' *CrT*, 5, 2002:407–44, analyses ll. 17–32 minutely; new intertextual evidence allows her to adjust her interpretation and propose a liturgical structural pattern. F. Zinelli, 'À propos d'une édition récente de Folquet de Marseille: réflexions sur l'art d'éditer les troubadours', *Romania*, 121:501–26, discusses Squillacioti's innovative application of ecdotic analysis, which results in a revision of Avalle's MS families. The third volume of the series *Intavulare, Venezia, Biblioteca Nazionale Marciana V (Str. App. 11 = 278)*, ed. Ilaria Zamuner, Modena, Mucchi, 188 pp., adds a study of sources to the index and codicological description of this troubadour *chansonnier*.

3. Cultural and Historical Background

Cynthia Robinson, *In Praise of Song: The Making of Courtly Culture in Al-Andalus and Provence, 1005–1134*, Leiden, Brill, 2002, 419 pp., once more proposes classical Arab poetry at the Zaragoza court as the origin of Occitan courtly lyrics. G. Peters, 'Urban minstrels in late medieval southern France: opportunities, status and professional relationships', *Early Medieval History*, 19, 2000:201–35, gives a picture of these professionals as respected, economically comfortable, and well-organized. F. R. P. Akehurst, 'Good name, reputation and notoriety in French customary law', pp. 75–104 of *Fama: The Politics of Talk and Reputation in Medieval Europe*, ed. Thelma Fenster and Daniel Lord Smail, Ithaca, Cornell U.P., 227 pp., uses legal texts (one Occitan *costuma*) and literature to assess the implications of having a 'good name'. G. M. Cropp, 'Felony and courtly love', *ICLS 9*, 73–80, investigates the criminal implications of the term *felon* in *romans* and in troubadour lyrics.

WOMEN AND COURTLY LOVE. A. Rieger, '*Trobairitz*, *domna*, mecenas: la mujer en el centro del mundo trobadoresco', *MSR*, 2:41–55, analyses the role of women as patrons, consumers, and creators of literature. A. M. Mussons, 'Dona, lírica i representació', *ib.*, 56–63, focuses on debates in order to return to the issue of real or fictional female authorship. L. Paterson, 'Women, property, and the rise of courtly love', *ICLS 9*, 41–55, refutes Bloch's sociological accounts of courtly love and defines courtliness as a 'locus of negociation'. M. Johnston, 'Gender as conduct in the courtesy guides for aristocratic boys and girls of Amanieu de Sescás', *EMS*, 20, 75–84, explains gender specific topics as examples of common imperatives, and different approaches as applications of theories on female knowledge acquisition. W. D. Paden, 'Gender in the world of William Marshal and Bertran de Born', *ib.*, 19, 2002:44–60, uses the data from the troubadour's work to correct Duby's male-biased account of William's world. K. A. Grossweiner, 'Implications of the female poetic voice in *Le Roman de Flamenca*', *ICLS 9*, 133–40, compares Flamenca's voice with that of *trobairitz* and *domnas* and suggests this is a cautionary tale for men. E. Jane Burns, *Courtly Love Undressed: Reading through Clothes in Medieval French Culture*, Philadelphia, Pennsylvania U.P., 2002, 326 pp., includes discussion of how Lombarda and Alamanda describe clothes as an important currency of courtly exchange. N. Frelick, 'Lacan, courtly love and anamorphosis', *ICLS 9*, 107–14, describes courtly love as a Lacanian model for desire in terms of an anamorphic game of mirrors. A. Leupin, 'L'expérience mentale des troubadours', *PerM*, suppl. 28:69–78, analyses the impossibility of troubadour love outside the boundaries of literature because of the lady's masculinization.

4. Poetry

M. Zink, 'Guiraut Riquier, du premier au dernier vers', *Cazauran Vol.*, 511–23, analyses several trajectories that can be tracked along

Riquier's *libre.* M.-A. Bossy, 'The ins and outs of court: Guiraut Riquier's poetics of ostracism', *ICLS 9*, 275–84, reads Riquier's *libre* as an account of a professional poetic career. M. Longobardi, 'Nomen omen — nom nombre: Guiraut Riquier e Alfonso X di Castiglia', *MedRom*, 26, 2002: 218–45, analyses encoded wordplay with the king's name in Guiraut's work, and suggests a numerical homage in the *libre.* L. Borghi Cedrini, 'L'enigma degli pseudonimi nel *débat* tra Raimbaut d'Aurenga, Bernart de Ventadorn e Chrétien de Troyes', Floris, *Il segreto*, 49–75, proposes a new order for the debate and calls for a systematic study of *senhals.* L. Rossi, 'Suggestion métaphorique et réalité historique dans la légende du cœur mangé', *Micrologus*, 11: 469–500, finds the court of Alfonso of Aragon as a likely centre of diffusion for the motif, found in a variety of Occitan and French texts. A. Guerreau-Jalabert, '*Aimer de fin cuer*: le cœur dans la thématique courtoise', *ib.*, 343–71, outlines the motifs related to heart and love and searches its Classical and Christian origins. C. Lucken, '*Chantars no pot gaire valer, si d'ins dal cor no mou lo chans*: subjectivité et poésie formelle', *ib.*, 373–413, re-examines the link between heart and song while surveying the notions that have ruled this analysis since Jeanroy. G. Passerat, 'Les outrances verbales d'un troubadour: le cas du spirituel Raimon de Cornet', *Cahiers de Fanjeaux*, 38: 135–58, presents the range of satiric poems in Cornet's corpus, the variety of which refutes the cliché of Consistori poetry.

ATTRIBUTIONS. S. Guida, 'L'autore della seconda parte della "Canso de la crotzada"', *CN*, 63: 255–82, proposes Gui de Cavalhon as a likely candidate, considering his biography and works. Id., 'La "biografia" di Aimeric de Peguilhan', *RSTe*, 3, 2001: 221–33, finds several clues to defend Uc de Sant Circ as the author. C. Lucken, '*Onqes n'amai tant que jou fui amee*: la chanson de femme à l'épreuve de la fin'amor', *PerM*, suppl. 28: 33–68, denies the authorship of Fournival, while considering attribution to a *trobairitz*.

SOURCES AND GENRES. F. Carapezza, 'Una *cobla* oscena di *G* (*BdT* 461.57) e il suo modello ritrovato', *RSTe*, 3, 2001: 97–111, proposes the *ensenhamen* of Garin lo Brun as the parodied model, which would imply a wider diffusion of the *ensenhamen* than its MS transmission suggests. J. T. Grimbert, 'Songs by women and women's songs: how useful is the concept of register?', *ICLS 9*, 117–24, re-examines Bec's genre classification, which fails to reflect a dynamic genre system, and women's contribution to it. E. Fidalgo, '"Tu es alva": las albas religiosas y una cantiga de Alfonso X', *MedRom*, 26, 2002: 101–26, reconsiders the corpus of *albas* and analyses the elements borrowed by the Castilian king. G. Avenoza, 'La *dansa*, corpus d'un genre lyrique roman', *RLaR*, 107: 89–129: classifies a corpus of 151 *dansas.*

METRICS AND MUSIC. *RLaR*, 107, has a special section on 'L'heritage des troubadours: la métrique': D. Billy, 'L'art des réseaux chez les néo-troubadours aux XIV-XV siècles' (1–40), finds Raimon de Cornet to be the chief model; and A. Solimena, 'Traditions métriques comparées: les troubadours et les poètes italiens du XIIIe siècle' (75–87), surveys what elements of troubadour versification are adopted or discarded by Sicilian and *siculotoscani* poets. I. Hardy and E. Brodovitch, 'Tracking the anagram: preparing a phonetic blueprint of troubadour poetry', *ICLS 9*, 199–211, describe their method of compiling phonetic inventories and its relevance to determining attribution. J. Schulze, 'Giacomino Pugliese und Gaucelm Faidit', *CN*, 63: 57–72, finds arguments in the metric and melodic analysis to support the existence of Pugliese's *contrafactum*. R. Castano, 'Sulla struttura della canzone trobadorica', *RSTe*, 3, 2001: 113–25, analyses the use of 'parole-guie', recurrent terms which create a semiotic fabric. Two articles in *Tenso*, 18, discuss Marcabru as a musician: V. Pollina analyses the variety of melodic patterns (39–49); and J. Haines points to the problems of interpreting monody (50–66). G. Le Vot, 'Réalités et figures: la plainte, la joie et la colère dans le chant aux XIIe–XIIIe siècles', *CCMe*, 46: 353–80, focuses on several troubadour genres within his discussion of emotion.

RECEPTION. A. Rieger, 'Aliénor d'Aquitaine et ses filles, détentrices des fils du réseau interculturel entre troubadours, trouvères et Minnesänger', Buschinger, *Aliénor d'Aquitaine*, 37–50, defines the moments when the courts of these three women could have favoured such contacts. Dominique Billy et al., *La lirica galego-portoghese: Saggi di metrica e musica comparata*, Rome, Carocci, 237 pp., study several aspects of troubadour metrics in relation to the Galician Portuguese tradition: D. Billy, 'L'arte delle connessioni dei *trobadores*' (11–111); P. Canettieri and C. Pulsoni, 'Per uno studio storico-geografico dell'imitazione metrica nella lirica galego-portoghese' (113–65). Also on the troubadour heritage in Galician Portuguese lyrics: Giuseppe Tavani, *Tra Galizia e Provenza. Saggi sulla poesia medievale galego-portoghese*, Rome, Carocci, 2002, 107 pp. S. Gutiérrez García and M. Souto Espasandín, 'Le *senhal* occitan et le secret de la dame en galicien-portugais', *RLaR*, 107: 411–28, describe the use of *senhal* in troubadours prior to studying the Galician-Portuguese counterpart. Several articles in *RVQ*, 15, deal with the reception and translation of troubadours: P. Canettieri, 'Pirandello, Folchetto e la Gaia Scienza' (73–91); M. De Conca, '*Un filo che si dipana senza fine*: tradurre i trovatori' (93–127), which mainly discusses Arnaut Daniel's translators; R. Capelli, 'Pound traduttore dei trovatori, tra esercitazione, tecnica e sperimentazione creativa' (129–86); and C. Pulsoni, 'I versi provenzali della *Commedia* e le loro traduzioni antiche'

(187–243), which finds unawareness of the Occitan language among early commentators. Id., 'I classici italiani di Aldo Manuzio e le loro contraffrazioni lionesi', *CrT*, 5, 2002: 477–87, detects Vellutello's source when commenting the presence of Arnaut in Dante and Petrarch. P. Allegretti, 'Il maestro de *lo bello stilo che m'ha fatto onore* (Inf. I 87), ovvero la matrice figurativa della sestina, da Arnaut Daniel a Virgilio', *StD*, 67, 2002: 11–55, proposes a mediating role of Virgil in Arnaut's rhetorical influence on Dante. B. Barbiellini Amidei, 'Dante, Arnaut e le metamorfosi del cuore: a proposito di *Sols sui qui sai lo sobrafan qe·m sortz*, vv. 26–28', *PaT*, 6, 2002: 91–108, uses the troubadour tradition to reinterpret Dante's heart images. Claudio Giunta, *Versi a un destinatario: saggio sulla poesia italiana nel medioevo*, Bologna, Il Mulino, 2002, 548 pp., touches on several aspects of troubadour lyrics, such as debate genres, within his wide analysis of how Italian poetry travels from objective to subjective.

NARRATIVE TEXTS. R. Lafont, 'Nouveau regard sur le "Fragment d'Alexandre"', *RLiR*, 66, 2002: 159–205, tries to reconstruct the language and metric of the Occitan Alexander antigraf, on the basis of the extant fragment, its derivations, and the early Romance narrative system. G. Gouiran, '*Tragediante*? Pis encore: jongleur! ou De l'art de déconsiderer un adversaire: la présentation de l'évêque Foulque de Toulouse, alias Folquet de Marseille par l'Anonyme de *La Chanson de la Croisade albigeoise*', *Cahiers de Fanjeaux*, 38: 111–33, reads the portrait of bishop Folc in the light of a reference to his 'jongleuresque' past. S. Kay, 'Singularity and spectrality: desire and death in *Girart de Roussillon*', *Olifant*, 22, 1998–2003: 11–38, uses the Derridean idea of spectrality to analyse the dynamics of singularity in terms of possession and death, and finds a counter narrative that allows for salvation instead of death. C. Lee, 'Le *chat rouge* de Guillaume d'Aquitaine', *Reinardus* 13, 2000: 123–34, relates the cat to a Southern European Arthurian tradition, which allows her also to read Jaufre as the Southern alternative to Northern heroes in 'Il simbolismo arturiano nel *Jaufre*', *Quaderni del Dipartimento di Scienze della Communicazione, Università di Salerno*, 2, 2002: 189–211.

BREVIARI D'AMOR. P. Ricketts, 'Knowledge as therapy: a comparison between the *Confessio Amantis* of Gower and the *Breviari d'Amor* of Matfre Ermengaud', *ICLS* 9, 57–69, outlines the main features of the *Breviari*, especially its diagrammatic structure and its purpose. V. Galent-Fasseur, 'Une expérience avec la lyrique: le *Perilhos tractat d'amor de donas* de Matfre Ermengau', *PerM*, suppl. 28: 169–92, describes Matfre's love treatise as a bait to lead the reader towards pure love.

5. Scientific, Doctrinal, and other Prose Texts

M. Jeay and K. Garay, 'Douceline de Digne: de l'usage politique de l'extase mystique', *RLaR*, 106, 2002:475–87, explores why Doucelina's life was written and why the manuscript was copied. G. Hasenohr, 'Quelques opuscules spirituels du XIIIe siècle en langue d'oc (ms. Egerton 945)', *Cazauran Vol.*, 493–510, edits seven Occitan treatises and evaluates the translation according to its aim. M. S. Corradini Bozzi, 'Per l'edizione di opere mediche in lingua d'oc e in catalano: un nuovo bilancio della tradizione manoscritta', *RSTe*, 3, 2001 : 127–95, edits and comments several Occitan medical recipe-books; and P. V. Davies, 'Le texte occitan d'un livre d'heures (Brunel n. 60; Médiathèque de Rodez, ms. 138): édition critique', *RLaR*, 107 : 343–428, offers a linguistic and liturgical commentary of the edited text. É. Gesbert, 'Les jardins du Moyen Âge: du XIe au début du XIV siècle', *CCMe*, 46 : 381–408, quotes from troubadours to analyse gardening terminology.

MODERN PERIOD

By Stanley F. Levine, *University of South Carolina at Aiken*

1. General

Dix siècles d'usages et d'images de l'occitan. Des troubadours à l'internet, ed. Henri Boyer and Philippe Gardy, pref. R. Lafont, Paris, L'Harmattan, 2001, 469 pp. + 12 pls. The ambitious goal of this volume is to constitute the first full sociolinguistic history 'of linguistic practices in the Occitan domain, of their social functioning, and of the images associated with them'. This is an important work, but an index and precise references would have made it more useful to the scholar. There is a bibliography of secondary sources, but in the text references are often given without page numbers; the only footnotes are French translations of Occitan passages. Four sub-chapters directly concern later literature: F. Gardy, 'XVIe–XVIIIe siècles: la littérature comme réaction à la situation sociolinguistique' (127–43), discusses a series of manifestos and defences of the Occ. language, usually linked to literary work. He speculates that the elimination of Occ. from official uses stimulated in some a compensatory desire to rescue the language through literature. Thus Pey de Garros, Guillaume Du Bartas, and others from Gascony, Languedoc, and Provence argued that Occ. was as good as, or superior to, other languages. After 1600, Occ. poets felt the need to imitate Fr. or classical models for legitimacy, but by the mid-17th c., all claims to equal other literatures were abandoned, and Occ. writers accepted their marginal status, writing parodies or burlesques of Virgil, Homer, and of Fr. texts. The 18th c. saw a revival however, which G. sees as a forerunner to the *Félibrige* movement of 1830–1850. J. Eygun, 'Les langues du sacré en pays occitan (XVIe–XIXe siècles)' (177–220), offers substantial excerpts from Occ. religious texts of great interest, including works by Pey de Garros, Arnaut de Salette, and Auger Gaillard, 17th-c. polemical texts such as *La detestaciu é coundannaciu del Calbinisme, Calvinisme de Bearn divisat en seys eglogues,* and the violently anti-Huguenot *Houros perdudos*, and several 'conversion Noëls' — supposedly addressed to the Jews but sometimes so aggressive and demeaning that they could only be meant to comfort the prejudices of a Christian audience. E. concludes that although the Church did not recognize Occ. in official usage, it had recourse to the language when spreading its doctrine among the humble who understood no other language; the early clerical contact with written Occ. may have prepared the way for the abundant religious literature during the *Félibrige* period. F. Gardy, 'La littérature occitane de l'époque moderne (XIXe et XXe siècles): les territoires d'une écriture' (292–304), argues first that Mistral created the 'topography' of Occ. poetry within which, or against which, most subsequent Occ. lit. is inscribed; he then devotes attention to the prose fiction of Félix Gras (*Li Rouge dóu Miejour*), Joseph d'Arbaud, Valère Bernard, Robèrt Lafont, Max Rouquette, Joan Bodon, and Bernat Manciet. Among younger writers, G. mentions only Joan-Claudi Forêt, in whose novel, *La Pèira d'azard*, he sees the culmination of the enterprise, begun with the *Félibrige*, of writing from within the 'absence' of language, and the double temptation 'du vide et du trop plein de la langue'. C. Alranq, 'Théâtre d'oc du XXe siècle' (311–17), is an excellent study of how Occ. theatre is evolving in response to changes in both ideology and the audience's familiarity with Occ.

Nivelle, *Écrivains*, contains papers read at a colloquium organized by members of the CNRS to mark the 26th centennial of Marseilles's founding, and devoted to writers who were born or lived in Marseilles, regardless of the language in which they wrote, and so implies interconnections which traditional treatments, addressing either Occ. authors or those who wrote in French, tend to hide. As is usual in a book of this sort, the quality of the articles varies; however, a few well-known authors are presented in a new light, and a useful introduction is provided to the work of several less well-known writers. In her own article, N. Nivelle, 'Masques et utopies. De quelques œuvres de quelques écrivains marseillais, de Victor Gelu à André Roussin' (57–65), the editor distinguishes various 19th-c. Occ. utopias: Gelu's pastoral, backward-looking utopia; Bernard's two utopias, one

Christian socialist, the other feminist; and Bertas's society built on love and friendship, all seen as a response to the suppression of Occ. language and culture, and she sees the same dynamic at work in the works of Edmond Rostand.

2. Sixteenth to Eighteenth Centuries

Premiers combats pour la langue occitane: manifestes linguistiques occitans XVIe–XVIIe siècles (Occitanas, 13), intro. and tr. J.-F. Courouau, Biarritz, Atlantica — Pau, Institut Occitan, 2001, 193 pp., reprints nine 'manifestos' for the Occ. language, dating from between 1555 and 1642, including works by Pey de Garros, du Bartas, Larade, Ruffi, Godolin, Dastros, and Bédout, and the anonymous 'Requeste [...] par les Dames de la Ville de Toulouse', preceded by a 19-page general introduction and followed by a brief but well-selected bibliography of recent criticism on each work or author and a 'répertoire thématique'. Texts are presented in the standardized spelling with facing translation, preceded by a biographical sketch and a five- to seven-page essay, and followed by a reference to the most dependable edition of the work and an explanation of the graphic system used by the author, reproducing two lines of the work in the original spelling. R. Lafont, 'L'institution "littérature française"', *Fest. Kirsch*, 120–36, looks at French literary history from an Occitan perspective, with two full sections 'De la Pléiade à Malherbe: l'enfermement français' and 'Comment se fait le "classicisme français"', demonstrating the gradual process of cooptation of major French authors by the court, ultimately resulting in self-censorship by these writers. Occitan literature, in contrast, remained multi-polar and in contact with social reality. J. Eygun, 'Occitan et Réforme protestante: l'histoire d'une absence', *Leng(M)*, 48, 2000: 27–91, starts from the paradox that the Reform, which adopted the vernacular languages for both liturgy and sacred works, nonetheless did not choose the Occ. language used by Calvinists of Southern France, but instead opted for French, the language of the élites. He demonstrates that despite Occ. being the official language of Béarn, and despite early efforts to preach and to publish catechisms, psalms, and other Protestant texts in Occitan, the beginnings of a diglossic situation already existed, and that most of the available clergy were exclusively francophone. He disputes the notion that Jeanne d'Albret actively favoured Occ. as a step toward greater autonomy, asserting that her long-term policy was rather to unite Béarn and France under her son's rule, noting that only a few Protestant polemic writings are in *béarnais*; however, a lively anti-Huguenot polemical literature developed in Occitan, which E. cites and analyses.

J. Eygun, 'Une littérature occitane de la gueuserie à Marseille au XVIIe siècle', *RLaR*, 105, 2001 : 263–84, focuses on two anonymous texts in rhymed verse from the anthology *Lou Jardin deys Musos prouvençalos* (Marseilles, 1665), both attributed to its putative editor, François de Bègue, *premier consul* of Marseilles (1645–46) and captain of a galley (1652–1653). *La farço de Juan dou Grau, à sieis Persounagis ou L'Assemblado dei paures mandians de Marseillo, per empacha de baistir la Charité* portrays a meeting of six beggars facing an impending catastrophe: the construction of an institution to house the poor. Beneath a light, picaresque surface the work participates in the political, social, and theological debate on the place of the pauper in society. *La souffranço et la miseri dei fourças que soun en galero* represents the lamentation of a man condemned to labour in the galleys. E. criticizes Zygsberg's 1988 edition of this work (*Provenço,* 2000, 6 : 12–35), and uses this case to criticize Gardy's theory that *ancien régime* Occ. texts were in themselves examples of Occ.'s diglossic situation, claiming that it would be anachronistic to see in the sufferings and ever-present death on the galley a metaphor for the discriminations and impending death of the Occ. language. On the contrary, he argues, *La Farço* and *La Souffranço* show that Occ. texts were related to larger European literary movements, and critics are wrong to exaggerate the *singularité* of Occ. literature. P. Gardy, 'Un disciple (rival?) de Pèire Godolin: l'auteur anonyme des *Stansos sur les faits de Louys le Juste, Rey de Franço et de Nabarro* (Toulouse, 1624)', *Ravier Vol.*, 475–91, after a discussion of the many parallels between Godolin's text and this one, provides a critical edition of the entire text and then a French translation.

GAILLARD. P. Millet, 'Auger Gaillard, poète de la paix au temps des guerres de religion', *RT,* 187 : 539–42, is a brief presentation of this 16th-c. Protestant poet who was forced out of his native Rabastens by the religious wars, took part in the siege of Chartres, and later became a champion of the cause of peace, addressing common soldiers, notables and even the king, preaching the horrors of war and the benefits of peace. Excerpts from his poems, addressing each of these moments, are quoted in their original spelling, followed by a prose translation.

RUFFI. Robert Ruffi, *Contradiccions d'amor / Contradictions d'amour* intro. and tr. J.-Y. Casanova (Occitanas, 8), Biarritz, Atlantica — Pau, Institut Occitan, 2000, 65 pp., is one of a useful series making hard-to-find classic (early-modern to 20th-c.) works accessible to a broader audience by offering the text in modern (occitanist) orthography, with facing Fr. translation, accompanied by a critical essay by an established scholar designed to help the non-specialist reader situate and better understand the text, in a very attractive format, and at a moderate price. The present work reprints Ruffi's complete cycle of 14 sonnets; a 12–page introduction describes the literary conventions and structure of the cycle, the political events of late-16th-c. Marseilles and R.'s role in them, the philosophical implications, and the literary tradition on which R. builds, with reference to works by Heraclitus, Plato, the Italian neo-Platonists, Petrarch, Scève, the Pléiade, and the contemporary Provençal poets Bellaud de la Bellaudière, Pierre Paul, and Michel Tronc.

3. Nineteenth Century

P. Gardy, 'La création littéraire occitane contemporaine dans les années 1870–1900 de la *Revue des Langues Romanes*. Une composante incongrue dans une publication d'études romanes?', *RLaR*, 105, 2001:335–66, argues that Occ. literary works were at first given a significant place in the journal, at a time when the literature was still trying to establish its viability; between 1870 and 1905, 350 contemporary literary texts by 74 different Occ. authors appeared in its pages, but after that first period *RLaR* devoted itself exclusively to academic articles. P. Blanchet, 'La littérature de langue provençale, ou écrire contre la censure et l'exclusion', pp. 175–81 of his *Langues, cultures et identités régionales en Provence: la métaphore de l''Aïoli'*, Paris, L'Harmattan, 2002, 235 pp., starts from the thesis that the speakers of the minority languages have bravely resisted the Fr. official and non-official effort to censure them by maintaining those languages alongside French, and particularly by maintaining a continued literary tradition which affirms the social legitimacy of the minority language. The most notable example, he argues, is Mistral; the texts 'manifestent presque tous explicitement ou implicitement leur relation à la censure qu'ils subissent et tentent de renverser'. He claims (as does Gardy from an occitanist perspective) that the determination to create high-status literature (epic and lyric poetry, the novel and short story) is inversely proportional to the social respectability of the language, claiming that this determination has decreased in the second half of the 20th c. as a result of the 'relegitimation of the language', or lessening of 'linguicide'. He concludes with polemical statements, perhaps displaced here. F. Pic, 'Du rapport entre les lettres occitanes et l'édition parisienne: Joseph d'Arbaud et les éditions Bernard Grasset', *Fest. Kirsch*, 137–50. Occitan scholars and activists have often commented on the fact that the most important literary works of the *Félibrige* were published in Paris, with a Fr. translation, implying perhaps that the primary audience addressed was not Provençal but Parisian. This study shows how two of d'Arbaud's major works, a novel and a short-story collection, came to be published by a Parisian house and d'Arbaud's insistence, at first resisted by the publisher, that the works not appear in Fr. unless accompanied by the Prov. original. There is a discussion of the market for Prov. books, an analysis of the economic background of their purchasers and an estimate of their numbers. D'Arbaud's relations with notable writers of his time are also noted. G. Barsotti, 'Lo music-hall Marselhés d'expression occitana', Nivelle, *Écrivains*, 298–303, traces Marseilles's Occ. music-hall tradition since the early 19th c., and notes a long list of celebrated singer-songwriters, many of whom achieved international recognition with an Occ. repertoire. Writers included such literary figures as Victor Gelu. P. Martel, 'Une touriste britannique face à l'occitan au milieu du XIXe siècle: Louise Stuart Costello', *Ravier Vol.*, 617–28, describes two travel journals of trips to the *Massif central* and to the Pyrenees. Both contain remarks on the various dialects of Occ. encountered, quotations of folksongs, and the second journal devotes over 60 pages to her two meetings with the Occ. poet, 'le perruquier d'Agen', Jasmin, to his charismatic poetry, his talent for declaiming his poetry, and his poetic production itself.

AUTHEMAN. S. Thiolier-Méjean, 'André Autheman, auteur des *Auvàri de Roustan*', *FL*, 135, 2002:57–91, includes a brief introduction which calls for reprinting overlooked works of Occ. popular literature that would otherwise be lost because of the cheap paper on which they were printed. She highlights their documentary value, as well as qualities of style, richness of language, and entertainment. She sums up the author's life and publications in one paragraph, characterizes the *Auvàri* as recounting the burlesque adventures of an unfortunate character from Palermo to 'Hindustan', to Spain, and ultimately to Marseilles where he dies of cholera, and compares it to a Prov. work from 1722. The 977-line poem is reprinted without comment, presumably from the original 1857 edition.

BERNARD. P. Nougier, 'Valère Bernard, poète social (1860–1936), "La Pauriho" (Les Miséreux)', Nivelle, *Écrivains*, 45–55, presents a working-class poet writing in the Marseilles dialect of Occ. through 'one of his least-known works', a collection of 51 poems, in three parts, which gradually descend down the ranks of misery from the proletariat to the completely destitute and marginalized. Like Mabilly (not mentioned by N.), B. not only depicted the misery of the masses, as did Gelu, but sought to play a social role. Since B. was perhaps better-known as an artist, N. concludes with a one-page discussion of his etchings, and lists the title and page number of those used to illustrate 'La Pauriho'.

GELU. G. Barsotti, 'Victor Gelu, le porte parole du peuple marseillais', Nivelle, *Écrivains*, 35–36, in two dense pages considers the social background of G.'s poetry: a time when 'northern' [French] capitalism was introduced to Marseilles, leading to the proletarization of artisans, and when French language and culture began to be generalized, reducing the functions available to Occ. His songs in the Marseilles dialect protest the injustices of society and allow those without a voice to be heard. In *Novè Granet*, published posthumously, the peasant is credited with intelligence and allowed to speak.

MABILLY. G. Barsotti, 'Felip Mabilly, écrivain engagé', Nivelle, *Écrivains*, 37–44, discusses an Occitan writer contemporary with Gelu, educated by the Church, but influenced by Proudhon and Blanqui, who edited republican newspapers in Avignon, Algiers, and Paris. In his longer, mock heroic poems ('Lei Braç-Nòus desonorats vo lo rei Maurèu' in six cantos, and 'Lei bancarotiers' in four books) he tells the story of unlikely characters: Maurèu who has sworn off work is elected king of the sect of 'braç-nòus' [virgin arms] because of the impressive number of spider webs that have accumulated under his idle arms; Victor, a labour union organizer who makes a fortune through a strategic bankruptcy, joins the corrupt financiers' 'sindicat dei bancarotiers'. These humorous satires against the leisured classes also have a didactic purpose, explaining for example the Marxist theory of surplus value. M. also wrote other work, including philosophical poems, and B. notes that he shares Gelu's identification with the poor, but whereas Gelu merely observes the injustice of society, M. intends his texts as weapons in the battle to change social conditions.

MISTRAL. Y. Gourgaud, 'Encore sur la strophe de *Mirèio*', *FL*, 135, 2002:51–55. In response to the claim of another scholar (*FL*, 129:301–16) that the stanzas in this poem and *Calendau* had no Prov. precedent and were modelled on Lamartine, G. cites a poem by le Marquis de La Fare-Alais, with seven stanzas of seven lines, each line having seven metrical feet. G. admits that this proves nothing, but offers the possibility of a Prov. influence, without diminishing 'l'éclatante nouveauté' of Mistral's stanza form. M. Décimo, 'Quand Michel Bréal, d'origine juive et berlinoise, alsacien, félibre et citoyen, écrivait à Mistral', *RLaR*, 104, 2000:187–218, presents information on this forgotten figure and on the situation of Prov. studies at the turn of the century, and then reprints 10 letters from Bréal to M. (as well as five from the Darmesteters, a Jewish family with close ties to M.). Despite Bréal's important civic functions, despite his favourable attitude to the languages of France and their integration into the school system, despite the fact that he was often cited by the *félibres* and addressed *Félibrige* ceremonies, he is oddly absent from the literature about M. and from the 60,000 letters to M. located in Maillane. Studies of M.'s relations with scholars focus on Gaston Paris and Paul Meyer. The ten letters, written from 1875 to 1904, show B. to have been a life-long admirer of Mistral and an ardent supporter of the *Félibrige*, and reveal how a French Jew of the time reacted to certain items published in M.'s *Aïoli* which seemed to contradict the ideal of tolerance in a time of growing intolerance. The Darmesteter letters are limited to social niceties and praise of the great poet; the last, however, solicits M.'s collaboration in the projected *Revue de Paris* and is interesting in revealing the strategy used to obtain M.'s consent as well as the negotiation over his remuneration.

MOUTIER. C. Magrini-Romagnoli, '*Lou Rose* de l'abbé Moutier', *FL*, 137: 161–77, proposes 'un simple parcours du *Rose*', a poem in seven parts published in 1896 (as was Mistral's *Pouèmo dóu Rose*). She depicts the poem as both a personal memoir and a veritable encyclopedia of the geography, mythology, anthropology, and history of the Rhone, from legendary origins through classical antiquity and the Middle Ages down to the time of the *félibres*. M.-R. notes that Moutier's efforts to preserve the linguistic specificities of the Drôme, as lexicographer and founder of *L'Escolo Dóufinalo*, motivate the composition of this poem. She notes that both Mistral's and Moutier's Rhone poems belong to the last years of the poets' careers, when the traditional way of life of those who worked the river was coming to an end, a fitting image of the decline of the culture to which they had devoted their lives.

4. Twentieth Century

A. Viaut, 'Le territoire de la mer dans la poésie gasconne contemporaine', *Ravier Vol.*, 577–606. After ten pages of general discussion of the ocean, its vocabulary, its place in oral literature, its possible symbolic weight, V. divides the oceanic theme into four types: 'la mer nécessaire' (the immediacy of the ocean in the daily life of the area), 'l'océan contemplé', 'la mer évocatoire', and 'la mer comme langage' (as an element in the poet's language). He cites examples of Gascon poetry illustrating each of these categories, which are further explicated or sub-divided, and ends with a few oceanic references from other Occ. poets. Among the poets he cites are Émilien Barreyre, Adrien Dupin, Justin Larrebat, l'abbé Césaire Daugé, Joseph and François Conord, Miquèu Camelat (*Belina*), André Berry, and l'abbé Daniel-Michel Bergey. The section on 'la mer comme langage' is devoted exclusively to Bernat Manciet, except for a brief reference to the author's own verse. J.-C. Latil, 'Le roman policier Marseillais aujourd'hui', Nivelle, *Écrivains*, 148–65, discusses seven authors who write in Fr. and three who write in Occ. (Florian Vernet, Glaudi Barsotti, and Amanda Biòt [Nicole Nivelle]). L. briefly notes each novel's manner of publication, narrative voice(s) or main character(s), geographical setting(s) (Marseilles or the back country) and suggests autobiographical analogies; he analyses the style, points out differences from the standard *roman policier* and the implied view of society, asserting that these novels share the common themes of opposition to authority, of the Mediterranean as a source of pleasure and poetry, and of linguistic self-affirmation.

BODON. C. Parayre, '*Lo Libre dels grands jorns* de Jean Boudou: poésie des troubadours et revendication culturelle', *Tenso,* 15, 2000: 118–26, asks to what effect B. uses quotations from medieval Occ. poetry in this novel of the last days of a dying man who symbolizes the fate of a dying language. She notes that the first group of quotations refer to the Crusade, and relate to the novel's setting in Clermont Ferrand, where the first Crusade was preached in 1095. They evoke the theme, central to this novel, of death. The second group, however, refer to renewal: the first three to its absence, and the final *alba* to the birth of a new day. This same ambivalence is seen in the third group, where a poem on courtly love is followed by one on mercenary love, reflecting the decline of Occ. from the noble language of the troubadours to a shameful patois. The final group of quotations refer once more to life: in the last one, the Occ. song of the blackbird persists, but feebly, after its death. P. remarks that the disparity within each group shows B.'s refusal of simplistic pronouncements. B., she concludes, relates the poetry of the troubadours, the *grand jour* of Occ. culture, to the contemporary question of Occ. identity. P. also contributes '*La Quimèra* de Jean Boudou', *FL,* 135, 2002: 29–43, analysing B.'s last completed novel, which narrates the period from the mid-17th c. to the start of the Camisard revolt; implicit however is the period of the 1960s and early 1970s. P. argues that this novel asks how to preserve the memory of a nation losing its language, how to oppose its marginalization, and how to narrate the loss of its heritage. Rémi Soulié, **Les chimères de Jean Boudou: écriture de la perversion*, Rodez, Fil d'Ariane, 2001, 192 pp., is a psychoanalytic study of B.'s psyche and writing, well reviewed by L. Gaubert, *RT,* 182, 2001: 348–49.

BOYER. C. Laux, 'Célestin Boyer (1888–1979)', *RT,* 182: 341–43. L'abbé Boyer ('Lou Pépi') wrote a weekly chronicle for the *Journal du Tarn.* Between 1924 and 1935, over 500 of these were printed, of which some 40 were reprinted in *Contes del Pepin,* IEO, 1993.

CONIO. R. Blanco, 'Un *troubaire marsihés,* Antòni Conio (1878–1947)', *FL,* 137: 179–94 gives a very detailed account of Conio's political activities (as an anarchist, then a federalist) and of the important role he played in numerous Occ. organizations and publications. He received honours and titles within the *Félibrige,* and had many contacts with other Marseillais Occ. poets such as

Mabilly, Bertas, and Valère Bernard. He later worked with Charles Camproux. Jordi Reboul who inspired the early Occitanist poets such as Lafont was his disciple. Blanco says very little, however, about Conio's creative works.

DELÈRIS. Cantalausa, '"Lo salvatge d'Avairon"', *Canta-grelh*, 58: 10–15, is on the Rouergat prose-writer Ferran Delèris, author of five works published in Fr. and four in Occitan.

DELPASTRE. Y. Rouquette, 'Delpastre: indigène, poète, ethnologue', pp. 7–11 of Marcelle Delpastre, *Le Bourgeois et le Paysan: les contes du feu*, Paris, Payot–Rivages, 2000, 360 pp., affirms that D., a major writer, is at her best not in her memoirs which appealed to such a wide audience, but in her poetry and in her reflections on the popular culture of the 'miniscule peasant and limousin society' of which she was both witness and participant. R. characterizes D.'s poetry as one of anguish and jubilation, celebrating 'son savoir, son imagination, sa pensée tout impregnée de christianisme, son exceptionnelle capacité à détecter l'archaïsme dans l'actuel, le mythe sous le burlesque ou le scatalogique, son intuition de poète femme'. *Plein Chant*, 71–72, 2001, is a special issue on D.

LAFONT. *Septimanie: le livre en Languedoc-Roussillon*, 9, April 2002, offers a series of articles assembled in a dossier under the collective title: 'Robert Lafont, voyage dans la logosphère en compagnie d'un septimanien d'exception': B. Pasobrola, 'Écrivain, linguiste, et géographe du temps' (26), P. Gardy, 'Le chant de la sève' (27), D. Julien, 'Ce multiple et mortel objet du désir' (28), P. Sauzet, 'Les mots et les lieux' (29), P. Siblot, 'Le praxématique, *qu'es aquò?*' (30), B. Pasobrola, 'Contre la Sensure' [sic]: entretien avec Robert Lafont' (31–33).

MELHAU. *ASc*, 4, 2001, under the title 'Jan dau Melhau poète paysan-païen', contains invaluable material on a writer who is both geographically and socially outside the major circuits of Occ. literature, and so is almost invisible in the critical literature. The issue opens with a 'Conversation' (8–12) with M.-H. Bonafé, of which only M.'s words are reproduced, making it read like a first-person essay acquainting the reader with his personality, ideas, and the sources of his creativity. There follows a well-chosen anthology of his writings, in Limousin and (the author's) French translation, in the genres of the *conte*, fable, song (*chanson-poème)*, 'monologues' (i.e. texts designed for delivery before a live audience), 'texts to read' (in contrast to most of his work which is meant to be spoken, in the oral tradition of the Limousin), aphorisms, and letters. Appreciations by several leading Occ. authors follow, as well as a few articles by literary scholars: 'Melhau dans les mémoires de Marcelle Delpastre' (122–28), is taken from unpublished writings by one of the greatest recent Occ. poets and a personal friend of M., who gives her personal as well as literary appraisal. Other articles are by A. Galan, 'Troubadour en colère' (130–32); P. Gardy, 'Le grand *reborsièr*' (133–35); M. Chapduelh, 'L'ex-fumeur de pipe ou de l'influence de la tradition orale sur l'œuvre écrite de Jan dau Melhau' (136–38); Y. Rouquette, 'Le Melhau, j'aime' (139–40), pointing out the urbanity and modernity of an author often thought of (including in the title of this issue) as a 'peasant poet'; R. Lafont, 'Le village, l'*èime* et la dérision' (142–44), devoting most of his article to a belated encomium for M.'s first novel *Los dos einocents*'; G. Dazas, 'Lo trobar de Melhau: faretz 'tencion pas vos entraupar / Le *trobar* de Melhau: faites attention de ne pas vous y perdre' (145–48).

MOUCADEL. M. Courty, 'Lou teatre de Reinié Moucadel', *FL*, 135, 2002:45–49, states that M.'s comedies are not farces but use current events to illustrate an idea. He recounts three plays which comment on contemporary issues before the main discussion of a new play, *Lou grand Embut*. In addition to its allusions to Proust, Mistral, Bernanos, Pagnol, this play includes the characters Simono Vibre (Simone Castor, i.e. de Beauvoir) and Wladimir (from *En attendant Godot*).

NELLI. W. Calin, 'René Nelli: poet of Occitan modernism', *Ravier Vol.*, 453–60, is almost identical to the excellent discussion of Nelli in Calin's book on modernism in minority languages reviewed in *YWMLS*, 64:237–38. C. describes Nelli's surreal poetic universe, the harrowing vulnerability of man facing a cruel or indifferent world and, ultimately, death.

PERBOSC. Antonin Perbosc, *Lo libre del campèstre / Le livre de la nature* (Occitanas, 9), Biarritz, Atlantica — Pau, Institut Occitan, 2000, 158 pp., part I: *Remembrança*, intro. and tr. Xavier Ravier (7–61); part II: *Invocacions*, intro. and tr. Georges Passerat (63–157). Each text is introduced by an essay skilfully placing it in its context and explaining its structure and meaning, followed by the full text in modernized ('occitan') spelling with a facing Fr. translation.

REBOUL. F. Mancebo, 'Jorgi Reboul: premiers itinéraires en poésie', Nivelle, *Écrivains*, 90–109, discusses the first three collections of a poet who influenced the course of 20th-c. Occ. poetry, and played a role in the Occ. movement (founder of *Lou Calen* and cofounder of the *Parti Provençal*, he was connected with the *félibrige* poets of *Marsyas*, before going over to the occitanist I.E.O.). M.'s approach is based on linguistic analysis and semantic structure.

ROQUETA. F. Gardy, 'Max Roqueta: naissença d'un bestiari', *Fest. Kirsch*, 673–83, investigates the earliest appearances and the significance of the animal world in two stories from *Verd Paradis*. Id., 'Le miroir des bêtes' pp. 87–92 of Max Rouquette, *Bestiari / Bestiaire* (Occitanas, 1), Biarritz, Atlantica — Pau, Institut Occitan, 2000,

94 pp., begins with a discussion of the importance of animals, real and mythical, in R.'s life and work and then characterizes this collection more particularly, concluding by seeing echoes in it of Mistral, Apollinaire, and the Occ. bestiaries by Camproux and Nelli. J.-C. Bouvier, 'Max Rouquette ou la parole retrouvée', pp. 367–76 of his *Espaces du langage: géolinguistique, toponymie, cultures de l'oral et de l'écrit,* Aix-en-Provence, Univ. de Provence, 411 pp., discusses the complex relationship between oral and written literature in R.'s short stories collected in the volumes of *Verd Paradis* and how this allows R. to attain his obsessive goal, the harmony of man and the universe. Unlike the duality which exists in Mistral, Bodon, Perbosc, and Galtier, in R. oral and written culture merge to form 'une dimension interculturelle et plus encore [. . .] une autre culture [. . .] qui assure la cohérence de la création et évite les pièges de la "provincialisation"'.

VERNET. M. Poitavin, 'Le feuilleton parodique de Florian Vernet', *Leng(M)*, 48:67–88, comments on V.'s five *romans policiers*, published first in feuilleton form in *La Marseillaise*. P. describes the characteristics of these works, many of which result from the episodic nature of their first publication and the (successful) effort to reach a broad audience, particularly among the young. He shows how V. parodies not only the genre of the *roman policier*, but also the *feuilleton* form, including the mock advertisements and imagined man-in-the-street interviews with readers preceding their publication, the résumé of past episodes, humour of repetition, humorous names, digressions with characters who never reappear, techniques to heighten suspense, concatenation of surprise revelations towards the end, and alternation between 'open' and 'closed' episodes, between portraits and action, between action and digression.

IV. SPANISH STUDIES

LANGUAGE

By Steven Dworkin, *University of Michigan*, and
Miranda Stewart, *University of Strathclyde*

1. General

Panorama de la linguistique hispanique, Lille 2000, ed. Yves Macchi, Villeneuve d'Ascq (Nord), Univ. Charles de Gaulle, 2001, 280 pp., is an eclectic collection of conference papers. Fernando Lázaro Carreter, *El nuevo dardo en la palabra*, M, Aguilar, 262 pp., is a new collection of articles published in the Madrid daily newspaper *El País* by the late former director of the RAE. *Studies in Contrastive Linguistics*, ed. Luis Iglesias Rábade and Susana María Doral Sánchez, Santiago de Compostela U.P., 2002, 1082 pp., contains the proceedings of the 2nd International Contrastive Linguistics Conference held in Santiago in 2001. *Nuevas tendencias en la investigación lingüística*, ed. Juan de Dios Luque Durán, Antonio Pamies Bertrán, and Francisco José Manjón Pozas, Granada, Granada Lingvistica, 2002, 650 pp., contains a number of articles relating to Spanish. *Cien años de investigación semántica: de Michel Bréal a la actualidad. Actas del Congreso Internacional de Semántica*, vols 1 and 2, ed. Marcos Martínez Hernández et al., M, Ediciones clásicas, 2000, 885, 873 pp., is a vast collection of papers; those relating specifically to Spanish can be found in both vols, pp. 169–976. *Alarcos Vol.* includes studies from the following areas: the works of Alarcos; synchronic grammar; diachronic grammar; discourse and text grammar; and philology and textual analysis. *Homenaje a Ofelia Kovacci*, ed. Elvira de Arnoux and Angela Di Tullio, Buenos Aires U.P., 2001, 541 pp., is a collection of articles with a predominantly Latin American focus. Félix San Vicente, *La lengua de los nuevos españoles*, Zaragoza, Pórtico, 2001, 270 pp., examines the phonology, morpho-syntax, and lexis of post-Franco Spain in a fairly general fashion.

2. Diachronic Studies

Several contributions to Ernst, *RS*, 1, offer useful overviews of different aspects of the history of the Spanish language: J. Kabatek, 'Bezeichnungen für die Sprachen der Iberoromania' (174–79) (see also his 'Las categorizaciones de las lenguas, del lenguaje y de los discursos — teoría y ejemplos iberorrománicos', *CILPR 23*, III, 253–66); J. Brumme, 'Historia de la reflexión sobre las lenguas románicas:

español' (265–79); B. Müller, 'Etymologische und wortgeschichtliche Erforschung und Beschreibung der romanischen Sprachen: Spanisch' (376–96); M. T. Echenique Elizondo, 'Substrato, adstrato y superstrato y sus efectos en las lenguas románicas: Iberorromania' (607–21); A. Martínez González and F. Torres Montes, 'Historia externa de la lengua española' (852–70). The question of the periodization of the history of Spanish is taken up again in C. Melis, M. Flores, and S. Bogard, 'La historia del español. Propuesta de un tercer período evolutivo', *NRFH*, 51 : 1–55. The authors argue for dividing the post-medieval period into 'español clásico' (16th to 18th cs) and 'español moderno', with the 19th c. constituting the beginning of a new evolutionary period in the history of Spanish, marked by the consolidation of the current syntax of the *gustar* construction, the increased use of *ir a* + inf. as a future, and the growing use of the reduplicative pronoun with an animate indirect object (*Le doy a Juan*).

Various specialists demonstrate the value of observation and analysis of linguistic variation observable in contemporary Spanish and in texts from earlier periods. In a major contribution to Spanish historical linguistics, Donald Tuten, *Koineization in Medieval Spanish*, Berlin–NY, Mouton de Gruyter, ix + 345 pp., critically analyses various definitions and approaches to koineization and applies these insights to key developments in the history of medieval Spanish during the Reconquest, which he divides into three historical moments: the Burgos phase, the Toledo phase, and the Seville phase. Many features of Castilian result from the levelling and reduction of variation associated with koineization brought about by dialect contact. The phenomena analysed include the morphology of the definite article, preposition + article contractions, apocope of *–e*, *leísmo*, reorganization of the possessive adjectives/pronouns, *seseo* and the origins of Andalusian. Juan A. Frago Gracia, *Textos y normas. Comentarios lingüísticos*, M, Gredos, 507 pp., discusses and illustrates through a linguistic analysis of selected texts issues of variation, norms, and periodization in medieval and Golden Age Spanish. Juan Andrés Villena Ponsoda, *La continuidad del cambio lingüístico*, Granada U.P., 2001, 151 pp., shows that contemporary variation observable in the comportment of Spanish fricatives continues processes begun in the past. Particular attention is paid to the ongoing deaffrication of *ch*. J. M. García Martín, 'Problemas que plantea el concepto de estado de lengua, con especial atención a algunos fenómenos del castellano medieval', *CLHM*, 24, 2001 : 11–25, discusses the Saussurean notion of 'état de langue' with regard to specific issues of Old Spanish (e.g. aspiration of *f-*, apocope of *–e*).

Perdiguero, *Lengua romance*, gathers together 18 papers presented at a conference which focused on the problems posed by the presence of

Romance elements in Latin texts and the relationship (as manifested in spelling practices) between the written and spoken language. Most papers accept the traditional distinction between Latin and Romance, challenged by R. Penny in his contribution, 'Ambigüedad grafemática: correspondencia entre fonemas y grafemas en los textos peninsulares anteriores al s. XIII' (221–28), in which he argues that the concept of Romance forms in Latin texts makes no sense, as speakers at the time did not conceptually distinguish Latin and Romance as distinct linguistic codes. What is at issue is the coexistence of two orthographic systems. Most of the papers, written by such specialists as R. Ciérbide, J. M. Díaz de Bustamante, P. Díez de Revenga Torres, M. C. Egido Fernández, E. Falque Rey, F. González Ollé, J. Gutiérrez Cuadrado, C. Hernández Alonso, J. R. Morala Rodríguez, J. A. Pascual Rodríguez, and R. Santiago Lacuesta, deal with the presence of Romance and Latin elements in specific early non-literary Leonese and Castilian documents. Valuable for their treatment of methodological issues concerning the interpretation of orthographic practices and the concepts of learned and semi-learned words are the following papers: A. García Valle, 'Revisión actualizada de la documentación medieval: ¿arcaísmo o cultismo?' (95–111), and M. Quilis Merín, 'Oralidad y representación gráfica de *f-* inicial latina en textos de orígenes del español' (229–42). Thematically related is R. Wright, 'A sociophilological approach to the earliest romance texts: [-t], -/t/ and *-t* in Castile (1206–08)', Goyens, *Vernacular*, 201–14, who seeks to explain from a 'sociophilological' perspective the presence of *-t* in 3rd person plural verb forms. The *-t* in texts from the first decade of the 13th c. reflect scribal attempts to make the relevant verb forms look more like the traditional unreformed (= Latin) orthography.

Several studies examine the linguistic nature of specific medieval texts. María Jesús Torrens Alvarez, *Edición y estudio lingüístico del Fuero de Alcalá (Fuero Viejo)*, Alcalá de Henares U.P., 2002, 687 pp., offers a traditional linguistic description of the chosen text. C. Matute Martínez, 'Interacción de sistemas lingüísticos en el *Libro de las Cruzes* (1259) de Alfonso X el Sabio', *CLHM*, 24, 2001: 71–99, describes the interaction of Latin, Castilian, Occitan, and Arabic elements in this text, which provides no evidence of an Alfonsine-inspired standard of linguistic correctness. I. Carrasco, 'La lengua de la *Crónica de Alfonso X*', *Bustos Vol.*, 401–11, surveys the linguistic features of this 14th-c. text. J. L. Girón Alconchel does the same for *La Celestina* in 'La lengua de *La Celestina*: notas para un estado de la cuestión', *López Vol.*, II, 997–1015. He concludes that the text displays both the polymorphism typical of the medieval language alongside the growing standardization and elimination of variants characteristic of the early modern language. A. J. Meilán García, 'La oracion simple en *La Celestina*', *AMal*, 25, 2002:479–544, demonstrates that the syntax of the simple sentence in that work shows a mixture of medieval and early modern linguistic features.

E. G. Miller, 'Legal language in Jewish and Christian documents of the fifteenth century', *La corónica*, 32:287–305, compares the language in the Jewish Statutes of Valladolid (1432) with various 15th-c. Christian legal texts. The legal language of both religions shows many similar lexical items and syntactic constructions. Beyond the medieval period note José Javier Rodríguez Toro, *Descripción y cosmografía de España (o Itinerario) de Hernando Colón: estudio lingüístico*, Seville U.P., 129 pp., and Miguel Ángel Puche Lorenzo, *El español del siglo XVI en textos notariales*, Murcia U.P., 170 pp. In both cases, the linguistic studies, based on doctoral dissertations, are very traditional in form and content. M. C. Gordillo Vázquez, 'Lengua/habla/jerga de moros', *RDi*, 1, 2002:29–49, gives an overview of the linguistic features of the speech of *moriscos* as portrayed (sometimes in a mocking way) in the work of Golden Age playwrights.

3. Diachronic Phonetics and Phonology

Juan Felipe García Santos, *Cambio fonético y fonética acústica*, Salamanca U.P., 192 pp., treats as lenition phenomena from the perspective of acoustic phonetics the voicing of Latin intervocalic stops in Spanish, as well as the transformation of the Old Spanish sibilants, *yeísmo*, and aspiration of *-s*. Taking as their starting point the phonetic bases of sound change, M. Batllori, S. Llach, and I. Puyol, 'Condiciones fonéticas de producción y percepción en segmentos consonánticos en la evolución de las lenguas romances', *CILPR 23*, 1, 189–202, examine phonetic factors involving speaker production and listener perception involved in the devoicing of obstruents (including the Old Spanish sibilants), epenthesis of postnasal homorganic consonants (OSp. *nomne* > *nombre*), postnasal voicing of stops, vocalization of syllable-final /l/ (SALTU > OSp. *soto*), r/l confusion, and sporadic metathesis of r (CREPARE > OSp. *crebar* > *quebrar*). The first part of M. Loporcaro, 'Due note sul raddoppiamento fonosintattico: 1. L'iberoromanzo in fase antica. 2. Fiorentino *tu*', *RPh*, 56:307–18, attempts to demonstrate that the transcription in Mozarabic texts of the final dental of the reflexes of Latin AD and of the third person verbal ending -T bespeaks the presence of syntactic doubling in early Ibero-Romance. J. Mondéjar, 'De copias, de originales y de grafías y sonidos: el "seseo-zezeo" en un legajo de documentos sevillanos (1495–1500)', *Bustos Vol.*, 175–84, shows that *seseo* was well established in Seville by the end of the 15th century. The documents examined here may offer the first documentation of *zezeo*. J. Moreno Bernal, 'Efectos de la síncopa en los futuros románicos', *ib.*, 247–57, discusses, within the broader context of the Romance languages, examples of epenthesis and metathesis resulting from the syncope of the theme vowel in the future of OSp. *–er* and *–ir* verbs. J. Perona, 'La venganza del estado latente: los anglicismos en español y el retorno de la apócope extrema', *ib.*, 185–95, describes the rise of new final consonants and consonant groups in Anglicisms.

4. Diachronic Morphology

D. Wanner, 'Pathways of change: 2nd person plural in Spanish', *HLS 6*, 102–20, wishes to demonstrate how the much-studied history of these verb endings in Spanish can illuminate the various pathways followed in such instances of morphological change. A. Enrique-Arias, 'From clitics to inflections: diachronic and typological evidence for affixal object agreement marking in Spanish', *Silexicales*, 3:67–74, claims that Romance clitic pronouns constitute an example of 'mixed properties' elements, i.e. elements which combine features of words and inflectional affixes. They have become object agreement markers in the modern language, a status they did not enjoy in the medieval language. This paper shows how inflectional agreement in verbs results from functionally-driven syntactic change. J. Elvira, 'Sobre la distribución columnar de la flexión incoativa medieval', *CLHM*, 24, 2001:167–79, re-examines some of the currently- accepted thinking on the history of the inchoative interfix /-sk-/ with regard to its semantic value and its role in creating columnar stress throughout the verb paradigm.

D. A. Pharies, 'The origin and development of the Spanish suffix *–azo*', *RPh*, 56:41–50, is a revised English version of the entry for this suffix in P.'s recent *Diccionario etimológico de los sufijos españoles* (see *YWMLS*, 64:251). The same suffix is studied by F. Rainer, 'Semantic fragmentation in word-formation: the case of Spanish *–azo*', Singh, *Explorations*, 197–211. The semantic fragmentation of this suffix, which originally designated 'blow, stroke', is seen as further evidence of the analogical conception of word-formation processes. R. stresses here the role in the semantic evolution of suffixes of what he calls 'metaphoric and metonymic approximation'. A. Puigvert Ocal, 'El enriquecimiento a través de la derivación adjetival en el *Cancionero de Baena*', *Bustos Vol.*, 653–66, describes the use of suffixes employed by the poets of the *Cancionero de Baena* to create derived adjectives.

5. Diachronic Syntax

The search for traces of the spoken language in the written record of earlier stages of Spanish occupies the attention of several workers. R. Cano Aguilar, 'Sintaxis histórica, discurso oral y discurso escrito', Bustos, *Textualización*, 27–48, is a methodological meditation on the tension between features of orality and written language in the analysis of questions of historical syntax. Illustrations are provided from Cano's previous work on the diachrony of sentence connectors. Similar issues are raised in R. Eberenz, 'Huellas de la oralidad en textos de los siglos xv y xvi', *ib.*, 63–83. The author seeks samples of orality in passages of dialogue taken from literary texts, argumentative texts, and the transcriptions of inquisitorial processes.

R. Cano Aguilar continues his work on grammatical discourse cohesion as manifested in intrasentential connectives: 'La cohesión gramatical del discurso en el castellano del siglo xv', *Alarcos Vol.*, 181–201, gives attention to the historical syntax of sentence connectives in prose texts. In 'Construcción del discurso en el siglo xiii', *CHLM*, 24, 2001:123–41, he challenges the traditional view of a unilineal development from older, simpler paratactic constructions to more complex hypotactic constructions; 13th-c. texts show the co-existence of differing discursive traditions and their syntactic manifestations. M. Barra Jover, 'Nuevas perspectivas sobre la historia de la subordinación española', *Alarcos Vol.*, 157–80, offers a detailed examination of the evolution of mechanisms of subordination. He notes that the major difference between subordination in the medieval and modern language is the fact that in the latter the subordinate clause must be governed by an element in the main clause, which was not always the case in the medieval language. J. Elvira, 'Sobre el origen de la locución concesiva "por mucho que" y similares', *Bustos Vol.*, 217–36, traces the evolution of this construction from a preposition + relative pronoun causal construction to a conjunction with concessive value. He stresses the importance of the negator, as in 'por mucho que grites, no te oirán'. J. M. Mendoza Abreu, 'La expresión de la causalidad en textos clásicos', *Alarcos Vol.*, 249–86, studies the syntax of causal conjunctions in selected Golden Age prose texts.

Issues of verbal syntax have attracted the attention of a number of scholars. B. Arias and M. L. Quaglia, 'La persistencia de la concordancia del participio con el clítico de objeto directo: una etapa en la gramaticalización de *haber + participio pasado*', *NRFH*, 50, 2002:517–29, claim that previous analyses of this agreement phenomenon have paid insufficient attention to the role of *haber*, its rivalry with *tener* as a full verb, and the grammaticalization processes it underwent in the creation of the compound past tenses in Hispano-Romance. M. L. Gutiérrez Araus, 'El uso de los perfectos simple y compuesto en *La Celestina*', *López Vol.*, II, 1035–51, concludes that the differences between Peninsular and American usage of these tenses can be seen at the end of the 15th century. A. S. Octavio de Toledo y Huertas, 'Auxiliación con *ser* de verbos intransitivos de movimiento (1450–1600): el caso de *ir(se)*', *RDi*, 1, 2002 : 257–69, examines the loss of the use of *ser* as an auxiliary verb with *ir* in compound past tenses. He works within the framework proposed by W. Croft in his *Explaining Language Change: An Evolutionary Approach* (2000). R. Aranovich, 'The semantics of auxiliary selection in Old Spanish', *StLa*, 27 : 1–37, traces the replacement of *ser* by *haber* (OSp. *aver*) as the auxiliary verb in compound tenses involving intransitive and reflexive verbs, claiming that verbs with 'a more patient-like subject' retain the longest (until the 17th c.) their ability to use *ser* as an auxiliary verb.

E. Douvier, 'L'iréel du passé exprimé par la forme verbale en *-ra*: étude d'un élément de l'état de langue de la *Première chronique générale* d'Alphonse le Savant', *CHLM*, 24, 2001 : 101–21, studies the use of this verb form to express contrary-to-fact conditions in the past in the selected text as a stage in the eventual grammaticalization of the *-ra* verb form as a subjunctive. A. Serradilla Castaño, 'Frecuencia de preposiciones en el régimen de construcciones transitivas: hacia una periodización lingüística de la Edad Media', *CLHM*, 24, 2001 : 143–65, examines the use and frequency of prepositions in transitive constructions governed by the verbs *fablar, pensar, creer, fiar* over time in 15 medieval texts. She claims that these constructions can help the researcher date a text or document. P. Arroyo Vega, 'La diátesis en el castellano del siglo XV de la Corona de Aragón', *CILPR 23*, II, 69–75, surveys the evolution of passive constructions found in literary and non-literary texts from the Crown of Aragon. Major factors are the triumph of *aver* over *ser* as the auxiliary verb in compound tenses, the evolution of *se*, and the development of *estar* + past participle constructions for the resultative passive. See also M. E. Castillo Herrero, 'Breve estudio comparativo de las construcciones del verbo *haber* como subcategorizador de predicaciones secundarias a lo largo de la historia del español', *ib.*, 235–47; A. Vera Luján, 'Sobre el origen de las construcciones estativo-atributivas con *hallar*', *Bustos Vol.*, 259–73; A. M. Coello Mesa, *'Funcionamiento de los tiempos simples de indicativo en el *Conde Lucanor*', *RFULL*, 20, 2002 : 25–36.

M. Bargalló and F. Roca Urgell, 'La extensión del artículo en español medieval y preclásico', *CILPR 23*, II, 99–113, offer a critique of C. Company's analysis of the spread of the definite article in the medieval language. They present an explanation based on the coexistence of two distinct systems of nominal determination; an etymological system in which the article functioned as a deictic, and an innovative system which represented the first steps toward the modern function of the article. Y. Congosto Martín, 'Presencia y ausencia del artículo en *El Corbacho*', *Alarcos Vol.*, 203–27, discusses the use of the article as an actualizer (*actualizador*) in that 15th-c. prose text. J. M. García Martín, 'Problemas previos en el análisis de las construcciones partitivas dependientes directamente del verbo', *Bustos Vol.*, 233–46, discusses issues related to the history of partitive constructions in Spanish.

C. Company Company, 'Reanálisis en cadena y gramaticalización. Dativos problemáticos en la historia del español', *Verba*, 29, 2002: 31–69, examines ten seemingly unconnected syntactic changes involving the dative pronoun *le*. According to C., these changes have in common an extensive reinforcement of dative marking at the expense of accusative marking. These changes constitute a grammaticalization process carried out by a multiple reanalysis. As a result, Spanish is gradually acquiring some of the features of a primary object language; also, by the same author, *'Gramaticalización y dialectología comparada: una isoglosa sintáctico-semántica del español', *Dicenda*, 20, 2002: 39–71. M. Flores, '*Leísmo, laísmo* y *loísmo* en español antiguo: caso, transitividad y valoraciones pragmáticas', *RPh*, 55, 2001[2003]: 41–74, argues that the choice of object pronoun was sensitive to various semantic and pragmatic factors, such as the degree of transitivity of the verbal event and the speaker's subjective attitude toward the referent of the pronoun.

A. M. Coello Mesa, '*Ende* en el *Poema de Mío Cid*: caracterización sintáctica y semántica', *RFE*, 83: 249–60, considers that *ende* is an adverbial capable of being used with anaphoric reference to another element in the discourse; see also her *'Función y valores del adverbio *i* en el castellano prealfonsí', *AEF*, 25, 2002: 57–68. M. Castillo-Lluch, 'Cronología lingüística y evoluciones pendulares: el caso de la construcción preposición + infinitivo + pronombre átono', *CLHM*, 24, 2001: 181–98, examines the chronology and the factors conditioning the varying pre- and postverbal placement of object pronouns with infinitives in Old Spanish (*por se vengar* vs *por vengarse*). Postverbal placement dominated in the 13th c. whereas preverbal placement dominated (especially with *de*, *por*, and *en*) in the 14th and 15th cs. Modern postposition placement became obligatory in the 17th c. The author claims that these patterns can help determine the date of a text. T. Berta, 'Sintaxis histórica del español: construcción de infinitivo en español medieval y en español moderno', *CILPR 23*, II, 125–31, concludes that the rules governing and restricting clitic climbing in Old Spanish are not the same as those operative in the modern language.

6. Diachronic Lexicology

The survey year saw the publication of fascicles 23 and 24 of *Diccionario del español medieval*, ed. B. Müller, Heidelberg, Winter, bringing the project up to the word *alidada.* Rafael Lapesa, *Léxico hispánico primitivo (Siglos* VIII *al* XII*). Version primitiva del 'Glosario del primitivo léxico iberorrománico'*, ed. Manuel Seco, M, Fundación Ramón Menéndez Pidal–Real Academia Española, 667 pp., has finally appeared. This compilation, with a long and complex history going back over 70 years, is based on documents used by Ramón Menéndez Pidal in preparing the first edition (1926) of his *Orígenes del español.* Each entry contains the word at issue, a modern Spanish gloss, orthographic variants, text locations, and identification of the etymon. Fabián González Bachiller, *El léxico romance de las colecciones diplomáticas calceatenses en los siglos* XII *y* XIII, Logroño, Univ. de la Rioja, 2002, 616 pp., offers a modern Spanish gloss, text locations with brief citations in context, linguistic and historico-cultural commentary of each word. Concepción Company and Chantal Melis, *Léxico histórico del español de México. Régimen, clases funcionales, usos sintácticos y variación gráfica*, Mexico, UNAM, 952 pp., offers 6756 entries in dictionary format, alphabetically arranged, of words in contexts which illustrate each item's syntactic and semantic features as well as orthographic and morphological variants. The corpus is drawn from Company's *Documentos lingüísticos de la Nueva España (Altiplano Central)*, UNAM, 1994. Félix Páramo García, *Anglicismos léxicos en traducciones inglés-español, 1750–1800.* Leon U.P., 362 pp., uses Anglicisms found in translations from English to measure British influence in Spain in the second half of the 18th century.

G. Clavería Nadal, 'Latinismos y ¿cultismos? en la documentación jurídica medieval', *ALH*, 15–16, 1999–2000[2003]: 11–30, proposes that the term *latinismo* be used to label borrowings from written Latin and that *cultismo* designate the use of words in certain formal and technical registers. She illustrates the analytic use of this distinction in analysing the vocabulary of medieval notarial documents. In her 'Notas lexicográficas y lexicológicas en torno a *sobre* (sustantivo) y *sobrescrito*: la formación de un acortamiento', *Moenia*, 7, 2001 : 343–70, she surveys the entries in the various editions of the *DRAE* and other dictionaries for the homographs *sobre* (preposition) = 'on' and *sobre* (noun) = 'envelope' to demonstrate that the noun is a shortened form of *sobrescrito.* S. N. Dworkin, 'The etymology of Sp. Ptg. *matar* revisited: an unpublished proposal by Yakov Malkiel', *Haensch Vol.*,

249–58, presents and discusses an unpublished hypothesis on the origin of *matar* proposed by the late Y. Malkiel. The Berkeley scholar claimed that It. *ammazzare* and Fr. *massue* are cognates of the Spanish verb and presuppose an earlier *MATTIARE. Analogy with such pairs as CAPTARE ~ *CAPTIARE led to the genesis of *MATTARE alongside *MATTIARE. D. then goes on to offer an alternative explanation of how documented MACTARE could have given *matar* (rather than the expected **mechar*). B. Pottier, 'Esp. *quizá(s)*', *BH*, 104, 2002:507–09, proposes that the affricate [ts] of OSp. *quiça(s)* results from the reduction of *qui lo sab* > **quilçab* > *quiçab*. He offers no explanation of nor parallels for the proposed phonetic evolution.

R. Kiesler, '¿Hay más arabismos en español o en portugués?', *CILPR 23*, III, 263–66, gives Portuguese as the answer to the question posed in the title. D. Fasla, 'La adopción de arabismos como fuente de creación sinonímica en español', *ALH*, 15–16, 1999–2000[2003]: 83–100, studies synonymic pairs in which one element is of Arabic origin. I. Carrasco, 'El léxico erótico del *Lapidario* alfonsí', *CILPR 23*, III, 49–60, discusses the vocabulary used to designate genitalia, copulation, and homosexuality in the chosen text. M. E. Azofra Sierra, 'Latinismos artificiales en el siglo XV', *BRAE*, 82, 2002:47–57, studies 28 pseudo-Latinisms created by Juan de Mena, especially in his prose. Most of these neologisms did not survive. F. Cortés Gabaudan and A. Kanaris de Juan, 'Los términos griegos del *Diccionario español de textos médicos antiguos (DETEMA)*', *CILPR 23*, III, 83–102, lists *c.* 500 items, most of which entered Spanish through Latin. F. Rainer, 'La terminología cambiaria castellana en la primera mitad del siglo XVI', *ib.*, 393–407, notes the predominance of loans and calques in Spanish *letras de cambio* of the period in question. Thematically related is J. Gómez de Enterría, 'Creación léxica en torno a la "Nueva Economía"', *ib.*, 203–15.

M. del Mar Espejo Muriel, 'Aproximación a la función creadora en los nombres de color', *Bustos Vol.*, 561–78, discusses, within the framework of cognitive semantics, the semantic evolution of selected colour terms. C. García Gallarín, 'Los gentilicios en la historia del español', *ib.*, 579–98, offers an historical overview of the formation of *gentilicios*, emphasizing the influence of Latinate models. M. T. Echenique Elizondo, 'Pautas para el estudio histórico de las unidades fraseológicas', *ib.*, 545–60, is a programmatic paper in which the author lays the foundations for a diachronic study of idiomatic expressions (*unidades fraseológicas*). P. Carrasco, 'El léxico de los oficios municipales en las ordenanzas andaluzas', *ib.*, 497–509, examines the lexicon pertaining to municipal administrative positions in medieval and modern Andalusian *ordenanzas*. P. Díez de Revenga Torres, 'Algunos oficios y léxico especializado en la Edad Media', *ib.*, 529–43, examines the lexicon pertaining to certain trades in medieval documents.

7. Phonetics and Phonology

C. González, 'Phonetic variation in voiced obstruents in North-Central Peninsular Spanish', *JIPA*, 32, 2002: 17–31, shows that stress has an effect on frication but not on voicing in the two varieties studied, suggesting that coda-devoicing is different in nature here than in other languages such as Catalan. I. Sánchez, 'Prosodic integration in Spanish complement constructions', pp. 201–13 of *Conceptual and Discourse Factors in Linguistic Structure*, ed. Alan Cienki, Barbara Luka, and Michael Smith, Stanford, CSLI, 2001, 276 pp., uses a corpus of casual spoken Madrid Spanish to argue that prosody plays a role in coding the semantic integration between two clausal constituents of complementation structures.

8. Morphology

Lluisa Gràcia Solé et al., *Configuración morfológica y estructura argumental: léxico y diccionario. Resultados del Proyecto de Investigación DGICYT, PB93–0546–CO4*, Zarautz, Univ. del País Vasco, 2000, 666 pp., analyses affixes in Catalan, Spanish, and Basque, subcategorizes these, and proposes additional categories of lexicographic information to be added now that on-line dictionaries are not so constrained by limitations on space. José Carlos Martín Camacho, *El problema lingüístico de los interfijos españoles*, Cáceres, Univ. de Extremadura, 2002, 266 pp., is sceptical about the existence of the use of infixation in Spanish. Mónica Cantero, *La morfopragmática del español*, Munich, Lincom, 2001, 136 pp., takes a relevance-theoretic approach to establishing the morphological rules governing the formation of lexemes. Elena Bajo Pérez, *La caracterización morfosintáctica del nombre propio*, Corunna, Toxosoutos, 2002, 243 pp., examines issues such as the pluralization or diminutivization of proper names (by, for example, infixation as in *Osquítar*).

9. Syntax

M. Jary, 'Mood in relevance theory: a re-analysis focusing on the Spanish subjunctive', *UCLWPL*, 14, 2002: 157–88, uses the indicative/subjunctive contrast in Spanish to question the assumption that what is encoded in these forms is simply actuality, possibility, or potentiality. José Ramón Losada Durán, *Los tiempos de futuro y la modalidad en español y en inglés*, Vigo U.P., 2000, 266 pp., uses a corpus of written and translated texts in Spanish and English to examine the different linguistic resources available in each language to express the abstract concept of future. Juan J. López Rivera, *El modo: la categoría gramatical y la cuestión modal*, Santiago de Compostela U.P., 2002, 172 pp., is an inconclusive attempt to provide an analytic framework for the discussion of modality. Luis García Fernández, *La gramática de los complementos temporales*, M, Visor, 2000, 380 pp., examines temporal adverbial complements in the light of tense, aspect, and mood. Henk Haverkate, *The Syntax, Semantics and Pragmatics of Spanish Mood*, Amsterdam, Benjamins, 2002, 235 pp., uses largely confected examples in his detailed analysis which allow him to make broad brush statements such as 'the Spanish imperative is commonly used to make a request'. María del Carmen Horno Cheliz, *Lo que la preposición esconde. Estudio sobre la argumentalidad preposicional en el predicado verbal*, Zaragoza U.P., 2002, 477 pp., takes a UG approach to a variety of prepositions and the verbs they accompany. María Kitova-Vasileva, *La 'verosimilitud relativa' y su expresión en español*, Santiago de Compostela U.P., 2000, 2190 pp., uses a corpus of literary Spanish to examine secondary means of conveying modality. María Jesús López Bobo, *La interjección. Aspectos gramaticales*, M, Arco Libros, 2002, 95 pp., covers grammatical aspects of interjections. Patrick Goethals, *Las conjunciones causales explicativas españolas 'como', 'ya que', 'pues', y 'porque'. Un estudio semiótico-lingüístico*, Leuven, Peters, 2002, 284 pp., is a speech act and semiotic study of these causal conjunctions using a corpus of written Spanish, arguing that the concept of 'framing' (as opposed to subordination or coordination) allows for a more coherent explicative framework in dealing with issues such as, for example, differences in word order position of *como*, *ya que* and *pues*. *Las construcciones con 'se'*, ed. Raúl Avila and Cristina Sánchez López, M, Visor, 2002, 413 pp., contains four parts: an overview; impersonal constructions; passive and middle constructions; and diachronic studies. Mario Barra Jover, *Propiedades léxicas y evolución sintáctica. El desarrollo de los mecanismos de subordinación en español*, Corunna, Toxosoutos, 2002, 421 pp., uses a corpus of predominantly medieval historical texts to examine the evolution of subordination in Spanish. L. Alonso Ovalle et al., 'Null vs. overt pronouns and the topic-focus articulation in Spanish', *ItJL*, 14, 2002, 151–69, is a restricted study of anaphora resolution. Alfonso Zamorano Aguilar, *Gramatografía de los modos del verbo en español*, Cordoba U.P., 2001, 209 pp. takes an historical view of mood, principally from Bello's grammar of 1847 to that of Bosque and Demonte of 1999.

10. Sociolinguistics and Dialectology

A special edition of *IJSL*, 155–56, 2002, contains a focus article by E. García, 'Bilingualism and schooling in the United States' (1–92), principally on instructional practices with Hispanic/Latino populations in the US, followed by comments by J. Crawford (93–99), M. Eisenstein Ebsworth (100–14), C. Faltis (115–24), O. García (125–30), K. Hakuta (131–36), N. Hornberger (137–42), S. Krashen (143–51), J. Llanes (152–60), T. McCarty (161–74), R. Otheguy (175–78), T. Skutnabb-Kangas (179–86), G. Valdés (187–95), and a rebuttal of the last essay by García (197–204). J. Toribio Almeida, 'Spanish-English code-switching among US Latinos', *IJSL*, 158, 2002:89–119, aims to examine how code-switching might function as a reflection or reconfiguration of Latino identity. H. Mejías, P. Anderson, and R. Carlson, 'Attitudes toward Spanish language maintenance or shift (LMLS) in the Lower Rio Grande Valley of South Texas', *ib.*, 121–40, examines self-reported attitudes to LMLS in 1982 and finds that they accurately predicted the observed reality in continued use of the Spanish language in this area. English is more frequently reported now in the home environment while Spanish has penetrated further into the business world. D. Suárez, 'The paradox of linguistic hegemony and the maintenance of Spanish as a heritage language in the United States', *JMMD*, 23, 2002:512–30, argues that an awareness of and a response to the paradox of linguistic hegemony are crucial to successful resistance to it and maintenance of the heritage language.

La Géolinguistique en Amérique Latine (*Géolinguistique*, Hors série, 2), Grenoble, Univ. de Stendhal–Grenoble 3, Centre de dialectologie, 2001–02, 276 pp., contains the following articles relating to Spanish: M. Vaquero de Ramírez, 'La géolinguistique hispanique aux Caraïbes' (7–31), C. Wagner, 'La géolinguistique au Chili (33–57), J. Montes Giraldo, 'Regards sur les études dialectologiques en Colombie (59–87), L. Montero Bernal, 'Variation phonodialectologique dans le parler rural de Cuba' (89–102), A. Quilis and C. Casado Fresnillo, 'Les travaux de l'Atlas Lingüístico Nacional del Ecuador' (103–26), J. Lope Blanch, 'Atlas lingüistique du Mexique' (127–41), R. Caravedo, 'L'espace dans une perspective sociogéographique. L'espagnol du Pérou' (143–68), H. Thun, 'L'atlas linguistique diatopique et diastratique de l'Uruguay (ADDU)' (169–85), A. Quilis, 'Les travaux de l'atlas lingüístico de Hispanoamérica' (187–95). *La Romania americana. Procesos lingüísticos en situaciones de contacto*, ed. Norma Díaz, Ralph Ludwig, and Stefan Pfänder, M, Iberoamericana, 2002, 446 pp., contains the following articles of interest to Hispanists: W. Dietrich, 'La situación actual del contacto lingüístico guaraní-castellano en la Argentina' (41–50), J. Lipski, 'Contacto de criollos y la génesis del español (afro)caribeño' (53–96), F. Boller, 'Sonorización en castellano vs. ensordecimiento en portugués en situaciones de contacto luso-español' (197–208),

S. Pfänder, 'Contacto y cambio lingüístico en Cochabamba (Bolivia)' (219–54), N. Díaz, 'La diáspora haitiana: desde la periferia hacia la periferia. Contactos en "Hispaniola"' (279–326), R. Ludwig, 'Urbanidad, migración e hibridación de la lengua: procesos de contacto en el español de Santiago de Chile' (357–86).

Angela Castellano Alemán, *Aspectos sociolingüísticos de la variación gramatical*, Las Palmas, Univ. de Las Palmas de Gran Canaria, 2001, 168 pp., examines the presence or absence of the personal pronoun *yo* in the Spanish of Gran Canaria showing that its use is more frequent among men and older speakers, and less frequent amongst the more highly educated. Antonio Carrasco Santana, *Los tratamientos en español*, Salamanca, Colegio de Salamanca, 2002, 212 pp., is a very general account of pronouns and terms of address in Spain and other Spanish-speaking countries. Adela Morín Rodríguez, *Las formas pronominales de tratamiento en el español de Las Palmas de Gran Canaria: variación y actitudes lingüísticas*, Granada, Granada Lingvistica, 2001, 326 pp., is a rigorous variationist study of T/V usage which shows, for example, the more important role of domain (as opposed to user or addressee variables) in the maintenance of mutual V usage. Juan Ramón Lodares, *Lengua y Patria. Sobre el nacionalismo lingüístico en España,* M, Taurus, 2002, 214 pp., looks at the economic, cultural, religious, and political circumstances framing Spanish attitudes towards the co-existence of different languages within the Spanish state. Antonio Martínez Gómez, *Las hablas andaluzas ante el siglo* XXI, Almería, Diputación de Almería, 2002, 402 pp., is a compilation of conference papers examining different aspects of these varieties of Spanish. José Antonio Galván Botella and Francisco Pedro Sala Trigueros, *Aspe: isla lingüística*, Alicante, Diputación Provincial de Alicante, 2002, 271 pp., is simply a collection of terms, expressions, and names which characterize this variety of Spanish. Rena Torres Cacoullos, *Grammaticalization, Synchronic Variation and Language Contact. A Study of Spanish Progressive -ndo Constructions*, Amsterdam, Benjamins, 2000, 252 pp., traces the evolution of these constructions showing reductive change in both form and meaning, for example, the extension of *estar* + *-ndo* to habitual uses occupying erstwhile *ir* + *-ndo* contexts (*andar* is maintained). Diachronic changes provide insights into synchronic variation and language contact phenomena. Analysis of New Mexican and Mexican data shows no evidence for convergence with English. Maitena Etxebarria Aróstegui, *Variación sociolingüística en una comunidad bilingüe*, Bilbao, Univ. del País Vasco, 2000, 525 pp., is a robust study of the phonological and syntactic variation in the use of Spanish of a socially-stratified group of informants. Specifically it examines the weakening of intervocalic

-/d/- and the verbal expression of hypotheses. It also reports on language attitudes.

Rosario Guillén Sutil, *Sociolinguística andaluza 12: Identidad linguística y comportamientos discursivos*, Seville U.P., 2001, 300 pp., contains the following: V. Lamíquiz, 'La identidad linguística' (13–20), M. Ropero Núñez, 'Sociolingüística andaluza: problemas y perspectivas' (21–48), M. Sedano, 'Los adverbios demostrativos en Madrid, Caracas y Buenos Aires ¿influencia de la direccionalidad?' (49–62), P. Carbonero Cano, 'Las construcciones con *lo que* y su uso en el habla de Sevilla' (63–98), R. Guillén Sutil, 'Varación funcional de los llamados verbos de habla' (99–118), J. Santana Marrero, 'Usos del gerundio en el habla urbana de Sevilla (nivel popular)' (119–40), J. Romero Heredia, 'De alguna diferencia entre construcciones con *sé* y construcciones con *conozco*' (141–48), C. Fuentes Rodríguez, 'Además, ¿un conector argumentativo?', (149–86), M. Martín Cid, 'Lo dicho y su reflejo: los interpretadores del discurso en el habla culta de Sevilla' (187–220), R. Díaz Aguilera, 'Elipsis y repeticiones en un texto oral: análisis de un debate televisivo' (221–32), R. Díaz Ortiz, 'Aproximación al texto radiofónico' (233–52), Y. Congosto Martín, 'Cambio lingüístico y variabilidad articulatoria en el subsistema de las palatales en Andalucía' (253–86), C. Montilla Vega, 'Análisis estadístico-sociológico de los comportamientos lingüísticos en la localidad de Pedrera' (287–300).

Estudios sobre lengua y sociedad, ed. Jose Luis Blas Arroyo et al., Castelló de la Plana, Univ. Jaume I, 2002, 251 pp., contains the following: H. Urrutia Cárdenas, 'Bilinguismo y educación en la comunidad autónoma vasca (CAV)' (7–52), J. R. Gómez Molina, 'Lenguas en contacto y actitudes linguísticas en la comunidad valenciana' (53–86), A. Briz, 'La atenuación en una conversación polémica' (87–104), J. Borrego Nieto, 'Niveles de lengua y diccionarios' (105–54), J. L. Blas Arroyo, 'Introduccion a los fenómenos del contacto de lenguas en las comunidades de habla castellonses' (155–68), L. Gimeno Beti, 'Espanyol i catala: dues llengues en contacte' (169–88), M. Porcar Miralles, 'Algunas consideraciones históricas sobre el contacto de las lenguas española y catalana' (189–200), S. Insa Sales, 'La interferencia de l'anglès sobre el català' (201–08), A. Hidalgo Navarro, 'El corpus de conversación coloquial elaborado por el grupo Val.Es.Co.' (209–16), J. Gómez Molina, 'El corpus de español hablado de Valencia: proyecto para el estudio sociolinguístico del espanol de España y América (PRESEEA)' (217–36), J. Blas Arroyo, 'Presentación del proyecto: laboratorio de sociolingüística de la UJI: materiales para la compilacion y estudio de un macrocorpus sociolingüístico del español en la comunidad de habla castellonense' (237–51).

Francisco Joaquín García Marcos, *Lenguaje e inmigración 1: Sociolingüística e inmigración*. Almeria U.P., 2002, 127 pp., provides a critical bibliography of works in this area, a number of which focus on Spanish and its contact languages. *El indigenismo americano: actas de las Primeras Jornadas sobre Indigenismo*, ed. Teodosio Fernández, Azucena Palacios, and Enrique Pato, M, Univ. Autónoma de Madrid, 2001, 173 pp., contains the following articles: A. Palacios Alcaine, 'El español y las lenguas amerindias. Bilingüismo y contacto de lenguas' (71–98), E. Martinell Gifre, 'La pervivencia del léxico americano prehispano en lenguas de Europa' (99–110), J. Calvo Pérez, 'Caracterización general del verbo en castellano andino y la influencia de la lengua quechua' (111–30), G. de Granda, 'Condicionamientos internos y externos de un proceso de variación morfosintáctica en el español andino. Potencial subjuntivo en estructuras condicionales' (131–46), A. Fernández Lávaque, 'Un caso de convergencia lingüística en el español del Noroeste Argentino' (147–57), R. Cerrón Palomino, 'J. J. Tschudi y los "Aymares del Cuzco"' (157–74). J. K. Choi, 'The genesis of *voy en el mercado*: the preposition *en* with directional verbs in Paraguayan Spanish', *Word*, 52, 2001 : 181–96, suggests that this construction should be analysed both as influence from Guaraní and as the tendency toward simplification within the Spanish linguistic system. M. C. Torras and J. Gafaranga, 'Social identities and language alternation in non-formal institutional bilingual talk: trilingual service encounters in Barcelona', *LSo*, 31, 2002 : 527–48, claim that language preference is itself a categorization device, a social identity. Mar Vilar, *El español, segunda lengua de los Estados Unidos*, Murcia U.P., 2000, 669 pp., examines, from a historical perspective, the role and status of Spanish language and literature within the US curriculum, especially in Higher Education (e.g. Harvard and Yale). Gracia Piñero Piñero, *Perfecto simple y perfecto compuesto en la norma culta de Las Palmas de Gran Canaria*, M, Iberoamericana, 2000, 185 pp., locates this variety, for example, as intermediary between standard Madrid Spanish and Latin American, both of which favour the preterite over the perfect tense. Florentino Paredes, *El habla de La Jara. Los sonidos*, Alcalá U.P., 2001, 230 pp., is a sociolinguistic study of language attitudes and phonological variation in this locality situated in the provinces of Toledo, Ciudad Real, Cáceres, and Badajoz. *Palenque, Cartagena y Afro-Caribe: historia y lengua*, ed. Yves Moñino and Armin Schwegler, Tübingen, Niemeyer, 2002, 284 pp., is a fascinating collection of articles comparing *palenquero* with other languages and investigating African influence both on it and on Spanish. Ana María de la Fuente García, *El habla de La Cepeda (León). 1: Léxico*. León U.P., 2000, 643 pp., is essentially a dictionary of terms used in this variety.

11. Lexis

Tendencias en la investigación lexicográfica del español. El diccionario como objeto de estudio lingüístico y didáctico, ed. Stefan Ruhstaller and Josefina Prado Aragonés, Huelva U.P., 2000, 571 pp., is a collection of conference papers on this topic. Eva María Iñesta Mena and Antonio Pamies Bertrán, *Fraseología y metáfora*, Granada, Granada Lingvistica, 2002, 286 pp., examine fixed expressions and metaphors for a variety of concepts (e.g. fear, anger) in Spanish and several other languages. Maurizio Fabbri, *A Bibliography of Hispanic Dictionaries*, Rimini, Panozzo, 2002, 613 pp., provides a bibliography of works published since the 1980s. Manuel Alvar, *Colectánea lexicográfica*, M, Agencia Española de Cooperación Internacional, 2001, 276 pp., contains reflections on disparate lexicographical issues, for example, animal noises and interjections. José Luis Aliaga Jiménez, *Aspectos de lexicografía española. El léxico aragonés en las ediciones de diccionario académico*, Zaragoza, Diputación de Zaragoza, 2000, 403 pp., gives an historical overview of the inclusion of Aragonese and other provincial terms in the DRAE over the last 300 years and the reasons (overt and covert) for their presence. It then includes a compendium of all the 800 Aragonese terms ever included from the *Diccionario de Autoridades* (1726–39) to the 1995 DRAE. Francisco Abad Nebot, *Cuestiones de lexicología y lexicografía,* M, Uned, 2000, 422 pp., is an extensive reworking of a previous volume and includes, for example, a review of the Academy's dictionaries. *Cinco siglos de lexicografía del español*, ed. Ignacio Ahumada, Jaén U.P., 2000, 441 pp., is a collection of conference papers looking at mono-, bi- and multi-lingual lexicography with a bibliography of works published in 1998–99. *Diccionarios y lenguas de especialidad,* ed. Ignacio Ahumada, Jaén U.P., 2002, 226 pp., is a collection of conference papers and a bibliography for 2000–01.

Léxico y gramática, ed. Alexandre Veiga, Miguel González Pereira, and Montserrat Souto Gómez, Lugo, Tris Tram, 2002, 372 pp., is a collection of conference papers on this topic. Catalina Jiménez Hurtado, *Léxico y Pragmática*, Frankfurt, Lang, 2001, 282 pp., employs a variety of approaches in lexical pragmatics to study verbs of saying and eating in Spanish and German. Roquelina Beldarrán Jiménez, *Das Kubaspanisch. Lexicalische Entwicklung seit der Revolution und ihre deutschen Entsprechungen*, Frankfurt, Lang, 2002, 243 pp., looks at influences on lexical creation in modern Cuba. Francisco Báez de Aguilar González, *Variaciones léxicas y morfosintácticas en el español de la prensa mexicana*, Malaga U.P., 2002, 116 pp., uses a corpus of Mexican newspapers to examine features such as lexis and morphosyntax, putting to rest easy assumptions that the particularities of Mexican practices are based on those of their northern neighbour. José Juan Arrom, *Estudios de Lexicología Antillana*, 2nd edn, San Juan de Puerto Rico, Univ. de Puerto Rico, 2000, 161 pp., is a re-edition of a study published by the Casa de la Américas in La Habana in 1980 but which was barely distributed outside Cuba. It has a mainly etymological focus. Juan Gómez Capuz, *Anglicismos léxicos en el español coloquial*, Cadiz U.P., 2000, 297 pp., uses a corpus of naturally-occurring spoken Spanish to look, for example, at the thematic areas where borrowings from English are most likely to occur. Enrique Jiménez Ríos, *Variación léxica y diccionario. Los arcaísmos en el diccionario de la Academia*, M, Iberoamericana, 2001, 310 pp., provides an historic overview of the inclusion of archaisms in these dictionaries and ends with proposals for how to mark variation in dictionaries. *Cuestiones de lexicografía*, ed. José Ignacio Pérez Pascual and Mar Campos Souto, Lugo, Tris Tram, 2002, 247 pp., is a collection of conference papers. *Diccionarios y enseñanza*, ed. Martín C. Ayala Castro, Alcalá U.P., 2001, 342 pp., is a collection of articles which examine the role of dictionaries within the school and the particularities of bilingual dictionaries.

Diccionarios: textos con pasado y futuro, ed. María Teresa Fuentes Morán and Reinhold Werner, M, Iberoamericana, 2002, 134 pp., contains the following articles of interest to Hispanists: C. Coello Villa, 'Ciro Bayo: lexicógrafo del español boliviano' (31–48), H. López Morales, 'América en el diccionario de la Real Academia Española: de la edición de 1992 a la de 2000. Indices de mortandad léxica' (65–74), R. Werner, 'Identidad nacional y regional de las palabras en los diccionarios españoles' (75–88), C. Chuchuy and A. Moreno, 'Diccionarios españoles en formato electrónico' (89–108). Cristina Fernández Bernárdez, *Expresiones metalingüísticas con el verbo decir*, Corunna U.P., 2002, 590 pp., takes a Coserian approach to the description of expressions which include *decir*.

12. Discourse Analysis and Pragmatics

Catalina Fuentes Rodríguez and Esperanza R. Alcaide Lara, *Mecanismos lingüísticos de la persuasión. Cómo convencer con palabras*, M, Arco Libros, 2002, 540 pp., look at argumentation strategies in a variety of written and oral texts (e.g. advertising, political debate, cinema reviews). María José Boyero Rodríguez, *Los marcadores conversacionales que intervienen en el desarrollo del diálogo*, Salamanca, Univ. Pontificia de Salamanca, 2002, 343 pp., is a poorly organized compilation of markers from a corpus largely composed of written texts, with little clear focus. Javier Gutiérrez-Rexach, *From Words to Discourse: Trends in Spanish Semantics and Pragmatics*, London, Elsevier, 2002, 356 pp., is an interesting collection of articles on this area preceded by a highly-focused introduction by the editor providing a useful survey of work in the field (1–20). Raquel Hidalgo Downing, *La tematización en el español hablado. Estudio discursivo sobre el español peninsular*, M, Gredos, 358 pp., uses two oral corpora to examine theme and topic, finding, for example, that pronominal themes (principally personal pronouns) account for almost 50% of all thematizations. Asunción Escribano, *Pragmática e ideología en las informaciones sobre contactos políticos*, Salamanca, Univ. Pontificia de Salamanca, 2001, 411 pp., takes a speech act approach to the study of headlines in the Spanish press from the 1996 general elections concentrating on features such as variation in lexis and word order. Daniel Jorques Jiménez, *Discurso e información. Estructura en la prensa escrita*, Cadiz U.P., 2000, 180 pp., provides a very general account of certain elements (e.g. headlines) of the Spanish press.

María Noemí Domínguez García, *El lenguaje jurídico-político: la constitución española de 1978*, Sta Cruz de Tenerife, La Página, 2000, 350 pp., provides a detailed lexical and syntactic study of this text, noting, for example, the proliferation of archaic future subjunctives, particularly in articles relating to the Crown. S. Hale, 'How faithfully do court interpreters render the style of non-English speaking witnesses' testimonies. A data-based study of Spanish-English bilingual proceedings', *DisSt*, 4, 2002: 25–47, shows how interpreters, while consistently respecting the propositional content of witnesses' answers, often disregard interpersonal features, thus affecting how the witness is perceived. María Angeles Torres Sánchez, *La Interjección*, Cadiz U.P., 2000, 163 pp., examines the multifunctionality of interjections from a pragmatic perspective. Miguel Peñarroya i Prats, *El lenguaje militar: entre la tradición y la modernidad*, M, Ministerio de Defensa, 2002, 283 pp., examines the different influences on and provides a glossary for this little-researched language variety. Delia Esther Suardiaz, *El sexo en la lengua espanola*, Zaragoza, Pórtico, 2002, 224 pp., contains a useful introduction to feminism and language, an up-to-date bibliography (15–108) on the Spanish language and gender followed by a reprint of Suardiaz's 1973 M.A. thesis.

MEDIEVAL LITERATURE

POSTPONED

ALJAMIADO LITERATURE

POSTPONED

LITERATURE, 1490–1700 (PROSE AND POETRY)

By Carmen Peraita, *Villanova University*

1. General

epistolography. Several studies of letter-writing and of specific correspondences examine hitherto neglected aspects of social practices implied in the writing of letters, paying attention to the letter as a vehicle for humanists', scholars' and scientists' self-representation and social identification, a way to define themselves as belonging to a specific group, to refashion a specific self-image. *Self-Presentation and Social Identification. The Rhetoric and Pragmatics of Letter Writing in Early Modern Times*, ed. Toon van Houdt et al., Leuven U.P., 2002, 478 pp., examines aspects of early modern writers' epistolary self-conciousnesss. It includes J.-R. Henderson, 'Humanist letter writing: private conversation or public forum?' (17–38); C. Fantazzi, 'Vives versus Erasmus on the art of letter writing' (39–56); E. George, 'Conceal or disclose? The limits of self-representation in the letters of Juan Luis Vives' (405–26). *La correspondencia en la historia. Modelos y prácticas de la escritura epistolar. Actas del* vi *Congreso Internacional de Historia de la Cultura Escrita*, ed. Carlos Sáez and Antonio Castillo, M, Calambur, 2002, 601 pp., comments on the history of written practices and their social dimensions, aspects such as the personal side of daily letter writing, practice enhanced by factors such as the cultural colonization of the New World; noteworthy are A. Castillo Gómez, 'Del tratado a la práctica. La escritura epistolar en los siglos xvi y xvii' (79–107), which studies the effects on letter writing of increased literacy, greater mobility due to military duties, and immigration to the New World, and the conscience of rootlessness; C. includes a valuable review of early modern epistolary manuals; J.-C. Galende Díaz, 'La correspondencia diplómatica: criptografía hispánica durante la Edad Moderna' (145–56); C. Espejo Cala, 'El origen epistolar de las Relaciones de Sucesos de la Edad Moderna' (157–67). *Correspondance d'un ambassadeur Castillan au Portugal dans les années 1530. Lope Hurtado de Mendoza*, ed. Aude Viaud, Lisbon–Paris, Centre Culturel Calouste Gulbenkian, 2001, 653 pp., edits 140 unpublished letters (1528–32) from the Castilian ambassador at John iii's Portuguese court, which delineate this negotiator's tasks for Charles v. *Epistolaris d'Hipòlita Roís de Liori i d'Estefania de Requesens (segle* xvi*)*, ed. Eulàlia de Ahumada Batlle, Valencia U.P., 453 pp., compiles business and family letters (1533–40), mostly between mother and daughter, recounting their different sensibilities in dealing with daily tasks in a period of transition from feudal to courtly society.

BIOGRAPHIES. Emilio Cotarelo y Mori, *El conde de Villamediana*, M, Visor, 242 pp., re-edits the extravagant poet and political satirist's biography. María Carmen Vaquero Serrano, *Garcilaso. Poeta del amor, caballero de la guerra.* M, Espasa, 2002, 355 pp., is a documented biography chronicling urban Toledo life, and detailing social, political, and economic relationships between its key families during Garcilaso's life and the *comuneros*' revolt.

LEXICOGRAPHY AND DICTIONARIES. *Nuevo Tesoro Lexicográfico de la Lengua Española*, M, Espasa, 2001, 2 CD-ROM, is an essential recompilation of early modern lexicographical works, such as fray Pedro de Alcalá's *Vocabulario arábigo en letra castellana*, Cristóbal de las Casas's *Vocabulario de las dos lenguas toscanas y castellana*, Richard Percival's *Bibliotheca Hispanicae pars altera containing a Dictionarie in Spanish, English and Latine* (1591), Juan Palet's *Diccionario muy copioso de la Lengua española y francesa* (1604), Cesar Oudin's *Tesoro de las dos lenguas francesa y española* (1607), and Girolamo Vittori's *Tesoro de las tres lenguas francesas, italiana y española* (1609). Some of the dictionaries edited here were never printed, such as Francisco del Rosal's *Origen y etimología de todos los vocablos originales de la Lengua Castellana*, and Juan Francisco Ayala Manrique's *Tesoro de la Lengua Castellana. En que se añaden muchos vocablos, etimologías y advertencias sobre el que escrivió el doctísimo Sebastián de Covarrubias*. Fray Alonso de Molina, *Aquí comienza vn vocabulario en la lengua castellana y mexicana*, ed. Manuel Galeote, Malaga U.P., 2001, 535 pp., a facsimile of the volume originally published in Mexico (1555), 17 years after the first printing press was installed in the New World. This first dictionary of an American language attests an uninterrupted influx of *indigenismos* or Amerindian words into Spanish. Influenced by Nebrija's lexicographic work, the Franciscan M.'s project encompassed two more dictionaries; missionary needs reshaped humanistic perceptions of language, privileging its oral dimension. In order to incorporate different socio-cultural realities from New Spain, Nebrija's methods were redefined, taking into account the difficulty of describing and normalizing languages radically different from Latin.

Atalayas del Gvzmán de Alfarache. Seminario internacional sobre Mateo Alemán. IV *Centenario de la publicación de Guzmán de Alfarache (1599–1999)*, ed. Pedro M. Piñero Ramírez, Seville U.P., 2002, 335 pp., includes J. Pérez, 'El tiempo del Guzmán de Alfarache' (29–44); M. Cavillac, 'Alemán y Guzmán ante la *Reformación de los vagabundos ociosos*' (141–67); L. López Grigera, 'La invención del *Guzmán de Alfarache* (1599) entre poética y retórica' (255–70).

Thomas J. Dandelet, *La Roma española (1500–1700)*, trans. Lara Vilà Tomàs, B, Crítica, 2002, 316 pp., is an extraordinarily documented study of the diplomats, courtiers, artists, and military men who represented in Rome diverse Spanish political interests. Barbara Simerka, *Discourses of Empire. Counter-Epic Literature in Early Modern Spain*, University Park, Pennsylvania State U.P., 223 pp., focusing mainly on the *comedia*, reviews counter-epic literary representations as discursive mediations questioning dominant ideologies, ways in which counter-epic texts contest imperialist practice and provide insights into the heterogeneity of early modern society. Theresa Ann Sears, *Clio, Eros, Thanatos. The Novela Sentimental in Context*, NY, Lang, 2001, 283 pp., analyses an erotic paradox in the *novela sentimental*, examining ways in which desire is ethically and aesthetically ennobling while at the same time morally subversive and destructive. Daniela Ventura, *Fiction et vérité chez les conteurs de la Renaissance en France, Espagne et Italie*, Lyons U.P., 2002, 255 pp., explores the poetics of verisimilitude and its distinctions between possible, impossible, and unlikely events narrated by European writers of *novellas*, and their concerns to offer plausible explanations. V. studies Antonio de Eslava (143–54), Cervantes (155–74), Lope de Vega (175–84), Alonso de Castillo Solórzano (185–92) and María de Zayas y Sotomayor (205–15).

Cortes del Barroco, de Bernini y Velázquez a Luca Giordano, M, Sociedad Estatal para la Acción Cultural Exterior, 395 pp., includes F. Checa, 'Del gusto de las naciones' (17–34); J. Portús, 'España y Francia: dos maneras de convivir con la pintura' (99–112).

2. Bibliography, Libraries, Printing, Reading, History of the Book

Historia de la edición y de la lectura en España, 1472–1914, ed. Víctor Infantes, François Lopez, and Jean-François Botrel, M, Fundación Germán Sánchez Ruipérez, 860 pp., is a comprehensive study of areas related to reading and printing, such as manuscript production and circulation; book production and trade; readers, reading and libraries. Noteworthy are V. Infantes, 'La tipología de las formas editoriales' (39–49); J. Moll, 'El impresor, el editor y el librero' (77–84); R. Chartier, 'El concepto de lector moderno' (142–50); N. Baranda, 'Las lecturas femeninas' (159–70); I. Urzainqui, 'Un nuevo sistema de escritura y lectura: la prensa periódica' (378–89). *Syntagma, Revista de historia del libro y de la lectura*, 0, 2002, includes F. Bouza, '*No puedo leer nada.* El corrector general Juan Vázquez del Mármol y la cultura escrita del Siglo de Oro' (19–45); F.-M. Gimeno Blay, '*Regola a fare lettere antiche.* A propósito de un tratado de caligrafía del *Quattrocento* italiano' (47–72); J. Moll, 'Un taller de imprenta en Sevilla a mediados del siglo XVI' (87–94). C. Peraita Huerta, 'Comercio de difuntos, ocio fatigoso de los estudios: libros y prácticas lectoras de Quevedo', *La Perinola*, 7:271–95, and I. Pérez-Cuenca, 'Las lecturas de Quevedo a la luz de algunos impresos de su biblioteca', *ib.*, 297–333. Asunción Rallo Gruss, *Los libros de antigüedades en el Siglo de Oro*, Málaga U.P., 2002, 209 pp. is an anthology and study of early modern texts dealing with antiquities and the representations of Classical antiquity. *El libro antiguo español* VI. *De libros, librerías, imprentas y lectores*, ed. Pedro M. Cátedra, María Luisa López-Vidriero, and Pablo Andrés Escapa, Salamanca U.P., 2002, 537 pp., includes P.-M. Cátedra, 'Notúnculas sobre impresores viejos y nuevos del siglo XVI' (67–72); L. López Grigera, 'Anotaciones al Quevedo lector' (163–92); V. Moreno Gallego, 'Sangre y tinta. Linajes y libros en el genealogista Pie de la Concha (1600): en torno a un índice de procedencias' (261–84); A. Rojo Vega, 'La biblioteca del maestro Pedro Simón Abril' (365–88). *Libro y lectura en la península ibérica y América, Siglo XIII a XVIII*, ed. Antonio Castillo Gómez, Valladolid, Junta de Castilla y León, 318 pp., includes a series of engaging studies: A. Castillo, 'De donoso y grande escrutinio. La lectura áurea entre la norma y la trasgresión' (107–28); P.-J. Rueda Ramírez, 'Libros a la mar: el libro en las redes comerciales de la carrera de Indias' (189–207); J.-M. Lucía Megías, 'Escribir, componer, corregir, reeditar, leer (o las transformaciones textuales en la imprenta)' (209–42); D. Navarro Bonilla, 'La huellas de la lectura: marcas y anotaciones manuscritas en impresos de los siglos XVI a XVIII' (243–87). Pedro M. Cátedra, *Nobleza y lectura en tiempos de Felipe II. La Biblioteca de don Alonso Osorio, marqués de Astorga*, Valladolid, Junta de Castilla y León, 2002, 643 pp., charts the formation, dispersion, and catalogues (43–104) of the library of Alonso Osorio (who died in 1592); the atmosphere and space of the books (105–51); their shapes (153–89), and subject-matter (191–234); and also analyses inventories and documents related to the marquis's activities (237–646). *Vivir en el Siglo de Oro. Poder, cultura e historia en la época moderna. Estudios en homenaje al profesor Ángel Rodríguez Sánchez*, Salamanca U.P., 316 pp., includes F. Bouza, 'Escribir en la Corte. La cultura de la nobleza cortesana y las formas de comunicación en el Siglo de Oro' (77–99); P.-M. Cátedra, 'El lugar o el orden de los libros en las bibliotecas femeninas del siglo XVI' (101–21).

Poesía manuscrita. Manual de investigadores, ed. Pablo Jauralde, M, Calambur, 223 pp., is a series of essays attempting to establish uniform criteria for transcribing and cataloguing poetic manuscripts.

Ángel de San Vicente, *Apuntes sobre libreros, impresores y libros localizados en Zaragoza entre 1545 y 1599*, I. *Los libreros*, Zaragoza,

Gobierno de Aragón, 260 pp., thoroughly documents the book trade in Zaragoza. María José Osorio Pérez, María Amparo Moreno Trujillo, and Juan María de la Obra Sierra, *Trastiendas de la cultura: librerías y libreros en la Granada del siglo XVI*, Granada U.P., 2001, 598 pp., examine contributions of the book trade to Granada intellectual life and the role of booksellers (such as Pedro Rodríguez de Ardila) as patrons of arts.

3. Humanism and Cultural Studies

Bartolomé Carranza de Miranda, *Tratado sobre la justicia*, Pamplona, EUNSA, 491 pp., is a bilingual edition of an unpublished commentary on Aquinas's passages on the virtue of justice. Carranza investigated law as object of justice, analysed facets of the virtue of justice, and issues related to usury and fair prices. *El gran debate sobre los pobres en el siglo XVI. Domingo de Soto y Juan de Robles 1545*, ed. Félix Santolaria Sierra, B, Ariel, 202 pp., edits and studies key texts of the debate on the *política de pobres* reform in the mid-16th century. Juan Luis Vives, *De subventione pauperum sive de humanis necessitatibus, libri II*, ed. Constant Mattheeussen and Charles Fantazzi, Leiden–Boston, Brill, 2002, 176 pp., is an essential bilingual edition of the first European tract to examine urban poverty and to propose suggestions for policies on social legislation.

Andrea Alciato, *Los emblemas de Alciato. Traducidos en rimas españolas 1549*, ed. Rafael Zafra, Mallorca, José J. de Olañeta — Univ. de les Illes Balears, 54 + 256 pp., is the first facsimile edition of this Spanish translation, influential in the process of formation of Alciatus's corpus of emblems, since it included ten new emblems that were later incorporated into the Latin original. Víctor Mínguez, *Los reyes solares*, Castellón, Univ. Jaume I, 2001, 345 pp., examines the spectacular dimensions of ephemeral constructions, political emblems, festive hieroglyphs, and cultural images celebrating Philip IV through an astrological iconographic programme.

Artful Armies, Beautiful Battles. Art and Warfare in Early Modern Europe, ed. Pia Cuneo, Leiden, Brill, 2002, 266 pp., gathers essays on warfare imagery, and on the relationships between image making and cultural production. Images of warfare are analysed within the processes of negotiating political, national, and social identities.

Ann Moss, *Renaissance Truth and the Latin Language Turn*, OUP, 306 pp., investigates the contrasting scholastic and humanist perspectives on language founded in two antagonistic idioms of Latin. Focusing on documents in Latin, M. argues that the turn to humanist Latin is of major significance in the intellectual history of the Renaissance, examining transformations in language strategies enforced by the humanists concerned with linguistic and cognitive difference.

Fray Agustín de Farfán, Tratado breve y mediçina, y de todas las enfermedades, que à cada paso se ofrecen, Valladolid, Maxtor, 353 ff., is a facsimile edition of a treatise addressed to readers in the New World, in remote areas with no access to physicians. In addition to describing symptoms and diagnosis, F. provided recipes for remedies, reflecting the hybrid medical conceptions of his time. Cristina Müller, *Ingenio y melancolía. Una lectura de Huarte de San Juan*, M, Biblioteca Nueva, 2002, 154 pp., is an engaging study of H.'s approaches to a new anthropology, his belief in creativity as a fundamental feature of any human activity and criticism of the myth of the homogeneity of ancient culture.

José Pellicer de Tovar, *Avisos, 17 de mayo de 1639 — 29 de noviembre de 1644*, ed. Jean-Claude Chevalier and Lucien Clare, 2 vols, Paris, Editions Hispaniques, 2002, xiv + 690, 489 pp., is a seminal, superb edition of an invaluable source of information for the reign of Philip IV.

Glyn Redworth, *The Prince and the Infanta. The Cultural Politics of the Spanish Match*, New-Haven–London, Yale U.P., 200 pp., re-examines the Prince of Wales's unexpected visit, accompanied by the duke of Buckingham, to the Madrid court in 1623 to marry the *infanta*, presenting an innovative analysis of the cultural politics involved in the marriage negotiations which ended in diplomatic disaster.

George Hugo Tucker, *Homo Viator. Itineraries of Exile, Displacement and Writing in Renaissance Europe*, Geneva, Droz, 395 pp., interestingly charts the complexities of early modern literary discourse of exile.

On *conversos* and *moriscos*: Alexandra Merle, *Le Miroir ottoman. Une image politique des hommes dans la littérature géographique espagnole et française (XVIe–XVIIe siècles)*, Paris, Univ. Paris-Sorbonne, 283 pp., focuses on travel and pilgrimage narratives, and cosmographical reports and treatises, to explore accounts of the nature and cultural idiosyncrasies of Turks. M. contrasts Spanish and French narratives to delineate how fluctuations in religious and political interests shaped the varied perceptions and representation of the Ottoman world and its different peoples (Turks, Moors and Arabs, Egyptians, Greeks, and Christian renegades). Juan Andrés, *Confusión o confutación de la secta Mahomética y del Alcorán*, pref. Elisa Ruiz García, transcription María Isabel García-Monge, Mérida, Editora Regional de Extremadura, 2 vols, 270 pp., 72 ff., is a facsimile of the Italian version of Andrés's translation in the Barcarrota library, a group of heterodox books found hidden in a wall in a village of Extremadura, edited here with Andrés's Spanish text and a study of anti-Islamic Peninsular literature. Amalía García Pedraza, *Actitudes ante la muerte en la Granada del siglo XVI. Los moriscos que quisieron salvarse*, 2 vols, Granada U.P., 2002, 531, 532–1059 pp.,

is an innovative study of *moriscos*' religious and social practices with engaging insights into life in the margins of early modern Spain. Miguel de Luna, *Historia verdadera del rey don Rodrigo*, ed. Luis F. Bernabé Pons, Granada U.P., 2001, 438 pp., is a facsimile edition of this chronicle by a morisco physician and royal Arab translator, suspected of participating in the falsified Sacromonte chronicles.

Juan Ignacio Pulido Serrano, *Injurias a Cristo. Religión, política y antijudaísmo en el siglo XVII*, Alcalá de Henares U.P., 2002, 357 pp., is a fascinating analysis recontextualizing the immigration of Portuguese *conversos* into Spain, and the disparate responses of rulers, inquisitors, Jesuits, and the general population to the issue. P.S. reflects on the nature and goals of politics which shaped the debates on *converso* treatment, and charts Inquisitors' political uses of heresy to counteract powerful rulers at court, receptive to *conversos*, such as Olivares. Norman Roth, *Conversos, Inquisition, and the Expulsion of the Jews from Spain*, Madison, Wisconsin U.P., 2002, 483 pp., includes an engaging afterword.

On the Inquisition, Joseph Pérez, *Breve historia de la Inquisición en España*, B, Crítica, 214 pp., provocatively challenges some deep rooted approaches, facts, and presuppositions. *Inquisition d'Espagne*, ed. Annie Molinié and Jean-Paul Duviols, Paris, Univ. Paris-Sorbonne, 185 pp., includes A. Molinié-Bertrand, 'Inquisition et secret en Espagne' (7–19); J. Gil, 'Judíos y conversos en los falsos cronicones' (21–43); A. Merle, 'L'Inquisition et les morisques: entre assimilation et répression' (79–93). Javier Pérez Escohotado, *Antonio de Medrano, alumbrado epicúreo. Proceso inquisitorial (Toledo, 1530)*, pref. Ricardo García Cárcel, M, Verbum–Gobierno de la Rioja, 651 pp., studies and transcribes the trial of Medrano, considered a member of the Toledo *Alumbrado* sect of 1525. It investigates Medrano's views held in common with the *Alumbrados* but also the wider Erasmiam ramifications of his thought, as well as Inquisitors' ways of manipulating language, adjusting witnesses' depositions to conform to the penal language of crimes of opinion or behaviour as the 1525 *Edicto* stipulated.

Several studies on cartography and atlases are worthy of attention. *El Atlas del Rey Planeta. La 'Descripción de España y de las costas y puertos de sus reinos' de Pedro Texeira (1634)*, ed. Felipe Pereda and Fernando Marías, Hondarribia, Nerea, 2002, 398 pp., reproduces a recently discovered superb manuscript atlas of the Spanish coasts addressed to Philip IV by the Portuguese cartographer best known for his Madrid map. It includes an excellent introduction to the Atlas (F. Pereda and F. Marías, 9–48), a study on Texeira's cartographic methods and techniques in this atlas (D. Marías, 293–303) as well as a series of noteworthy studies: R. L. Kagan, '*Arcana Imperii*: mapas,

ciencia y poder en la corte de Felipe IV' (49–70); F. Marías, 'Imágenes de ciudades españolas: de las convenciones cartográficas a la corografía urbana' (99–116). Geoffrey Parker, 'Felipe II, mapas y poder', pp. 99–122 of *El éxito nunca es definitivo. Imperialismo, guerra y fe en la Europa moderna*, trans. Marco Aurelio Glamarini and Pepa Linares, M, Taurus, 2001, 411 pp., examines specific maps as well as Philip II's cartographic interests. *España y América. Un océano de negocios. Quinto centenario de la Casa de la Contratación, 1503–2003*, M, Sociedad Estatal de Conmemoraciones Culturales, 558 pp., includes P.-E. Pérez-Mallaína Bueno, 'El arte de navegar: ciencia *versus* experiencia en la navegación transatlántica' (103–18); L.-C. Álvarez Santaló, 'El filtro ideológico: libros y pasajeros' (161–74); C. Rahn Phillips, 'Mercado, modas y gustos: los cargamentos de ida y vuelta en el comercio atlántico de España' (187–202). Josiah Blackmore, *Manifest Perdition. Shipwreck Narrative and the Disruption of Empire*, Minneapolis–London, Minnesota U.P., 2002, 186 pp., explores how shipwreck narratives — chronicles of death, survival, hunger, horror, and salvation — constructed a counter-discourse to the European colonial enterprise. The narratives challenged in unexpected ways state versions of those events, bringing to the fore an idea of imperial failure and wreckage. Richard Helgerson, 'The liberty of Spanish towns', pp. 123–49 of *Adulterous Alliances. Home, State, and History in Early Modern European Drama and Painting*, Chicago U.P. 2000, 238 pp., studies the early-17th-c. success of an artistic promotion of the non-aristocratic home and marriage, contextualizing Lope de Vega in an early modern European convergence of home, state, and history.

Manuel Jesús Izco Reina, *Amos, esclavos y libertos. Estudios sobre la esclavitud en Puerto Real durante la Edad Moderna*, Cadiz U.P., 2002, 146 pp., explores facets of the community of *personas sujetas a servidumbre*, investigating factors such as how New World trade in slavery increased in the Cadiz region when it was decreasing in the rest of the peninsula.

La teatralización de la historia en el siglo de oro. Actas del III coloquio del Aula-Biblioteca 'Mira de Amescua' celebrado en Granada del 5 al 7 de noviembre de 1999 y cuatro estudios clásicos sobre el tema, ed. Roberto Castilla Pérez and Miguel González Dengra, Granada U.P., 2001, 687 pp., includes noteworthy studies such as A. de la Granja, 'Teatro y propaganda ideológica: autos sacramentales al servicio de la monarquía española' (275–95), and E. R. Wright, 'Lope en el jardín de Lerma' (517–26).

4. Women's Studies

Walter Stephens, *Demon Lovers. Witchcraft, Sex, and the Crisis of Belief*, Chicago U.P., 2002, 451 pp., provocatively argues that theologians themselves were the real demon lovers, the persons who most ardently desired physical relationships with embodied devils. S. posits that the persecution of witches entailed a defence of central Christian principles, related not as much to moral or ethical questions about conduct, as to scientific problems of being and knowledge, concerning devils, angels, human souls, the truthfulness of the Bible, and the evidence of God's existence and presence in the world. Adelina Sarrión, *Beatas y endemoniadas. Mujeres heterodoxas ante la Inquisición, siglos* XVI *a* XIX, M, Alianza, 403 pp., focuses on 60 cases from the Cuenca Inquisition, starting in 1499, dealing with heterodox practices such as idolatry, prophetic revelations, pacts with devils, witchcraft, *alumbradas,* and *endemoniadas.* The study rehashes historical conditions for the Inquisition and religious heterodoxy, and does not always have a clear focus but presents a compelling panorama of female inquisitorial cases with insightful remarks. Manuel Fernández Álvarez, *Casadas, monjas, rameras y brujas. La olvidada historia de la mujer en el Renacimiento,* M, Espasa, 346 pp., a documented social history of women, which pays attention to female slaves, maids, prostitutes, *conversas, moriscas,* and witches. María Amparo Vidal Gavidia, *La Casa de Arrepentidas de Valencia. Origen y trayectoria de una institución de mujeres,* V, Generalitat, 2001, 195 pp., revises the role played by urban Valencian oligarchies in the increased importance of rehabilitation programmes for prostitutes. M. S. Brownlee, 'Genealogies in crisis: María de Zayas in seventeenth-century Spain', pp. 189–208 of *Generation and Degeneration. Tropes of Reproduction in Literature and History from Antiquity to Early Modern Europe,* ed. Valeria Finucci and Kevin Brownlee, Durham, Duke U.P., 2001, 327 pp., explores Zayas's complex treatment of traditionally marginal categories such as witchcraft, and homoerotic and lesbian desire.

5. Cervantes

David Quint, *Cervantes's Novel of Modern Times. A New Reading of Don Quijote,* Princeton–Oxford, Princeton U.P., 188 pp., is an innovative reading which examines the narrative geometries of the novel, its architectural and thematic unity, arguing that interlace techniques allowed C. to reflect upon the historical transition from feudalism to a moneyed, commercial, modern society, exploring the impact of crucial social and economic changes in the Castilian mentality. Q. charts the changes in the nature of erotic desire: DQ's relationship to modern times evolved from his love ideal for Dulcinea, which posits a feudal relationship, in which self-centered masculine lovers are caught in an absurd, selfish code of honour, to the story of DQ's marriage with Princess Micomicona, a modern type of relationship, characterized by the presence of money and social power. Barbara Fuchs, *Passing for Spain. Cervantes and the Fictions of Identity*, Urbana–Chicago, Univ. of Illinois, 142 pp., examines the intersections of identity, nation and literary representation, linking the use of disguise, of 'passing', to historical and social contexts, religious identities, and political ideologies in order to challenge and undermine a collective identity based on exclusion and difference. C.'s emphasis on the fluidity of certain subjects undoes the orthodox narratives of homogeneous and fully-realized national identity put forth by the Spanish Crown. Bénédicte Torres, *Cuerpo y gesto en el Quijote de Cervantes*, Alcalá de Henares, Centro de Estudios Cervantinos, 2002, 317 pp., explores the ironies created by disparity between gesture and context in C.'s construction of images of the body. José Manuel Lucía Megías, *Antología de libros de caballerías castellanos*, Alcalá de Henares, Centro de Estudios Cervantinos, 2001, 510 pp., is an anthology of a complete corpus of Spanish *libros de caballerías*, from *Amadís de Gaula* to Marcos Martínez's *Espejo de príncipes y caballeros* (printed in 1623). The selection pays attention to editorial criteria of genre and typographical display, and includes *Espejo de príncipes y caballeros* (after 1623) which never reached the printing press. Gonzalo Fernández de Oviedo, *Claribalte*, ed. Alberto del Río Nogueras, Alcalá de Henares, Centro de Estudios Cervantinos, 2001, 139 pp., is a brilliant re-edition of a characteristic *novela de caballería* penned by a humanist.

6. Quevedo

Poesía satírico burlesca de Quevedo, ed. Ignacio Arellano, M, Univ. de Navarra–Iberoamericana, 650 pp., is an erudite edition and key study of a significant corpus of complex sonnets. *Quevedo y la crítica a finales de siglo XX (1975–2000)* Vol. II, *Prosa*, ed. Victoriano Roncero and J.-Enrique Duarte, Pamplona, EUNSA, 335 pp., reprints noteworthy articles such as H. Ettinghausen, 'Ideología intergenérica: la obra existencial de Quevedo' (27–64); J. Riandière la Roche, 'Quevedo. Historiador y libelista' (205–26); Victoriano Roncero, 'La España defendida y la ideología quevedesca' (227–50). Diego Martínez Torrón, *Posibles inéditos de Quevedo a la muerte de Osuna*, Pamplona, EUNSA, 157 pp., edits a newly discovered manuscript containing a letter and a series of unpublished poems probably written by Quevedo, dealing with Osuna's death.

LITERATURE, 1490–1700 (DRAMA)

POSTPONED

LITERATURE, 1700–1823

By Gabriel Sánchez Espinosa, *Reader in Hispanic Studies, The Queen's University of Belfast*

1. Bibliography and Printing

P. Almarcegui, 'La biblioteca de Alí Bey', *Cuadernos de Estudios del Siglo xviii*, 10–11, 2000–01 : 5–16, studies a list of 48 books left in Cordoba in 1795 by the Catalan traveller and orientalist Domingo Badía y Leblich (1767–1818), who during his three-year stay in the Andalusian city, devoted all the free time not taken up by his job as a tobacco tax administrator to the construction of a hot-air balloon. Interestingly, among books of a scientific and orientalist nature, he owned three of P. Montengón's novels.

M.-J. García Garrosa, '*Días alegres*, de Gaspar Zavala y Zamora: recuperación de una obra perdida. 1. Historia editorial', *Dieciocho*, 26 : 199–222, illuminates the editorial and printing history of the translation of *Les Journées amusantes* by Madame de Gomez made by the popular novelist and playwright G. Zavala y Zamora. Zavala's hitherto lost *Días alegres* was published by the Imprenta Real between 1792 and 1798 in eight volumes, and its appearance coincided with the publication of another translation of Gomez's work by Baltasar Driguet, entitled *Jornadas divertidas*.

2. Thought and the Enlightenment

R. Haidt, 'A well-dressed woman who will not work: Petimetras, economics, and eighteenth-century fashion plates', *RCEH*, 28 : 137–57, interprets the *petimetra* as a dystopian figure, commenting on how her verbal — in *sainetes* and *tonadillas* — and visual representations — in fashion and costume plates — emblematize a relationship between women's desires for imported textiles and adornments, and the exercise of dangerous choices with regard to national economic development. In H.'s opinion, contemporary *petimetra*-images reiterate the depiction of the *petimetra* as a representation of women's idleness and desire.

G. Sánchez Espinosa, 'An episode in the 18th-century cultural reception of the exotic: the arrival in Madrid of an elephant in 1773', *Goya*, 295–96 : 269–86, relates how at the end of 1773 an Indian elephant, brought for the royal *ménagerie* at Aranjuez, was shown in the streets of Madrid. The resulting public fascination provoked by the intrusion of this exotic animal can be traced through poems (T. de Iriarte), short plays (R. de la Cruz), articles in the periodical press, popular and scientific prints representing the animal, and even in the *costumbrista* pastels of L. Tiepolo. The mythic and pre-modern knowledge of animal nature collides in a debate with the new scientific observation. In the final decades of the 18th c., the image of the captive elephant acquired in Europe a new symbolic meaning linked with the political fight against slavery.

3. Literary History

J. Álvarez Barrientos, 'Sociabilidad literaria: tertulias y cafés en el siglo xviii', Álvarez Barrientos, *Espacios*, 129–46, discusses some of the new spaces of literary sociability that appeared in the Spanish 18th c. — *tertulia, conversación, café* —, comparing them to their French and English models, and commenting on the presence or absence of women in them.

Y en el tercero perecerán. Gloria, caída y exilio de los jesuitas españoles en el siglo xviii. *Estudios en homenaje al P. Miquel Batllori i Munné*, ed. E. Giménez López, Alicante U.P., 2002, 701 pp., contains some contributions of special interest for Spanish 18th-c. literary history, such as E. Giménez López, 'Gregorio Mayans y la Compañía de Jesús: razones de un desencuentro' (163–93), E. Gallego Moya, 'Acercamiento a la biografía del jesuita Faustino Arévalo' (611–37), M.-J. Bono Guardiola, 'Una sátira antifilosófica: *Les philosophes à l'encan* de Juan Bautista Colomés' (639–60).

Imágenes del Quijote. Modelos de representación en las ediciones de los siglos xvii *a* xix, ed. P. Lenaghan, J. Blas, and J.-M. Matilla, M, Museo del Prado–Calcografía Nacional, 350 pp., is the catalogue of an exhibition on the illustrations of *Don Quixote* that took place in Madrid in the autumn of 2003 with rare and not often seen materials from the Hispanic Society of America, the Real Academia Española, and some Spanish private collectors. It features articles by P. Lenaghan, ' "Retráteme el que quisiere pero no me maltrate." Un recorrido por la historia de la ilustración gráfica del *Quijote*' (15–43), N. Glendinning, 'Venturas y desventuras del libro ilustrado: el caso del *Quijote*' (45–53), J. Krahe, 'Miscelánea grafica cervantina en la Biblioteca del Cigarral del Carmen. Coypel, Vanderbank y Hogarth' (55–71), and J. Blas and J.-M. Matilla, 'Imprenta e ideología. El *Quijote* de la Academia, 1773–1780' (73–117). The quality of the reproductions of preparatory drawings, copper plates, and prints is extraordinary. The *Don Quixote* materials of the Hispanic Society of America were collected in the late 19th c. by the Englishman Henry Spencer Ashbee.

J. Martínez Cuesta, *Don Gabriel de Borbón y Sajonia, mecenas ilustrado en la España de Carlos III*, V, Real Maestranza de Caballería de

Ronda–Pre-Textos, 501 pp., contains the work notes left by the prematurely deceased researcher, who planned a book on the cultural patronage of the *infante.* The title of the book is somewhat misleading, the first part of the text being mainly dedicated to don Gabriel's marriage to the Portuguese princess María Victoria, and the second being just an inventory of palace documents pertaining to the infante's very varied cultural expenses. This inventory could be very useful to anyone interested in studying the manifold aspects of high and low cultural life — from musical scores and books imported from Paris and London to carnival costumes and Punch and Judy shows — at Carlos III's palaces and court.

E. Palacios Fernández, *La mujer y las letras en la España del siglo XVIII*, M, Laberinto, 2002, 318 pp., devotes his study both to what was written at the time, mainly by men, on the topic of the social role of women, from Feijoo's widely influential essay of 1726, 'Defensa de las mujeres', to Josefa Amar y Borbón's 1790 *Discurso sobre la educación física y moral de las mujeres*, and the literature written by Spanish 18th-c. women themselves. Special attention is paid to the work of poet-playwrights Margarita Hickey and María Rosa Gálvez, and to the activity of women translators.

M.-A. Pérez Samper, 'Luces, tertulias, cortejos y refrescos', *Cuadernos de Estudios del Siglo XVIII*, 10–11, 2000–01: 107–53, attempts through an exemplary use of literary sources — mainly the periodical press, foreign travellers, and Jovellanos's diaries — a cultural history of these new 18th-c. ways of socialization among Spanish elites, analysing the role played by the different drinks — cocoa, coffee, and tea — and their specific connotations.

NARRATIVE. M. Cantos Casenave, 'El cuento en el siglo XVIII: una propuesta para el rescate y estudio de un género olvidado', *CDi*, 3, 2002: 112–32, is a useful consideration of recent critical and editorial approaches to this hitherto almost neglected genre and its different modalities in the Spanish 18th c., with special emphasis on its presence in the periodical press and miscellanies. Her study is completed with an inventory of not widely known primary texts, an up-to-date critical bibliography, and a proposal for further possible topics and avenues of research.

J.-F. de Saint-Lambert, *Colección de cuentos morales (los da a luz Francisco de Tójar)*, Salamanca U.P., 2002, 115 pp., is a well introduced edition by J. Álvarez Barrientos of the exotic short stories of the French writer J.-F. de Saint-Lambert, originally published in book form in Amsterdam in 1769. The enlightened printer and journalist, based in Salamanca, F. de Tójar, translated and published them in the mid 1790s, first in the *Semanario de Salamanca* that he directed, then in a small volume. *Zimeo*, the longest short-story, narrated by the

Quaker Jorge Filmer and the African prince Zimeo, is a strong denunciation of slavery set amid a slave rebellion in 18th-c. British Jamaica. *Zimeo* is followed by the *Cuentos orientales*, a collection of brief short-stories based on those by the Persian poet Sadi. The last story, *Abenaki*, is set among the American Indians. As a translator, F. de Tójar emphasized the enlightened content of the original. J. Álvarez Barrientos's research on Tójar's narrative and editorial work has opened a new avenue of approach to 18th-c. Spanish literature — the world of the exotic — that will, no doubt, prove very fruitful in all its different aspects.

POETRY. J. Checa Beltrán, 'La *Colección de poetas castellanos* (1786–1798)', Álvarez Barrientos, *Espacios*, 107–28, discusses how, under the cover name of Ramón Fernández, who financed the publication, P. Estala (vols. 1–13 and 19–20) and M.-J. Quintana (vols. 14–18) published between 1786 and 1798 a 20–volume anthology of *Siglo de Oro* poetry that extended from C. de Castillejo and the *Romancero* to J. de Jáuregui and L. de Góngora. Interestingly, the prologues to the different volumes acted as a debating arena for literary and political polemic among the anthologists, in which the government supporter Estala, a client of M. Godoy, the Príncipe de la Paz, attacked the introduction in Spain of a current of philosophical poetry of French origin, which the liberal Quintana defended. While Estala presented Góngora's poetry in a more favourable light, Quintana stressed the beauty and social relevance of the *Romancero*.

THEATRE. M.-E. Arenas Cruz, 'En desagravio de Estala. A propósito de una crítica contra *El filósofo enamorado* de Forner en el *Diario de Madrid* (1795)', *Cuadernos de Estudios del Siglo* XVIII, 10–11, 2000–01 : 17–41, devotes her study to the misunderstanding that broke up the friendship between J.-P. Forner and P. Estala amidst the polemic surrounding the Madrid premiere of *El filósofo enamorado* in January 1795.

Paisajes sonoros en el Madrid del siglo XVIII. *La tonadilla escénica*, ed. B. Lolo, M, Ayuntamiento de Madrid–Museo de San Isidro, 247 pp., is the richly-illustrated catalogue of an exhibition that took place in Madrid's Museo de San Isidro in the summer of 2003. The following introductory studies stand out amongst those included: B. Lolo, 'Itinerarios musicales de la tonadilla escénica' (15–30), G. Labrador López de Azcona, 'Una mirada sobre la tonadilla: música, texto e intérpretes al servicio de un nuevo ideal escénico' (39–59), A. Descalzo, 'Costumbres y vestimentas en el Madrid de la tonadilla' (73–91), and A. Aguerri Martínez, 'La Colección de Música y Teatro en la Biblioteca Histórica Municipal de Madrid: apuntes para su estudio' (93–107).

J. Tortella, *Boccherini. Un músico italiano en la España ilustrada*, M, Sociedad Española de Musicología, 2002, 534 pp., is a thorough, if somewhat overlengthy study on the life and work of this Italian musician who settled in Spain at the end of the 1760s, whose chapter 17, 'La pobreza: un mito que hay que desterrar' (422–69), could be methodologically very useful to anybody interested in taking into account the economic aspects of an artist's or writer's career against the background of the reigns of Charles III and Charles IV.

4. Individual Authors

FERNÁNDEZ DE MORATÍN. M. Ribao Pereira, 'Amor y pedagogía en el *Arte de las putas*, de N. Fernández de Moratín', *Cuadernos de Estudios del Siglo XVIII*, 10–11, 2000–01: 155–74, approaches this clandestine erotic treatise in verse, a parody of Ovid's *Ars amandi*, in the light of the Enlightenment's general principles of didacticism and utilitarianism.

ISLA. J.-F. de Isla, *Cartas familiares y escogidas*, León, Instituto Leonés de Cultura–León U.P., 297 pp., is a facsimile of the Barcelona, Biblioteca Clásica Española, edition of 1884 of Isla's letters to her sister and brother-in-law. Although welcome, a facsimile of the original 1786–89 edition would have been more useful to *dieciochistas*. R. Haidt, *Seduction and Sacrilege. Rhetorical Power in Fray Gerundio de Campazas*, Lewisburg, Bucknell U.P., 2002, 154 pp., characterizes Gerundio's preaching as rococo, instead of the standard baroque, assimilating it to contemporary practices and ways of life such as the *cortejo* and new social attitudes towards luxury.

PONZ. D. Crespo Delgado, 'Il giro del mondo: el *Viage fuera de España* (1785) de Antonio Ponz', *Reales Sitios*, 152, 2002: 64–81, connects Ponz's multivolume *Viage de España* (1772–94) with the published account of his tour in May-November 1783 of Northern Europe, in which he visited France, England, and the Low Countries. In England, besides London, Ponz visited Oxford, Bristol, Bath, Salisbury, Winchester, and Portsmouth, paying special attention to the state of the arts.

QUINTANA. J.-A. Valero, 'Manuel José Quintana y el sublime moral', *HR*, 71: 585–611, re-examines his literary — mainly poetic — production before Fernando VII's restoration to the throne as an absolute monarch in 1814, written at the crossroads of both the discourse on the moral sublime and the political tradition of republicanism.

SALVÁ Y PÉREZ. *Irene y Clara o La madre imperiosa*, ed. A. Rueda, Salamanca U.P., 299 pp., rediscovers an epistolary novel published in Paris in 1830 by the exiled liberal, bibliophile, and antiquarian bookseller V. Salvá, focusing on the negative influence on her daughters of a castrating mother named doña Isidora de Arcos.

LITERATURE, 1823–1898

POSTPONED

LITERATURE, 1898–1936

By K. M. Sibbald, *McGill University*

1. General

bibliography. To recoup material not included here the following are recommended: 'Bibliografía', *NRFH*, 51:279–366, in the Section 'Siglo xx' (347–66), with information on Gerardo Diego, García Lorca, Jiménez, Pérez de Ayala, Ramón J. Sender, and Unamuno; and the usual round-up contained in C. Byrne, 'Review of miscellanies', *BSS*, 80:275–81, and *ib.*, 645–56, with some useful additions on Rosa Chacel, Salinas, Valle-Inclán, and 20th-c. Spanish theatre.

literary and cultural history. *The Companion to Hispanic Studies*, ed. Catherine Davies, London, Arnold, 2002, viii + 109 pp., practises an interdisciplinary approach, integrating history and cultural analysis in equal treatment of peninsular and Latin American themes; student-oriented, it reflects well particular interests in Spanish studies in the UK. Eurocentric and targeting a very different audience, *Las influencias de las culturas académicas alemana y española desde 1898 hasta 1936*, ed. Jaime de Salas and Dietrich Briesemeister, M, Iberoamericana — Frankfurt, Vervuert, 2000, 287 pp., is a collection of 13 articles dealing with the unequal exchange of innovative methods of research in archaeology, medicine, the hard sciences, and political philosophy in which, predictably, Ortega dominates but, curiously, neither Helmut Hatzfeld nor Leo Spitzer are mentioned; of interest here, N. Werz (75–90) compares the diagnostic of time in E. R. Curtius's *Deutscher Geist in Gefahr* (1932), Karl Jaspers's *Die Geistige Situation der Zeit* (1930), and *La rebelión de las masas* (1930); J. Salas, 'Ortega y el ideal de una filosofía académica' (183–204), on Nietzsche, Husserl, and Heidegger as models; C. Strieder, 'Ortega entre culturas: conocimiento y modernización' (205–22), renovating the vision of medieval Spain; E. Menéndez Ureña, '*La Institución Libre de Enseñanza* y Alemania' (61–73), on Giner's practice of *krausismo*; while M. Tietz (32–53) analyses a very particular vision of Spain found in the conservative, catholic journal *Hochland* (1903–41), and W. L. Bernecker (112–27) looks at the differences between the Second Republic and Weimar through Luis Araquistáin's critique of National Socialism. Ricardo Krauel, *Voces desde el silencio: heterologías genérico-sexuales en la narrativa española moderna (1875–1975)*, M, Libertarias, 2001, 270 pp., expands the history of homosexuality in a discussion of homophobia that places *La Regenta* alongside Pérez de Ayala's *A.M.D.G.* (1910), Valle-Inclán's *Tirano Banderas* (1926), and Francisco Ayala's *Muertes de perro* (1958), an analysis of Giménez Caballero's view of Don Juan in 1928, together with a consideration of decadence and aestheticism punctuated by commentary on Gregorio Marañón, Kristeva, and James Joyce. Noël Valis, *The Culture of Cursilería. Bad Taste, Kitsch and Class in Modern Spain*, Durham, NC, Duke U.P., 2002, 406 pp., makes a contribution to cultural studies tracing *lo cursi* from romanticism until the postmodern context of the *movida madrileña* of the late 1970s and early 1980s, with input from the fashionable gurus Pierre Bourdieu, Raymond Williams, and Paul Ricoeur, while of special interest here: 'The dream of negation' (202–23), on Benavente's *Lo cursi* (1902); 'The margins of home: modernist cursilería' (224–27), with comments on Valle-Inclán's *Sonatas* and Gómez de la Serna's little known essay 'Lo cursi' of 1934 (see also R. Quance, *RCEH*, 28:71–85, below); and 'The culture of nostalgia or the language of flowers' (224–76), on García Lorca and *Doña Rosita.*

Modernity variously defined continues to be the key word in our period. Rosa Fernández Urtasun, *Poéticas del modernismo español,* Pamplona, Eunsa, 2002, 167 pp., takes *subjetivismo, fragmentarismo*, and *reflexión personal* as the main themes in the five chapters here that concentrate on the attempts made by Unamuno, Baroja, Azorín, and Valle-Inclán to show beauty in the world in a social and ideological context. Ana Aguado and María Dolores Ramos, **La modernización de España (1917–1939). Cultura y vida cotidiana*, M, Síntesis, 2002, 397 pp. The Roaring Twenties come under scrutiny: first, in *Temps de crise et 'années folles'. Les années 20 en Espagne (1917–1930). Essai d'histoire culturelle*, ed. Carlos Serrano and Serge Salaün, Paris, Univ. Paris-Sorbonne, 2002, 299 pp., that includes contributions from Paul Aubert, Jean-Michel Desvois, Evelyne López-Campillo, Élysée Trenc, Brigitte Maguien, and Claire Nicolle Robin, among others, in a comprehensive examination of the vanguard movements, new aesthetic directions in music and poetry, mass communication media, education, and the role of the intellectual at a time when Spain ardently wished to enter modernity; while, as a thumbnail sketch along similar lines, V. Trueba Mira, 'Paul Morand en la prensa periódica española: el cosmopolitanismo de los "happy twenties"', *RHM*, 55, 2002:302–19, characterizes the prototype of the new cosmopolitan whose work appeared in organs like *Alfar*, *Mediodía*, *España*, *La Pluma*, *La Gaceta Literaria*, *Revista de Occidente*, *Crisol*, *Heraldo de Madrid*, *El Sol*, *La Libertad*, and *La Voz*, praised by a long list of enthusiastic Spanish readers including Jorge Guillén, Max Aub, Jose Bergamín, Benjamín Jarnés, Antonio Espina, Antonio Marichalar, Corpus Barga, and Fernando Vela, all concerned with visions of the vanguard city in modernity. Continuing on with the vanguard: **Nacionalismo y vanguardias en las letras hispánicas*, ed. Eloy Navarro Domínguez and Rosa García Gutiérrez, Huelva U.P., 2002, 305 pp.;

and María Soledad Fernández Utrera, *Visiones de estereoscopio: paradigma de hibridización en el arte y la narrativa vanguardia española*, Chapel Hill, NC, Univ. of North Carolina, 2002, 229 pp., a well-researched, fundamental study which deserves wide dissemination; while, more specifically, A. Kent, 'Altered bodies that define surrealism: *La Revolution surrealiste* and *gaceta de arte*', *JRS*, 3:69–78, compares articles from both reviews to argue that the defining feature of the movement was the undermining of typical binary divisions of inclusion and exclusion in a surrealist synthesis. **Intermedialidad e hispanística*, ed. Angelica Rieger, Frankfurt, Lang, 257 pp., enquires into relations between different media in the modern Hispanic World: of interest here are the essays by Ingrid Simson on a little-known libretto by Gómez de la Serna; Miquel Visa on the evolution of the Dalí-Lorca friendship; and Dagmar Schmelzer on the cinema as the mass medium in Benjamín Jarnés.

There is strong critical interest in righting the imbalance in treatment between the sexes: dealing first with a precursor, R. Krauel, 'Hacia una redefinición de la sensualidad femenina en la modernidad: *La mujer fría* de Carmen de Burgos', *BHS*, 80:525–36, offers an example of the transition between the two major movements in the modern representation of female sexuality, first by *fin-de-siècle* (male) decadent poets, and then by (male and female) writers of the vanguard, in a close reading of this text of 1922, while A. Louis, 'Melodramatic feminism: the popular fiction of Carmen de Burgos', pp. 94–115 of *Constructing Identity in Contemporary Spain. Theoretical Debates and Cultural Practice*, ed. Jo Labanyi, OUP, 2002, goes even further to show how an example of the 'women's genre' of melodrama such as *El artículo 438*, published in the mass-produced *La Novela Semanal* for a readership that was decidedly not feminist in ideology, might serve the purposes of the feminist, pro-divorce lobby; Shirley Mangini, *La modernas de Madrid: las grandes intelectuales españolas de la vanguardia*, B, Península, 2001, 266 pp., presents the lives and works of those who strove to improve the status of women or become professional women themselves in a very conservative society; instead of literary criticism or socio-political analysis, the collective portrait is given in background comments to the precursors María Goyri, Carmen Baroja, and Carmen de Burgos, in some definitions of the new look 'mujer moderna' who emerged in the 1920s, and in a series of detailed biographies of Maruja Mallo, María Zambrano, and Rosa Chacel, together with outlines of the lives of Ernestina de Champourcin, Carmen Conde, Concha Méndez, Lucía Sánchez Saorni, and María Teresa León, and a long list of those involved in political activism, journalism, and republican politics; while two other women of our period finally come into their own, M. Dinverno, 'Gendered geographies: remapping the space of the woman intellectual in Concha Méndez's *Memorias habladas, memorias armadas*', *REH*, 37:49–74, challenging the literary canon by charting the diverse ways in which women living in an oppressive atmosphere could, and did, take to self-realization; and Zenaida Gutiérrez Vega, *Victoria Kent. Una vida al servicio del humanismo liberal*, Malaga U.P., 2001, 404 pp., which makes good use of the family archives to document how this prototype of the modern woman continued her activities in exile in NY after 1950, publishing *Ibérica* (1953–74), and forging friendships with Marianne Moore and Elizabeth Bishop, Victoria Ocampo, María de Maeztu, and Gabriela Mistral.

Exile as a topic has inspired various studies: Antonina Rodrigo, *Mujer y exilio 1939*, B, Flor de Viento, 342 pp., is an up-date of the 1999 publication, with 22 portraits and five *postales* of some better-known figures such as María Zambrano, Vicente Lorca (mother of Federico), and Ana Ruiz Hernández (mother of Antonio Machado), but many more hitherto anonymous women like Manuela Díaz Cabezas, Carmen Martín Belindon, Rosario Sánchez Mora, 'la dinamitera' (see also *YWMLS*, 54:332), Teófila Madroñal, and Sara Berenguer, who belonged to organizations supporting the Second Republic like *Mujeres Antifascistas*, the *UGT*, the *POUM*, or the *Milicias Populares*. Sebastiaan Faber, **Exile and Cultural Hegemony: Spanish Intellectuals in Mexico, 1939–1975*, Nashville, TN, Vanderbilt U.P., 2002, xviii + 322 pp., is a key text as the first study to place the exiles' ideological evolution in a broad historical context so that, by taking into account developments in both Spanish and Mexican politics from the early 1930s until the 1970s, particular attention is paid here to how the intellectuals' persistent nationalism and illusions of pan-Hispanist grandeur, typical of their hard-line Gramscian ideal of the intellectual as political activist but sadly misplaced in the increasingly authoritarian Mexican regime and the international climate of the Cold War, were eventually abandoned in favour of a more liberal and apolitical stance à la Ortega; this argument is also made in Id., 'Between Cernuda's paradise and Buñuel's hell: Mexico through Spanish exiles' eyes', *BSS*, 80:219–39, which identifies certain contradictions manifest in four representations of the host country written by José Moreno Villa, *Cornucopia de México* (1940), Juan Rejano, *La esfinge mestizo* (1945), Luis Cernuda, *Variaciones sobre tema mexicano* (1952), and Luis Buñuel, *Los olvidados* (1950), as each one lived out a precarious existence as an intellectual *voyeur* in a state of ideological ambivalence in a foreign country. **Los refugiados españoles y la cultura mexicana*, M, Residencia de Estudiantes — El Colegio de México, 2002, 142 pp., is dedicated to Emilio Prados.

Some obvious, and not so obvious, pairings are to be had. Marking the shared centenary year, Díez de Revenga, *Cernuda y Alberti*, contains three essays in comparatist vein: J. Cano Ballesta, 'Dos voces airadas del 27: Luis Cernuda y Rafael Alberti' (9–34), noting the dissonant notes struck by these two poets (with Prados and Hernández) in the lyrical harmony of the generation of the 'brilliant Pleiad' as a whole; F. J. Díez de Revenga, 'Desde Murcia: los inicios de Luis Cernuda y Rafael Alberti' (35–67), reviewing contributions to such poetry journals as *La Verdad*, *Verso y Prosa*, and *Sudeste*; and J. M. Balcells, 'El Mexico azteca en la poesía de Alberti y de Cernuda' (69–92), which contrasts Alberti's ethnographic focus with Cernuda's moral perspective but acknowledges the pro-indigenous solidarity of both. L. Estepa, 'Madrid 1906: Juan Gris y Francisco Villaespesa', *CHA*, 635:43–56, which explores 'la más negra, misérrima y pintoresca de las vidas bohemias madrileñas' in which Gris eked out a living by illustrating books by Dorio de Gadex, Pedro Luis Gálvez, and Alejandro Sawa, as well as Villaespesa. Ramón Gómez de la Serna, **Dali*, M, Espasa, 170 pp., is again available, and might be read together with Estrella de Diego, *Querida Gala. Las vidas ocultas de Gala Dalí*, M, Espasa, 232 pp., the first biography of Helena Diakonova who, as wife first of Paul Éluard, provides links between French Surrealism and Dalí's personal eccentricity.

Looking after the seventh art form: Emilio C. García Fernández, *El cine español entre 1896 y 1939*, B, Ariel, 2002, 364 pp., offers a carefully illustrated and well-documented history of the industry; while Juan Antonio Bardem, *Y todavía sigue*, B, Ediciones B, 2002, 370 pp., offers a personal memoir that doubles as cultural history.

In the currently favourable climate the encompassing cultural rather than the strictly literary approach gains ground. With an innovative disregard for the usual generic boundaries and formal conventions, *Crossing Fields in Modern Spanish Culture*, ed. Federico Bonaddio and Xon de Ros, Oxford, Legenda, 202 pp., provides insights into the bonding of society, politics, and culture in the text, and while not all 14 essays concentrate on poetics, the six of interest here do treat poets of the inter-war years: R. Quance, 'Norah Borges illustrates two Spanish women poets' (54–66), comments upon the formulation of a poetics of sexual difference when Norah Borges's drawings of androgynous, angelic child figures were combined with the poems of Concha Méndez' *Canciones de mar y tierra* (Buenos Aires, 1930) and, after, with Carmen Conde's *Júbilos* (Murcia, 1934); J. Cockburn, 'Gifts from the poet to the art critic' (67–80), explores García Lorca's entry in 1927 into the debate between Cubism and Surrealism, his relationship with Sebastià Gasch, and the part played by such of his drawings as *Teorema de la copa y la mandolina*, *Slavador Adil*,

Merienda, *La vista y el tacto*, *Manos cortadas*, *San Sebastián*, *Amor intelectualis*, and *Leyenda de Jérez* in this on-going dialogue; X. de Ros, 'Ignacio Sánchez Mejías blues' (81–91), traces the common elegiac mood in the 'Llanto' and the 'Harlem Renaissance' phenomenon, but underscores the significant politico-social and cultural disquiet of the latter that found some echo, but no resolution, in the turmoil of the Second Republic on the eve of war; D. G. Walters, 'Parallel trajectories in the careers of Falla and Lorca' (92–102), points up how both were inspired by the *cante jondo* in the early 1920s, although by the end of the decade both sought authenticity elsewhere; H. Laurenson-Shakibi, 'Angels, art and analysis: Rafael Alberti's *Sobre los ángeles*' (103–17), highlights the influence of Goya and Maruja Mallo on how Alberti replicated pictorial techniques in poetry to express the mental anguish of a nervous breakdown; while J. Rattray, 'The theory of surrealist collage through image and text' (118–34), analyses the four untitled collage-drawings by Ángel Planells that illustrate José María Hinojosa's poems of *La sangre en libertad* (1931) in order to explicate Surrealist theory and Hinojosa's love affair with the movement. Following a similar critical line, *RCEH*, 28, is a hefty special volume dedicated to 'Reproducciones y representaciones. Diálogos entre la imagen y la palabra', compiled and introduced by Claudine Potvin (5–8), as a desire to explore the profound connections in the semiotics of visual and verbal language, and of particular interest here are the following essays on the Spanish vanguard: R. Sarabia, 'Inter arte vanguardista y algunas cuestiones teórico-críticas a considerar' (45–69), revises the classical definitions of *poiesis* or art as perfection contemplated in tranquillity to deal with the dynamic, often shocking, 'creacionismo huidobreano trasuntado de ultraísmo madrileño-bonaerense' manifest in Huidobro's 13 painted poems exhibited in Paris in 1922, José Juan Tablada's *caligrammes* of 1918, Joan Miró's *tableaux-poèmes* from 1925–27, and Ernesto Giménez Caballero's literary posters of 1927–28; R. Quance, 'Norah Borges y Ramón Gómez de la Serna: revisions de lo cursi' (71–85), documents how Norah's later illustrations, *El herbario*, *Pablo y Virginia*, *Urbano y Simona*, all nostalgically feminine, rather melancholic museum pieces dedicated to some famous *novios*, might be read together with Ramón's essay as a *riposte* to the dominant Ortegan theory of dehumanization; M. S. Fernández Utrera, 'Esencia de verbena: saber popular y estética de minorías en la pintura de Maruja Mallo' (87–102), indicates how Mallo's painting *La verbena*, first exhibited in 1928, illustrates well the uneasy harmony between popular culture and minority aesthetics and, by an intelligent comparison with Salvador Dali's *Verbena de Santa Cruz* (1923), picks up on Mallo's realization of the limits of the vanguard dream of bourgeois intellectuals instituting change in the socio-political order; N. Dennis, 'Francisco de Ayala and Tintoretto: literature, painting, film' (103–18), focuses on a short prose piece of 1928 and *Susanna and the Elders* in the Prado Museum to highlight the filmic nature of Ayala's text.

2. Poetry

To be read together as introductory texts: **Antología de la poesía española del siglo* XX *(1900–1980)*, ed. José P. Ayuso, M, Castalia, 1080 pp.; and *Cien años de poesía. 71 poemas españoles del siglo* XX*: estructuras poéticas y pautas críticas*, ed. Peter Fröhlicher et al., Berne, Lang, 2001, 838 pp., which is, inevitably, an arbitrary construction but does illustrate the rich variety in 20th-c. Spanish poetry; all interpretations are directed 'al lector exigente' but preference is given to the semiotic focus of the Zurich School as the overall critical method, and although, again predictably, Unamuno, Valle-Inclán, the Machados, and the Guillén-Lorca Generation are all foregrounded, some useful consideration is given to Ernestina de Champourcín, Carmen Conde, and Gloria Fuertes. Various doyens of the discipline are honoured: **Federico García Lorca et cetera. Estudios sobre las literaturas hispánicas en honor de Christian de Paepe*, ed. Nicole Delbecque, Nadia Lie, and Brigitte Adriaensen, Louvain U.P., ix + 602 pp., is a meaty tribute to an influential voice in Lorca studies; while, from a particular critical stance, *The Discovery of Poetry: Essays in Honor of Andrew P. Debicki*, ed. Roberta Johnson, Boulder, CO, SSSAS, 174 pp., is a homage to Debicki's long service and rich contribution to Spanish studies in North America, and contains of interest here: personal reminiscing by Jonathan Mayhew (13–16); S. J. Fajardo, 'Plotting exile: self and community in post-civil war Spanish poetry' (17–33), using Pierre Bourdieu and Paul Ricoeur to plot the domain of exiles like José Moreno Villa, León Felipe, and Jorge Guillén; J. C. Wilcox, 'Ángel González's intertextualization of Juan Ramón Jiménez' (35–59), on the constant engagement with and subversion of Jiménez's *obra* by the younger poet in search of an intermittent source of inspiration; and S. Keefe Ugalde, 'Poetics of mid-century women poets of Spain' (87–102), considering how a cohort of 15 women poets born between 1924 and 1935 negotiated the limitations of the normative femininity enforced by Church and State to endorse a poetry of discovery and self-authentication. *José Bergamín tra avanguardia e barroco*, ed. Paola Ambrosi, Pisa, ETS, 2002, 266 pp., takes a hard look at an exemplary 'franco tirador' and explores his life, aesthetics, theatre, and poetry, and of special interest are: contributions from Alfonso Sastre (15–19), on the continuity with Lope; Yves Rouillère (33–45), on similarities with Tirso and Calderón; Maria Grazia Profeti (46–58), on 'le debolezze documentali'; Silvia Marti (77–86), with an analysis of *Los filólogos* (1925); N. Dennis (97–108), on the harmony here between communism and Roman Catholicism; Juan Cano Ballesta (121–36), championing an intellectual and verbal poetry in tune with the generation as a whole; general reminiscing by Gonzalo Santonja (137–41), Manuel Arroyo Stephens (143–56), and José Luis Barros (205–12); and Florence Delay (215–21), on *Beltenbros*. In comparative vein, Margarita Garbisu Buesa, **Purismo español y hermetismo italiano: coincidencias y divergencias en Jorge Guillén y Giuseppe Ungaretti*, M, Fundación Universitaria Española, 2002, 404 pp. Jacques Issorel collects and provides an introduction and the necessary notes to Fernando Villalón, *Semblanzas de matadores*, Fuentevaqueros, Museo Casa-Natal de Federico García Lorca, 2002, 62 pp., a bibliophile's delight that reproduces some unedited poems written between the end of 1917 and May 1920 that fleetingly describe 16 *toreros* in polymetric verse with the name in the last line in a *pie quebrado*; of them all only Joselito and Juan Belmonte escape the scathing comments and satirical humour of this knowledgeable *aficionado*.

INDIVIDUAL POETS

ALBERTI. The recent centenary is handsomely commemorated in the catalogue of the slightly different exhibitions at MNCARS and the Centro Andaluz de Arte Contemporaneo in Seville, **Entre el clavel y la espada. Rafael Alberti en su siglo*, ed. Juan Carlos Bonet, Carlos Pérez, and Juan Pérez de Ayala, M, Sociedad Estatal de Conmemoraciones Culturales, 571 pp. Gregorio Torres Nebrera, **Rafael Alberti. Un poeta en escena*, Seville, Renacimiento, 2002, 212 pp., concentrating on A.'s theatre. A. P. Debicki, 'Poemas tempranos de Rafael Alberti: los comienzos de una poesía social', *ALEC*, 28:61–75, corrects the usual view that A.'s socio-political stance dates back only to the 1930s, and reads *El alba del alhelí* to find evidence of A.'s compassion for fundamental human problems in a decadent world beset by corruption and gross materialism that prefigures the better known concerns of *El poeta en la calle* and *De un momento a otro*. Robert Havard, *The Crucified Mind: Rafael Alberti and the Surrealist Ethos in Spain*, London, Tamesis, 2001, 251 pp., focuses on the supersaturation in Catholicism of Spanish avant-garde poetry, art, and film of the late 1920s and early 1930s in order to show how A. resolved his repressive religious upbringing and deep-rooted sense of sexual guilt in a materio-mysticism that evolved from Surrealism to a commitment to Marxism; as might be expected, there is much that is innovative on A.'s relationship with Maruja Mallo, the dissolve device in *Un chien andalou* or *Tierra sin pan* as a surrealist documentary, and the particular use of syntax in *Sermones y moradas*, although poor proof-reading and false translations mar this provocative text. The double volume, Díez de Revenga, *Cernuda y Alberti*, has seven essays dedicated to A.: G. Torres Nebrera, 'Los sonetos de *Marinero en tierra*' (239–68); J. Neira, 'Gongorismo y vanguardia en Rafael Alberti: las metamorfosis iconoclastas de *Cal y canto*' (269–91); J. A. Pérez Bowie, 'Rafael Alberti y el cine: textos y contexto' (293–313); P. Guerrero Ruiz, 'Los modelos ekfrásticos en Rafael Alberti' (315–41); G. Morelli, 'Roma y la cultura italiana en Rafael Alberti' (343–66); M. de Paco, '*El hombre deshabitado* y "la podredumbre de la escena española"'(367–88); M. Aznar Soler, 'Rafael Alberti y la "guerra fría" teatral: la *Cantata por la paz y la alegría de los pueblos*' (389–416); C. Oliva, 'Alberti y el teatro: introducción a su práctica escénica' (417–48). (See also CERNUDA below).

CERNUDA. Another centenary makes even more of a splash. Various hands produce facsimile editions: José María Espinosa adds a preliminary study to **Variaciones sobre tema mexicano*, Mexico, Tezontle, 2002, 84 pp., Francisco Brines does the same for the 1958 edition of *La realidad y el deseo (1924–1956)*, Mexico, Tezontle, 2002, 334 pp., and Jordi Amat provides full critical apparatus for **Fuerza de soledad*, M, Espasa, 2002, 275 pp.; while, one of the better celebratory efforts, Antonio Carreira selects and adds a long introductory study to the anthology *Poesía del exilio*, M, Fondo de Cultura Económico, 345 pp., with, logically, most work coming from *La realidad y el deseo*, 24 pieces from *Ocnos*, and 11 from *Variaciones sobre tema mexicano*, in an altogether elegant collection. Interest is generated by the correspondence: **Páginas sobre una poesía. Correspondencia: Alfonso Reyes, Luis Cernuda (1932–1959)*, ed. Alberto Enríquez Perrea, Seville, Renacimiento, 212 pp., with an introductory study (11–30) contextualizing the letters and giving their provenance from, in the main, the archives of El Colegio de México; and the inclusive volume, *Epistolario 1924–1963*, ed. James Valender, M, Residencia de Estudiantes, 1273 pp., a detailed, autobiographical chronicle (if, of necessity, rather fragmentarily so) of the poet who shared in the early heyday of his generation, publishing in *Litoral*, *La Verdad*, and *Verso y Prosa* in the 1920s, and, finally, after the homage in *La Caña Gris* in 1960, whose poetic voice was rescued from silence and censorship; the letters show C. at his best and worst, with evidence of good relations with Rivas Cherif, Fernando Villalón, María Zambrano, Concha Méndez, Martínez Nadal, Nieves de Madariaga, and Salvador Moreno, among others, and memorable waspish comments against 'Alonso Desamado' or Dámaso Alonso, Prados, and the 'otra España' that first delighted C. but soon paled as he railed against 'La Fonda de Incultura Expensiva' and the 'burdel' known as UNAM in the 'insignificant' country of his final exile. Some familiar points of view are reiterated in the course of the festivities: Emilio Barón, **Luis Cernuda, poeta. Vida y obra*, Seville, Alfar, 2002, 316 pp.; José María Barrera López, *Luis Cernuda. Un destino a solas*, Seville, Ayuntamiento de Sevilla, 280 pp., and Bernard Sicot, *Exilio, memoria e historia en la poesía de Luis Cernuda*, Mexico, Fondo de Cultura Económico, 222 pp., to be read together with the earlier anthology co-ordinated by Id. and Rose Duroux, *60 ans d'exil républicain: des poètes espagnols entre mémoire et oubli*, Paris, Centre de recherches hispaniques du Centre d'études et de recherches interculturelles européennes, 2001, 341 pp. Close readings are the order of the day: Julio Neira and Javier Pérez Bazo, *Luis Cernuda en el exilio. Lecturas de 'Las nubes' y 'Desolación de la quimera'*, Toulouse, Univ. Toulouse-Le Mirail, 2002, 314 pp., offer a rather odd combination for didactic purposes in order, first, to illustrate the socio-cultural context of C.'s poetry between 1918 and 1936, and then to consider exile, of necessity, as the inspiration for C.'s later magisterial poetry (see also below); while J. M. Godoy, 'Luis Cernuda: historia y deseo en *Los placeres prohibidos*', *ETL*, 30, 2001–02: 104–19, presses Adrienne Rich, Walt Whitman, and Ángel Sahuquillo into service to explain that the freer socio-political climate of the Second Republic, with calls for greater licence for homosexuals, had at least as much effect on the writing of this particular collection of poetry as the personal references in the text to C.'s short-lived affair with a younger lover, Serafín, in this period; while, in exhaustive textual analysis, J. M. Serrano de la Torre, 'Sobre estética y poética cernudianas. Unas notas desde la lectura de Pierre Reverdy', *RLit*, 129: 167–97, highlights connections between Reverdy's novel *Le Voleur de Talan* (1917) and both *Perfil del aire* (1927) and the later work. Two centenary volumes appear in print: **Mondi de Luis Cernuda. Atti del Congreso Internationale nel I Centenario della nascita (Udine, 24–25 maggio 2002)*, ed. Renata Londero, Udine, Forum, 173 pp.; and Díez de Revenga, *Cernuda y Alberti*, which contains seven essays specifically on C.: J. L. Bernal Salgado, 'Cernuda en la vanguardia' (93–118); R. Reyes Cano, ' "Jardín antiguo": el primer exilio de Luis Cernuda' (119–32); J. Pérez Bazo, 'El proceso dialéctico de la afección en Luis Cernuda. De *Las nubes* a *Desolación de la quimera*, de Luis Cernuda' (133–74); M. J. Ramos Ortega, 'Nuevo y viejo canon: las antologías poéticas de Luis Cernuda' (175–202)'; J. M. Pozuelo Yvancos, 'La crítica literaria de Luis Cernuda' (203–20); and V. Serrano, '*La familia interrumpida* de Luis Cernuda: teatro y representación' (221–38). (See also ALBERTI above).

GARCÍA LORCA. C. Gala, 'Lorca's *Suites*: reflections on cubism and the sciences', *BHS*, 80: 509–24, reads the poems from the perspective of the then contemporary *avant-garde* preoccupations about form, space, dimension, simultaneity, colour, multiple planes, and disregard for the anecdotal to show how these paralleled and responded to the new science of Henri Bergson, Hermann Minkowski, and Albert Einstein. G. Basterra, 'The grammar of fate in Lorca's *Bodas de sangre*', *JRS*, 3:49–68, argues rather convolutedly that the characters both re-enact and disturb the inevitability of their fate, constructing in their very lamentations their own destiny through language. Juan Aguilera and Isabel Lizárraga, *Federico García Lorca y el teatro clásico: la versión escénica de 'La dama boba'*, Logroño, Univ. de la Rioja, 2001, 223 pp., is a welcome addition to the Lorcan *corpus;* divided into two parts, the first consists of five chapters covering G.L.'s part in contemporary attempts to place examples of the classical Spanish theatre at centre stage, the role of *La Barraca*, the collaboration with Eva Franco and the *estreno* of *La dama boba* in Buenos Aires, and the Lope tricentenary of 1935 and the Xirgu-Borràs *estreno* in Barcelona, while the second part is the most valuable, being the reproduction of the acting version of the play which enhances our view of G.L. as director and adapter. New perspectives come from: J. Huerta, '*La casa de Bernarda Alba* by national Asian American theatre company', *Gestos*, 34, 2002:183–84, describes the adaptation by Chay Yew to the Philippines with a multi-ethnic cast headed by the legendary Broadway hoofer, Chita Rivera, in the lead role, but which, nonetheless, as a play without its Andalusian roots could not, and did not, survive a long run; while M. T. García-Abad, 'García Lorca y Valle redivivos: *Arabilis (cuando estemos más tranquilos . . .)* de Laila Ripoll', *ib.*, 175–82, tells of the mix of *sainete costumbrista*, magic realism, horror novel, and obvious Lorcan inspiration in which four women — played by male actors — perform a grotesque *esperpento*.

HERNÁNDEZ. Jose María Balcells provides introduction and notes to *El rayo que no cesa*, M, SIAL, 2002, 128 pp. J. M. Pedrosa, '"Cuando paso por tu puerta . . ." Análisis comparatista de un poema de Miguel Hernández', *NRFH*, 50, 2002:203–15, is an exhaustive close reading of no. 41 of the series *Cancionero y romancero de ausencias*, written in 1939, partially published in 1969 and in full only in 1988, in order to elucidate the sexual image through painstaking recourse to the *Romancero*, Berceo, *La Celestina*, Hispanic popular songs, stellar researchers like Francisco Rodríguez Marín and Daniel Devoto, and the more contemporary collections compiled by Antonio Vallejo Cisneros (1988) and José Manuel Fernández Cano (1998).

JIMÉNEZ. J. Marchamalo García, 'La carpeta amarilla de Juan Ramón', *CHA*, 636:63–70, documents the details of the unhappy suicide of Marga Gil Roësset, a young sculptress who, on 28 July 1932, could no longer suffer her love for J., and tells, first, of the yellow file in which J. faithfully kept Marga's diary, poems, cuttings, and reproductions of her work, and then of how the file was lost when troops ransacked J.'s apartment in Padilla 38, not to reappear until Juan Guerrero's widow restored it to J.'s literary executor, Francisco Hernández Pinsón in the 1960s. T. Gómez Trueba, 'El libro de *Sueños* de Juan Ramón Jiménez y su problemática aproximación al surrealismo', *HR*, 71:393–413, quotes from the collection *Sueños* or *Viajes y sueños*, still partially unedited, which shows J. in 1915–16 intrigued by dreams and the unconscious and, even, in reference to two texts dated 7 and 9 April, respectively, putting into practice 'automatic writing' years before André Breton.

MACHADO, A. Jordi Doménech provides the critical apparatus and Rafael Alarcón Sierra the introduction to *Prosas dispersas (1893–1936)*, M, Páginas de Espuma, 2001, 890 pp., which is a handsome complement to the third volume of Oreste Macrì's compilation *Prosas completas (1893–1936)* (1988) in that more than 70 new ítems have been added, some writen under assumed names for the series 'Política y cultura' in *El Porvenir de Castilla* (Soria), co-founded by José María Palacios and M., others on Spain and WWI (1916), or as an open letter on poetry in 1928, all in a collection that evinces meticulous scholarship, rejoices in excellent notes that enlighten, correct, and verify, and contains a useful up-dated bibliography. Jacques Issorel, *Collioure 1939. Le derniers jours d'Antonio Machado*, Perpignan, Mare Nostrum, 2002, 172 pp., although in fact the third edition of this *plaquette* that first appeared in 1982, has significant revisions: both French and Spanish versions are now given, the bibliography has extensive additions, four new poems by Antón Carvial, Francisco Giner de los Ríos, Jean Cassou, and Carlos Álvarez have been added, although missing here is Manuel Andújar's original preface to this collection of haunting memories. H. Mattauch, 'Las "Galerías" de Antonio Machado: origen y evolución de una metáfora central de su poesía', *RLit*, 129:225–35, explicates a metaphor that, discovered in J.-K. Huysmans's *À rebours* sometime in 1903, appeared in M.'s poetry published in *Helios* and *Alma Española* between November 1903 and May 1904, and are a testimony to M.'s poetic journey through French Symbolism. In a neo-historicist approach to M.'s poetry, R. Vila-Belda, 'Pasajismo e impresionismo en *Campos de Castilla*, de Antonio Machado', *RCEH*, 28:281–97, reads M.'s *suites* to find notable connections with both artistic movements; while Araceli Iravedra Valea, **El poeta rescatado. Antonio Machado y la poesía del 'grupo de "Escorial"'*, M, Biblioteca Nueva, 2001, 252 pp., considers the re-discovery of M. after the War by younger poets centred on the review published between 1941 and 1945 by José María Alfaro. F. Bonaddio, 'Idealizing Lola: two film adaptations of the Machado brothers' play, *La Lola se va a los puertos*', *BHS*, 80:61–82, explores intertextualities between the original play of 1929, the first film version of 1947 made by Juan de Orduña, and the second by Josefina Molina in 1993, with Juanita Reina and Rocío Jurado, respectively, in the lead role, and shows how the first film maintained the Francoist political agenda in the idealization of the *patria*, the exaltation of family values, and the domestication of women, while the second overtly resexualized the *cantaora* and set flamenco back in a precise historical and economic context where class issues dominate in a refusal to 'sanitize' the folkloric genre.

SALINAS. *Cartas a Katherine Whitmore: el epistolario secreto del gran poeta del amor (1932–1947)*, ed. Enric Bou, B, Tusquets, 2002, 406 pp., is the painstaking selection and transcription of some 150 letters from the collection of 354 letters and 144 poems donated to Harvard University where, for so long, a respectful silence was maintained about the 'secreto a gritos' of the real life love affair behind *La voz a ti debida, Razón de amor,* and *Largo lamento*; therein S. shows himself a sharp-eyed observer and a writer of elegant prose as well as curiously insensitive to the feelings of his nearest and dearest, the paradox of a self-absorbed, egotistical man who composed perhaps the best of 20th-c. Spanish love poetry, while Bou documents clearly how such letters provide an invaluable gloss to that poetry. J. Pardo Pastor, 'La vida del "ser" en *La bomba increíble* de Pedro Salinas', *CH*, 25:129–47, is a close reading of the binary oppositions in S.'s *fabulación* to facilitate entry into the poet's 'other' reality.

3. Prose

Carlos Ramos, *Ciudades en mente. Dos incursiones en el espacio urbano de la narrativa española moderna (1887–1934)*, Seville, Fundación Genesian, 2002, 216 pp., explores the 'presencia incorporea' rather than the 'materialidad fisica' of the city as experienced by the characters in *Fortunata y Jacinta* and, of interest here, in the work of four vanguard writers, highlighting the association with the elusive female and an analogy between city and text in *Víspera del gozo* by Pedro Salinas, the moral opposition between city and countryside found in *Locura y muerte de Nadie* by Benjamín Jarnés, the new cinematographic techniques used in *Cazador del alba* by Francisco Ayala, and the loss of faith chronicled in *Hermes en la vía pública* by Antonio Obregón, all rounded off by a most useful bibliography. A. Zamora, '*El jardín de los frailes*: Azaña y la guerra simbólica', *HR*, 71:31–49, details Azaña's intuition that an autobiographical novel without the sadly typical dogmatism, intolerance, and manicheism of the period might be a better vehicle for ideological discussion in Spain. V. Trueba Mira,

'Lulú: el *extraño* personaje de *El árbol de la ciencia* de Pío Baroja', *ALEC*, 28:183–202, argues that Lulú was 'un ensayo de emancipación' and a true sister of Baroja's other female characters. J. A. Llera, 'Perspectivismo y contraste en las crónicas humorísticas de Julio Camba', *RHM*, 55, 2002:320–41, documents well the Spaniard's reactions to Harlem, the Wall Street Crash, and the pernicious double bind of technology and money in the 'Estados Engomados'. J. Pérez-Magallón, 'Leticia Valle o la determinación genérica', *ALEC*, 28:139–59, teases out the strategy whereby Chacel's character both hides and constructs her own identity as she moves the novel along. Eugenio d'Ors, **La vida breve*, V, Pre-Textos, 424 pp. M. T. Pao, 'Agustín Espinosa's *Crimen*: the avant-garde narrator as transgressor', *BSS*, 80:427–47, rights the neglect of this vanguard prose work and interprets well how the literal and literary transgressor is the author of a crime against the textual body of conventional 19th-c. narrative. J. J. Lanz, 'Entre deshumanización y rehumanización: perspectivas orteguianas en *Locura y muerte* de Benjamín Jarnés', *BH*:175–213, analyses in detail the three versions of this representative novel to evaluate exactly how Jarnesian narrative jibes with Ortegan ideas. E. Serrano Asenjo, 'Los Osuna de Antonio Marichalar (1): el malogrado', *RHM*, 55, 2002:342–56, outlines well the shift from 'novelized' biography to history 'literaturizada' à la Lytton Strachey in *Riesgo y ventura del duque de Osuna* (1930). Alan Wallis, *Modernidad y epifanía literaria en Miró y Azorín*, Alicante U.P., 144 pp., uses Baudelaire to set the Spanish writers within the European tradition. Á. A. Ayo, 'De las tinieblas a las cumbres: el humorismo de Pérez de Ayala a través de su visión de Cervantes y Galdós', *BSS*, 80:695–713, finds numerous affinities in art and temperament.

INDIVIDUAL WRITERS

AUB. The recovery of texts written in exile continues. Manuel Aznar Soler provides the critical apparatus for **Nuevos diarios inéditos (1939–1972)*, Seville, Renacimiento, 561 pp., the complete run from exile until A.'s death; L. Llorens Marzo, 'Génesis del *Laberinto mágico*: los autógrafos de Max Aub entre 1938 y 1942', *BSS*, 80:450–75, sifts through A.'s notebooks to elucidate *Campo de sangre*; M. P. Sanz Álvarez, 'Los relatos olvidados de Max Aub', *CHA*, 636:91–106, describes A.'s painful experiences with publishing in Mexico and unearths five short *relatos* from *La Vanguardia* (1938), Las Españas (1947), *Cuadernos Americanas* (1967), *Revista de Bellas Artes* (1968), and *Urogallo* (1970), which illustrate A.'s penchant for ludic writing; while, from the unpublished cache of correspondence, J. Rodríguez Richart, 'Correspondencia inédita Casona-Aub (1948–1960)', *ALEC*,

28:347–84, reproduces ten letters from Casona and three from A. over the period 1948–60 (369–84) that form part of a larger correspondence and deal with Casona's success in Argentina and A.'s desperate attempts at, and final realization of, the *estreno* of *Deseada*. R. Bonilla Cerezo, 'Max Aub y *La vida conyugal*: triángulo amoroso, drama policial, anarquismo en sombras plateadas de cine', *ALEC*, 28:275–304, draws parallels with Lauro Olmo, Fernando Fernán Gómez, Alfred Hitchcock, hardboiled detective fiction, Baroja, and Sartre by way of Saint-Simon.

ORTEGA Y GASSET. The *Revista de Estudios Orteguianos*, 7, continues the good work and a hasty pick of general interest for readers of this section might include: from the archives, José Ramón Carriazo et al.,'José Ortega y Gasset. Notas de trabajo sobre *El hombre* gótico' (5–31), which reproduces the two files containing, respectively, 54 and four notes and jottings dating from 1947 to 1951, while C. Asenjo and J. Zamora Bonilla, 'Caminos de ida y vuelta: Ortega en la *Residencia de Estudiantes*' (33–91), relive the golden era for 'Oxford y Cambridge en los Altos del Hipódromo' between 1923 and 1936, with details and illustrations of lectures and visits by H. G. Wells, G. K. Chesterton, John M. Keynes, Einstein, Valéry, Marinetti, and Count Keyserling, together with letters about projects and publications by Ortega himself; A. López Cobo, 'La narrativa del arte nuevo: Ortega y los límites de una influencia' (173–94), documenting O.'s philosophical strategy concerning the formation of a group of vanguard writers around the *Revista de Occidente* to produce 'la nueva novela' for the edification of the cultured minority; in comparatist vein, M. Campoamar, 'Nuevas y viejas generaciones argentinas. Entre el positivismo de José Ingenieros, el vitalismo de Ortega y Gasset y la renovación novecentista de Eugenio d'Ors' (195–246); a round-up of recently published doctoral theses (285–90), and the useful up-date for 2001–2002, 'Bibliografía orteguiana, 2002' (291–302), containing items not reviewed here.

SENDER. Texts become available: **Monte Ondina el pequeño teatro del mundo*, ed. Jean-Pierre Ressot, Seville, Renacimiento, 565 pp.; and Israel Rolón Barada selects and edits the exchange between the 'criaturas del desconcierto', *Carmen Laforet y Ramón J. Sender. Puedo contar contigo. Correspondencia*, B, Destino, 275 pp., that began with S.'s undisguised admiration for *Nada* (1947) and, despite Laforet's silences and rather diffident responses, S. continued with gusto through the late 1960s until his death in 1982. Francis Lough, *La revolución imposible. Política y filosofía en las primeras novelas de Ramón J. Sender (1930–1936)*, Huesca, Instituto de Estudios Altoaragoneses, 2001, 337 pp., is the revised Spanish version of the earlier English publication (*Politics and Philosophy in the Early Novels of Ramon J. Sender,*

1930–1936: The Impossible Revolution, Lewiston, NY, Mellen, 1996, 218 pp.), a serious commentary on S.'s efforts to develop the social novel of political commitment in the period immediately preceding the Civil War. The recent centenary celebrations have resulted in the mammoth *Sender y su tiempo. Crónica de un siglo. Actas del II Congreso sobre Ramón J. Sender (Huesca, 27–31 de marzo de 2001)*, ed. José Domingo Dueñas Llorente, Huesca, Instituto de Estudios Altoaragoneses, 2001, 622 pp., a grab-bag for all tastes; while *Sender 2001. Actas del congreso centenario celebrado en Sheffield*, ed. Anthony Trippett, Bristol U.P., 2002, xiv + 187 pp., is a rather uneven homage although with useful essays by Francis Lough, Shelley Godsland, and Jesus Vived Malral.

UNAMUNO. *Amor y pedagogía. Epistolario Miguel de Unamuno/Santiago Valentí Camp*, ed. Bénédicte Vauthier, M, Biblioteca Nueva, 2002, 535 pp., is a suggestive combination of novel and correspondence. Alison Sinclair, *Uncovering the Mind. Unamuno, the Unknown and the Vicissitudes of Self*, MUP, 2001, 248 pp., examines U.'s encounter with contemporary society and culture, applying D. W. Winnicott's object relations theory and Lacanian analysis in some original and controversial readings. Paul R. Olson, *The Great Chiasmus: Word and Flesh in the Novels of Unamuno*, West Lafayette, IN, Purdue U.P., vii + 264 pp., shows how U. uses grammar to reflect apparent contraries as freely reversible and thus identical in his exploration of the trope, suggesting that the reversal in the order of words or parts of speech in parallel phrases are to be found in both brief microstructures and the narrative structures of entire novels, and even encompasses whole stages in U.'s novelistic work.

VALLE-INCLÁN. Forming part of the revisionism exercised by biographers of Spain's Silver Age in resisting the legends and anecdotes that have hitherto constituted the myth of the public man, Manuel Alberca, *Valle-Inclán. La fiebre del estilo*, M, Espasa, 2002, 290 pp., aligns V.-I. unequivocably with 'el proyecto tradicionalista' while much of the 'autoficción' that has been endlessly repeated is exploded. Dru Dougherty, **Palimpsestos al cubo. Prácticas discursivas de Valle-Inclán*, M, Fundamentos, 266 pp., puts Genette, Barthes, and Derrida to work on intertextuality in this 'literatura mala bien hecha' as described by Corpus Barga. N. del Corno, 'Ramón del Valle-Inclán. Uno scrittore carlista', *Belfagor*, 58:281–94, takes a traditional view. J. Andújar Almansa, 'Del mundo galante al esperpento: dos farsas dieciochescas de Valle-Inclán', *BSS*, 80:203–18, highlights diverse literary codes in *La marquesa Rosalinda* (1912) and *Farsa italiana de la enamorada del rey* (1920) which together make up the recipe for the modern *esperpento*; while W. Johnson, 'Gaming and value structure in Valle-Inclán: a note on the *Sonata de estío*', *ib.*, 421–25, uses Huizinga's classic formulation to explain the transgression in the shark scene that leads to Bradomín's fixation with his 'amores desgraciados' and the Niña Chole's exorbitant erotic value. The third *Anuario Valle-Inclán* appears in *ALEC*, 28.3, and contains both original studies, unedited documentation, and a bibliographical up-date: in comparatist vein, D. Villanueva, '1902: Valle, Gide, Yeats' (7–32), deals with *Femeninas* and the *Sonata de estío*; L. Castro Delgado, 'Los personajes masculinos en el relato galante de Valle-Inclán' (33–52); S. Díaz Lage, 'Tiempo e historia en *La media noche*' (53–70); M. Filipczak-Grynbert, 'La arquitectura de la farsa valleinclaniana' (71–97), traces the essentially literary nature of the construction of the four farces subsumed in the *Tablado de marionetas para la educación de príncipes* and *La marquesa Rosalinda;* J. Núñez Sabarís, 'Las anotaciones autógrafas de *Femeninas*' (99–122), looks at the exception in V.-I.'s *obra*; J. Rubio Jiménez, 'La lógica de la superstición en *El embrujado* de Valle-Inclán' (123–54), a consideration of the typographical design and illustrations that accompany the text; C. Villarmea Álvarez, 'Una lectura irónica de *La pipa de Kif*' (155–81), highlights V.-I.'s instinct for parody; S. Domínguez Barreiro, 'Josefina Blanco, una mujer olvidada' (183–204), traces the subsidiary role played by actress and wife as reported in two forgotten interviews with Carmen de Burgos (1917) and Margarita Nelken in *El Día* (23 April 1917); J. A. Hormigón, 'Una cuestión personal y un duelo frustrado' (205–20), treats the 'lance moderaderamente rocambolesco' between V.-I. and Antonio Guzmán Pérez in 1906; R. Mascato Rey, 'Ramón del Valle-Inclán en el homenaje a Julio Antonio (1919): nuevas aportaciones de la prensa compostelana' (221–42), with details of V.-I.'s participation in the tribute to the sculptor as recounted in *El Eco de Santiago* of 22 March 1919; C. Míguez Vilas, '*Luces de bohemia* en Santiago de Compostela por la compañía *Ur Teatro*, dirigida por Helena Pimenta' (243–50), in praise of the original scene set by José Tomé and Susana de Uña in the December 2002 production; J. Serrano Alonso, 'Del epistolario de Valle-Inclán: otra carta a Manuel Azaña (1922)' (251–56), explicates the chronology of the publication of *Cara de plata* in *La Pluma* by reproducing a brief note dated 10 July 1922; J. Servera Baño, '"Flor de la tarde," de Valle-Inclán: propuesta de fijación textual' (257–70), considers all variants; while J. Serrano Alonso and A. de Juan Bolufer, 'Bibliografía de Ramón del Valle-Inclán' (257–70), concentrate particularly on primary material (collections, *sueltos*, translations, articles, and interviews as these appear) in order to update the general bibliography published in 1995 (see *YWMLS*, 57:355).

4. Theatre

Critical work on the drama of the period is also noted above under ALBERTI, AUB, CERNUDA, GARCÍA LORCA, SALINAS, and VALLE-INCLÁN. David George, *Theatre in Madrid and Barcelona, 1892–1936. Rivals or Collaborators*, Cardiff, Univ. of Wales, 2002, 235 pp., documents well the fluid relations between Spain's major centres, nosing out contacts, collaborations, and rivalries in both commercial and artistic productions, and is particularly good on the leading role of the Catalans in developing modern acting, stage design, and innovative direction in Madrid theatres; five major topics are covered, namely, the exploration of joint ventures, the migration to Madrid of Enrique Borràs and Margarita Xirgu and the consequences thereof, the reception of foreign plays in both cities, and similarities and differences in the reception of drama written and/or performed in Catalan and Spanish, all of which leads to the conclusion that indicates Madrid as the theatrical Mecca with greater financial opportunities, although audiences in both cities shared middle-class taste and values despite differences in language. E. Fernández, 'Modernización y muerte del género chico en la 2ª república', *Hispanófila*, 139:69–81, explicates clearly how practitioners tried to adapt the genre by incorporating references to new trades and professions, the *ateneo feminista* specializing in 'teorias onílicas', street violence, Freud, and pasteurized milk, but notes how this once popular theatre form finally succumbed not, in the end, to the competition in entertainment offered by the *variétés*, the cinema, and football, but because of the gradual separation of private and public space that began in the Second Republic and continued under Franco, which made the scene-sets so typical of the genre in the *corralas*, squares, and meadows of old Madrid a thing of the past. Some welcome scholarship in time to celebrate the centenary makes available lost or unedited work. María Teresa León, *Obras dramáticas. Escritos sobre el teatro*, ed. Gregorio Torres Nebrera, M, ADEE, 467 pp., contains an intelligent introductory study, three scrupulously edited texts in *Huelga en el puerto*, an emblematic example of agitprop based on a real event in Seville and first published in *Octubre*, *La libertad en el tejado*, a lay *auto sacramental* from the 1940s reminiscient of husband Alberti's *El hombre deshabitado*, and *Misericordia*, the adaptation of the Galdosian novel hitherto unedited, and, best of all, a wide selection of León's prose pieces, radio broadcasts, and reviews, some published under her pseudonym, Isabel Inghirami, in the *Diario de Burgos*, others from *Octubre*, *Heraldo de Madrid*, *El Mono Azul*, *Nueva Vida*, and *Defensa Nacional*, and, later, in the Mexican publication of 1935, *Todo*, and the Argentine *Latitud* of 1945; to be read together with *Teatro. La libertad en el tejado. Sueño y verdad de Francisco de Goya. Poesía y Teatro*, ed. Manuel Aznar Soler, Seville, Renacimiento, 405 pp., which augments the published drama.

LITERATURE, 1936 TO THE PRESENT DAY

POSTPONED

V. CATALAN STUDIES

LANGUAGE

POSTPONED

MEDIEVAL LITERATURE

By Lola Badia, *Professor of Catalan Literature at the Universitat de Barcelona* and Miriam Cabré, *Researcher at the Universitat de Girona*

1. General

research tools and historical background. *BBAHLM*, 16: 3–44, is an annotated list of publications for the year 2002. *Quern*, 5, covers publications in 2001–02; previous issues are available at <biblioteca.udg.es/qüern>. Carme Oriol and Josep M. Pujol, *Índex tipològic de la rondalla catalana*, B, Generalitat de Catalunya, 405 pp., classifies Catalan folklore, following the Aarne-Thompson system. M. Zimmermann, 'La représentation de la noblesse dans la vision primitive des *Usatges* de Barcelona (milieu du XIIe s.)', *CLCHM*, 25, 2002: 13–37, distinguishes nobility from *militia*. Albert Soler, *Literatura catalana medieval: un recorregut multimèdia pels grans autors i els seus textos*, B, Pòrtic–UOC, 236 pp., adds commentaries to the materials available at <www.editorialuoc.com/literaturacatalanamedieval/>. Joan Armangué Herrero, *Estudi sobre la cultura catalana a Sardenya*, B, IEC, 2001, 286 pp., collects 23 articles.

archival research and readership. Two new volumes of *Repertori de manuscrits (1474–1620)*, ed. Eulàlia Duran, B, Institut Joan Lluís Vives–IEC, have considerably expanded the libraries covered: vol ii, ed. Eulàlia Miralles and Maria Toldrà, 2001, 376 pp.; vol iii, ed. Maria Toldrà, Eulàlia Miralles, and Antoni Lluís Moll, 559 pp. *Diplomatari Borja 1*, ed. Miquel Batllori, V, 3 i 4, 2002, 624 pp., includes documents from as early as 1299. José Alcina Franch, *La Biblioteca de Alfonso v de Aragón en Nápoles: fondos valencianos*, 2 vols, V, Biblioteca Valenciana–Generalitat Valenciana, 248 + 558 pp., includes a historical study and the description of 216 volumes. J. A. Iglesias, 'Els llibres dels juristes: un record d'època universitària i una necessitat professional', Claramunt, *Món*, ii, 729–44, finds few literary works in lawyers' libraries. J. Guia, 'Dades documentals d'interès literari (València, s. xv)', *AISC* 7, 1, 201–22, offers archival data about several 15th-c. writers. *Le Statut du scripteur au Moyen Age: Actes du XII colloque scientifique du Comité international de paléographie latine*, ed. Marie Clotilde Hubert, Emmanuel Poule, and Marc H. Smith, Paris, École des Chartes, 2000, 388 pp., has articles by A. M. Mundó (21–28), J. Alturo (41–55), and J. A. Iglesias (229–66), covering the whole medieval period in Catalonia.

2. Lyric and Narrative Verse

lyrical poetry and ms transmission. M. Gómez Muntané, 'El canto de la Sibila: mil años de tradición', *Elx 6,* 159–74, studies evolution and reception within the context of eschatological literature. V. Beltran, 'Las formas con estribillo en la lírica oral del Medioevo', *Anuario Musical,* 57, 2002 : 39–57, includes examples from Cerverí de Girona's works. Isabel de Riquer and Maricarmen Gómez Muntané, *Las canciones de Sant Joan de les Abadesses: estudio y edición filológica y musical,* B, RABL, 94 pp., edit four *dansas* and their melodies. G. Avenoza, 'La *dansa*: introducción a la tipología de un género románico', *Baena 2,* ii, 89–105, offers the first results of a wider study on the *dansa* genre. C. Di Girolamo, 'La versification catalane médiévale entre conservation et innovation de ses modèles occitans', *RLaR,* 107 : 41–74, highlights the impact of using troubadour quotations in the Catalan metrical tradition. C. Licoccia, 'Innovazione e riuso delle fonti liriche nella poesia catalana medievale', *AISC 7,* i, 223–36, analyses the influence of Arnaut Daniel and Petrarch in Andreu Febrer. V. Orazi, '*Presoner* di Jordi de Sant Jordi: tra eredità medievale e fioritura umanistica nell'orizzonte mediterraneo della politica alfonsina', D'Agostino, *Corona,* ii, 1533–51, describes the historical, political, and literary context. J. Coll, '*I soliti ignoti*: errors de còpia (i presumptes errors) en uns versos de Jordi de Sant Jordi', *AISC 7,* ii, 187–228, uses textual theory to discuss one line of the *Estramps.* J. Clara i Resplandis, 'Aproximació a Bernat Estruç, poeta català del segle xv', *ATCA,* 22 : 621–31, provides archival data on the poet and his family. G. Avenoza, 'Una *dansa* de Mossén Jordi de Sant Jordi en el *Cancionero general* (1511)', Casas, *Iberia cantat,* 489–524, proposes Jordi Centelles as the author. L. Badia, 'De l'amor que educa a la passió culpable: Jordi de Sant Jordi, xi, versus Ausiàs March, iv', *Molas Vol.,* i, 85–97, compares the psychologic debates in both poems. R. Archer, 'Entre la preceptiva y la práctica: el concepto de la poesía según Ausiàs March', *MHRS 11,* 7–22, discusses M.'s lyrical style. C. Di Girolamo, 'Canti di penitenza da Stronski a Ausiàs March', *CN,* 62, 2002 : 191–209, explores probable Occitan sources for M.'s poem 105. J. L. Martos, 'Cuadernos y génesis del Cancionero O[1] de Ausiàs March (BUV, ms. 210)', *Baena 2,* ii, 129–42, offers a new hypothesis about the *stemma codicum* of M.'s corpus and the genesis of MS *O*[1]. X. Sánchez Parent, 'La trasmissione della lirica numero 86 attribuita ad Ausiàs March', *AISC* 7, II, 465–74, determines that the poem was not copied by Vilasaló. M. M. López Casas, '¿Quevedo, traductor de Ausiàs March?', Casas, *Iberia cantat*, 555–88, discusses the attribution of a marginal translation. J. Mahiques i Climent, 'D'Ausiàs March a Baltasar de Romaní: les al·lusions morals i teològiques en la *Cántica de amor* impresa en 1539', *Baena* 2, II, 107–28, finds that Romaní innovates mainly in religious passages. V. Beltran, 'Copisti e canzonieri: i canzonieri di corte', *CN*, 63: 115–62, draws a picture of *chansonniers* in the 15th-c. Trastamara courts. S. Martí, 'Escolios sobre impaginación y variantes redaccionales en Montserrat 992', *MHRS 11*, 67–76, contains a codicological description and the diplomatic edition of pieces with author emendations; and J. L. Martos, 'Los espacios en blanco y la estructura del Cançoner del Marquès de Barberà', *ib.*, 57–65, describes the MS as one of the first examples of a new type of miscellaneous codex. *Cançoner de París (París, Biblioteca Nacional, ms. esp. 225)*, ed. Joan Torruella, Bellaterra, La Caixa–Seminari de Filologia i Informàtica, 22 microfiches, is a new issue of *Els cançoners catalans: concordances.*

JAUME ROIG AND NARRATIVE POETRY. *Tres contes meravellosos del segle* XIV, ed. Lola Badia, B, Quaderns Crema, 182 pp., accompanies the Catalan translation of Torroella's *Faula*, *Fraire de joi*, and *Salut d'amor* with an introduction to the genre. A. I. Peirats, 'Analogies entre el *Livre des lamentations* de Matheolus i l'*Spill* de Jaume Roig', *AILLC 12*, 47–68, finds similarities in the treatment of autobiography, bigamy, etc; the same author's 'Jaume Roig: la comicitat de la moral o la moral de la comicitat?', *ER*, 25, 251–77, proposes a double reading of R.'s work. J. L. Martos, 'La presència de Boccaccio en les proses mitològiques de Joan Roís de Corella', *AISC* 7, I, 263–94, analyses the use of the *Genealogiae deorum*. J. Albertí Oriol, '*La vida de santa Magdalena en cobles*, de mossèn Jaume Gassull: anàlisi comparativa de l'obra', *RCat*, 170, 2002: 99–111, is a literary analysis. Two editions of utilitarian poems: O. Grapí Rovira, 'Un calendari català medieval: estudi i edició', *ATCA*, 22: 137–73; and J. Llobet i Portella, 'Poesia popular medieval: cinc oracions o conjurs extrets de manuals notarials cerverins del segle XV', *ELLC*, 45, 2002: 211–15.

3. Doctrinal and Religious Prose

RAMON LLULL AND LULLISM. New critical editions of L.'s works: *Raimundi Lulli Opera Latina 49–52: Liber de sancta Maria in Monte Pessulano anno* MCCXC *conscriptus, cui Liber de passagio Romae anno* MCCXCII *compositus necnon brevis notitia operum aliorum incerto tempore ac loco perfectorum adnectuntur*, ed. Blanca Garí and Fernando Domínguez Reboiras (Raimundi Lulli Opera Latina, 28; CCCM, 182), Turnhout,

Brepols, xxiv + 365 pp.; *Tabula generalis, in mari in portu Tunicii in medio septembris anno* MCCXCIII *incepta, et in civitate Neapolis in octavis Epiphaniae anno* MCCXCIV *ad finem perducta*, ed. Viola Tenge-Wolf (Raimundi Lulli Opera Latina, 53; CCCM, 181), Turnhout, Brepols, 2002, 204 + 262 pp.; and Ramon Llull, *Començaments de filosofia*, ed. Fernando Domínguez Reboiras and M. Eugènia Gisbert, Palma, Patronat Ramon Llull, xli + 194 pp. M. Vilà Bayerri, 'Per ço car es obra d'amor: Lluís Nicolau d'Olwer i alguns aspectes del lul·lisme de les primeres dècades del segle xx', *Randa*, 48, 2002 : 85–92, comments on L.'s works aesthetically and deals with the history of *ORL*. A. Bonner and L. Badia, 'Ramón Llull', pp. 511–14 of *Medieval Iberia: An Encyclopedia*, ed. E. Michael Gerli, NY–London, Routledge, 942 pp., offers a survey of L.'s life, thought, and works. Anthony Bonner and M. Isabel Ripoll, *Diccionari de definicions lul·lianes / Dictionary of Lullian Definitions*, Barcelona U.P. — Palma, Univ. de les Illes Balears, 2002, 293 pp., collects definitions contained in L.'s works and accounts for his methodology. A. Bonner, 'Notes per a la cronologia del cicle de l'*Art demostrativa*', *SLu*, 42, 2002 : 57–61, proposes a new chronology and accepts Perarnau's suggestion that *Quaestio de congruo* is not Lullian. Id., 'A background to the *Desconhort*, *Tree of Science*, and *Apostrophe*', *Hillgarth Vol.*, 122–33, studies L.'s confessions in the aftermath of his 1295 crisis and the creation of second-stage *Arts*. J. E. Rubio, 'L'evolució de les figures A, S, T de l'Art quaternària en el trànsit cap a l'Art ternària', *Taula*, 37, 2002 : 83–98, highlights the elements that anticipate the *Art ternària*. J. A. Grimalt, 'Notes sobre les fonts del *Llibre de les bèsties* de Ramon Llull', *Randa*, 48, 2002 : 37–46, analyses folk motifs in L.'s *Llibre de les bèsties*. D. Brancaleone, 'Il *Libro delle Bestie* di Raimondo Lullo nella versione trecentesca veneta', *Per leggere i generi della letteratura*, 2.2, 2002 : 17–62. H. Hames, 'Text, context, and interpenetration: Ramon Lull and the *Book of the Righteous*', *Hillgarth Vol.*, 134–57, points to possible borrowings from L. in *Sefer ha-Yashar*, a moral guide. C. Lohr, 'Chaos theory according to Ramon Llull', *ib.*, 158–65, discusses L.'s cosmological, ontological, and logical notions of chaos. Three publications on L.'s conversion strategies: V. Galent-Fasseur, 'Une solitude active: l'ermite et ses émules dans les romans de Raymond Lulle', *SLu*, 42, 2002 : 27–48; D. Abulafia, 'The apostolic imperative: religious conversion in Lull's *Blaquerna*', *Hillgarth Vol.*, 105–21; and Ramon Llull, *Darrer llibre sobre la conquesta de Terra Santa*, ed. Jordi Gayà, trans. Pere Llabrés, B, Proa, 2002, 228 pp., with a Catalan translation of some of his relevant texts. J. M. Ruiz Simon, '*En l'arbre són les fuyles per ço que y sia lo fruyt*: apunts sobre el rerafons textual i doctrinal de la distinció lul·liana entre la intenció primera i la intenció segona en els actes *propter finem*', *SLu*, 42, 2002 : 3–25, discusses the influence of Aristotle's *Physics*, II. T. Solà Simon, '*Nisi crediderítis non intelligetis*: lectura d'Is VII, 9 per Ramon Llull', *ATCA*, 22:579–95, studies the context of the biblical *locus* and its use by Church Fathers. P. Rigobon, 'Considerazioni sulla *Consolatio venetorum et totius gentis desolate* di Ramon Llull', *AISC* 7, II, 419–34, analyses structure, historical context, and transmission. J. Santanach, 'El Còdex miscel·lani de l'Arxiu de les Set Claus (Andorra la Vella, Arxiu Històric Nacional)', *AEM*, 33:417–62, gives a thorough codicological description; and Id., 'Un notari andorrà de final del segle XV, lector de Ramon Llull', *SLu*, 42, 2002:49–56, focuses on marginal notes.

ARNAU DE VILANOVA AND OTHER SCIENTIFIC TEXTS. Two bibliographic surveys: J. Mensa i Valls and S. Giralt i Soler, 'Bibliografia arnaldiana (1994–2003)', *ATCA*, 22:665–734; and A. Soler, 'Selecció d'edicions i d'estudis arnaldians recents', *LlLi*, 14:441–44. New editions: *Arnaldi de Villanova Tractatus Octo in Graecorum Sermonem Versi*, ed. Joan Nadal Cañellas, B, IEC, 2002, 446 pp.; and Arnau de Vilanova, *La prudència de l'escolar catòlic i altres escrits*, ed. Jaume Mensa i Valls, B, Proa, 2002, 208 pp., with an accessible introduction. M. R. McVaugh, 'Moments of inflection: the careers of Arnau de Vilanova', Biller, *Religion*, 47–67, surveys A.'s double career, as a doctor and as a mystic. Sebastià Giralt i Soler, *Arnau de Vilanova en la impremta renaixentista (segle XVI)*, B, Arxiu Històric de les Ciències de la Salut-Col·legi Oficial de Metges de Barcelona, 2002, 218 pp., is concerned, among other aspects, with the role of the Inquisition and the work of editors. *La 'Cirurgia Parva' de Lanfranc (segle XIV)*, ed. Pere Vallribera, B, Arxiu Històric de les Ciències de la Salut-Col·legi Oficial de Metges de Barcelona, 2002, 116 pp., edits the medieval Catalan translation. L. Cifuentes, 'La volgarizzazione della scienza alla fine del medioevo: un modello interpretativo a partire dal caso del catalano', Bray, *Filosofia*, 247–63, offers a wide survey of science vernacularization in the Crown of Aragon. S. Corradini Bozzi, 'Il ms. 215 della Biblioteca Classense di Ravenna: tradizione latina e testi volgari di materia medica', *SMV*, 48, 2002:1–15, describes this multilingual MS, which contains some texts by Arnau. L. Soriano, G. Sabaté, and A. M. Beltran, 'Textos mèdics inèdits medievals en català (s. XIV–XV)', *RPh*, 56:319–53, transcribe some recipe books. José Manuel Fradejas Rueda, *Bibliotheca cinegética hispánica: Suplemento 1. Bibliografía crítica de los libros de cetrería y montería hispano-portugueses*, London, Tamesis, 108 pp., includes more than 300 items.

FRANCESC EIXIMENIS AND OTHER MORAL TEXTS. Francesc Eiximenis, *Àngels e demonis*, ed. Sadurní Martí, B, Quaderns Crema, 247 pp., edits and provides a commentary on the fourth treatise of E.'s *Llibre dels Àngels*. X. Renedo, 'La vida conjugal segons Francesc Eiximenis', *MSR*, 2:7–20, focuses on consent, domestic life, and sexual morals. Three publications on aspects of E.'s political and social thought: D. J. Viera and J. Piqué-Angordans, 'Francesc Eiximenis (c. 1330–1409) i la Guerra dels Cent Anys', *ELLC*, 46, 111–21; Iid., 'Francesc Eiximenis i els reis medievals de França', *AILLC 12*, 23–30; and C. Wittlin, 'Francesc Eiximenis and the state secret of King Peter's ordinance for court officials', *CatR*, 16, 2002: 229–42. D. J. Viera, 'Francesc Eiximenis' brief compendium on medieval miracles: el *Primer del Crestià*, ch. 56–59', *ib.*, 221–28, discusses E.'s use of miracle stories. S. Gascón Uris, 'La *Crónica de Aragón* (València 1524) i les cartes autògrafes d'Eiximenis', *AILLC 12*, 31–45, relates the letters (edited here) to Lucio Marineo Siculo's chronicle. Two articles on the transmission of *Llibre de les dones*: J. Alturo, 'Noves dades sobre la difusió de *Lo libre de les dones* de Francesc Eiximenis', *Quaderns de La Selva*, 13, 2001: 255–64; and J. Perarnau, 'Un nou bifoli del *Llibre de les dones* de Francesc Eiximenis (ACA, Canc., Pergamins. Fragments, n. 420)', *ATCA*, 22, 269–308. R. Alemany Ferrer, 'Tradició i innovació en la *Disputa de l'ase* de Turmeda/Abdal·là', *Molas Vol.*, 1, 15–26, reviews narrative and parodic devices. Two editions of Vicent Ferrer's sermons: *Sermones: transcripción del manuscrito del Real Colegio y Seminario del Corpus Christi de Valencia*, ed. Francisco M. Gimeno Blay, M. Luz Mandigorra, and Francisco Calero, V, Valencia U.P.–Ajuntament–Estudi General, 2002, 826 pp.; and J. Perarnau, 'La (darrera?) quaresma transmesa de sant Vicent Ferrer: Clermont-Ferrand, BMI, ms. 45', *ATCA*, 22: 344–550. T. Martínez Romero, 'Expressions, gestos i textos: teatralitat en els sermons de Vicent Ferrer?', *Elx 6*, 211–29, discusses Ferrer's performance. G. Sabaté and L. Soriano, 'Literatura pietosa i edificant a la Corona d'Aragó: aportació de textos inèdits i nous manuscrits per al seu estudi (s. XIV i XV) (1)', *BBAHLM*, 16, 2002: 305–39, bring forgotten vernacular texts to life again. J. E. Ruiz-Doménec, 'El mapa de la devoción urbana en la Corona de Aragón (s. XIII, XIV y XV)', Claramunt, *Món*, 1, 35–57, uses data found in Llull, *Jaufré*, and Isabel de Villena. *Flors de virtut: facsímil de l'incunable de 1489 (Enric Botel, Lleida)*, ed. Julián Acebrón Ruiz, Lleida, Institut d'Estudis Ilerdencs, 2001, 51 pp., reproduces the only extant copy.

4. Historical and Artistic Prose, the Novel

V. Orazi, 'La *narratio brevis* in Catalogna', *QFRB*, 15, 2002: 301–29, surveys and classifies the corpus and highlights Llull's originality.

HISTORIOGRAPHY. *Diccionari d'historiografia catalana*, ed. Antoni Simon, B, Enciclopèdia Catalana, 1222 pp., provides an updated bibliography. J. M. Pujol, 'Jaume I, rex facetus: notes de filologia humorística', *ER*, 25:215–36, analyses humour and linguistic diversity. V. Orazi, 'Precisazioni ecdotiche sulla Crònica di Ramon Muntaner', *AISC 7*, II, 395–419, discusses the nine manuscripts. P. Quer, 'Una narració coetània llatina de la conquesta de Nàpols en una crònica de Jaume Marquilles', *ib.*, I, 467–84, gives details on Marquilles and transcribes the text.

BERNAT METGE. L. Badia, 'Bernat Metge medievale', *AISC 7*, II, 99–112, sets the adaptation of *Corbaccio* in *Lo somni* at the origin of 15th-c. prose. Three publications by J. Butinyà on M.'s sources and context: *Del 'Griselda' català al castellà*, B, RABLB, 2002, 100 pp.; 'La font més amagada i més externa de *Lo somni*: un altre somni', *ER*, 25:237–49; and 'Una nova font de *Lo somni* de Bernat Metge: Horaci', *Molas Vol.*, I, 215–33. F. Alexandri, 'Ramon de Perellós i la llegenda del Purgatori de Sant Patrici', *Auriga*, 29, 2001:14–19, helps contextualize Perellós's journey.

TIRANT LO BLANC and *CURIAL E GÜELFA*. Articles on specific aspects of *T.* and *Curial*: J. Anyó i Oliver, 'Entorn de *Tirant lo Blanc* a Constantinoble', *ELLC*, 47:65–83; R. Cantavella, 'Debate on women in *Tirant lo Blanch*', *Hassauer Vol.*, 45–57; A. Hauf, 'Segons que diu lo gloriós sant Luch: l'art d'interpretar els textos à la carte', *Molas Vol.*, I, 555–71, analyses the context for Martorell's statement that *militia* is fundamental to social cohesion; J. A. Aguilar Àvila, '*Posant les virtuts devant los vicis*: Joan de Gal·les, font del Tirant lo Blanch', *LlLi*, 14:241–82, compares John of Wales with *T.*, Corella and Antoni Canals, and G. Sabaté, 'Alegorías amorosas en la literatura catalana del siglo XV: el *Jardinet d'Orats* (BUB, ms. 151) y el *Curial e Güelfa*', *Baena 2*, II, 144–55. Several articles include *T.* and *Curial* in a wider survey: A. M. Espadaler, 'Política i ideologia en la novel·la catalana del segle XV', D'Agostino, *Corona*, II, 1419–30; R. Beltrán, 'Sobre el simbolismo profético de visiones y representaciones en libros de caballerías: de *Curial e Güelfa* y *Tirant lo Blanc* a la *Corónica* de Adramón', *Edad de Oro*, 21, 2002:481–98, compares the Catalan novels with the Castilian tradition, especially *Amadís de Gaula.* T. Martínez Romero, 'De *Lo somni de Joan Joan* a la *Vesita* d'Herèdia amb consideracions sobre Corella i el *Tirant*', *AISC 7*, II, 351–74, discusses and comparates prose style. V. Minervini, 'J. Martorell fra R. Llull e L. Manfredi: incontri, interferenze, traduzioni', *La lingua del mercoledì*, 5:51–60, compares *T.* with the *Llibre de l'orde de cavalleria* and Juan Manuel's *Libro del cavallero et del escudero.* E. Sales Dasí, 'Ver y mirar en los libros de caballerías', *Thesaurus*, 54, 1999[2002]:1–32. C. Alvar, 'Raíces medievales de los libros de caballerías', *Edad de Oro*, 21, 2002:61–84, re-examines the diffusion of Iberian texts linked to the Arthurian tradition. A. Varvaro, '*Tirant lo Blanch* nella narrativa europea del sec. xv', *AISC* 7, II, 487–500, highlights the similarities between *T.* and 14th-c. French romances.

5. Translations and other Genres and Texts

V. Minervini, 'Comunicare in letteratura fra XIV e XV secolo', *AISC* 7, I, 327–38, surveys the notion of 'translator' in medieval Catalan works. V. Martines, 'Traducció i contacte de llengües: bescanvis culturals i literaris d'àmbit romànic', pp. 447–98 of *Les claus del canvi lingüístic*, ed. Antònia Cano, Alacant, IIFV–Ajuntament de La Núcia–Caja de Ahorros del Mediterráneo, 2002, 500 pp., is a general survey. F. Montuori and F. Senatore, 'Lettere autografe di Ferrante d'Aragona', *AISC* 7, I, 367–88, edits and studies Ferrante's letters. J.-A. Ysern Lagarda, 'Sobre el fragment del *Valter e Griselda* contingut en el ms. 89 pertanyent a la Biblioteca de la Universitat de Barcelona', *RFR*, 17, 2000: 341–65, compares the translation in *Recull d'eximplis ordenat per alfabet* with that of Metge. J. M. Perujo, 'Jaume Conesa: afanys i paranys d'un traductor', *AISC* 7, I, 389–405, discusses how Conesa adapts Latin for his readers. *Llibre de Sent Soví; Llibre de totes maneres de potatges de menjar; Llibre de totes maneres de confits*, ed. Rudolf Grewe, Amadeu-J. Soberanas, and Joan Santanach (ENC), 327 pp., revises the critical edition of three cooking books. G. Ensenyat Pujol, 'Els Olesa: una família lletraferida de la Ciutat de Mallorca (s. XIV–XVI)', Claramunt, *Món*, II, 585–89, identifies three different authors who share the same name. M. Früh, '*Funus et eulogium*: Antonio Geraldinis Ode zum Tode König Johanns II. von Aragón', Czapla, *Lyrik*, 11–33, studies, edits, and translates Geraldini's panegyric distichs. M. G. Sanna, 'La morte di Mariano IV di Arborea nella corrispondenza di Pietro IV d'Aragona', *AISC* 7, II, 475–86, assesses the king's relationship with the Arborea Judge.

6. Drama

L. Rubio García, 'Consideraciones sobre el teatro medieval en la Corona de Aragón', *Elx 6*, 349–70, lists and classifies sacred plays written in the medieval Crown of Aragon. L. Kovàcs, 'Aquesta gran novetat . . . Els jueus en el teatre assumpcionista medieval', *ib.*, 195–208, analyses the role of Jews as antagonists. N. Leal, 'El misteri de la Selva del Camp de Tarragona i el Misteri d'Elx: apunts sobre la pràctica teatral', *AISC* 7, II, 303–16, discusses structure and performance. P. Mas i Usó, 'La representació del Misteri de Castelló. Els manuscrits del Misteri: La Consueta', *Elx 6*, 233–50, analyses the two MS witnesses and redates one of them.

MODERN LITERATURE

POSTPONED

VI. PORTUGUESE STUDIES

POSTPONED

VII. GALICIAN STUDIES

POSTPONED

VIII. LATIN AMERICAN STUDIES

SPANISH AMERICAN LITERATURE
THE COLONIAL PERIOD

POSTPONED

THE NINETEENTH CENTURY

By Annella McDermott, *Department of Hispanic, Portuguese and Latin American Studies, University of Bristol*

1. General

A. Acereda, 'Dos visiones del espacio marino como modernidad. Entre la poesía de Rubén Darío y la pintura de Joaquín Sorolla', *RHM*, 55, 2000: 281–301, contrasts the significance of the sea and the beach in the work of the two artists. Id., 'El antimodernismo. Sátira e ideología de un debate transatlántico', *His(US)*, 86: 761–72, looks at anti-*modernista* satires in Spain and Latin America and attempts to clarify the ideological stances underlying them. It is concerned particularly with the magazines *Caras y caretas*, in Buenos Aires, and the Spanish *Blanco y negro*. *CHA*, 639, has several articles on Argentinian women writers of the 19th century. L. Gálvez, 'La segunda mitad del siglo' (7–12), is an introductory article, outlining the historical background. L. Sosa de Newton, 'Las periodistas' (13–21), investigates both papers published for women, and the women who wrote in them. L. Fletcher, 'Las poetas' (23–29), focuses on poems published in women's magazines of the time. Three articles are general surveys of the work of a single author: M. G. Mizraje, 'Juana Manuela Gorriti' (31–39); L. F. Lewkowicz, 'Juana Mansó' (41–46); and M. R. Lojo, 'Eduarda Mansilla' (47–59). A. Fornet, 'De cerca, de lejos: dos intelectuales cubanos ante el desafío de la modernidad', *CAm*, 231: 75–84, is about José Martí and José María Heredia. C. Leante, 'Francisco y Juan Francisco', *CHA*, 641: 49–62, treats two works completed in the same year, 1839: Anselmo Suárez y Romero's novel *Francisco*, and Juan Francisco Manzano's *Autobiografía*. Similarities, both psychological and ideological, are noted between the two protagonists, though one is fictional and the other is not. *Literatura mexicana del otro fin de siglo*, ed. Rafael Olea Franco, México, Colegio de México, 2001, 691 pp., is a series of studies centred mainly on works from the period 1867 to 1910. J. A. Pastén B., 'Avatares del proceso de la institucionalización de la literatura en

Chile en las revistas literarias del siglo XIX', *RevIb*, 59:667–88, examines certain key concepts that reveal the ideology of these magazines from the late 19th century. B. Ruiz, 'Incorporaciones y exclusions al proyecto de la nación: el negro y el indio en la narrativa decimonónica venezolana', *ib.*, 883–94, looks at Manuel Vicente Romero García's *Peonía*, José Ramón Yepes's *Anaida* and (briefly) his *Iguaraya*, and mentions Rosina Pérez's *Guaicaipuro*. G. San Román, 'Eduardo Acevedo Díaz, Alejandro Magariños Cervantes y los orígenes de la novela histórica en el Uruguay', *BSS*, 80:323–46, compares and contrasts the two writers in their use of their country's history in their novels.

2. Individual Authors

ECHEVERRÍA, ESTEBAN. F. Opere, '*La cautiva* de Echeverría: el trágico señuelo de la frontera', *BSS*, 80:545–54, sees in the poem an early manifestation of Argentina's negative and pessimistic view of the significance of its frontier.

GÓMEZ DE AVELLANEDA, GERTRUDIS. J. C. Paulk, 'A new look at the strains of allegory in Gertrudis Gómez de Avellaneda's *Sab*', *RHM*, 50, 2002:229–41, argues that reading the novel in a way that allows the literal and abstract layers of meaning to react against each other, reveals a message in favour of equality. A. R.Selimov, 'El romanticismo y la poética de la cultura modernista', *HR*, 71:107–25, looks upon G. de A. as a pre-*modernista*, in her rejection of positivism. The article focuses on *El artista barquero, Dolores,* and *La ondina del lago.*

GROUSSAC, PAUL. P. G. Bruno, 'Paul Groussac y *La Biblioteca* (1896–98)', *Hispamérica*, 94:87–94, describes the magazine and its contents and explains the position it enabled Groussac to occupy in the intellectual life of Buenos Aires at the time.

HOSTOS, EUGENIO MARÍA DE. M. Reyes Dávila, 'Eugenio María de Hostos. El centenario ardiente', *CHA*, 640:113–18, marks the centenary of H.'s death with this article, which pays particular attention to his *Diario.*

MARTÍ, JOSÉ. J. Gomáriz, 'José Martí en las entrañas de la modernidad', *CAm*, 231:85–94, traces M.'s responses to modernity during his periods of exile in Spain and New York, particularly as expressed in his *Versos sencillos*. M. Fernández Lander, 'Familia, clase social y modernidad en *Lucía Jérez* de José Martí', *His(US)*, 86:751–60, sees the novel as emblematic of the transition from a traditional to a modern society, particularly in its treatment of patriarchal authority. R. Sarracino, 'Martí, el equilibrio internacional y la unidad latinoamericana', *CAm*, 229, 2002:44–57, traces the evolution of these two key concepts over the course of M.'s writing.

I. Schulman, 'Migraciones, viajes y la creación de la nación cubana', *RevIb*, 59:927–34, examines the importance of exile in the formation of M.'s thought and language.

MILLA Y VIDAURRE, JOSÉ. F. Solares-Larrave, 'Del archivo y la historia: textos y escritura en *Los nazarenos* (1867), de José Milla y Vidaurre', *REH*, 38:145–65, concerns the use of documents, real and invented, in this historical novel.

PALMA, RICARDO. I. Tauzin Castellanos, 'Refranes y tradiciones en la obra de Ricardo Palma', *BH*, 105:119–31, analyses the role of sayings in P.'s *Tradiciones peruanas*.

SILVA, MEDARDO ÁNGEL. R. Vallejo, 'Medardo Ángel Silva y la crónica de una edad de artificios', *CAm*, 232:38–49, proposes a revisionist version of *modernismo* in Ecuador.

THE TWENTIETH CENTURY

By Victoria Carpenter, *Senior Lecturer in Spanish, University of Derby*, and Fiona J. Mackintosh, *Lecturer in Hispanic Studies, University of Edinburgh*

1. General

Jorge Eduardo Arellano, *Literatura centroamericana: diccionario de autores contemporáneos: fuentes para su estudio*, Managua, Fundación Vida, 580 pp., focuses on contemporary Central American writers, presenting an exhaustive list from mainstream authors to what is (perhaps patronizingly) referred to as 'narrativa joven'. Another encyclopaedic study is *El pasado siglo XX: una retrospectiva de la literatura latinoamericana. Homenaje a Hans-Otto Dill*, ed. Dieter Ingenschay, Gabriele Knauer, and Klaus Meyer-Minnemann, Berlin, Tranvia, 212 pp., a collection of critiques of modern Latin American literature. Alejo Carpentier et al., **Los pasos recobrados: ensayos de teoría y crítica literaria*, Caracas, Biblioteca Ayacucho, 390 pp. Diana Taylor, **The Archive and the Repertoire: Performing Cultural Memory in the Americas*, Durham, Duke U.P., 326 pp. Fernando Ainsa, **Reescribir el pasado: Historia y ficción en América Latina*, Mérida, Otro, El Mismo, 190 pp.

G. Walas, *'Nostalgia, identidad y exilio: caras de la globalización en la literatura del cono sur', pp. 201–10 of *Proceedings of the 23rd Louisiana Conference on Hispanic Languages and Literatures*, Baton Rouge, Louisiana State Univ., vi + 218 pp., covers Uruguayan, Argentinian, and Chilean literature. José Amícola, **La batalla de los géneros: La novela gótica versus la novela de educación*, Rosario, Beatriz Viterbo, 318 pp. Christopher B. Conway, **The Cult of Bolívar in Latin American Literature*, Gainesville, Florida U.P., xii + 192 pp. A special issue of *STW*, 7.1, ed. Claire Lindsay and Tim Youngs, is on 'Latin American travel writing'. Z. Palermo, 'Una historia con variaciones: el mismo rostro, ¿distintas máscaras?', *REH*, 37:108–26, discusses intellectual colonialism and proposes a second historicism. **Heterotropías: Narrativas de identidad y alteridad lationamericanas*, ed. Carlos A. Jáuregui and Juan Pablo Dabove, Pittsburgh, Instituto Internacional de Literatura Iberoamericana, 500 pp. Dieter Reichardt and Carlos García, **Las vanguardias literarias en Argentina, Uruguay y Paraguay: Bibliografía y antología crítica*, Frankfurt, Vervuert — M, Iberoamericana, xxi + 538 pp. T. Escaja, *'Hacia una nueva historia de la poesía hispánica: escritura tecnetoesquelética e hipertexto en poetas contemporáneas en la red', *Espéculo: Revista de Estudios Literarios*, 24:[no pp.].

2. Gendered Writing

Laura Barbas-Rhoden, *Writing Women in Central America: Gender and the Fictionalization of History*, Athens, Ohio U.P., ix + 201 pp., links the history and gender foci in a comparative critique of the works of Claribel Alegría, Rosario Aguilar, Gioconda Belli, and Tatiana Lobo. *Latin American Women's Narrative: Practices and Theoretical Perspectives*, ed. Sara Castro-Klaren, Princeton, Wiener, 404 pp., presents a collection of essays on the works of major women writers, analysing the novel, the short story, and 'testimonio' writing of the second half of the 20th century. Other studies of the works of contemporary Latin American women writers include *Disciplines on the Line: Feminist Research on Spanish, Latin American, and U.S. Latina Women*, ed. Anne J. Cruz, Rosilie Hernández-Pecoraro, and Joyce Tolliver, Newark, Juan de la Cuesta, xv + 361 pp.; and Sonia Mattalía, *Máscaras suele vestir: pasión y revuelta: escrituras de mujeres en América Latina*, M, Iberoamericana — Frankfurt, Vervuert, 328 pp. A considerable contribution to the body of critique of Latin American women's writings is *Daughters of the Diaspora. Afra-Hispanic Writers*, ed. Miriam DeCosta-Willis, Kingston, Randle, xiii + 300 pp., which concentrates on a rather neglected aspect of Latin American literature — the works of Afro-Hispanic women writers. *Tortilleras: Hispanic and U.S. Latina Lesbian Expression*, ed. Lourdes Torres and Inmaculada Pertusa, Philadelphia, Temple U.P., 279 pp., presents an unconventional collection of close readings of lesbian writings from Spain, Latin America, and Chicana North America. This volume aims to fill the gap in literary gender studies, offering close readings of works spanning three continents, and challenging the existing notion that Hispanic lesbian expression can be termed a homogenous cultural entity. Among the writings analysed in the essays are the works of Magalí García Ramis, Cristina Peri Rossi, Ana María Moix, Emma Pérez, and Cherríe Moraga.

**The Canon Unplugged: Rethinking the Writer, the Reader and the Critic in Hispanic Women's Literature*, ed Immaculada Pertusa and Melissa Stewart, Greeley, Northern Colorado U.P., vi + 229 pp. Claire Lindsay, **Locating Latin American Women Writers: Cristina Peri Rossi, Rosario Ferré, Albalucía Angel and Isabel Allende*, NY, Lang, 162 pp. A. Forcinito, *'Señoras y señoritas: el género femenino y sus desencuentros', *LALR*, 31:41–57. Matthew C. Guttman, **Changing Men and Masculinities in Latin America*, Durham, Duke U.P., xi + 416 pp. M. Agosín, *'El lenguaje femenino frente a la violencia en la literatura latinoamericana', *Taller de Letras*, 32:125–26. Z. Moret, *'Voces y resonancias: diálogos con escritoras latinoamericanas', *AlAm*, 22:575–84.

3. Identity, Race, and History

Miguel Ángel Abellás González, *Jugando con estereotipos: los extranjeros y la identidad nacional en México y el área del Caribe hispano en el último cuarto de siglo*, M, Pliegos, 232 pp., offers a challenging analysis of national identity through late 20th-c. Mexican, Cuban, and Puerto Rican literature. The identity theme addresses the issue of race in Tace Hedrick, *Mestizo Modernism: Race, Nation, and Identity in Latin American Culture 1900–1940*, New Brunswick–London, Rutgers U.P., 252 pp., which combines studies of literature (César Vallejo and Gabriela Mistral), murals (Diego Rivera), and painting (Frida Kahlo). Unfortunately, such a choice of well-researched and often over-analysed artists suggests a traditional and therefore predictable approach to what could have been an unorthodox critique of the representation of race and nation in Latin American modernist art. Margaret Lindsay Morris, *An Introduction to Selected Afro-Latino Writers*, Lewiston–Lampeter, Mellen, 123 pp. Carlos Hiraldo, *Segregated Miscegenation: On the Treatment of Racial Hybridity in the North American Literary Traditions*, NY–London, Routledge, 144 pp., approaches the subject from a now-popular perspective of cultural hybridity and miscegenation, carrying out a comparative study of North American and Latin American contemporary literature. Similarly, Suzanne Bost, *Mulattas and Mestizas: Representing Mixed Identities in the Americas, 1850–2000*, Athens, Univ. of Georgia, 254 pp., concentrates on a variety of hybridities (racial and gender) as a catalyst of literary expression. F. Fahey, 'Pilgrimage as opposition in Latin American women's literature', *Mosaic*, 36.4:33–48. A logical progression of the theme is the study of subjectivity in the context of hybridized identity, carried out in Annegret Thiem, *Repräsentationsformen von Subjektivität und Identität in zeitgenössischen Texten lateinamerikanischer Autorinnen. Postmoderne und postkoloniale Strategien*, Frankfurt, Vervuert, 240 pp.

It is hardly surprising that there is an intrinsic link between Latin American literature and history, as the issue of Latin American identity, so often addressed in literature, arises from historical upheavals in the region. A number of volumes examine this connection: Silvia N. Rosman, *Being in Common: Nation, Subject, and Community in Latin American Literature and Culture*, Lewisburg, PA, Bucknell U.P. — Cranbury, London, AUP, 179 pp., contributes analyses of the works of Alejo Carpentier, Ezequiel Martínez Estrada, Octavio Paz, and Jorge Luis Borges, concentrating on the subject of national (non)belongingness and the resulting re-creation of texts as a means of self redefinition. Of particular interest is the chapter 'Borges: on reading, translation, and the impossibility of naming', which once again raises the topic of multiple spaces in Borges's works.

Unfortunately, the chapter 'Octavio Paz and the dialectics of universality' fails to contribute an original reading but restates the existing interpretation of the 'universality' of O.P.'s works.

Another critique examining the writings of Octavio Paz, among others, is Todd Oakley Lutes, *Shipwreck and Deliverance. Politics, Culture and Modernity in the Works of Octavio Paz, Gabriel García Márquez and Mario Vargas Llosa*, Lanham, U.P. of America, 233 pp. The readings focus on the writers' political and social views as presented in their works; the line-up is hardly innovative, considering the existing body of postcolonial comparative critiques. S. Hensel, 'Was there an age of revolution in Latin America? New literature on Latin American independence', *LARR*, 38:237–49. Fernando de Toro, *New Intersections. Essays on Culture and Literature in the Post-Modern and Post-Colonial Condition*, M, Iberoamericana — Frankfurt, Vervuert, 171 pp., continues the postcolonial theme in this year's publications. Patrick Collard and Rita de Maeseneer, *Murales, figuras, fronteras: narrativa e historia en el Caribe y Centroamérica*, M, Iberoamericana — Frankfurt, Vervuert, 286 pp., is a study of the historical aspect in the works of Francisco Herrera Luque, Julio Escoto, Sergio Ramírez, Olga Nolla, and Gabriel García Márquez.

As to the political focus in Latin American literature, Claudia Gilman, *Entre la pluma y el fusil: debates y dilemas del escritor revolucionario en América Latina*, BA, Siglo Veintiuno, 430 pp., is a study of writers' contribution to contemporary political thinking, with the focus on Cuban postrevolutionary intellectual history. *History and Histories in the Caribbean*, ed. Thomas Bremer and Ulrich Fleischmann, Frankfurt, Verwuert — Madrid, Iberoamericana, 2001, 271 pp., is a collection of papers presented at the Society of Caribbean Research Fourth International Conference in Berlin. Among the 14 essays, A. M. Cruz Benedetti, 'Ejemplos de la tradición narrativa (transmitida en forma oral) de los afroamericanos en el norte de Colombia' (161–69), and W. Binder, 'Un mundo enfermo? Manuel Zeno Gandía's *La charca* and national Puerto Rican discourse' (217–27), contribute to the body of postcolonial literary research.

4. Cross-Cultural Analyses

The theme of cross-cultural influences continues in a number of works. Anne Fountain, *José Martí and U.S. Writers*, Gainesville, Florida U.P., 153 pp., draws parallels between the works of José Martí, Walt Whitman, Henry Longfellow, and Ralph Waldo Emerson; the last chapter, 'Reading America', establishes a reciprocal relationship between José Martí's work and contemporary and subsequent writings by North American authors — a challenging conclusion, considering the popular perception of Latin American literature as the primary recipient of outside influences. Sabine Schlickers, *El lado oscuro de la modernización: estudios sobre la novela naturalista hispanoamericana*, M, Iberoamericana — Frankfurt, Vervuert, 429 pp., is an exhaustive study of the influence of naturalism in Hispanic novels. Julia A. Kushigian, *Reconstructing Childhood: Strategies of Reading for Culture and Gender in the Spanish American Bildungsroman*, Lewisburg, Bucknell U.P. — London, AUP, 267 pp., examines the 20th-c. Latin American *bildungsroman* in the postmodernist context as a record of the creation of the self and nation; the themes of identity displacement, collectivity, and cultural memory dominate the analysis. As far as Latin American literary counterculture is concerned, Manuel Luis Martinez, *Countering the Counterculture: Rereading Postwar American Dissent from Jack Kerouac to Tomás Rivera*, Madison, Wisconsin U.P., ix + 353 pp., is a refreshing comparative study of non-mainstream North American and Mexican literature, with the focus on dissent and liberal attitudes in the two countercultures. Unfortunately, this subject has been neglected by the majority of contemporary critics; however, this volume should reignite the interest in the works of La Onda and 'narrativa joven'.

5. Individual Countries

Argentina

GENERAL. Nicolás Rosa, **La letra argentina: crítica 1970–2002*, BA, Santiago Arcos, 221 pp. Cristina Iglesia, **La violencia del azar: Ensayos sobre literatura argentina*, BA, Fondo de Cultura Económica, 200 pp. Juan Pablo Neyret, *'Sombras terribles: la dicotomía civilización-barbarie como institución imaginaria y discursiva del Otro en Latinoamérica y la Argentina', *Espéculo: Revista de Estudios Literarios*, 24: [no pp.]. Bibiana Eguía, **Nuestra Babilonia: sobre la representación del paisaje de Córdoba*, Cordova, EMCOR, 71 pp.

ON MORE THAN ONE AUTHOR. *Ciberletras*, 9, is a special issue on 'Literatura y cultura argentinas de fin de siglo', including articles on Edgar Bayley, Luisa Futoransky, Néstor Perlongher, Luisa Valenzuela, Tomás Eloy Martínez, Reina Roffé, Alina Diaconú, and Héctor Murena. Jason Wilson, *'The mutating city: Buenos Aires and the avant-garde, Borges, Xul Solar and Marechal', *HRJ*, 4: 251–69. Fiona Mackintosh, *Childhood in the Works of Silvina Ocampo and Alejandra Pizarnik*, London, Tamesis, 199 pp., has a thematic and biographical approach. Marianella Collette, **Conversación al Sur: entrevistas con escritoras argentinas*, BA, Simurg, 180 pp.

POETRY. P. Venti, 'Las diversiones púbicas de Alejandra Pizarnik', *Espéculo*, 23: [no pp.], is on irony and metonymic logic. V. Melchiore, *'Amelia Biagoni: una identidad en fuga por el lenguaje errante', *ib.*, [no pp.].

THEATRE. Jorge Dubatti, **El convivio teatral: teoría y práctica del teatro comparado*, BA, Atuel, 190 pp. I. López-Calvo, *'Lesbianism and caricature in Griselda Gambaro's *Lo impenetrable*', *Journal of Lesbian Studies*, 7: 89–103.

FICTION. Adolfo Prieto, **La literatura autobiográfica argentina*, BA, Eudeba, 230 pp. G. Perrén de Jaquenod, *'La creación literaria de Arlt: una demanda de crítica futura', *AlAm*, 22: 157–69. M. I. Zwanck de Barrera, *'La carta: enigma y clave en la narrativa de Marco Denevi', *ib.*, 327–45. S. Godsland, *'Enajenadas, endiabladas, envidiosas: la mujer delincuente en los cuentos de Angélica Gorodischer', *ib.*, 263–75. Roberto Domínguez Cáceres, **Santa Evita: los entremanos del lector y sus obras*, Mexico, Miguel Angel Porrúa, 328 pp. Z. N. Martínez, *'Dangerous messianisms: the world according to Valenzuela', pp. 864–69 of *Twayne Companion to Contemporary World Literature Today*, ed. Pamela A. Genova, NY, Twayne-Thomson Gale, 1685 pp. Ksenija Bilbija, **Yo soy trampa: ensayos sobre la obra de Luisa Valenzuela*, BA, Feminista, 220 pp. Marcia Espinoza-Vera, **La poética de lo incierto en los cuentos de Silvina Ocampo*, M, Pliegos, 237 pp. Adriana Mancini, *Silvina Ocampo: escalas de pasión*, BA, Norma, 302 pp. S. Colás, 'Living invention, or, The way of Julio Cortázar', *REH*, 37: 189–212, is creative criticism in the manner of *Rayuela*. R. Roffé, 'Interview with Tomás Eloy Martínez', *CH*, 633: 101–06. E. V. Barenfeld, *'César Aira: realismo en proceso', *Espéculo*, 23: [no pp.]. J. P. Spicer-Escalante, *'Ricardo Güiraldes's Américas: reappropriation and reacculturation in *Xaimaca* (1923)', *STW*, 1: 9–28. Ana Camblong, **Macedonio: retórica y política de los discursos paradójicos*, Univ. Buenos Aires, 468 pp. C. Petit, *'Los roles sexuales represivos simbolizados por el encierro y la enfermedad en la obra de Manuel Puig (1932–1990)', *AlAm*, 22: 401–09.

BORGES. *Jorge Luis Borges (1899–1986) as Writer and Social Critic*, ed. Gregary J. Racz (Hispanic Literature, 76) Lewiston, Mellen, 175 pp., seeks the 'counter-monumental' Borges. Luis Kancyper, **Jorge Luis Borges, o La pasión de la amistad: Estudio psicoanalítico*, BA, Lumen, 190 pp. Lisa Block de Behar, *Borges: The Passion of an Endless Quotation*, Albany, NY State U.P., xvi + 206 pp. Jean-François Gérault, **Jorge Luis Borges: une autre littérature, parcours d'une œuvre*, Paris, Encrage, 175 pp. J. Serna Arango, *'Borges y el tiempo', *Espéculo*, 23: [no pp.]. J. L. Castillo, *'Pierre Menard and the school of the skeptics', *HR*, 71: 415–28. R. Jara, *'La lógica del deseo en Jorge Luis Borges: el ademán barroco', *AlAm*, 22: 317–25. A. J. Pérez,

*'Borges en la década del sesenta', *ib.*, 305–15. J. N. Goldsmith, 'Approaching a sacred center: narratives of origin and identity in the late fiction of Jorge Luis Borges', *Hispanófila*, 137:83–100, discusses his writing as an ontological project. *Variaciones Borges*, 15, contains ten essays on 'Tlön, Uqbar, Orbis Tertius'. R. Fiddian, 'Open bracket, close bracket: parenthetical statement in a selection of poems by Jorge Luis Borges', *HR*, 71:171–88. S. Petrilli, *'Translating with Borges', pp. 517–30 of *Translation, Translation*, ed. Susan Petrilli, Amsterdam, Rodopi, 660 pp.

CHILE

Maximino Fernández Fraile, **La crítica literaria en Chile*, Santiago, Edebé, 353 pp. Iván Carrasco, *'Etnicidad y canon literario en Chile', pp. 461–74 of *Texto social: estudios pragmáticos sobre literatura y cine: Homenaje a Manfred Engelbert*, ed. Annete Paatz and Burkhard Pohl, Berlin, Tranvía-Frey, 544 pp. O. Morales Benítez, *'Prosa y poesía de Gabriela Mistral en Colombia', *AlAm*, 22:173–94.

COLOMBIA

Carmiña Navia Velasco, **Guerras y paz en Colombia: miradas de mujer*, Cali, Univ. del Valle, 150 pp. Pablo González Rodas, **Colombia: novela y violencia*, Manizales, Secretaría de Cultura de Caldas, 187 pp. Eduardo Posada Carbó, **El desafío de las ideas: ensayos y historia intelectual y política en Colombia*, Medellín, Banco de la República–Univ. EAFIT, 294 pp. Jaime García Saucedo, **Diccionario de la literatura colombiana en el cine*, Bogota, Panamericana, 174 pp. Jaime Jaramillo Escobar, **El ensayo en Antioquia*, Medellín, Alcaldía de Medellín, 534 pp. Nelly S. González, **Bibliographic Guide to Gabriel García Márquez 1992–2002*, Westport, Praeger, xxvii + 498 pp. Guillermo Henríquez Torres, **El misterio de los Buendía: el verdadero trasfondo histórico de 'Cien años de soledad'*, Bogota, Nueva América, 393 pp. C. Lindsay, '"Clear and present danger": trauma, memory and Laura Restrepo's *La novia oscura*', *HRJ*, 4:41–58. Oscar Osorio, **Historia de una pájara sin alas*, Cali, Univ. del Valle, 137 pp.

COSTA RICA

Dorothy Mosby, *Place, Language, and Identity in Afro-Costa Rican Literature*, Columbia–London, Missouri U.P., 248 pp., analyses the construct of identity in Costa Rican black writings, examining the works of Quince Duncan, Eulalia Bernard, Delia McDonald Woolery, and Shirley Campbell Barr.

CUBA

Salvador Bueno, *Ensayos sobre literatura cubana*, Boulder, SSSAS, 84 pp., combines an overview of Cuban literary traditions spanning two centuries, and close readings of the works of Dulce María Loynaz, Alejo Carpentier, and Cirilo Villarde. Harald Irnberger, '*Nuestra América': literarische Streifzüge durch Kuba und die Karibik*, Düsseldorf, Artemis & Winkler, 279 pp., examines Caribbean literature from a historical perspective, an approach gaining popularity over the past years. S. Fernandes, 'Island paradise, revolutionary utopia or hustler's haven? Consumerism and socialism in contemporary Cuban rap', *JLACS*, 12:359–75, adds a countercultural perspective to the analysis of contemporary Cuban music. Jorge Domingo Cuadriello and Ricardo Luis Hernández Otero, *Nuevo diccionario cubano de seudónimos*, Boulder, SSSAS, 160 pp., presents a comprehensive list of over 2000 pseudonyms used by Cuban authors or by foreign writers who have worked and published their works in Cuba. The dictionary contains two indexes of the names and publications listed in the primary section. An intriguing cross-cultural study is Elina Miranda Cancela, *La tradición helénica en Cuba*, Havana, Grupo de Estudios Helénicos, 185 pp., concentrating on Greek influences and Hellenism in literature. This is a unique contribution to the field of Caribbean literary studies; with few critics working on this connection, it is hoped that such cross-cultural analyses will become more common in the near future.

MEXICO

Teresa Hurley, *Mothers and Daughters in Post-Revolutionary Mexican Literature*, Woodbridge, Tamesis, 212 pp., focuses upon a unique combination of testimonials, documentary narrative, and fiction in the works of Nellie Campobello, Rosario Castellanos, Elena Garro, and Elena Poniatowska, examining the mother-daughter relationship and the subsequent creation of the antithesis of 'madre abnegada' or 'mujer mala' in response to the mother's emotional distancing from the daughter. Rosa María Acero, *Novo ante Novo: un novísimo personaje homosexual*, M, Pliegos, 239 pp., revisits the works of Salvador Novo, a prominent member of the movement of Los Contemporáneos, analysing the representation of homosexuality. Close readings of individual works are presented in C. Taylor, 'Cities, codes and cyborgs in Carmen Boullosa's *Cielos de la tierra*', *BSS*, 80:477–93, and K. Ibsen, 'Dissecting the exquisite cadaver: on collections and colonialism in Fernando del Paso's *Noticias del Imperio*', *ib.*, 715–27. Marie-Agnès Palaisi-Robert, *Juan Rulfo: l'incertain*, Paris, Harmattan,

365 pp., offers an intriguing interpretation of the aspect of uncertainty in the works of the prominent Mexican author. Robert McKee Irwin, *Mexican Masculinities*, Minneapolis–London, Minnesota U.P., 282 pp., is a study of the representation of masculinity and homosexuality in Mexican literature, linking the gender self-definition with the specifics of Mexican national character. Considering that the topic of homosexual masculinity is by definition a potential controversy, this work deals with adversity in an intelligent and informed manner. On the subject of Mexican cinematography and its relationship with postmodern texts, the following articles are of particular interest: M. T. Martin and B. Paddington, 'On the cusp of postmodernity: *Lolo* and *Fibra Optica* in contemporary Mexican cinema — a conversation with Francisco Athié', *JLACS*, 12: 191–216; and P. J. Smith, 'Transatlantic traffic in recent Mexican films', *ib.*, 389–400.

PERU

**Heterogeneidad y literatura en el Perú*, ed. James Higgins, Lima, Centro de Estudios Literarios Antonio Cornejo Polar, 352 pp. Tito Cáceres Cuadros, **Literatura arequipeña*, Arequipa, UNSA, 341 pp. Federico Sánchez Cruz, **Voces y letras de Morropón*, Lima, Juan Gutemberg, 105 pp. C. de María, *'El teatro peruano en internet: a propósito de lo local y lo internacional', *LATR*, 36.2: 159–62. G. Geirola, *'La escritura indignada: entrevista a César de María', *ib.*, 95–102. J. Newmark, *'Language, absence and narrative impossibility in Mario Vargas Llosa's *El Hablador*', *LALR*, 31: 5–22. Eva María Valero Juan, **La ciudad en la obra de Julio Ramón Ribeyro*, Alicante U.P., 303 pp. César Augusto Angeles Caballero, **El cholo en la literatura peruana: el cholismo literario*, Lima, San Marcos, 238 pp. Jorge Bravo and Carmen María Pinilla Cisneros, **Primera Mesa Redonda sobre Literatura Peruana y Sociología: Del 26 de mayo de 1965*, Lima, Instituto de Estudios Peruanos, 111 pp. Several new Peruvian literary periodicals have started up in 2003: *El fingidor* (Lima, Pontificia Universidad Católica del Perú); *Cuadernos Literarios* (Lima, Universidad Católica Sedes Sapientiae); *Patio de Letras* (Lima, UNMSM Facultad de Letras y Ciencias Humanas); *Tierra Firme* (Tarma, Grupo Literario Kavilando).

PUERTO RICO

T. Peña-Jordán, 'The "multitude" in Luis Rafael Sánchez's *La Pasión según Antígona Pérez*: a genealogy of a future unknown', *JLACS*, 12: 377–88.

URUGUAY

CHA, 632:7–78, contains a dossier on 'Aspectos de la cultura uruguaya', including discussion of the visual arts, cinema, poetry, and narrative. P. Rocca, 'Marinetti en Montevideo: idas y vueltas de la vanguardia', *ib.*, 631:105–17. Marvin A. Lewis, **Afro-Uruguayan Literature: Post-Colonial Perspectives*, Lewisburg, Bucknell U.P. — Cranbury, AUP, 170 pp.

VENEZUELA

María del Rosario Jiménez Turco, **El relato humorístico tradicional en Venezuela: una aproximación a su estructura y tipología*, Caracas, Univ. Central de Venezuela, 233 pp. D. A. Medina, *'From keeping it oral to writing to mapping: the Kuyujani legacy and the De'kuana self-demarcation project', pp. 3–32 of *Histories and Historicities in Amazonia*, ed. Neil L. Whitehead, Lincoln, Nebraska U.P., xx + 236 pp. Benjamin Keith Belton, **Orinoco Flow: Culture, Narrative and the Political Economy of Information*, Lanham, Scarecrow, viii + 218 pp. Jesús María Herrera Salas and Miguel Izard, **El negro Miguel y la primera revolución Venezolana: la cultura del poder y el poder de la cultura*, Caracas, Vadell Hermanos, 359 pp.

6. Chicano/a literature

Reading U.S. Latina Writers: Remapping American Literature, ed. Alvina E. Quintana, NY–Basingstoke, Palgrave Macmillan, vi + 212 pp. is a collection of essays on the relationship between the 'Latina' text and the identity construct of its culture. Manuel M. Martín-Rodríguez, *Life in Search of Readers: Reading (in) Chicano/a Literature*, Albuquerque, New Mexico U.P., 268 pp., analyses the relationship between Chicano literature and its readership, concentrating on the nature of the Quinto Sol generation, and the issue of gender relating to the creation of an original text throughout the history of Chicano culture. The subject of the nature of the text is examined in Thorsten Thiel, *There is More than One Site of Resistance: Ironie und Parodie im zeitgenössischen Roman der Chicanos/as*, Heidelberg, Winter, viii + 392 pp.

BRAZILIAN LITERATURE

By Mark Dinneen, *Spanish, Portuguese and Latin American Studies, University of Southampton*

1. General

Fernando Cristóvão, *O romance político brasileiro contemporáneo e outros ensaios*, L, Almedina, 296 pp., contains 12 literary studies on a wide variety of themes. Most focus directly on Brazil, and are divided between writers of the colonial era, including Vieira and Anchieta, and those of the 20th c., with essays on Cecília Meireles and the changing nature of political writing during the last three decades. Mário Faustino, *De Anchieta aos concretos; poesia brasileira no jornal*, SPo, Companhia de Letras, 536 pp., is a collection of over 40 newspaper essays published in the 1950s, offering brief studies of a variety of Brazilian poets, which, though a little uneven, are all stimulating. The phases covered are the colonial period, modernism, the 1945 generation, concretism, and poets emerging in the 1950s. *Vozes femininas: gêneros, mediações e práticas da escrita*, ed. Flora Sussekind, Tânia Dias, and Carlito Azevedo, R, Sete Letras, 534 pp., gathers together an assortment of conference papers on the role of women in the arts in Brazil and beyond, in different historical periods. It includes articles on Clarice Lispector and Orides Fontela, the state of feminist criticism in Brazil, and the representation of women in the work of Guimarães Rosa and Caio Fernando Abreu. Moacyr Scliar, *Saturno nos trópicos*, SPo, Companhia das Letras, 274 pp., makes reference to writers such as Machado de Assis, Lima Barreto, and Clarice Lispector in an investigation into how melancholy has found expression in Brazilian culture throughout its history. M. A. M. C. Chaga, 'The circulation of literary ideas in the *Folhetim*', *JLACS*, 12.1: 119–56, is a detailed study of the role played by the cultural supplement of the *Folha de São Paulo* in the 1970s and 1980s, discussing how it provided an important space for the debate on literary theory and the state of literary production in Brazil. Alfredo Bosi, *Literatura e resistência*, SPo, Companhia de Letras, 2002, 297 pp., examines the varying ways in which writers of different historical periods expressed resistance to oppressive social or political conditions of their time. There are chapters on Antônio Vieira, Basílio da Gama, Cruz e Sousa, Lima Barreto, Euclides da Cunha, and Graciliano Ramos. Felipe Fortuna, *A próxima leitura: ensaios de crítica literária*, R, Francisco Alves, 248 pp., focuses chiefly on poetry, with studies on the work of Sebastião Uchoa Leite, Joaquim Cardoso, Cassiano Ricardo, and Cruz e Sousa, among others. *Diálogos literários luso-brasileiros*, ed.

Donísio Vila Maior, Coimbra, Pé de Página, 2002, 115 pp., consists of seven literary studies, which explore cultural relations between Portugal and Brazil and compare writers from the two countries. Those from Brazil discussed are Antônio Vieira, Gregório de Matos, Machado de Assis, Melo Neto, and Drummond de Andrade. Juan E. de Castro, *Mestizo Nations: Culture, Race and Conformity in Latin American Literature*, Tucson, Arizona U.P., 2002, 161 pp., includes reference to the work of José de Alencar and Gilberto Freyre in a study of the discourse of *mestizaje* which is traced through Latin American literature of the 19th and 20th cs, and in particular how that discourse has been used to construct a sense of national identity. It shows how both Brazilian writers sought to promote a homogeneous Brazilian cultural identity, moulded round an idealized conception of Portuguese cultural tradition. Gilberto Mendonça Telles, *Contramargem: estudos da literatura*, R, PUC, 2002, 374 pp., is a wide-ranging collection of essays of literary criticism which the author wrote over a 30-year period as journal articles, prefaces, and academic papers. The most significant articles focus on modern poets, including Manuel Bandeira, Oswald de Andrade, and Alphonsus de Guimaraens Filho.

2. Colonial

LBR, 40.1, is a special issue on Antônio Vieira, mainly discussing his life and work, but also the religious thought that underlies his writing. D. Alden, 'Some reflections on Antônio Vieira: seventeenth-century troubleshooter and troublemaker' (7–16), assesses V.'s attempt to protect the Brazilian Indian as well as his position regarding African slavery. F. A. Dutra, 'The Vieira family and the Order of Christ' (17–31), examines the role of religious practice in V.'s family history. S. B. Schwartz, 'The contexts of Vieira's toleration of Jews and New Christians' (33–44), explores the historical reasons for V.'s religious tolerance. M. V. Jordán, 'The empire of the future and the chosen people: Father Antônio Vieira and the prophetic tradition in the Hispanic World' (45–57), discusses V.'s prophetic millienarism through a study of his *Esperanças de Portugal e Quinto Império do Mundo* and *Livro anteprimario da história do futuro*. A. Pécora, 'Uma exegese do capital' (59–65), considers the writing V. produced whilst being tried by the Inquisition, to consider what it reveals about V.'s theological thought. T. Cohen, 'Judaism and the history of the church in the Inquisition trial of Antônio Vieira' (67–78), examines in detail what V.'s defence in the trial indicates about his position towards Judaism. M. B. N. da Silva, 'Vieira e os conflitos com os colonos do Pará e Maranhão' (79–87), studies V.'s arguments in favour of Indian protection during the dispute over the issue of Indian enslavement. J. Eisenberg, 'Antônio Vieira and the justification of Indian slavery' (89–95), shows the complexity and originality in V.'s thinking on the question of slavery. Teresa Domingues, **O múltiplo Vieira: estudos dos sermões indigenistas*, SPo, Annablume, 2002, 99 pp. *Dicionário de autores no Brasil colonial*, L, Colibrí, 502 pp., containing very brief entries on all the major writers of the colonial period, may be useful for rapid reference. Luis André Nepomuceno, *A musa desnuda e o poeta tímido*, SPo, Annablume — Patos de Minas, Unipam, 2002, 308 pp., analyses the influence of Petrarch on the *mineiro* poets, particularly Claudio Manuel da Costa, Tomás Antônio Gonzaga, and Silva Alvarenga, with particular attention to how they adapted that influence to express their own social and political concerns. Ricardo Martins Valle, 'Invenção da literatura brasileira: a recepção de Claudio Manuel da Costa no génese da crítica e do cânone literario brasileiro', *NovE*, 65: 125–40, reviews different critical interpretations of the poet throughout the 19th and 20th cs, and considers the role his work has played in the development of theories of national literature. Isabel Allegro de Magalhães, *Capelas imperfeitas*, L, Horizonte, 2002, 312 pp., includes studies on Antônio Vieira and Pêro Vaz de Caminha's *carta* in a collection of 15 essays on world literature.

3. Nineteenth Century

Luis Augusto Fischer, *Parnasianismo brasileiro: entre ressonância e dissonância*, Porto Alegre, Edipucrs, 332 pp., is a welcome and original study of a somewhat denigrated period of Brazilian poetry. It seeks to provide new understanding of the major Parnassian poets, especially the famous 'trinity' of Olavo Bilac, Alberto de Oliveira, and Raimundo Correia, through an examination of the social context of their work, and the specific conditions under which it was produced. Abel Barros Baptista, *A formação do nome: duas interrogações sobre Machado de Assis*, Campinas, UNICAMP, 271 pp., studies in detail M.'s *Instinto da nacionalidade* and *Memórias póstumas de Brás Cubas*, seen as representing two crucial phases in the development of his writing career. *Recortes machadianos*, ed. Ana Salles Mariano and Maria Rosa Duarte de Oliveira, SPo, Educ-Fapesp, 353 pp., contains 10 studies on M.'s work, both novels and short stories, from different theoretical approaches. There are essays on the hybridization of literary genres in M.'s writing, its philosophical dimension and its reception in France. Ana Cláudia Suriani da Silva, *'Linha reta e linha curva': edição crítica e genética de um conto de Machado de Assis*, Campinas, UNICAMP, 257 pp., is a study of the genesis of M.'s story, tracing its development through a play, a serialized newspaper story and finally the short story itself. Douglas Tufano, *Machado de Assis; questões éticas em discussão*, SPo, Paulus, 72 pp., aimed at students, briefly considers ethical questions raised in three of M.'s short stories. Dilson Ferreira da Cruz Júnior, **Estratégias e máscaras de um fingidor: a crónica de Machado de Assis*, SPo, Nankin, 2002, 240 pp. M. Grzegorczyk, 'Agoraphobia and modernity in *fin de siècle* Brazil: on *Dom Casmurro*', *JLACS*, 12.3:307–27, studies the protagonist's ambiguity towards modern urban life in Machado de Assis's novel. D. Treece, 'O indianismo romântico, a questão indígena e a escravidão negra', *NovE*, 65:141–51, examines how, in their writing, José Bonifácio, João Francisco Lisboa, Gonçalves Dias, Joaquim Manuel de Macedo, and José de Alencar all establish links between the conditions experienced by Indians and by black slaves in Brazil. Beatriz Berrini, *Brasil e Portugal: a geração de 70*, O, Campo das Letras, 369 pp., consists of an extensive collection of correspondence exchanged between major Brazilian and Portuguese writers of the late 19th c., including Machado de Assis, Joaquim Nabuco, and Eça de Queiroz, and an introductory study discussing the similarities and differences between them.

4. Twentieth Century

Poetry

Forçando os límites do texto, ed. Ana Cristina Chiara, R, Viveiro de Castro, 96 pp., includes two literary studies among six essays on Brazilian culture. A. C. de R. Chiara, 'Murilo Mendes, o poeta do futuro' (67–79), discusses salient features of M.'s work. F. C. D. Rocha, 'A representação lírica da cidade carioca na poesía de Drummond' (80–96), discusses the ambivalence evident in D.'s treatment of Rio de Janeiro in his poetry. E. V. Oliver, 'The machine world and the man-machine: cosmo-vision and individual consciousness in times of certainty and times of doubt', *PortSt*, 19, 122–44, offers an interesting and detailed analysis of Drummond's poem, *A máquina do mundo*, which is informed by consideration of different philosophical perceptions of the cosmos. V. Camilo, 'The social-lyrical cartography of *Sentimento do Mundo*', *ib.*, 145–62, studies Drummond's book of 1940 in its historical context, in order to discuss its central theme of alienation, and to consider what it indicates about the ideological choices made by the poet in the preceding years. Maria Veronica Aguilera, *Carlos Drummond de Andrade: a poética do cotidiano*, R, Expressão e Cultura, 2002, 273 pp., highlights the links between D.'s poetry and prose through a detailed study of his language and style, particularly in the chronicles he wrote. Sérgio Alcides et al., *Drummond revisitado*, SPo, UNIMARCO, 2002, 152 pp., consists of six essays by young Brazilian poets, presenting new and varied readings of D.'s work, and highlighting the impact it continues to make on current poetic writing. M. A. de Morães, 'Abrasileirar o Brasil (arte e literatura na epistolografia de Mário de Andrade)', *Caravelle*, 80: 33–47, examines the development of A.'s thinking on national literature through a study of his letters to other writers and artists in the 1920s. Douglas Tufano, *Modernismo: literatura brasileira (1922–1945)*, SPo, Paulus, 95 pp., offers students a brief introduction to the major characteristics of Brazilian Modernism. **Maria Antonieta d'Alkmin e Oswald de Andrade*, ed. Marília de Andrade and Esio Macedo Ribeiro, SPo, Edusp, 204 pp. *Querido poeta: correspondência de Vinicius de Moraes*, ed. Ruy Castro, SPo, Companhia das Letras, 372 pp., contains over 200 letters M. wrote or received from the 1930s to the late 1970s, which cast some light on his artistic tastes and his approach towards writing, though the book provides only limited context to guide the reader. Vera Lúcia de Oliveira, *Poesia, mito e história no modernismo brasileiro*, SPo, UNESP, 2002, 342 pp., discusses modernist attempts to create a new sense of national cultural identity through the study of three key works: *Pau Brasil* by Oswald de Andrade, *Martim Cererê* by Cassiano Ricardo, and *Cobra Norato* by Raul Bopp. Wilberth C. Ferreira Salgueiro, **Forças e formas: aspectos da poesia brasileira contemporânea, dos anos 70 aos 90*, Vitória, EDUFES, 2002, 268 pp. C. Slater, 'Terror in the Twin Towers: the events of September 11 in the Brazilian *Literatura de cordel*', *LARR*, 38.3: 37–59, shows how Brazil's tradition of popular poetry continues to defy predictions of its demise by fusing the traditional poetic conventions of the genre with modern innovations.

DRAMA

Elisa Larkin Nascimento, *O sortilégio da cor: identidade, raça e gênero no Brasil*, SPo, Summus, 412 pp., is an examination of varied aspects of Afro-Brazilian cultural identity, which includes an informative chapter on the work of the *Teatro Experimental do Negro*, with detailed discussion of Abdias Nascimento's play *Sortilégio (mistério negro)*. Cláudia Braga, *Em busca da brasilidade: teatro brasileiro na primeira república*, SPo, Perspectiva, 122 pp., sheds new light on the drama of the first decades of the 20th c., in an effort to show that it was not such a decadent period for the Brazilian theatre as many other critics have claimed. Bonnie S. Wasserman, **Metaphors of Oppression in Lusophone Historical Drama*, NY, Lang, 228 pp., examines the different ways in which a selection of late-20th-c. plays from Brazil, Portugal, and Angola debate the effects of political and social oppression, in both the past and the present.

PROSE

Cláudia Mendes Nina, *A palavra usurpada*, Porto Alegre, Edipucrs, 184 pp., discusses how changes in personal experience shaped the development of Clarice Lispector's writing. The concepts of exile, relating to the novels written outside Brazil, and of nomadism, linked to the works published after 1970, are used to provide insight into the creative process underlying L.'s fiction. Karl Posso, *Artful Seduction: Homosexuality and the Problematics of Exile*, Oxford, Legenda, 241 pp., contains highly sophisticated and original studies of Silviano Santiago's *Stella Manhattan* and Caio Fernando Abreu's *Bem longe de Marienbad* and *Onde andará Dulce Veiga?* Using theory provided by such thinkers as Baudrillard, Deleuze, and Guatarri, the author seeks to show how the two writers find new and subtle forms and techniques for challenging discrimination against homosexuals, both within contemporary Brazilian society and in global popular culture. José Luís Lira, *No alpendre com Rachel: ensaio biográfico de Rachel de Queiroz*, Fortaleza, Cidadania, 178 pp., sketches out the major moments in Q.'s life and career, outlining the context for her writing and the circumstances that help explain the changes it has undergone, but without detailed reference to particular works. Laura Cavalcante Padilha, **Novos pactos, outras ficções: ensaios sobre literaturas afro-luso-brasileiras*, L, Novo Imbondeiro, 2002, 322 pp. Roberto Ventura, *Euclides da Cunha: esboço biográfico*, SPo, Companhia das Letras, 349 pp., is the draft of a biography of C., unfinished because of the author's premature death, which offers new perspectives on the creation of *Os sertões*. *Juízos críticos: 'Os sertões' e os olhares de sua época*, ed. José Leonardo do Nascimento and Valentim Facioli, SPo, UNESP, 158 pp., is a collection of articles on *Os sertões*, originally published in the aftermath of the book's own publication in 1902. It provides a fascinating record of the controversy and debate the work provoked at the time. *Palavra de mulher*, ed. Alvaro Alves de Faria, SPo, Senac, 270 pp., consists of 20 brief interviews with major women writers, including Ana Miranda, Lya Luft, Lygia Fagundes Teles, Márcia Denser, and Nélida Piñon, in which they discuss their work and, more broadly, the role of women in the cultural and artistic life of Brazil. José Maria Cançado, **Memórias videntes do Brasil: a obra de Pedro Nava*, Belo Horizonte, Univ. Federal de Minas Gerais, 239 pp. L. Nagin, 'A língua da bala: realismo e violência em *Cidade de Deus*', *NovE*, 67, 181–91, analyses Paulo Lins's 1997 novel and its adaptation to film in 2002, emphasizing the techniques used to present the theme of violence. *CHA*, 633, contains four brief articles on Jorge Amado. B. Losada, 'Jorge Amado y Bahía' (7–11), discusses the Bahian roots of A.'s major novels. C. A. Pasero, 'Jorge Amado en Bueno Aires, capital de Hispanoamérica, 1935–1942' (13–22), refers to the impact made on A. and his work by his visits to the Argentine capital. M. Real, 'Los personajes en el funeral de Jorge Amado' (23–31), considers what A.'s funeral in 2001 indicates about his life and work. I. Soler, 'O destino é o mar' (33–41), discusses characterization within A.'s novel, *Mar morto*, particularly the differing attitudes of characters towards death. Igor Rossini, *Zen e a poética auto-reflexiva de Clarice Lispector*, SPo, UNESP, 2002, 258 pp., discusses the philosophical dimension of L.'s work, through a study of her major novels. Making use of Zen Buddhism, the author seeks to reach an understanding of the mystical tendency in L.'s writing. Luiz Fernando Medeiros de Carvalho, *Literatura e promessa: figuraçao e paradoxo na literatura brasileira contemporânea*, Niteroi, EdUFF, 2002, 82 pp., uses Derrida to analyse such writers as João Gilberto Noll, Silviano Santiago, and Sonia Coutinho, highlighting the ways in which their writing has broken with established literary practices. *Cartas de Caio Fernando Abreu*, ed. Italo Moriconi, SPo, Aeroplano, 534 pp., is a collection of A.'s correspondence, written over several decades, revealing much about his life and his approach towards his writing. Taísa Vilese de Lemos, **Graciliano Ramos: a infância pelas mãos do escritor. Um ensaio sobre a formação na psicologia socio-histórica*, SPo, Musa, 2002, 162 pp. Susana Kampff Lages, *João Guimarães Rosa e a saudade*, SPo, Ateliê, 2002, 188 pp., focuses on the notion of *saudade* evident in R.'s fiction in order to further understanding of its historical and ideological dimensions. Cida Golin, *Mulheres de escritores: subsídios para uma história privada da literatura*, SPo, Annablume, 2002, 198 pp., uses interviews with the wives of writers such as Suassuna, Borba Filho, Guimarães Rosa, and Dourado to try to shed light on the ways in which daily domestic and cultural life, and national political development, shaped the way they approached their writing. Cláudia Rejane Dornelles Antunes, **A poética do conto de Simões Lopes Neto: o exemplo de 'O negro Bonifácio'*, Porto Alegre, Edipucrs, 260 pp.

IX. ITALIAN STUDIES

LANGUAGE

POSTPONED

DUECENTO AND TRECENTO I
DANTE

By Paola Nasti, *Lecturer in Italian, University of Reading*

1. General

2003 has been a reasonable year for Dante studies: a fair number of volumes and studies have appeared covering various aspects of his œuvre. Gary P. Cestaro, *Dante and the Grammar of the Nursing Body*, Notre Dame U.P., 305 pp., is a fascinating and complex examination which considers the image of the nursing body as fundamental to the understanding of D.'s perception of Latin and the Italian vernacular. Based on Julia Kristeva's psychoanalytical studies on the semiotic body of the mother, C. explores the cultural paradigm that 'dictates the rejection of the nursing body as a prerequisite to rational language and selfhood' (2). C. explores D.'s reception of this idea and also its evolution as a paradigm from the *De Vulgari Eloquentia* to *Paradiso*. The first two chapters on the *De vulgari eloquentia* argue that the fear of the nursing body motivated and put an end to D.'s linguistic aspirations. Subsequent chapters investigate the evolution of the nurturing corporality in the *DC* with reference to the neo-Platonic representation of chaos as a wet nurse and also to neo-Platonic readings of Virgil. C. moves from the anti-nurse of *Inferno* (i.e. Circe), to the resurrection of the female nurse (and of selfhood) in *Purgatorio*. Chapter five takes us to *Paradiso*, where the pilgrim returns to a state of linguistic childhood thus celebrating a new subjectivity which embraces the fluid body as an anticipation of the resurrection. Massimo Seriacopi, *Bonifacio VIII nella storia e nell'opera di Dante*, pref. Antonio Lanza, F, Libreria Chiari, 276 pp., is a knowledgeable but light and accessible volume which illustrates the relationship between D. and Boniface VIII. It includes a general historical introduction to the second half of the 13th c. based on the studies of Davidsohn, Pirenne, and Salvemini. S. then proceeds to analyse the figure of Boniface as a political and religious leader, and also D.'s political thought. Great attention is devoted to D.'s representation of the pope and to the *loci* of the *DC* which deal with him. The final section of the book looks, with great competence and confidence, at the early *DC* commentaries and their treatment of Boniface. Politics is also the focus of Francesco Bruni, *La città divisa: le parti e il bene comune da Dante a Guicciardini*, Bo, Il Mulino, 620 pp. This is a commendable volume which illuminates the development or rather the disappearance of political parties in the passage from *comuni* to *signorie* in the Italian peninsula. B. achieves his aims not only by taking into account the political history of the peninsula but also more creative and intellectual forms of medieval and Renaissance Italian culture. In the first chapter, D. features among those who pursued the 'bene comune' against the 'spirito fazioso' that tore the cities apart. B. concludes that the only institution that sought to achieve peace and unity was the order of the Observants. Among these, D. was certainly the one who gained a really universal scope by addressing his poem to humanity as a whole.

The proceedings of the international conference held at Columbia University on 7–9 April 2000 are at last available to the general public. Barolini, *Dante*, is an excellent collection of papers which offers a valuable overview of the thriving world of D. studies and suggests new avenues of research in the field. The volume comprises six sections: 'Philologies', 'Appetites', 'Philosophies', 'Reception', 'Histories', and 'Rewritings'. Each section is followed by a useful bibliography. Most articles are discussed in the appropriate sections below. Two studies of a more general scope are worth mentioning here, however. The section 'Appetites' includes studies on issues such as gender, the body, and love in D.'s œuvre. T. Barolini, 'Beyond courtly dualism: thinking about gender in Dante's lyrics' (65–89), is an illuminating study which traces the development of D.'s poetics from his early courtly-love production to the *Commedia*. Through a vigilant analysis of 'Sonar brachetti', 'Poscia ch'Amor', and 'Doglia mi reca' B. describes the transition from a world which is polarized by gender to one in which 'women [. . .] are [. . .] much more complex [. . .] and human' (89) and can be considered as moral agents. G. P. Cestaro, 'Queering nature, queering gender: Dante and sodomy' 90–103, suggests that in spite of Virgil's scholastic grammar of sexuality disclosed in *Inf.* XI, in *Inf.* XV–XVI D.'s poetry 'is filled with images of flow and transformation from the natural world' that blur the line between procreative Nature and sodomy (95). On the basis of *Cvio* 2 : 13.9–10 C. comes to the conclusion that 'the grammar of sexuality for Dante must, like the moon, always remain mysterious' (101).

Battaglia, *Dante*, is another significant miscellany gathering the papers offered at two seminars organized by the editor at the University of Pisa in 2001–02. This is the Italian counterpart to Barolini, *Dante*, and it aspires to represent the vitality of D. studies within the Italian peninsula. It falls into two sections, each of which groups contributions under lengthy headings: 'Prolegomeni filologici', 'Il contributo dell'analisi formale', 'Il contributo di Dante (spiegar Dante con Dante)', 'Il contributo dei lettori', and finally 'Il contributo dell'analisi delle "fonti" e dei modelli (testuali e non)'. The majority of the articles are discussed in the appropriate sections below. A general study worth mentioning here is S. Marchesi, '"Intentio auctoris" tra *Purgatorio* XXII e *Convivio*. Poesia ed ermeneutica dantesca in movimento' (57–72), considers the Statius cantos in *Purgatorio* an expression of the contrast between exegesis based on the attempt to 'reconstruct' the *intentio auctoris* and exegetical practices focused around the intervention of the reader. The Statius episode is seen by M. as a clear celebration of 'un modello interpretativo in cui l'intervento attivo del lettore[. . .] dimostra di avere un più alto potere di penetrare il significato' (72). The position embraced by D. in this episode is in stark contrast to D.'s self-commentary practice in *VN* and *Cvio*, and can therefore be considered as another palinode of his earlier works.

2. Fortune

A great number of studies in 2002–2003 deal with D.'s European fortunes and with D. studies throughout the centuries. Haywood, *Dante*, collects a variety of interesting essays on D.'s *fortuna* among readerships of different ages and different countries. The essays cover the reception of the *DC* from the 15th to the 20th c. and range across a rather eclectic variety of issues. N. Round, 'Lovers in Hell: Inferno V and Íñigo López de Mendoza', *ib.*, 11–42, considers D.'s reception in 15th-c. Spain, focusing in particular on Mendoza's *Infierno de los enamorados*. R.'s analysis of the intertextual relationship between *Inf.* v and the Spanish text highlights the originality of Mendoza's work, which can by no means be considered a trivialization of D.'s canto. C. Salvadori, 'Landmarks in the fortunes of Dante in the Florentine Quattrocento', *ib.*, 43–70, discusses Dante's *fortuna* in humanist and Medici Florence from Salutati to Landino, arguing that by the beginning of the 16th c., while the Florentine humanists believed that the linguistic superiority of the Florentine vernacular had been proved once and for all by D.'s *florentinitas*, the publication of the *DC* in Venice, by Aldus in 1502, displayed a D. 'definitely lacking the linguistic veneer of the Florentine Quattrocento' (69): 'Dante had now become the poet of all Italy' (*ib.*) and the Florentine vernacular had become what Trissino and later generations were to define as *italiano*. Expanding on the notion of D.'s *florentinitas*, E. G. Haywood, 'Ariosto on Dante: too divine and Florentine', *ib.*, 44–104, maintains that it was to oppose D.'s attempt to 'highjack' the epic form for other-worldly aims, as well as Landino's claim to Florentine superiority, that Ariosto parodied D. in his *Orlando Furioso*. On an opposite note, the constant presence of D. in Campanella's works, shown in E. N. Girardi, 'Dante in the poetic theory and practice of Tommaso Campanella', *ib.*, 105–25, demonstrates Campanella's veneration for the Florentine poet. G. had previously devoted another article to the poet's appropriation of D. in 'Dante nel pensiero e nella poesia di Campanella, *CLett*, 30, 2002:423–40, highlighting above all the shortcomings of contemporary criticism, which has failed to see the merits of Campanella's discussion of Dante. N. R. Harvey, '"An Italian writer against the Pope?" Dante in Reformation England, c. 1560–c. 1640', *ib.*, 127–50, looks at the way in which English Protestant reformers appropriated both the *DC* (above all *Inf.* XIX) and *Mon.* to underpin their anti-papal stance. H. then moves on to discuss the close readings of D. attempted by Catholics 'in response to Protestant claims about him' (146). On a similar note, D. Wallace, 'Dante in England', Barolini, *Dante*, 422–34, looks at the positive reception of D.'s Catholicism in England, even during the Reformation when he was accepted as an anti-papal poet. F. Tieri, 'L'Italia e Dante: il centenario del 1865', *StD*, 68:211–32, looks at the presence of D. in the Italian Risorgimento and in the discussions that followed the unification of the peninsula. P. E. Crisafulli, '"Woe to thee, Simon Magus!". Henry Francis Cary's translation of *Inferno* XIX', Haywood, *Dante*, 151–84, analyses Cary's rendering of the *DC* in the light of contemporary debates on translation methodologies and approaches. C. illustrates Cary's fidelity to the original text to conclude that '*The Vision* is more than just a rendering of D. It is an act of literary criticism that expresses the poetics and the ideology of its author' (184) and whose significance cannot be underestimated considering that, in 19th-c. Italy, D.'s works still suffered heavy censorship. C. expands his treatment of Cary's translation in his *The Vision of Dante. Cary's Translation of the Divine Comedy*. Leicester, Troubador, 348 pp. The volume provides a case study focusing on the most influential and successful version of the *DC* in the British literary tradition. Cary has, in fact, a privileged place in the rediscovery of the *DC* in Romantic Britain. It was through Cary's translation that poets like Shelley and Coleridge grasped the beauty of the Italian poem. The book is interdisciplinary in character: it examines crucial aspects of British culture in the 19th c. and throws light on the manifold transformations of D.'s imagery in English poetry. There is also a thorough introduction to the main issues debated by translation scholars today. The main chapters deal with the fortunes of D. in British culture, the poetic and translation strategies in *The Vision*, and Cary's theological position and ideological interventions in the text. On the issue of translation, V. Jones, 'Dante the popular cantastorie: Porta's dialect translation of the *Commedia*', Haywood, *Dante*, 185–98, offers an attention-grabbing analysis of Porta's 19th-c. rendering of the *DC* into Milanese dialect. She looks at the practice of transformation used by Porta and concludes that 'the matter of Dante's poem is systematically filtered through a process of enhanced referentiality' which involves 'a lowering of the tone' and a 'modernization' of the poem (190). The study also traces the influence of the *linea lombarda* (Maggi, Balestrieri, and Parini) on Porta's rewriting of the *DC* and concludes that the revitalization of the Lombard tradition is the very rationale for such a translation. Finally, D. O'Grady, 'Francesca da Rimini from Romanticism to Decadence', *ib.*, 221–39, closes the panorama on D.'s *fortuna* offered in this volume with an overview of the metamorphoses of Francesca in the countless rewritings of *Inf.* v that appeared in the 19th c. Her investigation includes texts by Pellico (*Francesca da Rimini*), Hunt (*The Story of Rimini*), Phillips (*Paolo and Francesca*), and also D'Annunzio (*Francesca da Rimini*). Readers are the protagonists of: P. Hawkins and R. Jacoff, 'Still here: Dante after Modernism', Barolini, *Dante*, 451–64, dealing with the presence of D. in T. S. Eliot, Derek Walcott, Seamus Heaney, and Charles Wright, and of A. Cottignoli, 'Galileo lettore di Dante', *SPCT*, 64, 2002:83–91, a brief account of Galilei's defence of Antonio Manetti's thesis on D.'s cosmography, which had been criticized by Vellutello and many others. Galileo, however, seemed rather sympathetic towards Manetti's work. In particular, C. underlines Galileo's agreement with the author's view that Hell had the shape of an amphitheatre. M. Verdicchio, 'Dante at the end of the millennium', *ItQ*, 151–152, 2002:61–84, traces the most recent trends in D. studies. Particular attention is devoted to the work of Rino Caputo, Patrick Boyde, and Remo Fasani. The *Cambridge Companion to Dante* edited by R. Jacoff in 1993 is also taken into consideration as the English 'alternative' to the traditional Italian *Lectura Dantis*. V. concludes the article with a look at the future, pointing to the direction marked by Z. Barański's studies on D.'s experimentalism and plurilingualism. E. Sanguineti, 'Getto lettore di Dante', *LItal*, 55:327–34, studies Getto's approach to D. and concludes that the scholar's interest rested mainly on the *DC*'s theological and religious dimensions. **Divine Comedies for the New Millennium: Recent Dante Translations in America and the Netherlands*, ed. R. de Rooy, Amsterdam U.P., 143 pp., includes essays presented at a seminar at the University of Amsterdam organized by Professor de Rooy to celebrate the extraordinary number of D. translations brought out in the Netherlands between 1999 and 2002. The articles assembled in the volume look at the tradition of D. translation into Dutch as well as at the latest American translations of the *DC*.

COMPARATIVE STUDIES. P. Boitani, 'Moby-Dante', Barolini, *Dante*, 435–50, looks at the intertextual ties between D.'s *DC* and Melville's *Moby Dick*. In particular, B. offers a fascinating interpretation of Melville's Ahab as an 'ultra-Ulyssean' Ulysses (443). A. Thompson, 'Dante and George Eliot', Haywood, *Dante*, 199–220, focuses on the presence of Dantean intertext in three of Eliot's novel: *Romola*, *Middlemarch*, and especially *Daniel Deronda*. T. believes that characters such as Daniel Deronda and Felix Holt could be considered as Virgil-like figures, to whom Eliot attributed great responsibility in the 'battle against wrongs' (220). Ovid features in two studies on the *DC*. M. Picone, 'Ovid and the *Exul Inmeritus*, Barolini, *Dante*, 389–407, offers valuable insights into the intertexual relationship between D.'s *DC* and Ovid's poems of exile. One of the most striking points of contact, in P.'s view, is between the description of the endless cold in *Tristia* and D.'s representation of Cocytus. J. Levenstein, 'The re-formation of Marsyas in *Paradiso* I', *ib.*, 301–19, reads the episode of Marsyas in the sixth book of the *Metamorphoses* as an allegory of the fragmented self. Hence, in the L.'s view, D. rewrote the myth in order to present the image of the divided self as a central element of the canto. J. Luzzi, 'Literary lion: Alfieri's *Prince*, Dante and the Romantic self', *Italica*, 80: 175–94, assesses the impact of the figure of D. on Alfieri's creation of his autobiographical self in *Del principe e delle lettere* (1778–86), and concludes that Alfieri fully identified with the Florentine poet. K. Blanc, 'Una lettura dantesca: l'episodio di Bonconte ne *La disubbidienza* di Alberto Moravia', Battaglia, *Dante*, 291–305, considers the form and rationale of Moravia's quotation of the episode of Bonconte in his novel *La disubbidienza*. After a brief philological note on the text of the *DC* used by Moravia, B. examines the function of the Dantean intertext in the novel. The article concludes that the references to D. mirror the difficult situation of the young protagonist of Moravia's story. Like D., he is engaged in a journey, a passage from childhood to adulthood. B. Carletti, *'Presenze di Dante nella poesia di Vittorio Sereni', *SPCT*, 67: 169–95.

3. TEXTUAL TRADITION

The first section of Barolini, *Dante*, containing three articles, is entirely devoted to reviving philological studies as the foundation stage of D. scholarship. J. Ahern, 'What did the first copies of the *Comedy* look like?' (1–15), looks at the way D. was read and received soon after the poem started to circulate. He considers the strategies adopted by the poet to avoid the corruption of his written text and the format chosen by D. to circulate his verse in 'fascicoli'. A. hypothezises on the way they would have looked and finally mentions Brother Ilaro's *Epistle* to Uguccione della Faggiuola as a possible proof of the fact that D. had encouraged his learned readers 'to gloss the *Inferno* and send him the manuscript' (14). H. W. Storey, 'Early editorial forms of Dante's lyrics' (16–45), reflects on the effects the editorial choices of the scribes of D.'s lyrics have had on our interpretation and understanding of these texts. After a brief analysis based on several manuscripts, ranging from the *Memoriali bolognesi* to MS Barberiniano Latino 4036 and MS Magliabechiano Cl. VI 143, the article concludes that 'it is the scribe's relationship both to the use of the lyrics he has to copy and to the material mechanism of production in the context of his document that mediates the forms in which these poems were actually read by medieval readers' (33–34). Finally, G. Gorni, 'Material philology, conjectural philology, philology without adjectives' (56–64), is a witty essay written in defence of philological disciplines, which celebrates their conjectural nature and their relativism against the views of those who consider it a dry job for technicians. The job appears rather passionate in fact, if one looks at how F. Sanguineti, 'Esperienze di un editore critico della *Commedia*" ', Battaglia, *Dante*, 13–24, explains and, at times, defends the editorial choices made in his new critical edition of the *DC*. He discusses, among other things, his unprecedented rendering of *Purg.* XXIV, 57 (i.e. 'di qua dal dolce stil!/ e il novo ch'io odo'). Publication of Sanguineti's critical edition of the *DC* is still stimulating intense debate among D. scholars on the philological aspects of the poem. M. Veglia, 'Sul testo della *Commedia* (da Casella a Sanguineti)', *SPCT*, 66:65–119, is a substantial discussion of 'il problema ectodico della teodìa dantesca', which looks at past approaches as well as new ones in order to provide a better understanding of the complexity of the *DC* MS tradition. V. maintains that the contamination of the transmission, first assessed by Moore and Witte, has not been resolved by Sanguineti, who looks at this 'intermixture' with 'implacabile coerenza lachmanniana' (67). V. assesses the modalities of the *DC*'s transmission and also Casella's and Barbi's philological approaches to it. This rich and articulate study offers valuable examples and arguments to support the author's opinion that 'se stemmi si vogliono tracciare dovranno essere vari, e dovranno raggruppare non le tre cantiche, ma gruppi di canti, o almeno ciascuna cantica per volta; dovranno esprimere la situazione della *Commedia* nella sua mobilità' (118).

DANTE COMMENTARIES. Medieval and Renaissance commentaries are, without doubt, one of the topics most studied by contemporary D. scholars. *Chiose filippine: ms. CF 2 16 della Biblioteca oratoriana dei*

Girolamini di Napoli, ed. A. Mazzucchi, 2 vols, Ro, Salerno, 2002, 1355 pp., is a commendable critical edition of the Latin glosses on the *DC* in MS CF 2 16. The edition follows publication of a facsimile of the *Codice Filippino* in 2001 *(Il Codice Filippino della Commedia di Dante Alighieri*, Ro, Salerno, 2001, 239 pp.). A palaeographical study by G. Savino ('Stratigrafia del Dante filippino', 73–83) and A. Perriccioli's analysis of the MS's 146 miniatures ('Le miniature del Filippino', 85–95), follow M.'s introduction (1–53), which offers a comprehensive analysis of the MS, ultimately defined a 'collettore di materiali eterogenei' (p. 17). M. identifies five different strata which can be attributed to as many different authors or scribes. Some of the exegetical material is original, some reproduces previous glosses, such as Serravalle's and Pietro Alighieri's. On the basis of its relations with and dependence on other commentaries, M. hypothetically dates the composition of the *Chiose* to the period between 1344–49 and 1369. He also highlights the original contributions of the commentary to the exegetical tradition, such as the interpretation of the keys held by the angel in *Purg.* IX, 118, which, according to the commentator, are symbols for the Old and New Testaments. The illustrations that accompany the text are also examined and judged essential to an understanding of the exegetical project carried out in the *Codice Filippino*. The text also concludes with notes on the graphic and editorial criteria, as well as comprehensive and clear indexes. S. Bellomo, 'La *Commedia* attraverso gli occhi dei primi lettori', Battaglia, *Dante*, 73–84, starts from Giovanni del Virgilio's epitaph in honour of D. to give a knowledgeable and critical overview of early readers' perceptions of D. The Florentine poet was considered above all as 'sapientissimus' and often compared to the authors of the Bible as well as Virgil, appreciated for his theological and mystical qualities. But, as the exemplification given by B. shows, he was also exalted as a great poet, master of language and verse. M. Seriacopi, 'Il commento inedito del Laur. Gadd. XC sup. 128 a *Inferno* I–XVIII', *LIA*, 4: 161–76, announces the discovery of yet another commentary on the *Inferno* in the Biblioteca Mediceo-Laurenziana in Florence. The study provides a clear description of the MS. Usually dated to the end of 15th c., it belongs, according to S., to the beginning of the century. It includes the glosses on the *DC* from *Inf.* I, 22, to *Inf.* XVIII; it is written in Florentine vernacular possibly by an amanuensis from Emilia. A reproduction of the commentary is also provided. Focusing on the same glosses, Id., 'Questioni di esegesi dantesca: il caso della "lonza" in un commento del XIV–XV secolo', *SPCT*, 65, 2002: 133–46, offers an example of the exegetical approach adopted by this commentator. The glosses usually expand on the allegorical meaning of the text and refer to mythological as well as historical characters found in the poem. Here, S. copies only the glosses on the first canto of the *DC* and focuses on the commentary notes to the Dantean 'lonza'. Probably derived from Jacopo della Lana, the notes interpret the animal as a symbol of *vanitas*. R. Abardo, 'I commenti danteschi: i commenti letterari', pp. 321–76 of *Intorno al testo. Tipologie del corredo esegetico e soluzioni editoriali. Atti del convegno di Urbino (1–3 ottobre 2001)*, Ro, Salerno, 321–76, is a substantial study brimming with original and somewhat controversial interpretations of the early D. commentary tradition. A. puts forward the hypothesis that the 'Anonimo Lombardo' is one of the first commentaries on the *DC* and that probably the marginal glosses were added to D.'s text as soon as it started to circulate. A. also considers the difficult dating of Guido da Pisa's commentary and queries the latest proposals as to the existence of an early draft of the *Expositiones*. In the last section of his article, A. also considers the *Ottimo commento* and concludes that what is generally considered the first version of the commentary should in fact be regarded as a re-elaboration of the so-called second version of the Ottimo commento. The 30-page appendix includes a great amount of unpublished material, such as an unknown 'volgarizzamento' of Guido da Pisa's *Expositiones* and a *Prologo* to the *Inferno*. L. Miglio, 'I commenti danteschi: i commenti figurati', *ib.*, 377–401, aims at offering an overview of the different types of illustration that flourished around the *Commedia*. M. starts from the very first illustrated manuscripts to show the difficulty experienced by most of the early illustrators in finding figurations that could appropriately represent the novel narratives of *Purgatorio* and *Paradiso*. She then considers the illustrations that reproduce in a 'successione quasi filmica [. . .] i tempi del racconto' (394) and also the magnificent MS 597 of the Musée Condé at Chantilly. Focusing upon the latter, C. Balbarini, ' "Per verba" e "per imagines": un commento illustrato all'*Inferno* nel Musée Condé di Chantilly', *ib.*, 497–512, reports the discovery of black ink letters in alphabetical sequence in the bottom margins of the MS and advances the hypothesis that they were written by Guido da Pisa himself to serve as a 'riferimento, per l'illustratore, ad un menabò dove era stato stilato [. . .] il programma iconografico' (500). B. maintains that the illustrations not only display the influence of Guido's culture but also carry the mark of Francesco di Traino, the influential Pisan painter, who most probably carried out the plan devised by Guido. On a similar topic, C. Calenda, 'L'edizione dei testi: i commenti figurati', *ib.*, 419–34, lucidly reconsiders the close relationship between commentary and illustrations in four manuscripts: MS 597 of the Musée Condé, MS Riccardiano Braidense AG XII 2, *Codice Filippino*, MS CF 216 at the Biblioteca Oratoriana dei

Girolamini, Naples, and MS It. 2017 at the Bibliothèque Nationale, Paris. G. Pomaro, 'Forme editoriali nella *Commedia*', *ib.*, 283–319, is a competent palaeographical analysis of the *mise en page* of 67 MSS which have the text of the *DC* accompanied by the glosses of Jacopo della Lana, the 'Ottimo', and Francesco da Buti. P. classifies nine different types of *mise en page* and finds that the MSS including the commentary by Lana or 'Ottimo' often adopt the 'disposizione a cornice' (305). C. Rossignoli, 'Una possible fonte di Castelvetro: le postille dell'incunabolo ἀ κ ι 13 della Biblioteca Estense di Modena' *RSD*, 3:351–80, calls into question the traditional attribution to Castelvetro of the 1497 edition of Landino's commentary in the light of intratextual analysis and a reassessment of the annotator's handwriting. R. concludes that the annotations may well be a source for Castelvetro's own commentary on the *Commedia*. S. Gilson, 'Tradition and innovation in Cristoforo Landino's glosses on astrology in his *Comento sopra la Comedia* (1481)', *ItS*, 58:48–74, is a learned and interesting enquiry into Landino's exegetical personality and culture. After a close analysis of several passages, G. concludes that most of the astrological material in the commentary is derivative, and yet several passages show a much 'more personal blend of tradition and innovative accretion' which is perhaps justified by the late 15th-c. Florentine 'context of heightened concern with, and intense reflection upon, astrological texts' (74). Id., 'Plato, the platonici and Marsilio Ficino in Cristoforo Landino's *Comento sopra la Comedia*', *The Italianist*, 23.1:5–53, assessing Landino's neo-Platonism and his relationship to reception of Plato in Quattrocento Florence, is a substantial article divided into two main sections. The first traces the wide range of Neoplatonic ideas and concepts found in the *Comento* and the impact of the cultural *milieu* on Landino's thought. The second is a close analysis of five passages of the commentary. The author concludes that Landino's Platonism was mediated by many intertexts such as Augustine, Macrobius, and Cicero. He also underlines the overimposing presence of Ficino, who 'seems to take on the aura of a cultural and patriotic emblem' (25). The article includes two appendices collecting, respectively, Landino's references to Plato and the *platonici*, and his references to Ficino. Finally, L. Azzetta, 'Le chiose alla *Commedia* di Andrea Lancia, l'Epistola a Cangrande e altre questioni dantesche', *L'Alighieri*, 21:5–76, discusses MS II, I 39 at Florence's Biblioteca Nazionale Centrale,which contains a commentary on the *DC* compiled by Andrea Lancia between the late 1330s or 1340s and 1357. The commentary, so far unnoticed by D. scholars, has interesting bearings on the vexed questions of attribution affecting the *tenzone* with Forese Donati and the Letter to Cangrande della

Scala. P. Falzone, *'La chiosa di Boccaccio a *Inf.* II 61: "l'amico mio, e non de la ventura" ', Battaglia, *Dante*, 259–72.

4. Minor Works

Relatively little has appeared on D.'s minor works in 2003. Dealing with the self-commentary form of the *VN* and *Cvio*, S. Sarteschi, 'Uno scaffale della biblioteca volgare di Dante: dalla *Rettorica* di Brunetto alla *Vita Nuova*', *ib.*, 171–90, first highlights echoes of Brunetto Latini's *Rettorica* in *Inf.* xv, then moves on to analyse the impact of Brunetto's teachings on D.'s œuvre as a whole. S. argues that the *Rettorica* proved to D. the importance of a commentary for the understanding of the real meaning of poetry, thus inspiring him to follow the model of the *prosimetrum* in his *VN* and *Cvio.* She finally turns to collecting the possible echoes of the *Rettorica* in the *Vita Nuova.*

L. Peirone, *'Deissi temporale e testualità nella *Vita Nuova*', *EL*, 28.4:88–91. Dante Alighieri, *Vita Nuova*, ed. R. Pinto, trans. L. Martinez De Merlo, Madrid, Cátedra, 436 pp., is a valuable bilingual edition of the *libello* with Spanish translation. It also features an interesting and original introductory essay by P., who annotated the Italian text. **La Vita Nuova di Dante Alighieri*, ed. Corrado Gizzi, trans. Dante Gabriel Rossetti, Cinisello Balsamo, Silvano, 208 pp., is an illustrated exhibition catalogue.

On the *Rime*, L. Lazzerini, 'Osservazioni testuali in margine al discorso trilingue "Ai faus ris" ', *StD*, 68:140–65, is a brilliant textual analysis of "Ai faus ris" as it appears in De Robertis's new edition of D.'s *Rime* (2002). G. Baldissone, 'La tragedia di Beatrice. Una lezione su *Donne ch'avete intellecto d'amore*', *EL*, 28.3:71–79, is a textual analysis of the *canzone* grounded in traditional as well as new interpretations of the poem. Social history and biography are invoked by S. Noakes in her 'Virility, nobility, and banking: the crossing of discourses in the *tenzone* with Forese', Barolini, *Dante*, 241–58, a reconsideration of the *tenzone.* N. argues that the authenticity of these sonnets has been doubted because of their highly comic and sexually explicit content. Yet she claims that 'the *Tenzone* with Forese is better understood when the nuances of the languages of power employed in Florence in the 1290s [. . .] are permitted to emerge in their various shades of (blood-stained) gray' (248). Also on the *tenzone*: M. Zaccarello, 'L'uovo o la gallina? *Purg.* xxiii e la tenzone di Dante e Forese Donati', *L'Alighieri*, 22:5–26, is divided into three sections. The first hinges around *Purg.* xxiii, 115–17, which according to some critics allude to the *tenzone* and are traditionally invoked in support of its attribution to the two poet friends, whereas Z. does not believe *Purg.* xxiii to offer any evidence to corroborate this interpretation. The second section looks at sonnets III–IV of the *tenzone* and maintains that they are to be regarded as later additions or interpolations. In the third Z. looks at the *tenzone*'s stylistic features.

The *Cvio* is the focus of two interesting studies. A. Mazzucchi, 'Stategie patetiche ed emotive nella prosa scientifico-dottrinale del *Convivio*', *RSD*, 3:3–27, an excellent study of the prose of the *Convivio* based on a careful analysis of its rhetorical and stylistic features, demonstrates the metaphorical and 'poetic' dimensions of the philosophical language, thus proving, even at this level, the work's links with biblical and theological traditions. G. Brugnoli, 'Dante e l'*interpretatio Vergiliana*', *CrT*, 6, 2002:471–76, adds another *tessera* to B.'s study of intertextual phenomena in D. His analysis aims at highlighting the syncretist nature of intertextual quotations in D.'s œuvre. In this article, B. looks at the different textual strata that can detected behind *Cvio* 2, 5.13–14. The quotation of *Aeneid*, I, 664–65, is filtered, according to B, through Servius's commentary on Virgil, as well as the *Cento* by Proba Petronia.

M. Chiamenti, 'Il modulo della negazione sul filo di *Bibbia-Fiore-Commedia*', pp. 187–92 of *La scrittura infinita. Bibbia e poesia in età medievale e umanistica*, ed. F. Stella, Tavernuzze, Galluzzo, 2001, is a very interesting study on the use and abuses of the biblical text in the *Fiore*. In this text, whose authorship in C.'s view is still to be considered uncertain, quotations or uses of the Bible are transformed into parodies mainly through the use of adverbs which subvert the meaning of the original text. This consistent strategy of negation shows, in C.' s view, D.'s belief that there is an inescapable abyss between the Scriptures and earthly *mores*. The attribution of the *Fiore* to Dante is instead outrightly rejected as a 'vero e proprio *monstrum* critico' in Maurizio Palma di Cesnola, '*Fiore*: la battaglia attributiva', the first (pp. 13–42, already published but not noted in *YWMLS*) of the essays collected in his *Questioni dantesche: Fiore, Monarchia, Commedia*, Ravenna, Longo, 147 pp., which also includes a revised version of his paper dating the writing of the *Monarchia* to the period April–October 1314 and to an interruption between *Par.* V and VI (see *YWMLS*, 60:384).

5. Comedy

The theological concerns of the *DC* are the pivot of Giorgio Bárberi Squarotti's analysis in his *Il tragico cristiano: da Dante ai moderni*, F, Olschki, 251 pp., which collects essays on a variety of Italian authors ranging from D. to Caproni. The chapter from whose title that of the volume derives attempts to reach a definition of the tragic in Christian terms. The wide range of writers under scrutiny includes Dante,

Alfieri, Manzoni, and Caproni, each affording evidence to support B.'s hypothesis that Christian tragedy is based on the uncertainty of God's judgement and on man's inability to understand His ways. Four more chapters are dedicated to D.'s poetry. The opening chapter, 'L'inesistenza del personaggio', somewhat surprisingly subverts the view, shared by the majority of D. scholars, that the focus on individuality is one of the great 'revolutionary' features of the *DC*. B. maintains, in contrast to this, that 'funzioni [. . .] *exempla* sono le figure che Dante incontra nel suo viaggio escatologico, non "personaggi" secondo la concezione della letteratura che ha definito il valore poetico di un testo in base alla ricchezza irriducibile della personalità' (24). B. invites the reader to consider the *DC* as a poem which deals primarily with the mystery of divine justice. The second chapter, 'Esecrazione e condanna', attempts to follow precisely this line of enquiry as B. looks at all the instances in *Inf.* where 'Dante si arresta per intervenire direttamente [. . .] per meditare sul significato di quanto ha visto e conosciuto, oppure per trarne considerazioni e giudizi di carattere generale, che siano riassuntivi del valore del messaggio a lui dato' (27). The third chapter, 'Spiegazione e profezia', is an enlightening discussion on the two kinds of prophecy found in the *DC*: those usually called *post eventum* and those that seem authentic prophetic predictions (i.e. the prophecies of *Veltro* and the DXV). B. holds the former to have hitherto been considered prophecies on the basis of a very weak understanding of the nature of biblical prophecy. They are in fact explanations, of the kind one finds in the Bible, of the real significance of historical events from an eschatological/divine perspective. The latter, on the other hand, are real Christological prophecies written in the manner of St John and Joachim of Fiore. In 'Paradiso XIII e altro', the fourth chapter, B. analyses the opening simile of *Par.* XIII and the difficult tasks required of the reader in order to understand it. B. asserts that the conceptual difficulty of this image is preparatory to the last vision of the poem and to the imaginative as well as intellectual leap the reader is required to take in order to follow the poet. Chapter five, 'La preghiera alla Vergine: Dante e Petrarca', is an analysis of the prayers to the Virgin with which both the *DC* and the *Canzoniere* conclude. B. defines the prayer sung by St Bernard in the *DC* as an 'invocazione sacra e invocazione poetica' (91), dominated by the use of oxymoron, which echoes the paradoxical condition of D. the pilgrim who, still trapped in his mortal flesh, has achieved the divine vision of God. In conclusion, B. compares St. Bernard's prayer to the final *canzone* of the *Canzoniere*. For Petrarch, the Virgin is the object of poetry not a means to something else: 'la celebrazione della Vergine ha lo scopo di sostituire con infinito eccesso quell'altra lode mondana' (94), Laura and poetic fame.

Theology is also a key to the *DC* in Fernando Salsano, *Lecturae Dantis*, pref. A. M. Chiavacci Leonardi, Ravenna, Longo, 253 pp., which gathers the fruits of S.'s assiduous activity. Of the nineteen *lecturae* of various cantos of the *DC* collected in this volume, eight are dedicated to *Inf.* (III, IV, VI, XV, XVI, XVII, XXII, XXX), nine to *Purg.* (II, III, IV, XV, XVI, XVII, XVIII, XXIV, XXVIII) and five to *Par.* (XX, XXII, XXV, XXX, XXXIII). Only from A. Chiavacci's valuable introduction do we learn that some of these studies have never been published before, but which remains a mystery. S.'s approach is, however, consistent and clear throughout the volume in investigations which mainly address the intertextual dimensions of the text under scrutiny while continuously drawing attention to its religious and theological substance.

Massimo Verdicchio, *Della dissimulazione: allegoria e ironia nella Commedia di Dante*, Na, La Città del Sole, 2002, 260 pp., includes nine studies on different aspects of D.'s works, even though its main focus is on the *Commedia.* The overall intention of the author is to analyse the rhetorical strategy on which the poem is built and to prove that this strategy is grounded in allegory and irony. After an introductory discussion on the reasons that brought D. to break off abruptly the composition of the *Cvio*, V. analyses *Inf.* I (in particular the prophecy of the 'Veltro') and *Inf.* II, and emphasizes D.'s palinodic attempt to differentiate the *DC* from his own previous works and from the *Aeneid* and Bible. From this perspective, the choice of the title *comedia* is seen as an ironic reaction to the 'tragedy' of Virgil, a reaction which had moral and didactic aims. In a *lectura* of *Purg.* XXII, V. arguably attributes D.'s refusal to follow Virgil's authorial model to the classic poet's 'avidità' (215). The last two chapters of the book focus on *Paradiso* and in particular on the DXV prophecy and the poetics of the last *cantica.* V. rejects all possibility of considering *Par.* as the literary expression of an actual transcendental experience. Vittorio Russo, *Il romanzo teologico: seconda serie*, Na, Liguori, 2002, viii + 202 pp., includes writings collected by C. Calenda, author of the volume's introduction, which offer a clear and passionate profile of R.'s *dantismo* and pay tribute to his lifelong dedication to the subject. Some of the eleven essays included are *lecturae* of specific cantos, namely *Inf.* XII and XXIX, and *Pur.* IV. The opening essay deals with the use of the *DC* for theatrical purposes, whereas the concluding one considers the merits and limitations of Sapegno's commentary on the *Commedia.* In 'Virgilio autore di Dante' R. briefly looks at the relationship between D. and Virgil in the *Comedy*, also taking into consideration the contribution of the early commentators. In 'Musica e musicalità nella struttura della *Commedia* di Dante' he investigates, with clarity and competence, the presence of music as well as rhythmic patterns in the poem. In his conclusion he invites other scholars to take up the unfinished task of analysing and reconstructing the 'unità sinfonica della *Commedia*' (94). D.'s exile and its impact on contemporary views of the exilic condition are briefly considered in 'Dante *Exul inmeritus*: variazioni compositive sul/dal tema'. Two more studies deal respectively with the role of memory and writing in D. ('"O mente che scrivesti ciò ch'io vidi". Memoria – immaginativa – scrittura nella *Commedia* di Dante') and with the *exordium* in D. and in medieval rhetoric ('"Esordio" e/o "Proemio" nelle retoriche "volgari" e in Dante').

The constant battle between *eros* and *charitas* in D.'s poetry continues to stimulate critical responses. L. Pertile 'Does the stilnuovo go to heaven?', Barolini, *Dante*, 104–14, and R. Psaki 'Love for Beatrice: transcending contradiction in the *Paradiso*', *ib.*, 115–30, both deal with the concepts of love and sexuality in the *DC*, and yet come to rather different conclusions. Pertile argues that there is no space for exemplary earthly love in the *DC*, where the only positive passion is the love that elevates man to Heaven, the love of Saint Francis for example. The author knowledgeably argues that the Beatrice whom D. meets in *Purg.* 'goes already beyond *stilnuovo*', but that her replacement by Cacciaguida and then St Bernard perhaps signifies that he is pursuing 'an ideal of chastity, spirituality and mystical ardour' which he 'feels unable to fully associate with Beatrice – or any other woman for that matter' (113). Psaki, on the other hand, maintains, but perhaps only apparently, the opposite. She is convinced that there is no divide between *eros* and *agape* in D.'s mind and that the love Dante felt for Beatrice in the body is exactly the same as he feels for her in Paradise. G. Carugati, '"Quando amor fa sentir della sua pace"', *ib.*, 211–27, also devotes attention to the theme of love. C. considers D.'s neo-Platonic approach to amorous and erotic language and concludes that, in D., thinking of God and thinking of the lady are the same thing. Two studies deal with the impact of the figurative arts on D.'s imagination. C. Kleinhenz, 'On Dante and the visual arts', Barolini, *Dante*, 274–92, considers various elements in the *DC* that refer to, or may have been influenced by, the visual arts, such as the image of Henry VII's throne or St Francis's stigmata. He also envisages that D. might have learned much about narrative techniques while looking at the mosaics and frescoes of his day. L. Battaglia Ricci, 'Una biblioteca "visiva"', Battaglia, *Dante*, 191–215, investigates the influence of iconography on images such as the chariot of Elijah in *Inf.* XXVI or the Annunciation in *Par.* XXXII. In the absence of clear written intertexts, the details of D.'s narration could have been suggested by the iconographic tradition instead. B. looks with great care at the 'origins' of the 'nuvoletta' on which Elijah disappears (*Inf.* XXVI, 30) and establishes a link with the paintings of Giotto where, on the basis of biblical and mystical traditions, the cloud represents the border between the earth and heaven. R. L. Martinez, 'Dante's Jeremiads: the fall of Jerusalem and the burden of the New Pharisees, the Capetians, and Florence', Barolini, *Dante*, 301–19, in an intense analysis of the ways in which Florence and Jerusalem are compared in the *DC*, focuses on *Inf.* XIX and XXIII and *Purg.* XX and XXIII. M. concludes that 'Dante's troping of himself as one of the dispersed citizens of an ideal Rome or Jerusalem has thus come to resemble — more correctly to appropriate — the historical experience of the Jews after the Fall of Jerusalem' (315). Likewise focused on the theme of exile, A. M. Chiavacci Leonardi, 'Il tema biblico dell'esilio nella *Divina Commedia*', *La scrittura infinita*, 177–85, considers both the poet's historical exile from Florence and his spiritual pilgrimage to God and shows how both dimensions are intertwined in the *Commedia*. C. underlines the biblical and classical origins of exilic narratives but emphasizes the impact of the New Testament on D.'s treatment of the topic. In the light of the gospel message, exile on earth is 'trans-humanized' and projected towards the heavenly home to which the Christian soul aspires.

A number of studies concentrated on stylistic, rhetorical, and linguistic features of the *Commedia*. L. Blasucci, 'Sul canto come unità testuale', Battaglia, *Dante*, 25–38, examines the forms of the canto as a textual unit and investigates its relation and interaction with the unfolding of the fictional narrative. In particular, B. looks at the openings of cantos and finds two types of exordium: some cantos have a prologue, others do not. The latter are usually characterized by *rimas caras* and have strong links with the preceding canto. B. also notes how mimetic beginnings increase in the second *cantica*, perhaps reflecting the centrality of time and progression through space in *Purgatorio*. On much the same ground, M. C. Camboni, *'L'apertura e la chiusura dei canti: connessioni di tipo metrico retorico', *ib.*, 243–57. M. L. Palermi, '"A questo punto voglio che tu pense". Note di lettura intorno ad una serie rimica della *Commedia*', *CrT*, 6, 2002: 569–93, is an evocative study on the rhyme sequence 'spense-pense-offense', which appears three times in the *DC*, in *Inf.* V, 105–11, *Purg.* XXXI, 8–12, and *Par.* IV, 104–08. On the basis of Yates's and Weinrich's studies on the function of memory in the *DC*, P. shows how these three occurrences of the same set of rhyme words conceal a conceptual sequence. D. intentionally connects these three *loci* of the *DC* to underline a process of spiritual growth which begins with sinful approval of carnal passion, moves towards repentance, and ends with a clear understanding of the moral responsibility of the individual. Following a brief excursus on the presence and semantic evolution of the verb *abbandonare* in the romance lyric, F. Montuori, 'Tre luoghi di Dante e la semantica antica di "abbandonare"', *LS*, 38: 19–41, examines the semantics of the verb in three *loci* of the *DC*: *Purg*. VI, 97–99, *Par*. XVII, 106–11, and *Purg*. IX, 22–24, and finds that its respective meanings are: 'lasciar senza guida', 'lanciarsi all'assalto', and 'privarsi di qualcosa'. R. Fasani, 'L'apocope nel testo della *Commedia*', *SPCT*, 64, 2002: 63–82, is a dense and interesting study on the exceptions to the rule of apocopation in the *Commedia*. Usually used before a consonant in medieval poetry, vocalic apocope is at times ignored by Dante. F. lists and analyses all the exceptions to the rule and, having divided them into four groups, proceeds to a thoughtful analysis of their main features. Starting out from the early commentaries, F. Franceschini, 'Tra secolare commento e storia della lingua', Battaglia, *Dante*, 85–111, studies the semantic evolution of the adverb 'issa' found several times in the *DC*, showing how the commentaries, in combination with other medieval documents, can help one to trace the development and transformation of linguistic features, thus furthering one's understanding of both the *DC* and the Italian language. S. Gigli, *'Le preposizioni consecutive nella *Commedia*: osservazioni stilistiche', *ib*., 329–44.

On miscellaneous topics: W. Wehle, 'Ritorno all'Eden. Sulla scienza della felicità nella *Commedia*', *L'Alighieri*, 22: 27–68, discusses D.'s treatment, in the *DC*, of the science of happiness: the poem is said to be an effective manual on how to attain happiness and one which brilliantly summarizes Christian literature on the topic. W. believes that D. achieved a certain degree of originality thanks to his anthropocentric interpretation of the problem of happiness. G. Indizio, 'Gli argomenti esterni per la pubblicazione dell'*Inferno* e del *Purgatorio*', *StD*, 68: 17–47, analyses the references to the *DC* in early 14th-c. texts to establish possible dates for the publication of the poem. An attempt to date the start of the journey narrated in the *DC* is found in M. Managuerra, 'Una soluzione teologico-astronomica coerente per l'enigma della datazione del viaggio della *Commedia*', *L'Alighieri*, 21: 109–14. M. provides some evidence for 4 April 1300. G. Gorni, *'Epitaffi nella *Commedia*. Saggio sugli epitaffi nella *Commedia* di Dante', *StD*, 68: 1–16. B. Porcelli, *'Pluralità di tipologie onomastiche nella *Commedia*', Battaglia, *Dante*, 39–55. F. Veglia, *'Predoni e banditi nella *Commedia* (a proposito del bandito cortese), *ib*., 307–21.

Teodolinda Barolini, *La 'Commedia' senza Dio: Dante e la creazione di una realtà virtuale*, Mi, Feltrinelli, 381 pp., is an Italian version of her

The Undivine Comedy. Detheologizing Dante, Princeton U.P., 1992. I also note: Monica Cerroni, **Li versi strani: forme dell'allegoria nella Commedia di Dante*, Pisa, ETS, 209 pp., and Domenico Cofano, **La retorica del silenzio nella Divina Commedia*, Bari, Palomar, 121 pp.

INFERNO

General in scope is L. Battaglia Ricci, 'Per una lettura dell'Inferno. Strutture narrative e arte della memoria', *RSD*, 3:225–52, while F. Cacciafesta, 'Un'osservazione sulla geometria delle Malebolge', *LIA*, 4:397–400, considers two apparently contradictory *loci* of the *Inf.* regarding the shape and size of Malebolge, *Inf.* XVIII, 1–9, and *Inf.* XXX, 84–87. To resolve the *aporia*, C. argues in favour of a 'lezione erronea' in line 86: reading 'ventun' instead of 'undici' would in fact guarantee geometrical coherence.

Otherwise, contributions address individual cantos with more or less breadth of perspective. Dell'Aquila, *Nominanza*, included two previously published *lecturae*. In his reading of *Inf.* IV (9–25), D. believes that there is a clear progression in D.'s attitude towards the classics throughout the *DC*. Whereas his encounter with the Virtuous Infidels in Limbo shows a sort of humanistic awareness in exalting the glory of the great intellectuals of the past, in *Purg.* and *Par.* this same glory is in some sense belittled by the luminous glory of God. The *lectura* of *Inf.* X (26–43), summarizes traditional approaches to the canto of Farinata and then moves to a reassessment of the episode. It is the author's belief that the main functions of the drama staged by D. in this canto are moral and didactic. D.'s intent is to show the dangers of partisanship and political ideas for those who, like him, had been or were involved in political strife. M. Tavoni, *'Contributo sintattico al "disdegno" di Guido (*Inf.* X, 61–63). Con una nota sulla grammaticità e la leggibilità dei classici', Battaglia, *Dante*, 217–41. On the preceding canto, S. Barsella, 'The mercurial *integumentum* of the heavenly messenger (*Inferno, IX 79–103*)', *LIA*, 4:371–96, is an intricate and at times tortuous interpretation of the *messo celeste*. Bernardus Silvestris's criterion of *integumentum* provides the theoretical framework for an analysis which seeks to support Daniello's reading of the episode, i. e. that the messenger is a syncretistic figure bringing together the image of Mercury and that of an angel (the archangel Michael). B. offers additional iconographic evidence to support the existence of such syncretism in medieval culture. The paper also puts forward the hypothesis that the Horatian *Ode* XXIV is yet another literary source for the Dantean episode. S. Benini, '"Parole e sangue." Parola, fede e retorica in *Inferno* XIII', *L'Alighieri*, 22:69–82, is an interesting *lectura* which focuses on Pier delle Vigne's speech. The episode, in B.'s view, gave D. the possibility of investigating the difficult relationship between rhetoric, eloquence, and the language of Holy Scripture. B. shows how D. wished to demonstrate the shortcomings of rhetoric and eloquence, as opposed to the *sermo humilis* of the Bible. J. Stark, 'The Old Man of Crete', *FoI*, 37:5–19, believes that the importance and meaning of this symbolic figure can be explained by its relation to Rome and Damietta. The Old Man looks at the former and turns his back on the latter. In S.'s view, this incident is highly significant and strictly linked to the political stance of the *Monarchia*. Looking at the historical events that took place at Damietta in 1219 during the Fifth Crusade, S. deduces that they represented, in D.'s eyes, a striking example of the spiritual power meddling in secular affairs. In fact, the theme of the separation of the secular from the spiritual power is, in S.'s view, central to an understanding of the episode as a whole. J. Steinberg, 'Bankers in hell: the poetry of Monte Andrea in Dante's *Inferno* between historicism and historicity', *ISt*, 58:5–30, suggests the need to examine D.'s engagement, in *Inferno* (especially XVII, 118–21), with the lyrics of Monte Andrea in the light of the medieval reception of Monte's poetry. The notary public's work is skilfully analysed through a study of the physical aspects of the MS that transmits it, Vaticano latino 3793. The centrality of Monte's poetry in this MS clearly illustrates 'the significant role his poetry played for the emergent merchant-banker class' (6). D., on the other hand, was excluded from the collection, and S. concludes that in attacking Monte's poetry D. was not only criticizing the socio-political circumstances that 'dictated' the organization of the MS but, above all, seeking 'poetic legitimacy and literary authority' for himself (30).

Z. G. Barański, 'Scatology and obscenity in Dante', Barolini, *Dante*, 259–273, challenges traditional critical responses to *Inf.* XVIII which avoid its highly sexual and scatological elements. B. notes that whereas D. and his culture were not prepared to talk about the former they were more open towards the latter given the strong scatological elements present in the Bible. He considers much of the scatological imagery and language of *Inf.* XVIII to be biblical in origin. D.'s concern was to distinguish his divinely inspired work from the kind of 'low' sub-genres that treated the sexual and the excremental in an explicit manner for comical purposes. He, in contrast, rejected the 'false freedom of *turpiloqium*' (269). Having drawn attention to the linguistic preoccupations of this canto, B. moves on to consider medieval meditation on language and the *peccata linguae*. B. concludes that the *contrappassi* of the sinners in canto XVIII are 'moral assertion of the way in which their sinfulness had perverted the divine gift of speech' (270). This is put into stark contrast to the pilgrim's 'chiara favella' (*Inf.* XVIII, 53). D.'s language is the '*sermo purus* of the *prudens*' because he speaks when he ought to speak, that is to say he approaches language ethically and flexibly (272).

M. Picone, 'La carriera del libertino, Dante vs Rutebeuf (una lettura di *Inferno* XXII)', *L'Alighieri*, 21:77–94, is an interesting intertextual *lectura* which proposes original interpretations of several passages. P. believes that the poetry of the medieval French poet Rutebeuf is in fact the intertext that could help explain some of the obscurities of the canto. For instance, P. maintains that its main character, 'lo Navarrese', is to be identified with Rutebeuf himself. T. Keuker, 'L'acerbità di Vanni Fucci. Sul contrappasso del Caco dantesco', *LIA*, 4:401–06, considers D.'s presentation of the Virgilian character and compares it to St Augustine's. K. maintains that D. transformed Caco into a monstrous creature 'per mettere in opera il contrappasso da lui escogitato per il malfattore' (402). Caco in fact ardently desires companionship, but his horrible aspect precludes any possibility of social bonding. In the light of this, the disdain of Vanni Fucci, the man to whom Caco's attentions are directed, can be readily considered part of the punishment. Caco is *acerbo* (*Inf.* XXV, 15) because his soul is bitter, therefore, 'Dante [. . .] nega a Caco quella pace con se stesso che il ladro [according to Augustine] aveva, nel suo antro sull'Aventino, cercato e anche, in qualche misura, raggiunto' (406). E. Fenzi, 'Seneca e Dante: da Alessandro Magno a Ulisse', pp. 67–78 of *Studi sul Canone letterario del Trecento. Per Michelangelo Picone*, ed. J. Bartuschat and L. Rossi, Ravenna, Longo, sets out to demonstrate the fundamental influence of Seneca's writings on D.'s representation of Ulysses. Whereas Seneca's portrayal of Ulysses in the *Epistulae ad Lucilium*, LXXXVIII, 7, had little impact on D., F. believes that Seneca's representation of Alexander the Great may have shaped the infernal character. In particular, F. argues that D.'s Ulysses may have inherited the moral ambivalence of Seneca's Alexander.

A. Stazzone, '"Alla tua onta io porterò di te vere novelle": dérision et infamie dans le chant XXXII de l'*Enfer*', *Filigrana*, 7, 2002–03:9–32, considers how offence and derision in *Inf.* XXXII–XXXIV function as means of punishment. The study focuses on the 'offensive' techniques used by D. in *Inf.* XXXII and analyses the influences of contemporary painting on D.'s construction of the episode. C. Villa, 'Rileggere gli archetipi: la dismisura di Ugolino', Battaglia, *Dante*, 113–30, reads *Inf.* XXXII as an example of *renovatio* and *translatio* of the classics. The theme of Thebes and the myth of Tantalus shape the 'strutture significative' (123) of the canto, which 'renews' the tragic themes of starvation, hatred, cannibalism, and war, rewriting classical material in the process. V. Miele, *'La reazione della terra alla caduta di

Lucifero (*Inf.* XXXII, 121–126). Qualche appunto di carattere linguistico', Battaglia, *Dante*, 345–64.

PURGATORIO

Purg. has continued to attract a good number of studies. F. Bucci, 'Dante tra *iustificatio* e liturgia', *La Cultura*, 40, 2002 : 221–61, explores the liturgical dimension of D.'s journey through the afterlife, noting the sacred overtones of the imposition of Virgil's hands on D. in *Purg.* I, 120–29, as well as the liturgical meaning of the rite of purification which the pilgrim undergoes in lines 133–36, and considering these as the first steps in a *cursus rigenerationis* that ends in *Purg.*XXVII. The most important penitential 'stations' of the second *cantica* are brought to the fore in an interesting discussion which highlights the liturgical and catechetic aspects of D.'s process of *iustificatio impii.* E. Gragnolati and C. Holzey, 'Dolore come gioia. Trasformarsi nel *Purgatorio* di Dante', *Psiche*, 4 : 111–26, is a fascinating investigation, which analyses the nature and role of pain and suffering in *Purg.* within the context of changing 13th-c. attitudes towards pain. The authors conclude that 'è l'enfasi tardomedievale sull'umanità di Cristo e sulla sua passione a rendere possibile l'identificazione con Cristo al livello del corpo sofferente' (121). Joy becomes the result of the healing power of pain, so that pain, pleasure, and desire are all interwoven in D.'s representation of purgation.

Based on a close reading of the meteorological sections of *Purg.* V, A. Cornish, 'Vulgarizing science: vernacular translation of natural philosophy', Barolini, *Dante*, 169–82, shows how the *DC* could be regarded as an enterprise whose task was also that of vulgarizing natural science and make it available to D.'s original readers. Both R. M. Durling, 'The body and the flesh in the *Purgatorio*', *ib.*, 183–91, and E. Gragnolati, 'From plurality to (near) unicity of forms: embryology in *Purgatorio* 25', *ib.*, 192–210, look at the concept of the body in the *Commedia.* In a discussion focusing mainly on the first terrace of *Purg.* (cantos X–XII), D. highlights the importance of the bodily presence of the pilgrim for the successful completion of his journey. G., on the other hand, considers the difficult question of the formation of the airy bodies of the souls as described in *Pur.* XXV. Busnelli believed that D.'s idea of the generation of the soul was essentially Thomistic; Nardi, on the other hand, was convinced of D.'s independence on Aquinas. G. argues that D. deliberately left the matter unresolved or ambiguous and that the poet draws both from Bonaventure's and Aquinas's theories. There can be no doubt, according to G., about the importance D. attributed to the resurrected body. On a similar topic, V. Bartoli and P. Ureni, 'Controversie medico-biologiche in tema di generazione umana nel XXV del *Purgatorio*', *StD*, 68:83–111, examines lines 37–78 of *Purg.* XXV to discuss the problem of the generation of the soul and its embryological, philosophical, and theological implications.

Also relating to individual cantos are: M. Durante, *'Sul canto XI del *Purgatorio*', *StD*, 68:49–66, a *lectura* held in December 2002 at the Società Dantesca Italiana in Florence; A. Battistini, 'La "speranza de l'altezza". La retorica patetica in *Purgatorio* XII', *L'Alighieri*, 21:95–108, looking at the canto in relation to preaching's three aims, 'docere', 'delectare', and 'movere', and concluding that its formal complexity serves D.'s purpose of persuasion; L. H. Howard, 'Virgil the blind guide in *Purgatorio* XV–XVI and *Purgatorio* XXII–XXIII', *LIA*, 4:407–19; and for c. XXII M. Palma di Cesnola, 'La figlia di Tiresia', pp. 71–140 of his *Questioni dantesche*, already cit. under MINOR WORKS, where, following his essay on the Manto of *Inf.* XX (see *YWMLS*, 63:408), he suggests that the *Thebaid* itself holds the key to the episode of Statius's conversion to Christianity. Cantos XXIV–XXVI are at the centre of four articles. F. Brugnolo, 'Appendice a Cino (e Onesto) dentro e fuori la *Commedia*. Ancora sull'intertesto di *Purgatorio* XXIV, 49–63, Battaglia, *Dante*, 153–70, maintains that the memory of two sonnets by Cino da Pistoia and Onesto da Bologna underlies D.'s *terzine* on the 'dolce stil nuovo'. The sonnets are reproduced in an appendix. L. Peirone, 'Miglior fabbro del parlar materno', *EL*, 28.1:87–91, is a brief note on the semantics of 'fabbro' (*Purg.* XXVI, 117), which clarifies how the term, in this instance, is equivalent to the more general 'artista' and does not refer to any specific art or sector of the arts. F. Sberlati, 'Maestri e amici nel XXVI del *Purgatorio*', *SPCT*, 65, 2002:89–132, is a very dense and interesting study of the intertextual threads that enrich the canto. In particular, S. believes that the rhythmic pattern of lines 20, 22, and 24 are references to the rhetorical strategies of Cavalcanti's poetry. Linguistic, rhythmic, and stylistic analyses of the canto also bring to light D.'s intention to compare and contrast his poetry with the works of Guinizzelli, Guittone, and the troubadours. E. Fenzi, 'Dopo l'edizione Sanguineti: dubbi e proposte per *Purg.*, XXIV, 57', *StD*, 68:67–82, discusses the plausibility and consequences of Sanguineti's new reading of line 57 of *Purg.* XXIV, which upsets the historiography of early Italian literature and our understanding of the 'dolce stil nuovo'.

A. A. Iannucci, 'Already and not yet: Dante's existential eschatology', Barolini, *Dante*, 334–48, examines the apocalyptic overtones of the episode that unfolds in *Purg.* XXVIII–XXXIII and argues, on the basis of his view of eschatology, that although Dante 'participated in the millennial anxiety of his time, he did not embrace it' (p. 337).

Subsequently, I. offers an overview of the sources of D.'s eschatological thought, which range from St Paul to Thomas Aquinas. J. Nohrnberg, 'The autobiographical imperative and the necessity of Dante: *Purgatorio* 30.55', *MP*, 101:1–47, is a lengthy investigation into the different reasons that motivated D. to spell his own name in the Earthly Paradise. Each of its nine sections considers different reasons: historical, rhetorical, social, religious, cultural, eschatological, political, spiritual, and authorial. The conclusion of this at times rather confusing analysis is that 'the naming of his person is tantamount to the rebirth of his [D.'s] soul' (39): the 'reclamation of his eternal life' is strictly related to the 'textual apotheosis of the poet's name', which 'represents the individual's reclaiming of the author-function' (39).

PARADISO

S. Botterill, 'Mysticism and meaning in Dante's *Paradiso*', Barolini, *Dante*, 143–51, is an engaging reflection on the nature of D.'s mysticism. B. considers the reasons that have led Cupitt to exclude Dante from the canon of mystical writers and shows how fundamentally wrong they are. M. Marietti, 'L'agnello al centro', *ib.*, 435–44, offers a very competent analysis of the metaphors 'lupi rapaces' and 'agnus mansuetus' in *Paradiso*. M. shows how D.'s self-representation as the lamb who has been unjustly expelled from the 'bello ovile'(xxv, 5) puts him on a par with Jeremiah, whose figure 'è assunta in filigrana a modello, dando luogo ad un vero e proprio processo di identificazione' (438). After a complex numerological analysis of *Par.* xiv–xix, which brings together D. poet-prophet and Henry VII, M. concludes that, having lost all hope of returning to Florence, the only biblical model left to D. was David and his *teodia*. M. Ariani, ' "e sí come di lei bevve la gronda / de le palpebre mie" (*Par.* xxx, 88): Dante e lo Pseudo Dionigi Areopagita', Battaglia, *Dante*, 131–52, is a significant essay which aims at discovering a close interdiscursive and intertextual relationship between the *corpus* of Pseudo-Dionysus and a narrative sequence of the *Paradiso*. A. investigates the doctrine of the spiritual senses as found in a tradition which, starting with Origen and ending with St Bernard and Bonaventure, passed through the mediation of Pseudo-Dionysus. In *Par.* xxx, 88, A. finds a metaphorical typology which derives from Dionysus, but is also common in the texts of the medieval mystics. The article concludes that 'la possibile lettura del corpus pseudodionisiano permetteva a Dante di valorizzare [. . .] tutta una *traditio* di immagini, metafore, simboli che venivano a costituire i motivi formali stessi della scrittura paradisiaca' (151).

For individual cantos or episodes I note: M. Picone, '*Paradiso VIII*: il principe e il poeta', *LIA*, 4:421–34, a learned and articulate *lectura* of the encounter between D. and Charles Martel, focusing on their friendship, and the role of love in their lives, and also supporting some unfashionable yet perfectly reasonable interpretations such as (ll. 76–78) Torraca's: 'se Roberto riflettesse su quanto accaduto in Sicilia, già fuggirebbe quella sua avarizia degna di un catalano'. Three essays examine the complex narrative of the Heaven of the Sun as well as the philosophical and theological sympathies embedded in this episode of the *Commedia*. G. Mazzotta, 'Dante between Aquinas and Bonaventure', Barolini, *Dante*, 152–68, is a lucid and valuable investigation into D.'s philosophical-theological thought and his concept of wisdom. M. shows how, through the pilgrim's encounter with Saint Bonaventure and Saint Aquinas, D. confronts the major theological tendencies of his time, but 'he goes beyond them[. . .] By his poetry he opens up new vistas for theology' (167–68). R. Herzman, 'From Francis to Solomon: eschatology in the Sun', *ib.*, 321–33, pleasingly discusses the role of St Francis and Solomon in the heaven of the Sun and in the whole *DC*. According to H., St Francis fulfils *in bono* the apocalyptic events of *Purg.* XXXII, given that his marriage with Lady Poverty subverts the union between the papacy and wealth portrayed in the last cantos of *Purg.* Solomon, on the other hand, is celebrated as the author of the Book of Wisdom, which was believed to have engaged with the nature of Creation, the Incarnation and the Trinity, the fundamental notions that bring D., and indeed his readers, to the completion of the journey. M. Veglia, 'Da Sigieri al "venerabile Bernardo". Su *Par.*, X–XI', *StD*, 68:113–29, is a discussion of the way in which D. characterizes Boethius, Sigieri, and St Bernard in the heaven of the Sun. In particular, he looks at Boethius's 'pace', Sigieri's 'morir' and at the 'povertà' of Bernard. After considering issues relating to the structure of the entire episode (cantos XVIII–XX) and the symbolic meaning of the eagle that addresses D., B. Martinelli, 'La fede in Cristo. Dante e il problema della salvezza (*Paradiso* XIX)', *RLettI*, 20.2, 2002:11–39, looks at the biblical bearings of canto XIX. In particular, M. points out an interesting parallelism between the questions and answers that D. and the Eagle exchange and those exchanged by Job and God. M. notes, moreover, that D.'s questions are structured like a scholastic *quaestio*, whereas the answers of the eagle are founded on Christian theology and the Bible. S. Valerio, 'Lingua, retorica e poetica nel canto XXVI del *Paradiso*', *L'Alighieri*, 22:83–104, is a *lectura* of *Par.* XXVI which looks at the structural coherence and unity of the canto.

DUECENTO II (EXCLUDING DANTE)

POSTPONED

HUMANISM AND THE RENAISSANCE

By Nadia Cannata Salamone, *Università per Stranieri di Siena*

(This survey covers the years 2002 and 2003 for poetry and the theatre. The other three sub-sections are again postponed)

1. Poetry

Quondam, *Canone*, the *acta* of the fifth conference of ADI (Associazione degli Italianisti Italiani), contains several contributions on Renaissance poetry, ranging from general overviews on the canon and vernacular literature (Santagata), on ancients and moderns in baroque poetry (Guaragnella), women (Wood), as well as essays on specific authors or works: the Giuntina of 1527 (Vecchi Galli) and Tasso (Ardissino, Ruggiero). Two volumes in which some of Dionisotti's fundamental contributions on Renaissance poetry are republished have appeared lately, either with valuable explanatory notes, or just to make newly available Dionisotti's work: Carlo Dionisotti, *Scritti sul Bembo*, ed. Claudio Vela, T, Einaudi, 2002, xlviii + 277 pp., and *Boiardo e altri studi cavallereschi*, ed. Giuseppe Anceschi and Antonia Tissoni Benvenuti, Novara, Interlinea, 231 pp. Arnaldo Di Benedetto, *Poesia e comportamento. Da Lorenzo il Magnifico a Campanella*, Alessandria, Orso, 2002, 200 pp., collects 12 essays on Lorenzo, Niccolò da Correggio, Berni, Castiglione's *Cortegiano*, Della Casa's *Galateo* and other Cinquecento treatises on behaviour, and Tasso and the pastoral genre. Giulia Dell'Aquila, *La tradizione del testo. Studi su Cellini, Beni e altra letteratura*, Pisa, Giardini, 196 pp., is a useful collection of very recent critical studies which have appeared in various periodicals, mostly concerned with Paolo Beni and Cellini, but also dealing with Cinquecento Petrarchism and Muratori. Claudio Gigante, *Esperienze di filologia cinquecentesca. Salviati, Mazzoni, Trissino, Costo, il Bargeo, Tasso*, Ro, Salerno, 266 pp., collects several essays on the authors mentioned in the title. Relevant to this survey are the contributions on genesis and narrative structure in the epic poetry of Trissino, Costo, and Bargeo, and the second part of the volume entirely devoted to the textual history of the *Messaggiero*, the *Conquistata*, and its *Giudicio*, which afford new materials for the evaluation of the last phase of Tasso's poetry.

Similarly adopting a history of culture standpoint in her approach to research on the genre is Jane Everson, ' "Read what I say and not what I read": reading and the romance epic in fifteenth-century Ferrara', *ISt*, 58: 31–47, which identifies an interesting discrepancy between the ideal library as described in Decembrio's *Politiae Litterariae* and the Este library, which shows, conversely, a marked inclination towards romance literature in the everyday practice of reading. This trend is implicitly confirmed by evidence showing that towards the mid 16th c. chivalric epic and romances in the vernacular were indeed recommended as readers for schoolchildren. Italo Pantani, *'La fonte d'ogni eloquenzia'. Il canzoniere petrarchesco nella cultura poetica del Quattrocento ferrarese*, Ro, Bulzoni, 2002, 467 pp., is a very thorough survey of Quattrocento Petrarchism in Ferrara where the author (*rara avis*), setting out from the Trecento, also brings Latin verse into the argument in order to permit a comprehensive and coherent definition of this literary phenomenon. A rich and noteworthy anthology of verse by Petrarchan women poets (Gambara, Colonna, D'Aragona, Matraini, Terracina, Morra, Stampa, Battiferri, Franco, and Andreini), with updated bibliography and notes which may prove useful tools for the study of a topic which has recently enjoyed a welcome revival, is *Poetesse italiane del Cinquecento*, ed. Stefano Bianchi, introd. Giovanni Macchia, Mi, Mondadori, 234 pp. A useful collection of essays for the 16th-c. history of the anthology is **I più vaghi e soavi fiori: studi sulle antologie di lirica del Cinquecento*, ed. Monica Bianco and Elena Strada, Alessandria, Orso, 2001, xii + 208 pp.

Stefano Jossa, *La fondazione di un genere. Il poema eroico fra Ariosto e Tasso*, Ro, Carocci, 2002, 258 pp., surveys the narrative poetry produced between the times of Ariosto and Tasso (Trissino, Alamanni, Giraldi Cinzio, Bolognetti, Bernardo Tasso, and Giovan Battista Pigna) with a view to identifying the rhetorical structure of the genre and its itinerary from romance to heroic poem. Francesco Sberlati, **Il genere e la disputa: la poetica tra Ariosto e Tasso*, Ro, Bulzoni, 2001, 455 pp. Marco Praloran, *Il poema in ottava: storia linguistica italiana*, Ro, Carocci, 132 pp., is an anthology with individual commentaries on excerpts from Pulci, Boiardo, Ariosto, and Bernardo and Torquato Tasso, mainly intended for teaching purposes. Raffaele Morabito, 'Le lettere del *Cansonero* del conte di Popoli', *La Cultura*, 41 : 101–28, publishes 18 letters from the famous verse collection, one of the most important documents of 15th-c. Neapolitan poetry. The letters may prove instrumental for the historical interpretation of that document as well as for the history of early Renaissance poetry and book production. Giorgio Forni, *Forme brevi della poesia. Tra umanesimo e rinascimento*, Pisa, Pacini, 2001, xix + 259 pp., deals with a generally neglected sub-genre of lyric poetry falling outside the Bembian canon, and thus affords an extremely useful contribution to the study of Renaissance Petrarchism, surveying documents which normally receive only a passing mention when they are not altogether ignored. *Scrittura religiosa. Forme letterarie dal Trecento al Cinquecento*, ed. Carlo Del Corno e Maria Luisa

Doglio, Bo, Il Mulino, 2002, 170 pp., affords a literary and critical analysis of late medieval and early Renaissance religious writing extending from Giordano da Pisa's *prediche* to the high Cinquecento. The volume also contains an essay by G. Forni on the material qualities of the book of prayers 1530–70. M. Chiesa, 'Poemi biblici fra Quattro e Cinquecento', *GSLI*, 179, 2002, 161–92, urges the case for a census of epic poems written on biblical subject matter during the Renaissance. He deals exclusively with works in the vernacular that have a narrative structure (i.e. excluding translation from the Psalms and the like). The essays forms a preliminary survey of the material and its public, and also of the general cultural context in which the texts were received. Stefano Prandi, 'Letteratura e pietà (secc. XIII-XVI), *LItal*, 55:494–518, surveys the theme of piety as a means used by writers to define their literary identity. The article touches upon Guittone, Dante (both *Rime* and *Commedia*), Petrarch, Machiavelli, and Tasso, the only author to devote a whole treatise to piety.

Among volumes devoted to general issues but which also have a bearing on poetry, the *acta* of a conference on commentaries deserve mention. *Intorno al testo. Tipologie del corredo esegetico e soluzioni editoriali. Atti del convegno di Urbino*, Ro, Salerno, 584 pp., chiefly concerns Dante commentaries, but deals also with *cantari*, and in general with commentaries by and on individual authors and with their presentation and function. The parodic use of the commentary was the subject of a conference (Viterbo 2001), the proceedings of which were published as: **Cum notibusse et commentaribusse: l'esegesi parodistica e giocosa del Cinquecento*, ed. Antonio Corsaro and Paolo Procaccioli, Manziana, Vecchiarelli, 2002, 327 pp. On similar territory was **La fantasia fuor de' confini: Burchiello e dintorni a 550 anni dalla morte (1449–1999). Atti del Convegno, Firenze, 25 novembre 1999*, Ro, Storia e Letteratura, 2001[2002], xix + 260 pp.

As for relations between the arts, Claudio Scarpati, *Leonardo scrittore*, Mi, Vita e Pensiero, 2001, 263 pp., highlights the active presence, in Leonardo's writing, of an intense intertextual dialogue with the major texts of the Italian vernacular poetic and literary tradition, of substantial significance not only for Leonardo's writing, but — even more importantly perhaps — for the history of Renaissance culture with its complex and rich humus of contributions belonging to all fields of the arts. An interdisciplinary study on gender ambiguity in philosophy and the fine arts and its reflection and role in Renaissance comedy is to be found in Luciano Bottoni, *Leonardo e l'androgino. L'eros transessuale nella cultura, nella pittura e nel teatro del Rinascimento*, Mi, Angeli, 2002, 126 pp.

On miscellaneous minor figures or episodes: Simona Periti, 'L'edizione miscominiana della *Compagnia del mantellaccio* ed altre "giunte e correzioni" fiorentine a IGI', *MR*, 17, n.s. 14: 281–306, is a valuable bibliographical essay identifying two different editions of the *Compagnia del Mantellaccio*, both *sine notis*, but datable around 1492 and 1494, and attributing two further editions of vernacular verse to Bartolomeo dei Libri and four to the printing press of Morgiani & Petri. An excerpt from the translation of Lorenzo's *Canti Carnascialeschi* by Anthony Oldcorn, with a brief introduction, appears in *ParL*, 45–46–47: 70–97. Alessio Decaria, 'Spigolature manettiane. Spunti biografici da due liriche volgari', *Interpres*, 21, 2002: 253–85, illustrates some hitherto unknown details concerning Manetti's life and shows the two poems not to have been written by Manetti. T. Leuker, 'Ad Alessandro Cortesi rimasto in Italia. Un sonetto fiorentino (e non milanese) di Bernardo Bellincioni', *ib.*, 286–90, again provides a small but interesting detail on the author's writings. D. Chiodo, 'Di alcune curiose chiose a un esemplare delle *Rime* di Gandolfo Porrino custodito nel fondo Cian', *GSLI*, 180: 86–101, illustrates some interesting explanatory notes on the manuscript copy of the poems of an author closely associated with Molza, but who never enjoyed much critical attention. Editions of texts not mentioned below but which have been made newly available to scholars are as follows: Raniero Almerici da Pesaro, *Rime: Ravenna, Biblioteca Classense cod. 240*, ed. Nella Cacace Saxby, Bo, CTL, lxxxiii + 217 pp.; Luigi Cassola, *Il canzoniere del codice vaticano Capponiano 74*, ed. and comm. M. Giuliano Bellorini, Piacenza, TipLeCo, 2002, xxviii + 173 pp.; Galeazzo di Tarsia, *Canzoniere*, ed. Pasquino Crupi, Soveria Mannelli, Rubbettino, 2002, 120 pp., and also the anthology of poetry in Calabrese dialect *Rimatori del XV secolo: Roda, Coletta, Maurello*, ed. Pasquino Crupi, Soveria Mannelli, Rubbettino, 2002, 134 pp. A small bibliographical curiosity is the edition of *Cani di pietra: l'epicedio canino nella poesia del Rinascimento*, ed. Cristiano Spila, trans. Maria Gabriella Critelli and Cristiano Spila, Ro, Quiritta, 2002, xxxii + 94 pp., which collects Latin poems, mostly epigrams, on the death of dogs, preserved in Vatican MS collections.

INDIVIDUAL AUTHORS

ARIOSTO. *Ariosto Today. Contemporary Perspectives*, ed. Donald Beecher, Massimo Ciavolella, and Roberto Fedi, Toronto U.P., xi + 238 pp., assembles 11 essays — only one, by E. Weaver, already published — which range from analysing the cultural context in Ferrara (Looney, Franceschetti, Masi) to Ariosto's theatre and *Rime* (Bianchi and Fedi), the *Furioso*, its history, structure, and narrative devices (Casadei,

Farnetti, Javitch, Weaver), and modern readings and interpretations of Ariosto's masterpiece (Re on Calvino's relationship with A. and Bernardi on Luca Ronconi's theatre version of the *Furioso*). *Fra satire e rime ariostesche (Gargnano del Garda, 14–16 ottobre 1999)*, ed. Claudia Berra, introd. Cesare Segre, Mi, Cisalpino, 2000, 592 pp., the papers of a conference organized by Milan University's Dipartimento di Filologia Moderna, forms an analytical survey of Ariosto's poetry. Various contributions deal with the *Satire*; for the *Rime*, C. Bozzetti analyses the 48 poems preserved in Vatican MS Rossiano 639, C. Vela surveys previous contributions by Bozzetti himself, A. Comboni puts Ariosto's poetry in the context of lyric poetry in the *corti padane*, and S. Carrai discusses classicism in the *Rime*. Along similar lines are P. Vecchi Galli, 'Fra Ariosto e Tebaldeo: a proposito del capitolo XXVI "or che la terra di bei fiori è piena"' (355–78), C. Zampese, 'Presenze intertestuali nelle rime dell'Ariosto' (457–78), and M. Malinverni, 'Per una notte luminosa: fortuna di un topos da Properzio ad Ariosto' (499–513). On links between the *Rime* and the *Furioso* there are contributions by M. C. Cabani and R. Rinaldi. Ludovico Ariosto, *Satire*, ed. Alfredo D'Orto, Mi, Fond. Pietro Bembo – Parma, Guanda, 2002, lxxiv + 222 pp., publishes a new commentary on the *Satire* identifying the the *Furioso*'s dominant theme, the folly of love and its relation to the human condition, as that which also guarantees the cohesion of the *Satire*, where it is treated with just the same indulgence evident in the poem. L'Arioste, *Les Satires*, ed. and trans. Michel Paoli, Grenoble, ELLUG, 156 pp.

R. Ricci, 'La risemantizzazione del viaggio dantesco nell'*Orlando Furioso* fra allusione e parodia', *MC*, n.s., 1, 2002:35–55, is an interesting, if not original, reassessment of Ariosto's debt to Dante, with particular reference to his linguistic orientation. Similarly useful, albeit not ground-breaking, is L. Sannia Nowé, '*Bosco*, *foresta*, *selva* nell'*Orlando Furioso*. Indagine sulla parola ariostesca', *LingLett*, 28:15–32, an article in which the author indicates — on the basis of certain aspects of Ariosto's lexical usage — how the poet succeeded in building an intertextual discourse where the medieval and classical traditions blend into an entirely new literary model. H. Honnacker, 'Il κόσμος morale illustrato nei prologhi dell'*Orlando Furioso* di Ludovico Ariosto nelle edizioni del 1516 e del 1521: la *Weltanschauung* ariostesca fra Orazio ed Erasmo', *ib.*, 33–55, identifies Ariosto's debts towards two of his sources without, however, delving particularly deeply into them. Also on the *Furioso*: Marco Marangoni, **In forma di teatro: elementi teatrali nell'Orlando furioso*, Ro, Carocci, 2002, 126 pp., and for the *Cinque canti* we note Stella Larosa, *Poesia e cronologia nei Cinque canti: una nuova ipotesi*, Rende, University of Calabria, 2001, 205 pp.

BEMBO. *SFI*, 60, 2002, publishes two important contributions on Bembo's lyric poetry: T. Zanato, 'Indagine sulle *Rime* di Pietro Bembo' (141–216), a thorough and painstaking philological and critical study of the manuscript 1543 of the Bibliothèque Nationale, with an appendix of 16 newly edited texts; and A. Gnocchi, 'Un manoscritto delle *Rime* di Pietro Bembo (ms. L. 1347–1957, KRP. A. 19 del Victoria and Albert Museum di Londra)' (217–36), which contains a thorough description of the manuscript and reveals that Bembo worked for a long time on a form of *canzoniere* rather different from the one he was eventually to publish. Pietro Bembo, *Stanze*, ed. Alessandro Gnocchi, F, Società Editrice Fiorentina, clvi + 121 pp.

BOIARDO. Hard on the heels of the excellent critical edition Matteo Maria Boiardo, *Amorum Libri Tres*, ed. Tiziano Zanato, Ro, Storia e Letteratura, 2002, 318 pp., comes the volume *Gli 'Amorum Libri' e la lirica del Quattrocento. Con altri studi boiardeschi*, ed. Antonia Tissoni Benvenuti, Novara, Interlinea, 262 pp., gathering essays on the verse collection in relation to contemporary poetry and the *stilnovo*, to its metrical forms and to Boiardo's other works. *Schifanoja*, 22–23, 2002, groups several articles on Boiardo's poem, including: D. Boccassini, 'I libri di Orlando: saggezza ed erranza in Boiardo' (7–25), chiefly dealing with the narrative construction of the *Orlando*, and M. Villoresi, 'Boiardo e la produzione cavalleresca di consumo. Qualche riflessione a margine del nuovo commento a *L'Inamoramento de Orlando*' (27–30), centring on more general questions concerning the genre as such and, by extension, the cultural history of the Quattrocento.

CALMO. Andrea Calmo, *Le bizzarre, faconde e ingegnose rime pescatorie*, ed. Gino Belloni, Venice, Marsilio, 259 pp.

CARITEO. Beatrice Barbiellini Amidei, 'Il sogno nell'*Endimione* di Cariteo', *PaT*, 7:337–54, argues that in order to shed light on this complex author it is of vital importance to retrace the intertextual network of allusions to his neo-Platonic, humanistic, and classical culture, particularly evident in his treatment of the theme of dreams. Also by the same author see the article, 'L'età dell'oro nel Cariteo', pp. 221–37 of *Millenarismo ed età dell'oro nel Rinascimento. Atti del XIII Convegno Internazionale (Chianciano–Montepulciano–Pienza, 16–19 luglio 2001)*, ed. Lucia Secchi Tarugi, F, Cesati.

CASONI. We note the near-contemporaneous publication of two editions, the first following scholarly criteria, the second aiming at a more general public, of a Treviso poet's interesting love-treatise: Guido Casoni, *Della magia d'amore* ed. Elisabetta Selmi, T, Res, 2002, 174 pp., and *Della magia d'amore*, ed. Armando Maggi, Palermo, Sellerio, 203 pp.

CHIABRERA. L. Zuliani, 'Sull'origine delle innovazioni metriche di Gabriello Chiabrera', *SMI*, 3:91–128, reviews the sources in Quattrocento poetry of the innovations in Italian metrics (such as the use of short lines, *rime tronche*, *versi parisillabi* and so on) made acceptable and ultimately established by Chiabrera's poetry.

COLONNA. A. Brundin, 'Vittoria Colonna and the poetry of reform', *ISt*, 57, 2002:61–74, seeks to demonstrate that in the early 1540s Vittoria Colonna was working on a new form of *canzoniere spirituale* which turns away from the self-centredness of the Petrarchan model to address more contemporary and pressing spiritual issues.

COSMICO. Niccolò Lelio Cosmico, *Le Cancion*, ed. Silvia Alga, pref. G. Bárberi Squarotti, T, Res, xxiv + 118 pp., edits a work much read in the Quattrocento, the 18 *capitoli in terza rima* of the Paduan poet, written before his adoption of a more 'orthodox' (linguistically and thematically speaking) form of Petrarchan imitation. D. Chiodo, 'L'amico, l'ancella e il petrarchismo (?) di Niccolò Lelio Cosmico', *GSLI*, 180:260–65, reviews some critical assumptions about the poet and successfully challenges them in the light of the new critical text of his *Cancion*.

DELLA CASA. Giovanni Della Casa *Rime*, ed. Stefano Carrai, T, Einaudi, xxxvii + 272 pp., is an impeccable critical edition in which the 78 compositions are edited, commented upon, and each provided with an extensive introduction. The volume also includes an updated bibliography, a table of metrical forms, and cross references for all the authors and texts quoted in the poems. I also note the slightly earlier edition: Giovanni Della Casa, **Rime*, ed. Giuliano Tanturli, Mi, Fond. Pietro Bembo – Parma, Guanda, 2001, lviii + 242 pp.

MICHELANGELO. Claudio Scarpati, 'Michelangelo poeta dal *canzoniere* alle rime spirituali', *Aevum*, 77:593–613, analyses imitation and innovation within the literary tradition in Michelangelo's *Rime* and his gift for forcing his literary inheritance towards a unique near-expressionist style. Richard Bonanno, 'Sculptural form and the love theme in Michelangelo's *Rime*', *IQ*, 155–156: 5–16, notices a fusion, in M.'s poetry, of the formal, theoretical, and thematic elements of his painting, poetry, and sculpture.

POLIZIANO. Angelo Poliziano, *Due poemetti latini. Elegia a Bartolomeo Fonzio, epicedio di Albiera degli Albizzi*, ed. Francesco Bausi, Ro, Salerno, lvi + 132 pp., is a critical edition of the two poems (written around 1473) from a leading Poliziano scholar. The editor also provides Italian translations of the two texts. C. Storey, 'Ficino, Poliziano, and *Le stanze per la giostra*', *MLR*, 98:602–19, subjects P.'s 'Ficinian Platonism' in the *Stanze* to fresh scrutiny. Carlo Enrico Roggia, **La materia e il lavoro: studio linguistico sul Poliziano minore*, pref. Pier Vincenzo Mengaldo, F, Crusca, 2001, 275 pp.

PRODENZANI. Simone de' Prodenzani, *Rime*, ed. crit. Fabio Carboni, 2 vols, Manziana, Vecchiarelli, cxlix + 696 pp., and Simone de' Prodenzani, *Opere inedite in poesia e prosa*, ed. Massimo Seriacopi, Genoa, San Marco dei Giustiniani, 60 pp.

SERAFINO AQUILANO. Serafino Aquilano, *Strambotti*, ed. Antonio Rossi, Parma, Guanda – Fond. Pietro Bembo, 2002, cxix + 586 pp., makes available, now in an impeccable edition provided with an excellent introduction, a rich commentary and a painstaking analysis of the textual problems posed by the text of Serafino's *Strambotti*. The book also includes, though not in a critical edition, Colocci's *Apologia delle rime di Serafino aquilano*, a fundamental document for the early *questione della lingua*, which hitherto was only available in Menghini's edition dating back to 1894.

TANSILLO. Erika Milburn, *Luigi Tansillo and Lyric Poetry in Sixteenth-Century Naples*, Leeds, Maney/MHRA, x + 227 pp., a useful monograph, has chapters on the textual tradition and critical reception of T.'s works, on the structure and evolution of the various collections, on T.'s use of non-Petrarchan lexis in relation to reactions to Bembo's *Prose della volgar lingua* and contemporary Neapolitan theories of neologism, and on T.'s treatment of the theme of jealousy. Alien to earlier Petrarchism, this theme is also studied in the same author's '"D'invidia e d'amor figlia sì ria": jealousy and the Italian Renaissance lyric', *MLR*, 97, 2002: 577–91, highlighting the importance of Sannazaro's example in the proliferation of jealousy poems after 1530 and dwelling especially on the figure of T.

TASSO. Maria Luisa Doglio, *Origini e icone del mito di Torquato Tasso*, Ro, Bulzoni, 2002, 120 pp., collects three papers ('Tasso architetto dell'epica poesia nel dialogo di Camillo Pellegrino'; 'Tasso "principe della moderna poesia" nei discorsi accademici di Paolo Beni'; 'Tasso o "l'intelletto sempre luminoso" che vince le tenebre della malinconia nella *Vita* di Guido Casoni') delivered between 1995 and 2000 for the fourth centenary of Tasso's death. They are the outcome of Doglio's passionate but meticulous research on Tasso and are presented in a very cogent and useful introduction entitled 'L'immagine di se stesso. Tasso primo artefice del suo mito'. Emilio Russo, *L'ordine, la fantasia e l'arte. Ricerche per un quinquennio tassiano (1588–1592)*, Ro, Bulzoni, 2002, 302 pp., contributes insights into Tasso's later years, after his release from Sant'Anna, pointing to his growing interest in spiritual elevation as well as his impressive theoretical effort in support of his works: of particular interest, in R.'s analysis, are T.'s annotations to the so-called *Giuntina delle rime antiche* of 1527 and his *Discorsi del poema eroico*. *Sul Tasso. Studi di filologia e letteratura italiana offerti a Luigi Poma*, ed. Franco Gavazzeni, Ro–Padua, Antenore, 728 pp., collects the latest work of an group of scholars, linked to Luigi Poma, dealing with

T. from different perspectives over a wide range of themes: the *Rime* and the critical edition thereof, the *Aminta*, various aspects of the *Gerusalemme*, the *Satire*, and the critical attention devoted to T. by Apostolo Zeno, Leopardi, and Monti. Antonio Corsaro, *Percorsi dell'incredulità. Religione, amore, natura nel primo Tasso*, Ro, Salerno, 250 pp., a collection of essays already published in part, is a journey into the religious and philosophical convictions and contradictions troubling Tasso in his later years. *'Nel mondo mutabile e leggero'. Torquato Tasso e la cultura del suo tempo*, ed. Dante Della Terza, Pasquale Sabbatino, and Giuseppina Scognamiglio, Na, ESI, 194 pp., forms a general survey of T.'s writing in relation to the different genres in which he engaged and seeks to define the rationale underlying and linking his various literary choices. L. Borsetto, 'Commentare la *Gerusalemme*. Dall'esegesi a stampa al progetto della lettura ipertestuale', pp. 129–44 of *Il commento e i suoi dintorni*, ed. Bianca Maria Da Rif, con una nota di Guido Capovilla, Mi, Guerini, 2002, discusses the great advantages afforded by hypertext, use of which could provide a flexible system of reference in commentaries on the poem. G. Baldassarre, 'Dall'officina del commento tassiano: notizie e anticipazioni', *ib.*, 145–55, puts forward further suggestions for the publication of such commentares. R. Gigliucci, 'Materiali per la lettura del IX canto della *Liberata*', *PaT*, 6, 2002, 171–98, based on a Tasso reading delivered at the University of Padua, discusses the narrative function of the canto and the poetic devices used in the attempt to rewrite and reinterpret earlier poetic traditions. Maria Teresa Girardi, *Tasso e la nuova Gerusalemme. Studio sulla 'Conquistata' e sul 'Giudicio'*, Napoli, ESI, 2002, 286 pp., is a detailed study of the relationship between the *Liberata* and the *Conquistata* with a close analysis of the latter's genesis and composition. F. Ferretti, '*Quasi in un picciolo mondo dantesco*: allegoria e finzione nella *Liberata*', *LItal*, 55: 169–95, is an interesting exploration of the *Liberata* in search of the relationship between linguistic and literary signs and their real significance for the poet. *Borsellino Vol.* also contains contributions of interest for T.'s poetry: F. Pignatti, 'Le morti di Argante e Solimano: indagini intertestuali sulla *Liberata*' (307–34); and B. Alfonzetti, '*Oh vani giuramenti!* Tragico ed eroico in Tasso e Trissino' (355–86). For T.'s reworkings of metrical solutions afforded by near contemporaries, see R. Pestarino, ' "Nel numero di coloro che si lasciano cader le brache . . .". Scrupoli metrici tra Tansillo e Tasso', *SMI*, 3: 3–18, and M. C. Cabani, 'L'ariostismo mediato della *Gerusalemme Liberata*', *ib.*, 19–90.

On T.'s reception and influence, I note: Clara Borrelli, **Su Tasso e il tassismo tra Cinquecento e Ottocento*, Na, L'Orientale, 2001, 150 pp. The third 2003 issue of *Lettere italiane*, which is entirely devoted to the memory of Giovanni Getto, contains a survey of the deceased scholar's contributions on Tasso: M. L. Doglio, 'Getto e Tasso', *ib.*, 55:361–73.

2. Theatre

La maschera e il volto. Il teatro in Italia, ed. Francesco Bruni, Venice, Marsilio, 2002, ix + 497 pp., groups 23 lectures delivered in 2001 at the Fondazione Cini and ranging from 15th-c. *sacre rappresentazioni* to contemporary theatre. Some important contributions on Renaissance, and especially Venetian, theatre appear in the commemorative *Ricordo di Giorgio Padoan*, ed. Gino Belloni, Padua, Il Poligrafo, 112 pp. Contributions on late Renaissance and baroque theatre are also to be found in the Festschrift *Granteatro. Omaggio a Franca Angelini*, ed. Beatrice Alfonsetti, Daniela Quarta, and Mirella Saulini, Ro, Bulzoni, 2002, 591 pp. Renaissance theatre, with particular regard to Ferrara and Milan, is also dealt with in the miscellany *Corti rinascimentali a confronto. Letteratura, musica, istituzioni*, ed. Barbara Marx, Tina Matarrese, and Paolo Trovato, F, Cesati, 230 pp., where I note as being of particular interest S. Tichy, 'Cultura teatrale e rappresentazione del potere. Milano e Ferrara alla fine del XV secolo' (27–56); A. Neuschäfer, 'Le tragedie rinascimentali come manuali per i principi: dalla *Dido in Cartagine* di Alessandro de' Pazzi (1524) alla *Didone* di Lodovico Dolce (1547)' (57–84); F. Piperno, 'Solerti, Canigiani, i *nostri comedianti favoriti* e Stefanello Bottarga: sulla "prima" di *Aminta* a Ferrara' (145–60). On this subject I also note Mauro Canova, *Le lacrime di Minerva. Lungo i sentieri della commedia e della tragedia a Padova, Venezia e Ferrara fra il 1540 e il 1550*, Alessandria, Orso, 2002. Marina Longo and Nicola Michelassi, *Teatro e spettacolo nella Mirandola dei Pico (1468–1711)*, F, Olschki, 2001, 280 pp., aims at tracing the theatre history of Mirandola through the painstaking recovery and reconstruction of original sources (either direct or indirect). Particularly important (and useful) is the transcription provided of the documentation on which the research is based. Laura Riccò, *La 'Miniera' Accademica. Pedagogia, editoria, palcoscenico nella Siena del Cinquecento*, Ro, Bulzoni, 2002, 208 pp., on the one hand investigates the workings of the Sienese Academy in its efforts to maintain a homogeneous collective literary output in the period 1530–1600, while on the other it aims at producing a rigorous critique of the use of sources in previous works on the same subject.

Paola Cosentino, *Cercando Melpomene. Esperimenti tragici nella Firenze del primo Cinquecento*, Manziana, Vecchiarelli, 310 pp., traces the progressive appearance in Italy of Greek tragedies between the late Quattrocento and early Cinquecento — fostered by the massive arrival of Greek manuscripts and growing interest for Greek humanism in Florence — and the consequences that this revival had on contemporary Florentine theatre. S. Mammana, 'Il codice It. IX. 303 (=7006) della Biblioteca Nazionale Marciana di Venezia: nota sull'*Edipo tiranno* di Orsatto Giustinian', *StIt*, 30:87–102, identifies a new manuscript of G.'s translation (published in Venice in 1585) which bears significant variants perhaps documenting an earlier version of the text.

On Florentine theatre and its dynamics in relation to political power during the 16th c. I note F. Fido, 'La scena del principe a Firenze: commedie di Francesco d'Ambra', *Borsellino Vol.*, 261–80, while A. Gareffi, 'Una tragicommedia progressiva? L'*Adelonda di Frigia*', *ib.*, 399–412, deals with the Turin performance, in 1595, of Della Valle's first dramatic work, for which see also A. Bianchi, 'Il dolore che uccide e la femminilità pericolosa nell'*Adelonda di Frigia* di Federico Della Valle', *LItal*, 54, 2002:242–61.

Useful for the general availability of dramatic texts in this period are Lelio Manfredi, *Philadelphia*, ed. Leonardo Terrusi, Bari, Adriatica, 239 pp., an early Renaissance play; Bernardino Pino di Cagli, *Lo sbratta: commedia del XVI secolo*, ed. Stefano Termanini, Ravenna, Longo, 165 pp.; Angelo Ingegneri, *Danza di Venere*, ed. Roberto Puggioni, Ro, Bulzoni, 2002, 232 pp., a *favola pastorale* by an altogether more noted figure, presented in a respectable edition complete with bibliography and notes.

INDIVIDUAL AUTHORS

DELLA PORTA. The four-volume Edizione Nazionale of Giovanni Battista della Porta's *Teatro*, ed. Raffaele Siri, has now been brought to completion with the publication of the three vols of the *Commedie*: *Teatro*, II, Na, ESI, 2002, xxv + 546 pp., containing *L'Olimpia*, *La fantesca*, *La trappolaria*, *La Cintia*, and *La carbonaria*; *Teatro*, III, Na, ESI, 2002, viii + 516 pp., with *Gli duoi fratelli rivali*, *La sorella*, *La turca*, *L'astrologo*, and *Il moro*; and *Teatro*, IV, Na, ESI, 375 pp., with *La chiappinaria*, *La furiosa*, *I duo fratelli simili*, and *La tabernaria*.

GUARINI. L. Sampson, 'The Mantuan performance of Guarini's *Pastor Fido* and representations of courtly identity', *MLR*, 98:65–83.

MACHIAVELLI. Pasquale Stoppelli, 'Per il testo della *Mandragola*: l'edizione del Centauro', *Borsellino Vol.*, 195–206, puts forward new elements for the critical reconstruction of the text on the basis of a bibliographical analysis of the *editio princeps*. *'*La favola Mandragola si chiama': Machiavelli e il teatro comico del Cinquecento*, ed. Milena Montanile, Salerno, Edisud, 2002, 95 pp. Niccolò Machiavelli, *Mandragola*, ed. Eric Haywood, Dublin, UCD Foundation for Italian Studies,

2002, 165 pp., in its annotation of the text is particularly thorough and useful for the language of the comedy.

RINUCCINI. Anna Maria Testaverde, 'Nuovi documenti sulle scenografie di Ludovico Cigoli per l'*Euridice* di Ottavio Rinuccini (1600)', *MR*, 17, n.s. 14:307–21, provides a thorough reconstruction of the available documents regarding Ludovico Cigoli's sets for Rinuccini's *Euridice* and assesses its importance in the context of the festivities dedicated to Maria de' Medici, the new queen of France.

RUZANTE. Mauro Canova, *'E 'l riso e 'l pianto et la paura et l'ira'. L'opera di Angelo Beolco tra poetica e psicoanalisi*, F, Cesati, 374 pp., deals with the relationship, in Ruzante's work, between theatre and psychology, and aims at demonstrating that his dramatic production was, in fact, partially a projection of unconscious representations of the self. Id., 'Voci dall'*underworld*. Plurilinguismo nei personaggi teatrali del XVI secolo: Ruzante e Shakespeare', pp. 103–50 of *Eteroglossia e plurilinguismo letterario*, II: *Plurilinguismo e letteratura. Atti del XXVIII Convegno Interuniversitario di Bressanone (6–9 luglio 2000)*, ed. Furio Brugnolo and Vincenzo Orioles, Ro, Il Calamo, 2002, a long essay analysing the use of mistilingual devices in the two dramatists and identifying a common concern for the disruptive potential of such use together with a respect for social order which reflects on the 'order' of their theatrical discourse. Francesco Piovan updates earlier research in Paolo Sambin, **Per le biografie di Angelo Beolco, il Ruzante, e di Alvise Cornaro: restauri di archivio rivisti e aggiornati da Francesco Piovan*, Padua, Esedra, 2002, xi + 248 pp.

TASSO. Elisabetta Graziosi, *Aminta 1573–1580. Amore e matrimonio in casa d'Este*, Lucca, Pacini Fazzi, 2001, 234 pp., aims at demonstrating that the *Aminta* was written in 1573 in order to help the arrangement of a marriage engineered by Alfonso II d'Este; that T. was employed by the Este not merely as a court poet, but more importantly as an intellectual equipped to help the dynasty solve its major political problems in the years between 1570 and the end of the century; and lastly that T.'s mental disorders might well have been induced by the progressively less friendly context in which the duke's dislike forced him to live and work. This dislike was partly induced by political circumstances in which solutions T. himself had warmly supported turned out to be doomed. The latest results of a critical study of the text of the *Aminta*, soon to be incorporated in his announced new edition of the text, are presented in P. Trovato, 'Ancora sul testo dell'*Aminta*. Nuovi testimoni e vecchie macrovarianti', pp. 161–73 of *Corti rinascimentali a confronto*, noted earlier in this THEATRE sub-section. R. Gigliucci, 'Precipitando Aminta ascende', *Borsellino Vol.*, 335–54. Tasso's *fortuna* in Italian Romantic theatre is the subject of Giorgio Pullini, 'Tasso nel teatro romantico italiano', *LItal*, 54, 2002: 64–89.

TUCCIO. Mirella Saulini, *Il teatro di un gesuita siciliano*, Ro, Bulzoni, 2002, 219 pp., focuses on the dramatic activity of Stefano Tuccio, a Jesuit from Messina and author of five Latin tragedies: *Goliath*, *Juditha*, *Christus nascens*, *Christus patiens*, and *Christus iudex*.

SEICENTO*

By Letizia Panizza, *Royal Holloway College, London*, and Domenico Chiodo, *University of Turin*

(This survey covers the years 2002 and 2003)

1. General

Is it possible to define the baroque? Many contributions in this year's Seicento section afford tantalizing responses, the most all-embracing being A. Battistini, 'Il molteplice e l'uno. La cultura barocca tra vocazione al disordine e ricerca dell'ordine', *Intersezioni*, 22, 2002: 189–206, which takes the 'New Science' of the 17th c. as a paradigm for aesthetics. Just as the former calls into doubt Aristotelian certainties and an ordered universe from the lowest form of material existence to the Supreme Being with the human race in a privileged position, baroque art and literature, he argues, after fragmenting the classical canon and authoritative literary-critical criteria, attempt to re-establish an equilibrium and place us once more in control of our destinies. G. Baffetti, 'Retorica e cultura tridentina', *ib.*, 207–19, takes a more specific point of view. Controlling society by imposing strict moral discipline is the main purpose of the edicts of the Council of Trent, which made themselves felt in the late Cinque- and Seicento. Within the hierarchy, duties and responsibilities were spelled out at all levels, and likewise for all levels in society, beginning with the family.

Travel literature receives attention with the publication of Ottavio Bon, *Il seraglio del Gransignore*, Ro, Salerno, 2002, 146 pp., the account by a Venetian merchant and diplomat of his stay in Constantinople from 1604 to 1609 as ambassador of the Republic of Venice. His report is priceless as he was the first Westerner to gain access to the Sultan's palace and brought fine powers of observation to bear on social mores, ceremonial, art, and especially to the Islamic religion and its practices, and its relation to other religions using the Bible.

GENDER STUDIES. Virginia Galilei, *Lettere al padre*, ed. Bruno Basile, Ro, Salerno, 2002, 284 pp., is a modern critical edition of the letters written (1623–33) by Galileo's illegitimate daughter from a convent of Poor Clares outside Florence, where she was known as Suor Maria Celeste. Umberto Fortis has brought out a major biography of the only learned woman Jewish writer of Venice in the Seicento, *La bella ebrea: Sara Copio Sullam, poetessa nel ghetto di Venezia del*

* As in vols 62 and 63, subsections 2 and 3 have been translated from Italian by the editor.

'600, T, Zamorani, 165 pp (revised version of 1998 book). Tutored by the distinguished Hebrew scholar, Rabbi Leone of Modena, she engaged in literary correspondence with the epic poet Ansaldo Cebà, and disputed with Baldassare Bonifacio over the immortality of the soul. The book includes her poems. A. Jacobson-Schutte, 'Suffering from the stone: the accounts of Michel de Montaigne and Cecilia Ferrazzi', *BHR*, 64, 2002:21–36, compares the attitudes of the two very different personalities to a common illness and to successful outcomes: Montaigne by rational analysis of his condition found treatment in the spas of Italy; Ferrazzi a mystic, saw herself at the centre of dramatic struggles between the demonic and the sacred, with deliverance coming from divine intervention. N. Costa-Zalessow, 'La condanna all'*Indice* della *Semplicità ingannata* di Arcangela Tarabotti alla luce di manoscritti inediti', *NRLett*, 2002.1:97–113, presents a transcription and commentary of documents from the Archives of the Holy Office at the Vatican, with the reasons for placing on the Index Tarabotti's attack on the particularly Venetian custom of forcing young girls into convents against their wills to save on the dowry, and keep the birth-rate under control. T. is seen as impudent (therefore 'Protestant'), because critical of the religious life and its vows, sanctified by the Catholic church. A. Bianchi focuses on the analysis of a female heroine as a way of accessing women's social status in 'Il dolore che uccide e la femminilità pericolosa nell'*Adelonda di Frigia* di Federico Della Valle', *LItal*, 54, 2002:242–61. The most gifted tragedian of the age, Della Valle based his own piece on Euripedes's Greek tragedy, *Iphigenia in Taurus*. Bianchi interprets the emphasis on suffering and persecution as punishment for woman's sexuality, and sees the misogyny as particularly strong at the end of the 16th and beginning of the 17th c.

BIBLIOGRAPHY. C. Reale, 'La recente fortuna critica di Anton Giulio Brignole Sale (1995–2002)', *EL*, 27.2, 2002:109–18, surveys the secondary literature on the Ligurian novelist and essayist, author of a famous historical romance about Mary Magdalen. A. Mirto, 'Lettere di Cassiano dal Pozzo a Giovanni Filippo Marucelli', *StSec*, 43, 2002:279–312, reports on a short correspondence (18 letters 1653–55) between these two great scholars and bibliophiles, of interest because they comment on contemporary hostilities between Jansenists and Jesuits. Neither appears to have come down on one side or the other.

2. Poetry

Initiatives in the field of baroque studies — conferences, exhibitions, or seminars — have multiplied in recent years, and the *acta* and catalogues to which they give rise have come to be among the most important publishing events, not only in quantitative terms: in *YWMLS*, 63:469, we reported the proceedings of the Siena conference *I luoghi dell'immaginario barocco*; now other publications are to be pointed out and their individual contributions discussed. In Rizzo, *Identità*, especially noteworty for the Seicento is A. Quondam, 'L'identità (rin)negata, l'identità vicaria. L'Italia e gli italiani nel paradigma culturale dell'età moderna', 127–49, which develops the accepted critique of De Sanctis's idealism, and convincingly rejects the commonplace of a 17th-c. 'decadence' in Italian culture.

The catalogue *Sul Tesin piantàro i tuoi laureti. Poesia e vita letteraria nella Lombardia spagnola (1535–1706). Catalogo della mostra. Pavia, Castello Visconteo*, Pavia, Cardano, 2002, 560 pp., goes beyond the exhibition itself to attend to the indexing and illustration of a broader range of publications, and aims at reconstructing a sort of 'ideal library' which gives the fullest possible idea of literary culture in the Duchy of Milan under Spanish rule. It falls into four sections according to the languages used, i.e. books in Italian, Latin, Spanish, and Milanese. The *schede* for Italian books are edited by Quinto Marini, who has structured the material in the sections 'Poesia lirica, encomiastica e giocosa' (where the entries on Muzio Manfredi's *Cento sonetti* and Filippo Massini's *Rime* seem especially noteworthy). Religious poetry 'poesia sacra e borromaica' follows; and then come the 'Favole pastorali e idilli' efficiently dealt with by Uberto Motta. This, as Marini himself stresses, is the section that holds the biggest surprises thanks to the vitality with which the two genres spread in Counter-Reformation Milan and thanks to the rediscovery of various works of interest. The volume ends with sections devoted to the *poema* (long poem) and to 'Lo spettacolo fra scrittura e scena: gli Andreini, Maggi e Lemene'.

Atti (Lecce) cover a number of broad topics: P. A. Frare, 'Poetiche del Barocco' (41–70); A. Battistini, 'Retoriche del Barocco' (71–109); F. Guardiani, 'Polemiche secentesche intorno all'*Adone*' (177–97), M. Guglielminetti, 'Studi sul Barocco nel Novecento' (645–59), and, with more force and originality, A. Quondam, 'Il Barocco e la letteratura. Genealogie del mito della decadenza italiana' (111–75), which traces the formation of the image of *secentismo* as the historic 'disease' of Italian culture from Gravina to Tiraboschi and De Sanctis and right down to the controversy surrounding even Asor Rosa's timid attempted reaction thirty years ago. Among the general contributions we would particularly recommend the well-considered pages (25–40) of F. Croce's *Introduzione*, where, citing the conceit and *concettismo* as the hallmark of baroque writing, he acknowledges its 'conservative intent' and function of making transgression harmless by exaggerating its effects: in which remark lies the key to the baroque paradox of an art that is revolutionary in appearance and yet the official art of a conformist society such as existed in 17th-c. Italy. More specifically devoted to poetry are: A. Martini, 'Le nuove forme del canzoniere' (199–226), a full, well-documented examination of the evolution of the lyric-poetry collections of the first decades of the century, and G. Rizzo, 'Percorsi e immagini della lirica post-mariniana' (227–47), which almost responds to the previous author with a discussion of southern writers from the second quarter of the century onwards. In a related area I also note Id., 'Ancora su una polemica tardo-secentesca a Napoli: Baldassarre Pisani tra F. Meninni e G. Battista', *CLett*, 30, 2002:453–64, which explores in detail the reasons for the animosity between Battista and Meninni as being rooted in an aversion, on the former's part, for Marino, whose defence was take up by the latter, backed by the younger figure of Pisani, whose output of lyric poetry is examined in the article.

Atti (Lecce) are dedicated to Giorgio Fulco, and a further tribute is offered by *FC*, 27.1, 2002, an issue devoted to his memory and carrying a series of contributions (by Enrico Malato, Ottavio Besomi, Renzo Bragantini, and Martino Capucci) presented at a commemoration held at the University of Naples in May 2001 on the anniversary of Fulco's death. A heartfelt homage to the master is paid by a pupil in G. de Miranda, 'Il gioco segreto', *Aprosiana*, n.s. 9, 2001:11–5, while also recalling his activity in Id., 'Ha mai cantato Partenope a Napoli? Per un'aggiornata rassegna bibliografica sulla lirica napoletana del Seicento', *EL*, 28.2:105–14, which reflects on some recent and not-so-recent studies of Neapolitan baroque lyric poetry.

Knowledge of Seicento poetry progressed when reliance on anthologies gave way to republication of complete verse collections. The return to the anthological formula in *Antologia della poesia italiana*, ed. Cesare Segre and Carlo Ossola, v, *Il Seicento*, T, Einaudi, 2001, xxii + 326 pp. (the Pléiade ed. first publ. 1997), is not therefore beneficial, despite a number of innovative features such as the abandonment of the category 'marinismo'. Three poets, Chiabrera, Campanella, and Marino, are given the privilege of a whole section of their own; then follows a farrago entitled 'Poeti dell'"Hoggidì"', and two sections respectively of 'didascalica e giocosa' and 'dialettale e municipale' verse. The philological and 'bio-bibliographical' notes at the end of the volume are skimpy on the whole; those devoted to the three major poets (Chiabrera by M. Ariani, Campanella by S. Prandi, and Marino by V. De Maldé) are far better. Ossola's brief introduction contributes little to the study of Seicento poetry, and is notable for its heavily ideological approach: suffice it to say that the only poetry collections granted the honour of citation are Bartolomeo Cambi's *Praticello del Divino Amore* and Maria Alberghetti's *Giardino di poesie spirituali*. A pretty volume of devotional verse is *L'aspro sentiero. Poesia quaresimale di Pietro Cresci e Giulio Cesare Croce*, ed. Salvatore Ussia, Vercelli, Mercurio, 220 pp., bringing together two collections which achieved considerable success in the first decades of the Seicento. The publication of Pietro Cresci's *Sonetti Quadragesimali*, long (but wrongly) attributed to the preacher Francesco Panigarola, is particularly important.

L'onorato sasso. Un secolo di versi in morte di Torquato Tasso, ed. and ann. Domenico Chiodo, Alessandria, Orso, 192 pp., is an unusual type of anthology in that it gathers 77 poems (five of them previously unpublished) written by some 50 authors and devoted to the death of Tasso or to celebrating his tomb, which from the first became a place of pilgrimage for poets and *letterati*. The *schede* presenting the individual authors, some very famous, others completely unknown, offer a kind of muster of baroque poetic forces assembled to celebrate the 'onorato sasso' of the 'Principe de' Poeti'. G. P. Maragoni, *Il rigore dell'estro. Stilistica, tematologia e grammatica del racconto*, Bari, Di Canosa, 67 pp., brings together published essays on Stigliani and Capponi and adds his hitherto unpublished paper from the conference *Petrarca in Barocco* (Rome, 2002): '"Sogni e copule io fingo". Avventure secentesche del Petrarca onirico'.

M. Malavasi, 'Ancora sui "frutti dell'armi", tra "Polimnia" e "Clio": l'immagine della guerra nel Seicento dai generi letterari alla storiografia', pp. 121–45 of *Scrittori di fronte alla guerra*, Ro, Aracne, 285 pp., the *acta* of the two-day meeting organized by Roma-Tre University (7–8 June 2002), explores the perception of war in Seicento culture and its representation in the poetry of the period. It is not convincing, however, in its pursuit of homology whereby every specimen is marked by a 'forte stilizzazione iperbolica', whereas the critic ought rather to bring out the differences, which are already recognizable in the quotations provided by M. A 'war' text is also looked at in L. Giachino, 'Dalla storia al mito. La *Roccella espugnata* di Francesco Bracciolini', *StSec*, 44: 167–95.

I also note another disquisition on the term 'baroque' which does not yield any very significant results: M. Cerruti, 'Logica e retorica nella poesia barocca. Alcune considerazioni in margine all'edizione delle *Rime* di Scipione della Cella', *CLett*, 30, 2002: 11–34; and a more interesting study on the 'più famoso e prolifico cantore di piazza veneziano attivo nel XVII secolo': M. Visentin, 'Un cantore veneziano del XVII secolo: Paolo Briti il "Cieco da Venezia"', *QV*, 36, 2002[2003]: 45–76.

Also worthy of attention is A. Ziino, 'Riflessioni sul madrigale nel tardo Seicento', *Atti* (Lecce), 557–608, devoted to editions and MSS of vocal music from the latter half of the Seicento. L. Tufano, 'I testi per musica di Andrea Perrucci. Prime ricognizioni', *Aprosiana*, n.s. 9, 2001: 329–46, on the other hand, confines analysis to the author in question.

ANDREINI. Famed for her acting, Isabella also cultivated verse composition: less successfully, though her *Rime* (1601) present some interesting features, especially in the last two sections, the *versi funerali* (four poems in unrhymed hendecasyllables and *settenari* forming a single narrative) and the *egloghe boschereccie* in the same metre. But these are not discussed in L. Giachino, 'Dall'effimero teatrale alla quête dell'immortalità. Le rime di Isabella Andreini', *GSLI*, 178, 2001: 530–52, an article which scarcely gets beyond description and the use of banal formulae such as 'tardo petrarchismo manierista'.

BAZZANI CAVAZZONI. N. Costa-Zalessow, 'Le *Fantasie poetiche* di Virginia Bazzani Cavazzoni', *EL*, 27.2, 2002: 55–75, corrects a number of biographical errors perpetrated in histories of literature with regard to this obscure late-17th century poetess, before going on to attempt a reappraisal of her work, while taking issue over the scant critical interest shown for women's verse in the field of Seicento studies.

BRUNI. C. Perrone, 'Un poeta fra le Veneri: note sullo stile di Antonio Bruni', *Atti* (Lecce), 867–87, publishes and analyses two poems in *ottava rima* belonging to B.'s *Veneri* (1633), his last verse collection. B.'s important *Discorso intorno al titolo delle Veneri* has been edited by Domenico Chiodo in *Lo Stracciafoglio*, 3.5–6: 5–11.

CAMPANELLA. F. Giancotti, 'Tommaso Campanella: le poesie della *Scelta* e la loro disposizione', *StSec*, 43, 2002: 3–73, follows on from G.'s edition of the *Poesie*, as a third and final instalment of the ample supplement to the edition (see *YWMLS*, 62: 439 and 64: 473). He addresses the structure of the collection which he sees as having two parts (1–67, poems preceding the poet's imprisonment; 71–89, poems composed at Sant'Elmo) linked by a 'triad of distinctive sonnets' (68–70). The 'distinctive criterion' dominating the collection is defined as 'step-wise upward progression' and this is also recognized as the overall 'intent' of the work in as much as it 'signifies step-wise ascent' as the inner itinerary of the author and, at the same time, as the spiritual elevation of the reader.

The Giancotti edition is criticized in V. De Maldé, 'Su una nuova edizione delle *Poesie* di Campanella', *GSLI*, 179, 2002: 259–69, for its outdated idealist approach and its scant attention to C.'s poetic contemporaries in the commentary, but above all for its unjustified devaluation of the Firpo edition. A. Cerbo, '*Sub specie animalium*:

uomini e demonio nella poesia di Campanella e di Tasso', *BrC*, 8, 2002:85–111, distinguishes a tendency in C.'s poetry to make frequent use of allegorical figures *sub specie animalium* and sees it as being bound up with C.'s polemic against anthropocentrism. On the other hand, E. N. Girardi, 'Dante nel pensiero e nella poesia di Campanella', *CLett*, 30, 2002:423–40, reverts to the 'presence of Dante in the poetic practice of Tommaso Campanella', a theme which has already been amply discussed.

CHIABRERA. Taking his cue from the Chiabrera selection edited by Giulia Raboni (*YWMLS* 60:434–35), A. Donnini, 'In margine a una recente edizione di Gabriello Chiabrera', *GSLI*, 179, 2002:61–94, develops lengthy considerations on the current editorial situation of the Savonese poet, whose complete *corpus* of lyric poetry D. is personally in the process of editing. The comments on Raboni's work are detailed and precise, with regard both to her editing of the text and to her commentary, where one can fully share the reviewer's astonishment at her constant and methodical reference to Petrarch to justify minimal linguistic usage. This leads to her erroneous notion of C.'s 'Petrarchan orthodoxy': illuminating examples are adduced by D. to demonstrate the osmotic relationship between Chiabrera's verse and that of the Cinquecentisti (Bembo, Della Casa, Coppetta, Guidiccioni, etc.).

D'AQUINO. M. Leone, 'Pesci, mitili e crostacei: il *piscatus* di Taranto fra didascalismo barocco e simbologia municipale', Rizzo, *Identità*, I, 181–97, illustrates the poem *Deliciae Tarentinae* by Tommaso Nicolò D'Aquino, rightly drawing attention to Seicento Latin literature, which has been too hastily dismissed by students of baroque poetry. The same author returns more generally to the concept of 'delizia' in Seicento culture, in Id., 'Sulle *deliciae* barocche', *Atti* (Lecce), 817–36.

GALILEI. In A. Marzo, 'Galilei poeta', *Atti*, (Lecce), 837–55, the editor of G.'s few *Rime* (see *YWMLS*, 63:474) reverts to his claim of the 'importance and dignity' of the Pisan scientist's activity as a poet.

GIOVANETTI. The indefatigable L. Giachino, *'Amore è Maggio che non corre a verno'. Cinque saggi su lirici barocchi*, Alessandria, Orso, 168 pp., republishes writings on Rinaldi, Campeggi, and Michiel, adding a few pages on a short sonnet sequence by Tiberio Sbarra and a more elaborate descriptive essay on the poetry of Marcello Giovanetti from Ascoli.

IMPERIALE. G. V. Imperiale – G. Chiabrera, *Su 'La Gierusalemme di Torquato Tasso'. Con un sonetto di G. B. Marino e una lettera di Angelo Grillo. Tavole di Bernardo Castello*, ed. Stefano Verdino, Genoa, San Marco dei Giustiniani, 2002, 84 pp., an elegant little volume, contains not only Imperiale's 'arguments' for the Genoese edition (Pavoni,

1604) of Tasso's poem, which was illustrated with Bernardo Castello's plates, but also Chiabrera's *Fragmento de' tetrastichi per la Gierusalemme liberata*, as well as the sonnet and letter referred to in the title: the whole well explained in the editor's 'Nota al testo'.

LALLI. M. C. Cabani, 'La *Franceide* di Giovan Battista Lalli', *Atti* (Lecce), 693–716, examines L.'s mock-heroic poem, placing it in the context of the new 17th-c. genre, but also bringing out its links with the tradition of writing on the 'French disease' inaugurated by Fracastoro in *Syphilis* and with the fashion for poems devoted to the discovery and conquest of the Americas (the conquest of the *guaiacum*, or 'legno santo', is one of the central episodes of the work).

LEMENE. C. Fino, 'Francesco de Lemene poeta a San Colombano', *Archivio Storico Lodigiano*, 121, 2002[2003]: 75–81, briefly discusses two madrigals which De L. dedicated to Suor Serafina Ceserani, a painter and musician whom he knew.

LUBRANO. In I. Lubrano, *Scintille poetiche o Poesie sacre, e morali. Aggiunta la mutevolezza eloquente e una scelta di poesie sparse*, ed. Marzio Pieri, Trento, La Finestra, 2002, lxxviii + 406 pp., Pieri re-presents Lubrano's poetry, reproducing his edition of the *Scintille poetiche* after a lapse of 20 years but this time complete with all the odes and compositions for musical setting that were sacrificed in the earlier edition for reasons of space. The elegantly produced volume is enriched with other Lubrano texts (and a CD-ROM of the collected *Prediche quaresimali*) and with essays by the editor and Luana Salvarani. The complete republication of Lubrano's *œuvre* prompts obscure considerations from A. Ruffino, 'Nebbie edificate in mondi. Note su Iacopo Lubrano', *CLett*, 31: 359–66. Giacomo Lubrano, **In tante trasparenze: il verme setaiuolo e altre scintille poetiche*, ed. Giancarlo Alfano and Gabriele Frasca, Na, Cronopio, 2002, 176 pp.

MALATESTI. Two contributions in *Atti* (Lecce) are devoted to the whimsical Florentine: P. Cisternino, 'Aspetti della poesia burlesca del Seicento: gli *Enimmi* di Antonio Malatesti' (773–81), reads a poem from *La sfinge*, and rightly points out the ongoing vitality, in 17th-c. Florence, of 'a vast output of burlesque verse which continues that of the two preceding centuries and in some way seems another sign of the substantial extraneousness of Florentine culture to the more explosive novelties of Marino's poetry and poetics'. M. Masieri, '*La Tina*, ovvero i sonetti erotici di Antonio Malatesti' (857–66), in reading M.'s works applies, in my view too mechanically and with misplaced confidence, the interpretative keys of 16th-c. Bernesque poetry provided by J. Toscan.

MARINO. F. Guardiani, 'Marino lirico. L'apertura di *Madriali e canzoni*', *Aprosiana*, n.s. 9, 2001: 51–76, as a foretaste of the edition of *Lira II* he is preparing with Alessandro Martini offers the first 12 madrigals accompanied by a commentary too full, as he recognizes, for the edition itself. C. Caruso, 'Saggio di commento alla *Galeria* di G. B. Marino: 1 (esordio) e 624 (epilogo)', *Aprosiana*, n.s. 10, 2002: 71–89, is likewise a sample of another critical edition-cum-commentary, which C. has been working on for years. P. A. Frare, 'Marino al *Cannocchiale*', *ib.*, n.s. 9, 2001 : 97–107, examines the pages devoted to M. in Tesauro's treatise to conclude that the *Cannocchiale* 'preserves considerable traces' of T.'s early enthusiasm for M., but assayed and ordered 'by the touchstone of Barberini poetics'. M. Cerrai, 'A proposito del XVII canto dell'*Adone*: il poema del Marino e le descrizioni fiorentine delle feste per Maria de' Medici', *StSec*, 44 : 197–218, identifies the *Stanze* composed by Carlo Bocchineri for Maria de' Medici's wedding and departure for France as a source used by M. both for the *Tempio* (1615) and for c. XVII of the *Adone*. In c. XIX G. Bárberi Squarotti, 'Il tragico negato: *Adone*, XIX', *CLett*, 30, 2002 : 441–52, sees a revival of Tasso's *Rogo amoroso* and a disintegration of the tragic, which is dissolved through multiplication of fables and descriptions aimed at 'silencing the image of death'. In the same canto, and more specifically the episode of Giacinto, Id., 'Il Marino e gli sport moderni', *RLettI*, 21.3 : 187–94, sets out to show that even in the sporting arena M. tends towards exhaustiveness and therefore seeks to add modern sports to the classical ones given ample treatment in c. XX. In this he is reviving and exploiting Anguillara's eccentricity in his translation of Ovid, where in the myth of Hyacinth the original quoit-throwing contest is replaced with the game of *pallacorda*, the ancestor of modern tennis, described by Marino as 'sheer spectacle' and with all his customary virtuosity. G. P. Maragoni, 'Su un sonetto campestre del primo Seicento (Per la cronologia di uno stilema mariniano)', *GSLI*, 179, 2002: 53–60, interprets a pastoral sonnet by M. with minute and valuable observations on its compositional stylemes and the literary affinities they reveal. Also worth noting are the observations and erudite soundings in G. Sacchi, 'Schede mariniane', *StSec*, 43, 2002 : 313–29, and D. Conrieri e V. Guercio, 'Schede secentesche', *ib.*, 44 : 315–22. A. Cervone, *'L'estetica assenziale dell'*Adone*', *AASN*, 102, 2001[2002] : 91–104. D. Sbacchi, *'Polifemo: varianti del mito da Omero a Marino', *QI*, 23.1, 2002 : 49–64. V. Surliuga, *'La Galeria di G. B. Marino tra pittura e poesia', *ib.*, 65–84.

SEMPRONIO. L. Giachino, *Giovan Leone Sempronio tra 'lusus' amoroso e armi cristiane*, F, Olschki, 2002, x + 293 pp., a doctoral thesis, is of interest for factual and bibliographical information, albeit rather lacking in critical judgement and historiographical perspective.

STIGLIANI. A. Tirri, '*Canzone sulla Ragion di Stato* di Tommaso Stigliani a Raffaello della Torre', *Aprosiana*, n.s. 9, 2001 : 127–45, gives a (diplomatic?) transcription, commentary and analysis of an ill-written *canzone*, excluded from the 1623 *Canzoniere* but already published by Francesco Santoro in 1908.

TASSONI. Silvia Longhi, **Le memorie antiche: modelli classici da Petrarca a Tassoni*, Verona, Fiorini, 2001, ix + 207 pp.

TESTI. F. Pevere, *L'ingegnosa finzione. Saggi sulla letteratura del Seicento*, Alessandria, Orso, 181 pp., assembles various essays: those already published include a noteworthy contribution (49–82) devoted to Testi's poetry at the conference *Petrarca in Barocco*: ' "Mirti amorosi" ed "eterni lauri": forme del petrarchismo nella poesia di Fulvio Testi'.

3. Drama

THE THEATRE AND THEATRES. L. Mariti, 'Valore e coscienza del teatro in età barocca', *Atti* (Lecce), 419–55, starts from the assumption that 'the baroque age is the golden age of theatre' which sees the emergence of professional acting companies and publication of printed editions of plays, and in which the theatre takes on an extraordinary importance in society. But more heavily underscored is the affinity between the baroque age and the universe as theatre, 'finestra epistemologica e metafisica delle apparenze', locus *par excellence* of the gap between deceptive appearance and the world of authenticity, and hence also of the *meraviglia* that constitutes the essence of the baroque. In terms of its conceptual structure the essay is not always convincing, but there are noteworthy passages on the *meraviglia* produced by the first professional actresses and on Giovan Battista Andreini's unpublished 'interminable and hyperbaroque' text *Il convitato di pietra*, written 14 years before Molière's *Don Juan* and which, commendably, has been brought out in the critical edition: *Don Giovanni, o L'estrema avventura del teatro: Il nuovo risarcito convitato di pietra di Giovan Battista Andreini. Studi e edizione critica*, ed. S. Carandini and L. Mariti, Ro, Bulzoni, 734 pp.

F. Fiaschini, '*Negotium diaboli.* Approcci, valutazioni e ipotesi di ricerca intorno ai rapporti tra Chiesa post-tridentina e professionismo dello spettacolo', *Aprosiana*, n.s. 9, 2001, 309–28, summarizes a number of recent contributions on the church and professional acting in the Counter-Reformation. M. Brindicci, 'La pedagogia del teatro. Regole e prassi per una "civile conversatione" drammatica', *ib.*, 299–307, provides a succinct descripton of Manilio Pannelli, *Le regole della poesia drammatica o vero Dell'arte comica*, a short handbook intended for young tiroes wishing to perform or write plays and printed at Naples between 1634 and 1635.

N. Michelassi, 'Memorie dal sottopalco. Giovan Carlo de' Medici e il primo teatro della Pergola (1652–1663)', *StSec*, 43, 2002 : 347–55, sums up the programme of the Pergola as a theatre where 'poterono incontrarsi, in una fragile e costosa impresa, le nuove modalità spettacolari "alla veneziana", aggiornate dalle indicazioni torelliane, e la secolare tradizione scenografica medicea'.

COMEDY. G. Coluccia, 'Tradizione e parodia nel teatro di Gian Battista Della Porta', *Atti* (Lecce), 783–800, draws on some of his *prologhi* to illustrate the characteristics of D.'s comedies, stressing in particular the way his 'dramatist's sensibility' brings him to respond to the demands of his public: 'il Della Porta scrive pensando alla rappresentazione del testo. Le sue scelte linguistiche, strutturali e tematiche costruiscono un testo letterario in funzione del suo allestimento'. M. T. Lanza, 'Il cavaliere, la morte e il diavolo nelle *Bravure del Capitan Spavento*', *EL*, 28.4:47–57, looks briefly at actor-dramatist Giovan Battista Andreini's play and in particular at its thematic 'hallucinatory encounters' between Capitan Spavento and Death. Editions of less significant plays range from the anastatic reproduction of the 1724 edition of G. B. Ricciardi, *Trespolo podestà di Greve*, ed. Carlo Baldini, Greve in Chianti, 199 pp., to the Calabrese dialect comedy, published with a facing Italian translation, C. Quintana, *Organtino*, ed. Giulio Palange, Soveria Mannelli, Rubbettino, 117 pp., and to the republication of N. Barbieri, *L'inavertito*, ed. Giusi Baldissone, Novara, Interlinea, 2002, 174 pp., a text from the first half of the century and belonging to the tradition developed by the *commedia dell'arte* actors.

TRAGEDY. M. Sacco Messineo, 'Proteo a teatro', *Atti* (Lecce), 903–23, starting from the customary view that the language of the baroque theatre, as compared with other genres, is 'a closer heir to the past', points out that it reuses the past in a Counter-Reformation key by converting the mythology re-elaborated in tragedies into a useful 'sfondo per disamine moralistiche'. It should be noted, however, that the discussion focuses on the tragic genre and, as its essential point of reference, on the tragedies of Della Valle, on whose *Adelonda di Frigia* an article by A. Bianchi is noted above under GENDER STUDIES. Initiatives which expand the repertoire of available editions and contribute to fuller knowledge of the 17th-c. tragic canon are therefore particularly meritorious. Ansaldo Cebà, *Tragedie*, ed. Marco Corradini, Mi, Vita e Pensiero, 2001, lxviii + 284 pp., presents C.'s three texts, *La principessa Silandra, Alcippo spartano, Le gemelle capovane*, preceded by a very substantial introduction giving due attention not only to the plays themselves but also to the author's biographical vicissitudes and to the way they are reflected in those of the characters and plots. There are also pertinent observations on relations between C.'s tragic *œuvre* and the development of the 'spiritual tragedy' theorized by Bernardino Stefonio, and also on the political and ideological function of C.'s writing in his tragedies. Though they were much admired by Scipione Maffei, they are not entirely successful, particularly in the unfortunate choice of the *canzonetta* metre for the choruses. Another tragedian of the period enjoying scholarly interest at present is Tesauro: after the *Edipo* ed. Carlo Ossola and the *Alcesti* ed. Maria Luisa Doglio, his entire output of tragedies is now available thanks to the following two new editions. Emanuele Tesauro, *Ermegildo*, ed. Pier Antonio Frare and Michele Gazich, Manziana, Vecchiarelli, 2002, iv + 186 pp., offers T.'s last vernacular tragedy, written in 1659 after *Edipo* and *Ippolito* (1639–40), but the first to have been conceived (an unpublished Latin version, dated 1621, is extant). In his introduction F. maintains that *Ermegildo* is also the most important tragedy in that, more successfully than the others, it programmatically combines a 'classicizing framework' and modern elements: not only its choice of subject (historical and hagiographic, referring as it does to a recent beatification of some political moment for the alliance between the Spanish crown and the Holy See), but also its 'free inventiveness' and 'unusual stylistic choices [. . .] which can be traced back to *concettismo*'. Thus the project, which aimed at elaborating *modern* tragedy (F. rightly invokes the example of Corneille) achieved a landmark in *Ermegildo*: and what strikes one most as one reads it is the superabundance of ornament and a manifest infraction of the linear development expected in a tragedy in the classical mould, but also an exemplary demonstration of a new mode of 'feeling' the tragic genre. *Ippolito*, too, was drafted twice in different versions at different moments: in 1641 for performance and in 1661, with a substantial number of variants, for the printed edition (Turin, Zavatta). A copy of the original version has been found in a MS preserved at Leicester, and the discovery has provided the opportunity for a rich and unusual edition reproducing (with a double commentary!) both witnesses: E. Tesauro, *Ippolito. Una 'fabula' tirata da Seneca per i moderni teatri*, ed. S. Castellaneta, Taranto, Lisi, 2002, 240 pp.

I also note: M. Sarnelli, 'Note sulla scrittura tragica e tragicomica barocca italiana', *Atti* (Lecce), 925–42; M. T. Imbriani, 'Una presunta fonte di John Milton. L' *Adamo caduto*, tragedia sacra di Serafino della Salandra', *Aprosiana*, n.s. 9, 2001 : 77–83; A. Tantillo, *La Rosalia: tragedia sacra*, ed. Giovanni Bellini, Sala Bolognese, Forni, ccxxvi pp., facs. reprint of 1869 ed.; V. Gatti, **Giovan Battista Albéri: la vita e le opere del tragediografo cremasco dell'Accademia dei Sospinti*, F, Atheneum, 166 pp. T. Stein, '"Travestiti ne vanno". Note su *L'imagine difesa, overo la Sofronia* (1688) di Francesco Maria De Luco Sereni', *StSec*, 43, 2002 : 341–47, adds a fresh discovery to his earlier work on theatre adaptations of the Olindo and Sofronia episode in Tasso's *Gerusalemme liberata* (cfr. *YWMLS*, 63: 476).

OPERA. P. Besutti, 'L'identità nazionale in scena: il contributo degli attori e dei poeti alla nascita e alla prima affermazione dell'opera in musica', Rizzo, *Identità*, 165–80, starting from 16th-c. treatises and from the theoretical opposition between Vincenzo Galilei and Gioseffo Zarlino, argues that three distinct traditions can be seen to merge in the invention of opera: not only poetry and music but acting finds its 'ideal outcome' in the operatic sphere, as is well attested by the Andreini family's familiarity with music and music drama and by the fact that Virginia Andreini was entrusted with the role of Ariadne for the first performance of the Rinuccini–Monteverdi *Arianna*. Dating from 1661, when opera had fully established itself, and performed on the Venetian stage, G. Artale, *La Pasife, o vero l'impossibile fatto possibile*, ed. A. M. Razzoli Roio, Verona, Fiorini, 168 pp., is a perfect specimen of the libretto as a hybrid genre combining comic inserts in a 'low' style with attempts at a more elevated manner.

4. Prose

Several essays in the monumental collection *Atti* (Lecce) offer new points of view on Seicento prose. From the author of several key books and articles on the Seicento novel, M. Capucci, 'La narrativa del Seicento italiano' (249–70), is an indispensable essay for students of 17th-c. prose, reviewing editions and studies of the last half century, summarizing achievements, and offering a valuable guide to further research. D. Della Terza, 'Il barocco e la fiaba: il caso Basile' (271–86), examines the characteristics of the baroque fairy tale: what made the beautiful princess Zoza laugh for the first time in her life were the vulgar gestures and language of Naples's lower classes; with them lies the inventiveness that the writer needs. P. Guaragnella, 'Scrittura religiosa del Barocco' (207–309), revolves around Paolo Sarpi, taking as its starting point Getto's criticism that Sarpi sometimes showed only 'una esteriore bravura di polemista'. G. presents instead a stylistically rich, varied, and sophisticated Sarpi, capable of many tones and registers arising from a deeply thoughtful spirit. V. Marucci, 'L'Oratoria sacra' (311–32), seeks to rescue preaching from the prescriptions of the Council of Trent and heavy judgements of later critics to reveal a more complex picture in which preaching is a form of edifying entertainment meant to appeal to the emotions. G. Rabitti, 'Letteratura di viaggio nell'età barocca' (379–418), surveys the century's travel literature, examining travel accounts, as well as biographies, autobiographies, missionaries' reports, and histories of religious orders. Two essays concern specific discourses in prose. M. L. Altieri Biagi, 'Venature barocche nella prosa scientifica del Seicento' (507–55), is a fine linguistic analysis of the appropriation of non-scientific lexis for specific, technical use; of the creation of neologisms from Greek and Latin roots; and the semantic shifts of words from the realm of literary criticism — for example, *maraviglia, stupore, stravaganza, fantasia, capriccio, bizzarria* — to more rigorously intellectual domains. L. Bolzoni, 'Il "libro figurato" del Seicento: due esempi (Tesauro e Jacopone)' (479–506), examines the relationship between text and illustration/diagram in early books, giving most attention to Emanuele Tesauro's *Cannocchiale aristotelico* (1654). In the book's frontispiece, the telescope stands for human intelligence able to penetrate the secrets of nature in greater detail than ever before. But the figure observing is Poetry, and the knowledge is Rhetoric. Scientific discoveries serve as metaphors for poetics. G. L. Betti, 'Un elogio di Ferrante Pallavicino a Giovan Battista Manzini e una lettera di Giovan Francesco Loredan', *StSec*, 43, 2002: 265–75, addresses the apparent puzzle of a person hostile to Loredan and to Venice being praised alongside Loredan in the preface to Pallavicino's *Scena retorica* of 1640. Manzini had lent his talents to the praises of the Savoy royal family who wanted to take over Cyprus, dominated hitherto by the Venetians, supported France and the Pope in international relations, and were opposed to Venice's anti-Papal stance. Complex plays of self-interest, spelled out by B., may have induced P. to include Manzini in his praise. Another well-known member of the Accademia degli Incogniti is the subject of L. Spera, 'Su alcuni *Discorsi sopra la Poetica d'Aristotele* di Francesco Pona', *ib.*, 217–38. These were delivered in Verona at the Accademia Filarmonica and printed at Bologna in 1636, after Pona's famous novel *La lucerna*, of 1625. Spera reconstructs the biography of P., and the composition of the lectures, and provides transcriptions of excerpts from this rare publication. Pona's commentaries offer insights into early 17th-c. poetics, and include topics such as imitation, the chivalric romance (not of course touched on by Aristotle!), and tragedy. Spera notes that Pona's own predilections led him to hybrid genres, well beyond the Aristotelian pale. L. Giachino, '"Cicero libertinus". La satira della Roma barberiniana', *ib.*, 185–215, brings to light an almost forgotten novel in Latin by Vittorio Rossi, known as L'Eritreo (and also in the Latin form, Janus Nicius Erythraeus). The novel, *Eudemia* (1637), satirizes Papal Rome under the fiction of a shipwreck of aristocrats who have just enjoyed festivities resembling a Roman carnival at the time of the Emperor Tiberius (the paragon of wickedness and corruption in Tacitus and probably standing for Urban VIII), and now turn the island into another Rome. The author is shown around the island by Gallonius (probably the French libertine, Gabriel Naudé), a community where money is god, worshipped by usurers, corrupt bankers, swindlers, intriguers, and libellers. G. places the novel in the context of the satirical literature of Barclay, Casaubon, and Boccalini and his imitators, and especially of *romans à clef*.

For the baroque novel proper, Anna Maria Pedullà, *Il romanzo barocco ed altri scritti*, Na, Liguori, 2001, 183 pp., collects under one cover with updated bibliography seven essays published elsewhere: 'Il romanzo nel Seicento' (1–93); 'La novella del '600' (95–110); 'Epica del '600' (111–26); 'L'eloquenza del sacro' (127–46); 'Semiosi naturale e storia d'un anima in *Maria Maddalena peccatrice e convertita* di A. G. Brignole Sale' (147–64); 'Il gioco dello specchio: il *Calloandro*, tragicommedia di G. A. Marini' (165–76); 'La malinconia del Tasso nella biografia di G. B. Manso' (177–83). The first and longest chapter expands the chronology of the baroque novel (Asor Rosa would limit it to 1662, thereby excluding later works as not truly novels) and takes a sociological approach. The Seicento witnesses the arrival of 'letteratura di consumo': from 1634 to 1645, 75 first editions of novels, and a total of 230 for the century, with Venice as the centre, followed by Genoa and other cities. More people are writing novels than ever before, and the pocket-size books cost less and less. The novel, furthermore, is the most hybrid genre yet witnessed in Italian vernacular letters: it parodies, mixes, rewrites, and reinterprets other more 'classical' forms and linguistic registers, with combinatory capacity. The essay, with its annotated bibliography, serves as a good starting point for a course on the baroque novel, which is broadly classified into the Venetian 'libertine' novel, the spiritual novel, the historical/political novel, and the novel of manners and society. Special attention is given to the most popular novel of the century, G. A. Marini's *Calloandro*. Her chapter on *Maria Maddalena* emphasizes the tendency to glorify masochism in the novel: the saint is depicted as growing spiritually by punishing herself and inflicting ever greater destruction on her body. Here is no possibility for rewarding Platonic relationships.

Roberta Colombi, *Lo sguardo che s'interna. Personaggi e immaginario interiore nel romanzo italiano del Seicento*, Ro, Arachne, 2002, 263 pp., focuses on novels by five writers of the first half of the century: Luca Assarino's *Stratonica*, Giovan Francesco Biondi's *L'Eromena*, Ferdinando Donno's *L'amorosa Clarice*, Carlo della Lengueglia's *L'Aldimiro*, and Bernardo Morando's *La Rosalinda*. For C., the novels display a new kind of character in Italian prose, one given to introspection. In addition, the authors are more skilful at psychological analysis, she believes, spurred on by the search for new insights into human behaviour offered by science and medicine. Their works, it is argued, provide a bridge to the modern novel. She shows, too, how these novels often hold up strong female characters and promote decidedly Catholic values.

An entire volume of 20 essays brings an outstanding polymath into the foreground of cultural and literary life of the Venetian Seicento: *Girolamo Brusoni: Avventure di penna e di vita nel Seicento Veneto. Atti del 23. Convegno di Studi Storici, Rovigo, Palazzo Roncale, 13–14 novembre 1999*, ed. Gino Benzoni, Rovigo, Minelliana, 2001, 332 pp., divided into the four parts: 'Il caso Brusoni'; 'La narrativa brusoniana e l'immaginario barocco'; 'Sfondi libertini'; 'Suoni e scenari Veneto-rodigini'. In an inspired *tour de force*, Benzoni sets the main issues for a historian or any writer with moral principles in Venice in the Seicento in 'Istoriar con le favole e favoleggiar con le istorie' (9–28). Finding a patron was essential, but that compromised immediately one's independence. Marino, for Benzoni, is the model of the successful poet who sold his soul to become a slave of the court. Gian Francesco Loredan, founder of the Academy of the Incogniti, a powerful politician, novelist, and historian, learned how to survive surrounded by tyrannies. The answer lay in public dissimulation and pretence, and private freedom of expression and disagreement. His own secretary, the brilliant but impetuous Ferrante Pallavicino spoke out against the Pope too freely with his satires and was put to death at 28. B., a novelist of Venetian *mores*, is more cautious, but not enough. He writes an official *Vita* of Ferrante, changing the truth, to 'save' the Academy. At the end of his life at the court of Turin, he writes a truthful history, displeases his patrons, and dies in poverty. Benzoni's picture is dark — one has to write in code, hide behind a mask — yet sets the stage for understanding the heroic efforts needed to write at all. F. P. Franchi, '"Dietro una siepe di bosso": un'autobiografia trasposta' (29–57), proposes that B.'s main characters are repeated adaptations of himself, particularly of his childhood experiences of young love, and losing his mother. At the same time, B. is sensitive to female psychology and gives his female characters depth and complexity. The next three essays are predominantly biographical: M. Guglielminetti, 'Brusoni a Torino' (51–57), gives details of Brusoni's difficulties writing history at the court; L. Contegiacomo, 'Genealogie e documenti brusoniani in archivi veneti ed emiliani' (59–75), transcribes documents relating to the family and constructs a family tree; and C. Corrain, 'L'ambiente monacale dell'abbazia di Santa Maria della Vangadizza nel Seicento' (77–91). The abbey's land bordered on the Brusoni family estate and the abbey itself figures in several of B.'s narratives. M. Fantuzzi, 'La macchina meravigliosa: Girolamo Brusoni e la narrativa barocca' (95–106), opens the second section on literary and linguistic features. He brings V. Propp's

Morphology of the Tale to bear on Brusoni, especially his trilogy of Venetian manners and *mores*, unified by the main character, Glisomiro. He points out that the term 'macchina meravigliosa' is a Seicento one, used by another novelist of his own prose. Following on, F. Ambrosini examines the portrayal of women in 'Il cosmo femminile nella trilogia di Glisomiro di Girolamo Brusoni' (107–21). Numerous women fall in love passionately with Glisomiro, a literary relative of the arch-seducer, Don Giovanni; B. describes them and their attire in vast detail, with the eye of a painter, but presents most of them as submissive, needing to please men for their survival. Ambrosini picks out one heroine, Laureta (in *La gondola a tre remi*), who is the exception: a rebel who expresses her anger against social conventions. By asserting her wish to love but not to marry, she comes nearest to modern sensibilities. M. Cortelazzo, 'Spunti linguistici-etnografici nei romanzi di Brusoni' (123–30), picks out examples of Venetian dialect from B.'s prose and explains their meaning, while A. Bucella, 'Parlato-scritto e tracce di oralità ne *La gondola a tre remi* del Brusoni' (131–40), examines dialogue in this novel, looking for examples of lexis and syntax, of interjections, expressions, and repetition that betray oral discourse. Closing this section with an overview, M. Capucci, 'Qualche riflessione sulla storia letteraria del Seicento' (141–51), maps out the changes that have occurred in the study of Seicento literature in his lifetime and insists on the importance of close attention to historical contextualization that avoids facile generalizations. In the third section, the Incogniti come into their own. M. Miato, 'Accademia e autoprofilo: *Le Glorie degli Incogniti*' (155–61), studies the history and organization of the Academy, the close links of Loredan, as author and patron of other writers, with the press, the Academy's political leanings, and its cultural activities, and the possible authorship of the Academy's own biographies of its members. Taking as her title Gabriel Naudé's opinion of Venice, L. Coci, 'Venise est pleine de libertins et d'athées' (163–75), concentrates on two notorious members of the Incogniti, Ferrante Pallavicino (beheaded for blasphemy on the orders of the Pope) and Antonio Rocco, author of an open eulogy of Socratic love, of older men for young boys, *Alcibiade fanciullo va a scuola*, who lived a hidden life under the protection of Loredan. Brusoni is placed in between the two: he suffers imprisonment and condemnation but survives into old age. A trilogy of historical essays follows: S. Bertelli, 'Barocchismo e razionalismo nella storiografia secentesca' (177–87), reviews the passion for genealogies of illustrious families that historians had to invent, or at least take issue with. Brusoni rejected this practice and concentrated on contemporary history of the Savoy royal family. A. Tenenti, 'Botero, Brusoni e la Francia' (189–97), analyses the problems (particularly concerning religious divisions) encountered by Brusoni in updating Botero's *Relazioni universali* with his own *Istorie universali d'Europa* of 1657. M. Sarnelli, 'Biografie "libertine" del tardo rinascimento franco-italiano' (199–238), gives a historiography of the genre biography in the Seicento, going back to its antecedents in humanist collections of *De viris illustribus*. The last section contains essays on architecture and painting connected to Brusoni (B. M. Boccazzi), on opera (G. Novel and F. Passadore), and the rapport of Rovigo (Brusoni's home town) and Venice (R. Rugolo).

5. Thought

Tacito e tacitismi in Italia da Machiavelli a Vico, ed. Silvio Suppa, Na, Archivio della Ragion di Stato, 201 pp., contains nine articles, five of which examine the role of the Roman historian and political thinker Tacitus in shaping Seicento understanding of the amoral use of power, and especially of the concept of *ragion di stato*. The collection opens up little-known areas, and provides an extensive bibliography on letters and politics in this century. F. Barcia, 'Tacito e tacitismi in Italia tra Cinquecento e Seicento' (43–58), links the study of Tacitus to the interpretation of Machiavelli as a republican and a democrat (both reveal the actions of tyrants to the people) and focuses on Traiano Boccalini's *Ragguagli di Parnaso*. The satirist has Tacitus praised for revealing the real behaviour of princes, but then punished for allowing people to know what princes do, and thus endangering law and order. A. Tirri, 'Il Tacito di Boccalini tra i *Ragguagli* e i *Commentari a Cornelio Tacito'* (59–66), compares the prefaces and the contents of the two works to point out that the two are complementary (the former written in jest and the latter in earnest). M. Proto, 'Il tacitismo di Scipione Ammirato' (67–92), examines this author's *Discorsi sopra Cornelio Tacito nei quali si contiene il fiore di tutto quello si trova sparto nei libri delle attioni de' Principi et del buono e cattivo loro governo*, printed in 1607 and 1642. Tacitus was a weapon with which to attack the bad reputation of Machiavelli in France and at the same time make evident the workings of absolutist regimes. The article concludes with a valuable comparative table of Ammirato's chapters and the corresponding passages in Tacitus. G. Borrelli, 'Tacitismo e scienza politica nel regno di Napoli: Fabio Frezza e Ottavio Sammarco' (93–111), dwells on two unknown figures of the early Seicento in Naples. According to B., the fame of Campanella has obscured the significance of other writers who constitute an original current of Tacitus studies. D. Caruso, 'Tacitismo e "ragion di stato" nella riflessione politica di Giulio Cesare Capaccio' (113–27), examines an unusual Tacitus scholar, who rejected a Machiavellian interpretation of Tacitus for one supporting prince and Church. Capaccio wrote for the court and for the new kind of adviser in his *Secretario*; and for the prince using Alciato's *Emblemata* as a means of providing 'avvertimenti politici e morali utilissimi'.

Two volumes of Paolo Sarpi, *Consulti*, ed. Corrado Pin, I: *I Consulti dell'Interdetto (1606–1607)*; II: *(1607–1609)*, Pisa–Ro, IEPI, 2001, are the first fruits of the definitive edition of Sarpi's advice in the form of written *consulti* to the Senate of the Republic of Venice. The edition deserves special commendation as a model. The 87 'consulti' are accompanied by Sarpi's own notes of a legal, theological, and biblical nature, by Pin's notes, and by the textual variants. As Sarpi wrote about 1100 *consulti*, Pin's project is vast. These two Books deal with judgments about the fraught situation between Venice and Rome concerning jurisdiction over clergy who committed crimes in Venetian territory against lay people. Sarpi argued for Venice's right to try clergy and laity in secular courts by the same laws; Rome wanted to preserve its privileges of trying clergy in its own more lenient courts. Pin places all the *consulti* in the wider frame of Sarpi's moral and religious views.

Emanuele Zinato has brought together eight of his essays about followers of Galileo: *Il vero in maschera: Dialogismi Galileiani. Idee e forme nelle prose scientifiche del Seicento*, Na, Liguori, 179 pp. 'Ironia, parodia e dissimulazione nei *Discorsi* di Giovanni Alfonso Borelli' (19–44) illustrates how Borelli used indirect means of speech to put across new opinions on the causes of typhoid fever, and so avoid censure. The same strategies, Zinato explains in 'L'astuzia dialogica e ventriloqua del Malpighi polemista' (45–64), were needed by Marcello Malpighi, who collaborated with Borelli, and by Lorenzo Bellini, sympathetic to Gassendi (65–82). Zinato also examines Bellini's version of cosmogony (83–113), the *Dialogo* of Donato Rossetti, who followed Galileo, Campanella, and Bruno in his model of the solar system (115–39), and the letter-essay of G. Zambeccari on the effects of opium on sleep, insomnia, and sense perception (141–63). A final essay returns to deception: '"Maledetto sia Copernico!" Dissimulazione e menzogna nel *Dialogo* di Giuseppe Ferroni' (165–79). Ferroni, a Jesuit and disciple of Borelli, was nevertheless a Copernican and distorted known astronomical discoveries for the sake of biblical tradition.

In the field of *ekphrasis* is Stefano Benedetti, *Itinerari di Cebete: tradizione e ricezione della Tabula in Italia dal 15. al 18. secolo*, Ro, Bulzoni, 2001, 405 pp., a fascinating study, the most thorough to date, of the Italian reception of a detailed Greek description of a lost moral-allegorical painting about the Journey of Life, supposedly painted by the Greek Cebes, a contemporary of Plato. Numerous attempts were made to reconstruct and interpret the painting in the Renaissance; for the Seicento, the conviction that the Tablet expressed the sum of moral philosophy found its fullest elaboration in Agostino Mascardi's *Discorsi morali su la Tavola di Cebete Tebano*, published in 1627. B. traces the effect of Mascardi on later writers and moralists, including Ferrante Pallavicino and Giambattista Vico. Outside Italy, literature of journeys through moral landscapes like those of Comenius and Bunyan ensured the genre's flourishing.

BARTOLI. The relationship between science and letters is the subject of Giovanni Baffetti, *et al.*, *Alambicco e Calamaio. Scienza e letteratura fra Seicento e Ottocento*, Mi, Unicopli, 2002, 91 pp., to which Baffetti has contributed 'Daniello Bartoli tra antichi e moderni' (11–38). He places this Jesuit, who composed his scientific treatises late in life at the end of the century among the 'moderns', showing how Bartoli corresponded with the Royal Society in London, praised Galileo, studied Francis Bacon, and argued that there were no limits in the search for new knowledge. Another side of this enigmatic figure is portrayed by G. Sacchi, '"Letterato laico e savio cristiano": Daniello Bartoli e Giambattista Marino', *StSec*, 43, 2002:75–118, who places Bartoli at the heart of a shift in Seicento culture from a predominantly lay literature in the first half of the century (think of the Incogniti), to a predominantly clerical and Jesuitical one in the second half, beginning with Bartoli's *Dell'huomo di lettere difeso et emendato parti due* of 1645. Bartoli's attack on letters was a covert one on the rich, successful court poet Marino (and his followers), turned into the paragon of decadence and licentiousness. The true 'man of letters' stood outside the court, poor, austere, moral, and devoted to Christian values — a slap in the face to any lay man of letters. Sacchi's fine essay reveals the text that more than any other marks the triumph of Counter-Reformation culture in Italy. It's better to be miserable but moral than happy and immoral.

CAMPANELLA. The three short treatises by Tommaso Campanella in *Opuscoli astrologici: Come evitare il fato astrale, Apologetico, Disputa sulle bolle*, introd., trans. (with facing Latin text), and ann. Germana Ernst, Mi, Rizzoli, 277 pp., were written between 1628 and 1632, and are associated with the death of Barberini Pope Urban VIII, which some astrologers said they had predicted by reading malign astrological signs. Like many scientists of his age, C. believed in a 'natural' astrology, but not fatalism. In the first treatise, C. begins confidently with the statement: 'God would not allow any evil to befall the human race without a remedy', and then explains how one can avoid negative influences by practical remedies a physician would know. Accused of heresy and superstition, he wrote the second treatise, a defence of his advice on astrology as compatible with natural philosophy and the Christian tradition. When Pope Urban VIII himself condemned all divinatory practices in a Bull of 1631, C. returned again in the third treatise to the dispute and distinguished carefully between fatalism and predictions based on natural observation. Ernst's introduction provides an intelligent, readable cultural/historical contextualization of the treatises; and a vivid account of the turbulent events of the age. P. Caye, 'Campanella critique de Machiavel. La politique: de la non-philosophie à la métaphysique', *BrC*, 8, 2002:333–51, deconstructs the arguments of those who would make of M. a philosopher or even the founder of a new branch of knowledge. Neither is he in the vanguard of a lay 'modernity'. In his desire to 'theologize' politics and to reconcile the conflicts tearing Europe apart, C. saw clearly that Machiavelli was his main adversary. At the same time, Machiavelli's political pragmatism appealed to C., and he tried to bind it to a providential metaphysics. L. Guerrini, 'Osservazioni sul concetto di teocrazia universale nell'ultimo Campanella', *ib.*, 375–98, develops the above article by illustrating how the desire for a universal theocracy drove all C.'s political thought, especially during his stay in France. The article pays attention to C.'s arguments for the co-operation of Papal and princely powers in *De papatus bono ad principes orationes tres*; and also in *Consideratio de Regno Dei.* J. M. De Bujanda and E. Canone, 'L'Editto di proibizione di Bruno e Campanella. Un'analisi bibliografica', *ib.*, 451–79 + pl., examines the edict of 1603 of the prohibition of 55 books including all Bruno's and Campanella's. The discovery and edition are made possible with the opening of the Archivi Segreti della Congregazione per la Dottrina della Fede. M. Szentpéteri, 'Il Transilvano. The image of Zsigmond Báthory in Campanella's political thought', *ib.*, 9:217–25, looks for an answer to why C. in preparing the Calabrian revolt, had three portraits in his room: the Spanish king Philip III, the Turkish Emperor Mohamed III, and Z. Báthory, prince of Transylvania. By examining C.'s *La monarchia di Spagna* and other writings the author concludes that C. assigned to the prince a sacred mission of inaugurating the reign of Christ.

DELLA PORTA A. Paolella, 'La presenza di Giovan Battista della Porta nel *Carteggio Linceo*', *ib.*, 8, 2002:509–21, details the correspondence early in the century of one of the founders of the Accademia dei Lincei (aimed at the direct study of nature), Federico Cesi, with the famous older scientist Della Porta. Cesi wanted the membership of Della Porta for his fledgling group, and the latter needed the patronage of the wealthy, aristocratic Roman to help publish works condemned by the Inquisition. The respect and loyalty each had for the other lasted a lifetime. In the same years, Cesi was also involved with Galileo, towards whom Della Porta expressed hostile sentiments over who first discovered the telescope. The letters offer a glimpse into the scientific 'republic of letters' at Rome and Naples at the beginning of the Seicento.

GALILEO. F. Berretta, 'Une deuxième abjuration de Galilée ou l'inaltérable hiérarchie des disciplines', *ib.*, 9:9–43, explores in depth Galileo's oscillating pronouncements on Copernicus and heliocentrism, on the one hand, and the Bibical/Aristotelian cosmology requiring geocentrism on the other. Berretta shows how Galileo was caught up between changing interpretations of Scripture: one which 'accommodated' the Bible and another, used at the time of G's recantation, of the hierarchy of the disciplines, by which all natural science was subject to the 'higher' discipline, theology. S. Garcia, 'L'image de Galilée ou la trajectoire symbolique du portrait de 1635', *ib.*, 45–59, points out that Joost Sustermans' portrait of G., first sent to his friend in Paris, Elie Diodati, carried with it the aura of the martyr of free speech, of 'libertas philosophandi', especially after Diodati's defence of G. in 1636 after the scientist's condemnation. Twenty years later, Diodati returned the portrait to the Grand Duke of Tuscany, Ferdinand II, who planned to publish G.'s *Opera omnia.* But by then, G.'s image was tarnished and the portrait no longer cherished. L. Guerrini, '"Con fatiche veramente atlantiche". Il primato della scienza nella lettera a Cristina di Lorena', *ib.*, 61–81, places this essay/letter of 1615 at the heart of G.'s attempts to square his scientific discoveries with a 'broad', anti-literal, interpretation of biblical teaching. Guerrini discusses the letter in relation to other reconciliations of science and theology like the one of Cardinal Carlo Conti of 1612 which, according to some critics, anticipated G.'s own solution. L. S. Varanini, 'La *Dissertatio cum Nuncio Sidereo* fra Galileo e Bruno', *ib.*, 207–15, analyses the long letter of 1610 by the astronomer Kepler in the form of a dialogue between Kepler himself and the 'Starry Messenger' of G.'s treatise proclaiming the discovery of Jupiter's four moons. Kepler is full of praise for G., but at the same time wishes he would acknowledge more explicitly the achievements of predecessors like Giordano Bruno. Other exchanges between the two took place, including a confirmation of G's findings about Jupiter once Kepler had a telescope. M. Torrini, 'La biblioteca di Galileo e dei galileiani', *Intersezioni*, 21, 2001:545–58, presents an unexpected and much-discussed result of cataloguing the library left by Evangelista Torricelli, Galileo's secretary and disciple. At his death in 1647, he had only about a dozen books on mathematics, although he was the lecturer in mathematics at the Florentine Academy, but a much larger collection of classical texts. Torrini also reports that G. himself, to judge from what is known of his library, did not possess many books on mathematics and physics, preferring classical and vernacular literary texts. After Torricelli, the libraries of mathematicians and scientists belonging to the Academy grew in size and variety.

SETTECENTO

By G. W. Slowey, *Senior Lecturer in Italian, University of Birmingham*

1. General

R. Pasta, 'Centri e periferie: spunti sul mercato librario italiano nel Settecento', *Bibliofilìa*, 15:175–200, looks at various factors which influenced book publishing and distribution, including publishers' contacts with figures of the Enlightenment, the impact of religious printing, and the restricted nature of the bourgeois market in Italy. Alongside examination of the importance of the Church's strictures on reading novels, the article also looks at the popularity of Pietro Chiari's work. *Antonio Vallisneri: l'edizione del testo scientifico d'età moderna. Atti del seminario di studi, Scandiano, 12–13 ottobre 2001*, ed. Maria Teresa Monti, F, Olschki, xxi + 232 pp., discusses the editing and publication of 18-c. scientific texts under three main headings: 'Materiali di ricerca'; 'Tipologie del testo scientifico e criteri ecdotici'; and 'Edizioni e inventari elettronici'. G. Granata, *'La biblioteca del cardinale Stefano Borgia', *ASNP*, 2001:225–38. M. Catto, *'La "guerra dei catechismi" nel Settecento: il caso di Roberto Bellarmino', *AISIGT*, 28:95–131.

AnI, 21, is devoted to journeys, with the title *Hodoeporics revisited / Ritorno all'odeporica*, and for the 18th c. contains I. Crotti, 'Margini del viaggio: tra Marivaux e Goldoni' (137–59), which analyses Marivaux's *La surprise de l'amour*, Goldoni's *La locandiera*, and Algarotti's *Il congresso di Citera*. On travellers, too, is P. Bianchi, 'In cerca del moderno. Studenti e viaggiatori inglesi a Torino nel Settecento', *RSI*, 115:1021–51, which discusses the presence of the English as part of the *viaggio di formazione* that prepared many of them for high diplomatic careers, pointing out also their interest in broader cultural matters.

Matteo Ermini, *La cultura toscana del primo Settecento e l'origine della Società Colombaria Fiorentina*, F, Olschki, 95 pp., deals with the political situation and the general cultural climate at the beginning of the 18th c., tracing the origins of the society itself to meetings organized in the 1730s by Giovanni Girolamo de' Pazzi and Bindo Simone Peruzzi amongst others, and it finishes with an examination of the *Annali* of the society. B. Dooley, 'Accademie scientifiche venete nel Settecento', *SV*, 45:91–106, treats the development of academies, especially in Venice and Padua, examining in particular those institutions most interested in scientific discussion which led to a more critical approach to existing tradition and to an acceptance of notions of change. G. De Miranda, 'Tra storia politica e ragioni sociologiche.

Rassegna di studi per una definizione delle accademie italiane sei-settecentesche', *EL*, 28.4: 104–09, examines recent publications in Italy and elsewhere on the subject of academies in Italy. A. Gisondi, 'Ragione naturale e lumi per Alfonso de' Liguori e Antonio Genovesi', *Archivio di Storia della Cultura*, 16: 169–218, draws on recent historiography to dismiss the notion of Liguori as anti-Enlightenment, showing how he uses the concept of 'ragione naturale' to approach notions of the 'scienza dell'uomo', and examining similarities between Liguori and Genovesi on anthropological and other matters while emphasizing their differences in relation to such ideas as 'lumi divini'. A. Granese, 'Il riformismo politico-religioso di Pietro Giannone e Alberto Radicati', *EL*, 28.4: 3–25, describes Giannone's work in the *Istoria civile* as a deliberate challenge to the Church, continuing in the *Triregno* with his championing of primitive Christianity. His approach is compared to that of Alberto Radicati: both are seen as supporters of the lay state, which in the end did not live up to their expectations. R. Varese, 'La *Psiche* seconda: "ed ha un occulto magistero"', *SV*, 45: 263–334, sees Canova's *Psiche* (1789–1792) as representing the cultural ideal of such people as Mengs in the reconstruction of the classical. There is an extensive appendix of letters, including a number to and from Canova.

2. Prose, Poetry, Drama

Guido Morpurgo-Tagliabue e l'estetica del Settecento, ed. Luigi Russo, contains papers from a conference held in Palermo in 2002 which analyse various of Morpurgo-Tagliabue's writings on the Settecento and aesthetics. Guido Morpurgo-Tagliabue, *Il gusto nell'estetica del Settecento*, Palermo, Centro Internazionale Studi di Estetica, 2002, 254 pp., collects together from the 1960s a number of essays on aesthetics and notions of taste in 18th-c. Italy and Britain.

StSet, 22, 2002, under the title *Pace e guerra nella cultura italiana ed europea del Settecento*, contains the following articles on Italian topics: G. Ricuperati, 'Pace e guerra nella cultura europea del Settecento. Problemi di ricerca fra antitesi e dilemma' (25–40); E. Di Rienzo, 'Guerra civile e "guerra giusta" dall'antico regime alla Rivoluzione' (41–74); C. Donati, 'Stati, società, eserciti nel XVIII secolo: percorsi di ricerca' (75–87); P. Bianchi, 'Guerra e pace nel Settecento: alcune riflessioni sul caso sabaudo' (89–102); A. Dattero, 'Riforme militari e costituzionali nella Lombardia austriaca del Settecento' (103–21); A. M. Rao, 'Il Settecento italiano e la guerra' (123–39); C. Campa, 'Suoni della guerra e immaginario militare: evoluzione di una costante musicale nel segno del *pathos* eroico' (141–52); B. Danna,

'Goldoni e la guerra' (207–15); and G. Santato, 'Alfieri e la milizia. Dalla *Tirannide* alle *Satire*' (217–33).

Letteratura italiana e cultura europea tra illuminismo e romanticismo, ed. Guido Santato, Geneva, Droz, 384 pp., comprises the following items: G. Ricuperati, 'La cultura italiana nel secondo Settecento europeo' (33–64); S. Moravia, 'La filosofia degli "Idéologues". Scienza dell'uomo e riflessione epistemologica tra Sette e Ottocento' (65–79); L. Sozzi, 'L'idea dell'illusione tra la fine del Settecento e l'inizio dell'Ottocento' (81–93); M. Cerruti, 'Dalla "sociabilité" illuministica al mito del poeta solitario. La musa saturnina' (95–109); C. Capra, ' "l'opinione regina del mondo". Percorsi dell'evoluzione politica e intellettuale di Pietro Verri' (111–31); P. Del Negro, 'Rappresentazioni della guerra in Italia tra Illuminismo e Romanticismo' (133–60); M. Pastore Stocchi, 'Cenni su alcune tradizioni neoclassiche' (161–73); G. Baldassarri, 'Cesarotti fra Omero e Ossian' (175–207); G. Pizzamiglio, 'Illuminismo e Neoclassicismo a Venezia' (209–24); A. Fabrizi, 'Le discussioni sulla lingua nel secondo Settecento: da Baretti a Galeani Napione' (225–41); P. Adinolfi, 'L'idea della felicità tra la fine del Settecento e l'inizio dell'Ottocento' (243–52); A. Motta, 'I cambiamenti della forma-romanzo fra Illuminismo e Romanticismo: il caso Piazza' (253–74); F. Fido, 'La storia a teatro. Dalla tragedia settecentesca e alfieriana ai componimenti teatrali di Giovanni Pindemonte' (275–89); G. Santato, 'Un itinerario intellettuale tra Illuminismo e Romanticismo: Alfieri e Voltaire' (291–323); A. Di Benedetto, 'Da Goethe a Platen: momenti della fortuna di Alfieri in Germania' (325–35); E. Bonfatti, 'L'antologia tedesca di Aurelio de' Giorgi Bertola' (337–49); and E. Guagnini, 'Il viaggio, lo sguardo, la scrittura. Generi e forme della letteratura odeporica tra Sette e Ottocento' (351–66).

Le muse in loggia: massoneria e letteratura nel Settecento, Mi, Unicopli, 2002, 104 pp., is one of a series of occasional publications by the Dipartimento di Italianistica, Università di Parma, and contains: G. M. Cazzaniga, 'Massoneria e letteratura. Dalla *République des Lettres* alla letteratura nazionale' (11–32), which discusses the development of freemasonry from the beginning of the 18th c., together with literary movements where the idea of what is national runs alongside notions of internationalism; G. Tocchini, 'Frugoni e la Francia. Opere massoniche per Parma' (33–82), which deals with cultural developments in Parma under Don Filippo e Don Ferdinando di Borbone, examining attempts to reform the theatre and Frugoni's masonic contacts, revealed in his production of translations for the lyric theatre in Parma, in particular in *I Tindaridi*, Frugoni's version of Gentile Bernard's *Castor et Pollux*; R. Turchi, 'La "compagnia de galentomeni"' (83–104), examining the editorial principles underlying the Marsilio edition of Goldoni's *Le donne curiose*, which deals with freemasonry, and also of his *I morbinosi*, which according to Turchi has a masonic subtext.

Scritture di desiderio e di ricordo: autobiografie, diari, memorie tra Settecento e Novecento, Mi, Angeli, 2002, 444 pp., contains: M. C. Lamberti, 'Biografia di un'autobiografia. Riflessioni sulla *Vita di Francesco Bal (1766–1836)*' (73–81), on the historical accuracy of autobiography; S. Onger, 'Vita, viaggi e avventure del giovane conte Giuseppe Lechi (1766–1795)' (82–94), which looks at Lechi's autobiography and the diary of his journeys; R. Pasta, '"Ego ipse . . .non alius". Esperienze e memorie di un lettore del Settecento' (187–206), which deals with the *Efemeridi* of Giuseppe Pelli, a Florentine patrician and director of the Uffizi, whose diary covers the period 1759–1808; and N. Del Bianco, 'Un diario privato di Francesco Melzi d'Eril' (286–307), which covers 6–17 May 1796 and of which there are selections in an appendix.

Renato Barilli, *Dal Boccaccio al Verga. La narrativa italiana in età moderna*, Mi, Bompiani, 404 pp., contains brief writings on Goldoni, Gozzi, Casanova, and Alfieri. Mirella Agorni, *Translating Italy for the Eighteenth Century: Women, Translation and Travel Writing, 1739–1797*, Manchester, St Jerome, 2002, 169 pp., looks at writers such as Ann Radcliffe and translations of Algarotti's *Newtonianismo per le dame* by Elizabeth Carter, and at travel literature on Italy by women such as Hester Thrale Piozzi.

Settecento russo e italiano. Atti del Convegno, Genova 25–26 novembre 1999, ed. Maria Luisa Dondero and Maria Cristina Bragone, Bergamo, Facoltà di Lingue e Letterature Straniere, 2002, 232 pp., has the following articles of interest: P. Cazzola, 'Illuministi russi nell'Italia del Grand Tour' (1–13), which looks in particular at the links between the Bologna Accademia delle Scienze and its sister academy in St Petersburg; M. Di Salvo, 'Russia vecchia e nuova nelle memorie di Filippo Balatri' (15–22), which examines the six volumes of Balatri's *Vita e viaggi* describing his two-year stay in Russia; M. C. Bragone, 'Da Venezia a Mosca: storia di una traduzione di Fedor Polikarpov' (23–31), on a translation into Russian of an Armenian text printed in Venice; S. Rotta, 'Russia 1739: il filosofo sedentario e il filosofo viaggiatore' (33–71), which, in the first part, deals with Paolo Mattia Doria's *Politica alla moda* and in the second part with Algarotti's diary of his trip to Russia in 1739 on board Lord Baltimore's yacht; I. Volodina, 'Fr. Algarotti ed A. Kantemir (intorno alla storia di un'epistola in versi)' (73–85), which is concerned with a poem written by Algarotti to the Empress Anna Ivanovna on the occasion of Kantemir's translation of *Newtonianismo per le dame*. There are other articles on the relationship with the Church and on art. Guido Santato, *Letteratura italiana nel secondo Settecento: protagonisti e percorsi*, Modena, Mucchi, 318 pp., is a collection in revised form of already published articles.

A. Di Stefano, 'Cani e gatti. "Silhouette" favolistiche settecentesche', *Sincronie*, 13:227–38, looks at the use in poetry of images of the cat and the dog, drawn from fable, in order to comment on contemporary society. By the same author is 'Acqua, ruscelli, venti, palloni volanti e zefiretti amorosi', *ib.*, 12, 2002:239–48, which examines the use in 18th-c. fables of themes based on the observation of nature.

G. Camerino, 'Oltre la memoria e l'infanzia. Noia e non-vivere da Alfieri a Leopardi', *GSLI*, 180:191–205, analyses the approach of the two writers in their reliving of childhood through memory, showing also Leopardi's acquaintance with Alfieri's ideas. D. Vanden Borghe, 'Le *Annotazioni* alle *Canzoni* di Leopardi e la *Proposta* di Monti', *RLI*, 107:65–77, deals with the linguistic influence of Monti on Leopardi, especially of his *Proposta di alcune correzioni e aggiunte al Vocabolario della Crusca*. R. Zucco, 'Il sonetto anacreontico e altre sperimentazioni settecentesche sul sonetto', *SMI*, 1, 2001:223–58, points out some interesting technical aspects of the 18th-c. sonnet, drawing on poets as diverse as Francesco Gritti, Frugoni, and Paolo Rolli, examining too the poems written for music by Balestrieri and others. C. E. Roggia, 'Sintassi dell'*Ordo verborum artificialis*. Preliminari ad una indagine sulla poesia del Settecento', *SLI*, 29:161–82, draws widely for its examples on Parini and Algarotti. Pier Vincenzo Mengaldo, *Gli incanti della vita. Studi su poeti italiani del Settecento*, Padua, Esedra, 141 pp., gathers together articles which have appeared elsewhere.

Giovanna Zanlonghi, *Teatri di formazione. Actio, parola e immagine nella scena gesuitica del Sei-Settecento a Milano*, Mi, Vita e Pensiero, 2002, xxvi + 397 pp., has, for our period, an examination of work by Tommaso Ceva at the end of the 17th century and the beginning of the 18th, dealing primarily with work commissioned for special occasions, such as the death of Charles VI in 1740 and the installation of archbishop Giuseppe Pozzobonelli in 1744, who had himself taken part in dramatic productions during his time in the Collegio dei Nobili in Milan. The book finishes with an account of the theatrical presentations for the marriage between Archduke Ferdinand and Beatrice d'Este in 1771.

B. Brumana, 'Il componimento drammatico *San Benedetto al Monte-Casino* (1778) e la vita musicale nel monastero di S. Pietro a Perugia all'epoca di Francesco Zanetti (1762–1788)', *Benedictina*, 50:337–62, traces what the author refers to as 'paraliturgical' production of oratorios, using as an example this work by Cesare Orlandi, whose only libretto this appears to be. We know nothing of the music or its composer, though the writer argues that the latter may be identified with Francesco Zanetti who was responsible for various oratorios and melodramas in Perugia in the late 18th century. L. Verdi, 'Il Farinelli a Bologna', *NRMI*, 37:197–237, apart from discussing Farinelli's connections with Gluck and the young Mozart, also examines his contribution to cultural life in Bologna at the time of his debut there in 1727 and after his return to the city in 1760. *The Correspondence of Agostino Steffani and Giuseppe Riva, 1720–1728, and Related Correspondence with J. P. F. von Schönborn and S. B. Pallavicini*, ed. Lowell Lindgren and Colin Timms, *RMA Research Chronicle*, 36, 174 pp., publishes the interesting correspondence between Steffani and various diplomatic friends, which, amongst other matters, is concerned with Steffani's attempts to establish music in various cities in Europe. E. Bellotti, 'La vita musicale a Pavia nel Settecento', *NRMI*, 37:29–66, discusses the musical life of the city in the context of the wider cultural scene, particularly in relation to the theatre and the Church, examining the activities of various academies. In an appendix, there is a list of music manuscripts in the archives of the Seminario Vescovile.

3. Individual Authors

ALFIERI. A. Vigiani, 'Per una nuova considerazione del petrarchismo delle *Rime* alfieriane', *AFLUM*, 35, 2002:507–26, analyses A.'s indebtedness to Petrarch, while acknowledging that his use of Petrarch is in contrast with the dying Petrarchist school of the 18th century. The article points out the analogies between A.'s *Rime* and Petrarch's poetry and at the same time the clash between A.'s respect for Petrarch and his own 'proprio sentire'. G. Natali, *'Sulle tracce di Emma: presenze petrarchesche nei sonetti di Alfieri', *La Cultura*, 41:491–516.

C. Barbolani, 'Teneri accenti e languidi sospiri: su una traduzione spagnola inedita della *Mirra*', *EL*, 28.1:45–66, examines in detail the translation by Joaquin Roca y Cornet to show that A. was not simply considered in Spain as a writer of anti-tyrannical works. By the same author and on the same topic of Spanish translation is 'Alfieri stravolto: su una "Congiura de' Pazzi" spagnola', *CFI*, 9, 2002:49–77, which examines Francisco Rodrigues de Ledesma's *Lucrecia Pazzi* to see how closely it is influenced by A.'s play and points out the very different ideological standpoint of the two writers. S. Casini, 'Il ramo d'oro dell'antichità. Alfieri e la discesa agli inferi sulle orme di Seneca', *RLI*, 107:5–33, discusses A.'s somewhat ambivalent approach to Seneca, looking at his youthful reactions and the way he goes back to subjects from antiquity, and underlining

1779 as the year which marks the split between ancient and modern in the writing of *Rosmunda* and *Ottavia*; the article shows how these two tragedians of the universal have very different ways of dealing with the passions. A. Di Benedetto, '"Michelangiol, da' rei tempi costretto . . .". Alfieri e le arti figurative', *GSLI*, 180: 161–90, treats A.'s notable 'chiusura ai colori e insensibilità per la pittura' on the occasion of his first journey to Florence in 1766 and examines the influence on him of Luisa Stolberg, no mean painter herself, looking at what might be termed 'artistic' perception in other writings of A. Id., *Il dandy e il sublime. Nuovi studi su Vittorio Alfieri*, F, Olschki, 185 pp., collects together, with some revision, studies which have appeared before, together with three new ones: 'L'"orrendo a un tempo e innocente amore" di Mirra' (39–53); 'Nelle "regioni boreali". Varia fortuna di Alfieri in Germania' (117–35); and 'Genio o talento forzato? Vittorio Alfieri da autore a personaggio' (137–59). G. Luti, 'Vittorio Alfieri: attrazione e rifiuto della rivoluzione francese', in Id., *Letteratura e rivoluzione: saggi su Alfieri, Foscolo, Leopardi*, F, Pagliai Polistampa, 2002, 123 pp. G. P. Marchi, 'Tra cavalli e lettere: nota sul terzo viaggio in Inghilterra di Vittorio Alfieri', *LItal*, 55: 443–49, takes issue with A.'s description in the *Vita* of his life in London in this period, suggesting that it was not as isolated an existence as he would have us believe. *Letture alfieriane*, F, Edizioni Polistampa, 151 pp., contains: A. Battistini, '*Vita scritta da esso*' (13–34); M. Guglielminetti, '*Saul*' (35–42); A. Di Benedetto, 'L'"orrendo a un tempo e innocente amore" di Mirra' (53–68); R. Fedi, 'Le *Rime*' (69–84); M. Cerruti, 'Alfieri politico' (85–97); M. Sterpos, 'L'Alfieri comico dall'*Esquisse* alle commedie' (99–125); and A. Dardi, 'Alfieri e la lingua italiana' (127–46). *Alfieri e il suo tempo. Atti del Convegno internazionale, Torino–Asti, 29 novembre–1 dicembre 2001*, F, Olschki, xi + 486 pp., has three sections, divided as follows: I. 'Torino e gli stati sardi al tramonto dell'Antico Regime': G. Ricuperati, 'Vittorio Alfieri, società e stato sabaudo: fra appartenenza e distanza' (3–45); M. Cerruti, 'La letteratura' (47–54); P. Delpiano, 'Come si crea "lo spirito di nazione". Università ed educazione dell'élite nel Piemonte del Settecento' (55–88); P. Bianchi, '"Quel fortunato e libero paese". L'Accademia Reale e i primi contatti del giovane Alfieri con il mondo inglese' (89–112); M. T. Silvestrini, '"Sei anella della sacra catena". Politica e religione nel Piemonte settecentesco' (113–30); A. Merlotti, 'Il caso Dunand: vitalità e insidie della sociabilità nella Torino di Alfieri (1772–1777)' (131–77). II. 'Figure di rilievo dell'esperienza di Alfieri': W. Spaggiari, 'Paolo Maria Paciaudi' (181–212); G. P. Marchi, 'Tra storia e poesia. Alfieri e Pindemonte alla presa della Bastiglia' (213–41); G. Santato, 'Alfieri e Caluso' (243–74); M. Tatti, 'Alfieri e l'artificiosa rimozione dei modelli tragici: l'incontro a Roma con Jean-Gabriel La Porte Du Theil' (275–94); A. Chemello, 'Isabella Teotochi Albrizzi interprete di Mirra' (295–310); and T. Heydenreich, 'Ludwig Hain, traduttore della *Vita*' (311–19). III. 'Percorsi – sentimentali, intellettuali, politici – di Alfieri': L. Ricaldone, 'La donna "nuova" e il "genio": per un ritratto di Luisa Stolberg' (323–42); E. Strumia, 'Su *Il divorzio* e oltre' (342–65); F. Vazzoler, 'Alfieri fra drammaturgia italiana e drammaturgia europea' (367–87); G. Pagliero, 'Santi, martiri e "capi-setta": la religione ai tempi del Principato' (389–406); N. Mineo, 'Vittorio Alfieri nella crisi dell'Antico Regime' (407–44); and G. Schlüter, 'La bella repubblica settecentesca. Alfieri in confronto al contemporaneo repubblicanesimo tedesco. Uno schizzo' (445–61).

Cotteri, *Alfieri*, comprises: P. Trivero, '"Io tutti in me gli affetti / Sento di madre, e d'esser madre abborro": Giocasta in Alfieri' (1–18); H. Felten, 'Osservazioni intorno al discorso narcisista nella *Vita* di Alfieri' (19–29); C. Barbolani, 'Alfieri nella cultura spagnola: un approccio' (30–51); R. Reisinger, 'Vittorio Alfieri e André Chénier: tragedia di un'amicizia' (52–63); J. Lindon, 'Appunti sulla ricezione inglese dell'Alfieri nella prima metà dell'Ottocento' (64–77); K. Ley, 'Alfieri in der deutschen Literatur oder: warum las Schiller im Jahre 1803 italienische Tragödien?' (78–91); G. A. Camerino, 'L'Alfieri di Schlegel. Una polemica pregiudiziale' (92–107); E. Kanduth, 'A proposito di alcune traduzioni alfieriane in tedesco' (108–24); R. Scrivano, 'Mito e potere nelle tragedie del ciclo tebano' (125–40); G. Marchi, 'Voltaire, Lessing e Alfieri di fronte alla *Merope* di Scipione Maffei' (141–68); and A. Di Benedetto, 'Da autore a personaggio' (169–81).

BERTATI. R. Angemüller, 'Pasquale Anfossi's *Il curioso indiscreto* in Rovereto (1778)' *AARA*, 252, 2002: 119–45, deals with Giovanni Bertati as the possible librettist of this opera and with various productions of the work between 1777 and 1792.

CAMINER. *L'illuminismo e le donne. Gli scritti di Elisabetta Caminer: utilità e piacere*, ed. Mariagabriella Di Giacomo, Ro, La Sapienza, 2002, 297 pp., contains an anthology on various topics such as modern literature, education, and theatre, as well as material from C.'s own writings about herself.

CASANOVA. S. Ferri, 'L'impulso melancolico nei *Mémoires* di Casanova. La Charpillon', *Sincronie*, 11, 2002: 107–13, examines C.'s treatment of Charpillon alongside that of Pepita and Conchita. M. Lessona Fasano, 'Casanova sconosciuto', *Riscontri*, 25, 2–3: 21–28, attempts to rehabilitate C. for modern readers in the context of his elegant writing and his keen observation of the world around him. T. Iermano, '"Non oso afferrarmi al suo mantello rosso". Giacomo Casanova e la Napoli settecentesca negli studi di Salvatore Di

Giacomo', *CLett*, 31:441–77, discusses Di Giacomo's writings on Casanova and his translation of the *Fuga dai Piombi.*

CASTI. Giambattista Casti, '*Il pallone aerostatico*', *Sincronie*, 11, 2002:9–26, is the first publication of this verse novella, together with a critical apparatus by Lucia Rodler. On the same topic and by the latter is, 'Un volo di Giambattista Casti', *ib.*, 27–36, which deals with notions of flight in the 18th c. and looks at C.'s *Il pallone aerostatico.* A. Arce, '*Prima la musica, poi le parole*: "Divertimento" metateatral de G. B. Casti', *CFI*, 9, 2002:79–99, discusses aspects of the libretto which reflect the interests of musical society of the day, such as the clash between *opera seria* and *opera buffa.*

CONTI. Antonio Conti, *Lettere da Venezia a Madame la Comtesse de Caylus, 1727–29. Con l'aggiunta di un Discorso sullo stato di Francia*, ed. Sylvie Mamy, F, Olschki, 275 pp. R. Rabboni, 'Antonio Conti traduttore con una lettera inedita a Scipione Maffei', *AMAGP*, 115, 217–42, discusses this correspondence between the two men on such subjects as the rebirth of tragic theatre and deals with Maffei's negative response to C.'s *Cesare* (1723), presenting a letter in which C. discusses translating Homer and other classics.

DE COUREIL. A. Di Stefano, 'Un favolista cosmopolita del Settecento: Giovanni Salvatore De Coureil', *AMAT*, 68:227–57, is concerned with De C.'s *Favole, novelle e altre poesie* of 1787, which were modelled on La Fontaine and Lorenzo Pignotti, seeing the work as fitting in with the 18th-c. polemic against subjects such as false erudition.

GOLDONI. Carlo Goldoni, *Le bourru bienfaisant – Il burbero di buon cuore*, ed. Paolo Luciani, Venice, Marsilio, 345 pp. Id., *Il cavaliere e la dama*, ed. Franco Arato, Venice, Marsilio, 245 pp. *Problemi di critica goldoniana*, 9, 2002, has a couple of useful items: P. Ranzini, 'I canovacci goldoniani per il Théatre Italien secondo la testimonianza di un "Catalogo delle robbe" inedito' (7–168), which draws on a *catalogo delle robbe* dating from the late 1760s to illustrate the 155 titles produced for the theatre up to that date; and I. Crotti, 'I chiasmi teatrali della *Locandiera*' (169–227), which examines the complexity of the figure of Mirandolina. M. Arnando, 'La scena muta. Le illustrazioni settecentesche di Goldoni nel loro rapporto con i testi', *Intersezioni*, 23:467–98, discusses differences in illustration presentation between different editions, in particular those of Pasquali and Zatta, together with instances of the same images being used for different texts.

GOZZI, G. F. Soldini, 'Inventario dei manoscritti letterari di Gasparo Gozzi', *SV*, 46:355–91, presents a list of manuscripts, many of which have not been published.

KREGLIANOVICH. *A critical edition of Giovanni Kreglianovich's tragedy 'Orazio'*, ed. Michael Lettieri and Rocco Mario Morano, Lewiston, Mellen, cxxii + 350 pp., has an extensive introduction to this text of 1797 and includes in an appendix sources on which the play is based, including Corneille's *Horace*.

METASTASIO. *Metastasio nell'Ottocento*, ed. Francesco Paolo Russo, Ro, Aracne, xvii + 195 pp., includes: A. Ziino, '"Ritorna vincitor": proposte per una ricerca sulla fortuna di Metastasio nell'Ottocento' (1–11); M. Valente, 'L'Ottocento e Pietro Metastasio. Un modello di vita per la borghesia come nostalgia del Bello' (13–32); B. M. Antolini, 'Metastasio nella trattatistica musicale italiana del primo Ottocento' (33–41); F. Lippmann, 'Le revisioni dei drammi metastasiani nello sviluppo dell'opera seria dal 1770 al 1830' (43–60); F. P. Russo, 'Su alcuni libretti metastasiani intonati da Saverio Mercadante' (61–79); A. Lerro, 'L'*Achille in Sciro* da Pietro Metastasio a Rapisardi–Coppola' (81–93); G. Mascari, 'Il primo periodo artistico di Giovanni Pacini: *Temistocle* e *Alessandro nell'Indie*' (95–110); P. Petrobelli, 'Metastasio e il melodramma (alcuni spunti)' (111–20); R. Vlad, 'Metastasio e la scuola classica viennese' (121–26); M. Engelhardt, 'Metastasio "ottocentesco": la situazione nei paesi di lingua tedesca' (127–35); and L. Biancini, '*La Didona der Metastazzio:* Metastasio e il teatro popolare romano' (137–72).

MONTI. F. Favaro, 'Su Monti traduttore: versioni giovanili e misconosciute', *RLI*, 107:34–64, argues that for M. there is no clear distinction between a simple Italian version and the autonomous creative process, illustrating the argument from various of M.'s early works, including the *Degli endecasillabi di Dreso Cromonio* and discusses his links with Dionigi Strocchi.

PARINI. Giuseppe Parini, *Prose*, II: *Lezioni; Elementi di retorica*, ed. Silvia Morgana and Pietro Bartesaghi, Mi, Università degli Studi, 454 pp., contains the text from P.'s autograph of the *Lezioni di Belle Lettere* and other items, including students' notes, together with an excellent introduction, both historical and linguistic. Bartolo Anglani, *I lumi della notte. Progresso e poesia in Giuseppe Parini*, Ro–Bari, Laterza, 2002, 243 pp., examines how far P. can be considered an Enlightenment writer, emphasizing his belief in the dominance of the word, where the artist is the one who can best model the language, and arguing that *Notte* demonstrates P.'s view of history as something separate from 'contemporaneità' in a vision which is concerned with notions of a common humanity.

RISTORI. A. Cristiani, 'Una pagina poco nota di storia letteraria del Settecento: il "colpo d'occhio sullo stato presente della letteratura" di Giovanni Ristori', *LItal*, 55:267–92, analyses this work of R. which appeared anonymously in episodes between 1788 and 1789.

While pointing out idiosyncratic and at times totally inaccurate analyses, the author suggests that it is a work which reflects a tone both 'vivo e inquieto' in a typically Enlightenment perspective.

TIRABOSCHI. P. Simon, 'L'Italie et la France dans la *Storia della letteratura italiana* de Tiraboschi', *REI*, 48, 2002:347–58, shows how Tiraboschi was interested in mentioning Italian scientists and historians of France, while pointing out that Italian influence was much less evident in the 17th c. than in the 18th, and seeing much less French influence on Italy.

VERRI, P. A. Fabrizi, 'Rassegna bibliografica per Pietro Verri', *GSLI*, 180:414–26, is an good contribution on V., referred to as 'il nostro illuminista principale' and showing V.'s importance not just in Italy but throughout Europe.

OTTOCENTO

POSTPONED

NOVECENTO

By Roberto Bertoni, *Senior Lecturer in Italian, Trinity College Dublin* and Catherine O'Brien, *Professor of Italian, National University of Ireland, Galway*

1. General

Reflecting on Italian literature in the 20th c., Ezio Raimondi, *Novecento e dopo. Considerazioni su un secolo di letteratura*, Ro, Carocci, 168 pp., illustrates how in modernity the sublime cohabits with chaos and discontinuity prevails over linear chronology. Modernity is characterized by fragmentation, plural styles, and multiplicity, and modern literature is based on language but inevitably reflects life and history. **Storia della letteratura italiana contemporanea*, ed. Neuro Bonifazi, introd. Giorgio Luti, Arezzo, Helicon, 528 pp. *Italianistica*, 31, 2002, 2–3, is devoted to the 20th-c. as **Novecento letterario*, ed. Bruno Porcelli, Pisa, IEPI, 404 pp. *Thompson Vol.* examines a variety of fiction-writers and dramatists noted below under the individual authors Paola Capriolo, Carlo Levi, Natalia Ginzburg, Luigi Pirandello, Ignazio Silone, Italo Svevo, and Sebastiano Vassalli.

On the 20th-c. canon, Alfonso Berardinelli, 'Dove sta andando la letteratura?', *FAM*, 21, 2001 : 185–90, an interview given to P. Napoli, consists of a brief review of the most significant Italian texts in the 20th c. B. dismisses phenomena such as *dannunzianesimo* and futurism, but rescues a number of writers, especially Elsa Morante, whom he regards as a major Novecento figure. In contemporary Italy he sees poetry and prose as declining mainly because of what he calls a 'noiosità' prevalent in the 1990s and the fact that writers seem to take specific political sides instead of discussing things impartially. A. Riccio, 'Contro il canone', pp. 113–38 of *Oltrecanone. Per una cartografia della scrittura femminile*, ed. Anna Maria Crispino, Ro, Manifestolibri, 176 pp., in her gender analysis argues not only against the male-dominated canon in the history of literature, but also in favour of a deconstruction and rejection of the concept of canon itself.

On literary genres and movements, U. Dotti, 'Gli scrittori e la storia, da Silone a Elsa Morante', *Belfagor*, 58 : 125–58. Silvia Bellotto, *Metamorfosi del fantastico. Immaginazione e linguaggio nel racconto surreale italiano del Novecento*, Bo, Pendragon, 300 pp., sees Italian surrealism (as represented by Alberto Savinio, Giorgio De Chirico, Massimo Bontempelli, Tommaso Landolfi, and Antonio Delfini) as a modern form of fantasy, a new paradigm which does not require the reader's suspension of disbelief, portrays daily life, and insists on the themes of death and nothingness inherited from Schopenhauer, Nietzsche, and Leopardi. It thus becomes an allegory of the crisis of the individual in modernity, of the difficult balance between reason and fantasy, of the contradictions and conflicts between order and disorder, truth and metaphysics, dream and reality. On fantasy and the fantastic, especially in early 20th-c. work, *Poetiche*, 5.2, contains various articles: P. Pieri, 'Il simbolico nel racconto fantastico', 141–88, observes that modern symbols are partly linked to their ancient meanings but, in contrast to Junghian archetypes, develop historically and attempt to give shape to the world, represent world-visions, and create allegories: modern writers reinterpret archaic symbols in new ways according to social and personal inclinations, and this can be seen in a number of writers, including Aldo Palazzeschi in his poetry and prose. A. M. Mangini, 'Il maldestro demiurgo. Note sul "doppio" nel fantastico papiniano', 189–237, includes a discussion of Freud's concept of the *Unheimliche* in relation to the unsettling nature of *alter egos* and doubles created by the subconscious and found in Papini's stories. L. Weber, '"Una polveriera di fantasia". Esotismo, fiaba e fantascienza nel movimento futurista', 239–308, examines two novels, Paolo Buzzi's *L'ellisse e la spirale* and Bruno Corra's *Sam Dunn è morto*. S. Bellotto, '"Il demone in ogni cosa". Fantasma e fantasia in Alberto Savinio', 309–58, relates the theme of 'fantasmi' to Savinio's sense of 'mistero' investigated by 'intelletto' but open to exploration through 'fantasia', and also notes similarities in this respect between Alberto Savinio and his brother Giorgio De Chirico.

On postmodernism, *Tirature '04*, ed. Vittorio Spinazzola, Mi, Il Saggiatore, 320 pp., includes essays by F. Brioschi, A. Rollo, B. Pischedda, P. Giovannetti, and V. Spinazzola, where, among other things, the innovative style of postmodernism and its promotion of a pluralistic culture are highlighted, while reductionist views on modernism as simply based on grand narratives and utopian ideals are questioned. R. Bonavita, 'Il punto sul *pastiche*: *Santa Mira* di Gabriele Frasca e *Tutto il ferro della Torre Eiffel* di Michele Mari', *Il Verri*, 22:145–52, reads the two novels mentioned in the title as samples of postmodernist *pastiche*, and highlights Frasca's analysis of alienation and Mari's poetics of literature as 'artificio'. R. Donnarumma, 'Postmoderno italiano', *Allegoria*, 43:56–85, defines 'postmodernity' as the historical age which started in the 1950s and continues to the present, but considers both the aesthetics of 'postmodernismo' (dated 1965–90) and the cultural era of the 'postmoderno' now to be over. He argues that postmodernism proper never existed in Italy even though some critics (such as Achille Bonito Oliva) and creative writers (like Umberto Eco) came close to it. Works which may be considered postmodernist are Alberto Arbasino's *Fratelli d'Italia* and Giorgio Manganelli's *Hilarotragoedia* thanks to their nihilism, humour, perception of emptiness over ideology, and reduction of reality to metanarratives. Discussed against the background of postmodernism are the neoavantgarde and Pier Vittorio Tondelli's work in the 1980s. F. Muzzioli, 'Teoria e radicalità. Una rassegna non rassegnata tra le posizioni letterarie attuali', *Moderna*, 4.1 : 29–44, reflects on contemporary postmodernist, feminist, and postcolonial theories, and argues that a radical type of modernism is still possible. A. Tricomi, 'Crisi delle testualità, esplosione della biblioteca. La nascita del postmoderno in Italia', *Allegoria*, 44 : 35–60, in contrast to Barilli's views argues that postmodernism in Italy did not start with the Gruppo 63 but rather in the 1970s with what he calls a 'crisi delle testualità' and weakening of the coherence of the literary canon. He considers Gianni Celati and Pier Vittorio Tondelli as examples of this tendency, while Antonio Moresco is seen as coming at the end of the period. Matteo De Gesù, **La tradizione del postmoderno: studi di letteratura italiana*, Mi, Angeli, 128 pp.

On culture and politics, M. Paladini Musitelli, 'I nipotini di Padre Bresciani e la categoria del brescianesimo', *Problemi*, 121 : 138–59, examines Antonio Gramsci's approach to political ideologies as a critique of sectarian and clichéd literature, and sees the 'brescianesimo' identified by G. as a type of subjective propaganda which made Italian intellectuals resistant to the notion of what G. called 'national-popular'. Gabriele Turi, *Lo stato educatore. Politica e intellettuali nell'Italia fascista*, Ro–Bari, Laterza, vii + 392 pp., gathers a number of articles written between 1987 and 2000 on the reactions of intellectuals, such as Luigi Russo and the *Solaria* group, to fascism and the attempt of the regime to control the cultural field while arguing that the effort was doomed to failure.

On literature by and on women, *Presenze femminili del Novecento italiano. Letteratura, teatro, cinema*, ed. Graziella Pagliano, Na, Liguori, 268 pp., includes the essays: by F. Brezzi on the ideology of women futurists oscillating between non-conformist artistic values and conformity with traditional mother functions assigned to women (5–36), by G. Pagliano on American writers published by Sonzogno in Italy (65–86), by G. Sebastiani on the fashion magazine *Foemina* 1946–47 (103–36), by G. Taffon on figures of queens portrayed on stage by Dario Fo, Dacia Maraini, and Giovanni Testori (137–66), by A. T. Romano Cervone on letters exchanged between Sibilla Aleramo and Lina Galli (37–64), and by S. Parigi on Marco Ferreri's films *Storia di Piera* (1983) and *Il futuro è donna* (167–80). The last text, V. Cicogna, 'Rassegna bio-bibliografica: 1980–2002' (181–257), is a list of works published by women poets since 1980.

The relationship of a number of Italian writers (such as Corrado Alvaro, Alberto Moravia, Curzio Malaparte, Luigi Pirandello) with cinema is discussed by various critics in 'Letterati al cinema', *StN*, 28, 2001: 13–230.

On travel literature, 'Hodoeporics revisited / Ritorno all'odeporica', *AnI*, 21: 47–516, among other essays includes the following: L. Monga, 'The unavoidable "snare of narrative": fiction and creativity in hodoeporics' (7–46), on general concepts and in particular on the clash between 'truthfulness' and 'creativity'; S. Zatti, 'Viaggi sedentari' (57–70), on imaginary journeys including Italo Calvino's and Giacomo Leopardi's; J. J. Cachey Jr, 'The end of the journey from *Gilgamesh* to *Le città invisibili*' (71–92); and D. Papotti, 'Pubblicazioni recenti di argomento odeporico in italiano' (501–16). On landscape and literature: Vincenzo Bagnoli, *Lo spazio del testo. Paesaggio e conoscenza nella modernità letteraria*, Bo, Pendragon, 197 pp., examines landscape in literature as an aspect of the representation of the real world, but also as a metaphor for the form of texts. One chapter (61–113) is devoted to 'La mappa del labirinto. L'Ariosto di Calvino'.

On science and literature: Paolo Zublena, *L'inquietante simmetria della lingua*, Alessandria, Orso, 147 pp., examines the relationship between literature and the language of science in the 20th c.

On other topics: Fabio Todero, **Le metamorfosi della memoria: la grande guerra tra modernità e tradizione*, Udine, Del Bianco, 2002, 273 pp. *Anthony J. Tamburri, *Una semiotica della ri-lettura: Guido Gozzano, Aldo Palazzeschi, Italo Calvino*, F, Cesati, 114 pp. R. Ricci, 'Morphologies and functions of self-criticism in modern times: has the author come back?', *MLN*, 118: 116–46.

For local literatures: *Poesia, narrativa, saggistica in provincia di Trapani*, ed. Salvatore Mugno, Palermo, ISSPE, 2001, 142 pp., contains the papers of a conference held at Erice. **Piccola antologia di scrittrici campane*, ed. Anna Santoro, Na, Intra Moenia, 2001, 168 pp. Paolo Blasi, **Poeti dell'Istria tra le due guerre mondiali: 1914–1939*, Trieste, Italo Svevo, 2000, 210 pp. *Francesco De Nicola and Roberto Trovaso, *Parole e scene di un secolo in Liguria*, Alessandria, Orso, 2002, 242 pp.

On the history of criticism: Vittore Branca, *Protagonisti del Novecento*, T, Aragno, 442 pp., is part cultural autobiography and part recollections and critical appraisals of writers and critics such as Carlo Dionisotti, Giovanni Gentile, Attilio Momigliano, and Eugenio Montale. *Il carteggio di Benedetto Croce con la Biblioteca del Senato: 1910–1952*, ed. Giovanni Spadolini, Ro, Senato della Repubblica, 2002, 498 pp. **Benedetto Croce e gli studi di letteratura calabrese*, ed. Pasquino Crupi, Cosenza, Pellegrini, 167 pp. On Croce (and partly also on Gramsci) see also a number of essays in *La Cultura*, 41: M. Mustè, 'Carattere e svolgimento delle prime teorie estetiche di Benedetto Croce 1885–1913' (447–73); M. Reale, 'Sull'*Intuizione pura* *e il carattere lirico dell'arte* di Benedetto Croce' (405–45); G. Sasso, 'Croce nei suoi ultimi anni' (13–26); and Id., 'Gramsci e l'idealismo (Appunti e considerazioni)' (351–402). A. Borghesi, 'Il critico allo specchio. Giacomo Debenedetti e Francesco De Sanctis', *Allegoria*, 42, 2002 : 9–37, underlines the importance of De Sanctis's influence on Debenedetti in terms of ethical values, detachment of critical attitudes from the critics' own autobiography, and the concept of 'situation'. She also notes Debenedetti's dissent from orthodox Marxist views, which resulted in his resignation from the PCI newspaper *L'Unità* in 1947 and in his demand for the independence of intellectuals from political parties, or a type of 'impegno civile' similar to that of De Sanctis. Maria Corti, *I vuoti del tempo*, Mi, Bompiani, 220 pp., includes an essay on her, F. Caputo and A. Longoni, 'Quasi un autoritratto' (197–212), and her own biographical and cultural studies on Eugenio Montale (17–38), Sandro Sinigaglia (39–60), Gianfranco Contini (61–76), Benvenuto Terracini (107–36), and Italo Calvino (137–64), as well as letters from these authors to C. (167–95). N. Leone, 'Le carte di Maria Corti: il Novecento a nuovi crocevia', *NA*, 2226 : 280–88, underlines the importance of C.'s archive, and gives some examples of its content. A. Stella, 'Ricordo di Maria Corti', *StCrit*, 18 : 325–44, examines C.'s itinerary as a critic and argues that her legacy consists not only in her methods and discoveries but also in the duty of others to further investigate her intuitions. 'Per Guido Guglielmi', a section of *Allegoria*, 42, 2002 : 71–90, includes essays by R. Luperini on G.'s style (71–74); R. Donnarumma on G.'s *Prosa italiana del Novecento* (vol. 1, 1986, and vol. 2, 1998) (75–82); and N. Lorenzini on G.'s views on modernity as characterized by fragmented patterns and the decline of traditional literary models, and also by Utopian tendencies and a constant perception of the ever-changing meaning of time (83–90). M. L. Doglio, 'Ricordo di Giovanni Getto', *GSLI*, 180 : 36–55, appraises G. as one of the major critics of the 20th century, gives biographical details, goes through his main works on Italian classics, underlines his approach to multiple angles of interpretation, his attempt to illustrate their cohesive, interwoven dimensions, and his aversion for formulaic critical clichés. E. Guagnini, 'Per un maestro', *Problemi*, 121 : 131–37, commemorates Giuseppe Petronio, and in particular his founding and editorship of the journal *Problemi*. R. Luperini, 'Per Giuseppe Petronio', *Allegoria*, 43 : 141–43, underlines P.'s relation to Francesco De Sanctis, Antonio Gramsci, and György Lukács, his fundamentally materialist view of culture, and his interest in mass literature. M. Paladini Musitelli, 'Ricordo di Giuseppe Petronio', *Critica marxista*, 40.3–4 : 73–79, underlines P.'s demythologizing Marxist approach to criticism based on historical, sociological, and philosophical analysis of texts, his critique of formalism, and his debt to Antonio Gramsci within an attempt to propagate an alternative view of culture against the culture of the ruling classes. S. Pautasso, 'Letteratura come vita', *NA*, 2225:188–92, discusses Carlo Bo's role as a critic linked to hermeticism and his religious and spiritual interpretations of literature, and concludes that even though he became marginal in the 1960s his criticism was not so far from the *nouvelle critique* and its vision of literature as a 'fatto essenziale'. A section of *Allegoria*, 43:87–104, dedicated to Robert Dombrowski, includes N. Lorenzini, 'Per Robert Dombrowski' (90–91), on his interpretation of Carlo Emilio Gadda, and other essays by A. Andreini, R. Luperini, G. Nava, M. C. Papini, and M. Rebaudengo. *SpR*, 17, 2002[2003], 144 pp., is a special issue entitled *Studies in memory of Tom O'Neill.* In its preface, R. Bertoni, 'Some aspects of Tom O'Neill's work as a literary critic' (5–7), insists on the concepts of literariness, existential disquiet, and experimental novelty. Also included (8–14) is a list of O'Neill's publications. Other essays are listed later under individual authors.

On the state and functions of contemporary criticism, 'Dodici tesi sulla responsabilità della critica', *Allegoria*, 42, 2002:5–8, an unsigned text attributable to the editorial board, laments literature's loss of a central position in mass society, the scarcity of serious critical interpretation, the integration of some intellectuals into the culture industry and withdrawal of others into ivory towers. In opposition to this, the article proposes that critics should be interpreters of texts while coming to terms with society, and in particular with recent phenomena such as globalization and migration. M. Ganeri, 'Quattro domande sui destini degli studi letterari', *Allegoria*, 43:135–40, is a wide-ranging interview with Terry Eagleton touching, among other things, on recent developments, in criticism, of the themes of identity, otherness, and plurality in relation to postmodernism.

On periodicals, *Riga*, 21, ed. Anna Panicali, 305 pp., is devoted to *Gulliver*, the journal planned by Elio Vittorini and others. It includes an introduction by Panicali (17–55), and some of the editors' materials and authors' texts for *Gulliver* 1960–66, in part already published in *Il Menabò*, 7. 'Abbiamo cinquant'anni', *NArg*, 23:124–77, is dedicated to the 50th anniversary of *Nuovi argomenti* (2003) with subsections on its five series respectively by E. Siciliano, A. Colasanti, R. Manica, E. Trevi, and L. Pavolini. *Nuova corrente*, 131, likewise marks its 50th anniversary with the two commemorations G. Ferroni, 'Modernità civile' (11–14) and E. Pagliarini, 'Memoria' (69–70). It also carries an article by A. Rizzardi on *Nuova corrente*, 5–6, devoted to Ezra Pound, followed by a poem by Elisabeth Bishop and an article on Bishop by F. Rognoni (78–92); previously unpublished poems by Nanni Cagnone, Milo De Angelis, Luciano De Giovanni, Eugenio

De Signoribus, Marco Ercolani, Giovanni Giudici, Cesare Greppi, Mario Luzi, Cesare Viviani, and Andrea Zanzotto; and, within a section entitled 'Il forum delle riviste', the editorial article 'Messaggi in bottiglia' (5–9), probably by S. Mele and E. Tacchella, on *Nuova corrente* seen as a serious non-academic journal, situated on the border between literature and philosophy, which stands apart from the trends of the literary market. There are also essays by A. Cortellessa on contemporary journals in general (15–21), by A. Prete on his work on *Lacerba* and active participation in other literary journals (22–32), by G. Leghissa on '*Aut aut* e una certa idea di enciclopedia filosofica' (33–40), R. Luperini on *Allegoria*, its political / cultural intentions and recent work on two major topics (the canon and the crisis of contemporary criticism), and its partial continuity, in various ways, with *La Voce*, *Il Politecnico*, *Officina*, *Il Menabò*, and *Quindici* (41–43). We also note texts by Giovanni Mari, F. Andolfi, G. Bottiroli, and A. Casadei (44–67).

On publishing, Guido Davico Bonino, *Alfabeto Einaudi. Scrittori e libri*, Mi, Garzanti, 207 pp., is a piece of cultural history, based not only on intellectual references but also on the author's personal reminiscences of Einaudi writers and critics with whom he came into contact, including Calvino, Cassola, Contini, Carlo Levi, Sciascia, and others.

2. Poetry

Laura Mautone, *Che cos'è la poesia*, Mantua, Corraini, 2002, 180 pp., consists of a series of interviews with the poets Maria Luisa Spaziani, Antonio Manfredi, Edoardo Sanguineti, Giuseppe Conte, Valerio Magrelli, Nanni Balestrini, Roberto Mussapi, Roberto Carifi, Patrizia Valduga, and Mary de Rachewiltz on what they consider to be the nature of poetry in recent years. Davide Rondoni, *Non una vita soltanto. Scritti da un'esperienza di poesia*, Genoa, Marietti, 2002, 222 pp., discusses the way in which the writings of poets (including recent figures such as Betocchi, Montale, Ungaretti, Luzi, Caproni, Sereni, Bertolucci, Bigongiari, Sanguineti, Loi, Cucchi, Mussapi, Piersanti, and many others) impact in so many different ways on the public perception of poetry. Maria Antonietta Grignani, *La costanza della ragione. Soggetto, oggetto, testualità nella poesia italiana del Novecento*, Novara, Interlinea, 2002, 185 pp. Ronald De Rooy, *Il poeta che parla ai poeti: elementi danteschi nella poesia italiana ed anglosassone del secondo Novecento*, F, Cesati, 281 pp. E. Esposito, *Il verso. Forme e teoria*, Ro, Carocci, 200 pp., considers how theory and form are expressed in poetry. S. Colangelo, *Come si legge una poesia*, Ro, Carocci, 128 pp., offers various guidelines for reading individual poems. N. Merola, 'La

lettura del testo poetico come fatto personale', *EL*, 28.4:29–45, suggests that personal reaction to poetry is responsible for the wide range of interpretations that can be taken from the poetic text. G. Dotoli, 'La poesia, domani', *La Nuova Ricerca*, 12:387–94, ponders on the role of poetry now and attributes to it a salvific role for the future.

C. Calabrò, 'Tra poesia e re-velatio', *Testuale*, 33, 2002:23–33, discusses how poetry can convey subliminal dimensions. R. Nisticò, 'Dopo Auschwitz: trasformazioni della poesia a Firenze', *Il Ponte*, 58.12:136–52, examines the need for meaningful communication in the poetry of Franco Marescalchi (who began to write in the 1950s), Giuseppe Furati (active in the late 1960s), and Giuseppe Panella (writing from the 1990s onwards). *Testuale*, 33, 2002, contains two articles on different poets: S. Montalto, 'Poeti vegetali' (5–22), on the work of Pasquale Di Palmo, Raffaele Piazza, Andrea Zanzotto, Giacomo Affenita, and Pierluigi Bacchini, examines the representation of nature in their poetry and emphasizes the 'piccole cose quotidiane' that reflect the 'cosmici miracoli della natura' in their work; A. Vaccaro, 'Due poeti dell'*altra realtà*: Luigi Cannillo e Annamaria De Pietro' (47–61), looks at the depiction of the senses and beauty in C.'s work and contrasts it with the depiction of the 'io' in De P.'s poetry. A. Zattarin, *Tre storie d'amore e di sonetti. Gozzano, Saba, Caproni*, Venice, Supernova, 60 pp., outlines the depiction of love by these poets in sonnet form.

Leonardo Castellani, *L'uomo che passa. Scritti del Futurismo inediti e rari*, ed. Tiziano Mattioli, Pescara, Metauro, 2002, 258 pp., examines the work of C., painter, sculptor, ceramicist, and writer whose work collected in the Archivio Castellani shows his moderate stance and aversion for the extremes propounded by Marinetti. Antonio Lucio Giannone, *L'avventura futurista. Pugliesi all'avanguardia (1909–1943)*, Fasano, Schena, 2002, 124 pp., argues that the south of Italy, and Puglia in particular, made a significant contribution to the lively experimentation that characterized avantgarde movements in Italy in the early 20th c. *Italienisch*, 50, contains a series of articles on futurism, and particularly on its literary and artistic objectives, polemics, and achievements: W. Wehle, 'Einführung' (2–6); W. Asholt, 'Gesamtkunstwerk Futurismus' (8–24); P. Guaragnella, 'Il riso e l'allegria in Aldo Palazzeschi' (26–33); R. Behrens, 'Marinettis passatistische Stadt. Funktionen und Hintergründe eines polemischen Konzepts des frühen Futurismus' (34–57); and M. Bunge, 'Bildnerischer dynamismus versus pikturale Statik. Bemerkungen zur Bildauffassung im Futurismus' (58–82). *Gli anni '60 e '70 in Italia: due decenni di ricerca poetica*, ed. Stefano Giovannuzzi, Genoa, San Marco dei Giustiniani, 407 pp., is a series of collected essays which also contains a bibliography, bibliographic references, notes, and a name index.

P. Veronesi, 'Voci della poesia contemporanea: mezzo secolo di poesia italiana su compact disc', *Poesia*, 169:54–57, outlines the features of the CDs which present the work of Mario Luzi, Maria Luisa Spaziani, and Franco Loi. D. Piccini, 'I poeti visti da vicino. Una storia del Novecento tutta da guardare', *ib.*, 170:22–26, gives a critique of Niva Lorenzini's 2002 book, *Le parole esposte. Fotostoria della poesia italiana del Novecento. Poesia*, 176, contains two articles that pay tribute to Giacinto Spagnoletti (d. 2003) and his contribution as a critic, poet, and promoter of Italian literature (of poetry in particular) in the 20th c.: S. Ramat, 'Per Giacinto Spagnoletti: nel nome della poesia' (55–56), and P. Perilli, 'Novecento *adieu!* Per Giacinto Spagnoletti' (57–65).

On dialect poetry: Carmelo Aliberti, *Poeti siciliani del secondo Novecento*, Foggia, Bastogi, 198 pp., is an anthology of poems by Sicilian-born writers, some in the dialect, with brief biographies and a brief critical apparatus. *La poesia napoletana dal Novecento a oggi*, ed. Salvatore Palomba, Na, L'Ancora del Mediterraneo, 311 pp., an anthology of poems in Neapolitan, also includes bibliographical references, notes, and brief biographies of the poets.

On Italian poets in the U.S.A., Luigi Fontanella, *La parola transfuga. Scrittori italiani in America*, F, Cadmo, 267 pp., offers a precise overview that spans the 20th c., including the following: 'Letteratura ed emigrazione in America nel primo Novecento: Arturo Giovannitti, Emanuel Carnevali e altri. Questioni teoriche e metodologiche' (11–42); 'Autobiografia e letteratura: il caso di Pascal D'Angelo' (43–80); 'Il plurilinguismo di Joseph Tusiani' (81–100); 'Giose Rimanelli e il viaggio infinito' (101–74); 'Vita e poesia di Alfredo de Palchi' (175–237).

Further items in the ongoing series G. Langella, 'La parabola delle avanguardie (1895–1923)', include: XIX, 'Adelante con juicio', *Poesia*, 168:47–50, which deals with the cultural impact of Soffici's 1920 journal 'Rete Mediterranea'; XX, 'L'erma bifronte', *ib.*, 169:59–62, examining Croce's classicizing post-war revision of his aesthetics which stressed the contemplative, 'rasserenante' dimension of art; XXI, 'Approdi neoclassici', *ib.*, 171:45–47, detailing the appearance, side-by-side with the avantgarde movement, of a longing for neo-classicism prevalent particularly in the work of Carrà and De Chirico; XXII, 'La "gaia scienza" della *Ronda*', *ib.*, 172:73–75, which examines the classicism, 'metaforico e a doppio fondo', of this journal; XXIII, 'Tempo di lanci e di bilanci', *ib.*, 174:59–61, assessing the role of the

Turin journal *Primo Tempo* in the postwar debate on classical elements in Italian literature.

3. Narrative, Theatre

On narrative in general: *Il romanzo*, iv: *Temi luoghi, eroi*, ed. Franco Moretti, T, Einaudi, 866 pp., includes Italian contributions on topics relevant to the 20th and 21st c., such as C. Bertoni and M. Fusillo, 'Tematica romanzesca o *topoi* letterari di lunga durata?' (31–57), and D. Del Giudice, 'Meccanica e viaggi al limite del conosciuto' (293–317), on machinery in relation to human beings, technological imagery, flying carpets, and other mobile objects used in narrative. *Il romanzo*, v: *Lezioni*, ed. Franco Moretti, Pier Vittorio Mengaldo, and Ernesto Franco, T, Einaudi, 716 pp., includes essays on novels selected to represent the Italian narrative canon, i.e. A. Berardinelli on Italo Svevo, *La coscienza di Zeno* (457–70), M. Meriggi on Alberto Moravia, *Gli indifferenti* (471–90), C. Garboli on Carlo Emilio Gadda, *Quer pasticciaccio brutto de via Merulana* (539–70), and P. V. Mengaldo on Elsa Morante, *Menzogna e sortilegio* (571–84).

For the importance of history in 20th-c. narrative, U. Dotti, 'Gli scrittori e la storia, da Silone a Elsa Morante', *Belfagor*, 58:125–58, considers a variety of approaches, differentiating between Ignazio Silone's straightforward political and ideological message, Francesco Jovine's immersion in history and aspiration to tell historical events rationally and with an emphasis on civil society, and Carlo Levi's attention to folklore and myth. Also included are Elio Vittorini, Cesare Pavese, and Carlo Emilio Gadda, as well as Elsa Morante.

On narrative and regional identity, Massimo Onofri, *La modernità infelice. Saggi sulla letteratura italiana del Novecento*, Salerno, Avagliano, 192 pp., surveys a number of Sicilian writers, including Giuseppe Antonio Borgese, Vitaliano Brancati, Leonardo Sciascia, and Giuseppe Tomasi di Lampedusa, and adopts interpretations such as Sciascia's concept of 'sicilitudine', Sicilian insularity as felt by Gesualdo Bufalino, and alienation from Italian society as portrayed by Valerio Borgese.

On narrative genres, Luca Scarlini, *Equivoci e miraggi. Pratiche d'autobiografia oggi*, Mi, Rizzoli, and Scuola Holden, 180 pp., investigates recent fragmentation of identity in autobiographical writing and underlines the variety of ways in which modern autobiographies are written, arguing that autobiography is a plural genre. A. Carrera, '"Se tutti i mari fossero d'inchiostro". Aporie della testimonianza da Primo Levi a Derrida', *Intersezioni*, 23:51–66, has a title which originates from a saying attributed to Rabbi Eliezer and developed by a Polish Jew as 'even if the sky were paper and all seas were made of ink I could not describe my suffering and all I see around me', and hence argues that it is impossible to state the totality of the lager experience which, erupting unexpected and new into human history, generated narratives of a witnessing as well as fictional nature on a number of the lagers' dreadful aspects; but each witnessing narrative seems to confirm that total witnessing is impossible and that narratives of this kind may fail in their aim, lie, and either illuminate or obscure the past while trying to reveal personal and public truth.

On narrative and society, U. Dotti, 'Manzoni, la borghesia e il romanzo', *GSLI*, 180:1–35, examines both Alberto Moravia and Carlo Emilio Gadda as representatives of the bourgeoisie and, in their novels, of the quintessential bourgeois genre. He shows that they had contradictory relations with their class and how their characters, as previously Manzoni's characters, are related to the society around them.

On women's narrative, C. Gala, 'Identity and writing: a Lacanian reading of Alba De Céspedes' *Quaderno proibito* and Dacia Maraini's *Donna in guerra*', *FoI*, 37:147–60, explores the gap between reality and desire in women's identity as expressed through the diary form by the two writers mentioned.

On various topics relating to narrative, L. De Federicis, 'Il rapporto tra vita e letteratura nella nuova narrativa italiana', *Belfagor*, 58:582–88, discusses Elisabetta Rasy and Elena Ferrante in particular, but also other contemporary writers, partly in relation to the theme of death. Raffaele Manica, *La prosa nascosta. Narrazioni del Novecento italiano*, Cava de' Tirreni, Avagliano, 2002, 168 pp., contains essay-type reviews on 20th-c. authors such as Giovanni Comisso, Antonio Delfini, Alberto Moravia, and Goffredo Parise. *Dieci decimi. Sguardi a ritroso sulla nostra letteratura*, by various authors (no editor indicated), Mi, Rizzoli, 192 pp., published on behalf of Scuola Holden, a school of creative writing, includes texts by contemporary writers of a subjective and journalistic nature on works by Italian writers of the past: Bruno Arpaia on Giuseppe Berto and Luciano Bianciardi, Tommaso Giartosio on Tommaso Curradi, Diego De Silva on Dino Buzzati, Helena Janeczek on Giovanni Arpino, Davide Longo on Silvio D'Arzo, Domenico Starnone on Federigo Tozzi, Valerio Evangelisti on Emilio Salgari, and Antonio Moresco on Federico De Roberto.

On theatre, Paolo Puppa, **Il teatro dei testi: la drammaturgia italiana nel Novecento*, T, UTET, 234 pp. **Istituzione letteraria e drammaturgia: Mario Apollonio (1901–1971): i giorni e le opere. Atti del Convegno, Brescia–Milano, 4–7 novembre 2001*, ed. Carlo Annoni, Mi, Vita e Pensiero, 598 pp.

4. Individual authors

ACCROCCA. M. Armellino, *Elio Filippo Accrocca*, Ro, Fermenti, 2002, 310 pp., discusses A.'s place in the cultural and artistic life of Rome in the second half of the 20th c.

ANEDDA. F. Sepe, 'A colloquio con Antonella Anedda', *Italienisch*, 50:94–100, highlights A.'s link with the Sardinian literary tradition, her poetic models, and the relationship between her poetry, nature, and history.

ANTONIONI. S. Bernardi, 'Antonioni, narratore periferico', *RLI*, 107:149–56, discusses *Quel bowling sul Tevere* and finds it to be suspended on the border between diegetic and extradiegetic narrative, with changes in register, rather loose sequences of events, and similarities to cinematic procedures.

BALDINI. R. Ricchi, 'Intervista a Raffaello Baldini', *Gradiva*, 20–21:183–87, discusses the use and achievements of dialect poetry. D. Piccini, 'Raffaello Baldini: Santarcangelo, linea di confine del senso', *Poesia*, 177:2–16, details the importance of B.'s birthplace in Romagna in his dialect poetry.

BARICCO. Alessandro Scarsella, *Alessandro Baricco*, Fiesole, Cadmo, 138 pp. R. Rushing, 'Alessandro Baricco's *Seta*: travel, ventriloquism, and the other', *MLN*, 118:209–36.

BASSANI. F. Bausi, 'Il giardino incantato. Giorgio Bassani lettore di Thomas Mann', *LItal*, 55:219–48, stresses the symbolic, rather than the realist or historical, nature of *Il giardino dei Finzi-Contini*, argues that its main character acts as in a *Bildungsroman*, notes that the novel is related to Thomas Mann's *The Magic Mountain*, which is its model on the various levels of action performed by the protagonists, episodes, structure, and plot, and develops Mann's influence on B. also with reference to other works by the German writer, thus coming to the conclusion that the *Giardino* is not a late-naturalist or late-romantic novel but rather a book which conveys a vision of the world, portrays society, and is a metaphor for the passage from youth to maturity. R. Cotroneo, 'Memoria della vita, memoria della letteratura', *NArg*, 22:198–205, highlights B.'s interest in memory especially in *Storie ferraresi*. R. Manica, 'Bassani variantista', *ib.*, 206–16, sees B.'s variants as variations on a continuous line. Alessandro Roveri, *Giorgio Bassani e l'antifascismo (1936–1943)*, Sabbioncello San Pietro (Ferrara), 2 G Editrice, 187 pp., includes a preface by B.'s daughter Paola (5–9), dates B.'s antifascism to before the fascist racial laws and examines his 1936–43 ideology in the light of a 'Postilla' he wrote in 1948 on his support for 'Alleanza della Cultura' and the PSI.

BENEDETTI. C. Vinci-Orlando, 'Origine della poetica di Italo Benedetti', *Il Veltro*, 47:439–41.

BERTO. A. Vettori, 'Giuda tradito, ovvero l'ermeneutica parodica di Giuseppe Berto', *MLN*, 118:168–93.

BERTOLUCCI. A. Girardi, 'Le canzonette di Bertolucci', *Belfagor*, 58:327–36, shows how the 'canzonetta' form of medium and short lines, verse division, and rhyme variation are all present in different sections of *La capanna indiana*. Y. Gouchan, 'Brouillage syntaxique et traduction: *La camera da letto* d'Attilio Bertolucci', *ChrI*, 71–72:59–74, details syntactical and translation difficulties inherent in B.'s work when attempting to translate it into French. P. Lagazzi, '"Come lucciola" (Per un gruppo di inediti)', *NArg*, 22:54–71, introduces a number of unpublished B. poems and shows how the one referred to in the title (published posthumously and probably written in 1936) anticipates the theme of 'Lucertola di Casarola', B.'s final poem. R. Galaverni, 'Le pulsazioni e i lampi dell'amore. Situazione della poesia in Bertolucci', *ib.*,72–105, looks at B.'s poetry and examines how its presentation of love reflects the bitter-sweet highs-and-lows of life and reality.

BETOCCHI. L. Piantini, 'Il realismo estetico-visionario di Carlo Betocchi', *Il Cristallo*, 45.2:44–47. G. Fontana, '"Lo scavo che ai miei giorni migliori tento in me cercandomi . . .": alle radici del "realismo del corpo" di Betocchi', *StCrit*, 18:357–86, examines the prevalence of this factor in B.'s later collections such as *Diarietto invecchiando* and *Un passo, un altro passo*.

BIAMONTI. A. Viale and M. Camponovo present interviews with B., previously published in newspapers in 1999 and 2000, on pp. 37–43 of Francesco Biamonti, *Il silenzio*, T, Einaudi, 43 pp.

BIANCIARDI. J. Mastrogianakos, 'Embedded narratives of subversion in Luciano Bianciardi's *La vita agra*', *FoI*, 37:121–46, sets B.'s novel against the background of the Italian economic miracle, and sees it as a critique of capitalism achieved through transgressive literary strategies.

BIGONGIARI. D. Piccini, 'Nel labirinto della lingua. Conversazione con Piero Bigongiari', *Poesia*, 173:11–14, records B.'s ideas on movements like hermeticism and language as a 'labirinto della verità'.

BONTEMPELLI. V. Giordano, 'Realtà e *fiction* davanti agli specchi di Massimo Bontempelli', *EL*, 28.3:81–91, is about the image of the mirror in B.'s work and its meaning as a path towards fantastic realms where ordinary reality is distorted rather than imitated: thus mirrors are metanarrative symbols, deceptive objects, playful instruments which point to the complex relationship between reality and fantasy. Fabriano Fabbri, **I due Novecento. Gli anni Venti fra arte e letteratura: Bontempelli versus Sarfatti*, Lecce, Manni, 224 pp.

BUFFONI. G. Mesa, '"Nel profilo della rosa" di Franco Buffoni', *Testuale*, 33, 2002:41–45, outlines the varying roles of the rose, memory, animals, sorrow, and enigma in this work.

CALVINO. *Italo Calvino: uno scrittore pomeridiano*, ed. William Weaver and Damien Pettigrew, Ro, Minimum Fax, 77 pp., includes a short text by C., 'Pensieri prima di un'intervista' (31–34); a memoir by Weaver (25–30); and an essay by Pietro Citati (5–24) who underlines C.'s distrust of feeling and outlines his development from the trilogy to the 1980s, especially in pursuit of rhythm and style. The rest of this work is the Italian version of a 1983 interview in English by the two editors with Calvino. 'Calvino, Perec e l'Ou.Li.Po.', an interview between G. Nerli and Marcel Bénabou, *Allegoria*, 42, 2002:137–44, discusses, among other things, C.'s participation in Ou.Li.Po and his presentation to its members of an outline of *Se una notte d'inverno un viaggiatore*. G. Adamo, '*Limina* testuali nello sperimentalismo di Italo Calvino', *StCrit*, 18:1–27, examines the beginnings and endings of *Il barone rampante* and *Se una notte d'inverno un viaggiatore*. Roberto Bertoni and Bruno Ferraro, *Calvino ludico: riflessioni sul gioco in Italo Calvino*, introd. Remo Bodei, Viareggio, Baroni, 104 pp., discusses the concept of play in C.'s work, both as a theme throughout and as a series of structural procedures, but also opens perspectives on psychological and existential dimensions. Eugenio Bolongaro, *Italo Calvino and the Compass of Literature*, Toronto U.P., 240 pp., reappraises C.'s ideological commitment by looking at early articles, the trilogy, and *I giovani del Po* as socially significant texts and antecedents of later work. K. Pilz, 'A biography of the "intellettuale impegnato" Italo Calvino', *SpR*, 17, 2002 [2003]:117–32, highlights political orientation in works up to *Giornata di uno scrutatore* and a less clearly political reorientation in later works, or even at times disorientation (as in *Palomar*). G. Rizzarelli, 'Le *Lezioni americane* di Italo Calvino: il testamento apocrifo', *ParL*, 45–46–47:147–71, sees the *Lezioni* as a diary, or a witness: not only to C. but also to an entire generation of intellectuals. *Collezione di sabbia* is also examined, to show how different dimensions symbolized by 'cristallo' and 'fiamma' are integrated into these two works. Massimo Schilirò, **Le memorie difficili: saggio su Italo Calvino*, Catania, CUECM, 2002, 178 pp. Nicola Turi, *L'identità negata. Il secondo Calvino e l'utopia del tempo fermo*, F, Società Editrice Fiorentina, 126 pp., detects correspondence between existential and structural aspects, such as the flight of time and the precarious nature of becoming.

CAMILLERI. M. Pistelli, *'Montalbano sono'. Sulle tracce del più famoso commissario di polizia italiano*, F, Le Càriti, 154 pp., highlights C.'s cultural background, compares him to Luigi Pirandello, shows how his character Montalbano is linked to other writers of detective fiction, and considers his commercial success, but also his political questioning of the DC in *Forma dell'acqua* and of Berlusconi in *La paura di Montalbano*. J. Vizmuller-Zocco, 'I test della (im)popolarità: il fenomeno Camilleri', *QI*, 22.1, 2001:35–46, argues that current debate on C.'s books is mainly about three topics: his vision of Sicily, his plots and characters, and his language. Often snubbed by literary critics, he is widely read and popular as a best-selling author, while contrasting views on the literary quality of his work are due to the gap which exists in Italy between the intellectual elite and the public.

CAMPANA. Gianni Turchetta, *Dino Campana: biografia di un poeta*, Mi, Feltrinelli, 245 pp., previously published by Marcos y Marcos in 1990, reads C.'s life mainly in the light of his mental instability and argues that it is reason which may checkmate folly rather than viceversa.

CAMPO. M. Pieracci Harwell, 'Amicizie improbabili', *CV*, 58:459–71, discusses how the friendship between Cristina Campo and the American poet William Carlos Williams is apparent in the 2001 reprint of *Il fiore è il nostro segno*, which contains letters exchanged by Williams and Vanni Scheiwiller. This publication coincided with Giovanna Fozzer's *In forma di parole*, which also documents C.'s friendship with Andrea Emo. G. Fozzer, 'Postilla ad "Amicizie improbabili"', *ib.*, 472–76, provides further documentary evidence on the Campo–Emo friendship. M. Butò and R. Taioli, 'Cristina Campo tra chiarità e mistero', *Cenobio*, 52:234–44. Cristina De Stefano, *Belinda e il mostro. Vita segreta di Cristina Campo*, Mi, Adelphi, 222 pp., reconstructs C.'s life and work, uses some previously unpublished documents, and sees her as 'antimoderna' in her opposition to mass-society and alienation.

CAPASSO. S. Demarchi, 'Il manifesto e la poesia di Aldo Capasso', *Il Cristallo*, 45.1:107–09, argues that poetry must be communicative and accessible to a wider audience, as outlined by C. in his 1949 *Lettera aperta ai Poeti Italiani sul realismo della lirica*.

CAPRIOLO. G. Ania, 'Cara's "creative" writing: the fiction of originality in Capriolo's *Il doppio regno*', *Thompson Vol.*, 156–71, illustrates the protagonist's journey into herself as well as the author's disorienting narrative strategies.

CAPRONI. G. De Marco, 'Caproni poeta dell'antagonismo', *CLett*, 31:97–134, outlines the opposition, present in C.'s work, between the heroic and courageous, on the one hand, and 'tecnologismo' and 'mercificazione' on the other. J. Lindenberg, 'Le *Quaderno di traduzioni* de Giorgio Caproni', *ChrI*, 71–72:45–57, compares translations by C. to similar ones by Apollinaire, Prévert, Frénaud, and Char, and points to translation variations and similarities (such as suppression of repetition) in their work. Fabio Moliterni, *Poesia e pensiero nell'opera di Giorgio Caproni e di Vittorio Sereni*, Lecce, Pensa Multimedia, 2002, 243 pp., attempts, despite their individual characteristics of style and tone, to find common ground between the two poets. P. Zoboli, 'Caproni, Toba e il gibbone: la "Calata nel limbo" e la "Città dell'anima", *ON*, 27.1: 121–34, discusses the presence of these poems (which deal with the poet's family and his native Genoa) in the 1965 collection *Congedo del viaggiatore cerimonioso e altre prosopopee* and the connection between them and C.'s letter to Betocchi in 1961, which described his effort to 'descrivere una mia calata in limbo e un mio incontro con i morti, divenuto loro concittadino e fratello'.

COMISSO. Nico Naldini, *Vita di Giovanni Comisso*, Naples, L'Ancora del Mediterraneo, 352 pp. R. Liucci, 'Giovanni Comisso nella seconda guerra mondiale', *Belfagor*, 58: 295–311.

CONSOLO. F. Coassin, 'L'ordine delle somiglianze nel *Sorriso dell'ignoto marinaio* di Vincenzo Consolo', *SpR*, 17, 2002[2003]: 97–108, discusses various aspects of 'somiglianze' and the prominence in C.'s work of the metaphor of the 'chiocciola' and his 'plurilinguismo'. D. O'Connell, 'Consolo's "trista conca". Dantean anagnorisis and echo in *Il sorriso dell'ignoto marinaio*', pp. 85–106 of *Echi danteschi / Dantean Echoes*, ed. Roberto Bertoni, Dublin, Italian Dept., Trinity College — T, Trauben, 144 pp., is a study of the theme of recognition and of other motifs of C.'s novel in relation to Dante. E. Papa, 'Vincenzo Consolo', *Belfagor*, 58: 179–98.

CRISTINI. Giovanni Cristini, *Tutte le poesie: contesti inediti*, ed. Annamaria Vaccari, pref. Enzo Noè Girardi, Novara, Interlinea, 336 pp.

D'ARRIGO. Stefano D'Arrigo, *Horcynus orca*, introd. Walter Pedullà, Mi, Rizzoli, xxx + 1095 pp., is a new ed. incorporating D'A.'s unpublished corrections.

DELFINI. F. Santini, '*Il ricordo della basca*: Antonio Delfini tra surrealismo e surrealtà', *LetP*, 116–117: 38–46, argues that D. absorbed surrealism rather unconsciously than consciously, and that his characters are often weak and inept, acting in an aura of 'surrealtà' determined by the author's research into their interiority, provincial identity, and epiphanies.

DE LIBERO. Giuseppe Lupo, *Poesia come pittura. De Libero e la cultura romana (1930–1940)*, Mi, Vita e Pensiero, 2002, 263 pp., is the first monograph on DeL., one of the most important literary representatives of Roman culture in the 1930s.

DESSÌ. *Giuseppe Dessì: storia e catalogo di un archivio*, ed. Agnese Landini, F, Firenze U.P., 2002, 372 pp., within the electronic archive of the Biblioteca digitale of the Dept. of Italian, University of

Florence, and as part of the framework of a text research project (co-ordinated by Anna Dolfi) which aims at ordering and cataloguing a number of contemporary texts, includes D.'s published and unpublished works drawn from the files of the Gabinetto Vieusseux. **Le corrispondenze familiari nell'archivio Dessì*, ed. Chiara Andrei, F, Firenze U.P., 417 pp.

ECO. J. Francese, 'Eco's poetics of "the model reader"', *FoI*, 37:161–83. H. Strebel, 'Eco's stopwatch and narrative time in Puig, Jean-Renaud Camus, and Calvino', *MLR*, 98:335–52, is about the influence of Eco's theory of narrative time on the writers mentioned in the title.

ERBA. Luciano Erba, *Poesie (1951–2001)*, ed. Stefano Prandi, Mi, Mondadori, 2002, xxvii + 361 pp., provides a timely critical commentary on E.'s poetry.

FENOGLIO. 'Omaggio a Giuseppe Fenoglio, nel quarantesimo anniversario della morte', *Testo*, 45:9–133, includes several essays: G. Alfano, 'Presente assoluto e campo della scrittura nel *Partigiano Johnny* di Beppe Fenoglio' (9–38), is on the modern epic nature of this novel and its language; A. Casadei, 'Dagli *Appunti partigiani* al *Partigiano Johnny*' (39–54); O. Innocenti, '"Il nostro ordine sentimentale": quando la storia diventa *romance*. Lettura dei *Frammenti di romanzo*' (55–72), identifies some *romance* traits in the way in which history and characters are treated by F.; P. Ponti, 'Nomi di primavera. Ipotesi di onomastica fenogliana' (73–90), shows how names and their intertextual nature lead to some of the concepts in *Primavera di bellezza*, and in particular to its non rhetorical nature, literary aspirations, and difficulty with crossing the borders between youth and maturity; G. Rizzo, 'Le *Lettere* di Beppe Fenoglio' (91–102); A. Rondini, 'Dallo splendido isolamento al successo problematico. Fenoglio e la critica dell'ultimo decennio' (103–25). L. Bufano, 'Beppe Fenoglio e le cose sognate' and 'Nota ai testi', pp. vii-xx and 63–80 of Beppe Fenoglio, *Una crociera agli antipodi e altri racconti fantastici*, ed. Luca Bufano, T, Einaudi, xx + 83 pp., relates these previously unpublished fantastic short-stories to F.'s interest in Edgar Allan Poe. C. Milanini, 'Beppe Fenoglio: lettere ritrovate e carte neglette', *Belfagor*, 57, 2002:69–122.

FIRPO. Edoardo Firpo, *O grillo cantadö*, Genoa, San Marco dei Giustiniani, 100 pp., includes G. Devoto's Italian translation (*Il grillo canterino*) of the Genoese original.

FLAIANO. Margherita Mesirca, **Le mille e una storie impossibili. Indagine intorno ai racconti lunghi di Ennio Flaiano*, Ravenna, Longo, 280 pp.

FO. Andrea Bisicchia, *Invito alla lettura di Dario Fo*, Mi, Mursia, 271 pp., is a study of F.'s life and work which among other things underlines the fact that his theatre is a reflection of life, based on interaction of political aspects (especially exploitation, injustice, the family) and clownish motifs. This does not renew theatrical form but is innovative in content and avoids the limitations of a purely experimental type of drama.

FORTINI. Franco Fortini, *Saggi ed epigrammi*, Mi, Mondadori, 1850 pp.

GADDA. *Quaderni dell'ingegnere. Testi e studi gaddiani*, 2, 334 pp., includes information on the 'Fondo Pietro Citati' and the 'Fondo Giancarlo Roscioni' acquired by Milan city council and now at the Biblioteca Trivulziana together with essays by G. Stellardi ('Gadda tragico: miseria e grandezza della letteratura', 168–89), U. Salvafolta ('Paesaggi e architetture elettriche', 191–205), and E. Morsink ('Il gusto di donna Eleonora: la *Storia della letteratura inglese* di Mario Praz e l'antivittorianesimo ambrosiano di Carlo Emilio Gadda', 207–18). C. Fagioli, '*In limine*: rilettura della *Cognizione* attraverso il "saggio esplicativo" ', *Moderna*, 4.1 : 87–106, examines the dialogic structure of *La cognizione del dolore* and its critique of the bourgeoisie, and rescues G. from accusations of 'baroccaggine'. Franco Gàbici, *Gadda. Il dolore della cognizione. Una lettura scientifica dell'opera gaddiana con una sua riflessione 'dimenticata' sull'amore*, Mi, Simonelli, 121 pp., notes the importance of G.'s training as an engineer as well as his 'fantasia', discusses his interest in science, especially physics (which makes his work comparable to Robert Musil's *The Man without Qualities*), and underlines his concept of mathematical order set under the surface of his philosophical and literary sense of disorder. See also above under narrative and society in section 3. C. Garboli, '*Quer pasticciaccio* tra Gadda e Garzanti', *ParL*, 45–46–47 : 3–42, reconsiders some aspects of this novel (in particular its peculiar nature as a detective story written in difficult language, its apparently unfinished plot, and its metaphysical aspects) and examines the discussion of the novel in letters exchanged by G. and Livio Garzanti. N. Lorenzini, 'Il Carnevale nella *Cognizione del dolore*', *Il Verri*, 22 : 138–44, applies Bakhtin's concept of carnival as excess, and cohabitation of opposites, to G.'s novel where the motif of carnival underlines the monotony of the *petit-bourgeois* world, and the language uses the grotesque and other deforming procedures. P. Luxardo, 'Per una casistica dell'"auto-antologia". Antonio Baldini e Carlo Emilio Gadda', *StN*, 28, 2001: 391–400. Emanuele Narducci, **La gallina Cicerone: Carlo Emilio Gadda e gli scrittori antichi*, F, Olschki, xi + 151 pp. M. A. Terzoli, 'L'anima si governa per alfabeti. Note su Gadda scrittore di guerra', *ParL*, 45–46–47 : 98–120, compares G.'s writings on the first world war to Comisso's *Giorni di guerra* and other writings on the same topic, especially Ungaretti's.

GALLI. G. Baroni, 'La tremenda attualità di Lina Galli', *Gradiva*, 20–21:65–74, analyses the great humanity present in G.'s work from 1933 to 1989 and places it midway between the 'linea istriana' and the 'linea triestina'.

GINZBURG. S. Rizzardi, 'The theatre of Natalia Ginzburg between Chekhov and the Theatre of the Absurd', *Thompson Vol.*, 182–94, examines both the influences indicated in the title and G.'s compatibility with the theories of Sigmund Freud.

GIOVAGNOLI. A. Piromalli, 'Il mondo poetico di Guglielmo Giovagnoli', *Il Cristallo*, 45.2:70–76, pays particular attention to the influence of Pascoli on G.'s poetry.

GIUDICI. C. Marabini, 'Diario di lettura (Giovanni Giudici vince il premio Pascoli. Ottiero Ottieri, Ferruccio Ulivi. Le interviste di D'Annunzio. 50 anni dopo Silvio D'Arzo. Buzzati e i fumetti. Giuseppe Pontiggia)', *NA*, 2224, 2002:107–19.

GOZZANO. L. Pagnotta, '"Un sogno troppo a lungo sognato". L'ipotesi di Guido Gozzano in un'inedita redazione autografa', *ParL*, 45–46–47:43–69, outlines G.'s various editorial changes to this poem (a peripheral text in G.'s production), his hesitation as to whether he should publish it or not, the parallels between it and 'Signora Felicita' together with G.'s final text where he removed all direct parallels while emphasizing the external links between both texts. S. Bach, 'Un racconto al passato remoto: "Invernale" di Guido Gozzano', *Testo*, 46:61–75, examines the exclusive use of the 'passato remoto' in this text which features the relationship between man and nature and also highlights G.'s subtle and ironic depiction of the destiny of humankind. B. Porcelli, 'Maschere e nomi dell'"io" nella lirica di Gozzano', *La nuova ricerca*, 12:217–20, analyses the variety of doubles used by G. following his rejection of d'Annunzio and his belief that lack of authenticity was part of a historic existential condition.

GUERRA. S. Battaglia, 'I bu: un paradigma della letteratura italiana', *Poetiche*, 5.1:75–99, sees this 1972 work in Romagnol dialect as a key text which not only opened the way for dialect poetry but also made a significant contribution to the quality and content of such poetry.

GUIDACCI. M. Del Serra, 'Margherita Guidacci. La geometria della crescita', *Poesia*, 172:61–71, maps the growth of G.'s poetic strength throughout her life.

JOVINE. B. Moloney, 'Francesco Jovine's *Le terre del Sacramento* and the occupation of the land', *SpR*, 17, 2002[2003]:27–40, sees the protagonist of the novel, Luca Marano, as a Gramscian organic intellectual and illustrates the theme of class conflict.

KUBATI. A. C. Bova, 'La scrittura estranea nei romanzi di Ron Kubati', *Allegoria*, 43: 148–60, discusses K.'s language (the use of Italian by a non-native-speaker in a non-conventional and original way) and examines his existential concerns, especially the themes of 'profugo', 'straniero', and 'apolide'.

LA CAPRIA. Raffaele La Capria, *Opere*, ed. Silvio Perrella, Mi, Mondadori, xcii + 1753 pp., includes an introd. by Perrella on both La C.'s work in general and in particular his cosmopolitanism interwoven with his Neapolitan identity, and his combination of narrative and meditative aspects.

LAMARQUE. D. Piccini, 'Vivian Lamarque, cercando la maternità del mondo', *Poesia*, 168: 52–56, considers L.'s efforts to overcome the biographical dimension in her work in order to find a wider canvas for her concerns and sensibilities.

LEVI, C. D. Bini, 'Women of the South and the art of Carlo Levi', *FoI*, 37: 103–20, defines the feminine in L. as 'indistinto originario' after his own definition of the South of Italy, and compares Giovanni Verga's Gnà Pina to L.'s Giulia Venere. *Verso i Sud del mondo. Carlo Levi a cento anni dalla nascita (Convegno di Studi di Palermo, 6–8 novembre 2002)*, ed. Gigliola De Donato, Ro, Donzelli, 202 pp., includes several essays subdivided into sections on L.'s *meridionalismo*, his anthropology, southern Italian literature and on L. himself by a number of southern authors. Silvana Ghiazza, *Carlo Levi e Umberto Saba. Storia di un'amicizia*, Bari, Dedalo, 376 pp., outlines the friendship that existed between both men and especially L.'s positive role in the critical reception of S.'s poetry. B. Moloney, '*Fontamara* and *Cristo si è fermato a Eboli*: cases of intertextuality', *Thompson Vol.*, 133–45, discusses the possibility of mutual influence between the two authors. G. Russo, 'Carlo Levi e Umberto Saba', *NA*, 2226: 151–53.

LEVI, P. A. Baldini, 'Primo Levi e i poeti del dolore (da Giobbe a Leopardi), *NRLI*, 5: 161–203, highlights an increasing intertextual awareness in L.'s work, with particular reference to the Bible and Giacomo Leopardi, and examines the concept of sorrow ('dolore') as an ethical foundation.

LOY. P. Marzano, 'Diglossia, nomi e soprannomi in un romanzo di Rosetta Loy', *Il nome nel testo*, 5: 217–40, discusses the indeterminate use of place-names, as in fables, and the oscillation in the names of characters between their Italian, Piedmontese, and French forms according to the different social situations. Nicknames mostly reflect a 'motivazione affettiva'. Some paragraphs are devoted to the French and English translations of the names employed by L.

LUZI. F. de Napoli, '"Un sospiro profondo dalle foci alle sorgenti": l'opera poetica di Mario Luzi', *Gradiva*, 20/21: 57–64, argues that L.'s poetry is an ideal link between past, present, and future in the 20th c. *Mario Luzi da Ebe a Constant. Studi e testi*, ed. Daniele Maria Pegorari, Grottammare, Stamperia dell'Arancio, 2002, 264 pp., is a collection of articles which considers, among other topics, L.'s work as poet, dramatist, and critic. M. Veronesi, 'Luzi interprete di Mallarmé', *Testo*, 46: 137–40, details L.'s well-publicized debt to M. as poet, critic, and translator. *Mario Luzi cantore della luce*, ed. Stefano Verdino, Assisi, Cittadella, 218 pp., contains the following conference articles: S. Verdino, 'Prefazione' (7–9); M. Luzi, 'Parole di saluto' (11–14); A. Frattini, 'L'opera di Mario Luzi alle soglie del terzo millennio' (15–27); M. Marchi, 'Mario Luzi e il Novecento' (29–58); S. Verdino, 'Poeta civile' (59–91); E. Giachery, 'Il motivo della luce nella poesia di Mario Luzi' (93–102); G. Quiriconi, 'Le voci del "grande patema". La parola drammatica di Luzi' (103–22); G. Cavallini, 'L'ultimo Luzi: "Sotto specie umana"' (123–48); P. Tuscano, 'Impegno etico ed estetico in Mario Luzi critico di poesia' (149–66); and S. Verdino, 'Bibliografia' (167–215). Renzo Cassigoli, *Mario Luzi. Le nuove paure*, F, Passigli, 111 pp., records an interview between the author and L. where, starting with the violence of September 11, L. outlines his fears over the world-wide gulf between rich and poor, religious fundamentalism and Western errors, the separation of culture and politics, the accountability of science, the division between good and evil, the function of poetry today and its role as a harbinger of hope. M. Luzi, 'A ritroso, tra amici, nel lungo tornado del Novecento', ed. C. Trombetti and C. Ceccuti, *NA*, 2224, 2002: 156–72. Parts II-V respectively appear in *NA*, 2225: 166–79, 2226: 209–20, 2227: 143–52, and 2228: 152–66. M. Luzi, *Parlate*, ed. Stefano Verdino, Novara, Interlinea, 49 pp., contains a collection of poems but also extracts from *Hamlet* in an Italian translation by Luzi. See also Titone under intertextuality in the GENERAL section.

MALAPARTE. Luigi Martellini, **Comete di ghiaccio: Il sole è cieco di Curzio Malaparte: stesure e varianti*, Na, ESI, 131 pp.

MANGANELLI. Giorgio Manganelli, *L'impero romanzesco*, T, Aragno, 141 pp., introd. Viola Papetti, includes 111 'schede di lettura', or reports written by M. for a number of Italian publishers on novels by authors writing in English. R. Bertoni, 'Messaggi dall'inferno di Manganelli e Dante', pp. 31–46 of *Echi danteschi / Dantean Echoes*, ed. Roberto Bertoni, Dublin, Italian Department, Trinity College — T, Trauben, 144 pp., examines linguistic and psychological aspects, and in particular symbols and allegories as reworked by M. from Dante into modern configurations. R. Manica, 'Postfazione', pp. 197–205 of Giorgio Manganelli, *UFO e altri oggetti non identificati 1072–1990*, ed. Graziella Pulce, Ro, Quiritta, 224 pp., highlights the author's interest in fantasy and science fiction, and the paradox whereby reality presents itself under the guise of fiction. Id., *Costruire ricordi*, Mi, Archinto, 128 pp., includes M.'s letters to Giovanna Sandri and a memoir by her.

MARAINI. Maria Antonietta Cruciata, *Dacia Maraini*, Ro, Cadmo, 157 pp., examines M.'s theatre, poetry, and narrative under the main theme of the condition of women as portrayed in her work, and includes an interview with her (135–57). A. Brendler and F. Iodice, 'Intervista a Dacia Maraini sui nomi', *ItQ*, 155–156:81–89. E. Papp, '"Illuminismo al femminile". Le idee dell'Illuminismo nel romanzo *La lunga vita di Marianna Ucría* di Dacia Maraini', *Italianistica debreceniensis*, 9, 2002:160–68.

MASINO. T. Rorandelli, '*Nascita e morte della massaia* di Paola Masino e la questione del corpo materno nel fascismo', *FoI*, 37:70–102, surveys fascist ideologies on the role of women as mechanical procreators, and sees Masino's novel as questioning them while displaying perplexity and anxiety over the fascist approach to women in general.

MENEGHELLO. E. Guerrieri, 'Per Luigi Meneghello, omaggio breve', *Il Ponte*, 59.9:155–57.

MERINI. F. Parmegiani, 'La *folle* di Alda Merini', *QI*, 23.1, 2002:173–92. Alda Merini, *Dopo tutto anche tu*, ed. Angelo Guarnieri, Genoa, San Marco dei Giustiniani, 47 pp.

MICHELSTAEDTER. A. Perli, 'L'esilio e il regno: *I figli del mare* di Carlo Michelstaedter', *CLett*, 31:63–78, is a 'proiezione mitopoetica' of Itti and Senia, the 'figli del mare', whose extraneous nature was subsequently transfigured in the terrestrial world when they were exiled from the 'regno del mare'.

MONTALE. Tiziano De Rogatis, *Montale e il classicismo moderno*, Pisa–Ro, IEPI, 2002, 196 pp., collects various essays on M.'s cultural and poetic formation while offering a series of intertextual readings which show the influence on M. of Eliot, Alain, Valéry, Du Bos, Praz, Browne, and Baudelaire. G. Genco, 'Dante nella poesia di Montale', *Testo*, 46:77–94. G. Talbot, 'Montale's critical friendship with Henry Furst, "il falso cardinale"', *SpR*, 17, 2002[2003]:65–80. J. Butcher, 'Eugenio Montale and Italo Calvino: *Le cosmicomiche*, *Ti con zero* and the post *Bufera* verse', *FoI*, 36, 2002:411–37, investigates M.'s relationship with *Le Cosmicomiche* (1965) and *Ti con zero* (1967), and focuses on the importance of these works for the poetry of *Satura* (1971), *Diario del '71 e del '72* (1973), *Quaderno di quattro anni* (1977), *Altri versi* (1980), and *Diario postumo* (1996). T. C. Westphalen, 'Montale and the poetics of the discrete. A note on Eugenio Montale's *Collected Poems*, translated and annotated by Jonathan Galassi', *Gradiva*, 20–21:50–56, defines these translations of *Ossi di seppia*, *Le occasioni*, and *La bufera e altro* as ones that 'transpose the spare musicality and the integrity of Montale's corpus with care and conviction'.

P. Senna, 'Un mazzo di rose gialle nel pozzo delle memorie. Lettura della prima parte di *Farfalla di Dinard*', *RLettI*, 21.3:65–88, offers linguistic suggestions on specific stylistic traits that have tangential links with M.'s poetry. L. Surdich, 'Montale, gli oggetti, un'interpretazione', *RLI*, 107:119–26, argues that Luigi Blasucci's book *Gli oggetti di Montale* presents the poet as 'un classico' while emphasizing the centrality of M. in the 'rinnovamento dell'idea della poesia nella prima metà del Novecento'. T. Arvigo, ' "Casa sul mare" e "I morti": una lettura', *ib.*, 104–18, gives an incisive commentary on the compositional problems related to these two poems from *Ossi di seppia*. G. Burrini, 'La memoria del sole. Note e sottolineature sul giovane Montale', *LetP*, 116–117:3–8, analyses the 'Mediterraneo' section of *Ossi di seppia* and suggests that it provided an early introspective view of M.'s poetics.

Niccolò Scaffai, *Montale e il libro di poesia* (*'Ossi di seppia', 'Le occasioni', 'La bufera e altro'*), Lucca, Pacini Fazzi, 2002, 250 pp., does not consider the above collections as mere collections but rather as books with an internal coherence that was part of M.'s creative strategy at that time. Gianluigi Simonetti, *Dopo Montale. Le 'Occasioni' e la poesia italiana del Novecento*, Lucca, Pacini Fazzi, 2002, 424 pp., deals with the impact of M.'s 'strategia espressiva' on Italian poetry in the second half of the 20th c. C. Zanoni, 'Il pensiero religioso di Eugenio Montale', *RSLR*, 39:291–330. A. Zambardi, 'Montale tra realtà e metafisica', *Il Veltro*, 47:429–39. A. Roncaccia, 'L'antifrasi del postmoderno nella poesia di Montale', *Versants*, 41, 2002:27–45.

MORANTE. M. Barenghi, 'Tutti i nomi di Useppe. Saggio sui personaggi della *Storia* di Elsa Morante', *StCrit*, 28:363–89, analyses the novel's names on the basis of the importance of characters in M.'s fiction and in relation to her narrative strategy as both subjective and omniscient author, who assesses the characters' interiority and focuses on their daily lives rather than on history as such. As a result, this narrative may not be considered a historical novel proper as the title would suggest. Concetta D'Angeli, *Leggere Elsa Morante. Aracoeli, La storia e Il mondo salvato dai ragazzini*, Ro, Carocci, 142 pp., notes that some images recur throughout M.'s work and focuses in particular on death, a sense of history interwoven with literary aesthetics, sexuality linked to the family, and M.'s relation to other authors in the Italian canon. G. Dell'Aquila, 'Note di onomastica nell'*Isola di Arturo*', *Il nome nel testo*, 5:177–88, examines M.'s intentional strategies in choosing the characters' names in *L'isola di Arturo*, including ironic choices and the fact that some of the names anticipate the fate of the characters in the story. It also confirms, through an analysis of place- and character-names, that the novel presents a divergence between reality and myth. H. Serkowska, 'Percorsi androgini. *Aracoeli*: il romanzo definitivo di Elsa Morante', *LetP*, 115, 2002:3–28, sees *Aracoeli* in continuity with earlier works, especially *Menzogna e sortilegio*, and then highlights the myth of the 'androgino' as its central focus in relation to M.'s interest in psychoanalysis and oriental philosophy.

MORAVIA. R. Capec-Habecovic, 'Alberto Moravia revisited', *SpR*, 17, 2002[2003]: 109–16, examines relationships and their psychoanalytical and existential significance in his narrative. See also Dotti above in section 3.

MORETTI. *REI*, 48, 2002[2003], considers the 'Itinerari europei di Marino Moretti (1885–1979)'. Part One deals with M. and France and includes the following: M. Richter, 'Significato della presenza francese nella poesia italiana agli inizi del Novecento' (5–11); M. Ciccuto, 'Fra simbolisti e sognatori. Implicazioni artistiche d'oltralpe nella scrittura di Marino Moretti' (13–20); G. M. Bergamo, 'La vita parigina e le relazioni con gli ambienti letterari ed artistici italo-francesi: originarietà e originalità' (21–25); P. Pacini, 'Marino Moretti a Montparnasse. Dalla Closerie des Lilas al Café de Flore' (27–40); A. Nozzoli, 'La Francia di Pazzo Pazzi' (41–47); R. Campagnoli, '"A-t-on jamais entendu parler de Miss Kathleen Mowrer?": la ricezione di Moretti in Francia fino al 1930' (49–57); M. Ricci, 'Marino Moretti e Juliette Bertrand amica e traduttrice' (59–90); S. Magherini, '1925: "Due italiani a Parigi". Appunti di viaggio dal carteggio Moretti–Palazzeschi' (91–103); and A. Contò, 'Marino Moretti e Lionello Fiumi tra Italia e Francia' (105–38). Part Two considers his connection with Holland and Belgium and includes M. Guglielminetti, 'I fiamminghi, devozione e straniamento' (139–45); F. Livi, 'Marino Moretti e il mito di Bruges' (147–56); C. Farini, 'Georges Rodenbach e Marino Moretti: tra simbolismo e crepuscolarismo' (157–68); A. I. Villa, 'Moretti, Maeterlinck e il simbolismo: attrazioni e repulsioni del primissimo Moretti critico' (169–85); R. Gennaro, 'Le carte morettiane di Robert Van Nuffel' (187–96); D. Aristodemo, '"La dame en mauve". La stagione olandese di Marino Moretti' (197–210); J. Robaey, 'Dalla *Zélande* di De Coster alle *Fantasie olandesi*: la perdita del senso in Moretti' (211–28); and G. Farinelli, '*Le poverazze*: scelte per l'addio dell'ultimo Moretti' (229–36). *La fiera letteraria per Marino Moretti*, ed. Manuela Ricci, Bo, CLUEB, 2002, 158 pp., includes an essay by Guido Lopez.

NICCOLAI. R. West, 'Manganelli and Niccolai: the unlikely bond between a Junghian "bishop" and a Buddist nun', *Italica*, 80:73–78, points to the links that can be established between M. and N. in her Buddist phase as expounded in *Esoterico biliardo* (2001). By stressing the philosophy and creativity of each writer the author shows how in each case 'literature nurtures life as life in turn nurtures literature'.

PAGAN. A. Zambardi, 'Il mondo poetico di Roberto Pagan', *Il Veltro*, 46, 2002:567–73.

PALAZZESCHI. S. Vinall, 'Princes and Pierrots: Palazzeschi's early writing and Laforgue', *ISt*, 58:104–32, demonstrates P.'s early familiarity with the work of Laforgue, shows how he exploited it crucially in the emergence of his comic mask. Also highlighted are the analogies between P.'s 'saltimbanco' and Laforgue's Pierrot. M. Graffi, 'La parola trovata di Palazzeschi', *Il Verri*, 21:5–18, outlines P.'s use of linguistic devices in his writing, particularly his poetry. E. Ghidetti, 'Palazzeschi: piaceri e dispiaceri della memoria', *REI*, 48, 2002[2003]:293–308. Giovanni Capecchi, *Palazzeschi e la leggerezza*, F, Le Càriti, 94 pp. Giuliana Adamo, *Metro e ritmo del primo Palazzeschi*, Ro, Salerno, 216 pp., includes an introd. by C. Segre (9–10) and is a study of variants in the differing editions of P.'s early poems as he organized them himself. An appendix contains the texts of these poems and the variants are given in the footnotes.

PAPINI. G. Spadolini, 'Papini', *NA*, 2226:54–76, introd. C. Ceccuti, is an article written by Giovanni Spadolini in 1947 on P.'s political and religious itinerary as an intellectual. S. saw a significant change from P.'s role as a 'rivoluzionario moderno' after the writing of *Un uomo finito*, which eventually led to work published after World War II when P. became a 'profeta del nuovo cristianesimo'. See also A. M. Mangini under literary genres and movements in Section 1.

PARISE. G. Cavallini, 'L'onomastica nei *Sillabari* di Goffredo Parise', *Il nome nel testo*, 5:189–99, notes a contrast between indefiniteness and precision in P.'s designation of characters and places. He observes that definition, when it occurs, has the function of attaching concrete qualities to the prevalent mysterious and vague atmosphere of *Sillabari*, and he links this to the motif of memory. A. Gialloreto, 'Parise, "naufrago psicologico"', *Allegoria*, 42, 2002:105–14, reappraises 'Ricordi immaginari', 15 stories published in *Il Corriere della sera* (1983–84) and argues that they may have been an unfinished serial novel characterized by Darwinian motifs. Silvio Perrella, *Fino a Salgaredo. La scrittura nomade di Goffredo Parise*, Mi, Rizzoli, 204 pp., covers most of P.'s work and life, indicates, among other aspects, his skill in expressing nuances, and sees *Sillabari* as both emotionally charged and well written.

PARRONCHI. G. Ioli, 'Il "vivo lume" della prospettiva nella poesia di Alessandro Parronchi', *CFI*, 9: 151–64, highlights the need for familiarity with the historical background when approaching P.'s *Poesie*.

PASOLINI. A. Tricomi, 'Pier Paolo Pasolini', *Belfagor*, 58, 427–61, asks whether assessment of P.'s work in poetry, film, prose, and criticism has changed stance since the late 1970s. J. Khalip, 'Love's maturity: Pasolini's "La scoperta di Marx"', *FoI*, 36, 2002:360–92, details P.'s engagement with history and the manner in which Marxism impacted on P.'s work. D. Piccini, 'Pier Paolo Pasolini: la poesia, inseguimento della vita', *Poesia*, 172:2–12, discusses the passion for life discernible in P.'s poetry. 'Pasolini', *NArg*, 21:122–75, includes short essays by E. Siciliano on the variety of meanings of *Pilade*, by M. Raffaelli on F. La Porta's interpretation of P. (see below), by M. Belpoliti on P. the journalist and columnist, and by R. Ronchi on P.'s 'speculative mysticism' and 'ateologia', his relations with Georges Bataille, his sense of nothingness, and a vision of literature as democratically orientated towards the reader while rejecting any teaching functions. Angela Biancofiore, **Pasolini*, Palermo, Palumbo, 344 pp. Francesca Falchi, *'El Juanero'. Pasolini e la cultura spagnola*, F, Atheneum, 142 pp., outlines various influences on P. including Calderón, Garcia Lorca, and Picasso. Filippo La Porta, *Uno gnostico innamorato della realtà*, F, Le Lettere, 96 pp., values P. the essayist more positively than the narrator and reappraises his ideology and existential stance. G. Panella, 'Pier Paolo Pasolini: dal cinema di poesia ai film sul mito', *Gradiva*, 22, 2002:38–49, notes that cinema influenced P.'s work as a poet — and is itself a variety of poetry in P.'s poetics — and underlines the importance of myth, with its tragic impact on daily life apparent in films like *Medea*, especially through the image of the Centaur in scene 11. Sergio Parussa, **L'eros onnipotente: erotismo, letteratura e impegno nell'opera di Pier Paolo Pasolini e Jean Genet*, T, Tirrenia, 96 pp. F. Pisanelli, 'Per una religione degli odori: *Petrolio*. Geometrie di un disordine', *Poetiche*, 5:101–23, considers the cumulative poetics of P. in *Petrolio*, its corporal nature, its postmodern composite style, its anti-consumerist ideology, and the role assigned to smells and odours in the novel. Laura Zanella, **Dopo la favola del figlio cambiato: come rinasce una creatura innocente*, Olschki, 2002, xiii + 105 pp. Giuseppe Zigaina, **Pasolini e il suo nuovo teatro: senza anteprime né prime né repliche*, Venice, Marsilio, 213 pp.

PENNA. J. Butcher, 'Eros, enigma and euphemism in the poetry of Sandro Penna', *QI*, 23.1, 2002:105–32.

PIERRO. Emerico Giachery, *Albino Pierro grande lirico*, T, Genesi, 2002, 133 pp.

PILLONETTO. S. Tamiozzo Goldmann, 'La poesia interrotta di Giocondo Pillonetto: *Penultima fiaba. Poesie* (1935–1981)', *QV*, 36, 2002[2003]:117–27, presents a new edition of P.'s one poetry collection, which includes a certain number of previously unpublished poems, together with a critical presentation of the poet and his work.

PIRANDELLO. J. Lorch, 'Pirandello for the new Italy: Orazio Costa's production of *Sei personaggi in cerca d'autore*', *Thompson Vol.*, 104–16, is mainly on Costa's production but also, partly, on P.'s politics during fascism. I. Pupo, 'Una madre in più. Un soggetto cinematografico inedito di Stefano Pirandello', *FAM*, 21, 2001 : 119–46, argues that Stefano Pirandello's outline of a film script entitled *Le care ubbie di suo marito*, reproduced on pp. 141–46 from the original typescript and based on Luigi Pirandello's short story 'La balia', even though it derives, as Stefano wrote, from Luigi's own plot, is the result of collaboration and division of labour between father and son, with the son writing at least partly creatively, rather than under his father's direction. G. Quatriglio, 'Pirandello critico d'arte', *NA*, 2226 : 289–93, illustrates seven articles published in *Giornale di Sicilia* in 1895 on the Esposizione della Società degli Amatori e Cultori di Belle Arti held in Palermo. Franco Zangrilli, *Pirandello e il giornalismo*, pref. Giuseppe Costa, Caltanissetta, Sciascia, 130 pp. *Bibliografia pirandelliana 1936–1996*, ed. Cristina Angela Iacono, Palermo, Regione Sicilia, 2002, 351 pp.

PIZZUTO. M. Marchesini, '*Signorina Rosina*: Pizzuto e Beckett, ovvero la scrittura come pittogramma', *StCrit*, 18 : 183–201, notes that this novel differs both from the neorealist and hermetic trends and has more in common with Beckett's shifting writing and his suggestion that content and form coincide.

PONTIGGIA. Alberto Albertini, *Nascere due volte. Le straordinarie opportunità della scrittura di Giuseppe Pontiggia*, Brescia, L'Obliquo, 48 pp., argues that P. will become a 20th-c. classic thanks to his style, which avoids technical and specialized lexis and is based on careful revision, and thanks to his subject matter, especially the human and social aspects as seen in *Nati due volte*. Two sections are devoted to comments based on interviews with the German and English translators of *Nati due volte*, namely Karin Krieger (23–27) and Oonagh Stransky (28–33), while the work ends with a previously unpublished letter from P. to Albertini on the latter's essay.

POZZA. G. Pullini, 'L'autobiografismo di Neri Pozza', *StN*, 28, 2001 : 401–15.

POZZI. *Pozzi: la scrittura crudele. Atti del Convegno internazionale, Siena, Santa Maria della Scala, 24–26 ottobre 2002*, ed. Maria Antonietta Grignani, Pisa, IEPI, 269 pp., is the monographic issue *Moderna*, 4.2.

PRATO. M. Farnetti, 'L'antibiografia di Dolores Prato', pp. 33–58 of *Oltrecanone. Per una cartografia della scrittura femminile*, ed. Anna Maria Crispino, Ro, Manifestolibri, 176 pp., is about the novel *Giù la piazza non c'è nessuno* where description prevails and autobiography interacts with memory especially of the mother figure. Farnetti defines this work as 'antibiografia'.

PREZZOLINI. *Prezzolini e il suo tempo. Atti del Convegno internazionale di studi*, ed. Cosimo Ceccuti, F, Le Lettere, 332 pp., includes essays on Italian culture in the early 20th c. by G. Luti and M. Biondi, and on P. in relation to other authors: M. Richter on P. and Soffici, E. Giammattei on P. and Croce, S. Magherini on P. and Palazzeschi, and C. Ceccuti on P. and Spadolini. A section is devoted to P. and the U.S.A. (essays by L. Rebay and E. Gentile), and there are other texts by M. Apa, A. M. Russo, and D. Rüesch. Beppe Benvenuto, *Giuseppe Prezzolini*, Palermo, Sellerio, 172 pp., is largely an ideological biography of P. from his years at *La Voce* to his American period and his last phase; his sympathy for, but also independence on fascism, are discussed along with his attitudes towards Benedetto Croce, Giovanni Papini, and other intellectuals.

QUASIMODO. Natale Tedesco, *L'isola impareggiabile. Significato e forme di mito di Quasimodo*, Palermo, Flaccovio, 2002, 156 pp. *RLettI*, 21.1–2, 2002, for Q. contains the following articles: G. Finzi, 'Quasimodo; il tempo e le parole' (17–24); E. Guagnini, ' "La voce del poeta dentro il mondo". Sugli scritti di Quasimodo intorno alla poesia' (25–34); G. Bárberi Squarotti, 'Le lune di Quasimodo' (35–42); S. Pautasso, '*Poesie 1938:* un libro fantasma' (43–48); B. Martinelli, 'Quasimodo: rito e confessione nella *Lettera alla madre*' (49–61); G. Langella, 'Quasimodo, o della poesia come epitaffio' (63–67); A. Bellio, ' "Che giovinezza inganno/con nuvole e colori". La tavolozza del poeta' (69–78); F. Ghicopoulos, 'Quasimodo colpito dal dardo di Apollo' (79–83); A. Granese, 'L'inferno della violenza nelle dissonanze di Quasimodo' (85–95); B. Carle, 'Dall'antitesi al dialogo: le figure orfiche di Quasimodo' (97–102); A. Frattini, 'Tensioni e implicazioni ermetiche nella poesia di Quasimodo' (103–108); L. Fontanella, 'Quasimodo traduttore di E. E. Cummings' (109–16); P. Frassica, 'Quasimodo ludens' (117–27); C. Ferrari, 'Eros e morte in Salvatore Quasimodo' (129–32); G. Baroni, ' "Le parole della vita" ' (133–40); B. Van den Bossche, 'Nord e Sud nella poesia di Quasimodo' (141–47); A. L. Giannone, 'Quasimodo, Bodini e l'ermetismo meridionale' (149–58); G. Cavallini, 'Parole, stilemi, inflessioni del primo Quasimodo: alcuni esempi' (159–68); M. Cantelmo, ' "Azzurra siepe a me d'intorno". Sondaggi sulla riscrittura dello spazio letterario' (169–92); A. Rondoni, 'Viaggi e geografia dell'ultimo Quasimodo' (193–99); A. Iurilli, 'Quasimodo e Bocelli' (201–06); P. Paolini, 'Quasimodo critico della letteratura italiana delle origini' (207–20); F. Di Legami, 'Linguaggio presocratico in Quasimodo. Forme analogiche del moderno' (221–31); F. Russo, 'Quasimodo, le mani, la Sicilia mitica per Marguerite Yourcenar' (233–43); F. D'Episcopo, 'Salvatore Quasimodo e Alfonso Gatto' (245–49); R. Paternostro, 'Salvatore Quasimodo o della poesia come etica' (251–61);

T. Ferri, '*I Discorsi sulla poesia* e la lirica di S. Quasimodo: un dialogo tra testi' (263–67); M. C. Albonico, 'Il Catullo di Quasimodo' (269–73); F. D'Alessandro, 'Quasimodo e la coscienza critica degli anni trenta' (275–83); A. Guastella, 'Il muro metafisico e la siepe leopardiana. *Nell'isola* di Salvatore Quasimodo' (285–93); G. Lupo, 'Quasimodo a colori' (295–301); F. Millefiorini, 'Una giovenile prova futurista di Salvatore Quasimodo' (303–11); A. R. Romani, 'Intorno al "linguaggio universale": teorie e critiche teatrali di Salvatore Quasimodo' (313–20); R. Castelli, 'Quasimodo e il sentimento della solitudine' (321–28); C. Mauro, 'Nota in margine al carteggio Salvatore Quasimodo–Amelia Spezialetti' (329–36); C. Marchisio, 'Quasimodo e Neruda; il gioco del "dare" e dell'"avere"' (337–45); Ž. Djurić, 'Salvatore Quasimodo in Jugoslavia (fatti e momenti di una vita)' (347–51); P. Zovatto, 'La problematica religiosità di Quasimodo' (353–64); M. Ciccuto, 'Percorsi di cultura figurativa nella prosa di Salvatore Quasimodo' (365–74); M. G. Riccobono, 'Memoria delle poetiche e memoria poetica in Quasimodo: bilanci critici e sondaggi asistematici sui versi dell'autore' (375–405); R. Salsano, 'Critica dello stile e stile della critica nel *Discorso sulla poesia* di Salvatore Quasimodo' (407–16); G. Lavezzi, 'Il metro che si cala nella storia: l'endecasillabo di *Giorno dopo giorno*' (417–22); P. Ponti, 'Quasimodo illustrato. Versi e immagini nel *Falso e vero verde* del 1954' (423–37); E. Mezzetta, 'Salvatore Quasimodo e Francesco Messina' (439–53); P. Perilli, 'Salvatore Quasimodo dalla Sicilia all'Europa' (455–64); P. Senna, 'Prima che l'òboe sia sommerso. Quasimodo e Montale nelle lettere e nella critica fra 1930 e 1932' (465–74); F. De Nicola, 'Intorno a "Circoli": Descalzo e Quasimodo' (475–81); G. A. Brunelli, 'Salvatore Quasimodo nei *Poètes d'Italie*' (483–86); E. Ajello, 'Un poeta a teatro. Quasimodo spettatore di Goldoni' (487–95); and Z. Zografidou, 'Quasimodo e le sue traduzioni in Grecia' (497–505).

RABONI. 'Giovanni Raboni, '"Vivere almeno al 50 per cento"', *Poesia*, 168:2–14, records a general interview with Daniele Piccini; S. Ramat, 'Giovanni Raboni. L'esilio nella storia', *ib.*, 15–16; C. Di Franza, 'Un poeta nel purgatorio del tempo', *ib.*, 16–17.

RAGAZZONI. F. Lanza, 'Scapigliatura postuma: Ernesto Ragazzoni', *Cenobio*, 52:230–33.

REBORA. Roberto Cicala and Valerio Rossi, *Bibliografia reboriana*, F, Olschki, 2002, 232 pp.

ROSSELLI. *Trasparenze 17/19* concentrates on Amelia Rosselli's poetry and writings, and offers various critical assessents of her work. It includes the following pieces by R. and other writers and critics: 'Sandro Penna' (5–8), '*Metropolis* di Porta' (9–10), 'Introduzione a *Spazi metrici*"' (11–13) and 'Glossarietto esplicativo' (15–22); F. Caputo, 'Quattro scritti di Amelia Rosselli' (23–26); A. Rosselli,

'Emily scrive al mondo' (27–28); E. Dickinson, 'Poesie – traduzione di Amelia Rosselli' (29–35); A. Rosselli, 'Istinto di morte e istinto di piacere in Sylvia Plath' (37–42); S. Plath, 'Poesie – traduzione di Amelia Rosselli' (43–56); A. Rosselli, 'Lettera ad Antonio Porta' (57–58); G. Palli Baroni, 'Amelia Rosselli assetata d'amore: colloquio con Aldo Rosselli' (59–64); F. Vitelli, 'Amelia Rosselli e Scotellaro' (65–75); R. Scotellaro, 'Un lago nella memoria' (77–89); A. Rosselli, '[Carissimo Elio] – lettere da Londra a Elio Pecora' (91–101); E. Pecora, 'Nota alle lettere da Londra di Amelia Rosselli' (103–05); M. Venturini, 'Alla luce della critica: la poesia di Amelia Rosselli' (107–18); A. Baldacci, 'Amelia danza Kafka' (119–32); S. Giovannuzzi, 'Amelia Rosselli e la funzione Campana' (133–54); N. Lorenzini, 'Memoria testuale e parola "inaudita": Amelia e Gabriele' (155–71); E. Tandello, 'Alle fonti del lapsus: pun, portmanteau, wordscape. Appunti sull'inglese letterario di Amelia Rosselli' (173–92), and 'Un discorso appena un po' più largo: Scipione' (193–207); Scipione, 'Carte segrete – Versi' (209–14); F. Carbognin, 'La biblioteca personale di Amelia Rosselli' (215–25); M. Manera, 'Devianze intralinguistiche nella poesia italiana di Amelia Rosselli' (227–52); F. Fusco, 'Amelia Rosselli: la propagazione bloccata' (253–65); F. Carbognin, '"Non son mai stata così collettiva (però nella lingua)". Dall'"unità base del verso" allo "spazio metrico" di Amelia Rosselli' (267–88); P. Cairoli, 'Spazio metrico e serialismo musicale. L'azione dell'avanguardia postweberniana sulle concezioni poetiche di Amelia Rosselli' (289–300) and 'Suggestioni sonore evocate dalla poesia di Amelia Rosselli' (301–08); D. La Penna, 'La metafora ventosa nella poesia di Amelia Rosselli' (309–32); B. Frabotta, 'Le buone "intenzioni" di Amelia Rosselli: qualche riflessione su Documento' (333–42); G. Palli Baroni, 'La "casa buia" di Amelia Rosselli: peso di realtà e "fantastiche imprese" della poesia' (343–52); E. Testa, 'Per Amelia' (353–60); F. Carbognin, 'Bibliografia rosselliana' (361–81). G. Russo, 'Ricordo di Amelia Rosselli', *NA*, 2221, 2002:85–87.

SABA. See LEVI, C.

SANESI. *Il Confronto Letterario*, 39, contains E. Montagna, '*L'incendio di Milano*. Lettura di poesie di Roberto Sanesi', (181–82) and F. Sangermano, 'Note sulla lettura dei versi, e in particolare di quelli di Roberto Sanesi' (183–88).

SANGUINETI. E. Sanguineti, 'Il corpo è la poesia, e non si dà pace', *Poesia*, 171:3–6, details the restless image of the body that is especially present in S.'s *Il gatto lupesco*. D. Piccini, 'Edoardo Sanguineti. I piccoli fatti veri', *ib.*, 7–19, comprises a detailed interview with S. on his life, beliefs, and views on literature. J. Butcher, 'Da *Laborintus* a *Postkarten*',

Allegoria, 44: 123–32, is the text of an interview, given by S. in 2002, which includes a political interpretation of *Purgatorio de l'Inferno* (the author hoped that socialism would expand worldwide) and a reinterpretation of *Reisebilder* as an anticipation of the contemporary reality of globalization. Edoardo Sanguineti, *Faust. Un travestimento*, ed. Niva Lorenzini, Ro, Carocci, 142 pp., includes an essay by Lorenzini ('Il *Faust* di Sanguineti. La parola all'inferno', 7–47) which discusses S.'s genuine interest in the theme of 'inferno' but also his 'travestimento' in the reworking of Goethe's *Faust* through a deconstruction of the original *pathos* and a reorganized structure, all of which results in a 'fertile intertestualità'. An essay by P. de Meijer traces the presence of Goethe throughout S.'s work.

SAVINIO. A. Castronuovo, 'Alberto Savinio e il cristianesimo', *Belfagor*, 58, 37–42, examines S.'s initially hostile approach, and his later more objective one, to Christianity. P. E. Favalini, ' "Protogeo": neologismi e congetture saviniane', *RELI*, 17, 2001: 61–101, examines some aspects of S.'s innovative lexis. See also S. Bellotto under literary genres and movements in section 1 above.

SCIASCIA. *Sciascia autore editore, ovvero la felicità di far libri*, ed. Salvatore Silvano Nigro, Palermo, Sellerio, 316 pp., collects S,'s cover notes to several volumes published by Sellerio. 'Leonardo Sciascia', *NArg*, 22: 108–23, includes N. De Vita, 'Noi ci ricorderemo', on his meeting with S., and S. Ferlita, 'Leonardo Sciascia e la fotografia', discussing S.'s interest in photographs, and photo portraits, as discourse and narrative. Livia Barbella, **Sciascia*, Palermo, Palumbo, 334 pp. Bernardo Puleio, **I sentieri di Sciascia*, Palermo, Kalos, 175 pp. G. Traina, 'Le muse inquietanti di Leonardo Sciascia. Manichini, marionette, bambole sul palcoscenico di uno scrittore', *SpR*, 17, 2002[2003]: 41–57, expresses reservations about the theatrical nature of S.'s play and relates this, at least in part, to a Freudian interpretation and to the author's ambivalent attitude towards the 'teatro dei pupi'.

SCOTELLARO. *Rocco Scotellaro oltre il Sud: nel 50. anniversario della morte. Antologia letteraria*, ed. Francesco De Napoli, Venafro, Eva, 207 pp.

SERENI. S. Giovanuzzi, 'Sereni: dalla prosa agli *Immediati dintorni*', *FC*, 27, 2002[2003]: 399–429, outlines the difficulties experienced by Sereni in attempting to find a poetic vein, particularly in 1962 when he published the above work. J. Sisco, 'Sereni, de Staël e il linguaggio del fatto pittorico', *Il Verri*, 22: 91–111, describes similarities of expression in S.'s work and the paintings of the restless and reticent Nicolas de Staël. Francesca D'Alessandro, *L'opera poetica di Vittorio Sereni*, Mi, Vita e Pensiero, 2001, 252 pp., uses S.'s 1965 work (*Gli strumenti umani* and *Diario d'Algeria*) as a basis for a critical assessment of S.'s previous and later poetry collections. S. Giannini, 'Un'agra salita. Lettura di "Autostrada della Cisa" di Vittorio Sereni', *ItQ*, 155–156:27–36.

SGORLON. Carmelo Aliberti, *La narrativa di Carlo Sgorlon*, Foggia, Bastogi, 145 pp., shows how S., while keeping distance from literary fashions and the avantgarde, portrays social changes, ecological concerns, and existential motifs, thus offering a spiritual alternative to consumerism. Also examined is S.'s interest in archetypes.

SILONE. G. Baldi, 'Straniamento e comico antifrastico in *Fontamara.* Per una rilettura del primo romanzo di Silone', *Moderna*, 4.1:71–85, through an analysis of narrative procedures notes links between S. and Verga, and observes that S., unlike Verga, gives progressive perspectives to his characters. Francesco De Core and Ottorino Gurgo, *Silone, un alfabeto*, Na, L'Ancora del Mediterraneo, 160 pp., on concepts and motifs in alphabetical order, note especially the entries 'libertà', 'nichilismo' and 'verità'. See also B. Moloney on C. Levi, above.

SLATAPER. A. Cinquegrani, 'Certificazione negativa e vocativa ne *Il mio Carso* di Scipio Slataper', *QV*, 36:95–116.

SOLDATI. *Mario Soldati. Atti del Convegno 'Toscano, bretelle e papillon'*, ed. Graziella Colotto, La Spezia, Agorà, 100 pp., based on a Conference held at Lerici in 2003, includes pieces of institutional or commemorative nature by C. Bertieri, M. L. Eguez, M. Melley, M. Novaro, M. Piperno, S. Sandrelli, G. Soldati, and G. Tedoldi, and essays by F. Battolini on S. as an art critic (63–72), G. Benelli on S.'s education at a Jesuit school and the survival of various aspects of religiosity in his work (33–50), P. Bertolani on S.'s poetics of 'superficie profonda' (29–32), G. Bertone on *America, primo amore* (51–62), L. Faccini and B. Torri on S. the film director (73–80 and 89–99), and S. Verdino on S. and music (19–28).

SVEVO. Patrizia Biaggini, **Lo sguardo su di sé: Zeno e l'umorismo della coscienza*, Pisa, ETS, 158 pp. G. Guglielmi, 'Situazioni del racconto. Joyce e Svevo', *Moderna*, 4.1:57–70, notes that time and space belong together in narrative and gives examples of this from James Joyce's *Ulysses* and S.'s *La coscienza di Zeno*. D. De Ferra, 'Women, education and nationality in Svevo's Trieste', *Thompson Vol.*, 89–103, views S.'s novels from the angle of gender and shows, in particolar, how *La coscienza di Zeno* may be seen as critical of contemporary Italian patterns in bourgeois education and behaviour. Massimiliano Tortora, *Svevo novelliere*, Pisa, IEPI, 175 pp., includes some previously unpublished letters by and to Svevo. Fabio Vittorini, *Svevo: guida alla Coscienza di Zeno*, Ro, Carocci, 128 pp., is an introduction to the novel focusing on its narrative structures and themes.

TABUCCHI. Antonio Tabucchi, *Autobiografie altrui. Poetiche a posteriori*, Mi, Feltrinelli, 128 pp., in a mixture of styles, sometimes narrative, at other times epistolary or critical, goes into the reasons (realistic, allusive, or oniric) why he wrote some of his works. T. S. Kiss, 'Le investigazioni incongrue di un io latitante. Le "detective-story esistenziali" di Antonio Tabucchi', *Italianistica debreceniensis*, 9, 2002: 169.

TESTORI. Fulvio Panzeri, *Vita di Testori*, Mi, Longanesi, 245 pp.

TOMASI DI LAMPEDUSA. Gaetano G. Cosentini, *I miti, il tempo perduto, la grecità in Tomasi di Lampedusa*, Trapani, Coppola, 2002, 79 pp.

TONDELLI. Enrico Minardi, *Pier Vittorio Tondelli*, Fiesole, Cadmo, 155 pp.

TOZZI. *Federigo Tozzi fra tradizione e modernità (Atti del Convegno di Assisi, 2001)*, ed. Marco Marchi, Assisi, Cittadella, 2001, 234 pp. *Moderna*, 4.2, 2002, published separately as *Tozzi: la scrittura crudele*, ed. Maria Antonietta Grignani and Giada Mattarucco, 270 pp., contains the proceedings of a conference held in Siena in 2002: a memoir by Silvia Tozzi (105–11) and essays by P. V. Mengaldo on the language of T.'s *novelle* (33–45), F. Petroni on descriptive techniques in *Bestie* (77–88), R. Luperini on the interaction of psychology and religion, especially in 'Il crocifisso' (113–24), and F. Sanvitale on what she calls the 'psychological revolt' of the characters, or T.'s adoption of the characters' voices in his narrative. She also highlights T.'s modernity, consisting in his observation of psychological enigmas and his insistence on the sense of sight (comparable to surrealism) and mental solitude, and T.'s illustration of mental and physical disease which makes him similar to Luigi Pirandello and Italo Svevo. This volume also includes essays by R. Barzanti, R. Castellana, G. D'Elia, M. Fratnik, D. Garofano, M. A. Grignani, M. Lippi, B. Livi, M. Luzi, M. Maccari, M. Marchi, M. Martini, G. Nicoletti, A. Prete, M. Raffaelli, and E. Saccone. F. Sanvitale, 'Federigo Tozzi: la rivolta psichica del personaggio', is also in *NArg*, 21: 312–20. E. Saccone, 'Narrative di crisi. Sulla forma di alcuni romanzi e novelle di Federigo Tozzi', *MLN*, 118: 194–208.

TRILUSSA. M. Farkas, 'Trilussa, il poeta romanesco e il Centro Romanesco Trilussa', *Italianistica debreceniensis*, 7, 2000: 251–55.

TUROLDO. Giuseppina Commare, *Turoldo e gli organi divini*, F, Olschki, 208 pp., starting with the subtitle *Lettura concordanziale di 'O sensi miei'*, goes on to show that by using a mathematical system based on the 'frequenze concordanziali' T.'s spirituality and mysticism become apparent in his poetry.

UNGARETTI. V. Bagnoli, 'Frammenti di totalità: il paesaggio dell'*Allegria*', *Poetiche*, 1: 55–73. G. Bevilacqua, 'Ungaretti tradotto da

Celan', *RLMC*, 56:71–77. M. Petrucciani, 'Ungaretti. L'aurora (la poesia?) nell'esule universo', *La Nuova Ricerca*, 12:227–30, discusses the centrality of the 'aurora' in a number of U. poems and suggests it is a primary force in U.'s poetic symbolism. L. Paglia, 'L'"Incendio della terra a sera": lettura degli "Ultimi cori" ungarettiani', *ib.*, 231–46, considers the 'Ultimi cori' section of *Taccuino del Vecchio* and draws attention to its key themes of space, time, travel, and darkness.

VASSALLI. *La Chimera. Storia e fortuna del romanzo di Sebastiano Vassalli*, ed. Roberto Cicala and Giovanni Tesio, Novara, Interlinea, 110 pp., includes an introduction to the novel (7–26), an interview with V. (83–99), and previously published reviews by G. L. Beccaria, C. Bo, and M. Corti (34–49), and also an unpublished poem by V. Bellintani (50–51). G. Talbot, '"Le parole rombanti e le cose vili del mondo": Sebastiano Vassalli and the new historical novel', *Thompson Vol.*, 216–30, examines V.'s approach to language and the historical novel.

VIVIANI. D. Bisagno, 'L'orma dell'angelo. Prove di lettura dell'"Opera lasciata sola" e del "Silenzio dell'universo" di Cesare Viviani', *ON*, 27.1:39–94, highlights V.'s tendency to both evoke and evade the figure of the angel in his poetry by replacing it with the image of the dog.

VOLPONI. Elena Marongiu, *Intervista a Paolo Volponi*, introd. by Ernesto Ferrero, Mi, Archinto, 45 pp., is a 1990s interview in which V. discusses his roots in Urbino, and his views on industry, politics, and literature with predominant reference to his novel *Corporale*.

ZANZOTTO. M. Pacioni, 'Andrea Zanzotto, *Sovrimpressioni*: una lettura', *EL*, 28.3:57–69, provides an analysis linking this collection to Z.'s entire poetic corpus. *QV*, 36, 2002 [2003] contains the following articles on Zanzotto: M. Bordin, 'Zanzotto: *Sovrimpressioni* dalla colonia penale' (151–59); S. Bortolazzo, '"Temporalità" e "località" negli *incipit* di *Dietro il paesaggio* e *Sovrimpressioni*' (160–64); G. Turra, 'Gli aforismi improbabili di Zanzotto. Per una lettura di *Metéo* e *Sovrimpressioni*' (165–73). F. Carbognin, 'La materia del *corpus*: nota sulla poesia di Andrea Zanzotto', *Il Verri*, 22:112–37. J. Nimis, 'Le rythme comme élément de la "verbalisation du monde" dans la poésie d'Andrea Zanzotto', *REI*, 48, 2002[2003]:359–78, indicates links between the earlier and later phases of Z.'s work and concentrates on the rhythm present in his poetry up to *IX Ecloghe* and after *La beltà*. G. Frene, 'Incerte derive di natura in Andrea Zanzotto fra *Dietro il paesaggio* e *Sovrimpressioni*', *Testuale*, 33, 2002:35–39, looks for links between both texts and examines the 'figura-concetto' of the sun here.

ZOVATTO. *Trieste e un poeta: Pietro Zovatto*, ed. Giorgio Baroni, Trieste, Parnaso, 2002, 212 pp., presents an anthology, with critical assessments, of the work of a poet often considered the Triestine equivalent of David Maria Turoldo.

ROMANIAN STUDIES*

LANGUAGE

POSTPONED

LITERATURE

By Mircea Anghelescu, *Professor of Romanian Literature in the University of Bucharest*

1. Works of reference and of general interest

Probably the most important literary dictionary to come out this year is Florin Manolescu, *Enciclopedia exilului literar românesc, 1945–1989*, Compania, 778 pp., devoted to Romanian writers, publications, and literary institutions in exile. The author, a professor of Romanian literature at Bochum's Ruhr-Universität has been studying Romanian exile literature for many years and has benefited from the huge archive of the Romanian Library at Freiburg-im-Breisgau, the most complete collection of Romanian publications in exile after World War II; his dictionary is an excellent working tool rich in essential information. It lists almost 250 Romanian writers who lived abroad the entire, or just part of, the post-war period, and who were often translated in their adopted countries or became internationally renowned: among others, Emil Cioran, Andrei Codrescu, Mircea Eliade, Eugen Ionescu, Vintilă Horia, Norman Manea, and Elena Văcărescu. Also, the dictionary includes substantial articles on important publications such as *Revue des études roumaines* (Paris, 1956–88), *Revista scriitorilor români* (Munich, 1962–90), and *Apoziţia* (Munich, 1973–88). Without being exhaustive (it omits a few important writers in Israel who continue to write in Romanian, e.g. Alexandru Sever), the *Enciclopedia* is a serious, balanced, and well-documented work. Informative works for the wider public and for teachers' use are two dictionaries of literary works: *Dicţionar de opere literare*, IV, ed. Ion Pop, Cluj, Casa Cărţii de Ştiinţă, 721 pp., which comprises ampler articles about literary works whose titles begin with the letters Q-Z, including works of contemporary literature, and *Literatura română. Dicţionar de opere*, ed. Mircea Anghelescu, Litera Internaţional, 394 pp., comprising 188 articles limited to classical Romanian texts and giving special emphasis to the informative

* The place of publication is Bucharest unless otherwise stated.

elements (bibliographical data, the history of the text and its reception, its compositional structure, etc.).

A rich history of Jewish publications in Romanian, Yiddish, and other languages, with commentary, precious memories, and information, was published by Marius Mircu, *Povestea presei evreieşti din România*, Glob, Bat-Yam, 442 pp. illus. in text. The book is printed as a bibliophile's item in a limited edition of 101 copies and, regrettably, does not have an index of names.

Grid Modorcea, *Dicţionarul cinematografic al literaturii române*, Cartea românească, 412 pp., is a systematic presentation of those Romanian writers who had a special relationship with the cinema or whose work has been used as a starting point for films (Eminescu, Caragiale, Rebreanu, Petrescu, Agârbiceanu, Eliade, Preda, among others).

A recent bibliographical synthesis of Romanian literature, classifying the material in three long chapters: writers, journals, and 'concepts' (a hybrid chapter including heterogeneous fields such as anonymous literary works, literary trends and groups, and institutions like 'censorship') is *Bibliografia esenţială a literaturii române. Scriitori, reviste, concepte*, ed. and introd. Dan Grigorescu, and jointly published by the Institute for Literary History and Theory of the Romanian Academy and Editura enciclopedică, 349 pp.

Mircea Popa and Valentin Taşcu, *Istoria presei româneşti din Transilvania*, Tritonic, 365 pp., refers only to the period up to 1918. Adrian Dinu Rachieru, 'Există o literatură basarabeană?', Ichim, *Limba*, 362–66. *The Romanian Pilgrim* (in the 'Plural' collection), Institutul Cultural Român, 257 pp. + pls, is an anthology of texts of Romanian travellers abroad in the 17th–20th centuries, translated into English. Among them figure well-known writers like Nicolae Milescu, Ion Codru Drăguşanu, Mircea Eliade, George Călinescu, Virgil Nemoianu, and Mircea Cărtărescu.

2. Monographs, period syntheses, and criticism

Ichim, *Limba*, already referred to, gathers papers read at a symposium held at Iaşi in 2002, which include further items noted below. M. Joiţa, 'Venezia e il Levante. Riflessi nella letteratura romena', *AIRV*, 5:523–28. A. Duţu, 'La réception des écrivains français de l'âge classique en Roumanie (1750–1850)', pp. 277–84 of *Reception de autores franceses de la época clasica en los siglos XVIII y XIX en Espana y en el extranjero*, ed. Mercedes Boixareu and Roland Desné, Madrid, UNED, 2001; I. Mihaila, 'Voltaire dans les Pays Roumains aux XVIIIe et XIXe siècles', *ib.*, 285–91. Ioana Bot, *Histoires littéraires. Littérature et idéologie dans l'histoire de la littérature roumaine*, Cluj-Napoca, Institut Culturel Roumain, 292 pp., deals with the French model in 1848 patriotic poetry, the anatomy of the cultural myth of the national poet, the founding fathers of Romanian literary ideas, the two interwar critics Caracostea and Popovici, etc. *Symbolic Geographies*, ed. Sorin Antohi and Corin Braga (Caietele 'Echinox', 5), Cluj, Dacia, 296 pp., is a collection of studies in Romanian, English, and French. M. Spiridon, 'Confins réels, confins rêvés: les Balkans – fatalité ou provocation?', *ib.*, 80–85. A. Majuru, 'Bucharest: between European modernity and the Ottoman East', *ib.*, 92–103. On notes and books written by Romanian authors who visited Sicily in the 19th and 20th c.: Margareta Dumitrescu, *Viaggiatori romeni in Sicilia*, Sellerio, Palermo, 198 pp., ranges from Nicolae Bălcescu and Vasile Alecsandri to Ana Blandiana and Alexandru Balaci. *Simion Vol.* includes a *Pseudobiografie* by Mihaela Constantinescu with a selection of texts by the celebrated Eugen Simion, a selection of critical texts on the work of Simion, tribute articles, and a series of studies. D. Mănucă, 'Ficţiunea şi non-ficţiunea jurnalului', *ib.*, 211–17. Gheorghe Perian, *A doua tradiţie*, Cluj-Napoca, Dacia, 394 pp., is a monograph on naïve poetry in the 18th and 19th c., whether preserved in anonymous collections of party verse or written by known authors: among others Zilot Românul, Pitarul Hristache, Alexandru Beldiman, Ienăchiţă and Alecu Văcărescu, and Matei Millo, down to Anton Pann. It researches the interference of naive poetry with folklore, its relation with the jocular traditions (carnivals, popular festivals), the rhetoric of the genre, etc. Cornel Ungureanu, *Geografia literaturii române, azi*, 1: *Muntenia*, Piteşti, Paralela 45, 260 pp., has thematic chapters such as 'Bucureştii şi aşezarea centrului', 'Târgovişte şi supravieţuirea centrului', 'Sudul şi anarhia. Brăila ca reper', 'Arhipelagul Caragiale', focusing on well-known authors like Nicolae Filimon, Cezar Petrescu, Camil Petrescu, Ion Marin Sadoveanu, Panait Istrati, Ion Luca Caragiale, Anton Pann, and Mateiu Caragiale.

OLD ROMANIAN LITERATURE

Cărţi populare de prevestire: Cele douăsprezece vise în tîlcuirea lui Mamer and *Învăţătură despre vremea de apoi a prorocului Isaia*, ed. Alexandru Mareş, Fundaţia Naţională pentru Ştiinţă şi Artă, 243 pp. + 20 pls, is an edition of 17th-c. MSS, with studies and a glossary, in the series 'Cele mai vechi cărţi populare în literatura română'. It also comprises a complete philological and historical study on the old Slavonic intermediaries. In *Literatura română medievală*, ed. Dan Horia Mazilu and others, Academiei şi Univers Enciclopedic, cxx + 1118 pp., the texts are divided among 14 chapters: Letters; Hagiographic literature; Parenetic literature; Chronicles; Chronographs; Cosmographs; Juridical literature; Astrological and prediction literature; Oratory (lay and ecclesiastical); Ceremonial literature; Dramatic literature; the Novel; Religious poetry; and Popular books (chapbooks). *Marii cronicari ai Moldovei*, ed., with foreword and glossary, Gabriel Ştrempel, Academiei and Univers enciclopedic, xxxv + 1595 pp., includes the chronicles of Grigore Ureche, Miron Costin, Nicolae Costin, and Ion Neculce. L. Bănică, 'Raiul în imaginarul românesc din sec. al XVII-lea', *AUBLLR*, 52:21–24. M. Dinu, 'Dosoftei şi versul popular', *ib.*, 52:67–78. Dan Horia Mazilu, *Noi printre ceilalţi, sau despre literatura peregrinilor*, Ager, 238 pp., has chapters on the travels and writings of Petru Cercel, Luca Stroici, Nicolae Milescu, Miron Costin, Dosoftei, Constantin Cantacuzino, Dimitrie Cantemir, and Dumitru Corbea. Id., *Voievodul dincolo de sala tronului*, Iaşi, Polirom, 622 pp., explores princely ceremonials and traditions as reflected in old literature.

O. Pecican, 'Spaţiu imaginar în Evul Mediu românesc', pp. 86–91 of *Symbolic Geographies*, cit. above. Ion Aurel Pop, *Contribuţii la istoria culturii româneşti. Cronicile braşovene din secolele XVII-XVIII*, Cluj, Dacia, 338 pp., includes a chapter on 'Concept and historical method' in the Braşov chroniclers Radu Tempea, Dumitru and Teodor Corbea, Dimitrie Eustatievici, and others.

Neculai A. Ursu, *Contribuţii la istoria culturii româneşti în secolul al XVII-lea*, Iaşi, Cronica, 451 pp., comprises studies on the 'unknown literary activity' of Daniil Andrean Panoneanul, on the metropolitan bishop Dosoftei, translator of an old Byzantine chronograph, on the translations of N. Milescu Spătarul from the Old Testament, Herodotus, Emperor Ioan Cantacuzino and Agapie Landos.

EIGHTEENTH CENTURY

Texte uitate – texte regăsite, II, Fundaţia Naţională pentru ştiinţă şi Artă, 328 pp., is a collection of texts, translated or adapted in the 18th c., which circulated in manuscript among the masses: *Veşmîntul lui Hristos* (here ed. Silvia Marin-Barutcieff), *Ţara Preotului Ioan* (ed. Ileana Stănculescu), *Hexameronul* (ed. Manuela Anton), *Cugetările lui Oxenstiern* (ed. Adriana Mitu), *Întrebările lui Epifanie* (ed. Cătălina Velculescu), and *'Cercare asupra omului' de Alexander Pope* (ed. Andrei Nestorescu). Each text is preceded by a philological note, and the volume ends with a glossary. *Istoria lui Poliţion şi a Militinei*, ed., ann. and glossary Florina Racoviţă-Cornet, Fundaţia Naţională pentru Ştiinţă şi Artă, 143 pp., vol. VII of the series 'The oldest popular books in Romanian literature', is an end-of-18th-c. translation of a chivalric romance which develops a topic from the *Historia septem sapientum*, probably taken over from a Russian intermediary.

CANTEMIR. Dimitrie Cantemir, *Opere*, I: ed., ann., glossary, and introd. to *Hronic* Stela Toma, general foreword and introd. to *Divan*

V. Cândea, introd. to *Istoria ieroglifică* N. Stoicescu, Academiei Române and Univers enciclopedic, xlvii + 1655 pp. M. Cvasnîi-Cătănescu, 'Dimitrie Cantemir. Tehnici ale prozei eufonice', *AUBLLR*, 52:25–30.

NINETEENTH CENTURY

M. Anghelescu, 'În legătură cu cercetarea şi definirea începuturilor literaturii române moderne', *Simion Vol.*, 291–99; H. Fassel, 'Hugo Meltzl von Lomnitz (1846–1908) zum Verhältniss Regional- und Nationalliteratur. Das Beispiel rumänische Regionalliteratur in Siebenbürgen und Banat', Ichim *Limba*, 334–41; C. Moraru, 'Junimea şi Convorbiri literare', *Studia Universitatis 'Petru Maior'*, 1, 2002:5–16.

BARIŢ. *George Bariţ şi contemporanii săi*, x, ed., ann., and comm. Simion Retegan, Enciclopedică, 508 pp., gathers the letters sent by B., who between 1838 and 1849 edited the leading Romanian newspaper in Transylvania, *Gazeta de Transilvania*, and the journal *Foaie pentru minte, inimă şi literatură*.

CARAGIALE. 'Caragiale şi obsesia umbrei', pp. 45–73 of Mircea Braga, *Replieri interpretative*, Sibiu, Imago. N. Constantinescu, 'Posibile modele folclorice în proza lui I. L. Caragiale', *AUBLLR*, 52:41–48. Ion Derşidan, *Nordul caragialian*, Universul enciclopedic, 219 pp., includes chapters entitled 'Între biografie şi literatură', 'Climat caragialian', 'Familia de spirite' (among whom Poe, Chekhov, Mateiu Caragiale, Ionescu, Cioran, and Urmuz). Marta Petreu, *Filosofia lui Caragiale*, Albatros, 203 pp., attempts to find, in Caragiale's literary works and journalism, not only a pattern of practical philosophy, but also the structure of a thinker; for him 'philosophy is, first of all, a causal explanation', and 'the philosopher is a moralist who discovers the causes of human manias'.

CREANGĂ. Ilie Guţan and Victoria Murărescu-Guţan, *Ion Creangă. Treptele receptării operei*, Sibiu, Alma Mater, 225 pp., includes chapters on 'Ion Creangă în conştiinţa criticii' and 'Un posibil sistem de lectură'. V. Molan, 'Valorificarea folclorului în opera lui Ion Creangă', *LiL*, 48.3–4:76–86.

EMINESCU. Mihai Eminescu, *Opere*, VI and VII, ed., ann., and introd. Dimitrie Vatamaniuc, xii + 1620, 1550 pp., Academiei Române and Univers Enciclopedic ('Opere fundamentale' series). The former contains a rhyming dictionary, translations, lecture notes, reading notes, and correspondence (the correspondence between Eminescu and Veronica Micle); the latter includes, among other things, notes on national and world history, and on philosophy and the history of philosophy, translations of Kant's *Critique of Pure Reason*, and notes on physics and biology. I. Bot, 'L'immagine della Roma antica nella poesia patriotica di Mihai Eminescu', pp. 67–80 of *La ricerca antropologica in Romania. Prospettive storiche ed etnografiche*, ed. Cristina Papa, Giovanni Pizza, and Filippo M. Zerilli, Perugia, ESI. Sorina Creangă, *Arhetipuri, simboluri şi substanţă filosofică în creaţia eminesciană*, Semne, 314 pp. Constantin Cubleşan, *Eminescu în reprezentări critice*, Cluj-Napoca, Grinta, 252 pp., is a series of presentations and analyses of recently published Eminescu criticism. 'Ediţii şi editori [ai lui Eminescu]', pp. 176–83 of Gavril Istrate, *Studii şi portrete*, III, Iaşi, Cronica. George Lateş, *Gradul zero al interpretării eminesciene*, Iaşi, Junimea, 181 pp. D. M. Leca, 'Eminescu în traduceri germane şi italiene', Ichim, *Limba*, 352–56. S. Marcus, 'Asupra celor opt mituri eminesciene', *Simion Vol.*, 206–10. Rodica Marian, *Luna şi sunetul cornului. Metafore obsedante la Eminescu*, Piteşti, Paralela 45, 280 pp., discusses the motifs of longing, the moon, the forest, death, and the morning star in Eminescu's poetry. Luiza Marinescu, *Mihai Eminescu şi Jorge Luis Borges. Interferenţele lecturii postmoderne*, Fundaţia 'România de mâine', 225 pp. 'Eminescu. Poeticitatea formelor', pp. 17–53 of Cornel Munteanu, *Lecturi neconvenţionale*, Cluj, Casa cărţii de ştiinţă. 'Noi date despre bibliotecarul Eminescu', 'Eminescu, revizor şcolar', 'Eminescu la Ober-Döbling', 'Eminescu în germană', pp. 75–120 of Liviu Papuc, *Marginalii junimiste*, Iaşi, Timpul.

HASDEU. Bogdan Petriceicu Hasdeu, *Opere*, IV, ed. and ann. Stancu Ilin and Ionel Oprişan, Fundaţia Naţională pentru Ştiinţă şi Artă, 676 pp., contains the complete dramatic works (*Răzvan şi Vidra, Trei crai de la Răsărit, Femeia, Raposatul postelnic*), sketches and political dialogues, dialogic satires, etc. *Opere*, V, ed. and ann. Stancu Ilin, Floarea Darurilor, 526 pp., contains studies such as *Luca Stroici, Trei ovrei, Istoria toleranţei religioase în România*, the articles and conferences in the vol. *Sarcasm şi ideal*, etc.

MARCOVICI. Nicolae Isar, *Sub semnul romantismului. De la domnitorul Gh. Bibescu la scriitorul Simeon Marcovici*, Universităţii din Bucureşti, 252 pp., reproduces published texts by Marcovici dating from the years 1843–47, as well as various lectures given as professor.

TWENTIETH CENTURY

A whole crop of items relate to exile in different ways: *Caiete de dor. Metafizică şi poezie*, III, *1953–54*, ed. Mihaela Constantinescu-Podocea and Nicolae Florescu, Jurnalul literar, 263 pp., is a critical edition, with name index, of the journal published in Paris by Virgil Ierunca; Ion Cristofor, *Nicholas Catanoy sau avatarii unui peregrin*, Cluj, Napoca-Star, 170 pp., on the Braşov-born writer living in Germany; Nicolae Florescu, *Menirea pribegilor*, Jurnalul literar, 296 pp., with chapters on the exile journals *Luceafărul, Caiete de dor, Fapta*, etc., and dealing with

'Mitul Eliade', 'Regăsirea Soranei Gurian', 'Alexandru Ciorănescu', 'Emil Turdeanu', 'L. M. Arcade', 'Utopia narativă a lui Vintilă Horia', etc.); Nicoleta Sălcudeanu, *Patria de hârtie*, Braşov, Aula, 237 pp., with chapters on *De la exilul omului la depeizarea operei* and texts on Paul Goma, Dumitru Ţepeneag, Petru Dumitriu, Vintilă Horia, Monica Lovinescu, Virgil Ierunca, et al.

Miscellaneous aspects of the period are covered in: Mircea Opriţă, *Anticipaţia românească. Un capitol de istorie literară*, Viitorul românesc, 662 pp., an investigation into science fiction from the late 19th c. to the present day with reference to Victor Anestin, Felix Aderca, Victor Eftimiu, Mircea Eliade, Ion Marin Sadoveanu, Vladimir Colin, Mircea Cărtărescu, and others; M. Bulei, 'Studi critici sulla narrativa romena del Novecento apparsi in Italia', *AIRV*, 5:529–41; Liliana Corobca, *Personajul în romanul românesc interbelic*, Universităţii din Bucureşti, 212 pp., with chapters on 'Personaj şi limbaj', 'Lecturile personajului', 'Personajul scriitor', etc.; Ovidiu Morar, *Avangarda românească în context european*, Suceava, Universităţii Suceava, 270 pp., which covers 'Conceptul de avangardă', 'Premisele avangardismului', 'Mişcări internaţionale de avangardă' (Expresionismul, Futurismul, Dadaismul, Constructivismul, Suprarealismul european şi românesc, etc.); Id., *Avatarurile suprarealismului românesc*, Univers, 366 pp., covering 'Estetica suprarealismului', 'Suprarealismul interbelic' with reference to such important writers as Urmuz, Voronca, Tzara, Gugler, 'Suprarealismul postbelic', etc.); Eugen Negrici, *Literatura română sub comunism: Poezia*, I, Fundaţia Pro, 284 pp.; Marin Radu Mocanu, *Literatura română şi cenzura comunistă (1960–1971)*, Albatros, xxvi + 329 pp., a collection of chronologically arranged documents from the National Archives on the censorship of literary works; Gabriela Gavril, *De la 'Manifest' la 'Adio, Europa!' Cercul literar de la Sibiu*, Iaşi, Universităţii 'Al. I. Cuza', 323 pp., with chapters on Radu Stanca, Ion Negoiţescu, Ştefan Aug. Doinaş, Ion D. Sîrbu, Nicolae Balotă, and Cornel Regman; Petru Poantă, *Efectul 'Echinox' sau despre echilibru*, Cluj-Napoca, Apostrof, 173 pp., a study (*Precizări, Fenomenul 'Echinox', Eroii, Efectul*, etc.) of the journal *Echinox* and the young people who created a special climate in '60s and '70s Cluj; Diana Adamek, *Transilvania şi verile cu polen. Clujul literar în anii '90*, Piteşti, Paralela 45, 218 pp., consisting of brief essays attempting to put together the overall image of the Cluj literary world, with its main actors (Adrian Marino, Mircea Zaciu, Marian Papahagi, Liviu Petrescu, Eta Boeriu, et al.); Marian Popescu, *The Stage and the Carnival. Romanian Theatre after Censorship*, Piteşti, Paralela 45, 216 pp.

ARGHEZI. Tudor Arghezi, *Opere*, III and IV, ed. and ann. Mitzura Arghezi and Traian Radu, 1463, 1493 pp., contains his journalism from the years 1896–1913 and 1914–18; Petre Isachi, *Psalmii arghezieni*

şi problema devenirii creştine, Buzău, Psyhelp, 161 pp., has chapter on 'Spaţiul în *Psalmii* arghezieni'; 'Misticism şi poezie'; 'Muzicalitatea *Psalmilor*'.

BLAGA. R. Windisch, 'Este posibilă traducerea lui Lucian Blaga în limba germană?', *LiL*, 48.3–4: 51–58; E. Nistor, 'Lucian Blaga: apropieri şi disocieri între cultura minoră şi cea majoră', *Studia Universitatis 'Petru Maior'. Seria Philologia*, 1, 2002 : 64–71.

BUSUIOCEANU. Alexandru Busuioceanu, *Un roman epistolar al exilului românesc. Corespondenţa (1942–1950)*, I, ed., ann., and introd. Liliana Corobca, Jurnalul Literar, 303 pp., gathers his correspondence to and from Antoaneta Bodisco-Iordache, Victor Buescu, Mircea Eliade, Nicolae I. Herescu, Vintilă Horia, and others.

CĂRTĂRESCU. Alvaro Barbieri, 'Mircea Cărtărescu e il mito della reintegrazione', *AIRV*, 5 : 551–56.

CASSIAN. Nina Cassian, *Memoria ca zestre*, Institutului Cultural Român, 370 pp., contains diary fragments, memoirs, and comments of the famous poet on the years 1948–53 and 1975–79.

CIORAN. Simona Modreanu, *Cioran sau rugăciunea interzisă*, Iaşi, Junimea, 242 pp., has chapters on 'Cioran and irony', 'The temptation of the evil Creator', 'A comedian in the human comedy', etc.

CIORĂNESCU. George Ciorănescu, *Pagini de jurnal. Portrete. Amintiri*, ed. and introd. Crisula Ştefănescu, Institutului Cultural Român, 182 pp.

COMARNESCU. Petru Comarnescu, *Pagini de jurnal*, I-III, ed. Traian Filip, Mircea Filip, and Adrian Munţiu, foreword by Dan Grigorescu, 3 vols, Noul Orfeu, xxxvi + 328, 378, 379 pp., is an edition of the diary (1923–62) and travel notes (1966–68) of the essayist, literary and art critic, and former member of the Criterion group, who held a Ph.D. in philosophy from the University of Southern California.

COTRUŞ. Ion Cristofor, *Aron Cotruş, între revoltă şi rugăciune*, Cluj-Napoca, Societatea culturală 'Lucian Blaga', 316 pp., is a monograph of the 'life and works' variety, based on archive documents, with abundant data on the exile's times and activity;

CUGLER. Grigore Cugler, *Alb şi negru*, ed. and pref. Mircea Popa, Eforie, 256 pp., gathers the best-known prose-writings in Romanian by a precursor (1903–72) of the humour of the absurd, who died in exile at Lima (*Apunake şi alte fenomene*, *Afară de unu singur*, etc.).

ELIADE. *Mircea Eliade şi corespondenţii săi*, III, ed. and ann. Mircea Handoca, Fundaţia Naţională pentru Ştiinţă şi Artă, viii + 380 pp., comprises letters from correspondents K to P, including A. Marcu, C. Noica, Rudolf Otto, Giovanni Papini, Camil Petrescu, Cezar Petrescu. Ligia Monica Cristea, *Poetica timpului la Mircea Eliade*, Oradea, Abaddaba, 75 pp. Sabina Fânar, *Eliade prin Eliade*, Univers, 337 pp., covering 'Imaginarul mitic', 'De la imaginarul mitic la imaginarul literar', 'O perspectivă globală'; M. Mierlă, 'Mircea Eliade şi lumea profană ca receptacul al sacrului', *LiL*, 48.3–4:41–45; 'Mitul Eliade', pp. 102–21 of Nicolae Florescu, *Menirea pribegilor*, Jurnalul literar.

ERETESCU. Constantin Eretescu, *Periscop. Mărturiile unui venetic*, Eminescu, 251 pp., are memoirs of childhood and youth from a prose writer and ethnologist resident in the U.S.A. since the 1980s;

GOGA. Ilie Guţan, *Octavian Goga. Răsfrângeri în evantai*, Sibiu, Imago, 2002, 302 pp.

HORIA. Vintilă Horia, *Credinţă şi creaţie*, ed. and pref. Mircea Popa, Cluj-Napoca, 275 pp., comprises the essays and book reviews published in the interwar years. O. Ichim, 'Despre degradare şi risc în Europa, cu Vintilă Horia', Ichim, *Limba*, 438–44; 'Veşnicia actualităţii', pp. 87–91 of Cornelia Ştefănescu, *Traiectorii*, Jurnalul literar, concerns the novel *Dieu est né en exil.*

IONESCU. Marie-France Ionesco, *Portretul scriitorului în secol: Eugene Ionesco, 1909–1994*, transl. M. Ţepeneag, Humanitas, 152 pp., a biography by the writer's daughter, is enriched with her personal memories and includes chapters on 'Originile materne', 'Istorie şi politică', 'Exil', 'Relaţiile lui Eugene Ionesco cu România', and 'Ionesco, Cioran şi Mircea Eliade'. Laura Pavel, *Ionesco. Anti-lumea unui sceptic*, Piteşti, Paralela 45, 316 pp.

LOVINESCU, E. 'Noi date despre doctoratul lui E. Lovinescu'; 'Un moment din istoria criticii'; 'E. Lovinescu faţă cu trădarea'; 'Bătălia continuă', pp. 69–83 of Alexandru George, *Alte reveniri, restituiri, revizuiri*, Cartea Românească.

LOVINESCU, M. Monica Lovinescu, *Jurnal, 1990–1993*, Humanitas, 429 pp., offers an interesting panorama of the movements and activities of Romanian writers in Paris during the first years after the fall of communism.

MANEA. Norman Manea, *Întoarcerea huliganului*, Iaşi, Polirom, 360 pp., an autobiographical volume published simultaneously in English, puts special emphasis on return to the mother country and on private experience, his parents' and his own, at various times but always marred by pain: in his case as a Jew, bourgeois, and intellectual.

MARINO. 'Hermeneutica lui Adrian Marino', pp. 101–16 of Mircea Braga, *Teorie şi metodă*, Sibiu, Imago.

MUNTEANU. Cristian Florin Popescu, *Basil Munteanu, contemporanul nostru*, Muzeul Literaturii Române, 256 pp.

PAPADAT-BENGESCU. Liana Cozea, *Exerciţii de admiraţie şi reproş: Hortensia Papadat-Bengescu*, Piteşti, Paralela 45, 186 pp., is a traditional monograph.

PETRESCU, CAMIL. Irina Petraş, *Camil Petrescu. Schiţe pentru un portret*, Cluj-Napoca, Apostrof, 147 pp., has chapters on, *inter alia*, 'Luciditate şi febră', 'Starea de cumpănă', and 'Eros'.

POPESCU, D. R. Mirela Marin, *Universul prozei contemporane*, I (*Antiutopia and the utopia of value*), Viitorul românesc, 466 pp., a monographic presentation of Dumitru Radu Popescu's writings under the headings 'Structura complexă a personajului', 'Arta portretului', 'Onomastica personajului', 'Jocul titlurilor metaforice', etc.

PETRESCU, RADU. Ion Bogdan Lefter, *Primii postmoderni: 'Şcoala de la Tîrgovişte'*, Piteşti, Paralela 45, 196 pp.

REBREANU. Livio Rebreanu, *Opere*, XXII, ed. and ann. Neculai Gheran, Fundaţia Naţională pentru Ştiinţă şi Artă, 530 pp., comprises the correspondence (1908–1944) and an *addendum* of journalism omitted from the previous volumes. Ion Simuţ, *Liviu Rebreanu*, Braşov, Aula, 173 pp., in the 'Canon' collection intended for teaching/learning purposes, reviews and synthesizes the perspectives of two decades of research on Rebreanu.

SEBASTIAN. 'Un martor nu numai atât, Plecarea lui Mihail Sebastian', pp. 170–78 of Alexandru George, *Alte reveniri, restituiri, revizuiri*.

SIRBU. Antonio Patraş, *Ion D. Sîrbu — de veghe în noaptea totalitară*, Iaşi, Universităţii 'Alexandru Ioan Cuza', 303 pp., originally a Ph.D. thesis, discussed the personality of the writer through biography and analysis of his works, according to a rather classic formula, but used with an analytical and dissociative spirit. Gabriela Gavril, *De la 'Manifest' la 'Adio, Europa!'. Cercul literar de la Sibiu*, noted above, has the chapter 'I. D. Sîrbu'.

SORESCU. Marin Sorescu, *Opere*, III, ed. and ann. Mihaela Constantinescu-Podocea, Academiei Române and Univers Enciclopedic, vii + 1821 pp., gathers S.'s dramatic works: *Iona, Paracliserul, Matca, Pluta Meduzei, Există nervi, Casa evantai, Desfacerea gunoaielor, Lupoaica mea, Luptătorul pe două fronturi, Răceala, A treia ţeapă, Vărul Shakespeare.*

STĂNESCU. Anghel Dumbrăveanu, *Fenomenul Nichita Stănescu*, Excelsior Art, 161 pp. + 12 illus., includes chapters entitled 'Draptul la timp', 'Belgradul în cinci prieteni', 'Răspunsul prietenilor'. *Manuscriptum*, 33.1–2:33–239, and 33.3–4:13–255, respectively comprise hitherto unpublished poems (pref. A. Condeescu) and prose, journalism, and letters.

ŢEPENEAG. Dumitru Ţepeneag, *Clepsidra răsturnată. Convorbiri cu Ion Simuţ*, Piteşti, Paralela 45, 164 pp., contains *inter alia* confessions about his writings and his exile in Paris. 'Ţepeneag – omul care merge', pp. 123–55 of Nicoleta Sălcudeanu, *Patria de hârtie*, Braşov, Aula.

VOICULESCU. In Nicolae Oprea, *Magicul în proza lui V. Voiculescu*, Piteşti, Paralela 45, 176 pp., analysis of Voiculescu's stories is the starting point of a demonstration that the writer proceeds to re-mythicize literature.

XI. RHETO-ROMANCE STUDIES

By Ingmar Söhrman, *Göteborg University*

1. Bibliographical and General

A comparative study of addressing-pronouns in Romance languages where also the Rheto-Romance varieties are discussed, although only to a minor degree (pp. 165–69), is found in B. Coffen, *Histoire culturelle des pronoms d'adresse. Vers une typologie des systèmes allucutoires dans les langues romanes*, Paris, Champion, 2002, 319 pp. A recording, with booklet, of Swiss Romance linguistic varieties is given in **Enregistrements suisse — Ricordi sonori svizzeri — Registraziuns svizras*, comm. R. Liver, ed. J. Fleisch and T. Gadmer, Zurich, Verlag der Österreichen Akademie der Wissenschaften — Verlag des Phonogrammarchivs der Universität Zürich, 2002, 116 pp. G. Hoyer, *'Les désignations romanes de la libellule', *Atlas linguistique roman*, vol. II : a, Rome, IPZS, 2002, pp. 281–317. Id., *'Sur quelques toponymes romans et alémanniques d'origine celtique', *Allières Vol.*, 405–08. Celtic influence on Rheto-Romance is explored in T. MacNamee, 'Romanisch und Keltisch bei Joseph Planta', in *BM*, 2002 : 265–91. M. Pfister, 'Nuove scoperte redigendo il Lessico Etimologico Italiano', *AAA*, 95, 2001 : 21–32.

2. Friulan

Phonology and Morphology. S. Heinemann, 'Note sull'epitesi postnasale in friulano con speciale riguardo della nasale bilabiale (tipo omp)', *Ce fastu?*, 78, 2002 : 171–86, argues that while epenthesis is rare in Friulan, epithesis is more frequent and that this should be considered a regional feature of north-east Friuli rather than an archaism.

Onomastics and Lexis. Two interesting dictionaries of Friulan surnames have recently been published, E. Costantini, **Dizionario dei cognomi del Friuli*, publ. in instalments, from April 2002, with the newspaper *Messaggero veneto*, and E. Dal Cin, *Cognomi di Susegana*, Santa Lucia di Piave, Edizioni CSC, 2002, 300 pp. On Friulan toponyms I note C. C. Desinan, 'Divagazioni toponomastiche dal Friuli al mondo', *Sot la Nape*, 54.1, 2002 : 51–55, and Id., 'Toponomastica e giustizia in Friuli', *ib.*, 54.2–3, 2002 : 103–06, and now also the volume C. C. Desinan, *Escursioni fra i nomi di luogo del Friuli*, Udine, Società Filologica Friulana, 2002, 392 pp., collecting the linguist's many articles on the topic since 1998. Useful new editions are Antonio Di Prampero, *Saggio di un glossario geografico friulano dal VI al*

XIII secolo, ed. Giovanni Frau, Tavagnacco, Comune di Tavagnacco, 2001, lviii + 236 pp., and A. Gallas, *Toponimi e micro-toponimi della campagna e del colle di Medea. Vie e piazze del paese*, ed. C. C. Desinan, Medea, Comune di Medea, 2001, 32 pp. A new booklet on toponyms is A. M. Pittana, *I nons dai paîs dal Friûl di Mieç*, introd. Pierino Donada, Codroip, Progjet integrât Culture dal Friûl di Mieç, 2001, 48 pp.

J. B. Trumper, 'Friul. *muédul, Modolêt, Modoletto*: una proposta in termini di sostrato', *Ce fastu?*, 79, 2003: 7–11, sees in the common Friulan tree-name *muédul* (for *quercus cerris*) a possible Celtic original *MED-TU corresponding to Welsh *mess* and signifying '[tree] that produces acorns'. **Dizionario Italiano–Friulano — Furlan–Talian*, Pordenone, Biblioteca dell'Immagine, 2002, 172 pp., useful for practical purposes, will be of limited value to the linguist.

SOCIOLINGUISTICS AND LANGUAGES IN CONTACT. The complicated use of Veneto dialect and of Friulan in lower Friuli is studied in A. Buonocore and F. Finco, *Palmanova e le sue lingue. Inchiesta sociolinguistica* (Appunti di storia, 9), Mariano del Friuli (GO), Circolo di cultura 'Nicolò Trevisan' di Palmanova, 123 pp., which shows that Italian is gaining ground and Veneto losing considerably (from 14% among adults to 7.5 % in the younger generation), as is Friulan (50% to 39%). F. Angeli, 'Conservazione ed innovazione nella parlata germanofona di Sauris', *Ce fastu?*, 79: 183–204, outlines the results of an investigation, conducted for her *tesi de laurea*, into the way lexical innovation and neologisms are introduced into Saurano, a Germanic dialect supposedly spoken by 84% of the population of Sauris. An interesting comparison of Friulan and Catalan linguistic standardization is B. Pianca, 'Normalizzazione linguistica: i casi del catalano e del friulano', *ib.*, 205–26, which criticizes the lack of will to unify Friulan, giving Catalan as an example of how unification has created a useful and efficient instrument of communication. S. Trangoni, 'La comunità friulano-argentina a Maiano tra conservazione e innovazione', *Ce fastu?*, 78, 2002: 187–208, studies the language of homecoming Friulans who had emigrated to Argentina and shows clearly that they did not develop a Friulan *koiné*, while the diverse forms of Friulan which they continued to speak were heavily marked by Argentine Spanish influence.

3. LADIN

BIBLIOGRAPHICAL AND GENERAL. The volume *Il ladino o 'retoromanzo'. Silloge di contributi specialistici*, ed. G. B. Pellegrini, Alessandria, Orso, 2000, vii + 254 pp., is a collection of articles by different linguists on the problematic relationship between Ladin and Romansh.

ONOMASTICS AND LEXIS. **Dalla val Varúna alla val d'Ursé*, ed. S. Cazzaniga and L. Mengotti, Poschiavo, PGI Sezione di Poschiavo, 1998, 75 pp. R. Bracchio, 'Note etimologiche sul dialetto di Novate (XI)', *Clavenna*, 39, 2000: 235–46, offers some minor but interesting etymological remarks. S. Davatz, *'Meine Erfahrungen beim Sammeln der fanaser Flurnamen', *BM*, 2002: 216–20. G. Plangg, 'Nomi ladini e toponimi nelle leggende dolomitiche', *AAA*, 95, 2001: 53–64, gives an idea of the role of Ladin culture in Dolomitic folklore. C. Santi, **Famiglie originarie del Moesano o ivi immigrate*, Chiasso, Santi, 2001, xi + 272 pp.

4. Swiss Romansh

BIBLIOGRAPHICAL AND GENERAL. C. M. Lutta, *Der Dialekt von Bergün und seine Stellung innerhalb der rätoromanischen Mundarten Graubündens*, 2. unveränd. Aufl., Cuira / Chur, Societad retorumantscha, 2002, 356 pp., a reissue of an important work dating from 1923, is of great value, though an introduction updating the results of the original study would not have been out of place. Protestant ecclesiastical terminology has now been systematized into a dictionary, G. Tscharner, *Pledari da baselgia — Kirchliches Wörterbuch. Rumantsch–tudestg, tudestg–rumantsch*, Baselgia refurmada dal Chantun Grischun, 2002, 130 pp.

ONOMASTICS AND LEXIS. S. M. Berchtold, *'Zinrodel von 1501', *Monfort*, 54, 2002: 32–71. Two new fascicles have appeared of *Dicziunar Rumantsch Grischun*, ed. Felix Giger et al.: 147–148, LOCAL II – LUMBARD, and 149–150, LUMBARD – MACUBA, Chur, Societad Retorumantscha, 2002 and 2003 respectively. G. Hoyer, 'Les voix romanches construites sur le radical *magn-*', *ASR*, 116: 9–40, presents a hypothesis as to the origin and diffusion of the lexical root *magn-* and also seeks to interpret the originality of Rheto-Romance and its autochthonous linguistic history. H. Klausmann, 'Wortgeographische Besonderheiten Vorarlbergs (III). Das Rheintal', *Monfort*, 54, 2002: 81–94, continues the author's onomastic researches in the Vorarlberg. The Sutsilvan variety has always been the little brother of the Romansh varieties, and the publication of a fairly substantial Sutsilvan dictionary is therefore something of an event: *Pledari sutsilvan–tudestg — Wörterbuch Deutsch–Sutsilvan*, ed. Wolfgang Eichenhofer, Chur, Lehrmittelverlag, 2002, xxxvii + 840 pp., makes a very favourable impression and will surely become a valuable instrument for speakers, visitors, and linguists alike. W. Haas, 'Lichtensteiner Namenbuch: Zum Nutzen der Ortsnamnenforschung', *BM*, 2002: 228–34, outlines the advantages and consequences of onomastic studies applied to Lichtenstein. R. Hartmann, 'Vom blanken

Zettel zum bilderatlas. Arbeitstechniken eines lokalen Flur- und Ortsnamensammlers', *ib.*, 221–27, discusses methodological problems for onomastic research. J. Kuhn, *Die romanischen Orts- und Flurnamen von Wallenstadt und Quarten, St. Gallen, Schweiz* (Romanica Aenipontana, 18), Innsbruck, Institut für Romanistik der Leopold-Franzens-Universität, 2002, xlvi + 302 pp., is a meticulous onomastic investigation of the region north of the Rheto-Romance canton, where an earlier linguistic situation is reflected. A minor study on the same topic is to be found in P. Masüger, 'Das St. Galler Rheintal wird toponomastisch erschlossen. In Wartau entsteht das Werdenberger Namenbuch', *BM*, 2002: 201–05. Interesting contributions to the study of onomastics are E. Nyffenegger, 'Das Thurgauer Namenbuch', *ib.*, 205–15, and, over a longer period, H. Stricker, 'Namenforschung im Wandel. Von Robert v. Planta und Andrea Schorta bis zum Lichtensteiner Namenbuch', *ib.*, 171–200.

SOCIOLINGUISTICS AND LANGUAGES IN CONTACT. Language planning and language legalization are discusssed in B. Cathomas, 'Von der Kraft der Sprache und des Sprachenrechts', *Fest. Nay*, 239–48. The second report on the Swiss situation for the regional and so-called minority languages in Europe has been published in Romansh: *Charta europeica da las linguas regiunalas u minoritaras*, ed. R. Coray, C. Pitsch, and I. Berther, Bern, Uffizi federal da cultura, 57 + 8 pp. In a published dissertation, Anne-Marie Frese, *La lingua da minchadi*, Zuos, Verlag Exposiziun, 2002, 120 pp. + 2 CD, offers a detailed study of colloquial Romansh in Zuos. Early contacts between the languages in Switzerland is dealt with by N. Furrer in *Die viersprachige Schweiz. Sprachkontakte und Mehrsprachigkeit in der vorindustriellen Gesellschaft (15.–19. Jahrhundert)*, 2 vols, Zurich, Chronos, 2002, 699 + 478 pp. M. Grünert, 'Das Funktionieren der Dreisprachigkeit im Kanton Graubünden', *BM*, 2002: 84–89, gives a short overview of the present trilingual situation in the Grisons, the only Swiss canton where three of the now official languages are spoken. A first attempt to present the complex notion of ethnic and linguistic identity within the Romansh-speaking area after the introduction of the standardized variety Rumantsch Grischun is made by J. Joos, *Zum potentiellen Einfluss des Rumantsch grischun auf die rätoromanischen Identität. Betrachtung der Identitätssituation einer Sprachsituation im Ausnahmezustand*, Bern, Institut für Ethnologie der Universität Bern, 2002, 17 pp. The comprehension of other Romance languages in Switzerland among Romansh-speakers (who normally also speak German) is discussed by M. Killian, 'Tgei pudessan ils Romontschs emprender dils auters lungatgs minoritars en Svizra', *Fest. Nay*, 249–57. **Schlussbericht der Evaluation des Schulprojekts Samedan. Zu Handen des Erziehungs-, Kultur- und Umweltschutzdepartements Graubünden*, ed. J.-L. Gartner et al.,

Freiburg, Universität Freiburg, Departement Erziehungswissenschaften, 2000, 89 pp. The pros and cons of purism in the case of contemporary Romansh are weighed up in C. Solèr, 'Spracherhaltung, trotz oder wegen des Purismus. Etappen des Rätoromanischen', *BM*, 2002:251–64. Summary considerations on the impact of the unified Rheto-Romance language, Rumantsch Grischun, 20 years after its introduction, on the ways it has affected different linguistic areas, and on its future are offered by R. Steier et al., '20 onns rumantsch grischun', *Sulom*, 82:52–61.

3

CELTIC LANGUAGES

I. WELSH STUDIES

LANGUAGE

By Christine Jones, *Senior Lecturer in Welsh Language and Literature, University of Wales, Lampeter*

1. General

Brynley F. Roberts, 'Cymraeg Edward Lhwyd', *Y Traethodydd*, 158:211–29, demonstrates Edward Lhwyd's striking ability to adapt and create new Welsh words for his own purposes and those of modern science. Stefan Zimmer, 'A Medieval Linguist: Gerald de Barri', *EC*, 35:313–349, investigates Gerald of Wales' feelings of Welshness and his actual knowledge of the Welsh language. M. Wynn Thomas, 'Monica Lewinsky a Fi', pp. 24–43 of *Y Llyfr yng Nghymru 5*, ed. Andrew Green, Talybont, Y Lolfa 79 pp., discusses the problems inherent in translating literature. Using translations of Welsh hymns, T. shows how an awareness of cultural, political and linguistic issues can strengthen a translation.

1. Grammar

Yr Hen Iaith: Studies in Early Welsh, ed. Paul Russell, Aberystwyth, Celtic Studies Publications, 222 pp., is a varied and valuable collection of essays on aspects of the history of the Welsh language prior to 1500. These include: Peter Schrijver, 'The etymology of Welsh *chwith* and the semantics and morphology of PIE $*k(^{w})sweib^{h}\sim$' (1–24), which studies the etymology of *chwith* across the full range of Indo-European languages, concluding that it is related to a range of words meaning 'curved' or 'bent', which developed into 'amiss' or 'wrong' and therefore 'left'; Paul Russell, '*Rowynniauc, Rhufoniog*: the orthography and phonology of /μ/ in Early Welsh' (25–48), considers possible spellings of /μ/ in Early and Middle Welsh and discusses its phonological development; Peter Kitson, 'Old English literacy and the provenance of Welsh *y*'(49–66), suggests that *y* was adopted into the standard Welsh alphabet from Old English, particularly from the Cambridge Psalter of Winchombe; Simon Rodway, 'Two developments in medieval literary Welsh and their implications for dating texts' (67–74), analyses the different endings in use for the 3rd singular imperfect indicative and the 3rd singular present subjunctive in the works of the early Gogynfeirdd; Graham Isaac, 'The structure and typology of prepositional relative clauses in Early Welsh' (75–94), suggests that relative clauses are more widespread in the Celtic languages than has previously been thought. I. argues that the prepositional relative structure was replaced by the resumpative pronoun pattern within British; Alexander Falileyev and Paul Russell, 'The dry-point glosses in Oxoniensis Posterior'(95–102), concludes that none of the said glosses are definitely Brittonic and therefore not necessarily added in a bilingual environment; Pierre- Yves Lambert, 'The Old Welsh glosses on Weights and Measures' (103–134), provides a valuable new edition of the text on weights and measures, together with the Old Welsh glosses; Peter Busse, 'Are there elements of non-standard language in the work of the Gogynfeirdd?' (135–44), demonstrates that there are several colloquial elements in the generally elaborate poetry of the Gogynfeirdd. These elements are usually restricted to poems of a more personal nature and appear to indicate a Northern or North-Western dialect; Erich Poppe, 'The Progressive in *Ystorya Bown de Hamtwn*' (145–70), presents a detailed analysis of the use of the progressive in the above text and concludes that the progressive in Middle Welsh appears to have a wider functional range than has been previously acknowledged; John T. Koch, '*Marwnad Cunedda* a diwedd y Brydain Rufeinig' (171–98), is a comprehensive syntantical analysis of *Marwnad Cunedda* together with an in-depth discussion on the composition date.

Francesco Benozzo, *'Celtoromania: cinque note morfostintattiche', *QFRB*, 15:369–77, is a comparative analysis of a number of morphological features found in Celtic and Romance languages. Id. *'Ecdotica Celtica e Romanza: due modi diversi di non leggere i testi antichi', *Studi Celtici: An International Journal of History, Linguistics and Cultural Anthropology*, 1, 2002:21–65, compares the methodologies of text criticism in Romance and Celtic philology and considers specific linguistic problems in texts such as the *Gododdin* and the works of the Poets of the Nobility. Simon Rodway, 'What was the function of 3rd present indicative *-ydd* in Old and Middle Welsh?', *Studi Celtici 2*, 2003[2004]:89–132, uses a wide range of examples to show the various syntactical positions in which the verb ending *-ydd* occurs in Old and Middle Welsh. R. concludes that *-ydd* was generally, but not consistently, considered a relative form. From the perspective of comparative grammar, Stefan Zimmer, 'Twenty-nine notes on *Culhwch ac Olwen*', *ib.*, 143–74, suggests alternative interpretations and explanations to 29 phrases in the above text as edited by Rachel Bromwich and D. S. Evans (1988). Graham Isaac, 'Meaning and

Structure, Comparison and Representation: Readings from a Welsh construction', *ib.*, 265–75, discusses how phrase structure determines meaning in the case of *unig* and *gwahanol.* Ariel Shisha-Halevy, 'Juncture features in Literary Modern Welsh: Cohesion and Delimitation', *ZCP*, 53:230–58, attempts to formulate a typology of cohesion signals through extensive examples from the former weekly magazine *Y Faner* and the works of John Emyr and Kate Roberts.

3. Etymology and Lexicography

Iwan Wmffra, *Language and Place-names in Wales*, Cardiff, Univ. of Wales Press, 447 pp., is a thorough investigation of the written and oral forms of place names mainly in Ceredigion. The volume presents an interesting and wholly innovative contribution to the development of methodology for place name and dialect research. Adrian Room, *Penguin Dictionary of British Place Names*, London, Penguin, xxxix + 549 pp., explains the origins of a selection of the more familiar English and Welsh place names in Wales. A comprehensive introduction also makes several references to Welsh place names and includes a brief, general discussion on Welsh language place names. Andrew Breeze, 'Historia Brittonum and Arthur's Battle of Mons Agned', *Northern History*, 40:167–70, proposes that *agned* makes more sense if read as Old Welsh *agued* meaning death strait. B. goes on to suggest that this maybe Pennango near Hawick in southern Scotland. Patrizia de Bernado Stempel, 'Continental Celtic *ollo*: Early Welsh *(h)ol(l)*, Olwen, and Culhwch', *CMCS*, 46:119–28, contests the traditional interpretation of the name Olwen suggesting that it originated as Common Celtic *ollo-vinda*, the entirely white (i.e. fair) woman. V. Kalygin, 'Some archaic elements of Celtic cosmology,' *ZCP*, 53:70–76, looks at the concept of a dual universe consisting of white and black parts and discusses the etymology of *byd*, *dwfn*, *elfyd* and *Annwfn*. Stefan Zimmer, '*A uo penn bit pont*: Aspects of Celtic and Indo-European Leadership', *ib.*, 202–29, includes a discussion on the word *pont* and concludes that *a uo penn bit pont* is not a proverb, but rather has been born from a new interpretation of an old epithet reflecting aspects of leadership in Celtic and Indo-European. Alexander Falileyev, 'Old Welsh *y diruy hay camcul* and some problems related to Middle Welsh terminology', *Celtica*, 24:121–28, reviews the instances of *camgwl* and *camgylus* in Medieval Welsh Law Books and other Middle Welsh texts and suggests that *camgul* is an early term which was later replaced by *camlwrw*. Eric Hamp, *EC*, 35:167 has a further note on the name *Mona*.

C. Michiel Driessen and Caroline Aan de Wiel, 'British **sūðiklo-* and **kentunklo-*, two loan words from Latin', *SC*, 37:17–34, analyses the etymology and meaning of **sūðiklo* (Welsh *huddygl*) and **kentunklo-* (Middle Welsh *cynhwnghyl*). Robyn Léwis, *Geiriadur Newydd y Gyfraith*, Llandysul, Gomer Press, 1234 pp., is a substantial contribution to Welsh lexicography which contains a significant amount of newly coined Welsh legal terminology.

4. Sociolinguistics

Peter Garrett, Nikolaus Coupland and Angie Williams, *Investigating Language Attitudes: Social Meanings of Dialect, Ethnicity and Performance*, Cardiff, Univ. of Wales Press, 251 pp., provides an excellent critical review of the main methods employed in language attitudes research. Through a wide range of empirical studies, the authors demonstrate how varied research methods produce different insights into attitudes towards the Welsh language, Welsh-English dialect, bilingualism and Welshness amongst teachers and adolescents. Hywel Bishop, Nikolas Coupland, and Peter Garrett, 'Blood is Thicker than the Water that Separates Us!: Welsh Identity in the North American Diaspora', *The North American Journal of Welsh Studies*, *3.2*: 39–54, <spruce.flint.umich.edu/~ellisjs/journal.html>, uses extensive examples to indicate what Welsh identity means to 71 informants in the USA and Canada and how they engage with it outside Wales. Many comment on the importance of being able to speak the language in order to identify as a Welsh person. D. Ellis Evans, 'Iaith a Hunaniaeth', *Y Traethodydd* 158: 133–52, discusses the role of language as a symbol of identity and contains many references to the Welsh situation. *In-Migration, Yes, Colonisation, No*! Talybont, Y Lolfa, 40pp., is a bilingual volume produced by the organisation Cymuned, which discusses the main features of colonialism and suggests how colonialism can severely threaten the Welsh language and its culture. *Addysg Gymraeg Addysg Gymreig*, ed. Gareth Roberts and Cen Williams, Bangor, School of Education, 338 pp., is a wide-ranging volume on various theoretical and practical aspects of Welsh language teaching in Wales. Of particular relevance is Colin Baker and Jessica Chapman, 'Natur ac Anghenion Disgyblion Dwyieithog' (103–15), which presents a balanced picture of the advantages and disadvantages of bilingualism and summarizes the educational needs of such students. Trystan Owain Hughes, 'Croesi Ffiniau Diwylliannol? Pabyddion Gwyddelig, Mewnfudo a'r Iaith Gymraeg yn yr Ugeinfed Ganrif', *Cof Cenedl*, 18: 163–89, discusses the relationship between Catholicism and the Welsh language. J. Aaron, *The Welsh Survival Gene: The Despite Culture in the Two Language Communities of Wales*, Cardiff, Institute for Welsh Affairs, 19 pp., is a bilingual version of A.'s 2003 National Eisteddfod lecture in which she emphasises the importance of raising cultural awareness in Wales, thereby increasing confidence that a minority language and culture can survive successfully in a world of global capitalism. Cefin Campbell, 'Reviving Welsh As a Community Language', pp. 16–24 of *Language Revival in the Community*, Proceedings of the 2002 conference of the International Celtic Congress, Aberystwyth, Univ. of Wales, 41 pp., outlines the various socio-linguistic challenges facing present day Wales and discusses the role of the community based language enterprises known as *Mentrau Iaith*, in language planning and revitalization.

EARLY AND MEDIEVAL LITERATURE

By Owen Thomas,, *Lecturer in Welsh, University of Wales, Lampeter*

A further four volumes of poetry have appeared this year in the UWCASWC series, *Cyfres Beirdd yr Uchelwyr*, under the general editorship of Ann Parry Owen, all of which are germane to this section of the critical bibliography. *Gwaith Ieuan ap Llywelyn Fychan, Ieuan Llwyd Brydydd a Lewys Aled*, ed. M. Paul Bryant–Quinn, Aberystwyth, UWCASWC, xxii + 207 pp., is an edition of the poetry of three amateur 15th-c. poets, whose poetical interests reflect the richness and diversity of literature in the Vale of Clwyd during this period. *Gwaith Gruffudd ap Maredudd: 1 —Canu i deulu Penmynydd*, ed. Barry J. Lewis, Aberystwyth, UWCASWC, xvii + 171 pp., includes an annotated edition of seven eulogies and elegies sung by Gruffudd ap Maredudd ap Dafydd to the renowned Penmynydd family of Anglesey in the second half of the 14th c. *Gwaith Ieuan ap Rhydderch*, ed. Iestyn Daniel, Aberystwyth, UWCASWC, xviii + 231 pp., is a comprehensive edition of the work of the poet Ieuan ap Rhydderch (*c.* 1390–*c.* 1470) and includes an informative foreword about the poet's career, the themes and style of his work, together with a new edition of the texts of eleven poems in strict metre, detailed notes, and a glossary. *Gwaith Maredudd ap Rhys a'i Gyfoedion*, ed. Enid Roberts, Aberystwyth, UWCASWC, xvi + 157 pp., includes a comprehensive edition of the cywyddau of Maredudd ap Rhys, a 15th–c. poet to the gentry, together with poems by his peers, Ifan Fychan ab Ifan ab Adda and Syr Rhys o Garno, comprising informative introductions to the poets's lives, edited texts, detailed notes, and a glossary.

Peter Busse, *Cynddelw Brydydd Mawr—Archaismus und Innovation: Sprache und Metrik eines kymrischen Hofdichters des 12. Jahrhunderts*, Münster, Nodus Publikationen (2002), 160 pp., warns of the dangers of interpreting Cynddelw Brydydd Mawr's poetry monolithically and discusses the various poetic styles of the *Gogynfeirdd*. Joseph Falaky Nagy, *The Poetics of Absence in Celtic Tradition*, Aberystwyth, UWCASWC, 27 pp., brings to our attention the poetics of absence in Celtic literatures, namely the absence of one or more links in the chain of connection between poet, subject of the poem, and intended recipient of the poem. The examples cited include Rhiannon's horse-ride in the First Branch of the Mabinogi, Branwen's despair in the Second Branch of the Mabinogi and, more generally, medieval Welsh poetry which uses the *dyfalu* technique. Meinir Elin Harris, 'Dychwelyd at Gyfeiriadau, Termau a Chysyniadau Cyfreithiol yn y Mabinogi', *Y Traethodydd*, 158:17–39, considers the legal terms and aspects of the *Mabinogi* and concludes that the author was most familiar with medieval Welsh law and might even have belonged to the family of Iorwerth ap Madog. D. J. Bowen, 'Yr Ywen Brudd', *ib.*, 158: 153–56, discusses the conflicting evidence surrounding the location of Dafydd ap Gwilym's resting-place. Gwynfa M. Adam, 'Blodeuwedd: Ei Henw a'i Natur', *Dwned*, 9: 9–21, reconsiders the name of Blodeuwedd and concludes that her name should be construed as having a connection with mead. Nerys Ann Jones, 'Meilyr Gwalchmai–Rhithfardd!', *ib.*, 23–36, argues that the 12th–c. religious poet, whom we have come to know as Meilyr ap Gwalchmai, did not in fact exist but was an identity forged during the 17th c. Richard Glyn Roberts, 'Dalen Olaf Llawysgrif Peniarth 17', *ib.*, 37–42, consists of a list of proverbs with explanatory notes. Bleddyn Owen Huws, 'Rhan o Awdl Foliant Ddienw i Syr Dafydd Hanmer', *ib.*, 43–64, produces an annotated edition of an incomplete eulogy which appears in the Red Book of Hergest and reveals the subject to be Sir Dafydd Hanmer. Nicolas Jacobs, 'Nodiadau ar y Canu Gwirebol: I. "*Englynion*" y Misoedd: Testun A neu'r Fersiwn Cyffredin', *ib.*, 65–80, revisits Kenneth Jackson's edition of *Englynion y Misoedd* and provides additional commentary and notes. Gilbert E. Ruddock and Christine James, 'Englynion y Deg Gorchymyn', *ib.*, 81–90, is an edition of the medieval *englynion* based on the Ten Commandments, attributed in a some MSS to Dafydd Nanmor but which are now known not to be his work. Huw Meirion Edwards, 'Cnwd Iach y Canu Dychan: Golwg ar Rai o Ddychanwyr y Bedwaredd Ganrif ar Ddeg', *Barddas*, 274: 6–11, emphasizes the importance of satire for all grades of medieval Welsh poets.

R. Geraint Gruffydd, 'A Welsh Poet Falls at the Battle of Coleshill, 1157', *Flintshire Historical Society*, 36: 52–58 includes a translation and a text in modern Welsh orthography of Cynddelw Brydydd Mawr's elegy to Bleddyn Fawr who fell in a skirmish near Hawarden in 1157. Nerys A. Howells, 'Gwerful Mechain yn ei chyd–destun hanesyddol a llenyddol', *Cof Cenedl*, 18: 1–34, discusses the economic, social, cultural and personal factors which came together in 15th-c. Powys to make it possible for Gwerful Mechain to become a poet.

J. Cartwright, '*Buchedd Catrin*: A Preliminary Study of the Middle Welsh Life of Katherine of Alexandria and her Cult in Medieval Wales', pp. 53–86 of *St Katherine of Alexandria: Texts and Contexts in Western Medieval Europe*, ed. Jacqueline Jenkins and Katherine J. Lewis, Brepols, Turnhout, xiv + 257pp., provides a detailed overview of the cult of St Katherine in medieval Wales and synthesizes as many of the extant Welsh sources, including *Buchedd Catrin*, as possible. Sara Elin Roberts, 'Addysg Broffesiynol yng Nghymru yn yr Oesoedd Canol', *LlC*, 26: 1–17, offers invaluable insights into the education of poets and lawyers in medieval Wales, concluding that there were many similarities between them. Brynley F. Roberts, '*Breuddwyd Macsen Wledig*: Cymhellion yr Awdur', *ib.*, 18–26 examines the change of interpretation of *Breuddwyd Macsen Wledig* from the period when the earliest extant version of the tale was composed in MS Peniarth 16 to the period of the White Book of Rhydderch and the Red Book of Hergest.

Jane Cartwright, 'Virginity and Chastity Tests in Medieval Welsh Prose', pp. 56–79 of *Medieval Virginities*, ed. Anke Bernau, Ruth Evans and Sarah Salih, Cardiff, Univ. of Wales, xiv + 296 pp., focuses on the legal, mythological, and theoretical implications of the chastity test in medieval Wales. Andrew Breeze, '"Peredur Son of Efrawg" and Windmills', *Celtica*, 24: 58–64 deals with the reference to mills contained in *Peredur* and argues that this reference dates the tale to no earlier than *c.* 1200.

Celtic Hagiography and Saints' Cults, ed. Jane Cartwright, Cardiff, Univ. of Wales Press, xvi + 339 includes J. Wyn Evans, 'St David and St Davids: Some Observations on the Cult, Site and Buildings' (10–25) which traces the history and development of the cult of St David, focusing primarily on the cathedral site and its environs. He also points out that certain architectural features may in fact have more to do with the geology and topography of the site than they do with the shrine and cult of St David; Elissa R. Henken, 'Welsh Hagiography and the Nationalist Impulse' (26–44), argues that hagiographies have been used as political tools by both the Church and the State. The Latin Life of St David played a prominent role both in the struggle for an independent Welsh Church and in the attempt to establish the supremacy of St Davids over the other Welsh dioceses; Nerys Ann Jones and Morfydd E. Owen, 'Twelfth-century Welsh Hagiography: the *Gogynfeirdd* poems to the saints' (45–76), discuss the poems of Llywelyn Fardd, Cynddelw Brydydd Mawr, and Gwynfardd Brycheiniog to Cadfan, Tysilio, and David respectively and explain the circumstances which led to the commissioning of each poem and put forward arguments for the dates of each composition, the sources upon which the poets depended, the intended audiences for such compositions and their function within both secular and ecclesiastical contexts; Jane Cartwright, 'The Harlot and the Hostess: a Preliminary Study of the Middle Welsh Lives of Mary Magdalene and her Sister Martha' (77–101), examines Middle Welsh *bucheddau* of Mary Magdalene and Martha and argues that these *bucheddau* were intended for a lay, rather than an ecclesiastical, audience; Karen Jankulak, 'Alba Longa in the Celtic Regions? Swine, saints and Celtic Hagiography' (271–84), concentrates on one hagiographical motif and analyses its geographical distribution throughout the Celtic world.

Cyfoeth y Testun: Ysgrifau ar Lenyddiaeth Gymraeg yr Oesoedd Canol, ed. Iestyn Daniel et al., Cardiff, Univ. of Wales Press, xx + 396 pp., includes Daniel Huws, 'Llyfr Coch Hergest' (1–30), who gives an overview of the Red Book of Hergest's production. His article builds upon the earlier work of Gifford Charles-Edwards and there's a detailed exposition on Hywel Fychan's relationship with Hand A in the Red Book of Hergest. Jenny Rowland, 'Y Beirdd Enwog: Anhysbys a'i Cant' (31–49), discusses the anonymous bards and poetry associated with the period falling between the *Cynfeirdd* and the *Gogynfeirdd* eras and provides useful insights on authorship. Helen Fulton, 'Awdurdod ac Awduriaeth: Golygu'r Cywyddwyr' (50–76), warns of the dangers of overemphasizing the issue of authorship when editing medieval Welsh poetry. Rather than editing the *Cywyddwyr*, she suggests, we should edit the *cywyddau*. Patrick K. Ford, 'Agweddau ar Berfformio ym Marddoniaeth yr Oesoedd Canol (77–108), begins with the suggestion by the late Prof. J. E. Caerwyn Williams that the harpist could have been a servant to the *pencerdd*. Building on that suggestion Ford explores the available evidence for the performance of poetry. Peredur I. Lynch, 'Cynghanedd Cywyddau Dafydd ap Gwilym: Tystiolaeth y Llawysgrifau Cynnar' (109–47), scrutinizes the features of Dafydd ap Gwilym's *cynghanedd* by examining four of the earliest MSS in which collections of Dafydd ap Gwilym's poems appeared. Marged Haycock, 'Cadair Ceridwen' (148–75), analyses the different written forms of Ceridwen before turning to the five Gogynfeirdd references to her. Nerys Ann Jones, 'Marwnadau Beirdd y Tywysogion: Arolwg' (176–99), gives an overview of the 72 extant Poets of the Nobility elegies, emphasizing their exceptional variety in terms of their form, content, and style. Dafydd Johnston, 'Bywyd Marwnad: Gruffudd ab yr Ynad Coch' (200–19), counters the misconception that the works of the Poets of the Nobility were invariably from the outset set in stone and demonstrates that even one of the greatest poems in Welsh had an interesting and varied textual history. Iestyn Daniel, 'Awdl Saith Weddi'r Pader' (220–36), produces an annotated edition of a Red Book of Hergest poem, based on the Lord's Prayer. Ann Parry Owen, 'Cyfuniadau "hydref ddail" ym Marddoniaeth Beirdd y Tywysogion' (237–51), discusses the inverted syntax which frequently occurs in the work of the Poets of the Nobility. Peter Wynn Thomas, '("Gwnaeth"): Newidyn Arddulliol yn y Cyfnod Canol' (252–80), details the stylistic development of the verbs, *gwnaeth* and *gorug*. Proinsiais Mac Cana, 'Rhai Fformiwlâu Cypladol at Enwi Pobl' (281–303), details in a comparative study of Welsh and Irish texts how people are addressed. Patricia Williams,

'Golwg ar Ddatblygiad Semantaidd y Rhagenwau Cyfarch yn Gymraeg' (304–25), demonstrates the influence of French upon Welsh during the Middle Ages in relation to the formal pronoun in texts from the 13th c. onwards but concludes that English in the 16th c. was the predominant influence which invested *chi* with a formal connotation. Sioned Davies, 'O Gaer Llion i Benybenglog: Testun Llanstephan 58 o "Iarlles y Ffynnon"' (326–48), discusses the textual background to *Iarlles y Ffynnon.* Morfydd E. Owen, 'Prolegomena i Astudiaeth Lawn o Lsgr. NLW 3026, Mostyn 88 a'i Harwyddocâd' (349–84), gives a comprehensive account of MS Mostyn 88, its ecclesiastical tables and its astrological and medical content.

Catherine McKenna, 'Revising Math: Kingship in the Fourth Branch', *CMCS*, 46: 95–118, undermines the magnaminousness and sagacity usually associated with King Math's nature and foregrounds the blemishes in his character. Charles Thomas and David Howlett, '"Vita Sancti Paterni": The Life of Saint Padarn and the Original "Miniu"', *Trivium*, 33: 9–129, provides a comprehensively annotated edition of the Life of Padarn, authored by Ieuan ap Sulien and also includes a comparative discussion of this text and the Life of St David.

Prydwyn Piper, 'Filling Some Lacunae in "Mabinogi Iessu Grist"', *NLWJ*, 32: 241–74, revisits the *Mabinogi Iessu Grist* text in light of the publication of a new annotated edition of the Gospel of Pseudo-Matthew. Elissa R. Henken, 'Legendry of Owain Glyndŵr', *ib.*, 275–92, discusses the legends assocatied with Owain Glyndŵr. William Parker, 'Gwynedd, Ceredigion and the Political Geography of the Mabinogi', *ib.*, 365–96, re-examines the authorship of the Four Branches of the Mabinogi. Sara Elin Roberts, 'Creu Trefn o Anhrefn —Gwaith Copïydd Testun Cyfreithiol', *ib.*, 397–420, discusses in detail MS Q, Wynnstay MS 36 of the Welsh Laws and gives an indication of which manuscripts the scribe may have had in front of him when copying and compiling his text.

Brynley F. Roberts, 'Glosau Cymraeg *Historia Regum Britanniae* Dulyn, Coleg y Drindod, llsgr. 515 (E.5.12)', *SC* 37: 75–80, considers the nature of the Welsh glosses on a version of the *Historia Regum Britanniae.* Nerys Ann Jones, 'Ffynonellau Canu Beirdd y Tywysogion', *ib.*, 81–125, examines the 156 MSS which contains the 237 poems associated with the Poets of the Nobility, paying particular attention to the Hendregadredd MS, from which most extant versions of their poetry derive. Ned Sturzer, 'Inconsistencies and Infelicities in the Welsh Tales: Their Implications', *ib.*, 127–42, concerns himself primarily with the Four Branches of the Mabinogi and the Three Romances and concentrates on the quirks and inconsistencies of these texts, which reveals a great deal about the transmission of the texts themselves. Dafydd Johnston, 'Dafydd ap Gwilym and Oral

Tradition', *ib.*, 143–61, contends that Dafydd ap Gwilym's work contains some of the richest evidence of oral transmission and gives examples of such oral transmission via variation in line order, length of poems, line additions or absences, and variant readings, particularly the substitution of synonyms and minor words which make little difference to the sense. Sara Elin Roberts, '*Tri Dygyngoll Cenedl*: The Development of a Triad', *ib.*, 163–82, concentrates on a single triad, known as the three dire losses of kindred, which appears in all Blegywryd and Cyfnerth MSS of medieval Welsh law. The triad's title was more securely fixed in the legal tradition than were its contents and it had a clear textual development which Sara Elin Roberts traces in detail.

LITERATURE SINCE 1500

By A. Cynfael Lake, *Lecturer in Welsh, University of Wales Swansea*

Rh. Ifans, '"Cainc Dafydd Broffwyd": cyfeiriad cynnar?', *Canu Gwerin*, 26:58–73, discusses an interesting request poem by the Anglesey poet-priest, Syr Dafydd Trefor. D. J. Bowen, 'Y canu i deulu'r Penrhyn o gyfnod y Tuduriaid hyd 1628', *Dwned*, 9:91–107, plots the role of the Penrhyn family as patrons of the poets from the days of Sir Wiliam Gruffudd (died 1531) to 1628. *Y Canu Mawl i Deuluoedd Plastai Llangefni a Thregaean*, ed. Dafydd Wyn Wiliam, Llangefni, p.p., 42 pp., brings together 12 poems to two families in the parishes of Llangefni and Tregaean in Anglesey composed mainly in the 16th c. A. C. Lake, 'Cerdd ychwanegol i'r 'Barwn Owain' o Ddolgellau', *JMHRS*, 14:185–87, draws attention to one request poem to the notorious Lewis Owen who was murdered in 1555. Ceri Davies, 'Syr John Prise ac amddiffyn hanes Prydain', *Y Traethodydd*, 158:164–85, outlines the arguments presented by Prise in his *Historiae Brytannicae Defensio* and shows the use he made of Welsh sources, both historical and poetical. A. Price, 'Ar drywydd y "bigel phyrnig" — golwg ar fywyd a gwaith Morys Clynnog', *TCHS*, 64:15–32, offers details of Clynnog's activities both in Britain and on the continent, and his relationship with his fellow-Recusant, Gruffudd Robert. A. Breeze's contribution pp.260–73, of *British Rhetoricians and Logicians 1500–1660*, ed. Edward A. Malone, Detroit, Bruccoli Clark Layman, 473 pp., contains valuable bibliographical details of William Salesbury's works, and 'Llyfr Rhetoreg' in particular. B. F. Roberts, 'Edward Lhuyd a'r bywyd diwylliannol Cymreig', *Cof Cenedl*, 18:35–69, shows that Lhuyd's scientific, linguistic and cultural activities, and those of his aides, reflected the interests of the Welsh gentry class to which he belonged.

C. A. Charnell-White, 'Galaru a gwaddoli ym marwnadau Williams Pantycelyn', *LlC*, 26:40–62, considers the imagery in Pantycelyn's elegies and the author's attitudes to death. She also suggests that the elegies helped to forge the identity of the Methodist community.

E. W. James, '"A'r byd i gyd yn bapur..." rhan 2: topos yr anhraethadwy', *Canu Gwerin*, 26:46–57, lists examples of the topos of inexpressibility in prose and poetry.

Id., 'Galarnad delynegol orau'r iaith?', *Barddas*, 275:30–37, looks briefly at the connections between three Glamorgan hymn writers and comments on the merits of a well-known elegy by Thomas William. Id., 'Dafydd William, Llandeilo Fach: an eighteenth-century

Glamorgan hymn-writer', *Morgannwg*, 47:3–24, reminds readers of anecdotes connected with D.W.'s most well-known hymn and draws attention to his main themes. Like Pantycelyn he also composed elegies in honour of the converted. Dafydd Wyn Wiliam, *Cofiant Siôn Morris (1713–40)*, Llangefni, p.p., 86 pp., concludes his series of detailed biographies to the Morris brothers of Anglesey with his study of Siôn Morris, the least-known of the four brothers. He allocates one chapter to his literary activities. M. E. Jones, '"Gwaith prydydd da'i awenydd. . .": cerddi gwasael a phenillion telyn Lewis Morris', *Canu Gwerin*, 26:3–21, shows that although Morris played a major part in the literary renaissance of the 18th c., in his early years he was influenced by and contributed to the popular folk culture of his day. Ff. M. Jones, 'Cerddoriaeth yr anterliwtiau: golwg ar le'r caneuon mewn pedair anterliwt enghreifftiol', *LlC*, 26:63–86, looks at the contrasting use made of songs in 18th-c. interludes by Richard Parry and Twm o'r Nant and explains the musical significance of the songs in an earlier work attributed to Mathew Owen. G. Davies, '"Galar hen hil. . ."', *Ceredigion*, 14:91–93, draws attention to a ballad by Ellis Roberts concerning the death of 706 parishoners of Llanbadarn Fawr in 1784. *Cerddi Jac Glan-y-gors*, ed. E. G. Millward, Llandybïe, Barddas, 148 pp., is an annotated compilation of all Jac's known free-metre poetry; Carneddog in his 1905 collection omitted verses deemed to be objectable. E. W. James, 'Caethwasanaeth a'r beirdd, 1790–1840', *Taliesin*, 119:37–60, shows that poetry was one medium employed by opponents of the slave trade such as Iolo Morganwg and Morgan John Rhys but the missionary movement and the radicalisation of the Methodists also contributed to the change in attitudes. H. T. Edwards, 'Torri bara menyn cyn trin geiriau', *Taliesin*, 120:14–27, outlines the content of letters published in *Y Genedl Gymreig* in the year 1878 debating the appropriateness of literary pursuits by women. The names mentioned in the letters suggest that many women dabbled in this sphere. Glyn Tegai Hughes, *Islwyn*, Cardiff, Univ. of Wales Press, 354 pp., breaks new ground in this most welcome study which looks at both high and low points in Islwyn's poetic career. The poet's philosophical and theological ideas are discussed in detail and the poems, and the two 'Y Storm' in particular, are set not only in a Welsh but also English and European context. T. Robin Chapman, *Ben Bowen*, Cardiff, Univ. of Wales Press, 71 pp., sketches the personal characteristics and the external influences which shaped the poetry of Ben Bowen, and seeks to account for 'the appeal of this mediocre poet of immoderate self-belief'.

Alan Llwyd, *Rhyfel a Gwrthryfel*, Llandybïe, Barddas, 704 pp., contains a series of articles, previously published in *Barddas*, on the theme of modernism in Welsh poetry especially in the early decades of the 20th c. in the works of Cynan, E. Prosser Rhys, Gwenallt and Caradog Prichard. The extensive 350-page study of the work of Bobi Jones appears here for the first time. The chapter on Waldo Williams: '"O Bridd" gyda golwg ar rai cerddi eraill' featured in *Barddas*, 272: 40–5, *ib.*, 273: 8–17. Here Alan Llwyd shows the significance of the poem 'O Bridd' and sees parallels in the works of Henry Vaughan and William Blake. J. W. Davies, 'Waldo Williams: "Y Dderwen Gam"', *Barddas*, 271: 26–32, analyses one of Waldo's last poems to appear in print. R. Alun Evans, *Iorwerth C Peate*, Llandybïe, Barddas, 166 pp., is a full and interesting portrayal of the poet and prose writer whose inspiration led to the establishment of the Folk Museum at St Fagans. R. M. Jones, *Beirniadaeth Gyfansawdd*, Llandybïe, Barddas, 296 pp., summarizes the critical theories presented in the two preceeding volumes in this triology, and they concern primarily the relationship between 'langue' (*Tafod*) and 'parole' (*Mynegiant*). He also surveys current literary criticism in Wales with particular regard to Marxism, Feminism, and Post-Modernism. D. Densil Morgan, *Pennar Davies*, Cardiff, Univ. of Wales Press, 209 pp., focuses on P.D.'s theological viewpoint expressed directly in his religious writings and indirectly in the poetry and prose composed over a period of 45 years. His vivid imagination, his great learning and intellect also colour the creative works which have yet to receive due praise. G. Thomas, 'Alan Llwyd: bardd', pp. 91–105 of *Alan*, ed. Huw Meirion Edwards, Caernarfon, Barddas, 269 pp., deals briefly with the main themes in Alan Llwyd's poetry. J. Hunter, 'Ar drywydd y tragwyddol: golwg ar ddwy gerdd', *ib.*, 106–16, analyses two poems, 'Yr hebog uwch Felindre' and 'Van Gogh; hunan-bortread'. Huw M. Edwards, '*Barddas*: y chwarter canrif cyntaf', *ib.*, 63–90, traces the early history of the journal *Barddas* and the contribution of its editor, Alan Llwyd.

T. Robin Chapman's biography of Islwyn Ffowc Elis, *Rhywfaint o Anfarwoldeb*, Llandysul, Gomer, 245 pp., summarizes the themes in Elis's novels and short stories and discusses the circumstances surrounding their composition. He also comments on the author's comparative silence from the 1960s onwards and his mission as a writer, a theme expounded by Chapman in his monologue *Islwyn Ffowc Elis* (2000). Rh. Ifans, 'Rhai sylwadau ar grefydd yn y ddrama Gymraeg', *LlC*, 26: 87–105, remarks on the reluctance of dramatists, both early and modern, to make their religion the matter of their works. She refers briefly to the morality plays and to the works of Gwenlyn Parry. J. Hunter, 'Y traddodiad llenyddol coll', *Taliesin*, 118: 13–44, describes the Welsh in America in terms of an interpretive community and looks at ways in which they used literature to convey their identity. D. Williams, '"Cymry Ewythr Sam": creu hunaniaeth

Gymreig yn yr Unol Daleithiau *c.* 1860–1900', *Cof Cenedl*, 18:127–59, follows a similar trail but his study of three poems leads to the conclusion that contrasting identities were forged and promoted.

A. G. Jones, 'Politics and prophecy in the journalism of Gwilym Hiraethog', *THSC*, 2002 [2003]: 106–21, explains Hiraethog's commentary upon contemporary events in the light of his Calvinistic beliefs. M. Morton, 'Arolwg o hirhoedledd cyfnodolion Cymraeg', *WBS*, 5:54–66, charts the life-span of periodicals from 1735 onwards. P. Freeman, '*Baner y Groes*, a Welsh-language tractarian periodical of the 1950s', *NLWJ*, 32:305–16, deals mostly with the doctrines and viewpoints expounded in *Baner y Groes*, published between 1854–8, of editor, ab Ithel, and his correspondents. G. F. Nuttal, 'Welsh books at Bristol Baptist College (1795)', *THSC*, 2002 [2003]: 162–68, gives details of 38 Welsh volumes, mostly published in the 18th c., listed in the Baptist College catalogues. D. Morgans, 'Y Cerddor: cyfnodolyn y werin / periodical of the people', *Welsh Music History*, 5 [2002]: 105–34, shows that the variety of *Y Cerddor* — it included articles, biographical notes, musical transcripts, and a poetry section — made it unique during its 32 year lifespan.

D. E. Davies, 'Llyfrau a phamffledi Cymraeg a gyhoeddwyd yn yr Unol Daleithiau', *LlC*, 26:106–36, lists some 300 items published in America during the 19th c. The majority appeared between 1851–70 and many were connected either with the religious denominations or with the *eisteddfod* movement. G. Bowen, 'Gorsedd y Beirdd yn y Wladfa', *NLWJ*, 32:317–36, surveys the *eisteddfodau* and *gorsedd* ceremonies held in Patagonia over a period of fifty years. K. Bernard, 'The National Eisteddfod and the evolution of the all-Welsh' rule', *NAJWS*, 3:33–47, argues that the Welsh rule was instigated by 'vehement nationalists' such as Henry Lewis, Cynan and W. J. Gruffydd, and sees as insular attempts by its promoters to use the *eisteddfod* as a vehicle to promote the Welsh language.

BRETON AND CORNISH STUDIES

POSTPONED

III. IRISH STUDIES

EARLY IRISH

By Kevin Murray, *Department of Early and Medieval Irish, University College, Cork*

1. Language

G. R. Isaac, 'Prospects in Old Irish syntax', *ZCP*, 53:181–97, contextualizes the formal publication (over 20 years after his death) of P. Mac Coisdealbha's Ph.D. thesis, *The syntax of the sentence in Old Irish*. T. M. Charles-Edwards, '*Dliged*: its native and latinate usages', *Celtica*, 24:65–78, presents a very useful examination of the various meanings of the term *dliged* and suggests 'how a dictionary entry, restricting itself to Old Irish examples, might be set out'. K. McCone, 'Old Irish *na nní*: a case of *quid pro quo*?', *ib*., 168–81, presents a close analysis of certain aspects of P. Schrijver's 1997 study on Celtic pronouns and particles; elsewhere in the same volume, there are short notes by E. P. Hamp on 'Gaulish *ci*, *-c*, Old Irish *cé*, Ogam *koi*' (129) and by K. Murray on 'Lulgach "a milch cow"' (223–24).

L. Mac Mathúna, 'Lexical and literary aspects of "heart" in Irish', *Ériu*, 53:1–18, 'investigates the focus and dynamics of Old Irish *cride* "heart" within an overall lexical field framework'. L. Breatnach, 'On words ending in a stressed vowel in Early Irish', *ib*., 133–42, argues that 'there are no grounds for postulating a category of words ending in a short stressed vowel in Old Irish'. G.R. Isaac, 'Some Old Irish etymologies, and some conclusions drawn from them', *ib*., 151–55, takes issue with conclusions drawn by P. Schrijver in *ib*., 51. Elsewhere in *Ériu*, 53, there are short notes by R. Ó Maolalaigh on 'Vocal variation in *air-*, *aur-*' (163–69), by P. Mac Cana on '*lettáeb*', and 'Irish *leth-*, Welsh *lled* "quite, considerably"' (179–81) and by E. P. Hamp on '*immainse, immainsi*' and 'Addenda' (185–86).

2. Literature

The complete diplomatic texts of the famous 'Leinster poems' (which have been edited a number of times) are most usefully set out by J. Corthals, 'The rhymeless "Leinster poems": diplomatic texts', *Celtica*, 24:79–100 (this contribution complements his earlier article in *ib*., 21:113–25) while there is an examination of the sources for the BL MS Egerton 1782 copy of *Táin bó Cúailnge* (recension 1) in T. Ó Con Cheanainn, '*Táin bó Cúailnge*: foinsí an téacs atá in Egerton 1782', *ib*., 24:232–38.

E. Poppe, 'Personal names and an insular tradition of Pseudo-Dares', *Ériu*, 53:53–59, compares 'some names in the Early Irish *Togail Troí* and the Middle Welsh *Ystorya Daret*', noting some close relationships between varying recensions of both texts, and believing that 'this is an indication of a complex Insular transmission of Latin texts of the *De excidio Troiae historia*'. B. Smelik, 'The structure of the Irish Arthurian romance *Eachtra Mhacaoimh-an-Iolair*', *CMCS*, 45:43–57, argues that the Arthurian section within *Eachtra Mhacaoimh-an-Iolair* 'is the basis of the tale, without which there probably would not have been an Irish story at all'. C. Breatnach, 'The transmission and structure of *Immram curaig Ua Corra*', *Ériu*, 53:91–107, suggests that all versions of this *immram* 'derive from a composite narrative written some time after the mid-twelfth century' while E. Bhreathnach, 'Tales of Connacht: *Cath Airtig*, *Táin bó Flidhais*, *Cath Leitreach Ruibhe*, and *Cath Cumair*', *CMCS*, 45: 21–42, argues that the four tales listed in the article title 'belong to one medieval narrative: that of the "history" of Connacht'. K. Murray has a short note on the phrase *tongu do dia* in 'A reading from *Scéla Moshauluim*', *ZCP*, 53:198–201.

3. Other

Duanaire Finn: *Reassessments*, ed. J. Carey, London, Irish Texts Society, Subsidiary Series 13, xi + 123 pp., contains important new studies on this pivotal collection of *Fíanaigecht* material (originally edited by E. MacNeill and G. Murphy in three volumes between 1901 and 1953); in the 'Foreword' P. Ó Riain details the protracted problems involved in bringing *Duanaire Finn* through the press. The five other contributions to the volume are J. Carey, 'Remarks on dating' (1–18), D. E. Meek, '*Duanaire Finn* and Gaelic Scotland' (19–38), J. F. Nagy, 'The significance of the *Duanaire Finn*' (39–50), †M. Ó Briain, '*Duanaire Finn* XXII: Goll and the champion's portion' (51–78) and R. Ó hUiginn, '*Duanaire Finn*; patron and text' (79–106).

Prospect and retrospect in Celtic studies: *Proceedings of the Eleventh International Congress of Celtic Studies*, ed. M. Herbert and K. Murray, Dublin, Four Courts Press, 128 pp., contains six new contributions on the discipline that is Celtic Studies. These are: T. M. Charles-Edwards, 'Views of the past: legal and historical scholarship of the twentieth century' (15–27), M. Haycock, 'Between Cardiff and Cork: scholarship on medieval Welsh literature since 1963' (29–43), S. Ó Coileáin, 'Society and scholarship: Irish in the modern world' (45–56), A. Dooley, 'A view from North America: obstacles and opportunities for Celtic Studies' (59–73), J. T. Koch, 'Some thoughts on ethnic identity, cultural pluralism, and the future of Celtic Studies'

(75–92) and R. Ó hUiginn, 'Future directions for the study of Irish' (93–104).

J. Borsje and F. Kelly, '"The Evil Eye" in early Irish literature and law', *Celtica*, 24: 1–24, examines the representation of the 'evil eye' in legal texts and literature from medieval Ireland. J. Borsje returns to this topic in 'Het "boze oog" in middeleeuwse Ierse wetteksten', in *Arthur, Brigit, Conn, Deirdre . . . Verhaal, taal en recht in de Keltische wereld: Liber amicorum voor Leni van Strien-Gerritsen*, ed. I. Genee, B. Jaski, and B. Smelik (Nijmegen: De Keltische Draak), 38–50. T. Mikhailova and N. Nikolaeva, 'The denotations of death in Goidelic: to the question of Celtic eschatological conceptions', *ZCP*, 53: 93–115, state their belief in the 'peculiarity of the Celtic attitude towards death', with 'no boundary between . . . [their] . . . world and the Otherworld' arguing that 'the only barrier consists in perception'. R. Mark Scowcroft, '*Recht fáide* and its gloss in the pseudo-historical prologue to the *Senchus Már*', *Ériu*, 53: 143–50, suggests an alternative reading for a small section of this text, edited by J. Carey in *Ériu*, 45. B. Jaski, '"We are of the Greeks in our origin": new perspectives on the Irish origin legend', *CMCS*, 46: 1–53, concludes that the idea of Greek origin of the Irish was 'effectively written out of *Lebor Gabála*'.

In *Léachtaí Cholm Cille* 33, ed. R. Ó hUiginn, dedicated to the topic of Cearbhall Ó Dálaigh, P. Ní Chatháin, 'Máirín Bean Uí Dhálaigh: bean uasal agus scoláire' (89–101), paints an enlightening picture of the personality and scholarship of Máirín O Daly as well as including a complete list of her publications. In further matters bibliographic, R. Ó Maolalaigh, 'A title index of Brian Ó Cuív's publications 1942–71', *Celtica*, 24: 270–79, 'provides an alphabetically-arranged title index' of some of the late Prof. B. Ó Cuív's publications. D. McCarthy, 'On the shape of the insular tonsure', *ib.*, 140–67, presents a closely-argued study to support the view 'that the Insular tonsure was in the shape of a Greek "Δ"'. P. Ó Riain further sharpens his focus on the Irish martyrological tradition in 'A Northumbrian phase in the textual history of the Hieronymian Martyrology: the evidence of the Martyrology of Tallaght', *Analecta Bollandiana*, 120: 311–63 while in *Apocalyptic and eschatological heritage*, ed. M. McNamara, Dublin, Four Courts Press, xvi + 191pp., J. Carey, 'The seven heavens and the twelve dragons in Insular apocalyptic' (121–36), argues that 'the roots of *Fís Adomnáin*'s accounts of the seven heavens' lie in apocalyptic writings from Egypt.

With regard to manuscripts, C. Breatnach, 'Manuscript sources and methodology: Rawlinson B 502 and *Lebar Glinne Dá Locha*', *Celtica*, 24: 40–54, presents another paper in his ongoing debate with P. Ó Riain on whether the manuscript known as Lebor Glinne Dá Locha is to be identified with Rawlinson MS B. 502. G. Manning, 'The later marginalia in the Book of Leinster', *ib.*, 213–22, catalogues the 'hitherto unpublished late, marginal entries' in this important medieval Irish manuscript and P. Ó Riain, 'Dioscán lámhscríbhinní: a medley of manuscripts', *JCHAS*, 108:133–40, examines, *inter alia*, some of the material contained in MSS RIA 23 N 10 and Staatsbibliothek Preussischer Kulturbesitz, Berlin, Theol. Lat. Fol. 703.

MODERN IRISH

POSTPONED

IV. SCOTTISH GAELIC STUDIES

By Sheila M. Kidd, *Lecturer in Celtic, University of Glasgow*

B. Ó Buachalla, '"Common Gaelic" Revisited', Ó Baoill, *Rannsachadh*, 1–12, challenges Kenneth Jackson's arguments for Common Gaelic as a concrete and retrievable language, and argues for it existing as a theoretical construct instead with Northern and Southern Gaelic rather than Jackson's Western and Eastern. R. Ó Maolalaigh, '"Siubhadaibh a Bhalachaibh! Tha an suirbhidh ullamh agaibh": mar a dh'èirich do *-bh*, *-mh* gun chudrom ann an Gàidhlig Alba', Ó Baoill, *Rannsachadh*, 61–74, draws on the *Survey of the Gaelic Dialects of Scotland* and other dialect surveys in his examination of the vocalisation as /u/ or /i/ of what were originally unstressed labial fricatives, and suggests that the development of these syllables was related to the quality of the preceding consonant, while also considering exceptions to the rule he has posited. Evidence from the Book of the Dean of Lismore is drawn on to demonstrate that this vocalisation took place before the 16th c. R. Wentworth, 'Na bolaichean aig na Geàrrlaich 's an Loch Làn Diubh: fòineaman taobhach ann an dualchainnt Ghàidhlig an Ros an Iar', Ó Baoill, *Rannsachadh*, 91–99, discusses the retention of the velarised alveolar lateral consonant in the Gaelic of Alligin after it had been lost in surrounding districts. U. MacGill'Ìosa, '"Mo chreach-sa thàinig"', Ó Baoill, *Rannsachadh*, 45–59, discusses the origins of *-sa* in the title phrase and other sayings. S. Grant, 'Gaelic in Western Banffshire', Ó Baoill, *Rannsachadh*, 75–90, in considering 12 features of Banffshire Gaelic concludes that this area's dialect has most in common with that of Strathspey and to a slightly lesser extent with those of Aberdeenshire and East Perthshire. J. Grant, 'The Gaelic of Strathspey and its relationship with other dialects', *TGSI*, 61, 1998–2000 [2003]:71–115, examines some of the distinctive phonological, morphological, and lexical features of this dialect and concludes that it is closest to the dialects of Braemar and East Perthshire. S. Watson, ''N *Linnet* Mór: A window on language and community in 18th century Easter Ross', *ScL*, 21, 2002:43–59, discusses a mid 19th-c. elegy for seven drowned Easter Ross men, giving attention first to its socio-historical significance and then to the dialectal features which can be gleaned from it based on orthography and metre. N. MacKenzie, 'Scottish Gaelic *caismeachd*, Irish *caismirt*, and the emergence of cadenced marching', *ScL*, 21, 2002:60–71, discounts the possibility of *caismeachd* being derived from *cas* + *imeachd* based on the fact that cadenced marching was unknown before the middle of the 18th c. while the word *caismeachd* was in use before then. J. Heath, 'Liberty and tradition: Sound patterning in Hebridean prayer and preaching as poetic device and linguistic signal', Ó Baoill, *Rannsachadh*, 25–33, examines the acoustic patterning of Gaelic religious discourse based on research conducted for the most part among Free Church of Scotland congregations in Lewis and provides evidence of its use, sometimes unconsciously, by ministers as a marker of a shift in subject matter and in the significance of what is being said. This is shown to prompt both positive and negative responses from listeners. M. NicLeòid, 'An ceangal a tha eadar ceòl is faclan ann an òrain Ghàidhlig', Ó Baoill, *Rannsachadh*, 35–44, focuses on the way in which short syllables can be made long and long ones short in òran metre, tàlaidhean, puirt, and òrain luaidh.

Richard A. V. Cox, *The Gaelic Place-names of Carloway, Isle of Lewis. Their Structure and Significance*, Dublin, Dublin Institute for Advanced Studies, 2002, xii + 484 pp., is an invaluable study of nearly 3000 place names in this west-coast area of Lewis which draws on both documentary material and local informants. There is a thorough discussion of the structure of the names and of the onomasticon followed by a gazetteer of names which includes a phonetic transcription, translation, and derivation of each name. R. A. V. Cox, 'Les toponymes scandinaves dans le gaélique écossais', in *L'Héritage Maritime des Vikings en Europe de l'Ouest*, ed. Élisabeth Ridel, Caen U.P., 2002, 565 pp., 423–38, examines some of the Scandinavian elements which feature in the maritime nomenclature of the Hebrides. R. A. V. Cox, 'Clach an Truiseil', *JCLin*, 7, 1998[2002]: 159–66, suggests the possibility that the second element of this Lewis name may derive from Old Norse and have the sense of slow or trudging movement. A number of place names are discussed in A. Breeze, 'Some Celtic place names of Scotland, including Tain, Cadzow, Cockleroy and Prenderguest', *ScL*, 21, 2002: 27–42 and R. MacIlleathain, 'Ainmean-Aite Gàidhlig Inbhir Nis: dìleab phrìseil is thòimhseachanach', *TGSI*, 61, 1998–2000 [2003]: 236–50, surveys some Inverness place names.

D. Dumville, 'Ireland and North Britain in the earlier middle ages: Contexts for Míniugud Senchasa Fher nAlban', Ó Baoill, *Rannsachadh*, 185–211, fundamentally challenges previous understanding of the text, its construction and its significance. W. McLeod, 'Anshocair nam Fionnghall: Ainmeachadh agus ath-ainmeachadh Gàidhealtachd na h-Albann', Ó Baoill, *Rannsachadh*, 13–23, contrasts the frequent use of 'Fionnghall' to denote Scottish Gaels in classical poetry of the 16th and 17th centuries with its virtual absence in vernacular Gaelic verse except in the phrase 'Rìgh Fionnghall' to refer to the Lord of the Isles and suggests that this demonstrates the Gaels' sense of identity moving away from its Norse roots. M. Scott,

'Politics and poetry in mid-eighteenth century Argyll: *Tuirseach andiugh críocha Gaoidhiol*', Ó Baoill, *Rannsachadh*, 149–62, discusses Uilleam MacMhurchaidh's elegy to the 2nd Duke of Argyll and draws particular attention to the way in which the poet emphasises the Duke's status in both Scottish and British politics. S. Arbuthnot, 'A Context for Mac Mhaighstir Alasdair's *Moladh air Deagh Bhod*', Ó Baoill, *Rannsachadh*, 163–70, compares the poem with similar compositions from Scotland, Wales, and Ireland and suggests that these may be intended to deflate the traditional concept of panegyric. S. Fraser, '"The wheat/Grows tallest in well-dug fields": influence and innovation in some early poems by Alastair Mac Mhaighstir Alastair', Ó Baoill, *Rannsachadh*, 171–81, uses some of the poet's earliest work to demonstrate the potential benefits of applying theoretical frameworks to Gaelic literary texts. M. Newton, 'The MSS of Donald MacGregor', *TGSI*, 61, 1998–2000 [2003]: 280–305, reproduces part of the manuscript recorded by MacGregor in 1824 containing anecdotes on the Battle of Glen Fruin and other traditions relating to the Clan Gregor. M. Newton, 'Jacobite Past, Loyalist Present', *e-Keltoi*, 5, <www.uwm.edu/Dept/celtic/ekeltoi/volumes/vol5/5_2/newton_5_2.html> concludes that the response of Gaelic poets to the part which Highland soldiers played in North American warfare in the aftermath of Culloden remained highly consistent with their traditional rhetorical and ideological framework.

The Spoken Word. Oral Culture in Britain, 1500–1850, ed. Adam Fox and Daniel Woolf, Manchester U.P., 2002, x + 286 pp., contains two articles of relevance to Scottish Gaelic studies. M. MacGregor, 'The genealogical histories of Gaelic Scotland', 196–239, discusses the rise in the writing of clan histories from the 17th c. to the 19th c. as the learned Gaelic orders vanished and highlights the fact that these mainly English documents synthesised oral and literary sources. D. E. Meek, 'The pulpit and the pen: orality and print in the Scottish Gaelic world', 84–118, examines the influence which Gaelic-speaking Protestant clergy have had on oral and literary traditions with consideration of their roles as preachers, translators, writers, journal editors, and collectors of oral tradition. The Rev. Dr Norman MacLeod's literary activities in the 19th c. come under scrutiny in S. Kidd, 'Caraid nan Gaidheal and "Friend of Emigration": Gaelic emigration literature of the 1840s', *SHR*, 81 no. 211, 2002: 52–69, and in T. Mac Eachaidh, 'Caraid nan Gaidheal as discerned through the pages of *An Teachdaire Gaelach*, 1829–1831', Ó Baoill, *Rannsachadh*, 141–48. S. Kidd, 'The writer behind the pen-names: the Rev. Alexander MacGregor', *TGSI*, 61, 1998–2000 [2003]: 1–24, discusses this prolific 19th-c. writer in the context of contemporary trends and events.

North American Gaelic communities are the subect of three articles. M. Newton, '"Becoming cold-hearted like the Gentiles around them": Scottish Gaelic in the United States 1872–1912', *e-Keltoi*, 2, <www.uwm.edu/Dept/celtic/ekeltoi/volumes/vol2/2_3/newton_2_3.html>, examines the relatively sparse evidence for the survival of Gaelic in the United States and the largely unsuccessful attempts made by immigrant Gaels to revitalize their language. S. Watson, 'Ás a' Choillidh Dhuibh: cunntasan seanchais air a' chiad luchd-àiteachaidh an Eilean Cheap Breatainn', Ó Baoill, *Rannsachadh*, 271–77, uses material recorded from oral tradition to illustrate the experiences of early 19th-c. Highland settlers in Cape Breton. K. E. Nilsen, 'Some notes on pre-*Mac-Talla* publishing in Nova Scotia (with references to early Gaelic publishing in Prince Edward Island, Quebec and Ontario), Ó Baoill, *Rannsachadh*, 127–40, offers an overview of the development of 19th-c. Gaelic publishing in an emigrant context and demonstrates that Nova Scotian journals tended to draw heavily upon the periodicals of Norman MacLeod.

Dàin do Eimhir. Somhairle MacGill-Eain/Sorley MacLean, ed. Christopher Whyte, Glasgow, Association for Scottish Literary Studies, 2002, vii + 295 pp., brings together for the first time MacGill-Eain's cycle of 60 poems composed to 'Eimhir' with only one as yet unlocated poem omitted and including six not previously published. The introduction includes a discussion of the chronology of the poems' publication. The poems themselves are accompanied by translations, the editor's being used where the poet's own are not extant and the extensive commentary which follows offers invaluable information on the background to the individual poems. This volume re-opens the 'Eimhir' cycle, and indeed MacLean's work as a whole, to literary debate. D. E. Meek, 'An aghaidh na Sìorraidheachd? Bàird na ficheadamh linn agus an creideamh Crìosdail', Ó Baoill, *Rannsachadh*, 103–16, surveys the various attitudes to Christianity which appear in 20th-c. Gaelic verse and refutes the view that these modern poets are anti-religion and instead demonstrates the broad range of responses to and representations of religion which appear in their work. Modern poetry is also studied in M. Ní Annracháin, 'The force of tradition in the poetry of Aonghas MacNeacail', Ó Baoill, *Rannsachadh*, 117–26, which discusses the tension between tradition and modernity and demonstrates how MacNeacail adapts traditional imagery. *Eilein na h-Òige. The poems of Fr Allan McDonald*, ed. Ronald Black, Glasgow, Mungo Books, 2002, xvi + 527 pp., provides the most detailed study to date of the Eriskay priest's literary endeavours. Black brings together some 45 poems and hymns and ten translations by Fr Allan with detailed accompanying notes. The introduction which provides a brief biography and a general discussion of Fr Allan's verse is followed by John Lorne Campbell's 1956 biography of the priest.

4

GERMANIC LANGUAGES

I. GERMAN STUDIES

LANGUAGE

By Charles V. J. Russ, *Reader in the Department of Language and Linguistic Science, University of York*

1. General

Surveys, Collections, Bibliographies. The popularity of dealing with the linguistics of German is evidenced by the appearance of J. Boase-Beier and K. Lodge, *The German Language: A Linguistic Introduction*, Oxford, Blackwell, xi + 254 pp., which is aimed at second and final year students. Although there is no explicit statement about who wrote which chapter, the reader can guess from the authors' respective curricula vitae on the back cover. After an introductory chapter, bristling with linguistic terms, most of which the reader does not meet again, the predictable areas of syntax, morphology, phonetics, phonetics, phonology, lexis, stylistics, historical background, and contemporary variation are presented (or perhaps one should say, dangled briefly, since there is sometimes little time to take stock before the next example or theoretical point is laid out). All examples given in German are translated. At the end of each chapter there are exercises, but usually of an open-ended type so that no solutions are presented, and finally there is an index of terms. The emphasis is on linguistics, and especially Chomskyan linguistics. This surfaces chiefly in the introduction and the chapter on syntax. Here the authors are at home, but what about dependency and valency, widely followed in German-speaking linguistic circles? Chomskyan and traditional terminology fluctuate, complementizer alongside conjunction. The notions of subject, object, etc. are used but not explained. Some terms are not translated, e.g. *Vorfeld*, *Mittelfeld*, *Nachfeld*, nor is there any reference to their first use by E. Drach. The formation of the passive and wh-questions are used to illustrate syntactic processes, but passives with *bekommen* etc. are not mentioned nor yes/no-questions. Terms such as 'agent' and 'predicator' are not to be found in the index. In the morphology chapter the problem with German terms continues with *Fugen-s*, glossed only once or twice, when 'linking morpheme' is perfectly acceptable. In this chapter we are on more familiar ground yet allomorph is not illustrated clearly as being both phonologically and lexically conditioned. The concept of the word-form and lexeme do not seem to feature. The fuzzy boundary between inflexion and derivation is illustrated with the adjectival prefix *un-* which does not change the class of the word concerned, but the same effect produced by the nominal suffixes, *-lein/-chen* and *–in*, is not mentioned.The problems of the division between compounding and derivation are illustrated but the examples are not really fully explained, nor is the term affixoid mentioned at all. However, morphological processes are captured satisfactorily. There is a good discussion of the status of infinitives and conversion, with *-en* being regarded as an inflexional ending, but then *weit* > *weit* + *en* is still regarded as conversion, however the debate is open. The processes of ablaut and umlaut are illustrated but what about *e*>*i* as in *treffen, trifft*? Borrowing is dealt with under morphology and there is a discussion of the relationship between morphology and phonology/syntax which is rather inconclusive. Phonetics and phonology are covered in the normal fashion with the latter using modern syllabic phonology with the rather dubious treatment of extrasyllabic consonants (not in the index) which are ignored for certain processes. The bibliography for phonetics is rather meagre. It is interesting to note that as soon as speech with 'real' examples comes on the scene then variation, alternatives, and 'some speakers say' becomes important. The phonology closes with a good section on connected speech. Lexis starts with the lexical entry and theta roles, moving on to the structure of the vocabulary, e.g. lexical fields, which are not really explained very well, and concepts such as hyponymy, antonymy, etc. Phrases feature as well as words. The stylistics chapter shows the connection between language use and literature and deals with a variety of different concepts such as metaphor and ambiguity. This is a useful chapter for students studying literary texts. The historical background chapter functions more as a footnote explaining changes such as the Second Sound Shift, diphthongization, and umlaut, as well some morphological and syntactic changes. A brief overview of the development of standard German is given. This is an ill-conceived chapter. Far better would have been to have a section in each chapter about the relevant changes, some of which are ongoing. There are tantalizing historical 'hooks' in the other chapters. The final chapter on contemporary variation, describing variation according to use and user, should really have been put at the beginning of the book. This could have been combined with an account of synchronic and diachronic, and have set the scene for the presentation of the linguistic principles. The whole again largely neglected area of standardization could have been dealt with here, e.g. the role of instances such as

Duden, not mentioned. In general the authors are very familiar with general linguistic works but the bibliography lacks entries by W. König on pronunciation, J. Eichhoff on lexical variation, W. Fleischer on phraseology, and in some cases the editions are not the most up-to-date. What this signifies is that the volume would have been better entitled 'An introduction to linguistics, with reference to the German language'. If it is to be used with second and final year students of German then the teacher will have to be ready to explain concepts and provide a lot more illustrative material.

Germanistische Linguistik: Konturen eines Faches, ed. H. Henne et al. (RGL, 240), 183 pp., contains the following: A. Burkhardt, 'Worte und Wörter als Zeichen, (Be)Deutung und Handlung — Zum Stand der Sprachtheorie nach 1945' (1–23), pleading for a more fluid approach to speech acts; A. Linke, 'Sprachgeschichte — Gesellschaftsgeschichte — Kulturanalyse' (25–65), wanting to widen historical linguistics so that history is really the study of discourse; S. Wichter, 'Gesellschaftliche Kommunikation als linguistischer Gegenstand' (67–95), stressing that the quality of communication is important; G. Diewald, 'Viele Grammatikmodelle — eine Grammatik? Zur Spannung zwischen Theoriepluralismus und Einheit des Gegenstands' (97–116), who believes that the investigation of practical problems and reflection on theories will lead to a positive resolution of this dilemmma; P. Sieber, 'Hatte die germanistische Sprachwissenschaft Einfluss auf die Auffassungen von Sprache im Deutschunterricht?' (117–36), who answers first 'no' but then says that investigation, training, cooperation, and communication in the field of language learning would be beneficial; K.-P. Konerding, 'Lexikalische Semantik in der neueren Germanistik — Ein historischer Abriss' (137–58), who believes that cognitivism and structuralism can influence each other for good; J. Kilian, 'Alkmenes "Ach!" Die germanistische Linguistik entdeckt die dialogische Sprache' (159–83), who regrets that linguistics only came to dialogue research late and that literary scholars have ignored much research. The contours of the subject are that it is interdisciplinary. All the contributors give a research review of the work in their area. The tone is up-beat but rather specialized in terminology. There must be simpler ways to say what these scholars mean! The main criticism of this volume, perhaps unfairly, is that it is incomplete. There is no treatment of the internal linguistic communication between speakers in the German language community, i.e. what is normally dealt with under sociolinguistics and dialectology.

Also noted on standard and variation: '*Standardfragen.*' *Soziolinguistische Perspektiven auf Sprachgeschichte, Sprachkontakt und Sprachvariation*, ed. J. K. Androutsopoulos and E. Ziegler (VarioLingua. Nonstandard —

Standard — Substandard, 18), Frankfurt, Lang, 228 pp.; and L. Götze, 'Entwicklungstendenzen in der deutschen Gegenwartssprache — Normen — Deutsch als Fremdsprache', *DaF*, 40:131–34.

European language policy is becoming a topical matter, as illustrated by B. C. Witte, 'Die auswärtige Kultur- und Sprachpolitik des vereinten Deutschland. Erwartungen, Chancen, Probleme', *DaF*, 40:72–79; **Sprachenvielfalt und Demokratie in Deutschland. Dokumentation des Kongresses vom 16.–17. November 2001 in den Landesvertretungen Niedersachsen und Schleswig-Holstein, Berlin*, ed. A. G. H. Walker, Brussels, European Bureau for Lesser Used Languages. Komitee für die Bundesrepublik Deutschland, 2002, 131 pp.; **Sprache transdisziplinär*, ed. R. Emons (Forum angewandte Linguistik, 41), Frankfurt, Lang, 156 pp.; and U. Ammon, 'Sprachenpolitik in Europa — unter dem vorrangigen Aspekt von Deutsch als Fremdsprache', *DaF*, 40:195–209. German further afield features in L. Yéo, 'Fremdsprachen als Muttersprachen in Afrika — Chance oder Schande? Überlegungen zum Gebrauch von europäischen Idiomen als Verkehrs-, Literatur-, Unterrichts- und Amtssprachen im postkolonialen Afrika', *Muttersprache*, 113:328–40; M. A. Böhm, **Deutsch in Afrika. Die Stellung der deutschen Sprache in Afrika vor dem Hintergrund der bildungs- und sprachpolitischen Gegebenheiten sowie der deutschen auswärtigen Kulturpolitik* (Duisburger Arbeiten zur Sprach- und Kulturwissenschaft, 52), Frankfurt, Lang, 702 pp. Studies on language policy in Switzerland are: C. Ahokas, **Die Förderung der deutschen Sprache durch die Schweiz. Möglichkeiten und Einschränkungen* (Finnische Beiträge zur Germanistik, 8) Frankfurt, Lang, 193 pp.; **Living with Languages. The Contemporary Swiss Model*, ed. J. Charnley and M. Pender (Occasional Papers in Swiss Studies, 5), Frankfurt, Lang, 129 pp. Austrian German features in J. Grzega, 'Nonchalance als Merkmal des Österreichischen Deutsch', *Muttersprache*, 113:242–54; **Sprachenpolitik in Österreich. Eine Bestandsaufnahme*, ed. B. Busch and R. de Cillia, Frankfurt, Lang, 235 pp. Modern internal German trends are treated in F. Pfalzgraf, 'Recent developments concerning language protection organisations and right-wing extremism in Germany', *GLL*, 61:398–409, and **Deutsche Sprach- und Kommunikationserfahrungen zehn Jahre nach der "Wende"*, ed. G. Antos et al. (Wittenberger Beiträge zur deutschen Sprache und Kultur, 2), Frankfurt, Lang, 279 pp.

INTERDISCIPLINES

LEARNING AND TEACHING. H. W. Hess, 'Lerner als Kunden. Informationstechnologie im Alltagseinsatz', *DaF*, 40:14–23; G. Helbig, 'Kognitive Linguistik — Bemerkungen zu Anliegen und Ansätzen, zu Auswirkungen und Problemen (II)', *ib.*, 24–31;

R. Grotjahn, 'Der Faktor "Alter" beim Fremdsprachenlernen. Mythen, Fakten, didaktisch-methodische Implikationen', *ib.*, 32–41; J. Quetz, 'A1 — A2 — B1 — B2 — C1 — C2. Der gemeinsame europäische Referenzrahmen', *ib.*, 42–48; **Bilingualer Sachfachunterricht. Didaktik, Lehrer-/Lernforschung und Bildungspolitik zwischen Theorie und Empirie*, ed. S. Breidbach et al. (Mehrsprachigkeit in Schule und Unterricht, 1), Frankfurt, Lang, 2002, 276 pp.; J. Wenzel, '10 Jahre interDaF', *DaF*, 40:67–71; M. Hennig, '"Die hat doch Performanzschwierigkeiten." Performanzhypothese und Kompetenz(en)gegenthese', *ib.*, 80–86; E. Breindl and M. Thurmair, 'Wie viele Grammatiken verträgt der Lerner? Zum Stellenwert einer "Grammatik der gesprochenen Sprache" (nicht nur) für Deutsch als Fremdsprache', *ib.*, 87–93; N. Schumacher, 'Perspektiven für die Vermittlung von Tempusbedeutungen im Rahmen von DaF', *ib.*, 104–13; G. Liebscher, 'Ein Modell kooperativen Lernens für einen Fernlernkurs Deutsch als Fremdsprache', *ib.*, 135–40; B. Handwerker, 'Telizität im Deutschen — ein Lerngegenstand', ib., 141–47; G. Dietz, 'Zur Unterscheidung von "leichten" und "schweren" Regeln in der Zweitsprachenerwerbsforschung', *ib.*, 148–54; J. Möller Runge and R. Burbat, '"Collage": Sprachfragmente werden ein Gesamtwerk', *ib.*, 164–69; D. Blei, 'Aufgaben in einer konstruktivistischen Fernkultur', *ib.*, 220–27; B. Ahrenholz, 'Grammatik im Kontext von Zweitspracherwerbsforschung und Gesprochene-Sprache-Forschung', *ib.*, 228–32; I. Uzuegbu, **Ich kann nicht warten, eine "graduate" zu werden. Eine fehleranalytische Untersuchung schriftlicher Texte von Igbo Deutschlernenden mit Englisch als Zweitsprache* (Werkstattreihe Deutsch als Fremdsprache, 77), Frankfurt, Lang, 230 pp.; M. Niehoff, **Fremdsprachenlernen mit Multimedia. Anforderungen aus Sicht der Nutzerinnen. Eine qualitative Untersuchung zum selbstorganisierten Lernen* (Werkstattreihe Deutsch als Fremdsprache, 74), Frankfurt, Lang, 262 pp.; **Plurilingualität und Identität. Selbst- und Fremdwahrnehmung mehrsprachiger Menschen*, ed. I. De Florio-Hansen (StLi, 32), 198 pp.; **Deutsch als zweite Fremdsprache in Ostasien — neue Perspektiven*, ed. U. Wannagat et al. (Arbeiten zur angewandten Linguistik, 2), Tübingen, Narr, 230 pp.; **Didaktische Reflexionen. "Berliner Didaktik" und Deutsch als Fremdsprache heute*, ed. H. W. Hess (Arbeiten zur angewandten Linguistik, 3), Tübingen, Narr, 306 pp.; **Wissenschaftliches Schreiben im Deutsch als Fremdsprache*, ed. G. Starke and T. Zuchewicz (SST, 46), 132 pp.; D. Ohlinger, **Argumentation in der Erst- und Fremdsprache. Pragmalinguistische und grammatikalische Aspekte anhand von Argumentationen deutscher und litauischer Studierender* (Baltische Studien zur Erziehungs- und Sozialwissenschaft, 9), Frankfurt, Lang, 561 pp.; and I. Winkler, **Argumentierendes Schreiben im Deutschunterricht. Theorie und Praxis* (EH, XI, 890), 440 pp.

LANGUAGE AND LAW. H.-P. Schwintowski, 'Die Bedeutung interdisziplinären Arbeit von Rechts- und Sprachwissenschaft', *Muttersprache*, 113:1–14; C. Schendera, 'Verständlichkeit von Rechtstexten und ihre Optimierung', *ib.*, 15–22; C. Dern, 'Sprachwissenschaft und Kriminalistik', *ZGL*, 31:44–77; and E. Felder, 'Juristische Sprachnormierungskonflikte in Sitzblockadenentscheidungen', *LBer*, 194:153–82.

VARIOUS ASPECTS OF MEDICINE. U. Lürssen, **Untersuchung zum Wortschatz und phonologischen Gedächtnis bei Cochlear-Implant-versorgten Kindern* (Sprachentwicklung — Verlauf, Störung, Intervention, 4), Frankfurt, Lang, 298 pp.; **Neurokognition der Sprache*, vol. 1, ed. H. M. Müller and G. Rockheit, Frankfurt, Lang, vii + 368 pp.; M. Wenglorz, **Kreative Pathologie. Längsschnittliche Analyse der Lautproduktion eines autisch gestörten Mädchens, das nicht springt aber singt* (Sprachentwicklung — Verlauf, Störung, Intervention, 5), Frankfurt, Lang, 205 pp.; and T. Eitz, **AIDS. Krankheitsgeschichte und Sprachgeschichte* (Germanistische Linguistik, 12), Hildesheim, Olms, viii + 268 pp.

LANGUAGE AND GENDER. **Chancen und Grenzen des Dialogs zwischen den Geschlechtern. Beiträge zum 2. Tag der Frauen- und Geschlechterforschung an der Martin-Luther-Universität Halle-Wittenberg*, ed. E. Boesenberg, Frankfurt, Lang, 242 pp.

TRANSLATION STUDIES. M. Doherty, 'Topikalisierungsstrategien aus der Perspektive diskursadäquater Übersetzungen', *LBer*, 194:183–212; E. M. T. O'Connell, **Minority Language Dubbing for Children. Screen Translation from German to Irish* (EH, XL, 81), 211 pp.; **Linguistische Aspekte der Übersetzungswissenschaft*, ed. P. Colliander et al., Heidelberg, Groos, 258 pp.; and K. Kaindle, **Übersetzungswissenschaft im interdisziplinären Dialog. Am Beispiel der Comic-Übersetzung* (Studien zur Translation, 16), Heidelberg, Groos, x + 363 pp.

LANGUAGE AND BUSINESS. H. Ebert and M. Piwinger, '"Sie als Aktionär können sich freuen." Sprachstil und Imagearbeit in Aktionärsbriefen', *Muttersprache*, 113:23–35; R. Glahn, 'Unternehmenskommunikation: Geschäftsberichte des Jahres 2002', *ib.*, 36–50; M. Dannerer and G. Brunner, 'Wirtschaftskommunikation. Linguistische Analyse ihrer mündlichen Formen', *LBer*, 193:115–18; **Internationale Wirtschaftskommunikation auf Deutsch. Die deutsche Sprache im Handel zwischen den nordischen und den deutschsprachigen Ländern*, ed. E. Reuter and M.-L. Piitulainen (Nordeuropäische Beiträge aus den Human- und Gesellschaftswissenschaften, 23), Frankfurt, Lang, 416 pp.; and U. Kleiberger Günther, **Kommunikation in Betrieben. Wirtschaftslinguistische Aspekte der innerbetrieblichen Kommunikation* (ZGS, 57), 257 pp.

LANGUAGE AND LITERATURE. W. Mieder, '"Wir leben! Vor uns die Sintflut." Zu den sprichwörtlichen Aphorismen von Nikolaus

Cybinski', *Muttersprache*, 113:51–65; C. Bergmann, '"Hübsch" und "schön". Zum Wortgebrauch in Thomas Manns Roman *Die Bekenntnisse des Hochstaplers Felix Krull*', *ib.*, 66–76; C. Bergmann, '"Eine Herausforderung." Hans Castorp und Felix Krull im Schnittpunkt eines lexikalischen Vergleichs', *ib.*, 320–27; **Berührungsbeziehungen zwischen Linguistik und Literaturwissenschaft*, ed. M. Hoffmann and C. Kessler (SST, 47), 374 pp.; O. Havryliv, **Pejorative Lexik. Untersuchungen zu ihrem semantischen und kommunikativpragmatischen Aspekt am Beispiel moderner deutschsprachiger, besonders österreichischer Literatur* (Schriften zur deutschen Sprache in Österreich, 31), Frankfurt, Lang, 155 pp.; and V. Atabavikpo, **Sprichwörter im Volksmund und in der Literatur. Eine Studie über Sprichwörter in Sáxwe-Sprichwortliedern, im Roman 'Things Fall Apart' und in den Dramen 'Furcht und Elend des Dritten Reiches' und 'Die Gewehre der Frau Carrar' von Bertolt Brecht* (EH, I, 1868), 301 pp.

MEDIA. T. Kurzrock, **Neue Medien und Deutschdidaktik. Eine empirische Studie zu Mündlichkeit und Schriftlichkeit* (RGL, 239), ix + 335 pp.; H. K. Geissner and S. Wachtel, 'Schreiben fürs Hören. Aus dem Schreibtraining für Hörfunk- und Fernsehmoderatoren', *Muttersprache*, 113:193–207; T. Nehr, '"Hallo Karl-Josef, ich bin der 2.222 Besucher deiner Homepage." Linguistische Anmerkungen zum Umgang mit "Neuen Medien" in der politischen Kommunikation', *ib.*, 146–64; M. Soldo and C. Metzner, 'Gricesche Interaktionspostulate und Internetkommunikation', *ib.*, 165–80; S. Habscheid, 'Wie viel Rationalisierung verträgt die Sprache? Untersuchungen am Beispiel der Dienstleistungskommunikation', *ib.*, 208–24; R. Tenberg, 'Interaktionsformen und Neue Medien aus der Sicht des Fernlernens', *DaF*, 40:210–19; **Fachsprachenlinguistik, Fachsprachendidaktik und interkulturelle Kommunikation. Wirtschaft — Technik — Medien*, ed. J. Zhu and T. Zimmer (Angewandte Sprachwissenschaft, 12), Frankfurt, Lang, 289 pp.; and **Fachsprachen und Multimedia*, ed. F. Hebel et al. (Angewandte Sprachwissenschaft, 9), Frankfurt, Lang, 2002, 210 pp.

POLITICS. E. Ehtreiber, **Alles für Österreich. Das Bild Österreichs in den Regierungserklärungen der Zweiten Republik* (Sprache im Kontakt, 19), Frankfurt, Lang, 166 pp.; S. Pappert, **Politische Sprachspiele in der DDR. Kommunikative Entdifferenzierungsprozesse und ihre Auswirkungen auf den öffentlichen Sprachgebrauch* (Leipziger Arbeiten zur Sprach- und Kommunikationsgeschichte, 11), Frankfurt, Lang, 289 pp.; and **Sprache und politischer Wandel*, ed. H. Gruber et al. (Sprache im Kontext, 20), Frankfurt, Lang, 351 pp.

GENERAL LINGUISTICS, PRAGMATICS, AND TEXTLINGUISTICS

General studies include: J. Kuhlmann, **Angewandte Sprachwissenschaft in der Bundesrepublik Deutschland nach 1945* (TVS, 37), 348 pp.; I. Keim,

'Sprachvariation und sozialer Stil am Beispiel jugendlicher Migrantinnen türkischer Herkunft in Mannheim', *DSp*, 30, 2002:97–123; I. Bose, **Dóch da sín ja' nur mûster* II. *Kindlicher Sprechausdruck im sozialen Rollenspiel* (Hallesche Schriften zur Sprachwissenschaft und Phonetik, 9), Berlin, Lang, 437 pp.; R. Blankenhorn, **Pragmatische Spezifika der Kommunikation von Russlanddeutschen in Sibirien. Entlehnung von Diskursmarkern und Modifikatoren sowie Code-switching* (Berliner Slawistische Arbeiten, 20), Berlin, Lang, 263 pp.; **Diachronic Perspectives on Address Systems*, ed. I. Taavitsainen and A. H. Jucker (Pragmatics and Beyond, n.s., 107), Amsterdam, Benjamins, viii + 446 pp.; and H. J. Simon, **Für eine grammatische Kategorie 'Respekt' im Deutschen. Synchronie, Diachronie und Typologie der deutschen Anredepronomina* (LA, 474), xi + 236 pp.

Text studies include: E. Ockel, 'Vom hörenden Wahrnehmen — akustisch vermittelte Ästhetik des Textes', *Muttersprache*, 113:132–45; **Textallianzen am Schnittpunkt der germanistischen Disziplinen*, ed. A. Schwarz and L. A. Luscher, (Tausch — Textanalyse in Universität und Schule, 14), Berne, Lang, 570 pp.; **Textsorten und Textsortenvarianten*, ed. K.-E. Sommerfeldt (SST, 45), 117 pp.; M. Zirngibl, **Die fachliche Textsorte Bedienungsanleitung. Sprachliche Untersuchungen zu ihrer historischen Entwicklung* (RBDSL, 82), 262 pp.; **E-Text: Strategien und Kompetenzen. Elektronische Kommunikation in Wissenschaft, Bildung und Beruf*, ed. P. Handler (Textproduktion und Medium, 7), Frankfurt, Lang, 2001, ix + 315 pp.; **Vermittlungskulturen im Wandel. Brief — E-Mail — SMS*, ed. J. R. Höflich and J. Gebhardt, Frankfurt, Lang, 317 pp.; **Texttechnologie. Perspektiven und Anwendungen*, ed. H. Lobin and L. Lemnitzer, Tübingen, Narr, xxi + 480 pp.; **Sprachstil — Zugänge und Anwendungen. Ulla Fix zum 60. Geburtstag*, ed. I. Barz et al. (Sprache — Literatur und Geschichte. Studien zur Linguistik/Germanistik, 25), Heidelberg, Winter, xxviii + 380 pp.; M. Lisiecka-Czop, **Verstehensmechanismen und Lesestrategien von fremdsprachigen Fachtexten* (Danziger Beiträge zur Germanistik, 8), Frankfurt, Lang, 170 pp.; H.-S. Park, **Tempusfunktionen in Texten. Eine Untersuchung zu den Tempusfunktionen je nach Textsorte im Hinblick auf die Textrezeption und Textproduktion im Fremdsprachenunterricht* (Im Medium fremder Sprachen und Kulturen, 4), Frankfurt, Lang, x + 209 pp.; S. Stein, **Textgliederung. Einheitenbildung im geschriebenen und gesprochenen Deutsch: Theorie und Empirie* (SLG, 69), xxi + 479 pp.; and E. Felder, **Juristische Textarbeit im Spiegel der Öffentlichkeit* (SLG, 70), xii + 452 pp.

Discourse studies feature: **Gesprächsforschung. Tendenzen und Perspektiven*, ed. Z. Iványi and A. Kertész (Metalinguistica. Debrecener Arbeiten zur Linguistik, 10), Frankfurt, Lang, 2001, 260 pp.; S. Vater,

**Diskurs-Analyse-Intervention. Eine Methodologie der Diskursanalyse in illustrierten Redewendungen* (EH, XXII, 380), Frankfurt, Lang, 174 pp.; **Argumentieren in Gesprächen. Gesprächsanalytische Studien*, ed. A. Deppermann and M. Hartung (StLi, 28), 168 pp.; **Historical Dialogue Analysis*, ed. A. H. Jucker et al. (Pragmatics and Beyond, n.s., 66), Amsterdam, Benjamins, 1999, viii + 478 pp.; M. Wengeler, **Topos und Diskurs. Begründung einer argumentationsanalytischen Methode und ihre Anwendung auf den Migrationsdiskurs (1960–1985)* (RGL, 244), xiii + 573 pp.; S. Lee, **Chaos im Gespräch. Komplexitätstheoretische Betrachtung der chaotischen Gesprächsdynamik am Beispiel des Beratungsgesprächs* (EH, XXI, 252), 207 pp.; M.-S. Seo, **Direkt und Indirekt. Analyse des interkulturellen argumentativen Gespräches zwischen Deutschen und Koreanern* (Werkstatt Deutsch als Fremdsprache, 76), Frankfurt, Lang, 195 pp.; R. Branner, **Scherzkommunikation unter Mädchen. Eine ethnographisch-gesprächsanalytische Untersuchung* (Angewandte Sprachwissenschaft, 13), Frankfurt, Lang, xii + 381 pp.; S. Habscheid, **Sprache in der Organisation. Sprachreflexive Verfahren im systematischen Beratungsgespräch* (Linguistik — Impulse & Tendenzen, 1), Berlin, de Gruyter, 360 pp.; and **Wissenschaftlich schreiben — lehren und lernen*, ed. K. Ehlich and A. Steets, Berlin, de Gruyter, viii + 413 pp.

Contrastive studies include H. Kotthoff, 'Aspekte der Höflichkeit im Vergleich der Kulturen', *Muttersprache*, 113:289–06; and G. Rauh, 'Warum wir Linguisten "euch Linguisten", aber nicht "sie Linguisten" akzeptieren können. Eine personendeiktische Erklärung', *LBer*, 196:389–424.

2. History of Language

The tremendous work of the neogrammarians has had an overriding influence on studies of the history of the German language. Over a century after the first editions of the classical grammars the time has come for them to be revised. *Neue historische Grammatiken. Zum Stand der Grammatikschreibung historischer Sprachstufen des Deutschen und anderer Sprachen*, ed. A. Lobenstein-Reichmann and O. Reichmann (RGL, 243), xvi + 276 pp., contains contributions on revising these grammars and on general themes. O. Reichmann, 'Zur Schreibung historischer Grammatiken: einführende Bemerkungen' (VII-XVI) summarizes and reviews the conference. The general contributions are by V. Ágel, 'Prinzipien der Grammatik' (1–46), who wants to establish a dynamic grammar not bound by synchronicity and scriptism (reliance on the written word); T. Roelcke, 'Anforderungen des Typologen an Sprachstufengrammatiken des Deutschen'(47–58), for whom typological studies form a background to historical development; G. Zifonun, 'Sprachtypologische Fragestellungen in der gegenwartsbezogenen und der historischen Grammatik des Deutschen, am Beispiel des Relativsatzes' (59–85), who uses the modern language to view the parameters at different stages of historical development; V. M. Pavlov, 'Zur Entwicklung der Substantivdeklination im Deutschen' (87–109), who highlights the long term development emphasizing the switch to the importance of grammatical gender and the restitution of final *-e*. Then follow the articles by those revising the classic grammars: F. Heidermanns, 'Zur Neukonzeption der gotischen Grammatik' (111–22), who wants to expand the historical part and add word formation; H. Fix, 'Eine neue altisländische Grammatik auf Handschriftengrundlagen' (123–45), who flags up the need for a fresh study of the manuscripts; I. Reiffenstein, 'Zur Neubearbeitung der althochdeutschen Grammatik von Wilhelm Braune' (147–66), who wants to keep the familar structure but add a syntax section and drastically prune the older literature references; and H. Tiefenbach, 'Gedanken zur Bearbeitung einer Grammatik des Altsächsischen' (193–216), who discusses the problem of the sources, and the lack of a reliable dictionary, but realises that syntax and word formation just cannot be covered. The remaining contributions deal with OHG and MHG. The only author to deal in detail with OHG is R. Schrodt, 'Die Aporie der Deskription: Synchronie und Diachronie in der althochdeutschen Syntax' (167–91), who highlights the problem of describing grammatical constructions, not pushing syntactic/semantic differences too far in analysis. It is MHG that presents the most challenges. F. P. Knapp, 'Anforderungen eines Philologen an die neue *Mittelhochdeutsche Grammatik*' (217–30), looks at the whole problem of manuscripts and the accessibility of any grammar to literary scholars. He is in favour of a shortened, re-worked study edition of the classic MHG grammar and a larger linguistically aimed grammar. K.-P. Wegera, 'Grammatiken zu Sprachabschnitten. Zu ihren Grundlagen und Prinzipien' (231–40), treats such general topics as the size of the corpus and sets up principles of exactness (providing quantitively accurate statements of usage) and exhaustiveness (treating all the occurrences of a particular phenomenon). H.-P. Prell, 'Typologische Aspekte der mittelhochdeutschen Prosasyntax. Der Elementarsatz und die Nominalphrase' (241–56), highlights the neglect of MHG syntax and, using a specific corpus, treats the description of the basic sentence, which has both OV and VO features, and the noun phrase. An illustration from another language is provided by N. Cartagena, 'Leistung und Grenzen der traditionellen historischen Grammatik des Spanischen' (257–69).

The evergreen theme of the development of standard German written languages receives an airing in *Die deutsche Schriftsprache und die*

Regionen. Entstehungsgeschichtliche Fragen in neuer Sicht, ed. R. Berthele et al. (SLG, 65), viii + 285 pp. More theoretical contributions are: W. Haas, 'Die deutsche Schriftsprache und die Regionen — Die Regionen und die deutsche Schriftsprache' (1–3), who sets the scene and sketches the background, setting up the *Regionalmaxime*, i.e. region as a main factor in language use, as determining development in the period before 1500; W. Besch, 'Die Regionen und die deutsche Schriftsprache. Konvergenzfördernde und konvergenzhindernde Faktoren — Versuch einer forschungsgeschichtlichen Zwischenbilanz' (5–27), who emphasizes the antiregional role of the written language and discusses early statements on language variation in the German language area in some detail, setting up principles of how the *Regionalmaxime* became supraregional, with a differing timetable in different areas; O. Reichmann, 'Die Entstehung der neuhochdeutschen Schriftsprache: wo bleiben die Regionen?' (29–56), who uses the concept of 'Vertikalisierung', i.e the shift of primarily geographical variation to more social variation, to explain the development of the standard; E. Glaser, 'Zu Entstehung und Charakter der neuhochdeutschen Schriftsprache: Theorie und Empirie' (57–78), who devotes her attention to principles and exemplification of the relationship between manuscript and printed version in Augsburg; and A. Mihm, 'Schreibsprachliche und akrolektale Ausgleichsprozesse bei der frühneuzeitlichen Standardisierung' (79–110), who turns his attention to informal standardization in the pre-1500 period in the spoken language. He uses evidence from Duisburg sources to show how there is a development from 'top to bottom' with upper class linguistic behaviour being influential. There are also more data-driven contributions: N. R. Wolf, 'Gibt es althochdeutsche Sprachregionien? Oder: Warum gibt es keine althochdeutsche Schriftsprache?' (111–25), maintains that one can only talk about a region in the late Middle Ages; L. de Grauwe, 'Theodistik. Zur Begründung eines Faches und ein Plädoyer für eine kontinentalwestgermanische Sicht auf die neuzeitliche Bifurkation Deutsch/Niederländisch' (127–56), makes a plea for a discipline, *Theodistik*, which investigates all the varieties out of which both German and Dutch came; R. Peters, 'Ostmitteldeutsch, Gemeines Deutsch oder Hochdeutsch? Zur Gestalt des Hochdeutschen in Norddeutschland im 16. und 17. Jahrhundert' (157–80), shows how in the change of Low to High German there was a south-east to north-west spread with High German influencing eastern places such as Soest and Braunschweig, whereas it was Upper German which influenced the area from Cologne to Münster/Osnabrück; J. Macha, 'Regionalität und Syntax: Redewiedergabe in frühneuhochdeutschen Verhörprotokollen' (181–202), finds that use of subjunctive I or II was regionally conditioned. The south preferred subjunctive I whereas subjunctive II or a variable system of I and II characterized the north; T. Klein, 'Niederdeutsch und Hochdeutsch in mittelhochdeutscher Zeit' (203–29), demonstrates how LG authors followed the nearest HG when they translated their works; W. Hoffmann, 'Entregionalisierung im Kölner Buchdruck in den ersten Jahrzehnten des 16. Jahrhunderts?' (231–51), studies the decrease of regional forms in Cologne. After 1530 HG predominates but the printers had no real trend-setting function. Some printers, on the other hand, used deregionalized forms by 1509 and 1517. The later HG texts have a different reception audience with pilgrims coming from southern Germany; and G. Kettmann, 'Ostmitteldeutsch im 16. und 17. Jahrhundert (eine Standortbestimmung am Beispiel Wittenberg)' (253–72), shows how differentiated the language actually was. Scholars from different areas avoided regional forms and by the turn of the 17th c. there was a decrease in ECG forms and an increase in UG variables.

One of the scholars who has been instrumental in stimulating research on the development of standard German is W. Besch. His most important articles since 1961 have been collected together in *Deutsche Sprache im Wandel. Kleine Schriften zur Sprachgeschichte*, Frankfurt, Lang, 489 pp. This volume contains: 'Schriftzeichen und Laut. Möglichkeiten der Lautwertbestimmung an deutschen Handschriften des späten Mittelalters' (11–25); 'Zur Erschließung früheren Sprachstandes aus schriftlichen Quellen' (27–54); 'Zur Entstehung der neuhochdeutschen Schriftsprache' (55–75); 'Bemerkungen zur schreibsoziologischen Schichtung im Spätmittelalter' (77–90); 'Sprachnorm-Kompetenz des Bundestages? Das Beispiel der Handwerkernamen' (91–118); 'Dialekt als Barriere bei der Erlernung der Standardsprache?' (119–32); 'Zur Bestimmung von Regularitäten bei den sprachlichen Ausgleichsvorgängen im Frühneuhochdeutschen' (133–54); 'Einige Probleme empirischer Sprachforschung. Dargestellt am Beispiel des Erp-Projektes' (155–77); 'Sprachliche Änderungen in Lutherbibel-Drucken des 16.- 18. Jahrhunderts' (179–200); 'Zur Kennzeichnung sprachlandschaftlicher Wortvarianten im Duden-Wörterbuch und im Brockhaus-Wahrig' (201–20); 'Die Entstehung der deutschen Schriftsprache- Bisherige Erklärungsmodelle — neuester Forschungsstand' (221–56); 'Standardisierungsprozesse im deutschen Sprachraum' (257–84); ' ". . . und überhaupt die ganze Schreibart nach dem nun einmal in ganz Deutschland angenommenen Sprachgebrauche einzurichten" ' (285–308); 'Regionalität — Überregionalität. Sprachlicher Wandel zu Beginn der Neuzeit' (309–31); 'Martin Bucers deutsche Sprache. Beobachtungen zur Sprachform und zum Sprachstil' (333–60); 'Editionsprinzipien in interdisciplinärer Abstimmung. Annäherungen bei der Herausgabe deutscher Texte der frühen Neuzeit' (361–81); 'Hierarchie und Höflichkeit in der deutschen Sprache' (383–96); 'Wortschatzwandel in deutschen Bibeldrucken der frühen Neizeit' (397–412); '"...sein Licht (nicht) unter den Scheffel stellen"' (413–29); 'Wider den Stachel löcken (lecken)' (431–41); 'Zur sprachgeschichlichen Rolle Luthers' (443–57); 'Der *gemeine Mann* in Luthers Schriften' (459–79); and 'Variantentyp Hyperkorrektion' (481–86). Many of these articles were originally published in not very accessible places and it is good to have them all together in one place. B. not only pioneered work in this field but also initiated work by many other scholars. He has recently concentrated his research on Martin Luther, presenting a very positive picture of the latter's role in the history of German. The final article in the volume links up with the first in the fundamental question of the interpretation of written records. His dialectological work on Erp also finds its expression in one article. This volume is an important resource for libraries.

Sprachwissenschaft, 28, contains a number of articles on the development of a medical terminology in the history of German: J. Riecke, 'Über die volkssprachigen Anfänge des Schreibens über Körper, Krankheit, Heilung. Aspekte der Frühgeschichte der medizinischen Fachsprache im Deutschen' (245–71); J. G. Mayer and K. Goehl, 'Das Verhältnis der mittelalterlichen deutschen Kräuterbücher zu ihren lateinischen Quellen, dargestellt am "Älteren deutschen Macer", dem "Leipziger Drogenkompendium" (Leipzig UB, 1224) sowie dem "Gart der Gesundheit" (Mainz 1585)' (273–92); G. Hayer, Die deutschen *Problemata Aristotelis*' (293–311); L. Vanková, 'Der Anteil des Lateinischen als wichtiger Hinweis auf Autor und Adressat der medizinischen Fachprosa' (313–23); M. Habermann, 'Der Sprachenwechsel und seine Folgen. Zur Wissensvermittlung in lateinischen und deutschen Kräuterbüchern des 16. Jahrhunderts' (325–54). I. H. Warncke, 'Juristische Terminologisierung und Entterminologisierung zwischen 1500 und 1800. Zum Spannungsfeld Deutsch — Latein — Französisch in der deutschen Rechtsterminologie' (355–71).

A general volume on historical syntax is **Konnektoren im älteren Deutsch. Akten des Pariser Kolloquiums März 2002*, ed. Y. Desportes (GB, 15), 320 pp.

Germanic is represented by: H. Reichert, 'Personennamen bei antiken Autoren als Zeugnisse für die ältesten westgermanischen Endungen', *ZDA*, 132:85–100; and E. H. Antonsen, **Runes and Germanic Linguistics* (Trends in Linguistics. Studies and Monographs, 140), Berlin, de Gruyter, xxii + 380 pp.

Studies on Gothic include M. J. Jones, 'More on the "instability" of interdental fricatives: Gothic *þliuhan* "flee" and Old English *flêon* "flee" revisited', *Word*, 53, 2002:1–8; R. Woodhouse, 'Gothic *siuns*, the domain of Verner's Law and the relative chronology of Grimm's, Verner's and Kluge's Laws in Germanic', *BGDSL*, 125:207–222; M. Pierce, 'Prosody and Sievers' Law in Gothic', *ib.*, 223–41; and L. G. García, 'Valenzstruktur der gotischen Kausativa', *Sprachwissenschaft*, 28:374–94.

On OHG: D. Pasques, '"Ausdrucks- und Auslösungsfunktionen" der Nominalkomposita in Notkers Psalter', *Sprachwissenschaft*, 28:95–110; N. Kruse, 'Eine neue Schrift Notkers des Deutschen: der althochdeutsche Computus', *ib.*, 123–55; A. Gütter, 'Zur Chronologie des Primärumlauts von /a/ im Altoberdeutschen, vor allem im Altbairischen', *BGDSL*, 125:1–23; R. Froschauer, **Genus im Althochdeutschen. Eine funktionale Analyse des Mehrfachgenus althochdeutscher Substantive* (GB, 16), 529 pp.; and H. Eilers, **Die Syntax Notkers des Deutschen in seinen Übersetzungen: Boethius, Martianus Capella, Psalmen* (SLG, 336), 2002, 336 pp.

A sole MHG item is U. Bruchhold, 'Eine Admonter Konversenprofess? Zur Überlieferung und Pragmatik des deutschsprachigen Gelübdes (12. Jahrhundert) aus dem Benediktiner Stift Admont', *Sprachwissenschaft*, 28:157–93.

MLG is represented by *Mittelniederdeutsches Handwörterbuch*, vol. 2, fascs 29 and 30, *quâtdâdine — rêip*, Neumünster, Wachholtz, 2002, 1793–2048; and H. Weber, **Venlo — Duisburg — Essen. Diatopische Untersuchungen zu den historischen Stadtsprachen im 14. Jahrhundert* (Arbeiten aus dem Duisburger Graphemprojekt, 1), Heidelberg, Winter, xxxiv + 477 pp.

ENHG is as always well represented: *Flood Vol.* contains a number of contributions on the language of this period: P. Wiesinger, 'Das Frühneuhochdeutsche in Wien am Ende des Mittelalters' (747–71); J. West, 'Reassessing Serranus' (Jo(h)annes Serranus was a 16th-c. lexicographer) (773–91); I. H. Warncke, '"Consideryng that wordes ben perisshyng and writunges abide permanent' — Juristischer Wissenstransfer und kommunikativer Sprachwandel durch deutsche Rechtsspiegel des 15. und 16. Jahrhunderts' (793–816); N. McLelland, 'Schottelius, the notion of *Teutsch* and sleight of hand' (835–53); S. Watts, 'Caspar Stieler's false friends' (855–76); and W. J. Jones, 'From *aalbraun* to *zypressengrün*: German colour nomenclature during the modern period' (877–95). Items on Luther include: R. P. Ebert, 'Die Stellung des attibutiven Genitivs in Luthers Schriften', *Sprachwissenschaft*, 28:195–229; and T. Danilewitsch, **Zu den Complementizern dass und ob: Untersuchung im Neuhochdeutschen und in ausgewählten Schriften Luthers* (EH 1, 1843), 2002, ix + 209 pp. Also noted: U. Stelzel, **Aufforderungen in den Schriften Herzogin Elisabeths von Braunschweig-Lüneburg. Eine Untersuchung zum wirkungsorienten Einsatz der direktiven*

Sprachhandlung im Frühneuhochdeutschen (Documenta Linguistica, Studienreihe, 5), Hildesheim, Olms, x + 376 pp.

On the 17th and 18th cs we note: T. Roelcke, 'Die englische Sprache im deutschen Sprachdenken des 17. und 18. Jahrhunderts', *BGS*, 13:85–113; W. Dengler, **Johann Christoph Adelungs Sprachkonzeption* (EH, 1, 1866), 296 pp.; and C. Neis, **Anthropologie im Sprachdenken des 18. Jahrhunderts. Die Berliner Preisfrage nach dem Ursprung der Sprache (1771)* (SLG, 67), xiii + 656 pp.

On the 19th c.: W. Hüllen, 'Die Adaption von Rogets *Thesaurus* in Daniel Sanders' *Sprachschatz*', *Flood Vol.*, 897–919.

20th-c. items include **Das Deutsche Reich ist eine Republik. Beiträge zur Kommunikation und Sprache der Weimarer Zeit*, ed. H. D. Schlosser (Frankfurter Forschungen zur Kultur- und Sprachwissenschaft, 8), Frankfurt, Lang, 227 pp.; G. T. Horan, **Mothers, Warriors, Guardians of the Soul. Female Discourse in National Socialism* (SLG, 68), 350 pp.; and **Deutsche Sprachgeschichte nach 1945. Diskurs- und kulturgeschichtliche Perspektiven. Beiträge zu einer Tagung anlässlich der Emeritierung Georg Stötzels*, ed. M. Wengeler (Germanistische Linguistik, 169), Hildesheim, Olms, vi + 438 pp. A topical volume is P. Stevenson, *A Sociolinguistic History of East and West in Germany, 1945–2000*, OUP, 2002, 288 pp.

3. Orthography

The orthographic problems of German are further discussed again in: **Zur Reform der deutschen Rechtschreibung: Ein Kompromißvorschlag*, ed. Deutsche Akademie für Sprache und Dichtung, Darmstadt, Wallstein, 128 pp.; D. Nerius, 'Wie schreiben wir gegenwärtig? Stand und Probleme der Orthographiereform', *DaF*, 40:3–13; C. Stetter, 'Einige Bemerkungen zu Ideographie und Alphabetschrift', *ZS*, 21, 2002:82–97; J. Dittmann, 'Einige Probleme der deutschen Orthografie und Vorschläge zu ihrer Lösung', *Muttersprache*, 113:120–31; A. Wiebelt, 'Die Entwicklung der Symmetrie in der Schrift — Wie Objektkonstanz die Genese von Buchstabenformen beeinflusst', *LBer*, 195:295–324; D. Bernabei, **Der Bindestrich. Vorschlag zur Systematisierung* (Angewandte Sprachwissenschaft, 11), Berlin, Lang, 220 pp.; and K. Nettmann-Multanowska, **English Loanwords in Polish and German after 1945: Orthography and Morphology* (University of Bamberg Studies in English Linguistics, 45), Frankfurt, Lang, xv + 231 pp. Some historical issues feature in: G. Newton, '*Deutsche Schrift*: The demise and rise of German black letter', *GLL*, 56:184–211, and K. Rädle, **Die Entwicklung der Groß- und Kleinschreibung im Deutschen vor dem Hintergrund der Orthographiereformdiskussion des 19. Jarhunderts* (Sprache — Literatur und Geschichte, 24), Heidelberg, Winter, 247 pp.

4. Phonology

Phonetic and phonological items are: M. Neef and M. Neugebauer, 'Beschränkte Korrespondenz: zur Alternation von Schwa und silbischen Sonoranten im Deutschen', *ZS*, 21, 2002: 234–61; C. Ulbrich, 'Prosodische Aussprachebesonderheiten der deutschen, österreichischen und schweizerdeutschen Standardvarietät des Deutschen in gelesenen Äußerungen von Nachrichtensprechern', *DaF*, 40: 155–58; B. Primus, 'Zum Silbenbegriff in der Schrift-, Laut- und Gebärdensprache. Versuch einer mediumübergreifenden Fundierung', *ZS*, 22: 3–55; T. A. Hall and S. Hamann, 'Loanword nativization in German', *ib.*, 56–85; S. Rabanus, Intonation and syllable structure: a cross-linguistic study of German and Italian conversations', *ib.*, 86–122; R. Wiese, 'The unity and variation of (German) /r/', *ZDL*, 70: 25–43; C. Féry et al., '"Umlaut" in optimality theory. A comparative analysis of German and Chamorro', *LBer*, 193: 109–14; A. Kreuz, **Metaphonologische Fähigkeiten und Aussprachestörungen im Kindesalter* (Kölner Arbeiten zur Sprachpsychologie, 10), Frankfurt, Lang, 2000, 204 pp.

5. Morphology

Derivational morphology is the subject of G. Smith, **Phonological Words and Derivation in German* (Germanistische Linguistik, 13), Hildesheim, Olms, xiii + 236 pp.; J. Werner, '"Dankesgabe von seinen Dokoranten." Zur -and/ant und -end/ent-Konkurrenz im Deutschen', *Muttersprache*, 113: 355–64; H. U. Schmid, 'Zölibazis Lustballon. Wortverschmelzungen in der deutschen Gegenwartssprache', *ib.*, 265–78; A. Ogawa, 'Präfixverben im DaF-Unterricht', *DaF*, 40: 159–63; J. Meibauer, 'Phrasenkomposita zwischen Wortsyntax und Lexikon', *ZS*, 22: 153–88; H. Wegener, 'Entstehung und Funktion der Fugenelemente im Deutschen, oder: warum wir keine **Autosbahn* haben', *LBer*, 196: 425–58; G. A. Rich, **Partikelverben in der deutschen Gegenwartssprache mit durch-, über-, um-, unter, ab- an-*, Frankfurt, Lang, xi + 408 pp.; A. Feine, 'Fußballitis, Handyritis, Chamäleonitis: -itis Kombinationen in der deutschen Gegenwartssprache', *Sprachwissenschaft*, 28: 437–66; A. Klosa, '*gegen*-Verben — ein neues Wortbildungs-Muster', *ib.*, 467–94; and R. B. Maylor, **Lexical Template Morphology: Change of State and the Verbal Prefixes in German* (Studies in Language Commmunication, 58), Amsterdam, Benjamins, 2002, x + 273 pp.

Inflectional morphology features in I. Sonnenstuhl-Henning, **Deutsche Plurale im mentalen Lexikon. Experimentelle Untersuchungen zum Verhältnis von Speicherung und Dekomposition* (LA, 473), x + 199 pp.

6. Syntax

General items on various aspects of syntax include: **Dependenz und Valenz. Ein internationales Handbuch zur zeitgenössischen Forschung*, ed. V. Ágel et al., Vol. 1, Berlin, de Gruyter, xvi + 849 pp.; **Funktionale Syntax. Die pragmatische Perspektive*, ed. L. Hoffmann, Berlin, de Gruyter, 400 pp.; **Bibliographie zur deutschen Grammatik*, ed. H. Frosch et al. (SDG, 68), 506 pp.; U. Detges and R. Waltereit, 'Grammaticalization vs. reanalysis: A semantic-pragmatic account of functional change in grammar', *ZS*, 21, 2002: 151–95; T. Vierhuff et al., 'Effiziente Verarbeitung deutscher Konstituentenstellung mit der Combinatorial Categorial Grammar', *LBer*, 194: 213–38; **Funktion und Bedeutung. Modelle einer syntaktischen Semantik des Deutschen. Festschrift für François Schanen*, ed. D. Baudot and I. Behr (Eurogermanistik, 20), Tübingen, Narr, xi + 359 pp.; **Valency in Practice*, ed. A. Cornell et al. (German Linguistic and Cultural Studies, 10), Frankfurt, Lang, 279 pp.; and S. Miyake, **Aufbau der deutschen Sprache. Vom Standpunkt des Sprechers aus*, Frankfurt, Lang, 173 pp.

Sentences and clauses are dealt with in: R. Lühr, 'Konzeptionierungen des Prädikativums in der Indogermania', *ZS*, 21, 2002: 4–24; A. Holler-Feldhaus, 'Zur Grammatik der weiterführenden *w*-Relativsätze', *ZGL*, 31: 78–98; U. Schade, 'Relativsatzproduktion', *LBer*, 193: 33–56; K.-P. Konerding, **Konsekutivität als grammatisches und diskurs-pragmatisches Phänomen. Untersuchungen zur Kategorie der Konsekutivität in der deutschen Gegenwartssprache* (SDG, 65), 2002, vii + 362 pp.; and Y.-S. Yang, **Aspekte des Fragens. Frageäußerungen, Fragesequenzen, Frageverben* (Beiträge zur Dialogforschung, 24), Tübingen, Niemeyer, xi + 327 pp.

Features of nouns, noun phrases, and their members are treated in D. Bittner, 'Semantisches in der pronominalen Flexion des Deutschen', *ZS*, 21, 2002: 196–233. C. Dürscheid, '"Polemik satt und Wahlkampf pur" — Das postnominale Adjektiv im Deutschen', *ib.*, 57–81; R. Joeres, 'Noch einmal: *der Friede* oder *der Frieden?*', *Sprachwissenschaft*, 28: 231–38; B. Menzel, 'Genuserwerb im DaF-Unterricht', *DaF*, 40: 233–37; N. Fuhrhop, '"*Berliner*" *Luft* und "*Potsdamer*" *Bürgermeister*: zur Grammatik der Stadtadjektive', *LBer*, 193: 91–108; A. Ogawa, **Dativ und Valenzerweiterung. Syntax, Semantik und Typologie* (SDG, 66), ix + 254 pp.; and J. Ballweg, **Quantifikation und Nominaltypen im Deutschen* (SDSp, 28), 160 pp.

Features of verbs and verb phrase find treatment in: M. Hundt, 'Formen und Funktionen des Reflexivpassivs im Deutschen', *DSp*, 30, 2002: 124–66; A. Golato, 'Grammar and interaction: reported discourse and subjunctive in German', *ZS*, 21, 2002: 25–56; F.-J.

d'Avis and H. Lohnstein, 'Satzmodus — kompositionell. Zur Parametrisierung der Modusphrase im Deutschen', *LBer*, 196:501–06; M. Rödel, 'Die Entwicklung der Verlaufsform im Deutschen', *Muttersprache*, 113:97–107; B. Sieberg, 'Zur Unterscheidung der Tempuskategorien Perfekt und Imperfekt', *ib.*, 108–19; H. Weiss et al., 'Prätertumschwund und Diskursgrammatik', *LBer*, 193:119–24; I. Kaufmann, 'Das Verb "legen"', *ib.*, 195:375–82; L. Gunkel, **Infinitheit, Passiv und Kausativkonstruktionen im Deutschen* (SDG, 67), xii + 286 pp.; **Tempus/Temporalität und Modus/Modalität im Deutschen — auch in kontrastiver Perspektive*, ed. O. Leirbukt (Eurogermanistik, 18), Tübingen, Narr, xi + 258 pp.; **Aspekt und Aktionsarten im heutigen Deutsch*, ed. L. Gaudier and D. Haberkorn (Eurogermanistik, 19), Tübingen, Narr, vii + 230 pp.; **Arbeiten zur Reflexivierung*, ed. L. Gunkel et al. (LA, 481), vii + 304 pp.; and **Diathese, Modalität, Deutsch als Fremdsprache. Festschrift für Oddleif Leirbukt zum 65. Geburtstag*, Tübingen, Narr, iv + 266 pp.

Particles are dealt with in A. Molnár, **Die Grammatikalisierung deutscher Modalpartikeln. Fallstudien* (Metalinguistica, 12), Frankfurt, Lang, 2002, 129 pp.

Contrastive studies include the following: T. Oya, 'Überlegungen zu zwei Unterschieden zwischen der Mittelkonstruktion des Deutschen, Englischen und Niederländischen', *ZS*, 22:213–42; H.-M. Gärtner and M. Steinbach, 'What do reduced prominals reveal about the syntax of Dutch and German? Part 1: Clause-internal positions', *LBer*, 195:257–94, and 'Part 2: Fronting', *ib.*, 196:459–90; **Die kleineren Wortarten im Sprachvergleich Deutsch-Portugiesisch*, ed. H. Blühdorn and J. Schmidt-Radefeldt (Rostocker romanistische Arbeiten, 17), Frankfurt, Lang, 260 pp.; A. Pilarski, **Die Operation Merge im Verbalkomplex des Polnischen und des Deutschen* (Danziger Beiträge zur Linguistik, 4), Frankfurt, Lang, 163 pp.; J. Choe, **Adjektivphrasen im Deutschen und Koreanischen* (LA, 482), viii + 134 pp.; A. Frühwirth, **Strategies of Reflexivisation and the Meaning of Predicates. A Contrastive Study of English, German and French* (Aachen British and American Studies, 16), Frankfurt, Lang, xviii + 333 pp.; M. Ahn, **Wortartenzugehörigkeit der Kardinalzahlwörter im Sprachvergleich* (EH, XXI, 262), 203 pp.; and **Verb Constructions in German and Dutch*, ed. P. A. M. Seuren and G. Kempen (Current Issues in Linguistic Theory, 242), Amsterdam, Benjamins, vi + 316 pp.

Historical studies include M. L. Kotin, **Die werden-Perspektive und die werden-Periphrasen im Deutschen. Historische Entwicklung und Funktionen in der Gegenwartssprache* (Danziger Beiträge zur Linguistik, 6), Frankfurt, Lang, 180 pp.

7. Semantics

General items are: S. Löbner, **Semantik. Eine Einführung*, Berlin, de Gruyter, xv + 387 pp.; C. Römer and B. Matzke, **Lexikologie des Deutschen: eine Einführung* (Narr Studienbücher), Tübingen, Narr, 250 pp.; **Sinnformeln. Linguistische und soziologische Analysen von Leitbildern, Metaphern und anderen kollektiven Orientierungsmustern*, ed. S. Geideck and W.-A. Liebert (Linguistik — Impulse & Tendenzen, 2), Berlin, de Gruyter, 300 pp.; and H. Schemann, *'*Kontext'* — *'Bild'* — *'idiomatische Synonymie' mit einer Darstellung der Synonymie in der deutschen Idiomatik* (Germanistische Linguistik: Monographien, 14), Hildesheim, Olms, xii + 337 pp.

Phraseology is treated in **Europhras 2000. Internationale Tagung zur Phraseologie vom 15.–18. Juni in Aske/Schweden*, ed. C. P. Meister (StLi, 25), 545 pp.

Lexicography continues to feature largely with *Untersuchungen zur kommerziellen Lexikographie der deutschen Gegenwartssprache* 1, ed. H. E. Wiegand (Lexicographica Series Maior, 113), Tübingen, Niemeyer, xii + 463 pp., which contains a plethora of contributions: W. Martin, 'Definitions and collocations in dictionaries: the *GWDS* compared to the *Van Dale Groot Woordenboek der nederlandse Taal*' (3–23); A. J Fraczek, 'Das *GWDS* und das *Slownik Jezyka Polskiego*, 2. Aufl. 1996–1997' (25–36); F.-J. Hausmann, 'Das *GWDS* und *Le Grand Robert de la langue française*' (37–45); M. T. Fuentes Morán, 'Das *GWDS* und das *Diccionario del Espanol actual*' (47–59); G. Rovere, 'Das *GWDS* und der *Grande dizionario italiano dell'uso (GDU)*' (61–80); H. Bergenholtz, 'Die Entwicklung der Lemmaselektion' (83–97); M. Schlaefer, 'Die Entwicklung der Wörterbuchbasis' (99–107); S. Nielsen, 'Changes in dictionary subject matter' (109–14); P. O. Müller, 'Das *Grosse Duden-Fremdwörterbuch* und das *GWDS*: ein Vergleich' (115–23); P. Kühn, 'Das *Duden-Universalwörterbuch* und das *GWDS*: ein Vergleich' (125–65); N. Weber, 'Bedeutungsparaphrasenangaben zu den nennlexikalischen Lemmazeichen im *GWDS*' (169–84); T. Roelcke, 'Ausmaß und Rolle von Synonymangaben in den semantischen Kommentaren des *GWDS*' (185–95); G. Augst, 'Die Rolle von Wortfamilien in den semantischen Kommentaren des *GWDS*' (197–217); F. Geeb, 'Diatechnische Markierungen im *GWDS*' (209–17); U. Ammon and M. Schlossmacher, 'Nationale und regionale Varianten im *GWDS*: Übersicht und Kritik' (221–31); J. Ebner, 'Die Lexik des österreichischen Deutsch im *GWDS*' (233–43); H. Bickel and L. Hofer, 'Die Lexik des schweizerischen Deutsch im *GWDS*' (245–57); N. R. Wolf, 'Elemente der gesprochenen Sprache im *GWDS*' (259–66); N. Fries, 'Gefühlswortschatz im *GWDS*' (267–82); K.-D. Ludwig, 'Die Lexik der Sprache der ehemaligen

DDR im *GWDS*' (283–92); H. Kämper, 'Rechtlich relevante Lexik im *GWDS*' (293–301); W. Müller, 'Wörter und Bezeichnungen für Sexuelles im *GWDS*' (303–16); J. Kubczak, 'Die Grammatik der Verben im *GWDS*' (319–36); S. J. Schierholz, 'Die Grammatik der Substantive im *GWDS*' (337–52); J. E. Mogensen, 'Die Grammatik der Adjektive im *GWDS*' (353–74); R. Hessky, 'Movierung im *GWDS* — deskriptive und normative Aspekte' (375–82); I. Barz, 'Affixe im *GWDS*' (383–93); E. Schafroth, 'Kollokationen im *GWDS*' (397–412); and W. Mieder, 'Sprichwörter im *GWDS*' (413–36). The *GWDS* has established itself and will represent a benchmark for dictionaries for some years. 29 contributors in 31 contributions devote detailed studies to comparisons with other dictionaries and with investigation of aspects of its microlexicography. H. E. Wiegand, the editor, emphasizes that the commercial aspect of lexicography is not something negative but is a positive contribution to a general cultural background of dictionary use.

H.-D. Kreuder, *Metasprachliche Lexikographie* (Lexicographica Series Maior, 114), Tübingen, Niemeyer, x + 271 pp., traces the history of dictionaries of linguistics against their social and historical background, concentrating on those published between 1967 and 1990. He then examines theoretical aspects of metalinguistic lexicography, treating the definitions and structure of articles. He shows how there are gaps in the coverage of terms. As an example he surveys the treatment of *freie Angabe* from valency theory in 19 dictionaries. The result is not satisfactory, six dictionaries have no entry and four only an entry with its meaning as used by H. Glinz. Many aspects, e.g. pronunciation, etymology, foreign equivalents, antonyms, etc. do not occur. K. then makes a plea in future work for the target group to be made clear, also which aspects of linguistics are being covered, e.g. generative syntax or general topics, for clearer definitions and exemplification, and for good cross-referencing. All this leads to the necessity of team work. While the discussion of principles and history is good, the exemplification is on a rather meagre basis. Also one major consideration is almost entirely lacking, that of whether there should be a corpus of works underlying any dictionary. This is a challenging and timely work. Linguists should be very careful before burdening lexicographers with new word creations!

Also noted: G. Harras and K. Proost, 'Strategien der Lemmatisierung von Idiomen', *DSp*, 30, 2002: 167–83; and **Wissenschaftliche Lexikographie im deutschsprachigen Raum*, ed. T. Städtler, Heidelberg, Winter, xii + 548 pp.

Foreign words are the subject of J. Grabowski, 'Fremdsprachige Fachbegriffe in deutschen Texten. Systematische Probleme und Lösungsmöglichkeiten, aufgezeigt an einem Beispiel', *DSp*, 30,

2002:184–91; E. O'Halloran, 'Scheinentlehnungen in der deutschen Modesprache', *Muttersprache*, 113:225–41; H. P. Althaus, *Zocker, Zoff & Zores. Jiddische Wörter im Deutschen*, Munich, Beck, 2002, 159 pp., and Id., *Kleines Lexikon deutscher Wörter jiddischer Herkunft*, Munich, Beck, 216 pp. **Eurospeak. Der Einfluss des Englischen auf europäische Sprachen zur Jahrtausendwende*, ed. R. Muhr and B. Kettemann (Österreichisches Deutsch — Sprache der Gegenwart, 1), Frankfurt, Lang, 2002, 236 pp.; **Internationalismen* II. *Studien zur interlingualen Lexikologie und Lexikographie*, ed. P. Braun et al. (RGL, 246), Tübingen, Niemeyer, vi + 297 pp.; and D. N. Yeandle, '"Handy callboy seeks evergreen dressmann for flipper fun" or "pseudo-anglicisms" in Modern German', *Flood Vol.*, 955–82.

Historical studies include a pioneering work by A. Burkhardt, *Das Parlament und seine Sprache. Studien zu Theorie und Geschichte parlamentarischer Kommunikation* (RGL, 241), xiii + 608 pp. B. covers an amazing amount of ground. He sets the scene for his study by examining seven different types of parliament from 1848 onwards which have used different types of linguistic behaviour. However, all of them have a central function of reflecting the power struggle between executive and legislative. He then goes on to cover political language and communication, of which parliamentary language is a part. Parliament is also an institution so institutional linguistics comes into play. Even the shape of the parliamentary chamber plays a semiotic role. Parliamentary communication and the media is examined. In chapter 7 B. reaches the exemplification of parliamentary language with an investigation of the debate in 1982 which signalled the transition from Helmut Schmidt's government to Helmut Kohl's. He examines such topics as key-words, metaphors, allusions, the play on proper names, and forms of address. He then continues to treat two exemplary debates, one in the Paulskirche, Frankfurt am Main, in 1848 and the debate about the move to Berlin in 1991. Finally he deals with the linguistic sources, the stenographic reports of the proceedings and how they have been changed from direct to indirect speech. There is an index of names, with politicians italicized, and topics. All in all this is a fascinating book for both linguists and scholars interested in politics and history.

Another important work is T. Gloning, *Organisation und Entwicklung historischer Wortschätze. Lexikologische Konzeption und exemplarische Untersuchungen zum deutschen Wortschatz um 1600* (RGL, 242), ix + 471 pp., which aims to present the history of vocabulary in a new way. G. treats vocabulary in a dynamic way, embracing a much wider range of lexical phenomena than the traditional word. He starts with speech acts and how they are realized. His theoretical framework is elaborated in chapter 2, while chapters 3 and 4 form the main exemplification of his approach. The positive side to his approach is that it is based on texts which range from 1500 to 1677, 1600 is thus really a mean date. He treats these historical texts according to communicative tasks and lexical means, thematic vocabulary and semantic fields, text types and their lexical profile, frames and communicative acts, apocalyptic vocabulary and presentient knowledge, foreign words, and finally, obsolescence and innovation. The treatment of foreign words is then dealt with according to their contemporary view of foreign words, their functional and thematic use, their role in individual lexical areas (e.g. military), their conditions of use and their immediate and continued use, first and early attestations, and the languages that play a role in borrowing. Further, Turkish words are taken as an actual example. The insights gained by this approach are deeper than some approaches and the emphasis is synchronic, treating all the words at that time, not just those that have survived to the present. The downside is that the work needs a detailed index of words. This is rather a utopian demand, given the size of the volume, but in an ideal world would have made the work much more user-friendly. The system of cross-references in the structure of texts is treated in chapter 4. These had their hey-day in the 16th and 17th cs but declined after that. The connection with the whole topic is that of the history of elements in texttypes. This is a stimulating work and shows how little we know about the vocabulary of Early NHG.

Also noted: D. Brückner, **Geschmack. Untersuchung zu Wortsemantik und Begriff im 18. und 19. Jahrhundert. Gleichzeitig ein Beitrag zur Lexikographie von Begriffswörtern* (SLG, 72), xi + 431 pp.; D. Felbick, **Schlagwörter der Nachkriegszeit*, Berlin, de Gruyter, xii + 602 pp.; and R. Keller and I. Kirschbaum, **Bedeutungswandel. Eine Einführung*, Berlin, de Gruyter, ix + 168 pp.

Individual words are treated in M. Egbert, 'Die interaktionelle Relevanz einer gemeinsamen Vorgeschichte: zur Bedeutung und Funktion von *übrigens* in deutschen Alltagsgesprächen', *ZS*, 22:189–212; B. Paraschkewow, 'Nhd. *kitzeln*: ein Germanismus oder ein Indogermanismus?', *ZGL*, 31:105–08; and E. Grab-Kempf, 'Zur Etymologie von dt. *Wismuth*', BGDSL, 125:197–206.

Contrastive studies include: P. Storjohann, **A Diachronic Contrastive Lexical Field Analysis of Verbs of Human Locomotion in German and English* (EH, XXI, 260), 265 pp.; J. Parad, **Biblische Verbphraseme und ihr Verhältnis zum Urtext und zur Lutherbibel. Ein Beitrag zur historisch-kontrastiven Phraseologie* (Danziger Beiträge zur Germanistik, 5), Frankfurt, Lang, 251 pp.; and M. Plominska, **Farben und Sprache. Deutsche und polnische Farbbezeichnungen aus kontrastiver Sicht* (Danziger Beiträge zur Germanistik, 7), Frankfurt, Lang, 208 pp.

8. Dialects

General items include: R. Möller, 'Zur diatopischen Gliederung des alltagsprachlichen Wortgebrauchs. Eine dialektometrische Auswertung von J. Eichhoff: *Wortatlas der deutschen Umgangssprachen* (Bd. 1–4; 1977, 1978, 1993, 2000)', *ZDL*, 70:259–97; G. Grober-Glück, **Beiträge zur sprachliche Volkskultur. Nach Materialien des Atlas der deutschen Volkskunde* (GASK, 43), 316 pp.; and S. Wilking, **Der Deutsche Sprachatlas unter dem Nationalsozialismus. Studien zu Dialektologie und Sprachwissenschaft zwischen 1933 und 1945* (Germanistische Linguistik, 173), Hildesheim, Olms, viii + 269 pp.

There are several items on individual dialectologists: V. Hellfritsch and H. Steinmüller, 'Der Dialektologe Emil Gerbet (1867–1919)', *ZDL*, 70:1–24; E. Weider, 'Marthe Philipp zum 80. Geburtstag', *ib.*, 52–54; H. J. Dingeldein, 'Reiner Hildebrandt zum 70. Geburtstag', *ib.*, 325–33.

Low German features in quite a number of publications: T. A. Francis, 'Perceptions of Low German to Schottelius: a chronological overview and review', *Flood Vol.*, 817–34; B. Kellner, **Zwischen Anlehnung und Abgrenzung. Orthographische Vereinheitlichung als Problem im Niederdeutschen* (Sprachgeschichte, 7), Heidelberg, Winter, 2002, 367 pp.; F. W. Michelsen, **Plattdeutsche Bibliographie. Verzeichnis der in den Jahren 1945 bis 1970 selbständig erschienen plattdeutschen Schriften und Tonträger* (Schriften des Instituts für niederdeutsche Sprache, 23), Leer–Hamburg, Schuster, 2002, 352 pp.; **Studien zum Ostfälischen und zur ostfälischen Namenlandschaft*, ed. D. Stellmacher (Veröffentlichungen des ostfälischen Instituts der Deuregio Ostfalen, 4), Bielefeld, Vlg für Regionalgeschichte, 2001, 95 pp.; W. Beckmann, **Suppletion im Niederdeutschen* (NdS, 47), 2002, xiv + 210 pp.; and R. Schophaus, **Zur Lautentwicklung im Hiat in den westfälischen Mundarten* (NdS, 48), xviii + 250 pp.

There are a few items on West and East Central German: K.-H. Mottausch, 'Die Flexion des Adjektivs in den Mundarten um Lorsch. Systematik und Vorgeschichte', *ZDL*, 70:129–54; Id., **Das Verb in der Mundart von Lorsch und Umgebung* (DDG, 95), 2002, xii + 102 pp.; A. N. Lenz, **Struktur und Dynamik des Substandards. Eine Studie zum Westmitteldeutschen (Wittlich/Eifel)* (*ZDL* Beiheft, 125), Stuttgart, Steiner, 443 pp.; M. Selting, 'Treppenkonturen im Dresdenerischen', *ZGL*, 31:1–43; and **Beiträge zur Dialektforschung in Thüringen 2001*, ed. W. Lösch, Jena–Quedlinburg, Bussert & Stadeler, 2001, 143 pp.

On Upper German, general studies include J. M. Denton, 'Rhotic articulation and the early UG gemination of *r', *BGDSL*, 124, 2002:385–410, and G. Seiler, **Präpositionale Dativmarkierung im Oberdeutschen* (*ZDL* Beiheft, 124), Stuttgart, Steiner, 283 pp.

Swiss German is the subject of *Gömmer MiGro? Veränderungen und Entwicklungen im heutigen Schweizerdeutschen*, ed. B. Dittli et al. (Germanistica Friburgensia, 18), Fribourg U.P., 261 pp., which was produced to celebrate the 75th birthday of P. Dalcher, a veteran editor of the *Schweizerisches Idiotikon.* The volume contains the following contributions: H.-P. Schifferle, 'Schweizerdeutsch in seiner lexikographischen Erfassung. Brüche, Neuansätze im Wortschatz' (7–23); H. Christen, '*Uu fein, welts guet* und *rüüdig schöön.* Überlegungen zu lexikalischen Aspekten eines Schweizerdeutsch der Regionen' (25–38); E. Glaser, 'Schweizerdeutsche Syntax. Phänomene und Entwicklungen' (39–66); B. Siebenhaar, 'Variation im heutigen Schweizerdeutschen. Analysemethoden, Befunde und Interpretationen der Entwicklungen in den Regionen Aarau und Basel im Vergleich' (67–83); R. M. Kully, 'Neue Entwicklungen in den deutschschweizerischen Orts- und Flurnamen' (85–109); U. Fischer, 'Sprachen aus verschiedensten Ländern einer unheilen Welt. Sprachbegegnungen in der deutschen Schweiz im Umfeld von anerkannten Flüchlingen' (113–22); F. Rash, 'Die Entwicklung des Schweizerdeutschen aus angelsächsischer Sicht' (123–30); R. Watts, 'Flexibilität oder Sterilität? Englische Entlehnungen im Schweizerdeutschen und ins schweizerische Standarddeutsch' (131–40); R. Schmidlin, 'Vergleichende Charakteristik der Anglizismen in den standardsprachlichen Varietäten des Deutschen' (141–60); A. Rowley, 'Zur Wörterbucharbeit an einem süddeutschen Dialekt — aus der Sicht des Englischen' (161–70); L. Hofer, 'Dialektmusik und Subkultur' (173–92); C. Schmid, '"Bach- und Wöschtag." Deutschschweizer Mundartliteratur am Ende des 20. Jahrhunderts' (193–204); H. J. Kupper, '"Überlupfe." Schweizerdeutsche Übersetzungsliteratur aus dem Englischen' (205–22); P. von Matt, 'Schweizerdeutsch als Literatursprache?' (223–37); K. Schnidrig, 'Sprache und Persönlichkeit. Vorvernissage für den ersten Band einer wissenschaftlichen Buchreihe' (241–54); and 'Verzeichnis der sprachwissenschaftlichen Publikationen von P. Dalcher' (257–60). This book covers a great variety of topics and themes. It shows how linguistic identity through the use of Swiss German is very much alive and well.

Also noted: A. Kraehenmann, **Quantity and Prosodic Asymmmetries in Alemannic. Synchronic and Diachronic Perspectives* (Phonology and Phonetics, 5), Berlin, de Gruyter, xii + 262 pp., and F. Rash, 'Opening and closing rituals in Swiss German', *Flood Vol.*, 941–54.

Bavarian items include **Bairisch in Bayern, Österreich, Tschechien. Michael-Kollmer-Gedächtnis-Symposium*, ed. A. Wildfeuer and L. Zehetner (Regensburger Dialektforum, 1), Regensburg, Vulpes, 2002, 306 pp.; U. Kanz, **Drent und herent. Bayerisches und östrreichisches Bairisch in der Region Burghausen-Hochburg-Ach* (Regensburger

Dialektforum, 2), Regensburg, Vulpes, 2002, 258 pp.; E. H. Antonsen, 'Bairisch *uns/ins* und die Doppelentwicklung von Wurzelmorphem', *HSp*, 115, 2002: 308–12; C. Maiwald, **Das temporale System des Mittelbairischen. Synchrone Variation und diachroner Wandel* (Schriften zum Bayerischen Sprachatlas, 6), Heidelberg, Winter, 2002, 163 pp.

Speech islands and multilingual situations are treated in **Die Siebenbürgischen Landler. Eine Spurensicherung*, ed. M. Bottesch et al., Vienna, Böhlau, 2002, 967 pp.; C. Földes, 'Dialektalität und Variation des Deutschen unter Mehrsprachigkeitsbedingungen', *ZDL*, 70: 177–92; A. Plewnia, **Sätze, denen nichts fehlt. Eine dependenzgrammatische Untersuchung elliptischer Konstruktionen. Am Beispiel des mitteldeutschen Dialekts des Ermlands* (Germanistische Linguistik, 11), Hildesheim, Olms, vi + 206 pp.; H. Tyroller, **Grammatische Beschreibung des Zimbrischen von Lusern* (*ZDL* Beiheft, 111), Stuttgart, Steiner, 291 pp.

DIALECT DICTIONARIES. General principles are treated in J. Fournier, 'Vorüberlegungen zum Aufbau eines Verbundes von Dialektwörterbüchern', *ZDL*, 70: 155–76. Completed dictionaries are: *Wallisertitschi Weerter. Walliser Wörterbuch*, vol. 1, ed. A. Grichting, Brig, Radio Rottu Oberwallis–Walliser Bote, 1999, 303 pp.; **Oberharzer Wörterbuch. Die Mundart der Oberharzer Sprachinsel*, ed. K.-H. Weidemeier, vol. 7, *U — Z*, Clausthal-Zillerfeld, Schriftenreihe des Oberharzer Geschichts- und Museumsvereins, 2002, 404 pp.; **Wörterbuch der donauschwäbischen Landwirtschaft*, ed. H. Gehl (Schriftenreihe des Instituts für donauschwäbische Geschichte und Landeskunde, 12), Stuttgart, Steiner, 1122 cols; and W. Lösch, **Dialektwörterbuch von Biberschlag im Thüringer Wald*, Berlin, Dyck & Westerheide, 2002, 278 pp. The following dictionaries continue on their way: *Brandenburg-Berlinisches Wörterbuch*, vol. 3, fasc. 5 *tun — Verzierung*, Berlin, Akademie, 1998, cols 513–640, fasc. 6, *verzischen — weiß*, 1999, 641–768; *Preußisches Wörterbuch*, vol. 1, fasc. 5, *Backeber — Beiert*, Neumünster, Wachholtz, 2002, cols 513–640, fasc. 6, *Beiertag — beziepsen*, 2002, cols 641–768, fasc. 8, *Bornbalken — Bulle*, 2003, cols 893–1024; *Schweizerisches Idiotikon*, vol. 16, fasc. 206, *Fëder-Ge-wand — Ober-Wind*, Frauenfeld, Huber, 2002, cols 385–512, fasc. 207, *Ober-Wind — wunderig*, 2002, cols 513–640; *Südhessisches Wörterbuch*, vol. 6, fasc. 21, *U-Wesen*, Marburg, Elwert, 2002, cols 1–480; *Hamburgisches Wörterbuch*, fasc. 21, *möten* — orn(t)lich, Neumünster, Wachholtz, 2003, cols 385–640, fasc. 22, *Örn(t)lichkeit — Püttenfeger*, cols 641–896; *Niedersächsisches Wörterbuch*, vol. 6, fasc. 7, *in — Instmann*, Neumünster, Wachholtz, cols 769–928; *Westfälisches Wörterbuch*, vol. 2, fasc. 6, *düt — Ende*, Bielefeld, Vlg für Regionalgeschichte, 2002, pp. 133–264; *Wörterbuch der bairischen Mundarten in Österreich*, vol. 5, fasc. 4, *(Dach)tropfen — Tschischkel*, VÖAW, cols 577–768.

The following atlases continue publication: **Sprachatlas von Oberösterreich*, ed. S. Gaisbauer and H. Scheuringer, fasc. 6, maps 159–204, Linz, Adalbert-Stifter-Institut des Landes Oberösterreich, 2002; and **Südwestdeutscher Sprachatlas*, ed. U. Knoop et al., fasc. 7, 48 maps, Marburg, Elwert.

9. Onomastics

General items are: V. Blanar, **Theorie des Eigennamens. Status, Organisation und Funktionieren der Eigennamen in der gesellschaftlichen Kommunikation* (Germanistische Linguistik, 164), Hildesheim, Olms, 2002, 208 pp.; A. Weste, 'Wahl und Funktion von E-Mail-Adressen. Onomastische Betrachtungen zu einem jungen Namenstypus', *Muttersprache*, 113:307–19; S. Oelkers, **Naming Gender. Empirische Untersuchungen zur phonologischen Struktur von Vornamen im Deutschen* (EH, 1, 1870), 315 pp.; R. Köster, **Eigennamen im deutschen Wortschatz. Ein Lexikon.* Berlin, de Gruyter, 196 pp.

Forenames and personal names are treated in W. Seibicke, **Historisches Deutsches Vornamenbuch. Sc-Z*, Berlin, de Gruyter, xv + 540 pp.; V. Kohlheim, 'Bremer Rufnamen im späten Mittelalter', *BNF*, 38:249–61; H. E. H. Lenk, **Personennamen im Vergleich. Die Gebrauchsformen von Anthropymen in Deutschland, Österreich, der Schweiz und Finnland* (Germanistische Linguistik, Monographien, 9), Hildesheim, Olms, 2002, xvi + 490 pp.; R. Schrimpf, **Vornamengebung in Braunschweig 1871–1945* (Braunschweiger Beiträge zur Geschichte der deutschen Sprache und Literatur, 6), Bielefeld, Vlg für Regionalgeschichte, 2002, 206 pp.; D. L. Gold, 'Real or fictitious people whose names have come to designate their publications and, in some cases, similar publications too (English, French, German, Italian, Portuguese, and Spanish)', *Sprachwissenschaft*, 28:111–21; E. Pieciul, **Literarische Personennamen in deutsch-polnischer Translation. Eine kontrastive Studie aufgrund von ausgewählten Prosawerken von Thomas Mann* (Danziger Beitrâge zur Germanistik, 5), Frankfurt, Lang, 251 pp.; and A. Warner, 'Familiennamen deutscher Forscher für physikalisch-technische Maßeinheiten. Ohm — Siemens — Hertz — Weber — Gauß — Röntgen — Clausius', *Muttersprache*, 113:341–58. Also noted: T. Lénárd, **Der ostgermanische Aspekt in der Frühgeschichte des Volksnamens 'deutsch'*, Vienna, Praesens, 2002, xii + 127 pp.

A major work on Swiss placenames is the detailed lexicon of the *Thurgauer Namenbuch. Die Siedlungsnamen des Kantons Thurgau*, ed. E. Nyffenegger and O. Bandle, Frauenfeld, Huber, 2 vols, 1445 pp. This volume contains several contributions: U. Moor, 'Der Kulturraum Thurgau' (11–33); E. Nyffenegger, 'Zur Geschichte des Thurgauer Namenbuches' (35–48); Id., 'Kleine Einführung in die

Namenkunde' (71–99); J. de Luca, 'Die Sammlung der historischen Namen' (49–69); O. Bandle, 'Ortsname und Siedlungsgeschichte. Zur Schichtung der thurgauischen Ortsnamen' (101–26); and M. H. Graf, 'Siedlungswüstungen im Kanton Thurgau aus namenkundlicher Sicht' (127–62). The entries contain dialect variants of the name together with its interpretation, medieval recordings, and its possible etymology. This is a beautifully produced book with a number of maps. What is striking is the financial support given to the project both locally and nationally. An example to be followed! Also noted: **Südhessisches Flurnamenbuch*, ed. H. Ramge et al. (Arbeiten der Hessischen Historischen Kommisssion, n.F., 23), Darmstadt, Hessische Historische Kommisssion, 2002, 1024 pp.; **Perspektiven der thüringischen Flurnamenforschung*, ed. E. Meinecke, Frankfurt, Lang, 288 pp.; R. Harnisch, 'Zum Ortsnamen Liebengrün', pp. 10–12 of *Festschrift zur 625-Jahrfeier des Marktfleckens Liebengrün 1377–2002*, ed. by the Gemeinde Liebengrün, 2002; V. Hellfritzsch, 'Schadeneck. "Burg"-Namen im Umkreis der Stadt Altdorf im Vogtland', pp. 395–98 of *Methodische Vielfalt Im Dienste der historischen Landeskunde. 40 Beiträge zur Archäologie, Mittelalterforschung und Museumsarbeit vornehmlich in Sachsen. Festgabe für Gerhard Billig zum 75. Geburtstag*, ed. R. Aurig et al., Beucha, Sax, 2002, 532 pp.; P. Glasner, **Die Lesbarkeit der Stadt. Kulturgeschichte der mittelalterlichen Straßennamen Kölns*, Cologne, DuMont, 2002, 480 pp.; and K.-H. Mottausch, 'Was uns der Name "Lorsch" erzählt', *Geschichtsblätter Kreis Bergstraße*, 34, 2001 : 27–34.

MEDIEVAL LITERATURE

By Nigel W. Harris, *University of Birmingham*, Linda Archibald, *Liverpool John Moores University*, and Will Hasty, *University of Florida**

I. General

A Companion to Philosophy in the Middle Ages, ed. Jorge J. E. Gracia and Timothy B. Noone (Blackwell Companions to Philosophy, 28), Malden MA, Blackwell, xx + 739 pp., is a valuable and well organized guide to this massive subject. It begins with a series of chapters on the historical context (covering topics such as the School of Chartres, Scholasticism, and the religious orders), and then presents articles of appropriately varying length on some 138 thinkers. Many of these will be of interest to Germanists, not least those on Albertus Magnus (by R. Dreyer), Eckhart (J. A. Aertsen), Hildegard von Bingen (B. Milem), and Nicolaus Cusanus (L. Dupré and N. Hudson).

Aderlass und Seelentrost. Die Überlieferung deutscher Texte im Spiegel Berliner Handschriften und Inkunabeln, ed. Peter Jörg Becker and Eef Overgaauw, Mainz, von Zabern, xiii + 473 pp., is a remarkably handsome and richly illustrated volume designed to accompany an exhibition organized in Berlin and then Nuremberg between June 2003 and February 2004. The aim of the event was to use the outstanding MS collection of the Staatsbibliothek zu Berlin — Preussischer Kulturbesitz, along with exhibits from a few other libraries, to illustrate the extraordinary range of literary production in medieval Germany. Accordingly, both exhibition and catalogue consist of some 12 sections, ranging from early glosses through numerous works of imaginative and religious literature, legal and other specialized texts, and chronicles, to early printed books. Elucidatory material for all 211 entries is provided by a team of experts, and there are longer articles by E. Overgaauw and R. Bresler on the Staatsbibliothek's MS acquisitions before and after 1945 (1–12), by B. Braun-Niehr and J. Ott on ways of reading illuminated MSS (13–26), and by H. Nickel on the influence of printing on German literature (446–59).

Das Mittelalter, 7, 2002, contains several studies of medieval MS culture, and in particular the role of scribes. J. Wolf (92–109) surveys attitudes towards both the contents and the physical appearance of

* Linda Archibald is primarily responsible for the sections on 'Germanic and Old High German' and 'Early Middle High German'; Will Hasty for the books covered under 'Middle High German Heroic Literature', 'The Courtly Romance', and 'Lyric Poetry'; and Nigel Harris for the articles covered under these sections, all of the remaining sections, and the co-ordination and editing of the contribution as a whole.

books evinced in various scriptoria; M. J. Schubert (125–44) constructs a typology of scribal interventions; K. O. Seidel (145–56) discusses the value of colophons as indicators of scribal self-consciousness and self-assessment; C. Fasbender (110–24) considers recent research on the MS workshop of Diebolt Lauber, focusing especially on the role of its scribes; and M. Baisch (74–91) discusses the decidedly interventionist scribal practices of Gabriel Sattler, who wrote numerous MSS for Johann Werner d.Ä. von Zimmern (1423–83).

Several new studies discuss and demonstrate the considerable potential of regionally-oriented literary historiography. Perhaps the most striking example is Ralf G. Päsler, *Deutschsprachige Sachliteratur im Preußenland bis 1500. Untersuchungen zu ihrer Überlieferung* (Aus Archiven, Bibliotheken und Museen Mittel- und Osteuropas, 2), Cologne, Böhlau, 452 pp. This is the first serious attempt to document and characterize literary activity within Prussia as a whole between approximately 1250 and 1500. P. bases his work on descriptions of some 114 relevant MSS from the region which transmit vernacular works of a not primarily theological or belletristic nature. These reveal a notable predominance of legal texts, though works of a historiographical and medical orientation are also well represented. The accompanying chapters analysing the development of these genres show perhaps above all how misguided it is to equate the literary culture of medieval Prussia in general with that of the Teutonic Order in particular. This is true not least with regard to legal texts, many of which seem for example to have been geared towards protecting secular urban interests against the claims of the Order.

Many interesting new perspectives on regionally-based literary history are found also in Tervooren, *Literaturgeschichtsschreibung*, which contains, along with studies of particular texts, a number of more general articles. H. Tervooren (7–30) discusses the possibilities of writing a medieval literary history of the Rhine-Maas region, including a case study of the differing reactions of lyric as against narrative poets to impulses from France around 1200; C. Kirschner (57–73) examines the differing priorities of historiography written in medieval Cleves as against Geldern; B. Bastert (74–80) seeks to account for the greater popularity of Charlemagne in the vernacular literature of North and Central, as against Southern Germany; H. Freytag (81–101) sketches various aspects of the literary history of medieval Lübeck; C. Fasbender (143–57) examines ways in which MHG poets constructed their own version of a literary region (in this case Thuringia); N. F. Palmer and H.-J. Schiewer (178–202) outline a research project aimed at describing the literary profile of the

Alemannic region in the 14th c., with special reference to MS transmission; F. Löser (245–65) considers how one might write a history of MHG religious literature which emphasized the role of specific towns (such as Würzburg) and monasteries (such as Melk); and H. Brunner (308–12) pleads for an encyclopaedia of MHG literary history which would promote understanding of its regional dimensions, not least by providing articles on individual courts, monasteries, towns, universities, and scribes. Elsewhere Haustein, *JIG*, 34.2, 2002:164–80, further explores the literary history of medieval Thuringia; Tervooren, *Fest. Honemann*, 277–93, discusses what literature is likely to have been read in Lower Rhenish towns in the 15th and 16th cs; H. Endermann, *Flood Vol.*, 173–93, shows the importance of Nikolaus von Bibra's *Carmen satiricum* for students of the literary (and social) history of Erfurt; and M. Backes, *OGS*, 31, 2002:1–16, argues, on the basis of a study particularly of the Alemannic area, that the reception of French literature in medieval Germany depended less on geographical proximity to France than on the effectiveness of networks of social and literary communication. Meanwhile F. Fürbeth, *Das Mittelalter*, 7, 2002:125–46, investigates the role of episcopal cities (especially Würzburg and Constance) in the production and reception of vernacular literature; and N. Staubach, Lehmann-Benz, *Schnittpunkte*, 19–40, surveys the literary production of the 'Devotio moderna', which he characterizes as a 'textual community'. More generally, T. Bein, Schiewer, *Forschungsberichte*, 9–53, discusses various aspects of the theory and practice of literary historiography; and in *JIG*, 34.2, 2002:89–104, he also surveys recent research on the nature of textuality, authorship, and MS transmission in the Middle Ages. In the same volume M. Baisch (105–25) problematizes the concept of a 'work' in relation to medieval literature.

Roloff, *Editionsverfahren*, contains several articles on editorial theory and practice of interest to Germanists. These include Roloff himself on the methodology and influence of Karl Lachmann (63–81), and A. Corbillari on those of Joseph Bédier (83–121). Moreover M. Thumser (265–86) discusses the editing of medieval historical sources, and W. Ott (329–55) various relevant applications of information technology. D. Pravida, *Gabler Vol.*, 43–52, also examines Lachmann's method, comparing in particular his *Nibelungenlied* edition to Richard Bentley's 1732 text of *Paradise Lost*; and in the same volume N. H. Ott (113–26) discusses the role of illustrations as sources of non-verbal commentary in MSS of the *Sachsenspiegel*, *Willehalm*, Seuse's *Exemplar*, and Otto von Passau's *Vierundzwanzig Alten*. In *Editio*, 17, J. Heinzle (1–15) defines and problematizes the concepts of reconstruction, linguistic standardization, and MS variants in editions of MHG literature; and M. Springeth and M. E. Dorninger (207–20) update their critical bibliography of publications on the editing of MHG texts, this time covering 2000 and 2001.

Monika Schulz, *Beschwörungen im Mittelalter. Einführung und Überblick*, Heidelberg, Winter, 184 pp., is if anything an even more ambitious project than Verena Holzmann's 2001 catalogue of charms (see *YWMLS*, 63:617). Like Holzmann, S. prints a large quantity of these short pieces, but offers rather more explication and analysis, and categorizes them not by form, but by subject-matter. Successive chapters deal with charms against the demonic worm, wounds, bleeding, fever, gout, epilepsy, eye disease, and lameness, as well as for horses and the safe delivery of children; and each category is further sub-divided according to particular motifs or historiolae. An introductory chapter on the power of the magical word completes a particularly well-conceived and worthwhile volume. In *LiLi*, 130, V. Holzmann (25–47) surveys and interprets various examples of magic spells in OHG and MHG texts, and D. Faraci (48–71) analyses the German charm against worms found in the 13th-c. Codex Vaticanus Pal. Lat. 1227.

Meinolf Schumacher, *Ärzte mit der Zunge. Leckende Hunde in der europäischen Literatur. Von der patristischen Exegese des Lazarus-Gleichnisses (Lk. 16) bis zum 'Romanzero' Heinrich Heines* (Aisthesis Essay, 16), Bielefeld, Aisthesis, 87 pp., fills a gap in research, and does so admirably. It is the first detailed survey of the numerous literary appearances of the motif of the healing properties of a dog's tongue — generally compared to one aspect or another of human speech. S. focuses on, amongst other things, the use of canine metaphors in the construction of both positive and negative images of preachers, the lasting influence of the biblical image of dogs licking Lazarus's wounds, and various ways in which a dog's licking was creatively contrasted with its barking or biting. The vast majority of his examples are medieval; inevitably, most are taken from Latin literature (in which S. is extraordinarily well versed), but he also makes appropriate references to vernacular authors such as Hugo von Trimberg, Der Meissner, and Heinrich der Teichner.

Dichterbilder von Walther von der Vogelweide bis Elfriede Jelinek, ed. Frank Möbus and Friederike Schmidt-Möbus, Stuttgart, Reclam, 206 pp., is an arresting large-format volume which presents full-page portraits of some 90 German authors, each accompanied by a page of interpretative commentary. It includes pictures of Walther von der Vogelweide (from the Codex Manesse), Oswald von Wolkenstein (from MS B), and Sebastian Brant (the portrait by Hans Burgkmair

d. Ä). The texts discussing Walther and Oswald are by G. Dicke, that on Brant by M. Schnyder.

2. Electronic Media

Deutsche Literatur im Mittelalter. Geschichte — Kultur — Gesellschaft (Digitale Bibliothek, 88), Berlin, Directmedia, 1 CD-ROM, contains electronic versions of some five DTV volumes: the standard three-volume history of medieval German literature (by Dieter Kartschoke for the early, Joachim Bumke for the high, and Thomas Cramer for the later Middle Ages), and Bumke's classic two-volume work *Höfische Kultur*. The disc is very easy to install, use, search, and print from; and the quality of the scholarship in the writings offered is enormously high. These factors, along with the disc's commendably low price (cheaper than the five volumes in book form), make it strongly recommendable to specialist and non-specialist alike.

Sigrid Krämer, *Scriptores codicum medii aevi. Ein Katalog von Schreibern mittelalterlicher Handschriften aus der Zeit um 500 bis ins 16. Jahrhundert*, Augsburg, Rauner, 1 CD-ROM, is potentially one of most useful research tools to have appeared for a long time. K.'s database, built up over a period of some 40 years, contains 33,000 entries listing scribal names culled from MSS, MS catalogues, and secondary literature. It also includes the corpus published between 1965 and 1982 by the Benedictines of Bouveret. Sadly, however, the review copy could not be successfully loaded on to any of the three (normally reliable) computers in which it was tried. Elsewhere R. Giel, *MJ*, 38:291–93, introduces the 'Manuscripta mediaevalia' database <http://www.manuscripta-mediaevalia.de>, which, as he stresses, amounts to a searchable digitized library of MS catalogues; G. Giertz, *ZDA*, 132:421–23, describes a project to digitize rubbings of blind tools from the bindings of 15th-c. and 16th-c. books kept in the principal libraries of Berlin, Stuttgart, and Wolfenbüttel <http://www.hist-einband.de/projekt.shtml>; and H. T. M. van Vliet, *Fest. Gärtner*, 269–88, discusses some possibilities and problems of electronic editions.

3. Germanic and Old High German

Bernhard Maier, *Die Religion der Germanen. Götter — Mythen — Weltbild*, Munich, Beck, 206 pp., examines a good range of historical and literary references to the religion of Germanic peoples, whilst admitting that the definition of both 'Religion' and 'Germanen' in this context is problematic. Citations from Roman historians including Caesar and Tacitus vilify the Germanic tribes in accordance with contemporary views of barbarians generally, whilst later evidence, including almost every literary piece such as the *Heliand* and the *Edda*, are to be seen as attempts either to promote or resist the advance of Christianity. More modern interpretations by Jacob Grimm, Wagner, and the movement known as 'neugermanisches Heidentum' are shown to be misguided attempts to create a mythology to rival Classical traditions. In summary, the author warns against the temptation to indulge in 'speculative reconstruction' when hard evidence is scarce.

The Continental Saxons from the Migration Period to the Tenth Century. An Ethnographic Perspective, ed. D. H. Green (Studies in Historical Archaeology, 6), Woodbridge, Boydell and Brewer, 393 pp., provides a number of useful essays on the scant historical, archaeological, and even geological evidence which indicates the early history of the Saxon peoples. It highlights the unified structures of Frankish society in contrast to the more flexible allegiances of the Saxons. A paper on Saxon legislation (G. Ausenda, 113–19) is followed by a lively discussion (119–31) about runes and early alphabets, and how far these can constitute evidence for literacy. Green himself (247–63) examines three aspects of the *Heliand*: the delivery mode is described as 'paraliturgical'; the pagan concept of fate is replaced by the Christian notion of providence; and there is a repudiation of the warrior ethos in favour of a more passive acceptance of suffering.

Tineke Looijenga, *Texts and Contexts of the Oldest Runic Inscriptions* (The Northern World, 4), Leiden, Brill, xiii + 383 pp., lists and describes nearly all of the older fuþark inscriptions from the period AD 150 to AD 700, and researches their use, spread, and purpose. This exhaustive study concentrates less on Scandinavian examples and more on the Germanic, or — as L. prefers — 'continental' corpus from England, the Netherlands, Denmark, and Germany, and seeks to trace connections with Greek/Etruscan as well as Latin origins. L. argues that in the early phase objects were inscribed in order to express ownership or prestige, and that only much later does the influence of MS culture become evident. Elsewhere R. Schützeichel, *Fest. Honemann*, 27–29, finds traces of OHG in an erotic 7th-c. runic inscription from Bülach.

Roswitha Wisniewski, *Deutsche Literatur vom 8. bis 11. Jahrhundert* (GL, 28), 372 pp., is a thorough and readable overview presented in three chronological sections: pre-800, 800–900, and 900 until the time of Williram. Within each section the content is arranged by genre, which results in some topics such as glosses and legal texts appearing in a somewhat fragmented format. The author strikes a good balance between description of the major texts and discussion of critical works. Informative summaries of historical events are provided, along with clear contextualization of the pieces. There is very little quotation from OHG and Latin originals, and these small extracts are heavily edited. Everything comes with a modern German translation. This makes the book much more accessible, though also less authentic, than Schlosser's classic *Die literarischen Anfänge der deutschen Sprache* of 1977 (see *YWMLS*, 39:624), which it aims to replace.

Wolfgang Beck, *Die Merseburger Zaubersprüche* (IMA, 16), 454 pp., is a distillation of the secondary literature on these perplexing short items. It rests heavily on Jacob Grimm and the older scholars, but covers also an eclectic mix of later work from many discipline areas. There is exhaustive word-by-word commentary covering all the old debates on the MSS and etymology of disputed words, including the names 'Balderes' and 'Phol', followed by some thematic discussions of genre, function, reception, and religion. Though there are few new insights in this monograph, it is a balanced and useful summary of the field. In addition H. Eichner and R. Nedoma, *Die Sprache*, 42, 2000–01[2003]:1–195, provide a detailed linguistic and literary commentary on the *Zaubersprüche*, preceded by a critical edition of the poems, and by discussion of their date, phonology, structure, and possible lexical parallels with a song from the *Atharva Veda*. This latter question is addressed also by two other contributions in the volume, by A. Griffiths (196–210) and by Eichner (211–33).

Notker der Deutsche von St. Gallen. Lateinischer Text und althochdeutsche Übersetzung der Tröstung der Philosophie (De consolatione philosophiae) von Anicius Manlius Severinus Boethius. Diplomatische Textausgabe, Konkordanzen und Wortlisten, ed. Evelyn Scherabon Firchow with Richard Hotchkiss and Rick Treece, 3 vols, Hildesheim, Olms, xlviii + 1778 pp., is a monumental contribution to Notker studies. It represents the culmination of some 30 years of editorial work on the four main MSS, presenting for the first time a true diplomatic edition which pays as much attention to the Latin variants as to Notker's interspersed Alemannic dialect sections. The 165-year history of Notker editions is complex, and the introduction spells out the weaknesses in the early editions, not least the strange habit of printing the OHG text as if it were a single entity, and the failure to adopt systematic editorial processes. The introduction clarifies with great precision the rigorous method adopted for this three-volume effort, and the concordances are an invaluable reference aid for future scholars. The use of bold and normal text to distinguish the Latin from the German, though more a product of the computer age, is a very helpful tool to modern readers struggling with the bilingual presentation and the plethora of glosses and notes.

Christopher Schlembach, *Wort Raum Heil. Architektur, Übersetzung und Unterricht im frühen Mittelalter: Notker Labeos 'Consolatio' (2. Buch)*, Vienna, Praesens, 207 pp., sets out to be an empirical investigation of the syntax and semantics of Notker's translation, though it focuses on only five poetic and two prose sections. There are passing references to Foucault, Eliade, Bourdieu, and McLuhan, but also some useful insights in the more traditional domains. It traces literary, architectural, and religious themes, and demonstrates how the Irish-Scottish tradition, with its love of bilingualism, reinstates the binary opposition of Latin and vernacular which had become somewhat blurred in the context of late Latin and early Romance languages.

Helge Eilers, *Die Syntax Notkers des Deutschen in seinen Übersetzungen. Boethius, Martianus Capella und Psalmen* (SLG, 66), xvi + 302 pp., presents a thorough analysis of the Boethius and Martianus Capella texts, and of about one third of the Psalms (Psalms 21–70 inclusive). The author demonstrates that Notker's technical virtuosity as a translator is intended to promote understanding of the content of these works, rather than simple manipulation of the Latin and vernacular languages, or training in rhetorical methods. The additions to the originals (particularly the Christian interpretations added to the Psalms) lean on patristic examples, such as Augustine, and reflect an emergent OHG to EMHG tendency towards verbal rather than nominal constructions, active rather than passive mood, and a more concrete and personal focus to the narrative. A brief comparison with Tatian, Isidore, Williram, and Otfrid is made, but there is no attempt to trace chronological development in translation theory from these isolated surviving texts.

Also on Notker, N. Kruse, *Sprachwissenschaft*, 28:123–55, reports on the exciting recent discovery of an 11th-c. fragment of what is plainly an OHG *Computus* by him in the archives of the former monastery of Isny (OSB). K. edits the fragment, compares it to the equivalent passage in Notker's Latin *Computus* (the end of which the fragment also transmits), and analyses its language. In the same volume D. Pasques (95–110) examines the compound nouns coined in Notker's Psalter, arguing that they perform either an interpretative, or an evaluative, or a hypostatic function; and, using the example of a passage from his *Categoriae*, E. Hellgardt and H. Saller, *Gabler Vol.*, 313–29, suggest an editorial approach to Notker's works which would make them more accessible to a non-specialist readership. Elsewhere in *Sprachwissenschaft*, 28, E. Glaser (1–27) outlines a set of criteria for differentiating between various forms of OHG entries (including glosses) in Latin MSS; R. Bergmann (29–55) discusses the implications of the fact that much glossography of the OHG period was essentially monolingual (i.e. in Latin), with only a sprinkling of

German words; and H. Tiefenbach (57–85) edits and interprets the OS glosses to Prudentius's *Psychomachia* in Paris, BNF, Cod. lat., 18554 (10th c.), and suggests that the MS belonged to the Abbey of St Mihiel in Lorraine as early as the 11th century. Furthermore, N. Wagner (87–94) argues that the word 'frono' in the OHG *Würzburger Markbeschreibung B* should be rendered 'dominicus' or 'dominicalis'; and J. Rieck (245–71) examines aspects of the vocabulary of OHG medical texts.

On women authors, S. Gäbe, *AKG*, 85:437–69, re-examines the use of modesty topoi in the works of such writers as Hugeburc von Heidenheim and Hrotsvit von Gandersheim, problematizing the idea that this reflects the direct influence of misogynistic discourses; J. K. Schulmann, *GN*, 34:13–26, argues that Hrotsvit's presentation of Christian martyrs shows that she knew the *Heliand*; and both C. Cardelle de Hartmann, *Gabler Vol.*, 137–47, and R. Finckh and G. Diehl, *Fest. Honemann*, 53–72, discuss Conrad Celtis's 1501 edition of Hrotsvit's works and its instrumentalization of her as a cultural icon. Meanwhile J. M. Jeep, *Mediävistik*, 14, 2001[2003]:95–123, surveys the various roles played by women in OHG literature.

In an introductory article, P. Scardigli, *JIG*, 34.2, 2002:598–74, lists the OE, Old Icelandic, and OHG poems which feature alliterative rhyme, and suggests various lines of research into this field. In the same volume U. Groenke (75–86) problematizes the idea that alliterative and end rhyme are mutually exclusive, taking Notker's *De arte rhetorica* as one of his examples; and R. D. Fulk and K. E. Gade (87–186) provide a thorough bibliography of work on Germanic alliterative metres, including a section on OHG. Other articles on OHG include C. Búa's reflections (*BGDSL*, 125:24–35) on the forms 'ero', 'stein', and 'liuhta', as they appear in the *Wessobrunner Schöpfungshymnus*; M. Stolz's discussion (*Fest. Gärtner*, 511–34) of the text and function of the *Wessobrunner Gebet* in the context of its MS; J. L. Flood's analysis (*ib.*, 289–314) of the lexical field of 'to answer' in the OHG *Tatian*; and H.-J. Schiewer's contention (*Fest. Honemann*, 73–88), that some of the *Cambridge Songs* (not least *De Heinrico*) bear witness to an 'adaptatio clericalis', a Latinization of orally transmitted vernacular literature. Finally C. L. Gottzmann, *ZDP*, 122:1–19, re-examines the traditional view that the *Hildebrandslied* is about kinship and vassalage, depicting Hildebrand's departure from family and nation as a pragmatic and defensible action in the face of an unworthy lord.

Ruodlieb, con gli epigrammi del Codex Latinus Monacencis 19486. La formazione e le avventure del primo eroe cortese, ed. and trans. Roberto Gamberini (SISMEL, Per Verba, 19), lxxx + 203 pp., makes this late Latin verse poem accessible to readers of Italian. The introduction explains the difficulties of dealing with a fragmentary text, and situates it neatly within the epic and courtly traditions, highlighting its significance to both Germanic and Romance literature. The edition itself presents a synthesis of all previous, mostly German, editorial contributions, with textual variations in the footnotes and useful endnotes indicating sources and a few references to the secondary literature.

4. Middle High German

GENERAL. Michael Graf, *Mittelhochdeutsche Studiengrammatik. Eine Pilgerreise*, Tübingen, Niemeyer, 304 pp., is a student-oriented grammar of MHG with a difference. It differs from its predecessors not least in that it describes the language of, and draws its examples from, a discrete corpus of ten narrative texts, of which the earliest is *Erec* and the latest Konrad von Würzburg's *Pantaleon*. It is also unusual, however, in its consistent focus on helping the student to translate from MHG; and, more controversially, in being organized according to the conceit of a pilgrimage, complete with pictures, cultural-historical excursuses, and even a guide in the form of a character called Tragemund. These features, along with G.'s informal, droll, and sometimes self-indulgent style will doubtless attract some students and put off others. The actual grammatical material, however, is full and well presented, and is supported by good introductions to the history of the German language and to the tools of a medievalist's trade, as well as by an excellent bibliography and index.

Helmut Birkhan, *Geschichte der altdeutschen Literatur im Licht ausgewählter Texte, Teil III: Minnesang and Sangspruchdichtung der Stauferzeit; Teil IV: Romanliteratur der Stauferzeit* (Edition Praesens Studienbücher, 8–9), 2 vols, Vienna, Praesens, 271, 277 pp., are the texts of lectures given by B. in 2002–03. The first of these volumes begins with an introduction to courtliness and chivalry and general remarks about 'Minnesang' (melodies, MSS, form, personal experience versus social conventions), and then considers examples of the love lyric from the early poets to Ulrich von Liechtenstein. Only a brief section (152–65) is devoted to political and didactic poetry, specifically to the 'Sangspruchdichtung' of Walther von der Vogelweide. The second volume divides the romances into the 'matière de Rome' (Heinrich von Veldeke's *Eneit*), and the 'matière de Bretagne'. This latter section (52–250) concentrates on Hartmann, Wolfram, Gottfried, and their relationships to their sources.

Timo Reuvekamp-Felber, *Volkssprache zwischen Stift und Hof. Hofgeistliche in Literatur und Gesellschaft des 12. und 13. Jahrhunderts* (KGS, n.s., 4), viii + 414 pp., explores the role played by clerics and monks in the production of the courtly-chivalric literature of the high Middle Ages. R.-F. questions the traditional view of this literature as a manifestation of cultural emancipation on the part of the noble laity and argues, following the general direction of the research of C. Stephen Jaeger, for an appreciation of the constitutive role played by clerics and monks in its production. The relationship of clerics and monks to noble courts remained — and this insight is the specific contribution made by R.-F.'s study — dynamic and open-ended. Historical evidence suggests that religious men generally remained at courts only on a temporary basis, which had implications for the production of court literature that have yet to be fully considered.

Elsewhere Jaeger himself (*Speculum*, 78:1151–83) problematizes the concept of the 'Twelfth-Century Renaissance' by showing that the age's historiography, intellectual life, poetry, and ideas about love were permeated by a sense of pessimism and decline; and W. M. Sprague, *ABäG*, 58:93–122, re-evaluates the evidence suggesting the reception of Andreas Capellanus in MHG literature.

Bertelsmeier-Kierst, *Umbruch*, contains 18 essays on a wide variety of topics pertaining to 13th-c. medieval writing in the vernacular. In addition to those referred to below, D. H. Green (1–22) explores terminological aspects of hearing and reading; C. Bertelsmeier-Kierst herself (23–44) argues for a more rigorous cultural contextualization of German court literature; E. C. Lutz (45–72) considers the heuristic value of illuminations of authors represented in situations of complex communication; P. Kern (175–93) examines the reception of Ovid's *Metamorphoses* in German poetry of the 13th c.; K. Ridder (221–48) studies anger, affect, and physical force in medieval German epics and romances; B. Schnell (249–65) surveys 13th-c. German literature as a whole; and F.-J. Holznagel (291–306) presents a typology of shorter verse narratives of the 13th century.

A similar sense of the 13th c. as a time of profound cultural change is one of the preoccupations that inform Walter Haug, *Die Wahrheit der Fiktion. Studien zur weltlichen und geistlichen Literatur des Mittelalters und der frühen Neuzeit*, Tübingen, Niemeyer, xii + 708 pp. This volume reproduces — often in significantly revised form — no fewer than 39 essays published by H. since 1994, along with a substantial introduction and a new piece about 'Innerlichkeit', corporeality, and language in Mechthild von Magdeburg and Elsbeth von Oye. Partly because it culls the essence of a relatively short period of intensive research, the book is more cohesive than many of its type. The range of topics covered is admittedly very wide, with much on 'Blütezeit' narratives and on Eckhart, but also pieces focusing on, for example, Bonaventure, Boccaccio, Elisabeth von Nassau-Saarbrücken, and Giordano Bruno, as well as on various aspects of literary theory and the history of scholarship. Nevertheless one can discern a variety of recurring themes, prominent among which are the multi-faceted relationships between truth and fiction, tradition and innovation, continuity and discontinuity, similarity and dissimilarity, and, not least, personal encounter and the experience of transcendence. Unity is conveyed also by H.'s unfailingly erudite yet provocative style.

Gutram Haag, *Traum und Traumdeutung in mittelhochdeutscher Literatur. Theoretische Grundlagen und Fallstudien*, Stuttgart, Hirzel, 233 pp., H.'s doctoral thesis (Tübingen, 2001), considers, first, the significance of dreams in the writings of numerous antique and medieval sources (including poetry, philosophy, and medicinal tracts). Here he focuses in particular on the tension between typological meanings (Macrobius) and individual (psychological) understandings of dream content. He then undertakes a systematic and instructive analysis of dreams as depicted in a few representative literary texts: *Wolfdietrich*, *Salman und Morolf*, and Walther von der Vogelweide's L94,11. In a final section, H. offers questions about the interpretation of dreams in MHG literature which have presented themselves in his study and point in directions of future research.

Michael Müller, *Namenkataloge, Funktionen und Strukturen einer literarischen Grundform in der deutschen Epik vom hohen Mittelalter bis zum Beginn der Neuzeit* (DOLMA, B, 3), xviii + 574 pp., is an analysis of structures and functions of catalogues of names in selected works of literature from the beginning of the 13th c. to the early modern period. Although is it frequently somewhat tedious — perhaps rather like the catalogues of names themselves — Müller's study sheds light on the catalogues as a constitutive element of medieval poetry that can have different historiographical, theological, intellectual, and exemplary functions.

Simone Loleit, *Ritual und Augenschein. Zu Gedächtnis und Erinnerung in den deutschen Übersetzungen der 'Navigatio Sancti Brendani' und der deutsch-niederländischen Überlieferung der 'Reise'-Fassung* (Essener Beiträge zur Kulturgeschichte, 3), Aachen, Shaker, 180 pp., is a perhaps surprisingly rare comparative study of these two main branches of the medieval Brendan tradition. L. concentrates particularly on Johannes Hartlieb's version of the *Navigatio*, and on the text of the *Reise* found in the Berlin MS Mgo 56 (recently edited by R. Hahn and C. Fasbender, see *YWMLS*, 64:588). She deals with various thematic and structural issues, but especially with the two branches' conceptions of memory and use of mnemonic techniques. The *Reise* version emerges as taking a systematic approach to these questions which relates it to early Scholasticism, whereas the *Navigatio* favours a more meditative approach which relies heavily on allegorical techniques. Moreover the latter also is more obviously indebted to oral culture, whereas the former lays particular emphasis on the motif of reading, not least in its characterization of Brendan. Overall L.'s analysis is fruitful, sensible, and balanced.

Articles on MHG literature in general include J.-D. Müller's discussion (*ZDP*, 122:118–32) of problems associated with the interpretation of gestures and other forms of non-verbal communication; J. E. Godsall-Myers's assessment (Godsall-Myers, *Speaking*, 1–19) of the possibilities of a sociolinguistic approach to the study of speech in literary texts; C. Lechtermann's examination (Harms, *Ordnung*, 81–95) of various literary conceptions of the courtly regulation of speech; U. Friedrich's analysis (Dilg, *Natur*, 70–83) of the understanding of nature and order in various works; and P. Hörner's survey (*Euphorion*, 97:327–48) of variations and developments in the concept of martyrdom. Elsewhere A. Classen, *ABäG*, 58:123–49, argues that anti-Semitism was not as common or virulent in 12th-c. and 13th-c. literature as it became in the later Middle Ages; J. D. Martin, Harms, *Ordnung*, 179–91, surveys some relatively positive presentations of Jews in MHG works such as Konrad von Würzburg's *Silvester*, Boner's *Edelstein*, and Hugo von Trimberg's *Renner*; and D. A. Wells, *Mediävistik*, 14, 2001[2003]:179–224, discusses the Latin tradition of dialogues between Christians and non-Christians, and its reception and development in several vernacular works. Moreover A. Sager, *GSl*, 24:5–23, examines the use of the chivalric tournament to illustrate perceived differences between Western and Eastern Europeans in *Biterolf und Dietleib*, Ottokar von Steiermark's *Österreichische Reimchronik*, and Ludwig von Eyb d. J.'s *Turnierbuch*; E. Feistner, *ZDA*, 132:281–94, examines the instrumentalization of Prussians, Lithuanians, and Mongols as representatives of alterity in various MHG texts, not least those written for the Teutonic Order; H. Kästner, *Poetica*, 34, 2002:307–22, considers literary presentations of love between children in songs by Walther and Morungen, and in some 'Blütezeit' narratives; D. Klein, *Fest. Gärtner*, 633–51, writes on family roles and conflicts in *Der arme Heinrich*, *Kudrun*, and Ruprecht von Würzburg's *Treueprobe*; K. Philipowski, *GSR*, 26:81–104, discusses the themes of deception and the incomprehensibility of the world in Eleonore von Österreich's *Pontus und Sidonia*, and in several other works; and H. Brunner, *Fest. Gärtner*, 775–86, reflects on the presentation of war in *Willehalm*, in Wittenwiler's *Ring*, and in a selection of modern texts. Also noted: Renate Laszlo, *Germanische Rätsel in der Literatur des Mittelalters*, Marburg, Tectum, 123 pp.

EARLY MIDDLE HIGH GERMAN. *Ava's New Testament Narratives. 'When the Old Law Passed Away'*, ed. and trans. James A. Rushing, Jr. (MGTBE, 2), 235 pp., is a much needed edition of this little-known author's work with a faithful yet readable translation into modern English. The introduction is a balanced summary of some rather extreme early criticism, arguing for greater appreciation of Ava's liturgical knowledge and literary skills. Discussion of the scant information on Ava's biography raises interesting questions regarding her lifestyle and family relationships.

Martin Embach, *Die Schriften Hildegards von Bingen. Studien zu ihrer Überlieferung im Mittelalter und in der frühen Neuzeit* (Erudiri Sapientia, 4), Berlin, Akademie, 595 pp., traces the MS history of this most fascinating author. The book covers everything except the discussions of music and fine art, and deliberately excludes the Cistercian branch of the MS tradition. The earliest surviving MSS may not, in Hildegard's case, always be the most authentic. Many intermediate stages of the later copying and editing work have been lost, leaving scholars with real difficulty when trying to identify where Hildegard ends and Pseudo-Hildegard begins. E. maintains that the prolific output of glosses and translations over several centuries places Hildegard firmly in the German literary canon. There are many original Latin extracts, without translation, and the 62-page bibliography is eclectic, including a strong focus on the contribution of the 'propagator of Hildegard', Johannes Trithemius. Also on Hildegard, S. El Kholi, Dilg, *Natur*, 294–310, discusses the use of nature imagery in her letters; M. Bažil, *Fest. Gärtner*, 535–48, comments on the cloud imagery of her *Ordo Virtutum*; and B. K. Vollmann, *Sudhoffs Archiv*, 87:159–72, argues that the longer text of her *Physica* in the recently discovered Florence MS represents an 'authentic' version, and as such should form the basis of an overdue new edition of the work.

S. Müller, Tervooren, *Literaturgeschichtsschreibung*, 230–45, questions modern conceptions of EMHG literature having been produced in two separate stages, namely composition (by an author) and copying (by a scribe); and L. Deutsch, *Poetica*, 35:69–90, uses the example of *König Rother* to problematize the perception of a close link between the textual poetics of EMHG epics and the beginnings of a written literary culture. Meanwhile P. Hörner, *ABäG*, 58:39–54, argues that the idea of the imitation of Christ became important in German literature during the EMHG period; U. Bruchhold, *Sprachwissenschaft*, 28:157–93, examines and places in its historical context a 12th-c. vernacular formula of profession from Admont (OSB), which he establishes as being the oldest of its type; and O. Neudeck, *GRM*, 53:273–94, examines the attempts of the *Kaiserchronik* to synthesize learned and popular literary traditions in its presentation of Charlemagne. Finally, on *Herzog Ernst B*, E. A. Andersen, *Flood Vol.*, 3–22, examines the use of time as a compositional element; and C. Morsch,

Harms, *Ordnung*, 109–28, discusses questions of perception and observation, particularly in the prologue and Gryppia episode.

MIDDLE HIGH GERMAN HEROIC LITERATURE

'Das Nibelungenlied.' Mittelhochdeutsch / Neuhochdeutsch. Nach dem Text von Karl Bartsch und Helmut de Boor, ed., trans., and comm. Siegfried Grosse, Stuttgart, Reclam, 1045 pp., is a hardcover edition of the text originally published by Reclam in 1997 (see *YWMLS*, 59:681–82). Beside G.'s dependable prose translations of the individual strophes, readers will benefit from his detailed commentary on the MHG text (719–935), his respectable bibliography covering important critical literature (938–69), his 'Nachwort', which introduces the most important aspects of the medieval poem (970–1027), and an index of the names of figures in the work along with maps showing the geography of its action (1028–37).

Rudolf Kreis, *Wer schrieb das Nibelungenlied? Ein Täterprofil. Die Grimassen des Sakralen und der 'große Mord'*, Würzburg, Königshausen & Neumann, 113 pp., places the *Nibelungenlied* specifically, and courtly-chivalric literature generally, in the socio-historical context of the Crusades. Kreis's unconventional thesis is that the unknown author of the *Nibelungenlied* belonged to the Jewish community of Worms, the same community that had been destroyed in the fanaticism of the First Crusade. Seen from this Jewish perspective, the poem expresses the ultimate, tragic consequences of Siegfried's, and later the Burgundians' crusader-like fanaticism and disregard for the traditional roots of political and social authority. While it may not garner widespread scholarly support in the near future, K.'s study is thought-provoking in its consideration of the relationship of courtly-chivalric culture and medieval Jewish communities in the time of the Crusades.

Die Nibelungen. Sage — Epos — Mythos, ed. Joachim Heinzle et al., 656 pp. + 130 pls, is the latest of numerous books published in recent years dealing with the Nibelungen material in its medieval and modern manifestations. This collection of essays in German, which will be of interest both to Nibelungen scholars and educated non-specialists, is impressive with respect both to the quality of the contributions and to the scope of the material covered. The first section of the volume focuses on the *Saga*, and includes contributions by Heinzle (3–27) on the *Saga* as a European heroic song, and by H. Reichert (29–88) on the *Saga* in medieval Scandinavia (29–88). A second section on the *Nibelungenlied* as poetry of the high Middle Ages includes contributions by E. Lienert (91–112) on interpretative approaches to the epic, N. Henkel (113–33) on the *Klage* and MS C, A. Wolf (135–59) on the literary constitution and ambition of the

Nibelungenlied, and E. Brügge (161–88) on courtly spaces and encounters. In the third section, on the transmission of the *Nibelungenlied*, the medieval MSS are covered by Heinzle (an overview, 191–212), K. Klein (a descriptive index of all *Nibelungenlied* and *Klage* MSS, 213–38), U. Obhof (MS C, 239–51), B. Schirok (MS B, 253–69), K. Schneider (MS A, 271–82), and L. Voetz (MSS of the 15th and 16th cs, 283–305). A fourth section on the nationalistic employment of the *Nibelungenlied* in modern times includes an essay by K. von See on the *Nibelungenlied* as a possible 'Nationalepos' (309–43), by W. Wunderlich on Nibelungen pedagogy (345–73), and by P. Krüger on Göring's Nibelungen speech in 1943 (375–403). A fifth section looks at modern versions of the Nibelungen story: U. Müller presents a survey of literature, music, and film in the 19th and 20th cs (407–44), H. Glaser focuses on Hebbel's *Nibelungen* trilogy (445–57), V. Mertens on Richard Wagner (459–96), H. Heller on Fritz Lang's Nibelungen films (497–509), W. Hoffmann on Walter Jansen's *Das Buch Treue* (511–21), C. Thiede on Reinhold Schneider's *Tarnkappe* (523–30), and B. Greiner on Heiner Müller's employment of the *Nibelungenlied* material (531–44). The final section examines visual representations: C. Hallendorff and M. Kiefer look at the paintings of the Swiss artist Johann Heinrich Füssli (547–60); F. Büttner surveys Nibelungen pictures in the context of German Romanticism (561–82); H.-T. Wappenschmidt examines the relationship of the *Nibelungenlied* to 'Historienmalerei' of the 19th c. (583–602); E. von Hagenow and S. Wernsing study images relating to the *Nibelungenlied* in the popular press (603–19); J. Schmoll gen. Eisenwerth looks at the Nibelungen wall paintings in Worms (621–35); and H. Kimpel and J. Werckmeister examine motifs of suffering in the artistic rendering of the Nibelungen material since 1945 (637–56). The volume ends with 130 black and white prints of visual renderings of the Nibelungen material, ranging from 11th-c. stone carvings in Scandinavia, to medieval MS illuminations, to the works of modern artists such as Füssli, Ernst Barlach, and Anselm Kiefer.

In *ZDA*, 132, U. Obhof (177–88) discusses the provenance of the 13th-c. *Nibelungenlied* fragment S1, and its relationship to fragments S2 and S3; Obhof and B. Knödler-Kagoshima (546–47) report on a digitized copy of *Nibelungenlied* MS C at <http://www.blb-Karlsruhe>; J. Heinzle and K. H. Staub (443–52) describe and print a newly discovered fragment of MS L; and E. Lienert (3–23) discusses the work's constructions of gender and violence. Elsewhere D. Buschinger, *ICLS* 9, 81–89, interprets the *Nibelungenlied* as a work from which God is largely absent; M. Jönsson, *SN*, 75: 186–97, discusses the function of signs and symbols in the epic; A. Suerbaum, *Flood Vol.*, 23–37, examines the motif of crying, pointing especially to its use as a means of challenging cultural assumptions and expectations; A. Classen, *GSR*, 26:295–314, argues that, in the *Nibelungenlied*, the depiction of heroism in general, and of Siegfried in particular, is more differentiated and critical than is often allowed; A. Kuklinski, *NBG*, 2:179–94, considers the relationship between its inconsistencies (especially those relating to the characterization of Hagen) and its origins as an orally delivered text; B. Hasebrink, Henkel, *Dialoge*, 7–20, writes on its 37th 'Aventiure', with regard particularly to its presentation of modes of courtly interaction; T. Tomasek and A. Iskhakova, *Fest. Honemann*, 125–36, contrast the epic's presentation of the Huns with that found in 19th-c. and 20th-c. works based on it; N. Henkel, *Fest. Honemann*, 137–48, investigates a lost wall painting featuring Siegfried which was made at the Town Hall in Worms around 1545; and J. Heinzle, *Fest. Janota*, 15–30, examines the evidence suggesting the survival into the late Middle Ages of orally transmitted stories about the Nibelungs.

Dietrichs Flucht. Textgeschichtliche Ausgabe, ed. Elisabeth Lienert and Gertrud Beck (Texte und Studien zur mittelhochdeutschen Heldenepik, 1), Tübingen, Niemeyer, xxx + 352 pp., is a welcome edition of the story of Dietrich von Bern's exile and battles surrounding his attempt to return. At the bottom of each page is a critical apparatus, and also a detailed commentary organized by verse numbers that sheds light on the significance of specific words and phrases. The edition includes an introduction to the poem and its MSS (ix-xxx), a list of the names of characters and places (301–36), and a bibliography of critical literature (339–52).

In Bertelsmeier-Kierst, *Umbruch*, B. Bastert (91–110) undertakes a comparative analysis of Konrad's *Rolandslied* and Stricker's *Karl der Große*; E. Lienert examines the staging of narration in the heroic epic (123–37); and V. Millet examines generic aspects of German heroic poetry in a broader European context (139–53). In Harms, *Ordnung*, C. Bornholdt (129–41) points to various parallels between *Ortnit* and *Waltharius*, and draws conclusions from these about the origins and literary-historical position of the former work; A. Krass (165–78) reads the *Großer Wolfdietrich* as seeking to deconstruct conventional notions of courtly identity; and U. Störmer-Caysa (21–39) evaluates the ritualized dialogues between heroes, as these appear in *Biterolf und Dietleib*. In Lehmann-Benz, *Schnittpunkte*, H. Sievert (109–23) reads *Karl und Galie* as a playful, indeed joyful work, which takes delight in combining elements from both narrative and lyric traditions; and B. Bastert (125–43) examines the structure of the *Karlmeinet* compilation, and points to the tension within it between heroic and hagiographical elements. Finally in *BGDSL*, 125, M. Siller (36–56) argues that *Der Rosengarten zu Worms* was based on a now lost saga describing the conflict between the Burgundians and the Ostrogoths in Lombardy around AD 500; and T. Reuvekamp-Felber (57–81) discusses the thematic and structural significance of letters in the *Virginal.*

THE COURTLY ROMANCE

Wolfzettel, *Das Wunderbare*, contains proceedings from the meeting of the German section of the International Arthurian Society held in February 2002. The book is divided into three sections dealing respectively with the phenomenology, the reception and influence, and the function and structure of the marvellous. W.'s own essay evaluates Francis Dubost's seminal 1991 study of the fantastic in the Middle Ages (3–21). K. Ridder considers the relationship of fiction, perfection, and the marvellous in the case of the courtly romance (23–43); U. Ernst surveys 'mirabilia mechanica', technical wonders in medieval Arthurian romances (45–77); E. Schmid examines the marvellous as a means of bringing about literary reflection by confronting the reader with different possibilities of meaning (79–94); M. Meyer studies the fairy youth of the heroes of Ulrich von Zatzikhoven's *Lanzelet*, the *Prosa-Lancelot*, and *Wigamur* (95–112); U. Wyss offers a general consideration of the values of the term 'marvellous' and posits that it is a manner rather than an object of narration (129–39); J. Eming surveys depictions of sorcery in MHG and OF romances (141–157); and W. Haug examines the use of the marvellous in post-classical romances to produce comical effects (159–174).

Anette Sosna, *Fiktionale Identität im höfischen Roman um 1200: 'Erec', 'Iwein', 'Parzival', 'Tristan'*, Stuttgart, Hirzel, 303 pp., examines the complex dynamics of identity and individuality as represented in the chivalric romances of Hartmann, Wolfram, and Gottfried. The analysis focuses on significant figures in the romances, proceeding sequentially from one to the next, as S. argues that individuality is constituted on the basis of interaction (conflict), reflection, memory, and narration. Her book contributes to an appreciation of identity as a concern of court literature *c.* 1200, and to the understanding of the historically specific ways in which the question of identity was addressed by these significant medieval poets.

Timothy R. Jackson, *Typus und Poetik. Studien zur Bedeutungsvermittlung in der Literatur des deutschen Mittelalters* (*Euphorion*, Beihefte, 45), xii + 326 pp., assembles revised and greatly extended versions of papers originally given at conferences between 1976 and 1986. They are concerned not least to demonstrate that stylistic and structural elements do not merely adorn, but also convey meaning in medieval texts; and they focus in particular on ways in which poetic devices and fixed character types combine to construct identity in MHG narratives. The individual essays deal with Hartmann's use of *contradictio in adiecto* to present character in *Erec*, *Gregorius*, and *Iwein*; on questions of truth, credibility, and sainthood specifically in *Gregorius*; on the construction of ideals of female beauty in Gottfried's *Tristan* and Konrad von Würzburg's *Engelhard*; and on the communication of meaning through rhyme in various narratives. Particular strengths of J.'s approach are the lucidity of his exposition, and his scrupulous, painstaking attention to textual detail.

Rosemarie Deist, *Gender and Power. Counsellors and Their Masters in Antiquity and Medieval Courtly Romance*, Heidelberg, Winter, 259 pp., deals mainly with OF works, but also contains chapters on *Tristan* (96–107) and *Parzival* (151–70). The former is primarily concerned with Brangäne (especially her role as confidante to Tristan), and the latter with Herzeloyde and her influence on Parzival.

Barbara Sabel, *Toleranzdenken in mittelhochdeutscher Literatur* (IMA, 14), x + 350 pp., has a somewhat narrower focus than its title implies. It deals almost exclusively with high-medieval narratives, and indeed concentrates for two thirds of its length on just three closely related works: Wolfram's *Willehalm*, Ulrich von Türheim's *Rennewart*, and Ulrich von dem Türlin's *Arabel*. Nevertheless S. provides a lucid and well-argued account of the nature and extent of 'tolerance' in these works — defining the term primarily but not solely as a readiness to allow non-Christians the possibility of finding their own route to salvation. Not surprisingly, she presents *Willehalm* as uniquely ahead of its time in this respect; *Rennewart*, by contrast, is seen as resorting to the levels of intolerance associated with, for example, the *Rolandslied*; and *Arabel* is interpreted as partly adopting, and partly developing or problematizing Wolfram's model. S.'s final, more general chapter finds examples of tolerance especially in *Graf Rudolf*, *Herzog Ernst B*, *Flore und Blanscheflur*, and *Die Heidin* IV.

Other studies of romance include J. Wolf's examination (Bertelsmeier-Kierst, *Umbruch*, 205–20) of the transmission of Arthurian romances in France and Germany; V. Honemann's discussion (*ICLS* 9, 27–39) of the figure and role of the king in various MHG narratives; J. Schulz-Grobert's analysis (Dilg, *Natur*, 243–53) of the presentation of storms and their thematic significance in several works; and V. Bok's article (*Fest. Honemann*, 113–23) on the use of names of characters from MHG romances as Christian names in medieval Bohemia and Moravia.

HARTMANN VON AUE. Articles on *Erec*: I. Gephart, *AKG*, 85:171–99, examines gender relationships in the romance, especially the tensions between patriarchal or matriarchal consciousness and the search for personal identity; R. W. Fisher, *Mediävistik*, 14, 2001[2003]: 83–93, analyses Hartmann's re-definition of manhood and manliness; H. Wandhoff, Harms, *Ordnung*, 45–60, discusses Hartmann's use of ekphrasis in his description of Enite's horse; W. C. McDonald, *BGDSL*, 125: 460–68, criticizes the conventional editorial emendation of 'also' to 'saelde und' in line 2438; and E. Rolf and F. H. Roolfs, *Fest. Honemann*, 89–103, evaluate various narratorial statements using the present tense, which they see as proposing a theory of courtly behaviour. Meanwhile H. Graser, *Fest. Janota*, 265–98, describes the language and rhymes of the 16th-c. Lindau MS of *Iwein*, comparing it with its source text in the early 13th-c. MS B.

K. Gärtner, *Editio*, 17: 89–99, uses the critical reaction to his recent edition of *Der arme Heinrich* (see *YWMLS*, 63: 631) to illustrate the extent to which the prior existence of a generally accepted 'received' text can influence assessments of the textual-critical value of subsequently discovered MSS. Also on *Der arme Heinrich*, A. Classen, *Mediävistik*, 14, 2001[2003]: 7–30, sees in the unnamed maiden a personification of Heinrich's soul, supporting this view with references to the *Klagebüchlein* and to mystical literature; and in the same volume D. Duckworth (31–82) explores the important part played by love in Heinrich's conversion — a thesis which he illuminates by detailed reference to William of St Thierry and Bernard of Clairvaux. Furthermore J. Dewhurst, *ArLit*, 20: 43–83, examines numerous aspects of generic hybridity in the work, focusing particularly on its affinities to romance, its intertextual relationships, and the role of the maiden as a source of narrative plurality; and A. C. Gow, *Sudhoffs Archiv*, 87: 129–58, refers to it in the course of his study of the perceived healing qualities of blood in the Middle Ages.

WOLFRAM VON ESCHENBACH. Sonja Emmerling, *Geschlechterbeziehungen in den Gawan-Büchern des 'Parzival.' Wolframs Arbeit an einem literarischen Modell* (Hermaea, 100), Tübingen, Niemeyer, ix + 358 pp., is a slightly revised version of E.'s doctoral thesis (Augsburg, 2001). Her focal point is an examination of the Gawan books, but she also looks at the story of Gahmuret and at Parzival's initial series of adventures, arguing as she does that Wolfram seeks to recast conventional gender roles and gender relations. The traditional literary model, oriented towards heroism and combat on the part of the male, and patient suffering on the part of the female, is replaced in Wolfram's text — and in the Gawan books in particular — by an increased emphasis on the knight as a 'Minneritter', for whom fame and honour based on combat are no longer the primary concerns. E. persuasively argues that Wolfram's Gawan books manifest new possibilities of (inter-)action for male and female characters, thus reinforcing an increasing tendency in the scholarship of recent years to regard the Gawan sections of Wolfram's romance on their own terms. Also on *Parzival*, N. Kaminski, *DVLG*, 77:16–44, reads the 'Bogengleichnis' as a polemic directed against impatient or insensitive audience members; B. Quast, *DVLG*, 77:45–60, examines Wolfram's sophisticated use of narrative signs; A. Tiplady, Henkel, *Dialoge*, 61–74, comments on the form and function of various constructions using 'wellen' in the work's dialogues; K. Philipowski, *ZGer*, 13:9–25, considers the function of Cunnewâre's laughter; J. Reichert, *Mediävistik*, 14, 2001[2003]: 149–78, analyses Wolfram's description of the attempt to heal Anfortas using *trachontê* in the light of medieval alchemy and of Parzival's development; D. N. Yeandle, *Fest. Gärtner*, 249–63, discusses his CD-ROM 'Stellenbiographie' to *Parzival* (see *YWMLS*, 64:581); H. Rölleke, *WW*, 53–58, finds extensive and remarkable evidence of the reception of *Parzival* in Gotthelf's *Kurt von Koppingen*; and J. E. Godsall-Myers, Godsall-Myers, *Speaking*, 93–102, compares Parzival's, Feirefiz's, and Rennewart's use of language.

There are two articles on *Willehalm* by M. H. Jones: in *Flood Vol.*, 71–89, he examines the treatment of dead bodies and its significance for the interpretation of the work; and in *Fest. Honemann*, 193–207, he discusses the allusions to the Cross made by Gyburc, Bertram, and Willehalm himself. S. Ghosh, *Euphorion*, 97:303–25, focuses on the unresolved tensions in *Willehalm* caused by Wolfram's awareness of several forms of kinship, including that between the Christian and Muslim religions; and U. Müller, *JIG*, 34.2, 2002:207–25, argues that the elopement and marriage of Willehalm and Gyburc would have seemed plausible to Wolfram's contemporaries.

Wolfram von Eschenbach, 'Titurel.' Studienausgabe, ed., trans. and comm. Helmut Brackert und Stephan Fuchs-Jolie, Berlin, de Gruyter, vii + 297 pp., makes one of the most fascinating poems of the German high Middle Ages accessible to a broader audience by providing an introduction to the poem's unique content and form, the MHG text, and the editors' reliable strophe-by-strophe prose translation of Wolfram's verses. The edition contains a helpful, detailed commentary that explains passages of the poem in view of the critical literature (145–274), and a short bibliography (284–93).

GOTTFRIED VON STRASSBURG. *A Companion to Gottfried von Strassburg's 'Tristan'*, ed. Will Hasty, Columbia SC, Camden House, viii + 319 pp., contains 13 essays aimed at making Gottfried's romance more easily accessible and explicable to English-speaking readers (English translations, for example, are helpfully provided for all MHG and NHG quotations). Following an introductory essay by H. on the challenge of *Tristan* (1–20), A. Wolf (23–54) presents the work as a remarkable example of high-medieval Humanism, and M. S. Batts (55–69) outlines relevant aspects of life in Gottfried's

Strasbourg. A sequence of pieces on figures, themes, and episodes covers aspects of the 'Vorgeschichte' (D. Buschinger, 73–86), of the love potion (S. M. Johnson, 87–112), of the presentation of God and religion (N. Harris, 113–36), of the female characters (A. M. Rasmussen, 137–57), of performative aspects of the lovers' behaviour at court (W. Hasty, 159–81), and of the episodes involving Isolde of the White Hands (N. Thomas, 183–201). Thereafter D. Rocher (205–21) contributes an analysis of Gottfried's narrative art which foregrounds especially his movingly persuasive lyricism; and A. Stevens (223–56) investigates the relationship between his romance, Thomas's *Tristan*, and earlier treatments of the 'matter of Britain'. The volume concludes with surveys of both the medieval and the modern reception of *Tristan*, by M. E. Gibbs (261–84) and U. Müller (285–304) respectively.

Anna Sziráky, *Éros Lógos Musiké* (WAGAPH, 38), 545 pp., S.'s doctoral thesis, is a lengthy textual analysis of *Tristan*. Her argument is that Gottfried's work rests on a 'symbiotic-dialectical' relationship of love, language, and music. S.'s analysis of Gottfried's poem and the critical literature about it is impressive in its scope, though it sometimes lacks great depth of analysis and covers territory that will already be quite familiar to many Gottfried scholars.

Philippa Hardman et al., *The Growth of the Tristan and Iseut Legend in Wales, England, France, and Germany* (Studies in Mediaeval Literature, 24), Lewiston NY, Mellen, xii + 214 pp., includes a chapter by N. Thomas (149–84) on 'Tristan in Germany between Gottfried von Strassburg, Wagner and Thomas Mann'. T.'s analysis of Gottfried stresses his romance's multiplicity of voices and viewpoints, not least concerning love; and there is brief reference also to Eilhart and the other MHG Tristan texts. Of the mere ten pages devoted to German romances in Derek Pearsall, *Arthurian Romance. A Short Introduction*, Maldon MA, Blackwell, viii + 182 pp., no fewer than eight are devoted to Gottfried's *Tristan* — the sophistication and narrative style of which are seen as precursors of Chaucer and Fielding.

Other work on *Tristan* includes W. Sayers's analysis (*OGS*, 32: 1–52) of the scene describing the breaking of the deer, which considers in particular its structure, vocabulary, sources, and provocative novelty; R. A. Wisbey's reading of the romance (*MLR*, 98: xxxi-lx) as a study of love as a powerful, ill-starred passion; L. Auteri's discussion (*ABäG*, 58: 73–91) of Gottfried's presentation of the dichotomy between death in general and the death of individuals; and R. Schmidt-Wiegand's article (*Fest. Honemann*, 164–74) on legal aspects of the ordeal scene. Moreover S. Glauch, *ZDA*, 132: 148–76, comments on the function of the apparently conventional assertions of inexpressibility and indescribability made by Gottfried's narrator;

A. Schulz, *DVLG*, 77:515–47, discusses the instrumentalization of mythic elements in Gottfried's, Eilhart's, and Béroul's descriptions of the lovers' life in the wilderness; and E. Brüggen and H.-J. Ziegeler, Lehmann-Benz, *Schnittpunkte*, 237–67, publish (in colour) and assess the nine illustrations of the Cologne MS of *Tristan* (MS B, dated 1323), which they see as focusing the reader's attention particularly on Tristan's knightly career. Meanwhile J. Rùžičková, *Fest. Gärtner*, 653–68, compares the text of the recently discovered St Paul fragment of Eilhart's *Tristrant* with relevant passages from the related Czech *Tristram*.

OTHER ROMANCES AND SHORTER NARRATIVES. On Wirnt von Gravenberg's *Wigalois*, C. Dietl, Wolfzettel, *Das Wunderbare*, 297–311, looks at the work's presentation of magic and the marvellous, and Y. Yokogama, *Fest. Gärtner*, 131–56, examines and interprets Wirnt's use of the forms 'quam', 'kam', and 'kom'. R. Banschke, Bertelsmeier-Kierst, *Umbruch*, 155–74, analyses the relationship of learned discourse and historical truth in Herbort von Fritzlar's *Liet von Troye*; N. McLelland, Henkel, *Dialoge*, 41–59, associates the stylistic diversity of the dialogues of Ulrich von Zatzikhoven's *Lanzelet* with the author's conscious engagement in dialogue with various literary traditions; S. Plausmann, *ZGer*, 13:26–40, discusses the theatricality of the tournament presented in *Mauritius von Craûn*; M. Hagby, *Fest. Honemann*, 149–66, examines differing perceptions of the hero and his significance in the late-medieval reception of Otte's *Eraclius*; and W. Layher, Harms, *Ordnung*, 61–80, seeks to reconstruct the lost *Herzog Friedrich von der Normandie*, which he believes was an early 13th-c. *Brautwerbungsepos*.

On Heinrich von dem Türlin's *Diu Crône*, N. Thomas, Henkel, *Dialoge*, 75–94, examines Heinrich's use of motifs from French and German sources to construct his own new interpretation of the Arthurian and Grail worlds; U. Störmer-Caysa, *Fest. Honemann*, 209–24, discusses the interplay he creates between linear and cyclical time structures; and J. Keller, Wolfzettel, *Das Wunderbare*, 225–48, considers his presentation of the fantastic. Elsewhere M. Waltenberger, Harms, *Ordnung*, 25–43, discusses the construction of culture in Konrad Fleck's *Flore und Blanscheflur* and in his French source.

German Romance. Volume 1: Daniel von dem blühenden Tal, ed. and trans. Michael Resler (Arthurian Archives, 9), Cambridge, Brewer, 435 pp., is a welcome combination of R.'s 1995 edition of Der Stricker's romance (see *YWMLS*, 57:683) and — printed in parallel — a revised version of his 1990 translation of it into English prose (see *YWMLS*, 52:619). These texts are supported by an introduction dealing with Der Stricker's biography, sources and influence, and artistic achievement, as well as by 30 pages of notes, a bibliography, and an index of names. R.'s division of the romance into 15 chapters is controversial and arguably unnecessary; but his overall approach is sensible, scholarly, and considerate towards the needs of non-specialist readers — who one hopes will be numerous. Also on Der Stricker, Helmut Dworschak, *Milch und Acker. Körperliche und sexuelle Aspekte der religiösen Erfahrung. Am Beispiel der Bussdidaxe des Strickers* (DLA, 40), 411 pp., is an innovative if somewhat eccentric study of two *bîspel* concerning penitence and confession, namely *Die Milch und die Fliege* and *Säen und Ernten*, both as embedded in the context of the 13th-c. Vienna MS CPV 2705. D. concentrates on certain of their key images, such as the pouring of milk, the ploughing of a field and, in particular, the symbolic representation of their reader as a vessel. On the basis of a range of psychoanalytical and psychosomatic theories, he argues that these images, with their marked sexual implications, activate a powerful range of unconscious thought processes both in their readers and indeed in those responsible for the grouping together of texts within a *Sammelhandschrift*. Other work on Der Stricker includes W. Freytag's examination (*Flood Vol.*, 117–35) of the sententia and exemplum which begin *Der Kater als Freier*; and M. Hagby's employment of the same fable (*ZDA*, 132:35–61) to illustrate ways in which the poet treated the Latin sources of his short narratives. Moreover G. Wolf, *Flood Vol.*, 91–115, interprets Stricker's *Karl der Große* as a hybrid work which combines a variety of discourses and exemplifies its author's preoccupation with the theme of *list*; F.-J. Holznagel, *JIG*, 34.2, 2002:127–45, contends that research on the *Reimpaardichtungen* attributed to Der Stricker should concentrate less on the author and more on the works' MSS (especially CPV 2705); and in Henkel, *Dialoge*, 159–73, Holznagel compares Stricker's *Der Richter und der Teufel* to other 'devil and advocate' stories by Caesarius von Heistersbach and Chaucer.

On the *Prosa-Lancelot*, S. Fuchs-Jolie, Wolfzettel, *Das Wunderbare*, 313–40, explores the poet's treatment of the fantastic in terms of breaks and gaps in meaning which bring about experiments of signification; and in Lehmann-Benz, *Schnittpunkte*, 193–214, the same scholar sees the descriptions of dreams in the German, Dutch, and French versions of the *Prosa-Lancelot* as loci of playful poetic experimentation. Meanwhile I. Hahn, *Fest. Honemann*, 225–36, discusses the interplay of the individual will, self-knowledge, and social norms in the *Prosa-Lancelot*; N. von Merveldt, Harms, *Ordnung*, 1–23, compares constructions of order and disorder in the *Prosa-Lancelot* and in the OF *Voyage de Charlemagne*, focusing especially on the motif of promise; and J. Margetts, *Flood Vol.*, 209–26, comments on Agravain and Mordred's revelation to Arthur of Guinevere's adultery, as presented in the Heidelberg *Prosa-Lancelot* and in Malory's *Morte d'Arthur*. Bart

Besamusca, *The Book of Lancelot. The Middle Dutch 'Lancelot' Compilation and the Medieval Tradition of Narrative Cycles* (Arthurian Studies, 53), Cambridge, Brewer, x + 210 pp., contains a brief discussion of Ulrich Füetrer's *Buch der Abenteuer* as a narrative cycle comparable to, but different from, the Middle Dutch *Lancelot* and Malory.

On Rudolf von Ems, H. Bluemer, Henkel, *Dialoge*, 95–112, discusses the tensions between narrative structures and the presentation of ethical values in *Der guote Gêrhart*; C. Stollinger-Löser, *ASNS*, 240:347–54, evaluates Rudolf's reception of Pseudo-Methodius's *Revelationes* in his *Alexanderroman*, and provides an edition of the relevant section of the *Revelationes* from a 15th-c. German translation; and S. Schmitt, *ZDA*, 132:307–20, suggests that the 700-line verse adaptation of part of the *Buch der Könige* which follows the *Alexanderroman* in its Munich MS, Cgm 203, constitutes a continuation of Rudolf's work. Meanwhile in Henkel, *Dialoge*, M. Stock (113–34) and B. Kellner (135–58) discuss the nature and function of intertextuality in relation to the montage techniques of Ulrich von Etzenbach's *Alexanderroman* and *Friedrich von Schwaben* respectively; and R. Finkch, Dilg, *Natur*, 386–407, examines Ulrich's conception of nature and his use of it as a form of political slogan in the *Alexanderroman*.

On Konrad von Würzburg, W. Hoffmann, *ASNS*, 240:354–60, discusses semantic and interpretative problems raised by lines 744–53 of *Heinrich von Kempten*, concentrating especially on Konrad's use of *tiuren*; and K. Gärtner, *Fest. Honemann*, 105–12, identifies and explains the use of the first line of *Gregorius* in a sequence of pen trials at the head of the Trier MS of Konrad's *Silvester*. Moreover J. Eming, *ICLS 9*, 153–60, examines the relationships in *Partonopier und Meliur* and in *Mai und Bêaflôr* which Freud and Lévi-Strauss would define as incestuous. *Mai und Bêaflôr* is also discussed by V. Honemann, *Flood Vol.*, 155–71, who sees it as a work which, whilst ultimately failing in its attempt to depict a truly Christian courtly lifestyle, is important for the development of MHG romance through its thematization of communication, emotionality, and money.

Begriffsglossar und Index zu Albrechts 'Jüngerem Titurel' (IDL, 32–35), 4 vols, xi + 2221 pp., is the latest set of volumes resulting from work on the 'Mittelhochdeutsche Begriffsdatenbank' (MHDBDB), a collaborative venture involving the Christian-Albrechts-Universität in Kiel, Bowling Green State University, and the Paris Lodron Universität in Salzburg. (Earlier glossaries on, for example, Ulrich von Liechtenstein and *Kudrun* have already appeared — see *YWMLS*, 55:721–22 and 56:740–41). The goal of the project is to offer experts and a general audience data about MHG. The glossaries in particular contain precise information on the locations and frequency of given terms, as well as data about the different meanings a particular term is given. This comprehensive glossary will enhance philological work with Albrecht's text and with the MHG language more generally. Elsewhere R. Barber and C. Edwards, *ArLit*, 20:85–102, translate into English and discuss the description of Albrecht's description of the Grail temple; and T. Neukirchen, *ZDA*, 132:62–76, argues that the so-called 'Hinweis- und Kunststrophen' in 'Branch 1' of the *Jüngerer Titurel* MSS refer not to Wolfram's *Titurel*, but to his *Parzival*.

Work on other narratives includes H. Linke's discussion (*Fest. Janota*, 1–13) of the relationship between appearances and reality in the stories of Herrand von Wildonie; W. Schröder's analysis (*JIG*, 34.2, 2002:183–205) of tragic elements in Wernher der Gartenaere's portrayal of Helmbrecht senior; A. Classen's examination (Godsall-Myers, *Speaking*, 65–92) of the relationship between gender conflicts and problems of communication in various narratives; and D. Blamires's comments (*Flood Vol.*, 629–42) on the seven early prints of Egenolf von Staufenberg's *Peter von Staufenberg*. On later romances, W. Achnitz, *ZDA*, 132:453–59, describes and prints a fragment from Amorbach which transmits some 144 lines of Heinrich von Neustadt's *Apollonius von Tyrland*, of which it appears to be the work's oldest surviving witness; K. Speckenbach, *Fest. Honemann*, 249–62, examines cosmological aspects of Johann von Würzburg's *Wilhelm von Österreich*; S. Emmerling, *Fest. Janota*, 31–49, looks at the epilogue of the *Rappoltsteiner Parzifal*, reflecting particularly on its thematization of love; and R. Hahn, *Daphnis*, 31, 2002:1–31, argues that the *Berner Pontus* was written independently of the two better known 15th-c. German versions of the romance, constituting instead a generally faithful adaptation of the French *Pontus et Sidoine*. In Lehmann-Benz, *Schnittpunkte*, U. Zellmann (145–66) suggests that the MLG *Valentin und Namelos* may have had a Dutch source that reflected the preoccupations and cultural interests of the Bruges mercantile class; and R. Schlusemann (269–87) discusses the lightly 'Germanized' Brussels MS of the Dutch *Roman van Limborch*, seeing it as an example of the mediating role played by the Rhine-Maas region in 15th-c. literary culture.

S. Coxon, *OGS*, 31, 2002:17–62, surveys the poetic treatment of literate protagonists, and of their story-telling, in a variety of late-medieval comic tales, which he sets against the background of other contemporary literary traditions; and in *Flood Vol.*, 243–61, Coxon studies the form and function of authorial signatures in various late-medieval *Schwankmären*. Moreover K. Grubmüller, *BGDSL*, 125:469–93, discusses the problematic relationship between orality and textual variability in MHG *Mären*, especially *Der Striegel*; and S. Westphal, *LiLi*, 130:72–87, examines the theme of magic, and especially its relationship to the law, in Hermann von Sachsenheim's *Mörin*.

LYRIC POETRY

Research on 'Minnesang' up to and including Walther von der Vogelweide is surveyed by H. Haferland, Schiewer, *Forschungsberichte*, 54–160. Elsewhere A. L. Klinck, *Neophilologus*, 87:339–59, examines markers of an author's or speaker's gender in various love laments, including Der von Kürenberg's *Falkenlied*; A. Touber, *ZDA*, 132:24–34, argues that Rudolf von Fenis's song *MF* 80,1 reflects a knowledge of the songs of Folquet de Marseille which must have been gained from personal acquaintance on Rudolf's part with MS P (now in the Medici Library in Florence); D. A. Traill, *MJ*, 38:189–98, interprets *Carmina Burana* 59 not as a plea for chastity, but as a 'tour-de-force of double-entendres'; and K. Schneider, *Fest. Gärtner*, 241–47, discusses palaeographical questions relating to the *Weingartner Liederhandschrift*.

On Walther, R.-H. Steinmetz, *LJb*, 44:19–46, demonstrates the influence on his re-evaluation of courtly love of classical and medieval perspectives on friendship; and in *ZDA*, 132, 425–42, Steinmetz argues that Walther's praise of mutual, requited love in L69,1 constitutes a strategem used in the context of an otherwise largely conventional wooing song. Elsewhere S. Ranawake, *Fest. Honemann*, 175–92, surveys Walther's career and assesses his importance for modern German culture; H. Wandhoff, Dilg, *Natur*, 360–72, argues that a textual variant in L8,28 exemplifies the existence of differing medieval conceptions of how the animal kingdom should be subdivided; T. Bein, *Fest. Gärtner*, 579–99, uses the example of Walther L39,1 to discuss ways in which a developed understanding of textual variation would influence both editors and literary historians; and C. Rozier, *MA*, 109:493–528, examines the poetic functions of Walther's landscape descriptions.

R. Brandt, *Fest. Gärtner*, 601–31, comments on Neidhart's *Sommerlied* 18, and especially on the image of the two cradles, which he interprets as a metonymy for twins; and J. Haustein, Bertelsmeier-Kierst, *Umbruch*, 307–16, explores the literary-historical implications of Neidhart's request for a house. Focusing especially on his presentation of the singer in three songs, C. Laude, *GRM*, 53:1–26, argues that Ulrich von Winterstetten proposes a radical re-evaluation of conventional Minnesang as a locus of aesthetic emancipation and intellectual experiment; and S. Ranawake, Henkel, *Dialoge*, 175–88, discusses wooing songs in dialogue form by Ulrich and by other MHG poets.

In *Queeste*, 10:115–26, J. Goossens and F. Willaert provide a new edition of the songs of Duke Jan (or Johann) I of Brabant, as transmitted in the Codex Manesse. In the same volume F. Willaert (97–114) interprets the songs, stressing their conventionality and indebtedness to Gottfried von Neifen; W. van Arooij (127–45) discusses a MHG paeon to Jan composed in response to his death at a tournament in 1294; and R. Stein (162–81) considers the images of him constructed in late-medieval historiographical writings from Brabant. Meanwhile in *Fest. Honemann*, 237–47, Goossens argues that the language of Jan's songs as transmitted is a South-Western dialect of MHG with traces of Middle Dutch from the Brabant area.

U. Müller, Ertzdorff, *Erkundung*, 163–77, comments on several of Oswald von Wolkenstein's *Reiselieder*; F.-J. Holznagel and H. Möller, Tervooren, *Literaturgeschichtsschreibung*, 102–33, compare the transmission of the text and melody of Kl.101 in Oswald's own MS A, and in the 'Lochamer' and 'Rostocker Liederbücher'; and N. R. Wolf, *Flood Vol.*, 195–207, argues that motifs which reflect Oswald's own individuality and biography occur in the MSS in which his songs are transmitted, but not in the songs themselves. Meanwhile M. Schiendorfer, Tervooren, *Literaturgeschichtsschreibung*, 203–29, re-examines the (for him, misleading) claim that Freiherr Walther von Klingenberg led a literary circle for the cultivation and promotion of Minnesang in 15th-c. Basle.

On *Sangspruchdichtung*, D. Gade, *ZDP*, 122:143–46, interprets Bruder Wernher's *Sangspruch* 2/11 as a warning against parsimony; N. Miedema, Henkel, *Dialoge*, 189–212, examines various forms of dialogue between singer and audience in the *Sprüche* attibuted to Konrad von Würzburg; R. Schöller, *ZDP*, 122:416–24, makes textual-critical observations about the new edition of the (Pseudo-) Frauenlob song V,204 (see *YWMLS*, 62:624), and suggests it might after all be genuine; and B. Wachinger, *Fest. Janota*, 93–107, discusses genre divisions in respect of late-medieval religious songs.

Die kleineren Dichtungen Heinrichs von Mügeln. Zweite Abteilung, ed. Karl Stackmann (DTM, 84), lx + 294 pp., represents the completion of the critical edition of Heinrich's collected work that began with the publication of Stackmann's first volume in 1958. This volume includes political and didactic strophes not contained in the Göttingen collection, the *Libri tocius Biblie* (a summary in Latin of books from the Old Testament), and *Der Meide Kranz* (an allegorical discourse on the arts and Christian virtues). A further section including short Latin texts by Heinrich on the characteristics of the Liberal Arts is edited not by Stackmann but by Michael Stolz. The volume includes a substantial glossary (213–91). Meanwhile H. Brunner, *Fest. Janota*, 109–23, examines the structure of Mügeln's *Spruchtöne*; and F. Löser, *Fest. Gärtner*, 689–708, argues that the Psalm commentary sometimes erroneously attributed to him is not the work of the 'Österreichischer Bibelübersetzer' either.

A. Volfing, Schiewer, *Forschungsberichte*, 161–96, contributes an authoritative survey of research into pre-Reformation *Meisterlieder*. V. Zapf, *Gabler Vol.*, 127–36, discusses the possibilities of editions documenting the reception and development of *Sangspruchtöne* (such as Stolle's *alment*), also in *Meisterlieder*; and H. Bierschwale, *Fest. Honemann*, 879–94, discusses the late-medieval genre of *Meistersprüche*, and assesses the relationship between the nine MLG or Middle Dutch MSS containing them.

DIDACTIC, DEVOTIONAL, AND RELIGIOUS LITERATURE

Ulrich von Liechtenstein, *Das Frauenbuch. Mittelhochdeutsch / Neuhochdeutsch*, ed. and trans. Christopher Young (UB, 18290), 240 pp., is only the third edition of Ulrich's *Minnerede* to have appeared, and the first which is remotely student-friendly — thanks not least to its highly competent and reliable parallel NHG translation. Y. has made a number of sensible choices which make the volume in many ways a model of its kind: his edition of the *Frauenbuch* sticks closely to the version of the work in the Ambraser Heldenbuch, but features normalized spelling and punctuation; his extensive commentary concentrates mainly on providing information not readily available elsewhere; and his introduction contains not only the expected material on author, date, and MSS, but also a well presented survey of the *Minnerede* tradition, and an interpretative essay — though, strangely, no explanation of Y.'s own approach to translation. There are also several new studies of Ulrich's *Frauendienst*: Young and K. Kellermann (Bertelsmeier-Kierst, *Umbruch*, 317–44) and also T. Gutwald (Harms, *Ordnung*, 143–63) examine the work's mixture of written and unwritten communication; Lisa Perfetti, *Women and Laughter in Medieval Comic Literature*, Ann Arbor, Michigan U.P., xiv + 286 pp., includes a chapter (126–67) which focuses on the mocking laughter of Ulrich's lady (seen as a means of ridiculing courtly literature), and on performative aspects of gender; and S. Linden, *ZDP*, 122:409–15, argues that the absence of a double leaf in the main MS of *Frauendienst* (Cgm 44) is attributable to a conscious decision on the part of a medieval user to remove one version of a song originally written out twice.

Michael Mareiner, *Mittelhochdeutsche Minnereden und Minneallegorien der Wiener Handschrift 2796 und der Heidelberger Handschrift Pal. germ. 348. 2. Band: 'Von einem Schatz'. Wörterbuch und Reimwörterbuch* (EH, 1, 1863), 466 pp., complements M.'s 1988 edition of *Von einem Schatz* (see *YWMLS*, 50:717). Astonishingly, it includes entries, sometimes very detailed ones, for every single word and rhyme in the poem. W. Achnitz, Schiewer, *Forschungsberichte*, 197–255, surveys research on 'Minnereden'; and in *ASNS*, 240:360–70, he identifies the Johannes cited as an authority on love in *Der Schüler von Paris B* as Johann von Konstanz, author of the *Konstanzer Minnelehre*. Similarly D. Huschenbett, *Flood Vol.*, 227–41, argues that Johann's work acted as a source for Hermann von Sachsenheim's *Mörin*.

Also on didactic literature, C. Bertelsmeier-Kierst, *ZDP*, 122:20–47, argues that the so-called 'A-prologue' of the *Lucidarius* formed part of an early version of the work which originated at the court of Henry the Lion; W. P. Gerritsen, Lehmann-Benz, *Schnittpunkte*, 215–22, perceives a compositional unity between the three didactic works that make up the late-12th-c. 'Niederrheinisches Moralbuch'; S. Höfer, *Fest. Honemann*, 865–77, discusses the views on education and learning expressed in *Der welsche Gast*, and especially Thomasin's recommendation that scholars should be valued integral members of court society; F. Löser, Bertelsmeier-Kierst, *Umbruch*, 267–89, examines the use of Daniel 2. 31–45 in 13th-c. religious and didactic poetry; I. Heiser, *ZDA*, 132:239–48, presents evidence suggesting the reception of Freidank in 14th-c., 15th-c., and 16th-c. inscriptions; M. Temm, *Fest. Honemann*, 895–915, introduces and prints the text of a late-15th-c. fragment of Stephan von Dorpat's *Schachbuch* now in Cracow; H. Lähnemann, *ICLS 9*, 99–106, considers the didactic strategies of Johannes Rothe's *Ritterspiegel*; A. Classen, *FCS*, 28:65–79, surveys the social and moral functions of wisdom in medieval German literature, with particular reference to Erhart Gross's *Witwenbuch*; R. Günthart, Dilg, *Natur*, 373–85, discusses the characterization of nature in the Cyrillus fables and their German translations; and G. Roth and V. Honemann, *Fest. Gärtner*, 175–239, provide a parallel edition of the two versions of the MLG *Geistliche Minnejagd*, and discuss various problems associated with the work and its MS transmission.

Rebecca L. R. Garber, *Feminine Figurae. Representations of Gender in Religious Texts by Medieval German Women Writers 1100–1375* (Medieval History and Culture, 10), NY, Routledge, xviii + 295 pp., fills an important gap in research by offering a detailed analysis of representatives of three related literary forms much practised by nuns: cycles of visions, accounts of personal revelations, and sorority books. G. illuminates in particular the complex inter-textual relationships which often obtained between such works, and the sophisticated and notably diverse ways in which their authors re-fashioned conventional ideas, such as the polarities between Mary and Eve and the *vitae activa et contemplativa*, and the conception of the soul as bride of Christ. She also examines in detail various constructions of authority and of specifically feminine exemplarity. Of the 12 authors covered, particular attention is paid to Hildegard von Bingen, Margarethe Ebner, and Adelheid Langmann; there is perhaps surprisingly little on Mechthild von Magdeburg and Gertrud von Helfta. Dinshaw, *Companion*, whilst a valuable handbook, contains disappointingly little on German women authors. It is symptomatic that its brief sections on Hildegard and on the 'Helfta women' (by A. Barnett) deal mainly with their reception in England.

Theresia Heimerl, *Frauenmystik — Männermystik? Gemeinsamkeiten und Unterschiede in der Darstellung von Gottes- und Menschenbild bei Meister Eckhart, Heinrich Seuse, Marguerite Porete und Mechthild von Magdeburg* (Mystik und Mediävistik, 1), Münster, LIT, 2002, iv + 321 pp., is a readable and intelligent attempt to relativize the importance often ascribed to gender when accounting for differences between types of medieval mysticism. H. compares perspectives on divine and human nature, gender, ethics, and the Church, as these are expressed in the works of the four mystics named in her title; in practice, however, Eckhart is compared specifically to Porete, and Seuse to Mechthild. She concludes that, between each pair, there are not only many similarities, but also several differences that can be explained more convincingly with reference to levels of education, social and religious status, contemporary realities, and personal disposition, than to gender. Especially given the close relationship between gender and all of these other criteria, her analysis is obviously selective and partial, but it is also interesting and thought-provoking.

Ralph Frenken, *Kindheit und Mystik im Mittelalter* (Beihefte zur *Mediävistik*, 2), Frankfurt, Lang, 2002, 344 pp., is a fascinating contribution to research on medieval *Erlebnismystik*, written from the perspective of a psychologist. F. suggests that mystical experience arose ultimately out of childhood traumas, and represented a form of self-therapy aimed at re-integrating traumatized and hence disassociated parts of the mystic's personality. Moreover he sees mystics as having frequently suffered from 'borderline syndrome' (the borderline in question being that between neurosis and psychosis). Inevitably many readers will find some of F.'s interpretations hard to swallow — including, for example, his argument that Seuse was a victim of child abuse, which in turn led him to develop infanticidal and paedophiliac fantasies. F. himself, however, has no illusions as to the difficulties and limitations inherent in his approach, and his book as a whole provides many worthwhile insights to set alongside those of Germanists and theologians. Moreover the range of mystics he covers is impressive: most are women, but these include not only the usual suspects, but also figures like Christina von Retters, Liutgard von Wittichen, Dorothea von Montau, and Elisabeth Achler von Reute.

Dorothea is also the subject of an article by W. Williams-Krapp, *Fest. Honemann*, 711–20, who edits and discusses a *Sendbrief* in which Nikolaus von Nürnberg (I) pleads for her canonization.

Much work continues to be done on Mechthild von Magdeburg. Above all, Elizabeth A. Andersen, *Mechthild of Magdeburg: Selections from 'The Flowing Light of the Godhead'. Translated from the Middle High German with Introduction, Notes, and Interpretive Essay*, Cambridge, Brewer, ii + 170 pp., valuably complements A.'s important 2000 monograph on Mechthild (see *YWMLS*, 62 : 628). As in that volume, her approach reflects a consistently sound appreciation of the needs of the non-specialist English-speaking reader. Here she offers approximately 45% of the *Fliessendes Licht* in a clear and well-annotated English translation. Appropriately, the extracts are chosen to illuminate several of Mechthild's main themes, notably her conception of *unio mystica*, her self-presentation, her relationships to various contemporaries, and her visionary experiences; and they are introduced in an order which respects Mechthild's own arrangement of her material. They are also supported by salient biographical and literary-historical material, and by an essay that focuses particularly on the motif of the eyes of the soul. Many will be grateful for this volume, though it complements, rather than supersedes, Frank Tobin's 1998 translation of Mechthild's entire work. Four articles on *Das fliessende Licht* appear in Henkel, *Dialoge*. E. A. Andersen (225–38) studies the intertextual relationship between Mechthild's work and the Psalter; A. Suerbaum (239–55) examines her constructions of identity in the work's dialogues, especially those not primarily concerned with mystic union; A. Volfing (257–66) analyses the dialogues involving Mechthild's various 'brides'; and G. Dicke (267–78) considers semantic and pragmatic aspects of the dialogues between God and the soul.

Lectura Eckhardii II. Predigten Meister Eckharts von Fachgelehrten gelesen und gedeutet, ed. Georg Steer and Loris Sturlese, Stuttgart, Kohlhammer, viii + 251 pp., continues this enormously promising series devoted to Eckhart, in which individual sermons (printed in their original language with a facing translation into modern German) are interpreted by distinguished scholars in the field. The present volume covers six German sermons, nos 1 (A. Beccarisi), 6 (K. Flasch), 10 (R. Schönberger), 37 (M. J. F. M. Hoenen), 72 (W. Haug), and 86 (D. Mieth); and two Latin ones, XXV (N. Largier) and XXIX (B. McGinn). The approaches of the scholars inevitably differ; all, however, seek to combine detailed textual analysis with a sensitivity towards the structures of Eckhart's arguments, and towards the cultural contexts in which they were produced.

Gabriele Hille-Coates, *'Lux' und 'lumen' in den Bibelkommentaren Meister Eckharts*, Göttingen, Cuvillier, x + 441 pp., is a thorough study of some of the most important metaphors of Eckhart's Latin Bible commentaries: H.-C. calculates that forms of *lux* or *lumen* occur nearly 500 times in this corpus alone, and also demonstrates that the many nuances they convey are central to his construction of both the unity and the difference between God and man. She shows not least that Eckhart creatively combines various biblical and patristic conceptions of light with Neo-Platonic theories of emanation, and in so doing uses the Latin language more imaginatatively and flexibly that is often allowed. Elsewhere W. Haug, *Fest. Janota*, 73–92, argues that the song *Granum sinapis* is not by Eckhart; W. Williams-Krapp, Lehmann-Benz, *Schnittpunkte*, 41–53, describes and accounts for the limited reception of Dutch mystical writings in late-medieval Southern Germany; H. E. Keller, *Das Mittelalter*, 7, 2002: 157–82, offers a semiotic analysis of the 'IHS' monogram which Seuse describes himself, in his *Vita*, as having cut into his chest; G. Warnar, Lehmann-Benz, *Schnittpunkte*, 55–66, discusses the nature and extent of contact between Tauler and Ruusbroec; and E. Senne, *Gabler Vol.*, 149–60, examines the German versions of mystical texts by Elisabeth von Schönau transmitted in the early-16th-c. 'Codex Wolhusensis'.

Rudolf Wintnauers Übersetzung der 'Legenda maior de beata Hedwigi'. Text und Untersuchungen zu einem Frühwerk der Wiener Übersetzungsschule unter Herzog Albrecht III, ed. Jelko Peters (Edition Praesens Textbibliothek, 1), Vienna, Praesens, xvi + 303 pp., is the first reliable and generally available edition of the earliest of five German translations of the Latin life of the confessor St Hedwig of Silesia (1174/78–1243), which was commissioned by Duke Albrecht of Austria around 1380. P.'s edition is in essence a diplomatic one, with the orthography, punctuation, and even line divisions of the work's sole surviving MS preserved almost unchanged, and its many scribal corrections documented in no fewer than 1269 footnotes. Given that the MS (Brussels, Bibliothèque Royale, MS 4300) was written and corrected by Wintnauer himself, this approach is defensible, even desirable; but it does not make for easy reading. P.'s extensive chapters on the historical Hedwig, on Wintnauer's Latin source and translation techniques, and on the early years of the 'Vienna School' are, however, exemplary, as are the Latin-German glossary and analysis of the MS's language which he also provides. Also on legends, F. P. Knapp, *GRM*, 53: 133–54, examines characteristic narrative structures of the lives of Judas, Albanus, and Gregory the Great, and looks at medieval attempts to legitimize their 'scandalous' aspects; K. Klein, *ZDA*, 132: 332–34, describes and prints a previously unknown fragment of *Das Passional* from Louny; and V. Bok, *Fest. Janota*,

159–66, suggests Hedwig von Schauenberg, wife of Count Wok I von Rosenberg, as the patroness who commissioned the *Märterbuch*. Specifically on Mary, W. Schröder, *Fest. Gärtner*, 43–73, prints part of Priester Wernher's *Driu liet von der maget* from MS F, and discusses various problems associated with the work's origins, MSS, and interpretation; P. Ochsenbein, *Fest. Gärtner*, 125–30, comments on a recently discovered fragment of Bruder Philipp's *Marienleben* from the Cistercian convent Mariastern in Panwitz-Kuckau; A. Otto, *FCS*, 28: 184–98, looks at the forms and functions of biblical quotations in the Marian verse attributed to Johannes der Weise; and R. Peters, *Fest. Honemann*, 809–24, looks at both the circumstances of composition and the much later MS transmission of the *Bordesholmer Marienklage*.

Kurt Otto Seidel, *'Die St. Georgener Predigten.' Untersuchungen zur Überlieferung und Textgeschichte* (MTU, 121), x + 370 pp., brings a new clarity to the complex textual history of this early-13th-c. Alemannic corpus, which seems to have been perceived above all as an anthology for public and private reading in a monastic context. If one includes a diverse *Streuüberlieferung*, it is found in over 80 MSS, all of which S. carefully describes and analyses. He shows that, whilst numerous MSS reproduce the original corpus with few alterations, many others change and, above all, add to it freely. This textual 'openness' is no doubt one reason why the *Predigten* appear to have remained popular in all monastic orders down to 1500; but they were never printed. Nor is there a reliable modern edition — an enterprise which, however, will be a much more manageable one thanks to S.'s exhaustive groundwork. Elsewhere V. Mertens and W. Scheepsma, Lehmann-Benz, *Schnittpunkte*, 67–81, discuss the reception of the *St. Georgener Predigten*, Seuse, and Tauler in the late-medieval Netherlands; D. Neuendorff, *JIG*, 34.2, 2002: 147–66, uses examples from Berthold von Regensburg's vernacular sermons to argue that both editors and literary historians should take greater account of the textual history of medieval works; and H.-J. Schiewer, *MSS*, 47: 83–87, provides a bibliography of German-language publications on medieval sermons from the Germanic area which appeared between 1998 and 2002.

Other studies of religious literature include four contributions to *Fest. Gärtner*: W. J. Hoffmann (101–24) edits and discusses the Munich fragment of Konrad von Heimesfurt's *Urstende*; V. Bok (131–68) prints and introduces a newly discovered MS of the vernacular *Evangelium Nicodemi D* found in the Franciscan monastery at Cheb; H. Boková (169–74) examines this MS's language; and G. Kornrumpf (677–88) assesses the MS tradition of the 'Österreichischer Bibelübersetzer''s *Klosterneuburger Evangelienwerk*. In *Fest. Janota*, U. Williams and

W. Williams-Krapp (167–89) edit and introduce a misogynistic *Sendbrief vom Betrug teuflischer Erscheinungen* written in Nuremberg around 1450, and C. Roth (191–210) discusses an early-15th-c. bilingual (Latin and German) text of and commentary on the *Song of Songs*. In *Fest. Honemann*, H.-J. Spitz (661–73) looks at Tilo von Kulm's treatment of his Latin source material in *Von siben Ingesigeln*, and J. Splett (675–86) assesses the various renderings of Latin *phariseus* in the *Alemannische Evangelienübersetzung*. In Tervooren, *Literaturgeschichtsschreibung*, V. Honemann (134–42) discusses the strong regional flavour and inter-regional importance of Heinrich von Hesler's *Apokalypse* (which he dates to *c.* 1260), and C. Tuczay (280–93) considers a range of Southern German texts which imply a particular concern to combat superstition in that area from the 14th c. onwards. Elsewhere A. Volfing, *Flood Vol.*, 137–54, points to various aspects of fictionality in Brun von Schönebeck's *Das Hohe Lied*, and suggests that the role of its narrator reflects a particular enthusiasm for Wolfram on Brun's part; M. Sherwood-Smith, Henkel, *Dialoge*, 213–24, examines the dialogues between the members of the Trinity presented in *Das Anegenge* and *Die Erlösung*; and G. C. Shockey, *ABäG*, 58: 151–70, discusses aspects of the complementarity of Judaism and Christianity as shown in *Die Erlösung*.

DRAMA

Eckehard Simon, *Die Anfänge des weltlichen deutschen Schauspiels 1370–1530. Untersuchung und Dokumentation* (MTU, 104), xii + 492 pp. + 12 pls, is an important book by one of the leading scholars in the field. S. edits some 521 short documents concerning the performance of secular drama in Germany, thereby complementing Bernd Neumann's still more extensive 1987 collection of documents relating to religious plays (see *YWMLS*, 49: 650). His work offers much more than this, however. The documentary material is analysed in a sequence of seven chapters, each relating to a particular town or area; and S. concludes from a careful reappraisal of the MS evidence that the Osnabrück play *Septem mulieres: Sieben Frauen und ein Mann* almost certainly dates from around 1370, roughly the same time therefore as the generally accepted 'first' German secular play, the *St. Pauler Neidhartspiel*. Moreover his emphasis on records of performance leads him to problematize the accepted sub-divisions of religious plays according to subject-matter, and instead to suggest performance-related categories such as *Einkehrspiel*, *Rathaus- oder Saalspiel*, *Marktspiel*, or *Umzugsspiel*.

Dunbar H. Ogden, *The Staging of Drama in the Medieval Church*, Newark, Delaware U.P., 2002, 251 pp., inevitably contains little on the texts of vernacular dramas, but affords many fascinating insights into performance practices at places such as Benediktbeuren, Klosterneuburg, Bozen, Magdeburg, Essen, and Regensburg. In *Fest. Janota*, U. Schulze (211–32) considers ways in which the St Gall, Frankfurt, and Donaueschingen Passion Plays reflect and promote emotional experience of the divine; K. Vogelgsang (233–54) edits and comments on the scene involving the Devil in the *Hessisches Weihnachtsspiel*; and K. Wolf (255–64) discusses problems associated with reconstructing the costumes used in medieval plays. In Lehmann-Benz, *Schnittpunkte*, C. Dauven-von Knippenberg (95–107) suggests that the *Maastrichter (ripuarisches) Passionsspiel* may have been used for private devotional reading; and H. R. Velten (331–52) examines aspects of the characterization of fools in secular German and Dutch plays (especially *Fastnachtspiele*) from between 1400 and 1600. Elsewhere K. Scheel, Braet, *Laughter*, 195–205, discusses the variations introduced to the story of Neidhart and the violet in the 'St. Pauler', 'Großes' and 'Kleines' Neidhart plays, and draws conclusions from them about the three plays' likely target audiences; J. Haustein and W. Neumann, *Fest. Gärtner*, 385–94, locate the so-called 'Innsbrucker (thüringische) Spielhandschrift' to Eastern Thuringia, between Altenburg and the Saale; H. Freytag et al., *ZDA*, 132:189–238 and also *NdW*, 43:287–90, demonstrate that the *Redentiner Osterspiel* drew from the paintings of the Dance of Death in the Lübeck Marienkirche, and was probably performed in Lübeck; and E. E. Du Bruck, *FCS*, 28:1–36, lists and assesses publications on late-medieval drama which appeared between 1998 and 2000.

SCIENTIFIC AND SPECIALIZED LITERATURE

History as Literature. German World Chronicles of the Thirteenth Century in Verse, ed. and trans. R. Graeme Dunphy (MGTBE, 3), 186 pp., presents excerpts from three major works. From Rudolf von Ems's *Weltchronik*, there is the creation and the fall of mankind; from the *Christherre-Chronik* there is part of the story of Jacob; and from Jans Enikel's *Weltchronik* a much longer section on the prophet Job, corrupt popes, and then Frederick II and other contemporary figures. The introduction and notes are informative, and the English translation is elegant with a rather liturgical flavour.

Gabriel Viehhauser, *Die Darstellung König Salomos in der mittelhochdeutschen Weltchronistik*, Vienna, Praesens, 205 pp., is a useful study of a relatively little explored aspect of the medieval reception of the story of Solomon, namely its treatment in the *Weltchroniken* of Rudolf von Ems and Jans Enikel, in Petrus Comestor's *Historia Scholastica*, and in the *Historienbibeln*. The core of V.'s work is a thorough comparative analysis of these works' presentation of the principal motifs concerning Solomon which were handed down in the biblical and legendary accounts. In it, he points not least to the consistently exemplary role of Solomon in Rudolf's work, to the techniques of rationalization and sensationalization that pervade Enikel's, and to the importance of non-narrative biblical sources (such as the *Song of Songs* and *Ecclesiastes*) in the *Historienbibeln*. Elsewhere D. Klein, Bertelsmeier-Kierst, *Umbruch*, 73–90, surveys the rise of vernacular world chronicles in the 13th century.

Several articles are concerned with Nikolaus von Jeroschin's *Kronike von Pruzinlant*. In *Fest. Janota*, G. Vollmann-Profe (125–40) examines Nikolaus's strategies of translation, and E. Feistner (141–58) studies the construction of various identities in the *Kronike* and other works produced for the Teutonic Order. Moreover in *ZDA*, 132, K. Klein and R. G. Päsler (77–84) describe two 14th-c. fragments of the *Kronike* recently discovered in Amberg and in Toruń, and G. Vollmann-Profe (295–306) discusses the function of the work's reports of miracles.

Fama. The Politics of Talk and Reputation in Medieval Europe, ed. Thelma S. Fenster and Daniel Lord Small, Ithaca NY, Cornell U.P., x + 227 pp., includes a chapter by M. H. Caviness and C. G. Nelson (47–72) dealing with male speech and female silence in medieval courts, referring particularly to the pictorial cycle of the Dresden *Sachsenspiegel* MS. R. Schmidt-Wiegand, *Fest. Gärtner*, 825–38, compares representative images from the four illustrated MSS of the *Sachsenspiegel*; and in *NdW*, 43:221–33, she discusses the terms *mundel* and *herwede* as used and depicted in the work's Oldenburg MS. Elsewhere J. Wolf, *Fest. Gärtner*, 839–74, discusses what 13th-c. vernacular *Judeneide* reveal about the interplay between oral and written legal traditions; and G. Roth, *Fest. Honemann*, 403–11, studies the complex relationship between the *Meißner* and *Leobschützer Rechtsbücher*.

Nine Robijntje Miedema, *Rompilgerführer in Spätmittelalter und Früher Neuzeit. Die 'Indulgentiae ecclesiarum urbis Romae' (deutsch/niederländisch). Edition und Kommentar* (FN, 72), x + 554 pp., is the third distinguished volume which this author has devoted to medieval descriptions of Rome. In many ways it is both a continuation of M.'s 1996 edition and study of the *Mirabilia Romae* tradition (see *YWMLS*, 58:760) and a companion to her systematic catalogue of medieval accounts of Roman churches: *Die römischen Kirchen im Spätmittelalter nach den 'Indulgentiae ecclesiarum urbis Romae'*, Tübingen, Niemeyer, 2001. The present volume is centred around a readable and solidly documented edition of some 12 vernacular texts from within the extremely complex and variable *Indulgentiae* tradition. The editorial part is accompanied by textual histories of the tradition's three main branches, studies of its sources and influence, and cultural-historical chapters that seek to situate it within late-medieval discourses on pilgrimage, relics, and indulgences. Also on travel literature, M. Przybilski, *MJ*, 37, 2002:295–330, examines the foreign language alphabets recorded in the MSS of Otto von Diemeringen's translation of Mandeville's *Travels*, and analyses their contribution to the construction of alterity; P. Johanek, *Fest. Honemann*, 455–80, discusses Gabriel Tetzel's report of the travels undertaken in the mid-1460s by Lev von Rožmital on behalf of the Bohemian King Georg von Podiebrad; W. Rösener, Ertzdorff, *Erkundung*, 87–108, considers accounts of travels and countries in late-medieval autobiographies by aristocrats; and in the same volume (109–33) S. Heimann-Seelbach discusses the nature of subjectivity in Stephan von Gumpenberg's *Warhafftige Beschreybung der Meerfart*.

Jürgen Fröhlich, *Bernhard Hirschvelders Briefrhetorik (Cgm 3607). Untersuchung und Edition* (DLA, 42), 349 pp., provides the first edition of this late-15th-c. example of the 'modus epistolandi', and of several letters and other contemporary documents relevant to it. As such his work neatly complements Knape and Röll's recent *Rhetorica deutsch* collection (see *YWMLS*, 64:617–18). It is also notable, however, for the lucid and thorough way in which F. sets Hirschvelder's work in its cultural-historical context. A brief history of the relevant ancient and medieval rhetorical traditions is followed by an account of Hirschvelder's main deviations from it, and by a stimulating short essay on his position at an important crossroads in media history.

Der deutsche 'Macer'. Vulgatfassung. Mit einem Abdruck des lateinischen Macer Floridus, 'De viribus herbarum', ed. Bernhard Schnell and William Cossgrove (TTG, 50), xii + 509 pp., is an outstandingly erudite and clear-headed volume which will be of value to anyone with even a basic interest in herbals. It is far more than an edition: indeed, its text of the German *Macer* (edited from an early-14th-c. Berlin MS) occupies a mere 60 pp. Alongside it, S. and C. offer a detailed textual history of the work (which originated around 1220 in Thuringia or Upper Saxony), a comprehensive glossary to it, an analysis of its origins, sources, *Mitüberlieferung*, and techniques of adaptation, a full version of the text of its principal source (the *Macer Floridus*), and excerpts from three other Latin sources, the *Spuria Macri*, Gargilius Martialis's *Medicinae ex oleribus et pomis*, and Constantinus Africanus's *Liber de gradibus*. They also include a chronological survey of all Western herbals from before the 15th c., which gives particular emphasis to those which had most influence on the vernacular *Macer*. Elsewhere J. G. Mayer and K. Goehl, *Sprachwissenschaft*, 28:273–92, examine the relationships between the German *Macer*, the *Leipziger*

Drogenkompendium, and the *Gart der Gesundheit*; L. V. Gerulaitis, *FCS*, 28:138–47, surveys the presentation of medicinal plants in the *Gart der Gesundheit* and other herbals printed in the late 15th c.; and B. Schnell, Dilg, *Natur*, 442–61, discusses the conception of plants, and of nature in general, underlying vernacular German herbals, especially the *Kräuterbuch* of Johannes Hartlieb. Also noted: Christoph Gerhardt and Bernhard Schnell, **In verbis et herbis et in lapidibus est deus: Zum Naturverständnis in den deutschprachigen illustrierten Kräuterbüchern des Mittelalters* (Mitteilungen und Verzeichnisse aus der Bibliothek des Bischöflichen Priesterseminars zu Trier, 15), Trier, 2002, 40 pp.

Konrad von Megenberg, *Das 'Buch der Natur'. Band II: Kritischer Text nach den Handschriften*, ed. Robert Luff and Georg Steer (TTG, 54), iv + 529 pp., has appeared, rather confusingly, in advance of the accompanying parts of a four-volume set. Nevertheless it is enormously welcome, offering as it does a superb modern edition of Megenberg's seminal work, based on Munich, Bayerische Staatsbibliothek, Cgm 38. It maintains an exemplary balance between fidelity and readability, and as such immediately supersedes Franz Pfeiffer's edition, which has done invaluable but imperfect service for over 140 years. Elsewhere O. Riha, Dilg, *Natur*, 111–23, looks at the conception of nature underlying medieval medicine, referring in particular to the *Buch der Natur* and to Ortolf von Baierland's *Arzneibuch*.

Other work on medical texts includes B. Schnell's edition and study (*Fest. Gärtner*, 75–99) of the *Benediktbeurer Rezeptar*, and L. Vaňková's discussion (*Sprachwissenschaft*, 28:313–23) of the widely differing degrees to which Latin is used in the *Olmützer medizinisches Compendium*, *Olmützer Chirurgie*, and *Olmützer Wundarznei*. Moreover M. Giese, *BGDSL*, 125:494–523, examines the MS traditions and dates of, and relationships between the *Ältere* and *Jüngere deutsche Habichtslehre*, the *Beizbüchlein*, and the *Wiener* and *Heidelberger Falkenheilkunde*; and C. Baufeld, *Fest. Gärtner*, 709–45, discusses the reception of Volmar's *Steinbuch* in the verse lapidary of Greifswald 8⁰ Ms 875.

OTHER LATER MEDIEVAL LITERATURE

Die Bibliothek Konrad Peutingers. Edition der historischen Kataloge und Rekonstruktion des Bestandes. Bd. I: Die autographen Kataloge Peutingers. Der nicht-juristische Bibliotheksteil, ed. Hans-Jörg Kunast and Helmut Zäh (Studia Augustana, 11), Tübingen, Niemeyer, x + 755 pp., provides valuably detailed information about the remarkably extensive collection of the Augsburg Humanist, historian, and Imperial servant Konrad Peutinger (1465–1547). Two catalogues of its contents have been preserved in Peutinger's own hand, both divided into legal texts and others — he plainly had a considerable interest in theology, philosophy, the Liberal Arts, and Classical literature, as well as historiography. The non-legal parts of these catalogues are edited here, and also form the basis of an exhaustive attempt to identify the precise editions to which Peutinger's entries refer. In addition the volume contains clear introductory material on Peutinger, his books, and his catalogues. Meanwhile in *Marginalien*, 169:32–42, S. Knackmus considers the library and reading habits of Caritas Pirckheimer, and prints some letters of the three Pirckheimer sisters to their brother Willibald.

On Johannes von Tepl's *Der Ackermann aus Böhmen*, U. Kühne, *ASNS*, 240:371–77, discusses textual problems associated with the dedicatory epistle to Peter Rother; J. M. Clifton-Everest, Henkel, *Dialoge*, 279–98, suggests that the *Ackermann* was read in early modern times as an *ars bene moriendi* — a factor which accounts in part for its remarkable popularity; and A. Hausmann, *BGDSL*, 125:292–323, places the work in the context of an ongoing debate between Christian and Jewish scholars in late-medieval Prague, and postulates (extraordinarily but not implausibly) that the work seeks to portray to a Jewish audience the inadequacy of a religion without Christ.

On Sebastian Brant, E. E. Du Bruck, *FCS*, 28:97–110, examines the education, mentality, and cultural significance of late-medieval merchants as evinced in *Das Narrenschiff*; and F. Küenzlen, *Fest. Honemann*, 825–40, establishes and interprets the fact that one of Brant's two Marian prayers in Latin prose is based on material from the *Golden Ass* of Apuleius. Moreover W. Röcke, *Fest. Janota*, 51–71, discusses the thematization of violence and its avoidance in late-medieval folly literature (notably the *Salomon und Markolf* tradition).

G. Signori, *MJ*, 38:249–66, discusses aspects of the reception of Aristotle in late-13th-c. and early-14th-c. Europe, including Germany; and G. Hayer, *Sprachwissenschaft*, 28:293–311, considers the two German translations of the late-14th-c. *Problemata Aristotelis*, focusing especially on questions concerning their sources and reception. Meanwhile D. Roth, *ZDP*, 122:359–82, argues that the *Mitüberlieferung* of two German translations of the *Sieben Weise Meister* implies that the work was understood as having a marked moral-theological dimension; S. S. Poor, Harms, *Ordnung*, 193–205, assesses the principles underlying the choice and ordering of the texts of a mid-15th-c. *Sammelhandschrift*, University of Pennsylvania, Cod. 824; and U. Friedrich, *ZDP*, 122:73–92, examines the forms of social and political order adumbrated in the *Epistola presbiteri Johannis*, stressing the work's mythic potential.

Peter Schmidt, *Gedruckte Bilder in handgeschriebenen Büchern. Zum Gebrauch von Druckgraphik im 15. Jahrhundert* (Pictura et poesis, 16), Cologne, Böhlau, x + 511 pp. + 53 pls, offers a fascinating collection of case studies concerning the use of woodcuts, copper engravings, and other new pictorial techniques in MSS dating from between 1400 and 1470. S. begins by examining the development of this phenomenon in three important South German monastic libraries, at Nuremberg (OP), Tegernsee (OSB), and Inzighoven (CRSA), all of which became increasingly keen to acquire printed images from the 1440s onwards, in the wake of observantist reform. He then analyses ways in which such images were used to rationalize the process of MS production in codices written by two identifiable scribes, Leonhard Taichstetter von München and Konrad Bollstatter von Öttingen; and he traces technical developments which occurred in the production of a particular type of 15th-c. illustrated book, namely collections of Passion prayers. In this chapter one becomes particularly aware of the important role played by printed images in the gradual transition from manual to mechanical book production. Notable features of S.'s book are his use of almost exclusively unpublished material, his detailed descriptions of the MSS he discusses, and the 243 black and white illustrations which conclude the volume. On a similar theme, S. Griese examines, in Henkel, *Dialoge*, 315–35, the dialogic relationships between text and image, and between artist and viewer, in 15th-c. single-leaf woodcuts; and in *Fest. Honemann*, 783–801, she interprets the woodcuts depicting saints in 15th-c. prints as signs and symbols characteristic of an increasingly visual culture. Also in *Fest. Honemann*, F. Eisermann (481–502) discusses the importance of printing for the production and reception of open letters, proclamations, and other public notices in the late 15th c.; U. Rautenberg (503–12) outlines changes in the ways in which knowledge was organized and presented in books as a consequence of the invention of printing; and M. Ostermann (551–67) discusses the contemporary publication in printed form of letters documenting a political conflict between Hans von Tratt and Eitel Schelm von Bergen. In *Flood Vol.*, H. Nickel (579–90) surveys the incunabula commissioned by Emperor Maximilian I; P. Naylor (591–613) studies the activities of several men who worked as both printers and authors in Germany between 1470 and 1540; and J. Schulz-Grobert (615–28) examines the career and reputation of Johannes Gruninger against the background of more general criticisms of printing and printers around 1500.

M. Bärmann, *ABäG*, 58:209–14, uses a hitherto unconsidered entry in the Freiburg council minutes of 1495 to shed light on the biography of Johannes Pauli; and A. Classen, *Fabula*, 44:209–36, examines Pauli's reception of exempla from late-medieval sermons in his *Schimpf und Ernst*. Meanwhile M. Bärmann and M. Prosser,

Daphnis, 31, 2002: 32–54, assess the significance for our understanding of Anton von Pforr's biography of his being mentioned alongside Margrave Rudolf IV von Hochberg in the so-called 'Großer Dingrodel' of the Abbey of St. Peter im Schwarzwald; A. Simon, Henkel, *Dialoge*, 299–313, examines dialogue in *Der Ritter von Turn* in the light of the work's constructions of gender identity and of the interaction between its text and woodcuts (in the 1493 edition); K. Grubmüller, *Fest. Gärtner*, 885–98, investigates the use of German at 15th-c. and 16th-c. schools; and D. Klein, *Fest. Janota*, 299–316, considering the question of when the late-medieval period of German literature ended, suggests that a caesura can be observed in respect of the years 1500–1520.

THE SIXTEENTH CENTURY

By Mark Taplin

1. General

Hans-Gert Roloff, *Kleine Schriften zur Literatur des 16. Jahrhunderts. Festgabe zum 70. Geburtstag*, ed. and introd. Christiane Caemmerer et al. (Chloe, 35), Amsterdam, Rodopi, 434 pp., is a useful collection of 21 essays and lectures published by R. over the past 35 years. In their introduction, the editors pay tribute to R. for developing the concept of 'Mittlere deutsche Literatur', which radically expanded the range of early modern texts considered worthy of attention by Germanists and paved the way for more recent interdisciplinary approaches. The contributions themselves are grouped to reflect R.'s principal research interests: the early modern prose novel, 16th-c. drama, the literature and propaganda of the Reformation, and the works of Thomas Naogeorg. The final essay in the volume, on the biographical and bibliographical lexicon *Die Deutsche Literatur*, illustrates R.'s contribution to efforts to place the study of early modern literature on a sounder empirical basis. *Venezianisch-deutsche Kulturbeziehungen in der Renaissance. Akten des interdisziplinären Symposions vom 8. und 10. November im Centro Tedeschi di Studi Veneziani in Venedig*, ed. Klaus Arnold, Franz Fuchs, and Stephan Füssel (Pirckheimer Jahrbuch für Renaissance- und Humanismusforschung, 18), Wiesbaden, Harrassowitz, 178 pp., deals with three aspects of cultural exchange between southern Germany and northern Italy in the early modern period: printing and the traffic in books; the role of teachers and scholars; and Venetian influences on the painting of Albrecht Altdorfer. C. Reske, 'Erhard Ratdolts Wirken in Venedig und Augsburg', *ib.*, 25–43, provides an overview of Ratdolt's career as a printer, noting his use of innovative techniques but also the decline in quantity and quality of his output from around 1500. H. Stein-Kecks, *ib.*, 143–63, contests the traditional view of Altdorfer as an exponent of the 'Danube school' of painting and identifies points of contact between his work and that of Italian artists such as Jacopo Bellini and Giorgione. Wilhelm Kühlmann and Walter E. Schäfer, *Literatur im Elsaß von Fischart bis Moscherosch. Gesammelte Studien*, Tübingen, Niemeyer, 2001, ix + 436 pp., brings together articles published by the authors between 1970 and 2000. Of particular relevance are K.'s essays on Fischart (1–24) and a Paracelsian poem by Michael Toxites (25–40), and S.'s study of the 17th-c. reception of Fischart's works (389–408). Christa Grössinger, *Humour and Folly in Secular and Profane Prints in Northern Europe, 1430–1540*, London, Harvey Miller, 2002, xiv + 227 pp., analyses the treatment of non-religious themes in early modern Dutch and German prints. G. argues that the development of printing enabled profane, bawdy, and scatological subjects to move from hidden locations such as the margins of manuscripts and the corbels of buildings into the cultural mainstream. With the onset of the Reformation, the representation of human vice took on an increasingly didactic tone. Woodcut depictions of pious bourgeois life were counterbalanced with images of drunken, violent peasants and domineering wives, which illustrated the consequences of deviation from the new Protestant moral order (in Nuremberg broadsheets, the message was often underlined by an accompanying text by Hans Sachs). G. concludes that unlike later 'popular prints', which had a subversive character, the publications of this period 'affirmed social norms, making them acceptable to a conservative, urban population'. Ertzdorff, *Erkundung*, presents essays on travel accounts by Byzantine, Jewish, Arab, European, and Far Eastern writers from the High Middle Ages through to the present day. Two contributions of particular interest are U. Seelbach (135–62), on the Rhineland nobleman Roland von Waldenburg's description of his study tour of Italy during the late 1560s; and X. von Ertzdorff (335–63), on Sigmund von Herberstein's Latin and German accounts of Muscovy, which he visited as Imperial ambassador in 1516–17 and 1526. E. notes the combination of accurate observation and humorous anecdote in Herberstein's portrayal of Russian society and customs. Petra Schöner, **Judenbilder im deutschen Einblattdruck der Renaissance*, Baden-Baden, Koerner, 2002, 438 pp. R. Seidel, '"Parodie" in der Frühen Neuzeit—Überlegungen zu Verbreitung und Funktion eines intertextuellen Phänomens zwischen Humanismus und Aufklärung', *WRM*, 27:112–34.

2. Humanism and the Reformation

Die Musen im Reformationszeitalter, ed. Walther Ludwig (Schriften der Stiftung Luthergedenkstätten in Sachsen-Anhalt, 1), Leipzig, Evangelische Verlagsanstalt, 2001, 323 pp., consists of papers from a 1999 conference on the relationship between early German Protestantism and humanism. Contributions include W. Ludwig, on the significance of the muses for Melanchthon and his circle (9–51); J. Leonhardt, 'Drucke antiker Texte in Deutschland vor der Reformation and Luthers frühe Vorlesungen' (97–129); F. Rädle, on post-Reformation Catholic humanism (131–49); U. Mennecke-Haustein, on the importance of the *studia humanitatis* for Luther's theology (151–65); R. Wetzel, on Melanchthon's defence of Classical learning during the early years of the Reformation (167–87); R. F. Glei, 'Sed pudenter et raro?

Lateinische Dichtungen Melanchthons' (189–208); J. Loehr, 'Melanchthons Übersetzungen griechischer Dichtungen' (209–45); M. Rener, on Melanchthon's reaction to the sack of Rome (247–63); L. Mundt, on bucolic poetry published in Germany between 1540 and 1570 (265–88); and G. Huber-Rebenich, on Eobanus Hessus's Latin translation of the psalter, first published in 1537 (289–303). Ilonka von Gülpen, *Der deutsche Humanismus und die frühe Reformations-Propaganda 1520–1526. Das Lutherporträt im Dienst der Bildpublizistik* (Studien zur Kunstgeschichte, 144), Hildesheim, Olms, 2002, 517 pp., highlights the contribution of humanist circles to the early success of the Reformation. The author suggests that humanist-inspired propaganda played a crucial role in bringing Luther's protest to public attention and in building sympathy for his cause. This was done partly by associating Luther's image with familiar humanist themes, such as the reform of learning, and by portraying him as the champion of a revived German nation against the papacy. Of particular benefit to Luther was the support that he received from Nuremberg and Augsburg, cities where artists, writers and printers were used to working together and had learned to combine images and texts effectively in the service of imperial propaganda. Later, Ulrich von Hutten took up the cudgels on Luther's behalf, turning his refuge at the Ebernburg into a centre for the production and distribution of pro-Lutheran works. The alliance of reformers and humanists began to unravel only after Hutten's death, as the fundamental differences in outlook and priorities between the two groups gradually became apparent. The result was a decline in the production of Reformation pamphlet literature and in the use of Luther's image as a propaganda tool. Horst Brunner et al., *Dulce bellum inexpertis — Bilder des Krieges in der deutschen Literatur des 15. und 16. Jahrhunderts* (Imagines medii aevi, 11), Wiesbaden, Reichert, 2002, xiv + 711 pp., is a collaborative study by members of the Würzburg research group 'Das Bild des Krieges im Wandel vom späten Mittelalter zur frühen Neuzeit'. The texts discussed include Luther's *Türkenschriften*, Latin poems and plays, biblical dramas, *Flugschriften* concerning the Peasants War, works by Hans Sachs, and Georg Rollenhagen's *Froschmeuseler* (1595). The authors contrast the literature of the late medieval period, which does not call into question the legitimacy of war, with the much more varied discourse of the 16th c. Thomas Haye, **Humanismus in Schleswig und Holstein. Eine Anthologie lateinischer Gedichte des 16. und 17. Jahrhunderts*, Kiel, Ludwig, 2001, 248 pp. U. Muhlack, 'Das Projekt der Germania illustrata. Ein Paradigma der Diffusion des Humanismus?', pp. 142–58 of *Diffusion des Humanismus. Studien zur nationalen Geschichtsschreibung europäischer Humanisten*, ed. Johannes Helmrath, Ulrich

Muhlack, and Gerrit Walther, Göttingen, Wallstein, 2002, 464 pp., compares German and Italian humanist historiography. T. Maissen, *ib.*, 210–49, charts attempts by various 16th-c. writers to construct a distinct 'Helvetic' identity for the Swiss. **Turicensia Latina. Lateinische Texte zur Geschichte Zürichs aus Altertum, Mittelalter und Neuzeit*, ed. Peter Stotz, Zurich, Verlag Neue Zürcher Zeitung, 355 pp.

Ingvild Richardsen-Friedrich, *Antichrist-Polemik in der Zeit der Reformation und der Glaubenskämpfe bis Anfang des 17. Jahrhunderts. Argumentation, Form und Funktion*, Frankfurt, Lang, 500 pp., examines Protestant and Catholic treatments of the figure of Antichrist. R.-F. provides a detailed account of the process by which Luther came to designate the papacy as Antichrist and analyses the rhetorical strategies that he used to support this identification, notably antithesis. As she makes clear, Luther's doctrine of the Antichrist developed independently of medieval tradition and was grounded in his reading of scripture. Subsequent Protestant writers popularized the theme through *Flugschriften*, drama, and sermons (works discussed include Naogeorg's *Pammachius* and Rudolf Gwalther's *Der Endtchrist*). It also featured in works by religious radicals, who identified mainstream Protestants as well as Catholics with the church of Antichrist. Similar accusations were directed against supporters of the Interim and against Andreas Osiander during the intra-Lutheran conflicts of the late 1540s and early 1550s. In the later 16th c., the identification of the papacy with Antichrist became central to Protestant ecclesiology; Catholic writers responded by making similar claims about Luther and, to a lesser extent, Calvin. As confessional tension increased, this debate took on a political dimension, with Catholics denouncing the Protestant view of the papacy as a 'Schmähung' that breached the terms of the Peace of Augsburg. Thomas Kaufmann, *Das Ende der Reformation. Magdeburgs 'Herrgotts Kanzlei' (1548–1551/2)* (Beiträge zur historischen Theologie, 123), Tübingen, Mohr Siebeck, xvii + 662 pp., is a systematic study of Magdeburg printing during the period of the Augsburg Interim. According to K., Magdeburg's emergence as the main centre of Lutheran opposition to the Interim is attributable in the first instance to the political stance adopted by the city authorities, who encouraged prominent refugees to settle there and provided support for their publishing efforts. These new arrivals were responsible for the bulk of the works printed in Magdeburg at the time; the most energetic propagandist, Matthias Flacius, had a hand in more than 40 per cent of texts published in 1549 and 1550. After examining a representative selection of works, K. attempts to sketch out the 'mental world' of the Herrgotts Kanzlei. This, he argues, was characterized by fervent loyalty to the memory of Luther and a sharp dualism pitting God, Christ, and true believers against the devil, Antichrist, and Protestant 'apostates' such as the Wittenberg professors. It also had a strong apocalyptic and local dimension: the Schmalkaldic War and the subsequent siege of Magdeburg were seen as ushering in the end times prophesied by Luther, during which the faith of Christians would be tested. The volume includes a bibliography of works published in Magdeburg between 1548 and 1552, together with statistical tables that break down the data by printer, genre, and language. Bruce Gordon, *The Swiss Reformation*, MUP, xxiv + 368 pp., has a useful chapter on the intellectual culture of Reformed Switzerland. *Preachers and People in the Reformation and Early Modern Period*, ed. Larissa Taylor, Leiden, Brill, 2001, xviii + 397 pp., includes an essay by B. Kreitzer on the Lutheran sermon (35–63). K. discusses Luther's approach to preaching, Melanchthon's rhetorical homiletics and invention of the *genus didascalicum*, and the different forms of Lutheran sermonic literature (postils, funeral sermons, wedding sermons, and sermons on the passion). This last theme is developed in S. C. Karant-Nunn's contribution on preaching in Germany (193–219). John L. Thompson, *Writing the Wrongs: Women of the Old Testament among Biblical Commentators from Philo through the Reformation*, OUP, 2001, xv + 288 pp., analyses the treatment of the stories of Hagar, Jephthah's daughter, the family of Lot and the Levite's concubine by Jewish and Christian exegetes from the 'pre-critical' era. Among the 16th-c. writers considered are Luther, Bucer, Johannes Brenz, and several Swiss reformers. Reference is also made to dramatic adaptations of the Jephthah story, including those by Hans Sachs (1555), Bruno Seidel (1568), Johannes Pomarius (1574), and Georg Dedeken (1594). R. Kolb, *Church History*, 72:504–24, notes the use of Melanchthon's *loci* method as the organizing principle for the index to the Book of Concord (1580). H. Claus, 'Subversion in den Alpen. Früher Reformationsdruck im alpenländischen Bergwerksgebiet', *Fest. Scheible*, 41–59, discusses Lutheran works published at Schwaz in the Tyrol.

3. Genres

DRAMA AND DIALOGUE. G. Mecky Zaragoza, *Daphnis*, 31, 2002: 107–26, compares Sixt Birck's portrayal of the figure of Judith with that of the Croatian dramatist Marko Marulić. Whereas in Marulić's play, dated 1501, Judith takes on the character of a Renaissance Madonna, Birck depicts her as the embodiment of masculine virtues. F. de Michele, 'Der "Capitano" der Commedia dell'arte und seine Rezeption und Entwicklung im deutschsprachigen

Theater', *ib.*, 529–91, includes a consideration of Panphilus Gengenbach's plays *Der Gouchmat* (1516) and *Nollart* (1517), and the *Comoedia von Vincentio Ladislao* (1594) by Duke Heinrich Julius of Brunswick-Wolfenbüttel.

PROSE AND VERSE. Charlotte Woodford, *Nuns as Historians in Early Modern Germany*, Oxford, Clarendon, 2002, xv + 229 pp., is a well-researched and illuminating study, focusing on 16th and 17th-c. texts from Bavaria and south-west Germany. W. links the establishment of a tradition of history writing in convents to the late medieval monastic reform movement, which saw historiography both as a means of recalling religious institutions to their founders' ideals and as an act of *memoria* for the benefit of subsequent generations. During the turmoil of the Reformation, researched history gave way in the main to eye-witness writing, the best-known example of which is Caritas Pirckheimer's *Denkwürdigkeiten.* W. cautions against reading this work as an autobiography, despite its use of the first-person narrator, and relates it instead to the historiographical tradition of the convent of the Poor Clares in Nuremberg, over which Pirckheimer presided. She argues that Pirckheimer's intention in the *Denkwürdigkeiten* was to illustrate the effects of the Reformation on her convent and to strengthen its nuns' determination to resist attempts to persuade them to leave. The work also served an apologetic function: by emphasizing the unity of the nuns and their obedience to her, Pirckheimer was able to make clear that she had done all in her power to ensure the convent's survival.

Christoph J. Steppich, *Numine afflatur. Die Inspiration des Dichters im Denken der Renaissance* (Gratia, 39), Wiesbaden, Harrassowitz, 2002, 435 pp., explores the development of ideas concerning the divine origin of poetry, first in Italy and then in Germany, from the 14th to the 16th c. According to S., early Italian humanists such as Coluccio Salutati defended their interest in Classical literature by arguing that it was not the work of demons, as Christians since Tertullian had maintained, but rather a form of *praeparatio evangelica*, inspired by the Holy Spirit in much the same way as the writings of the Old Testament prophets. Others, taking their cue from Cicero's *Pro Archia Poeta*, described poetry as a divine gift, manifested in the writer's *ingenium*. From here it was a short step to seeing the poet as a creator (ποιητής) acting in imitation of God. In the writings of Marsilio Ficino, this notion was combined with the Platonic motif of the 'furor poeticus', so that writing became an act of anamnesis, through which the soul was restored to its primal unity with God. In part 2 of the book, S. examines the reception of these ideas by 16th-c. German writers. He suggests that in Germany the notion of inspiration 'from above' was combined with an emphasis on the *imitatio* of ancient models. Through technical virtuosity and the use of topoi from Greek and Roman mythology, poets such as Celtis, Vadian, and Paul Schede Melissus sought to provide evidence of the *translatio studii* and the rebirth of Classical learning on German soil.

Czapla, *Lyrik*, presents papers given at the first colloquium of the Deutsche Neulateinische Gesellschaft, each of which is accompanied by the text and translation of the principal works discussed; J. Robert (35–73), links Konrad Celtis's defence of erotic poetry in the *Amores* to Neoplatonist thought, noting specifically his indebtedness to the Propertius commentaries of Antonio Volsco and Filippo Beroaldo; H. Wiegand (74–95), discusses hodoeporica by Heinrich Glarean and Balthasar Nusser; C. Wiener (96–131), identifies the *Parthenice Mariana* of Baptista Mantuanus as the model for the verses by Benedictus Chelodonius that accompany Dürer's *Life of Mary*; L. Poelchau (159–79), provides an overview of the Latin poetry of Christian Schesaeus; M. Korenjak (181–205), discusses an epithalamium by the Catholic priest Johannes Leucht, written to celebrate the marriage in 1582 of Archduke Ferdinand II of Tyrol and Anna Caterina Gonzaga; R. G. Czapla (217–55), examines Paul Schede's use of poetry as a means of securing political patronage while travelling in Italy in the late 1570s.

Jordan, *Lyrik*, is concerned with Dutch-German literary relations during the early modern period. Although the majority of contributors to the volume focus on the Dutch 'Golden Age', when cultural exchange between the Netherlands and Germany was at its peak, several essays are of relevance to the 16th c. L. de Grauwe (21–34), shows that speakers of Dutch and German continued to see themselves as sharing a common language, albeit one that existed in two distinct variants. J. Oosterman (37–55), examines the reception of songs from Antwerp in 16th-c. manuscripts from the Dutch-German border region. Two of the songs discussed, together with corresponding texts from the 1544 *Antwerps Liedboek*, are appended. T. Naaijkens, '"Undern wîben ûf gestanden." Ansätze zur Frühgeschichte der Lyrikübersetzungen aus dem Niederländischen ins Deutsche' (157–76), notes the influence of the Dutch humanist Johannes Secundus on 16th and 17th-c. German Neo-Latin verse. H. E. Stiene, *NJb*, 4, 2002: 227–52, presents Latin and Greek poems published along with the 1573 edition of *De incendio Tuitiensi* by Rupert of Deutz. N. Thurn, 'Deutsche neulateinische Städtelobgedichte. Ein Vergleich ausgewählter Beispiele des 16. Jahrhunderts', *ib.*, 253–69, compares encomia by Eobanus Hessus (on Nuremberg), Erasmus Michael Laetus (on Nuremberg and Hamburg), Michael Barth and Matthäus Behem (on Annaberg), and Johannes Bocer (on Freiberg and Minden). T. Haye, *ib.*, 5:135–61, edits poems written at the Bordesholm grammar school to mark the death of Duke Adolf of Schleswig-Holstein-Gottorf.

4. Other Work

Peter van der Coelen, *Bilder aus der Schrift. Studien zur alttestamentlichen Druckgrafik des 16. und 17. Jahrhunderts*, trans. Astrid Tümpel and Sabine Noack (Vestigia Bibliae, 23), Berne, Lang, 2002, 441 pp., examines the development of biblical illustration as an art form during the early modern period. The author characterizes the Renaissance as a time of increased engagement with the stories of the Old Testament, which ceased to be portrayed merely in typological terms. Much of the book is concerned with developments in the Netherlands and France, but the first two chapters focus on the origins of the tradition of Old Testament illustration in Germany. C. suggests that the initial impetus was provided by Luther's *Passional*, published in 1529 with his *Betbüchlein*, which was intended as the prototype for a new 'Bible of the laity'. However, the key role in the emergence of the new genre of the *Bilderbibel* was played not by theologians or artists, but by printers, who found it a profitable way of recycling woodcuts commissioned for other purposes. C. illustrates this point with reference to an important early example of such a work, Hans Holbein's *Historiarum Veteris Testamenti Icones* (1538). Thanks to the efforts of printers such as Sigmund Feyerabend, the genre enjoyed widespread popularity in Protestant Europe during the second half of the 16th c., with Strasbourg and Frankfurt among the main centres of production. C. notes that, unlike Luther, who valued illustration solely for its usefulness as a teaching aid, the producers of *Bilderbibeln* attached a high premium to aesthetic considerations, emphasizing the quality of the images selected as part of their marketing strategy. Jouko Parad, *Biblische Verbphraseme und ihr Verhältnis zum Urtext und zur Lutherbibel* (Finnische Beiträge zur Germanistik, 9), Frankfurt, Lang, 463 pp., analyses 151 verbal idioms drawn from the Luther Bible. Forty of these phrases are examined in detail and compared with equivalent passages in the original Hebrew or Greek text, the Latin Vulgate, earlier High and Low German Bibles, and early modern Swedish translations, which were modelled on that of Luther. By highlighting differences between Luther's formulation of the idioms considered and the versions that appear in modern German Bibles and dictionaries, P. is able to establish that such phrases were not 'standardized' by the Luther Bible.

Werner Wilhelm Schnabel, *Das Stammbuch. Konstitution und Geschichte einer textbezogenen Sammelform bis ins erste Drittel des 18. Jahrhunderts* (FN,

78), xiii + 715 pp., is a comprehensive and sophisticated study of the *Stammbuch* and its place within early modern European culture. In parts A and B of the book, S. defines the characteristics of the genre and sets out his methodology, which combines textual analysis of inscriptions with attention to 'mediale Aspekte' (e.g. format, binding, and decoration) and to the intended and actual use of *Stammbücher*. Part C is given over to an analysis of the historical development and functions of the *album amicorum*. S. distinguishes between an aristocratic form of the genre, which incorporated features of the late medieval noble guestbook, and one associated with the 'Bildungsmilieu' of humanists, students, and clerics. The latter tradition had its origins in Wittenberg, where Luther's followers collected inscriptions in order to provide themselves with a material link to the leaders of the Reformation. Wittenberg students transmitted the custom to other centres of learning throughout Europe, although outside Germany it became established only in Lutheran and Calvinist territories. By the end of the 16th c., the 'academic' variety of *Stammbuch* had largely subsumed its 'aristocratic' rival, remaining the dominant form until the genre's decline in the late 18th c. A selection of introductory texts and inscriptions from *Stammbücher* is appended. M. Braun, *Daphnis*, 31, 2002: 413–67, highlights contradictions and compromises in the early modern discourse of marriage, which limited its effectiveness as a tool for imposing social discipline. J. J. Hurwich, *SCJ*, 34: 701–27, examines the portrayal of illegitimacy in the Zimmern Chronicle. A. Murray, *ZWL*, 61, 2002: 145–57, finds evidence of the adaptation of medieval sources by the Zimmern Chronicle's authors in order to exaggerate the German role in the First Crusade. R. Walinski-Kiehl, *Reformation*, 6, 2002: 49–74, highlights the importance of pamphlets as a means of disseminating learned ideas about witches in late 16th and early 17th-c. Germany, and suggests that they may have helped prompt outbreaks of persecution. R. Gamper, 'Der Adel in den Zürcher Chroniken', pp. 125–41 of *Alter Adel — neuer Adel? Zürcher Adel zwischen Spätmittelalter und früher Neuzeit*, ed. Peter Niederhäuser (Mitteilungen der antiquarischen Gesellschaft in Zürich, 70), Zurich, Chronos, 232 pp., examines the negative portrayal of the Swiss nobility in late medieval and 16th-c. Swiss chronicles, especially the works of Heinrich Brennwald and Johannes Stumpf. T. Burkard, *NJb*, 5: 5–58, discusses early modern approaches to the punctuation and accentuation of Latin texts, with particular reference to Leonhard Culmann's *De Orthographia* (1549), Joachim Camerarius's *Tractatus de Orthographia* (1553), and Aldus Manutius's *Interpungendi Ratio* (1561).

5. Individual Authors

BODENSTEIN VON KARLSTADT, ANDREAS. N. R. Leroux, *SCJ*, 34:73–105, analyses the rhetoric and arguments of B.'s tract *Von Abtuhung der Bilder und Das keyn Bedtler unther den Christen seyn sollen* (1522). Id., *Church History*, 72:102–37, discusses K.'s *Christag Predig* as an example of 'prophetic rhetoric', noting his use of Classical rhetorical devices such as prolepsis and anaphora.

BUCER, MARTIN. *Martin Bucer zwischen Luther und Zwingli*, ed. Matthieu Arnold and Berndt Hamm, (Spätmittelalter und Reformation, n.s., 23), Tübingen, Mohr Siebeck, vii + 167 pp., presents papers from a conference held in June 2001 to mark the publication of volume IV of the critical edition of B.'s correspondence, covering the period January to September 1530. The focus of the volume is on B.'s role as an advocate of Protestant unity in the period leading up to the Diet of Augsburg. A. Mathieu (9–29), compares B.'s and Luther's interpretations of events at the Diet through an analysis of their correspondence. R. Liebenberg (30–48), examines the ways in which B. attempted to rationalize and smooth over Protestant divisions in the period following the Marburg colloquy. R. Friedrich (49–65), and A. Noblesse-Rocher (67–83), consider aspects of B.'s involvement in the Eucharistic dispute between Lutherans, Zwinglians, and Catholics. B. Hamm (85–106), explains B.'s eirenic approach as 'das Ergebnis einer Synthese von Ingredienzen des erasmischen Humanismus und eines reformatorisch-biblischen Denkens'. A. Puchta (107–25), discusses B.'s attitude to the visual arts, with particular reference to his correspondence with Zwingli and his work *Das einigerlei Bild bei den Gotgläubigen* (1530). V. Ortmann (127–46), chronicles B.'s attempts to reach agreement with senior Catholic churchmen prior to and during the 1541 Diet of Regensburg. N. de Laharpe (147–56), notes the characterization of B. in Luther's *Tischreden* as untrustworthy and as a 'sacramentarian'.

BULLINGER, HEINRICH. C. Euler, *SCJ*, 34:367–93, discusses B.'s *Der Christlich Eestand* (1540) and its reception in England under Henry VIII and Edward VI. W. P. Stephens, *RRR*, 3, 2001:96–107, compares B.'s *Von dem unverschämten Frevel* (1531) with Zwingli's writings against the Anabaptists. U. B. Leu, *Zwingliana*, 30:5–29, provides an overview of B.'s private library, 217 works from which have now been identified. C. Moser, '"Papam esse Antichristum." Grundzüge von Heinrich Bullingers Antichristkonzeption', *ib.*, 65–101. Id., 'Ratramnus von Corbie als "testis veritatis" in der Zürcher Reformation. Zu Heinrich Bullingers und Leo Juds Ausgabe des "Liber de corpore et sanguine Domini" (1532)', *Fest. Stotz*, 235–309. E. Campi, 'Über das Ende des Weltzeitalters. Aspekte der

Rezeption des Danielbuches bei Heinrich Bullinger', pp. 225–38 of *Europa, Tausendjähriges Reich und Neue Welt. Zwei Jahrtausende Geschichte und Utopie in der Rezeption des Danielbuches*, ed. Mariano Delgado, Klaus Koch, and Edgar Marsch (Studien zur christlichen Religions- und Kulturgeschichte, 1), Fribourg U.P., 483 pp.

CELTIS, KONRAD. Gernot Michael Müller, *Die 'Germania generalis' des Conrad Celtis. Studien mit Edition, Übersetzung und Kommentar* (FN, 67), 2001, xvii + 536 pp. In the first part of this impressive monograph, M. reconstructs the textual history of the *Germania generalis* and analyses its style, syntax, and versification. The edited text of the poem is accompanied by a German prose translation and extensive commentary. In the *Studien* section, M. relates the *Germania generalis* to C.'s ambitious project for a 'Germania illustrata'. Flavio Biondo's 'Italia illustrata', which served as a model for the project, and the writings of Aeneas Silvius Piccolomini, who first defined Germany in ethnic and linguistic terms, are identified as key influences on C. Piccolomini was also the source for one of the principal themes of the *Germania generalis*, Germany's cultural *mutatio* from barbarism to civilization. M. suggests that the poem was designed to be read as 'additiones' to Tacitus's *Germania*, hence its emphasis on topography, to which Tacitus paid little attention, and on the high cultural level attained by Germany in C.'s time, which was to counterbalance Tacitus's portrayal of the ancient Germans as barbarous and primitive. Jörg Robert, *Konrad Celtis und das Projekt der deutschen Dichtung. Studien zur humanistischen Konstitution von Poetik, Philosophie, Nation und Ich* (FN, 76), xviii + 564 pp., traces the development of C.'s conception of poetry and the poet's role from the *Ars versificandi et carminum* of 1486 through to the *Amores* of 1502. For R., the *Amores* represents the culmination of C.'s attempts to construct a synthesis of philosophy and poetry, *sapientia* and *eloquentia*. This is reflected in the way in which the cycle brings together serious and playful elements, and in its dual character as a collection of erotic verse and the precursor to a projected national topography of Germany. The work is unified around the personality of C. himself, whose birthplace in the 'silva Hercynia' serves as the geographical and symbolic centre of a four-sided *Germania*. Above all, the *Amores* is to be seen as a 'literarisches Memorial des Dichters Celtis', combining autobiography and rhetorical stylization in order to project the poet's self-image as a teacher of wisdom to Germany's youth. **Amor als Topograph. 500 Jahre 'Amores' des Conrad Celtis. Ein Manifest des deutschen Humanismus. Kabinettausstellung 7. April-30. Juni 2002*, ed. Claudia Wiener et al., Schweinfurt, Bibliothek Otto Schäfer, 2002, 191 pp.

CHYTRAEUS, DAVID. O. Czaika, *Historisches Jahrbuch*, 123:93–110, highlights C.'s contacts with John III of Sweden and the influence of the university of Rostock on Swedish Lutheranism.

DRACH, JOHANNES. J. Schilling, *Fest Scheible*, 381–410, republishes D.'s *Oratio de pia morte Doctoris Martini Lutheri* (1546).

EBER, PAUL. M. Rössler, *Fest. Scheible*, 339–80, offers an in-depth analysis of E.'s German hymns.

EULENSPIEGELBUCH. R. Heinritz, 'Erde zu Erde. Fäkalmotivik im *Dyl Ulenspiegel*', *Eulenspiegel-Jb.*, 42, 2002:17–33. M. Ampferl, *ib.*, 43:19–52, highlights changes to the language of *Till Eulenspiegel* in editions published over the course of the 16th c.

FABRICIUS, GEORG. Walther Ludwig, **Christliche Dichtung des 16. Jahrhunderts — Die 'Poemata sacra' des Georg Fabricius*, Göttingen, Vandenhoeck & Ruprecht, 2001, 78 pp.

FISCHART, JOHANN. Johann Fischart, *Sämtliche Werke*, continues with vol. II, *Eulenspiegel reimenweis*, ed. Ulrich Seelbach and W. Eckehart Spengler, Stuttgart–Bad Cannstatt, Frommann-Holzboog, 2002, 436 pp. The text is based on the original 1572 edition, published in Frankfurt by Johannes Schmidt, and includes reproductions of 82 woodcuts by Tobias Stimmer. The critical apparatus provides details of variant readings in the surviving copies of the work and of editorial corrections, with cross-references to the 19th-c. edition published by Adolf Hauffen. The 1569 version of the *Eulenspiegelbuch*, which corresponds most closely in structure and wording to F.'s text, is identified as his likely prose source. A. Bässler, 'Ein "Diogenischer Spottvogel" in Johann Fischarts *Eulenspiegel reimensweis* (1572)', *Eulenspiegel-Jb.*, 42, 2002:63–79.

FRANCK, SEBASTIAN. R. Häfner, *Euphorion*, 97:349–78, discusses F.'s use in *Die Guldin Arch* of the Church Fathers (especially Cyril of Alexandria) to demonstrate the compatibility of Platonic and Hermetic thought with Christianity.

FRIES, JOHANNES. U. B. Leu, 'Die Privatbibliothek von Johannes Fries (1505–1565)', *Fest. Stotz*, 311–329.

FRISCHLIN, NIKODEMUS. Nicodemus Frischlin, *Sämtliche Werke. Dritter Band. Dramen iii: 1. Teil*, ed. and trans. Christoph Jungk and Lothar Mundt, Stuttgart–Bad Cannstatt, Frommann-Holzboog, 668 pp., presents two humanist comedies by F.: *Priscianus vapulans* (1578), a satire on traditional scholastic learning, and *Iulius redivivus* (1585), which celebrates the *translatio studii* from Italy to Germany. The volume includes the Latin text of each play, along with a clear German prose translation, prefaces, and other relevant material. Bibliographical details of 16th-c. editions of the plays and variant readings are appended.

HISTORIA VON D. JOHANN FAUSTEN. J.-M. Valentin, *EG*, 57, 2002:441–58, relates Faust's condemnation to the orthodox Lutheran understanding of grace.

LUTHER, MARTIN. *Luther's Lives. Two Contemporary Accounts of Martin Luther*, trans. Elizabeth Vandiver, Ralph Keen, and Thomas D. Frazel, MUP, 2002, vii + 408 pp., presents English translations of Melanchthon's *Historia de vita et actis Lutheri* (1548) and the much longer *Commentaria de Actis et Scriptis Martini Lutheri* (1549), by the Catholic polemicist Johannes Cochlaeus. Each text is accompanied by an introductory essay and extensive notes. *Luther on Women. A Sourcebook*, ed. and trans. Susan C. Karant-Nunn and Merry E. Wiesner-Hanks, CUP, 246 pp., contains translated extracts from L.'s works illustrating his views on women in the Bible, marriage and the family, sexuality, childbirth, his wife, other contemporary women, and witchcraft and marriage. Neil R. Leroux, **Luther's Rhetoric: Strategies and Style from the Invocavit Sermons*, St Louis, Concordia Academic, 2002, 240 pp. Id., 'Luther's use of doublets', *Rhetoric Society Quarterly*, 20, 2000:35–54. T. A. Fudge, *SCJ*, 34:319–45, considers the reaction to L.'s marriage by Catholic polemicists in Germany (Johann Hasenberger, Joachim von der Heyden) and England (Thomas More). F. Posset, *LutherJb.*, 69, 2002:71–78, identifies a reference to Bernard of Clairvaux's *Sermo in annuntiatione* 1 in L.'s *Dictata super Psalterium*.

MELANCHTHON, PHILIPP. C. Augustijn, 'Melanchthons Editionen der Akten von Worms und Regensburg 1540 und 1561', *Fest. Scheible*, 25–39. J. M. Estes, *ib.*, 83–101, interprets M.'s *De officio principum* (1539) as a response to the 'Erasmian' policies of confessionally neutral German princes and their advisers in Albertine Saxony, Cologne, Brandenburg, the Palatinate, and Jülich-Cleves during the 1530s. G. Franck, *ib.*, 103–18, assesses M.'s contribution to the intellectual life of Europe during the early modern period. B. R. Jenny, *ib.*, 147–69, discusses perceptions of M. in Reformed Switzerland. J. Loehr, 'Pindars Begriff der Charis als Resonanzraum für Melanchthons Lektüre der Epinikien', *ib.*, 267–76. C. Peters, *ib.*, 277–311, examines M.'s correspondence with Johannes Brenz. Á. Ritoók-Szalay, *ib.*, 325–37, reconstructs the content of M.'s lectures on Sophocles's *Electra* from statements by his students. B. Stolt, *ib.*, 425–31, questions the tradition that M. translated the two books of Maccabees for the *Lutherbibel*.

**Melanchthon und Europa. 1. Teilband: Skandinavien und Mittelosteuropa*, ed. Günter Franck and Martin Treu (Melanchthon-Schriften der Stadt Bretten, 6.1), Stuttgart, Thorbecke, 2001, 305 pp.

MÜNSINGER VON FRUNDECK, JOACHIM. W. Ludwig, *NJb*, 4, 2002: 215–26, corrects biographical details for M. given in the critical edition of the *Stammbuch* of Abraham and David Ulrich.

MÜNTZER, THOMAS. A. Bradstock, *Reformation*, 5, 2000: 27–53, analyses the language of M.'s writings, which combines apocalyptic and mystical elements.

PEUCER, CASPAR. **Zwischen Katheder Thron und Kerker. Leben und Werk des Humanisten Caspar Peucer 1525–1602. Ausstellung 25. September bis 31. Dezember 2002*, ed. Stadtsmuseum Bautzen, Bautzen, Domowina, 2002, 216 pp. W. Ludwig, *WRM*, 27: 97–111, corrects the translation by the editors of the above catalogue of a Latin epigram that accompanies the contemporary woodcut portrait of Peucer. L. refutes the suggestion, based on a serious misreading of the text, that it alludes to P.'s fall from grace and imprisonment, and identifies the author of the verses as Martinus Henricus Sanganensis.

PIRCKHEIMER, WILLIBALD. The edition of P.'s correspondence continues with vol. 5, ed. Helga Scheible, Munich, Beck, 2001, xxviii + 530 pp.

PRAETORIUS, STEPHAN. Eckhard Düker, *Freudenchristentum. Der Erbauungsschriftsteller Stephan Praetorius* (Arbeiten zur Geschichte des Pietismus, 38), Göttingen, Vandenhoeck & Ruprecht, 360 pp., assesses P.'s contribution to the development of German devotional literature during the second half of the 16th c. In part 1, the author provides an overview of P.'s career and discusses his writings, both Latin and German. D. attributes the predominantly Melanchthonian orientation of P.'s thought first to the influence of the Rostock professor David Chytraeus, under whom he studied between 1558 and 1565, and secondly to his experiences as a pastor in Salzwedel over more than 30 years. Familiarity with the daily difficulties faced by his parishioners led P. to emphasize the consolatory aspects of Protestant teaching, especially the 'gegenwärtige Seligkeit der Gläubigen' and the importance of active piety. Part 2 of the book examines the subsequent history of P.'s works in Germany and Scandinavia, beginning with the publication of his German tracts by Johann Arndt in 1622. Particular attention is given to Martin Statius's reworking of the Arndt edition, the *Geistliche Schatzkammer* (1636), which was censured by the church authorities in Danzig and by other representatives of Lutheran orthodoxy, but enthusiastically received in pietist and spiritualist circles. A full bibliography of P.'s works (including translations into Danish, Norwegian, Swedish, Finnish, and Lithuanian) is appended.

REUCHLIN, JOHANNES. Johannes Reuchlin, *Briefwechsel*. Vol. II: *1506–1513*, ed. Matthias Dall'Asta and Gerald Dönner, Stuttgart–Bad Cannstatt, Frommann-Holzboog, lxv + 727 pp., presents 95 letters from R.'s personal correspondence, including five previously unpublished items. The letters contain a wealth of information on R.'s intellectual activities during this period, showing his support for the development of Greek and Hebrew studies in Germany. Particularly noteworthy in this regard are R.'s prefaces to the combined Hebrew grammar and dictionary *De rudimentis Hebraicis* (1506), and to his Latin translation of the seven penitential psalms (1512). Also of interest is R.'s correspondence with the Basle printer Johannes Amerbach, which documents his work on the great edition of the works of Jerome published in 1516. However, the letters are dominated by the controversy over Reuchlin's defence of Jewish books and his increasingly bitter exchanges with Johannes Pfefferkorn and the theology faculty in Cologne. Like its predecessor, the volume is a model of critical scholarship; detailed descriptions of the main manuscript and published sources for the correspondence are provided, and each letter is accompanied by a synopsis in German and exhaustive notes. A very different aspect of R.'s activity is highlighted by appendices I-III, which present summaries of a further 144 letters arising from his work as judge to the Swabian League. Other texts published in the volume include the imperial decrees ordering the confiscation of R.'s *Augenspiegel* (1511) and *Defensio* (1513). There is a useful index listing biblical, Classical, rabbinical, and other texts cited in the letters. U. Roth, 'Die philologische Freiheit des Humanisten Johannes Reuchlin. Interpretation und Edition von Reuchlins Übersetzung der Psalmen 110–115', *Daphnis*, 31, 2002:55–105.

RHENANUS, BEATUS. J.-L. Charlet and J. Hirstein, *NJb*, 5:59–102, describe R.'s annotated copy of the *Castigationes Plinianae* of Ermolao Barbaro, now held at the municipal library of Aix-en-Provence.

SCHALLENBERG, CHRISTOPH VON. G. Hübner, *Daphnis*, 31, 2002:127–86, considers the influence of Italian and Neo-Latin models on S.'s verse.

SIEDER, JOHANNES. R. Häfner, *BGDSL*, 125:94–136, discusses S.'s translation into German of Apuleius's *Golden Ass*, together with the first published version of the work, which appeared in 1538. Appended to the essay is the text of S.'s preface, addressed to Johann von Dalberg, bishop of Worms.

SPERATUS, PAUL. M. Brecht, *AR*, 94:105–33, assesses S.'s contribution to the early Reformation as an author of *Flugschriften* and hymns and as the translator of several important works by Luther, including the *Formula Missae et Communionis* (1523).

TSCHUDI, AEGIDIUS. Aegidius Tschudi, **Chronicon Helveticum. 4. Registerband zum 9.–13. Teil (sog. Urschrift von 1418–1470)*, ed. Bernhard Stettler, Basle, Allgemeine Geschichtforschende Gesellschaft der

Schweiz, 2001, 115 pp. **Aegidius Tschudi und seine Zeit*, ed. Katharina Koller-Weiss and Christian Sieber, Basle, Krebs, 2002, 400 pp.

WICKRAM, GEORG. Georg Wickram, *Sämtliche Werke*, continues with vol. 9, *Losbuch*, ed. Hans-Gert Roloff, Berlin, de Gruyter, 268 pp. D. Kartschoke, *Daphnis*, 3, 2002:469–89, questions the traditional attribution of *Ritter Galmy* (1539) to W.

ZWINGLI, HULDRYCH. Olivier Bangerter, *La Pensée militaire de Zwingli* (Zürcher Beiträge zur Reformationsgeschichte, 21), Berne, Lang, viii + 287 pp., places Z.'s approach to war in the context of his wider theology and political thought. B. focuses principally on two groups of texts: the works against mercenary service, which date from the early 1520s; and the military strategies prepared by Z. in order to defeat the Swiss Catholic states. Z.'s position on war is distinguished from both the pacifism of Erasmus and the medieval Christian doctrine of the 'just war', as developed by Augustine and Thomas Aquinas. B. relates it closely to Z.'s emphasis on the sovereignty of God, which informed both his denunciation of mercenary service and pensions (as corrupting influences on the Zurich polity) and his belief that war, whilst evil in itself, is a legitimate means of securing the free preaching of the gospel. Of particular relevance to scholars of literature are B.'s discussion of the early allegorical poems 'Der Ochse' (1510) and 'Das Labyrinth', which illustrate Z.'s growing opposition to Swiss involvement in the Italian wars.

THE SEVENTEENTH CENTURY

By Anna Linton, *University of Oxford*

1. General

Two comprehensive volumes are devoted to genres often neglected in literary research: Gabriele Schramm, *Widmung, Leser und Drama. Untersuchungen zu Form- und Funktionswandel der Buchwidmung im 17. und 18. Jahrhundert* (Studien zur Germanistik, 2), Hamburg, Kovač, 718 pp., investigates the changing function and structure of book dedications from early modern handbooks of rhetoric and from examples taken from works by Lohenstein, Moscherosch, Gottsched, and Klopstock. Werner Wilhelm Schnabel, *Das Stammbuch. Konstitution und Geschichte einer textsortenbezogenen Sammelform bis ins erste Drittel des 18. Jahrhunderts* (FN, 78), xiii + 715 pp., argues that *Stammbücher* constitute a genre in their own right, and therefore deserve greater critical attention than they have received in the past. Based on the collection in the Nuremberg Staatsbibliothek, the work considers the albums from a number of angles: S. looks at how the entries are structured, the poems they contain, the physical form of the books, their function within friendship networks, and their reception. He argues that the genre undergoes varying developments amongst different social groups, and finally evolves into the 18th-c. *Poesiealbum*. L. Martin, 'Female reformers as gatekeepers of Pietism: the example of Johanna Eleonora Merlau and William Penn', *MDLK*, 95:33–58. Ralph Häfner, *Götter im Exil. Frühneuzeitliches Dichtungsverständnis im Spannungsfeld christlicher Apologetik und philologischer Kritik (ca. 1590–1736)* (FN, 80), xxxi + 716 pp., is a detailed and scholarly study of the changes which the concept of poetry underwent in its position between Christian apologetics and the reception of Classical literature in early modern Europe. H. does justice to the complexities of this issue, and in the final section he shows what he describes as 'comparative polymathy' in practice in the works of the Hamburg philologists Johann Albert Fabricius and Barthold Heinrich Brockes.

2. Poetry

The first symposium of the Deutsche Neulateinische Gesellschaft, hosted by the Werner-Reimer-Stiftung in Bad Homburg, has produced the volume Czapla, *Lyrik*. In addition to those articles cited below on Bidermann, Opitz, and Fleming, one other touches on the 17th c.: R. Seidel, 'Die "tote Sprache" und das "Originalgenie". Poetologische und literatursoziologische Transformationsprozesse in der Geschichte der deutschen neulateinischen Lyrik' (422–48). The volume is valuable to Germanists, not least because each contribution is followed by the text with a German translation. Another collection of essays, Jordan, *Lyrik*, deals with the literary influence of the Netherlands on the German-speaking area. S. Kiedroń, 'Deutsch-niederländische "poetische" Beziehungen im 17. Jahrhundert: der Fall Schlesien' (57–74), discusses the particularly close links between Silesia and the Netherlands, and draws attention to some lesser-known poets. C. Niekus Moore, 'Gelegenheitspoesie von Frauen in den Niederlanden und Deutschland im 17. und 18. Jahrhundert' (109–26), examines occasional poetry by women, which she argues grew out of their religious verse. T. Naaijkens, '"Undern wîben ûf gestanden." Ansätze zur Frühgeschichte der Lyrikübersetungen aus dem Niederländischen ins Deutsche' (157–78), considers the translation of Dutch poetry into German. Two further contributions are concerned with translations of Jacob Cats: F. van Ingen on Zesen (see p. 553 below), and M. A. Schenkeveld-van der Dussen and D. Schipperheyn, 'Johann Peter Titz als Übersetzungstheoretiker und Cats-Übersetzer' (193–205). Anthony J. Harper, *German Secular Song-Books of the Mid-Seventeenth Century. An Examination of the Texts in Collections of Songs Published in the German-Language Area between 1624 and 1660*, Aldershot, Ashgate, viii + 354 pp., claims that studies of early modern German poetry and song have tended to focus on religious works, and he sets out to redress the balance. The parameters of the work are set at the one end by Opitz's *Poeterey*, and at the other by the publication of song-books by Stieler and Schoch. The study opens with a discussion of the song in the work of Opitz and Fleming. The subsequent division of the material into geographical areas, arranged broadly chronologically, results in motifs being covered several times, a problem which the author discusses in the concluding review, but this approach means that H. can introduce the reader to some less well-known poets as well as to the usual suspects. The work is supplemented by a useful bibliography of primary sources. S. Kyora, 'Erotischer Genuß, religiöses Ergriffensein. Körperinszenierungen in barocker Lyrik', *Euphorion*, 97:405–17, draws on poems by Fleming, Andreas Gryphius, Hoffmannswaldau, and Greiffenberg.

INDIVIDUAL AUTHORS

BALDE. Jakob Balde, *Panegyricus Equestris (1628)*, ed., trans., and introd. Veronika Lukas, comm. Stephanie Haberer (Documenta Augustana, 8), Institut für Europäische Kulturgeschichte der Univ. Augsburg, Wissner, 2002, 200 pp. In her analysis of one of B.'s earliest works, written to commemorate Philip IV of Spain's award of the Order of the Golden Fleece to Count Ott Heinrich Fugger, L. considers the somewhat unflattering implications of B.'s choice of Classical model, Claudian's panegyrics, especially the one on the Fourth Consulate of Honorarius.

BEER. M. Beetz, 'Johann Beers deutsche und lateinische Epigramme', Ingen, *Beer*, 457–85, considers the epigrams for which Beetz argues B. was best known before Alewyn's monograph (1932) established him in the literary canon as a novelist. This is borne out by the fact that Beetz's contribution is the only one to focus on the poetry in a collection of 30 essays.

BIDERMANN. M. Baumbach, 'Der Heilige Meinrad und die Protestanten. Jacob Bidermanns politisch-religiöse Dichtung am Beispiel der Meinradvita', Czapla, *Lyrik*, 304–29, shows, in his discussion of the epigram 'Sanctus Menradus, familiaribus corvis usus', how B. co-opts the story of the murder of the 9th-c. hermit, who befriends and reforms a couple of ravens, into a thorny confessional debate about the lives of the saints and the value of the ascetic monastic life.

FLEMING. B. Czapla, 'Erlebnispoesie oder erlebte Poesie? Paul Flemings *Suavia* und die Tradition des zyklusbildenden Kußgedichts', Czalpa, *Lyrik*, 356–97, traces the history of the kiss poem through Classical literature and the Renaissance, and places F.'s cycle within the context of social occasional poetry. She argues that it is an intellectual exercise which reflects the process of writing poetry, and she claims that F.'s comparison of Rubella and Salvie in a German poem written during his time in Persia is an assessment of the Latin and German love-poems in favour of the former.

GERHARDT. Alain Bideau, **Paul Gerhardt (1607–1676): pasteur et poète* (Contacts: Série 3: Études et Documents, 60), Berne, Lang, viii + 318 pp., is divided into two sections. The first provides biographical background and the second discusses the form and theological content of G.'s hymns.

GRYPHIUS. J. Schmidt, 'Die Opposition von *contemplatio* und *curiositas*. Ein unbekanntes Denkmuster, seine Tradition und seine poetische Gestaltung durch Andreas Gryphius im Sonnett *An die Sternen*', *DVLG*, 77:61–76, sets this opposition in the context of early modern attitudes towards astronomy: wondrous contemplation of the stars can contribute to a knowledge of God, but *curiositas* focused on the connections between them is overweening and sinful. Framing the discussion are St Augustine's *Confessions* and Francis Bacon's *Advancement of Learning*.

KNORR. Although most of the articles in *Morgenglantz*, 13, are devoted to K.'s prose, two consider his poetry: I. M. Battafarano, '"Licht vom unerschöpften Lichte": Knorr von Rosenroth zwischen

Böhme und Schelling. Versuch einer Deutung der ersten Strophe von *Morgen-Glantz der Ewigkeit*', *Morgenglantz*, 13:369–98; and R.-G. Bogner, 'Nekrolog als kontroversielle Legitimation und Apologie der Profan-Wissenschaften. Christian Knorrs von Rosenroth Nachruf-Ode auf Andreas Gryphius', *ib.*, 351–66.

OPITZ. S. Arend, 'Zu Topik und Faktur von Martin Opitzens Panegyricus auf Ludwig Camerarius', Czapla, *Lyrik*, 330–55, analyses O.'s poem to Camerarius, statesman of the Palatine court, and considers whether the term panegyric is apposite. It is followed by the poem and a prose German translation. O. features in P. Béhar's article on the connections between the Rosicrucians and the Bohemian court of Friedrich V: 'Okkultismus, Politik, Literatur und Astronomie zwischen Prag und Heidelberg', *Morgenglantz*, 13:22–46. He is also the subject of several essays in Gerhard Kosellek's collection on literary activity in Silesia, **Silesiaca: Literarische Streifzüge*, Bielefeld, Aisthesis, 367 pp.

SCHIRMER. Anthony J. Harper's facsimile edition of S.'s *Singende Rosen oder Liebes- und Tugend-Lieder* (1654) and the *Poetische Rosen-Gepüsche* (1657) (Deutsche Neudrucke, Reihe Barock, 42), Tübingen, Niemeyer, 2 vols, 16 + lxviii + 126, xlii + 506 pp., is accompanied by an account of S.'s life and circle. H. discusses the parallel genesis of the two works, and his thorough appendices provide bibliographical descriptions of the various editions and references for the original sources where songs first appeared as occasional publications.

SPEE. Frank Rustemeyer, *'*Nur zun Himmelpforten Verweisets allen ton.' Allegorie im Werk Friedrich Spees*, Paderborn, Mentis, 302 pp., analyses S.'s *Trutznachtigall* and the *Güldenes Tugend-Buch*.

ZESEN. Z.'s translation of a popular Dutch medical work by Johan van Beverwijck, which contains copperplate engravings with verse by Jacob Cats, is the subject of F. van Ingen, 'Philipp von Zesen als Übersetzer von Jacob Cats (1671)', Jordan, *Lyrik*, 177–92. This coincides with the publication of the volume *Cats-Übersetzungen* in Philipp von Zesen, *Sämtliche Werke*, vol. 3.2: *Weltliche Lyrik*, ed. F. van Ingen (Ausgaben deutscher Literatur des 15. bis 18. Jahrhunderts), Berlin–NY, de Gruyter, 428 pp.

3. Prose

S. Trappen, 'Jugendtorheit, Brötchenarbeit, Heilsbemühung. Erzählmotivationen und ihre sozialgeschichtliche Fundierung beim niederen Roman von Beer, Dürer, Grimmelshausen, Reuter und Riemer', Ingen, *Beer*, 401–19.

INDIVIDUAL AUTHORS

ANDREAE. *Theca Gladii Spiritus.* ed. Frank Böhling and Carlos Gilly (Gesammelte Schriften, 5), Stuttgart–Bad Cannstatt, Frommann-Holzboog, 316 pp., presents a parallel text Latin-modern German edition of A.'s collection of *sententiae* and is prefaced by an introduction in which B. considers the reasons for the originally anonymous publication of the work and the Rosicrucian influence to which it testifies.

BEER. Andreas Solbach, *Johann Beer. Rhetorisches Erzählen zwischen Satire und Utopie* (FN, 82), vii + 456 pp., searches for the unifying narratological practice in B.'s *œuvre.* Ingen, *Beer,* is a collection of papers from the symposium held in Weissenfels in 2000 to mark the tercentenary of B.'s death. 30 contributions cover B.'s intellectual and political context, his novels and epigrams, and his work as a composer. Some link these areas, for example H. Thomke, 'Musikerfiguren und musikantisches Erzählen in Johann Beers Romane' (235–54). A number of contributions address moral questions in B.'s works: G. van Gemert, 'Johann Beer und die geistliche Literatur. Beobachtungen zum Stellenwert des geistlichen Moments in den autobiographischen Aufzeichnungen und in einigen in der pikaresken Tradition stehenden Erzählwerken' (115–29); A. Solbach, 'Unehrlichkeit: Spuren einer sozialhistorischen Kategorie in Texten Johann Beers' (131–68); M. Kremer, 'Die ambivalente Verwendung der Transgression in Beers satirischen Erzählstrategien' (203–16); P. Rusterholz, 'Scherz und Ernst bei Grimmelshausen und Johann Beer. Zur Typologie der Moralisation' (327–41). Other papers with a specifically literary focus are R. Zeller, 'Beers "Rittergeschichten", der *Amadis* und die Volksbücher. Zur Unterhaltungsliteratur des 18. Jahrhunderts' (377–99); A. Wicke, 'Beer und die Bestseller: historische und literaturtheoretische Überlegungen zu den Politischen Romanen' (421–42); K. Kiesant, 'Das Reise-Motiv in den Romanen Johann Beers — "Das Narrenspital" und "Jucundi Jucundissimi Wunderliche Lebensbeschreibung" (343–63); B. Becker-Cantarino, 'Johann Beers *Weiber-Hächel* und die Tradition der Ehe- und Frauensatire' (443–56); U. Breuer, 'Herz und Kleid — Melancholie der Kommunikation in Johann Beers Romandilogie' (487–504); A. Keller, ' "Confuse" oder "artige" Ordnung? Zum Spannungsverhältnis von forensischer Disposition und adressatenorientierter Dissimulation der oratorischen Kunst bei Johann Beer am Beispiel der *Weiber-Hächel* (1680)' (517–73); I. Wirtz, 'Mausköpf, Fuchsschwänz und Bärenhäuter — Schimpfreden und Picarofiguren in Johann Beers Romanen' (615–30).

BÖHME. B. Andersson, 'Jacob Böhmes Denken in Bildern', *Morgenglantz*, 13:303–19, applies Lakoff's and Johnson's theories of metaphor to B.'s *Morgen Röte im auffgang* (1612).

GRIMMELSHAUSEN. *A Companion to the Works of Grimmelshausen*, ed. Karl F. Otto (SGLLC), xiv + 400 pp., is a collection of invited essays in English on various aspects of G.'s work. The target readership is not clear from O.'s introduction; a certain familiarity with the battles and generals of the Thirty Years' War is assumed, but glosses are provided for literary figures such as Tieck. The first part rehearses some of the more fundamental issues facing anyone reading G. for the first time: I. M. Battafarano, 'Grimmelshausen's "autobiographies" and the art of the novel' (45–91); C. E. Schweitzer, 'Problems in the editions of Grimmelshausen's works' (25–42); and Id., 'Grimmelshausen and the picaresque novel' (147–64). K. Haberkamm, 'Allegorical and astrological forms in the works of Grimmelshausen with special emphasis on the prophecy motif' (93–145), discusses the different levels on which G.'s novels may be (and have been) interpreted, and presents the astrological reading with clarity and useful background information. Later sections include welcome discussions of some of the less well-known works: R. Zeller, 'Grimmelshausen's *Ewig-währender Calender*: a labyrinth of knowledge and reading' (167–99), and A. Solbach, 'Grimmelshausen's non-Simplician novels' (201–27). The relation of the text to the engravings is the topic of S. Keenan Greene, '"To see from these black lines": the mise en livre of the phoenix copperplate and other Grimmelshausen illustrations' (333–56). Two contributions discuss the importance of clothing in the Simplician novels: P. Hess, 'The poetics of masquerade: clothing and the construction of social, religious, and gender identity in Grimmelshausen's *Simplicissimus*' (299–331); and L. Tatlock, 'Engendering social order: from costume autobiography to conversation games in Grimmelshausen's Simpliciana' (269–96). The notion of propriety and transgression in *Simplicissimus* is examined from a linguistic perspective in A. Stevens, '*Simplicissimus Teutsch*: Grimmelshausen and the art of writing German novels', *Flood Vol.*, 353–69; and vice and virtue is the focus of another article: R. E. Schade, 'A war story of deceit, gambling and sex: Simplicissimus at the siege of Magdeburg (1636)', *GRM*, 53:155–81. *Simpliciana*, 25, contains papers delivered at the colloquium 'Grimmelshausen in seiner regionalen Umwelt' held in Renchen in July 2003: W. Kühlmann, '"Baldanders" — Grimmelshausen und die "altdeutsche" Bewegung am Oberrhein' (15–32); F. Gaede, 'Die Inselhöhle in der Ortenau. Das selbstreferentielle Substrat des *Simplicissimus*' (33–45); A. Aurnhammer, 'Simplicius zwischen Herzbruder und

Olivier, 'Historizität und Überzeitlichkeit der Konfigurationsstrukturen im *Simplicissimus Teutsch*' (47–62); H. T. Gräf, 'Landschaft und Schauplätze: Grimmelshausens Jugendjahre und ihre Spiegelung im *Simplicissimus Teutsch*'(105–24); M. Ruch, 'Realität und Fiktion in der simplicianischen Landschaft: Grimmelshausen auf der Moos' (125–42); D. Breuer, 'Grimmelshausen und das Kloster Allerheiligen' (143–75); W. E. Schäfer, 'Grimmelshausen und Burg Hohenrod' (177–86); P. Hesselmann, '"Es gung so Kurraschy her!" — Die Literarisierung der Griesbacher und Peterstaler Sauerbrunnen bei Moscherosch und Grimmelshausen' (187–220); R. Zeller, 'Die Wallfahrt nach Einsiedeln: zum Kontext simplicianischer Frömmigkeit' (221–37); D. Martin, 'Grimmelshausens Ortssagen' (239–54). The volume also contains articles apparently not connected to the topic of the conference, amongst them P. Hesselmann, 'Das "Bauernlied" bei Grimmelshausen und in Johann Georg Schielens Zeitschrift *Historische Politische und Philosophische Krieg- und Friedens-Gespräch* (1683)' (379–88); J. J. Berns, 'Zum Grimmelshausen-Biographismus und der Nachlaß-Frage' (85–103); and I. M. Battafarano, 'Literarische Variationen der biblischen Parabel vom verlorenen Sohn: Grimmelshausens *Stoltzer Melcher* und Marinos *Figliuol Prodigo*' (63–83). Italo Michele Battafarano and Hildegard Eilert, *Courage. Die starke Frau der deutschen Literatur. Von Grimmelshausen erfunden, von Brecht und Grass variiert* (FEK, 21), 264 pp., is divided into two parts. The first considers Courasche's self-presentation and how she is seen by other characters in the novels, while the second examines her afterlife in the hands of editors with particular agendas and in Brecht's *Mutter Courage* and Grass's *Das Treffen im Telgte*. This volume would appeal to an undergraduate reader, or to someone wanting to understand Brecht and Grass's model, but makes few new contributions to G. scholarship.

HARSDÖRFFER. H. as a mediator of neo-Platonic thought is the subject of P. Hess, 'Neoplatonismus und Bacon-Rezeption: Naturphilosophie bei Harsdörffer', *Morgenglantz*, 13:321–49, and H. appears as a mediator in another context in J. Konst, '"Galathe gehab dich wol!" Roemer Visschers *Sinnepoppen* (1614) und die *Frauenzimmer Gesprächspiele* (1641–49) von Georg Philipp Harsdörffer' Jordan, *Lyrik*, 75–107.

KNORR. The first part of *Morgenglantz*, 13, contains the papers delivered at the 12th conference of the Christian K. von Rosenroth-Gesellschaft in June 2002: 'Naturwissenschaften, Medizin, Kabbala und Alchemie am Sulzbacher Hof. Der Kontext von Knorrs wissenschaftlichem Werk'. Articles include: R. Zeller, 'Naturwissenschaften und Kabbala am Sulzbacher Hof und ihr kultureller Kontext' (11–19); I. M. Battafarano, 'Die Imagination in Hexenlehre, Medizin und Naturphilosophie' (73–96); A. Weeks, 'Theorie und Mystik in der Nachfolge des Paracelsus' (283–302); and A. B. Kilcher, 'Cabbala chymica. Knorrs spekulative Verbindung von Kabbala und Alchemie' (97–119). Two articles focus on K.'s translations: U. Lindgren, 'De Magnete' (137–47); and E. Achermann, 'Ordnung im Wirbel. Knorr von Rosenroth als Kompilator und Übersetzer von Thomas Browne, Jean d'Espagnet, Henry More, Gottfried Wilhelm Leibniz und Antoine Le Grand' (205–82).

MEYFART. O. Pfefferkorn, 'Imagination der ewigen Herrlichkeit. Johann Matthäus Meyfart und sein Buch *Vom himmlischen Jerusalem*', *Euphorion*, 97:379–403, compares M.'s work (1627) with his sermon cycle *Tuba novissima* (1626) and with other edifying books which attempt to describe eternal life: Philipp Nicolai's *Spiegel deß ewigen Lebens* (1599) and Johann Lassenius's *Ewig währende Freuden-Saal der Kinder Gottes* (1698).

MOSCHEROSCH. Jürgen Donien, *'Wie jener Weise sagt . . .' Zitatfunktionen in Johann Michael Moscheroschs Gesichten Philanders von Sittewalt* (Mikrokosmos, 70), Berne, Lang, 228 pp., based on the author's doctoral dissertation, considers M.'s engagement with texts by a range of authors Classical to contemporary.

SCHWARZBURG-RUDOLSTADT. J. P. Aikin continues her examination of the writings of Aemilie Juliane of S.-R. in 'Gendered theologies of childbirth in early modern Germany and the devotional handbook for pregnant women by Aemilie Juliane, Countess of Schwarzburg-Rudolstadt (1683)', *Journal of Women's History*, 15:40–67, in which she compares the onerous handbooks written by men with the much more practical, proactive, and empathetic one by Aemilie Juliane, herself a wife and mother.

4. Drama

Stefanie Arend, *Rastlose Weltgestaltung. Senecaische Kulturkritik in den Tragödien Gryphius' und Lohensteins* (FN, 81), ix + 349 pp., explores the confrontation between 17th-c. theories of how to live and Stoic philosophy in early modern tragedy. Her detailed analysis shows that the influence of Seneca in the works of G. and L. extends far beyond the neo-Stoic emphasis on *constantia* to a programme of living in accordance with nature. A. emphasizes the tension in which G. and L.'s characters find themselves as they struggle to live in this way in a world which no longer recognizes it as viable. Karin Kelping also turns her attention to G. and L., to whom she adds Hallmann, in *Frauenbilder im deutschen Barockdrama. Zur literarischen Anthropologie der Frau* (Poetica. Schriften zur Literaturwissenschaft, 73), Hamburg, Kovač, 352 pp. K.'s stated intention is to examine these dramas in the light of anthropological discussions about the social construct of 'woman' and to use psychohistorical theories. She considers the roles in which women find themselves in the dramas, dividing them into the private/family sphere and political/public roles, but her conclusions are at times naïve, and a firmer theoretical basis and deeper analysis would have made this a more convincing study.

INDIVIDUAL AUTHORS

BALDE. Heidrun Führer, *Studien zu Jacob Baldes Jephtias. Ein jesuitisches Meditationsdrama aus der Zeit der Gegenreformation*, Dissertationsschrift am Klassischen und semitischen Institut der Univ. Lund, 209 pp., offers a detailed discussion of this Latin Jesuit drama (1654). The main interest of the work lies in the allegorical use of the biblical account in which the daughter Menulema (an anagram of Emmanuel) prefigures Christ's passion.

GRYPHIUS. Alan Menhennet, *The Historical Experience in German Drama. From Gryphius to Brecht* (SGLLC), 198 pp., is concerned with dramas which convey a historical experience. In his first chapter, which focuses on *Carolus Stuardus* with references to *Papinian* and *Leo Armenius*, M. argues that G. is certainly concerned with a historical perspective, but that this perspective differs from that of later historical dramatists because G. regards history as part of an eternal framework. A section of Lothar van Laak, *Hermeneutik literarischer Sinnlichkeit. Historisch-systematische Studien zur Literatur des 17. und 18. Jahrhunderts* (Communicatio. Studien zur europäischen Literatur- und Kulturgeschichte, 31), Tübingen, Niemeyer, ix + 309 pp., discusses G.'s *Papinian* and *Carolus Stuardus* (90–109). Van Laak argues that Schöne's model, where the *Reyen* perform the same explanatory function as the *subscriptio* in an emblem, is an over-simplification. He is much more interested in the interaction of the *Reyen* and the stage action, which results in multiple interpretations of an image.

HARSDÖRFFER. Danielle Brugière-Zeiss, **Seelewig de G. Ph. Harsdörffer et S. Th. Staden (1644): un opéra?* (Contacts Série 3: Études et Documents, 59), Berne, Lang, xxiv + 630 pp.

HOFFMANN. Gottfried H. (1658–1712) was first deputy headmaster and then headmaster at the Gymnasium in Lauban (and later Weise's successor in Zittau). He wrote a number of plays for his pupils to perform, and this is the first to be made available in a modern edition: *Die gefallene und wieder erhöhete Eviana. Ein Schauspiel aus dem Jahr 1696*, ed. and comm. Ulrike Wels (Bibliothek seltener Texte, 9), Berlin, Weidler, 254 pp., illus. Through the story of a servant-girl's transgression, punishment, restoration, and eventual marriage to a prince, H. offers a parable of salvation. His own preface to the printed text also includes a defence of school drama which was under threat from Pietist critics.

THE CLASSICAL ERA

By Matthew Bell, *Senior Lecturer in German, King's College London*

(This survey covers the years 2001–2003)*

1. General

Historical revisionism continues to make itself felt. Recent trends, whether post-structuralist, New Historicist, or focused on issues of gender or colour, have weighed the Enlightenment's master ideas of autonomy, the public sphere, secularism, and toleration against its apparent endemic prejudices, which, it is argued, caused many writers to fail to recognize the claims of gender and ethnicity alongside the more general claims of humanity. The debate continues. U. Daniel, 'How bourgeois was the public sphere of the eighteenth century? Or: Why it is important to historicize *Strukturwandel der Öffentlichkeit*', *Das achtzehnte Jahrhundert*, 26, 2002: 9–17, makes telling points against Habermas's conception of the *Verbürgerlichung* of politics in the 18th c. In opposition to the current trend for limiting the scope of the Enlightenment's aims and achievements, M. L. Davies, 'Wissenschaft und Ambivalenz: zur Rezeption der Aufklärung in Großbritannien', *ib.*, 18–34, criticizes the tendency in recent British writing to assume that the Enlightenment project is over and counters this with the Enlightenment's own promise of a constantly actualized self-criticism.

From the maintenance of a living tradition to the rediscovery of a dead one: the flood of interest in 18th-c. anthropology shows no sign of abating. Anthropology continues to arouse interest for the light it sheds on literature and for its prominent role in philosophy. To some extent a distinctive German product, it forms a tradition to which all the major movements of the century contributed, from the Rationalism of the early Enlightenment to the Idealism of the end of the century. Now, in what one might call the second phase of interest in 18th-c. anthropology and in keeping with the revisionist trend, it is the discontinuities and deferrals in the tradition that are coming to light. C. J. Minter, 'Literary *Empfindsamkeit* and nervous sensibility in eighteenth-century Germany', *MLR*, 96, 2001: 1016–28, illustrates the persistent conflation of physical and moral realms in the anthropology of *Empfindsamkeit*, whilst her '"Die Macht der dunkeln

* The author acknowledges his gratitude to the late Derek Glass, from whose long experience of compiling the German Literature 1830–1880 section of *The Year's Work* and wisdom in all matters bibliographical he was fortunate to benefit. Derek is sadly missed.

Ideen": a Leibnizian theme in German psychology and fiction between the late Enlightenment and Romanticism', *GLL*, 54, 2001: 114–36, emphasizes the caution with which the German Rationalist tradition accommodated and subsumed the irrational mind in the later 18th c. R. Godel, '"Eine unendliche Menge dunkeler Vorstellungen." Zur Widerständigkeit von Empfindungen und Vorurteilen in der deutschen Spätaufklärung', *DVLG*, 76, 2002: 542–76, adds further detail to Panajotis Kondylis's seminal account of the paradoxes of Enlightenment (*Die Aufklärung im Rahmen des neuzeitlichen Rationalismus*, Stuttgart, Cotta, 1981) by highlighting the problematic relation between the Enlightenment's rehabilitation of the 'dunkel', irrational senses, and its campaign against prejudice.

Aufklärung, 14, 2002, collects essays on the theme of 'Aufklärung und Anthropologie' spanning literary and philosophical texts. These include H.-E. Friedrich, '"Geordnete Freiheit." Zur anthropologischen Verankerung der Verslehre in der poetologischen Diskussion des 18. Jahrhunderts' (7–22); M. Willems, 'Der Verbrecher als Mensch. Zur Herkunft anthropologischer Deutungsmuster der Kriminalgeschichte des 18. Jahrhunderts' (23–48); K. Mellmann, '"Ich fühle mich! Ich bin!" Zur literarischen Anthropologie des Sturm und Drang' (49–74); F. Jannidis, 'Die "Bestimmung des Menschen". Kultursemiotische Beschreibung einer sprachlichen Formel' (75–96); G. D'Alessandro, 'Der Moralmensch. Anthropologie und Kantianismus in der Theologie und der Moralphilosophie am Ende des 18. Jahrhunderts' (97–122); M. Oberhausen, 'Dunkle Vorstellungen als Thema von Kants Anthropologie und A. G. Baumgartens Psychologie' (123–46); C. Schweiger, 'Klugheit bei Kant. Metamorphosen eines Schlüsselbegriffs der praktischen Philosophie' (147–60); J. Garber, 'Die "Bestimmung des Menschen" in der ethnologischen Kulturtheorie der deutschen und französischen Spätaufklärung' (161–204); R. Godel, 'Der Wilde als Aufklärer? Kulturanthropologisch vermittelte Rezeptionssteuerung in Joseph von Sonnenfels' *Mann ohne Vorurtheil*' (205–32); N. Hinske, 'Kant und Alexander Gottlieb Baumgarten. Ein leider unerledigtes Thema der Anthropologie Kants' (261–74).

RGI, 18, 2002, makes a significant contribution to the understanding of psychological and ethical thinking in the later 18th c. by showing how the concept 'Trieb' developed from its British empiricist origins into a key component of Idealism; articles include S. Buchenau, '*Trieb*, *Antrieb*, *Triebfeder* dans la philosophie morale prékantienne' (11–24); J.-P. Paccioni, 'Le terme *Trieb* et l'homme comme fin dernière et ultime' (25–44); P. Pénisson, '*Trieb* et énergie chez Herder' (45–52); C. Couturier-Heinrich, '"Tendance naturelle au rhythme" et "observation instinctive de la mesure": l'inscription du rhythme dans le domaine du spontané chez Johann Georg Sulzer et August Wilhelm Schlegel' (53–70); N. Waszek, 'La "tendance à la sociabilité" (*Trieb der Geselligkeit*) chez Christian Garve' (71–86).

Caroline Torra-Mattenklott, *Metaphorologie der Rührung. Ästhetische Theorie und Mechanik im 18. Jahrhundert*, Munich, Fink, 2002, 384 pp., makes a noteworthy contribution to the history of aesthetics in the tradition of M. H. Abrams's *The Mirror and the Lamp*, by analysing the evolution of the master tropes of affect in 18th-c. psychology and aesthetics. The important discursive role of analogies, which has been well-known in Herder's persistently metaphorical writing, is here traced back through key works by Sulzer, Mendelssohn, and Baumgarten, to Wolff. I. Stöckmann, 'Traumleiber. Zur Evolution des Menschenwissens im 17. und 18. Jahrhundert. Mit einer Vorbemerkung zur literarischen Anthropologie', *IASL*, 26.2, 2001 : 1–55, interprets a series of literary dreams as reflections of society's 'kommunikative Ordnungen'.

Die Grenzen des Menschen. Anthropologie und Ästhetik um 1800, ed. Maximilian Bergengruen, Roland Borgards, and Johannes Friedrich Lehmann, Würzburg, Königshausen & Neumann, 2001, 206 pp., includes the following: J. F. Lehmann, 'Vom Fall des Menschen. Sexualität und Ästhetik bei J. M. R. Lenz und J. G. Herder' (15–36); M. Bergengruen, 'Das neue Recht und der neue Körper. Wagners *Kindermörderin* zwischen Anthropologie und Rechtstheorie' (37–50); G. Vickemann, 'Verschiebungen zwischen Leib und Seele. Populärmedizinisches Sprechen über Verführung im 18. Jahrhundert' (51–64); H. Neumeyer, '"Ich bin einer von denjenigen Unglückseligen . . ." Rückkopplungen und Autoreferenzen. Zur Onaniedebatte im 18. Jahrhundert' (65–96); B. Thums, 'Moralische Selbstbearbeitung und Hermeneutik des Lebensstils. Zur Diätetik in Anthropologie und Literatur um 1800' (97–112).

AUFKLÄRUNG. The focus on Kant as the standard-bearer of Enlightenment in Germany is fading, and other important figures are receiving deserved recognition. *Aufklärung* 12, 2001, carries a series of essays on Christian Wolff and his influence, including: H.-M. Gerlach, 'Eklektizismus oder Fundamentalphilosophie? Die alternativen Wege von Christian Thomasius und Christian Wolff im philosophischen Denken der deutschen Frühaufklärung an der Universität Halle' (9–26); B. Paź, 'Christian Wolffs Ontologie. Ihre Voraussetzungen und Hauptdimensionen' (27–50); D. Döring, 'Der Wolffianismus in Leipzig. Anhänger und Gegner' (51–76); G. Mühlpfordt, 'Christian Wolffs Lehre im östlichen Europa' (77–100). Celebrating the tenth anniversary of the return of a university to Frankfurt an der Oder, A. Haverkamp, '"Wie die Morgenröthe zwischen Nacht und Tag."

Alexander Gottlieb Baumgarten und die Begründung der Kulturwissenschaften in Frankfurt an der Oder', *DVLG*, 76, 2002 : 3–26, makes major claims for the historical importance of Baumgarten's *Aesthetica*. Steffen W. Gross, *Felix Aestheticus. Die Ästhetik als Lehre vom Menschen. Zum 250. Jahrestag des Erscheinens von Alexander Gottlieb Baumgartens 'Aesthetica'*, Würzburg, Königshausen & Neumann, 2001, 282 pp., undertakes to rescue and relocate Baumgarten's work within the tradition of anthropology, arguing that the tendency to see the *Aesthetica* as a work about art has led to its real significance being underestimated. R. Bezold, 'Baumgartens Tod', *Fest. Schings*, 19–28. Another rescue attempt, from deeper obscurity, is Michael Kempe and Thomas Maissen, *Die Collegia der Insulaner, Vertraulichen und Wohlgesinnten in Zürich, 1679–1709. Die ersten deutschsprachigen Aufklärungsgesellschaften zwischen Naturwissenschaften, Bibelkritik, Geschichte und Politik*, Zurich, Vlg Neue Zürcher Zeitung, 2002, 453 pp.

Political theory is the subject of *Aufklärung* 13, 2001, with the following analyses: S. Pott, 'Gemeinwohl oder "schöner Schein". Staatszwecke und Staatsideen bei Christoph Martin Wieland und in der Weimarer Klassik' (211–42); M. Fuhrmann, 'Die Politik der Volksvermehrung und Menschenveredelung. Der Bevölkerungsdiskurs in der politischen und ökonomischen Theorie der deutschen Aufklärung' (243–82); K. Tribe, 'Natürliche Ordnung und Ökonomie' (283–302). Sigrid Habersaat, *Verteidigung der Aufklärung. Friedrich Nicolai in religiösen und politischen Debatten*, 2 vols, Würzburg, Königshausen & Neumann, 2001, 224, 286 pp., maps Nicolai's retreat from offensive polemic, for instance against the Catholic Church, to defensive polemic, as the Enlightenment came under political suspicion after the French Revolution. Vol. 2 comprises an annotated edition of Nicolai's correspondence with J. G. Zimmermann and C. F. von Blanckenburg.

EMPFINDSAMKEIT, STURM UND DRANG. *Aufklärung*, 13, 2001, returns to the vexed question of the relation of *Empfindsamkeit* to *Verbürgerlichung*, with the following contributions: L. Pikulik, 'Die Mündigkeit des Herzens: über die Empfindsamkeit als Emanzipations- und Autonomiebewegung' (9–32); L. Danneberg and F. Vollhardt, 'Sinn und Unsinn literaturwissenschaftlicher Innovation. Mit Beispielen aus der neueren Forschung zu G. E. Lessing und zur Empfindsamkeit' (33–69); D. Till, '"Der Gräber Todesnacht ist nun nicht mehr! erwacht!" Pietismus, Neologie und Empfindsamkeit in Klopstocks Bearbeitung von Nicolais "Wächterlied"' (70–102); K. Mellmann, 'Güte — Liebe — Gottheit. Ein Beitrag zur Präzisierung des 'utopischen' Gehalts von Goethes *Stella*' (103–47); H.-E. Friedrich, '"Ewig lieben", zugleich aber "menschlich lieben"? Zur Reflexion der empfindsamen Liebeskonzeption von Gellert und

Klopstock zu Goethe und Jacobi' (148–90); Y.-G. Mix, 'Männliche Sensibilität oder die Modernität der Empfindsamkeit. Zu den *Leiden des jungen Werther*, *Anton Reiser*, *Buddenbrooks* und den *Verwirrungen des Zöglings Törless*' (191–208). The volume ends with a valuable survey of recent work by the doyen of *Empfindsamkeit* studies Gerhard Sauder, 'Empfindsamkeit. Tendenzen der Forschung aus der Perspektive eines Betroffenen' (307–38).

Jan Engbers, *Der 'Moral-Sense' bei Gellert, Lessing und Wieland. Zur Rezeption von Shaftesbury und Hutcheson in Deutschland* (*GRM*, Beiheft, 16), Heidelberg, Winter, 2001, 161 pp., corrects the assumption that *Empfindsamkeit* accepted British moral sense theory uncritically and differentiates between the phases of its reception. A useful documentation of German translations of British moral sense philosophy is included. D. Oschmann, '"Versinnlichung" der Rede. Zu einem Prinzip aufklärerischer Sprach- und Dichtungstheorie', *MDLK*, 94, 2002 : 286–305, contextualizes the poetics of the *Sturm und Drang* and Weimar Classicism by showing that the lament of Herder, Goethe, and others that language had lost its sensuous component was a familiar Enlightenment theme. U. Hentschel, '". . . da wallfahrte ich hin, oft mit der neuen Héloïse in der Tasche." Zur deutschen Rousseau-Rezeption im 18. und beginnenden 19. Jahrhundert', *Euphorion*, 92, 2002 : 47–74, studies accounts of pilgrimages to Swiss sites associated with Rousseau. R. Behrens, '"Sens intérieur" und meditierende Theoriesuche. Jacob Heinrich Meisters *Lettres sur l'imagination*', *Fest. Schings*, 149–66. R. Krebs, 'Wer ist die Schönste im ganzen Land? Über die Relativität des Schönen bei Riedel, Wieland und Heinse', *Fest. Jacobs*, 129–48.

CLASSICISM. Dimitri Liebsch, *Die Geburt der ästhetischen Bildung aus dem Körper der antiken Plastik. Zur Bildungssemantik im ästhetischen Diskurs zwischen 1750 und 1800*, Hamburg, Meiner, 2001, 211 pp., pursues the historical link between earlier notions of outer, physical *Bildung* and the later 18th c.'s use of *Bildung* as a term for the cultivation of the inner self. In studies of Winckelmann, Wieland, Herder, Forster, Wilhelm von Humboldt, and Schiller, Liebsch finds this link in the idea that inner *Bildung* is to be had from an engagement with the outer *Bildung* of ancient sculpture. *Fest. Schings* contains three essays on the concept of the 'pregnant moment' in classicism: R.-P. Janz, 'Ansichten der Juno Ludovisi. Winckelmann — Schiller — Goethe' (357–72); N. C. Wolf, '"Fruchtbarer Augenblick" — "prägnanter Moment": zur medienspezifischen Funktion einer ästhetischen Kategorie in Aufklärung und Klassik (Lessing, Goethe)' (373–404); M. Jaeger, 'Kairos und Chronos — oder: Der prägnante Moment ist flüchtig. Antike Philosophie, klassische Lebenskunstlehre und moderne Verzweiflung' (405–20). Weimar has boomed as a tourist destination since unification, reaching a peak in 1999. Studies of the culture of classical Weimar are being produced in corresponding quantities. Biographies of Weimar figures include Jochen Klauss, *Der 'Kunschtmeyer'. Johann Heinrich Meyer: Freund und Orakel Goethes*, Weimar, Böhlau, 2002, vii + 358 pp.; Walter Steiner and Uta Kühn-Stillmark, *Friedrich Justin Bertuch. Ein Leben im klassischen Weimar zwischen Kultur und Kommerz*, Weimar, Böhlau, 2002, vii + 321 pp.; Karsten Hein, *Ottilie von Goethe (1796–1872). Biographie und literarische Beziehungen der Schwiegertochter Goethes*, Berne, Lang, 2001, 698 pp. The essays collected in *Das Archiv der Goethezeit. Ordnung — Macht — Matrix*, ed. Gert Theile (Jb. der Stiftung Weimarer Klassik), Munich, Fink, 2001, 312 pp., analyse the role of archives and museums in past and present. Essays include G. Theile, 'Die Akten des Goethesangs. Selbstverwaltung und Individualität im Zeichen des Archivs' (11–30); M. Wetzel, 'In Mignons Mausoleum. Das Bildersaal als Archivschrift' (63–82); W. Ernst, 'Zwischen Imagination und multimedialem Gedächtnis. Bildarchive der Goethezeit' (83–116); R. Bärwinkel, 'Ordnung durch Selektion. Die Weimarer Bibliothek' (117–30); G. Arnold, '*Adrastea* — Quellen zur Rezeption einer kulturgeschichtlichen Zeitschrift' (197–252).

Goethe's interest in collecting commemorative coins and medals began in Rome in 1787 and was sustained until his death. Jochen Klauss, *Die Medaillensammlung Goethes*, 2 vols, Berlin, Deutsche Gesellschaft für Medaillenkunst– Goethe-Nationalmuseum der Stiftung Weimarer Klassik, 2000, 482, 258 pp., catalogues Goethe's collection of over 1900 items. Vol. I presents good quality plates and descriptions and transcriptions. Vol. II contains documentation, chiefly extracts from Goethe's correspondence, including everything Goethe ever said about coins or medals. In several places, especially on what are listed as imitations of ancient coinage, the lettering is incorrectly transcribed, and in one case a head of Agrippa is described as female; consultation with a classical numismatist would have prevented these errors. *Unwrapping Goethe's Weimar. Essays in Cultural Studies and Local Knowledge*, ed. Burkhard Henke, Susanne Kord, and Simon Richter, Rochester, NY, Camden House, 2000, xi + 339 pp., approaches aspects of the written, visual, and aural culture of Weimar Classicism from a cultural studies perspective with the aim if not of dethroning then (to quote the title of one of the contributions) of 'decentering' Goethe. The generously illustrated volume includes B. Henke, 'Goethe®. Advertising, marketing, and merchandising the classical' (15–35); D. Purdy, 'Weimar Classicism and the origins of consumer culture' (36–62); C. MacLeod, 'Floating heads: Weimar portrait busts' (65–96); A. Janeiro Randall, 'Music in Weimar circa 1780: decentering text, decentering Goethe' (97–144); K. Schutjer,

'War and dramaturgy: Goethe's command of the Weimar theatre' (147–65); S. E. Gustafson, 'From Werther to Amazons: cross-dressing and male-male desire' (166–87); E. Krimmer, 'Sartorial transgressions: re-dressing class and gender hierarchies in masquerades and travesties' (191–212); L. Dietrick, 'Women writers and the authorization of literary practice' (213–32); S. Kord, 'The hunchback of Weimar: Luise von Göchhausen and the Weimar grotesque' (233–69); S. Hammer, 'Creation and constipation: *Don Carlos* and Schiller's blocked passage to Weimar' (273–94); W. D. Wilson, 'Skeletons in Goethe's closet: human rights, protest, and the myth of political liberality' (295–309); G. Theile, 'The Weimar myth: from city of the arts to global village' (310–27). The sort of view of Weimar Classicism that the authors of the volume wish to 'decentre' is represented by T. J. Reed, 'Weimar Classicism: Goethe's alliance with Schiller', Sharpe, *Goethe*, 101–15. Elizabeth M. Wilkinson and L. A. Willoughby, *Models of Wholeness. Some Attitudes to Language, Art and Life in the Age of Goethe*, ed. Jeremy Adler, Martin Swales, and Ann Weaver, Berne, Lang, 2002, 271 pp., brings together a range of stimulating essays on Goethe and Schiller from various published sources. Karl Robert Mandelkow, *Gesammelte Aufsätze und Vorträge zur Klassik- und Romantikrezeption in Deutschland*, Berne, Lang, 2001, 380 pp., brings together a number of his shorter essays. K. F. Gille, '"Glückliches Ereignis." Zum Freundschaftsbund zwischen Goethe und Schiller', *WB*, 48, 2002: 520–30.

GENRES. Stefan Trappen, *Gattungspoetik. Studien zur Poetik des 16. bis 19. Jahrhunderts und zur Geschichte der triadischen Gattungslehre* (Beihefte zum *Euphorion*, 40), Heidelberg, Winter, 2001, x + 303 pp., ranges from Renaissance Humanism to 1800. On the premise that the classification of literature into lyric, epic, and dramatic genres represents as much of a problem as it does a solution for the analysis of genre, T. argues that the triadic division has no basis in logic and can only make sense as a historical phenomenon. The assumption of e.g. A. W. Schlegel and Goethe that there were three 'Naturformen der Poesie' is shown here to be grounded in attempts in the last decade of the 18th c. to rationalize the increasingly unstable generic classifications developed in the Enlightenment.

VERSE. *Literatur und Kultur des Rokoko*, ed. Matthias Luserke, Reiner Marx, and Reiner Wild, Göttingen, Vandenhoeck & Ruprecht, 2001, 328 pp., attempts to rehabilitate a much-maligned fashion. Key questions are addressed. How much more was *Rokoko* than a style or even a cluster of motifs? Did *Rokoko* extend beyond lyric poetry and the visual and plastic arts? To what extent and how seriously did *Rokoko* engage with intellectual trends? In what ways did writers 'grow out of' *Rokoko* and to what extent were their trajectories already presupposed by the evolution of *Rokoko* itself? Mainly concerned with lyric *Kleinformen*, it contains M. Luserke, '*O vis superba formae!* Über die Basia-Gedichte des Johannes Sekundus (1511–1536) und ihr Nachspiel bei Goethe' (9–32); M. Beetz, 'Von der galanten Poesie zur Rokokolyrik. Zur Umorientierung erotischer und anthropologischer Konzepte in der ersten Hälfte des 18. Jahrhunderts' (33–62); W. Promies, 'Liebesspiel. Zeiten um den Rokoko herum' (79–94); L. Lütteken, 'Gibt es ein musikalisches Rokoko?' (95–108); A.-M. Lohmeier, '*Arte aut Marte*. Über Ewald Christian von Kleist, Dichter und Soldat' (121–34); R. Marx, 'Anakreontik als lyrische Initiation. Zu Lessings *Kleinigkeiten* und Goethes *Annette*' (135–46); H. Blinn, 'Shakespeare im Rokoko. *Natur* und *Grazie* in Wielands Shakespeare Übersetzungen' (147–66); J.-U. Fechner, 'Matthias Claudius: *Tändeleyen und Erzählungen*. Ein Erstlingswerk im Spannungsfeld der Geistesgeschichte um 1760' (167–76); S. Bonacchi, 'Ewald Christian von Kleist und J. M. R. Lenz im Kontext der Rokokolyrik' (177–96); C. Zelle, 'Zwischen Gelehrtendichtung und Originalgenie. Barrieren der Ramler-Rezeption in der Germanistik' (197–210); Y.-G. Mix, 'Das Ende des Rokoko und die Formierung eines autonomen Lyrikmarktes in Deutschland (J. G. Herder, J. W. L. Gleim, G. A. Bürger)' (211–22); U. Leuschner, 'Anmerkungen zu Maler Müllers Rokokolyrik' (223–34); S. Kiefer, ' "Gesellige Bildung." Ein Ideal des Rokoko und seine Fortschreibung in Goethes *Unterhaltungen deutscher Ausgewanderten*' (235–50); K. Richter, 'Rokoko-Reminiszensen in Goethes *West-östlichem Divan*' (277–88). H. D. Irmscher, 'Naturwissenschaftliches Denken und Poesie in der deutschen Literatur des 18. Jahrhunderts', *Fest. Schings*, 167–92, sees the beginning of C. P. Snow's *Two Cultures* in the poetry of the 18th c. A. Košenina, 'Schönheit im Detail oder im Ganzen? Mikroskop und Guckkasten als Werkzeuge und Metaphern der Poesie', *Fest. Jacobs*, 101–28. H. Kurzke, 'Proscribirt und castigirt. Kirchenliedbearbeitungen der Aufklärung', *Fest. Schings*, 49–62.

DRAMA. *Dramenlexikon des 18. Jahrhunderts*, ed. Heide Hollmer and Albert Meier, Munich, Beck, 2001, 351 pp., contains short articles on over 250 plays in German and aims to raise awareness of the full range of what was read and performed in the 18th c. Bibliographical details, the date and place of premiere, brief plot summaries, comments on thematic contours, and suggestions for further reading are given for both canonical and forgotten works, with the former receiving longer articles. An alphabetical listing of work titles is the only index; a subject index might have been helpful. The volume largely achieves its aims and will be a useful aid to research. However, translations and works published in Germany in foreign languages are not covered, so that this remains a partial picture and one that reinforces the myth that an independent German literary tradition existed in the 18th c. Peter Hesselmann, *Gereinigtes Theater? Dramaturgie und Schaubühne im Spiegel deutschsprachiger Theaterperiodika des 18. Jahrhunderts (1750–1800)*, Frankfurt, Klostermann, 2002, xi + 512 pp., analyses the structure, organization, and critical premises of the vehicles of theatre criticism. This forms a prelude to a sociologically and anthropologically orientated account of the 'new' theatre of the latter part of the century and its role as 'Erziehungsinstitut mit dem Ziel der Einübung bürgerlicher Tugenden und Affektmodellierung' (p. 422). Elias's model of the process of civilization is at work here. Addressing a similar field, *Theater und Publizistik im deutschen Sprachraum im 18. Jahrhundert*, ed. Raymond Heitz and Roland Krebs, Berne, Lang, 2001, xviii + 274 pp., the product of a conference in Metz in 2000, shows just how central theatre reviews were to cultural life and how seriously they were taken as a form of public utterance by major figures whom one might not normally associate with the theatre. We shall need to reflect more critically on the notion that the likes of Lessing, Goethe, and Schiller were trying to create a public discourse about the theatre *ex nihilo*. Papers include W. F. Bender, 'Theaterperiodika als Forum des öffentlichen Diskurses über eine nationalen Bühne und eine neue Schauspielkunst' (1–18); C. Juillard, 'La condamnation de l'opéra dans les *Critische Beyträge* (1732–1744): Gottsched et ses sources françaises' (19–38); M. Grimberg, 'La discussion sur le théâtre dans la revue zurichoise *Freymüthige Nachrichten von neuen Büchern, und andern zur Gelehrtheit gehörigen Sachen* (1744–63)' (39–56); J. Moes, 'D'Aristote à Shakespeare: le théâtre dans les revues de Justus Möser' (57–88); J. Clédière, 'Le théâtre dans la *Deutsche Chronik* de Schubart (1774/1777–1787/1791)' (89–122); G.-M. Schulz, 'Die moralische Anstalt als eine medizinische Angelegenheit betrachtet' (123–40); G. Sauder, 'Otto Heinrich von Gemmingens *Mannheimer Dramaturgie* (1778–1779)' (141–60); R. Heitz, 'Theater und Publizistik in Bayern: *Der dramatische Censor* (1782–1783)' (161–90); R. Krebs, 'La réception du théâtre du *Sturm und Drang* dans les périodiques des années 1770' (221–240). K. A. Wurst, 'Women dramatists in late eighteenth-century Germany: the hazards of a love match', *Seminar*, 38, 2002:313–31, argues that the complex and sensitive treatments of this familiar theme by a selection of women dramatists have been unfairly neglected. K. S. Guthke, 'Dodd hat euch ganz verdorben. Der europäische Kontext der Shakespeare-Kenntnis des jungen Goethe', *JFDH*, 2002: 1–30, illuminates affinities in English and German Shakespeare reception in the middle of the 18th c. P. Hesselmann, 'Kranke Heiler. Zum ästhetischen, anthropologischen und medizinischen Diskurs über Schauspielkunst im späten 18 Jahrhundert', *Fest. Jacobs*, 73–100.

PROSE. The 18th-c. novel continues to elicit attempts to explain its 'rise', although there is still little agreement over the premisses of the debate: are the conditions for the rise of the novel of a social, a philosophical, or an aesthetic nature? The triumph of the prose medium can also be seen to have its limits. F. Krause's wide-ranging and purposeful article 'Von der Theodizee-Krise zur ästhetischen Anthropodizee: literarische Modernität in Romanen der Aufklärung', *GLL*, 55, 2002: 1–23, traces the development of aesthetic autonomy in the novel. B. Herrmann, 'La vie comme roman. Transformations médiales du fictif entre classicisme et romantisme', *RGI*, 16, 2001: 47–68, illuminates changing attitudes towards realism. R. S. Bledsoe, 'Empathetic reading and identity formation', *LY*, 33, 2001: 201–31, traces the debate about novel-reading in the late 18th c. back to changes in the conception of the nature of human individuality. Y. Birumachi, 'Von der lauten zur stillen Lektüre. Zum Buchmedium und Leseverhalten in der Goethezeit', *DB*, 107, 2001: 82–98, revisits the topic of the paradigm shift from an oral to a reading culture. U. Hentschel, '"Briefe sind Spiegel der Seelen." Epistolare Kultur des 18. Jahrhunderts zwischen Privatheit und Öffentlichkeit', *LY*, 33, 2001: 183–200, emphasizes the popularity of published letters in the second half of the 18th c., but also notes concerns surrounding privacy that set a limit on the *empfindsam* attempt to open fully the soul to public gaze. S. Martus, '"Man setzet sich eben derselben Gefahr aus, welcher man andre aussetzt." Autoritive Performanz in der literarischen Kommunikation am Beispiel von Bayle, Bodmer und Schiller', *ZDP*, 120, 2001: 481–501, suggests that in the course of the 18th c. criticism developed into an art-form as a means of self-legitimation.

THEMES. Ruth P. Dawson, *The Contested Quill. Literature by Women in Germany, 1770–1800*, Newark, Delaware U.P., 2002, 415 pp., argues that the great expansion in numbers of women authors in the final third of the 18th c. is accompanied by their growing self-assertiveness. The role of women writers in the period, however, can only be properly recognized if literary history promotes the status of *Empfindsamkeit.* On this basis D. conducts an examination of the context of female literary production and representations of the female in works by Friderika Baldinger, Sophie von La Roche, Philippine Engelhard, Marianne Ehrmann, and Sophie Albrecht. Ha-Jo Maier, *Zwischen Bestimmung und Autonomie. Erziehung, Bildung und Liebe im Frauenroman des 18. Jahrhunderts. Eine literatursoziologische Studie von Christian F. Gellerts 'Leben der schwedischen Gräfin von G***' und Sophie von La Roches 'Geschichte des Fräuleins von Sternheim'*, Hildesheim, Olms–Weidmann, 2001, 406 pp., shows, by means of largely sociological analysis, that conceptions of the female broke free of traditional, male projections, but that this occurred outside the normal bourgeois family milieu and hence did little to extend the possibilities for self-realization available to women in their everyday lives. P. U. Hohendahl, 'Die Krise der Männlichkeit im späten 18. Jahrhundert', *ZGer*, 12, 2002: 275–86, surveys canonical texts for signs of discomfort about the social role of masculinity and reinterprets the theme of anti-patriarchal rebellion in gendered terms. K. A. Wurst, 'Spellbinding: the body as art/art as body in the cultural practice of *Attitüden*', *LY*, 33, 2001: 151–82, sees 'attitudes', which allowed their consumers freely to indulge the 'erotic gaze', as the trivial counterpart in 'everyday culture' to Schiller's aesthetic state. F. Nelle, 'Im Wechselbad der Gefühle — Materialisationen der Leidenschaft in der Theater- und Gartenkunst des 18. Jahrhunderts', *GRM*, 52, 2002: 327–41, examines the ways these two newly respectable art-forms dealt with problems in the representation of emotions. Stephan K. Schindler, *Eingebildete Körper. Phantasierte Sexualität in der Goethezeit*, Tübingen, Stauffenburg, 2001, 258 pp., moves in the opposite direction, arguing that the Enlightenment increasingly spiritualizes sex but that in the *Goethezeit* the sexual imagination takes its revenge. Y.-G. Mix, 'Nationale Selbst- und Fremdbilder in der Mode- und Alamodekritik des *Hinkenden Boten* und anderer populärer Kalender des 18. Jahrhunderts', *IASL*, 26.2, 2001: 56–71, contributes to the revision of the internationalist image of the Enlightenment by tracing the growth of the idea of the 'fatherland' in popular almanacs up to 1789. I. Sahmland, 'Gibt es ein deutsches Nationaltemperament? Die Temperamentenlehre und ihr Beitrag zur Frage der nationalen Identität im 18. Jahrhundert', *GRM*, 52, 2002: 103–28, shows that the ancient theory of temperaments continued to be attractive as it provided a means of constructing national identities. Literature is influenced by all manner of non-literary media. Linda Simonis, *Die Kunst des Geheimen. Esoterische Kommunikation und ästhetische Darstellung im 18. Jahrhundert*, Heidelberg, Winter, 2002, 456 pp., applies insights from the study of 18th-c. freemasonry and other secret societies to several works including Moritz's *Andreas Hartknopf*, Mozart's *The Magic Flute*, and texts by Hamann and Herder. Stefan Kister, *Text als Grab. Sepulkrales Denken in der deutschen Literatur um 1800*, Bielefeld, Aisthesis, 2001, 250 pp., traces imagery of the grave in the writing of Lessing and Herder and in Goethe's *Die Wahlverwandtschaften*.

2. Goethe

General. Thorsten Valk, *Melancholie im Werk Goethes. Genese — Symptomatik — Therapie*, Tübingen, Niemeyer, 2002, viii + 325 pp., is the first general study of melancholy in G.'s writing and deserves to be widely read. The approach is traditional: the early chapters establish a historical context for subsequent readings of *Werther*, *Tasso*, *Lila*, *Wilhelm Meisters Lehrjahre*, *Die Wahlverwandtschaften*, and *Faust*. It should be stressed that V.'s subject is melancholy in G.'s writing (indeed a fairly narrow range of his writings), not his life, though in G.'s case it is hard to exclude biographical considerations at the best of times, and an argument could be made, for instance, for having included the 'Tagebuch der italienischen Reise', in which G. undertakes a cure for his own melancholy. V. rightly identifies the influence of the Halle school of medicine, mediated through J. F. Metz, who 'cured' G. in 1768/69. V. does not promise a systematic account of G.'s exposure to theories of melancholy, which might have included an analysis of the English literary sources that lay behind e.g. the melancholic poses in his early Leipzig correspondence. Equally a separate account of G.'s dealings with Moritz would shed light on the period after 1788 and in particular the theme of 'religious melancholy' in *Faust*. The final chapter on *Faust* makes the crucial point that the wager is in part the product of Faust's melancholy. It would be interesting to consider in more detail how the formulation of the wager and in particular the issue of 'Sorge' relates to melancholy. If the focus on five major and one minor texts — necessary for reasons of space — does not reveal the full range of G.'s literary engagement with melancholy, V.'s monograph establishes the framework within which much of G.'s writing will now have to be seen. Karl-Heinz Hahn, *'Dann ist Vergangenheit beständig . . .' Goethe-Studien*, Cologne, Böhlau, 2001, 215 pp., republishes essays by H. in commemoration of his untimely death in 1990.

BIBLIOGRAPHY, EDITIONS, CORRESPONDENCE, BIOGRAPHY. *Gedichte*, ed. Bernd Witte, Stuttgart, Reclam, 2001, 1166 pp., is a handy, chronologically ordered *Studienausgabe* containing all of the commonly-read shorter poems and cycles, with a critical apparatus and a commentary on textual and contextual matters. Other new editions include *J. F. Reichardt — J. W. Goethe Briefwechsel*, ed. Volkmar Braunbehrens, Gabriele Busch-Salmen, and Walter Salmen, Weimar, Böhlau, 2002, x + 239 pp. Fascicles 5 to 7 of vol. 4 of *Goethe Wörterbuch*, ed. Wilhelm Kühlmann, Heimo Reinitzer, and Hartmut Schmidt, Stuttgart, Kohlhammer, 2001 and 2002, 514–640, 641–769, 770–895 pp., cover *Grundähnlichkeit* to *herandrohen*.

Luserke, *Goethe*, contains papers given at the anniversary symposium 'Goethe 99 — zwischen Edition und Deutung' held in Darmstadt. It takes as its starting point the traditional techniques of textual criticism, genetic criticism, and *Rezeptionsforschung*, and attempts to move these in new directions. T. Zabka, ' "Von einem Wort läßt sich kein Jota rauben." Zur Überinterpetation von Buchstaben und

Satzzeichen in der neueren Goethe-Philologie' (9–22), criticizes interpretations of Goethe's writing based on punctuation or the lack of it. This is well timed given the recent spate of new editions, although Z.'s position implies a less favourable view of Albrecht Schöne's *Faust* edition than he actually takes. H. Wender, 'Probleme der *Werther*-Edition' (23–30), reviews recent computerized editions of Goethe and raises questions about current trends in textual criticism and in particular Schöne's opposition to editorial intervention and conjectural emendations. Issues of publication and reception history are addressed in F. Herboth, '"Das will er aber nicht drucken lassen." Anmerkungen zur Druck- und Rezeptionsgeschichte von Goethes Personalsatire *Götter Helden und Wieland*' (67–78). T. Richter, 'Zur Kenntnis der "Doppelhandschriften" von Goethe und Zelter', *Editio*, 15, 2001:136–48, shows how Zelter's notes on the MSS of letters he received from G. reflect the various modalities of their friendship. V. C. Dörr, 'Zwischen Intertextualität und Kolportage. Das Deutungspotential von *Briefen, Tagebüchern und Gesprächen* im Falle der Zusammenarbeit Goethes mit Schiller', Luserke, *Goethe*, 57–66. Johannes Anderegg, '". . . wenn ich dir es nicht mittheilen könnte": zu Goethes Briefen an Charlotte von Stein auf der Reise nach Rom', *GY*, 10, 2001:84–98. A vigorous attempt to defend Goethe against the charge of callousness in the matter of the execution of Anna Catharina Höhne is mounted by W. Wittkowski, 'Hexenjagd auf Goethe. November 1783: Hinrichtung einer Kindesmörderin und "Das Göttliche"', *OGS*, 31, 2002:63–102. T. J. Reed, 'Existence and transcendence: premisses and judgements in Nicholas Boyle's *Goethe*', *ib.*, 30, 2001:157–82.

POETRY. The idea of G.'s early poetry as verbalized spontaneity seems ever more implausible. C. Zelle, 'Die Geburt der Natur aus dem Geiste der Rhetorik. Zur Schematisierung von Natur und Genie bei Dennis und Goethe', *JIG*, 66, 2001:145–68, finds traditional rhetoric in the supposed spontaneity of Goethe's early poetry. U. Renner, 'Eros, Melancholie und Medien: Goethes "Amor als Landschaftsmaler"', *JFDH*, 2001:1–29, offers a very fine analysis of the poem in the context of G.'s evolving interest in the visual and plastic arts. A. Binder, '"Amors Tempel." Zu Goethes Elegie "Saget Steine mir an"', *GJb*, 119, 2002:120–31, undertakes a detailed numerical analysis of the metre and structure of the first *Römische Elegie*. C. Louth, 'Goethe's Sonnets', *PEGS*, 72, 2002:15–24, lucidly relates the uncertainty of the poems to their knowingness and self-reflexive character. S. Kiefer, 'Wortmusik und mystische Erfahrung. Anmerkungen zu Goethes Gedicht "Selige Sehnsucht"', *WB*, 47, 2001:403–17, gives a rich and detailed reading of G.'s poem in the (sadly now seldom encountered) manner of New Criticism. W. D.

von Lucius, 'Buchherstellung im Cotta'schen Verlag. Eine Fallstudie: die Herstellung des *West-oestlichen Divans* in den Jahren 1817/19', *AGB*, 56, 2002: 125–46, sheds interesting light on the mechanics and economics of publishing poetry. J. Williams, 'Goethe the poet', Sharpe, *Goethe*, 42–65, uses metrical questions as a starting point for his survey. M. Lohner, 'Vom "geistigen Handel und Wandel". Zur Poetologie des *West-östlichen Divans*', *Fest. Fiedler*, 17–28. K. Jesiorkowski, 'Die Grammatik der Architektur. Zum Rhythmus bei Goethe und Palladio', *ib.*, 29–37. G. Kluge, 'Der Schelm — ein Ästhet. Goethes *Reineke Fuchs*', *ib.*, 193–204. G. Oesterle, 'Maskerade und Mystifikation im *Tiefurter Journal*: Prinz August von Gotha — Johann Wolfgang Goethe — Jacob Michael Reinhold Lenz', *Fest. Bormann*, 43–54. B. Witte, '"Hegire." Transkulturelle Übersetzung in Goethes *West-oestlichem Divan*', *ib.*, 83–92. A. Aurnhammer, 'Unzeitgemäße Zeitdichtung. Strukturale Intertextualität und latente Gegenwartsbezüge im *West-östlichen Divan*', *Fest. Schings*, 421–38. W. Keller, 'Variationen zum Thema: "Wär' nicht das Auge sonnenhaft . . ."', *ib.*, 439–57. E. Powers, 'From genre to gender: on Goethe's "Der Wandrer"', *GY*, 10, 2001: 31–49.

FAUST. Ulrich Gaier, *Erläuterungen und Dokumente. Johann Wolfgang Goethe, 'Faust. Der Tragödie erster Teil'* (UB, 16021), 2001, 301 pp., and Id., *Kommentar zu Goethes 'Faust'*, Stuttgart, Reclam, 2002, 350 pp., rework material published in Gaier's two-volume Reclam commentary of 1999, and readers who own the latter will be unlikely to need the present volumes. Moreover, there is considerable overlap between the two new volumes, with the explanatory commentary that traditionally opens Reclam green series here duplicating much of the material in the commentary on *Faust I* in the other (yellow) volume. Having said this, both volumes offer much important material. Gaier is especially alert to intertextuality, and he emphasizes the role of the visual arts as influences on G. more than previous commentators have done, to good effect. The *Erläuterungen und Dokumente* volume contains examples of some of the most important of what Gaier terms G.'s 'Textvorlagen', with, however, only minimal indications of how the texts relate to *Faust*. A. Bohm, 'Margarete's innocence and the guilt of Faust', *DVLG*, 75, 2001: 216–50, argues from the provocative premise that *Faust* 'was conceived according to the rules of the epic [tradition]' to the much less provocative conclusion that Faust himself is partly to blame for the fate of his and Gretchen's child. Id., 'Typology and history in the "Rattenlied" (*Faust I*)', *GY*, 10, 2001: 65–83, seeks to identify the plague that Faust recalls in 'Vor dem Tor' as syphilis. F. Harzer, '"Hinweg zu Proteus!" Goethes "poetische Metamorphosen" in der *Klassischen Walpurgisnacht*', Luserke, *Goethe*, 31–44, shows by means of an exemplary genetic analysis how Homunculus replaces Faust as the protagonist of Act II and relegates the latter to the status of a failed Prometheus. An early plan has Wagner's attempt at creating life succeeding, whereupon Wagner and Homunculus accompany Faust to the classical witches' sabbath. In 1830 Goethe conceived of the idea of ending Act II with Proteus, the spirit of metamorphosis, leading Homunculus to the marine source of life, so that 'aus literarischen Verwandlungsscherzen wird [. . .] wieder evolutionstheoretischer Ernst' (p. 40). Widening the perspective, Harzer argues that with this gradual metamorphosis Goethe stands apart from the Ovidian tradition of disjunctive poetic metamorphoses. S. Schneider, 'Mnemonische Imaginationen in Goethes *Faust II*. Eine Lektüre der Klassischen Walpurgisnacht', *GJb*, 119, 2002:66–77, analyses G.'s method of integrating extrinsic elements in the text often in very visible form. A less enthusiastic view of G.'s art in *Faust II* can be found in R. Reichstein, 'Über himmlische und irdische Liebe. Betrachtungen zur Bergschluchten-Szene in Goethes *Faust*', *JFDH*, 2001:30–40. C. A. Grair, 'Seducing Helena: the court fantasy of *Faust II*, Act III', *GY*, 10, 2001:99–114, tries to turn the tables on Dorothea Hölscher-Lohmeyer's argument that politics is a metaphor for human desires in *Faust II* by arguing that Faust's desire for and 'conquest' of Helen is a metaphor for political power. Not a companion in the traditional sense, *A Companion to Goethe's 'Faust': Parts I and II*, ed. Paul Bishop, Rochester, NY, Camden House, 2001, xliv + 319 pp., contains thoughtful interpretative essays of an introductory and a more advanced nature covering a range of topics. J. K. Brown, '*Faust*', Sharpe, *Goethe*, 84–100, continues the tradition of reading the work as an allegory of secularization. M. Spohr, 'Das Problem der Vanitas. Goethes *Faust* und das Faust-Sujet im populären Musiktheater', *MK*, 45, 2001:71–92.

DRAMA. D. V. Pugh, 'Goethe the dramatist', Sharpe, *Goethe*, 66–83, is refreshing in its normative approach and clear judgements. L. Sharpe, 'Goethe and the Weimar theatre', *ib.*, 116–28, gives a detailed and balanced appreciation of G.'s not inconsiderable achievements in this field. J. K. Brown, 'Der Drang zum Gesang: on Goethe's dramatic form', *GY*, 10, 2001:115–24, sees music as a form of transcendence of subjectivity and argues that G. may well have preceded Wagner and Nietzsche in seeing opera as the modern successor of classical tragedy. In H. Lange, 'Wolves, sheep, and the shepherd: legality, legitimacy and Hobbesian political theory in Goethe's *Götz von Berlichingen*', *ib.*, 1–30, Götz, who is normally seen as a mouthpiece of Goethe's presumed Möserian conservatism, emerges as an ambivalent, Hobbesian character. L.'s conclusion that, as Götz himself remains free of modern taint, the play voices no general critique of modernity seems to overlook the meaning of the satirical Bamberg scenes and the figure of Weislingen, who is thoroughly modernized and, in the process, emasculated. J. Heimerl, 'Egmont und Ferdinand — Träger des Goetheschen Prometheussymbols', *WB*, 48, 2002:202–25, interprets *Egmont* in terms of G.'s notions of 'Systole' and 'Diastole'.

NARRATIVE. It is pleasing to see critics turning their back on the earlier tendency to shoe-horn G.'s prose into the dominant 19th-c. realist tradition of fiction. This is leading to a re-evaluation of the *Wanderjahre* in particular. M. Swales, 'Goethe's prose fiction', Sharpe, *Goethe*, 129–46, establishes a framework for reading the works in the light of recent theory. Perspective and self-reflexivity continue to be the preeminent themes of work on G.'s prose. I. Egger, 'Eíkones: zur Inszenierung der Bilder in Goethes Romanen', *GJb*, 118, 2001:260–73, brings out the latter. A. Anglet, 'Das "ernste Spiel" der Kunst — Anmerkungen zum ästhetischen Perspektivismus im Romanwerk Goethes', *ZDP*, 121, 2002:187–202, sees this much discussed notion as a strategic positioning between claims of aesthetic autonomy and the rational utility that comes to typify G.'s later fiction. The early fiction, on the other hand, benefits from being set in its context, as in T. Valk, 'Poetische Pathographie. Goethes *Werther* im Kontext zeitgenössischer Melancholie-Diskurse', *GJb*, 119, 2002:14–22, which argues that the novel offers an account of melancholy both sympathetic and critical. A. Bohm, ' "Klopstock!" Once more: intertextuality in *Werther*', *Seminar*, 38, 2002:116–33, adds a new dimension to the argument that W.'s misreadings of literary texts show a characteristic lack of care on his part. H.-J. Kim, 'Rituelle Identitätsbildung. Zur Lossprechung Wilhelm Meisters', *GJb*, 119, 2002:42–51, moves the debate about Wilhelm's *Bildungsweg* from the traditional emphasis on socialization to the theme of identity. R. Brinkmann, 'Kennst du das Buch? Oder: Die Vertreibung der Musiknoten aus *Wilhelm Meisters Lehrjahren*', *ib.*, 118, 2001:289–303, makes an appeal for the reinstatement of the musical scores of Reichardt's *Vertonungen* in new editions of the novel. K. Yamamoto, 'Die literarische Selbstreflexion in Goethes *Wilhelm Meisters Lehrjahre*', *DB*, 106, 2001:101–11, analyses intertextual relations to other genres in the novel. Jane V. Curran, *Goethe's 'Wilhelm Meister's Apprenticeship': A Reader's Commentary*, Rochester, NY, Camden House, 2002, vii + 328 pp., is an unusual attempt at continuous commentary on the novel, in the manner of e.g. Stuart Atkins's *Goethe's 'Faust': A Literary Analysis* (Cambridge, Mass., Harvard U.P., 1958). The commentary effectively paraphrases the novel, interspersing comments on imagery, structure, narrative perspective, context, etc. It does so with delicacy and tact, illuminating small-scale structural features and showing the discipline of cleaving close to the text it discusses, whilst also rising to a sufficient level of conceptual abstraction. The themes of reading and realism are foregrounded. Secondary literature is cited in good measure, for its insights and not for the sake of point-scoring or the pathos of pretended dialectic. H. Ammerlahn, 'Der Strukturparallelismus von Wilhelms kreativer, bildender und tätiger Vergangenheitsbewältigung in Goethes Meister-Romanen', *GY*, 10, 2001 : 154–90, uncovers similarities between the *Lehrjahre* and the *Wanderjahre* in the way they treat childhood emotional traumas. R. Campe, 'Continuing forms: allegory and *translatio imperii* in Caspar von Lohenstein and Johann Wolfgang von Goethe', *GR*, 77, 2002 : 128–45, discusses the *Unterhaltungen deutscher Ausgewanderten*. B. Jahn, 'Das Hörbarwerden des unerhörten Ereignisses. Sinne, Künste und Medien in Goethes *Novelle*', *Euphorion*, 95, 2001 : 17–38, reads the *Novelle* as a 'Kritik' (in the Kantian sense) of the senses and sensory media. D. Hoffmann, '"Der Löwe brüllt, wer sollte sich nicht fürchten?" Zur utopischen Restauration der alten Stammburg in Goethes *Novelle*', *ZDP*, 120, 2001 : 527–39, uses parallels with the Book of Amos to bring out the text's moralizing undertones. R. Schellenberg, 'The genesis of Goethe's last novel: *Wilhelm Meisters Wanderjahre* (1821)', *NGR*, 17, 2001–02 : 47–63, explains the very marked differences between the 1821 and 1829 versions of the novel. G. Sasse, '"Die Zeit des Schönen ist vorüber." Wilhelm Meisters Weg zum Beruf des Wundarztes in Goethes Roman *Wilhelm Meisters Wanderjahre oder die Entsagenden*', *IASL*, 26.2, 2001 : 72–97, reads the novel as a positive response to the claims of modernity, in contrast to the negative responses of *Faust II* and Wilhelm's failed self-realization in the *Lehrjahre*. N. C. Wolf, '"Die Wesenheit des Objektes bedingt den Stil." Zur Modernität des Erzählkonzepts in *Wilhem Meisters Wanderjahren*', *GJb*, 119, 2002 : 52–65, emphasizes the proto-modernist character of the novel with its discontinuity, perspectivism, and renunciation of narrative personality. G. Sasse, 'Der Gesang als Medium der Sozialdisziplinierung in Goethes Roman *Wilhelm Meisters Wanderjahre*', *ib.*, 118, 2001 : 274–88, returns to the theme of socialization and shows that the organization of musical performance has an educational function. I. Egger, '"Verbinden mehr als Trennen": Goethe und die plastische Anatomie', *GRM*, 51, 2001 : 45–53, sets Wilhelm's dislike of dissection in the context of the history of anatomy. N. Puszkar, '"Scheide Blick." Abschluß und Ausschluß in Goethes *Italienischer Reise*', *EG*, 57, 2002 : 649–70, has G. grappling with the problem of representing the conflicting feelings of consummation and exclusion at the end of his stay in Rome. Other work on the non-fictional prose includes D. F. Mahoney, 'Autobiographical writings', Sharpe, *Goethe*, 147–59; O. Kramer, 'Ein Leben schreiben. Goethes *Dichtung und Wahrheit* als

Form autobiographischer Selbstüberredung', *Rhetorik*, 20, 2002: 117–30; T. O. Beebee, 'Ways of seeing Italy: landscapes of nation in Goethe's *Italienische Reise* and its counter-narratives', *MDLK*, 94, 2002: 322–45. H. Reinhart, 'Ästhetische Geselligkeit. Goethes literarischer Dialog mit Schiller in den *Unterhaltungen deutscher Ausgewanderten*', *Fest. Schings*, 311–42. P. Michelsen, 'Wilhelm Meister liest Shakespeare', *ib.*, 343–56. L. Bluhm, 'Goethes "incalculable Productionen". Zur Kontextualität von *Wilhelm Meisters Lehrjahren* und den *Unterhaltungen deutscher Ausgewanderten*', *Fest. Jacobs*, 35–50. D. Vincent, 'Text as image and self-image: the contextualization of Goethe's *Dichtung und Wahrheit* (1810–1813)', *GY*, 10, 2001: 125–43.

PHILOSOPHY, NATURAL SCIENCE, AESTHETICS. Attempts to win G. for the Enlightenment continue. Paul E. Kerry, *Enlightenment Thought in the Writings of Goethe. A Contribution to the History of Ideas*, Rochester, NY, Camden House, 2001, xi + 243 pp., is a less general study than its title suggests, focusing in fact on one strand of Enlightenment thought, the idea of tolerance. Kerry makes a strong and coherent attempt to rescue Goethe for a kind of confessional liberalism. He proceeds chronologically through a range of major and minor texts, giving particularly committed and sensitive accounts of the latter, such as the *Sankt-Rochus-Fest zu Bingen*. The *Divan* is the subject of a strong and persuasive argument that the focus of criticism should move away from the idea of the reception of Persian models and towards the idea of cultural bridging. Also dealing extensively with the *Divan*, Katharina Mommsen, *Goethe und der Islam*, Frankfurt–Leipzig, Insel, 2001, 527 pp., argues that mere toleration, whilst increasingly characteristic of European views of Islam in the 18th c. and undoubtedly forming a necessary condition for G.'s attitudes, is not enough to explain his lifelong engagement with Islam. G.'s 'tief begründete Sympathie' for aspects of Islam stemmed from his own (religious) conviction that there is one God who manifests himself in nature and has revealed his truth to mankind through a number of prophets. That is to say, G.'s is a version of Islam that comports well with Enlightenment Spinozism and deism. *GJb*, 118, 2001, attempts to situate G. in relation to the Enlightenment, the general view of the following papers being that it makes good sense to do so: H. Friedrich, 'Vom Nutzen und Nachteil der Aufklärung für das Leben' (22–30); J. Bauer and G. Müller, 'Lehr- und Wanderjahre: Goethes Weg durch die Geheimgesellschaften' (31–45); K. Manger, 'Goethe und die deutschen Aufklärer' (46–57); T. J. Reed, 'Goethe und Kant: Zeitgeist und eigener Geist' (58–74); J. Mondot, 'Goethe und die französischen *Lumières* oder Voltaire und kein Ende' (75–90); O. Hildebrand, 'Im "Irrgarten" der Paradoxien. Goethe, Diderot und *Le neveu de Rameau*' (91–107); G. Sauder, 'Aufklärerische Bibelkritik und

Bibelrezeption in Goethes Werk' (108–25); W. Frick, 'Die Schlächterin und der Tyrann: Gewalt und Aufklärung in europäischen Iphigenie-Dramen des 18. Jahrhunderts' (126–41); U. Diederichsen, 'Goethes *Wahlverwandtschaften* — auch ein juristischer Roman' (142–57); M. Bollacher, 'Aufklärungspositionen des jungen Goethe' (158–70); P. Gülke, 'Verschwiegene Humanität: Mozarts *Entführung* und Goethes *Iphigenie*' (171–75); P. Øhrgaard, 'Anmerkungen zum Reden und Schweigen in *Wilhelm Meisters Lehrjahren*' (176–86); W. Busch, 'Die Rolle der englischen Kunst für Goethes Kunstbegriff' (187–201); U. Pörksen, 'Die Selbstüberwachung des Beobachters. Goethes Naturwissenschaft als Brückenschlag zwischen menschlicher Erfahrung und wissenschaftlicher Methode' (202–16); E. Boa, 'Die Geschichte der O oder die (Ohn-)Macht der Frauen: *Die Wahlverwandtschaften* im Kontext des Geschlechterdiskurses um 1800' (217–33); H. R. Vaget, '"Mäßig boshaft": Fausts Gefährte. Goethes Mephistopheles im Lichte der Aufklärung' (234–46). H. B. Nisbet, 'Religion and philosophy', Sharpe, *Goethe*, 219–31, is as lucid and well-balanced a summary of G.'s reception of philosophy and theology as one could wish for. D. Steuer, 'In defence of experience: Goethe's natural investigations and scientific culture', *ib.*, 160–78, mounts a defense of Goethe's science as methodologically advanced, even if scientifically unsuccessful. A. Gnam, '"Geognosie, Geologie, Mineralogie und Angehöriges". Goethe als Erforscher der Erdgeschichte', Luserke, *Goethe*, 79–88, reveals the *weltanschaulich* underpinnings of G.'s geological studies, whilst arguing for their importance in the history of scientific method. On G.'s aesthetics, *DVLG*, 75, 2001, devotes a number to the theme of seeing, including K. Calhoon, 'The Gothic imaginary: Goethe in Strasbourg' (5–14); H. R. Vaget, 'The "Augenmensch" and the failure of vision. Goethe and the trauma of dilettantism' (15–26); R. Nägele, 'The pure gaze' (27–38); K. Weimar, 'Der Blick und die Gewalt der Stimme. Zu *Die Natürliche Tochter*' (39–59); B. Hahn, 'Augen. Blicke. Augenblicke. Metaphern des Sehens zwischen Charlotte von Stein und Goethe' (60–70); F. Zika, 'Color theory beyond Wittgenstein's Goethe' (71–86); E. Förster, Goethe and the "Auge des Geistes"' (87–101); H. J. Schneider, 'Das Licht der Welt. Geburt und Bild in Goethes Faustdichtung' (102–22). G. Sauder, 'Goethes Ästhetik der Dämmerung', Luserke, *Goethe*, 45–56, contributes to the view of Goethe as a poet of gradualism and mediation by reading the Strasbourg cathedral essay and the Sulzer review in terms of the 'helldunkel' states of fog and twilight. Benjamin Bennett, *Goethe as Woman: The Undoing of Literature*, Detroit, Wayne State U.P., 2001, 274 pp., which consists mainly of essays already published elsewhere, focuses on G.'s problematic attitude towards the German reading public and, by means of the notion of 'the undoing of literature', highlights his resistance to the modern German national literary tradition. Y. Takahashi, 'Goethes *Farbenlehre* und der Ausdruck der Natur', *GJb*, 118, 2001 : 247–59, mounts an attempt to defend G.'s scientific methodology as stimulating artistic practice, rather than science as such. D. Barry, 'Faustian pursuits: the political-cultural dimension of Goethe's *Weltliteratur* and the tragedy of translation', *GQ*, 74, 2001 : 164–85, discusses the extrinsic obstacles facing G.'s quixotic internationalism and the intrinsic problems in a project that relies on the Mephistophelean art of translation. Further pieces on aesthetics include H. Geulen, '"Und was ist Schönheit?" Marginalien zu Goethes Brief an Friederike Oeser vom 13. Februar 1769', *Fest. Jacobs*, 161–78; S. Lulé, 'L'opéra comme modèle esthétique chez Goethe et E. T. A. Hoffmann', *RGI*, 16, 2001 : 123–40.

INFLUENCE, RECEPTION. Much can be inferred from G.'s reception of other writers. J. Jølle, 'Goethe's translation of Pindar's Fifth Olympian Ode', *GY*, 10, 2001: 50–64, emphasizes the experimental character of G.'s translations and situates the method of them between the Enlightenment and Hölderlin. The essay also sheds interesting light on G.'s lyrics of the early 1770s. In general what emerges from the following studies is his lifelong interest in the unorthodox, adversarial, and obscure: S. Sbarra, 'Der junge Goethe und Jean-Jacques Rousseau', *GJb*, 119, 2002 : 23–41; J. Rees, 'Das Tagebuch einer Reise nach Italien von Richard Payne Knight. Anmerkungen zum wiedergefundenen Originalmanuskript und zu Goethes Übersetzung', *ib.*, 78–95; Y. Wübben, '"... und dennoch spukt's in Tegel" — Zu Goethes Cagliostro-Rezeption', *ib.*, 96–119. Karl S. Guthke, *Goethes Weimar und 'Die große Öffnung in die weite Welt'* (Wolfenbütteler Forschungen, 93), Wiesbaden, Harrassowitz, 2001, 202 pp., analyses two phenomena: G.'s reading of English travel literature, and visits by English travellers to Weimar. The former disproves the conventional view that G. was not interested in reports of newly explored lands. English travel literature also featured prominently in G.'s preparatory reading for the *Divan*. The continuous presence of English visitors in Weimar, on the other hand, provided a point of contact between two cultures, the 'Weltkenntnis' of the English and the 'innere Kultur' of the Germans, which G. himself was uniquely able to balance. P. Brandes, 'Goethes Na(h)me', *WB*, 47, 2001 : 540–58, offers a rather subtle meditation on G.'s debts to Gleim, Klopstock, and Herder. K. F. Gille, '"...und nun ist die Betrachtung so viel bequemer gemacht." Goethes Lektüre des *Nibelungenlieds*', *Fest. Bormann*, 71–82.

Treating G.'s reception of earlier writers and his reception of them as two aspects of one process has become fashionable. This can be fruitful as long as the two aspects are clearly defined and delineated. Hartmut Fröschle, *Goethes Verhältnis zur Romantik*, Würzburg, Königshausen & Neumann, 2002, 564 pp., does not distinguish, in its structure or indeed its argumentation, between G.'s reception of the German Romantics and their reception of him, although given its largely prosopographical approach this is not a serious problem. An exhaustive book-length *Forschungsbericht* and an account of G.'s interest in and use of Romantic advances in philology and oriental studies frame the main body of the study, a series of self-contained essays on the main figures of German Romanticism. These confine themselves largely to biographical data, which will no doubt form an extremely useful resource for (future) literary studies of the subject, such as are contained in *Goethe und das Zeitalter der Romantik*, ed. Walter Hinderer, Würzburg, Königshausen & Neumann, 2002, 524 pp., a collection of papers given at the 1999 Princeton conference of the same title. Papers by an international cast include D. Borchmeyer, 'Zur Typologie des Klassischen und Romantischen' (19–30); J. le Rider, 'War die Klassik farbenfeindlich und die Romantik farbengläubig? Von Lessings *Laokoon* zu Goethes *Farbenlehre* und deren Nachwirkung' (31–50); G. Oesterle, 'Das Faszinosum der Arabeske um 1800' (51–70); G. Neumann, ' "Mannigfache Wege gehen die Menschen." Romananfänge bei Goethe und Novalis' (71–90); I. Oesterle, ' "Es ist an der Zeit!" Zur kulturellen Konstruktionsveränderung von Zeit um 1800' (91–120); W. Vosskamp, ' "Jeder sey auf seiner Art ein Grieche! Aber er sey's." Zu Goethes Romantikkritik in der Zeitschrift *Ueber Kunst und Altertum*' (121–32); A. von Bormann, ' "Sie grüßen den alten Held." Zur Goetherezeption in der Hochromantik' (133–48); G. Motzkin, 'Goethe's theory of memory' (151–62); L. Weissberg, 'Weimar and Jena: Goethe and the New Philosophy' (163–74); D. E. Wellbery, 'Goethes Lyrik und das frühromantische Kunstprogramm' (175–92); G. Brandstetter, 'Schreibszenen — Briefe in Goethes *Wahlverwandtschaften*' (193–212); M. Osten, ' "Alles veloziferisch": Goethes Ottilie und die beschleunigte Zeit' (213–30); S. Moses, ' "Natur! Natur!": Sigmund Freuds Goethe-Traum' (231–41); P. Chiarini, ' "Alte Meister" in klassisch-romantischem Kontext. Goethe, Friedrich Schlegel und die "Deutsche Renaissance" ' (245–64); W. Vaughan, 'Goethe, line and outline' (265–80); N. Boyle, 'Goethe's later cycles of drawings' (281–306); C. Grewe, 'Mignon als Allegorie des poetischen: Goetherezeption und Kunsttheorie in der deutschen Maleri der Spätromantik' (307–44); D. Ottmann, 'Gebändigte Natur. Garten und Wildnis in Goethes *Wahlverwandtschaften* und Eichendorff's *Ahnung und Gegenwart*' (345–95); C. Lubkoll, ' "Neue Mythologie" und musikalische Poetologie. Goethes Annäherungen an die Romantik' (399–412); D. Borchmeyer, 'Eine Art Symbolik fürs Ohr." Goethes Musikästhetik' (413–46); H. J. Kreutzer, 'Über die Musik in Goethes *Faust*' (447–58); G. Lanza Tomasi, 'Goethe-Lieder: a challenge for Romantic composers' (459–71); M.-C. Hoock-Demarle, 'Europa, die Frühromantik und der "europäische" Goethe' (475–88); W. Hinderer, 'Goethe und Amerika' (489–506); J. Willms, 'Goethe und die Folgen' (507–14).

'*Von Pol zu Pol Gesänge sich erneun . . .' Das Europa Goethes und seine Nationalautoren*, ed. Jochen Golz and Wolfgang Müller, Cologne, Böhlau, 2001, 221 pp., comprises papers given at the 1999 conference of Goethe societies in Weimar. It offers studies of G.'s reception of some 18th-c. writers and of the reception of G. in 19th-c. Europe, as well as more general attempts to situate G. in relation to European literature, with special emphasis on Eastern Europe, including J. Lehmann, 'Die Literaturen Osteuropas im Dichten und Denken Goethes' (47–63); P. Chartier, 'Goethe und Diderot. Die Übersetzung des *Neveu de Rameau*' (76–83); H. Urbahn de Jauregui, 'Goethe und das literarische Frankreich des 18. Jahrhunderts. Goethe, Voltaire und Diderot' (84–114); R. Danilevski, 'Goethe und Pushkin. Eine vergleichende Betrachtung' (115–25); R.-D. Keil, 'Mickiewicz bei Goethe' (126–34); R. Paulin, 'Wilhelm Meister liest Shakespeare. Über Wilhelm Meisters Shakespeare-Verständnis' (179–90). A general survey of reception is given in G. Hoffmeister, 'Reception in Germany and abroad', Sharpe, *Goethe*, 232–55. In *GJb*, 119, 2002, three papers investigate the reception of Goethe in Germany: M. Ventzke, 'Der Weimarer Musenhof und seine ungeratenen Kinder — zur Entwicklung eines kulturellen Exportmodells' (132–47); G. Jäckel, 'Dresden als Erinnerungsort für Goethe' (148–64); G. Körner and M. Sielaff, 'Goethe und die Volkswirtschaftlehre' (165–82).

Goethe in German-Jewish Culture, ed. Klaus L. Berghahn and Jost Hermand, Rochester, NY, Camden House, 2001, xiii + 190 pp., contains K. L. Berghahn, 'Patterns of childhood: Goethe and the Jews' (3–15); E. Bahr, 'Goethe and the concept of Bildung in Jewish emancipation' (16–28); B. Hahn, 'Demarcations and projections: Goethe in the Berlin salons' (31–43); J. Hermand, 'A view from below: H. Heine's relationship to Johann Wolfgang von Goethe' (44–62); C. König, 'Cultural history as Enlightenment: remarks on Ludwig Geiger's experiences of Judaism, philology, and Goethe' (65–83); H. Hague, B. Machosky, and M. Rotter, 'Waiting for Goethe: Goethe biographies from Ludwig Geiger to Friedrich Gundolf' (84–103); R. C. Holub, 'From the pedestal to the couch: Goethe, Freud and Jewish assimilation' (104–20); G. Hoecherl-Alden, 'Upholding the ideals of the "other Germany": German-Jewish Goethe scholars in U. S. exile' (123–45); W. D. Wilson,

'"Humanitätssalbader": Goethe's distaste for Jewish emancipation, and Jewish responses' (146–64); K. L. Schultz, 'The insufficient as event: Goethe lesson at the Frankfurt School' (165–80). K. L. Berghahn, 'Ein klassischer Chiasmus: Goethe und die Juden, die Juden und Goethe', *GY*, 10, 2001 : 203–21.

I. E. Fry, 'Authorizing the proto-feminist Bettine von Arnim: gender dichotomies and feminine authority in Goethe's "beautiful Amazon" and La Roche's Sternheim', *LY*, 34, 2002 : 125–44. A. Gerhard, 'Goethes "herrliche Dichtungen" und Schuberts "große Freiheit". Ein Spannungsverhältnis — einmal anders betrachtet', *GJb*, 118, 2001 : 304–14. N. Kimura, 'Goethes *Wahlverwandtschaften* und die japanische Romantik', *Fest. Jacobs*, 51–62. D. John, 'The first black Gretchen: Fritz Bennewitz's *Faust I* in New York', *MDLK*, 94, 2002 : 447–63.

3. Schiller

EDITIONS, LETTERS, AND REFERENCE WORKS. *Gedichte*, ed. Norbert Oellers (UB, 18061), 2001, 213 pp., is an annotated selection. N. Oellers, 'Fünf Briefe Schillers an Friederike Juliane Griesbach', *JDSG*, 45, 2001 : 25–38, presents hitherto unknown letters.

LITERARY WORKS, THOUGHT, RECEPTION, BIOGRAPHY. If S.'s relative unpopularity at the present time results from the perception of him as a narrowly intellectual writer, Peter-André Alt, *Schiller. Leben — Werk — Zeit*, 2 vols, Munich, Beck, 2000, 737, 686 pp., is likely, if anything, to confirm his status. As its title indicates, this massive biography is not simply a 'life', but also a study of Schiller the writer in his time, which for A. means fully detailing S.'s dealings with his intellectual environment. Whilst much of the material is well known, e.g. the content of the teaching S. received at the Karlsschule, A. also adds much, and the synoptic perspective brings into focus the breadth and variety of S.'s interests in a way that no previous study of S. has done and in a manner that manages to be both exhausting and refreshing. Much of the recent literature on S.'s work is concerned less with its aesthetic qualities than with its political, social, or psychological content. The essays on S. in *Fest. Schings* exemplify the tendency: W. Riedel, '"Weltgeschichte ein erhabenes Object." Zur Modernität von Schillers Geschichtsdenken' (193–214); P.-A. Alt, 'Auf den Schultern der Aufklärung. Überlegungen zu Schillers "nationalem" Kulturprogramm' (215–38); A. Costazza, '"Wenn er auf einen Hügel mit euch steiget / Und seinem Auge sich, in mildem Abendschein,/ Das malerische Tal — auf einmal zeiget." Das ästhetische Theorie in Schillers Gedicht *Die Künstler*' (239–64); D. Borchmeyer, '"Zustand des Gemüts" versus "Gegenstand".

Schillers Musikästhetik und das Problem des klassischen Stils' (265–74); W. Müller-Seidel, 'Schiller im Verständnis Max Kommerells. Nachtrag zum Thema "Klassiker in finsteren Zeiten"' (275–310). J. Barkhoff, 'Tanz der Körper — Tanz der Sprache. Körper und Text in Friedrich Schillers Gedicht "Der Tanz"', *JDSG*, 45, 2001 : 147–63, which shows that the label *Gedankenlyrik* does injustice to the physical character of S.'s poetry of the mid-1790s, is an exception to this rule. M. T. Jones, 'Schiller trouble: the tottering legacy of German aesthetic humanism', *GY*, 10, 2001 : 222–45, locates the problem in S.'s notion of *Bildung*. Vigorously rebutting some of S.'s recent critics, Jones is nonetheless unsparing in his analysis of S.'s evasion of politics in favour of morality. Interest in S.'s psychology shows no sign of abating. S. Neuhaus, '"Daß die Zärtlichkeit noch barbarischer zwingt als Tyrannenwut!" Zur Problematisierung von Familienstrukturen in Schillers Dramen', *JIG*, 33, 2001 : 98–111, attempts to show that S. intuits a finding of modern family psychology, namely that errors in parenting are to blame for the bad behaviour of children. Stephanie Hammer, *Schiller's Wound: The Theater of Trauma from Crisis to Community*, Detroit, Wayne State U.P., 2001, 172 pp., reads a selection of S.'s dramas in the light of Freudian and more recent theory of trauma in a manner that if anything detracts from S.'s psychological insight. The starting point is the supposed trauma S. suffered at leaving Württemberg. There follow analyses of *Die Räuber*, *Don Carlos*, *Wallenstein*, *Die Braut von Messina* and *Demetrius*. The argument, which relies on tenuous implications, is hard to summarize. Matthias Hurst, *Im Spannungsfeld der Aufklärung. Von Schillers 'Geisterseher' zur TV-Serie 'The X-Files': Rationalismus und Irrationalismus in Literatur, Film und Fernsehen, 1789–1999*, Heidelberg, Winter, 2001, 609 pp., also pairs S. with some unlikely bedfellows. As part of a more ambitious attempt to link the rational and the irrational in a range of media, Hurst undertakes an extended analysis of *Der Geisterseher*. Christian Begemann's thesis that the Enlightenment's application of reason brought with it anxiety serves as the starting point. Enlightenment theories of the sublime show how Gothic terror can be the logical corollary of the rational analysis of superstition. Marquis Posa is introduced to show that S. had concerns about rationality's tyrannical excesses. Employing these methods to get behind the rational façade of S.'s writing, H. is able to find in *Der Geisterseher* a strikingly modern awareness of irrationality as the symptom of a rational age. E. Kleinschmidt, 'Brüchige Diskurse. Orientierungsprobleme in Friedrich Schillers *Die Verschwörung des Fiesko zu Genua*', *JFDH*, 2001 : 100–21, views the inconsistencies of the play as symptoms of the as yet unformed character of the German political arena. M. C. Foi, 'Schillers *Wilhelm Tell*: Menschenrechte, Menschenwürde und die Würde der Frauen', *JDSG*, 45, 2001:193–223, reads *Tell* as a novel response to the issue of how to ground natural law. B. Sandkaulen, 'Die "schöne Seele" und der "gute Ton". Zum Theorieprofil von Schillers ästhetischem Staat', *DVLG*, 76, 2002:74–85, argues that in S.'s aesthetics the element of freedom associated with social good manners (*guter Ton*) ultimately loses out to his concern with the sublime. E. Ostermann, 'Christian Wolfs Kampf um Anerkennung: eine anerkennungstheoretische Deutung von Schillers Erzählung *Der Verbrecher aus verlorener Ehre*', *LWU*, 23, 2001:211–24, reads S.'s narrative in the light of Hegel's theory of the process by which individual and society grant one another recognition. A section of Peter Nickl, *Ordnung der Gefühle. Studien zum Begriff des habitus*, Hamburg, Meiner, 2001, x + 247 pp., reconsiders S.'s critique of Kant in terms of the notion of *habitus*. Further articles include P.-A. Alt, '"Arbeit für mehr als ein Jahrhundert." Schillers Verständnis von Ästhetik und Politik in der Periode der Französischen Revolution (1790–1800)', *JDSG*, 46, 2002:102–33; U. Port, '"Künste des Affekts." Die Aporien des Pathetischerhabenen und die Bildrhetorik in Schillers *Maria Stuart*', *ib.*, 134–59; Y. Shirasaki, 'Schiller und Verdi. Wie wird klassisches Drama zur Oper?', *DB*, 107, 2001:13–22; F. Piedmont, 'Wallensteins "schwankendes Charakterbild". Schillers Drama auf der Bühne in der zweiten Hälfte des 20. Jahrhunderts', *JDSG*, 45, 2001:164–92; T. Esaka, 'Zur Entstehungsgeschichte von Schillers *Dom Karlos*', *ib.*, 131–46; H. Krah, '". . . der Freiheit ewig Zeichen." Schillers *Wilhelm Tell* als klassische Lösung revolutionärer Probleme', *RG*, 32, 2002:1–26; M. Beetz, 'Vom "selbsttätigen Widerstand" des Schönen. Schillers Dramaturgie des Publikums in *Wallenstein*', *Fest. Jacobs*, 205–30. Rüdiger Zymner, *Friedrich Schiller. Dramen*, Berlin, Schmidt, 2002, 187 pp.

4. Lessing

GENERAL STUDIES AND ESSAY COLLECTIONS. S. D. Martinson, 'Chaos and comedy: Lessing's theory and practice', *LY*, 34, 2002:21–33, helpfully emphasizes the thematics of chaos in L.'s writing, which he (perhaps unnecessarily) reads in terms of modern chaos theory. W. Wilms, 'Im Griff des Politischen. Konfliktfähigkeit und Vaterwerdung in *Emilia Galotti*', *DVLG*, 76, 2002:50–73, presents L.'s play as political in the sense of Carl Schmitt's *Begriff des Politischen*: the Galotti family is reconfigured as a political entity through a Schmittian process of the recognition of friend and foe. Similarly his 'The universalist spirit of conflict: Lessing's political Enlightenment', *MDLK*, 94, 2002:306–21, reads *Nathan der Weise* and *Ernst und Falk* as evidence for L.'s Schmittian 'political realism', which sees division and conflict as necessary in order to retain space for 'a legitimate Other within'. R. Stauf, '"O Galotti, wenn Sie mein Freund, mein Führer, mein Vater, seyn wollten!" Über die versäumte Fürstenerziehung in Lessings *Emilia Galotti*', *GRM*, 52, 2002: 129–52, sees the political import of L.'s drama not in any critique of systems, but in the failure of the individual to recognise the ruler as merely a human being. The possibility that this might have systemic causes is not considered. M. Erlin, 'Urban experience, aesthetic experience, and Enlightenment in G. E. Lessing's *Minna von Barnhelm*', *MDLK*, 93, 2001: 20–35, connects L.'s representation of Berlin with social and aesthetic themes of the Enlightenment. H. M. Schlipphacke, 'The dialectic of female desire in G. E. Lessing's *Emilia Galotti*', *LY*, 33, 2001: 55–78, sees Emilia's behaviour in the final act as symptomatic of a psychologically grounded masochistic tendency that is heightened by separation from her family. Further articles on L.'s writings include K. J. Kenkel, 'Monstrous women, sublime pleasure, and the perils of reception in Lessing's aesthetics', *PMLA*, 116, 2001: 545–61; I. Karg, 'Familie als Metapher? Überlegungen zu Wolfram, zu Lessing, zur Kinderliteratur und zum Literaturunterricht', *JIG*, 33, 2001: 63–81; W. F. Bender, 'Ikonenbildung und Affirmation: Lessing in der Theaterpublizistik des 18. Jahrhunderts', *LY*, 33, 2001: 79–96; J. Pizer, 'Confusion or transcendent illumination? Lessing and Wieland on music and its interface with poetry', *ib.*, 97–114; K. Bohnen, 'Grumbach, Struensee und die anklagende "Nachtigall". Lessings Politik-Rezeption: ein deutsch-dänischer Problemfall', *ib.*, 115–26; Y.-M. Quester, 'Lessing als deutscher Voltaire. Zu einer Übersetzung der *Bijoux indiscrets* von Diderot aus dem 18. Jahrhundert', *ib.*, 34, 2002: 35–39. W. Düsing, 'Wandlungen des Literaturbegriffs in der *Laokoon*-Debatte zwischen Lessing und Herder', *Fest. Schings*, 63–80.

BIOGRAPHY, RECEPTION. In Willi Jasper, *Lessing. Aufklärer und Judenfreund. Biographie*, WBG, 2001, 471 pp., L. is made yet again to do service as the 'good German' in a biography that is heavy on pathos. To be fair, the subtitle suggests a less nuanced picture than Jasper in fact delivers. A rich knowledge of the social context, above all of Jewish life in Prussia and Saxony, allows Jasper to modify some of the legends surrounding L., for instance that of his relationship with Moses Mendelssohn. B. Siwczyk, '"Erhält dieser einzige Augenblick durch die Kunst eine unveränderliche Dauer." Johann Christoph Frisch und seine bildnerische Interpretation zweier Schlüsselszenen aus Lessings *Nathan der Weise*', *LY*, 34, 2002: 41–56. N. Rennie, '"Schilderungssucht" and "historische Krankheit": Lessing, Nietzsche, and the body historical', *GQ*, 74, 2001: 186–96.

V. Nölle, 'Der Widerpart eines aufklärerischen Diskurses. *Das Fossil* von Carl Sternheim im Spiegel der *Minna von Barnhelm*', *LY*, 34, 2002: 7–20.

5. Individual Authors (excluding Goethe, Schiller, and Lessing)

BROCKES. K. Richter, 'Teleskop und Mikroskop in Brockes' *Irdischem Vergnügen in Gott*', *Fest. Schings*, 3–18.

BÜRGER. P. Cersowsky, '"Wunderbare Welt." Zu Bürger und Shakespeare', *Fest. Schings*, 105–26.

CLAUDIUS. J.-U. Fechner, 'Datierung und Kommentar von zwei Briefen von Matthias Claudius oder ein Umweg oder Abweg zu Goethes Gedicht "Selige Sehnsucht"?', *Euphorion*, 96, 2002: 437–48.

EHRMANN. Marianne Ehrmann, *Die Einsiedlerinn aus den Alpen*, ed. Annette Zunzer, Berne–Stuttgart–Vienna, Haupt, 2002, 341 pp., reproduces the periodical edited by the Swiss writer and journalist Marianne Ehrmann in 1793–94.

FORSTER. T. Fischer, 'Wie Reisebeschreibungen zu schreiben und zu lesen sind. Georg Forsters Gattungsreflexion in seinen Rezensionen und Vorreden', *DVLG*, 76, 2002: 577–607. L. Uhlig, 'Mitbürger unserer Gelehrtenrepublik. Georg Forsters Beiträge zu den zeitgenössichen deutschen Zeitschriften', *ZDP*, 121, 2002: 161–86. J. Esleben, 'Georg Forster's dialect of desire', *Seminar*, 37, 2001: 305–22.

GELLERT. S. Hilger, 'The feminine performance of class in Chr. F. Gellert's *Leben der schwedischen Gräfin von G****', *Seminar*, 37, 2001: 283–304.

GERSTENBERG. Y.-P. Alefeld, '"Der Simplizität der Griechen am nächsten kommen" — Entfesselte Animalität in Heinrich Wilhelm von Gerstenbergs *Ugolino*', *HY*, 2002: 63–82.

GOTTSCHED. C. Wild, 'Geburt der Theaterreform aus dem Geist der Theaterfeindlichkeit: der Fall Gottsched', *LY*, 34, 2002: 57–77. F. Krause, 'Stoische Ungeduld. Johann Christoph Gottsched: *Der sterbende Cato* (1732)', *GLL*, 54, 2001: 191–209. S. Hilger, 'The "weibliche Geschlechte" in the mirror of the early German Enlightenment: class and gender in Johann Christoph Gottsched's *Die vernünftigen Tadlerinnen*', *LY*, 33, 2001: 127–50.

HAGEDORN. Reinhold Münster, *Friedrich von Hagedorn. Personalbibliographie. Mit einem Forschungsbericht und einer Biographie des Dichters*, Würzburg, Königshausen & Neumann, 2001, 126 pp.

HAMANN. *Metacritique. The Linguistic Assault on German Idealism*, ed. Jere Paul Surber, Amherst, NY, Humanity Books, 2001, 172 pp., contains translations of texts by Hamann, Herder, Salomon Maimon, and others. Oswald Bayer, *Vernunft ist Sprache. Hamanns Metakritik Kants*, Stuttgart–Bad Cannstatt, Frommann-Holzboog, xiv + 504 pp. R. Kany, 'Tiefblickende Augen, wunderliche Phantasien. Ein Hamann-Fund und seine Bedeutung', *JDSG*, 45, 2001:11–24. H. Graubner, 'Kinder im Drama. Theologische Impulse bei Hamann, Lindner und Lenz', *ib.*, 46, 2002:73–101.

HEBEL. *TK*, 7, 2001, is a special issue on H. and contains J. Knopf, '"... und hat das Ende der Erde nicht gesehen." Heimat, die Welt umspannend — Hebel, der Kosmopolit' (3–10); G. Bevilacqua, '"... wie sind die Worte richtig gesetzt." Zwei unveröffentlichte Hebel-Kommentare Ernst Blochs' (11–22); Y.-G. Mix, 'Mediale und narrative Interdependenz. Zur Raum- und Zeitsemantik in Johann Peter Hebels Kalendertexten' (23–31); C. Pietzcker, 'Wie der Hebel-Frieder und ZundelPeter dem Consistorio auf ein kurzes entwichen und dem geneigten Leser den Boden unter den Füßen wegstahlen. Eine literarische Lumpengeschichte' (32–46); A. Geisenhanslüke, 'Barocke Aufklärung. Tod und Vergänglichkeit in Hebels Alemannischen Gedichten und Kalendergeschichten' (47–56); Johann Peter Hebel, 'Die Vergänglichkeit' (57–60); A. Stadler, '"Und wemme nootno gar zweytusig zehlt, isch alles z'semme g'keit." Zu einem Vers aus Johann Peter Hebels Gedicht "Die Vergänglichkeit" in Jahr 2001' (61–68); J. A. Steiger, '"... und fällt deswegen auch in Gottes Sprache." Johann Peter Hebels Kalendererzählung "Baumzucht" als Beispiel biblischer Volksaufklärung' (69–81); R. Gillett, 'Hebel der Briefschreiber. Prolegomena' (82–95); W. Thoeben, 'Auswahlbibliografie Johann Peter Hebel' (100–07).

HERDER. J. G. Herder, *Werke*, vols III.1 and 2, ed. Wolfgang Pross, Munich, Hanser, 2002, 1185, 1031 pp., contain the text of the *Ideen zur Philosophie der Geschichte der Menschheit* and, in the second volume, an enormous commentary on the *Ideen*, which will be treasured by those who admire Pross's style of *wissenssoziologisch* analysis and his stupendous range of reference. V. Buchheit, 'Sendungsbewußtsein beim frühen Herder', *Euphorion*, 95, 2001:1–16, shows how H.'s allusive style points to his sense of his own mission to change the course of German literature. Michael Zaremba, *Johann Gottfried Herder: Prediger der Humanität. Eine Biographie*, Cologne, Böhlau, 2002, 270 pp., styles itself as 'populärwissenschaftlich'. Arno Sonderegger, *Jenseits der rassistischen Grenze. Die Wahrnehmung Afrikas bei Johann Gottfried Herder im Spiegel seiner Philosophie der Geschichte (und der 'Geschichten' anderer 'Philosophen')*, Berne, Lang, 219 pp., finds stereotypical but also non-stereotypical images of Africa in Herder's writing. E. A. Menze, 'Herder and prejudice: insights and ambiguities', *HY*, 2002:83–96. G. Sauder, 'Herders Gedanken über lyrische Sprachen und Dichtkunst', *ib.*, 97–114. W. Stellmacher, 'Herders Fabeln,

Parabeln, Legenden als Versuche einer "abgerissenen" und "verstummenden" Poesie', *ib.*, 115–28. G. Arnold, 'Monboddo die Palme? Zur Monboddo-Rezeption J. G. Herders', *ib.*, 7–20. G. Bockwoldt, '"Mein Prinz" — Johann Gottfried Herders Mission in Eutin. Mit drei bislang unbekannten Briefen im Anhang', *ib.*, 21–42. U. Gaier, 'Ein unseliges Mittelding zwischen Hofstadt und Dorf. Herder und Weimar', *ib.*, 43–62. S. Reynolds, 'A scandal in Bohemia: Herder, Goethe, Nasaryk, and the 'war of the manuscripts', *PEGS*, 72, 2002:53–68. H. Gaskill, '"Aus der dritten Hand": Herder and his annotators', *GLL*, 54, 2001:210–18. T. Pago, '"Aus der Welt hinaussrückt." Aspekte der Querelle des Anciens et des Modernes bei Herder', *Fest. Jacobs*, 149–60.

HIPPEL. Anke Lindemann-Stark, *Leben und Lebensläufe des Theodor Gottlieb von Hippel*, St. Ingbert, Röhrig, 2001, 384 pp. G. Shaw, 'Theodor Gottlieb von Hippel (1741–1796) als Wegbereitung der Frauenbewegung in Deutschland: "Lachender Philosoph" oder "Prophet"?', *GLL*, 54, 2001:273–90.

HIRSCHFELD. J. P. Heins, 'Characters of environments, peoples, and nations in C. C. L. Hirschfeld's *Theorie der Gartenkunst* (1779–85)', *LY*, 33, 2001:277–95.

JACOBI. M. Nenon, 'Freundschaft und literarische Kooperation: Friedrich Heinrich Jacobi und Christoph Martin Wieland (1770–1776)', *LY*, 33, 2001:261–75.

JUNG-STILLING. G. Schwinge, 'Jung-Stilling und seine Verleger. Von Deinet in Frankfurt bis Raw in Nürnberg', *AGB*, 56, 2002:109–24.

KALB, CHARLOTTE VON. E. Kleinschmidt, '"Wie ein Aug im Gewölk." Die vergessene Autorschaft Charlotte von Kalbs', *JDSG*, 46, 2002:160–83.

KLINGER. T. Salumets, 'Ein "etablierter Außenseiter": Friedrich Maximilian Klinger und die *Geschichte eines Teutschen der neuesten Zeit*', *Euphorion*, 96, 2002:421–36.

KLOPSTOCK. S. Busch, 'Blasphemisches Lachen in Klopstocks *Messias* und Lessings *Minna von Barnhelm*. Zur Herausbildung eines literarischen Leitmotivs der Moderne', *LY*, 33, 2001:27–55. H. Bosse, 'Klopstocks "Kriegslied" (1749). Militärische Poesiepolitik im 18. Jahrhundert', *JFDH*, 2001:41–99.

LA ROCHE. B. Scherbacher-Posé, 'Aux origines du journalisme féminin en Allemagne. Sophie von La Roche (1730–1807)', *EG*, 57, 2002:35–62, gives a detailed account of La Roche's journalistic career that shows how central this activity was to writers of the late 18th century. E.-M. Russo, 'More than the consummate libertine? Sophie von La Roche's seducer figure in *Geschichte des Fräuleins von Sternheim*', *LY*, 34, 2002:101–24. H. Brown, 'Sarah Scott, Sophie von

La Roche, and the female utopian tradition', *JEGP*, 100, 2001:469–81.

LAVATER. E. Kocziszky, 'Ein Leib-Sein. Lavaters Dialog mit Hamann', *Seminar*, 38, 2002:1–18.

LENZ. L. has become markedly more central to late 18th-c. literary history in recent years, thanks in part to new discoveries that have allowed a fuller and more rounded picture of his work to emerge. Lenz, *Werke in zwölf Bänden*, ed. Christoph Weiss, St. Ingbert, Röhrig, 2001, presents facsimiles of all the works that appeared during L.'s lifetime, including those recently rediscovered by W. himself. H. Tommek, 'Lenz und das Tatarische. Skizze einer großen Konstruktion aufgrund einiger bislang ungedruckter Briefstellen aus Moskau', *LY*, 34, 2002:145–96, presents the text of several unpublished letters from L.'s time in Moscow and argues for L.'s engagement in Russian national political debates of the time. Georg-Michael Schulz, *J. M. R. Lenz*, Stuttgart, Reclam, 2001, 351 pp., is a judicious and well-documented account of the life and works. Beginning with a brief biography, S. analyses all of the writings, including the prose essays and letters, and ends with a short account of L.'s reception. The emphasis is on L. within his social, literary, and linguistic milieu. Sharp and well-balanced analyses relate L. closely to his audience. There is no attempt to hide the failures or attribute them to L.'s having been misunderstood. In three articles, J. Gibbons argues against the now discredited view of L. as the 'wild child' of the *Sturm und Drang*: in 'Politics and the playwright: J. M. R. Lenz and *Die Soldaten*', *MLR*, 96, 2001:732–47, Gibbons reads the play as an implicit critique of some of the values of the *Sturm und Drang*; 'J. M. R. Lenz's *Der Landprediger*: an adaptation of *The Vicar of Wakefield* "tradition"?', *ColGer*, 34, 2001:213–36, argues that, far from being an idyll in the manner of its model, L.'s story ironizes the writer's own idealism; 'Laying the moral foundations: writer, religion and late eighteenth-century society — the case of J. M. R. Lenz', *GLL*, 54, 2001:137–54, analyses two of L.'s moral-theological texts and brings out the complexity and uniqueness of L.'s position. H. Steinhorst, 'Antinomien und Affinitäten der Aufklärung — Lenz und Wieland', *Euphorion*, 96, 2002:371–85, finds similarities in the two writers' responses to problems of subjectivity and objectivity. Matthias Luserke, *Lenz-Studien. Literaturgeschichte — Werke — Themen*, St. Ingbert, Röhrig, 2001, 292 pp., gathers various articles already published by Luserke plus three new pieces. D. Ende, 'Empfindsame Selbst- und Fremdinszenierungen. *Das Tagebuch* und die *Moralische Bekehrung eines Poeten von ihm selbst aufgeschrieben* von Jakob Michael Reinhold Lenz', *Euphorion*, 96, 2002:387–420. G.-M. Schulz, 'Wie das liebende Ich verweht wird und das lyrische Ich sich behauptet.

Zu Jacob Michael Reinhold Lenz' Gedicht "Ich suche sie umsonst" ', *Fest. Jacobs*, 179–92. W. Hinck, 'Der Grenzgänger Jakob Michael Reinhold Lenz. Zu einigen seiner Gedichte', *Fest. Schings*, 81–90. Albert Koschorke, 'Der prägnante Moment fand nicht statt. Vaterlosigkeit und heilige Familie in Lenz' *Hofmeister*', *ib.*, 91–104. *Jakob Michael Reinhold Lenz. Vom Sturm und Drang zur Moderne*, ed. Andreas Meier (Beihefte zum *Euphorion*, 41), Heidelberg, Winter, 2001, 145 pp., contains R. Zymner, 'Shakespeare und Lenz' (11–22); J.-U. Fechner, 'Ein wiedergefundener Brief von Lenz aus Weimar 1776 an Friedrich Leopold Graf Stolberg' (23–36); A. Martin, 'Die Nobilitierung der Krankheit. Zu einer Linie der Lenz-Rezeption im 19. Jahrhundert' (61–74); A. Meier, 'Ankunft in die Moderne. Franz Bleis Lenz-Ausgabe' (75–96).

LICHTENBERG. S. Metzger, 'Guter Rat. Konsensualismus, Autorisierung und Experiment bei Lichtenberg', *DVLG*, 76, 2002 : 608–42. S. Braese, ' "Ihr seids selbst." Subjektgeschichte und Literatur. Lichtenbergs Diskurskritik am Sturm und Drang', *LY*, 34, 2002 : 79–99. L. Olschner, 'The allegoresis of visual perception: the London of Georg Christoph Lichtenberg', *PEGS*, 72, 2002 : 39–52, analyses L.'s visual reading of the city in terms of a 'perceived dense network of double meanings' that produce 'allegorical intimations'.

MENDELSSOHN. C.-F. Berghahn, 'Mendelssohn als Leser Montesquieus. Zur Rekonstruktion einer Denkfigur der europäischen Aufklärung', *GRM*, 52, 2002 : 153–74.

MERCK. Walter Schübler, *Johann Heinrich Merck, 1741–1791. Biographie*, Cologne, Böhlau, 2001, 439 pp.

MORITZ. Oliver Cech, *Das elende Selbst und das schöne Sein. Autonomie des Individuums und seiner Kunst bei Karl Philipp Moritz*, Freiburg, Rombach, 2001, 287 pp., attempts a psychoanalytical interpretation of *Anton Reiser* and the other autobiographical writings that is hampered by a sketchy knowledge of the psychological theory of Moritz's time. H. Hollmer and A. Meier, ' "Die Erde ist nicht überall einerlei!" Landschaftsbeschreibungen in Karl Philipp Moritz' Reiseberichten aus England und Italien', *JIG*, 66, 2001 : 263–88, shows the stylistic differences in M.'s portrayal of 'subjective' England and 'objective' Italy. B. Thums, 'Paradigmes classiques et romantiques d'une esthétique de la distance chez Karl Philipp Moritz et Wilhelm Heinrich Wackenroder', *RGI*, 16, 2001 : 101–22. A. Simonis, 'Die "neue Mythologie" der Aufklärung. Karl Philipp Moritz' Mythenpoetik im diskursgeschichtlichen Kontext', *JDSG*, 45, 2001 : 97–130. A. Košenina, ' "Die Universität war die Klippe, an welcher er scheiterte." Karl Philipp Moritz' Erzählung *Aus K . . .s Papieren*', *Fest. Schings*, 127–48.

NICOLAI. A. Košenina, 'Friedrich Nicolai's satires on philosophy', *MDLK*, 93, 2001 : 290–99, offers a reappraisal of Nicolai's polemical writings.

SEUME. Urs Meyer, *Politische Rhetorik. Theorie, Analyse und Geschichte der Redekunst am Beispiel des Spätaufklärers Johann Gottfried Seume*, Paderborn, Mentis, 2001, 292 pp.

WIELAND. Reinhard Ohm, *'Unsere jungen Dichter.' Wielands literaturästhetische Publizistik im 'Teutschen Merkur' zur Zeit des Sturm und Drang und der Frühklassik*, Trier, WVT, 2001, 198 pp., shows on the one hand that W.'s generally antagonistic relationship with the younger generation of poets was important in historical terms, and on the other that the antagonism was often pursued for its own sake, which explains the ease with which, for instance, Goethe and Lenz became close friends of Wieland. G. Thuswaldner, 'Verbotene Liebe: Inzest, Narzißmus und Homoerotik in Wielands *Geschichte des Agathon*', *LWU*, 34, 2001 : 307–19, considers the hero's love for Psyche and Danae as dysfunctional stages that must be overcome in the process of socialization. R. Campe, '"Improbable probability": on evidence in the eighteenth century', *GR*, 76, 2001 : 143–61, reads *Agathon* against the background of 18th-c. debates on mathematical probability. C. Niekerk, 'Wieland und die Irrwege der Aufklärung: Öffentlichkeitskritik in der *Geschichte der Abderiten*', *LY*, 33, 2001 : 233–60. F. Siepe, 'Wieland und der prodikeische Herkules. Zu einem Detail in Kraus' Gemälde *Wieland im Kreis seiner Familie* und zu Wielands lyrischem Drama *Die Wahl des Herkules*', *JDSG*, 45, 2001 : 73–94.

WINCKELMANN. E. Décultot, 'Theorie und Praxis der Nachahmung. Untersuchungen zu Winckelmanns Exzerptheften', *DVLG*, 76, 2002 : 27–49.

THE ROMANTIC ERA

By Carol Tully, *University of Wales, Bangor*

1. General Studies

This year has seen the publication of updated versions of two valuable reference works dealing with the period as a whole. *Romantik-Handbuch*, ed. Helmut Schanze (KTA, 363), xxviii + 810 pp., which draws on the expertise of a number of established scholars in the field including Gerhart Hoffmeister, John Fetzer, and Markus Schwering, is wide-ranging and well-structured, providing contextual studies in relation to philosophical, theological, and historical issues, as well as detailed analyses of individual thinkers. Those sections examining the influence of other European cultures and also those focusing on issues of genre are of particular interest. The volume also offers a valuable assessment of the reception of Romantic thought in scholarly circles. Detlef Kremer, *Romantik*, Stuttgart, Metzler, viii + 341 pp., also offers a comprehensive overview of the period. Aimed at a different audience, clearly intended as a teaching aid, this volume nevertheless provides a valuable range of information on both genre and context, as well as focusing on key writers and texts. Structured according to themes and genres, the chapters are clearly presented and contain detailed material, easily accessible to new and established scholars alike.

The reception of Romanticism in both the 19th and 20th cs provides the impetus for two substantial volumes. *Romantik und Vormärz. Zur Archäologie literarischer Kommunikation in der ersten Hälfte des 19. Jahrhunderts*, ed. Wolfgang Bunzel, Peter Stein, and Florian Vassen (Vormärz-Studien, 10), Bielefeld, Aisthesis, 465 pp., focuses on comparative and reception issues, highlighting the clear tensions but also revealing certain affinities between the two periods. Worthy of particular mention is R. Rosenberg, 'Das Junge Deutschland — die dritte "romantische" Generation?' (49–65), which discusses generational and ideological issues in a reassessment of the influence of Romantic thought in the mid-century and the reliance of *Vormärz* writers on their Romantic forebears; P. Stein, ' "Die gute alte Zeit" — ein Zeitkonstrukt zwischen Romantik und Nachmärz' (185–97), traces the usage of the term 'die gute alte Zeit' back to 1800, revealing it not to be an ancient topos but instead a modern development with continually shifting significance. Other contributions dealing with influence and tensions are U. Landfester, ' "So kommt das Volk zur Welt." Politische Konzepte der Romantik im Vormärz' (67–86); C. Weckwerth, 'Anthropologie im Spannungsfeld zwischen Romantik und Vormärz' (87–107); O. Briese, 'Herrschaft über die Natur. Ein Topos in Vormärz und Romantik. Versuch einer Legitimierung' (109–43); M. Podewski, 'Fragment und Journal: romantische und jungdeutsche Sprechorte' (145–61); N. O. Eke, 'Moderne Zeit(en). Der Kampf um die Zeit in Romantik und Vormärz' (163–83); G. Oesterle, 'Zum Spannungsverhältnis von Poesie und Publizistik unter dem Vorzeichen der Temporalisierung' (199–211); and D. Göttsche, '"Auf der Brücke zweier Zeiten." Traditionen und Neuansätze des Zeitromans in Romantik und Vormärz' (213–33). In the second half of the volume attention turns to the reception of Romanticism during the *Vormärz* period. There are three contributions devoted to the role of Heine: C. Liedtke, '"Mondglanz" und "Rittermantel". Heinrich Heines romantische Masken und Kulissen' (237–56); G. Höhn, 'Weder "Passionsblumen" noch "nutzloser Enthusiasmusdunst". Heine — Romantik — Vormärz' (257–74); and S. Bierwirth, 'Deutscher Vormärz und westeuropäische Romantik. Heinrich Heine und Victor Hugo' (275–91). Other studies focus on literary responses to the social changes of the period: M. E. Goozé, 'Utopische Räume und idealisierte Geselligkeit: die Rezeption des Berliner Salons im Vormärz' (363–90); U. Köster, 'Frauenherrschaft, Zeitenwende. Über das Verhältnis von Mythos und Geschichte in Romantik und Vormärz am Beispiel der Bearbeitungen des Libussa-Stoffes bei Brentano, Ebert, Mundt und Grillparzer' (391–411); M. Perraudin, '"Poesie" ist keine "Trivialschule der sogenannten Realien": Eichendorff als systematischer Anti-Realist. Zu *Dichter und ihre Gesellen* und *Geschichte der poetischen Literatur Deutschlands*' (413–31); and J. Strobel, 'Nach der Autonomieästhetik. Zur Reaktion romantischer Autoren auf Veränderungen des Literatursystems in der Zeit des Vormärz' (433–59). Finally, direct responses to Romanticism are dealt with in: W. Wülfing, '"Die jrine Beeme." Einige Bemerkungen zur Romantik-Kritik im Vormärz, speziell bei Börne, Heine und den Jungdeutschen' (293–312); W. Bunzel, '"Der Geschichte in die Hände arbeiten." Zur Romantikrezeption der Junghegelianer' (313–38); and F. Vassen, 'Rhein contra Themse. Georg Weerths Beziehung zur Romantik' (339–61).

A later period of reception is the subject of Anja Hagen, *Gedächtnisort Romantik. Intertextuelle Verfahren in der Prosa der 80er und 90er Jahre*, Bielefeld, Aisthesis, 523 pp., which centres mainly on the reception of Hoffmann but also considers the role of Romantic aesthetics in modern literature, in particular the fascination with the *Kunstmärchen* and the figure of the Romantic artist. Modern authors discussed include Süsskind, Strauss, Morgner, Hilbig, and Handke. This is a detailed study which also includes an extensive discussion of issues of intertextuality. Also noted: **Hans Eichner. Against the Grain: Selected*

Essays / Gegen den Strich: Ausgewählte Aufsätze, ed. Rodney Symington (CSGLL, 47), 411 pp.; M. Chaouli, 'The politics of permanent parabasis', *StRom*, 42:323–40.

THEMES. The politics of the age and their relation to issues of identity, both national and individual, have provided the material for a number of studies. Stefan Nienhaus, *Geschichte der deutschen Tischgesellschaft* (UDL, 115), 405 pp., provides a long-overdue comprehensive study of the controversial society, offering a record of the formation of the group as well as analysis of its textual output, including discussion of the group's anti-Semitic views. The individual members discussed include Arnim, Brentano, Fichte, Müller, and Schleiermacher. There is a detailed analysis of the reception of the society by literary scholars plus a new evaluation which ties the anti-Semitic, nationalistic era of the group to the period of the Wars of Liberation, as well as identifying a reforming tendency in the group's work. N. also provides detailed bibliographical information. This valuable study is essential for any scholar of Romantic politics. Responses to the French Revolution are discussed in Ulrike Dedner, *Deutsche Widerspiele der Französischen Revolution. Reflexionen des Revolutionsmythos im selbstbezüglichen Spiel von Goethe bis Dürrenmatt* (Hermaea Germanistische Forschungen, n.F., 101), Tübingen, Niemeyer, 322 pp. Of particular interest in this wide-ranging study is the extensive discussion of Tieck's *Der gestiefelte Kater* and *Die verkehrte Welt*. D. focuses on dualities and ambivalences, and rejects a reading of the texts as simply pro- or anti-revolutionary works. The Romantic response to the revolution is seen as an inherent part of the artistic process and not as a political phenomenon.

Romantische Identitätskonstruktionen: Nation, Geschichte und (Auto-)Biographie. Glasgower Kolloquium der Internationalen Arnim-Gesellschaft, ed. Sheila Dickson and Walter Pape, Tübingen, Niemeyer, x + 302 pp., covers three key areas. The first is that of national identity, and worthy of note here is K. Peter, 'Die alte Bäuerin: zur Identität des "Volkes" in Brentanos "Geschichte vom braven Kasperl und dem schönen Annerl"' (13–30), which examines how B. develops a notion of 'Volk' in his tale, extending a practice already seen in *Des Knaben Wunderhorn* and the Grimms' *Kinder- und Hausmärchen*. The author is seen to strive for an ideal of the 'Volk' which no longer existed in the contemporary proto-capitalist world. Also of note is R. Robertson, 'Antisemitismus und Ambivalenz: zu Achim von Arnims Erzählung "Die Majoratsherren"' (51–63), which examines A.'s attitude to Jews, highlighting a fascination with Jewish physicality and the Jew as the embodiment of a feared modernity. R. also explores the possibility of a link between the figure of Esther and A.'s response to the death of his mother. National identity is also the focus of

D. Martin, 'Vom Beistand altdeutscher "Biederleute" bei der romantischen Suche nach nationaler Identität' (3–11); J. Knaack, 'Achim von Arnim, die britischen und die preußischen Freiwilligen in den Kriegen gegen Napoleon' (31–36); R. Moering, 'Reisespuren in Arnims englischen Lyrik-Heften' (37–50); and H. Schwinn, 'Arnims Orientalinnen' (65–86). History and biography are the focus of the following section: C. Nitschke, 'Die Erreichbarkeit von Gemeinschaft: die Konstruktion von "Volk" und Individualität im "Wintergarten"' (89–103); Y. Pietsch, 'Von einem der auszog, das Dienen zu lernen: Arnims Posse "Janns erster Dienst" und John Lockes Vertragstheorie' (105–16); U. Ricklefs, ' "Was war ich? was bin ich? was werde ich?" Identität als Progression: Romantische Identitätskonzepte bei Arnim' (117–37); and S. Dickson and C. Wingertszahn, ' "Selig sind Deine Selbsttäuschungen": Carl Otto Ludwig von Arnim (1779–1861)' (139–59). The final section focuses on biography, autobiography, and the notion of a constructed identity. Of particular interest is B. Becker-Cantarino, 'Erotisierte Freundschaft in der Konstruktion romantischer Identität am Beispiel Bettina von Arnims' (229–45), which traces B.v.A.'s concept of friendship as a paradigm from the author's early Romantic construction of an identity to her later development of the ideal, via the literary process, into an eroticized notion which circumvents traditional gender relations. Other contributions include: M. Andermatt, 'Wer erzählt? Erzähltes Erzählen und Identitätskonstruktion bei Achim von Arnim' (163–73); G. Schulz, 'Anmerkungen zur Interaktion von Leben und Literatur bei Heinrich von Kleist oder: Über die Schwierigkeiten, eine Biographie über Kleist zu schreiben' (175–91); R. Schmidt, 'Biographie, Autobiographie, Fiktion: Die Funktion von Rousseaus "Confessions" für die Konstruktion von Identität in E. T. A. Hoffmanns "Kater Murr"' (193–216); U. Japp, 'Die Identität des Künstlers: Arnims Erzählung "Raphael und seine Nachbarinnen"' (217–27); W. G. Schmidt, 'Der Sammler, der Dichter und die verlorene Jugend: Arnims Poetik im Kontext seiner Beschäftigung mit Macphersons "Ossian"' (247–69); and R. Littlejohns, 'Marbot und Wainewright: zum Verhältnis von Identität und Authentizität in der Biographie' (271–77).

Madame de Staël und die Internationalität der europäischen Romantik. Fallstudien zur interkulturellen Vernetzung, ed. Udo Schöning and Frank Seemann (Göttinger Beiträge zur Nationalität, Internationalität und Intermedialität von Literatur und Film, 2), Göttingen, Wallstein, 255 pp., offers an excellent overview of the influence of de S. in Europe, including J. von Rosen, 'Deutsche Ästhetik in *De l'Allemagne*: eine Transferstudie am Beispiel der Kant-Interpretation Mme de Staëls' (173–202), which examines the dissemination of the ideals of early Romanticism via de S.'s text and also traces the emergence of the term 'romantique'. R. argues that de S.'s process of dissemination itself 'romanticizes' these ideals through the various connections she makes with other ideals and traditions, and in particular via her emphasis on emotion and enthusiasm. The study focuses on her reception of Kant which is found to be flawed, leading to a partial, specifically Romantic redefinition.

Charles I. Armstrong, *Romantic Organicism. From Idealist Origins to Ambivalent Afterlife*, Basingstoke–NY, Palgrave Macmillan, 233 pp., devotes a substantial section to German Idealism and *Frühromantik*. Attention focuses on concepts of unity and fragmentation in 'Romanticism's often underestimated inheritance from the Enlightenment'. The concepts are traced from German Idealists following Kant to early Romanticism and Friedrich Schlegel, and are seen to reappear in Coleridge and Wordsworth. Their continuing significance is found in the modern critical theory of Gadamer and Derrida. The study is clearly presented and, although perhaps aimed more at an audience concerned with philosophy than literary studies, is a valuable contribution to the study of interaction between German and British Romanticism.

Monika Schmitz-Emans, *Seetiefen und Seelentiefen. Literarische Spiegelungen innerer und äußerer Fremde* (Saarbrücker Beiträge zur vergleichenden Literatur- und Kulturwissenschaft, 22), Würzburg, Königshausen & Neumann, 429 pp., traces the trope of the water dweller as a representative of 'otherness' through a period of three centuries in world literature. The study opens with a discussion of Kleist's essay 'Wassermänner und Sirenen' and devotes ch. 4 to the German Romantic use of the trope as a vehicle for the notion of otherness represented by 'Elementargeister' with references to the work of Brentano, Fouqué, Tieck, Hoffmann, and Eichendorff. Studies of individual works offer little new insight, in particular those dealing with Fouqué's *Undine* and Tieck's *Die Elfen*, but the various *excurse* are more thought-provoking, notably the discussion of notions of form and formlessness.

Corina Caduff, *Die Literarisierung von Musik und bildender Kunst um 1800*, Munich, Fink, 386 pp., provides a detailed examination of literary responses to art and music in the Romantic period, including references to August Wilhelm Schlegel and the role of music in his aesthetic theories. A number of writers are discussed including Tieck, Hauff, Heinse, and Fouqué. Of particular note, however, is the discussion of the role of art in Wackenroder's work where works of art are seen to occupy a 'Nicht-Ort', subsumed into the world of the artist himself. Also interesting is the discussion of music in the work of Hoffmann, which reveals the so-called 'serapiontische Prinzip' whereby the author sees music as integral to otherwise visual means of conceptualization. There is also an innovative discussion of depictions of gender.

Meike Hillen, *Die Pathologie der Literatur. Zur wechselseitigen Beobachtung von Medezin und Literatur* (BSDL, 61), 296 pp., includes a discussion of the aestheticization of illness in Friedrich Schlegel and Novalis, in particular the notion of 'Tranzendentalmedezin' in N.'s work. Here physical disharmony is seen as a stepping stone to a higher harmony thus legitimizing the aesthetic role of illness. There is also a discussion of the concept of insanity as 'otherness' in Hoffmann. Hillen does not argue for a link with the author's own mental state, proposing instead that the interest of the material itself led H. to exploit it in his work. The volume closes with an examination of madness in life and art in relation to Hölderlin. This study necessarily relies on a medical register which may impact upon the accessibility of the text.

Also noted: Ronald Dietrich, **Der Gelehrte in der Literatur* (Ep, 425), 530 pp.; **Darstellbarkeit. Zu einem ästhetisch-philosophischen Problem um 1800*, ed. Claudia Albes and Christiane Frey (Stiftung für Romantikforschung, 23), Würzburg, Königshausen & Neumann, 280 pp.; Stefan Willer, **Poetik der Etymologie. Texturen sprachlichen Wissens in der Romantik*, Berlin, Akademie, xii + 348 pp.; D. Kremer, 'Idyll oder Trauma. Kindheit in der Romantik', *E. T. A. Hoffmann Jb.*, 11:7–18.

GENRES. Studies of genre have continued to prove popular this year with three major studies appearing. Two of these are concerned with the often neglected area of Romantic drama. Stefan Scherer, *Witzige Spielgemälde. Tieck und das Drama der Romantik* (QFLK, 26), viii + 652 pp., is an extensive study which not only focuses on Tieck as an experimental dramatist, but also offers a discussion of drama as a Romantic genre, tracing its development with reference to works by Brentano, Arnim, and Friedrich Schlegel and their responses to T.'s work. The study also examines the subsequent reception of Romantic drama in the 19th c. and looks forward to its influence in the present day. This is an excellent, erudite and well-structured study. Yifen Tsau Beus, *Towards a Paradoxical Theatre. Schlegelian Irony in German and French Romantic Drama, 1797–1843* (The Age of Revolution and Romanticism: Interdisciplinary Studies, 32), NY, Lang, 170 pp., considers the means by which the theatre of the age seeks to 'redefine the mission of the genre' whilst forwarding the ideals of Romantic poetics via Schlegelian irony. B. discusses F.S.'s notion of Romantic irony, A.W.S.'s related comparatist work, and Tieck's use of irony. The study ends by highlighting the modernity of notions of irony during the Romantic age.

Hutchinson, *Landmarks*, presents a series of lectures delivered at Cambridge, including C. Woodford, 'Kleist, *Michael Kohlhaas*' (29–43), which examines narrative strategies and inconsistencies in

K.'s novella, centring on the themes of justice, trust, and morality. W. highlights the juxtaposition of source material and invention, and shows how the resulting contradictions create suspense. Also included in this volume is R. Robertson, 'Eichendorff, *Aus dem Leben eines Taugenichts*' (45–60), which focuses on allegory and makes reference to Lukács reception of the text. B. Theisen, 'χα absolute chaos: the early Romantic poetics of complex form', *StRom*, 42:301–21, examines the work of the Schlegel brothers, Jean Paul Richter, Brentano, and Bonaventura.

2. Individual Authors

ARNIM, BETTINE VON. Ulrike Growe, *Das Briefleben Bettine von Arnims — Vom Musenanruf zur Selbstreflexion. Studie zu 'Goethes Briefwechsel mit einem Kinde', 'Die Günderrode' und 'Clemens Brentanos Frühlingskranz'* (Ep, 434), 264 pp. + 3 pls, is a thought-provoking study which examines B.v.A.'s three semi-fictional correspondences and discusses the Romantic nature of the texts and the narratives employed. The interrelation of the three texts is discussed, as is the author's rationale. G. detects a contradiction in the work which suggests self-reflection as a means to self-creation but also an element of self-distancing. As such, B.v.A.'s writing represents a means of creating space for the self which facilitates a shifting stance.

ARNIM, LUDWIG ACHIM VON. *Ludwig Achim von Arnim, Bettina von Arnim, Clemens Brentano. 'Anekdoten, die wir erlebten und hörten'*, ed. Heinz Härtl, Göttingen, Wallstein, 109 pp., represents the first publication of anecdotes recorded by the writers at Wiepersdorf. The texts provide an insight into family life and emphasize the individuality of these figures. Their respective reflections on their grandparents are prompted by the events of the Napoleonic Wars and perhaps suggest a search for self in the past. B.v.A.'s anecdotes concerning 'Großmutter Laroche' are particularly interesting. Context and commentary are provided in the editor's afterword.

Tobias Bulang, *Barbarossa im Reich der Poesie. Verhandlungen von Kunst und Historismus bei Arnim, Grabbe, Stifter und auf dem Kyffhäuser* (Mikrokosmos, 69), Frankfurt, Lang, 349 pp., includes a lengthy chapter on *Die Kronenwächter* (55–129), which presents the work as part of the historicizing movement of later Romanticism. The novel is seen as a literary parallel to the developing philological trend of the period, epitomized in the guarding of cultural history through the use of chronicles. This is a useful study of A.'s text which reveals both his sources and the rationale behind its conception. C. Drösch, 'Johann Heinrich Jung-Stillings Theorien und Achim von Arnims Novelle *Die Majorats-Herren*', *EG*, 58:5–27, highlights the influence of J.-S.'s

Theorie der Geisterkunde on A.'s novella. Traces of J.-S.'s theory of 'Entbindung' are readily found in A.'s narrative with a similar message evident in both texts, namely the need for an intermediate position between the naive belief in ghosts and the rationalistic critique of such a belief.

BONAVENTURA. Noted: L. Katritzky, *'Decoding anonymous texts. The case of the "Nightwatches" of Bonaventura', *MDLK*, 95:458–502.

BRENTANO, CLEMENS. There has been a degree of interest in B. this year. *Auf Dornen oder Rosen hingesunken? Eros und Poesie bei Clemens Brentano*, ed. Hartwig Schultz, Berlin, Saint Albin, 237 pp., accompanies the Frankfurt exhibition of the same name and is accordingly well-illustrated. The volume also contains five essays, each focusing on B.'s relationships with women and how these affected his work and, conversely, how a relationship with the poet affected each of the women concerned. The women discussed are Minna Reichenbach, Auguste Bussmann, Luise Hensel, and Emilie Linder. H. Rölleke, ' "Zu Straßburg auf der Schanz." Clemens Brentanos Kreation eines "Wunderhorn"-Liedes', *Fest. Perels*, 161–68, traces B.'s reworking of the 'Straßburg'-*Lied* for the *Wunderhorn*, a process which created one of the most popular songs in the collection; H. Schultz, ' "Und das Märchen schien am Ende." Zur Spätfassung von Brentanos "Märchen von Gockel, Hinkel und Gackeleia"', *ib.*, 169–76, criticizes attempts to read B.'s text in the context of Friedrich Schlegel's theories in the *Athenäum*. C. Tully, 'Saving the self: tradition and identity in Clemens Brentano's *Rheinmärchen*', *Spalding Vol.*, 118–25, examines B.'s creation of identity, both national and individual, in response to national and personal crises. Two parallel heroes emerge: Radlauf, the stylized mythological hero of the tales who is able to unite and thus save the German nation with the help of Father Rhine, and Achim von Arnim, B.'s own personal 'Mittler mit der Welt', who provides an anchor for the vulnerable poet during the first two decades of the century. Radlauf and Arnim are both discussed in relation to B.'s response to a dual sense of crisis and are as such co-dependent constructs in B.'s search for self-definition. Also noted: J. M. Snook, 'A tale of two monuments: social criticism in Brentano's *Geschichte vom braven Kasperl und dem schönen Annerl*', *Seminar*, 39:187–202; K. Plonien, 'Von Jena über Heidelberg nach Dülmen. Die Krise "ästhetischer Subjektivität" bei Clemens Brentano in der "Geschichte vom braven Kasperl und dem schönen Annerl"', *MDLK*, 95:76–96; H. Rölleke, 'Der Götze "Holzebock". Zur Herkunft eines Namens in Brentanos *Fanferlieschen Märchen*', *WW*, 53:179–80.

DE LA MOTTE FOUQUÉ, CAROLINE. Elisa Müller-Adams, *'Dass die Frau zur Frau redete.' Das Werk der Caroline de la Motte Fouqué als Beispiel*

für weibliche Literaturproduktion der frühen Restaurationszeit (SBL, 74), 499 pp., examines thoughtfully and with a wealth of detail how F. deals with the issue of marginalization as a writer excluded from the canon by her gender, and her approach to the notion of a specifically feminine literature. Discussion of issues surrounding the expanding professional market for writing demonstrates how F. is often typical in her choice of material but nevertheless manages to contribute to both 'high' and also trivial literature. A.-B. Renger, 'Zur Bestimmung von Genre und Geschlecht um 1800: Caroline Fouqués "Briefe über die griechische Mythologie" — ein Werk für Frauen?', *JFG*, 47–60, places F.'s text in the context of contemporary studies of world mythology, including that of Joseph Görres, and in particular those aimed at a female readership. F. is seen to comply with the *Geschlechterideologie* of the period in her depictions, whilst nevertheless ascribing the feminine a positive influencing role.

DE LA MOTTE FOUQUÉ, FRIEDRICH. This year's *JFG* contains a number of contributions dealing with F. and his relations with contemporary scholars, including P. Hasubek, 'Immermanns erste literarische Beziehungen (mit besonderer Berücksichtigung Friedrich de la Motte Fouqués)' (29–46), and T. Witt, 'August Ludwig Hülsen und Friedrich de la Motte Fouqué — Nähe und Distanz zweier Romantiker'(61–80), which provides an overview of H.'s life, tracing his gradual move away from the traditional, Christian Romantic movement, and consequently also from his former pupil and friend, F. Also included in the *Jb.* are M. Schmidt, 'Fouqué schlägt Goethe. Caroline und Friedrich de la Motte Fouqué und die Präsenz ihrer Texte in den Leihbibliotheken des deutschen Biedermeier' (7–28), and U. Schuch, 'Norman Douglas' "Nerinda". Eine capresisch-pompejanische Undinen-Erzählung' (81–124). Also noted: D. A. F. Salama, *'Die Frau aus der anderen Welt. Der Undine-Stoff in der deutschen Romantik (Friedrich de la Motte-Fouqués "Undine") und in den orientalischen Märchen aus "Tausendundeiner Nacht" ("Die Geschichte von Dschanschâh")', *KGS*, 13:247–96.

EICHENDORFF, JOSEPH VON. Katja Löhr, *Sehnsucht als poetologisches Prinzip bei Joseph von Eichendorff* (Ep, 461), 464 pp., examines the concept of 'Sehnsucht', not in relation to E.'s own statements or historical context, but rather focusing on issues of being and consciousness with some reference to the history of ideas. A number of texts are given individual attention, including detailed readings of the poems 'Wehmuth' and 'Sehnsucht'. These are also read in the context of the novels in which they appear, *Ahnung und Gegenwart* and *Dichter und ihre Gesellen*, and the significance of Italy is highlighted in both cases. This is a well-structured and erudite study. E.'s poetry is also the subject of Rolf Krafft Ligniez, *Das Bild des Dichters in*

Eichendorffs Lyrik, ed. Roger Schöntag, Munich, Utz, x + 78 pp. Rather unusually, this is the first publication of a dissertation presented to the University of Frankfurt in 1943, now also revised and updated. K.L. examines E.'s poetry from 1802 to 1815 and traces the development of the depiction of the poet from a chosen, God-given talent to a leader bringing order. The poet's role as 'Mittler' is seen to fail in reaction to historical events. Despite its late emergence, this is still a valuable study. H.-P. Niewerth, 'Eichendorffs *Zauberei im Herbste*: die Neisser Manuskripte sind wieder greifbar', *Aurora*, 62, 2002: 143–57, reports on the availability of the Neisser manuscripts and reproduces the fragment 'Die Zauberei im Herbste'; V. Stein, 'Zwanzig Jahre später: *Dichter und ihre Gesellen*', *ib.*, 159–70, outlines observations made over 20 years working on the *HKA* of E.'s novel; R. Klausnitzer, 'Taugenichts im real existierenden Sozialismus. Aspekte der Eichendorff-Rezeption in der DDR', *ib.*, 171–95, focuses on the DEFA film and looks at E.'s reception in academic, media, and school/publishing circles. Also noted: J. Enklaar, 'Fenster und Ferne. Einige Bemerkungen zu Eichendorffs Lyrik', *Neophilologus*, 87:605–15.

FICHTE, JOHANN GOTTLIEB. A further five volumes in the series *Fichte-Studien* appeared this year: **Zur Wissenschaftslehre. Beiträge zum vierten Kongress der Internationalen Johann-Gottlieb-Fichte-Gesellschaft in Berlin vom 03.–08. Oktober 2000*, ed. Helmut Girndt (Fichte-Studien, 20), Amsterdam–NY, Rodopi, 284 pp.; *Fichte und seine Zeit. Beiträge zum vierten Kongress der Internationalen Johann-Gottlieb-Fichte-Gesellschaft in Berlin vom 03.–08. Oktober 2000*, ed. Hartmut Traub (Fichte-Studien, 21), Amsterdam–NY, Rodopi, 235 pp., which contains essays examining F.'s interaction with other writers and thinkers of the age. Of note is G. Florschütz, 'Mystik und Aufklärung — Kant, Swedenborg und Fichte' (89–107), a fascinating appraisal of Kant's engagement with Swedenborg and F.'s notion of 'Geisterreich'. Also of interest is E. Gareewa, 'Die Bedeutung der Populärphilosophie bei J. G. Fichte und A. Schopenhauer' (183–92), which examines the drive for an accessible popular philosophy in early F. and late Schopenhauer. A number of essays focus on the relations between F. and Schelling: K. Okada, 'Fichte und Schelling' (45–52); R. Marzalek, 'Das Poetische in der späten Wissenschaftslehre aus dem Blickpunkt von Schellings Philosophie der Mythologie' (53–61); and H. Minobe, 'Die Stellung des Seins bei Fichte, Schelling und Nishida' (63–72). Other contributions include: H. Eidam, 'Die Identität von Ideal- und Realgrund im Begriff der Wirksamkeit. Fichtes Begründung des kritischen Idealismus und ihr Problemzusammenhang' (29–44); Y. Kubo, 'Transformation der Deduktion der Kategorien. Fichte in Hegel' (73–87); A. V. Lukjanow, 'Die Beziehung zwischen Geist und

System bei Fichte und Reinhold' (111–16); S. Kahlefeld, 'Standpunkt des Lebens und Standpunkt der Philosophie. Jacobis Brief an Fichte aus dem Jahr 1799' (117–30); H. Traub, 'J. G. Fichte, der König der Juden spekulativer Vernunft — Überlegungen zum spekulativen Anti-Judaismus' (131–50); C. Dierksmeier, 'Fichtes kritischer Schüler. Zur Fichtekritik K. C. F. Krauses (1781–1832)' (151–62); and M. Kossler, 'Phantasie und Einbildingskraft. Zur Rolle der Einbildungskraft bei Fichte und Solger' (163–81). **Geschichte und Gegenwart. Beiträge zum vierten Kongress der Internationalen Johann-Gottlieb-Fichte-Gesellschaft in Berlin vom 03.–08. Oktober 2000*, ed. Helmut Girndt (Fichte-Studien, 22), Amsterdam–NY, Rodopi, 270 pp.; **Praktische und angewandte Philosophie* I. *Beiträge zum vierten Kongress der Internationalen Johann-Gottlieb-Fichte-Gesellschaft in Berlin vom 03.–08. Oktober 2000*, ed. Helmut Girndt and Hartmut Traub (Fichte-Studien, 23), Amsterdam–NY, Rodopi, 232 pp.; **Praktische und angewandte Philosophie* II. *Beiträge zum vierten Kongress der Internationalen Johann-Gottlieb-Fichte-Gesellschaft in Berlin vom 03.–08. Oktober 2000*, ed. Helmut Girndt and Hartmut Traub (Fichte-Studien, 24), Amsterdam–NY, Rodopi, 177 pp. Also noted: R. T. Gray, 'Economic Romanticism: monetary nationalism in Johann Gottlieb Fichte and Adam Müller', *ECS*, 36:535–57.

FRIEDRICH, CASPAR DAVID. Noted: R. Zimmermann, '"Kommet und sehet." Caspar David Friedrichs Bildverständnis und die Frage des "offenen Kunstwerks"', *Aurora*, 62, 2002:65–93.

GRIMM, JACOB AND WILHELM. An expanded second edition of Maria Tatar, *The Hard Facts of the Grimms' Fairy Tales*, Princeton–Oxford, Princeton U.P., xxxvi + 325 pp., reiterates the significance of this seminal study. A new preface has been added which places the tales in a modern context, making reference to their continued literary, pedagogical, and psychological importance. However, perhaps the most significant addition is the inclusion of translations of six tales, each furnished with an incisive commentary which explores the interpretative history and cultural dissemination of the stories. This year saw the publication of the *Jahrbuch der Brüder Grimm-Gesellschaft* for 1999. The volume includes two essays devoted to the brothers' travels in Germany: B. Lauer, 'Wilhelm Grimms Rheinreise im Sommer 1853. Aus den unveröffentlichten Tagebuchnotizen' (7–48); and R. Fischer, '"Wissenschaftliche Stimmung" des Geistes — die Brüder Grimm im "romantischen" Marburg' (49–74). This year also saw the publication of *Brüder-Grimm-Gedenken*, 15, which included the following contributions: B. Schäfer and L. Denecke, 'Die Brüder Grimm als Bibliothekare. Unter besonderer Berücksichtigung der Erwerbungs- und Katalogisierungspraxis während ihrer Amtszeit in der Kurfürstlichen Bibliothek zu Kassel' (16–35); J. E. Sennewald,

'Die Kunst, Naturpoesie zu sammeln. Zu den poetischen Konstruktionen der "Kinder- und Hausmärchen, gesammelt durch die Brüder Grimm"' (64–79); A. Dimitriou, C. Scheibe, and J. Stahlkopf, 'Spuren der Brüder Grimm. Handschriftliche Rückentitel in der Grimm-Bibliothek' (80–99); B. Friemel et al., 'Die Bibliothek der Brüder Grimm. Nachträge und Berichtigungen zum annotierten Verzeichnis. Zweite Folge' (100–18); L. Kawaletz and B. Friemel, 'Aus Briefen der Familie Reimer über die Brüder Grimm. Mit einer Einführung in die Beziehungen zwischen den Brüdern Grimm und Georg Reimer' (119–31); Id., 'Aus der Berliner Umwelt der Brüder Grimm', (132–67); H. Rölleke, 'Die Ehrenmitgliedschaft der Brüder Grimm in Bechsteins "alterthumsforschendem Verein". Ungedruckte Briefe und Dokumente' (168–71); and T. Erb, 'Die Revolte des Bauern Einochs. Betrachtungen zu einer von Jacob Grimm entdeckten mittellateinischen Dichtung' (186–200). Also noted: **Das deutsche Wörterbuch von Jacob und Wilhelm Grimm. Ein wissenschaftliches Symposium der Brüder Grimm-Gesellschaft e.V. aus Anlaß des 150-jährigen Jubiläums des Erscheinens der ersten Lieferung (1852) im Brüder Grimm-Museum Kassel am 25. Oktober 2002* (Schriften der Brüder Grimm-Gesellschaft, 35), Kassel, Brüder Grimm-Gesellschaft, 96 pp.; Erika Timm, **Frau holle, Frau Percht und verwandte Gestalten. 160 Jahre nach Jacob Grimm aus germanistischer Sicht betrachtet*, Stuttgart, Hirzel, ix + 370 pp.; Eugen Drewermann, **Schneewittchen, Die zwei Brüder. Grimms Märchen tiefenpsychologisch gedeutet*, DTV, 448 pp.; H. Rölleke, 'Grimms Märchen in Eduard Mörikes *Wald-Idylle*', *WW*, 53:369–72.

GÜNDERRODE, KAROLINE VON. Noted: J. Heimerl, 'Dem Tode verfallen. Die Ballade *Piedro* im Kontext des literarischen Werks der Karoline von Günderrode', *WW*, 53:401–16.

HEBEL, JOHANN PETER. Peter Grathwol, *Mutmaßungen über Johann Peter Hebel. 'Der Spaziergang an den See' als Schlüsselerzählung zu seiner Frömmigkeit*, Frankfurt, Cornelia Goethe Literaturverlag, 116 pp., presents an interesting theological discussion of H.'s poem which is read as a means to interpreting the significance of piety to the poet. G. also examines H.'s critique of academic theology and considers the notion of the text as catechism.

HEGEL, GEORG WILHELM FRIEDRICH. Noted: Evelin Kohl, **Gestalt. Untersuchungen zu einem Grundbegriff in Hegels Phänomonologie des Geistes*, Munich, Utz, 346 pp.; Hans Friedrich Fulda, **Georg Wilhelm Friedrich Hegel* (Beck'sche Reihe Denker, 565), Munich, Beck, 345 pp.

HOFFMANN, E. T. A. Birgit Röder, *A Study of the Major Novellas of E. T. A. Hoffmann*, NY, Camden House, xii + 193 pp., is a solid study which focuses on eight novellas with three key themes: madness, love, and death. The study aims to explore the relationship of the individual to ideal and reality, often expressed through the artist figure.

R. considers the impact of social factors as well as the intellectual and emotional ostracization of the artist. Considerable attention is also paid to gender relations, the feminine often found to be a source of disillusionment as an embodiment of the fractured ideal. Also with a focus on the theme of madness is Karin Preuss, *The Question of Madness in the Works of E. T. A. Hoffmann and Mary Shelley* (EH, XVIII, 107), 289 pp. In this worthwhile study, P. seeks to analyse the depiction of madness in the transition from Romanticism to Realism. She explores the depiction of the individual and the critique and subversion of social structures and mores. In so doing, the interdependency of the German 'Schauerroman' and the British Gothic novel is brought to the fore. The main focus of the study falls on *Der Sandmann* and *Frankenstein* as P. examines the two authors' approaches to scientific experimentation. Issues of style, narrative technique and context are also explored. Two studies explore H.'s relationship to different art forms: Olaf Schmidt, *'Callots fantastisch karikierte Blätter.' Intermediale Inszenierungen und romantische Kunsttheorie im Werk E. T. A. Hoffmanns* (PSQ, 181), 272 pp., discusses the relationship between image and text through H.'s integration of art and artists into his work. This is seen as part of a complex poetological programme which can be linked to the notion of *Universalpoesie* in early Romantic aesthetic theory. S. provides a chronological analysis of image-text relations in aesthetic theory from the Renaissance to the Romantic period, before focusing on H.'s 'Callot' essay, *Doge and Dogeresse* and *Prinzessin Brambilla*. Christian Mattli, *Der Tod der Primadonna. Der Mensch als Instrument im literarischen Werk E. T. A. Hoffmanns* (EH, I, 1853), 156 pp., examines the aestheticization of the feminine death trope in H.'s work, often appearing in the figure of a singer or the death of a muse. The survival of the male singer is highlighted in contrast to the death of the female as M. attempts to link H.'s treatment of his characters to contemporary notions of gender. The wider issue of music and art in H.'s work is discussed, notably through analysis of the analogy of the woman as instrument in the *Nachtstück*, *Das Sanctus*. Music also features in B. Neymeyr, 'Musikalische Mysterien. Romantische Entgrenzung und Präfiguration der Décadence in E. T. A. Hoffmanns *Rat Krespel*', *E. T. A. Hoffmann Jb.*, 11:73–103. Other contributions to the *Jb.* include J. Löffler, 'Das Handwerk der Schrift. Autorschaft und Abschrift bei Hoffmann und Arnim' (19–33); C. Lieb and A. Meteling, 'E. T. A. Hoffmann und Thomas Mann. Das Vermächtnis des "Don Juan"' (34–59); B. Besslich, 'Apokalypse 1813. E. T. A. Hoffmanns "Vision auf dem Schlachtfelde bei Dresden"' (60–72); M. M. Müller, 'Phantasmagorien und bewaffnete Blicke. Zur Funktion optischer Apparate in E. T. A. Hoffmanns *Meister Floh*' (104–21); and H. Steinecke, '"Dem humoristischen Dichter muß es freistehen ...'' Hoffmanns "Erklärung" vom Februar 1822 als poetologischer und literarischer Text' (122–33). Also noted: R. Schmidt, 'Heroes and villains in E. T. A. Hoffmann's "Ritter Glück",' *BJR*, 84:49–66; R. Vilain, 'Bringing the villains to book: Balzac and Hoffmann as antecedents of the modern detective story', *ib.*, 105–23; D. Darby, 'The unfettered eye: glimpsing modernity from E. T. A. Hoffmann's corner window', *DVJS*, 77:274–94.

HÖLDERLIN, FRIEDRICH. This year saw the publication of a major contribution to the study of H.'s life and work: *Hölderlin und der deutsche Idealismus. Dokumente und Kommentare zu Hölderlins philosophischer Entwicklung und den philosophisch-kulturellen Kontexten seiner Zeit*, ed. Christoph Jamme and Frank Völkel (Specula, 3.1–4), 4 vols, Stuttgart–Bad Cannstatt, Frommann-Holzboog, xii + 452, viii + 448, viii + 436, viii + 543 pp. This monumental study brings together documents related to H.'s life and work. These are thematized chronologically with careful commentaries, focusing on five key phases of the poet's life: his time in the Tübinger Stift (1788–93), Jena (1794–95), Frankfurt and Homburg (1796–1800), Stuttgart, returning to Homburg (1800–06), and the final years in the tower at Tübingen (1806–43). Three key philosophical constellations are identified and characterized according to location: Tübingen, Jena, and Frankfurt/Homburg. Two key influences, Kant and Rousseau, are then identified as impacting upon the period around 1800. Of central importance throughout is the interdependence and parallel development of H.'s literary and philosophical work. As well as tracing the emergence of H.'s own thought, the four volumes also aim to provide a new perspective on both H. and the period by demonstrating the close affiliation between contemporary philosophical and literary debates. In this respect, H. provides the editors with a case study which covers topics and figures as wide-ranging as Kantian philosophy, Pietism, Fichte's political thought, Spinoza, early Romanticism, Schelling, Napoleon, and Hegel, as well as H.'s relations and correspondence with lesser known, intimate acquaintances. The editors have adopted a selective approach, collating excerpts from a wide variety of relevant texts from H.'s correspondence and literary and philosophical writings, as well as a wealth of material from friends and contemporary thinkers. This study might almost overwhelm the reader with its vast array of material and detail. However, the careful structure and well-organized overview of the content provide essential guidance to a significant resource for scholars of Hölderlin and German Idealism alike. Further exploration of H.'s work in the context of his time is offered in Jochen Bertheau, *Hölderlins französische Bildung* (Heidelberger Beiträge zur deutschen Literatur, 14), Frankfurt, Lang, 203 pp. This study outlines H.'s experiences of

France and his reception of French culture, examining in particular his responses to the French Revolution and the impact of Rousseau, taking to task a number of assumed truths surrounding H. and France. B. provides a series of interpretations of individual poems and texts and includes an interesting discussion of H.'s position between Pietist and Huguenot ideals. Also concerned with H.'s position in the wider contemporary debate is Martin Jörg Schäfer, *Szenischer Materialismus. Dionysische Theatralität zwischen Hölderlin und Hegel*, Vienna, Passagen, 262 pp. Drawing on Derrida and modern discussions on performative writing, this study responds to the current questioning of cultural evaluations by examining another earlier period of upheaval, that surrounding the year 1800. S. seeks to reassess the responses of H. and Hegel to the theatrical via the figure of Dionysus, as both react to the application of Kantian concepts. The texts under scrutiny are H.'s *Empedokles* and his *Anmerkungen zu Sophokles*, and Hegel's *Phänomenologie des Geistes*.

H.'s *Hyperion* is the subject of two studies. Hansjörg Bay, *'Ohne Rückkehr.' Utopische Intention und poetischer Proceß in Hölderlins Hyperion*, Munich, Fink, 431 pp., discusses the possible presence of a specific structure for the text and reads H.'s work as a quest for unity and completeness via friendship with Alabanda, the love of Diotima, and the attempt at revolutionary renewal of Greece, all of which fail. Emphasis is placed on the cyclical process of attempt and failure in this fascinating study. Katharina Jeorgakopulos, *Die Aufgabe der Poesie. Präsenz der Stimme in Hölderlins Figur der Diotima* (Ep, 432), 255 pp., examines how H. exploits the figure of Diotima in the development of his own work. Possible affinities with modern theory are also explored, in particular in relation to Derrida. *Friedrich Hölderlin. Neue Wege der Forschung*, ed. Thomas Roberg, WBG, 328 pp., presents a collection of articles and chapters which offer a valuable overview of the often overwhelming variety of research into H.'s work over the last 25 years, including structuralist and deconstructionist readings. Areas covered include poetics, poetry, philosophy, and H.'s work as a whole. Also noted: C. Louth, 'The Frankfurt edition of Hölderlin's hymns: a review article', *MLR*, 98:898–907; C. Mackrodt, 'Haltloser Entwurf, haltlose Konstitution: die Nymphe/Mnesosyne in der Frankfurter Hölderlin-Ausgabe', *DVJS*, 77:183–96; T. Schestag, 'Vom Abgrund angefangen. Zur Frage der Gespräche. Im Hinblick auf Robert André, Gespräche von Text zu Text. Celan — Heidegger — Hölderlin', *MLN*, 118:755–70; A. Honold, *' "Schön und lieblich ist es zu vergleichen." Hölderlin und der Kalender', *JDSG*, 47:240–65.

KLEIST, HEINRICH VON. Interest in K. continues to be buoyant with a number of general studies of his life and work. Rudolf Loch,

Kleist. Eine Biographie, Göttingen, Wallstein, 540 pp., provides an extensive study with careful consideration of the critical literature, placing K.'s work in historical and biographical context. The text is well-written with many illustrations, providing a wealth of detail which offers an insight into the author's life beyond his writing. The volume is less concerned with analysis of the works than with the man himself. *A Companion to the Works of Heinrich von Kleist*, ed. Bernd Fischer, NY, Camden House, vi + 258 pp., provides a valuable introduction to K.'s work with contributions from a number of eminent scholars. Some attention is paid to K.'s works in the context of modern critical theory in J. L. Sammons, 'Jupiterists and alkmenists: *Amphitryon* as an example of how Kleist's texts read interpreters' (21–41); and J. Hermand, 'Kleist's *Penthesilea*: battleground of gendered discourses' (43–60). Issues of language and form are discussed in four contributions. Of note here is B. Theisen, 'Strange news. Kleist's novellas' (81–102), which looks at his novellas within the tradition of the genre and draws parallels with his journalistic work. Also included are A. Stephens, 'On structures in Kleist' (63–79); H. C. Seeba, 'The eye of the beholder: Kleist's visual poetics of knowledge' (103–22); and B. Greiner, 'The performative turn of the beautiful: "free play" of language and the "unspeakable person"' (123–37). K.'s responses to contemporary thought are also explored: H. J. Schneider, 'The facts of life: Kleist's challenge to Enlightenment humanism (Lessing)' (141–63); and T. Mehigan, '"Betwixt a false reason and none at all": Kleist, Hume, Kant, and the "thing in itself"' (165–88). Finally, themes and motifs are explored. S. Zantop, 'Changing color: Kleist's "Die Verlobung in St Domingo" and the discourses of miscegenation' (191–208), examines K.'s possible race politics and focuses on the symbolism and significance of skin, especially facial, colouring. Also included are H. M. Brown, 'Ripe moments and false climaxes: thematic and dramatic configurations of the theme of death in Kleist's works' (209–26), and S. Allan, '"Mein ist die Rache spricht der Herr": violence and revenge in the works of Heinrich von Kleist' (227–48). *Heinrich von Kleist. Neue Wege der Forschung*, ed. Anton Philipp Knittel and Inka Kording, WBG, 299 pp., draws together the last two decades of research on K., providing a useful overview of an arguably over-researched area.

A variety of monographs dealing with themes and genres have also appeared. Jochen Schmidt, *Heinrich von Kleist. Die Dramen und Erzählungen in ihrer Epoche*, WBG, 312 pp., provides a detailed examination of K.'s work in its historical context. S. assesses the writer's work as both a response to and a manifestation of a changing society. Each work is dealt with individually and the reader is offered an overview of K.'s own experience of historical events. This is a well-researched and insightful study. Pierre Kadi Sossou, *Römisch-Germanische Doppelgängerschaft. Eine 'palimpsestuöse' Lektüre von Kleists Hermannsschlacht* (EH, 1, 1858), 191 pp., is a fascinating study which examines K.'s text via those texts which inform and underlie it, with references to Cicero and Ovid as sources. The concept of the 'Doppelgänger' is linked to the historical and literary/mythical pre-texts which informed K.'s work. Issues of national identity and double identities are key, the latter especially in the figure of Thusnelda. Erika Berroth, *Heinrich von Kleist. Geschlecht — Erkenntnis — Wirklichkeit* (STML, 58), 144 pp., is a frank and thought-provoking reassessment of notions of gender order and its relationship to knowledge in K.'s work. B. examines the presence of the 'feminine' and the depiction of gender relations in his work, employing feminist theories as well as psychoanalytical ideas. The study focuses for the most part on *Die Marquise von O . . .* and *Der Findling*. Dieter Heimböckel, *Emphatische Unaussprechlichkeit. Sprachkritik im Werk Heinrich von Kleists. Ein Beitrag zur literarischen Sprachskepsistradition der Moderne* (Palaestra, 319), Göttingen, Vandenhoeck & Ruprecht, 383 pp., introduces K. as a forerunner of the modern challenge to notions and validity of language, a view which, the author claims, takes the entire debate back to a new genesis. H. challenges research to date as having failed to address the issue adequately. The study focuses on issues of expression and the limits of language, as well as the correlation between language and identity. It is K.'s poetic innovations which are seen to undermine accepted concepts of expression. Sybille Peters, *Heinrich von Kleist und der Gebrauch der Zeit. Von der Machart der Berliner Abendblätter* (Ep, 445), 237 pp., focuses on the making of the *BA* as a newspaper and 'Volksblatt'. The study highlights K.'s individual stance in the aesthetic and political debate of the time and points to the experimental nature of his journalism. Attention is drawn to the diverse content of the publication and the strong focus on issues of national identity. This study is a valuable contribution to the knowledge of areas once regarded as peripheral but undoubtedly crucial to appreciation of the period as a whole.

Also noted: Anett Lütteken, **Heinrich von Kleist — Eine Dichterrenaissance*, Tübingen, Niemeyer, vi + 426 pp.; **Politik, Öffentlichkeit, Moral. Kleist und die Folgen:* 1. *Frankfurter Kleist-Kolloquium 18.–19. Oktober 1996*, ed. Peter Ensberg and Hans-Jochen Marquardt (SAG, 408), 2002, 162 pp.; E. Block jr., 'Heinrich von Kleist: "On the Puppet Theater", "The Broken Jug", and tensions in the Romantic theatrical paradigm', *ERR*, 14:65–79; E. Colbey, 'Ambivalence and dialectics: Mann's *Doktor Faustus* and Kleist's "Über das Marionettentheater"', *Seminar*, 39:15–32; V. Kaiser, 'Epistemological breakdown and passionate erruptions: Kleist's *Die Verlobung in St Domingo*', *StRom*, 42:341–67.

NOVALIS. W. G. Schmidt, '". . .in weinender Entzückung": die Ästhetisierung der *joy of grief* bei Novalis', *LJb*, 44:125–45, examines what is regarded as the underestimated influence of *Ossian* on Romanticism, focusing on the paradigm of the introspective poet and the obsession with night and light. Two groups of writers are identified, those concerned with issues of authenticity and those concerned with aesthetic issues. S. focuses on N.'s adoption of the 'joy in grief' trope and pinpoints its source in *O.*, as well as in *Werther*. Intertextual references to *O.* are identified in N.'s work, in particular in connection with issues surrounding death, grief, and loneliness. F. Schmidt, 'Identität und Darstellung bei Keats und Novalis: Endymion und Hyazinth auf dem Weg zum Ideal', *LWU*, 36:3–17, examines K.'s romance and N.'s *Märchen*, highlighting similarities in theme and structure centred around the real and the ideal. S. identifies a triadic structure and uncovers a variation in philosophical approach, K. tending to notions of explicit identity, with N. favouring the concept of difference in identity. Also noted: Ralf Liedke, **Das romantische Paradigma der Chemie. Friedrich von Hardenbergs Naturphilosophie zwischen Empirie und alchemistischer Spekulation*, Paderborn, Mentis, 390 pp.; H. F. Weiss, 'Entdeckungen zu einem verschwundenen Schloß und seinen Rittergütern. Schlöben und die Familie von Hardenberg', *WW*, 53:17–35; M. Tokarzewska, *'Bewusstsein, Sprache und Individualität. Zu Novalis' Auseinandersetzung mit Fichte', *Convivium*, 2002:193–202.

RICHTER, JEAN PAUL. Brigitte Langer, *Jean Pauls Weg zur Metapher. Sein 'Buch' Leben des Quintus Fixlein* (EALS, 15), xxiii + 203 pp., promotes a comprehensive assessment of R.'s text, moving beyond previously fragmentary responses. Emphasis is placed on the discovery and invention of metaphor in R.'s work, a strategy by means of which the author acknowledges and challenges the societal changes of his time. Ulrike Hagel, *Elliptische Zeiträume des Erzählens. Jean Paul und die Aporien der Idylle* (Ep, 463), 288 pp., is a fascinating study which seeks to reveal narrative as a means to structure time, moving from the idyll to narrative texts. Particular attention is paid to the interrelation of the temporal and the perpetual. The study is divided into three sections, the first focusing on R. as narrator, the second on heroes in the idyll, and the third on the various forms of narrative time construct identified.

This year's *Jahrbuch der Jean Paul Gesellschaft* contains material from two previously unpublished texts: '"Der Poet träumt, der Leser schläft." Materialien aus Jean Pauls unveröffentlichter Satiren- und Ironiensammlung', ed. B. Sick (2–8), and '"Aus diesen Verwirrungen einen Roman zu machen." Aus den unveröffentlichten Vorarbeiten zum *Hesperus*', ed. B. Hunfeld (9–13). The *Jb.* also contains the following contributions: G. Sauder, '"Komet"(en)-Autorschaft' (14–29); S. Eickenrodt, 'Sinesische Sprachgitter: Jean Pauls Schriftbilder der anderen Welt' (30–77); H. Pfotenhauer, 'Empfindbild, Gesichterscheinung, Vision. Zur Geschichte des inneren Sehens und Jean Pauls Beitrag dazu' (78–110); M. Schmitz-Emans, 'Engel in der Krise. Zum Engelsmotiv in der romantischen Ästhetik und in Jean Pauls Roman *Der Komet*' (111–38); W. G. Schmidt, '"Zweifellicht" und "Sphärenmusik". Jean Pauls *Ossian*-Rezeption' (139–62). Also noted: Maximilian Bergengruen, **Schöne Seelen, groteske Körper. Jean Pauls ästhetische Dynamisierung der Anthropologie* (Studien zum achtzehnten Jahrhundert, 26), Hamburg, Meiner, x + 262 pp.

RUNGE, PHILIPP OTTO. Noted: R. Littlejohns, 'Philipp Otto Runge's *Tageszeiten* and their relationship to Romantic nature philosophy', *StRom*, 42:55–74.

SCHLEGEL, DOROTHEA. Noted: C. Ujma, 'Zwischen Kunst, Religion und "Avantgarde" — Dorothea Schlegels Briefe aus Rom', *Jb. der Brüder Grimm-Gesellschaft*, 9, 1999[2003]:75–90; F. C. Roberts, 'The perennial search for paradise: garden design and political critique in Dorothea Schlegel's "Florentin"', *GQ*, 75, 2002:265–81.

SCHLEGEL, FRIEDRICH. Astrid Keiner, *Hieroglyphenromantik. Zur Genese und Destruktion eines Bilderschriftmodells und zu seiner Überforderung in Friedrich Schlegels Spätphilosophie* (Ep, 459), 238 pp., explores ancient, Enlightenment, and Romantic responses to hieroglyphics before taking a detailed look at their role in F. S.'s later philosophy, in particular his 'Hieroglyphenlied', and specifically Christian interpretation. A. Erlinghagen, 'Poetica in nuce. Friedrich Schlegels poetologisches Vermächtnis: die Elegie *Herkules Musagetis*. Historisch-kritische Ausgabe / editorischer und exegetischer Kommentar', *Euphorion*, 97:193–234, provides a detailed analysis of S.'s poem, the first critical account of this previously unknown elegy. Also noted: S. Matuschek, 'Winckelmänner der Poesie. Herders und Friedrich Schlegels Anknüpfung an die *Geschichte der Kunst der Altertums*', *DVJS*, 77:548–63; J. Gulddal, *'Das "bessere" und das "gerade so gut" Verstehen. Friedrich Schlegels hermeneutischer Doppelblick', *TeK*, 25.1–2:65–94.

SCHOPENHAUER, ARTHUR. L. Pikulik, 'Schopenhauer und die Romantik', *Aurora*, 62 2002:95–111, considers the links between S. and the Romantic school. This fascinating essay identifies affinities even though S. distanced himself from his contemporaries. However, P. also pinpoints key differences. The areas under consideration are experience and interpretation of the world, anthropology and psychology, and art and the artist.

SCHOPENHAUER, JOHANNA. Noted: Carola Stern, **'Alles, was ich in der Welt verlange.' Das Leben der Johanna Schopenhauer*, Cologne, Kiepenheuer & Witsch, 320 pp.

TIECK, LUDWIG. *Ludwig Tieck. Märchen aus dem 'Phantasus'*, ed. Walter Münz, Stuttgart, Reclam, 351 pp., presents the prose elements of T.'s collection, preserving also the relevant 'Zwischengespräche', an approach which arguably leads to further fragmentation. The volume benefits, however, from a substantial concluding essay in which the editor examines T.'s sources and discusses the reception of his work. Also noted: W. Schmitz and J. Strobel, 'Teleskop und Briefverkehr. Ein ungedruckter Brief Ludwig Tiecks an Wilhelm Heinrich Wackenroder', *Aurora*, 62, 2002: 127–42.

WACKENRODER, WILHELM HEINRICH. B. Tautz, 'Wackenroder's "Ein wunderbares morgenländisches Mährchen von einem nackten Heiligen": autopoiesis of world, rhetoric of the Orient', *MDLK*, 95: 59–75, examines the tale in the context of other works by W. The 'self-proclaimed' rhetoric of the Orient is not only linked to autopoiesis but also relies on a response to the Enlightenment tradition which perceived Asia as a text and presumed a unity of the world. W.'s use of visuality and aurality mark his tale as different, as images are erased through listening. The 'sensual field' defines the autopoietic act which emerges as a new universal ideal of Romanticism.

LITERATURE, 1830–1880

By Barbara Burns, *Lecturer in German, University of Strathclyde*

1. General

reference works and general studies. *Philosophy and German Literature, 1700–1990*, ed. Nicholas Saul, CUP, 2002, xii + 324 pp., includes a substantial chapter on our period: J. Walker, 'Two realisms: German literature and philosophy 1830–1890' (102–49), refers to a broad range of 19th-c. writers and will provide students with a valuable contextualized overview of the developments in German thought which lay behind the major works of literary realism.

themes. Uwe Hebekus, *Klios Medien: Die Geschichtskultur des 19. Jahrhunderts in der historistischen Historie und bei Theodor Fontane*, Tübingen, Niemeyer, ix + 313 pp., is a Constance dissertation which includes discussion of the perception of history in Fontane's texts on the Franco-German war of 1870–71 and in the novels *Die Poggenpuhls* and *Der Stechlin*. Bettina Plett, *Problematische Naturen? Held und Heroismus im realistischen Erzählen*, Paderborn–Munich, Schöningh, 2002, 450 pp., is a Cologne Habil.-Schrift with analysis of Spielhagen (*Problematische Naturen*, *Durch Nacht zu Licht*, *In Reih und Glied*), Stifter (*Witiko*), Meyer (*Jürg Jenatsch*), Vischer (*Auch einer*) and Raabe (*Alte Nester*, *Das Odfeld*, *Hastenbeck*). Tobias Bulang, *Barbarossa im Reich der Poesie: Verhandlungen von Kunst und Historismus bei Arnim, Grabbe, Stifter und auf dem Kyffhäuser*, Frankfurt–Berlin, Lang, 349 pp., is a dissertation from the Techn. Univ. Dresden. *Vom Salon zur Barrikade. Frauen der Heine-Zeit*, ed. Irina Hundt, Stuttgart–Weimar, Metzler, 2002, 460 pp. Bernd Stiegler, *Philologie des Auges. Die photographische Entdeckung der Welt im 19. Jahrhundert*, Munich, Fink, 2001, 472 pp., is a Mannheim Habil.-Schrift examining the interaction between 19th-c. photography, aesthetics, and literature; it includes reference to Heyse, Raabe, Hackländer, and Stifter. Stefan Neuhaus, *Literatur und nationale Einheit in Deutschland*, Tübingen–Basle, Francke, 2002, 587 pp., is a Bamberg Habil.-Schrift with some coverage of 19th-c. texts. Klaus R. Scherpe, *Stadt, Krieg, Fremde: Literatur und Kultur nach den Katastrophen*, Tübingen–Basle, Francke, 2002, xviii + 353 pp., has material on Fontane. Martina Rebmann, **'Das Lied, das du mir jüngst gesungen . . .' Studien zum Sololied in der ersten Hälfte des 19. Jahrhunderts in Württemberg. Quellen — Funktion — Analyse*, Frankfurt–Berlin, Lang, 2002, 473 pp., is a Tübingen dissertation. **Geistliches Lied und Kirchenlied im 19. Jahrhundert: theologische, musikologische und literaturwissenschaftliche Aspekte*, ed. Irmgard Scheitler, Tübingen–Basle, Francke, 2000, 254 pp.

G. Niggl, 'Die deutsche Autobiographie in der Restaurationszeit', *Immermann-Jb.*, 4: 13–22. H. Steinhorst, 'Aspekte weiblichen autobiographischen Schreibens im frühen 19. Jahrhundert', *ib.*, 85–97. R. Kolk, ' "Rollenaustheilungen." Zur Darstellung von Lebensläufen bei den Grimms, Heine und Gutzkow', *ib.*, 117–30. H. G. von Arburg, 'Archäodermatologie der Moderne. Zur Theoriegeschichte der Tätowierung in der Architektur und Literatur zwischen 1830 und 1930', *DVLG*, 77: 407–45. K. Belgum, 'Tracking the liberal hero in the nineteenth century', pp. 15–34 of *Heroes and Heroism in German Culture. Essays in Honour of Jost Hermand, April 2000*, ed. Stephen Brockmann and James Steakley, Amsterdam, Rodopi, 2001, 259 pp. S. Elspass, 'Sprache und Geschlecht in Privatbriefen "einfacher Leute" des 19. Jahrhunderts', pp. 89–108 of *Vertextungsstrategien und Sprachmittelwahl in Texten von Frauen. Internationale Fachtagung, Dresden 10.–12.9.2001*, ed. Gisela Brandt, Stuttgart, Heinz, 2002, 194 pp. C. Schuppenhauer, " ' "Scheet die doot!" seggt Buurlala . . ." Anmerkungen zur Tradition niederdeutscher Kriegsdichtung', pp. 41–74 of *Niederdeutsch. Sprache und Literatur der Region*, ed. Ursula Föllner, Frankfurt–Berlin, Lang, 2001, 198 pp. J. Voss, ' "Sklaverei im Ameisenstaat." Die darwinistische Tiergeschichte als gattungstheoretischer Problemfall in *Das Ausland*', *BHGLL*, 4, 2001: 101–16. M. Wagner, 'Lebensgefühl des Biedermeier — wie es Künstler bezeugen', Dürhammer, *Witz*, 11–30.

LYRIC. *Poetry Project: Irish Germanists Interpret German Verse*, Oxford–Berne, Lang, 276 pp., contains 40 interpretations of German poems from 1663 to 1991. The following are relevant to this section: J. Fischer, 'August Heinrich Hoffmann von Fallersleben, "Lied der Deutschen" (1841)' (59–66); K.-B. Bödeker, 'Annette von Droste-Hülshoff, "Am Turme" (1841/42)' (67–71); S. H. Harris, 'Annette von Droste-Hülshoff, "Der Knabe im Moor" (1842)' (73–79); J. Fischer, 'Georg Weerth, "Deutscher und Ire" (ca. 1845/46)' (81–87); E. Bourke, 'Heinrich Heine, "Die schlesischen Weber" (1847)' (89–94); Id., 'Heinrich Heine, "Jammertal" (1857)' (95–101); F. Krobb, 'Friederike Kempner, "Drei Schlagworte" (1880)' (103–07); E. Bourke, 'Theodor Fontane, "Die Brück' am Tay" (1880)' (109–16). R. Berbig, 'Die Gelegenheit im Gelegenheitsgedicht des 19. Jahrhunderts', *BHGLL*, 4, 2001: 7–24. H. P. Althaus, ' "In jüdischer Mundart." Lyrikparodien des 19. Jahrhunderts zwischen Witz und Diffamierung', *Akten* (Wien), IX, 223–28.

NARRATIVE PROSE. Hutchinson, *Landmarks*, continues a useful series of brief studies on key literary texts and contains the following within our period: A. Bunyan, 'Heine, *Die Harzreise*' (61–77); E. Swales, 'Büchner, *Lenz*' (79–94); M. Minden, 'Grillparzer, *Der arme Spielmann*' (95–110); J. Guthrie, 'Droste-Hülshoff, *Die Judenbuche*'

(111–24); N. Saul, 'Keller, *Romeo und Julia auf dem Dorfe*' (125–40). *Kunstautonomie und literarischer Markt: Konstellationen des Poetischen Realismus*, ed. Heinrich Detering and Gerd Eversberg, Berlin, Schmidt, 199 pp., addresses the complex relationship between artistic demands and market conditions and contains the following: S. S. Tschopp, 'Kunst und Volk. Robert Eduard Prutz' und Gottfried Kellers Konzept einer zugleich ästhetischen und populären Literatur' (13–30); S. P. Scheichl, 'Selbstaussagen von Autoren des Realismus. Karl Emil Franzos' Sammlung *Die Geschichte des Erstlingswerks* (1894)' (31–46); R. Helmstetter, '"Kunst nur für Künstler" und Literatur fürs Familienblatt. Nietzsche und die Poetischen Realisten (Storm, Raabe, Fontane)' (47–63); R. Fasold, 'Romantische Kunstautonomie versus Realismuskonzept um 1864. Über die Bedeutung von Storms Märchen für seine realistische Poetik' (65–81); J. L. Sammons, 'Zu den Erzählungen Theodor Fontanes und Friedrich Spielhagens anlässlich des Ardenne-Skandals: Fragen an das Kanonisierungswesen' (83–95); H. Denkler, 'Die Verwandlung des Marktgängigen ins Marktwidrige: Raabe schreibt Jensen um' (97–109); A.-B. Gerecke, 'Fontanes *Unwiederbringlich*: das Ende des historischen Romans?' (111–22); J. Royer, 'Erziehung zur Zweisamkeit in Storms *Waldwinkel* und Raabes *Stopfkuchen*' (123–35); P. Goldammer, 'Halligfahrt und Mondschein. Storms und Raabes Reaktionen auf die Gründung des deutschen Reiches' (137–44); D. Jackson, 'Wilhelm Raabes Reise in das Mondgebirge. Politische Tendenz und verfehlte Publikumswirksamkeit am Beispiel des Romans *Abu Telfan*' (145–70).

Gunter H. Hertling, *Bleibende Lebensinhalte. Essays zu Adalbert Stifter und Gottfried Keller*, Berne–Berlin, Lang, 240 pp., brings together six essays on Stifter, previously published between 1967 and 1985, and one new essay on Keller's Märchen *Spiegel, das Kätzchen*. The discussions of S. cover the *Studien*, *Abdias*, *Turmalin*, and *Der beschriebene Tännling* and provide close readings of the texts in a traditional stlye. O. Jahraus, 'Unrealistisches Erzählen und die Macht des Erzählers. Zum Zusammenhang von Realitätskonzeption und Erzählinstanz im Realismus am Beispiel zweier Novellen von Raabe und Meyer', *ZDP*, 122:218–36, has analysis of Raabe's *Zum wilden Mann* and C. F. Meyer's *Die Hochzeit des Mönchs*. E. Dangel-Pelloquin, 'Im Namen des Vaters. Romaneingänge bei Stifter und Keller', *ib.*, 526–43. M. Andermatt, 'Konfessionalität, Identität, Differenz. Zum historischen Erzählen von Conrad Ferdinand Meyer und Gottfried Keller', *IASL*, 27, 2002:32–53. Id., 'Historisches Erzählen und der Kulturkampf im 19. Jahrhundert. Zur Konstruktion von konfessioneller Differenz bei Conrad Ferdinand Meyer und Gottfried Keller', *Akten* (Wien), IX,

375–81. D. Göttsche, 'Kanonrevision und Gattungsgeschichtsschreibung am Beispiel des Zeitromans im 19. Jahrhundert', *ib.*, VIII, 119–29.

DRAMA. Alan Menhennet, *The Historical Experience in German Drama: From Gryphius to Brecht*, Rochester, NY–Woodbridge, Camden House, 186 pp., is a scholarly investigation of plays that are historical not only in terms of the source of the subject matter, but also in that they create a dramatic experience that is both historical and political. The study has a general introduction outlining the aesthetic context and includes two chapters of relevance to our period: 'The emergence of Austria: Franz Grillparzer' (99–123), and '"Non-Austrian" historical drama: C. F. Hebbel' (124–48). The analysis, which takes account of literary history, the philosophy of history and German history, will be appreciated more by academics than by undergraduates for whom the scope and pitch may prove rather challenging. W. C. Reeve, 'Kleist, Büchner, Grillparzer: three dramatists' archetypal representations of the body', *ABNG*, 55:393–407.

MOVEMENTS AND PERIODS. The ongoing wave of interest in the Vor- and Nachmärz is evidenced by the significant number of volumes of collected essays that have appeared this year. *Formen der Wirklichkeitserfassung nach 1848. Deutsche Literatur und Kultur vom Nachmärz bis zur Gründerzeit in europäischer Perspektive* 1, ed. Helmut Koopmann and Michael Perraudin, Bielefeld, Aisthesis, 276 pp., contains: M. Perraudin, 'Sinn und Sinnlichkeit im deutschen Vor- und Nachmärz' (13–42); H. Lengauer, 'Der Dichter, der Revolutionär und das Soziale im Übergang von Vormärz zum Nachmärz. Zu Sigmund Engländer' (43–70); I. Hilton, 'Reaction to 1848 in England' (71–92); J. Rignall, 'From revolutionary enthusiasm to realism. A. H. Clough's and George Eliot's responses to the revolutions of 1848' (93–103); B. Anton, 'Jane Francesca Elgee — "Speranza" — Lady Wilde — "Mother of Oscar": before and after the revolution' (105–16); W. Mercer, 'The failure of French feminism in 1848 and its reflections in women's writing 1848–1860' (117–28); L. Schneider, 'Symbol eines Volkes oder Darstellung einer Pathologie? Friedrich Theodor Vischer und Robert Zimmermann zu Shakespeares *Hamlet*' (129–46); A. Wirsching, 'Liberale Historiker im Nachmärz: Georg Gottfried Gervinus und Heinrich von Sybel' (147–65); W. Wülfing, '"Luft ist kein leerer Wahn." Theodor Fontane und die Berliner Luft als Metapher für das politisch-gesellschaftliche Klima im nachmärzlichen Preußen; unter besonderer Berücksichtigung des Briefwechsels mit Theodor Storm im Jahre 1853' (167–88); C. Haug, '"Populäres auch populär vertreiben [. . .]" — Karl Gutzkows Vorschläge zur Reform des Buchhandels und zur Beschleunigung des Buchabsatzes. Ein Beitrag zur Geschichte der Buchdistribution und Buchwerbung im 19. Jahrhundert' (189–215); H. Ridley, '"Der Halbbruder des Vormärz": Friedrich Spielhagen. Reflexionen zu den Kontinuitäten seines Werkes' (217–31); L. Schneider, 'Die Verabschiedung des idealistischen Realismus. Friedrich Spielhagens Romanpoetik und ihre Kritiker' (233–44); H. Lengauer, 'Spielplatz für Helden. Thomas Carlyle in der deutschen Literatur' (245–70). *Kulturkritik, Erinnerungskunst und Utopie nach 1848. Deutsche Literatur und Kultur vom Nachmärz bis zur Gründerzeit in europäischer Perspektive* II, ed. Anita Bunyan and Helmut Koopmann, Bielefeld, Aisthesis, 356 pp., has the following within our period: H. Koopmann, 'Kulturmodelle in Romanform' (41–56); W. Wülfing, 'Wider die "Wächter des großen geschichtlichen Welt-Harem": zu Nietzsches "vormärzlicher" Kritik am Ungang mit der "Historie"' (57–82); H. Ridley, 'Nietzsche and Wienbarg. A consideration of parallels between Nietzsche and the Young Germans' (83–104); Id., 'Das Fehlen eines Zentrums — noch einmal Natur / Kultur' (105–19); J. Rignall, 'Nietzsche's *Vom Nutzen und Nachteil der Historie für das Leben* and English fiction in the later nineteenth century' (121–31); J. Eder, 'Schopenhauer-Rezeption nach 1848' (133–48); L. Schneider, 'Die Gründung der Universität Straßburg aus dem Geiste des Realismus' (149–63); E. Sagarra, '"Entfamter Jesuwiter!" Zur Dämonisierung der Jesuiten in der Literatur des Vor- und Nachmärz bzw. der Gründerzeit' (165–82); A. Bunyan, 'Cultural criticism and anti-semitism: the "Berliner Antisemitismusstreit" of 1897' (183–200); H. Koopmann, 'Eduard Mörike: Erinnerungskunst und Utopie' (229–48); H. Brandes, 'Utopische Momente in der Memoirenliteratur der Malwida von Meysenbug' (295–307).

Deutsch-französischer Ideentransfer im Vormärz, ed. Gerhard Höhn and Bernd Füllner (Forum Vormärz Forschung, 8), Bielefeld, Aisthesis, 2002, 486 pp., contains: G. Höhn, 'Vormärz: Sternstunde des deutsch-französischen Ideentransfers. Einleitung' (19–47); J. A. Kruse, 'Deutsch-französische Erfahrungen und/oder Erfindungen. Heines Besucher in Paris von 1831 bis 1848' (51–78); I. Rippmann, '"Aimer dieu et Lisette." Ludwig Börnes europäische Vision' (79–114); A.-R. Meyer, 'Jeune France und Junges Deutschland' (115–40); M. Podewski, 'Das Subjekt zwischen zwei Nationen. Figurationen von Interkulturalität in Heinrich Heines *Über die französische Bühne*' (141–58); B. Kortländer, '"Diesseits und jenseits des Rheins." Das Bild des Rheins in Deutschland und Frankreich' (159–80); I. Fellrath, 'Vielschreiberin und Vermittlerin deutscher Klassiker: die Baronin Carlowitz in Paris in den Jahren 1830 bis 1850' (181–207); M. Werner, 'Deutsch-französische Verflechtungen im Pariser Musikleben der Julimonarchie' (211–27); E. Décultot, 'Die französische Rezeption deutscher Ästhetik, 1830–1848'

(229–48); G. Höhn, '"Wahlverwandtschaften." Programme einer deutsch-französischen Allianz von Heine bis Ruge und Marx' (251–86); M. Espagne, 'Von der Philologie zur Naturphilosophie. Victor Cousins deutscher Bekanntenkreis' (287–310); J. Nickel, '"... um den Cadaver einen kurzen teutschen Rock." Anmerkungen zum Nachleben des Saint-Simonismus in Deutschland' (311–31); M. Hundt, 'Junghegelianer in Paris' (333–51); P. Régnier, 'Références et interférences allemandes à l'intérieur du saint-simonisme avant 1848' (353–70); B. Füllner, 'Mund: *gewöhnlich*, Gesichtsfarbe: *gesund*. Zwei Reisepässe Georg Weerths in Moskau' (373–77).

1848 und das Versprechen der Moderne, ed. Jürgen Fohrmann and Helmut J. Schneider, Würzburg, Königshausen & Neumann, 191 pp., contains, after the editors' introduction (7–14); R. Kolk, '"Ja, begeisternd ist der Anblick aufstrebender Jünglinge." Das Versprechen der Jugend zwischen Vormärz und Moderne' (15–32); K. Stüssel, 'Punkt, Punkt, Komma, Strich ... — Revolution(en) und die Geschichte von "Gegenwartsliteratur"' (33–48); N. Oellers, 'Dichter in der Paulskirche' (49–63); V. Kaiser, 'Karl Marx: Darstellung und Kritik als Versprechen zur Moderne' (65–84); F. Breithaupt, 'Homo Oeconomicus (Junges Deutschland, Psychologie, Keller und Freytag)' (85–112); J. Fohrmann, 'Die Erfindung des Intellektuellen' (113–27); K. S. Calhoon, 'The moon, the mail, and the province of German literature' (129–46); B. Fischer, 'Jüdische Emanzipation und deutsche Nation: von Mendelssohn zu Auerbach' (147–64); J. Grossmann, '"Die Beherrschung der Sprache": Funktionen des Jiddischen in der deutschen Kultur von Heine bis Frenzel' (165–78); B. Hahn, 'Prekäre Kontinuitäten — oder vom Ort der "Frau"' (179–91).

A Companion to German Realism, 1848–1900, ed. Todd Kontje, Rochester, NY–Woodbridge, Camden House, 2002, vi + 412 pp., contains: T. Kontje, 'Introduction: reawakening German Realism' (1–28); R. C. Holub, 'Adalbert Stifter's *Brigitta*, or the lesson of Realism' (29–51); B. O. Peterson, 'Mühlbach, Ranke, and the truth of historical fiction' (53–84); L. Tatlock, '"In the heart of the heart of the country": regional histories as national history in Gustav Freytag's *Die Ahnen* (1872–80)' (85–108); T. C. Fox, 'A woman's post: gender and nation in historical fiction by Louise von François' (109–31); J. L. Sammons, 'Friedrich Spielhagen: the demon of theory and the decline of reputation' (133–57); J. Pizer, 'Wilhelm Raabe and the German colonial experience' (159–81); H. J. Rindisbacher, 'From national task to individual pursuit: the poetics of work in Freytag, Stifter, and Raabe' (183–221); I. S. Di Maio, 'Das Republikanische, das Demokratische, das Pantheistische: Jewish identity in Berthold Auerbach's novels' (223–57); K. Belgum, 'E. Marlitt: narratives of virtuous desire' (259–82); N. Berman, 'The appeal of Karl May in the Wilhelmine empire: emigration, modernization, and the need for heroes' (283–305); R. Tobin, 'Making way for the third sex: liberal and antiliberal impulses in Mann's portrayal of male-male desire in his early short fiction' (307–38); R. A. Berman, '*Effi Briest* and the end of Realism' (339–64). **Wirkungsgeschichte als Kulturgeschichte. Viktor von Andrian-Werburgs Rezeption im Vormärz. Eine Dokumentation. Mit Einleitung, Kommentar und einer Neuausgabe von 'Österreich und dessen Zukunft (1843)'*, ed. Madeleine Rietra, Amsterdam, Rodopi, 2001, 356 pp. W. Lukas, '"Entzauberter Liebeszauber." Transformation eines romantischen Erzählmodells an der Schwelle zum Realismus', *Fest. Wünsch*, 137–66, examines Franz von Gaudy and Hermann Kurz. H. Aust, 'Trilaterale Positionen in der Literatur des Realismus', Dethloff, *Realismen*, 391–415. A. Böhn, '"Zwischen Klassik / Romantik und Realismus." Eine notorisch "schwierige" Epoche und neue Ansätze zu ihrer Bestimmung', *Akten* (Wien), VI, 87–92. M. Fauser, 'Literatur des Historismus. Ein Epochenbegriff in der Lyrik des 19. Jahrhunderts', *ib.*, 93–101. G. Butzer, 'Epochen als Problemkonstellationen. Zur deutsch-österreichischen Realismus-Diskussion im 19. und frühen 20. Jahrhundert', *ib.*, 103–08.

LITERARY LIFE, JOURNALS, AND SOCIETIES. P. Wruck, 'Gelegenheitsdichtung und literarische Geselligkeit. Das Beispiel der Berliner *Mittwochsgesellschaft* und des *Tunnel über der Spree* und ihrer Liederbücher. Im Anhang Moritz Saphir: "Der Gelegenheitsdichter"', *BHGLL*, 4, 2001:36–59. G. Jelitto-Piechulik, '"Heil, Schweizer, Euch und Dank!" Der Schlesier Theodor Opitz als Chefredakteur der polnischen Exilschrift *Der weiße Adler*', Rudolph, *Polenbilder*, 195–223. W. Bunzel, 'Politische Lyrik in Musenalmanachen des Vormärz. Ein Beitrag zur Gattungs- und Mediengeschichte der dreißiger und vierziger Jahre des 19. Jahrhunderts', *Rückert-Studien*, 13, 2001:9–37. J. A. Kruse, '"...weil die Musen nie in Prosa sprechen": Almanache und Taschenbücher aus dem Heine-Kontext', *ib.*, 53–74. T. Stamm-Kuhlmann, 'Zeitschriften und Almanache als Mittel der Netzwerkbildung. Eine Projektskizze', *ib.*, 139–55. P. S. Ulrich, 'Pankratius Brüllers Vermächtnis. Der Souffleur und seine Theateralmanache und -journale', *ib.*, 157–81. K. Hack, 'Verzeichnis der Illustrationen in den Almanachen und Taschenbüchern der Bibliothek Otto Schäfer 1810–1850. I: Aglaja — Novellenkranz', *ib.*, 183–244. M. Hirai, 'Das deutsche Pressewesen nach der Märzrevolution (2) — Das Verlagswesen zwischen 1848 und 1871', *DB*, 44, 2000:111–28, is in Japanese with a German summary.

REGIONAL LITERATURE. Primus-Heinz Kucher, *Ungleichzeitige / verspätete Moderne: Prosaformen in der österreichischen Literatur 1820–1880*,

Tübingen–Basle, Francke, 2002, x + 464 pp., is a valuable investigation which engages in some detail with the socio-political background to Austrian literature in this period and traces literary influences from elsewhere in Europe. A broad range of authors is covered in three main sections: 'Roman- und Erzählprosa im literatursoziologischen Kontext in der Restaurationszeit' (17–158), 'Reiseprosa, pikturale Prosa, Genreskizzen und ihr Beitrag zur Ausbildung der Romanprosa' (159–272), and 'Historischer Roman — Zeitroman — Gesellschaftsroman: europäische Modelle und österreichische Anlaüfe' (273–428). *Geistiges Preußen — Preußischer Geist,* ed. Gabriele Hundrieser and Hans-Georg Pott, Bielefeld, Aisthesis, 217 pp., contains: W. Engel, 'Geistiges Preußen — Preußischer Geist. Zur Einführung' (7–11); H. Hecker, 'Preußen — Staat der Grenzen. Ein Versuch über Voraussetzungen und Wirkungen staatsbedingter Tugenden' (13–25); T. Namowicz, 'Berlin versus Weimar. Zu einem Phänomen deutscher Kulturgeschichte' (27–43); W. Zientara, 'Reiseberichte über Preußen und Polen' (45–59); Y.-P. Alefeld, 'Die Souveränität des Geistes und die Souveränität der Macht — Voltaire und Friedrich der Große' (61–82); M. Rohrwasser, 'Lessings Verhältnis zu Preußen' (83–106); A. Kusborska, 'Literatur und Deutsche im Werk von Donelaitis und Vydunas' (107–19); R. Hartmann, 'Willibald Alexis — ein dichterischer Biograph Preußens. Geschichtskonstruktionen auf märkischem Sand' (121–34); H. Orlowski, 'Die Geburtsstunde der "ost-preußischen" Literatur' (135–50); H.-G. Pott, 'Fontane und Preußen' (151–68). *Literature in Vienna at the Turn of the Centuries. Continuities and Discontinuities around 1900 and 2000*, ed. Ernst Grabovszki and James Hardin, Rochester, NY–Woodbridge, Camden House, viii + 232 pp., has brief references to a number of writers from our period including Ebner-Eschenbach, Engels, Nestroy, Nietzsche, Stifter, and Wagner.

2. Individual Authors

ALEXIS. Thierry Carpent, **W. A., intellectuel du 'juste milieu'. Histoire, droit et politique dans l'Allemagne du XIXe siècle,* pref. Bernard Cottret, Berne–Berlin, Lang, 2002, xvi + 351 pp., is a Nancy dissertation. B. Balzer, 'Realität und Geschichte bei Alexis, Freytag und Fontane', Dethloff, *Realismen*, 81–98.

BAUERNFELD, EDUARD VON. C. Menger, 'Biedermann und Brandstifter. Der erfolgreichste Wiener Theaterautor des 19. Jahrhunderts E. v. B.', Dürhammer, *Witz*, 49–70.

BECKER, NIKOLAUS. G. van Gemert, 'Frei und deutsch. N. B. und die Tradition der politischen Rheindichtung', pp. 185–202 of *Wessen*

Strom? Ansichten vom Rhein, ed. Leopold Decloedt and Peter Delvaux, Amsterdam, Rodopi, 2001, 229 pp.

BÖRNE, LUDWIG. Christa Walz, **Jeanette Wohl und L. B.: Dokumentation und Analyse des Briefwechsels*, Frankfurt–NY, Campus, 2001, 290 pp. U. Stuhr, '". . .wer mit dem Herzen spricht ist allen gegen verständlich . . .": L. Bs publizistisches Programm', *CEtGer*, 42, 2002 : 59–67.

BÜCHNER. *G. B., 'Leonce und Lena'*, ed. Burghard Dedner and Thomas Michael Mayer (UB, 18248), 88 pp. Gerald Funk, *Erläuterungen und Dokumente: G. B., 'Dantons Tod'* (UB, 16034), 2002, 208 pp. Helmut Müller-Sievers, *Desorientierung: Anatomie und Dichtung bei G. B.*, Göttingen, Wallstein, 199 pp., appears in the series 'Wissenschaftsgeschichte' which is concerned with bridging the gap between science and the arts, and is a sophisticated study on the problem of orientation in B.'s work. Three 'concentrically structured' chapters focus on the relationship between spacial and philosophical orientation in the thought of Kant, on B.'s scientific work, the anatomical thesis *Mémoire sur le système nerveux du barbeau*, and finally on B.'s literary achievement. Arguing that B.'s use of unmarked quotations is not a rhetorical device, but a 'Faktum der Sprache', and that it represents his most revolutionary contribution to literature, M.-S. seeks to demonstrate the significance of the 'zitathaften Entankerung und Entortung der Sprache' as a key stage in the development of modern prose. Jean-Louis Besson, **Le Théâtre de G. B. Un jeu de masques*, Belfort, Circé, 2002, 316 pp. V. C. Dörr, '"Melancholische Schweinsohren" und "schändlichste Verwirrung". Zu G. Bs "Lustspiel" *Leonce und Lena*', *DVLG*, 77 : 380–406. R. Taylor, 'B.'s critique of Platonism in *Dantons Tod*', *Neophilologus*, 88 : 281–97. J. Schwann, 'Analoge Intentionalitätsstrukturen: Bs, Baudelaires und Zolas Teilhabe an einem ästhetischen Diskurskontinuum', *Euphorion*, 97 : 73–83. A. Burckhardt, 'Politische Sprache in der Literatur — Am Beispiel G. Bs', *Muttersprache*, 112, 2002 : 387–407. F. Cercignani, '*Leonce und Lena* e il teatrino del mondo', Cercignani, *Wieland*, 95–115. A. Härter, 'Der Untergang des Redners. Das Dementi der Rhetorik in Bs Drama *Dantons Tod*', *Rhetorik*, 21, 2002 : 84–101. R. Köhnen, 'Kulturelle Codes in Bild und Text. G. Bs *Dantons Tod* im Spiegel der Malerei', *LU*, 2, 2001 : 211–31. K. Sanada, 'Der abwesende Andere. G. Bs *Lenz* im Licht von Descartes und Jacobi', *Fest. Hirao*, 431–48. I. Waragai, 'Die Funktion des pietistischen Sprachgebrauchs in Bs *Lenz*', *ib.*, 421–30. J. Schröder, 'Restaurationszeit — Komödienzeit — Narrenzeit. G. B. als "enfant du siècle" ', *Brummack Vol.*, 259–73.

BURCKHARDT. L. A. Burckhardt, 'Das Bild der Griechen in J. Bs *Griechischer Culturgeschichte*', Aurnhammer, *Antike*, 113–34. Z. Moros,

'Kultur als ständige Potenz der Menschheit in J. Bs *Weltgeschichtlichen Betrachtungen*', *Studniem*, 24, 2002: 279–90.

BUSCH. A warm welcome will be extended to the first truly critical edition of the pictorial series: *Die Bildergeschichten*, Historisch-kritische Gesamtausgabe im Auftrag der W.-B.-Gesellschaft, ed. Herwig Guratzsch and Hans Joachim Neyer, comp. Hans Ries, Hanover, Schlütersche, 2002, 3 vols, Vol. 1, *Frühwerk*, xvi + 8 + 1819 pp., ends with *Schnurrdiburr* (1868/69); vol. 2, *Reifezeit*, viii + 9–24 + 1729 pp., covers the years 1868–77; vol. 3, *Spätwerk*, viii + 25–48 + 1889 pp., goes up to *Maler Klecksel* (1884) and includes *Hernach* (1892–94) and *Inedita* (1878–95). Frank Pietzcker, *Symbol und Wirklichkeit im Werk W. Bs. Die versteckten Aussagen seiner Bildergeschichten*, Frankfurt–Berlin, Lang, 2002, 174 pp. D. Poncin, 'W. B. ou la "canonisation" d'un humoriste', *EG*, 58: 467–73. D. Horvat, 'Zur Rezeption W. Bs in Kroatien', *ZGB*, 11, 2002: 157–67.

DAHN, FELIX. H.-R. Schwab, 'Helden, hoffnungslos. F. Ds *Ein Kampf um Rom* als gründerzeitliche Schicksalstragödie', *WW*, 51, 2001: 211–34.

DROSTE-HÜLSHOFF. *A. v. D.-H., Liebesgedichte*, ed. Werner Fritsch, Frankfurt–Leipzig, Insel, 126 pp. *A. v. D.-H., Darf nur heimlich lösen mein Haar: ein Lesebuch*, ed. Dieter Borchmeyer, DTV, 254 pp. Martina Ölke, **'Heimweh' und 'Sehnsucht in die Ferne'. Entwürfe von 'Heimat' und 'Fremde' in der westfälischen und orientalischen Lyrik und Prosa A. v. D.-Hs*, St. Ingbert, Röhrig, 2002, 266 pp., is a Freiburg dissertation. L. Kalago, 'Das Gedicht "Der kranke Aar" von A. v. D.-H. in der Vertonung der Autorin. Zum Dialog zwischen sprachlichen und musikalischen Strukturen', *Studniem*, 24, 2002: 131–63. G. Bonheim, 'Von der Würde der Lebenden und der Toten. A. v. D.-Hs *Die Judenbuche*', *JFDH*, 2002: 212–39. W. Woesler, '"Das Eselein." Interpretation eines D.-Gedichtes', *ib.*, 367–80. W. Gössmann, '*Die Judenbuche* — zum dritten Mal neu angeeignet', *Fest. Windfuhr*, 183–98.

EBNER-ESCHENBACH. P. C. Pfeiffer, 'Im Kanon und um den Kanon herum: M. v. E.-E.', *Akten* (Wien), VIII, 113–18.

FONTANE. Theodor Pelster, *T. F., 'Effi Briest'* (UB, Lektüreschlüssel für Schüler, 15327), 85 pp. *T. F., 'Unwiederbringlich': Roman*, ed. Christine Hehle, Berlin, Aufbau (vol. 13 of *Das erzählerische Werk*), 514 pp. *T. F., Meine Kinderjahre: autobiographischer Roman*, Düsseldorf–Zurich, Artemis & Winkler, 217 pp., has a 'Nachwort' by Rüdiger Görner. Isabel Nottinger, *Fs Fin de Siècle: Motive der Dekadenz in 'L'Adultera', 'Cécile' und 'Der Stechlin'*, Würzburg, Königshausen & Neumann, 234 pp., is a Bochum dissertation which adds an articulate contribution to the recent discussion on F.'s relationship to decadence (see *YWMLS*, 64: 678). Arguing that F. in his late work goes beyond

Realism and anticipates writers such as T. Mann, Hofmannsthal, and Rilke, N. devotes the first half of her study to a contextualization of F.'s creative output in late 19th-c. Berlin, tracing the cultural and aesthetic background to literary decadence and considering the influence on F. of Schopenhauer, Nietzsche, and Nordau, as well as the role of his own nervous constitution in shaping his world-view. The second half of the volume offers close analysis of motifs of decadence in the three selected novels, of which his final work, *Der Stechlin*, with its theme of deterioration and death, receives particular attention. *'Erschrecken Sie nicht, ich bin es selbst': Erinnerungen an T. F.*, ed. Wolfgang Rasch and Christine Hehle, Berlin, Aufbau, 318 pp., brings together for the first time 58 short texts by contemporaries of F., composed for anniversaries and special occasions, which were originally published in newspapers, periodicals, and various collections. Although at first glance the volume may seem to be little more than an entertaining assortment of F. anecdotes for the general reader, closer inspection reveals much that will be of interest also to scholars, for the contributions demonstrate aspects of F.'s personality not generally illuminated in the secondary literature, as well as offering a lively insight into the attitudes of the writers, publishers, and other prominent individuals with whom he mixed. Each text is prefaced by a brief biography of the writer which also often includes comments from F.'s own pen on his association with the person concerned. T. F., *Glückliche Fahrt: Impressionen aus England und Schottland*, ed. Gotthard Erler, Berlin, Aufbau, 294 pp., consists of spontaneous impressions and historical accounts recorded by F. during his three-year period in London, during which time he also travelled to Scotand. *Fs 'Wanderungen durch die Mark Brandenburg' im Kontext der europäischen Reiseliteratur*, ed. Hanna Delf von Wolzogen, Würzburg, Königshausen & Neumann, 528 pp., publishes the proceedings of an international conference held in Potsdam in September 2002, devoted exclusively to a work that has been widely read by the public but neglected by academics. The contributions by 25 prominent scholars from across Europe are interdisciplinary in nature, approaching the topic from a literary, cultural, and historical perspective, and are arranged in three sections entitled 'Reisen, Wandern, Sehen' (41–227), 'Werkstatt, Quellen, Kommerz' (231–393), and 'Geschichten, Strukturen, Spuren' (397–501). The volume is a substantial achievement which fills a gap in F. studies and offers many fresh angles of interpretation. Paul Irving Anderson, *Ehrgeiz und Trauer. Fs offiziöse Agitation 1859 und ihre Wiederkehr in 'Unwiederbringlich'*, Stuttgart, Steiner, 2002, 239 pp. Helen Chambers, *T. Fs Erzählwerk im Spiegel der Kritik. 120 Jahre F.-Rezeption*, trans. Verena Jung, Würzburg, Königshausen & Neumann, 201 pp., is a revised edition in German translation of *The Changing Image of T. F.* (1997; see *YWMLS*, 59:794). Humbert Settler, *'*Der Stechlin.' Fs preußisches Altersepos neu interpretiert*, Scheeßel, Heimatverein Niedersachsen, 176 pp. Id., **Fs 'Irrungen Wirrungen'. Der Titel als Deutung des Stils der Sprache und des Lebens*, Scheeßel, Heimatverein Niedersachsen, 2001, 112 pp. Id., *'*L'Adultera.' Fs Ehebruchsgestaltung, auch im europäischen Vergleich*, Flensburg, Baltica, 2001, 184 pp.

Fontane Blätter, 75, contains: ed. H. Delf von Wolzogen, '"Sie haben die Geschichte zur Verfügung . . ." oder: Ein Geburtstagsbrief. Pierre-Paul Sagave zum Neunzigsten' (8–13); ed. W. Rasch and H. Olejnik, 'Aus den Berliner Korrespondenzen Fs für das *Danziger Dampfboot* 1851/52' (14–25); K.-P. Möller, '"Bin ich's denn wirklich?" F.-Porträts und -Bildnisse (1)' (26–40); J. Osborne, 'Aus Schottland und Frankreich. Überlegungen zum Gattungscharakter von Fs Kriegsberichten' (42–63); G. Weiss-Sussex, 'F. und die englische Malerei: die *Briefe aus Manchester*' (64–79); G. Wolpert, '"Es war eine traurige Auktion" — ein bislang unbekannter zeitgenössischer Bericht zu der Versteigerung des schriftlichen Nachlasses T. Fs 1933' (92–111); '". . . um mehr als zehn Jahre zu spät." Eine unbekannte Rezension zu Fs *Stechlin* von Maksymilian Kohlsdorfer', trans A. Grundke, ed. J. Pacholski (112–17). *Fontane-Blätter*, 76, contains: C. Hehle, 'T. F.: "Wir lernen das." Ein unveröffentlichter Novellenentwurf. Mit einem Geburtstagsgruß an Eda Sagarra und Gotthard Erler' (12–25); K.-P. Möller, 'Der Neuruppiner "Gedächtnis-Ofen". Fs Provokation und die Berliner Bildhauerzunft' (26–42); E. Sagarra, 'Geschichte als Prozeß. Von der Honoratiorenpartei zur Massendemokratie: Wahlen und Wähler beim späten F.' (44–61); C. Buffagni, 'Aspekte der Reise in *Vor dem Sturm* und dem *Stechlin*' (62–79); S. Källström, '"Das Eigentliche bleibt doch zurück." Eine linguistisch-literaturwissenschaftliche Untersuchung der semantischen Unbestimmtheit in T. Fs *Effi Briest*' (80–94); A. Kliems, 'Zwischen Schlachtfeldern und Wirtshaus: T. F. in Böhmen' (95–103).

B. Breggin, 'F.'s aesthetics of the Slavic race', *GLL*, 56:213–22. J. Schneider, 'Masculinity, male friendship and honor in F.'s *Effi Briest*', *GQ*, 75:265–81. P. I. Anderson, '"Interpredition." Verpfuschte Klassikerpflege am Beispiel Fs', *LiLi*, 33:123–37. C. Sittig, 'Gieshüblers Kohlenprovisor. Der Kolonialdiskurs und das Hirngespinst vom spukenden Chinesen in T. Fs *Effi Briest*', *ZDP*, 122:544–63. R. Berbig, 'Dichtungs-, aber nicht gratulationsunfähig. Ein unbekannter Brief von T. F. an Friedrich Eggers mitgeteilt von Roland Berbig', *BHGLL*, 5:127–29. H. Ester, 'Günter Grass und T. F.: ein genüßlicher Irrtum', *DK*, 52:171–85. R. Berbig, '"Auf den ersten Blättern standen die Namen Warschau und Fehrbellin." Der

"Osten" in Fs *Wanderungen durch die Mark Brandenburg*', *ZGer*, 13:53–66. H. Fischer, '"Marseillaise des preußischen Gardelieutenants." Fritz von Gaudy, der Prinz von Preußen und ein vergessenes F.-Lied', *WW*, 51, 2001:26–41. H.-K. Jeong, 'Das Problem des Kalküls in Fs Romanen', *ib.*, 362–74. E. Fiandra, 'Dietro la storia. Metafore di adulterio in *Cécile* di T. F.', *CTed*, 19, 2002:125–36. D. Mugnolo, 'Romanzo come "Zeitbild": F. da *Vor dem Sturm* a *Der Stechlin*', *ib.*, 109–24. C. Blod-Riegl, 'Aurora und Marinelli — Zitierunfähigkeit und verweigertes Zitat in T. Fs *Cécile*', Gutenberg, *Fähigkeit*, 104–22. W. Wülfing, '"Trinkspruch reihte sich an Trinkspruch." Bemerkungen zur Rhetorik des Toasts bei T. F.', *BHGLL*, 4, 2001:60–78. W. Nehring, '"Das Glück rennt hinterher" — nicht nur bei Brecht: Glückserwartungen und Glücksenttäuschungen in den Romanen T. Fs.', *Fest. Knobloch*, 91–99. W. Hettche, '"Schafe" und "Nachplapperer". T. F. und die Goethe-Rezeption des 19. Jahrhunderts', Eibl, *Kritiker*, 87–99. U. Lang, 'T. Fs *Stine*: ein Werk des poetischen Realismus?', *MBA*, 20, 2001:21–34. G. Radecke, 'Für eine textgenetische Edition von T. Fs *Mathilde Möhring*', Haslinger, *Textgenese*, 28–45. G. Catalano, 'Archeologia del presente. Collezionismo e narrazione nel romanzo di T. F. *Vor dem Sturm*', pp. 117–37 of *Simmetria e antisimmetria. Due spinte in conflitto nella cultura dei paese di lingua tedesca*, ed. Luciano Zagari, Pisa, ETS, 2001, 358 pp. E. Erdmann, 'Der Sprachvergleich im literarischen Text. Am Beispiel T. F.', pp. 30–50 of *Sprachvergleich und Übersetzungsvergleich. Leistung und Grenzen, Unterschiede und Gemeinsamkeiten*, ed. Jörn Albrecht and Hans-Martin Gauger, Frankfurt–Berlin, Lang, 2001, 447 pp. A. Heitmann and C. Öhlschläger, 'Macht — Spiel — Plagiatur. Zitat und Weiblichkeit bei Ibsen und F.', Gutenberg, *Fähigkeit*, 187–212. U. Helduser, '*Pater incertus*. Zum Motiv von "Unfruchtbarkeit" in T. Fs *Irrungen Wirrungen*', pp. 161–77 of *Krankheit und Geschlecht. Diskursive Affären zwischen Literatur und Medizin*, ed. Tanja Nusser and Elisabeth Strowick, Würzburg, Königshausen & Neumann, 2002, 217 pp. W. Hettche, 'Die Tenzonendichtung im *Tunnel über der Spree*', *BHGLL*, 4, 2001:24–35. P. Kofler, 'Die Anekdote im Roman bei T. F.: *Schach von Wuthenow*, *Graf Petöfy*, *Frau Jenny Treibel*', pp. 79–101 of *Die kleinen Formen in der Moderne*, ed. Elmar Locher, Innsbruck, Studien-Vlg, 2001, 304 pp.

FRANZOS. **Georg Brandes — K. E. Franzos. Ein Briefwechsel*, ed. Karin Bang, Roskilde, Univ. Centre for østrigst-nordiske kulturstudier, 2001, 44 pp. Hermann Böhm, *Ein Dichter aus Halb-Asien. K. E. Franzos*, Roskilde, Univ. Centre for østrigst-nordiske kulturstudier, 2000, 28 pp., includes a 'Nachwort' by Karin Bang. A. Corbea-Hoisie, 'Ein deutsch-österreichischer Missionär in "Halb-Asien": K. E. F.', Csáky, *Ambivalenz*, 151–64. J. Doll, 'Judaïsme oriental, culture allemande et antisémitisme dans *Der Projaz* de K. E. F. (1847–1904)', Doll, *Écrivains*, 57–68.

FREILIGRATH. A. Schulze-Weslarn, 'F. und die Düsseldorfer Malerschule', *Grabbe-Jb.*, 21, 2002: 119–42. K. Roessler, 'F. F. und die rheinischen Lyriker 1848–1849', *ib.*, 143–59. Id., 'Drei Kölner Bauten mit Bedeutung für Robert Blum und F. F.', *ib.*, 189–96. Id., 'F. an seinem 125. Todestag am 18. März 2001 und im Jahr der Rheinromantik 2002', *ib.*, 197–204. Id., 'Fs Beziehungen zu Weimar — eine Ergänzung', *ib.*, 205–16. J. Hiller von Gaertringen, 'F.-Bibliographie 2001, mit Nachträgen', *ib.*, 245–49. K. Roessler, 'F. 1848 — 1953 — 1989', *ib.*, 22: 126–30. E. Fleischhack, 'Poesieerfülltes Wiedersehen. Fs Besuch der alten Heimat 1869', *ib.*, 131–43. M. Walz, 'F. Fs Lebensabend in Cannstadt und Stuttgart (1868–1876). 2: Weshalb es F. nach Stuttgart zog', *ib.*, 144–62. V. Giel, 'F. und seine Briefe. Das Reportorium *F. F.: Briefe. Kritisches und kommentiertes Gesamtverzeichnis* als Online-Präsentation', *ib.*, 163–67. J. Hiller von Gaertringen, 'F.-Bibliographie 2002, mit Nachträgen', *ib.*, 231–35.

FREYTAG. B. Balzer, '1200 Jahre Slawenkriege. Die Prägung des deutschen Polenbildes durch G. F.', Grucza, *Beziehungen*, 527–36. L. Stockinger, 'Das Bild Polens in G. Fs *Soll und Haben* mit einem Ausblick auf *Die Ahnen*', *ib.*, 537–50.

GERSTÄCKER, FRIEDRICH. A. Corkhill, 'Reiseabenteuer in Australien. F. G.', pp. 269–83 of *Abenteurer als Helden der Literatur oder: wie wurden oder machten sich Schwindler, Spione, Kolonialisten oder Militärs zu großen Gestalten der europäischen Literatur?*, ed. Horst Albert Glaser and Sabine Kleine-Rossbach, Stuttgart, Metzler, 2002, 307 pp.

GRABBE. Jörg Aufenanger, **Das Lachen der Verzweiflung. Grabbe. Ein Leben*, Frankfurt, Fischer, 2001, 282 pp. T. Scamardi, 'Don Giovanni incontra Faust. C. D. G. *Don Giovanni e Faust* (1829)', pp. 175–89 of *Il convitato di pietra. Don Giovanni e il sacro dalle origini al Romanticismo*, ed. Monica Pavesio, Alessandria, Ed. dell'Orso, 2002, 268 pp. *Grabbe-Jb.*, 21, 2002, contains: P. Schütze, '"Komponiere mich! ...": C. D. G. und die Oper' (57–69); Id., 'Originelles und Originales — Über Gs Shakespeare-Verständnis' (70–76); A. Schulze-Weslarn, 'Skulpturen — Büsten — Reliefs — Objekte zu G.' (98–114); J. Hiller von Gaertringen, 'G.-Bibliographie 2001 — mit Nachträgen' (224–44). *Grabbe-Jb.*, 22, contains: P. Schütze, 'Wann ist Geschichte? Wo wohnt sie? Über Gs *Hannibal* und seine Stuttgarter Inszenierung' (47–75); J. Popig, 'Eine doppelte Ausgrabung. *Hannibal* am Schauspiel Staatstheater Stuttgart' (77–82); W. Broer, 'Gs Vaterland' (83–98); K. Roessler, 'G. und die Rheinromantik' (99–106). J. Hiller von Gaertringen, 'G.-Bibliographie 2002, mit Nachträgen' (214–30). See also under FREILIGRATH and WEERTH.

GRILLPARZER. Armin Gebhardt, *F. G. und sein dramatisches Werk*, Marburg, Tectum, 2002, 140 pp., principally offers 5–10-page plot summaries of the dramatic works with a minimal element of critical commentary, but contains no bibliography or notes. S. Wodianka, '"(Un-)Männliches" und "(Un-)Weibliches": das Spiel der Geschlechter in den Dramen F. Gs', *Raabe-Jb.*, 44:117–46. B. Prutti, 'Sapphos Todessprung bei G. oder: Wie tötet man eine Diva?', *GJb*, 11, 2002:279–305. G. Scheit, 'Depressionen in Krähwinkel. Das Theater als neurotische Anstalt. Der verborgene Staat bei G. und Nestroy', Dürhammer, *Witz*, 169–80. W. Schmidt-Dengler, 'Vorgriff auf die Moderne. G. als Satiriker', *ib.*, 205–16. T. G. Waidelich, '"Geisterreich und entfesselte Phantasie." Conradin Kreutzers *Melusina* (1833) nach Gs Opern-Libretto für Beethoven', *ib.*, 181–204.

Grillparzer-Jb., 20, 1997–2002[2003], contains: J. Grosse, 'Kritik der Ästhetik im Namen der Kunst. Über Kunst-Platonismus bei Jacob Burckhardt und F. G.' (11–83); K. Bohnert, 'Bildnis in Aktion. Zur dramatischen Dynamik von Porträts bei G.' (84–124); J. Kost, 'Zwischen Napoleon, Metternich und habsburgischem Mythos. Überlegungen zum Gegenwartsbezug des Geschichtsdramas am Beispiel von Gs *König Ottokar*' (125–58); S. Enzinger, 'Kausale Verknüpfung der Geschehnisse und Raum-Zeit-Struktur in *König Ottokar*' (159–87); B. Hoffmann, 'König Ottokar und kein Ende. Zur Anthropologie F. Gs' (188–220); K. Schaum, 'Kritische Geschichtsbetrachtung und historische Tragödie. Zu Gs *Ein Bruderzwist in Habsburg*' (221–39); J. Neissl, 'Frauen, die das Geschick des Staates lenken. Geschlechterpositionen bei *Libussa* und *Penthesilea*' (240–77); D. Scharmitzer, 'Nicht Auersberg. Tant mieux. F. G. und Anastasius Grün: Protokoll einer komplizierten Beziehung' (278–318); I. F. Roe, 'Britische G.-Forschung der neunziger Jahre' (319–31).

GRIMM, HERMAN. K. Grzywka, '"Es könnte mir nie ein schönerer Ruhm gewährt werden." Zu H. Gs Erinnerungen an seine Familie und ihre kulturgeschichtliche Bedeutung', *Studniem*, 25:187–200.

GROTH. *Jahresgabe der K.-G. Gesellschaft*, 45, contains: U. Bichel and I. Bichel, 'Vor 150 Jahren. K. G. im Jahre 1853' (9–76); D. Runge et al., '"Wie eine Oase in der Wüste." Ein Podiumsgespräch über Gedichte von K. G. am 20. April 2002 in Heide' (77–97); D. Lohmeier, 'K. G. und die Plattdeutschen in den USA. Auch ein Beitrag zur Wirkungsgeschichte des "Quickborn"' (99–122); 'K. G. und Hans Christian Andersen: ein fast vergeblicher Briefwechsel. Vorgestellt von H. Egge' (127–44).

GUTZKOW. Ute Promies, *K. G. — Romanautor und kritischer Pädagoge*, Bielefeld, Aisthesis, 332 pp., is a Bremen dissertation which charts new ground in its focus on the educational theme in *Blasedow und seine Söhne* (1838) and *Die Söhne Pestalozzis* (1870). P. argues that these two largely neglected novels, to each of which she devotes around 100 pages, not only reveal much about G.'s socio-political agenda, but also demonstrate the continuity in his views throughout his writing career. A shorter section on *Die Zeitgenossen* (1837) sheds further light on G.'s critique of education through the medium of essays, and a closing chapter presents a summation of G.'s pedagogical ideal. In its examination of the reception of the educational constructs of Basedow and Pestalozzi in the early and later parts of the 19th c. respectively, the volume offers a stimulating interdisciplinary approach and highlights the extent to which G. incorporated subject matter of topical intellectual debate in his literary work. Armin Gebhardt, *K. G.: Journalist und Gelegenheitsdichter*, Marburg, Tectum, 235 pp., consists of some 70 pages of 'Lebenslauf' followed by plot summaries of all the main *Novellen* and plays. It may be of limited use to those looking at G. for the first time, but is a disappointing volume which contains no critical apparatus whatsoever. **K. G., Briefe eines Narren an eine Närrin*, ed. Herbert Kaiser, Berlin, Kadmos, 2001, 224 pp. A. Hummel, '*Die Polen lieben?* K. Gs Polenbild zwischen Respekt und Ressentiment', Rudolph, *Polenbilder*, 261–80.

HARRING, HARRO. W. Seidel-Höppner, 'Carl Georg Allhusen und H. H.: Landsleute, Zeitgenossen, Antipoden', *CEtGer*, 42, 2002 : 7–15.

HEBBEL. Wolfgang Ranke, *Erläuterungen und Dokumente: F. H., 'Maria Magdalena'* (UB, 16040), 135 pp. Alexandra Tischel, *Tragödie der Geschlechter: Studien zur Dramatik F. Hs*, Freiburg im Breisgau, Rombach, 2002, 197 pp., is a Munich dissertation which investigates H.'s drama from a gender studies angle. The volume consists of five main chapters on *Judith*, *Herodes und Mariamne*, *Gyges und sein Ring*, *Die Nibelungen*, and *Moloch*, examining the confrontation between men and women as a key feature of H.'s tragedy which differentiates it from earlier approaches of German classicism and anticipates the modern battle of the sexes portrayed by Ibsen and Strindberg. Drawing on a broad range of both primary and secondary literature, T. locates H.'s work at a point of transition in the 19th c. when the issue of women's emancipation was gaining momentum in society. N. Brieskorn, 'F. Hs *Judith* und *Genoveva*. Von der Versuchung des Menschen durch Gott und Gottes durch den Menschen', Tschuggnall, *Perspektiven*, 246–62. E. Brüns, 'Geschlecht als Material: Staat, Revolution und Fürsorge in Hs *Agnes Bernauer*', *Akten* (Wien), x, 31–36.

Hebbel-Jb., 58, contains: H. Kaiser, '"Der schöne Tod." H. und die Tragödientheorie des jungen Georg Lukács' (11–26); R. Gnosa, 'Paul Ernsts Auseinandersetzung mit F. H.' (27–46); H. Scheible, '". . .völlig getrennten Haushalt . . ." F. H. und Arthur Schnitzler' (47–64); A. Rudolph, 'Zum H.-Bild in Gottfried Benns Gedicht *Der junge Hebbel*' (65–90); H. Koopmann, '". . .immer fesselnde Lektüre, wenn auch viel Dekoration und die Gefühle überinszeniert." Zu Hs Tagebüchern' (91–112); C. Scholz, '"Darüber kann kein Mann weg"? Zwei unbekannt gebliebene Halbbrüder F. Hs' (113–22); U. H. Gerlach, 'H.-Bibliographie 1990–2000' (123–58); K. Sadkowska, 'H. im galizischen Gymnasium 1890–1939' (159–93); H. Thomsen, 'Theaterbericht' (195–207).

HEINE. The *Säkularausgabe* of H.'s *Werke, Briefwechsel, Lebenszeugnisse* (Berlin, Akademie), has added vol. 16–17, *De L'Allemagne: Kommentar,* II, ed. Dirk Fuhrig, 2002, viii + 290–1044 pp., and vol. 6, *Reisebilder,* II, *1828–1831*, ed. Christa Stöcker, 733 pp. *H. Hs Werk im Urteil seiner Zeitgenossen*, Stuttgart–Weimar, Metzler, has added vol. 9, *Rezensionen und Notizen zu Hs Werken aus den Jahren 1846 bis 1848*, ed. Sikander Singh, 747 pp. Bernd Kortländer, *Heinrich Heine* (UB, 17638), 366 pp. *H. H., Buch der Lieder*, ed. Bernd Kortländer (UB, 2231), 412 pp. Wolfgang Kröger, *H. H., 'Deutschland. Ein Wintermärchen'* (UB, Lektüreschlüssel für Schüler, 15325), 78 pp. Hong-Kyung Yi, *H. Hs Vermittlungsversuch zwischen Kunst und Politik in ausgewählten Werken von 1837–1840*, Heidelberg, Winter, 229 pp., is a Siegen Univ. dissertation which focuses on *Über die französische Bühne. Vertraute Briefe an August Lewald* (1837), the introduction to *Miguel Cervantes de Saavedra. 'Der Sinnreiche Junker Don Quixote von la Mancha'* (1837), and the notes to *Shakespeares Mädchen und Frauen* (1839). Peter Waldmann, **Der verborgene Winkel der sterbenden Götter: Temporalisierung als ästhetischer Ausdruck im Werk von H. H.*, Würzburg, Königshausen & Neumann, 302 pp., is a Mainz dissertation.

A Companion to the works of H. H., ed. Roger F. Cook, Rochester, NY–Woodbridge, Camden House, 2002, xiv + 373 pp., contains: R. F. Cook, 'Introduction' (1–33); M. Perraudin, 'Illusions lost and found: the experiential world of H.'s *Buch der Lieder*' (37–53); P. Peters, 'A walk on the wild side: H.'s eroticism' (55–103); R. F. Cook, 'The riddle of love: Romantic poetry and historical progress' (105–35); W. Goetschel, 'Nightingales instead of owls: H.'s joyous philosophy' (139–68); G. Höhn, 'Eternal return or indiscernible progress? H.'s conception of history after 1848' (169–99); P. Reitter, 'H. H. and the discourse of mythology' (201–26); R. C. Holub, 'Troubled apostate: H.'s conversion and its consequences' (229–50); J. Grossman, 'Heine and Jewish culture: the poetics of appropriation' (251–82); A. Phelan, 'Mathilde's interruption: archetypes of modernity in H.'s later poetry' (285–313); J. A. Kruse, 'Late thoughts: reconsiderations from the 'Matratzengruft' (315–41); G. F. Peters, 'H. and Weimar' (345–60).

Heine-Jb., 42, contains: A. Böhn, 'Erinnerungswelten. Geschichte und Exotik im *Romanzero*' (3–13); O. Briese, 'Exil auf Erden. Facetten einer Zumutung in Hs Spätwerk' (14–36); J. Nickel, 'Grabgeschichten. Zur Besichtigung einer Ortschaft im *Romanzero*' (37–58); R. Steegers, '"Indezent und *dégoutant* zugleich." Intertextuelles in Hs *Romanzero* — am Beispiel August von Platen' (59–72); K. Sousa, 'Wahrheit und Widersprüche in H. Hs *Buch der Lieder*' (73–87); H. Gössmann, 'H. Hs *Harzreise* und *Die Tänzerin von Izu* von Kawabata Yasunari. Eine literarische Gegenüberstellung' (88–104); J. Bernig, 'Vergessenheit und Instrumentalisierung. Die deutsche H.-Rezeption im ersten Nachkriegsjahrzehnt' (105–23); S. Singh, '"Schickt einen Philosophen nach London; bey Leibe keinen Poeten!" H. H. und Georg Christoph Lichtenberg' (140–49); G. Seybert, 'Hs "Loreley" und Puschkins "Sing mir nicht, schöne Frau". Dekonstruktiv-linguistische Analyse von zwei Gedichten der Romantik' (150–57).

M.-C. Boerner, '"Je ne fais que rêver Italie": H. Hs Verfahren der Fiktionalisierung in den italienischen *Reisebildern*', *GRM*, 53:205–19. S. Boyer, '"Das Mark aus meinem Rückgrat trank / Ihr Mund mit wildem Saugen": le corps vampirique chez H. H. ou l'échange symbolique de l'amour et de la mort', *ABNG*, 55:195–210. K. Fingerhut, '"Wenig Blätter Freuden, / Ganze Hefte Leiden." Hs Liebeslyrik', *MDG*, 50:24–43. P. Wapnewski, 'Dichtergott. H. H. und die Tradition seiner Schöpfungsgedichte', *WW*, 53:37–52. H. Kiba, 'Ein Lichtstrahl aus dem Dunkeln. Zur Judenkritik in Hs "Lutezia"', *Fest. Windfuhr*, 107–42. H. Steinecke, '"Auf Requisition unserer Regierung konfisziert." H. und der Zensurfall Hoffmann', *ib.*, 88–106. J. Brummack, 'Zweifaches Exil. Über die Schwierigkeiten der Deutschen mit ihrem Heine', pp. 73–89 of *Humanität in einer pluralistischen Welt? Themengeschichtliche und formanalytische Studien zur deutschsprachigen Literatur. Festschrift für Martin Bollacher*, ed. Christian Kluwe and Jost Schneider, Würzburg, Königshausen & Neumann, 2000, 349 pp. L. Calvié, 'Henri Heine et les dieux de la Grèce', *Romantisme*, 31, 2001:29–42. U. Dedner, '"Meine Nase ist nicht abtrünnig geworden." H. Hs *Rabbi von Bacherach* als Zeugnis erschriebener Identität', *Brummack Vol.*, 275–95. A. Fambrini, 'H. a Lucca', Cercignani, *Wieland*, 63–80. G. Häntzschel, 'Das Ende der Kunstperiode? H. H. und Goethe', Eibl, *Kritiker*, 57–70. M. Haslé, 'Coeur croisé de Heine. Gastronomie politique et jeux linguistiques', *CEtGer*, 41, 2001:91–104. R. Hartmann, 'Selbst- und Fremdbild von Deutschland: H. Hs *Harzreise* (1826) und Hans Christian Andersens *Schattenbild von einer Reise in den Harz [. . .]* (1831)', *WW*, 51, 2001:183–94. S. Jaeger, 'Das Zerrbild Apollons: Hs künstlerische Erschreibung der Gegenwart durch Literaturgeschichte', pp. 195–218 of *Kunst und Wissenschaft um 1800*, ed. Thomas Lange and Harald Neumeyer, Würzburg, Königshausen & Neumann, 2000, 297 pp. D. F. Mahoney, 'H. Hs ikonoklastischer Exilpatriotismus in

Deutschland. Ein Wintermärchen', pp. 136–46 of *Exil. Transhistorische und transnationale Perspektiven = Exile*, ed. Helmut Koopmann and Klaus Dieter Post, Paderborn, Mentis, 2001, x + 316 pp. J.-J. Pollet, 'Au-delà du romantisme: l'image de la mine selon H. H.', pp. 45–53 of *Mélanges offerts à Paul Cologne*, ed. Pierre Vaydat, Villeneuve d'Ascq, Univ. Charles-de-Gaulle — Lille 3, 2001, 214 pp. C. Trautmann-Waller, 'La science du judaïsme au risque du roman. H. H. et George Eliot', *Romantisme*, 31, 2001 : 61–69. S. B. Würffel, 'Von Bacherach nach Bimini. Hs religiöses Denken im Lichte unserer Erfahrung', Tschuggnall, *Perspektiven*, 287–302.

HERWEGH, GEORG. W. Büttner, 'Der andere H. — über sein Verhältnis zur internationalen Arbeiterbewegung', *Heine-Jb.*, 42 : 124–39. K.-L. König, 'G. H. wird von Adolf Widmann attakkiert', *CEtGer*, 42, 2002 : 69–84.

HOFFMANN VON FALLERSLEBEN. Peter Rühmkorf, '*Das Lied der Deutschen*', Göttingen, Wallstein, 2001, 46 pp. J. Vromans, 'La longue vie d'un titre anachronique: *Die Hexe*', pp. 19–22 of *Wahlverwandtschaften in Sprache, Malerei, Literatur, Geschichte. Festschrift für Monique Boussart*, ed. Irene Heidelberger-Leonard and Mireille Tabah, Stuttgart, Heinz, 2000, 314 pp.

IMMERMANN. H. Roland, 'K. I. und der tierische Magnetismus: "Fetische, Amulette und Poltergeister"', pp. 183–204 of *Traces du mesmérisme dans les littératures européennes du XIXe siècle / Einflüsse des Mesmerismus auf die europäische Literatur des 19. Jahrhunderts*, ed. Ernst Leonardy, Brussels, Facultés universitaires Saint-Louis, 2001, 284 pp.

KELLER. The HKA of K.'s *Sämtliche Werke*, ed. Walter Morgenthaler, Basle–Frankfurt, Stroemfeld, has added vol. 29, *Studien- und Notizbücher. Apparat zu Band 16.1 und 16.2*, ed. Walter Morgenthaler, 2002, 412 pp.; vol. 18, *Nachgelassene Prosa und Dramenfragmente*, ed. Peter Stocker, 699 pp.; and vol. 31, *Nachgelassene Prosa und Dramenfragmente. Apparat zu Band 18*, ed. Walter Morgenthaler and Dominik Müller, 401 pp. G. K., *Der grüne Heinrich*, ed. Jörg Drews (UB, 18282), 953 pp. *G. K., Der grüne Heinrich* (IT, 2944), 944 pp. Klaus-Dieter Metz, *G. K., Romeo und Julia auf dem Dorfe* (UB, Lektüreschlüssel für Schüler, 15324), 85 pp. U. Henry Gerlach, *G. K. Bibliographie*, Tübingen, Niemeyer, xix + 339 pp., is a comprehensive and clearly presented volume which will be welcomed by K. students as it fills a gap that has existed since the last such reference work, by Charles C. Zippermann, appeared in 1935. It lists editions of K.'s works and secondary literature published all over the world between 1930 and 2000.

M. Swales, 'G. K's *Der grüne Heinrich* and the poetics of the nineteenth-century European novel', *Flood Vol.*, 411–25. A. Dunker,

'Ein "historisch-ethnographischer Schneiderfestzug". Die Ikonographie der Fortuna als Reflexionsfigur in G. Ks Erzählung *Kleider machen Leute*', *WW*, 52, 2002:361–71. H. Rölleke, '"Alas! poor Yorick." Ein verdecktes Shakespeare-Zitat bei G. K.', *ib.*, 51, 2001:323–24. G. Kaiser, 'Experimentieren oder erzählen? Zwei Kulturen in G. Ks *Sinngedicht*', *SchillerJb.*, 45, 2001:278–301. S. F. Kern, 'Fortschritt zurück — Rückschritt nach vorn', *Welfengarten*, 11, 2001:84–96. A. Rudolph, 'Ideale Polenbilder als Kritik an der Moderne. G. Ks Novelle *Kleider machen Leute*, Rudolph, *Polenbilder*, 225–59. T. Schestag, 'Novelle. Zu G. Ks *Romeo und Julia auf dem Dorfe*', pp. 197–222 of *Anführen — Vorführen — Aufführen. Texte zum Zitieren*, ed. Nils Plath, Bielefeld, Aisthesis, 2002, 291 pp. M. Swales, 'From Goldach to Güllen', *Fest. Butler*, 69–76. D. Wiederkehr, 'Sterbende und tote Liebe bei G. K.: Lesarten eines Theologen', pp. 39–51 of *'Das poetischste Thema der Welt'? Der Tod einer schönen Frau in Musik, Literatur, Kunst, Religion und Tanz*, ed. Ute Jung-Kaiser, Berne–Berlin, Lang, 2000, 334 pp.

KERNER, JUSTINUS. W. J. Hanegraaff, 'Versuch über Friederike Hauffe: zum Verhältnis zwischen Lebensgeschichte und Mythos der *Seherin von Prevorst* (1)', *Suevica*, 8, 1999–2000:17–45.

KOBELL, FRANZ VON. B. Lautenbacher, 'Vom Tod und Leben des Brandner Kaspar', Tschuggnall, *Dialog*, 73–80.

KRUSE, HEINRICH. S. Schwabach-Albrecht, 'H. K. — ein Journalist und Schriftsteller', *AGB*, 57:287–96.

LENAU. *Temeswarer Beiträge zur Germanistik*, 4, marks the L. bicentenary of 2002 by publishing the proceedings of a conference held near the writer's birthplace of Csatád (now Lenauheim in Romania) on the subject of L. in a European context. The volume contains: H. Steinecke, 'L. und Europa' (13–27); K. Stocker, 'N. L.: ein lyrisches Vermächtnis für das Europa des 21. Jahrhunderts? Versuch einer Prognose' (29–52); J. Holzner, 'Abkehr vom Vaterland — Gedichte zur Geschichte Österreichs: von L. bis Artmann' (53–65); W. Kriegleder, 'N. Ls *Albigenser* oder: Wozu dichten in dürftiger Zeit?' (67–86); A. Meyer-Schubert, 'Politik — Poesie — Natur. Ls poetisches Wirken zwischen Politik und Natur. Eine philosophische Reflexion' (87–95); H. Fassel, 'L. in deutschen und österreichischen Gedichten. Sonderformen produktiver Rezeption' (97–156); C. A. Leibiger, '"Habent sua fata libelli": der Inhalt der Bibliothek N. Ls als Hinweis auf die bellettristischen und philosophischen Einflüsse auf sein Werk' (157–71); M. Fischer, '"Das sinnende Meer" — Fahrt-, Zug- und Wandermotive in Ls Lyrik' (173–82); M. Zaharia, 'Zur Metapher der Fremde bei N. L.' (183–92); F. Spadini, '"Mitten im dem Maienglück / Lag ein Kirchhof innen": die problematische Idyllenkonzeption bei N. L.' (193–207); I. Crăciun-Fischer, '"Wie echte Wollust nur selbander lodert / So werden zwei zum rechten Tod erfordert." Eros und Thanatos in N. Ls dramatischem Gedicht *Don Juan*' (209–24); J. Dama, 'Philosophische Grundzüge bei L. und Eminescu' (235–49); E. Pascu, 'Ls *Schilflieder* in der Vision des Komponisten Richard Oschanitzky' (251–62).

**Europäische und regionale Bezugssysteme im Spiegel von Ls Dichtung: Beiträge der Stuttgarter L.-Tagung vom 25. und 26. Mai 2000*, ed. Horst Fassel and Annemarie Röder, Tübingen, Inst. für Donauschwäbische Geschichte und Landeskunde, 2002, 118 pp. Hartmut Steinecke, **Von Lenau bis Broch: Studien zur österreichischen Literatur — von außen betrachtet*, Tübingen–Basle, Francke, 2002, 215 pp. J. Holzner, 'Polenlieder — Projektionen für Österreich und Europa', Grucza, *Beziehungen*, 736–45.

LEWALD. Vanessa Van Ornam, *F. L. and Nineteenth-Century Constructions of Femininity*, NY, Lang, 2002, 192 pp., offers a well-researched insight into the 19th-c. context of L.'s work in respect of gender definitions and limitations. The study is divided into four sections focusing on the discursive domains of medicine, law, education, and the family respectively. In each chapter a substantial introduction drawing on primary sources and social histories illustrates the dominant ideas that contributed to the construction of 'femininity' in that period, and this is followed by analysis of the manner in which characters in selected works by L. both adhere to gendered norms and at the same time manifest 'strategies of dissent'. The strength of the book lies in the writer's skill in incorporating a broad range of informative background texts into a work of literary criticism which will be welcomed both by L. scholars and by a wider readership interested in the ongoing debate surrounding the portrayal of conformity to and potential subversion of social norms in 19th-c. women's writing. Ulla Schacht, **Geschichte in der Geschichte. Die Darstellung jüdischen Lebens in F. Ls Roman 'Jenny'*, Wiesbaden, Deutscher Universitätsverlag, 2001, viii + 275 pp., is a Bremen dissertation. R. Calabrese, '"Si respira il sud con tutti i sensi . . ." Il viaggio in Sicilia di F. L.', pp. 35–59 of *Viaggio nel tempo. Studi dedicati alla memoria di Maria Teresa Morreale*, ed. Ute Schwab and Guiseppe Dolei, Catania, CUEM, 189 pp.

MARX, KARL. H. Meyer, 'K. M. et al.: "Die großen Männer des Exils." A literary satire and a London spy story', *Flood Vol.*, 427–46. R. Sperl, 'Probleme der Autorschaft, Autorisation und Authentizität bei der historisch-kritischen Edition der publizistischen Texte von K. M. und Friedrich Engels', *Editio*, 16, 2002:86–104. H. Jeanblanc, 'K. M. à la découverte des mystères de Paris', *CEtGer*, 42, 2002:135–53. H. Pelger, '"Das Gespenst des Kommunismus." Die Genese einer Phrase bei K. M. 1842–1848', *ib.*, 177–85. R. Sperl,

'Die Marx-Engels-Gesamtausgabe: editorische Konsequenzen literarischer Zusammenarbeit zweier Autoren', Plachta, *Zusammenarbeit*, 141–55. M. Zuckermann, 'Der Kulturbegriff bei M.', pp. 85–94 of *Arche Noah. Die Idee der 'Kultur' im deutsch-jüdischen Diskurs*, ed. Bernhard Greiner and Christoph Schmidt, Freiburg, Rombach, 2002, 413 pp.

MEINHOLD, WILHELM. M. Pólrola, 'Übersetzerische Lektüreerfahrungen mit W. Ms Roman *Maria Schweidler. Die Bernsteinhexe: Der interessanteste aller bisherigen Hexenprozesse, nach einer defekten Handschrift ihres Vaters, des Pfarrers Abraham Schweidler in Coserow auf Usedom* (1843)', Rudolph, *Polenbilder*, 127–50.

MENZEL, WOLFGANG. L. Calvié, 'W. M. (1798–1873) ou la gallophagie comme passion', *CEtGer*, 41, 2001 : 117–28.

MEYER. E. Weber, 'Bildende Kunst und Selbstthematisierung der Literatur — Zu C. F. Meyers Gedicht "Michelangelo und seine Statuen"', *Fest. Gebhard*, 129–43. R. Zeller, 'Betsy Meyer, Sekretärin, Kopistin, Mitarbeiterin. Ihre Selbstdarstellung im Briefwechsel mit dem Verleger', Plachta, *Zusammenarbeit*, 157–66. H. Zeller, 'Betsy Meyers Mitautorschaft an C. F. Ms Werk', *ib.*, 167–95.

MÖRIKE. The Stuttgart (Klett-Cotta) edition of M.'s *Werke und* Briefe, ed. Hubert Arbogast et al., has added vol. 1.1, *Gedichte*, ed. Hans-Henrik Krummacher, 388 pp. E. M.: *Mozart's Journey to Prague, and a Selection of Poems*, trans., introd., and ann. David Luke, Penguin, London, xxxvi + 216 pp. H. Ester, 'M. und Mozart. Die Faszination des Nächtlichen', *DK*, 52:53–72. L. L. Albertsen, 'Zeit und Ewigkeit bei M.', *ZKB*, 9, 2000:65–68. M. Mandelartz, 'Zeit und Form. Ms "Um Mitternacht" und "Am Rheinfall"', *DB*, 108, 2002:141–50. I. Wild and R. Wild, '"Ein köstliches Liedchen": Rokoko-Elemente in der Lyrik E. Ms', pp. 289–307 of *Literatur und Kultur des Rokoko*, ed. Matthias Luserke, Göttingen, Vandenhoeck & Ruprecht, 2001, 328 pp. T. Wolf, '"Apropos was halten Sie von Gespenstern?" Ms Beziehung zu Kerner im Schwarzlicht privater Geisterkunde', *Suevica*, 8, 1999–2000:47–110.

MÜHLBACH, LUISE (MUNDT, KLARA). J. E. Martin, '*Oroonoko* in nineteenth-century Germany: race and gender in L. M.'s *Aphra Behn*', *GLL*, 56:313–26.

MUNDT, THEODOR. Petra Hartmann, *'Von Zukunft trunken und keiner Gegenwart voll.' T. Ms literarische Entwicklung vom 'Buch der Bewegung' zum historischen Roman*, Bielefeld, Aisthesis, 323 pp., is a Hanover dissertation which differs from most M. scholarship in that it explores the lifetime achievement of the artist, rather than focusing mainly on the work published before the federal denunciation of Junges Deutschland in 1835. Challenging the commonly held view that M.'s writing lost its liberal or 'radical' quality following the ban, H. examines the 26-year period of M.'s later career in which some 40 titles and numerous periodicals appeared, arguing with conviction that M. continued to develop and refine his Young-German themes and ideals, and that a true break does not manifest itself until the failed revolution of 1848. Taking account of M.'s position vis-à-vis the other Young-German writers as well as tracing the progression in his aesthetic, political, and theological thinking, the study is a valuable contribution that opens up largely unexplored areas of M.'s work to critical debate.

NESTROY. Jürgen Hein and Claudia Meyer, **Theaterg'schichten. Ein Führer durch Ns Stücke. Eine Veröffentlichung der Internationalen N.-Gesellschaft*, Vienna, Lehner, 2001, 352 pp. *Johann Nepomuk Nestroy. Tradizione e transgressione*, ed. Gabriella Rovagnati, Milan, CUEM, 2002, 218 pp., contains: G. Rovagnati, 'Letteratura e calendario. Omaggio a J. N. nel bicentenario della nascita' (13–22); J. Hein, '"Aus'n Begeisterungstempel in's schnöde Wirtschaftsleben" oder "Bretter- und Leinwand-zusammengeflickte Coulissenwelt" als Geschäft und Profession — J. N. und sein Theater' (23–42); M. Stern, 'Die N.-Polemik des deutschen Vormärz — Vorspiel des "Poetischen Realismus"' (43–60); A. Destro, 'Il cronista sulla scena. N. tra cronaca e storia' (61–74); R. Urbach, 'N. — der Schauspieler: Herkunft, Merkmale und Wirkung seiner Rollengestaltung' (75–93); S. P. Scheichl, 'Flora Baumscheer oder: Was ist das eigentliche satirische Objekt Ns?' (95–108); F. Cambi, '"Aber ob realistisch oder nicht. Er sagte die Wahrheit." La ricezione di N. nell'opera di Jura Soyfer' (109–22); W. Obermaier, '"...dann geht das maschinenmäßige Werckstatt-Leben fort." Ns literarische Arbeitsbedingungen als Autor des Wiener Vorstadttheaters' (123–44); J. Benay, 'Johann Nestroys / Jean Nestroys Werk als frankophone und deutsche Kulturwaffe im annektierten Lothringen (1871–1918)' (145–77); G. Rovagnati, 'Fedele intenzione e coatta violazione: tradurre Nestroy' (179–94). R. Reichensperger, 'J. N. und die französische Moderne 1830–1860', Csáky, *Ambivalenz*, 113–34. P. Branscombe, 'Die Musik bei N. als Flucht in bessere (?) Welten', Dürhammer, *Witz*, 153–61. J. Hüttner, 'J. N.: verschlagene Sprache', *ib.*, 135–42. C. Krauss, 'N. im Zug seiner Zeit. Anmerkungen zu den *Eisenbahnheirathen*', *ib.*, 143–52. A. Pfabigan, 'Dämonie, Humor und Kulturindustrie. Das "Über"-Lebenssystem des Johann Nepomuk Eduard Ambrosius Nestroy', *ib.*, 117–33.

Nestroyana, 23, contains: W. Pape, '"Überall mehr Zufall als Schicksal zu finden": Tragödie und Possenstruktur am Beispiel von Schiller und N.' (5–18); M. Wagner-Egelhaff, 'Vom Nachäffen. Menschen und Affen in der Literatur' (19–34); P. Branscombe, 'Erstausgabe der Musik zu *Lumpacivagabundus*?' (35–41); F. Walla, 'Zu Ns Quodlibet-Vorspielen' (42); M. Giesing, 'Ein Stündchen in der Schule der schlimmen Buben. Eine Hamburger Vorlage zu Ns

Schulburleske' (43–52); Y.-K. Ra, 'Die N.-Rezeption in der Literaturgeschichtsschreibung' (69–84); P. Branscombe, 'Erstveröffentlichungen von Adolf Müllers Gesängen zu N.-Stücken. Aus dem Verlagsverzeichnis Anton Diabellli & Co. (1824 bis 1840)' (101–05); U. Helmensdorfer, 'Nachdrucker Nestroy. Das *Patent* vom 16. Oktober 1846' (106–19); R. Theobald, 'Zur Pressepolitik des Carl-Theaters. Noch ein N.-Brief aus der Sammlung Theobald' (120–23); F. Walla, 'Affen, Bräutigame, Buben, der fliegende Holländer, zwei Juden oder (k)einer, Lumpen und liebe Anverwandte. Zur Titelgebung der Stücke Ns' (124–39); G. Stieg, 'Übersetzen als Prozeß der Ent- und Aufwertung' (140–46); G. Rovagnati, 'Launen des Einfalls. Die italienischen Übersetzungen von Ns *Zu ebener Erde und erster Stock*' (149–57); P. Schweinhardt, 'N. und die Remigranten. Die musikalische *Höllenangst*-Fassung des Neuen Theaters in der Scala (Wien, 1948)' (160–78); J. R. P. McKenzie, '"*Judith und Holofernes* kann und soll leider derzeit nicht gespielt werden." Zur Wiener Inszenierung des Werks 1972 im Theater im Palais Erzherzog Karl' (179–92); A. Ludewig, 'N., Horváth, Loher und die Volksstücktradition. Nur das Lachen ist uns vergangen' (193–202).

NIETZSCHE. The Berlin HKA of N.'s *Werke*, ed. Giorgio Colli et al., de Gruyter, has produced Part I, vol. 5, *Nachgelassene Aufzeichnungen Frühjahr 1868 — Herbst 1869*, ed. Katherina Glau, xvi + 440 pp, and Part V, vol. 3, *Nachbericht zum ersten Band der fünften Abteilung: Morgenröthe*, ed. Marie-Luise Haase, vii + 915 pp. The Berlin HKA of N.'s *Briefwechsel*, ed. Giorgio Colli et al., de Gruyter, has added Part III, vol. 7, *Nachbericht zur 3. Abteilung, Teilband 1, Briefe von und an F. N.: Januar 1880 — Dezember 1884*, ed. Renate Müller-Buck and Holger Schmid, viii + 1051 pp.; Part III, vol. 7, *Nachbericht zur 3. Abteilung, Teilband 2, Briefe von und an F. N.: Januar 1885 — Dezember 1886*, ed. Holger Schmid, vi + 572 pp.; Part II, vol. 7, *Nachbericht zur 2. Abteilung, Teilband 3, Briefe von und an F. N.: Januar 1875 — Dezember 1879*, ed. Andrea Bollinger and Annemarie Pieper, *Halbband 1*, 2001, vii + 444 pp., and *Halbband 2*, 2001, pp. 446–1406; Part II, vol. 7, *Nachbericht zur 2. Abteilung, Teilband 2, Breife von und an F. N.: Mai 1872 — Dezember 1874*, ed. Andrea Bollinger and Annemarie Pieper, 2000, vi + 835 pp. *Ns persönliche Bibliothek*, ed. Giuliano Campioni and Renate Müller-Buck, Berlin, de Gruyter, 736 pp., offers a comprehensive and long overdue index of all the works and notes from N.'s personal library up to the beginning of January 1889, replacing the 1942 work by Max Oehlers. The volume, which will provide an important tool for future N. research, covers stock from both the Herzogin Anna Amalia Bibliothek and the Goethe- und Schiller Archiv in Weimar. It lists around 2,200 titles and also catalogues some 20,000 traces of N.'s reading such as marginal notes

and underlinings. *Ecce opus: N.-Revisionen im 20. Jahrhundert*, ed. Rüdiger Görner and Duncan Large, Göttingen, Vandenhoeck & Ruprecht, 240 pp., contains: V. Gerhardt, 'N., Goethe und die Humanität' (11–24); N. Martin, 'Extremes of N.: "wo sind die *Barbaren* des 20. Jahrhunderts?"' (25–35); M. Liebscher, 'Die "unheimliche Ähnlichkeit". Ns Hermeneutik der Macht und analytische Interpretation bei Carl Gustav Jung' (37–50); C. Diethe, 'N. emasculated: postmodern readings' (51–63); D. Large, '"Zerfall der Werte": Broch, N., nihilism' (65–82); F. Krause, 'Kaiser's *Der gerettete Alkibiades*: an Expressionist revision of N.'s *Die Geburt der Tragödie*' (83–110); D. Midgley, 'Experiments of a "free spirit": Musil's explorations of creative morality in *Der Mann ohne Eigenschaften*' (111–24); R. Furness, 'N. in the work of Christian Morgenstern' (125–37); H. G. Hödl, 'Die N.-Rezeption in Österreich im frühen 20. Jahrhundert' (139–64); P. Dávidházi, '"Was Europa den Juden verdankt": a revaluation of N. by the Hungarian novelist Lázló Németh' (165–80); P. Sedgwick, 'The "N. legend": a genealogy of myth and enlightenment' (181–92); R. Görner, '"Wie ich N. überwand." Zu einem Motiv der N.-Rezeption bei Rilke, Döblin und Hugo Ball' (193–203); K. Kohl, '"Die Rhetorik ist das Wissen der Philosophie Ns." (Hans Blumenberg). Klassische Tradition moderner Wirkung' (205–25).

Alfons Reckermann, *Lesarten der Philosophie Ns: ihre Rezeption und Diskussion in Frankreich, Italien und der angelsächsischen Welt 1960–2000*, Berlin, de Gruyter, xvi + 336 pp., offers an erudite and wide-ranging assessment of N. reception outside the German-speaking countries. The study falls into three main sections on France (1–98), Italy (99–128), and America (129–296), covering Foucault, Derrida, Colli, Montinari, de Man, Eagleton, and Rorty among many others, and has a substantial critical apparatus. Aldo Venturelli, *Kunst, Wissenschaft und Geschichte bei N.: Quellenkritische Untersuchungen*, trans. Leonie Schröder, Berlin–NY, de Gruyter, vii + 359 pp. Carol Diethe, *N.'s Sister and the 'Will to Power': A Biography of Elisabeth Förster-Nietzsche*, Champaign, Illinois U.P., xiii + 214 pp. Mazzino Montinari, *Reading N.*, trans. Greg Whitlock, Urbana, Illinois U.P., 176 pp., is a translation of the German original of 1982 (see *YWMLS*, 44:929–30). Carsten Bäuerl, *Zwischen Rausch und Kritik* I: *Auf den Spuren von N., Bataille, Adorno und Benjamin*, Bielefeld, Aisthesis, 409 pp., is a Bielefeld dissertation which includes analysis of *Menschliches, Allzumenschliches*, *Der Fall Wagner*, and *Die Geburt der Tragödie*. Lee Spinks, *Friedrich Nietzsche*, London, Routledge, x + 184 pp. Yong-Soo Kang, *Ns Kulturphilosophie*, Würzburg, Königshausen & Neumann, 192 pp.

James D. Stewart, *N.'s 'Zarathustra' and Political Thought*, NY–Lampeter, Mellen, viii + 237 pp. Michael Weber, *Textura: Ns 'Morgenröthe' — Versuch über ihre Struktur*, Frankfurt–Berlin, x + 217 pp., is a Heidelberg dissertation. Josef M. Werle, *Ns Projekt 'Philosoph des Lebens'*, Würzburg, Königshausen & Neumann, 191 pp. R. Kevin Hill, *N.'s Critiques: The Kantian Foundations of his Thought*, OUP, xvi + 242 pp. F. N.: *Writings from the Late Notebooks*, ed. Rüdiger Bittner, trans. Kate Sturge, CUP, xliii + 286 pp. *N. and the Divine*, ed. Jim Urpeth and John Lippitt, Manchester, Clinamen, 2000, xxvii + 315 pp. Matthew Rampley, *N, Aesthetics and Modernity*, CUP, 2000, xi + 286 pp., is a Cambridge dissertation. Josef Rattner, *N.: Leben — Werk — Wirkung*, Würzburg, Königshausen & Neumann, 2000, 399 pp. **Ns 'Also sprach Zarathustra'. 20. Silser N.-Kolloquium 2000*, ed. Peter Villwock, Basle, Schwabe, 2001, ix + 241 pp. Gerd Schank, **'Rasse' und 'Züchtung' bei N.*, Berlin–NY, de Gruyter, 2000, x + 480 pp. Timo Hoyer, **N. und die Pädagogik. Werk, Biografie und Rezeption*, Würzburg, Königshausen & Neumann, 2002, 693 pp., is a Kassel dissertation. Hubert Thüring, **Geschichte des Gedächtnisses. F. N. und das 19. Jahrhundert*, Munich, Fink, 2001, 391 pp., is a Basle dissertation.

I. Almond, 'N.'s peace with Islam: my enemy's enemy is my friend', *GLL*, 56:43–55. A. Erwin, 'Rethinking N. in Mann's *Doktor Faustus*: crisis, parody, primitivism, and the possibilities of Dionysian art in a post-Nietzschean era', *GR*, 78:283–99. T. Körber, 'Thomas Manns lebenslange N.-Rezeption', *WW*, 52, 2002:417–40. A. Geisenhanslüke, '"Zu lange ist schon die Ohrfeige fällig, die schallend durch die Hallen der Wissenschaft gehen soll." Zum Widerstreit von Philologie und Philosophie in F. Ns *Geburt der Tragödie* und Walter Benjamins *Ursprung des deutschen Trauerspiels*', *DVLG*, 77:77–90. N. Martin, '"Fighting a philosophy": the figure of N. in British propaganda of the First World War', *MLR*, 98:367–80. J. Riou, 'Historiography and the critique of culture in Schiller, N. and Benjamin', pp. 35–52 of *Cultural Memory: Essays on European Literature and History*, ed. Edric Caldicott and Anne Fuchs, Oxford–Berne, Lang, 422 pp. L. Bluhm, 'Die "zitternde Nadel". Herkunft, Genese und Variation einer N.-Zuschreibung bei Thomas Mann, Ernst Jünger und Alfred Baeumler', *WW*, 51, 2001:48–55. P. van Tongeren, 'Freundschaft, Selbsterkenntnis und Einsamkeit', *CP*, 51, 2002:5–20. R. Müller-Buck, '"Una sua parola mi farebbe felice." N. scrittore di lettere', *CTed*, 20, 2002:7–30. G. W. Most, 'On the use and abuse of ancient Greece for life', *ib.*, 31–53. V. Vivarelli, '"Aggiungo una punta di comicità alle cose più serie": aspetti delle ultime lettere di N.', *ib.*, 55–67. O. Ponton, 'Il tema dell' "alleggerimento della vita" in *Umano, troppo umano* e nei manoscritti preparatori

(1875–1880)', *ib.*, 69–83. P. D'Iorio, 'L'annuncio dell'eterno ritorno in *Così parlò Zarathustra*', *ib.*, 85–97. K. Kropfinger, 'Beethoven in N.', *ib.*, 99–142. T. Ward, 'Los possibiles caminos de N. en el modernismo', *NRFH*, 50, 2002:489–515. L. Szabó, '"Die Worte liegen uns im Wege": zum Kunstsprachstil Ns in *Also sprach Zarathustra*', *SGUV*, 6, 2002:35–52. F. Ulfers and M. D. Cohen, 'F. N. as bridge from nineteenth-century atomistic science to process philosophy in twentieth-century physics, literature and ethics', *WVUPS*, 49, 2002[2003]:21–29. J. Lehmann, 'Bachtin und N.', *Akten* (Wien), VIII, 257–63. R. Müller-Buck, 'Nihilismus und Melancholie. Ns Denken im Spiegel Sigmund Freuds', *ib.*, X, 261–68. F. Wistuba, 'Leben als Experiment oder der "Doppelblick" aufs Dasein. F. Ns *Ecce homo*', pp. 105–21 of *Selbstpoetik 1800–2000. Ich-Identität als literarisches Zeichenrecycling*, ed. Ralph Köhnen, Frankfurt–Berlin, Lang, 2001, 355 pp. K. Xantinidis, 'Die Kunst als Konjektur. Anmerkungen zur editorischen Problematik des späten Nachlasses F. Ns', pp. 361–79 of *Literarische Trans-Rationalität. Für Gunter Martens*, ed. Wolfgang Wirth and Jörn Wegner, Würzburg, Königshausen & Neumann, 548 pp. A. Aichele, 'Erlebnis ohne Erfahrung. Ns Bestimmung der Grenze aller Kunst', pp. 47–62 of *Grenzsituationen. Wahrnehmung, Bedeutung und Gestaltung in der neueren Literatur*, ed. Dorothea Lauterbach, Göttingen, Vandenhoeck und Ruprecht, 2002, 335 pp. K. Fliedl, 'Ns Vogel. Zur Kritik eines Motivs', pp. 131–46 of *Gender Revisited: [Subjekt- und Politikbegriffe in Kultur und Medien]*, ed. Katharina Baisch, Stuttgart–Weimar, Metzler, 2002, viii + 331 pp. G. Maisuradze, '(Nietzsche), die Genealogie, die Biographie', pp. 107–12 of *Grundlagen der Biographik. Theorie und Praxis des biographischen Schreibens*, ed. Christian Klein, Stuttgart–Weimar, Metzler, 2002, vi + 282 pp. M. Landfester, 'Ns *Geburt der Tragödie*: Antihistorismus und Antiklassizismus zwischen Wissenschaft, Kunst und Philosophie', Aurnhammer, *Antike*, 89–111. J. Le Rider, 'Un siècle de réception française de N.', *ChrA*, 9, 2001–2002:43–65. Id., 'N. — ein Jahrhundert französische N.-Rezeption', pp. 79–93 of *Geist und Macht. Schriftsteller und Staat im Mitteleuropa des 'kurzen Jahrhunderts' 1914–1991*, ed. Marek Zybura and Kazimierz Wóycicki, Dresden, Thelem, 2002, 426 pp. A. M. Haas, 'Ns Begriff der Mystik', *Fest. Ruberg*, 207–19. D. von Petersdorff, 'Die Freiheit und ihr Schatten. F. Ns Subjektkritik', Detering, *Autorschaft*, 142–60. M. Stingelin, '"Er war im Grunde der eigentliche Schriftsteller, während ich bloß der Autor war." F. Ns Poetologie der Autorschaft als Paradigma des französischen Poststrukturalismus (Roland Barthes, Gilles Deleuze, Michel Foucault)', *ib.*, 80–106. P. Memmolo, 'Goethes Auge und Ns Kunst', pp. 221–37 of *'Nachdenklicher Leichtsinn.' Essays on Goethe and Goethe Reception*, ed. Heike Bartel and Brian Keith-Smith, Lewiston, NY, Mellen, 2002, xiv + 288 pp.

'F. N.: Perspektivismus als Herausforderung. N.-Tagung am Goethe-Institut Kopenhagen vom 20.–22.9.2000', *TeK*, 23, 2001:5–155, comprises a preface and nine articles.

ORTLEPP, ERNST. Hermann J. Schmidt, **Der alte O. war's wohl doch oder für mehr Mut, Kompetenz und Redlichkeit in der Nietzscheinterpretation: in Aufnahme von Nietzsches 'Album', des als verschollen geltenden Skandalpoems 'Fieschi' (1835), der ungekürzten Druckfassung des 'Vaterunser des neunzehnten Jahrhunderts' (1834) und weiterer Texte E. Os sowie von Klassenkameraden Nietzsches und in Wiedergabe von Autographen*, Aschaffenburg, Alibri, 2001, 440 pp.

PAOLI, BETTY. K. S. Wozonig, 'B. P., die Lykerin als Journalistin', *GQ*, 76:56–67.

RAABE. Brigitte Dörrlamm, *Gasthäuser und Gerüchte. Zu integrativer Polyphonie im Werk W. Rs*, Frankfurt–Berlin, Lang, 184 pp., is a Mainz dissertation which focuses on three elements associated with R.'s experimentation with narrative perspective, namely inns, newspapers, and rumours. The study identifies references to over 140 inns in R.'s work, stressing their importance as centres of semi-public discourse in the 19th c., and has brief analyses of their function in *Gutmanns Reisen*, *Pfisters Mühle*, *Der Dräumling*, and *Villa Schönow*. After a short digression on R.'s exploitation of journalistic media as a narrative device, the volume concludes with detailed examinations of the role of rumour as a polyphonic, non-linear form of communication in *Horacker* and *Stopfkuchen*. Karin Kluger, *'Der letzte Augenblick der hübschen Idylle'. Die Problematisierung der Idylle bei W. R.*, NY–Washington, Lang, 2001, viii + 199 pp. is a New York City Univ. dissertation. *Von W. R. und anderen. Vorträge aus dem Braunschweiger R.-Haus*, ed. Herbert Blume, Bielefeld, Vlg für Regionalgeschichte, 2001, 292 pp., contains: R. G. Czapla, 'Ein Porträt des Künstlers als alter Mann. Zur Ikonographie des R.-Porträts in der zeitgenössischen Photographie und Malerei' (11–43); R. Parr, 'Wie die Burenkriege durch *Stopfkuchen* in die Leonhardstraße kamen — auch ein Stück R.-Rezeption' (45–93); H. Blume, 'Blaugelb und Schwarzweißrot. Wilhelm Brandes als Schriftsteller' (95–129); G. Henkel, 'Ein Autographenfund in der R.-Bibliothek. Nachträge zum Thema "W. R. und Westermann"' (131–40); J. Eckhoff, 'Schwefelwasserstoff und Gänsebraten. Moderne und Tradition in W. Rs *Pfisters Mühle*' (141–70); J. Kilian, 'Private Gespräche im 19. Jahrhundert. Am Beispiel von W. Rs *Pfisters Mühle*' (171–90); E. Rohse, 'Wie R. den Tod gebildet. Zur Ikonographie von Zeitlichkeit und Tod in späten Texten und Zeichnungen W. Rs' (191–239); H.-J. Behr, '"Des Reiches Krone." Anmerkungen eines Mediävisten zum Mittelalter-Bild W. Rs' (241–57); A. Vierhufe, 'Fritz Mauthner und W. R.' (259–82).

Raabe-Jb., 44, contains: S. Doering, 'Standhafte Krieger und sittenlose Verführer. Konfessionelle Stereotypen in Reformationsdichtungen bei W. R., Conrad Ferdinand Meyer und Gottfried Keller' (1–20); C.-M. Ort, '"Stoffwechsel" und "Druckausgleich". Rs *Stopfkuchen* und die "Diätetik" des Erzählens im späten Realismus' (21–43); J. Sammons, 'W. R. und Friedrich Spielhagen. Eine kontrafaktische Spekulation' (44–56); C. Blasberg, 'Jugend in Zeiten des Krieges. Überlegungen zu W. R. und Herman Bang' (57–76). E. Joseph, 'Melancholie und Metaphorik des Gesteins. W. Rs Erzählungen *Holunderblüte*, *Meister Anton*, *Zum wilden Mann* und *Frau Salome*', *WW*, 51, 2001 : 195–210.

RAIMUND. Günter Holtz, *F. R. — der geliebte Hypochonder. Sein Leben, sein Werk*, Frankfurt–Berlin, Lang, 2002, 280 pp., turns the spotlight back on an increasingly neglected dramatist. The work falls into two parts: the first traces the development of R. as an actor, writer, and private individual, as well as exploring the political and cultural context in Vienna after 1814, the tradition of the Volkstheater, and in particular the *Zaubermärchen* in which R. specialized. The second part comprises analyses of the dramatic structure and effect of all eight of R.'s plays.

REDWITZ(-SCHMÖLZ), OSKAR VON. M. Jakubów, 'Literatur aus dem Geist der Romantik?', *Studniem*, 24, 2002 : 591–604.

REUTER. Volker Griese, *F. R.: Chronik seines Lebens*, Husum, Husumer Druck- und Verlagsgesellschaft, 165 pp., is, as the title suggests, an account of R.'s life in the form of brief, chronologically arranged entries drawing substantially on the writer's correspondence and literary works. The volume offers fascinating insights into R.'s strained relationship with his father who pressured him to study law, the privations of his seven-year imprisonment for treason, his struggle with alcoholism and with frustrated attempts to find his true vocation, and his eventual path to success as a pre-eminent exponent of northern German culture. While the book may prove useful to scholars wishing to check the events of a particular month or year, a disadvantage is that only a general list of sources is included, and citations are not credited individually. This renders it more suitable for readers interested in a lively introduction to R. than for those seeking a full critical apparatus. *Fritz Reuter, John Brinckmann, Dethloff Carl Hinstorff und Rostock*, ed. Christian Bunners im Auftrag der F.-R.-Gesellschaft, Rostock, Hinstorff, 2002, 135 pp., includes material on the Rostock student fraternities between 1831 and 1834, on R.'s and Brinckmann's narrative techniques, and on the reception of R. in Sweden. K. Malsch, 'Der Einfluß des Französischen auf das Mecklenburgische bei F. R.', *NdJb*, 124, 2001 : 135–54.

RÜCKERT. The HKA of R.'s works, ed. Rudolf Kreutner and Hans Wollschläger, Göttingen, Wallstein, has added vol. 5–6, *Liedertagebuch. Werke der Jahre 1850–1851*, ed. Rudolf Kreutner et al., 424 pp. A. Geisenhanslüke, 'Der Kanon der Theorie. Mallarmé in Deconstruction. Mit einer Anmerkung zu F. R. und dem Gespenst des Biedermeier', Arnold, *Kanonbildung*, 259–73. E. Stuck, 'Die Rolle des literarischen Kanons an der Universität. Überlegungen zu impliziten und expliziten Wertungen bei der Selektion am Beispiel von F. R.', *Akten* (Wien), VIII, 105–11. *Rückert-Studien*, 13, 2001, contains: G. Häntzschel, 'Die deutschsprachigen Lyrikanthologien des 19. Jahrhunderts: Chancen oder Barrieren für die Popularisierung F. Rs?' (39–52); M.-V. Leistner, 'F. R. im Urteil Wilhelm Müllers' (75–88); F. Schüppen, 'F. Rs Beiträge zum Deutschen Musenalmanach. Das Jahrzehnt der "Weisheit des Brahmanen"' (111–38); P. Bachmann, 'R. als Übersetzer al-Mutanabbīs' (245–72). See also under LITERARY LIFE above.

SACHER-MASOCH. Lisbeth Exner, *Leopold von Sacher-Masoch*, Hamburg, Rowohlt, 160 pp., achieves a balanced examination of the life and work of an author whose image has become distorted by stereotypes. The study documents S.-M.'s background, family life, and literary career and paints a broad picture of an achievement extending beyond *Venus im Pelz* with which he is predominantly associated. It offers insights into the disturbed personality and problematical relationships of a gifted and prolific writer, focusing also on his wife Wanda whose revelations in her notorious *Meine Lebensbeichte* (1906) shaped S.-M. criticism for better or worse. A concluding chapter traces the enduring literary and media interest in the theme of masochism. Karin Bang, *Aimez-moi! Eine Studie über L. v. S.-Ms Masochismus*, Frankfurt–Berlin, Lang, 358 pp., takes its title from S.-M.'s last words which B. interprets as being indicative of a search for a love he never found. This interdisciplinary work combines insights from psychology and literary studies and is divided into three parts. The first describes the research of Richard von Krafft-Ebing into sexual behaviour which led to his coining of the term 'masochism' in 1890, and examines the sociopolitical context of S.-M.'s writing in a period of revolution, incipient communism, and the early women's movement. The second part adopts a psychoanalytical approach to the evaluation of seven works by S.-M. which exhibit the psychic conflict of his inner world; and in the third the phenomenon of masochism is explored through a focus on S.-M.'s life and literary career, including aspects of his correspondence and of his first marriage. G. Leisten, 'Bildnisbegegnung — Fetischismus — Schrift: L. v. S.-Ms Novelle *Venus im Pelz*', pp. 101–13 of *Behext von Bildern? Ursachen, Funktionen und Perspektiven der textuellen Faszination durch*

Bilder, ed. Heinz J. Drügh and Maria Moog-Grünewald, Heidelberg, Winter, 2001, xix + 312 pp.

SAPHIR, MORITZ GOTTLIEB. S. P. Scheichl, 'Saphir — Kein Wiener Heine', Doll, *Écrivains*, 27–41.

SCHEFFEL, JOSEPH VICTOR VON. K. Gantert, '*Neigung zieht mich nach der Wartburg, Pflicht hält mich an der Donau stillem Quell.* J. V. v. Ss nie verwirklichter Wartburgroman', *Euphorion*, 96, 2002: 469–93.

SCHOPENHAUER. A. S., *Aphorismen zur Lebensweisheit* (IT, 2959), 253 pp., includes a 'Nachwort' by Hermann von Braunbehrens. G. Steven Neeley, **S. — A Consistent Reading*, NY–Lampeter, Mellen, xvii + 205 pp. Rüdiger Safranski, **S. und die wilden Jahre der Philosophie. Eine Biographie*, Frankfurt, Fischer, 2001, 556 pp. L. Pikulik, 'S. und die Romantik', *Aurora*, 62, 2002: 95–111.

SCHUMANN, ROBERT. *R. S.: Neue Ausgabe sämtlicher Werke*, Mainz, Schott, has added vol. 8,2: *Literarische Vorlagen der ein- und mehrstimmigen Lieder; Gesänge und Deklamationen*, ed. Helmut Schanze and Krischan Schulte, 2002, xliv + 470 pp. I. Knechtges-Obrecht, 'Die doppelte Wort-Text-Unterlegung bei vier Liedern aus R. Ss Sammlung *Fünf Lieder für eine Singstimme und Pianoforte* op. 40 nach Texten von Hans Christian Andersen übersetzt durch Adalbert von Chamisso', *Editio*, 16, 2002: 182–95.

SEALSFIELD. *C. S., Das Kajütenbuch, oder, Nationale Charakteristiken*, ed. Günter Schnitzler (Jb. der C. S.-Gesellschaft, 15), Munich, Langen Müller, 384 pp.

SPITZER, DANIEL. U. Tanzer, 'Mit kolonialem Blick und spitzer Feder. Thematisierung des Nationalitätenkonflikts in den Feuilletons D. Ss', Csáky, *Ambivalenz*, 135–49.

STELZHAMER, FRANZ. **Nur fort zu Dir. F. S. und Betty Stelzhamer: Briefwechsel*, ed. Silvia Bengesser and Günther Achleitner, Salzburg, Müller, 2002, 592 pp.

STIFTER. *Adalbert Stifter*, ed. Heinz Ludwig Arnold, TK, 115 pp., contains: S. Schiffner, 'S. als Comic' (4–9); M. van Aerschot, 'Cartoons zu *Abdias*' (10–17); M. Göritz, 'Vom Lesen in der Landschaft. Topografie und Wissen in A. Ss *Bunte Steine*' (21–35); R. Koch, 'Das kalte Gesetz. Zu Ss *Der Waldbrunnen* und meinem Roman *Das braune* Mädchen' (40–47); M. Donhauser, 'Kritik des reinen Verlusts. Zu A. S.' (48–55); F.-J. Czernin, 'Zu A. Ss *Witiko*' (56–72); N. Hummelt, 'Über die Liebe bei S. und Proust' (73–90); M. Scheffel, 'S.-Studien im Wandel der Zeit. Eine kleine Forschungs- und Rezeptionsgeschichte' (91–108); N. Hummelt, 'Vita A. S.' (109–13). Eugen Banauch, **S. und Doderer. Harmonik in erzählender Prosa*, Vienna, Braumüller, 2001, 102 pp. **Waldbilder. Beiträge zum interdisziplinären Kolloquium 'Da ist Wald und Wald und Wald' (Adalbert Stifter), Göttingen, 19. und 20. März 1999. Veranstaltet vom Fachbereich*

Forstwirtschaft und Umweltmanagement der Fachhochschule Hildesheim/Holzminden/Göttingen, ed. Walter Hettche and Hubert Merkel, Munich, Iudicium, 2000, 157 pp. Günter Sasse, '"Um gewisse Linien und Richtungen anzugeben." Zur symbolischen Ordnung in Ss Erzählung "Der beschriebene Tännling"', *ZDP*, 122:509–25. F. Schösser, 'Zwischen romantischer Verlockung und dämonischer Rationalität. Zu Ss Erzählung *Der Waldsteig*', *Aurora*, 62, 2002:113–25. A. Doppler, 'A. S. als Briefschreiber. Dargestellt vor allem an Briefen an Amalia Stifter', pp. 133–46 of *'Ich an Dich.' Edition, Rezeption und Kommentierung von Briefen*, ed. Werner M. Bauer, Innsbruck, Inst. für deutsche Sprache, Literatur und Literaturkritik, 2001, 278 pp. Id., '*Witiko*, der Wald und die Waldleute', *Fest. Vizkelety*, 393–402. W. Wiesmüller, 'Die abgebrochene Korrektur. Zur Textgenese von Ss *Witiko* als "Perfektionsdrama"', Haslinger, *Textgenese*, 8–27.

STORM. Clifford Albrecht Bernd, *T. S.: The Dano-German Poet and Writer*, Oxford–Berne, Lang, 233 pp., is a significant study which offers a genuinely new understanding of S.'s literary achievement in the light of his strong Danish heritage. The work questions some of the received ideas about S., examining the way in which his daughter Gertrud, who wrote her authoritative biography in a period of marked German nationalism, altered or omitted facts which would have revealed the formative influence of Danish culture on her father's writing. In three convincingly argued sections, B. traces S.'s exposure to Danish literature and ideas at school and university, revisits the poems — today often sadly neglected —, highlighting the inspiration S. derived from Danish verse melody, and considers elements of the Danish novella form apparent in four works: *Immensee*, *In St. Jürgen*, *Aquis submersus*, and *Der Schimmelreiter*. Ingrid Schuster, *Tiere als Chiffre: Natur und Kunstfigur in den Novellen T. Ss*, Berne–Berlin, Lang, 182 pp., investigates an aspect of S.'s narrative technique that, although perhaps obvious, has hitherto not been fully explored. The study offers 24 very readable new interpretations of Novellen in which animals play an emblematic role, highlighting the interaction of these creatures with the protagonists and probing their poetic function as a mirror and catalyst of human behaviour. The chapters on *Immensee* and *Der Schimmelreiter* in particular analyse this complex relationship with some skill and represent a noteworthy contribution to S. scholarship. Christine Geffers Browne, *T. S.: Das Spannungsverhältnis zwischen Glauben und Aberglauben in seinen Novellen*, NY–Washington, Lang, 2002, xii + 155 pp., brings together for the first time the familiar subjects of faith and superstition which have previously been examined separately by S. scholars. This relatively short but insightful study, which benefits from the author's theological training, presents a definition of the two terms and traces S.'s personal development with respect to both dispositions before turning to the literary works. B. argues that while the elements of faith and superstition coexist unproblematically in many *Novellen*, five examples can be identified in which conflict results from a tension between the two positions. The main body of the volume is devoted to a detailed and penetrating analysis of *In St. Jürgen*, *Aquis submersus*, *Renate* (the focal point of the inquiry), *Im Brauerhause*, and *Der Schimmelreiter*. *T. S.: The Lake of the Bees*, trans. Jonathan Katz, London, Hesperus, 112 pp. Heiner Mückenberger, **T. S. — Dichter und Richter. Eine rechtsgeschichtliche Lebensbeschreibung*, Baden-Baden, Nomos, 2001, 255 pp.

T. A. Kamla, 'Transitoriness and Christian transcendence in S.'s *Aquis submersus*', *FMLS*, 39:27–52. B. Malinowski, 'Mimesis als Transgression. Gattungsdiskursive Untersuchungen zu T. Ss Bekenntnisnovelle *Ein Bekenntnis*', *Raabe-Jb.*, 44:77–116. C. A. Bernd, 'Die Entstehung von T. Ss Dichtung in Zusammenhang mit der dänischen Kultur', *Akten (Wien)*, XII, 153–58. A. Meier, '"Wie kommt ein Pferd nach Jevershallig?" Die Subversion des Realismus in T. Ss *Der Schimmelreiter*', *Fest. Wünsch*, 167–79. K. E. Laage, 'T. S. — ein literarischer Vorfahr von Thomas Manns *Buddenbrooks*?', *TMJb*, 15, 2002:15–33. H. Rölleke, 'Kinderszenen. Ss Novellenskizze *Die Armensünder-Glocke* und Kellers *Romeo und Julia*', *WW*, 51, 2001:1–3. Id., '"Letzter Zweck aller Krüppeley." Volksliterarische Subtexte zu T. Ss Novelle *Eine Malerarbeit*', *JFDH*, 2002:240–48. *STSG*, 52, contains: G. Eversberg, 'T. Ss Bibliothek' (9–29); K. E. Laage, '30 Jahre S.-Haus. Vom privat genutzten Wohnhaus zum Dichter-Museum' (31–33); R. Fasold, 'Eine Dichterliebe in Husum. Anmerkungen zum Briefwechsel T. S. — Constanze Esmarch' (43–52); C. Neumann, 'Ein Text und sein Doppelgänger. Eine plurale Lektüre von T. Ss Novelle *Ein Doppelgänger*' (53–73); H. Beckwenn, '"*Aquis submersus.*" Das Motiv des ertrinkenden Kindes in Ss Novelle und in Goethes Roman *Die Wahlverwandtschaften*' (75–83); P. Goldammer, 'Eine eigentümliche Freundschaft. T. S. und Ludwig Graf zu Reventlow' (85–105); K. E. Laage, 'T. Ss Besuch bei der Familie Jacobs in Gotha (mit unveröffentlichten Briefen)' (107–13); E. A. Prjanischnikov, 'Über den Zweifel. Ein literarisch-psychologisches Paradox' (115–17); E. Jacobsen, 'S.-Bibliographie' (119–25); G. Eversberg, 'S.-Forschung und S.-Gesellschaft' (127–34).

VISCHER, FRIEDRICH THEODOR. A. Baillot, 'F. T. Fs Auseinandersetzung mit der Solgerschen Kunstphilosophie. Unveröffentlichte Exzerpte aus Karl Wilhelm Ferdinand Solgers *Vorlesungen über Ästhetik*', *SchillerJb.*, 46, 2002:3–22.

WAGNER. Udo Bermbach, *'Blühendes Leid': Politik und Gesellschaft in R. Ws Musikdramen*, Stuttgart–Weimar, Metzler, vii + 363 pp., takes as its starting-point W.'s emotive words 'keiner kann dichten, ohne zu politisieren' and offers from the perspective of the political scientist a weighty investigation of the relationship between politics, society, and art on which W. himself insisted. The opening chapter traces the biographical context of the operas and examines important aspects of W.'s theoretical essays, including the influence of Feuerbach and the interest in Classical Greece. By pursuing a chronological approach in the main part of the study and devoting a chapter to each opera, B. illustrates his conviction that W.'s works can be seen as 'eine schrittweise Einlösung seines politisch-ästhetischen Programms' leading up to the appearance of *Der Ring des Nibelungen* in which politics is the dominant theme. A final chapter addresses the controversial debate on anti-semitism in W.'s work. Eva Rieger, *Minna und Richard Wagner: Stationen einer Liebe*, Düsseldorf, Artemis und Winkler, 444 pp., offers a detailed and fascinating account of the 30-year marriage of R. and M. W., drawing frequently on letters which illuminate the reality of their relationship in both its joys and strains. R. challenges the stereotypes perpetuated by a series of W. biographers who have contrasted Minna unfavourably with W.'s second wife Cosima, branding her an unintelligent, second-rate actress who was insensitive to her husband's creative genius. Instead she is revealed to be a charming, competent woman who coped loyally with adverse domestic circumstances and was closely involved in the artistic process behind W.'s early works before eventually capitulating under the pressure of his profligate, promiscuous lifestyle. The volume contains perceptive observations on the socio-economic norms surrounding marriage in the 19th c. which W. was temperamentally incapable of meeting, and amply fills a gap in scholarship with regard to the central woman in W.'s life. Dieter Borchmeyer, *Drama and the World of R. W.*, trans. Daphne Ellis, Princeton U.P., 376 pp., presents W. primarily as a man of letters rather than a composer. The study examines W.'s complete works from the standpoint of literary and theatrical history and traces W.'s relationship to King Ludwig II, Bismarck, Nietzsche, and Thoman Mann. Id., **R. W.: Ahasvers Wandlungen*, Frankfurt–Leipzig, Insel, 2002, 647 pp. Heiko Jacobs, **Die dramaturgische Konstruktion des Parsifal von R. W.: Von der Architektur der Partitur zur Architektur auf der Bühne*, Frankfurt–Berlin, Lang, 2002, 230 pp., is a Hanover dissertation. Ulrich Drüner, **Schöpfer und Zerstörer: R. W. als Künstler*, Cologne–Weimar, Böhlau, ix + xvi + 361 pp. Christian Merlin, **Le Temps dans la dramaturgie wagnérienne. Contribution à une étude dramaturgique des opéras de R. W.*, Berne–Berlin, Lang, 2001, xi + 448 pp. **R. W.: Points de départ et aboutissements. Anfangs- und Endpunkte. Actes du colloque d'Amiens 19, 20, 21, 22 octobre 2001*, ed. Danielle Buschinger, Amiens, Centre d'Etudes Médiévales, Univ. de Picardie Jules Verne, 2002, iii + 400 pp.

W.-D. Hartwich, 'Künstler, Arier und Mysterien: "Griechenland" im W.-Kreis', Aurnhammer, *Antike*, 59–87. C. Merlin, 'Présence des juifs dans les opéras de W.', pp. 73–82 of *Images de l'altérité*, ed. André Combes, Villeneuve d'Ascq, Univ. Charles-de-Gaulle — Lille 3, 2002, 216 pp. R. Perlwitz, 'W.-Rezeption in *À la recherche du temps perdu*. Ein deutscher Komponist in einem französischen Roman: Okkultierung und Evidenz', pp. 327–67 of *Die Macht der Differenzen. Beiträge zur Hermeneutik der Kultur*, ed. Reinhard Düssel, Heidelberg, Synchron, 2001, 423 pp.

WEERTH. B. Füllner, ' ". . . nichts ist langweiliger und uninteressanter als die Unschuld." Der Prozeß gegen G. W. wegen Verleumdung des Fürsten Lichnowsky in "Leben und Thaten des berühmten Ritters Schnapphanski" ', *Fest. Windfuhr*, 143–59. F. Melis, 'Neue Aspekte in der politischen Publizistik von G. W. und Ferdinand Freiligrath 1848/49. Ihre Wohn- und Wirkungsstätten in Köln', *Grabbe Jb.*, 21, 2002: 160–88. J. Hiller von Gaertringen, 'W.-Bibliographie 2001 — mit Nachträgen', *ib.*, 250–54. G. Gadek, 'Zur Rezeption G. Ws in Deutschland. Aus Anlass des Todes des Verlegers Siegfried Unseld', *Grabbe-Jb.*, 22: 175–86. B. Füllner, ' ". . .ich bin ja ein halber Rheinländer!" Eine biographische Skizze zur Mutter G. Ws', *ib.*, 187–95. J. Hiller von Gaertringen, 'W.-Bibliographie 2002 mit Nachträgen', *ib.*, 236–37.

ZSCHOKKE. W. Bänziger, 'Pestalozzi, Z. und Wessenberg. Ein Vergleich der autobiographischen Lebensentwürfe', *Immermann-Jb.*, 4: 39–53. R. Charbon, 'Autobiographisches Schreiben bei H. Z.', *ib.*, 55–70. M. Prescher, 'Magdeburger Jugend in den Autobiographien von Z., Immermann und Schütze', *ib.*, 71–83.

LITERATURE, 1880–1945

By Malcolm Humble, *formerly Lecturer in German, University of Saint Andrews*

1. General

Matthew Jefferies, *Imperial Culture in Germany, 1871–1918*, Houndsmills, Palgrave Macmillan, 338 pp., has sections on literature in all the cultural phases of the period. F. Wefelmeyer, 'From nature to modernism: the concept and discourse of culture in its development from the nineteenth into the twentieth century', Niven, *Politics*, 23–42. S. Parkes, 'The German "Geist und Macht" dichotomy. Just a game of Red Indians?', Niven, *Politics*, 43–62. **Deutsche Geschichte des 20. Jahrhunderts im Spiegel der deutschsprachigen Literatur*, ed. Moshe Zuckermann (Conferences 2. Tagungsbände des Instituts für deutsche Geschichte der Universität Tel Aviv), Göttingen, Wallstein, 205 pp. Klaus Johann, **Grenze und Halt: der Einzelne im 'Haus der Regeln'. Zur deutschsprachigen Internatsliteratur* (BNL, 201), xiv + 727 pp.

LYRIC. *Lyrik des Expressionismus*, ed. Hansgeorg Schmidt-Bergmann, Stuttgart, Reclam, 344 pp.

NARRATIVE. Kerstin Barndt, *Sentiment und Sachlichkeit. Der Roman der Neuen Frau in der Weimarer Republik* (Literatur, Kultur, Geschlecht, 19), Cologne, Böhlau, 234 pp., includes chapters on Vicki Baum, *stud.chem. Helene Willfüer*, and Irmgard Keun, *Gilgi — eine von uns* and *Das künstliche Mädchen*. R. Hahn, 'Der Erfinder als Erlöser — Führerfiguren im völkischen Zukunftsroman', Esselborn, *Utopie*, 29–47.

DRAMA. Sarah Colvin, *Women and German Drama. Playwrights and Their Texts 1860–1945*, Woodbridge, Camden House, 218 pp. Annette Bühler-Dietrich, **Auf dem Weg zum Theater. Else Lasker-Schüler, Marieluise Fleisser, Nelly Sachs, Gerlind Reinshagen, Elfriede Jellinek* (Ep, 444), 240 pp. M. Pirro, 'Dramentheorien im Rahmen der deutschen neuklassischen Bewegung um die Jahrhundertwende', *LJb*, 44:251–70. Shu-Mei Shieh, *Kleinbürgerin und Kleinbürger im Drama der Jahrhundertwende. Studie zu den Dramen männlicher und weiblicher Autoren* (EH, 1, 1856), 264 pp., deals with Hauptmann's *Der Biberpelz* and *Die Ratten*, Sternheim's *Die Hose*, Juliane Déry's *D'Schand'*, Clara Viebig's *Fräulein Freschbolzen*, and Johanna Wolff's *Die Meisterin*. **Hundert Jahre Kabarett. Zur Inszenierung gesellschaftlicher Identität*, ed. Joanne McNally and Peter Sprengel, Würzburg, Königshausen & Neumann, 240 pp. Helmut Kreuzer, **Deutschsprachige Hörspiele 1924–33. Elf Studien zu ihrer gattungsgeschichtlichen Differenzierung* (FLK, 73), 172 pp. D. Martin, '"Ein Buch für Schwächlinge." "Werther"-Allusionen in Dramen des Naturalismus', *ZDP*, 122:237–65.

MOVEMENTS AND PERIODS. Rosa B. Schneider, '*Um Scholle und Leben': Zur Konstruktion von 'Rasse' und Geschlecht in der kolonialen Afrikaliteratur um 1900*, Frankfurt, Brandes & Apsel, 295 pp. *Sprache im technischen Zeitalter*, 168, contains a section entitled: '"Hic sunt leones." Der deutsche Kolonialismus in Südwestafrika in der Literatur', 388–471. **Mädchenliteratur der Kaiserzeit. Zwischen weiblicher Identifizierung und Grenzüberschreitung*, ed. Gisela Wilkending, Stuttgart, Metzler, 300 pp. M. E. Humble, '*Das Reich der Erfüllung*: a theme in Wilhelmine counter-culture', Giles, *Counter-Cultures*, 105–20. D. Midgley, '"Los von Berlin!" Anti-urbanism as counter-culture in early twentieth-century Germany', *ib.*, 121–36. M. Kohlenbach, 'Walter Benjamin, Gustav Wyneken and the *Jugendkulturbewegung*', *ib.*, 137–54. C. Riordan, 'The Green alternative in Germany 1900–1930', *ib.*, 155–70. S. Busch, 'Bluthochzeit mit Mutter Erde: Repression und Regression in der Blut-und-Boden-Literatur', *ib.*, 193–212. E. Fuchs, 'Räume und Mechanismen der internationalen Wissenskommunikation und Ideenzirkulation vor dem Ersten Weltkrieg', *IASL*, 27.1, 2002: 125–43. H. Müller, 'Verlagswesen und europäische Massekommunikationsgesellschaft um 1900', *ib.*, 170–97. K. Maase, 'Die soziale Bewegung gegen Schundliteratur im deutschen Kaiserreich. Ein Kapitel aus der Geschichte der Volkserziehung', *ib.*, 27.2, 2002: 45–123.

Carsten Strathausen, **The Look of Things. Poetry and Vision around 1900* (UNCSGL, 126), 321 pp. Simone Winko, **Kodierte Gefühle. Zu einer Poetik der Emotionen in lyrischen und poetischen Texten um 1900*, Berlin, Schmidt, 456 pp. Rainer Rumold, *The Janus Face of the German Avant-Garde. From Expressionism towards Postmodernism*, Evanston, Northwestern U.P., 2002, 245 pp., covers the development of the avant-garde through crisis to stasis with attention to Expressionism, Dadaism, Carl Einstein, Benjamin, George Grosz, Brecht, and Benn. Jan Christoph Metzler, **De/Formationen. Autorenschaft, Körper und Materialität im expressionistischen Jahrzehnt*, Bielefeld, Aisthesis, 388 pp., concentrates on Gottfried Benn. André Bucher, **Repräsentation als Performance. Walter Serner, Robert Müller, Hermann Ungar, Joseph Roth, Ernst Weiss*, Munich, Fink, 282 pp.

ABNG, 53, 'Von Richthofen bis Remarque: deutschsprachige Prosa zum 1. Weltkrieg', ed. Thomas F. Schneider and Hans Wagener, contains, after the editors' introduction (11–16): H. Wagener, 'Wandervogel und Flammenengel. Walter Flex: *Der Wanderer zwischen beiden Welten. Ein Kriegerlebnis* (1916)' (17–30); R. Parr, 'Reisender "sportsman" im Krieg. Gunther Plüschow: *Die Abenteuer des Fliegers von Tsingtau. Erlebnisse in drei Erdteilen* (1916)' (31–49); M. Hettling, 'Arrangierte Authentizität. Philipp Witkop: *Kriegsbriefe gefallener Studenten* (1916)' (51–69); W. Fähnders, '"Das leidenschaftlichste Buch gegen den Krieg." Leonhard Frank: *Der Mensch ist gut* (1917)' (71–84); A. Barker, ' "Ein Schrei, vor dem kunstrichterliche Einwendungen gern verstummen." Andreas Latzko: *Menschen im Krieg* (1917)' (85–96); J. Bernig, 'Anachronistisches Kriegsbild, Selbstinszenierung und posthume Heroisierung. Manfred von Richthofen: *Der rote Kampfflieger* (1917)' (97–111); M. Pöhlmann, ' "Das große Erleben da draußen." Die Reihe *Schlachten des Weltkrieges* (1921–1930)' (113–31); H. Peitsch, 'Wenig "Licht" im "Rachen der Schlange." Hans Carossa, *Rumänisches Tagebuch* (1924)' (133–64); M. Baumeister, 'Ästhetik der Abschreckung. Der Versuch einer pazifistischen Kriegsdarstellung. Bruno Vogel: *Es lebe der Krieg! Ein Brief* (1925)' (165–79); J. Vollmer, 'Gift/Gas oder das Phantasma der reinigenden Gewalt. Johannes R. Becher: *(CH Cl = CH)3As (Levisite) oder Der einzig gerechte Krieg* (1926)' (181–93); J. Hermand, 'Arnold Zweig: *Der Streit um den Sergeanten Grischa* (1927). Eine "systemkritische" Analyse' (195–205); U. Broich, ' "Hier spricht zum ersten Male der gemeine Mann." Die Fiktion vom Kriegserlebnis des einfachen Soldaten in Ludwig Renn: *Der Krieg* (1928)' (217–16); T. F. Schneider, ' "Krieg ist Krieg schließlich." Erich Maria Remarque: *Im Westen nichts Neues* (1928)' (217–32); B. Hüppauf, 'Zwischen Metaphysik und visuellem Essayismus. Franz Schauwecker: *So war der Krieg* (1928)' (233–48); B. Murdoch, 'Tierische Menschen und menschliche Tiere. Ernst Johannsen: *Vier von der Infanterie und Fronterinnerungen eines Pferdes* (1929)' (249–60); U. Fröschle, ' "Radikal im Denken, aber schlapp im Handeln?" Franz Schauwecker: *Aufbruch der Nation* (1929)' (261–98); H. Ehrke-Rotermund, ' "Durch die Erkenntnis des Schrecklichen zu seiner Überwindung?" Werner Beumelburg: *Gruppe Bösemüller* (1930)' (299–318); R. Schafnitzel, 'Die vergessene Collage des Ersten Weltkrieges. Edlef Köppen: *Heeresbericht* (1930)' (319–41); H. Orlowski, 'Krieg der Reiter. Karl Benno von Mechow: *Das Abenteuer. Ein Reiterroman aus dem großen Krieg* (1930)' (343–58); M. Sargeant, 'Roman der deutschen Kriegsflotte oder Roman der geschundenen deutschen Arbeiter? Theodor Plievier: *Des Kaisers Kulis* (1930)' (359–73); U. Dittmann, 'Das erste Kriegsbuch eines Arbeiters. Adam Scharrer: *Vaterlandslose Gesellen* (1930)' (375–86); H. Schreckenberger, ' "Über Erwarten grauenhaft." Der 1. Weltkrieg aus weiblicher Sicht. Adrienne Thomas: *Die Katrin wird Soldat* (1930)' (387–98); W. Delabar, ' "Aufhören, aufhören, he, aufhören — hört doch einmal auf!" Hans Zöberlein: *Der Glaube an Deutschland* (1931)' (399–421). T. Schneider, 'Pazifistische Kriegutopien in der deutschen Literatur vor und nach dem Ersten Weltkrieg', Esselborn, *Utopie*, 12–28.

**Das Deutsche Reich ist eine Republik. Beiträge zur Kommunikation und Sprache der Weimarer Zeit*, ed. Horst D. Schlosser (Frankfurter Forschungen zur Kultur- und Sprachwissenschaft, 8), Frankfurt, Lang,

227 pp., includes contributions on Ernst Jünger's *In Stahlgewittern*, Remarque's *Im Westen nichts Neues*, Kästner's *Emil und die Detektive*, Thomas Mann's *Von deutscher Republik*, the Agitprop theatre, and Tucholsky.

Die Weltbühne. Zur Tradition und Kontinuität demokratischer Publizistik. Dokumentation der Tagung 'Wieder gilt: Der Feind steht rechts!', ed. Stefanie Oswalt (Schriftenreihe der Kurt Tucholsky-Gesellschaft, 1), St. Ingbert, Röhrig, 225 pp., includes: H. Pross, 'Die *Weltbühne* im Kampf gegen Hitler und gegen Rechts' (9–26); M. Messerschmidt, 'Militärkritik in der *Weltbühne*' (27–38); B. Schrader, 'Literatur- und Kunstdebatten in der *Weltbühne.* Oder: Der schwierige Weg des Siegfried Jacobsohn im Umgang mit Expressionismus und Revolution' (39–50); V. Otto, 'Kulturkritik zwischen Chaplin und Jazz. Die *Weltbühne*, die USA und der Amerikanismus' (51–64); G. Kraiker, 'Kurt Tucholsky als politischer Publizist der *Weltbühne*' (65–74); G. Fülberth, 'Aktivismus, Sozialismus, Pazifismus. Herrschaft der "Geistigen". Kurt Hillers politische Interventionen in der *Weltbühne*' (75–84); S. Neuhaus, 'Erich Kästner zwischen Literatur und Journalismus. Konzeptionelle Gemeinsamkeiten der *Weltbühnen*-Beiträge bis 1933' (85–98); W. Boldt, '"Ein runder Tisch wartet." Zu Ossietzkys Aufsatz von 1932' (99–128); D. Schiller, 'Die *Weltbühne* im Prager Exil' (129–42); U. Wiemann, 'Paradigmenwechsel oder literarische Mimickry: Kurt Tucholsky und die Politisierung des Kabaretts' (185–98); M. Düsberg, '"Soll ich aufstehn und das Schreiben lassen?" Kurt Tucholsky und Franz Kafka im Vergleich' (199–206); E. Jäger, 'Ernst Tollers späte Dramen' (207–14); P. Kabus, 'Hätte Tucholsky für die DDR-Weltbühne geschrieben? Zur Geschichte einer Zeitschrift zwischen humanistischer Tradition und Parteijournalismus' (215–22).

Thomas Achternkamp, **Das Schattenjahr 1932. Subjekt zwischen Krise und Katastrophe im Roman der späten Weimarer Republik* (Cursus. Texte und Studien zur deutschen Literatur, 21), Munich, Iudicium, 2002, 268 pp. Hans-Peter Rüsing, **Die nationalistischen Geheimbünde in der Literatur der Weimarer Republik. Joseph Roth, Vicki Baum, Ödön von Horváth, Peter Martin Lampel* (HKADI, 33), 315 pp. **Autorinnen der Weimarer Republik*, ed. Walter Fähnders and Helga Karrenbrock (Studienbuch, 5), Bielefeld, Aisthesis, 297 pp., includes contributions on Gertrud Kolmar, Anna Seghers, Marieluise Fleisser, Vicki Baum, Irmgard Keun, and Gabriele Tergit. S. Becker, 'Literatur der Weimarer Republik. Literaturgeschichte als Mediengeschichte', *DUS*, 55.6:54–65. Id., 'Die literarische Moderne der zwanziger Jahre. Theorie und Ästhetik der Neuen Sachlichkeit', *IASL*, 27.1, 2002:73–95. K. Grosse Kracht, '"Ein Europa im kleinen." Die Sommergespräche von Pontigny und die deutsch-französische

Intellektuellenverständigung in der Zwischenkriegszeit', *ib.*, 144–69. D. Barnouw, 'Postmodernism and Weimar culture', *Arcadia*, 38:23–38.

Kathleen Coudray, **Women Writers of the Journal 'Jugend' from 1919–1940: 'Das Gehirn unsrer lieben Schwestern'* (SGLL, 34), 340 pp. *JKLWR*, 8, includes contributions on Kästner's *Emil und die Detektive* and Joseph Roth's *Das Spinnennnetz* (and its film version of 1989), the state architecture of the period, the portrayal of the November revolution 1918 in novels of the time, and previously unpublished texts by Heinrich Eduard Jacob and Annemarie Schwarzenbach. Hans-Albert Walter, *Deutsche Exilliteratur 1933–1950*, Vol. 1. *Die Vorgeschichte des Exils und seine erste Phase*, part 1.1. *Die Mentalität der Weimardeutschen/Die 'Politisierung' der Intellektuellen*, Stuttgart, Metzler, 782 pp. Although only incidentally concerned with creative literature, this represents the most thorough survey to date of the continuities in the German mentality from the Kaiserreich through World War I to the later years of the Weimar Republic in relation to the now familiar cultural and political divisions which emerged at the same time. Without giving emphasis to the right (whether new conservative or Nazi) it traces the effect of authoritarian socialization on intellectuals of the left and republican centre as well as on the general public.

F. Trapp, 'Der Geist der "völkischen Bewegung" und die Bücherverbrennungen vom Mai 1933', *Exil*, 23.1:5–15. **Goethe im Exil. Deutsch-amerikanische Perspektiven*, ed. Gert Sautermeister and Frank Baron, Bielefeld, Aisthesis, 207 pp. *Deutschsprachige Exilliteratur seit 1933. 3. USA*, part 3, ed. John M. Spalek, Konrad Feilchenfeldt, and Sandra H. Hawrylchak, Zurich, Saur, 2002, 541 pp. While of the nine figures represented by essays only Claire Goll is likely to be known to most readers, the thematic contributions cover such topics as female poets, the aphorism, public lecturing, anti-Nazi films, and the American Guild for German Cultural Freedom; Part 4 of the same work, Zurich, Saur, 557 pp., consists of articles on authors in various fields, including Richard Coudenhove-Kalergi, George Grosz, Siegfried Kracauer, Paul Tillich, Eric Voegelin, and on a range of themes including book illustration, children's literature, cabaret, right-wing immigrants, and anti-Stalinist political renegades. A fifth volume is due to complete this section of a major project (thus the statement in *YWMLS*, 63:739, that the USA section had been completed with vol. 2, has proved to be premature).

Christina Thurner, *Der andere Ort des Erzählens. Exil und Utopie in der Literatur deutscher Emigrantinnen und Emigranten 1933–1945*, Cologne, Böhlau, viii + 309 pp., has chapters on Anna Seghers, *Transit*, Irmgard Keun, *Kind aller Länder*, Alice Rühle-Gerstel, *Der Umbruch oder Hanna und die Freiheit*, Klaus Mann, *Der Vulkan*, Lion Feuchtwanger,

Exil, and offers a reading which aims to show that exile literature, through the development of a utopian discourse through the act of writing, contains signs of modernism for which it is not usually given credit. Joseph P. Strelka, *Exil, Gegenexil und Pseudoexil in der Literatur* (Patmos, 8), Tübingen, Francke, x + 172 pp., includes essays on Jacob Klein-Haparasch, *...Der vor dem Löwen flieht* (1961), Alfred W. Kneucker, Robert Pick, *The Terboven File* (1944), Soma Morgenstern, *Flucht in Frankreich* (1998), Ernst Lothar, Ernst Schönwiese, Hitler in novels by Ernst Weiss and Bruno Brehm, Broch's *Der Tod des Vergil,* Ernst Glaeser, and Theodor Plievier.

ABNG, 54, 'Ästhetiken des Exils', ed. Helga Schreckenberger, after the editor's introduction (9–13), includes: H. Peitsch, '"Das Politische zur Natur werden lassen": vom Umgang mit dem Vorwurf der "Tendenz" in der Exilliteratur' (15–36); B. Englmann, 'Exil und Expressionismus — Kontinuitäten eines kunsttheoretischen Diskurses nach 1933' (37–54); R. Cohen, 'Brechts ästhetische Theorie in den ersten Jahren des Exils' (55–70); J. Vinzent, 'Aesthetics of internment. Art in Britain during the Second World War' (71–92); R. Neugebauer, 'Anti-Nazi-Cartoons deutschsprachiger Emigranten in Großbritannien: ein spezielles Kapitel Karikaturengeschichte' (93–122); D. Vietor-Engländer, 'Alfred Kerr's unknown film scripts written in exile. The famous critic and his change of genre' (123–39); R. Zachau, 'Der "kleine Mann" als Übermensch in Stefan Heyms Thriller *Hostages* (1942): zur Genese eines sozialistischen Stereotyps' (141–55); K. von Tippelskirch, 'Mimicry als Erfolgsrezept: Mascha Kalékos Exil im Exil' (157–71); T. Schneider, 'Das Exil als biographischer und ästhetischer Kontinuitätsbruch: von Hans Sochaczewer zu José Orabuena' (173–85); P. Weckerl, '"Light from our past" — Rückbesinnung auf jüdische Traditionen im amerikanischen Exil am Beispiel der Künstlerin Lulu Kayser-Darmstädter' (187–207); W. Koepke, 'Hölderlin in einer gottverlassenen Zeit' (209–33); H. Häntzschel, 'Macht und Ohnmacht der Wörter. Die Innenansicht des nationalsozialistischen Alltags im Exilroman *Nach Mitternacht* von Irmgard Keun' (235–49); K. Kröhnke, 'Wurde Lion Feuchtwanger durch das Exil zum Trivialautor?' (251–65); J. Thunecke, 'Der große Einschnitt: drei Exil-Gedichte Erich Frieds aus den frühen 40er Jahren' (265–85); H. Doane, 'Die wiedergewonnene Identität: zur Funktion der Erinnerung in Anna Seghers' Erzählung "Der Ausflug der toten Mädchen"' (287–300); J. Vogt, '*Damnatio memoriae* und "Werke von langer Dauer." Zwei ästhetische Grenzwerte in Brechts Exillyrik' (301–17); H. Krauss, 'Reise-Erinnerungen — die nachgetragenen Exilerfahrungen Fred Wanders' (319–32); U. Seeber, 'Der unheimliche Dichter. Zur deutschsprachigen Rezeption von Jakov Lind' (333–51); D. Sevin, 'Hilde Domin: Rückkehr aus dem Exil als

Ursprung und Voraussetzung ihrer Poetologie' (353–64); L. Olschner, 'Poetiksplitter des nicht abgelegten Exils. Paul Celans Bremer Rede (1958)' (365–85); G. Stern, 'The impact of rescued artists on European and American culture' (387–403).

Brita Eckert, **Deutsches Exilarchiv 1933–1945 und Sammling Exilliteratur. Katalog der Bücher und Broschüren*, vol. 2, Stuttgart, Metzler, 600 pp. *Zwischenwelt*, 20.1, has a section on exile cabaret (17–79). E. Bahr, 'Exiltheater in Los Angeles: Max Reinhardt, Leopold Jessner, Bertolt Brecht und Walter Wicclair', *Exilforschung*, 21:95–111. *Die Rezeption des Exils: Geschichte und Perspektiven der österreichischen Exilforschung*, ed. Evelyn Adunka and Peter Roessler, Vienna, Mandelbaum, 374 pp. *Die totalitäre Erfahrung: Deutsche Literatur und Drittes Reich*, ed. Frank-Lothar Kroll (Literarische Landschaften, 5), Berlin, Dunckler & Humblot, 315 pp., includes: G. Scholdt, 'Deutsche Literatur und "Drittes Reich". Eine Problemskizze' (13–36); C. Koepcke, 'Konservative Schriftsteller im Nationalsozialismus. Eine (preußische) Alternative' (37–54); R. Mossbach, 'Die Ohnmacht der Verzweiflung. "Innere Emigration" am Beispiel Otto von Taubes' (55–74); B. Röhrl, 'Die revidierte Moderne. Siegfried von Vegesack — Das gescheiterte Experiment einer "neuen Heimatliteratur" im Dritten Reich' (75–102); N. L. Hackelsberger, 'Das Wort als Waffe. Werner Bergengruen, Carl Muth und der Kreis um die Zeitschrift "Hochland" im Dritten Reich' (103–16); H. Siefken, 'Totalitäre Erfahrungen aus der Sicht eines christlichen Essayisten. Theodor Haecker im Dritten Reich' (117–52); J. Pottier, 'Erlebte und gedeutete Geschichte. Gertrud von le Forts "Weg durch die Nacht" im Dritten Reich' (153–72); W. Halder, 'Sehnsucht nach universaler Gerechtigkeit. Zum Verhältnis von "Innerer Emigration" und Exil während des Dritten Reiches' (173–96); J. M. Ritchie, 'Stimmen von außen. Exilautoren und ihr Bild vom Nationalsozialismus' (197–214); M. Klaussner, 'Vom Traum der Vernunft und vom Geldbeutel. Kurt Hillers Wollen und Exil' (215–34).

Karl-Heinz Schoeps, *Literature and Film in the Third Reich*, Woodbridge, Camden House, 400 pp. *Reflexe und Reflexionen der Modernität 1933–1945*, ed. Erhard Schütz and Gregor Streim (Publikationen zur *ZGer.*, n.F., 6), Berne, Lang, 366 pp., includes, of relevance to literature: H. Kiesel, 'Nationalsozialismus, Modernisierung, Literatur. Ein Problemaufriß' (13–28); E. Schütz, 'Flieger — Helden der Neotenie. Jugendlichkeit und Regeneration in Literatur, Massenmedien und Anthropologie. Eine Studie zur unspezifischen Modernität des "Dritten Reiches"' (83–108); R. Klausnitzer, '"Überstaatliche Mächte." Verschwörungsphantasien und -theorien in Publizisitik, Literatur und Film des "Dritten Reiches"' (125–72); W. Delabar, 'Goebbels' Moderne. Versuch über die Modernität der Literatur des

"Dritten Reiches" und ihres ersten Repräsentanten' (173–92). *Literaturwissenschaft und Nationalsozialismus*, ed. Holger Donat and Lutz Danneberg (STSL, 99), viii + 452 pp., includes a contribution on Hans Friedrich Blunck. **Hamburg 1943 — Literarische Zeugnisse zum Feuersturm*, ed. Volker Hage (FT, 16036), 329 pp. A. Schalk, 'Schockerfahrung ist nicht erzählbar. Zum Problem des Luftkriegs in der Literatur', *LitL*, 2003.2:117–26. B. Jahn, 'Bombenkrieg und Kulturbunker. Distanzierungsrhetorik und ihr Scheitern in Texten Carossas und Langgässers', pp. 85–103 of *Krieg und Rhetorik*, ed. Thomas Rahn (Rhetorik, 22), Tübingen, Niemeyer, 180 pp. B. Dodd, 'Die Spachglosse als Ort des oppositionellen Diskurses im "Dritten Reich". Beispiele von Dolf Sternberger, Gerhard Storz und Wilhelm Süskind aus den frühen 1940er Jahren', *WW*, 53:241–52. *DUS*, 55.4, is devoted to the Third Reich and contains, relevant to literature: H. Scheuer, 'Editorial: das "Dritte Reich" im Literaturunterricht' (2–6); K. Bruns, ' "Mann — du alles auf Erden!" Topographien des Mütterlichen im Nationalsozialismus' (37–47); P. Siebert, 'Der Film — "Kunst für das Volk bis zu seinen primitivsten Regungen." Film und Literatur im Nationalsozialismus' (74–88). M. Jaeger, 'Lektüre und "Hochverrat". Literaturgeschichtliche Anmerkungen zur "Weißen Rose" ', *JDSG*, 47:303–28.

Flight of Fantasy: New Perspectives on 'Inner Emigration' in German Literature, 1933–1945, ed. Neil H. Donahue and Doris Kirchner, NY, Berghahn, 318 pp., includes: S. Brockmann, '*Inner Emigration*: the term and its origins in Postwar Debates' (11–26); R. Grimm, 'In the thicket of *Inner Emigration*' (27–45); H. D. Schäfer, 'The Young Generation's non-National Socialist literature during the Third Reich' (46–81), and 'Culture as simulation: the Third Reich and postmodernity' (82–112); F. Trommler, 'Targeting the reader, entering history: a new epitaph for the inner emigration' (113–30); L. Olschner, 'Absences of time and history: poetry of inner emigration' (131–51); C. Riordan, 'Depictions of the state in works of the inner emigration' (152–67); V. Dahm, 'The limits on literary life in the Third Reich' (168–75); G. R. Cuomo, 'Opposition or opportunism? Günter Eich's status as inner emigrant' (176–87); K.-H. Schoeps, 'Conservative opposition: Friedrich Reck-Malleczewen's antifascist novel *Bockelson: A History of Mass Hysteria*' (188–98); D. Orendi, 'Luise Rinser's escape into inner emigration' (199–210); G. Stern, 'Exile *honoris causa*: the image of Erich Kästner among writers in exile' (223–34); W. Koepke, 'Günther Weissenborn's ballad of his life' (235–47); G. Funk, 'Between apocalypse and arcadia: Horst Lange's visionary imagination during the Third Reich' (248–57); D. Basker, ' "I mounted resistance, though I hid the fact": versions of Wolfgang Koeppen's early biography' (258–68); C. S.

Gelbin, 'Elisabeth Langgässer and the question of inner emigration' (269–76).

GERMAN-JEWISH STUDIES. Hannah Burdekin, *The Ambivalent Author. Five German Writers and their Jewish Characters, 1848–1914* (British and Irish Studies in German Language and Literature, 29), Oxford, Lang, 2002, 338 pp., includes Thomas Mann in a study of the antisemitic images and language evident in the work of authors not normally associated with antisemitism. Karlheinz Rossbacher, **Literatur und Bürgertum. Fünf Wiener jüdische Familien von der liberalen Ära bis zum Fin de Siècle* (Literatur und Leben, 64), Vienna, Böhlau, 664 pp. E. Schwarz, 'Das jüdische Selbstverständnis jüdischer Autoren im *Fin de siècle*', Betten, *Judentum*, 21–31. J. Sonnleitner, 'Völkische Literatur und Antisemitismus in der Zwischenkriegszeit', *ib.*, 84–92. Anatol Schenker, **Der Jüdische Verlag 1902–1938. Zwischen Aufbruch, Blüte und Vernichtung* (CJ, 41), vii + 605 pp. Brigitte Dalinger, **Quellenedition zur Geschichte des jüdischen Theaters in Wien* (CJ, 42), vi + 282 pp. F. Krobb, 'Gefühlssozialismus und Zionsgefühle: zum Palästina-Diskurs bei Schnitzler, Herzl, Salten und Lasker-Schüler', *Ridley Vol.*, 149–64. Franka Marquart, **Erzählte Juden. Untersuchungen zu Thomas Manns 'Joseph und seine Brüder' und Robert Musils 'Der Mann ohne Eigenschaften'* (Literatur, Kultur, Medien, 4), Münster, LIT, 400 pp. *Jüdische Intellektuelle im 20. Jahrhundert: literarische und kulturgeschichtliche Studien*, ed. Ariane Huml and Monika Rappenecker, Würzburg, Königshausen & Neumann, 296 pp., has contributions on Karl Kraus and Selma Stern. A. Levenson, 'The problematics of philosemitic fiction', *GQ*, 75, 2002:379–93, is on Heinrich Johann Siemer, Emil Jakob Felden, Alfred Knobloch, and Ernst Püschel.

ANGLO-GERMAN LITERARY RELATIONS. **Uncanny Similitudes. British Writers on German Literature*, ed. Rüdiger Görner, Munich, Iudicium, 71 pp. *Intellectual Migration and Cultural Transformation. Refugees from National Socialism in the English-Speaking World*, ed. Edward Timms and Jon Hughes, Vienna, Springer, vi + 267 pp., includes: N. Hubble, 'Franz Borkenau, Sebastian Haffner and George Orwell: depoliticisation and cultural exchange' (109–28); N. Warr, 'Siegfried Kracauer's extraterritorial critique' (129–38). C. Brinson, '"In the exile of internment" or "Von Versuchen, aus einer Not eine Tugend zu machen": German-speaking women interned by the British during the Second World War', Niven, *Politics*, 63–88.

AUSTRIA, BUKOVINA. Alice Bolterauer, **Selbstvorstellung. Die literarische Selbstreflexion der Wiener Moderne*, Freiburg, Rombach, 184 pp. *Die Teile und das Ganze: Bausteine der literarischen Moderne in Österreich*, ed. Bernhard Fetz and Klaus Kastberger (Profile, 10), Vienna, Zsolnay, 299 pp., includes: W. Schmidt-Dengler, 'Auf halbem Weg mit ganzen Mitteln. Zum Fragment in der österreichischen Literatur' (83–89);

B. Fetz, '"Nichts als das Unvollendete." Der Fall Hermann Broch' (90–112); U. Ott, 'Kafkas unterbrochener Prozeß' (157–64); W. M. Hemecker, '"Das System des Teilbaus." Die Gestalttheorie und Franz Kafka' (165–73); J. Seng, '"Das Halbe, Fragmentarische aber, ist eigentlich menschliches Gebiet." Der *Andreas*-Roman von Hugo von Hofmannsthal' (174–86); H. Böhm, 'Ein vollendetes Fragment: *Die letzten Tage der Menschheit* von Karl Kraus' (187–97); C. Eggenberger, 'Zu Elias Canettis Aufzeichnungen' (198–206); W. Fanta, 'Der Feinmechaniker. Robert Musils Arbeit am *Mann ohne Eigenschaften*' (207–15); E. Gartner and K. Kastberger, 'Das ganze Fräulein — ein Stück. Von den Geschichten vom Mädchenhandel zu den *Geschichten aus dem Wiener Wald*' (216–22). **Glück und Unglück in der österreichischen Literatur und Kunst* (Internationales Kolloquium an der Universität des Saarlandes, 3.–5. Dezember 1998), ed. Pierre Béhar (Musiliana, 9), Berne, Lang, 292 pp., has contributions on Hofmannsthal and Musil. Marianne Fischer, **Erotische Literatur vor Gericht. Der Schmutzliteraturkampf im Wien des beginnenden 20. Jahrhunderts* (Untersuchungen zur österreichischen Literatur des 20. Jahrhunderts, 16), Vienna, Braumüller, xii + 204 pp. **Radikalismus, demokratische Strömungen und die Moderne in der österreichischen Literatur*, ed. Johann Dvorák (BBLI, 43), 311 pp., has contributions on Bahr and Karl Kraus. **Verflechtungsfiguren. Intertextualität und Intermedialität in der Kultur Österreich-Ungarns*, ed. Endre Hárs, Wolfgang Müller-Funk, and Magdolna Orosz (Budapester Studien zur Literaturwissenschaft, 3), Frankfurt, Lang, 240 pp., has contributions on Rilke, Musil, Joseph Roth, and Hofmannsthal. R. Duhamel, 'Zu den philosophischen Grundlagen der österreichischen Literatur um und nach 1900', *GM*, 58:5–18. J. Holzner, 'Österreichische Literatur im Exil', Betten, *Judentum*, 93–105.

*'*Blaueule Leid.' Bukowina 1940–1944.* Eine kommentierende Anthologie, ed. Bernhard Albers (Texte aus der Bukowina, 10), Aachen, Rimbaud, 160 pp. M. Kublitz-Kramer, 'Czernowitz, die "himmlische Stadt". Eine allegorische Lektüre deutschsprachiger Gedichttexte aus der Bukowina', *ZDP*, 122:582–99. S. Marten-Finnis and K. Jastal, 'Presse und Literatur in Czernowitz 1918–1940. Vom kolonialen Diskurs zum eigenständigen Feld der kulturellen Produktion. Eine Forschungsskizze', *IASL*, 28.1:181–231.

MISCELLANEOUS. **Textualität und Rhetorizität*, ed. Kálmán Kovács (Debrecener Studien zur Literatur, 10), Frankfurt, Lang, 192 pp., has contributions on Rilke's 'Stundenbuch' and 'Buch der Bilder', Kafka, Musil, and Benn. *Die biographische Illusion im 20. Jahrhundert. (Auto-)Biographien unter Legitimierungszwang*, ed. Izabela Sellmer (Posener Beiträge zur Germanistik, 1), Frankfurt, Lang, 226 pp., includes: J. Golec, 'Auf der Suche nach sozialer und politischer Identität: Ernst

Tollers *Eine Jugend in Deutschland*' (23–34); J. Kalazny, 'Die biographische Erfahrung der Heimatlosigkeit bei Theodor Lessing' (59–71); C. Karolak, '"In die Geschichte hinabgraben ..." Ina Seidels erzählerische Selbstdarstellung' (73–79); W. Kunicki, 'Lebensläufe schlesischer Autoren in den Personalakten der Reichskulturkammer' (81–97); A. Runge, 'Marieluise Fleisser. Biographie — Konstruktionen an der Schnittstelle zwischen "Leben" und "Werk"' (179–96); I. Sellmer, 'Nachdem der Dornbusch verbrannt ist: Manès Sperber erzählt von seinem Bruch mit dem Kommunismus' (199–208); K. Wagner, 'Von den Erfindungen der biographischen Wahrheit: Freud/Zweig/Dostojewski' (209–26). **Russische Studien zur deutschen Literatur des 20. Jahrhunderts*, ed. Paul Gerhard Klussmann, Frank Hoffmann, and Silke Flegel (Schriften zur Europa- und Deutschlandforschung, 9), Frankfurt, Lang, xiv + 277 pp., has contributions on George's *Algabal*, Novalis and Trakl, Eduard von Keyserling's *Beate und Mareile*, Thomas Mann's *Tristan*, and 'Zur Technik des Auslassens in der Erzählkunst Thomas Manns'. **Lust am Kanon. Denkbilder in Literatur und Unterricht*, ed. Susanne Knoche, Lennart Koch, and Ralph Könen, Frankfurt, Lang, 358 pp., has contributions on Rilke's *Die Aufzeichnungen des Malte Laurids Brigge*, Heinrich Mann's *Der Untertan*, Kafka's *In der Strafkolonie*, Döblin's *Berlin Alexanderplatz*, Musil's *Nachlaß zu Lebzeiten*, the figure of the father in the work of Thomas Mann, and Brecht's *Der kaukasische Kreidekreis*.

2. Individual Authors

ANDRIAN, LEOPOLD VON. **Leopold von Andrian 1875–1951. Korrespondenzen, Notizen, Essays, Berichte*, ed. Ursula Prutsch and Klaus Zeyringer (Veröffentlichungen der Kommission für neuere Geschichte Österreichs, 97), Cologne, Böhlau, 904 pp.

ASCHER, OTTO. A. Goodbody, 'A life among gypsies and wolves: Otto Aschler's quest for an alternative to modern civilisation', *GMon*, 57:181–208.

BAHR, HERMANN. H. B., *Tagebücher, Skizzenbücher, Notizhefte*. Vol. 5: *1906 bis 1908*, ed. Moritz Csáky with Kurt Ifkowitz and Lukas Mayerhofer, Vienna, Böhlau, 563 pp., like the previous volumes in this series, has much to tell of literary plans, meetings with contemporary cultural figures (here especially Reinhardt), and theatre performances, but its main interest lies in the detailed account in the diaries of the intense love affair with Anna Mildenburg, the singer whom Bahr married in 1909. Helene Zand, **Identität und Gedächtnis. Die Ausdifferenzierung von repräsentativen Diskursen in den Tagebüchern Hermann Bahrs* (Kultur, Herrschaft, Differenz, 3), Tübingen, Francke, 207 pp.

BALL, HUGO. Hugo Ball, *Briefe, 1904–1927* (Sämtliche Werke und Briefe, 10. Veröffentlichungen der deutschen Akademie für Sprache und Dichtung, 81), ed. and comm. Gerhard Schaub and Ernst Teubner, 3 vols, Göttingen, Wallstein, 1816 pp. Christoph Schmidt, **Die Apokalypse des Subjekts. Ästhetische Subjektivität und politische Theologie bei Hugo Ball*, Bielefeld, Aisthesis, 166 pp.

BARLACH, ERNST. Ernst Barlach, *Sämtliche Werke. Kritische Ausgabe, Das literarische Werk. 1. Dramen 1. Der tote Tag*, ed. Ulrich Bubrowski, Leipzig, Seemann, 2002, 1055 pp. G. Schmidt-Henkel, 'Verboten und vergraben. Ernst Barlachs posthumer Roman *Der gestohlene Mond*', Wild, *Bücher*, 39–46.

BECHER, JOHANNES R. Alexander Behrens, *Johannes R. Becher. Eine politische Biographie*, Cologne, Böhlau, 296 pp.

BEER-HOFMANN, RICHARD. G. Vassiliev, 'Das Konzept der Erwählung in Richard Beer-Hofmanns Drama "Jaakobs Traum" 1918', *ÖGL*, 47.4: 228–39.

BENJAMIN, WALTER. Peter Garloff, **Philologie der Geschichte. Literaturkritik und Historiographie nach Walter Benjamin* (Ep, 452), 342 pp. Christian Schulte, **Ursprung ist das Ziel. Walter Benjamin über Karl Kraus* (Ep, 439), 226 pp. G. R. Kaiser, 'Eduard Koloff, Walter Benjamin: Paris — "Mikroskop der Gegenwart"', *Fest. Brandt*, 213–28. D. Oschmann, 'Gestalt und Naturgeschichte. Benjamins *Erzähler*-Aufsatz im Horizont der zeitgenössischen Gattungspoetologie', *ib.*, 299–318. M. Sagnol, 'Walter Benjamin, Archäologe der Moderne', *WB*, 49, 260–73.

BENN, GOTTFRIED. *Sämtliche Werke*, ed. Gerhard Schuster and Ilse Benn, vol. VII.1–2: *Szenen und andere Schriften. Nachlaß und Register*, Stuttgart, Klett-Cotta, 1400 pp., completes the Stuttgart edition of his works. *Ich bin nicht innerlich: Annäherungen an Gottfried Benn*, ed. Jan Bürger, Stuttgart, Klett-Cotta, 210 pp., consists of responses by contemporary creative writers. *Benn-Jb.*, 1, ed. Joachim Dyck et al, Stuttgart, Klett-Cotta, 240 pp. Susan Ray, **Beyond Nihilism. Gottfried Benn's Postmodernist Poetics* (SMGL, 96), 205 pp. Ursula Kirchdörfer-Bossmann, **"Eine Pranke in den Nacken der Erkenntnis." Zur Beziehung von Dichtung und Naturwissenschaft im Frühwerk Gottfried Benns* (SBL, 79), 341 pp. M. Stern, '"Solipsistischer Nihilismus" und nationalsozialistisches Engagement. Der Fall Gottfried Benn', *JDSG*, 47: 329–41. O. Briese, 'Pathologie der Pathologie. Gottfried Benns "Schöne Jugend"', *DUS*, 55.5: 64–70. N. Creighton, 'Gottfried Benn: "Schöne Jugend" (1912)', Krobb, *Project*, 143–48. *BHGLL*, 5: 7–126, consists of four contributions on Benn.

BLEI, FRANZ. Helga Mitterbauer, **Die Netzwerke des Franz Blei. Kulturvermittlung im frühen 20. Jahrhundert* (Kultur, Herrschaft, Differenz, 4), Tübingen, Francke, iv + 163 pp.

BLUNCK, HANS FRIEDRICH. W. Scott Hoerle, *Hans Friedrich Blunck. Poet and Nazi Collaborator, 1888–1961* (SMLG, 97), 271 pp.

BORCHARDT, RUDOLF. *R. B., *Anabasis, Aufzeichnungen, Erinnerungen und Dokumente 1943–1945*, ed. Cornelius Borchardt, Munich, Hanser, 352 pp. Meike Steiger, **Textpolitik. Zur Vergegenwärtigung von Geschichte bei Rudolf Borchardt* (Ep, 468), 210 pp. Kai Kauffman, **Rudolf Borchardt und der 'Untergang der deutschen Nation'. Selbstinszenierungen und Geschichtskonstruktion im essayistischen Werk* (SDL, 169), 480 pp. Alexander Kissler, *'Wo bin ich denn behaust?' Rudolf Borchardt und die Erfindung des Ich*, Göttingen, Wallstein, 289 pp., constructs, on the foundation of the facts of B.'s personal and family life and his complex relation to his Jewish heritage, an inner biography which defines the roots of his creativity by tracing in all genres, with the emphasis on the prose fiction, key concepts and images: metamorphoses, the mask, the villa and the garden, mysticism, relations between the sexes, in order to present the process of self- and world fashioning in his work. G. Seibt, 'Rudolf Borchardt während des Dritten Reiches', *Merkur*, 57:465–79. G. Schuster, 'Borchardt besucht Konrad Burdach. Ein unveröffentlichter Nekrolog von 1936 und seine Vorgeschichte', *ib.*, 480–83.

BRECHT, BERTOLT. *Brecht-Handbuch*, vol. 4: *Schriften, Journale, Briefe*, ed. Jan Knopf, Stuttgart, Metzler, 547 pp. *Brecht-Handbuch*, vol. 5: *Register, Chronik, Materialien*, ed. Jan Knopf, Stuttgart, Metzler, 233 pp. *Brecht on Art and Politics*, ed. Tom Kuhn and Steve Giles, London, Methuen, viii + 354 pp. Günther Thimm, **'Das Chaos war nicht aufgebraucht.' Ein adoleszenter Konflikt als Strukturprinzip von Brechts Stücken* (Freiburger Studien, 6), Würzburg, Königshausen & Neumann, 202 pp. Matthew Philpotts, **The Margins of Dictatorship. Assent and Dissent in the Work of Günter Eich and Bertolt Brecht* (British and Irish Studies in German Language and Literature, 34), Oxford, Lang, 377 pp. Werner Wutrich with Stefan Hufeld, *Bertolt Brecht und die Schweiz* (Theatrum Helveticum, 10), Zurich, Chronos, 600 pp. Stefan Schallenberger, *Bertolt Brecht — 'Mutter Courage'* (Lektüreschlüssel), Stuttgart, Reclam, 94 pp. Peter Langemeyer, *Bertolt Brecht — 'Mutter Courage und ihre Kinder'* (Erläuterungen und Dokumente), Stuttgart, Reclam, 208 pp. A. Todorow, 'Ästhetik der Gemeinplätze: Topik und Synkretismus in Bertolt Brechts "Der Lebenslauf des Boxers Samson-Körner"', *Fest. Müller*, 297–310. W. Hecht, 'Brecht als Pygmalion? Sein Modell der Weigel', *ib.*, 311–22. J. Kopf, 'Nachgereichte Aufklärungen. Zwei Fälle bei Bertolt Brecht', *ib.*, 323–28. H.-P. Bayerdörfer, 'Galy Gay im Medienkommerz — oder das "B-Movie" als 'B. B.'-Movie?', *ib.*, 329–42. B. Banoun, 'Le lyrisme de Brecht dans la pléiade italienne', *EG*, 58:479–83. B. Gaston, 'Brecht's pastiche history play: Renaissance drama and modernist theatre',

GLL, 56:344–62. H. Kaulen, 'Brecht und die Liebeslyrik der Anakreontik', *MDG*, 50:44–58. J. Köster, 'Brecht als Schulautor. Bilanz und Perspektiven', *WW*, 53:459–72. F. Hofmann, 'Literatur des Vergessens. Brechts Strategie für Städtebewohner und die Kritik der Erinnerung', *Germanica*, 33:79–96. W. Gerhardt-Schmidt, 'Zwischen Bücherverbrennung und sozialistischer Utopie. Bertolt Brecht, die Furcht vor dem Vergessen und das Problem adequater Kunstproduktion', *Sprachkunst*, 34:51–70. J. Barkhoff, 'Bertolt Brecht: vom Schwimmen in Seen und Flüssen (1919)', Krobb, *Project*, 167–74. W. G. Schmidt, '"Tod" und "Leben" des Bertolt Brecht. Kulturpoetische Strategien in der Nachkriegsrezeption eines Klassikers', Wild, *Bücher*, 59–68.

BREITBACH, JOSEF. Jochen Meyer, *Josef Breitbach oder Die Höflichkeit des Erzählers* (*MaM*, 102), 110 pp. R. Paulus, '"Gegen politische und persönliche Selbstbeweihräucherung" — Josef Breitbachs: *Rot gegen Rot*', Wild, *Bücher*, 69–76.

BROCH, HERMANN. Hermann Broch, *Visionary in Exile. The 2001 Yale Symposium*, ed. Paul Michael Lützeler et al., Woodbridge, Camden House, 286 pp., contains, after an introduction by the editor: R. Klüger, 'Kitsch and art: Broch's essay "Das Böse im Wertsystem der Kunst"' (13–20); E. Schürer, 'Erneuerung des Theaters: Broch's ideas on drama in context' (21–36); B. Fetz, '"Der Rhythmus der Ideen": on the workings of Broch's cultural criticism' (37–54); W. Schmidt-Dengler, '"Kurzum die Hölle": Broch's early political text "Die Straße"' (55–66); P. M. Lützeler, 'Visionaries in exile: Broch's cooperation with G. A. Borgese and Hannah Arendt' (67–88); W. Müller-Funk, 'Fear in culture: Broch's *Massenwahntheorie*' (89–106); K. L. Komar, 'Inscriptions of power: Broch's narratives of history in *Die Schlafwandler*' (107–24); J. Ryan, 'The German colonial aftermath: Broch's *1903. Esch oder die Anarchie*' (125–36); G. Brude-Firnau, 'Neither sane nor insane: Ernst Kretschmer's influence on Broch's early novels' (137–46); G. Roethke, 'Non-contemporaniety of the contemporaneous: Broch's novel *Die Verzauberung*' (147–58); R. Rizzo, '"Great theater" and "soap bubbles": Broch the dramatist' (159–86); J. Heizmann, 'A farewell to art: poetic reflection in Broch's *Der Tod des Vergil*' (187–200); P. Y. Paik, 'Poetry as perjury: the end of art in Broch's *Der Tod des Vergil* and Celan's *Atemwende*' (201–16); J. Hargraves, '"Beyond words": the translation of Broch's *Der Tod des Vergil* by Jean Starr Untermeyer' (217–30); T. Ziolkowski, 'Between guilt and fall: Broch's *Die Schuldlosen*' (231–44); K. Yamaguchi, 'Broch reception in Japan: Shin'ichiro Nakamura and *Die Schuldlosen*' (245–52). Judith Sidler, **Literarisierter Tagtraum. Einheitskonstruktionen in Hermann Brochs 'Tierkreis-Erzählungen'*, Würzburg, Königshausen & Neumann, 210 pp. **Hermann Broch — Neue Studien. Festschrift für Paul*

Michael Lützeler zum 60. Geburtstag, ed. Michael Kessler et al. (Stauffenburg Colloquium, 61), Tübingen, Stauffenburg, 603 pp. *Austriaca*, 55, is devoted to Broch. See also under SAHL.

BRUCKNER, FERDINAND. *Werke, Tagebücher, Briefe*, ed. Hans-Gert Roloff, vol. 1: *Schauspiele* 1, Berlin, Weidler, x + 521 pp.

CANETTI, ELIAS. E. C., *Party im Blitz: Die englischen Jahre*, Munich, Hanser, 240 pp. Karoline Naab, **Elias Canettis akustische Poetik. Mit einem Verzeichnis von Tondokumenten und einer Bibliographie der akustischen Literatur* (Frankfurter Forschungen zur Kultur- und Sprachwissenschaft, 7), Frankfurt, Lang, 156 pp. Kristina Michaelis, **Dimensionen einer europäischen Identität. Studien zu Elias Canetti* (EH, 1, 1862), 369 pp. Stefanie Wieprecht-Roth, **'Die Freiheit in der Zeit ist die Überwindung des Todes.' Überleben in der Welt und im unsterblichen Werk. Eine Annäherung an Elias Canetti* (Ep, 478), 238 pp. W. H. Sokel, 'The love affair with the mother tongue: on the relation between autobiography and novel in Elias Canetti', *GR*, 78: 39–48.

CANETTI, VEZA. E. Meidl, 'Der Schmerz des Vertriebenwerdens: Veza Canettis Roman *Die Schildkröten*', *AUMLA*, 99: 104–14. A. Kosenina, ' "Wir erheben uns über das Land und verlassen es mit Verachtung." Veza Canettis Exilroman *Die Schildkröten*', Wild, *Bücher*, 77–86.

DÖBLIN, ALFRED. *Internationales Alfred Döblin-Kolloquium, Berlin 2001*, ed. Hartmut Eggert and Gabriele Prauss (*JIG*, Reihe A, Kongreßberichte, 51), Berne, Lang, 2002, 320 pp., contains: H. Eggert and G. Prauss, 'A. D. und die künstlerische Avantgarde in Berlin' (9–12); H. Eggert, 'Eine Topographie zwischen "Alter Westen" und "Neuer Westen". A. D. und die Berliner Literaturszene' (13–27); S. Becker, 'Mit der "Straßenbahn" durch die Moderne: A. D. — Leitfigur der literarischen Moderne 1910–1933' (30–39); W. Stauffacher, 'Umrisse einer Begegnung: A. D. und Ernst Ludwig Kirchner' (41–50); G. Scimonello, 'Futuristische Avantgarde um 1912 in Berlin. A. D. zwischen F.T. Marinettis ästhetisch-künstlerischer Rebellion und F. Mauthners sprachkritischen Bemerkungen *Beiträge zu einer Kritik der Sprache*' (51–62); M. Hofmann, 'Avantgarde, kulturelle Differenz und europäischer Blick. Carl Einsteins Analyse der afrikanischen Kunst und Döblins Romanpoetik' (63–76); L. Grevel, ' "Mensch, det is knorke" — oder: Kunst ist nicht heilig. A. D. als Kunst- und Theaterkritiker' (77–95); E. Ribbat, ' "Menschlicher, kantiger, zottiger." Karl Kraus und Linke Poot' (97–106); W. Köpke, 'Zur Ethik der Avantgarde. Zur Rezeption von Döblins ersten Romanen' (107–22); E. Kleinschmidt, 'Semiotik der Aussparung. "Vergessenes" Erzählen bei A. D.' (123–39); K. R. Scherpe, 'Krieg, Gewalt und Science Fiction. A. Ds *Berge, Meere und Giganten*' (141–56); H. Kiesel, 'Noch einmal "Benjamins Erzähler":

nicht Nicolai Lesskow, sondern Alfred Döblin!' (157–65); R. Dollinger, 'Ds Stellung zwischen avantgardistischer Technikeuphorie und naturphilosophischer Romantik' (167–78); G. Bauer, 'Glitzern und Platzen. Impressionsexerzitien von und an dem staunenden Personal einiger "neusachlicher" Romane' (179–90); A. Honold, 'Der Krieg und die Großstadt. *Berlin Alexanderplatz* und ein Trauma der Moderne' (191–211); F. Wambsganz, 'Widerstand statt Demut. Neue Thesen zu A. D. *Berlin Alexanderplatz*' (213–29); H.-D. Tschörtner, '"Er wird vielleicht noch mal Klassiker." Döblin versus Hauptmann' (231–45); S. Sanna, 'Ars aurifera. Die Verwandlung des Königs in A. Ds *Wallenstein*' (247–69); P. K. Neguié, 'A. D. und Ethnographie-Diskurs: zur Inszenierung des Dialogs zwischen Eigen- und Fremdkulturalität am Beispiel des *Wadzek*-Romans' (271–82); M. Mattick, '"Von Gesichtern Bildern und ihrer Wahrheit" — Überlegungen zur Portraitkunst August Sanders und A. Ds Figurenkonzeption in *Pardon wird nicht gegeben* und *November 1918*' (283–90); P. Krause, 'Ars militans: A. Ds Ideal von Kunst und dessen Umsetzung im Roman *Hamlet oder die lange Nacht nimmt ein Ende*' (291–310).

Thorsten Hahn, **Fluchtlinien des Politischen. Das Ende des Staates bei Alfred Döblin* (KGS, 5), 448 pp. Simonetta Sanna, *Selbststerben und Ganzwerdung: Alfred Döblins grosse Romane* (IRIS. Forschungen zur europäischen Kultur, 20), Berne, Lang, 368 pp. Michael Braun, **Kontingenz und Gewalt. Semiotische Strukturen und erzählte Welt in Alfred Döblins Roman 'Berlin Alexanderplatz'* (Ep, 429), 266 pp. Meike Mattick, **Komik und Geschichtserfahrung. Alfred Döblins komisierendes Erzählen in 'November 1918. Eine deutsche Revolution'*, Bielefeld, Aisthesis, 300 pp. Dagmar Heinze, **Kulturkonzepte in Alfred Döblins Amazonas-Trilogie. Interkulturalität im Spannungsverhältnis von Universalismus und Relativisimus*, Trier, Wissenschaftlicher Vlg, 228 pp. E. Horn, 'Literary research, narration and the epistomology of the human sciences in Alfred Döblin', *MLN*, 118:719–39. B. Kohn, 'Döblin und das Problem des Bösen. Eine Forschungsdiskussion', *RG*, 33:106–28. M. Luserke-Jaqui, '"Doeblin, Alfred; alles außer: *Wallenstein*." oder: Lasst uns wieder mehr Döblin lesen', Wild, *Bücher*, 87–94.

DOMINIK, HANS. J. Hermand, 'Weiße Rasse — gelbe Gefahr. H. Dominiks ideologisches Mitläufertum', Esselborn, *Utopie*, 48–57.

EDSCHMID, KASIMIR. E. D. Becker, 'Erna Pinner und Erich Reiss lesen Kasimir Edschmid *Das gute Recht*', Wild, *Bücher*, 95–104.

EINSTEIN, CARL. German Neundorfer, **'Kritik an Anschauung.' Bildbeschreibung im kunstkritischen Werk Carl Einsteins* (Ep, 453), 270 pp. **Die visuelle Wende der Moderne. Carl Einsteins Kunst des 20. Jahrhunderts*, ed. Klaus H. Kiefer, Munich, Fink, 350 pp. Liliane Meffre, **Itinéraires* *d'une pensée moderne — Carl Einstein 1885–1940* (Monde Germanique, Histoires et Cultures), Paris, Univ. Paris-Sorbonne, 344 pp.

ERNST, PAUL. Alexander Reck, **Briefwechsel Paul Ernst — Will Vesper 1919–1933. Einführung — Edition — Kommentar*, Würzburg, Königshausen & Neumann, 148 pp.

EWERS, HANNS HEINZ. Ulrike Brandenburg, **Hanns Heinz Ewers (1871–1943). Von der Jahrhundertwende zum Dritten Reich. Erzählungen, Dramen, Romane 1903–1932. Von der Genese des Arioheros aus der Retorte: Die Gestaltwerdung einer 'deutschen Reichsutopie'* (SDLNZ, 48), 381 pp. A.-M. Lohmeier, 'Warum Pg. Ewers trotzdem auf den Index kam', Wild, *Bücher*, 105–12.

FALLADA, HANS. Geoff Wilkes, *Hans Falladas Crisis Novels 1931–1947* (ANZSGLL, 19), 2002, 167 pp., argues that Fallada's concept of individual values, influenced by the upheavals of the Third Reich, is much more ambivalent and mutable than scholars have yet recognized and that it is radically redefined in *Jeder stirbt für sich allein.* H. A. Turner, Jr, 'Fallada for historians', *GSR*, 26:477–92.

FLEISSER, MARIELUISE. Carmel Finnan, **Eine Untersuchung des Schreibverfahrens Marieluise Fleissers anhand ihrer Prosatexte* (EH, I, 1852), 205 pp.

FRIED, ERICH. S. Lawrie, '"Ein Urviech und seine Seele von Mensch": Erich Fried at the BBC', Brinson, *Broadcasting*, 117–38.

FRIEDLÄNDER, SALOMO. **S. F., Ich (1871–1936). Autobiographische Skizze.* Aus dem Nachlaß, ed. Hartmut Geerken (Aisthesis Archiv, 3), Bielefeld, Aisthesis, 151 pp.

GEORGE, STEFAN. M. Elliott, 'Beyond left and right. The poetic reception of Stefan George and Rainer Maria Rilke, 1933–1945', *MLR*, 98:908–28. B. Böschenstein, 'Der junge Stefan George am Genfer- und am Luganersee', *Fest. Perels*, 307–12. U. Oelmann, 'Anklänge. Stefan George und Ernest Dowson', *ib.*, 313–38. E. Landmann, 'Stefan Georges Auffassung von den Griechen', *CP*, 258–59:5–44. J. D. Todd, '"Poetry is praise." Beobachtungen zu Stefan Georges Dichtung', *ib.*, 45–66. T. Kölling, 'Stefan Georges letztes Lied. Eine Meditation', *CP*, 260:55–60. N. Deeney, 'Stefan George: der Widerchrist (1907)', Krobb, *Project*, 131–36.

GOLDSTEIN, MORITZ. Irmtraud Ubbens, **'Aus meiner Sprache verbannt . . .' Moritz Goldstein, ein deutsch-jüdischer Journalist und Schriftsteller im Exil* (Dortmunder Beiträge zur Zeitungsforschung, 59), Munich, Saur, 315 pp.

GOLL, IWAN. H. Lafaut, '"Basis für alle kommende Kunst ist das Kino." Iwan Golls Auseinandersetzung mit dem Medium des Films in den 20er Jahren des zwanzigsten Jahrhunderts', *MK*, 49.3–4:137–54.

GRAF, OSKAR MARIA. D. Bousch, 'Synthesen der Zukunft im Roman: *Die Erben des Untergangs* von Oskar Maria Graf', Esselborn, *Utopie*, 95–106.

HARDEN, MAXIMILIAN. Helga Neumann and Manfred Neumann, **Maximilian Harden (1861–1927). Ein unerschrockener deutsch-jüdischer Kritiker und Publizist*, Würzburg, Königshausen & Neumann, 214 pp. H. Neumann, 'Maximilian Harden. Förderer und Wegbegleiter der Brüder Mann', *ZDP*, 122 : 564–81.

HASENCLEVER, WALTER. H. Blinn, '"...auf einem *Ochsenkarren* zum Richtplatz geschleift." Phasen der Walter-Hasenclever-Rezeption 1914–2002', Wild, *Bücher*, 125–34.

HAUPTMANN, GERHART. Mario Leis, *Gerhart Hauptmann — 'Bahnwärter Thiel'* (Lektüreschlüssel), Stuttgart, Reclam, 72 pp. M. Stewart, 'Hauptmann, *Bahnwärter Thiel*, Hutchinson, *Landmarks*, 141–55. P. Mellen, '*Bahnwärter Thiel* and the railway: a historical note', *GN*, 34.2 : 103–07. H.-D. Tschörtner, 'Drei Briefe zu H. Hs "Tiberius"-Drama von 1884', *ZGer*, 13 : 378–82.

HAUSMANN, RAOUL. Corinna Hübner, **Raoul Hausmann. Grenzgänger zwischen den Künsten*, Bielefeld, Aisthesis, 176 pp.

HERRMANN-NEISSE, MAX. *'*Ich gehe wie ich kam: arm und verachtet.' Leben und Werk M. H.-Ns. (1886–1941)*, ed. Klaus Schuhmann, Bielefeld, Aisthesis, 276 pp.

HESSE, HERMANN. *Hermann Hesse, Emmy Ball-Hennings, Hugo Ball. Briefwechsel*, ed. Bärbel Reetz, Frankfurt, Suhrkamp, 612 pp. *Hermann Hesse 1877 — 1962 — 2002*, ed. Cornelia Blasberg, Tübingen, Attempto, 146 pp., contains: P. Moog, 'Opfertode. Hs *Unterm Rade* und die literarische Schulkritik der Jahrhundertwende' (13–25); H. Heselhaus, 'Hs *Demian* — Adoleszenz als Utopie' (27–42); A. V. K. Findeis, 'H. Hs Indienbild — Dichtung und Wahrheit' (43–66); B. Kümmerling-Meibauer, 'H. H. als Crosswriter — ein Autor für Erwachsene und für Jugendliche' (67–85); D. Niefanger, 'Harry Haller und die großen Männer. H. Hs *Steppenwolf* im Kontext der Biografien-Mode' (87–102); W. Erhart, 'Narzissmus und Goldmund' (103–19); K.-P. Philippi, 'H. H., *Das Glasperlenspiel*: "Zerfall der Werte" und Flucht in die Legende' (121–46). Heiko Gröger, **Hermann Hesses Kunstauffassung auf der Grundlage seiner Rezeptionshaltung*, Frankfurt, Lang, 311 pp. Joseph Mileck, **Hermann Hesse. Between the Perils of Politics and the Allure of the Orient* (Berkeley Insights in Linguistics and Semiotics, 55), NY, Lang, xiv + 199 pp. Beate Petra Kory, *Hermann Hesses Beziehung zur Tiefenpsychologie: traumliterarische Projekte* (Studien zur Germanistik, 4), Hamburg, Kovac, 307 pp. B. Schottler, '*Das Glasperlenspiel* von Hermann Hesse', Esselborn, *Utopie*, 67–82.

HESSEL, FRANZ. Magali Laure Nieradka, *Der Meister der leisen Töne. Biographie des Dichters Franz Hessel*, Oldenburg, Igel, 231 pp.

HODDIS, JAKOB VAN. Anne-Christin Nau, **Schizophrenie als literarische Wahrnehmungsstruktur am Beispiel von Jakob Reinhold Lenz und Jakob van Hoddis* (Mäander, 4), Frankfurt, Lang, 494 pp. S. Strümper-Krobb, 'Jakob van Hoddis: *Weltende* (1911)', Krobb, *Project*, 137–42.

HOFMANNSTHAL, HUGO VON. *Hofmannsthal-Jb. zur europäischen Moderne*, 11, Freiburg, Rombach, 432 pp., contains: 'H. von H. und Rudolf Kassner, Briefe und Dokumente samt ausgewählten Briefen Kassners an Gerty und Christian von Hofmannsthal', ed. Klaus E. Bohnenkamp, part I, 1901–1910 (7–136); H. Bosse, 'Die Erlebnisse des Lord Chandos' (171–208); S. Schneider, 'Das Leuchten der Bilder in der Sprache. Hofmannsthals medienbewußte Poetik der Evidenz' (209–48); K. Fliedl, 'Unmögliche Pädagogik. Chandos als Vater' (249–66); A. Assmann, 'Hofmannsthals Chandos-Brief und die Hieroglyphen der Moderne' (267–80); D. E. Wellbery, 'Die Opfer-Vorstellung als Quelle der Faszination. Anmerkungen zum Chandos-Brief und zur frühen Poetik Hofmannsthals' (281–310); H.-J. Schings, 'Lyrik des Hauchs. Zu Hofmannsthals "Gespräch über Gedichte"' (311–40); H. Rölleke, 'Die durchschnittene Laute. Zu einem Motiv in Hofmannsthals "Ur-Jedermann"' (341–50). Martin E. Schmid with Regula Hauser and Severin Perrig, **Hugo von Hofmannsthal. Briefchronik.* Regest-Ausgabe, Heidelberg, Winter, vol. I (1874–1911), xvii + 719 pp., II (1912–1929), v + 714 pp., III (*Registerband*), v + 128 pp. Heinz Hiebler, **Hugo von Hofmannsthal und die Medienkultur der Moderne* (Ep, 416), 500 pp. Kristin Uhlig, *Hofmannsthals Anverwandlung antiker Stoffe* (Litterae, 104), Freiburg, Rombach, 395 pp. Heike Grundmann, **'Mein Leben zu erleben wie ein Buch.' Hermeneutik des Erinnerns bei Hugo von Hofmansthal* (Ep, 447), 240 pp. Timo Günther, *Hofmannsthal, *Ein Brief*, Munich, Fink, 209 pp. R. Helmstetter, 'Entwendet. Hofmannsthals *Chandos-Brief*, die Rezeptionsgeschichte und die Sprachkrise', *DVLG*, 77:446–80. K. Neumann, '"Nur sehe ich, im bürgerlichen Sinn, keinen präcisen Weg vor mir." Hofmannsthal 1895. Mit einem unveröffentlichten Brief an Heinrich Gomperz', *JFDH*: 235–62. G. Schulz, 'Noch-nicht und nicht-mehr. Zum Fragment bei Hofmannsthal und Novalis', *Fest. Perels*, 377–90. A. Bosse, '"Dichter steht gegen Dichter und Epoche gegen Epoche." Hofmannsthal zwischen Goethe und Moderne', *ib.*, 391–404. M. Reich-Ranicki, '"Also spielen wir Theater." Hugo von Hofmannsthal und Richard Strauss', *ib.*, 405–12.

HORVÁTH, ÖDÖN VON. Peter Baumann, **Ödön von Horváth: 'Jugend ohne Gott' — Autor mit Gott? Analyse der Religionsthematik anhand ausgewählter Texte*, Berne, Lang, 555 pp. J. Schräder, 'Ödön von Horváths kleiner Totentanz "Glaube Liebe Hoffnung"', *Fest. Müller*, 283–96.

HUELSENBECK, RICHARD. M. Kane, 'Richard Huelsenbeck: Ende der Welt (1916)', Krobb, *Project*, 161–66.

JACOB, HEINRICH EDUARD. E. Faul, 'Krieg und Kino, Heinrich Eduard Jacobs Roman *Blut und Zelluloid*', Wild, *Bücher*, 145–54.

JUNG, CARL GUSTAV. P. Bishop, 'C. G. Jung and "Naturmystik". The early poem "Gedanken in einer Frühlingsnacht"', *GLL*, 56:327–43.

JUNG, FRANZ. *Vom Trottelbuch zum Torpedokäfer. Franz Jung in der Literaturkritik 1912–1963*, ed. Walter Fähnders and Andreas Hansen, Bielefeld, Aisthesis, 297 pp.

JÜNGER, ERNST. Ernst Jünger and Gerhard Nebel, **Briefwechsel*, ed. Ulrich Froschle and Michael Neumann, Stuttgart, Klett-Cotta, 750 pp. Nicolai Riedel, **Ernst Jünger — Bibliographie. Wissenschaftliche und essayistische Beiträge zu seinem Werk 1928–2002* (Personalbibliographien zur neueren deutschen Literatur, 5), Stuttgart, Metzler, 430 pp. Axel Holm, **Grenzgänger der Moderne: Ernst Jüngers Aufbruch zur Individuation 1939–1943. Eine tiefenpsychologische Untersuchung mit C. J. Jung*, Würzburg, Königshausen & Neumann, 100 pp. Hans Verboven, **Die Metapher als Ideologie. Eine kognitiv-semantische Analyse der Kriegsmetaphorik im Frühwerk Ernst Jüngers* (BNL, 200), 194 pp. Michael Gnädinger, **Zwischen Traum und Trauma. Ernst Jüngers Frühwerk*, Frankfurt, Lang, 360 pp. Thomas Weitin, **Notwendige Gewalt. Die Moderne Ernst Jüngers und Heiner Müllers* (Cultura, 34), Freiburg, Rombach, 422 pp. H. Segeberg, '*Wir irren vorwärts*. Zur Funktion des Utopischen im Werk Ernst Jüngers', Esselborn, *Utopie*, 58–66.

KAFKA, FRANZ. **Synoptische Konkordanz zu Franz Kafkas 'Nachgelassene Schriften und Fragmente'*, ed. Ralf Becker et al. (IDL, 36–38), 3 vols, xlii + 1603 pp. Michael Wood, **Franz Kafka* (Writers and their Work), Tavistock, Northcote House, viii + 104 pp. John Zilcowsky, *Kafka's Travels. Exoticism, Colonialism, and the Traffic of Writing*, NY–Houndmills, Palgrave, xviii + 289 pp., has chapters on the early fragment *Richard and Samuel*, the three novels, 'In der Strafkolonie', the correspondence with Milena, and 'Der Jäger Gracchus', and places Kafka in the context of *fin de siècle* exoticism by examining his fascination with popular German colonialist literature and the travel writings of Goethe and Flaubert. The author combines political, psychoanalytical, and post-structural readings which bring to attention, where appropriate, the element of the erotic, including sado-masochism, in the writing in what amounts to an extended meditation on images and tropes of travel, circulation, traffic, movement, and displacement.

Patrick Bridgwater, *Kafka, Gothic and Fairytale* (IFAVL, 66), viii + 198 pp., and Id., *Kafka's Novels. An Interpretation* (IFAVL, 67), viii + 365 pp. Basing himself on the scholarly consensus that Kafka's work is a projection of his inner life, and that allegorical and political interpretations are therefore inappropriate, the author presents with conviction the debatable view that the court represents Kafka/K.'s conscience and that he is guilty of original sin. However, the ingenuity with which this thesis is supported in an examination of the texts in all their ramifications cannot fail to impress. The commentary, probably more detailed than any other, is completed without a conclusion which might have considered the literary value of such radical solipsism and elaborate libido punishment fantasies. **Die Gesetze des Vaters. Hans und Otto Gross, Sigmund Freud, Franz Kafka*, ed. Gerhard M. Dienes and Ralf Rother, Cologne, Böhlau, 360 pp. Marek Nekula, **Franz Kafkas Sprachen: '. . .in einem Stockwerk des innern babylonischen Turmes . . .'*, Tübingen, Niemeyer, xiii + 397 pp. Sonja Dierks, **Es gibt Gespenster. Betrachtungen zu Kafkas Erzählung* (Ep, 449), 132 pp. Elfie Poulain, **Kafka: Einbahnstraße zur Hölle. Oder die unmögliche Selbstrechtfertigung des Daseins* (M & P Schriftenreihe), Stuttgart, Metzler, 400 pp. Michael L. Rettinger, **Kafkas Berichterstatter. Anthropologische Reflexionen zwischen Irritation und Reaktion. Wirklichkeit und Perspektive* (TSL, 40), 353 pp. Paul M. Malone, **Franz Kafka's 'The Trial': Four Stage Adaptations* (GSC, 13), xi + 289 pp. Bill Dodd, *Kafka — Das Schloss* (CGGT, 18), 100 pp. **Kafkas Betrachtung. Lektüren*, ed. Hans Jürgen Scheuer et al. (HKADL, 34), xiv + 213 pp.

J. Brummack, 'Beobachtungen zur Parabel bei Kafka', *Fest. Müller*, 247–58. B. Greiner, 'Im Umkreis von Ramses: Kafkas *Verschollener* als jüdischer Bildungsroman', *DVLG*, 77:637–58. K.-P. Philippi, '"K. lebte doch in einem Rechtsstaat . . ." Franz Kafkas "Der Proceß": ein Prozeß des Mißverstehens', *Fest. Müller*, 259–82. S. Nerad, 'Das teuflische Früchtchen und die widerliche Gans. Wer ist wer in Kafkas Erzählung *Das Urteil*?', *LitL*, 2003.2:63–81. A. Webber, 'Kafka, *Die Verwandlung*', Hutchinson, *Landmarks*, 175–90. T. Valk, '"Und heilt er nicht, so tötet ihn!" Subjektzerfall und Dichtertheologie in Kafkas Erzählung "Ein Landarzt"', *Hofmannsthal-Jb. der europäischen Moderne*, 11:351–73. C. Albert and A. Disselnkötter, '"Inmitten der Strafkolonie steht keine Schreibmaschine." Eine Relektüre von Kafkas Erzählung', *IASL*, 27.2, 2002:168–84. K. S. Yee, '*In der Strafkolonie*: Kafka's mouth of justice', *GN*, 34.2:128–34. G. Mein, 'Ablenkung. Kafkas Idee des literarischen Suizids', *ZDP*, 122:266–86. V. Liska, 'The gap between Hannah Arendt and Franz Kafka', *Arcadia*, 38:329–33. G. Sander, 'Neuere Forschungsliteratur zu Franz Kafka und seinem Werk', *WW*, 53:501–10. G. Shahar, 'Der Erzähler auf der Galerie. Franz Kafka und die dramaturgische Figur', *WB*, 49:517–33.

GR, 78.3, is a special issue on Kafka and the theatre, which contains, after an introduction by M. Puchner (163–66): M. M. Anderson, '"[. . .] nicht mit großen Tönen gesagt": On theater and the theatrical in Kafka' (167–76); M. Puchner, 'Kafka's antitheatrical gestures' (177–93); W. Kittler, 'Heimlichkeit und Schriftlichkeit: das österreichische Strafprozessrecht in Franz Kafkas Roman *Der Proceß*' (194–222); K. Mladek, 'Radical play: gesture, performance, and the theatrical logic of the law in Kafka' (223–49); S.-M. Garrett, 'The Kafka theater of New York' (250–60); M. Puchner, 'Interview with JoAnne Akalaitis' (261–64).

KÄSTNER, ERICH. *Erich Kästner Jb.*, 3, ed. Volker Ladenthin, 200 pp., contains: V. Ladenthin, 'E. K. , the innovator: modern books for modern kids'; M. Dahrendorf, 'E. K. und die Zukunft der Jugendliteratur oder Über die Neubewertung einer Besonderheit des Erzählens für Kinder und Jugendliche bei K.'; R. Reichstein, 'E. Ks Werke im Ausland'; J. Glötzner, '"Ich wollte kein Held sein oder werden."'; A. Wittenberg, 'E. K. und das Kabarett — ein Forschungsbericht'; J. Zonneveld, 'Bibliographie — E. K. in Rundfunk und Fernsehen'. C. Albert, 'Konstruierte Autorrollen: Erich Kästner zwischen Moral und Unterhaltung', *LitL*, no. 2:82–101. F. T. Grub, '"Werdet anständiger, ehrlicher, gerechter und vernünftiger als die meisten von uns waren!" Erich Kästners *Pünktchen und Anton* zwischen Utopie und Wirklichkeit', Wild, *Bücher*, 155–66.

KAISER, GEORG. Miyung Chu, **Natur und Modernität: Untersuchungen zu den Frauengestalten in den Dramen Georg Kaisers*, Marburg, Tectum, 2002, 206 pp.

KALÉKO, MASCHA. Andreas Nolte, *'*Mir ist zuweilen so als ob das Herz in mir zerbrach.' Leben und Werk Mascha Kalékos im Spiegel ihrer sprichwörtlichen Dichtung* (Sprichwortforschung, 23), Berne, Lang, 2002, 327 pp. H. Korte, '"Jeder ein seliger Singular." Mascha Kalékos Liebeslyrik', *MDG*, 650:60–72.

KAUS, GINA. M.-L. Roth, 'Gina Kaus. Ein "gestohlenes Leben"', Wild, *Bücher*, 167–74.

KERR, ALFRED. S. Kerschbaumer, '"Die Willkür des freien Menschen." Verteidigt von Alfred Kerr', Wild, *Bücher*, 175–82.

KEUN, IRMGARD. H. Häntzschel, '"Ist Gilgi eine von uns?" Irmgard Keuns Zickzackkurs durch die NS-Zensurbarrieren', Wild, *Bücher*, 183–92.

KLAGES, LUDWIG. P. Bishop, 'The reception of Friedrich Nietzsche in the early work of Ludwig Klages', *OGS*, 31, 2002:129–60.

KLEPPER, JOCHEN. Oliver Kohler, *Wir werden sein wie die Träumenden: Jochen Klepper — eine Spurensuche*, Neukirchen-Vluyn, Neukirchner Verlagshaus, 199 pp.

KOLMAR, GERTRUD. Gertrud Kolmar, *Das lyrische Werk*, ed. Regina Nörtemann, 3 vols, Göttingen, Wallstein, 1080 pp.

KOMMERELL, MAX. *Max Kommerell. Leben — Werk — Aktualität*, ed. Walter Busch and Gerhard Pickerodt, Göttingen, Wallstein, 408 pp., contains: D. Hölscher-Lohmeyer, 'Geist und Buchstabe der Briefe M.Ks. Anmerkungen zu ihrer Gesamtedition' (15–29); E. Geulen,

'Aktualität im Übergang: Kunst und Moderne bei M.K.' (32–53); P. Fleming, 'Die Moderne ohne Kunst: M.Ks Gattungspoetik in *Jean Paul*' (54–73); U. Port, 'Die "Sprachgebärde" und der "Umgang mit sich selbst". Literatur als Lebenskunst bei M.K.' (74–97); I. Schiffermüller, 'Gebärde, Gestikulation und Mimus. Krisengestalten in der Poetik von M.K.' (98–117); M. Massalongo, 'Versuch zu einem kritischen Vergleich zwischen Ks und Benjamins Sprachgebärde' (118–61); M. Weichelt, 'Gedicht, Symbol und Augenblick. Zu M.Ks lyriktheoretischen Überlegungen' (162–93); G. Pickerodt, 'Ks Philosophie des Verses' (194–206); K. Köhler, 'Ks dramatisches Werk' (207–33); C. Albert, 'Eine Welt aus Zeichen — Ks Calderón' (234–48); E. Locher, 'Die Sprache und das Unaussprechliche. Kleist bei K.' (249–77); W. Busch, 'Ks Hölderlin: von der Erbschaft Georges zur Kritik an Heidegger' (278–99); H. Schmidt-Bergmann, 'M.Ks Weg von George zu Rilke' (300–13); M. Vialon, 'Die Konstellation M.K. und Werner Krauss. Schreiben als Sprechen über Literatur in finsteren Zeiten' (314–48); R. Nägele, 'Vexierbild einer kritischen Konstellation. Walter Benjamin und M.K.' (349–67); M. Bormuth, 'M.K. und die Psychologie der Moderne' (368–90); A. Müller, 'Forschungsbibliographie zu M.K.' (391–402). K. emerges as a deeply conservative figure, who nevertheless was firmly opposed to the régime after 1933. The collection offers much incidental information on German intellectual life during this period.

KRACAUER, SIEGFRIED. Helmut Stalder, **Siegfried Kracauer. Das journalistische Werk in der 'Frankfurter Zeitung' 1921–1933* (Ep, 438), 280 pp. Harald Reil, **Siegfried Kracauers Jacques Offenbach. Biographie, Geschichte, Zeitgeschichte* (Exil-Studien/Exile Studies, 5), NY, Lang, 168 pp. S. Giles, 'Limits of the visible: Kracauer's photographic dystopia', Giles, *Counter-Cultures*, 213–40.

KRAUS, KARL. Friedrich Rothe, *Karl Kraus. Die Biographie*, Munich, Piper, 423 pp. Irmgard Schartner, **Karl Kraus und die Musik. Musik nach Angabe des Vortragenden, Bearbeiters und Verfassers. Musik zum Zweck des Vortrags*, Frankfurt, Lang, 2002, 424 pp. L. Simonis, 'Die Maske des Menschenfeinds. Karl Kraus und die Tradition der Moralistik', *GRM*, 53:321–38.

KRAUSS, WERNER. *Werner Krauss. Literatur. Geschichte Schreiben*, ed. Hermann Hofer, Thilo Karger, and Christa Riehm, Tübingen, Francke, 222 pp., includes, of relevance to the period: H. Coppi, 'W. K. und der Schulze-Boysen/Harnack-Widerstandskreis' (41–54); O. Ette, 'Der Romanist als Romancier. *PLN* — eine Literatur der Grenze' (69–98).

KUBIN, ALFRED. Gerlinde Gehrig, **Sandmann und Geierkind: Phantastische Diskurse im Werk Alfred Kubins* (Dissertationen zur Kunstgeschichte, 40), Cologne, Böhlau, 224 pp.

KURZ, ISOLDE. *'In der inneren Heimat oder nirgends.' Isolde Kurz (1853–1944)* (*MaM*, 104), 92 pp.

LAMSZUS, WILHELM. Wilhelm Lamszus, *Antikrieg. Die literarische Stimme des Hamburger Schulreformers gegen Massenvernichtungswaffen*, ed. Andreas Pehnke, Frankfurt, Lang, 349 pp., includes *Das Menschenschlachthaus*, *Das Irrenhaus*, *Der verlorene Sohn*, *Genius am Galgen*, and *Der große Totentanz*.

LANGNER, ILSE. P. Davies, 'Ilse Langner's *Amazonen* and the reception of J. J. Bachofen's *Das Mutterrecht*', *GLL*, 56:223–43.

LASKER-SCHÜLER, ELSE. *Else Lasker-Schüler Jahrbuch zur Klassischen Moderne*, 2, ed. Lothar Bluhm and Andreas Meier, Trier, Wissenschaftlicher Vlg, 232 pp. Betty Falkenberg, **Else Lasker-Schüler: A Life*, Jefferson, NC, McFarland, 256 pp. Thomas Höfert, **Signaturen kritischer Intellektualität. Else Lasker-Schülers Schauspiel 'Arthur Aronimus'*, St. Ingbert, Röhrig, 2002, 428 pp. F. Krobb, 'Else Lasker-Schüler, *Mein Volk* (1905)', Krobb, *Project*, 125–30.

LE FORT, GERTRUD VON. Roswitha Goslich, **Orientierungsssuche im Zeitalter der Angst. Gertrud von le Forts Weg zur Mystik* (GTS, 71), 246 pp.

LERNET-HOLENIA, ALEXANDER. C. Wingertszahn, 'Blaue Stunde im Krieg. Alexander Lernet-Holenias fantastisches Zwischenreich', Wild, *Bücher*, 221–30.

MANN, ERIKA. *BHGLL*, 5, contains four reportages by Erika Mann for the magazine *Ford im Bild*.

MANN, HEINRICH. Stephen A. Grollmann, *Heinrich Mann. Narratives of Wilhelmine Germany, 1895–1925* (STML, 64), 2002, viii + 162 pp., deals with the editorship of *Das Zwanzigste Jahrhundert* and the novels *Im Schlaraffenland*, *Der Untertan*, and *Der Kopf*. Hanjo Kesting, **Heinrich Mann und Thomas Mann: Ein deutscher Bruderzwist* (Göttinger Sudelblätter), Göttingen, Wallstein, 80 pp. Hilaire Mbakob, **Normen und Grenzen der Kritik und des Engagements in den politischen Schriften von Heinrich Mann und André Gide zwischen 1923 und 1945* (EH, I, 1875), 185 pp. M. E. Humble, 'Heinrich Mann and Arnold Zweig: left-wing Nietzscheans?', pp. 245–62 of *Nietzsche and the German Tradition*, ed. Nicholas Martin, Oxford, Lang, 314 pp. H. Schlobach, '*Geist und Tat.* Zu drei frankophilen Essays von Heinrich Mann', Wild, *Bücher*, 251–60. W. B. Berg, 'Frankreich, du hast es besser . . .! Liebe und Vollendung des Königs Henri Quatre in der Sicht Heinrich Manns', Wild, *Bücher*, 261–72.

MANN, KLAUS. Arwed Schmidt, **Exilwelten der 30er Jahre. Untersuchungen zu Klaus Manns Emigrationsromanen 'Flucht in den Norden' und 'Der Vulkan. Roman unter Emigranten'* (Ep, 460), 320 pp. U. Leuschner, '"Wir sind eine Generation, und sei es, daß uns nur unsere Verwirrtheit vereine." Die *Anthologie jüngster Lyrik* von Willi R. Fehse und Klaus Mann', Wild, *Bücher*, 273–84.

MANN, THOMAS. Thomas Mann, *Briefe an Richard Schaukal*, ed. Claudia Gerardi with Sibylle and Andrea Traxler (TMS, 27), 242 pp. **Man erzählt Geschichten, formt die Wahrheit. Thomas Mann — Deutscher, Europäer, Weltbürger*, ed. Michael Braun and Birgit Lermen, Frankfurt, Lang, 335 pp. Angelika Abel, *Thomas Mann im Exil: zum zeitgeschichtlichen Hintergrund der Emigration*, Munich, Fink, 281 pp. Yahya Elsaghe, **Thomas Mann und die kleinen Unterschiede. Zur erzählerischen Imagination des Anderen* (Literatur — Kultur — Geschlecht, Große Reihe, 27), Cologne, Böhlau, 400 pp. Kikuko Kashiwagi, **Festmahl und frugales Mahl. Nahrungsrituale als Dispositive des Erzählens im Werk Thomas Manns*, Freiburg, Rombach, 197 pp. Ingeborg Robles, **Unbewältigte Wirklichkeit. Familie, Sprache, Zeit als mythische Strukturen im Frühwerk Thomas Manns*, Bielefeld, Aisthesis, 239 pp. Astrid Roffmann, *'*Keine freie Note mehr.' Natur im Werk Thomas Manns* (Ep, 420), 271 pp. Jacques Darmaun, **Thomas Mann, Deutschland und die Juden*, trans. from the French by the author (CJ, 40), x + 319 pp. Claudia Gremler, *'*Fern im dänischen Norden ein Bruder': Thomas Mann und Hermann Bang. Eine literarische Spurensuche* (Palaestra, 320), Göttingen, Vandenhoeck & Ruprecht, 384 pp. Frithjof Haider, **Verkörperungen des Selbst: Das bücklige Männlein als Übergangsphänomen bei Clemens Brentano, Thomas Mann und Walter Benjamin* (EH, 1, 1869), 263 pp. **Thomas und Heinrich Mann im Spiegel der Karikatur*, ed. Thomas Sprecher and Hans Wisskirchen, Munich, Fink, 208 pp. *Resounding Concerns*, ed. Rüdiger Görner (PIGS, 79), 202 pp., includes: L. Dreyfus, 'Music and motive in Thomas Mann's *Wälsungenblut*' (86–113); and J. Reiber, 'Hans Pfitzner, Thomas Mann und ein deutsches Problem' (114–34).

Ellis Shookman, *Thomas Mann's 'Death in Venice'. A Novella and its Critics*, Woodbridge, Camden House, 320 pp., represents one of the most exhaustive reception studies of a single text (in this instance also of the film and the opera based on it) ever undertaken, tracing the response through five chronological phases and in relation to all relevant stylistic and thematic aspects, politics, philosophy, psychoanalysis, homoeroticism, and music, as well as comparisons to other authors. *Thomas Mann: Der Tod in Venedig. Wirklichkeit, Dichtung, Mythos*, ed. Frank Baron and Gert Sautermeister, Lübeck, Schmidt-Römhild, viii + 200 pp., includes: E. Bahr, 'Imperialismuskritik und Orientalismus in T. Ms *Der Tod in Venedig*' (1–16); T. Schultz, 'Aschenbach und Savonarola' (17–26); S. Henry, 'August Graf von Platen und *Der Tod in Venedig*' (27–50); M. Pearson, 'Platon-Interpretationen des Erzählers und seines Helden' (51–57); F. Baron, 'Das Sokrates-Bild von Georg Lukács als Quelle' (81–91); G. Hudspeth, 'Von Goethe zu Wagner und Aschenbach. Gedanke und Gefühl im Schaffensprozeß' (93–100); H. Koopmann, 'Faust reist an den Lido' (101–17); C. Petzer, 'Die Stadt als Verführerin' (119–24); R. Jones, 'Die

Rezeption von Thomas Manns *Der Tod in Venedig* bei D. H. Lawrence' (125–33); A. Neumann, 'Alfred Kubins *Die andere Seite* und *Der Tod in Venedig*. Apokalypse, Verfall und Untergang' (173–87); T. Koebner, 'Eine Passions-Geschichte. *Der Tod in Venedig* als Film' (189–200). P. Hutchinson, 'Mann, *Der Tod in Venedig*', Hutchison, *Landmarks*, 157–73.

Ulla Stemmermann, *'*Ein einfacher junger Mensch reiste . . .' Thomas Manns Transposition des 'Candide' Voltaires in den 'Zauberberg'* (Ep, 472), 200 pp. Simone Seider, **Richard Wagner im Sanatorium und im alten Orient. Thomas Manns Wagner-Sicht im Zauberberg und in Joseph und seine Brüder* (EH, 1, 1874), 326 pp. Eva Schmidt-Schutz, *'Doktor Faustus' zwischen Tradition und Moderne. Eine quellenkritische und rezeptionsgeschichtliche Untersuchung zu Thomas Manns literarischem Selbstbild* (*TMS*, 28), 357 pp. *Thomas Mann's Addresses Delivered at the Library of Congress*, ed. Don Heinrich Tolzmann (New German-American Studies, 25), Oxford, Lang, xiv + 132 pp.

K. R. Scherpe, '100 Jahre Weltanschauung, was noch? Thomas Manns *Buddenbrooks* noch einmal gelesen', *WB*, 49:570–84. L. K. Worley, 'Girls from good families: Tony Buddenbrook and Agathe Heidling', *GQ*, 76:195–211. C. Bergmann, ' "Hübsch" und "schön". Zum Wortgebrauch in Thomas Manns Roman *Die Bekenntnisse des Hochstaplers Friedrich Krull*', *Muttersprache*, 113:66–76. A. Classen, 'Der Kampf um das Mittelalter im Werk Thomas Manns: *Der Zauberberg*: die menschliche Misere im Kreuzfeuer geistesgeschichtlicher Strömungen', *SN*, 75:32–46. S. Besser, 'Mynheer Peeperkorn's fever', *Arcadia*, 38:257–63. H. Rudloff with H. Liche, 'Wer hat das Bild der Charitas geküßt? Die "heiter-criminologische Angelegenheit" in Thomas Manns Roman *Lotte in Weimar*', *WW*, 53:59–84. E. K. Paefgen, 'Erzählen über Äußeres, Erzählen über Inneres. Funktionen von Farbwerten in den Josephsromanen von Thomas Mann', *WW*, 53:429–46. K. L. Crawford, 'Exorcising the devil from Thomas Mann's *Doktor Faustus*', *GQ*, 76:168–82. A. Erwin, 'Rethinking Thomas Mann's *Doktor Faustus*: crisis, parody, primitivism, and the possibilities of Dionysian art in a post-Nietzschean era', *GR*, 787:283–99. U. Erichsen, 'Klangchiffren und Schmetterlinge: Robert Schumann in Thomas Manns *Doktor Faustus* — eine Nachlese', *LJb*, 44:271–88. S. Ireton, 'Die Aufzeichnung der Memoria in *Buddenbrooks* und *Der Erwählte*', *GQ*, 76:183–94.

Y. Elsaghe, 'Die "Judennase" in Thomas Manns Erzählwerk', *JEGP*, 102:88–104. A. Bance, 'Has Thomas Mann run out of steam? Did Hans ever finish reading *Ocean Steamships*? The Ida Herz lecture 2002', *PEGS*, 72:1–14. E.-M. Fleissner, 'Thomas Mann in retrospect', *GN*, 34.2:137–41. M. O. Huber, 'Heimwehlieder und Zukunftsgeist. Romantik und Nation bei Thomas Mann

(1914–1925)', *WB*, 49:553–69. W. Haefs, '"Verhunzter Geist, Groschen-Intellektualismus." Thomas Mann, *Deutsche Ansprache*', Wild, *Bücher*, 285–96.

MARTENS, KURT. V. Hansen, 'Das Goethe-Bild von Kurt Martens und Thomas Mann', *Fest. Perels*, 239–50.

MORGENSTERN, CHRISTIAN. Anthony T. Wilson, **Über die Galgenlieder Christian Morgensterns* (Ep, 448), 346 pp.

MÜHSAM, ERICH. *Schriften der Erich-Mühsam-Gesellschaft*, fasc. 22, 'Das Tagebuch im 20. Jahrhundert, E. M. und andere', includes: 'Aus den Tagebüchern E. Ms' (7–29); R. Görner, 'Orte intimer Selbstgewisserung. Das Tagebuch im frühen 20. Jahrhundert' (31–42); C. Hirte, 'Selbsterziehung eines Anarchisten. Die Tagebücher E. Ms' (43–52); B. Reetz, 'Die Moritat von Finny Morstadt. E. Ms Notizen vom Rande der Boheme' (53–69); B. Hamacher, 'Bleistiftschnitzel und letzte Geheimnisse: Thomas Manns Tagebücher' (70–83). *Mühsam-Magazin*, fasc. 10, includes, besides texts by Mühsam: C. Knüppel, 'Antisemitische Hetze gegen E. M. in der Endphase der Weimarer Republik' (45–48); C. Piens, 'Eine alte Truhe in Südtirol. Eine Episode im Leben E. Ms und bisher unbekannte Gedichte' (70–84); I. M. Battafarano, 'E. M., Mignon 1925: Kennst du das Land, wo die Faschisten blühn' (104–109); A. Götz von Olenhusen, 'Der Satiriker E. M. als Objekt von Satire und Karikatur' (110–15).

MUSIL, ROBERT. Karl Corino, *Robert Musil. Eine Biographie*, Reinbek, Rowohlt, 2026 pp. Herbert Kraft, *Musil*, Vienna, Zsolnay, 356 pp. Joseph P. Strelka, **Robert Musil. Perspektiven seines Werks* (New Yorker Beiträge zur Literaturwissenschaft, 5), Frankfurt, Lang, 183 pp. Timothy Mehigan, **The Critical Response to Musil's 'The Man without Qualities'*, Woodbridge, Camden House, 180 pp. Peter Deibler, **Ist der Mann ohne Eigenschaften ein Gottsucher? Die Erfahrung der Fraglichkeit als Element moderner Weltwahrnehmung* (EH, 1, 1834), 301 pp. Annette Gies, **Musils Konzeption des 'Sentimentalen Denkens'. 'Der Mann ohne Eigenschaften' als literarische Erkenntnistheorie* (Ep, 446), 230 pp. Oliver Pfohlmann, **Eine finster drohende und lockende Nachbarmacht? Untersuchungen zu psychoanalytischen Literaturdeutungen am Beispiel von Robert Musil* (Musil-Studien, 32), Munich, Fink, 383 pp. David S. Luft, *Eros and Inwardness in Vienna. Weininger, Musil, Doderer*, Chicago U.P., xiv + 257 pp., sees the significance of these writers in their understanding of eros and inwardness and the part that they play in ethical experience and the formation of meaningful relations to the world, against the background of the clash between scientific rationalism and irrational idealism under the impact of Schopenhauer and Nietzsche. The role of Freud is deliberately de-emphasized in order to bring out neglected aspects of the liberal Viennese milieu. N. C.

Wolf, '". . .einfach die Kraft haben, diese Widersprüche zu lieben." Mystik und Mystizismuskritik in Robert Musils Schauspiel *Die Schwärmer*', *IASL*, 27.2, 2002:124–67. E. C. Hamilton, 'Imaginary bridges: politics and film art in Robert Musil's *Die Verwirrungen des Zöglings Törleß* und Volker Schlöndorff's *Der junge Törleß*', *ColGer*, 36:69–85. F. Lönker, 'Der Fall Moosbrugger. Zum Verhältnis von Psychopathologie und Anthropologie in Robert Musils *Der Mann ohne Eigenschaften*', *JDSG*, 47:280–302. C. Erhart, 'Le poids de la mémoire. Quelques réflexions sur la nouvelle *Tonka* de Robert Musil', *Germanica*, 33:57–77. O. Pfohlmann, '"Ein Mann von ungewöhnlichen Eigenschaften." Robert Musil, die "Neue Rundschau", der Expressionismus und das "Sommererlebnis im Jahre 1914"', *WB*, 49:325–60.

NORDAU, MAX. Petra Zudrell, **Der Kulturkritiker und Schriftsteller Max Nordau. Zwischen Zionismus, Deutschtum und Judentum* (Ep, 421), 296 pp.

PRZYBYSZEWSKI, STANISLAUS. S. P., *Studienausgabe. Werke, Aufzeichnungen und ausgewählte Briefe in acht Bänden und ein Kommentarband*. Vol. 9. *Kommentarband*, ed. Hartmut Vollmer, Oldenburg, Igel, 256 pp., contains, after an editorial introduction: H. Vollmer, '"Meine Seele verblutet an der Sehnsucht nach dem verlorenen Paradies." S. Ps "Pentateuch"' (15–35); W. Fähnders, '"Wie ein blutiger Meteor . . ." S.Ps Anfänge: "Zur Psychologie des Individuums"' (36–61); K. Tebben, 'Von der Herrschaft des Bösen — und der Bürde, es darzustellen. S. Ps "Homo Sapiens" und "Satans Kinder"' (62–89); A. Opyrchal, 'S. Ps Romane "Erdensöhne" und "Das Gericht"' (90–110); W. Olma, 'S. Ps später Roman "Der Schrei"' (111–56); J. Marx, 'Das intime Schicksalsdrama S. Ps' (157–91); U. Steltner, 'Harlekin als Theoretiker. S. Ps kritische und essayistische Schriften' (192–208); M. M. Langner, 'Momente und Strategien der Selbstinszenierung eines Schriftstellers. S. Ps "Ferne komm ich her . . ."' (209–32); T. Recke, 'Die Briefe S. Ps' (233–56).

REGLER, GUSTAV. H. Gätje, '"Das Exil begann mit dem Verpacken der Bücher." Gustav Regler — Die Bücherverbrennung und seine Entwicklung im Exil', Wild, *Bücher*, 323–32.

REMARQUE, ERICH MARIA. *Erich Maria Remarque-Jb.*, 13, ed. Thomas F. Schneider, includes: S. Stephanie, '". . .weil wir Funken in einem unbekannten Wind sind." E. M. R.: *Arc de Triomphe*' (42–77). Haim Gordon, **Heroism and Friendship in the Novels of E. M. R.* (STML, 63), 168 pp.

RILKE, RAINER MARIA. *'Sieh dir die Liebenden an.' Briefe an Valerie von David-Rhonfeld*, ed. Renate Scharffenberg and August Stahl, Frankfurt, Insel, xxvi + 334 pp. Sandra Kluwe, **Krisis und Kairos. Eine Analyse der Werkgeschichte Rainer Maria Rilkes* (Schriften zur Literaturwissenschaft,

20), Berlin, Duncker & Humblot, 472 pp. Martina Kurz, **Bild-Verdichtungen. Cézannes Realisation als poetisches Prinzip bei Rilke und Handke* (Palaestra, 315), Göttingen, Vandenhoeck & Ruprecht, 391 pp. Sascha Löwenstein, **Poetik und dichterisches Selbstverständnis. Einführung in Rainer Maria Rilkes frühe Dichtungen (1884–1906)* (Ep, 488), 282 pp.

W. Donahue, 'Ein politisch fortschrittlicher Rilke: Kunst als Politik in den *Zwei Prager Geschichten*', *RG*, 33:81–105. M. Krings, 'Ästhetische Inkarnation. Zur formalen Struktur von Rilkes *Malte Laurids Brigge*', *DVLG*, 77:619–36. J. Metz, '"Eine eigentliche Durchdringung." Literature and national identity, gender and body in Rilke's "Stifter Letter" to August Sauer', *GQ*, 76:314–28. H. Graubner, 'Rilkes Christus und das Erhabene der Zeit', *MDLK*, 95:583–602. F. Malkain, 'Figures de la mémoire et du progrès dans l'œuvre de Rilke: du Cornette à Orphée', *Germanica*, 33:37–55. T. R. Jackson, 'Rainer Maria Rilke: *Der Panther* (1902/03)', Krobb, *Project*, 117–24. T. J. Casey, 'Rainer Maria Rilke: *Tränen, Tränen, die aus mir brechen* (1934)', Krobb, *Project*, 175–81. See also under GEORGE.

ROTH, JOSEPH. G. vom Hofe, 'Das Ausmaß des "furor teutonicus" — Vorspiel zu einer Tragödie der Literatur? Zu den Folgen für Joseph Roths Selbstverständnis als Exilautor und zum "Schicksal" seiner Bücher nach 1933', Wild, *Bücher*, 333–42. W. Müller-Funk, 'Landnahme und Schiffbruch: Carl Schmitt, Theodor Herzl, Joseph Roth. Eine Forschungsskizze', Betten, *Judentum*, 32–47.

SAHL, HANS. A. Reiter, 'Hans Sahl und Hermann Broch: ein Briefwechsel im Exil 1941–1950', *Exil*, 23.1:36–49. R. Müller, 'Drei Briefe Hans Sahls an Willi Schlamm', *ib.*, 50–61.

SANZARA, RAHEL. G.-M. Schulz, 'Vom Bösen und im gleichen Maße auch vom Guten. Rahel Sanzara: *Das verlorene Kind*', Wild, *Bücher*, 343–52.

SCHICKELE, RENÉ. *R.S., *Blaue Hefte*, ed. Anne-Marie Post-Martens, Stroemfeld, 2002, 522 pp. E. Nährlich-Slatewa, 'Die Pariser Erzählungen von René Schickele', *Fest. Brandt*, 271–98.

SCHNITZLER, ARTHUR. Andrew C. Wisely, **Arthur Schnitzler and Twentieth-Century Criticism. More Than Viennese Charm*, Woodbridge, Camden House, 256 pp. *A Companion to the Works of Arthur Schnitzler*, ed. Dagmar C. G. Lorenz (SGLLC), 320 pp., contains, after an introduction by the editor: G. K. Schneider, 'The social and political context of A. S.'s *Reigen* in Berlin, Vienna, and New York: 1900–1933' (27–57); E. Deutsch-Schreiner, '"...nothing against Arthur Schnitzler himself...": interpreting Schnitzler on stage in Austria in the 1950s and 1960s' (59–75); E. Loentz, 'The problem and challenge of Jewishness in the city of Schnitzler and Anna O.' (79–102); I. Bruce, 'Which way out? Schnitzler's and Salten's conflicting responses to cultural Zionism' (103–26); D. C. G. Lorenz, 'The self as process in an era of transition: competing paradigms of personality and character in Schnitzler's works' (129–47); F. Tweraser, 'Schnitzler's turn to prose fiction: the depiction of consciousness in selected narratives' (149–86); E. B. Ametsbichler, 'A century of intrigue: the dramatic works of Arthur Schnitzler' (187–204); G. J. Weinberger, 'Arthur Schnitzler's puppet plays' (205–26); H. H. Herzog, '"Medizin ist eine Weltanschauung": on Schnitzler's medical writings' (227–41); K. Arens, 'Schnitzler and the discourse of gender in *Fin-de-siècle* Vienna' (243–64); J. Neubauer, 'The overaged adolescents of Schnitzler's *Der Weg ins Freie*' (265–76); I. Meyer, '"Thou shalt not make unto thee any graven image": crises of masculinity in Schnitzler's *Die Fremde*' (277–300); S. C. Anderson, 'The power of the gaze: visual metaphors in Schnitzler's prose works and dramas' (303–24); E. Kuttenberg, 'Suicide as performance in Dr. Schnitzler's prose' (325–45); M. Konzett, 'The difficult rebirth of cosmopolitanism: Schnitzler and contemporary Austrian literature' (349–69). The collection makes good the editor's promise that the essays are representative of the current tendencies in Schnitzler scholarship, that they emphasize texts neglected in the past (*Die Fremde*, *Spiel im Morgengrauen*, the puppet plays, *Frau Berta Garlan*, *Doktor Gräsler, Badearzt*, *Der letzte Brief eines Literaten*), examine topics previously considered inappropriate to Schnitzler, and offer new theoretical perspectives, especially on gender and Jewish studies.

**Arthur Schnitzler im zwanzigsten Jahrhundert*, ed. Konstanze Fliedl, Vienna, Picus, 384 pp. *'*Seh'n Sie, das Berühmtwerden ist doch nicht so leicht!' Arthur Schnitzler über sein literarisches Schaffen*, ed. Irène Lindgren, Frankfurt, Lang, 2002, x + 705 pp. Oliver Neun, **Unser postmodernes Fin de Siècle. Untersuchungen zu Arthur Schnitzlers 'Anatol'-Zyklus* (Ep, 490), 270 pp. B. Besslich, 'Intertextueller Mummenschanz. Arthur Schnitzlers Brieferzählung *Die kleine Komödie* (1895)', *WW*, 53:223–40. W. L. Cunningham, 'Arthur Schnitzler: an unrecognized feminist?', *GN*, 34.2:134–37. J. Heimerl, 'Die "anima humana". Arthur Schnitzlers Adaptation des Geniegedankens am Beispiel der Komödie "Professor Bernhardi"', *WB*, 49:534–52. K. Richter, 'Die Regel und die Ausnahme. Urteile über Arthur Schnitzler und seinen Roman *Der Weg ins Freie*', Wild, *Bücher*, 353–66.

SCHREYER, LOTHAR. *Prose Works, Selections, Frühe Prosa*, ed. and introd. Brian Keith-Smith (Bristol German Publications), Lewiston, Mellen, 220 pp.

SCHWITTERS, KURT. S. Lichtenstein, 'Listening to Kurt Schwitters' *Ursonate*. A dadaistic-romantic *transposition d'arts*?', *Arcadia*, 38:276–84.

SEGHERS, ANNA. A. S., **Und ich brauch doch so schrecklich Freude. Tagebuch 1924/25. Legende von der Reue des Bischofs Jehan d'Aigremont von St. Anne in Rouen*, ed. Christiane Zehl Romero, Berlin, Aufbau, 90 pp. Christiane Zehl Romero, *Anna Seghers. Eine Biographie 1947–1983. Mit Anmerkungen, Personenregister und Bibliographie*, Berlin, Aufbau, 479 pp. S. Komfort-Hein, '"Inzwischenzeit": Erzählen im Exil. Anna Seghers' "Der Ausflug der toten Mädchen" und Peter Weiss' "Der Schatten des Körpers des Kutschers"', *Fest. Müller*, 343–56. G. Loster-Schneider, '"Unwünschbar fremd?" Zu Anna Seghers' "anderem" Identitätsroman *Transit*', Wild, *Bücher*, 377–86. *Argonautenschiff*, 12 ('Bilder von Anna Seghers im 20. und 21. Jahrhundert'), 352 pp.

SPERBER, MANÈS. Mirjana Stancic, **Manès Sperber: Leben und Werk*, Frankfurt, Stroemfeld, 687 pp.

STEINER, FRANZ BAERMANN. *From Prague Poet to Oxford Anthropologist. Franz Baermann Steiner Celebrated. Essays and Translations*, ed. Jeremy Adler, Richard Fardon, and Carol Tully (PIGS, 80), 265 pp., includes: R. B. Pynsent, 'F.B.S.'s first work, *Die Planeten*, in its Czech literary context' (89–104); P. J. Conradi, 'F.B.S.'s influence on Iris Murdoch' (122–32); C. Tully, 'F.B.S. and Spain: "The Prayer in the Garden" and Manrique's "Coplas a la muerte de su padre"' (133–50); N. J. Ziegler, '"To find a language where no neighbours call": reflections on the reception of F.B.S.'s poetry' (187–98).

STRAMM, AUGUST. B. Bigge, 'August Stramm: *Blüte* (1914)', Krobb, *Project*, 155–60.

STUEBS, ALBIN. I. Wallace, '"Lob der Emigration": Albin Stuebs', *GMon*, 57:119–80.

SUDERMANN, HERMANN. A. Corkhill, 'Zeitkritik in Hermann Sudermanns Roman *Der tolle Professor* (1926)', *LitL*, 2003, 1:15–27.

SUTTNER, BERTHA VON. G. Häntzschel, '"Das Buch wirkte wie eine Bombe." Bertha von Suttners pazifistische Kampfschrift *Die Waffen nieder!*', Wild, *Bücher*, 387–94.

THIESS, FRANK. Yvonne Wolf, **Frank Thiess und der Nationalsozialismus. Ein konservativer Revolutionär als Dissident* (UDL, 114), ix + 339 pp. U. Kittstein, '"Soldatische Männlichkeit" als Prinzip der Geschichtskonstruktion. Zu Frank Thiess' *Tsushima. Der Roman eines Seekrieges*', *WW*, 53:447–58.

TRAKL, GEORG. Hartmut Cellbrot, **Trakls dichterisches Feld*, Freiburg, Rombach, 148 pp. K. Bosse, 'Auf den Spuren von Georg Trakl', *Fest. Perels*, 323–90. A. Witte, 'Georg Trakl: *In den Nachmittag geflüstert* (1913)', Krobb, *Project*, 149–54.

TRAVEN, BEN. *B. T.: frühe Romane und mediale Adaptionen*, ed. Gunter Helmes, Siegen, Boschen, 140 pp., includes: W. Olma, '*Die Baumwollpflücker*. Abenteuer, Exotik und Arbeitsverhältnisse in einer deutschen Vorabendserie der sechziger Jahre' (911–36); E. Dietrich, '"...die Waage schlagt in Scherben ..." Musikwissenschaftliche Überlegungen zu Hanns Eislers *Ballade von den Baumwollpflückern*' (37–46); G. Helmes, 'Literatur und Literaturtransformationen. B. Ts Roman *Das Totenschiff* (1926) und mediale Adaptionen (Hörspiel und Film)' (47–70); T. Köster, '"Gold ist eine verteufelte Sache." John Huston verfilmt *Der Schatz der Sierra Madre* (1927)' (71–84); A. Martin, 'Intermediale Schwarz-Weiß-Malereien. B. Ts mexikanische Erdöl-Roman *Die weiße Ros*e (1929) und dessen Transformationen in Film und Hörspiel' (85–104); W. W. Wende, '"Es gibt keine Macht, die aus sich heraus besteht ..." B. Ts Dschungel-Romane über die Zwangsarbeit der Ureinwohner Mexikos im Medienwechsel vom Buch zum Film' (105–28); D. Roll, '*Die Rebellion der Gehenkten* (1936) — *La rebellión de los colgados*. Die Verfilmung des Traven-Romans aus dem Jahr 1954' (129–40).

TUCHOLSKY, KURT. S. Becker, 'Vorweggenommene Bücherverbrennung. Kurt Tucholskys *Deutschland, Deutschland über alles*', Wild, *Bücher*, 395–406.

UNRUH, FRITZ VON. D. Kemper, '*Politeia.* Splitter zur Exilgeschichte Fritz von Unruhs aus einem Moskauer Teilnachlaß', Wild, Bücher, 407–18.

WALSER, ROBERT. R. W., *Feuer — unbekannte Prosa und Gedichte*, ed. Bernhard Echte, Frankfurt, Suhrkamp, 140 pp. Robert Machler, *Das Leben Robert Walsers: eine dokumentarische Biographie* (ST, 3486), 273 pp. Marius Neukomm, *Robert Walsers Mikrogramm 'Beiden klopfte das Herz': eine psychoanalytisch orientierte Erzähltextanalyse*, Giessen, Psychosozial-Vlg, 274 pp.

WASSERMANN, JAKOB. S. Michaud, 'Humanität versus Messianismus. Jakob Wassermann und *Die Juden von Zirndorf*', Wild, *Bücher*, 419–24.

WEDEKIND, FRANK. A. Finger and G. Kathöfer, 'A reputation reassessed: unravelling Wedekind's early writings', *ColGer*, 36:27–44.

WEINERT, ERICH. C. T. Fischler, 'Zwischen Nacht und Tag. Erich Weinerts sowjetische Exilzeit im DDR-Spielfilm der 70er Jahre', *Exilforschung*, 21:155–69.

WERFEL, FRANZ. H. F. Pfanner, 'Zweimalige Vergangenheitsbewältigung. Franz Werfels Roman *Eine blaßblaue Frauenschrift* und ihre Verfilmung durch Axel Corti', *LitL*, no. 1:28–36. S. Fraimann-Morris, 'Verdrängung und Bekenntnis. Zu Franz Werfels jüdischer Identität', *GRM*, 53:339–54. D. Meyer, 'Vom mentalen Schlaraffenland zur Apokalypse: Franz Werfels Roman *Der Stern der Ungeborenen*', Esselborn, *Utopie*, 83–94. H. Kernmayer, '"Fremdheit ..., auf ihren Grund nun konnte ich tauchen." Zur Thematisierung jüdischer

Identität in Franz Werfels Erzählung *Pogrom*', Betten, *Judentum*, 62–83.

WIECHERT, ERNST. Manfred Franke, **Jenseits der Wälder. Der Schriftsteller Ernst Wiechert als politischer Redner und Autor*, Cologne, SH-Vlg, 248 pp.

WOLF, FRIEDRICH. M. Horn, '"Früchte vom Baum des Lebens der Weltliteratur." Friedrich Wolf und seine Bibliothek', *Marginalien*, 170.2:43–60.

ZUCKMAYER, CARL. *C. Z. — Annemarie Seidel. *Briefwechsel*, ed. Günther Nickel (Zuckmayer-Schriften), Göttingen, Wallstein, 328 pp. *C. Z.: *Briefe an Hans Schiebelhuth 1921–1936 und andere Beiträge zur Zuckmayer-Forschung*, ed. Günther Nickel, Erwin Rotermund, and Hans Wagener (Carl Zuckmayer-Gesellschaft, Zuckmayer-Jb., 2003), Göttingen, Wallstein, 448 pp. M. C. Denman, 'Nostalgia for a better Germany: C. Z.'s *Des Teufels General*', *GQ*, 76:369–80.

ZUR MÜHLEN, HERMYNIA. D. Vietor-Engländer, 'Hermynia Zur Mühlen and the BBC', Brinson, *Broadcasting*, 43–56.

ZWEIG, ARNOLD. V. Riedel, 'Die zögerliche Entdeckung eines bekannten Autors. Probleme der Arnold-Zweig-Edition', *BHGLL*, 5:148–60. S. Kiefer, '"Ein Kriegsbuch? Ein Friedensbuch." Arnold Zweigs *Der Streit um den Sergeanten Grischa* (1927)', Wild, *Bücher*, 433–40.

ZWEIG, STEFAN. Gert Kerschbaumer, *Stefan Zweig: Der fliegende Salzburger*, Salzburg, Residenz, 350 pp. *Stefan Zweig im Zeitgeschehen des 20. Jahrhunderts* (3. S.Z.-Kongreß, 2002, Dortmund), ed. Thomas Eicher, Oberhausen, Athena, 316 pp., contains: K. Beck, 'Politik — die wichtigste Sache im Leben? S. Zs Haltung zum Zeitgeschehen' (13–42); H.-A. Koch, 'Ästhetischer Widerstand oder politischer Eskapismus? Vom Erasmus-Buch zur *Schachnovelle*' (43–58); G. Kerschbaumer, 'Der Festspieldichter S. Z.' (59–76); R. Görner, 'Schweigsame Dissonanzen. Anmerkungen zum Verhältnis zwischen Richard Strauss und S. Z.' (77–92); M. H. Gelber, 'Wandlungen in S. Zs Verhältnis zum Zionismus' (93–108); G. Rovagnati, 'Mussolinis "reaktionäre und ahistorische Politik": S. Z. und der italienische Fascismus' (109–28); I. Schwamborn, 'S. Zs ungeschriebenes Buch: *Getúlio Vargas*' (129–58); B. Hamacher, 'Das Verschwinden des Individuums in der Politik. Erasmus, Luther und Calvin bei S. Z. und Thomas Mann' (159–78); T. Eicher, 'Der Kriegsheimkehrer als Verbrecher: S. Zs *Rausch der Verwandlung* und Hugo Bettauers *Hemmungslos*' (179–208); F. Hackert, 'S. Zs Universum. Die Wunder von Geschichts- und Lebenswelt der Sternstunden' (209–24); M. Birk, 'S. Zs Humanitätsgedanke während des Ersten Weltkrieges und seine Fiktionalisierung in der Novellistik' (225–42); G. Rademacher, 'Absolution für einen Königsmörder? Zu S. Zs *Joseph Fouché*' (243–58); L. Decloedt, 'S. Z. im Spiegel der Wiener Presse der dreißiger Jahre' (259–80); M. Reffet, 'S. Zs historische Biographien und die Gegner der "bürgerlichen Literatur"' (281–92); M.-V. Lazarescu, 'Zur Rezeption S. Zs im Wandel der politischen Verhältnisse in Rumänien' (293–304); V. Vertlib, 'Der doppelte Bruch' (305–12). D. Baldes, 'Liberales Weltbürgertum und humanes Menschenbild. Stefan Zweig im Kontext der Säuberungsaktion "wider den undeutschen Geist" am Beispiel seiner Novelle *Der Amokläufer*', Wild, *Bücher*, 441–48.

LITERATURE FROM 1945 TO THE PRESENT DAY

By Joanne Leal, *Lecturer in German, Birkbeck College, University of London*

I. General

Frank Thomas Grub, *'Wende' und 'Einheit' im Spiegel der deutschsprachigen Literatur. Ein Handbuch*, 2 vols, Berlin, de Gruyter, ix + 689, xiv + 349 pp., explores from a variety of perspectives literary treatments of the 'Wende'. The first volume offers a framework for the substantial number of textual readings with chapters on changes in the publishing industry in the former GDR, definitions of 'Wendeliteratur' and an examination of 'Wendesprache'. These are followed by a section on the 'Debatten und Auseinandersetzungen' which surrounded the 'Wende' and re-unification and their manifestation in literature (this section includes a reading of Grass's *Ein weites Feld*), and a chapter on '"Ich" und die "Wende"', which looks at diaries and autobiographical writings, including Günter de Bruyn's *Zwischenbilanz* and Heiner Müller's *Krieg ohne Schlacht. Leben in zwei Diktaturen.* Three further chapters are devoted to prose, poetry, and drama where representative readings help the author to identify recurring themes and forms in 'Wendeliteratur'. A final section deals with the literary exploration of issues such as the depiction of the IM, stereotype images of 'Ossis' and Wessis', and 'Ostalgie'. The second volume contains a detailed bibliography of primary and secondary literature. **Zehn Jahre nachher. Poetische Identität und Geschichte in der deutschen Literatur nach der Vereinigung*, ed. Fabrizio Cambi and Alessandro Fambrini, Trento, Dipartimento di Scienze Filogiche e Storiche, 2002, 365 pp.

Recasting German Identity. Culture, Politics, and Literature in the Berlin Republic, ed. Stuart Taberner and Frank Finlay, Rochester, NY, Camden House, 2002, vii + 276 pp., is an interdisciplinary collection of essays exploring issues of self-understanding in the new Germany, particularly in relation to questions of a 'normalization' of German identity in the post-'Wende' period and the ability of the Berlin Republic to embrace the differing self-understandings of the varied groups within it. Essays which focus on these issues in relation to literature include K. Schödel's account of the 'Walser-Bubis debate' and her reading of *Ein springender Brunnen* (67–84); K. Leeder's examination of the motif of the angel in the poetry of Heiner Müller, Andreas Koziol, and Thomas Martin in an exploration of the changing attitudes to history of writers from the GDR (87–103); S. Ward's analysis of the image of the train in the post-1989 fiction of

Brigitte Struyzk, Reinhard Jirgl, and Wolfgang Hilbig (173–89); R. Skare's exploration of 'the function of the foreign' in Grit Poppe's *Andere Umstände* and Kerstin Jentzsch's *Seit die Götter ratlos sind* (191–203); M. Littler's examination of Turkish-German identity in Emine Sevgi Özdamar's *Mutterzunge* (219–34); K. Gerstenberger's comparison of Zafer Şenocak's *Gefährliche Verwandschaft* and Monika Maron's *Pawels Briefe* (235–49); and S. Parkes's overview of developments in contemporary German literature in which he demonstrates German writing's move out of the 'national ghetto' and 'closer to other western literatures' (251–66). **Erinnerte und erfundene Erfahrung. Zur Darstellung von Zeitgeschichte in deutschsprachiger Gegenwartsliteratur*, ed. Edgar Platen, Munich, Iudicium, 2002, 202 pp. C. Poore, 'Who belongs? Disability and the German nation in postwar literature and film', *GSR*, 26:21–42.

German Writers and the Politics of Culture. Dealing with the Stasi, ed. Paul Cooke and Andrew Plowman, Basingstoke, Palgrave Macmillan, xxi + 262 pp. This volume's first chapter provides a brief but fascinating historical overview of the work of the Stasi (M. Dennis, 3–12). Subsequent chapters concentrate on the depiction of the Stasi in fiction by writers from both East and West and the ways in which a focus on this theme is often coupled with an exploration of German identity as well as issues around narrative and representation. The volume's first part contains essays on works written before 1989 and includes reflections on the figure of Rohlfs as the 'acceptable face of the GDR's secret police' in Uwe Johnson's *Mutmassungen über Jakob*, with a comment on his 'misrepresentation' in Margarethe von Trotta's *Jahrestage* (D. Tate, 25–39); Stefan Heym's *Collin* (R. K. Zachau, 41–55); Martin Walser's *Dorle und Wolf* (M. Butler, 57–70); and Hans Joachim Schädlich's *Tallhover* with a note on the novel's influence on Günter Grass's *Ein weites Feld*. The second part concentrates on post-Wende depictions of the Stasi, opening with G. Paul's insightful account of Wolf's treatment of this theme in relation to her 'politics of self-analysis', which explores the reading public's failure to interpret *Was bleibt* in terms of Wolf's own self-understanding as an author (87–106). C. A. Costabile-Heming examines the structure of Jürgen Fuchs's *Magdalena*, analysing the combination of memory, documentation, and fiction that makes up his autobiographical struggle to come to terms with the legacy of the secret police (221–26). A. Plowman examines Monika Maron's *Pawels Briefe* as a response to the revelation of her contact with the Stasi (227–42). Other contributions focus on Erich Loest's *Fallhöhe* (S. J. Evans, 107–20); Uwe Saeger's *Die Nacht danach und der Morgen* (O. Evans, 121–38), Wolfgang Hilbig's '*Ich*' (P. Cooke, 139–53), Brigitte Burmeister's *Unter dem Namen Norma* (A. Lewis, 155–72);

Thomas Brussig's *Helden wie wir* (K. Foell and J. Twark, 173–94), and Günter Grass's *Ein weites Feld* (J. Preece, 195–212). Franz Huberth, **Aufklärung zwischen den Zeilen: Stasi als Thema in der Literatur*, Cologne, Böhlau, ix + 412 pp. **Die Stasi in der deutschen Literatur*, ed. Franz Huberth, Tübingen, Attempto, 180 pp. A. Lewis, 'Reading and writing the Stasi file: on the uses and abuses of the file as (auto)biography', *GLL*, 56:377–97.

Coming Home to Germany? The Integration of Ethnic Germans from Central and Eastern Europe in the Federal Republic, ed. David Rock and Stefan Wolff, NY–Oxford, Berghahn, 2002, xviii + 234 pp., explores the consequences of post-war mass migration in the old Federal Republic and the new reunited Germany. After an introductory essay providing an historical overview of the topic (S. Wolff, 1–15), the volume's first section examines from a variety of historical perspectives the integration of ethnic German migrants into German society. The second part focuses on the literary thematization of the migration process. Two chapters are concerned with Richard Wagner: D. Rock explores continuities and discontinuities in his work since his arrival in West Germany (121–38) and G. Jackman discusses his portrayal of the figure of the 'Aussiedler' in relation to the themes of 'the difficulty of integration, loneliness and the fluidity of identity' (157–70). J. J. White examines issues of 'ethnic and ideological identity' in the work of Herta Müller (171–87). J. Preece explores Günter Grass's works in the light of his own evaluation of his status as a 'Heimatvertriebener' (188–98). K. Tonkin considers the significance of Gudrun Pausewang's Sudeten German identity for an understanding of her work (199–212). The volume also includes interviews with Richard Wagner and the artist Walter Grill. Kirsti Dubeck, **Heimat Schlesien nach 1945. Eine Analyse deutscher, polnischer und tschechischer Prosatexte*, Hamburg, Kovac, 568 pp. Metin Buz, *Literatur der Arbeitsemigration in der Bundesrepublik Deutschland. Eine literatursoziologische Studie zu Thematik, Schreibweise und Sprachgebrauch in Texten der 1. und 2. Generation der Arbeitsemigranten sowie Überlegungen zur Definitions- und Differenzierungsproblematik der Literatur ausländischer Autoren in der Bundesrepublik*, Marburg, Tectum, 160 pp. Simplice Agossavi, **Fremdhermeneutik in der zeitgenössichen deutschen Literatur. An Beispielen von Uwe Timm, Gerhard Polt, Urs Widmer, Sibylle Knauss, Wolfgang Lange, Hans Christoph Buch* (SBL, 77), 186 pp.

B. Salzmann, 'Literatur als Widerstand. Auf der Spur eines poetologischen Topos' der deutschsprachigen Literatur nach 1945', *DVLG*, 77:330–47. W. Emmerich, 'German writers as intellectuals: strategies and aporias of engagement in East and West from 1945 until today', *NGC*, 88:37–54. Astrid Schau, **Leben ohne Grund. Konstruktion kultureller Identität bei Werner Söllner, Rolf Bossert und Herta*

Müller, Bielefeld, Aisthesis, 380 pp. J. Magenau, 'Literature as a generation's medium for self-understanding', *NGC*, 88:97–106, looks at literary developments since 1989. Andrei Corbea-Hoisie, George Gutu, and Martin Hainz, **Stundenwechsel. Neue Perspektiven zu Alfred Margul-Sperber, Rosa Ausländer, Paul Celan, Immanuel Weissglas*, Konstanz, Hartung-Gorre, 2002, 470 pp. S. Kyora, 'Postmoderne Stile. Überlegungen zur deutschsprachigen Gegenwartsliteratur', *ZDP*, 122:287–302, identifies different concepts of authorship in contemporary fiction and uses these to define two distinct postmodern styles, illustrating the argument with reference to the work of Rainald Goetz, Benjamin von Stuckrad-Barre, Elfriede Jelinek, and Thomas Meinecke.

Pop-Literatur, ed. Heinz Ludwig Arnold (*TK*, special number), 328 pp. Alongside more general essays on the development of 'Pop-Literatur' in Germany since 1960, including discussions of British and American influences on German literature (A. Kramer, 26–40, and M. Büsser, 149–57), 'Pop und Neues Hörspiel' (M. Maurach, 104–15), and the distinctions between 'trash, social beat and slam poetry' (E. Stahl, 258–78), this volume includes analyses of the works of specific authors, amongst them Rolf Dieter Brinkmann (J. Schäfer, 69–80), Hubert Fichte (A. Erb and B. Künzig, 116–32), Rainald Goetz (E. Schumacher, 158–71), Thomas Meinecke and Andreas Neumeister (C. Goer, 172–82), and Christian Kracht and Benjamin von Stuckrad-Barre (M. Mertens, 201–17). N. Werber, 'Der Teppich des Sterbens. Gewalt und Terror in der neusten Popliteratur', *WB*, 49:55–69. C. Berger, 'Pop-Identitäten 2001: Thomas Meineckes *Hellblau* and Christian Krachts *1979*', *Gegenwartsliteratur*, 2:197–225. J. Daiber, 'Digitale Literatur — Kulturelles Phantasma und technologische Wirklichkeit', *DeutB*, 33:277–89. Annette Blühdorn, **Pop and Poetry — Pleasure and Protest: Udo Lindenberg, Konstantin Wecker, and the Tradition of German Cabaret* (GLCS, 13), 374 pp.

K. Gerstenberger, 'Play zones: the erotics of the New Berlin', *GQ*, 76:259–72. C. Cosentino, 'Die Hauptstadt als dritter Ort: Anmerkungen zur Berlin-Literatur der neunziger Jahre', *GN*, 34:2–10, provides a brief overview of a number of works by an older generation of 'Berlin-writers': Volker Braun, Hans Joachim Schädlich, Klaus Schlesinger, Richard Wagner, and Christoph Hein, as well as commenting on texts by two younger writers, Alexander Osang's *Die Nachrichten* and Marko Martin's *Der Prinz von Berlin*.

C. Cosentino, 'Anti-Amerikanismus in der Literatur um die Jahrtausendwende?' GN, 34:95–102, considers works by Ingo Schulze, Angela Kraus, Bernhard Schlink, Judith Hermann, Jakob Hein, and Bernd Wagner written between 1999–2003, a period of 'strapazierten politischen Beziehungen' with the US and comes to the conclusion that contemporary fiction's 'Amerikabild [. . .] hat sich nicht radikal gewandelt'.

Christine Frisch, **Von Powerfrauen und Superweibern: Frauenpopulärliteratur der 90er Jarhe in Deutschland und Schweden*, Huddinge, Södertörn, 198 pp. Emily Jeremiah, *Troubling Maternity: Mothering, Agency, and Ethics in Women's Writing in Germany of the 1970s and 1980s* (BSD, 26), 198 pp. Drawing on the work of Judith Butler, this densely-argued study develops a concept of 'maternal perfomativity' as a way of exploring 'maternal subjectivities' in works by ten women writers (Gisela Elsner, Margot Schroeder, Karin Struck, Barbara Frischmuth, Elfriede Jelinek, Anna Mitgutsch, Andrea Wolfmayr, Maja Beutler, Erica Pedretti, and Irmtraud Morgner) which have mothers as central figures and which were written at a period of social change with implications for the understanding of motherhood. Five chapters explore the texts in relation to different aspects of the maternal experience: community, the maternal body, the mother-child relationship, and the family. Taken together these literary works, which generally portray the experience of motherhood negatively, are read as providing evidence of 'the need for maternal agency to be developed and enabled if the maternal position is to be rendered no longer abject'. Susanne Lackner, **Zwischen Muttermord und Muttersehnsucht. Die literarische Präsentation der Mutter-Tochter-Problematik im Lichte der écriture féminine* (Ep, 457), 312 pp. Stephanie Bird, *Women Writers and National Identity. Bachmann, Duden, Özdamar*, CUP, x + 246 pp., is an illuminating study of 'the way in which national identity manifests itself at the individual level and how it relates to female identity'. It is concerned particularly with the unique possibilities literature offers to explore, without needing to resolve, the complexities, tensions, and ambiguities that can surround issues of self-understanding and in the process it reflects on feminist theory's ability to deal with the existence of such ambiguity. The first section examines the narrative complexity of Bachmann's *Todesarten* prose and considers the relationship between its exploration of female self-understanding and its questioning of Austrian identity. The second section examines the image of the suffering woman in Anne Duden's short stories before analysing the relationship between this theme and issues of German national identity in *Das Judasschaf*. The final part explores the ways in which works by Emine Sevgi Özdamar 'concurrently celebrate and question the role that tradition plays in identity formation'. E. Ludwig Szalay, 'Norms of femininity and their "transformation": gender identity in Kaschnitz, Bachmann, and Wolf', *Seminar*, 39:114–34. R. Wilczek, 'Familienkonflikte als Thema der Gegenwartsliteratur. Prosatexte von Treichel, Vanderbeke, Jenny', *DUS*, 56.1:21–25.

Fractured Biographies, ed. Ian Wallace (*GMon*, 57), Amsterdam–NY, Rodopi, 249 pp., contains biographical studies of Germans active in various fields, including a photographer, a physical chemist, and a cabaret artist, who have in common 'a biography fractured by the Nazis' accession to power'. Two essays offer fascinating accounts of writers who continued their literary work in the post-war period: Albin Stuebs, who, forced to flee in 1933 because of his communist convictions, returned to Germany but failed to achieve literary success with his post-war novels; and Georg Kreisler, prominent in the field of German cabaret but less well-known as a writer of plays and novels, an area on which this essay in part focuses. Gary Schmidt, **The Nazi Abduction of Ganymede. Representations of Male Homosexuality in Postwar German Literature*, NY–Oxford, Lang, 307 pp. Marcel Atze, *'Unser Hitler'. Der Hitler-Mythos im Spiegel der deutschsprachigen Literatur nach 1945*, Göttingen, Wallstein, 493 pp., examines the construction of a 'Hitler-Mythos' during the Nazi period and explores its various facets before turning to the way in which attempts have been made to deconstruct this myth in the post-war fiction in which Hitler appears as a character.

Susanne Vees-Gulani, **Trauma and Guilt. Literature of Wartime Bombing in Germany*, Berlin, de Gruyter, ix + 217 pp. Volker Hage, **Zeugen der Zerstörung. Die Literaten und der Luftkrieg. Essays und Gespräche*, Frankfurt, Fischer, 304 pp. A. Schalk, 'Schockerfahrung ist nicht erzählbar. Zum Problematik des Luftkriegs in der Literatur', *LitL*, 26:117–26, explores aspects of the controversy surrounding W. G. Sebald's *Luftkrieg und Literatur* and Jörg Friedrich's *Der Brand* and identifies evidence of the difficulty of writing about aerial bombardment in works which take this as their theme, such as Hans Erich Nossack's *Der Untergang*.

J. Hell, 'Eyes wide shut: German post-Holocaust authorship', *NGC*, 88:9–36, focuses particularly on Uwe Johnson, Martin Walser, Wolfgang Hilbig, and W. G. Sebald. Klaus Briegleb, *Mißachtung und Tabu. Eine Streitschrift zur Frage: 'Wie antisemitisch war die Gruppe 47?'*, Berlin, Philo, 322 pp. *Handbuch zur deutsch-jüdischen Literatur des 20. Jahrhunderts*, ed. Daniel Hoffmann, Paderborn, Schöningh, 2002, 488 pp., includes two essays relating to the post-war period: H. Gehle, 'Schreiben nach der Shoah. Die Literatur der deutsch-jüdischen Schriftsteller von 1945 bis 1965' (401–40) and A. A. Wallas, 'Deutsch-jüdische Schriftsteller und die Literatur Israels' (441–79). Daniel Ganzfried, * . . . *alias Wilkomirski — Die Holocaust Travestie. Enthüllung und Dokumentation eines literarischen Skandals*, Berlin, Jüdische Verlagsanstalt, 2002, 270 pp. A. Huyssen, 'Diaspora and nation: migration into other pasts', *NGC*, 88:147–64, offers a reading of Zafer Şenocak's

Gefährliche Verwandschaft in relation to issues of diasporic and national memory.

I. Cornils, 'Long memories: the German student movement in recent fiction', *GLL*, 56:89–101, includes readings of Leander Scholz's *Rosenfest*, Erasmus Schöfer's *Ein Frühling irrer Hoffnung*, and Uwe Timm's *Rot*.

J. Preece, 'Between identification and documentation, "Autofiction" and "Biopic": the lives of the *RAF*', *GLL*, 56:363–76, examines the work of older writers and film-makers such as Uwe Timm, Peter O. Chotjewitz, Eva Demski, Margarethe von Trotta, and Volker Schlöndorff, as well as that of their younger counterparts Leander Scholz, Andreas Dresen, Dea Loher, Judith Kuckart, and Andreas Veiel, exploring the way in which generational affiliation and the gender of both author and terrorist subject affect the depiction of the lives of members of the RAF.

S. Richter '"Hic sunt leones." Die Kolonialkriege in Deutsch-Südwestafrika und die deutschsprachige Gegenwartsliteratur', *StZ*, 41:428–43. D. Göttsche, 'Der neue historische Afrika-Roman: Kolonialismus aus postkolonialer Sicht', *GLL*, 56:261–80.

Gundula M. Sharman, *Twentieth-Century Reworkings of German Literature. An Analysis of Six Fictional Reinterpretations from Goethe to Thomas Mann*, Rochester, NY, Camden House, 2002, xii + 221 pp., examines a number of literary pairings in which a later text is based explicitly on an earlier one in such a way that the two works become mutually illuminating, allowing a 'third narrative' to arise through the process of comparison in the mind of the reader. The study examines the methodological implications of a concept of 'literary reworking' and identifies an underlying principle at work in each of the pairings it explores: thus, for instance, 'ironic reproduction' is identified as the defining link between Franz Xaver Kroetz's *Maria Magdelena* and Hebbel's original version; a process of 'fragmentation' connects Wolfgang Koeppen's *Tod in Rom* to Thomas Mann's *Tod in Venedig*; Georg Büchner's and Peter Schneider's *Lenz* are shown to provide an example of 'integration'; while 'quotation' provides the primary point of connection between Goethe's *Die Leiden des jungen Werther* and Ulrich Plenzdorf's *Die neuen Leiden des jungen W*. **Grenzsituationen. Wahrnehmung, Bedeutung und Gestaltung in der neueren Literatur*, ed. Dorothea Lauterbach, Uwe Spörl, and Uli Wunderlich, Göttingen, Vandenhoeck & Ruprecht, 2002, 335 pp., contains essays on Paul Celan, Franz Fühmann, and Hubert Fichte. Heinz-Peter Preusser, **Letzte Welten. Deutschsprachige Gegenwartsliteratur diesseits und jenseits der Apokalypse* (BNL, 193), 321 pp. **The Culture of German Environmentalism. Anxieties, Visions, Realities*, ed. Axel Goodbody, NY–Oxford, Berghahn, 2002, 240 pp. Hans-Jürgen Krug, **Kleine Geschichte des Hörspiels*,

UVK, 166 pp. Ruthild Kropp, **Konstanz und Wandel der Pferdedarstellung in der neueren deutschen Literatur. Ein Beitrag zur Motivgeschichte des Pferdes* (SDLNZ, 47), 2002, 299 pp.

AUSTRIA. Franz Haas, Hermann Schlösser, and Klaus Zeyringer, *Blicke von außen. Österreichische Literatur im internationalen Kontext*, Innsbruck, Haymon, 203 pp. Bianca Theisen, **Silenced Facts: Media Montages in Contemporary Austrian Literature* (APSL, 152), xi + 199 pp. Margarete Lamb-Faffelberger, **Literature, Film and the Culture Industry in Contemporary Austria* (Austrian Culture, 33), NY–Oxford, Lang, 2002, x + 205 pp. **Glück und Unglück in der österreichischen Literatur und Kunst*, ed. Pierre Béhar (Musiliana, 9), Berne, Lang, 292 pp., includes essays on Ingeborg Bachmann and Michael Haneke, Elfriede Jelinek and Marlene Streeruwitz, Peter Rosei, and Thomas Bernhard. *Literature in Vienna at the Turn of the Centuries. Continuities and Discontinuities around 1900 and 2000*, Ernst Grabovszki and James Hardin, Rochester, NY, Camden House, viii + 232 pp. M. Lamb-Faffelberger, 'Beyond *The Sound of Music*: the quest for cultural identity in modern Austria', *GQ*, 76:289–99, examines the connections between national and cultural identity in Austria, first by exploring 'Austria's founding myths' (including 'the myth of Austria as Hitler's first victim'), and then by demonstrating how writers and dramatists have attempted to deconstruct these myths and the notion of 'Heimat' they have helped to perpetuate.

SWITZERLAND. Pia Reinacher, *Je Suisse. Zur aktuellen Lage der Schweizer Literatur*, Zurich, Nagel & Kimche, 184 pp, documents a shift in the concerns of two different generations of Swiss writers, those defined by the experience of 1968 who wrote a specifically political literature concerned above all with concepts of nationhood and national identity, and a younger generation who no longer seem to be concerned with the theme of 'Heimat' but are interested instead in less nationally specific and more obviously personal themes like 'die eigene Biographie [. . .], Liebe, Sex und Partnerstress'. The first part of the volume explores the nature of and the reasons for this shift, while the second offers short readings of recent novels by authors from both generations, including Adolf Muschg, Urs Widmer, Peter Bichsel, Thomas Hürlimann, Gertrud Leutenegger, Ruth Schweikert, Zoë Jenny, and Peter Stamm. Vesna Kondrič Horvat, *Der eigenen Utopie nachspüren. Zur Prosa der deutschsprachigen Autorinnen der Schweiz zwischen 1970 und 1990, dargestellt am Werk Gertrud Leuteneggers und Hanna Johansens*, Berne, Lang, 2002, 248 pp.

EAST GERMANY. Gert Reifarth, **Die Macht der Märchen: zur Darstellung von Repression und Unterwerfung in der DDR in märchenhafter Prosa (1976–1985)* (Ep, 423), 320 pp. Simone Barck, **Antifa-Geschichte(n). Eine literarische Spurensuche in der DDR der 1950er und 1960er Jahre*,

Cologne, Böhlau, 275 pp. Helmut Fuhrmann, **Vorausgeworfene Schatten: Literatur in der DDR, DDR in der Literatur. Interpretationen*, Würzburg, Königshausen & Neumann, 203 pp. Anna Maria Weise, **Feminismus im Sozialismus. Weibliche Lebenskonzepte in der Frauenliteratur der DDR, untersucht an ausgewählten Prosawerken* (EH, I, 1867), 284 pp. Alison Lewis, *Die Kunst des Verrats. Der Prenzlauer Berg und die Staatssicherheit*, Würzburg, Königshausen & Neumann, 272 pp. N. O. Eke, '"Kein neues Theater mit alten Stücken." Entgrenzung der Dramaturgien in der DDR-Dramatik seit den 70er Jahren (Müller, Braun, Brasch, Trolle)', *ABNG*, 52, 2002: 307–46, traces, with reference to four representative dramatists, processes of aesthetic modernization in GDR theatre from the 1970s onwards. H.-C. Stillmark, 'Der Arbeiter — die zentrale Nebengestalt der DDR-Literatur', *ib.*, 347–69, examines the portrayal of the figure of the worker in texts by a range of authors including Brecht, Heiner Müller, Volker Braun, and Wolfgang Hilbig. C. Stenger, '"Simple storys" aus dem Osten? Wie eine Generation junger Autoren und Autorinnen ihre Erfahrungen in Literatur verwandelt', *ib.*, 389–415, explores attitudes to the old GDR and the new BRD as they emerge in the work of Thomas Brussig, Johannes Jansen, Kerstin Jentsch, Marko Martin, and Ingo Schramm. K. McPherson, 'Rückblicke — Briefe und Tagebücher von Autorinnen aus der DDR', *ib.*, 417–32, focuses primarily on editions of letters and diaries written in the 1960s and early 1970s. M. Lüdecke, '"Jeder von uns ist einmalig . . ." Zum Wandel des Bildes vom kindlichen Helden in der Kinderliteratur der DDR', *ib.*, 433–54. B. Dahlke, 'Berlin — Frontstadt, Mauerstadt, Metropole? Zum literarischen Zusammenhang von Stadtbild und Gesellschaftsutopie', *ib.*, 455–72, explores the changing symbolic function of depictions of Berlin in GDR literature and film. L. R. Whitmore, 'Transcending conspirational interpretations of the East German avant-garde', *ib.*, 473–93, examines the possibilities offered by aesthetic and socio-political perspectives for understanding the work of the GDR's avantgarde with particular reference to Bert Papenfuss. M. Bircken, 'Über die Notwendigkeit kultureller Brücken im eigenen Land', *ib.*, 95–114, explores possibilities of reading GDR writing within the context of a socialist literature and within a 'generational context' with specific reference to Anna Seghers's *Drei Frauen aus Haiti*. M. Westdickenberg, '"Es ist zu empfehlen, dem Buch ein Nachwort über die Alternative beizugeben." Veröffentlichungsstrategien und Literaturzensur westdeutscher belletristischer Literatur in der DDR am Beispiel von Thomas Valentins Roman *Die Unberatenen*', *IASL*, 28: 88–110.

LYRIC POETRY. **Interpretationen: Liebesgedichte der Gegenwart*, ed. Hiltrud Gnüg (UB, 17520), 173 pp. M. Braun, '"Allein zu zweit /

sind sie im Einen": Liebe in der Gegenwartslyrik', *Gegenwartsliteratur*, 2:103–27. Hans G. Huch, **Phantasie und Wirklichkeit. Phänomene dichterischer Imagination in der Poesie der Moderne. Gespräche mit Gedichten von Ezra Pound bis Durs Grünbein*, Würzburg, Königshausen & Neumann, 2002, 120 pp. R. J. Owen, '"Eine im Feuer versunkene Stadt": Dresden in poetry', *Gegenwartslitertur*, 1, 2002:87–106. A.-R. Meyer, 'Physiologie und Poesie: zu Körperdarstellungen in der Lyrik von Ulrike Draesner, Durs Grünbein und Thomas Kling', *ib.*, 107–33. L. M. Sager, 'German unification: concepts of identity in poetry from the East and West', *GQ*, 76:273–88. E. Grimm, 'Fathoming the archive: German poetry and the culture of memory', *NGC*, 88:107–40, focuses particularly on the poetry of Michael Krüger, Paul Celan, and Durs Grünbein. B. Preckwitz, 'Ready — steady — slam! Notizen zum Poetry Slam', *WB*, 49:70–79.

DRAMA. **Postwar Austrian Theater. Text and Performance*, ed. Linda C. DeMeritt and Margarete Lamb-Faffelberger, Riverside, California, Ariadne, 2002, 377 pp. Birgit Haas, **Modern German Political Drama 1980–2000*, Rochester, NY, Camden House, vii + 239 pp. Ulrike Dedner, **Deutsche Widerspiele der französischen Revolution: Reflexionen des Revolutionsmythos im selbstbezüglichen Spiel von Goethe bis Dürrenmatt*, Tübingen, Niemeyer, vii + 322 pp. Annette Bühler-Dietrich, **Auf dem Weg zum Theater: Else Lasker-Schüler, Marieluise Fleisser, Nelly Sachs, Gerlind Reinshagen, Elfriede Jelinek* (Ep, 444), 232 pp. Friedericke Emonds, **Gattung und Geschlecht. Inszenierungen des Weiblichen in Werken deutscher Dramatikerinnen*, Würzburg, Königshausen & Neumann, 230 pp. J. Birgfeld, 'Nur das Leben eben? Tendenzen im deutschen Drama der Gegenwart oder Anmerkungen zu Texten von Düffel, Reffert, Loher und Hensel', *DeutB*, 33:91–114. P. Bekes and V. Frederking, 'TheaterSpiel. Moderne Dramen im Deutschunterricht', *DUS*, 56.4:4–9.

PROSE. **Utopie, Antiutopie und Science Fiction im deutschsprachigen Roman des 20. Jahrhunderts*, ed. Hans Esselborn, Würzburg, Königshausen & Neumann, 189 pp. **Der 'gesamtdeutsche' Roman seit der Wiedervereinigung*, ed. Hans-Jörg Knobloch and Helmut Koopmann (Colloquium, 59), Tübingen, Stauffenburg, 212 pp. Anja Hagen, **Gedächtnisort Romantik. Intertextuelle Verfahren in der Prosa der 80er und 90er Jahre*, Bielefeld, Aisthesis, 2002, 522 pp. Volker C. Dörr, **Mythomimesis. Mythische Geschichtsbilder in der westdeutsche (Erzähl-) Literatur der frühen Nachkriegszeit (1945–1952)* (PSQ, 182), 584 pp. C. Könneker, 'Dupliks, ULOs und Upgrades des Menschen: Romanliteratur im Zeichen der neuen Biotechnologie', *Gegenwartsliteratur*, 1, 2002:134–54. L. Federmair, 'Und dann ist der Erzähler ding. Über die Sprache zeitgenössischer Kriminalromane', *Merkur*, 57:1150–53.

2. Individual Authors

ALONIS, JENNY. Petra Renneke, **Das verlorene, verlassene Haus. Sprache und Metapher in der Prosa J. A.* (Veröffentlichungen der Literaturkommision für Westfalen, 8), Bielefeld, Aisthesis, 343 pp.

AMANSHAUSER, GERHARD. G. Stocker, 'Die Subversion der Zauberer. Anmerkungen zu G. A.', *LK*, 377–78:57–61.

ANDERS, GÜNTHER. M. A. Hainz, '*Trojanisches Pferd*, Negativ, oder: G. A. als *falscher Feind* Paul Celans', *Arcadia*, 38:66–76.

ARTMANN, HANS CARL. Sonja Kaar, Kristian Millecker, and Alexandra Millner, **Donauweibchen, Dracula und Pocahontas. H. C. As Mythenspiele*, Vienna, Praesens, 159 pp.

BACHMANN, INGEBORG. *Werke von I. B.*, ed. Matthias Mayer (UB, 17517), 2002, 260 pp., includes chapters on major prose works like *Malina* (S. Weigel, 220–46), on stories like *Das dreißigste Jahr* (B. Bannasch, 140–55), and *Undine geht* (R. Neubauer-Petzoldt, 156–75), and the radio play *Der gute Gott von Manhattan* (C. Lubkoll, 122–39), but also individual readings of a number of B.'s best known poems, including 'Früher Mittag' (L. Olschner, 43–57), 'Reklame' (L. Reitani, 67–80) and 'Böhmen liegt am Meer' (C. Ivanović, 108–21). Bettina von Jagow, **Ästhetik des Mythischen: Poetologien des Erinnerns im Werk von I. B.* (Literatur, Kultur, Geschlecht: Studien zur Literatur- und Kulturgeschichte, 25), Cologne, Böhlau, vi + 280 pp. Kirsten A. Krick-Aigner, *I. B.'s Telling Stories. Fairy Tale Beginnings and Holocaust Endings*, Riverside, California, Ariadne, 2002, 215 pp. Ingvild Folkvord, **Sich ein Haus schreiben. Drei Texte aus I. Bs Prosa*, Hanover, Wehrmann, 224 pp. Patricia Preuss, **I. B. Zu ihren Essays, Gedichten und Briefen an den Akzente-Herausgeber Walter Höllerer*, Sulzbach-Rosenberg, Literaturarchiv Sulzbach-Rosenberg, 2002, 63 pp. Christian Bielefeldt, **Hans Werner Henze und I. B. Die gemeinsamen Werke. Beobachtungen zur Intermedialität von Musik und Dichtung, Kultur- und Medientheorie*, Bielefeld, Transcript, 250 pp. Nathalie Amstutz, **Autorschaftsfiguren: Inszenierung und Reflexion von Autorschaft bei Musil, B. und Mayröcker*, Cologne, Böhlau, 176 pp. *'Im Geheimnis der Begegnung': I. B. und Paul Celan*, ed. Dieter Burdorf, Iserlohn, Institut für Kirche und Gesellschaft, 100 pp. D. Burdorf, '"Alles verloren, die Gedichte zuerst." I. Bs nachgelassene Lyrik', *MDG*, 50:74–85. S. Ogawa, 'Die Produktivität der Hysterie. I. Bs Roman *Malina*', *DB*, 110, 2002:209–20. S. Weiler, 'Und nicht nur "Trotta kehrt zurück" (Jean Améry). I. Bs Revision des kulturellen Gedächtnisses Österreichs in ihrer Erzählung *Drei Wege zum See*', *GM*, 58:67–85. F. Pilipp, 'Die Banalität des Guten: I. Bs Erzählung *Unter Mördern und Irren*', *LitL*, 26:37–51. C. Kanz, 'Intertextuelle Bezüge: W. H. Audens *The Age of Anxiety* und I. Bs *Malina*', *Gegenwartsliteratur*, 2:128–53. E. Boa,

'Musings on muses: poems by Goethe, Rilke and B. and an essay by Anne Duden', *Spalding Vol.*, 86–93, explores the issue of the gendering of cultural creativity in relation to three poems which contain reflections on the motif of the muse: Goethe's Fifth Roman Elegy; the second poem in Rilke's first cycle of sonnets to Orpheus; and B.'s 'Dunkles zu sagen'. The conclusion makes reference to Duden's essay 'Vom Versprechen des Schreibens und vom Schreiben des Verprechens'.

BECKER, JUREK. Sander L. Gilman, **J. B. Die Biografie*, Berlin, Ullstein, 2002, 380 pp. B. Prager, 'The West German East German novel: J. B.'s *Schlaflose Tage* in context', *Gegenwartsliteratur*, 1, 2002: 191–214.

BECKER, JÜRGEN. *J. B.*, ed. Heinz Ludwig Arnold (TK, 159), 130 pp.

BERNHARD, THOMAS. Stefan Krammer, '*Redet nicht von Schweigen —': zu einer Semiotik des Schweigens im dramatischen Werk T. Bs* (Ep, 436), 202 pp. Susanne Gillmayr-Bucher, *Die Psalmen im Spiegel der Lyrik T. Bs* (Stuttgarter Biblische Beiträge, 48), Stuttgart, Katholisches Bibelwerk, 2002, 412 pp. R. Steingröver, '"The most sharp-witted fool": the genius, Glen Gould, and Schopenhauer in T. B.'s prose', *Seminar*, 39: 135–52. G. Jansen, 'Die Uneigentlichkeit der Literatur: wie die Texte der Weltliteratur im Werk T. Bs ihr Unwesen treiben', *Runa*, 29, 2001–02: 169–94. D. W. Price, 'Thoughts of destruction and annihilation in T. B.', *JEGP*, 102: 188–210. P. Höyng, 'Plays of domination and submission in T. B.'s *Ritter, Dene, Voss* (1986) and Werner Schwab's *Die Präsidentinnen*', *GQ*, 76: 300–13. S. Stockhorst, 'Zwischen agitierter Depression und melancholischen Peripatos. Diskursgeschichtliche Anmerkungen zu T. Bs *Gehen* (1971) and Karl Krolows *Im Gehen* (1981)', *ASNS*, 155: 1–19. J. Doll, 'Die Grenzüberschreitung nach Steinhof. Zu T. Bs Erzählung *Gehen*', *Germanica*, 32: 109–22. A. Hettiger, 'T. Bs "Auslöschungs-Musik" — zu Sprache und Stil im Roman *Auslöschung. Ein Zerfall*', *LWU*, 36: 113–20. P. Bozzi, 'Der Traum als Wiederkehr des Körpers: zum anderen Diskurs im Werk T. Bs', pp. 128–48 of *Dream Images in German, Austrian and Swiss Literature and Culture*, ed. Hanne Castein and Rüdiger Görner (PIGS, 78), 2002, 183 pp. See also SCHMIDT, ARNO, WOLF, CHRISTA.

BEYER, MARCEL. U. Baer, '"Learning to speak like a victim": media and authenticity in M. B.'s *Flughunde*', *Gegenwartsliteratur*, 2: 245–61.

BIENEK, HORST. Thomas B. Ahrens, **Heimat in H. Bs Gleiwitzer Tetralogie. Erinnerungsdiskurs und Erzählverfahren* (STML, 66), ix + 236 pp.

BOBROWSKI, JOHANNES. P. Jentzsch, 'Antikes Erbe in neuem Gewand: J. Bs "Der Soldat an der Birke"', *Spalding Vol.*, 166–73, identifies the humanitarian nature of the 'Kulturvorstellung' underpinning B.'s re-working of Petronius's 'The Widow of Ephesus'.

BÖLL, HEINRICH. Heinrich Vormweg, **Der andere Deutsche. H. B. — Eine Biographie*, Cologne, Kiepenheuer & Witsch, 2002, 416 pp. J. H. Reid, 'Some issues of tradition: H. B. and John Henry Newman', *Spalding Vol.*, 159–65, examines B.'s reading of Newmann's theological novel of 1848, *Loss and Gain: The Story of a Convert*. R. Schnell, 'German debates: H. B. and the GDR', *NGC*, 88:55–69. F. Finlay, '"Ein krampfhaftes Augenzumachen"; H. B. and the *Literaturbetrieb* of the early post-war years', *MDLK*, 95:97–115. W. Bellmann, 'Die Akten der Nürnberger Kriegsverbrecherprozesse als Quelle für H. Bs Roman *Gruppenbild mit Dame*', *Euphorion*, 97:85–97.

BORCHERT, WOLFGANG. Gordon J. A. Burgess, *W. B. His Life and Works*, Rochester, NY, Camden House, 300 pp., provides the first comprehensive account in English of B.'s life and works and also updates existing biographies available in German by drawing on newly available material. Just over half the book is taken up with a very readable account of B.'s life. This is followed by chapters analysing a selection of poems (identifying elements of continuity in the early and late pieces), and short stories (grouped thematically under headings such as 'Prison Stories', 'War Stories', 'Stories of the Ruins', and 'Stories of Childhood'), and offering a reading of *Draussen vor der Tür* with a comment on the film *Liebe 47*. The volume concludes with some remarks on the reception of B.'s life and works, exploring and questioning some of the clichés that have arisen from it.

BRAUN, VOLKER. Chung Wan Kim, **Auf der Suche nach dem offenen Ausgang. Untersuchungen zur Dramaturgie und Dramatik V. Bs*, Marburg, Tectum, 210 pp. C. Cosentino, 'Das Eigentliche, das Nichtgewollte: V. Bs Kurzprosa *Das Wirklichgewollte*', *Seminar*, 39:50–61.

BRINKMANN, ROLF DIETER. Jan Röhnert, *Meine erstaunliche Fremdheit! Zur poetischen Topographie des Fremden am Beispiel von R. D. Bs Reiselyrik*, Munich, Iudicium, 150 pp. Thomas Bauer, *Schauplatz Lektüre. Blick, Figur und Subjekt in den Texten R. D. Bs*, Wiesbaden, Deutscher Universitäts-Verlag, 2002, x + 259 pp. A. Chiarloni, 'Was anfällt. Lyrische Strategien in R. D. Bs *Gedicht*', *JIG*, 34.2:229–38.

DE BRUYN, GÜNTER. S. Pak, 'Liebe, Seitensprünge oder die Anpassung an die Gesellschaftsnorm. Thesen zu G. d. Bs *Buridans Esel*', *LitL*, 26:102–16.

CELAN, PAUL. Simone Schmitz, **Grenzüberschreitungen in der Dichtung P. Cs* (BNL, 202), 411 pp. Martin Jörg Schäfer, **Schmerz zum Mitsein. Zur Relektüre Cs und Heideggers durch Philippe Lacoue-Labarthe und Jean-Luc Nancy* (Ep, 456), 408 pp. *Die Zeitlichkeit des Ethos. Poetologische Aspekte im Schreiben P. Cs*, ed. Ulrich Wergin and Martin Jörg Schäfer,

Würzburg, Königshausen & Neumann, 232 pp. Ingeborg Ackermann, *Am Rande seiner selbst: zu P. C., 'Einem, der vor der Tür stand . . .'* (LU, 35), 116 pp. J. Trinks, 'Sinnbildung in P. Cs Gedichten — Sprachphänomenologische Interpretationen', *ZDP*, 122:600–17. M. Fauser, 'Reizaufnahmen. P. C. und die Liebeslyrik', *MDG*, 50:86–96. A. Richter, 'Die politische Dimension der Aufmerksamkeit im *Meridian*', *DVLG*, 77:659–76. A. Bohm, 'Landscapes of exile: C.'s "Gespräch im Gebirg"', *GR*, 78:99–111. J. Voellmy, 'P. C. révise les traductions allemandes des poèmes de René Char', *ColH*, 33, 2002:325–51. L. Norfolk, 'The hunt for Celan's boar', pp. 9–20 of *Uncanny Similitudes: British Writers on German Literature*, ed. Rüdiger Görner, Munich, Iudicium, 2002, 71 pp. S. G. Williams, 'The Deukalion and Pyrrha myth in P. C. and Christoph Ransmayr', *GLL*, 56:142–55. S. Mosès, 'Else Lasker-Schüler, Rosa Ausländer, P. C. Drei Jerusalem-Gedichte', *EG*, 58:197–209. See also ANDERS, GÜNTHER, BACHMANN, INGEBORG.

DELIUS, FRIEDRICH CHRISTIAN. G. L. Jones, 'On revering the old and espousing the new: F. C. D. *Die Birnen von Ribbeck*', *Spalding Vol.*, 200–06.

DOMIN, HILDE. Stephanie Lehr-Rosenberg, **'Ich setzte den Fuss in die Luft, und sie trug': Umgang mit Fremde und Heimat in Gedichten H. Ds*, Würzburg, Königshausen & Neumann, 413 pp.

DONHAUSER, MICHAEL. M. Pajević, 'Die Ungewißheit der Natur. Zur Dichtung M. Ds und Hans-Ulrich Treichels', *EG*, 58:63–81.

DREWITZ, INGEBORG. M. Mattson, 'D.'s *Eis auf der Elbe* and *Gestern war heute*', *GQ*, 76:38–55.

DUDEN, ANNE. *A. D. A Revolution of Words. Approaches to her Fiction, Poetry and Essays*, ed. Heike Bartel and Elizabeth Boa (*GMon*, 56), Amsterdam–NY, Rodopi, 191 pp. E. Boa's introduction (1–18) provides a chronology of D.'s life and publications and examines her poetological essay 'Vom Versprechen des Schreibens und vom Schreiben des Versprechens' before exploring 'places and spaces as poetic motifs' in the essay 'A mon seul désir' and the volume of poems *Hingegend*. D. Göttsche (19–42) examines short prose from the volumes *Wimpertier*, *Der wunde Punkt im Alphabet*, and *Zungengewahrsam*, showing how D. transcends and transforms traditional genres. M. Littler (43–61) explores the representation of violence in *Übergang*. S. Bird (62–71) considers the ethical issues raised by the depiction of pain and suffering in D.'s short stories. T. Ludden (72–87) examines the philosophical influences on conceptions of the relationship between self and world in D.'s work. J. Wigmore (88–101) argues for the significance of the portrayal of nature in D.'s writing. W. Sievers (102–22) examines translation issues in relation to *Übergang*. G. Paul (123–48), C. Roth (149–58), and H. Bartel (159–81) all offer close readings of the poem-cycle *Steinschlag* from different and mutually illuminating perspectives.

DÜRRENMATT, FRIEDRICH. Annette Mingels, *D. und Kierkegaard. Die Kategorie des Einzelnen als gemeinsame Denkform* (Literatur und Leben, 62), Cologne, Böhlau, 2002, x + 400 pp.

EICH, GÜNTER. Sabine Buchheit, **Formen und Funktionen literarischer Kommunikation im Werk G. Es* (SBL, 75), 278 pp. Matthew Philpotts, **The Margins of Dictatorship. Assent and Dissent in the Work of G. E. and Bertolt Brecht* (British and Irish Studies in German Language and Literature, 34), Oxford, Lang, 377 pp.

ELSNER, GISELA. Dorothe Cremer, **'Ihre Gebärden sind riesig, ihre Äußerungen winzig.' Zu G. Es 'Beitrag' 'Die Riesenzwerge'. Schreibweise und soziale Realität in der Adenauerzeit* (Frauen in der Literaturgeschichte, 13), Herbolzheim, Centaurus, 93 pp.

ENZENSBERGER, HANS MAGNUS. Kyung-Nan Kim, **Es medienkritische Positionen im Spiegel seiner Essays über Medien. Eine literaturwissenschaftliche Untersuchung*, Herzogenrath, Shaker, 2002, 258 pp.

ERPENBECK, JENNY. N. Nobile, '"So morgen wie heut": time and context in J. E.'s *Geschichte vom alten Kind*', *Gegenwartsliteratur*, 2:283–310.

FICHTE, HUBERT. R. Heinritz, '"Mehrstimmigkeit" als transkulturelle Erzählform? Zu Reiseberichten Alexander von Humboldts und H. Fs', *ZGer*, 13:41–52.

FRISCH, MAX. Paola Albarella, *Roman des Übergangs. M. Fs 'Stiller' und die Romankunst um die Jahrhundertmitte* (Ep, 443), 192 pp., offers a comparative analysis of *Stiller* with reference to Italo Calvino's *I nostri antenati* as well as works by Vladimir Nabokov, Carlo Emilio Gadda, and André Gide, exploring the way in which the self-reflexivity of F.'s text acts as an ironic commentary on the novel form itself. Meike Heinrich-Korpys, *Tagebuch und Fiktionalität. Signalstrukturen des literarischen Tagebuchs am Beispiel der Tagebücher von M. F.* (SBL, 76), 289 pp. Youngsil Lee, **'Die Selbstverwirklichung' und 'das existentielle Vakuum' in M. Fs Roman 'Mein Name sei Gantenbein' im Lichte der Jaspersschen Existenzphilosophie und der Franklschen Logotherapie*, Marburg, Tectum, 214 pp. G. Kaiser, 'Endspiel in Tessin. M. Fs unentdeckte Erzählung *Der Mensch erscheint im Holozän*', *SchwM*, 82.12–83.1, 2002–03:46–52.

FRITSCH, WERNER. Stefan Prokroppa, **Sprache jenseits von Sprache. Textanalysen zu W. Fs 'Steinbruch', 'Fleischwolf', 'Cherubim' und 'Chroma'*, Bielefeld, Aisthesis, 135 pp.

FUCHS, GERD. J. Heizmann, 'In den Wäldern die Feuer: Geschichte und Aktualität im *Schinderhannes*-Roman von G. F.', *Gegenwartsliteratur*, 1, 2002:215–46.

FÜHMANN, FRANZ. **Dichter sein heißt aufs Ganze aus sein. Zugänge zu Poetologie und Werk F. Fs*, ed. Brigitte Krüger, Frankfurt, Lang, 253 pp.

U. Heukenkamp, 'Ein Kontrahent des Hoffens. F. F. und seine Kriegserzählungen', *ZGer*, 13:101–12. W. Jung, 'Klassiker und Romantiker, oder Rainer Kirsch und F. F.', *ABNG*, 52, 2002:179–90.

GENAZINO, WILHELM. H. Böttiger, 'W. Gs Spiel mit der Verborgenheit', *SuF*, 55:403–10.

GRASS, GÜNTER. *G. G.: Stimmen aus dem Leseland*, ed. Klaus Pezold, Leipzig, Militzke, 232 pp., collects together a series of commentaries on G.'s works which appeared in the GDR between 1957 and 1989 (including articles by Johannes Bobrowski, Heiner Müller, and Stephan Hermlin) and in the new federal states between 1990 and 1999 (including contributions by Hermann Kant, Volker Braun, and Christoph Hein). These are set in context in Pezold's introduction which provides a history of G.'s reception in the East. Fritz J. Raddatz, **G. G. Unerbittliche Freunde. Ein Kritiker. Ein Autor*, Zurich–Hamburg, Arche, 2002, 114 pp. Marcel Reich Ranicki, **Unser G.*, Munich, Deutsche Verlags-Anstalt, 220 pp. D. Reynolds, 'Blinded by the Enlightenment: G. G. in Calcutta', *GLL*, 56:244–60. K. Fieberg, '*Im Krebsgang*. Einführung in die Medien: Spezial zu G. Gs' Novelle', *DUS*, 56.3:34–41. S. Taberner, '"Normalization" and the new consensus on the Nazi past: G. G.'s *Im Krebsgang* and the problem of German wartime suffering', *OGS*, 31, 2002:161–86. A. Höfer, 'Die Entdeckung der deutschen Kriegsopfer in der Gegenwartsliteratur. Eine Studie zur Novelle *Im Krebsgang* von G. G. und ihrer Vorgeschichte', *LitL*, 26:182–97. T. W. Kniesche, '"Distrust the ornament": G. G. and the textual / visual imagination', *Gegenwartsliteratur*, 1, 2002:1–20. J. Heinz, 'G. G.: *Ein weites Feld*: "Bilderbogen" and oral history', *ib.*, 21–38. M. Shafi, '"Gezz will ich ma erzähln": narrative and history in G. G.'s *Mein Jahrhundert*', *ib.*, 39–62. A. Eshel, 'The past recaptured? G. G.'s *Mein Jahrhundert* and Alexander Kluge's *Chronik der Gefühle*', *ib.*, 63–86. S. Braese, '"Tote zahlen keine Steuern": Flucht und Vertreibung in G. Gs *Im Krebsgang* and Hans-Ulrich Treichels *Der Verlorene*', *ib.*, 2:171–96.

GRÜNBEIN, DURS. A. De Boever, 'Innerhalb / Außerhalb der textlichen Falte / Falle. D. G. anno 2003', *GM*, 57:41–58.

HACKS, PETER. F. Dieckmann, 'Die Verteidigung der Insel. Der Artist und sein Asyl. Über P. H.', *SuF*, 55:411–20.

HANDKE, PETER. Georg Pichler, *Die Beschreibung des Glücks. P. H. Eine Biografie*, Vienna, Ueberreuter, 2002, 208 pp. Martina Kurz, *Bild-Verdichtungen: Cézannes Realisation als poetisches Prinzip bei Rilke und H.*, Göttingen, Vandenhoeck & Ruprecht, xvi + 390 pp., demonstrates primarily with reference to the poetry of Rilke and the prose writing of H. the extent of the influence exerted by Cézanne's aesthetic on writers in the 20th c. The first part offers a detailed reading of H.'s *Die Lehre der Sainte-Victoire* exploring its understanding of Cézanne's specific view of reality. This understanding then provides a basis in the second part for the exploration of Rilke's reception of Cézanne, which includes a detailed analysis of the 'Neue Gedichte'. Roland Borgards, *Sprache als Bild. Hs Poetologie und das 18. Jahrhundert*, Munich, Fink, 287 pp. Christoph Parry, **P. H.'s Landscapes of Discourse. An Exploration of Narrative and Cultural Space*, Riverside, California, Ariadne, 251 pp. K. J. Fickert, 'P. H.'s prolonged journey home', *GN*, 34:116–21. C. Zelle, 'Parteinahme für die Dinge. P. Hs Poetik einer literarischen Phänomenologie (am Beispiel seiner *Journale*, 1975–1982)', *Euphorion*, 97:99–117. C. Mondon, 'Erinnerung und Form bei P. H.: zum phänomeno-poetischen Verfahren des Autors', *Gegenwartsliteratur*, 1, 2002:155–74.

HÄRTLING, PETER. B. Röder, 'P. Hs *Hoffmann oder Die vielfältige Liebe*. Ein Plädoyer für Mischa?', *GLL*, 56:168–82.

HASLER, EVELINE. **E. H. in Porto. Akten des Workshops über E. H. in Anwesenheit der Autorin Porto / Mai 2001*, ed. Teresa Martins de Oliveira, Coimbra, Centro Interuniversitário de Estudos Germanísticos, 2002, 87 pp.

HASLINGER, JOSEF. H. Harbers, '"Losing my religion": J. Hs Roman *Das Vaterspiel*', *LitL*, 26:52–61.

HAUSHOFER, MARLEN. A. Friedrichsen, '"Damals war ich glücklich gewesen" — über Kindheit und Mutterschaft als komplementäre Pole bei M. H.', *TeK*, 25:95–124.

HEIN, CHRISTOPH. David Clarke, *'Diese merkwürdige Kleinigkeit einer Vision.' C. H.'s Social Critique in Transition* (APSL, 150), 2002, 339 pp. A. Köhler, 'Facettenreicher Widerhall. C. Hs Erzählwerk vor und nach der deutschen Wiedervereinigung', *WB*, 49:585–98. P. McKnight, 'Geschichte und DDR-Literatur. (Amnesie, Fragmentierung, Chronik, Kritisches Bewußtsein und Weichenstellung im Rückblick auf die Mitte der 50er Jahre: Mankurt, Horn und *Horns Ende*)', *ABNG*, 52, 2002:191–219, examines the way in which H. explores in *Horns Ende* literature's potential for providing ways of remembering that run counter to official historiography. B. Krüger, '"Ein Spiel, nicht selbst gewählt, doch seinen Regeln unterworfen [. . .]." Zum Spiel-Begriff bei C. H.', *ib.*, 221–52. M. Krol, 'C. H.: "Die Vergewaltigung": Kalender der "großen Geschichte" versus Kalender der "kleinen Geschichte"', *Gegenwartsliteratur*, 1, 2002:268–88.

HENISCH, PETER. Craig Decker, **Balancing Acts. Textual Strategies of P. H.*, Riverside, California, Ariadne, 2002, 308 pp. **P. H.*, ed. Walter Grünzweig and Gerhard Fuchs, Graz, Droschl, 320 pp. F. Schuh, 'Ohne Widerruf. Zu den "letzten Dingen" im Werk von P. H.', *Wespennest*, 132:67–71. W. Grünzweig, 'Österreich von innen und außen. Über P. H.', *LK*, 379–80:19–22.

HEYM, STEFAN. Regina U. Hahn, **The Democratic Dream: S. H. in America* (Exile Studies, 10), NY–Oxford, Lang, 148 pp. **S. H.: Socialist — Dissenter — Jew*, ed. Peter Hutchinson and Reinard K. Zachau (British and Irish Studies in German Language and Literature, 32), NY–Oxford, Lang, 220 pp.

HILBIG, WOLFGANG. Jens Loescher, *Mythos, Macht und Kellersprache: W. Hs Prosa im Spiegel der Nachwende* (APSL, 151), 360 pp. Sabine Sistig, **Wandel der Ich-Identität in der Postmoderne? Zeit und Erzählen in W. Hs 'Ich' und Peter Kurzecks 'Keiner stirbt'* (Ep, 407), 147 pp. G. Fischer, 'Arbeiter — Schriftsteller: Dichotomien einer Daseinsform. Zu W. Hs Roman *Eine Übertragung*', *Seminar*, 39:316–28. R. R. Duffaut, 'The function of poststructuralism in W. H.'s novel *"Ich"*', *ABNG*, 52, 2002:371–88. See also WOLF, CHRISTA.

HILDESHEIMER, WOLFGANG. Christine Chiadò Rana, **Das Weite suchen. Unterwegs in W. Hs Prosa*, Würzburg, Ergon, 356 pp.

HOCHHUTH, ROLF. H. L. Arnold, 'Gäbe es ihn nicht — man müsste ihn erfinden. R. H. ist in der deutschen Literatur das Salz in der Suppe', *SchwM*, 83.2:39–43.

HONIGMANN, BARBARA. P. S. Fiero, 'Life at the margins of East German society: B. H.'s epistolary novel *Alles, alles Liebe!*', *Gegenwartsliteratur*, 2:81–102.

HUCHEL, PETER. *P. H.*, ed. Heinz Ludwig Arnold (TK, 157), 98 pp., includes essays on H.'s relationship to politics (P. Walther, 7–22), the reception of his work in the francophone world (M. Jacob, 71–77), and an analysis of his writing in relation to that of Ingeborg Bachmann, Reiner Kunze, Ludvík Kundera, and Jan Skácel (H. D. Zimmermann, 51–60). S. Parker, 'Visionäre Naturbilder. Literarische und autobiographische Züge der Privatmythologie P. Hs', *SuF*, 55:257–66. K. Schumann, 'Vom Gedichtenschreiben in "schwerer Lage". Bertolt Brechts "Böser Morgen" und P. Hs "April 63"', *NDL*, 51.3:168–73.

HÜRLIMANN, THOMAS. J. Dewulf, 'Calderón in der Innerschweiz. Über T. Hs Stück: *Das Einsiedler Welttheater*', *Runa*, 29, 2001–2002:124–30.

JELINEK, ELFRIEDE. *Die Nestbeschmutzerin. J. und Österreich*, ed. Pia Janke, Salzburg–Vienna, Jung und Jung, 2002, 252 pp. J. J. Rosellini, 'Js Haider: Anmerkungen zur literarischen Populismus-Kritik', *TeK*, 25:125–38. B. Kallin, 'Jörg Haider as a contemporary Orestes: Aeschylus's *Oresteia* in E. J.'s *Das Lebewohl*', *Seminar*, 39:329–49.

JOHNSON, UWE. Ulrich Krellner, **'Was ich im Gedächtnis ertrage': Untersuchungen zum Erinnerungskonzept von U. Js Erzählwerk* (Ep, 430), 403 pp. Katja Leuchtenberger, **'Wer erzählt, muss an alles denken': Erzählstrukturen und Strategien der Leserlenkung in den frühen Romanen U. Js*

(Johnson-Studien, 6), Göttingen, Vandenhoeck & Ruprecht, 349 pp. Manfred Windfuhr, **Erinnerung und Avantgarde. Der Erzähler U. J.* (BNL, 195), 84 pp. M. Hofmann, 'Zur Aktualität einer Poetik des Erhabenen. Schiller, Hugo, J., Tabori', *WB*, 49:202–18. L. Koepnick, 'Zapping channels: U. J., Margarethe von Trotta, and the televisual aesthetics of *Jahrestage*', *Gegenwartsliteratur*, 1, 2002: 175–90. See also SCHÄDLICH, HANS JOACHIM.

KASCHNITZ, MARIE LUISE. A. Bushell, 'The poet between war and peace: M. L. K.'s essays *Menschen und Dinge 1945*', *Spalding Vol.*, 192–99. Ruta Eidukeviciene, **Jenseits des Geschlechterkampfes. Traditionelle Aspekte des Frauenbildes in der Prosa M. L. K., Gabriele Wohmann und Brigitte Kronauer* (SBL, 80), 351 pp.

KEMPOWSKI, WALTER. M. Rutschky, 'Unbelebte Erinnerung. Der Schriftsteller W. K.', *Merkur*, 57: 127–40.

KERN, ELFRIEDE. U. Schütte, 'Unausschöpfbare Vieldeutigkeit. Zum Romanwerk der E. K.', *Sprachkunst*, 34:71–86.

KERSCHBAUMER, MARIE THÉRÈSE. K. Zeyringer, '"SIE Erwachen": M. T. Ks Erzählgeflechte', *Gegenwartsliteratur*, 2:154–170.

KIPPHARDT, HEINAR. B. Bach, 'H. K.: *März* (1976). La folie, protestation contre une société malade', *Germanica*, 32:91–107.

KIRSCH, SARAH. W. Bunzel, '"... dankbar daß ich entkam." S. Ks Autorexistenz im Spannungsfeld von DDR-Bezug und "Exil"-Erfahrung', *GM*, 57:7–27.

KLEMPERER, VICTOR. R. H. Watt, '"Ich triumphiere sozusagen": the publication history of V. K.'s "Zion-Kapitel" in *LTI* (1947–1957)', *GLL*, 56:132–41.

KLING, THOMAS. T. Lehmkuhl, 'Gedächtnisspeicher. Zu T. Ks Zyklus *Der Erste Weltkrieg*', *WB*, 49:44–54.

KLUGE, ALEXANDER. **Ks Fernsehen: A. Ks Kulturmagazine*, ed. Christian Schulte and Winfried Siebers (ESk, 2244), 2002, 265 pp. See also MÜLLER, HEINER.

KROLOW, KARL. Neil H. Donahue, *K. K. and the Poetics of Amnesia in Postwar Germany*, Rochester, NY, Camden House, 2002, ix + 285 pp., explores K.'s activities in the Third Reich and his literary output before 1945 and from this basis offers a reassessment of his literary career in the post-war period, establishing the way in which K. developed a 'notion of literariness' which became 'a refuge from the past' and identifying as the element of continuity in his work the remarkable avoidance of an engagement with personal or political history. See also BERNHARD, THOMAS.

KRONAUER, BRIGITTE. J. Bertschik, 'Die Einöde und ihre Propheten. Demonstrative Legendenbildung bei B. K.', *JIG*, 34.2:75–86. See also KASCHNITZ.

KUNERT, GÜNTER. K. Dunne, 'The symbolic function of Medusa, Clio, and the "Fee" in G. K.'s work', *GQ*, 76: 155–67.

KUSZ, FITZGERALD. A. De Winde, '"naa ä lebkoung mechädi ned saa." F. K. und die neue deutsche Mundartdichtung', *GM*, 58: 19–47.

LANGE, HARTMUT. **Der Dramatiker und Erzähler H. L.*, ed. Manfred Durzak, Würzburg, Königshausen & Neumann, 261 pp.

MARON, MONIKA. K. von Oppen, '"Genügend Berühmtheit, wenigstens aber Prominenz": M. M. and the feuilleton', *ColGer*, 35, 2002: 155–74. A. Bolterauer, '"Manche sagen, ich bin irre ..." Anmerkungen zu M. Ms Roman *Die Überläuferin*', *Germanica*, 32: 123–35. Julia Petzl, **Realism and Reality in Helga Schubert, Helga Königsdorf and Monika Maron* (HKADL, 35), 179 pp.

MAYRÖCKER, FRIEDERIKE. S. Bani, 'F. M. oder Das Herumzigeunern im Text', *Manuskripte*, 160: 124–27. See also BACHMANN, INGEBORG.

MEIER, GERHARD. Jan Watrak, *G. Ms Lyrik und Kurzprosa*, Frankfurt, Lang, 2002, 177 pp.

MENASSE, ROBERT. Verena Holler, **Felder der Literatur. Eine literatursoziologische Studie am Beispiel von R. M.* (EH, 1, 1861), 341 pp. M. Rutschky, 'Sänftigung der Glaubensmächte. R. Ms *Die Vertreibung aus der Hölle*', *Merkur*, 57: 529–34.

MONÍKOVÁ, LIBUŠE. Alfrun Kliems, **Im 'Stummland'. Zum Exilwerk von L. M., Jiří Gruša and Ota Filip* (EH, XVI, 67), 2002, 249 pp.

MÜLLER, HEINER. *H. M. Handbuch: Leben-Werk-Wirkung*, ed. Hans-Thies Lehmann and Patrick Primavesi, Stuttgart, Metzler, 525 pp. Marcus Kreikebaum, *H. Ms Gedichte*, Bielefeld, Aisthesis, 399 pp. Sabine Pamperrien, *Ideologische Konstanten — Ästhetische Variablen. Zur Rezeption des Werks von H. M.* (Schriften zur Europa- und Deutschlandforschung, 10), Frankfurt, Lang, 220 pp. Corinna Mieth, **Das Utopische in Literatur und Philosophie. Zur Ästhetik H. Ms und Alexander Kluges*, Tübingen, Francke, 403 pp. Thomas Weitin, **Notwendige Gewalt. Die Moderne Ernst Jüngers und H. Ms* (Cultura, 34), Freiburg, Rombach, 422 pp. D. Hensing, 'Wenn der Stein der Geschichte zurückrollt. Über einen glücklichen und vor allem einen unglücklichen Sisyphos — über Albert Camus und H. M.', *ABNG*, 52, 2002: 253–305, explores M.'s reflections on history and literature in *Gesammelte Irrtümer* with reference to Camus's philosophy.

NIZON, PAUL. Doris Krockauer, **P. N. Auf der Jagd nach dem eigenen Ich*, Munich, Fink, 260 pp. H.-J. Heinrichs, 'Mit dem Schreiben geht es. Über P. N.', *Merkur*, 57: 721–25.

NOSSACK, HANS ERICH. P. Prochnik, 'H. E. N.: new beginnings', *Spalding Vol.*, 186–91, explores the genesis of N.'s *Der Untergang* and the significance of this piece and the events that inspired it for N.'s subsequent writings.

ÖZDAMAR, EMINE SEVGI. B. Venkat Mani, 'The good woman of Istanbul: E. Z. Ö.'s *Die Brücke vom Goldenen Horn*', *Gegenwartsliteratur*, 2:29–58.

SAEGER, UWE. O. Evans, '"The most painful poetry I know": U. S. and Georg Trakl's "Grodek"', *Spalding Vol.*, 214–19, examines intertextuality in S.'s autobiographical *Die Nacht danach und der Morgen*.

SCHÄDLICH, HANS JOACHIM. T. Buck, 'Verhinderte Innovation. Die in der DDR ungedruckt gebliebenen Bücher von Uwe Johnson und H. J. S.', *ABNG*, 52, 2002:11–44. D. Pilz, 'Die Schrift bleibt verwischt. Überlegungen zur Aktualität von H. J. Ss Band *Versuchte Nähe* anhand des Textes "Lebenszeichen"', *ib.*, 45–69.

SCHLAG, EVELYN. Riccarda Novello, **Das Leben in den Worten — die Worte im Leben. Eine symptomatische Lektüre als Literatur- und Lebenserforschung zu Evelyn Schlag, Marianne Fritz, Marlene Streeruwitz*, Milan, Cooperativa Universitaria Editrice Milanese, 286 pp. K. Zeyringer, 'Das Lieben und das Dichten. E. Ss poetisches Netz', *LK*, 375–76:41–46.

SCHLINK, BERNHARD. B. Niven, 'B. S.'s *Der Vorleser* and the problem of shame', *MLR*, 98:381–96. U. Mahlendorf, 'Trauma narrated, read, and misunderstood: B. S.'s *The Reader*: "... irrevocably complicit in their crimes"', *MDLK*, 95:458–81. D. Reynolds, 'A portrait of misreading: B. S.'s *Der Vorleser*', *Seminar*, 39:238–56. M. Matsunaga, 'Ein zufälliger Bestseller? Die Rezensionen von B. Ss *Der Vorleser* in Japan', *DB*, 114:147–49. J. Desch, 'Uneasy journey into the past: B. S.'s *Der Vorleser*', *Spalding Vol.*, 242–49. H. M. Schlipphacke, 'Enlightenment, reading, and the female body: B. S.'s *Der Vorleser*', *Gegenwartsliteratur*, 1, 2002:310–28.

SCHMIDT, ARNO. Volker Langbehn, **A. S.'s 'Zettels Traum'. An Analysis*, Rochester, NY, Camden House, 192 pp. *Wiederholte Spiegelungen: elf Aufsätze zum Werk A. Ss*, ed. Robert Weninger (*BaB*, special number), TK, 190 pp. I. Garnier, 'Die Verführungsstrategie war / ist erfolgreich. Ein Lektürebericht vom *Steinernen Herz*', *BaB*, 266:9–11. K. Piperek, '"Jene abstoßend-unbekannte Sprache." A. S. und das Sorbische', *ib.*, 267–268:17–34. J. Süsselbeck, 'Die neue Ess-Klasse oder: Warum die A.-S.-"Gemeinde" dringend Thomas Bernhard lesen sollte', *ib.*, 266:6–9. Id., '"Geschichte? Schicksal?" In einer Nebenrolle: Fouqué. Das Restaurationspanorama "Goethe und Einer seiner Bewunderer"', *ib.*, 269–270:3–26.

SCHMIDT, KATHRIN. F. Eigler, '(Familien-)Geschichte als subversive Genealogie: K. Ss *Gunnar-Lennefsen-Expedition*', *Gegenwartsliteratur*, 2:262–82.

SCHNEIDER, PETER. R. W. Williams, '"Er klammerte sich an alle Gegenstände": Büchner, P. S. and the uses of Germanistik', *Spalding Vol.*, 228–34, examines the reasons for and the uses of intertextuality in the writings of the student generation of 1968 with particular reference to S.'s *Lenz.*

SCHNEIDER, ROBERT. Mark Werner, **Die Konzeption des Genies in R. Ss 'Schlafes Bruder'*, Marburg, Tectum, 147 pp.

SCHULZE, INGO. P. Cooke, 'Beyond a *Trotzidentität.* Storytelling and the postcolonial voice in I. S.'s *Simple Storys*', *FMLS*, 39:290–305. I. Urupin, '*33 Augenblicke des Glücks.* Überlebenschancen im Raum von Sankt Petersburg', *GM*, 57:29–40.

SCHWAB, WERNER. Harald Miesbacher, *Die Anatomie des Schwäbischen: W. Ss Dramensprache*, Graz–Vienna, Droschl, 270 pp. H. Miesbacher, 'Hoch vom Hochschwab an . . . Entgrenztes Sprechen — W. Ss Suche nach einer *anderen* Sprache', *Manuskripte*, 160:128–31. See also BERNHARD, THOMAS.

SEBALD, W. G. *The Anatomist of Melancholy. Essays in Memory of W. G. S.*, ed. Rüdiger Görner, Munich, Iudicium, 93 pp., contains contributions to the 'W. G. S. Memorial Day' held at London University's Institute of Germanic Studies in January 2003. These include a fascinating account by A. Bell of the experience of translating S. (11–18), and a long contribution by J. Catling in which an attempt is made to explore themes that recur throughout S.'s *œuvre*, such as the use of landscapes and journeying motifs (19–50). A number of shorter essays focus on specific aspects of S.'s writing: E. Shaffer writes on the way S. deploys photographs in his work (51–62); U. Schütte examines his critical essays on Austrian literature (63–74); R. Görner contributes reflections on S.'s poetry (75–80); and M. Swales offers a brief but insightful attempt to determine the nature of the characteristic voice in evidence in S.'s fiction and to identify the nature of 'the metonymy of melancholy' which characterizes his work as a whole (81–87). Mark R. McCulloh, *Understanding W. G. S.*, Columbia, South Carolina U.P., xxiv + 193 pp. *W. G. S.*, ed. Heinz Ludwig Arnold (TK, 158), 119 pp. K. Sibelewski, 'Vom Erzählen nach der Katastrophe. Über W. G. S.', *SuF*, 55:117–28. A. Köhler, 'W. G. Ss Gesichter', *Akzente*, 50:15–20. R. Tabbert, 'Max in Manchester. Außen- und Innenansicht eines jungen Autors', *ib.*, 21–30. R. Görner, 'Begehungen in drei Stätzen. W. G. Ss gedenkend', *ib.*, 31–34. S. Meyer, 'Das Fähnlein auf der Brücke', *ib.*, 51–55. U. Schütte, 'Ein Lehrer. In memoriam W. G. S.', *ib.*, 56–62. A. Shields, 'Neun Sätze aus *Austerlitz*', *ib.*, 63–72. C. Scholz, 'Photographie und Erinnerung. W. G. S. im Porträt', *ib.*, 73–80. T. Steinfeld, 'W. G. S.', *ib.*, 81–87. S. Sontag, 'Ein trauernder Geist', *ib.*, 88–95. C. Hitchen, 'Die Deutschen und der Krieg. W. G. S. schrieb über die Qual, zu einem Volk zu gehören, das, in Thomas Manns Worten "sich nicht sehen lassen kann"', *NRu*, 114.1:116–26. J. M. Coetze, 'Erbe einer düsteren Geschichte. Zu W. G. Ss *Nach der*

Natur', *ib.*, 127–35. A. Fuchs, '"Phantomspuren": zu W. G. Ss Poetik der Erinnerung in *Austerlitz*', *GLL*, 56:281–98. A. Eshel, 'Against the power of time: the poetics of suspension in W. G. S.'s *Austerlitz*', *NGC*, 88:71–96. J. J. Long, 'History, narrative, and photography in W. G. S.'s *Die Ausgewanderten*', *MLR*, 98:117–37. C. Albes, 'Die Erkundung der Liebe. Anmerkungen zu W. G. Ss "englischer Wallfahrt" *Die Ringe des Saturn*', *JDSG*, 46, 2002:279–305. P. C. Pfeiffer, 'Korrespondenz und Wahlverwandschaft: W. G. Ss *Die Ringe des Saturn*', *Gegenwartsliteratur*, 2:226–44. U. Schütte, 'Der Hüter der Metaphysik. W. G. Ss Essays über die österreichische Literatur', *Manuskripte*, 155, 2002:124–28.

ŞENOCAKS, ZAFER. **Z. Ş.*, ed. Tom Cheesman and Karin Yesilada, Cardiff, Univ. of Wales Press, x + 187 pp. K. Hall, '"Bekanntlich sind Dreieckbeziehungen am kompliziertesten": Turkish, Jewish and German identity in Z. Ş.'s *Gefährliche Verwandtschaft*', *GLL*, 56:72–88. R. Dollinger, '"Stolpersteine": Z. Şs Romane der neunziger Jahre', *Gegenwartsliteratur*, 2:1–28.

SPERBER, MANÈS. Mirjana Stancic, *M. S.. Leben und Werk*, Stroemfeld, Frankfurt, 687 pp.

STRAUSS, BOTHO. Michael Wiesberg, **B. S.*, Dresden, Antaios, 2002, 144 pp. F. Schössler, 'Die Aufhebung des Bildungsromans aus dem Geist Nietzsches. Zu B. S.' Roman *Der junge Mann*', *GRM*, 53:75–93.

STREERUWITZ, MARLENE. G. Eckart, 'M. S.' *Majakowskiring*: ein kritischer Beitrag zur Debatte über die deutsche Wiedervereinigung', *Seminar*, 39:153–70. H.-P. Bayerdörfer, 'Nebentexte, groß geschrieben: Zu M. S.' Drama *New York. New York*', *Gegenwartsliteratur*, 1, 2002:289–309. See also SCHLAG, EVELYN.

STRITTMATTER, ERWIN. A. Schalk, '"Bericht zu mir! Gerade Linie! Durch!" Überlegungen zu E. Ss *Ochsenkutscher* und *Ole Bienkopp* und einem deutschen Literaturstreit', *ABNG*, 52, 2002:71–91.

SÜSKIND, PATRICK. Frank Degler, **Aisthetische Reduktion: Analysen zu P. Ss 'Der Kontrabass', 'Das Parfum' und 'Rossini'* (QFLK, 24), vii + 386 pp.

TIMM, UWE. R. Parr, 'Nach Gustav Frenssens Peter Moor. Kolonialisten, Herero und deutsche Schutztruppen bei Hans Grimm und U. T.', *StZ*, 41:395–409. M. Hielscher, 'Sprechende Ochsen und die Beschreibung der Wolken. Formen der Subversion in U. Ts Roman *Morenga*', *ib.*, 463–71. M. Hielscher, 'Der Kannibalismus des Erzählens: zu U. Ts Roman *Kopfjäger*', *Gegenwartsliteratur*, 1, 2002:247–67.

TREICHEL, HANS-ULRICH. G. Henschel, 'Emsfelde regiert. Der Erzähler H.-U. T.', *Merkur*, 57:344–48. See also DONHAUSER, MICHAEL and GRASS, GÜNTER.

WAGNER, RICHARD. D. Rock, '"Ungeist" in East and West: representations of Ceausećcu's Romania and pre-unification West Germany in two works by R. W.', *Spalding Vol.*, 220–27, examines W.'s representation of the experience of the Romanian German 'Aussiedler' in the first two stories he wrote after coming to the West, 'Ausreiseantrag' and 'Begrüßungsgeld'.

WALSER, MARTIN. *Der Ernstfall: M. Ws 'Tod eines Kritikers'*, ed. Dieter Borchmeyer and Helmuth Kiesel, Hamburg, Hoffmann & Campe, 288 pp., is a collection of essays offering readings of W.'s novel and assessing the literary scandal which preceded its publication. B. Niven, 'M. W.'s *Tod eines Kritikers* and the issue of anti-Semitism', *GLL*, 56:299–311. A. Mathäs, 'M. W. und der Sinn des Lesens: zur Ästhetik von *Tod eines Kritikers*', *Gegenwartsliteratur*, 2:311–36. H. Verboven, 'M. W. und die Öffentlichkeit. Die Tragik des Missverstehens', *GM*, 57:59–73. M. Hofmann, 'M. W. und die deutsche Vergangenheit', *ib.*, 58:49–65. Wolfram Burkhardt, **Intellektuelle und Politik. Jürgen Habermas — M. W. — Daniel Cohn-Bendit*, Marburg, Tectum, 2002, 7 microfiches, 685 pp. Hilmar Grundmann, *Berufliche Arbeit macht krank. Literaturdidaktische Reflexionen über das Verhältnis von Beruf und Privatsphäre in den Romanen von M. W.* (Beiträge zur Literatur- und Medienkritik, 4), Frankfurt, Lang, 256 pp. Ralf Oldenburg, *M. W.: bis zum nächsten Wort. Eine Biographie in Szenen*, Meerbusch bei Düsseldorf, Lehrach, 217 pp.

WEISS, PETER. Olaf Berwald, *An Introduction to the Works of P. W.*, Rochester, NY, Camden House, vii + 170 pp. A brief biographical overview is followed by three chapters on W.'s theatre, covering the early grotesque plays, the documentary dramas from the 1960s, and the later plays. Four further chapters cover the early prose, the autobiographical fictions, his writings on art and politics, and finally a slightly more detailed analysis of 'Die Ästhetik des Widerstands'. With its tracing of developments and continuities in his writing the volume provides a useful introduction to W.'s work. Karen Huidtfeldt Madsen, **Widerstand als Ästhetik. P. W. und 'Die Ästhetik des Widerstands'*, Wiesbaden, Deutscher Universitäts-Verlag, 228 pp.

WINKLER, JOSEF. H. L. Ott, 'Les délires verbaux de J. W. — du cri à l'incantation rituelle?', *Germanica*, 32:137–50. B. Mariacher, 'Zwischen Statik und Bewegung. Anmerkungen zum poetischen Verfahren in J. Ws Erzählung *Wenn es soweit ist* (1998)', *ÖGL*, 47:375–80.

WOLF, CHRISTA. Jörg Magenau, *C. W. Eine Biographie*, Berlin, Kindler, 2002, 496 pp. Stefanie Gödeke-Kolbe, *Subjektfiguren und Literaturverständnis nach Auschwitz: Romane und Essays von C. W.*, Frankfurt, Lang, 338 pp., examines various contextualizing perspectives from which to explore W.'s work, including the influence of Anna

Seghers and the romantic, communist, and anti-fascist tradition she represents and W.'s essays after 1989 in the light of her changing understanding of what it means to be a socialist author. It then offers a detailed analysis of W.'s major prose works, *Nachdenken über Christa T.*, *Kindheitsmuster*, *Kassandra*, and *Medea*, particularly as responses to Germany's Nazi past. Mi-Kyeung Jung, **Fremde und Ambivalenz. Die Fremdheit als literarischer Topos im Werk C. Ws im Vergleich mit Thomas Bernhard* (EH, 1, 1864), viii + 184 pp. Katharina Theml, *Fortgesetzter Versuch — Zu einer Poetik des Essays in der Gegenwartsliteratur am Beispiel von Texten C. Ws* (SDLNZ, 49), 305 pp., explores the history and the historical understanding of the essay form from Montaigne onwards in an international context and with particular reference to the neglected history of women essayists. An attempt is then made to re-explore definitions of and theoretical considerations surrounding the essay in the light of poststructuralist literary theory, which is shown to be particularly appropriate to 'eine Beschreibung des Grenzcharakters, der Offenheit der Form, des essayistischen Spiels und des trotzdem bewußten und reflektierten Umgangs mit Sprache' characteristic of this genre. This historical and theoretical section provides the context in which a selection of C. W.'s essays written between 1968 and 1993 are explored. The study provides a useful contribution to the history of the essay as a form of 'Gegenöffentlichkeit' in the GDR and also to the theoretical understanding of the essay form in general. S. Wilke, 'Die Konstruktion der wilden Frau: C. W.'s *Medea. Stimmen*', *GQ*, 76:11–24. A. Pinkert, 'Myth, holocaust, and dissidence in C. W.'s *Kindheitsmuster*', *GQ*, 76:25–37. U. Merkel, 'Selbstreferenz und Selbsterschaffung aus dem Möglichkeitssinn. Beobachtungen zu Struktur und Sprache des Romans der Neuzeit (Moderne, Postmoderne) am Beispiel von Grimmelshausens *Simplicissimus*, C. Ws *Kindheitsmuster*, Wolfgang Hilbigs *Ich*', *WB*, 49:80–95. C. Cosentino, 'C. Ws *Leibhaftig* und Wolfgang Hilbigs *Das Provisorium*: zwei "Krankenberichte" an der Jahrtausendwende', *GN*, 34:121–27. A. Chiarloni, 'Nachdenken über C. W.', *ABNG*, 52, 2002:115–54, explores the Italian reception of W. as a socialist and a feminist writer and examines whether in the post-Wende period these still provide appropriate perspectives from which to view her work, with particular reference to prose works from the 1960s to the 1980s. Y. Delhey, 'Kunst zwischen Mythos und Aufklärung — *Littérature engagée* im Zeichen des Humanen. Zur Mythosrezeption C. Ws mit einer Fußnote zu Franz Fühmann', *ABNG*, 52, 2002:155–77.

WÜHR, PAUL. Reinhard Kiefer, **Gottesurteil. P. W. und die Theologie*, Aachen, Rimbaud, 80 pp.

ZÜRN, UNICA. Helga Lutz, *Schriftbilder und Bilderschriften: Zum Verhältnis von Text, Zeichnung und Schrift bei U. Z.*, Stuttgart, Metzler, 180 pp.

II. DUTCH STUDIES

LANGUAGE

By Reinier Salverda, *Professor of Dutch Language and Literature, University College London*

(This survey covers the years 1997–2003)

1. General

To bridge the gap that has occurred in this section I have selected the most significant publications on Dutch (and Frisian) language and linguistics of the past seven years, about 200 in total.

The field of Dutch language and linguistics is served by a good range of bibliographic tools, a survey of which is given in Smedts, *Taalkunde.* The three opening chapters, on bibliographies, linguistics journals, and electronic resources respectively, are followed by bibliographic surveys of 26 subdomains, ranging from 'Taalplanning' (language planning) by Roland Willemyns, 'Afrikaans' by F. A. Ponelis, and 'Tekstwetenschap' (discourse studies) by W. Van Belle and A. Maes, to 'Taalbeheersing' (stylistics) by W. Braet. The book does not yet cover the new fields of variation studies, speech technology, or contact linguistics, however. Neither does it have an index. See also the critical review by J. Noordegraaf in *TsNTL*, 117, 2001: 398. The three main bibliographies are now all available online. The international *Bibliographie Linguistique*, which started in 1948, offers online access to its records from 1993 onwards via the Royal Library in The Hague at <www.kb.nl/blonline>. The records of the *MLAIntBibl*, which began in 1921, are now available from 1963 onwards at <www.ucl.ac.uk/Resources/Arts/Dutch.htm>. The Dutch-language *Bibliografie van de Nederlandse Taal- en Letterkunde* (*BNTL*) gives complete access, at <www.niwi.knaw.nl> (click on 'Neerlandistiek'), to works on Dutch language and literature, and also on Frisian, which have been published in the periods 1940–45 and 1960–2001. The *BNTL* habitually includes publications in English, which is now one of the established languages of scholarly exchange in the field. It is continuously updated, and can be searched for publications under name, title, subject, and year of publication; titles also have handy links to the relevant reviews.

For news on work in progress there is the electronic bulletin for Dutch language and literature, *Neder-L*, founded in 1992, which offers announcements of conferences and new publications (including Ph.D. theses); a useful monthly survey of journals, listing the titles of all new articles; and a regular column (*Linguistische Miniatuurtjes*),

devoted to little-studied and intriguing features of the Dutch language. *Neder-L* comes out three times a month and can be consulted at <www.neder-l.nl>. Other useful discussion forums and mailing lists are provided by the *Linguist List* (at <cf.linglist.org>) and *Lowlands-L* (at <www.lowlands-l.net>). In addition there are the informative websites of various associations and institutions such as the *Algemene Vereniging voor Taalwetenschap* (*AVT*, at <odur.let.rug.nl/orgs/avt>); the *ANeLA* (Association Néerlandaise de Linguistique Appliquée, at <www.anela.nl>); the *Koninklijke Akademie voor Nederlandse Taal- en Letterkunde* (KANTL, in Ghent, Flanders, at <www.kantl.be>) and the Belgian Linguistic Society (BKL, Belgische Kring voor Linguistiek, at <bkl-www.uia.ac.be/bkl>). Much solid information is also available from research centres such as the *Landelijke Onderzoeksschool Taalwetenschap* (LOT, the Dutch Graduate School in Linguistics, at <www.lot.let.uu.nl>, including a useful list of the Ph.D. dissertations it publishes); the Utrecht Centre for Language and Speech (OTS, Onderzoekscentrum voor Taal en Spraak, at <www.uilots.let.uu.nl>), the University of Leiden Centre for Linguistics, ULCL (at <www.ulcl.leidenuniv.nl>), and the Antwerp Centrum voor Nederlandse Taal en Spraak, CNTS (at <www.cnts.ua.ac.be>).

More and more periodicals in the field are becoming available online. The journal *Onze Taal* has an attractive and informative website at <www.onzetaal.nl>. The E-journal for Dutch Studies can be read at <www.neerlandistiek.nl>. Since 2000, the *Tijdschrift voor Nederlandse Taal- en Letterkunde* (*TsNTL*) publishes all its reviews online at <www.leidenuniv.nl/host/mnl/tntl>. From the same year onwards, *Linguistica Antverpiensia* is also published online at <www.hivt.be/publicaties>; the series 'Antwerp Papers in Linguistics' (APIL) is at <apil-www.uia.ua.ac.be/apil>. The *Linguistics in the Netherlands* yearbooks of the Algemene Vereniging voor Taalwetenschap (AVT), with their cutting-edge contributions to Dutch linguistics, are published online, from volume 17, 2000, onwards, at <www.benjamins.nl>, the website of John Benjamins Publishers in Amsterdam.

The new *Digitale Bibliotheek voor de Nederlandse Letteren* website (DBNL, at <www.dbnl.org>) offers, under the heading 'De Nederlandse taal', 100 classic articles published during the 20th c. This website now also contains complete out-of-print books such as C. H. den Hertog, *Nederlandsche spraakkunst* (3 vols, 1903), Jac. van Ginneken, *Handboek van de Nederlandsche taal* (2 vols, 1917), G. S. Overdiep, *Stilistische grammatica van het moderne Nederlandsch* (1949), M. Schönfeld, *Historische grammatica van het Nederlands* (1947), and A. A. Weijnen, *Nederlandse dialectkunde* (1966). New online resources are reviewed in

the *DigiTaal* section of the journal *Nederlandse taalkunde* (*NTk*). *DigiTaal* is edited by Matthias Huening and accessible at <www.niederlandistiek.fu-berlin.de/digitaal>.

In book form there are a number of collective volumes on Dutch linguistics from around the world. In 1997, 15 leading scholars from the Netherlands, Flanders, Poland, Great Britain, and the USA gathered in Berkeley for a conference on the Dutch language. Their papers have been published in *The Berkeley Conference on Dutch Linguistics 1997. The Dutch Language at the Millennium*, ed. Thomas F. Shannon and Johan P. Snapper, Lanham, MD, Univ. Press of America, 2000, 290 pp. Some 30 important studies by Jan Goossens on historical, social, and geographic linguistic variation across the Flemish, Dutch, and Low German-speaking area have been collected in Jan Goossens, *Ausgewählte Schriften zur niederländischen und deutschen Sprach- und Literaturwissenschaft*, ed. Heinz Eickmans et al., Münster, Waxmann, 2000, 564 pp. Similarly, a selection of Stefan Morciniec's articles on Dutch, German, and Polish grammar, phonology, dialectology, and contrastive linguistics have been brought together in Stefan Morciniec, *Studia Philologica. Ausgewählte Schriften zur Germanistik und Niederlandistik*, ed. Leslaw Cirko and Stefan Kiedron (Orbis Linguarum Beihefte, 16), Wroclaw, Oficyna Wydanicza ATUT, 316 pp.

Meanwhile, the genre of the *Festschrift* is alive and well. In 1997 a volume in honour of I. Schermer-Vermeer appeared, *Grammaticaal spektakel*, ed. E. H. C. Elffers et al., Amsterdam, Vakgroep Nederlandse Taalkunde UvA, 1997, 254 pp. This was followed by one for Jos Wilmots, *Kanwelverstaan*, ed. Bruno de Soomer et al., Diepenbeek, Limburgs Universitair Centrum, 1999, 344 pp.; for Georges De Schutter, *Met taal om de tuin geleid*, ed. Steven Gillis et al., Wilrijk, Universitaire Instelling Antwerpen, 2000, 495 pp.; *Samengevoegde woorden: voor Wim Klooster bij zijn afscheid als hoogleraar*, ed. Hans den Besten et al., Amsterdam U.P., 2000, 289 pp; for Jan W. de Vries, *Kerven in een rots*, ed. Berry Dongelmans et al., Leiden, Stichting Neerlandistiek Leiden, 2001, 285 pp.; *Polyfonie. Opstellen voor Paul van Hauwermeiren*, ed. W. Vandeweghe et al., Ghent, Mercator Hogeschool, 2001, 236 pp.; and most recently *Waar gaat het Nederlands naartoe? Panorama van een taal*, ed. Jan Stroop, Amsterdam, Bakker, 362 pp.; and the e-book *Germania et alia. A Linguistic Webschrift for Hans den Besten*, ed. Jan Koster and Henk van Riemsdijk, which can be read at <odur.let.rug.nl/-koster/DenBesten>.

At Nijmegen Catholic University, A. M. Hagen took his leave with the valedictory lecture *De lof der Nederlandse taal*, Nijmegen, Katholieke Universiteit Nijmegen, 1999, 22 pp. At Utrecht University H. J. Verkuyl did the same with *Woorden, woorden, woorden*, Utrecht U.P., 36 pp.; he was interviewed in *NTk*, 8.3. A collection of interviews with leading Dutch and other linguists, *Het vermogen te verlangen. Gesprekken over taal en het menselijk brein*, ed. Liesbeth Koenen, 2nd edn, Amsterdam, Atlas, 1997, 338 pp., is a much expanded version of the 1990 first edition, with useful indexes to names and subjects.

The changing of the guard is marked also by the inaugural lectures delivered by the new professors of Dutch language and linguistics in the Netherlands: Arie Verhagen, *Achter het Nederlands*, Leiden U.P., 2000, 29 pp., Vincent van Heuven, *Boven de klanken*, Leiden U.P., 2001, 32 pp., Hans Bennis, *Tegengestelde krachten in de taal*, Amsterdam U.P., 2001, 34 pp., Fred Weerman, *Dynamiek in de taal en de explosie van de neerlandistiek*, Amsterdam U.P., 2002, 32 pp., Norbert Corver, *Taal in zicht*, Utrecht U.P., 2002, 48 pp., and Pieter Muysken, *Waar is de taalwetenschap?*, Nijmegen, Katholieke Universiteit Nijmegen, 2002, 23 pp. Weerman's inaugural was combined with a symposium at which his fellow professors in Dutch linguistics in the Netherlands lectured on the future of the Dutch language. The texts, by Norbert Corver, Theo Janssen, Anneke Neijt, and Arie Verhagen, were published together with a reaction from Fred Weerman in a special theme issue of *NTk*, 8.4, December 2002.

2. Linguistics: Grammar, Phonology, Morphology, Syntax, and Semantics

Both in Dutch Grammar, our first domain here, and in the various subdomains that follow — phonology, morphology, syntax, and semantics of Dutch — many good descriptions, monographs, handbooks, studies of detail, databases, analyses, and theories have been published over the past seven years. The descriptive grammar of Dutch is a thriving field. In 1997 the second, heavily revised and expanded edition was published of the *ANS* or *Algemene Nederlandse Spraakkunst*, ed. Walter Haeseryn et al., Groningen, Nijhoff — Deurne, Wolters Plantyn, 2 vols, 1997, 1717 pp. The many reviews of the first edition (1984) of this comprehensive reference grammar of modern standard Dutch are listed on the *ANS*-website at <www.kun.nl/~e-ans>. Amongst the critical reactions to this new edition, see in particular the special *ANS*-issue of *NTk*, 3.3, September 1998, which contains eight contributions on various aspects of this grammar, by A. van Santen (morphology); H. Bennis (verbs); W. Vandeweghe (subclauses and subordination); A. Verhagen (word order); T. van der Wouden (modality and negation); H. van de Velde (norms and variation); R. Salverda (international aspects); H. Broekhuis and H. van Riemsdijk (Modern Grammar of Dutch, MGD). In 2002 an electronic version of the *ANS* went online. This was reviewed in 'De Elektronische ANS' by Reinier Salverda in *NTk*, 8:255–61.

Another major grammar is the project for *A Modern Grammar of Dutch* (*MGD*) available online at <fd/www.kub.nl/-broekhuis/ mgd>. This project, carried out at the University of Tilburg up until 2001, resulted in a number of massive studies, on generative principles, and on specific subjects: Hans Broekhuis et al., *Adjectives and Adjective Phrases (MGD* Occasional Paper, 2), Tilburg Univ. Models of Grammar Group, 1999, 500 pp., and Id., *Nouns and Noun Phrases* (*MGD* Occasional Paper, 4), Tilburg Univ. Models of Grammar Group, 2001, 2 vols, 950 pp. See the review of the latter by S. Barbiers, *NTk,* 6, 2001 : 133–48.

A number of new Dutch grammars were published in book form by the *Staatsuitgeverij* in The Hague. Functionally oriented is that by F. Balk-Smit Duyzentkunst, *Grammatica van het Nederlands*, The Hague, Sdu, 2000, 244 pp. W. G. Klooster, *Grammatica van het hedendaags Nederlands. Een volledig overzicht*, The Hague, Sdu, 2001, 411 pp., is a traditional grammar enriched with many generative insights. From a generative pont of view, an introductory course book is Peter van Bart, Johan Kerstens, and Arie Sturm, *Grammatica van het Nederlands. Een inleiding*, Amsterdam U.P., 1998, 262 pp. Finally, Jelle de Vries offers an extensive grammatical description of spoken Dutch, *Onze Nederlandse spreektaal*, The Hague, Sdu, 2001, 563 pp.

In addition, three new Dutch grammars were published in English: Carol Fehringer, *A Reference Grammar of Dutch. With Exercises and Key*, CUP, 1999, 185 pp.; Gerdi Quist and Dennis Strik, *Teach Yourself Dutch Grammar,* London, Hodder Headline, 2000, 244 pp.; and W. Z. Shetter and Inge Van der Cruysse-Van Antwerpen, *Dutch. An Essential Grammar*, 8th edn, London–NY, Routledge, 2002, 322 pp., a greatly expanded and improved edition of the Dutch grammar which Shetter first published in 1957; even so, the new one does not give a rule for the diminutive in *-kje.*

In the subdomain of Dutch phonology there is the new handbook by Jan Kooij and Marc van Oostendorp, *Fonologie: uitnodiging tot de klankleer van het Nederlands*, Amsterdam U.P., 236 pp. This introduction to the phonology of Dutch contains nine main chapters, on phonetics and phonology; syllables, vowels, and consonants; features; feet and words; stress and dynamics; allomorphs; and sentence phonology. The book also contains a number of short biographies of leading Dutch phonologists of the past, such as B. van den Berg, A. Cohen, Jac. van Ginneken, Louise Kaiser, Petrus Montanus, William Moulton, and N. van Wijk. For current debate see also the volume **Fonologische kruispunten*, ed. G. De Schutter and S. Gillis, Ghent, KANTL, 249 pp.

A basic description of the phonetics of Dutch is given in the chapter 'Dutch', by Carlos Gussenhoven, pp. 74–78 of the *Handbook of the*

International Phonetics Association. A Guide to the Use of the International Phonetic Alphabet, ed. International Phonetics Association, CUP, 1999, 214 pp. Another such description is given by John Wells at <www.phon.ucl.ac.uk/home/sampa/dutch.htm>. A comprehensive contrastive description is given by Beverley Collins and Inger M. Mees, *The Phonetics of English and Dutch*, 5th edn, Leiden–Boston, Brill, 376 pp.

For the pronunciation of Dutch there is now the new *Uitspraakwoordenboek*, ed. J. Heemskerk and W. Zonneveld, Utrecht, Spectrum, 2000, 857 pp. What they did not put into this dictionary is discussed in their article '(not the) Uitspraakwoordenboek', *Gramma*, 9, 2002 : 23–44. An interesting study of the teaching of pronunciation in schools in Flanders is Hanne Kloots, *Uitspraakonderwijs in het Vak Nederlands in Vlaanderen en Nederland op het einde van de twintigste eeuw* (APIL, 104), 128 pp. R. van Hout et al., 'De uitspraak van het Standaard-Nederlands: variatie en varianten in Vlaanderen en Nederland', pp. 133–86 of *Artikelen van de derde sociolinguistische conferentie*, ed. E. Huls and B. Weltens, Delft, Eburon, 1999, 522 pp. The pronunciation of Dutch by foreigners is the subject of the very interesting Ph.D. dissertation by Rianne Doeleman, *Native Reactions to Non-Native Speech*, Tilburg U.P., 1998, 320 pp., in which she investigates how native speakers of Dutch evaluate and react to the Dutch of non-natives from Morocco, Turkey, the Caribbean, Germany, and England. Non-native speech features often trigger negative evaluations and attitudes, especially when combined with stereotypic views and social distance towards the ethnic group involved.

For the intonation of Dutch, the wonderful online PRAAT-program for doing phonetics by computer, developed between 1992 and 2003 by Paul Broersma and David Weenink of the University of Amsterdam, is available at <www.praat.org>. Vincent van Heuven, *Boven de klanken*, <www.let.leidenuniv.nl/ulcl/faculty/vheuven>, 2001, offers a very informative and readable experimental study of stress in Dutch. A further empirical study is the Ph.D. dissertation of C. S. Gooskens, *On the Role of Prosodic and Verbal Information in the Perception of Dutch and English Language Varieties*, Nijmegen, Katholieke Universiteit Nijmegen, 1997, 221 pp. A special mention, finally, for the excellent Ph.D. dissertation, shortlisted for the *AVT's* annual prize for the best Ph.D. dissertation in linguistics, J. J. M. Haan-Van Ditzhuyzen, *Speaking of Questions. An Exploration of Dutch Question Intonation*, Utrecht, LOT, 2001, 254 pp.

A very important development is the joint Dutch-Flemish effort in the field of language and speech technology. One of the major resources here is the *Corpus Gesproken Nederlands* (CGN) at <lands.let.kun.nl/cgn/ehome.html>, which contains about 800 hours of speech, or 9 million words, with orthographic transcriptions, lemmatization, part-of-speech tagging, an automatic time alignment and phonetic transcription for the entire corpus, plus relevant information about speakers and recordings. For smaller parts of the corpus there are also syntactic and prosodic annotations available, all to a very high standard. This basic resource, the fruit of large-scale, multidisciplinary, and high-tech co-operation, is due to be completed in 2004. For the midterm evaluation of the CGN-project in 2001 see the report by Reinier Salverda et al., *Mid-Term Evaluation, Dutch Spoken Corpus project*, at <lands.let.kun.nl/cgn/publs/mid_term_eval.pdf>. See also the special theme issue on language technology, *NTk*, 7.3, September, 2002.

In the domain of morphology, we now have two new handbooks: Geert Booij and Ariane van Santen, *Morfologie. De woordstructuur van het Nederlands*, Amsterdam U.P., 1998, 211 pp., and the new standard work, Geert Booij, *The Morphology of Dutch*, OUP, 2002, 253 pp., which explains the intricacies of Dutch morphology for the international scholarly community.

A series of excellent Ph.D. dissertations have been devoted to morphological topics: Matthias Huening, *Woordensmederij: de geschiedenis van het suffix –erij*, The Hague, Holland Academic Graphics, 1999, 319 pp.; Priscilla Heynderickx, *Relationele adjectieven in het Nederlands*, Antwerp, Lessius Hogeschool, 2000, 267 pp. For ongoing research in this domain see also the annual *Yearbook of Morphology* (*YM*), ed. Geert Booij and Hans van Marle. International in scope, it regularly features articles on the morphology of Dutch, such as A. van Kemenade and B. Los, 'Particles and prefixes in Dutch and English', *YM*: 79–117, on the so-called 'separable compound verbs' in Dutch. Another article of interest is M. Ernestus and H. Baaijen, 'Predicting the unpredictable: interpreting neutralized segments in Dutch', *Language*, 79: 5–38, reporting on an experiment with Dutch pseudoverbs, the choice of *-te* or *-de* as past tense suffix, and what this can tell us about the underlying knowledge of the rules by which native speakers operate. The Dutch diminutive is the subject of the Ph.D. dissertation of Peter Bakema, *Het verkleinwoord verklaard. Een Morfosemantische Studie over Diminutieven in het Nederlands*, Leuven, Katholieke Universiteit Leuven, 1998, 249 pp. On the same subject see also S. Theissen, 'De vorming van de diminutief', *Neerlandica Wratislawiensia*, 12, 1999: 87–97, which critically evaluates the treatment of the diminutive in the *ANS*, and suggests ways of improving and simplifying this account.

In the field of syntax, a new handbook has been published by Hans Bennis, *Syntaxis van het Nederlands*, Amsterdam U.P., 2000, 255 pp., an attractive and stimulating course book within Chomsky's minimalist framework. It comes with a CD, 'De Zin', containing exercises.

The dominant theoretical framework for syntactic research is the formal-theoretical approach of the Chomskyans, led by Henk van Riemsdijk (Tilburg) and Jan Koster (Groningen). A very good sense of their achievements is given in the 16 articles in the e-book *Progress in Grammar. Articles at the Twentieth Anniversary of the Comparison of Grammatical Models Group in Tilburg*, ed. Marc van Oostendorp and Elena Anagnostopoulou, <meertens.library.uu.nl/progressingrammar/toc.htr>. Among others, it contains the article by the defender of the radical autonomy of syntax, J. Koster, 'Mirror symmetry in Dutch'. Two further articles by K., 'Volledige unificatie', in the *Festschrift* for Wim Klooster, 159–68 (see above, p. 709) and 'All languages are tense second', in the *Webschrift* for Hans den Besten (see above, p. 709), also mark significant theoretical progress. Of particular interest is the Ph.D. thesis of C. Jan-Wouter Zwart, *Morphosyntax of Verb Movement. A Minimalist Approach to the Syntax of Dutch*, Durdrecht, Kluwer, 1997, 328 pp., as well as his article, 'The Germanic SOV languages and the universal base hypothesis', pp. 246–67 of *The New Comparative Syntax*, ed. Liliane Haegeman, London, Longman, 1997, 294 pp., in which Z. concludes that Dutch is head-initial, and not a head-final language. In other words, Dutch is SVO, and here Z. takes issue with Koster's classic article, 'Dutch as an SOV language' (1975), which is now accessible online in the *DBNL*.

Zwart's ideas have been applied to the study of Afrikaans by E. Vriendt, 'Morphosyntax of verb movement and Afrikaans verbal constructions', *SPIL*, 31, 1998:95–124, and by T. Biberauer, 'Verb second in Afrikaans: is there a unitary phenomenon?' *ib.*, 34, 2002:19–70. Vriendt's conclusion is that Zwart's theory fails to predict that in Afrikaans embedded inversion is possible — something which scholars working from a different perspective might explain as a case of spoken creole information structure taking precedence over formal grammatical structure. Other generative studies are available in two important collections, *Materials on Left Dislocation*, ed. Elena Anagnostopoulou et al., Amsterdam, Benjamins, 1997, 349 pp., and **Verbal Complexes*, ed. Hilda J. Koopman and Anna Szabolcsi, Cambridge, Mass., MIT, 2000, 245 pp.

As an alternative to the Chomskyan approach, Pieter Seuren has developed his theory of *Semantic Syntax* (1996), which is tested in the Nijmegen Ph.D. dissertation of Lisanne M. Teunissen, *Semantic Syntax: Evaluation by Implementation*, Utrecht, LOT, 2001, 219 pp. Yet another theory is the discourse-functional-cognitive and corpus-based approach of the collection *Usage-Based Approaches to Dutch. Lexicon, Grammar, Discourse*, ed. Arie Verhagen and Jeroen van de Weijer,

Utrecht, LOT, 207 pp., which contains six corpus-based studies of words and constructions in Dutch grammar and discourse, by A. van Santen (on non-feminine names such as *pedagoog*), A. Verhagen (on constructions involving 'weg' ('way/a way'), R. S. Kirsner (on the interjections *hè* and *hoor*); T. F. Shannon (on pronominal order in the middle part of sentences and the historic drift in Dutch, from pragmatic to grammatical word order), J. Loewenthal (on Dutch causative constructions without 'causee'), and H. Pander Maat and L. Degand (on causal connectives in Dutch and French). An attractive course book in discourse studies is the volume *Communiceren. Over taal en taalgebruik*, ed. T. Janssen, The Hague, Sdu, 1997, 231 pp.

Important Ph.D. dissertations have been published on a range of individual topics in Dutch grammar. The so-called 'balansschikking' is the subject of Ad Welschen, *Duale syntaxis en polaire contractie. Negatief gebonden 'of'-constructies in het Nederlands*, Amsterdam, Stichting Neerlandistiek VU — Münster, Nodus, 1999, 512 pp. In the same year, the Nijmegen Ph.D. dissertation of E. M. van der Heijden, *Tussen nevenschikking en onderschikking. Een onderzoek naar verschillende vormen van verbinding in het Nederlands*, The Hague, Holland Academic Graphics, 1999, 228 pp., approached the the same problem from a rather different angle. Also of note are Louise H. Cornelis, *Passive and Perspective*, Amsterdam, Rodopi, 1997, 295 pp.; Liesbeth Degand, *Form and Function of Causation: A Theoretical and Empirical Investigation of Causal Constructions in Dutch*, Leuven, Peeters, 2001, 218 pp.; Justine A. Pardoen, *Interpretatiestructuur. Een onderzoek naar de relatie tussen woordvolgorde en zinsbetekenis in het Nederlands*, Amsterdam, Stichting Neerlandistiek VU — Münster, Nodus, 1998, 467 pp. (but see the very critical review by Els Elffers in *TsNTL*, 117:77–83); and Monique Lamers, *Sentence Processing Using Syntactic, Semantic and Thematic Information*, Groningen, RUG, 2001, 237 pp.

The diversity of theoretical approaches in the field of Dutch syntax highlights the need for a critical, comparative evaluation of the conflicting claims and assumptions underpinning different research projects. Here there is not nearly enough being done, and too many linguists are happily beavering away within their once-chosen framework. An attempt at critical comparison of four different theories is made by R. Salverda, 'On topicalization in modern Dutch', pp. 93–111 of *The Berkeley Conference* (see above, p. 709). Similarly, the volume *Verb Constructions in German and Dutch*, ed. Pieter Seuren and Gerard Kempen, Amsterdam, Benjamins, 316 pp., contains eight contributions from various different schools of linguistic thought, such as Head-Driven Phrase Structure Grammar, Lexical Functional Grammar, and Semantic Syntax, with a view to stimulating critical comparison and evaluation of their different formalisms and theoretical frameworks.

In the field of semantics we now have the introduction by H. J. Verkuyl, *Semantiek. Het verband tussen taal en werkelijkheid*, Amsterdam U.P., 2000, 96 pp. A number of studies have been devoted to problems of verbs, time, tense, and aspect: Angeliek van Hout, *Event Semantics of Verb Frame Alternations. A Case Study of Dutch and its Acquisition*, NY–London, Garland, 1998, 407 pp.; Anna L. Oppentocht, *Lexical Semantic Classification of Dutch Verbs. Towards Constructing NLP and Human-Friendly Definitions*, Utrecht, LED, 1999, 291 pp.; and R. J. U. Boogaart, *Aspect and Temporal Ordering in a Contrastive Analysis of Dutch and English*, The Hague, Holland Academic Graphics, 1999, 293 pp. An intriguing phenomenon is the use of past tense imperatives in modern Dutch, which is studied by H. Wolf, 'Imperatieven in de verleden tijd', *Taal en tongval*, 55:168–87.

Going beyond lexical semantics, we have the studies by Henny Klein, *Adverbs of Degree in Dutch and Related Languages*, Amsterdam, Benjamins, 1998, 232 pp., and, on the use of modal particles, R. Vismans, 'Modal particles in Dutch: reinforcement, mitigation and the layered structure of the clause in functional grammar', *Neerlandica Wratislawiensia*, 12, 1999:73–81; H. Smessaert, *Perspectief en vergelijking: aspectuele partikels in het Nederlands*, Leuven, Peeters, 1999, 176 pp., about the particles *al* (already) and *nog* (still); and T. van der Wouden, 'Naar een partikelwoordenboek voor het Nederlands', *NTk*, 7, 2002:20–43, on the dictionary of Dutch modal particles that is being prepared. And finally there is the thorough historical-comparative investigation of tense prepositions by Mariet Raedts, *Een taalvergelijkend onderzoek naar de temporele voorzetsels 'in', 'op', 'om', 'bij' en 'met' in elf Indo-Europese talen* (APIL, 97), 2000, 162 pp.

3. History of the Dutch Language and of Dutch Linguistics

A sound introductory survey of the sociocultural history of the Dutch language is given in the chapter 'Dutch' by Roel Vismans, pp. 129–36 of the *Encyclopedia of the Languages of Europe*, ed. Glanville Price, London, Blackwell, 1998, 499 pp. The historical relations between Dutch and English are explored by R. Salverda, 'English = Dutch. A dossier of compelling evidence', *The Low Countries*, 11:124–33.

Over the past few years a number of important handbooks have appeared. First of all, there is the comprehensive *Geschiedenis van de Nederlandse taal*, ed. M. C. van den Toorn et al., Amsterdam U.P., 1997, 697 pp., reviewed by R. Salverda, *Dutch Crossing*, 23, 1999:172–77. Secondly, we have the thorough monograph on the

Dutch language in the 20th c., *Geschiedenis van het Nederlands in de twintigste eeuw*, ed. Joop and Kees van der Horst, The Hague, Sdu — Antwerp, Standaard, 1999, 498 pp., a well-documented study of changes in the vocabulary, parts of speech, verbs, pronouns, word order, morphology, and pronunciation of standard Dutch. The third book worth mentioning here is the attractive, decade-by-decade survey of developments in 20th-c. Dutch in *Taalboek van de Eeuw*, ed. Peter Burger and Jaap de Jong, The Hague, Sdu — Antwerp, Standaard, 1999, 262 pp.

A long-term analysis of the two key forces of analysis and synthesis governing the historical development of Dutch syntax is given by A. M. Duinhoven, *Analyse en synthese in het Nederlands*, Assen, Van Gorcum, 2001, 243 pp., who brings together a wide range of his original semantico-diachronic insights into unusual Dutch constructions. D. has also published Part II, 'De werkwoordgroep', of his *Middelnederlandse Syntaxis, synchroon en diachroon*, The Hague, Nijhoff, 1997, 611 pp. A comparative Germanic study is *DO in English, Dutch and German: History and Present-Day Variation*, ed. Ingrid Tieken-Boon van Ostade et al., Münster, Nodus, 1998, 170 pp.

Not long ago, the history of Dutch did not go back in time much before the year 1100. But recent new discoveries have changed this situation rather drastically, and we now have the new, well-documented, introductory course book *Inleiding Oudnederlands*, ed. A. Quak and J. M. van der Horst, Leuven U.P., 2002, 111 pp., which sets out very clearly the historical context, the available often fragmentary material, dialect variation, and clear analyses of forms, sounds, and syntax. Another important contribution here is the scholarly volume *ABÄG*, 57, 'Quod vulgo dicitur. Studien zum Altniederländischen', ed. W. E. Pijnenburg et al., containing the proceedings of a symposium in Leiden. The explicit aim of this volume is to promote the new term 'altniederländisch' for what used to be called 'alt(west)niederfränkisch'.

The historical distribution of the Dutch language in the world as a consequence of Dutch maritime and colonial expansion has been the subject of a range of studies: Kees Groeneboer, *Gateway to the West. The Dutch Language in Colonial Indonesia 1600–1950. A History of Language Policy*, Amsterdam U.P., 1998, 400 pp.; Lila Gobardhan-Rambocus, *Onderwijs als sleutel tot maatschappelijke vooruitgang. Een taal- en onderwijsgeschiedenis van Suriname 1650–1975*, Zutphen, Walburg, 2001, 553 pp., particularly relevant since Surinam joined the Dutch Language Union in December 2003. An important collection of 11 articles on Dutch colonial language policy is found in *Koloniale taalpolitiek in Oost en West. Nederlands-Indië, Suriname, Nederlandse Antillen, Aruba*, ed. Kees Groeneboer, Amsterdam U.P., 1998, 304 pp.

For the history of Afrikaans see the solid and comprehensive contribution by F. A. Ponelis, pp. 597–645 of *Geschiedenis van de Nederlandse Taal*, see above, p. 716. Closer to home, H. M. C. Ryckeboer, *Het Nederlands in Noord-Frankrijk: sociolinguistische, dialectologische en contactlinguistische aspecten*, Ghent, Vakgroep Taalkunde, 1997, 300 pp., discusses the Dutch language in the North of France. In addition, there is the collection of papers presented at a conference at the Gerhard Mercator Universität, Duisburg in 1997, *Niederländisch am Niederrhein*, ed. H. Bister-Broosen, Frankfurt, Lang, 1998, 171 pp. Of related interest are three books about Yiddish, first *Hebreeuwse en Jiddisje woorden in het Nederlands: spelling, uitspraak, verbuiging, herkomst, betekenis*, ed. Henk Heikens et al., The Hague, Sdu, 2002, 333 pp.; then, at a more popular level, *Jofel Jiddisj, van achenebbisj tot zwansen*, ed. M. van der Valk, Amsterdam, Veen, 160 pp.; and finally the solid Ph.D. dissertation of Ariana D. Zwiers, *Kroniek van het Jiddisj: taalkundige aspecten van het achttiende-eeuws Nederlands Jiddisj*, Delft, Eburon, 602 pp.

A special theme issue appeared on the language of Flanders in the 19th c., 'De taal in Vlaanderen in de negentiende eeuw. Historisch-sociolinguistische onderzoekingen', ed. Roland Willemyns, *VMKA*, 112.3, 2002; Id. and R. Haeseryn, 'Taal', pp. 2931–46 of the *Nieuwe Encyclopedie van de Vlaamse beweging*, vol. 3, ed. Reginald De Schryver, Tielt, Lannoo, 1998. Roland Willemyns and Wim Daniels, *Het Verhaal van het Vlaams. De geschiedenis van het Nederlands in de Zuidelijke Nederlanden*, Antwerp, Standaard — Utrecht, Spectrum, 399 pp., is important. The use of the term 'Vlaams' in the title of this book was noticed, not least because it is Dutch (and not Flemish) that is mentioned in the Belgian constitution as one of the official languages. On current and future development of Dutch in Flanders see further J. Goossens, 'De toekomst van het Nederlands in Vlaanderen', *Ons Erfdeel*, 43, 2000: 2–13; and J. Cajot, 'Nieuwsnederlands en verkavelingsvlaams: de zorgen in een binationaal taalgebied', pp. 41–62 of the *Festschrift* for Jos Wilmots, see above, p. 709.

The history of the personal pronouns and forms of address in Dutch (and also in Afrikaans and Frisian) is described in the solid historical-comparative monograph of Stephen Howe, *The Personal Pronouns in the Germanic Languages. A Study of Personal Pronoun Morphology and Change in the Germanic Languages from the First Records to the Present Day*, Berlin–NY, de Gruyter, 1996, 390 pp. Of related interest is the article on the disappearance of *du* from Dutch by A. Van Berteloot, 'Van *du* naar *ghi*. Waarom het pronomen *du* uit het Nederlands verdween', *TsNTL*, 119: 204–17. Changes in the Dutch forms of address between 1200 and today are discussed in the Leiden Ph.D. dissertation by J. A. M. Vermaas, *Veranderingen in de Nederlandse aanspreekvormen van de dertiende tot en met de twintigste eeuw*, Utrecht, LOT, 2002, 239 pp., although this is certainly not the last word on the subject.

Over the past few years a number of new editions have been published of important linguistic studies by Dutch and Flemish linguists of previous generations. The oldest of these, *Wie komt daar aan op die olifant? Een zestiende-eeuws taalgidsje voor Nederland en Indië, inclusef het verhaal van de avontuurlijke gevangenschap van Frederik de Houtman in Indië*, ed. Nicoline van der Sijs, Amsterdam–Antwerp, Veen, 2000, 220 pp., is a colonial language guide, originally published in 1602 by the Dutch naval commander Frederik de Houtman who adapted the famous *Dialogues* of Noel Van Berlaimont for use in the Malay world. For the 17th and 18th cs we now have new text editions of Adriaen Verwer, *Schets van de Nederlandse taal, grammatica, poetica en retorica/Idea Linguae Belgicae grammatica, poetica et rhetorica*, ed. T. A. J. M. Janssen and J. Noordegraaf, Amsterdam, Stichting Neerlandistiek VU, 1996, 140 pp.; Lambert ten Kate Hermansz, *Aenleiding tot de Kennisse van het Verhevene Deel der Nederduitsche Sprake* (1723), ed. Jan Noordegraaf and Marijke van der Wal, 2 vols, Alphen aan den Rijn, Canaletto–Holland-Repro, 2001, 743, 748 pp., with a solid historical-linguistics introduction and comprehenisve bibliograpy. For Ten Kate see also R. Salverda, 'Newtonian linguistics: the contribution of Lambert ten Kate (1674–1731) to the study of language', pp. 115–32 of Maire Davies et al., *'Proper Words in Proper Places.' Studies in Lexicology and Lexicography in Honour of William Jervis Jones*, Stuttgart, Heinz, 2001, 420 pp. Our third 18th-c. grammarian is Balthasar Huydecoper, whose grammar of Dutch was reissued by R. J. G. de Bonth under the title *'De Aristarch van 't Y': de grammatica uit Balthazar Huydecopers Proeve van taal- en dichtkunst (1730)*, Maastricht, Shaker, 1998, 419 pp. At the end of the 18th c. there was, finally, Jan Baptiste Verlooy, the great fighter for the Dutch language in the Southern Netherlands, who is the subject of the monograph by Paul De Ridder, *Nieuw licht op J.B.C. Verlooy (1746–1797), vader van de Nederlandse beweging*, Ghent, Stichting Mens en Kultuur — Brussels, Vereniging Brusselse Geschiedenis, 2001, 126 pp.

For the 19th c. we now have a monograph on the Dutch schoolmaster and dictionary-maker Van Dale: Lo van Driel, *Een leven in woorden. J.H. van Dale, schoolmeester — archivaris — taalkundige*, Zutphen, Walburg, 448 pp. In addition, we have two collections of articles in this domain, *Voorlopig verleden: taalkundige plaatsbepalingen 1797–1960*, ed. Jan Noordegraaf, Münster, Nodus, 1997, 234 pp., and *Taal kundig geregeld: een verzameling artikelen over Nederlandse grammatica's en grammatici uit de zestiende, de zeventiende en de achttiende eeuw*, ed.

G. R. W. Dibbets, Amsterdam, Stichting Neerlandistiek VU — Münster, Nodus, 242 pp.

Finally, we should mention the well-informed, firsthand account of the history of dialectography in the Netherlands, Jo Daan, *Geschiedenis van de dialectgeografie in het Nederlandse taalgebied. Rondom Kloeke en het Dialectenbureau*, Amsterdam, KNAW, 2000, 139 pp., in which she defends the National Dialect Office against the devastating attack in the seven-volume novel *Het Bureau* by J. J. Voskuil (cf. also S. Leinbach, *Dutch Crossing*, 27:45–72). Two further historical studies are the survey article, W. van Anrooij and E. Ruijsendaal, 'Honderdvijfien delen Tijdschrift Nederlands(ch)e Taal- en Letterkunde (1881–1999)', *TsNTL*, 116, 2000: 295–367, and the reconstruction of key developments in 20th-c. Dutch linguistics in R. Salverda, 'Old paradigms never die: on the development of linguistics in the Netherlands in the twentieth century', *Flood Vol.*, 921–40.

4. Sociolinguistics and Dialectology

Several useful survey articles have appeared in the various subfields of this domain. A general overview is given by T. Koole and J. Nortier, 'Sociolinguistics in the Dutch speaking community in 2003', *Thema's en trends in de sociolinguistiek*, 4: 1–19, ed. Tom Koole et al. (*Toegepaste Taalwetenschap in Artikelen*, 70, 2), Tilburg, AneLA, 168 pp. See also J. Goossens, 'Nederlandse sociodialectologie', *Neerlandica Wratislaviensia*, 14: 51–63. A survey of gender and language studies is given by M. Gerritsen, 'Dutch. Towards a more gender-fair usage in Netherlands Dutch', pp. 81–108 of vol. 2 of *Gender across Languages*, ed. M. Hellinger and H. Bussmann, 3 vols, Amsterdam, Benjamins, 2001–03, 329, 349, 391 pp. For Dutch research in contact linguistics see C. van Bree and J. W. de Vries, 'Netherlands', pp. 1143–52 in vol. 2 of *Contact Linguistics: An International Handbook of Contemporary Research*. ed. H. Goebl et al., 2 vols, Berlin, de Gruyter, 1997, 2171 pp. For multilingualism in the Netherlands see R. Salverda, 'The other languages of the Netherlands', *The Low Countries*, 8, 2000: 245–52. Standardization in the Dutch language area is surveyed by R. Willemyns, 'Dutch', pp. 93–125 of *Germanic Standardizations, Past to Present*, ed. A. Deumert and W. Vandenbussche, Amsterdam, Benjamins, 362 pp. These and many other subjects — such as street language, contact phenomena in Dutch-language schools in Brussels, the varieties of stress in Dutch, the dialect of Ameland, the ongoing diphthongization in Dutch, or the Dutch spoken by people from the Moluccas — also feature in the more than 50 contributions to *Artikelen voor de vierde sociolinguistische conferentie*, ed. Tom Koole et al., Delft, Eburon, 570 pp. For students there is now the attractive course book on Dutch from an interactional perspective, *Taal in gebruik. Een inleiding in de taalwetenschap*, ed. Theo Janssen, The Hague, Sdu, 2002, 295 pp., which has 15 chapters on communication, cognition, and culture; on words, sentences, and text structure; on language change and language norms; and on politeness, verbal interaction, and communication in a plurilingual society.

The enormous variation within the Dutch language area (Netherlands and Flanders) is reflected in *Taal in stad en land*, a series of books edited by Nicoline van der Sijs and published by the Staatsuitgeverij in The Hague. In 2002, 13 volumes were published, on the dialects of Amsterdam, Groningen, The Hague, Leiden, Maastricht, Rotterdam, Oost-Brabant, Utrecht, de Veluwe and Flevoland, Venlo, Roermond and Sittard. Each volume describes, in about 120 pages, the relevant city or regional dialect, with good attention to its history and literature. On the series website at <www.taalinstadenland.nl> one can listen to recordings, read dialect word lists, and find useful links. A 'talking map' of some 100 Dutch dialects is online at the Meertens-instituut in Amsterdam at <www.meertensinstituut.knaw.nl>.

A general survey of Dutch dialects is given by C. and G. Hoppenbrouwers, *De indeling van de Nederlandse streektalen: dialecten van 156 steden en dorpen geklasseerd volgens de FFM*, Assen, Van Gorcum, 2001, 210 pp. A descriptive tour of 20 city dialects from all the provinces of Flanders and the Netherlands, and their development over the past century, each extensively documented with language data, vocabularies and references, is offered in the collection *Honderd jaar stadstaal*, ed. Joep Kruijsen and Nicoline van der Sijs, Amsterdam–Antwerp, Contact, 1999, 336 pp. Of particular interest is also S. Tol, 'The dialect of Volendam — fifty years after van Ginneken: preliminary data', pp. 603–28 of *Productivity and Creativity. Studies in General and Descriptive Linguistics in Honor of E. M. Uhlenbeck*, ed. M. Janse, Berlin, Mouton de Gruyter, 1998, 632 pp., and also S. De Vriendt, *Grammatica van het Brussels*, Ghent, KANTL, 110 pp.

Research at the Meertens-institute now operates under the new paradigm of Variation Linguistics, as witness the collection of articles 'De toekomst van de variatielinguistiek', a special issue of *Taal en Tongval*, 52, 2000, ed. Hans Bennis et al., for Jo Daan's 90th birthday. Amongst the major resources that are being produced in this domain are two innovative atlases of Dutch dialects. The first of these is the *Fonologische Atlas Nederlandse Dialecten* (FAND), vols I-III, ed. J. Goossens et al., Ghent, KANTL, 2000. Alongside it there is the massive study of A. C. M. Goemans, *T-deletie in Nederlandse dialecten: kwantitatieve analyse van structurele, ruimtelijke en temporele variatie*, The Hague, Holland Academic Graphics, 1999, 500 pp., and the special theme issue of

Taal en tongval, 14, 2001, 'De variabiliteit van de -(sjwa)n in het Nederlands', ed. I. Draye, H. Ryckeboer, and J. Stroop, which deals with the issue of apocope versus insertion of -n after schwa, and the geographical distribution of this alternation across the Dutch language area. The second new atlas is the *Syntactische Atlas van de Nederlandse Dialecten* (SAND), which, under the direction of Sjef Barbiers, is under construction at the Amsterdam Meertensinstituut: <www.meertens.knaw.nl>. Here again, this is accompanied by a special theme issue of *Taal en tongval*, 15–16, 'Dialectsyntaxis in bloei', ed. S. Barbiers, M. Devos, and G. de Schutter.

Faced with all this variation, the question arises, 'What about the Dutch standard language?' This is the subject of the 43 contributions in *Waar gaat het Nederlands naartoe? Panorama van de taal*, ed. Jan Stroop, Amsterdam U.P., 362 pp. In 1998, Jan Stroop first drew attention to the demise of Standard Dutch due to the rise of new varieties in his *Poldernederlands: waardoor het ABN verdwijnt*, Amsterdam, Bakker, 1998, 120 pp. See also his website at <www.janstroop.nl>. A complicating factor is the arrival of the European Charter for Regional Minority Languages, the recognition of which, in the Netherlands, but not in Belgium, has led to a chaotic situation, where Limburgs is now officially a regional minority language in the Netherlands, whereas in Belgium it has no status beyond that of a dialect. So the question is: when do we speak of a dialect, and when of a regional language? This issue is dealt with in the perceptive and critical article by R. van Bezooijen, 'Wat is een streektaal?', *Taal en tongval*, 53, 2001: 154–74. See also below, p. 731.

Over the past ten years there has been a significant increase in immigrant multilingualism in the Dutch language area. In recent years a number of studies have been devoted to this subject, especially by researchers of the Babylon Centre at Tilburg University (see <www.tilburguniversity.nl/babylon>). In 1999 a popular survey was published by Gaston Dorren, *Nieuwe tongen. De talen van migranten in Nederland en Vlaanderen*, The Hague, Sdu, 1999, 280 pp. A collection of articles on 15 major immigrant communities and their acquisition of Dutch is given in *Babylon aan de Noordzee. Nieuwe talen in Nederland*, ed. Guus Extra and Jan Jaap de Ruijter, Amsterdam, Bulaaq, 2001, 336 pp. An account of the multicultural and multilingual borough of Lombok in Utrecht is given in *Een buurt in beweging. Talen en culturen in het Utrechtse Lombok en Transvaal*, ed. H. Bennis et al., Amsterdam, Aksant, 2002, 373 pp. A comprehensive inventory of the 96 other languages of the Netherlands and their use by children in the Dutch school system is reported, with many interesting data about language preferences, choice, and attitudes in *De andere talen van Nederland thuis en op school*, ed. Guus Extra et al., Bussum, Coutinho, 2002, 377 pp.

In Flanders, the new immigrant multilingualism in Brussels is the subject of Rudi Janssens, *Taalgebruik in Brussel. Taalverhoudingen, taalverschuivingen en taalidentiteit in een meertalige stad*, Brussels, VUB, 2001, 312 pp. A survey of other languages spoken by school children in Flanders is given by Annick De Houwer, 'Home languages spoken in officially monolingual Flanders', pp. 71–87 of *Methodology of Conflict Linguistics*, ed. Klaus Bochmann et al., St Augustin, Asgard, 193 pp.

Against this background, we can identify three main research focuses in contact linguistics in the Low Countries. The first of these has to do with Flanders and the language border with French, the subject of a special issue of *JMMD*, 23.1–2, 2002, also published as a book, *Language Contact at the Romance-Germanic Language Border*, ed. Jeanine Treffers-Daller and Roland Willemyns, Clevedon, Multilingual Matters, 2002, 149 pp., with four chapters that are directly concerned with Dutch: L. van Durme, 'Genesis and evolution of the Romance/Germanic border' (9–21); H. Ryckeboer, 'Dutch/Flemish in the north of France' (22–35); R. Willemyns, 'The Dutch-French language border in Belgium' (36–49); and J. Treffers-Daller, 'Language use and language contact in Brussels' (50–64).

A second focus of contact linguistic research is on so-called Diaspora Dutch, the consequence of the historical expansion of the Dutch language in the colonial era. Here we have the stimulating collection of articles by researchers around Guus Extra's Babylon Centre in Tilburg, *Dutch Overseas. Studies in Maintenance and Loss of Dutch as an Immigrant Language*, ed. Jetske Klatter-Folmer and Sjaak Kroon, Tilburg U.P., 1997, 272 pp. Another volume published by researchers at Peter Nelde's Centre for Multilingualism Research in Brussels, *Recente studies in de Contactlinguistiek*, ed. Wim De Geest, Bonn, Dümmler, 1997, 164 pp., contains 25 contributions on Afrikaans, Brussels, Friesland, the European Union, Dutch-German language contact, and West-Flemish language conflicts in the 19th century. See also the article by Kees de Bot, 'Nelde's Law revisited: Dutch as a diaspora language', pp. 51–59 of *Recent Studies in Contact Linguistics*, ed. W. Wölck and A. de Houwer, Bonn, Dümmler, 1997, 484 pp. Of particular importance in this subdomain is the new standard work by Michael Clyne, *Dynamics of Language Contact*, CUP, 282 pp. Building on the theoretical insights of Frans Van Coetsem and on Pieter Muysken's recent typology of code-mixing, Clyne studies the dynamics of the contact with English of Australian immigrants, with very interesting data on the language use of the Dutch who settled there after the second world war.

A third focus of research in Dutch contact linguistics has to with the spread of English as the global language. As Tom McArthur put it, in his book *The English Languages*, CUP, 1998, English is *de facto* the second language in the Low Countries today. Extrapolating from this there is the recent suggestion in the valedictory lecture of T. J. M. van Els, *De Europese Unie, haar Instituties en haar Talen. Enkele taalpolitieke beschouwingen*, Nijmegen, Catholic Univ., 2000, 106 pp., that the Netherlands should take the lead on this and propose the adoption of one single official language for the European Union, viz. English. This is in line with the main thrust of a recent study of the political economy of the world language system by the Amsterdam sociologist Abram de Swaan, *Words of the World. The Global Language System*, Cambridge, Polity, 2001, 253 pp., which generated a lot of debate in the Netherlands, see the critical review by R. Salverda, 'Taal is meer dan taal', *Ons Erfdeel*, 45, 2002: 177–85. The impact of English is the subject of Mark van Oostrom, *Steenkolen-Engels. Een pleidooi voor normvervaging*, Amsterdam, Veen, 2002, 159 pp. As against this there is the highly instructive (and entertaining) study of the often deplorable English of Dutch academics in the Ph.D. dissertation of Joy Burrough-Boenisch, *Culture and Conventions. Writing and Reading Dutch Scientific English*, Utrecht, LOT, 2002, 357 pp. See also the cross-cultural comparison of Dutch and English question behaviour in B. C. Hendriks, *More on Dutch English . . . Please? A Study of Request Performance by Dutch Native Speakers, English Native Speakers and Dutch Learners of English*, Nijmegen U.P., 2002, 277 pp. Their findings should come as no surprise to anyone familiar with the chapter on the English errors of Dutch native speakers in the second, revised, and expanded edition of *Learner English: A Teacher's Guide to Interference and Other Problems*, ed. Michael Swann et al., CUP, 2001, 362 pp.

The general cultural, societal, and academic developments sketched above define the context within which Dutch language policy and Dutch language maintenance have to operate. On language maintenance see the collection of odes to the Dutch language, from Johannes Goropius Becanus (1569) to Mark Insingel (1995), *O schone moedertaal. Lofzangen op het Nederlands 1500–2000*, ed. A. M. Hagen, Amsterdam, Contact, 1999, 123 pp. A more scholarly counterpart is the collection on purism in some 40 different languages, *Taaltrots. Purisme in een veertigtal talen*, ed. Nicoline van der Sijs, Amsterdam–Antwerp, Contact, 1999, 447 pp., which, in addition to an important chapter on minority languages in Europe and one on Frisian, also has five contributions on varieties of Dutch (regional, provincial, urban) in the Netherlands, in Flanders, in Surinam, and in South Africa.

New developments in the Dutch language area, such as globalization and the resultant proliferation of English and many other immigrant languages, were addressed in a series of perceptive strategy papers presented at a conference in Ghent in May 2000 to mark the

20th anniversary of the Dutch Language Union, and subsequently published in *Taalvariatie en taalbeleid. Bijdragen aan het taalbeleid in Nederland en Vlaanderen*, ed. Johan De Caluwe et al., The Hague, Taalunie — Antwerp–Apeldoorn, Garant, 2002, 308 pp. The *Nederlandse Taalunie* (Dutch Language Union, with a very informative website at <www.taalunieversum.org>, published its five-year action plan in the policy document *De taalgebruiker centraal. Nederlandse Taalunie 2003–2007*, The Hague, Nederlandse Taalunie, 17 pp. One regrettable consequence is that grammatical research for the *Algemene Nederlandse Spraakkunst,* mentioned above p. 710, will not be continued.

As a reminder of how different the Netherlands and Flanders can be when it comes to matters of language and language policy, see R. B. Howell, 'The Low Countries: a study in sharply contrasting nationalisms', pp. 130–50 of *Language and Nationalism in Europe,* ed. Stephen Barbour and Catie Carmichael, OUP, 2000, 319 pp. See also Lode Wils, *Waarom Vlaanderen Nederlands spreekt*, Leuven, Davidsfonds, 2001, 71 pp.

5. Orthography

As the Leuven linguist Guido Geerts has memorably remarked, spelling is perhaps the only thing that the Dutch and the Flemish really do have in common. The standardization of Dutch spelling is part of the official remit of the intergovernmental Dutch-Flemish *Nederlandse Taalunie* (Dutch Language Union). The last round of spelling reform was in 1995. An electronic version of J. Renkema, *Woordenlijst van de Nederlandse taal,* also known as *Het Groene Boekje,* which contains the official spelling for all Dutch words, is now available, since 1998, on CD from Sdu publishers in The Hague. A good overview of this subdomain is given in Anneke Neijt's informative bibliographic survey of Dutch spelling, its principles, reform and history, as well as research, in Smedts, *Taalkunde*, 249–56. See also A. Neijt and A. M. Nunn, 'The recent history of Dutch orthography. Problems solved and created', *LB,* 86, 1997: 1–26; and J. van Megen and A. Neijt, 'Niederländische und deutsche Orthographie im Vergleich', *DSp,* 26, 1996: 193–217.

A solid outcome of systematic research into spelling, standardization, the problem of phonetic representation, its relation to the linguistic system, and its use by readers is the Nijmegen Ph.D. dissertation of Anneke M. Nunn, *Dutch Orthography. A Systematic Investigation of the Spelling of Dutch Words*, Katholieke Universiteit Nijmegen, 1998, 223 pp. A stimulating new development is the interdisciplinary collection of articles by phonologists, psycholinguists, special education researchers, and theoretical linguists, *The*

Relation of Writing to Spoken Language, ed. Martin Neef, Anneke Neijt, and Richard Sproat, Tübingen, Niemeyer, 2002, 210 pp.

6. Dutch Language Acquisition

In the field of first language acquisition, there is the network of researchers and projects in universities across the Dutch language area, entitled NET-werk, at <pcger33.uia.ac.be/joris/NET>. Two major publications in this field are *The Acquisition of Dutch*, ed. S. Gillis and Annick De Houwer, Amsterdam, Benjamins, 1998, 437 pp., and *Kindertaalverwerving. Een handboek*, ed. S. Gillis and A. M. Schaerlaekens, Groningen, Nijhoff, 2000, 564 pp. For recent research into the early stages of Dutch see the Ph.D. dissertations of N. J. van Kampen, *First Steps in Wh-Movement. Eerste stappen in vraagwoordverplaatsing*, Utrecht U.P., 1997, 218 pp., and Elma Blom, *From Root Infinitive to Finite Sentence: The Acquisition of Verbal Inflections and Auxiliaries*, Utrecht, OTS, 300 pp.

In the field of Dutch as a second language (NT2), there is the informative website of the NT2–expertise centre at <millennium.art.kuleuven.ac.be/steunpunt>. An important handbook is *Nederlands als tweede taal in de volwasseneneducatie: handboek voor docenten*, ed. J. H. Hulstijn et al., Amsterdam, Meulenhoff Educatief, 1996, 281 pp. See also Juliane House et al., *Interculturele communicatie*, Amsterdam, VU, 1997, 172 pp. An interesting collection of articles is *Perspectives on Foreign-Language Policy: Studies in Honour of Theo van Els*, ed. T. Bongaerts et al., Amsterdam, Benjamins, 1997, 223 pp.

Research into bilingualism has resulted in several Ph.D. dissertations: Petra Bos, *Development of Bilingualism: A Study of School-Age Moroccan Children in the Netherlands*, Tilburg U.P., 1997, 192 pp.; M. Woutersen, *Bilingual Word Perception*, Katholieke Universiteit Nijmegen, 1997, 163 pp.; and B. J. H. Schulpen, *Explorations in Bilingual Word Recognition: Cross-Modal, Cross-Sectional and Cross-Language Effects*, Nijmegen, NICI, 261 pp.

For Dutch as a foreign language (*Nederlands als Vreemde Taal*, NVT) there is the so-called *Steunpunt Nederlands als Vreemde Taal* of the University of Amsterdam (SNVT, at <www.snvt.hum.uva.nl>), which offers an up-to-date bibliography of relevant publications. New publications are regularly reviewed in the journal *Neerlandica Extra Muros* of the *Internationale Vereniging voor Neerlandistiek* (IVN, at <www.ivnnl.com>). The IVN has published two conference volumes, *Nederlands 200 jaar later*, ed. H. Brems et al., Woubrugge, IVN, 1998, 575 pp., with 16 articles on Dutch language, language acquisition, and linguistics; and *Perspectieven voor de internationale neerlandistiek in de 21ste eeuw*, ed. G. Elshout et al., Woubrugge, IVN, 2001, 457 pp., containing nine contributions on the linguistics of modern Dutch. In Indonesia, the 30th anniversary of the Dutch Department at the Universitas Indonesia was celebrated in the volume *Tiga Puluh Tahun Studi Belanda/Dertig Jaar Studie Nederlands in Indonesië*, ed. Yati Suhardi et al., Depok, Fakultas Sastra Universitas Indonesia, 2001, 426 pp., which contains five useful articles on teaching and learning Dutch as a source language for disciplines such as Law and History.

For research into intercultural aspects of Dutch as a foreign language see the Ph.D. dissertation on relational strategies in the Dutch of German learners, Veronika Wenzel, *Relationelle Strategien in der Fremdsprache. Pragmatische und interkulturelle Aspekte der niederländischen Lernersprache von Deutschen*, Münster, Agenda, 320 pp., and G. Quist, 'Culture in the university foreign language curriculum: some theoretical considerations', *Dutch Crossing*, 24, 2000: 3–28, which discusses the results of the London project *Critical Language Awareness*, on such higher-level skills as reading between the lines and dealing with implicit cultural meanings.

An interesting question for further research and debate is, finally, whether NT2 and NVT are really that different, and what sort of synergies are possible between these two domains. See in particular A. van Kalsbeek, 'NT2–NVT: synergie of scheiding der wegen?', *Neerlandica Extra Muros*, 39.1, 2001: 23–33.

7. Lexicology

A five-page list of Dutch dictionaries is included in the introductory survey by A. Dalby, 'Dutch', pp. 99–104 of Id., *A Guide to World Language Dictionaries*, London, Library Association, 1998, 480 pp. The same year also saw the publication of the revised and expanded *A Bibliography of Dutch Dictionaries*, ed. F. Claes and P. Bakema, Tübingen, Niemeyer, 1998, 470 pp. 1998 was an important year also in that finally, after almost one and a half centuries of sustained lexicographic activity, the great *Woordenboek der Nederlandsche Taal* (WNT) was completed. With 40 volumes, this is the largest dictionary in the world; it is now also available on CD. Its completion was accompanied by the volume *Het grootste woordenboek ter wereld. Een kijkje achter de kolommen van het Woordenboek der Nederlandsche Taal (WNT)*, ed. F. Heyvaert et al., The Hague, Sdu — Antwerp, Standaard, 1998, 434 pp. It was the subject of a special theme issue of *Nederlandse taalkunde*, 6.1, 1999, a very useful survey article by M. C. van den Toorn, 'Om en bij de voltooiing van het WNT', *TsNTL*, 115, 1999: 261–67, and also of M. Mooijaert, 'Niet bedacht op onderduikers. Het WNT in revisie', *Neerlandica Wratislaviensia*, 13, 2001: 73–85.

Major lexicographic resources, corpora, and databases are available online at the Leiden Instituut voor Lexicologie (INL, at <www.inl.nl>) and at CELEX, the Centre for Lexical Information of the Catholic University of Nijmegen, at <www.kun.nl/celex>.

In a regular flow of new dictionaries, the year 2000 brought the 14th much expanded edition of *Van Dale Groot Nederlands Woordenboek*, Utrecht, Van Dale Lexicografie, 3 vols + CD. In Flanders a counterpoint was made with the publication of the *Vlaams-Nederlands Woordenboek: Van Ambetanterik tot Zwanzer*, ed. Peter Bakema et al., Antwerp, Standaard — Utrecht, Spectrum, 395 pp. In addition there is now the useful *Idioomwoordenboek: verklaring en herkomst van uitdrukkingen en gezegden*, ed. H. de Groot et al., Utrecht, Van Dale Lexicografie, 1999, 1049 pp., and the excellent *Combinatiewoordenboek van Nederlandse substantieven (zelfstandige naamwoorden) met hun vaste verba (werkwoorden)*, ed. Piet de Kleijn, Amsterdam, Rozenberg, 774 pp., which describes, with many example sentences, the fixed combinations of some 3,000 nouns with their verbs, and explains why in Dutch a coffee cup 'stands' and a knife 'lies'. This matter was traditionally handled very incompletely and arbitrarily in existing Dutch dictionaries.

For foreign learners there are the two new Dutch-English dictionaries, *The New Routledge Dutch Dictionary*, ed. N. J. Osselton and R. Hempelman, London, Routledge, 2001, 907 pp., and the *Teach Yourself Dutch Dictionary*, ed. Gerdi Quist and Dennis Strik, London, Hodder & Stoughton, 397 pp.

For the history of Dutch words there is now the massive volume by Nicoline van der Sijs, *Chronologisch woordenboek. De ouderdom en herkomst van onze woorden en hun betekenissen*, Amsterdam, Veen, 2001, 1164 pp. Using the oldest known sources, she traces the origin of many Dutch words, establishing their chronology, and explores a range of themes with extensive Dutch word material concerning the weather, plants, animals, the senses, drinks, time, religion, shipping, trade, art, music, games and sports. Of great scholarly importance is the new *Etymologisch Woordenboek van het Nederlands* (EWN), vol. 1 (A-E), ed. Marlies Philippa et al., Amsterdam U.P., 728 pp., also available online at <www.etymologie.nl>, which is expected to be complete in four volumes by 2009.

Finally there is a range of studies on the more informal aspects of the Dutch lexicon. Nicoline van der Sijs has prepared the new edition of J. G. M. Moormann, *De Geheimtalen*, Amsterdam, Veen, 2002, 863 pp. But see the critical review by P. van Hauwermeiren, *Taal en tongval*, 54, 2002: 183–90. A very interesting study of swearing in Dutch is P. G. J. van Sterkenburg, *Vloeken. Een cultuurbepaalde reactie op woede, irritatie en frustratie*, The Hague, Sdu, 2001, 715 pp. This is the second and much revised edition of a monograph first published in

1997, from which we learn that *shit!* is now the most common and frequently used expletive in Dutch. In this connection one should also read the fascinating article on the Dutch expression of anger by E.-J. Kuiper, 'Als blikken konden doden. Over de conceptualisering van woede in vaste woordverbindingen in het Nederlands', *Neerlandica Wratislaviensia,* 10, 1998: 195–207, and on how the Dutch, by way of insult, may wish all kinds of terrible diseases upon each other, W. H. Fletcher, 'Come down with the cholera! Disease names in Dutch strong language', *CJNS,* 17.1–2, 1996: 231–39. There is an enormous linguistic creativity here, as also in the standard work on language at play by Battus (Hugo Brandt Corstius), *Opperlans! Taal- en letterkunde,* Amsterdam, Querido, 2002, 676 pp., the completely revised second edition of a work first published in 1981.

8. Frisian

For bibliographic access to this domain, the helpful booklet *Orientation in Frisian Studies,* ed. P. H. Breuker et al., 1996, is now available online on the website of the Fryske Akademy in Ljouwert (Leeuwarden) at <www.fa.knaw.nl> (click under 'Universitêr ûnderwiis'). A full record of publications in the field of Frisian linguistics is included in the *Bibliografie van de Friese Taal- en Letterkunde* (*BFTL*), which is part of the *BNTL* mentioned above p. 707.

An introductory survey is given by R. Salverda, 'Frisian', pp. 177–84 of *Encyclopedia of the Languages of Europe,* ed. Glanville Price, Oxford, Blackwell, 1998, 499 pp. A more touristic account is offered in chapter six of Helena Drysdale, *Mother Tongues. Travels through Tribal Europe,* London, Picador, 2001, 401 pp. Basic information on Frisian, including texts, recordings, and English translations, is available at <www.tiersma.com> from Pieter Meijes Tiersma, whose *Frisian Reference Grammar* (1985) was reissued in 1999 in Ljouwert, Fryske Akademy, 147 pp.

The journal *Us Wurk* published a special issue, 46, 1997, containing nine articles by leading Frisianists, as a *Festschrift* for Bo Sjölin. It includes a very interesting article on interference phenomena from Dutch into Frisian by G. J. de Haan, 'Contact-induced changes in modern West Frisian' (61–89). The proceedings of the 15th Conference of Frisian Philologists were edited by P. Boersma et al., *Philologia Frisica anno 1999,* Ljouwert, Fryske Akademy, 2000, 296 pp. A critical review was published by S. Dijk, *Us Wurk,* 50, 2001: 147–53.

The single most important publication in Frisian linguistics is the bilingual *Handbuch des Friesischen/Handbook of Frisian Studies,* ed. Horst Haider Munske, Tübingen, Niemeyer, 2001, 845 pp. An international team of 45 Frisianists contributed 79 articles in four main sections: I: The Study of Frisian (10 articles, pp. 1–72); II: Frisian Languages and Literatures today — in the Netherlands (17 articles, pp. 73–262) and in Germany (14 articles, pp. 263–478); III: History of Frisian Languages and Literatures — Prehistory (7 articles, pp. 479–537), Old Frisian (14 articles, pp. 538–670), and Modern Frisian (9 articles, pp. 671–766); and IV: General and Comparative Aspects of Frisian (4 articles, pp. 767–804). The book has two solid indexes, one on Subjects (813–28) and one on Names (829–45). The standard of writing, information, and bibliographic references is very high throughout. It is to be noted that for Dutch linguistics there is nothing comparable as yet. For the synchronic study of Frisian, G. J. de Haan has opened interesting perspectives in his article 'Recent trends in Frisian linguistics', *ib.*, 32–47.

Ongoing research has resulted in several English-language Ph.D. dissertations: S. Dijk, *Noun Incorporation in Frisian*, Ljouwert, Fryske Akademy, 1997, 231 pp.; Jarich Hoekstra, *The Syntax of Infinitives in Frisian*, Ljouwert, Fryske Akademy, 1997, 169 pp.; and Willem Visser, *The Syllable in Frisian*, The Hague, Holland Academic Graphics, 1997, 405 pp. Jarich Hoekstra also published a monograph on morphology, *Fryske wurdfoarming*, Ljouwert, Fryske Akademy, 1998, 183 pp.

For the history of Frisian the late Dirk Boutkan prepared the important *Old Frisian Etymological Database*, as part of the Leiden Indo-European Etymological Dictionary Project, online at <iiasnt/leidenuniv.nl/ied>. The volume of *ABÄG*, 49, 'Approaches to Old Frisian philology', ed. Rolf H. Bremmer et al., has a stimulating introduction by Bremmer, 'Old Frisian philology: the way ahead' (vii-xvi). An important volume on historical contact linguistics is *ABÄG*, 54, 'Language contact. substratum, superstratum, adstratum in Germanic languages', ed. D. Boutkan and A. Quak, which includes etymological studies by R. S. P. Beekes, A. Quak, and W. de Vaan, plus articles by C. van Bree on syntax, and by J. Hoekstra and N. van Koppen on the Dutch/Frisian dialect of Het Bildt. A useful historical survey of Frisian language studies is *In Skiednis fan 'e Fryske taalkunde*, ed. Anne Dykstra and Rolf H. Bremmer, Ljouwert, Fryske Akademy, 1999, 372 pp. But see the critical review by G. J. de Haan, *Taal en tongval*, 54, 2002: 76–80.

The domain of Frisian sociolinguistics is dominated by a series of important contributions by Durk Gorter. In 1997 he discussed the struggle about place names in the province of Fryslân in 'Naamgeving in Friesland: contact en conflict = consensus?', pp. 35–46 of *Recente studies in de Contactlinguistiek*, ed. Wim De Geest, Bonn, Dümmler, 164 pp. In 2001, in the very informative contribution 'Frisian in the Netherlands' by Durk Gorter et al., pp. 103–18 of the conference volume *The Other Languages of Europe. Demographic, Sociolinguistic and*

Educational Perspectives, ed. Guus Extra and Durk Gorter, Clevedon, Multilingual Matters, 2001, 454 pp., the authors report that 'today 74% of the population is able to speak Frisian. This implies an absolute number of roughly 400,000 speakers of Frisian'. Of particular interest, finally, is G.'s 'A Frisian update of reversing language shift', pp. 215–33 of *Can Threatened Languages be Saved? Reversing Language Shift, Revisited. A 21st-Century Perspective*, ed. Joshua Fishman, Clevedon, Multilingual Matters, 2001, 503 pp.

In language contact studies, the *Stadsfries* citylect continues to be a focus of interest. Following P. Jonkman's Ph.D. dissertation *It Leewarders* (1993), we now have Pieter Duijff, *Fries and Stadsfries*, The Hague, Sdu, 2002, 120 pp. A number of penetrating articles were published by C. van Bree: 'Die Syntax des Stadtfriesischen im Vergleich zum Friesischen, Niederländischen und Niederdeutschen', pp. 1–48 of *Friesische Studien III, Beiträge des Föhrer Symposium zur Friesischen Philologie*, ed. Volkert F. Faltings et al. (*NOWELE*, Suppl. 18), Odense U.P., 1997, 205 pp.; and 'De morfologie van het Stadsfries', *TsNTL*, 117, 2001: 41–58, 133–50.

In 1997 Bertus Mulder published a book-length contribution on the politics of language, *Fryske taalpolityk*, Bolsward, Koperative Utjowery, 134 pp. Against the background of the European Charter for Regional and Minority Languages, the position of Frisian and Irish in their respective school systems have been compared by J. Effemey, 'Treading softly and dreaming. Frisian and Irish at school', *Dutch Crossing*, 25, 2001: 53–77. A solid exploration of policy making for these European regional and minority languages is undertaken in the Ph.D. dissertation of Piet Hemminga, *Het beleid inzake unieke regionale talen. Een onderzoek naar het beleid en de beleidsvorming met betrekking tot een drietal unieke regionale talen: het Fries in Nederland, en het Noordfries en Sorbisch in Duitsland*, Ljouwert–Leeuwarden, Fryske Akademy, 2000, 521 pp. The Declaration of Oegstgeest, which formulates a set of principles for a sensible language policy for the minority languages of Europe, is included at pp. 447–49 of *The Other Languages of Europe*, see above pp. 730–31. A relevant official document in language policy making is the *Bestuursafspraak Friese Taal en Cultuur*, agreed in 2001 between the provincial authorities and the national government, online at <www.minbzk.nl/pdf/bi/bzkbil/bestuursaf spraak_friese_taal_6–01.pdf>.

As for Frisian lexicography, the Fryske Akademy continues to produce the large-scale *Wurdboek fan de Fryske Taal/Woordenboek der Friese taal*. Since 1997 a further six volumes of this large-scale dictionary have been published, from 14 ('mudde-oansnije') through to 19 ('siedstale-skogje'). Further important publications are the legal dictionary *Juridisch Woordenboek Nederlands-Fries, met een index Fries-Nederlands*, ed. P. Duijff, Leeuwarden–Ljouwert, Fryske Akademy, 2000, 677 pp., the Frisian-English dictionary *Frysk-Ingelsk wurdboek, with a corresponding English-Frisian word list*, ed. A. Dijkstra, Ljouwert, Fryske Akademy, 2000, 1153 pp., and the *Eilander wèzzenbuek. Woordenboek van het Schiermonnikoogs*, ed. W. Visser and S. Dijk, Ljouwert, Fryske Akademy, 2002, 844 pp. F. van der Kuip discusses the Frisian lexical material included in the *Woordenboek der Nederlandsche Taal*, in 'Fries in het WNT', in the electronic journal *Trefwoord* (www.fa.knaw.nl, see under 'Publikaasjes'). A well-informed survey of Frisian lexicography is given by S. Dijk, 'De Fryske wurdboekskriuwerij om 'e millennium-wiksel hinne: stân fan saken en perspektiven', *Us Wurk*, 50, 2001 : 107–26.

Finally, a number of important new digital resources which are being developed at the Fryske Akademy, such as the Corpus of Spoken Frisian and databases containing all available language material for the history of Frisian, are surveyed by E. Hoekstra, 'Taaldatabanken op het gebied van het Fries', *NTk*, 9 : 58–62.

II. DUTCH STUDIES

LITERATURE

By WIM HÜSKEN, *Stedelijke Musea Mechelen*

1. GENERAL

One of the most prominent scholars of Dutch literature in Flanders, Karel Porteman, was offered a *Festschrift* on the occasion of his retirement as professor at the University of Leuven. *De steen van Alciato: Literatuur en visuele cultuur in de Nederlanden: Opstellen voor prof. dr. Karel Porteman bij zijn emeritaat / The Stone of Alciato: Literature and Visual Culture in the Low Countries: Essays in Honour of Karel Porteman*, ed. Marc van Vaeck, Hugo Brems, and Geert H. M. Claassens, Leuven, Peeters, xx + 1131 pp., presents 56 essays on various topics divided over five categories, reflecting the areas of research Porteman focused on during the years of his academic career. The first section, 'Op het snijvlak van taal, denken en visuele expressie' (On the cutting edge of language, thought, and visual expression), includes, among other articles, an essay by R. Lievens, 'Middelnederlandse letter-allegorese' (55–76), in which the medieval practice of expanding on the symbolic meaning of names and words by seeing them as contractions of certain phrases (e.g., *deus* being short for *dans eternam vitam suis*) is discussed. Sections two and three in the book both have the Horatian dictum *Ut pictura poesis* in their titles, thus alluding to Porteman's important contributions to the study of emblem literature. Their subtitles, 'De dichter en de schilder' (poet and painter) and 'De dichter als schilder' (the poet as painter), reveal the different points of view taken in these sections. Articles worthwhile mentioning here are M. Janssens, ' "In Flanders Fields" in woord en beeld' (79–89), on a well-known poem by the 20th-c. poet Hugo Claus; J. Weisgerber, 'Ut pictura poesis. Hugo Claus in het teken van Corneille' (249–57), on the discovery, *c.* 1947, of French surrealism in art and literature; and L. van Gemert, 'Verreziende helden. Visualiteit in het Nederlandse epos' (387–403), on the way the 17th-c. and 18th-c. authors Joost van den Vondel and Lucretia van Merken attempted to depict subject matter verbally, so as to be able to recreate visual images. Section four is entitled 'Boek en prent: woord naast beeld' (Book and print: words alongside images). Where art historians and cultural historians have been making extensive study of 19th-c. book illustrations, to literary historians this topic is relatively unknown. P. Couttenier, ' "Verbeeld U." Illustraties in de Vlaamse historische romans van de negentiende eeuw' (633–53), embarks on a journey exploring illustrations in 19th-c. Flemish historical novels. The fifth section in this *Festschrift* concentrates on the genre of the emblem itself: 'Het embleemgenre: van Alciato tot Mutsaers'. Although most essays here focus on 16th-c., 17th-c., and 18th-c. emblem books, there is also one by E. Brems, 'Een boek om traag te lezen. Over de *Emblemata* van Charlotte Mutsaers' (23–43), on a 20th-c. Flemish poetess who, in 1983, published a book entitled *Het circus van de geest*, in which she shows herself to have been inspired by one of the masters of the genre in the 17th c., Jacob Cats. The concluding subsection looks at issues related to emblem book bibliography and the book trade. M. De Schepper, '"Amblemata voor de uldinge." Een zestigtal "onbekende" Zuid-Nederlandse embleemdrukken in de Brusselse Koninklijke Bibliotheek' (1085–118), supplies a short bibliography of some 60 hitherto unknown emblem books kept in the Royal Library at Brussels, not included in John Landwehr's 'notoriously defective' *Emblem and Fable Books Printed in the Low Countries, 1542–1813: A Bibliography* (1988). This voluminous *Festschrift* for Karel Porteman ends with his extensive list of publications written between 1967 and the year of his retirement (1119–31).

Burger, ed. Joost Kloek and Karin Tilmans (Reeks Nederlandse begripsgeschiedenis, 4), Amsterdam U.P., 2002, vii + 387 pp., is the fourth volume in a series on the history of cultural concepts in the Netherlands (see *YWMLS*, 63:783–84). Central to this volume is the concept of the 'citizen'. Contributions include, among others, essays by Herman Pleij on the idea of the citizen in late medieval texts, by Maaike Meijer Drees on 17th-c. middle-class literature, by Evert van Uitert on 19th-c. middle-class art, and by Remieg Aerts on the way the concept was undermined during the 20th c.

2. The Middle Ages

After having been professor of Medieval Dutch literature at the University of Leiden, Frits van Oostrom was appointed University Professor at Utrecht. In *Academische kwesties: Van middeleeuwse literatuur naar universiteit en maatschappij*, Utrecht Univ., Faculteit der Letteren, 44 pp., his inaugural lecture, he reflects on the historiography of medieval Dutch literary studies, concentrating on W. J. A. Jonckbloet (1817–85), Jan te Winkel (1847–1927), Gerrit Kalff (1856–1923), Jozef van Mierlo (1878–1958), and Gerard Knuvelder (1902–82). Since 1970, the year in which Knuvelder published volume I, on medieval Dutch literature, in the fifth edition of his *Handboek tot de geschiedenis der Nederlandse letterkunde*, many new views on Middle Dutch literature have emerged and previouosly unknown text fragments have been found. A new history of Middle Dutch literature, shortly to appear as part of an new multi-volume history of Dutch literature, is expected to include these new views and discoveries as well as to broaden the horizon of the hitherto mainly aesthetic-inspired observations on medieval literature towards a multi-disciplinary approach.

Paul Wackers, *Terug naar de bron*, Utrecht Univ., Faculteit der Letteren, 2002, 48 pp., is the inaugural lecture, given on 26 April 2002, by the recently appointed professor of medieval Dutch literature at the University of Utrecht. W. concentrates on a manuscript, now in the Hessisches Hauptstaatsarchiv, Wiesbaden (sign. 3004 B 10), containing 50 religious texts, some of them mystical, others more of a didactic nature, and 37 drawings. Until well into the 19th c., scholars were inclined to deny texts like these literary status but, W. argues, the idea of 'literature' is post-medieval. Rather than studying texts labelled 'literary' we should concentrate on texts held important by medieval people themselves.

W.'s predecessor, Willem P. Gerritsen, was offered the prestigious Scaliger chair at the University of Leiden. *Het alfabet als zoekinstrument: Een beschouwing over de geschiedenis van de alfabetische index* (Scaliger-lezingen, 2), Leiden, Primavera, 40 pp., is his inaugural lecture. G. studies the introduction of alphabetical indexes during the 12th c. Indexes dramatically changed the manner of reading, allowing readers to use texts as reference books. G. also discusses J. C. Scaliger, the latinized name for Joseph de l'Escale (1540–1609), who supplemented Janus Gruterus's *Inscriptiones antiquae* (1603), a collection of inscriptions from Classical antiquity, with an index. Mainly thanks to this index Gruterus's work was for over 250 years the standard book on ancient inscriptions. Marieke van Delft et al., *Bibliopolis: Geschiedenis van het gedrukte boek in Nederland*, Zwolle, Waanders — The Hague, Koninklijke Bibliotheek, 317 pp., presents a history of the printed book in the Netherlands. Frederik Kwakkel, *Die dietsche boeke die ons toebehoeren: De kartuizers van Herne en de productie van Middelnederlandse handschriften in de regio Brussel (1350–1400)*, Leuven, Peeters, 2002, x + 316 + [60] pp., comes to the conclusion that the Brussels Rooklooster, one of the most famous scriptoria active in the Low Countries, was less important than scholars have until now believed. They come to this conclusion on the basis of a list of books included in a manuscript, copied in 1390, attributed to a scribe who was identified as the *librarius* of this monastery. K.'s codicological approach now shows that it was in fact a Carthusian monk from Herne who composed the list, in it simply giving a list of books they had on their shelves instead of suggesting they had been copied by them. The use of a small correction mark in manuscripts copied at

Herne allows us to identify a considerable number of manuscripts as originating from this monastery, the monks of which belonged to a contemplative religious order, rather than from the Augustinian abbey of Rooklooster that housed a secular religious order. K.'s theory greatly upsets literary historians' ideas on the pivotal position this monastery allegedly had as one of the most productive centres of medieval literature.

Jos Huls, *'Seuen maniren van minnen' van Beatrijs van Nazareth: Het mystieke proces en mystagogische implicaties* (Miscellanea Neerlandica, 28), 2 vols, Leuven, Peeters, 2002, xx + 1063 pp., concentrates on the 13th-c. treatise, *Seven Ways to Love*, attributed to the nun Beatrijs van Nazareth (1200–68). Three manuscripts of the text survive. H. studies all three but mainly looks at the one at the Hague Royal Library, since this manuscript is believed to provide the oldest version. Special attention is paid to analysing the text, an edition of which and translation into modern Dutch are also given. Finally the way the treatise tries to explain seven ways of spiritual growing are elaborated upon as well. Rob Faesen, *Lichaam in lichaam, ziel in ziel: Christusbeleving bij Hadewijch en haar tijdgenoten* (Mystieke teksten & thema's, 21), Baarn, Ten Have — Ghent, Carmelitana, 158 pp., focuses on the way the mystic poetess Hadewijch and her contemporaries perceived Christ in their works. Geert Warnar, *Ruusbroec: Literatuur en mystiek in de veertiende eeuw*, Amsterdam, Athenaeum-Polak–Van Gennep, 398 pp., is a biography of the other great Dutch mystic, Jan van Ruusbroec. Much of our knowledge of the man was written by Henricus Pomerius, one of the monks of Groenendael monastery, the first prior of which was Ruusbroec. Further information is taken from Ruusbroec's works. W. also looks at matters of vocabulary and style as well as at the images evoked in his treatises. Ruusbroec attempted to make available to a wider audience what was only accessible to those who were able to read Latin. Jan van Ruusbroec, *Van seven trappen*, introd. and ed. R. Faesen; transl. into English H. Rolfson; transl. into Latin L. Surius as *De septem gradibus amoris* (1552) (Studiën en tekstuitgaven van Ons geestelijk erf, 20.9; Opera Omnia, 9; Corpus Christianorum, Continuatio Mediaevalis, 109), Turnhout, Brepols, 274 pp., is a trilingual edition of a tract by the same famous mystic author on how to become one with God in seven steps. For sermons, a rich source for didactic texts in the Low Countries, providing also enjoyable stories, see Maria Sherwood-Smith and Patricia Stoop, *Repertorium van Middelnederlandse preken in handschriften tot en met 1550 = Repertorium of Middle Dutch Sermons Preserved in Manuscripts from before 1550* (Miscellanea neerlandica, 29), 3 vols, Leuven, Peeters, x + 1478, iv + 407, iv + 450 pp.

Soetje Oppenhuis de Jong, *De Middelnederlandse Perceval-traditie: Inleiding en editie van de bewaarde fragmenten van een Middelnederlandse vertaling van de 'Perceval' of 'Conte du Graal' van Chrétien de Troyes, en de 'Perchevael' in de 'Lancelotcompilatie'* (Middelnederlandse Lancelotromans, 9), Hilversum, Verloren, x + 558 pp., presents an edition, accompanied with a detailed study of the relationship between the extant fragments with their original source, of the Middle Dutch translations of Chrétien de Troyes's *Conte du Graal*. The oldest Arthurian novel in Dutch literature, *Ferguut*, written between 1240 and 1250, has been edited in a modernized prose translation by Willem Kuiper, **Ferguut, of De Ridder met het Witte Schild* (Griffioen), Amsterdam, Athenaeum-Polak & Van Gennep, 2002, 139 pp.

Van Madelgijs tot Malagis: Een bundel opstellen verzameld n. a. v. de tachtigste verjaardag van Gilbert de Smet, ed. Georges de Schutter and Jan Goossens (Studies op het gebied van de oudere Nederlandse letterkunde, 1), Ghent, KANTL, 2002, 97 pp., is a collection of essays in honour of Gilbert de Smet, former professor at the University of Ghent, on the occasion of his 80th birthday. Madelgijs is the name of a great-uncle of the legendary four children of Aymon. The book also includes an article by De Smet himself, 'De Nederlandse 'Madelgijs': Schets van een geschiedenis' (11–21). Further contributions include B. Duijvestijn, 'Madelgijs, zwerftocht van een epische stof' (23–34), J. D. Janssens, 'Madelgijs en de 14de-eeuwse ridderroman: een literairhistorische verkenning' (35–52), M. J. Schubert, R. Bentzinger, and A. Haase, 'Nederlands-Duitse betrekkingen op gebied van taal en literatuur in de late Middeleeuwen: over de manier waarop "Malagis", "Ogier"en "Reinolt"vertaald zijn' (53–64), and B. Besamusca, 'Humor in "Malagis"' (65–76).

Anne Reynders, *De Middelnederlandse 'Parthonopeus van Bloys' en zijn Oudfranse origineel: Een studie van de vertaal- en bewerkingstechniek* (Antwerpse studies over Nederlandse literatuurgeschiedenis, 8), Leuven, Peeters, 2002, x + 329 pp., studies the way the miraculous story of *Partonopeus de Blois*, narrated by the mid-12th-c. French author Denis Pyramis, was adapted and translated into Dutch.

Ghi Fransoyse sijt hier onteert: De Guldensporenslag, Lodewijk van Velthem: Kritische editie van de Middelnederlandse tekst uit de Voortzetting van de 'Spiegel historiael' met inleiding en vertaling, ed. Ludo Jongen and Miriam Piters, Leuven, Davidsfonds, 2002, 232 pp., commemorates the Battle of the Spurs of 11 July 1302. This heroic event in the history of Flanders was described by Lodewijk van Velthem in his continuation of Jacob van Maerlant's *Spiegel historiael*. Along with a modern translation Jongen and Piters present a new edition of the text. The famous 19th-c. novel about this battle, Hendrik Conscience's *De Leeuw van Vlaenderen, of De slag der Gulden Sporen*, has also been given a new edition by Edward Vanhoutte, Tielt, Lannoo, 2002, 537 pp., with an introduction by Karel Wauters.

Wim van Anrooij et al., *Al t'Antwerpen in die stad: Jan van Boendale en de literaire cultuur van zijn tijd* (Nederlandse literatuur en cultuur in de middeleeuwen, 24), Amsterdam, Prometheus, 2002, 205 pp., focus on Antwerp in the first half of the 14th c., when the scribe Jan van Boendale was one of the most important authors in town. The 'Antwerp School', as it had become known in literary history (but the expression is no longer supported in recent scholarship), produced ten texts, seven of which can be attributed to Boendale. The nine contributions to the book, by W. van Anrooij, R. van Uytven, G. Warnar, M. Piters, J. van Leeuwen, S. Corbellini, A. B. Mulder-Bakker, and J. Reynaert, attempt to study these texts from a multidisciplinary perspective. Reynaert holds the opinion that two of the hitherto anonymous titles belonging to this corpus of texts, *Melibeus* and *Dietsche doctrinale*, are also by Boendale. Jan van Boendale, *Lekenspiegel*, ed. Ludo Jongen and Miriam Piters (Griffioen), Amsterdam, Athenaeum-Polak & Van Gennep, 229 pp., is an abbreviated edition in modern Dutch of Boendale's best known work, a long didactic poem in four books for ordinary people, hence its title, *Lekenspiegel*, or 'Lay Persons' Mirror'. The poem was composed between 1325 and 1330; books I and II include stories from the Bible and Church history; book III is of a didactic nature, teaching the reader how to live according to God's rules; Book IV deals with matters related to the day of the Last Judgement. In their afterword Jongen and Piters elaborate on the genre to which this book belongs, the structure of the work, and the sources Boendale used.

One of the longer allegorical poems in the famous *Gruuthuse* manuscript has been studied and newly edited by Kees Lassche, *Die weghe der conste: Verkenningen in en rond de eerste allegorie van het Gruuthuse-handschrift (contextuele studie, editie en interpretatie)*, Ommen, Lassche, 2002, 301 pp. In this poem the speaker describes a dream he recently had. He saw a castle, the allegorical representation of a woman, set in an idyllic environment. Before he could enter this castle the man had a number of adventures. After he had lived in it for a year he was forced, by way of punishment for his misbehaviour, to leave the building. Lassche discusses all hitherto given explanations of the text, finally interpreting this allegorical poem himself by viewing it in the light of the remaining poems in the manuscript.

Een wereld van kennis: Bloemlezing uit de Middelnederlandse artesliteratuur, ed. Erwin Huizenga, Orlanda S. H. Lie, and L. M. Veltman (Artesliteratuur in de Nederlanden, 1), Hilversum, Verloren, 2002, 237 pp., presents a selection of texts on various scientific topics, now, because of their scholarly background, referred to as '*artes* literature'.

Three types of texts belong to this genre, related to the *artes liberales*, the *artes mechanicae*, and the *artes magicae*. Topics discussed in these texts, more often than not reflecting rather strange ideas about man and his environment, cover areas such astronomy, alchemy, and medicine, but also including cooking and language teaching, as well as travel accounts. Erwin Huizenga, *Tussen autoriteit en empirie: De Middelnederlandse chirurgieën in de veertiende en vijftiende eeuw en hun maatschappelijke context* (Artesliteratuur in de Nederlanden, 2), Hilversum, Verloren, 635 pp., focuses on one particular field of '*artes* literature', surgery.

Karel ende Elegast, ed. Geert Claassens (Alfa), Amsterdam U.P., 2002, 56 pp., is a new edition of one of the most popular stories about Charlemagne in Dutch medieval literature. In it the emperor is given an angelic command to go on a foray in which he discovers that an assault on his life is being prepared. A previously disgraced knight proves to be still loyal to his lord and is restored to his former honourable position.

3. The Rhetoricians' Period

Most essays in *De macht van het schone woord: Literatuur in Brussel van de 14e tot de 18e eeuw*, ed. Jozef Janssens and Remco Sleiderink, Leuven, Davidsfonds, 270 pp., concentrate on the literature produced in Brussels by Rhetoricians. The introductory chapter by J. Janssens (13–105) discusses the entire period this book attempts to cover. J. gives an impression of the richness of cultural expression the town harboured within its walls. From the time the Burgundian court moved its seat from Dijon to Brussels, *c.* 1433, until 11 August 1695, when the town was sacked by troops of the French king, Louis XIV, Brussels was one of the main centres for art and literature as it developed in monasteries, at the many noble courts, and in town. However, most attention in this essay is focused on the 15th and 16th cs. R. Sleiderink, 'Grootse ambities: Culturele initiatieven van de stad Brussel ten tijde van Filips de Goede' (107–23), limits himself to the earlier period of the 15th c. In 1430, Philip the Good had been elected as successor to the Duke of Brabant; with an eminent ruler of his reputation in town the Brussels aristocracy showed itself worthy of his presence by organizing events attracting large crowds to the new capital. In addition, the town's magistrates commissioned artists, such as Rogier van der Weyden, to create majestic works of art and authors to compose poetry or to complete, as in the case of Wein van Cotthem (identified as such by Sleiderink), an account of Brabant's glorious history (the *Brabantsche yeesten*), begun by Jan van Boendale in the 14th-c. A.-L. Van Bruaene, 'Minnelijke rederijkers, schandelijke spelen: de rederijkerskamers in Brussel tussen 1400 en 1585' (125–39), provides a survey of Rhetoricians' activities during 200 years of their greatest productivity. The oldest chamber of rhetoric in the Low Countries is to be found in Brussels. In 1401, the company of 'The Book' (*Den boeck*) was inaugurated here, possibly to function as a counterbalance to the Paris 'Cour Amoureuse'. Both noble institutions entertained a special cult with respect to their membership lists, thus implicitly establishing a symbolic link with the Book of Life (Revelation 3. 5). By the end of the 15th c., Emperor Maximilian of Austria, regent on behalf of his young son, Philip the Fair, was a true patron for one of the other chambers in town, 'Het Mariencransken' (The Rosary). In later years, after the Reformation had reached Brussels, the third chamber, 'De Corenbloem' (The Corn Flower) dominated the town's literary circles. Further chapters in this volume are S. S. Sutch, 'Dichters van de stad: De Brusselse rederijkers en hun verhouding tot de Franstalige hofliteratuur en het geleerde humanisme (1475–1522)' (141–59), on interaction between Dutch and French culture at the ducal court and in a humanist environment; R. Jacobs, 'De sneeuwpoppen zijn terug in de stad: de plaatsaanduidingen in *Dwonder van claren ijse en snee* van Jan Smeken (1511)' (161–79), on the identification of geographical locations in a text describing a festival, held during the cold winter of 1511, when 46 ice sculptures, some on mythological themes others with a folkloristic background, decorated the streets and squares of Brussels; P. De Ridder, 'De mythe van de vroege verfransing: taalgebruik in Brussel van de 12e eeuw tot 1794' (181–212), on the alleged frenchification of Brussels. De Ridder arrives at the conclusion that French language and culture were held in high esteem but they only served as a thin varnish on top of a basically Dutch foundation. In the concluding chapter D. Coigneau, 'Van de *Bliscappen* tot Cammaert: vier eeuwen toneelliteratuur in Brussel' (213–33), returns to the town's theatrical heritage, stretching from the famous cycle of seven plays on the Joys of Our Lady, dating back to the mid-15th c., to the much more modest products of 17th-c. and 18th-c. playwrights who no longer received the generous support of the nobility and the town's magistrates which the 16th-c. rhetoricians had enjoyed.

Werner Waterschoot, *Schouwende fantasye: Opstellen* (Studia Germanica Gandensia Libri, 2), Ghent, Academia, 2002, iv + 275 pp., is a selection of articles previously published by one of the leading scholars on the poetry of the Rhetoricians. Authors studied in these essays include Anthonis de Roovere, Lucas d'Heere, J. B. Houwaert, and Jan van der Noot.

Symon Andriessoon, *Duytsche Adagia ofte Spreecwoorden: Antwerp, Heynrick Alssens, 1550: In Facsimile, Transcription of the Dutch Text and*

English Translation, ed. Mark A. Meadow and Anneke C. G. Fleurkens, Hilversum, Verloren, 334 pp., is a complete edition of a book published in 1550, listing hundreds of proverbs and verbal expressions current at the time. Most are accompanied with explanations by Andriessoon, giving the meaning of the proverb or expression of the day. Some are still in use in modern Dutch. The edition is preceded by introductory chapters: M. A. Meadow, 'A preface of proverbs' (7–8), and 'On sixteenth-century proverbs and proverb collections: a contextual introduction' (13–35); H. Roodenburg, 'Historical proverb scholarship in Flanders and the Netherlands' (9–12); S. A. C. Dudok Van Heel, 'Symon Andrieszn Bonijn (1565): an Amsterdam schoolmaster and notary' (37–50), on the author of the collection; and A. C. G. Fleurkens, 'The *Duytsche Adagia*: description and provenance' (51–55). The edition concludes with extensive word indices to the Dutch and English translations.

E. Hofman, *Het lied van Oranje en Nederland: Nieuw licht op het Wilhelmus en zijn dichters*, Kampen, Kok, 317 + [20] pp., researches the oldest versions of the strophic poem 'Wilhelmus van Nassoue', the Dutch national anthem. Hofman thinks the order in which the stanzas were originally written was distorted. A rearrangement was implemented so as to present the text as an acrostic poem. Hofman also establishes a link with the genre of scriptural poem, popular at the time of emerging Protestantism in the Netherlands. Impossible to avoid, of course, is the question of the poem's author. The author suggests the poem was a cooperative enterprise between William the Silent's army chaplain, Adriaen Saravia, who composed the original version, and Philips van Marnix van Sint-Aldegonde, who remodelled it resulting in the present-day version.

4. The Seventeenth Century

René van Stipriaan, *Het volle leven: Nederlandse literatuur en cultuur ten tijde van de Republiek (circa 1550–1800)*, Amsterdam, Prometheus, 2002, 351 pp., presents a richly illustrated history, aimed at a wide audience, of Dutch literature and culture between 1550 and 1800. The first chapter, on the 16th and early 17th cs, concentrates on the revolutionary era during which the Republic liberated itself from Spanish oppression. In 'Schrijvers en drukkers', Van Stipriaan discusses the position of authors and printers, among other topics focusing on the famous Antwerp 'Landjuweel' of 1561. In 'De kleine wereld' he describes the way in which men, poets in particular, saw the microcosmos of the surrounding world as a reflection of a wider macrocosmos. Further topics include explorations and distant territories, readers, buyers and collectors of books, and, finally, the dream of a better world ('Dromen van betere tijden'), a chapter in which the start of the Enlightenment period and the increasing influence of French culture on Dutch civilisation are discussed.

'Teeckenrijcke woorden' voor Henk Duits: Opstellen over literatuur, toneel, kunst en religie, meest uit de zestiende en zeventiende eeuw, ed. Fred de Bree, Marijke Spies, and Roel Zemel (Uitgaven Stichting Neerlandistiek VU, 38), Amsterdam, Stichting Neerlandistiek VU — Münster, Nodus, 2002, 289 pp., is a collection of essays in honour of Henk Duits, former lecturer at the Free University of Amsterdam. Riet Schenkeveld-Van der Dussen, *Vondel en 't vrouwelijke dier: Vondels visie op vrouwen en enkele aspecten van de receptie daarvan*, Utrecht Univ., Faculteit der Letteren, 2002, 31 pp., is the valedictory lecture by the former professor of historical Dutch literature at the University of Utrecht. In it she looks at the way the poet and playwright Joost van den Vondel approaches women by focusing on specific types; she pays attention to Badeloch as the typical spouse in *Gijsbrecht van Aemstel*, to Filopaie as the suffering mother in *Jeptha*, to female martyrs in the *Brieven der heilige maeghden* (rhyming letters to their friends, relatives, or acquaintances, e.g., Mary Magdalen to Saint John), and, among others, to the temptress Jempsar in *Joseph in Egypte*. It is this last-mentioned type in particular that dominates in Vondel's works, revealing the poet's rather hostile attitude towards women. S.-Van der D. argues that this remarkable aspect of his works may have been one of the reasons for the constant changes in appreciation the author was subject to over time. *In de boeken, met de geest: Vijftien studies van M. A. Schenkeveld-van der Dussen over vroegmoderne Nederlandse literatuur, uitgegeven bij haar afscheid als hoogleraar van de Universiteit Utrecht op 31 oktober 2002*, ed. A. J. Gelderblom et al., Amsterdam U.P., 2002, 312 pp., is a re-edition of 15 articles, mainly on 17th-c. literature, previously published by the same retiring professor of historical Dutch literature. Some of the areas represented in this collection are poetics and rhetoric, genre theory, and Classicist drama, as reflected in the works of Constantijn Huygens, Daniël Heinsius, Dirk Rafaëlsz Camphuysen, Pieter Corneliszoon Hooft, Joost van den Vondel, and Matthijs van de Merwede van Clootwijck, in addition to a number of female authors, such as Anna Roemersdochter Visscher, Aagje Deken, and A. L. G. Bosboom-Toussaint. The book ends with an extensive bibliography of S.-van der D.'s publications (287–301).

J. W. H. Konst, *Fortuna, Fatum en Providentia Dei in de Nederlandse tragedie, 1600–1720*, Hilversum, Verloren, 384 pp., focuses on the development of the connected complex of motifs of fate, fortune, and divine providence in Dutch tragedies written between 1600 and 1720. Pieter Moelans, *'En spreekt mij van geen sterven meer': Over de dood in het wereldlijke volkslied van de Zuidelijke Nederlanden (17de-18de eeuw)*, Leuven–Leusden, Acco, 171 pp., researches the way people handled death in the 17th and 18th cs, by focusing on secular songs in the Southern Netherlands. One of the observations in this monograph relates to the fact that death was often seen as a penalty for lustful people. A further area of study undertaken by M. is the change of attitude over time towards the death of animals. Another popular theme in these songs was the violent death of heroes and enemies.

In 1678, almost 82 years old, the poet Constantijn Huygens, one of the secretaries of the Princes of Orange, described his life in two long poems, composed in Latin, entitled *De vita propria sermonum inter liberos libri duo*, addressed to his children, four of whom were still alive. Constantijn Huygens, *Mijn leven verteld aan mijn kinderen: In twee boeken*, ed. Frans R. E. Blom (Nederlandse klassieken), 2 vols, Amsterdam, Prometheus–Bakker, vol. 1: *Inleiding, teksteditie en vertaling*, 191 + [34] pp., vol. 2: *Commentaar en annotatie*, 628 pp., is a new edition of this text, with a prose translation into modern Dutch. A much earlier rendering of a biographic account of events by the same poet and diplomat, then 23 years old, originally written in French, has also been given a new edition; the French text is accompanied by a translation into modern Dutch: Constantijn Huygens, *Journaal van de reis naar Venetië*, transl. and introd. Frans R. E. Blom (Nederlandse klassieken), Amsterdam, Prometheus–Bakker, 191 pp., narrates adventures during a voyage H. made in 1620, as part of a diplomatic mission, to Venice. In Strasbourg, the young man put his life at risk by climbing the cathedral's spire, almost getting killed during the descent. In 1651, H. wrote a long poem on building and rebuilding his luxurious country estate, *Hofwijck*. In a modern Dutch translation, Ton van Strien, Kees van der Leer, and Ad Leerintveld, *Hofwijck: Het gedicht en de buitenplaats van Constantijn Huygens*, Zutphen, Walburg, 2002, 160 pp., present a new edition.

Jacob Cats, *Verhalen uit de Trou-ringh*, ed. Johan Koppenol (Alfa), Amsterdam U.P., v + 135 pp., is an edition of a selection of rhymed stories from a famous collection entitled *'s Werelts begin, midden, eynde, besloten in den trou-ringh, met den proefsteen van den selven* (1637), the wedding ring or *Trou-ringh* as it is commonly referred to, by one of the most popular poets of the 17th c., Jacob Cats (1577–1660). Koppenol's edition includes five of these stories. The original work had them embedded in prose dialogues of the elderly widower Sophroniscus, a man who has certain reservations towards marriage, and a young man, eager to marry, Philogamus. The dialogues connected with the five selected stories put the narrated events in a didactic setting but Koppenol decided to omit these prose texts. The first story deals with the wedding of Adam and Eve (17–41), the so-called 'Gronthouwelick' or fundamental wedding. This is followed by an adaptation of a classic rhetorical exercise, a *controversia* by Seneca rhetor, entitled 'Twee verkracht, en beyde getrout' (43–59). Its remarkable contents read as follows: on the same day a man rapes two women. The legislation of the imaginary country where this happened gives women, victims of such a defiant act, the right to choose between marrying their attacker or having him beheaded. One of the girls chooses to marry him but the other wants him killed. Thanks to the rhetorical strength of the speech delivered by the perpetrator he is saved. Moreover, the vigour displayed by the girl who wanted the man's head, inspires a nobleman, present at the court case, to ask for her hand in matrimony. Hence the title of the story: 'Two raped and yet two married'. The next two stories deal with the miraculous love of Odatis and Zariadres, who fall in love by dreaming about one another, and with the daughter of Charlemagne, Emma, who, according to legend, fell in love with the emperor's scribe Eginard. The next story, 'Liefdes vossevel' (107–31), appeared in print for the first time in a later edition of the collection, published in 1658. It may have been based on a genuine event that happened shortly before Cats issued his first edition of 1637, the reason why he initially suppressed it. In The Hague, early one morning a certain Faes compromised a widow named Aletta by standing in her door opening, thus suggesting an amorous affair between the two. Eventually Aletta agrees to marry the man on the condition that he admits to having resorted to a trick. The final text in this edition consists of the dedicatory poem Cats wrote for his daughters Anna and Elisabeth, preceding his long 'Lofsangh op het geestelick houwelick van Godes sone', a poetic summary of stories taken from the Bible with which the *Trou-ringh* concluded.

Michiel de Swaen, *De gekroonde laars: Een vastenavondspel*, ed. Hubert Meeus (Griffioen), Amsterdam, Athenaeum-Polak & Van Gennep, 108 pp., is a translation into modern Dutch of the best-known play by an author who lived and worked in Dunkirk, a town still within the Dutch language border during the years of De Swaen's life (1654–1707). In his postface to the edition Meeus pays attention to De Swaen's biography, the structure of his plays and the genre of the shrovetide play to which it belongs.

Inger Leemans, *Het woord is aan de onderkant: Radicale ideeën in Nederlandse pornografische romans 1670–1700*, [Nijmegen], Vantilt, 2002, 411 + [32] pp., studies ten late-17th-c. pornographic novels, a new genre in Dutch literature introduced in 1670. Apart from juicy stories these novels also present serious criticism of a hypocritical society and certain individuals and institutions in it. The philosophical background of a number of these books is Cartesian or Spinozian. After the the turn of the century, this type of novel was replaced by the less subversive genre of the moralistic novel.

Wat wonders, wat nieuws!: De zeventiende eeuw in pamfletten, ed. Marijke Meijer Drees and Els Stronks (Griffioen), Amsterdam, Athenaeum-Polak & Van Gennep, 2002, 143 pp., gives modern translations of a number of pamphlets published during the 17th c. In the oldest text, dating back to 1598, Anna Uitenhove, a Protestant woman who was buried alive, addresses the reader in a fictitious speech in which she openly attacks the Roman Catholic Inquisition. The last pamphlet, published in 1704, is a poem in which the Stadtholder-minded government is criticized. Despite their political intent many pamphlets of the time, instead of being presented as treatises, were given literary formats. Their distribution was not only in the hands of booksellers but also of pedlars, travelling from one fair to the other, who played an important role in spreading information as well. In their afterword the editors also give a brief summary of the political developments in the Dutch Republic over the 17th c.

De Kaap: Goede Hoop halverwege Indië: Bloemlezing van Kaapteksten uit de Compagniestijd, ed. Marijke Barend-Van Haeften and Bert Paasman, Hilversum, Verloren, 192 pp., presents a selection of text fragments dealing with the Cape of Good Hope, where Dutch ships on their way to the East Indies took in fresh water, vegetables, and other food. Some fragments are by colonists who settled there permanently, one text was even written by someone, Jodocus Hondius, who never visited the area. The time span covered in this edition is between 1595, when the first Dutch expedition under Cornelis Houtman sailed to the East, and 1803 when, for a couple of years only, the Cape was returned to the Dutch, after it had been in English hands since 1795. *De wereld van Hendrik Hamel: Nederland en Korea in de zeventiende eeuw*, ed. Vibeke Roeper and Boudewijn Walraven, Amsterdam, SUN, 192 pp., presents the text of an account by one of 38 fortunate shipwrecked sailors who, in 1653, reached the coast of Korea on a boat made out of the wreckage of their ship, the 'Sperwer', on its way from Taiwan to Nagasaki. After having been imprisoned there for 13 years, eight of them managed to escape to Japan. One of them, Hendrick Hamel (1630–92), wrote an account of the events, describing the country, the rulers of which did not want to have any contact with the rest of the world, the reason why they did everything to prevent the Dutch from fleeing. The edition, translated into modern Dutch, is accompanied by four essays: Leonard Blussé reflects on similar discoveries made by employees of the Dutch East Indies Company on their journeys to the East; Boudewijn Walraven elaborates on the little information on Korea available at the time; W. J. Boot looks at Hendrick Hamel's return to Japan in 1666 and how he composed his account; Vibeke Roeper concentrates on the crew of the 'Sperwer'. In an appendix are included some notes on Korea by Nicolaas Witsen, written in 1705. The book has also been published in English as *Hamel's World. A Dutch-Korean Encounter in the Seventeenth Century*, ed. Vibeke Roeper and Boudewijn Walraven, trans. Jean-Paul Buys et al., Amsterdam, SUN, 192 pp. A second edition of the same text, also in modern translation, is Hendrick Hamel, *Het journaal van Hendrick Hamel: De verbazingwekkende lotgevallen van Hendrick Hamel en andere schipbreukelingen van het VOC-schip de Sperwer in Korea (1653–1666)*, ed. Henny Savenije, Rotterdam, Donker, 168 pp., with H.'s biography and a description of his native town of Gorinchem by Rien Robijns.

5. The Eighteenth Century

André Hanou, *Verlicht Amsterdam* (Marollenreeks, 2), Leuth, Astraea, 34 pp., is the text of a valedictory lecture by a former lecturer at the University of Amsterdam, now appointed professor at the University of Nijmegen. H. concentrates on Amsterdam in the 18th c. as reflected in literary texts of the time by authors such as Betje Wolff (1738–1804) and Aagje Deken (1741–1804), Pieter Langendijk (1683–1756), Justus van Effen (1684–1735), Jacob Campo Weyerman (1677–1747), Jan van Gijsen (1668–1722), and Johan Christoph Ludeman (1683–1757). André Hanou, *Nederlandse literatuur van de Verlichting (1670–1830)*, [Nijmegen], Vantilt, 2002, 287 pp., mostly containing reprints of previously published essays, contains studies on authors who focus on the position of humankind in society: Cornelis de Bruijn, Jacob Campo Weyerman, Gerrit Paape, and Johannes Kinker. Further topics are the theatre, theory and practice of tolerance and freedom, and freemasonry. Further essays deal with the periodical *Janus* (1787) and the genre of imaginary travel stories.

Achter slot en grendel: Schrijvers in Nederlandse gevangenschap, 1700–1800, ed. Anna de Haas and Peter Altena, Zutphen, Walburg — [Amsterdam], Stichting Jacob Campo Weyerman, 2002, 255 pp., presents a collection of 20 essays on 18th-c. authors, all of whom spent some time in prison. Among the better known are Jacob Campo Weyerman, Pieter Boddaert Jr., and Franciscus Lievens Kersteman. The book's intention is to draw more attention to Dutch culture and literature of the 18th c., a time traditionally judged to belong to the least interesting periods of Dutch literature. Many of the authors discussed have been overlooked by later literary historians because of their social, political, religious, or ethical radicalism. Admittedly, not all were great literary geniuses.

P. J. H. M. Theeuwen, *Pieter 't Hoen en De Post van den Neder-Rhijn (1781–1787): Een bijdrage tot de kennis van de Nederlandse geschiedenis in het laatste kwart van de achttiende eeuw*, Hilversum, Verloren, 2002, 842 pp., takes us back to the late-18th-c. Patriot period during which a periodical, *De Post van den Neder-Rhijn*, tried to influence political views of Dutch citizens by proposing a democratic government. When, in 1787, the Orange party won a clear victory over the Patriots, the journal was banned. T. not only studies and analyses the essays published in it by concentrating on their social and political background, but he also devotes a great deal of attention to the biography of the author of the essays, Pieter 't Hoen.

Pieter van Woensel, *De lantaarn*, ed. André Hanou (Griffioen), Amsterdam, Athenaeum-Polak–Van Gennep, 2002, 164 pp., is an edition in modern Dutch of an anthology of texts published between 1792 and 1802 in *De lantaarn.* This almanac, four volumes of which appeared in print, was entirely filled with essays by Amurath-Effendi, Hekim-Bachi, pseudonym of Pieter van Woensel (1747–1808). From a political point of view Van Woensel was very critical of his time, judging by the titles of the essays such as 'Is mijn natie geschikt voor democratie?' (Is my country fit for democracy?). Van Woensel was an early advocate of birth control, advising the use of contraceptive methods yet still describing them in masked terms.

6. The Nineteenth Century

Rhetoricians had their finest days in the 15th and 16th cs but they continued to work, long after literary circles had turned their backs on them, until well into the 19th c. Oscar Westers, *Welsprekende burgers: Rederijkers in de negentiende eeuw*, [Nijmegen], Vantilt, 525 pp., concentrates on this late period in their history, when Rhetoricians focused on delivering eloquent speeches. More than 1,000 different chambers were active at the time. W. depicts the ideological foundations of these companies by studying their cultural, religious, and political positions. Though the art of eloquence was held in high esteem, representatives of 19th-c. official ('high') literature were reluctant to show any sign of appreciation for what these Rhetoricians stood for.

Dik van der Meulen, *Multatuli: Leven en werk van Eduard Douwes Dekker*, Nijmegen, SUN, 2002, 912 pp., is a much applauded biography of Multatuli, pseudonym of Eduard Douwes Dekker (1820–87), the author of *Max Havelaar* (1860). The book has three parts: 'Jeugd' (Youth) is mainly based on autobiographical elements in *Woutertje Pieterse*, a 'novel' reconstructed from Dekker's multi-volume collection, *Ideeën*; 'Indische jaren' (Life in the Dutch East Indies) deals with the traumatic events Dekker's experienced in the 1850s when he served as a deputy resident in the district of Lebak. Being an idealist rather than a civil servant, after having discovered his predecessor had been killed by the regent, the highest representative of the indigenous population, Dekker wanted to stop corruption in his district. The affair would eventually lead him to resign, hoping that he would be listened to and consequently reinstated in his former high position. When this did not happen, Dekker, disillusioned, returned to the Netherlands where he recounted his tribulations in a book named *Max Havelaar*. Part three, 'Schrijversjaren' (Creative Years), reviews Dekker's life as a writer of essays and of thousands of letters, revealing many details regarding his financial and marital problems, his addiction to gambling, and his complex personality. Even though Multatuli is one of the most widely studied 19th-c. Dutch authors, surprisingly enough Van der Meulen's book is the first complete biography.

Published as a book in 1867, Paaltjens's *Snikken en grimlachjes* were originally intended for his fellow students of theology at the University of Leiden. The collection brought the author great fame — Piet Paaltjes is pseudonym of François HaverSchmidt (1835–94) — but this did not prevent him from eventually committing suicide. Piet Paaltjens, *Snikken en grimlachjes: Academische poëzie*, ed. Marita Mathijsen and Dick Welsink (Delta), Amsterdam, Athenaeum-Polak & Van Gennep, 157 pp., presents a new edition of this collection of poems. In their afterword M. and W. present a coherent picture of HaverSchmidt's life and literary environment as well as a detailed analysis of the texts.

E. J. Potgieter, *Uit de nalatenschap van een dromer*, ed. Jan Oosterholt (Griffioen), Amsterdam, Athenaeum-Polak & Van Gennep, 136 pp., presents an anthology of shorter poems written by E. J. Potgieter (1808–75), co-founder of the famous periodical *De Gids* (1837 to the present day). As a poet, P., together with a number of his literary friends, attempted to modernize Dutch poetry. In his critical essays he refused to be superficial, proposing a thorough analysis of a work under scrutiny. O.'s edition is in modern spelling and with revised punctuation. It concludes with a brief impression of the reception P.'s works met over time. In a famous story, *Jan, Jannetje en hun jongste kind*, published in 1842 in *De Gids*, P. invented, among others, the now proverbial characters of 'Jan Salie', 'Jan Soldaat' and 'Jan Crediet', sons of a couple named Jan and Jannetje, 'Jan Salie' being the most miserable of all. Nobody wants to get involved with him. Maartje Janse, *De geest van Jan Salie: Nederland in verval?* (Verloren verleden, 17),

Hilversum, Verloren, 2002, 95 pp., describes the background of this story and the atmosphere from which it emerged, during an era viewed as nothing compared to the powerful and grand 17th c. In 1842, the Netherlands were seen as politically insignificant and all ranks of society suffered the lack of their country's former greatness.

Jacob van Lennep, *De roos van Dekama: Een verhaal*, ed. Joke van der Wiel (Delta), Amsterdam, Athenaeum-Polak & Van Gennep, 632 pp., is a new edition of a historical novel, initially published in 1836, by Jacob van Lennep (1802–68). Set against the historical context of a mid-14th-c. expedition by Count Willem IV against Frisian rebels, the novel narrates the love of two knights for Madzy Dekama, or the Rose of Dekama, a Frisian girl of noble birth. Van der Wiel supplies her readers with an extensive afterword in which she pays attention to Van Lennep's other historical novels, to the different versions of the text, its historical precision, and the novel's 19th-c. reception.

The general idea historians hold about early-19th-c. theatrical life of Amsterdam is that, after the period of the French occupation, a bourgeois, well-informed, and erudite audience was replaced by a public consisting of ordinary people. As a consequence, the repertoire was adjusted to the taste of the new theatregoer. According to 19th-c. and 20th-c. critics, the Amsterdam 'Schouwburg' would eventually suffer a serious devaluation in literary and aesthetic quality as a result. Henny Ruitenbeek, *Kijkcijfers: De Amsterdamse Schouwburg 1814–1841*, Hilversum, Verloren, 2002, 526 pp., researches whether this impression is based on fact or fiction. After having studied the type of plays performed, the audiences they drew, and the reasons why critics disapproved of what they saw in the theatre, R. comes to the conclusion that the negative attitude towards the achievements of the new theatre makers was mainly expressed by critics from one particular political and religious background, the antirevolutionaries.

Guido Gezelle, *Poëzie en proza*, ed. P. Couttenier and A. De Vos (Delta), Amsterdam, Bakker, 2002, 536 pp., is an anthology from the works of the most important Flemish poet of the 19th c. G. was also active as a translator and his translation of 'The song of Hiawatha' is included. Romain Vanlandschoot, *Albrecht Rodenbach: Biografie*, Tielt, Lannoo, 2002, 758 pp., wrote a biography of one of Gezelle's pupils, the poet and playwright Rodenbach who died in 1880 at the tender age of 23. Rodenbach's influence on the emerging Flemish Movement has been widely acknowledged.

7. 1880 TO 1945

Mathijs P. J. Sanders, *Het spiegelend venster: Katholieken in de Nederlandse literatuur 1870–1940*, [Nijmegen], Vantilt, 2002, 405 pp., studies the contributions Roman Catholic authors made to Dutch literature between 1870 and 1940. The central topic of Helleke van den Braber, *Geven om te krijgen: Literair mecenaat in Nederland tussen 1900 en 1940*, [Nijmegen], Vantilt, 2002, 411 pp., is literary patronage during the first four decades of the 20th c. The author attempts to answer four questions: what types of patronage can be identified? What did the phenomenon of patronage do to the patrons themselves, to the authors and to literary production? What is the relationship, if any, between patronage and processes of competition and co-operation in literary circles? What circumstances — literary, political, and social — influenced the growth of patronage during the period under scrutiny? Two patrons in particular are concentrated upon, Frans Mijnssen (1872–1954) and Matthieu René Radermacher Schorer (1888–1956). In 1905, a special fund (the 'Ondersteuningsfonds van de Vereeniging van Letterkundigen') was established to support authors financially as well as in kind.

Harry G. M. Prick, *Een vreemdeling op de wegen: Het leven van Lodewijk van Deyssel vanaf 1890*, Amsterdam, Athenaeum-Polak & Van Gennep, 1430 pp., is the sequel to *In de zekerheid van eigen heerlijkheid*, the first part of a comprehensive biography of Lodewijk van Deyssel, pseudonym of Karel Alberdingk Thijm (see *YWMLS*, 59:871). Since Van Deyssel no longer lived in Amsterdam (in 1889, he moved to Bergen op Zoom and from there to Baarn) he was forced to maintain his literary contacts by correspondence. In 1918, he divorced his wife. After his naturalistic period, Van Deyssel moved into the direction of a lyrical-realistic style. He also published books on his father J. A. Alberdingk Thijm and on Multatuli. Apart from fictional prose texts, such as *De Adriaantjes* (1902) and *Uit het leven van Frank Rozelaar* (1911), Van Deyssel published his *Gedenkschriften* (1924), memoirs, and a large number of critical reviews. In 1935, the University of Amsterdam acknowledged the great value of these reviews by granting him an honorary doctorate. Van Deyssel died in 1952.

One of Van Deyssel's contemporaries, Louis Couperus, was one of the most prolific authors of his time. Ineke Sluiter, *Hoogmoed en ironie: Couperus' Xerxes* (Couperus cahier, 7), The Hague, Louis Couperus Genootschap, 2002, 44 pp., concentrates on the sources C. used for his novel *Xerxes* (1919). S. denies that the author followed Herodotus too slavishly, seeing rather a distinct irony added to the account of the Greek historian, thus picturing Xerxes as an immature and a haughty character. Marco Goud, *Ziende verbeelding: Over zien en (on)zichtbaarheid in poëzie en poëtica van P. C. Boutens*, [Leuven, Peeters], viii + 384 pp., studies the theme of vision and (in)visibility in P. C. Boutens's (1870–1943) poetic works. G. mainly limits his observations to five poems by analysing them in great detail. In addition, B.'s symbolist poetry is compared with the ideas of fellow poets and artists such as Maurice Maeterlinck and Jan Toorop.

Rob Delvigne and Leo Ross, *Een uitmuntend letterkundig kunstenaar: Opstellen over Jacob Israël de Haan*, Assen, Servo, 2002, 147 pp., is a collection of previously published essays on the question how literary critics have judged the personality of Jacob Israël de Haan (1881–1924), author of a semi-pornographic novel, *Pijpelijntjes* (1904). According to D. and R., many misconceptions related to De Haan distort an honest view of the man and his works.

Avant-garde! Voorhoede?: Vernieuwingsbewegingen in Noord en Zuid opnieuw beschouwd, ed. Hubert F. van den Berg and Gillis J. Dorleijn, [Nijmegen], Vantilt, 2002, 254 pp., unites 12 essays on the topic of modernist and avant-garde movements in early-20th-c. Dutch and Flemish literature, alternatively labelled futurist, cubist, constructivist, surrealist, dadaist, and expressionist. A. H. den Boef and S. van Faassen discuss the contacts the Groningen 'Kunstkring De Ploeg' maintained with Antwerp constructivists; J. Poot concentrates on Hendrik Werkman, and W. Fähnders on the relations Dutch and Flemish avant-gardist authors entertained with Germany and the periodical *Der Sturm*; K. Humbeeck focuses on the periodicals *Staatsgevaarlik* and *De Nieuwe Wereldorde*; H. F. van den Berg looks at Dadaism, and M. G. Kemperink at mathematics in the works of Theo van Doesburg; G. J. Dorleijn discusses the overwhelming Dutch dislike of historical avant-garde movements.

One of the best-known and best-loved Flemish avant-garde poets is Paul van Ostaijen (1896–1928). Jef Bogman, *Professoren hier is de laatste gnostieker: Paul van Ostaijen tussen schilderkunst en mystiek*, [Nijmegen], Vantilt, 2002, 174 pp., stresses the importance of shape and colour in the text of Van Ostaijen's posthumously published cycle of poems, 'Feesten van angst en pijn', written in Berlin between 1918 and 1922. In addition to interpreting this cycle from the biographical background of Van Ostaijen's life in exile in Berlin, B. pays special attention to the delicate borderline between the subject expressing himself in these poems and the author himself. Van Ostaijen was not the only Flemish or Dutch writer or artist in Berlin after the Great War, a town where many of them lived for longer periods. August Hans den Boef and Sjoerd van Faassen, *'Verrek, waar is Berlijn gebleven?': Nederlandse schrijvers en hun kunstbroeders in Berlijn 1918–1945* (Schrijversprentenboek, 47), Amsterdam, Bas Lubberhuizen — The Hague, Letterkundig Museum, 2002, 245 pp., give an impression of their lives and what life was like in this metropolis between the Wars by looking at diaries, letters, and other documents related to various Dutch poets and artists. Among them are Herman Gorter, Henriëtte

Roland Holst-Van der Schalk, Hendrik Marsman, Theo van Doesburg, and Paul Citroen.

Anny E. M. Albers, *Betreft Bint: 'Bint' van Bordewijk modernistisch bekeken*, p.p., 2002, 233 pp., studies Ferdinand Bordewijk's short novel *Bint*, written in 1934, from a modernist point of view. Bint, the main character in this functionalist story, is the name of the headmaster of a secondary school where discipline rules the roost. One group of pupils, gathered together in a classroom, seems refractory but when, after the suicide of a pupil of a different group, the school starts a revolt against Bint, it is this particular group of seemingly unmanageable pupils that restores law and order. Huib G. van den Doel, *Maar dat is tot daaraan toe: Benaderingen van gedichtenuitleg toegepast op 'Het uur U' van Martinus Nijhoff*, Haarlem, Stichting Hoofd-Hart-Handen, 2002, 119 pp., gives a summary of interpretations by various authors of one of Nijhoff's most famous poems, 'Het Uur U' (1936, revised in 1941). Van den Doel attempts a new interpretation in a line-by-line analysis of the two versions of the poem, from the point of view of the interaction between observer and observed objects. The critic is in favour of a subjective approach to poetry, so as to be able to acknowledge the importance of the creativity of the reader rather than exclusively concentrating on the creativity of the poet.

Jan van der Vegt, *Zes winters aan zee: Liefde en rekenschap bij A. Roland Holst: Over inhoud, ontstaan en compositie van de bundel 'Een winter aan zee'*, Baarn, Prom, 2002, 126 pp., discusses a collection of poems the 'Prince of Dutch Poets', Adriaan Roland Holst (1888–1976) published in 1937. Roland Holst had been working on them for six years. The volume comprises 63 poems, each having eight lines and based on the same rhyme scheme. In them the poet gives an account of how he managed to say farewell to a certain woman who had played an important role in his life. Van der Vegt describes the genesis of *Een winter aan zee* and analyses the text. Many poems testify to Roland Holst's emotional engagement with nature.

A. L. Sötemann, *Dichters die nog maar namen lijken*, Amsterdam, Meulenhoff — Rekkem, Stichting Ons Erfdeel, 213 pp., is a posthumously published collection of essays by the former professor of modern Dutch literature at the University of Utrecht, all previously printed in the periodical *Ons erfdeel*. Even though some of the 12 poets S. writes about are still seen as important representatives of poetic expression of their times, most are seldom read nowadays. It is this S. would like to see changed. Among the poets discussed are Albert Verwey, P. C. Boutens, Henriëtte Roland Holst, Adriaan Roland Holst, Jan Engelman, Marnix Gijsen, and J. W. F. Werumeus Buning.

Schepelingen van De Blauwe Schuit: Brieven van Bertus Aafjes, K. Heeroma, M. Nijhoff, S Vestdijk en Hendrik de Vries aan F. R. A. Henkels, 1940–1946,

ed. Gillis Dorleijn, Sjoerd van Faassen, and Ageeth Heising (Achter het boek, 36), The Hague, Letterkundig Museum — Amsterdam, Lubberhuizen, 338 pp., presents an edition of letters between five poets and novelists and one of the leading men behind the clandestine presses of the 'Blauwe Schuit' series, active during the years of the German occupation.

8. 1945 TO THE PRESENT DAY

Arnold Heumakers, *De schaduw van de vooruitgang*, Amsterdam, Querido, 224 pp., concentrates on the way cultural criticism influences cultural perception. In line with Martin Heidegger's philosophical views, H. is very critical of cultural criticism, and illustrates his ideas by looking at Eduard du Perron whose individualism is seen as a type of cultural criticism. Further chapters deal with two autobiographical novels, one by Charlotte Mutsaers, *Rachels rokje* (1994), and one by Nicolaas Matsier, *Gesloten huis* (1995). *Het lied van Orpheus: De antieke hellevaart in de moderne Nederlandse literatuur*, ed. Rudi van der Paardt, Amsterdam, De Bezige Bij, 176 pp., focuses on the theme of a descent into hell, borrowed from Classical literature, as it occurs in modern Dutch literature.

Anneke Reitsma, *Het woord te vondeling: Een eeuw Nederlandse poëzie in zeventien portretten: Essays*, Amsterdam, De Prom, 2002, 277 pp., is a collection of 17 essays on various poets living between 1850 and the present. Apart from discussions on some of the best known poets in Belgium and the Netherlands, such as Guido Gezelle, Hélène Swarth, Jacqueline E. van der Waals, Henriëtte Roland Holst, J. C. Bloem, Hendrik Marsman, Martinus Nijhoff, Gerrit Achterberg, Ida Gerhardt, M. Vasalis, Hans Lodeizen, Judith Herzberg, C. O. Jellema, Gerrit Komrij, and Eva Gerlach, R. also pays attention to works by authors who are normally seen as writers of prose texts: Marcellus Emants, Gerard Reve, and Harry Mulisch.

Jos Joosten, *Onttachtiging: Essays over eigentijdse poëzie en poëziekritiek*, [Nijmegen], Vantilt, 320 pp., discusses current trends in modern poetry such as poetic conservatism without the distinct move away from the idealistic principles of the 19th-c. 'Tachtigers' movement. Authors criticized by J. include Leonard Nolens and Arnon Grunberg. Even J. C. Bloem, one of the most widely acclaimed post-War poets, is regarded as overrated by this critic. On the other hand, J. admires H. H. ter Balkt and, not surprisingly, Hugo Claus. The book has been given a theoretical foundation in an essay on the literary struggle for power as seen through the eyes of the cultural sociologist, Pierre Bourdieu. Further books on post-War poetry in general are Yvan De Maesschalck and Herman Henderickx, *Naakt en*

wit, een ademende steen: Thematische verkenning van de Nederlandse poëzie van na 1945 tot omstreeks 2000 (Literatuur in veelvoud, 16), Antwerp–Apeldoorn, Garant, 157 pp., and Thomas Vaessens and Jos Joosten, *Postmoderne poëzie in Nederland en Vlaanderen*, [Nijmegen], Vantilt, 271 pp.

H. U. Jessurun d'Oliveira, *Het gedicht als wereld: Essays over Lucebert, Leo Vroman en Rutger Kopland*, Amsterdam, Uitgeverij 521, 103 pp., focuses on three of the best known Dutch poets. Lucebert is one of the most important representatives of experimental poetry of the 'Vijftigers' period, whereas Vroman published his works during the same years yet without belonging to a distinctly identifiable group. Kopland is a leading poet from the post-'Vijftig' era. By profession, the last mentioned of the three, Rutger Kopland (pseudonym of R. H. van den Hoofdakker), is a biological psychiatrist. In *Twee ambachten: Over psychiatrie en poëzie*, Amsterdam, Van Oorschot, 197 pp., he reflects on the two sides of his life, his professional career as a scientist and his artistic 'hobby' as a poet. Seven essays in this book deal with the former, ten with the latter.

Nico Keuning, *Angst voor de winter: Het leven van Jan Arends*, Amsterdam, De Bezige Bij, 368 pp., is a biography — with a tendency to the hagiographical — of the poet Jan Arends (1925–74), who, during most of his life, suffered from mental depression. Mieke Koenen, *Stralend in gestrenge samenhang: Ida Gerhardt en de klassieke oudheid*, Groningen, Historische Uitgeverij, 2002, 286 pp., presents a biography of Ida Gerhardt, one of the most interesting female Dutch poets of the post-War period, focusing in particular on the role of Classical authors and antiquity in her works. K. has used recently discovered letters, notes, oral accounts by former pupils, and transcripts of lectures and talks. Classical authors whose impact on Gerhardt's poetry are discussed include Lucretius, Epicurus, Virgil, Homer, Sappho, Socrates, and Plato. Special attention is given to the poet Jan Hendrik Leopold, one of Gerhardt's teachers when she was a young student herself.

Tegen alle bloedvergieten en kanariepieten in: Hans Verhagen, dichter, filmer, schilder, ed. Daan Cartens et al. (Schrijversprentenboek, 48), Amsterdam, Nijgh & Van Ditmar — The Hague, Letterkundig Museum, is a catalogue published on the occasion of a retrospective exhibition on the poet, film maker, and painter, Hans Verhagen (1939–). In 1963, Verhagen published his first poetry collection, entitled *Rozen & motoren: 7 cyclussen naar nu*. He belongs to the first generation of poets emerging after the wave of 'Vijftigers', who turned their backs on the unintelligibility of the products of this movement. The catalogue contains four articles: one by fellow poet Hans Sleutelaar on Verhagen's poetry, one by Jan Mulder on his artwork, one by Hans

Keller (creator of television documentaries) on his personality, and one by Ilja Leonard Pfeijffer on his latest poems. In addition to this catalogue Bob Visser and others have also issued a DVD (113 min.) showing selections from Verhagen's work for television.

Freddy de Vree, *De aardigste man ter wereld: Willem Frederik Hermans*, Amsterdam, De Bezige Bij, 2002, 343 pp., describes his long friendship with W. F. Hermans (1921–95), one of the most important post-War novelists and essay writers in the Netherlands. Rather than giving a chronological account, De Vree builds his book around certain themes in Hermans's life and works, mostly based on tape-recorded interviews he conducted over many years. The first chapter, 'Parijs', concentrates on H.'s life in the French capital where he lived from 1973. Further chapters carry titles derived from the titles of some of H.'s books: 'Een heilige van de horlogerie' (1987), 'Ruisend gruis' (1995), 'De tranen der acacia's' (1949), 'Au pair' (1989), 'De God denkbaar' (1956), and 'Dood en weggeraakt' (1980). Arno van der Valk, *Hermans: Het grootste gelijk buiten Nederland*, Soesterberg, Aspekt, 2002, 224 pp., reprints six interviews with Hermans, translated into Dutch, originally published in foreign newspapers and journals from Norway, Sweden, Lebanon, Poland, Spain, and South Africa. Compared to his Dutch interviews, Hermans shows himself much milder in these talks and less critical towards the Netherlands. Ronald Havenaar, *Muizenhol: Nederland volgens Willem Frederik Hermans*, Amsterdam, Van Oorschot, 214 pp., tries to explain the rationale behind H.'s negative, at times even cynical attitude towards his home country. Topics addressed in this respect relate to moral issues, politics, language, literature, and the War. H. once referred to the Netherlands as a mousehole, hence the title of this book. *Uit de donkere kamer: Essays over en interpretaties van Hermans' Donkere kamer van Damokles*, ed. Arthur Kooyman, Utrecht, Alexandria, 2002, 126 pp., contains previously published essays by D. Betlem, Coen Bersma, G. J. P. van Hoeke and C. B. M. Wingen, A. Kooyman, and René Marres. All focus on one single question: how the motif of the look-alikes Osewoudt and Dorbeck functions in H.'s novel *De donkere kamer van Damokles* (1958). In this fascinating novel, set during World War II, a timid young man, Osewoudt, is believed to be the same person as Dorbeck who, at the beginning of the occupation, killed a German. The one and only proof Osewoudt hoped to be able produce of the real existence of Dorbeck, a photo with both men on it, went wrong. Is Dorbeck a figment of Osewoudt's imagination?

Chris de Zoeten, *Ander water: Een herlezing van Gerard Reve's De Avonden* (SNL-reeks, 10), Leiden, SNL [Stichting Neerlandistiek Leiden], 118 pp., pays special attention to the position of dreaming in Gerard Reve's anti-novel *De avonden* (1947). A further remarkable aspect of this dark story, so far insufficiently explained by critics and literary scholars, is its positive conclusion. De Zoeten is of the opinion that the novel is more soundly constructed than has been admitted so far. The main character's psychological development shows an evolution from inertia to movement.

Annie van den Oever, *'Fritzi' en het groteske*, Amsterdam, De Bezige Bij, 571 pp., concentrates on the grotesque in the works of F. ten Harmsen van der Beek, who is best known for her collection of poems, *Geachte Muizenpoot en achttien andere gedichten* (1972). Ute Langner, *Zwischen Politik und Kunst: Feministische Literatur in den Niederlanden, die siebziger Jahre* (Niederlande-Studien, 30), Münster, Waxmann, 2002, 281 pp., concentrates on feminist literature in the 1970s including observations on Anja Meulenbelt, Hannes Meinkema, Hella S. Haasse, Andreas Burnier, and Monika van Paemel.

Martien J. G. de Jong, *Een klauwende muze: De tussenwereld van Maurice Gilliams*, Ghent, KANTL, 2001, 138 pp., discusses aspects of Gilliams's life (1900–82) and works. De Jong studies the Flemish author's relationships with artists such as James Ensor and Henri de Braekeleer, and literary celebrities such as Karel van de Woestijne and Paul van Ostaijen. Georges Wildemeersch, *Vrome wensen: Over het literaire werk van Hugo Claus*, Amsterdam, De Bezige Bij, 206 pp., pays special attention to three works by the Flemish poet, playwright and novelist: his collection of poems *De Oostakkerse gedichten* (1955), his play *Vrijdag* (1969), and the novel *Het jaar van de kreeft* (1972). According to W., the three works share a common background in the influence detectable in them of the ideas of various psycho-analytic scientists. Gerard Walschap, *Brieven*, ed. Harold Polis, Bruno Walschap, and Carla Walschap, vols 2 and 3, Amsterdam, Nijgh & van Ditmar, 2002, 1027, 899 pp., are the final volumes in the edition of the complete correspondence (see *YWMLS*, 60 : 794) of the Flemish novelist Gerard Walschap (1898–1989), and cover the years 1951 to 1965 (vol. 2) and 1965 to 1989 (vol. 3). Apart from letters to his children these volumes also include letters to Frank Baur (1887–1969), Raymond Brulez (1895–1972), Ernest Claes (1885–1968), and Herman Teirlinck (1879–1967).

'Je bent een onmogelijk man!': De briefwisseling tussen Simon Vestdijk en Johan van der Woude, 1939–1969, ed. Tim Duyff (Achter het boek, 31), Amsterdam, Lubberhuizen, 225 pp., is the edition of the correspondence between Johan van der Woude (1906–79), a lesser-known novelist and writer of short stories, and Simon Vestdijk (1898–1971), one of the most successful authors of his day. Despite the fact that Van der Woude published no less than 53 books, he is nearly completely forgotten. His letters show a greater talent than most people would believe him to have had. *Vervolg je weg en laat de lui maar*

dazen!: Theun de Vries, getuige van een eeuw, ed. Daan Cartens and Muriël Steegstra (Schrijversprentenboek, 49), Amsterdam, Querido — The Hague, Letterkundig Museum, 182 pp., was published to accompany an exhibition in the Hague held in honour of the novelist Theun de Vries (1907–). Chapters in the book present a survey of his life and works, an essay on a debate, held in literary circles of the 1930s, on the low international level of Dutch literature, and four essays on particular novels by De Vries.

Onno-Sven Tromp, *Labyrintische genoegens: Een literaire wandeling door het Amsterdam van A. F. Th. van der Heijden*, Amsterdam, Lubberhuizen, 2002, 96 pp., is a literary guide for those who want to explore Amsterdam through the eyes of A. F. Th. van der Heijden (1951–). The author's cycle of novels *De tandeloze tijd* is almost entirely set in Amsterdam. Tromp offers three different tours of the town passing locations where Van der Heyden's heroes lived their adventures.

III. DANISH STUDIES*

LANGUAGE

By Tom Lundskær-Nielsen, *Senior Lecturer in Danish, Department of Scandinavian Studies, University College London*

1. General

**Oversigt over dansksystemet — kortlægning af danskfaget i alle uddannelsesniveauer* (Uddannelsesstyrelsens temehæfteserie, 2), Undervisningsministeriet, 302 pp., formed the basis for a discussion of the future of the teaching of Danish in Denmark in **Fremtidens danskfag — en diskussion af danskfaglighed og et bud på dens fremtid* (Uddannelsesstyrelsens temehæfteserie, 1), Undervisningsministeriet, 338 pp., which contains discussions of the principles for the study of Danish in the future and a number of suggestions for innovation in the teaching of Danish at different levels. The retirement of Professor Erik Hansen, after many years as Chairman of the Danish Language Council (Dansk Sprognævn) is mentioned, and his achievements in that role celebrated, in *Nyt fra Sprognævnet*, 2001.3, but he himself sums up his career as a linguist in E. Hansen, 'Mit liv som sprogmand', *Nyt fra Sprognævnet*, no. 1:2–10.

Sprog & Samfund contains two short articles on the influence, if any, of literature on language: E. Hansen, 'Litteraturen og sproget', 21.1:6–7, and S. Sørensen, 'Litteraturen og sproget', 21.2:11, plus a rejoinder from E. Hansen, 'Svar', 21.2:11. A proposal for a language policy for Danish is found in **Sprog på spil — et udspil til en dansk sprogpolitik*, Kulturministeriet, 70 pp., and in a presentation by the Danish Language Council, 'Dansk Sprognævns forslag til retningslinjer for en dansk sprogpolitik', *Nyt fra Sprognævnet*, no. 2:1–5, which is an edited version of the proposal submitted to the Danish Parliament. This topic is picked up by R. Phillipson, 'Behovet for en mere aktiv sprogpolitik', *Sprog & Samfund*, 21.1:9–10, and to a lesser degree by H. F. Kragh, 'Jeres høvle bliver sløve', *ib.*, 12, and P. Højholt, 'Skyd virkeligheden!', *ib.*, 13–15. A much more substantial contribution to this discussion is Jørn Lund, **Den sproglige dagsorden. Dansk sprogpolitik i perspektiv*, Gyldendal, 136 pp.

A recurring topic in later years has been the establishment of new rules for using commas in Danish, known as the 'new comma', which formed an alternative (recommended by the Language Council) to

* The place of publication of books is Copenhagen unless otherwise stated.

the 'traditional comma'. The attempt to promote the 'new comma' has now been abandoned, mainly because so few public media were willing to use it, and instead a unified system (albeit with one optional area) has been adopted. Articles about this development include a brief summing-up of the current position by the new Chairman of the Language Council in N. Davidsen-Nielsen, 'Ændrede kommaregler', *Nyt fra Sprognævnet*, no. 4:1–2, and H. Galberg Jacobsen, 'Det nye kommas "fald"', *Sprog & Samfund*, 21.4:9.

Hans Arndt, **Sproget. Hverdagens mirakel*, Aarhus U.P., 304 pp., examines language in general, including structure, use, sounds, writing, words, sentences, and utterances, and touches on its history and the scientific study of language. *Take Danish — for instance*, ed. Henrik Galberg Jacobsen et al., U.P. of Southern Denmark, 314 pp., is a *Festschrift* in honour of the eminent Danish phonetician Hans Basbøll which includes the following contributions: L. Brink, 'En upåagtet tonal kommutation i dansk' (9–15); J. Durand, 'The vowel system of Danish and phonological theory' (41–57); E. Engberg-Pedersen, 'Udtryk for perspektivskift i døve børns fortællinger på tegnsprog' (59–73); G. Fellows-Jensen, 'Thingland and Fingland: the Danish tongue in contact with French, English and Gaelic' (75–82); M. Fortescue, 'Some thoughts on the functionality of *stød* and the acquisition of Danish' (99–105); F. Gregersen, 'Some notes on historicity' (107–14); K. Gregersen, 'Et essay om stødets (u)nødvendighed. Brudstykker af en udtalelærers dagbog' (115–17); N. Grønnum, 'Why are Danes so hard to understand?' (119–30); E. Hansen, 'Nominale tidsadverbialer' (131–36); P. Harder, 'Produktivitet, kognition og strukturel lingvistik' (137–47); M. Herslund, 'Remarks on the Danish *stød*' (149–57); B. Le Fevre Jakobsen, 'Aspekter af en Functional Grammar-analyse af satelitter i moderne dansk som L_1. — Nogle kvalitative betragtninger' (159–71); P. Kihl, 'Some frequent phonological processes observed in Danish children with language impairment' (173–80); K. Kristensen, 'En lille test af lydskrift' (181–87); G. Laureys, 'The use of lexical databases and of corpora within bilingual lexicography. The case of the Dutch-Danish dictionary' (217–29); and J. Rischel, 'The Danish syllable as a national heritage' (273–81). **Kognitiv semiotik. En antologi om sprog, betydning og erkendelse*, ed. Peer Bundgård, Jesper Engholm, and Martin Skov, Haase, 638 pp., contains a number of articles (old and new) about the ability of human beings to understand and categorize their surrounding world and to express this in language. *Hermes*, 31, ed. H. Bergenholtz et al., has 'business communication' as its theme. Among its articles are: S. Vandermeeren, 'German language needs in Danish companies' (13–29), and K. Pedersen, 'The construction of a genre: the case of service information pamphlets in a Danish county' (31–45).

2. History of the Language, Phonology, Morphology, Lexis, Syntax, Semantics, and Pragmatics

Vibeke Sandersen, **Jeg skriver dig til for at lade dig vide. Skrivefærdighed og skriftsprog hos menige danske soldater i treårskrigen 1848–50*, 2 vols, Reitzel, 986 pp., is a doctoral thesis, analysing the language of ordinary private soldiers through their letters from the frontline in the middle of the 19th century. Henrik R. Wulff, **Lægevidenskabens sprog — fra Hippokrates til vor tid*, Munksgaard, 194 pp., is a description of medical language from ancient Greece to modern times, with an analysis of present usage and a look towards the future. **Rigtigt kort. Anbefalede forkortelser*, ed. Jørgen Nørby Jensen and Marianne Rathje (Dansk Sprognævns skrifter, 30), Gyldendal, 120 pp. J. N. Jensen and M. Rathje, 'Rigtigt kort', *Nyt fra Sprognævnet*, no. 4:3–6, is an article based on this book. Andrzej Szubert, *Englische Entlehnungen im Dänischen. Morphologie und Wortbildung*, Poznań, ad rem, 108 pp. M. Cristofoli and L. Stage, 'DET BLEV EN MUS. Fraseologismer i dansk, fransk og italiensk', *Sprint*, no. 2:19–56. E. Hansen, 'Jammen altså . . .', *Sprog & Samfund*, 21.3:3. B. Pedersbæk, 'Ordet racisme', *ib.*, 7, and concerning the same word, E. Hansen, 'Højeste ret og rimelighed', *ib.*, 21.4:8.

3. Dialectology, Contrastive Linguistics, Bilingualism, and Applied Linguistics

Ord & Sag, 23, contains the following articles: O. Rasmussen, 'Gærde — ord & sag' (4–8); T. Arboe, 'Om haspetræer og andre garnvinder' (9–20); I.S. Hansen, 'Dialekt på skrift — Jens Thises vendelbomål' (21–31); and N. K. Grøftehauge and V. Sørensen, 'Jamen, så lad os gå halvt om det' (32–39). I. Carlsen, 'Længe leve dialekter', *Sprog & Samfund*, 21.1:10–11. I. L. Pedersen, 'Traditional dialects of Danish and the de-dialectalization 1900–2000', *IJSL*, 159:9–28. K. M. Pedersen, 'Et nordisk sprog uden for Norden — dansk i Sydslesvig', *Sprog i Norden*, 7–25, and Id., 'Sydslesvisk — et dansk mindretalssprog', *Nyt fra Sprognævnet*, no. 3:4–10.

A few articles deal with the influence of English on Danish: M. H. Andersen, 'Fra ungdomssprog til Sprognævn. Om holdninger til brugen af engelske lån i dansk', *Nyt fra Sprognævnet*, no. 1:11–15; A. Hamburger, 'Kamuflerede ord fra engelsk', *ib.*, no. 4:10–13; and K. B. Olsen, 'Om bøjning af engelske ord i dansk', *ib.*, no. 2:6–11.

J. S. Arnfast and J. N. Jørgensen, 'Code-switching as a communication, learning, and social negotiation strategy in first-year learners of Danish', *International Journal of Applied Linguistics*, 13:23–53. R. Brodersen, 'Analyse af leksikalsk og fonetisk akkomodation. Et ph.d-projekt om sprogbrug, sproglig akkomodation og sprogholdninger blandt danskere i Norge', Akselberg, *Dialektologi*, 263–77. Id., 'Purismen i Danmark — en succes?', pp. 111–46 of **Purt og reint. Om purisme i dei nordiske språka*, ed. Randi Brodersen, Helge Sandøy, and H. Brunstad (Skrifter frå Ivar Aasen-instituttet, 15), Volda, 237 pp. A. Jensen, 'Ordene mange og meget. Et par eksempler på ordgeografi i nordisk perspektiv', Akselberg, *Dialektologi*, 359–73. T. Kristiansen, 'Danish', pp. 69–91 of **Germanic Standardizations. Past to Present*, ed. Ana Deumert and Wim Vandenbussche, Amsterdam–Philadelphia, Benjamins, 480 pp. Id., 'Language attitudes and language politics in Denmark', *IJSL*, 159:57–71. Id., 'Reflektioner omkring sprogvidenskabens rolle og muligheder i sprognormeringsspørgsmålet — med Danmark som eksempel', pp. 155–64 of **Krefter og motkrefter i språknormeringa. Om språknormer i teori og praksis*, ed. Helge Omdal and Rune Røsstad, Kristiansand, Høyskoleforlaget, 305 pp. Id., 'Sproglig regionalisering', Akselberg, *Dialektologi*, 115–49. J. N. Jørgensen and T. Kristiansen, 'The sociolinguistics of Danish', *IJSL*, 159:1–7. I. L. Pedersen, 'Da danskerne lærte bilen at kende. Et causeri om hjemlige og fremmede ord i fortid og nutid', pp. 9–14 of **Med 'bil' i Norden i 100 år. Ordlaging og tilpassing av utlandske ord*, Oslo, Novus, 153 pp. P. Quist and J. S. Møller, 'Research on youth and language in Denmark', *IJSL*, 159:45–55.

Veje til dansk — forskning i sprog og sprogtilegnelse, ed. Anne Holmen, Esther Glahn, and Hanne Ruus, Akademisk, 248 pp., contains the following articles: N. Grønnum, 'Dansk intonation' (15–38); N. M. Andersen, 'Det forstår jeg ikke — om det fremmede ord i fremmedsprogsperspektiv' (39–53); J. S. Arnfast and J. N. Jørgensen, '[ˈjærmə ˈgåd mæn ˈu:ð ˈbæsd] — om udviklingen af dansk udtalefærdighed hos unge med henholdsvis tyrkisk, amerikansk-engelsk og polsk modersmål' (55–90); D. Duncker, 'Børnenes ord — om det danske ordforråd hos børn med dansk og tyrkisk som modersmål' (91–124); E. Glahn, 'Hvem fører ordet? — om initiativ-respons-analyse af indfødte og ikke-indfødte samtaler' (125–40); C. E. Brouwer, 'Hvad???' — om opfordringer til gentagelse i NS-NNS-samtaler' (141–68); A. Hauksdóttir, 'Dansk som fremmedsprog i Island — tradition og nytænkning' (169–218); P. V. Vedel, 'På sporet af en andetsprogspædagogik — en undersøgelse af metodeudviklingen i dansk som andetsprog' (219–44).

4. Lexicography, Grammars, Stylistics, and Rhetoric

A number of dictionaries have appeared. The most significant one is the first of six volumes of **Den Danske Ordbog*, 1, ed. Ebba Hjort et al. (Det Danske Sprog- og Litteraturselskab), Gyldendal, 752 pp. Among the others are **Gads stribede italiensk-dansk, dansk-italiensk small*, ed. Flemming Forsberg and Olivia Schmitt Jensen, Gad, 774 pp.; **Gads stribede kombi dansk-engelsk, engelsk-dansk*, ed. Eva Jørgensen, Gad, 1064 pp.; **Ordbog for social- og sundhedsuddannelserne*, Munksgaard, 123 pp.; **Ordbog over ismer*, ed. Bodil Kjær, Sesam, 144 pp.; **Spansk-dansk erhvervsordbog*, ed. Anna-Lis Laursen, Virginia Hvid, and Sven Tarp, Gad, 435 pp.; **Politikens tyskordbog*, Politiken, 846 pp. + CD-ROM; **Dansk-fransk, fransk-dansk ordbog*, ed. Niels Christian Sørensen, Gyldendals elektroniske ordbøger; **Juridisk Ordbog*, ed. Dorthe Christensen and Thomas Fich, Gad, 350 pp. + CD-ROM.

Niels Holck, **Sprogets univers*, Alinea, 388 pp., is a substantial handbook on Danish language, which is divided into three parts: Language and Function; Language and Structure; Language and Pedagogics. Knud Paasch Almar, **Grammatik på dansk — adgang til fremmedsprog*, Roskilde U.P., 139 pp. Ole Togeby, *Fungerer denne sætning? Funktionel dansk sproglære*, Gad, 365 pp., is a functional description of Danish in areas such as morphology, syntax, semantics, text-linguistics, and the function of language in communication (for a previous version see *YWMLS*, 63:811). Hélène Wagn, *Skeletter i skabet*, Politiken, 80 pp., is a book about Danish idioms. *Samtalen på arbejde — konversationsanalyse og kompetenceudvikling*, ed. Birte Asmuss and Jakob Steensig, Samfundslitteratur, 358 pp. Pia Hardy and Kåre Thomsen, *Skriv korrekt*, Gad, 68 pp.; Id., *Skriv og bliv forstået*, Gad, 72 pp.; and Id., *Sæt nyt komma*, Gad, 62 pp. K. Kjøller, *Aschehougs store bog om at holde tale*, Gyldendal, 346 pp.

5. Onomastics

Navnet er trofast (Modersmål-Selskabets årbog), C. A. Reitzel, 183 pp. The yearbook is this time devoted to names and contains the following contributions: E. V. Meldgaard, 'Hvad hedder barnet og hvorfor?' (11–24), and Id., 'Dyrenavne i Danmark' (43–53); B. Jørgensen, 'Du danske navn' (25–32); G. Søndergaard, 'Om højtidelige og uhøjtidelige personnavne' (33–42); J. Jørgensen, 'Danske navne på insekter og andre hvirvelløse dyr' (55–67); J. Schack, 'Lægemiddelnavne' (69–79); K. Rifbjerg, 'Hvad ligger der i et navn?' (97–101); K. M. Pedersen, 'Navne i Sønderjylland' (111–22); S. Novrup, 'Øgenavne i Kerteminde — ikke kun folkevid'

(123–36); G. Leffers, 'Reersøs marknavne' (137–47); S. Pind, 'Vejen til navnet' (149–59); and A. J. Hermann, 'Huse med sjæl og identitet i Gladsaxe Kommune' (161–83). J. Schack, 'Anbefalede Plantenavne', *Nyt fra Sprognævnet*, no. 3 : 1–4.

NORNA-rapporter, 76, 'Nordiske torp-navne', ed. P. Gammeltoft and Bent Jørgensen, contains a number of articles on place-names ending in *-torp*: G. Fellows-Jensen, 'Torp-navne i Norfolk i sammenligning med torp-navne i andre dele af Danelagen' (47–59); P. Gammeltoft, 'Stednavne på -torp i Sydvestjylland' (61–78); B. Holmberg, 'Sakrale torp-navne i Danmark?' (109–20); B. Jørgensen, 'Torpens størrelse og status. Hvordan kan en vikingetidig udflyttergård blive til 44 gårde i matriklen 1664?' (155–66); M. L. Nielsen, 'Sognekriteriets betydning for vurderingen af torp-navnenes alder' (177–202); Id., 'Fra Hellerup til Klattrup. En præsentation af begrebet "nyere torpnavne"' (243–52); R. S. Olesen, 'Unge torp-navne i Danmark' (253–63); and B. Eggert, 'Torp-navne som skabelon for efternavneforslag' (265–74).

V. Dalberg, 'Navneforskning — del af sprogvidenskaben', pp. 127–33 of *Saga och Sed. Kungl. Gustav Adolfs akademiens årsbok, 2002. B. Holmberg, 'Gudarnas platser', *Namn och bygd: Tidskrift för nordisk ortnamnsforskning*, 91 : 35–57. B. Jørgensen, 'Sprog, tekst, udgave, navn', *Historisk Tidsskrift*, 103.1 : 195–215. M. L. Nielsen, 'Bornholms bebyggelsesnavne i Østersøperspektiv', *NORNA-rapporter*, 78 : 115–42.

LITERATURE

By Jens Lohfert Jørgensen, *Lecturer in Danish, Department of German and Nordic Studies, The University of Iceland*

1. General

Torben Brostøm, *Uden titel*, ed. Christian Lund, Gyldendal, 254 pp., is a collection of essays written over 31 years by one of Denmark's leading modernist critics. As a successor to the collection of Broström's reviews, *Underspil* (see *YWMLS*, 64:767), the book demonstrates his ability to create non-traditional connections between literature and literary conceptions. *Uden titel* includes essays reflecting on general subjects, such as 'Poesiens indre lyd' (9–30); essays on literary genres and periods, such as 'Eventyr er ikke for børn. Folkeeventyrets brug af børn' (56–68); essays dealing with specific authors, such as 'Varitéens sprog hos Johannes V. Jensen' (148–54); and essays on specific works, such as 'Kærlighedens forrykte tale i Sanct Hansaften-Spil' on Adam Oehlenschläger's play (112–24).

The Centre for *Børnelitteratur* and Roskilde U.P. have published two works on Danish children's literature: Nina Christensen, *Den danske billedbog 1950–1999*, 397 pp., is the result of her Ph.D. dissertation, the first on picture books in Denmark, thus contributing to the establishment of a new research area by discussing theoretical, methodological, and historical points of view on the picture book. C.'s study is characterized by an impressive thoroughness and clarity. The first part discusses the picture book in literary, paedagogical, artistic, social, and oral narrative contexts, and forms the basis of the establishment of an analytical method in the second part, which is used to interpret ten works in the third part. These works are chosen as representatives of the five decades between 1950 and 2000, the interpretation of them thereby creating a literary historical point of view on the picture book. *Nedslag i børnelitteraturforskningen 4*, Centre for *Børnelitteratur* — Roskilde U.P., 197 pp., includes three articles which discuss the concept of the literary canon in relation to children's literature: T. Weinreich, 'Litteraturens kanon — og børnelitteraturens' (11–33), presents four different principles according to which canons are created and concludes by proposing one for Danish children's literature; T. Jørgensen writes about the role librarians play in creating a canon in 'Skolebibliotekets kanon' (35–52); H. Høyrup's essay 'Børnelitteratur og kanon — Nogle teoretiske problemstillinger i forbindelse med 1800-tallets børnelitteratur' (53–84) is primarily a theoretical description of the canonizing processes, taking as her example children's literature of the 19th c.

T. Grünbaum, 'Fortælling og indlevelse. En teori om synligheden i det litterære værk', *Kritik*, 164:59–69, is an attempt to formulate a theory on the pictorial effect of literature, using as examples among others J. P. Jacobsen's *Fru Marie Grubbe*, Jens Baggensen's *Labyrinten*, and Herman Bang's *Les Quatre Diables*. Marie Louise Kjølbye, *Med andre øjne. Fem nydanskere læser danske klassikere*, Dansklærerforeningen, 113 pp., is a compound of political debate and literary interpretation. Five prominent second generation immigrants interpret Hans Kirk's *Fiskerne*, Henry Nathansen's *Inden for Murene*, Ludvig Holberg's *Jean de France* and *Erasmus Montanus*, Leif Panduro's *Rend mig i traditionerne*, and Morten Korch's *Fruen paa Hamre*, works that are all considered Danish literary classics which thereby define national identity. The aim of the book is to effect an alternative or 'other' view on Danish culture, thereby elucidating both the normal conception of it and of their own cultural background.

Frank Kjørup, *Sprog versus Sprog. Mod en versets poetik*, Museum Tusculanum, 416 pp., is a discussion of the peculiarity of the poetic line of verse in its combination of meaning, sound, graphics, and prosody. K.'s fundamental thesis is that a metrical line creates its own kind of meaning. He investigates this by focusing on the tension between the 'normal' linguistic meaning of an utterance, manifesting itself in an oral version of a poem, and the disturbance of this by an unconventional metrical division of the utterance disclosed in the written version, using poems from Danish literary history as his empirical material. The book is divided into three parts. In the first, K. creates the basis for his discussion by reflecting upon a number of juxtaposed theoretical complexities related to his thesis, such as rhythm vs. metre, aesthetics vs. cognition, and audition vs. visuality. In the second, he presents his aesthetic and cognitive conception of a line of verse, evolving around what he names 'V-punktet', the turning-point where one breaks off and a new one starts; and in the third part he attempts to generalize this conception into a 'poetics of the verse'. L. Korsbek, 'Dialogiske strukturer i den lyriske genre', *Kritik*, 164:43–49, attempts to refute the general assumption that poetry is monological, i.e. that there is always only one voice in a poem, and that this voice melts together with the subject matter.

Two text books on literary analysis, targeted at university and teacher training college level, have been published this year. Peter Heller Lützen, *Analyse og relevans — grundbog i litterær analyse og fortolkning*, Dansklærerforeningen, 183 pp., is a readable, basic book, which emulates a number of other works in the field, thereby helping to establish an interpretative tradition. Focusing on the concept of relevance throughout the book, L. presents a model for literary analysis in seven chapters dealing with the relationship between text and reader, with genre, with motive and theme, with the narrator, with composition, and with character and language, adding to these a chapter on different schools of criticism. As empirical material, five works are discussed in detail: Herman Bang's short story 'Irene Holm', Johannes Jørgensen's documentary text 'Vesterbro', Emil Bønnelycke's and Dan Turèll's poems 'Vesterbrogade' and 'Livet i Istedgade', and Tom Kristensen's novel *Hærværk*. The anthology *Om litteratur. Metoder og perspektiver*, ed. Leif Søndergaard, Aarhus, Systime, 315 pp., is a more ambitious, theoretically-founded discussion of a number of central literary conceptions, meant as an elaborating supplement to works such as the above mentioned. The difference between *Om litteratur* and *Analyse og relevans* can be illustrated by comparing the books' treatment of the concept of the literary motive: where Lützen in the former defines it as the concrete occurrences in the text, R. Thorning Hansen discusses it by involving eight different theoretical points of view in his essay in the latter. The volume includes the following essays: L. Søndergaard, 'Indledning: Hvorfor læser vi litteratur?' (5–16), 'Fiktion' (99–117), 'Paratekst' (133–52), and 'Kontekst' (170–89); K. Hvidtfeldt Madsen, 'Hvad er litteratur' (17–34); H. Goldbæk, 'Det litterære værk' (35–53); J. Dines Johansen, 'Indgange til tekstanalyse' (54–76), and 'Forfatterskab'(209–29); O. Lund Nielsen, 'Strukturer i teksten' (77–98); A. Gemzøe, 'Metafiktion' (118–32); M. Marnarsdóttir, 'Intertekstualitet' (153–69); H. M. Davidsen, 'Tekst og læser' (190–208); A. Ballegaard Petersen, 'Periode' (230–47); L. Korsbek, 'Genre' (248–67); R. Thorning Hansen, 'Motiv, tema og stof' (268–92); and M. Nøjgaard, 'Litterær vurdering' (293–315).

Olsen, *Essays*, is a collection of O.'s essays published for his 60th birthday. C. Skovbjerg Paldam, 'Ombord. Drikkevisen og den danske drukkultur', *Passage*, 46:73–77, is a critical analysis of the Danish drinking-song tradition, comparing it to the Swedish tradition, which is said to have greater literary qualities. *Passage*, 45, discusses the construction of literary periods: S. E. Larsen, 'En nødvendig omvej. Strøtanker om litteratur og perioder' (21–35), points out a series of antonymic conceptions one should consider when studying literary periods, such as synchronism vs. diachronism and homogenization vs. atomization; M. Rosendahl Thomsen, 'Modernismens postmoderne kanon' (63–69), considers the consequence of the increasing use of postmodern reading strategies in the critique of the canonical works of modernism. Paul, *Schriften*, is a collection of P.'s essays published on the occasion of his 60th birthday.

K. Wentzel, 'Dansk litteraturhistorie — en politisk sag', *Kritik*, 166:57–61, discusses the need for a new view on Danish literary history, because of the undermining of the concept of Danish culture, which forms its foundation, by globalization and multiculturalism. Mette Winge and Bo Tao Michaëlis, *Forfatternes Danmark*, Politikens håndbøger, 233 pp., guide readers through the authors' Denmark. The book is a literary topography, a work of reference exploring Danish authors' resorts and these resorts' occurrences in their works. The book is geographically structured, starting in the Northern part of Jutland and finishing on Bornholm, and each of the 10 chapters describes a part of the country. However, references to Copenhagen are excluded, since all Danish authors at a given time have left their marks in the city and the retracing of these would be impossible to contain within the framework of the book. The book is rich in factual information and is beautifully illustrated. It is well structured and contains a detailed author and place-index. The only apparent lack is an index of titles.

2. The Eighteenth Century

HOLBERG, L. P. Olsen, 'Litterære utopier mellem rationalisme og romantik — med særlig henblik på Holbergs "Niels Klim"', Olsen, *Essays*, 67–80, discusses the concept of utopia in relation to the author's famous novel of 1741.

3. The Nineteenth Century

Maria Helleberg, *Vilde kvinder, milde kvinder. 12 kvindeliv fra guldalderen*, Samleren, 371 pp., portrays nine Danish women from the Danish 'golden age' 1770–1830. It is H.'s claim that the golden age, compared with both former and later periods, valued femininity, which found expression in the fact that women belonging to the aristocracy, despite not possessing any formal power, were cultural trendsetters and performers. According to H., these positive circumstances for women have been ignored by the present-day feminist movement, a neglect she tries to remedy with portraits of, for instance, the authors Thomasine Gyllembourg, Frederikke Brun, and Louise von Stolberg. The style of the book bears resemblances to the historical novel. Other important figures in the period are also discussed, such as Jens Baggensen, Peter Andreas Heiberg, his son Johan Ludvig Heiberg, and Adam Oehlenschläger. J. Hougaard, 'Harem, odalisker og erotik', *Kritik*, 162–63: 141–147, is a short presentation of orientalism in Danish romanticism, focusing on the appearance of the harem in the works of Steen Steensen Blicher, Frederik Paludan-Müller, Bernhard Severin Ingemann, Carsten Hauch, Meïr Aron Goldschmidt, and Søren Kierkegaard. Jørgen Dines Johansen, *Litteratur og begær* (Univ. of Southern Denmark

Studies in Scandinavian Language and Literature, 55), Odense, Syddansk U.P., 341 pp., investigates the relation between sexuality and death in inspiring interpretations of the works of ten 18th-c. authors, largely from a psychoanalytical point of view. It includes essays on works by Bernhard Severin Ingemann, H. C. Andersen, Fredrik Paludan-Müller, Emil Aarestrup, J. P. Jacobsen, Herman Bang, and Johannes V. Jensen. F. Paul, 'Akromanie. Zur Tradition und Innovation ein literarischen Motivs bei Goethe, Baggensen, Heine, Andersen und Ibsen', Paul, *Schriften*, 101–22, discusses the occurrence of a mountaineering motif and its psychological and existential implications in, among others, Jens Baggensen's *Labyrinthen* and H. C. Andersen's *Skyggebilleder*. Marie-Louise Svane, *Formationer i europæisk romantik* (Teori & Æstetik, 15), Museum Tusculanum, 286 pp., is a collection of essays on romantic aesthetics between 1800–1830. Inspired by Roland Barthes, S. views romantic art not as secluded, remote and idealistic, but as inclusive, comprising traditional oppositions such as mind/body and sense/sensibility. Placing special focus on the German Jena romantics, the book includes essays of general interest for the scholar dealing with romanticism, such as 'Arabesk. En romantisk grænsefigur' (13–39) and 'Stilens aktivisme i romantisk prosafiktion' (41–59). Of particular interest in this context is the book's central essay 'Mellem nær og fjern. Det poetisk landskab' (61–148), in which S. interprets, among others, H. C. Andersen's *Skyggebilleder*, and 'Landskab og luftsyner hos St. St. Blicher' (215–33), in which she discusses Steen Steensen Blicher's short stories 'Røverstuen', 'Hosekræmmeren', and 'Himmelbjerget'.

ANDERSEN, H. C. The paramount literary event in 2005 will be H. C. Andersen's 200th anniversary. Gyldendal has anticipated the celebration by publishing *Andersen — en biografi*, 968 pp., a biography in two volumes written by the leading biographer of Danish authors, Jens Andersen. The book is gripping, well written, and characterized by thorough preliminary studies, not only of the posthumous papers of Andersen and his acquaintances, but also of the social, psychological, and aesthetic conventions of the 19th c., resulting in a nuanced representation of the author's life and work. This expresses itself in, for instance, the book's discussion of Andersen's unconventional sexuality, where A., supported by his knowledge of relationships between men at the time, convincingly argues against the author's asserted homosexuality. A. focuses on the curious mixture of extreme sensitivity and immoderate ambitions that characterized Andersen during his whole life, and which found its expression in his consistent battle against suppression by various teachers and critics, and his never-ending pursuit of his main goal: to become a famous and loved poet. U. Hansen, 'H.C. Andersens *Skyggen* i en overset idehistorisk sammenhæng', *Kritik*, 165:63–70, is a new interpretation of 'Skyggen' — perhaps the tale by Andersen which has generated most academic critique — in the light of the interest in hypnotism that arose in Europe at the time when Andersen wrote the tale.

BANG, H. Dag Heede, *Herman Bang. Mærkværdige læsninger. Toogfirs tableauer*, Odense, Syddansk U.P., 275 pp., is a 'cross interpretation' of Bang's work in 82 short 'tableaux' or scenes. With a theoretical basis in the writings of Sigmund Freud, Michel Foucault, and Judith Butler, H. takes as his starting point B.'s own words from *Realisme og Realister* that any book must be a confession about the author and the one he loves. The question H. poses is, logically, the consistency between the occurrence of the many female protagonists in the works — the ones B. according to himself loved — and the author's self-proclaimed homosexuality. H.'s thesis, which he pursues in the following tableaux, is that B. effected an allegorical 'gender conversion', so that his female protagonists are to be understood as homosexual men, and his masculine, heterosexual protagonists as homosexual men surrounded by women who 'really' are men. In H.'s own words, his project in the book is to 'queer the queer': to reveal the homosexual tendencies in the homosexual writer's work.

CLAUSSEN, S. P. Olsen, 'Sophus Claussen', Olsen, *Essays*, 9–26, is a general introduction to the author's work, whereas his essay 'Studenterjubilæum, erindring — og Sophus Claussens "Ekbatàna"', *ib.*, 137–52, is a close-reading of one of Claussen's most famous poems.

JACOBSEN, J. P. F. Paul, 'Bild — Dichtung — Übersetzung. J.P. Jacobsens "Michelangelo-Arabeske" in den Übertragungen Georges og Rilkes', Paul, *Schriften*, 153–73, compares Stefan George's 1893 translation of Jacobsen's famous poem to that of Rainer Maria Rilke in 1914.

KIERKEGAARD, S. S. Bektovic, 'Kierkegaard og sufismen', *Kritik*, 162–63:117–23, is an inspired essay on the relation between K.'s existential notion of Christianity and the mystical Muslim movement, Sufism. F. Paul, 'Kierkegaards Verführer, Don Juan und Faust', Paul, *Schriften*, 132–52, discusses K.'s use of the Faust and Don Juan figures in the creation of his seducer Johannes, the main character in *Forførerens Dagbog*.

4. The Twentieth Century

A. Borup, 'Avantgarden og den litterære institution', *Vandfanget*, 2:18–23. *Passage*, 46, an issue devoted to literature and drugs, contains L. Bukdahl, 'At styre en lyre på syre' (45–59), on Danish authors' use of LSD in 1969–75, focusing on the works of Dan Turèll,

Johannes L. Madsen, and the children's author Knud Holten. J. Cramer, 'Mellemkrigstidens kulturdebat og tidsskrifter', *Vandfanget*, 3:6–13.

Two anthologies have been published as a result of the collaborative project between Danish universities on modernism: *Betydende former. Modernismens retorik. Modernismens historie*, ed. Anker Gemzøe and Peter Stein Larsen (Modernismestudier, 2), Akademisk, 334 pp., focuses on the historical development of notions of modernism, and on the relation between modernism and concepts such as avant-garde and postmodernism, with the aim of remedying the lack of studies concerning Danish modernism in an international context. The book includes P. Stein Larsen, 'Modernisme som strukturelt og funktionelt begreb' (20–48); A. Gemzøe, 'Modernisme og mimesis' (49–75), and 'Modernismen som norm, spændetrøje og litteraturhistorisk kategori' (285–311); E. Svendsen, 'Johannes V. Jensen — en modernist? (76–107); G. Larsen, 'Modernismekonstruktioner. Æstetiske og sociologiske synsvinkler på modernisme' (151–76); P. Madsen, 'Da modernismen kom til Danmark' (177–96); T. Ørum, 'De eksperimenterende tressere' (197–212); M. Stidsen, 'Nye brændpunkter — om senfirsernes danske lyrik' (213–33); and C. Falkenstrøm, 'Avantgarde og avantgardelyrik' (258–84). *Modernismens betydende former*, ed. Gorm Larsen and John Thobo-Carlsen (Modernismestudier, 3), Akademisk, 331 pp., claims that modernism is characterized by form becoming the intermediary of meaning, whereby the focus shifts from content to performance, i.e. from what is pointed out to the pointing itself. The essays discuss a number of different modernistic form-related concepts such as intertextuality, stream of consciousness, and polyphonic writing, metaphorical strategies, the role of the author and the role of the reader, apostrophe in poetry, and the status of the character. The anthology includes M. Stistrup Jensen, 'Nye former for intertekstualitet' (64–87), on among others Svend Åge Madsen's *Sæt verden er til* and Inger Christensen's *Det malede værkelse*; G. Larsen, 'Stream of consciousnes og polyfoni' (88–121), on H. C. Branner's *To minutters stilhed* and Peer Hultberg's *Requiem*; P. Stein Larsen, 'Tre metaforiske strategier inden for ny dansk lyrik' (122–56), discussing a number of Danish poets from J. P. Jacobsen to Simon Grotrian; J. Thobo-Carlsen, 'Læsningens (an)svarlighed' (203–27), which takes Per Højholt's *6512* as its starting point; and P. Krogh Hansen, 'Det nye ved den nye realisme. Til den fortsatte diskussion af relationen mellem realisme og modernisme' (252–74), on the works of Jan Sonnergaard and Helle Helle.

Arne Herdis, *Æresretten. Dansk Forfatterforening og udrensningen af de unationale 1945–52*, Lindhardt & Ringhof, 259 pp., is a historical account of a subject which hitherto has attracted very limited discussion: the 'court of honour' that the Danish Writers' Union appointed in 1945 to pass judgement on 26 authors, who — in various ways — had shown Nazi sympathies during World War II. The book is written as an attempt to introduce light and shade into the proceedings, which H. claims was characterized by the need for a quick and powerful release from the hateful atmosphere towards pro-Germans in Denmark straight after the war. H. does so by adding the accused authors' responses to the material of the court of honour, which in reality worked as a legislative, prosecutive, and judging institution. Among the authors discussed are Jacob Bech Nygaard, Valdemar Rørdam, and Ole Sarvig, and also Hans Kirk as member of the court of honour.

M. Ipsen, 'Teksten og bogsiden', *Passage*, 48:5–12, discusses the relationship between content and the printed page, with examples from works by authors within the Danish literary avant-garde movement of the 1960s. P. Stounbjerg, 'Verdensrevolutionen og Valby-parnasset. Lidt om avantgarden i dansk og international litteraturhistorie', *Vandfanget*, 2:13–17. The anthology *Virkelighed, virkelighed! Avantgardens realisme*, ed. Karin Petersen and Mette Sandbye, Tiderne Skifter, 336 pp., is published in continuation of *Virkelighedshunger. Nyrealismen i visuel optik* (see *YWMLS*, 64:764). Whereas the latter describes the occurrence of new realistic tendencies in the art of the 1990s, the aim in *Virkelighed, virkelighed!* is to create an explanatory context for these tendencies by investigating the historical relationship between avant-garde and realism. Thus, some of the contributors claim that a normative discrimination between realism, modernism, and avant-garde is problematic, and that it is more rewarding to consider them as different expressions of the same historical period.

ANDERSEN, B. P. Olsen, 'Her er — ja, hér er Benny Andersen', Olsen, *Essays*, 31–36, celebrates the author's 70th birthday.

BRANDT, J. G. Lotte Thyrring Andersen, *Gentagelsens poesi. Virkelighedsopfattelsen i Jørgen Gustava Brandts digtning*, Gads, 260 pp., is the first discussion of Brandt's work in full, based on A.'s Ph.D. dissertation of 2002. She represents Brandt, whose work expands into all genres and constitutes one of the most momentous of the present day, as a religious modernist, and defines and discusses the directing principle in his writings: repetition understood not as reiteration, but as reclaiming something lost, and its basis in B.'s 'dialogical' conception of the world. A. puts this concept into perspective by implicating Martin Buber's dialogical thinking, which he presents in *Ich und Du* in the discussion of B.'s work. According to A., the existential-religious dialogue between the I and God in B.'s works exceeds the subjectivism of modernism, but carries this excess into effect with the very same means modernism itself makes use of: self reflection and linguistic consciousness. In six chapters, A. discusses these principles and related subjects in the work of B., with special focus on the collections of poetry 'Fragment af imorgen', 'Janushoved', 'Der er Æg i mit Skæg', 'Ateliers', and 'Ansigt til ansigt', and the poetics 'Hvad angår poesi'.

GROTRIAN, S. S. Kjerkegaard, 'Jeg vil vise mig påklædt for Abraham / gerne i shorts. Guddommelig avantgarde? — en mindre opsang til mig selv', *Vandfanget*, 2:24–27.

HULTBERG, P. In the essay 'Peer Hultberg' in his book *Så hvad er et menneske? Tre kapitler om P.O. Enquist, Peer Hultberg og Jan Kjærstad*, Samleren, 2002, 256 pp., Thomas Thurah investigates the appearance of human nature in Hultberg's *Mytologisk landskab med Daphnes forvandling*, *Desmond!*, *Requim*, *Slagne veje*, *Præludier*, and *Byen og verden*. T. 's point of view is that throughout his works, H. discusses how conscience perceives itself in relation to other consciences and their self-perception. This relation is never unproblematic in H.'s works; rather, the self always seems estranged from its surroundings, an estrangement T. recognizes in the myth of the Fall of Man, which he places as the founding narrative in H.'s works.

KRISTENSEN, T. S. Klitgaard Povlsen, 'Delerium III mens — Ordets alkymi. Omkring Hærværk', *Passage*, 46:15–22, is a comparative study of Tom Kristensen's *Hærværk* and James Joyce's *Ulysses*, pointing out that K. not only describes intoxication in his novel, but that the language itself seems to be intoxicated, as is the case in *Ulysses*.

MICHAËLIS, K. Merete von Eyben, *Karin Michaëlis. Incest as Metaphor and the Illusion of Romantic Love* (Studies on Themes and Motifs in Literature, 65), Berne, Lang, 133 pp., investigates the thematically provoking and stylistically renewing writings of the author. Through psychoanalytically-inspired interpretations of the novels *Justine*, *Bogen om Kærlighed*, and *Lillemor*, E. discusses the occurrence of incest, masochism, and faulty motherhood as metaphors for the limitation of female existential conditions in a patriarchal society, concluding that a successful relationship between man and woman is impossible. The interpretations make use of works by, for instance, Jan Cohn, Judith Lewis Herman, the marquis de Sade, Johann Wolfgang von Goethe, David Celani, Amalie Skram, and H. C. Andersen.

MUNCH-PETERSEN, G. Martine Cardel Gertsen's Ph.D. dissertation *Gustafs ansigter — selvfremstilling i Gustaf Munch-Petersens forfatterskab* (Centrum för Danmarksstudier, 2), Makadam, 383 pp., is a thematic investigation of the identity theme in the works of M.-P. Central to the study is the face metaphor, which appears throughout the works of M.-P., but which G. also assigns to express different, re-occurring self-representations and perspectives on the world, which M.-P. experimented with in his works. After an opening chapter in which she presents the face metaphor and introduces different contexts, which she implies in the analysis, and a chapter on M.-P.'s dramatic biography, G. goes on to discuss five 'faces' in chapters named 'Det nye menneske', 'Sønnen', 'Elskeren', 'Frelseren', and 'Kunstneren', the latter possessing a concluding quality as this face appears as the sum of all the rest.

MUNK, K. Per Stig Møller, *Mere Munk*, Gyldendal, 101 pp. In 2000, the Danish Minister of Foreign Affairs published a biography on the priest and poet Munk's life and work. As a result, Møller was presented with the Rosenkjærprisen by Danmarks Radio 2001, which required him to give a series of lectures on Munk. *Mere Munk* is the result of these lectures. It consists of five chapters, dealing with the role Munk played during World War II as one of the strongest adversaries, not only of the German occupation, but also of the political collaboration of the Danish government. It also discusses the attempts, by his opponents, to 'demythologize' Munk after the war in order to reach their political goals, as well as Munk's literary influence before and primarily after his death in 1944.

NIELSEN, H.-J. T. Hvid Kromann, 'Et slag for et overset monster', *Kritik*, 164:50–58, presents a new interpretation of N.'s experimental novel *Den mand der kalder sig Alvard*, which includes a discussion of the relationship between the novel and Michel Foucault's essay 'La pensée du dehors'.

RIFBJERG, K. *Kærligheden er alt — en bog om Klaus Rifbjerg*, ed. Jakob Kramhøft and Janus Kramhøft, Tiderne Skifter, 198 pp., is a portrait of the author, told in an intimate collage-like form combining interviews with his friends and colleagues Fredrik Dessau, Jesper Jensen, Jørgen Leth, Palle Kjærulff-Schmidt, and Hanne Marie Svendsen, letters to these from Rifbjerg, exemplifying excerpts from his works, and interviews with him throughout the years. Torben Broström's contributions are of special interest, in that they form an ongoing, insightful characterization of Rifbjerg's work from 1951 to 2003. P. Olsen, 'Klaus Rifbjerg: Portræt, 17', Olsen, *Essays*, 27–30, interprets the poem '17'.

SONNE, J. P. Olsen, 'Denne Sonne — en introduktion', Olsen, *Essays*, 37–44, is a general presentation of the author's work.

SØRENSEN, V. Finn Hauberg Mortensen, *Bibliografi over Villy Sørensens forfatterskab*, Gyldendal, 123 pp., is a complete bibliography of Sørensen's work, including not only his fictional, essayistic, and intermediary writing, but also sketches, lectures, speeches, etc. The works are both ordered alphabetically and according to the year in which they were written.

IV. NORWEGIAN STUDIES*

LANGUAGE

By Arnstein Hjelde, *Lecturer in Norwegian, Department of Education, Östfold University College*

(This survey covers the years 2001–2003)

1. General

Mons 9: utvalgte artikler fra Det niende møtet om norsk språk i Oslo 2001, ed. Inger Moen, Hanne Gram Simonsen, Arne Torp, and Kjell Ivar Vannebo, Novus 2002, 255 pp., contains 23 papers presented at the ninth MONS conference in 2001, and, to some extent, the selected articles reflect the focus this conference had on corpus linguistics, diachronic linguistics, and Norwegian as a second language. *Krefter og motkrefter i språknormeringa: om språknormering i teori og praksis*, ed. Helge Omdal and Rune Røsstad, Kristiansand, Høyskoleforlaget, 305 pp., is a collection of articles focusing on planning and standardization of language. The articles are based on papers presented at a conference held in Kristiansand in 2001. Most, but not all, of these articles focus on the specific language situation in Norway: H. Dyvik deals with the antagonism between public and private standardization of the written norm (25–39); O. Nygaard writes about the conservative norm used by the newspaper *Aftenposten* (57–67); G. Akselberg has studied which optional forms high-school students with Nynorsk as their first language tend to use (69–92); J. O. Askedal, T. Guttu, A. O. Sandved, and O. M. Selberg write about norms and their usage in Bokmål/Riksmål (93–119); E. Brunstad reflects on the influence which the 'national know-all', Finn-Erik Vinje, has had on language standardization (121–33); J. O. Fretland sums up the situation for the language, as well as for the Norwegian Language Council, at the present stage (135–44); K. Johansen writes about gender in Bokmål/Riksmål (145–54); A. R. Linn gives a brief presentation of the philologist Johan Storm (175–86); R. Lockertsen writes about determinism in the standardization of written Norwegian (187–93); S. Lomheim has studied the language used by the national news bureau NTB and its influence on the language used by the press (195–207); E. Maagerø focuses on the use of nominalizations in textbooks and in the work of pupils (209–20), while H. Omdal deals with the teacher's role in the implementation of language norms

* The place of publication of books is Oslo unless otherwise stated.

(221–38); E. Papazian focuses on standardization of spoken language (247–57); H. Sandøy writes about different mechanisms in the standardization of Norwegian (259–71), K. I. Vannebo about Bokmål (285–94), and L. S. Vikør about Nynorsk (295–305); finally, K. Slet-thei reflects on language technology (273–83).

Helge Omdal and Lars Vikør, *Språknormer i Norge*, Cappelen akademisk, 2002, 191 pp., is published in a new edition. It provides an introduction to theories on language planning and standardization, and applies these to the language situation in Norway. The authors aim especially at students at university and college level, and each chapter is provided with exercises. *Med 'bil' i Norden i 100 år: Ordlaging og tilpassing av utalandske ord*, ed. Helge Sandøy, Novus, 152 pp., is the result of a project initiated by the Nordic Language Council on how foreign words are treated in the Nordic languages, and the articles (in Norwegian, Swedish, Danish) are based on papers presented at a conference in Bergen in 2001. Since this book has a Nordic perspective, only a few of the articles deal with the specific situation for such words in Norwegian: A. Skjeseth presents a journalist's personal view on how the press should deal with English words and phrases when translating international news bulletins into Norwegian (59–63); J. Myking presents a study on terminology related to the oil industry, a domain where English and Norwegian terms compete (82–91); T. Lie writes about the use of Norwegian and English in Norwegian pop music, trying to find explanations for why so many Norwegian artists have avoided using their mother tongue — the introduction of rap music seems however to represent a change in this trend (95–110); S. Johansson writes about different aspects of how English words are integrated into Norwegian, in particular how English words compete with Norwegian substitutes (123–37); J. Hoel (138–43), D. F. Simonsen (144–49), and A. H. Aarflot (150–52), all contribute short articles dealing with 'Ordsmia', The Norwegian Language Council's discussion forum on Internet, where the aim is to come up with new Norwegian substitutes for imported foreign words. Two articles compare the situation in each of the Nordic languages: E. Brunstad compares the use in newspapers of different Nordic countries of imported words (111–19), while L. S. Vikør presents a comparative study on language attitudes in the Nordic countries, focusing especially on attitudes toward English and the influence from this language (42–51). H. Sandøy also has an article on modern imported words in Scandinavia in *Språk i Norden*, 2002: 73–100. Another book dealing with some of these questions is that of Stig Johansson and Anne-Line Graedler, *Rocka, hipt og snacksy: om engelsk i norsk språk og samfunn*, Kristiansand, Høyskoleforlaget, 2002, 318 pp., which is a study of different phenomena related to the contact between Norwegian and English over the years, with a special focus on loanwords.

Three books focus on Nynorsk: Ottar Grepstad, *Det nynorske blikket*, Samlaget 2002, 575 pp., contains a number of essays dealing with different aspects of the Nynorsk language and culture, such as its creator Ivar Aasen, some of its famous, as well as forgotten authors, users, advocates, and institutions supporting Nynorsk. *Kampen for språket: Nynorsken mellom det lokale and globale*, ed. Håvard Teigen and Elisabeth Bakke, Samlaget 2001, 251 pp. *Modernity, Nation, Written Culture*, ed. J. Peter Burgess and Odd Monsson, Kristiansand, Høyskoleforlaget — Norges forskningsråd, 2002, 173 pp., presents papers given at a conference at Volda University College in 2000. Scholars with a wide variety of backgrounds have contributed, focusing on different aspects of Nynorsk.

Egil Børre Johnsen, *Vårt eget språk*, Aschehoug 2002, 335 pp., is about different aspects of the Norwegian language, including history of the language, dialects, the use of Norwegian in different settings, as well as grammar and spelling. This is a revised and updated edition of the 1987 three-volume series with the same title. Sylfest Lomheim, *Språkteigen*, Samlaget 2002, 262 pp., covers a wide range of topics, such as etymology, dialects, slang, and swearing, and is based on questions asked by listeners of a radio programme of which Lomheim is the editor. Several books are published with the intention of offering users of Norwegian advice on how to improve their writing: Ruth Vatvedt Fjeld, **Norsk til kontorbruk: god norsk i administrasjon og forvaltning*, 4th edn, Universitetsforlaget, 2002, 259 pp., is intended as a help for administrators and clerks at different levels; Lars Aarønæs, **Presse-språket: oppslagsbok for journalister og andre skribenter*, Aneholmen, 204 pp., aims especially at journalists. *Språkvett: skriveregler, grammatikk og språklige råd fra a til å*, ed. Dag Gundersen, Jan Engh, Ruth E. Vatvedt, and Elin Anita Frysjøenden, 2nd edn, Kunnskapsforlaget, 2001, 393 pp., is a useful handbook covering a number of topics in relation to written Norwegian. Finn-Erik Vinje, *Moderne norsk: en veiledning i skriftlig framstilling: morfologske og syntaktiske vanskeligheter*, 5th edn, Bergen, Fagbokforlaget, 2002, 506 pp., presents the author's continuing knowledge and personal views on what should be considered correct and good Norwegian. Ivar Aasen, *Norske Ordtak*, 4th edn, Bergen, Vigmostad og Bjørke, 378 pp., first published in 1856, collects approximately 5,000 Norwegian proverbs; the present edition uses a slightly modernized spelling with å for aa. Jon Winge, **For bare stumpene; arven fra de hvite seil og det svarte kull ; sjømannsuttrykk i norsk dagligtale*, NKS-forlaget, 2001, 140 pp., focuses on how expressions related to the maritime world have entered everyday speech. Helge Svare, *Livet er en reise: metaforer i filosofi, vitenskap og dagligliv*, Pax, 2002,

208 pp., deals with the use of metaphors in everyday life. Øyvind Pålshaugen, *Språkets estetiske dimensjon: vitenskapskritiske essays*, Spartacus, 2001, 213 pp., reflects on the aesthetic dimension of language. Lars S. Vikør, *The Nordic Languages: Their Status and Interrelations*, Novus, 2001, 254 pp., is released in a third and updated edition. Jan Svennevig, *Språklig samhandling: innføring i kommunikasjonsteori og diskursanalyse*, Cappelen akademisk — Landslaget for norskundervisning, 2001, 288 pp., is an introduction to the disciplines of communication theory and discourse analysis. The book is especially aimed at students at university and college level, as well as at teachers who feel the need to extend their knowledge in this field.

**New Directions in Nordic Text Linguistics and Discourse Analysis: Methodological Issues, ed.* Wenche Vagle and Kay Wikberg, Novus, 2001, 264 pp., and Eli Glomnes, *Alt jeg kan si: Språk, virkelighet og subjektets stemme*, Cappelen akademisk, 2001, 160 pp., are two books covering the same field. Helene Valvatne and Margareth Sandvik, *Barn, språk og kultur: språkutvikling fram til sjuårsalderen*, Cappelen akademisk, 2002, 342 pp., is a textbook on children and language development. Geirr Wiggen, *Quando corpus morietur: Dødsannonser i Norge gjennom det 20. hundreåret. Et bidrag til norsk språk- og mentalitetshistorie med internasjonalt utblikk*, Novus, 2001, 204 pp., contains a study of the language used in 20th-c. Norwegian death announcements. Oskar Bandle, *Schriften zur nordischen Philologie: Sprach-, Literatur- und Kulturgeschichte der skandinavischen Länder*, ed. Jürg Glauser and Hans-Peter Naumann, Tübingen, Francke, 2001, 622 pp., is a collection, made in honour of his 75th birthday, of articles written by B., demonstrating the diversity of his academic interests, ranging from modern literature to linguistics, and several of these articles deal with aspects of the Norwegian language.

B. Mæhlum, *NLT*, 2002: 177–99, offers a critical view of the idea proposed by the linguist Sylfest Lomheim that in 100 years time English will be the dominating written language in Norway. M. demonstrates that L.'s prophecy will find little support in modern linguistic theory and that it should be regarded as nothing but guesswork. J. O. Askedal, *NLT*: 121–33, focuses on how different languages are represented in *NLT*'s published articles. The figures presented here show that Norwegian is still the dominant language in *NLT*, and Nynorsk is also well represented. English is the most frequent foreign language, while the use of Swedish, Danish, and especially German is more sporadic. A recent proposal for funding of university institutions emphasizes the importance of publishing internationally, and A. reflects on what consequences this might have on the use of Norwegian in scholarly work. As part of the project 'Cultural Identity in Academic Prose', K. Fløttum, *NLT*: 21–55, investigates differences between Norwegian, English, and French when it comes to pronominal manifestation of the author in research articles. F. has studied the language used in the fields of linguistics, medicine, and economics, and finds that Norwegian writers tend to prefer the first person plural pronoun, in contrast to English writers, who seem to prefer first person singular, and French the indefinite pronoun. The life and language of Georg Sauerwein is discussed in two articles in *MM,* 2001, no. 2: K. Venås (135–49), deals with the biographical aspect, and a special focus is given to S.'s attitude towards Ivar Aasen and the *landsmål*; A. Bjørkum (151–60), presents a systematic study on how S. used the Norwegian Dovre dialect in written texts.

2. History of the Language and Textual Studies

Språk i endring: Indre norsk språkhistorie, ed. Jan Terje Faarlund, Novus, 309 pp., is a collection of nine articles, and is the fruit of a project directed by F. on the linguistic transition from Old Norse to Modern Norwegian. M. Christoffersen writes about the three Old Norse conjunctions 'ok', 'en', and 'nema' (13–28). H.-O. Enger focuses on the verbal suffix '-st' in Old Norse (29–56). J. T. Faarlund writes about infinitive constructions, covering the period from Old Norse to Modern Norwegian, and the evolution of the infinitive marker also gets attention from him (57–79). N. G. Garmann offers a new explanation of the change of the quantity system in Norwegian phonology, basing her ideas on Joan Bybee's theory of cognitive phonology (81–110). K. Ottosson studies developments in the inflexion system from Old Norse and up to the 16th c. (111–83). L. Sakshaug writes about changes in reflexive reference from Old Norse to Modern Norwegian, using a theoretical framework of autolexical syntax and government and binding (185–217). A. Torp reflects on why very frequent words do not always follow traditional sound laws, but instead show a strong tendency to be victims of pure phonological simplifications (219–54). K. I. Vannebo writes about pseudo-coordinations with the verb 'ta' (255–78), while Å. Wetås deals with the disappearance of the case system in the transitional stage between Old Norse and Modern Norwegian (279–309). All articles are written in Norwegian. Olaf Almenningen, Thore A. Roksvold, Helge Sandøy, and Lars S. Vikør, *Språk og samfunn gjennom tusen år: ei norsk språkhistorie*, 6th edn, Universitetsforlaget, 2002, 208 pp., has been the standard textbook on language history at many Norwegian colleges and universities for several decades, and it does not seem very likely that it will disappear from the student's desk in the near future either. Gustav Indrebø's famous *Norsk målsoga*, ed. Johan A. Schulze, Bergen, Norsk bokreidingslag, 2001, 511 pp., first published posthumously in 1951, appears in a new and extended edition; the discovery of further unpublished manuscripts has made it possible to extend the period beyond 1525, bringing the book to be more in accordance with I.'s intentions. Jan Ragnar Hagland, *Språkhistorisk årstalsliste*, 2nd edn, Trondheim, Tapir, 2002, 48 pp., gives a brief chronological overview of incidents relevant to the history of Norwegian, thus providing students with a useful tool when being introduced to the history of the language. Two books containing writings by Ivar Aasen have been published: *Målsamlingar 1855–1861 av Ivar Aasen*, ed. Jarle Bondevik, Oddvar Nes, and Terje Aarset, Bergen, Norsk Bokreidingslag, 2001, 222 pp.; and *Ord, uttrykk og inntrykk frå Hallingdal og Valdres*, introd. Kjell Venås, Ål, Boksmia, 2002, 318 pp., contains a variety of material such as letters, diary entries, and collections of words with information on meaning etc., recorded by Aa. from the region of Hallingdal and Valdres. One of Knud Knudsen's main works, *Haandbok i dansk-norsk sproglære*, Samlaget, 2002, 411 pp., first publised in 1856, is again made available.

The Nordic Languages: An International Handbook of the History of the North Germanic Languages, Vol. 1, ed. Oskar Bandle et al., Berlin–NY, de Gruyter, 2002, 1057 pp., is a very impressive work which contains 118 articles written by leading scholars in this field, covering the period up to the mid-14th c. The content in divided into 12 sections, covering previous research, Nordic as a branch of Old Germanic, ancient Nordic, as well as Old Nordic and its grammar. Gudleiv Bø and Magne Myhren, *Draumkvedet: Diktverket og teksthistoria*, Novus, 2002, 135 pp., presents a new version of Draumkvedet based on how Landstad wrote it down in the 1840s; this version deviates considerably from that of Moltke Moe. The text is commented, and the reconstruction work discussed. In addition, a literary analysis is given. Martin Syrett, *The Roman-Alphabet Inscriptions of Medieval Trondheim*, Vols I-II, 2 vols, Trondheim, Tapir, 2002, 456, 132 pp., provides a full account of medieval inscriptions in the Roman alphabet from the city of Trondheim. These inscriptions cover a period from about 1150 to 1520, and the major part of this book consists of a presentation of the different inscriptions, discussing points of linguistic and historical interest.

M. Christoffersen, *NLT*, 2002: 153–76, presents a study of subordinate clauses as used in an authentic Old Norwegian legal text, finding that there are no clear-cut distinctions between the two fronting processes of 'stylistic inversion' and 'topicalization', hence there may be no point in trying to distinguish them. M. Schulte, *NLT*: 163–94, writes about the early and almost complete prefix loss in Nordic as compared to Gothic and West Germanic, explaining this change by means of metrical phonology. M. Myren, *MM*, 2001, no.1 : 29–32, discusses the interpretation of the verb ‘hanga’ used in *Hávamál*, stanza 138, concluding that it should be understood as ‘hold on to while in an upright position’, and not as ‘hanging (with a rope around the neck)’. H. Bjorvand, *MM*, 2002, no.2 : 167–78, discusses the etymology of the Norwegian noun ‘hale’: while rejecting the reconstructed Germanic form *halan-, he argues for the base *hálhan-. F. O. Lindemann, *ib.*, 179–80, has a note on the word ‘folk’, rejecting the thought that it could have been borrowed from Celtic. M. Myren, *ib.*, 181–86, discusses the relationship between Islandic ‘gljúf(u)r’, Old Norse ‘gjúf’, and Nynorsk ‘djuv’ and ‘gjuv’. K. J. Myrvold, *MM*, no.2 : 156–69, reflects on the etymology of the noun ‘nisse’, relating it to the personal name Nils.

3. Runology

Terje Spurkland, *I begynnelsen var fuþark: norske runer og runeinnskrifter*, Cappelen akademisk — Landslaget for norskundervisning, 2001, 224 pp., is an insightful presentation of Norwegian runes and runic inscriptions. The book treats the evolution in the fuþark script system from its first appearance around 100 AD until it vanished some 1300 years later. Many of the documented runic inscriptions are interpreted and discussed in detail; the discussion of the famous Eggja stone, to which the author devotes a whole chapter, is very thorough. Here the problems of decoding and interpreting runic inscription are discussed in depth, and the new interpretation which is suggested here departs radically from the way this inscription had earlier been understood. The use and function of runes and runic inscriptions are also dealt with, and the wide span of content is demonstrated, from their religious function to the more prosaic messages found on wooden sticks, like ‘Gyda tells you to go home!’.

O. Grønvik, *NLT*: 3–19, writes about a runic inscription found on a wooden plate in a boat grave in Wremen, Germany, dating back to around 430 AD. G. challenges the traditional interpretation, suggesting that this is a defamatory inscription directed against Odin. Furthermore G. claims that this inscription was made after Germanic split into Gothic, North Germanic, and West Germanic, and that it represents an example of the latter.

4. Dialectology and Sociolinguistics

Språkmøte: Innføring i sosiolingvistikk, ed. Brit Mæhlum, Gunnstein Akselberg, Unn Røyneland, and Helge Sandøy, Cappelen Akademisk, 279 pp., is a new textbook on sociolinguistics. As such, it contains many of the elements expected, a chapter on methodology, two on multilinguism and language contact, one on language and identity, while different aspects of linguistic norms, variation, and change are dealt with in several chapters. Covering an international field, this book of course also has such an orientation, but a pedagogical advantage is that to a great extent it uses studies on Norwegian to exemplify more general theories. Of special interest is a chapter focusing on variation in written language. As a textbook, each chapter has exercises and suggestions for further reading, and the bibliography should prove helpful for anyone seeking insight into sociolinguistics. A book focusing on bilingualism and language contact is *Jallaspråk: slanguage og annet ungdomsspråk i Norden*, ed. Eli-Marie Drange, Ulla-Britt Kotsinas, and Ana-Brita Stenstrøm, Kristiansand, Høyskoleforlaget, 2002, 152 pp., is the result of an inter-Nordic research project on language contact and youth language, and the articles found here are based on papers presented at a conference in Lammi, Finland, in 2000. These articles deal with different aspects of youth language, and several of them focus on the situation for Nordic languages other than Norwegian. Contributions dealing with the situation in Norway are: E.-M. Drange on slang words borrowed from other languages and used by Norwegian youths, presenting information on from which languages such words are imported, as well as documenting regional differences in this process within Norway (9–18); T. Opsahl studies the use of the discourse marker 'bare' as used by young Norwegians (63–71); U.-B. Kotsinas writes about the use of English words in Nordic slang, describing and comparing this phenomenon in Scandinavia (37–61). One of the articles in this book is in English, the rest are in Norwegian, Danish, and Swedish. *Meetings at the Crossroads: Studies of Multilingualism and Multiculturalism in Oslo and Utrecht*, ed. Anne Hvenekilde and Jacomine Nortier, Novus, 2001, 340 pp., is a collection of articles dealing with different issues related to cultural and linguistic contact between the minority and the majority populations in The Netherlands and Norway. As such, both Dutch and Norwegian scholars have contributed to this book. Among the contributors dealing with contact situations in Norway are A. B. Nilsen, 'Linguistic minorities and communication in the Norwegian administration of justice' (91–105), J. Svennevig, 'Institutional and interpersonal frames of talk bureaucratic consultations' (106–35), J. Frøili, 'Signals at the transition place: the interpreter's turn-taking in dialogues' (136–57), A. Golden, 'To agree or not to agree — expressed metaphorically' (198–214), B. A. Svendsen, 'Can a social network approach contribute to the explanation of eight to nine-year-old children's behavior?' (280–95), and A. Hvenekilde and E. Lanza,

'Applying social network analysis to the Filipino community in Oslo' (296–313). All articles are in English.

Agnete Nesse, *Språkkontakt mellom norsk og tysk i hansatidens Bergen*, Novus, 2002, 291 pp., is a historical study of the dialect of Bergen, with emphasis on features that can be explained as results of language contact with Low German during the Hanseatic period. Part I gives the theoretical and methodological foundation for the study. Part II discusses the sociolinguistic situation in Bergen during the Hanseatic era. Part III describes and analyses five dialectal features of the Bergen dialect which are interpreted as results of language contact. These features are genitive constructions with 'sin', the use of 'te' as an infinitive marker, the use of '-et' as a past tense suffix for a number of weak verbs, the merging of masculine and feminine gender, and finally the use of definite suffix in connection with proper names. Criticism of some of N.'s claims, as well as her defence, is found in *NLT*: 21–55.

Sonja Kibsgaard and Olaf Husby, *Norsk som andrespråk i barnehage og småskole*, Universitetsforlaget, 2002, 192 pp., is a new textbook covering Norwegian as a second language. This book is especially well suited for courses at teacher training colleges, and it should also prove useful for teachers in pre-school and elementary school. *Global Eurolinguistics: European Languages in North America — Migration, Maintenance and Death*, ed. P. Sture Ureland, Tübingen, Niemeyer, 2001, 490 pp., contains three articles dealing with different aspects of the Norwegian language in America: P. Hallaråker writes about the use of surnames and place names among Norwegian-Americans and how this reflects a triple identity (231–41); A. Hjelde discusses the problem of distinguishing borrowing from code switching in bilingual speech, as well as giving a brief description of a bilingual Norwegian-American community in Wisconsin (209–29); P. Moen studies Norwegian substrata at a syntactic and idiomatic level in the English speech of Norwegian-Americans (243–64). Among the articles in *Språk i Norden 2003*, is K. Tenfjord's brief presentation of a study on how a small group of young Vietnamese immigrants are acquiring Norwegian (27–40).

In *Kontakten mellom Agder og Holland på 1600– og 1700–tallet. Seminarrapport*, Flekkefjord museum, 2001, 139 pp., M. Skjekkeland (100–13) has an article comparing the dialect of coastal Agder with that of inland Telemark. He finds that loanwords with a Low German origin are more common in Agder than in Telemark, a likely explanation being the close economic contact between the Southern coast of Norway and the Low Countries from the 16th c. onwards.

Tor Erik Jenstad, *Ein repetis i obligadur: folkemusikkterminologi i norske dialektar med vekt på feletradisjonen*, Novus, 2001, 379 pp., is about folk music terminology in Norwegian dialects and is based on the author's doctoral thesis. It focuses especially on the distribution of such terms, and this distribution is seen in comparison with boundaries for other dialectal features. Some of the more interesting terms are also subjected to etymological and morphological analysis. Id. and Jan Ragnar Hagland have edited *Spor i Trønderord: Festskrift til Arnold Dalen*, Trondheim, Tapir, 2001, 265 pp., a collection of previously-published articles written by Dalen, covering topics such as dialectology and word geography with a special focus on the Trønder dialects. Ola Stemshaug, *Norske innbyggjarnemningar i overført tyding*, Trondheim, Tapir, 2002, 139 pp., deals with how names for inhabitants of different geographical places can be used metaphorically, for example the word 'Rørosing', originally denoting a person from the town Røros, can also be used for a copper coin. S. has recorded instances of such use, and offers explanations. Traditional Norwegian dialectology has to a great extent focused on special features in phonology and morphology, while syntactic variation has not attracted the same interest: *Dialektsyntaktiska studier av den nordiska nominalfrasen*, ed. Øystein Alexander Vangsnes, Anders Holmberg, and Lars-Olof Delsing, Novus, 207 pp., within a generative grammar framework exploring variations in NPs in Nordic dialects, presents five articles of which the editors are authors or co-authors.

E. Heide, *MM*, no.1 : 23–35, gives a new explanation for the reduction from a three to a two gender system in the dialect of Bergen. H. claims that due to language contact with Low German in the Middle Ages, the Bergen dialect lost the quantity distinction in unstressed positions, causing many of the masculine and feminine gender markers to merge. E. Papazian, *MM*, 2002, no.2 : 113–34, presents a study of the singular definite form of nouns in the Halling dialect and in standardized East-Norwegian speech, pointing to differences in these two speech variants regarding the formation of this particular inflected form, and also discussing how phonology and morphology interact in this process. K. Bakken, *MM*, 2001, no.2 : 183–209, focuses on how the Old Norse *l* has evolved in West Telemark dialects.

5. Onomastics

Kjell Venås, *Norske innsjønamn* IV*: Telemark fylke*, Novus, 2002, 480 pp., is the fourth volume in a series about Norwegian lake names, this time covering Telemark county in southern Norway. After a general introduction, the lake names are listed in alphabetical order, commented on, and explained. Kåre Hoel, *Bustadnamn i Østfold 4. Spydeberg*, ed. Marit Harsson, Solum, 2001, 312 pp., is the fourth volume in this series on place names in Østfold, this time dealing with the Spydeberg area. *Nordiske torp-navne*, ed. Peder Gammeltoft and Bent Jørgensen (Norna-rapporter, 76), Uppsala, 288 pp., contains two articles on Norwegian onomastics: G. Akselberg (11–46) writes about the occurrence of the name 'Torp' in Østfold county, while O.-J. Johannesen (121–54) focuses on 'Torp' as used in farm names in the region west of the Oslo fjord. Johan Hammond Rosbach, *Stedsnavn*, Pax, 2002, 119 pp., offers information on the etymology and background for a number of national as well as international place names.

I. Særheim, *MM*, 2001, no.1:1–16, discusses the impact Hans Krahe's theory on hydronymia has had in Scandinavia. O. Grønvik, *ib.*, 17–22, M. Rindal, *ib.*, 23–24, and G. Widmark, *ib.*, 25–27, write each their comment on the origin of the name Oslo, while F. Korslund, *ib.*, 33–39, replies to Gösta Holm's view presented in *MM*, 1997, no.2, on the origin of Vinland, claiming that it is related to 'vin' in the meaning 'grazing land', and not to 'vine', thus Vinland does probably refer to Newfoundland, and not Maine as some have suggested. Holm defends his original view in *MM*, 2002, no.2:76–78, claiming that the form 'vin', meaning 'grazing land' was no longer productive in the formation of place names at that time, pointing to the fact that place names with 'vin' are not documented on Iceland or on the Ferry Islands. F. Korslund, *MM*, no.2:180–95, writes about farm names in Bohuslän, and in comparison with farm names in Norway, there are few compounds with '-vin', '-staðir', or '-heimr' in this Swedish province. I. Særheim, *Namn och bygd*, 89, 2001:29–51, writes on the 'staðir' names as found in the south-western parts of Norway. T. Schmidt, *ib.*, 91:5–34, deals with changes in farm names. T. Eskeland, *Namn og nemne*, 18, 2001:65–78, discusses the relationship between geographical names and cultural history; I. Utne, *ib.*, 79–98, deals with surnames and homonyms of surnames as first name and how naming has been regulated by the authorities; while A.-K. Pedersen, *ib.*, writes about place names and language contact. Personal names found in runic inscriptions is the theme for an article by K. F. Seim, *ib.*, 7–13. B. Helleland, *Namn och bygd*, 90, 2002:53–107, discusses how place names can serve as a source of information on social conditions and mentalities during the transition from pagan religion to Christianity.

6. Phonology, Morphology, Syntax

Per Moen and Per-Bjørn Pedersen, *Norwegian Grammar*, Kristiansand, Høyskoleforlaget, 151 pp., covers topics such as pronunciation, phrase structure, word classes, and clauses, and there is a special section with exercises. The reader would greatly benefit from fluency in English since many characteristics in Norwegian are explained through comparison with English. This textbook focuses on the Bokmål standard, but it has a useful appendix where some special dialectal features in Norwegian are taken into account.

G. Kristoffersen, *MM,* 2001, no.1:65–83, discusses the quantity system found in the Norwegian and Swedish sound system by using generative theories. Compounding is a widely used word formation process in Norwegian, and J. B. Johannessen, *NLT*, 2001:59–91, writes about this type of word. According to her study, a stem analysis has an advantage over the more traditional word-based analysis.

The problem of gender in Norwegian has been addressed in several articles: T. Trosterud, *NLT*, 2001:29–57, writes about gender assignment, claiming that gender in not arbitrary, but governed by rules. By exploring a huge corpus of Norwegian nouns, the author has been able to identify a set of semantic, morphological, and phonological rules, by which gender is correctly assigned to approximately 94% of all these nouns. H.-O. Enger, *MM,* 2002, no.2:135–51, comments on the rules Trosterud has proposed for gender assignment in Norwegian, arguing especially against the somewhat Freudian idea that nouns referring to objects with a physical shape similar to the male or female genitals are assigned masculine or feminine gender according to this. The problem of conflicting gender assignment rules is also discussed. E. has also written two other articles on gender: in *Norskrift*, 104, 2002:3–33, E. discusses gender and inflectional class, while in *NLT*, 2001 : 163–83, he gives a broad presentation of the gender problem in Norwegian. In *MM*, 2002, no.1, J. T. Faarlund (38–42), K. E. Kristoffersen (43–46), and E. Papazian (47–56), discuss the distinction between pronouns and determinatives in Norwegian. J. O. Askeland, *ib.*, 57–75, also focuses on pronouns, giving a morphological analysis of this particular word class in modern Norwegian. M. Julien, *NLT*: 135–61, studies the double supine, claiming that it is different from pseudo-coordination and that none of the previous analyses of the double supine are adequate. J. also points to the connection between supine form and *irrealis* mood. H.-O. Enger, *MM*, no.1:81–105, writes about agreement in constructions like 'Pannekaker er godt', where the subject 'pannekaker' is plural while the adjective 'godt' is neuter singular. A. Sveen, *NLT*, 2002:3–26, discusses aspects of meaning found in the sentence structure itself. J. Orešnik, *NLT*: 57–70, uses a theory of natural syntax developed at the University of Klagenfurt, applying it to Norwegian examples. A. L. Andersen, *NLT*, 2001 : 185–206, presents a psycho-linguistic study on how easily children are able to understand different syntactic structures.

7. Lexicography and Dictionaries

The fourth volume of the large dictionary *Norsk ordbok*, Samlaget, 2002, 800 pp., is finally available, covering entries from 'gigle' to 'harlemmerolje'. When finished, this dictionary will consist of 12 volumes; the aim is to have it complete in 2014, in time for the bicentennial celebration of the Norwegian constitution. *Nynorskordboka*, Samlaget, 2001, 848 pp., is once again published in a new edition, updated and with an extended number of entries. Ivar Aasen's *Norsk Ordbog*, Samlaget, 883 pp., first published in 1873, is now available in a new edition, this time in Roman type and with an introduction by Kristoffer Kruken and Terje Aarset. Tor Erik Jenstad and Arnold Dalen, *Trønderordboka*, Trondheim, Tapir, 2002, 382 pp., is published in a new and extended edition, the number of entries is much increased, and like the first edition, it is furnished with information on local variation in pronunciation, distribution, etymology, and meaning. Tor Erik Jenstad, *Norge rundt med ord*, Ål, Boksmia, 2003, 239 pp., documents variation in the vocabulary of Norwegian dialects, and the content is organized according to themes, e.g. human body, health, family relations, and games. The book should be of interest to scholars, as well as to the general public. Johan Hammond Rosbach, **Ord og begreper: norsk tesaurus*, Pax, 2001, 325 pp., is a Norwegian thesaurus, divided into 22 chapters with altogether 801 articles. Vigleik Leira and Ståle Løland, *Norsk forkortingsordbok*, 2nd edn, Cappelen, 2001, 207 pp., is a dictionary of Norwegian abbreviations. Jacob Dybwad's 1943 dictionary on rhyme, *Norsk rimleksikon*, is now published as *Norsk rimordbok*, ed. Tor Guttu, 5th edn, Kunnskapsforlaget, 2001, 256 pp. It contains more than 32,000 rhymes, arranged in accordance with pronunciation. Audun Øyri, *Norsk medisinsk ordbok*, 7th edn, Samlaget, 1421 pp., contains more than 25,000 entries in Norwegian, most of them are in addition linked to English entries. The dictionary is also equipped with a list of relevant Internet addresses. Karl Arne Utgård, **Juridisk og administrativ ordliste. Bokmål — nynorsk*, Samlaget, 2002, 109 pp. is a dictionary with 3,700 entries covering the vocabulary of law and administration, offering translations from bokmål to nynorsk, as well as general advice on how to write nynorsk within these two domains. Thus this book could be of great help to users of nynorsk within two fields where bokmål is very dominating. Two small dictionaries deal with the vocabulary used for SMS and chat: Gaute Hopland, *SMS-bbln*, Kagge, 2001, 96 pp. and *Qlt: sms-ordboken*, ed. Ina C. Sandberg, Schibsted, 2001, 80 pp.

Evalda Jakaitienë and Terje Mathiassen, **Litauisk-norsk ordbok*, Vilnius, Baltos lankos, 2001, 628 pp., is a new Lithuanian-Norwegian dictionary which contains *c.* 22,000 entries. Arne Halvorsen, **Rumensk-norsk ordbok,* Sypress, 2001, 518 pp., is a Rumanian-Norwegian dictionary with *c.* 25,000 entries. Liv Nilsen Garras, **Norsk-gresk ordbok,* Ad Infinitum, 2002, 640 pp., is a Norwegian-Greek dictionary containing 40,000 entries, as well as a section on grammar. Gerda Moter Erichsen, *Tyske synonymer,* Fagbokforlaget, 2001, 321 pp., is a collection of approximately 14,000 German synonyms with Norwegian translation.

Most dictionaries printed during the period under review are on Norwegian-English / English-Norwegian. Willy A. Kirkeby has published several such dictionaries: *Stor engelsk ordbok: engelsk-norsk,* Kirkeby, 1599 pp., and *Stor engelsk ordbok: norsk-engelsk,* Kirkeby, 1484 pp., both with 90,000 entries; *Norsk-engelsk / engelsk-norsk ordbok,* Kirkeby, 2001, 1086 pp., with *c.* 60,000 entries, *Norsk-engelsk blå ordbok,* Kunnskapsforlaget, 2002, 976 pp., with approximately 65,000 entries, and **Engelsk ordbok: engelsk-norsk / norsk-engelsk,* eBok, 2001, 1381 pp., this last also available on CD-ROM. The publishing house Kunnskapsforlaget has also published an *Engelsk-norsk blå ordbok,* 2002, 1280 pp., with 65,000 entries and the much larger *Engelsk stor ordbok,* 2001, 767 pp., with more than 200,000 entries and over 500,000 translations, covering British, as well as American English. Petter Henriksen and Vibecke C. D. Haslerud have edited two large dictionaries aiming for the advanced user, *Norsk-engelsk stor ordbok,* Kunnskapsforlaget, 2002, 1296 pp., with 94,000 entries and *Engelsk-norsk stor ordbok,* Kunnskapsforlaget, 2002, 2048 pp., with 123,000 entries. Jan Erik Prestesæter, **Norsk-engelsk teknisk ordbok,* Kunnskapsforlaget, 2002, 1017 pp., is a Norwegian-English dictionary focusing on the vocabulary of technology. Gerd Moter Erichsen, *Ord og uttrykk på fire språk: norsk, engelsk, tysk, fransk,* Cappelen akademisk, 256 pp., contains *c.* 1,300 Norwegian words and phrases translated into German, English, and French.

LITERATURE SINCE THE REFORMATION

POSTPONED

V. SWEDISH STUDIES

POSTPONED

5
SLAVONIC LANGUAGES
I. CZECH STUDIES
LANGUAGE

By Marie Nováková and Jana Papcunová,
Ústav pro jazyk český Akademie věd České republiky, Prague

1. General and Bibliographical

The Polish Bohemicist Ewa Siatkowska has published a collection of her essays on Czech, *Czeszczyzna widziana z boku*, Wa, Instytut Filologii Slowiańskiej, 314 pp., in which she covers a wide spectrum of topics: the development of the language, the question of its norm and codification, lexicology, morphology, semantics, word formation, and language contacts with Polish and Slovak. F. Daneš, *IJSL*, 162:9–18, concentrates on the present-day situation of Czech, especially on the specificities of the Czech diglossia and the process of functional differentiation in Czech; J. Hasil, *PLS*, 46:49–55, discusses the changes in Czech at the turn of the 20th and 21st cs, and J. Kraus, *ib.*, 81–89, writes on the evolutionary dynamics in contemporary standard Czech and on its relationship to common Czech in modern communication. Galina Parfenevna Neščimenko, pp. 174–221 of her book *Языковая ситуация в словянских странах: опыт описания: анализ концепций*, Mw, Nauka, 277 pp., refers to the conception of the description of the Czech language situation.

BIBLIOGRAPHIES. Jana Papcunová and Alena Nejedlá, *Bibliografie české lingvistiky 1996*, Prague, Ústav pro jazyk český AV ČR, 240 pp., is a thematically ordered and annotated bibliography (1004 entries on Czech). Marie Nováková, Zdeněk Tyl, and Milena Tylová, *Bibliografie české lingvistiky 1961–1963*, vol. 1, Prague, Ústav pro jazyk český AV ČR, 227 pp., have prepared a retrospective bibliography of general, Indo-European, Slavonic, and Czech linguistics (1551 entries). E. Golková, *Firbas Vol.*, 9–22, has produced a bibliography for Jan Firbas (for the years 1951–2000). Bibliographies for Radoslav Večerka and Jan Chloupek have appeared in *SPFFBU-A*, 52:257–58 and 259 respectively. J. Nekvapil, *Sociolinguistica*, 17:217–19, has compiled a bibliography of Czech sociolinguistics.

2. History of the Language

N. Kvítková, Čechová, *Okraj*, 35–40, focuses on the question of the centre and periphery of the lexicon in the chronicle of the so-called Dalimil (14th c.); M. David, *ib.*, 60–62, examines word borrowings in the translation of *Theatrum Mundi Minoris* by Nathanaël Vodňanský z Uračova; M. Janečková, *ib.*, 27–34, is on neologisms in the lexicon of Jan Amos Komenský; M. Homolková, Janyšková, *Studia Etymologica*, 191–200, reconstructs two parallel parts of the verb *přěmoci* and explains the function of the suffix *přě-*; H. Karlíková, *ib.*, 201–07, submits a study of Church Slavonic expressions of Croatian redaction in Old Czech collected in Klaret's dictionary (*holet, hradobit*); M. Janečková, *Studia Comeniana et historica*, 33:69–70, 150–95, analyses the language of the legend *Muž apoštolský aneb Život a ctnosti pátera Albrechta Chanovského* (from 1680) by Jan Tanner (focusing on phonetic, morpological, syntactic, and lexical features); V. Koblížek, *Čeština̋ř*, 14:6–10, 29–36, examines the state of Czech in East Bohemia in the Renaissance and Baroque period. Pavel Kosek, *Spojovací prostředky v češtině v období baroka*, Ostrava, Ostravská Univ., 180 pp., is a characterization of Baroque Czech and an analysis of Baroque compound sentences and conjunctions.

3. Phonetics and Phonology

M. Krčmová, Šimková, *Tradícia*, 53–59, deals with the description of acoustic means in the language and points out its difficulty; I. Balkó, Čechová, *Okraj*, 229–33, follows the spatio-temporal qualities of a spoken discourse and the speech tempo and its stylistic functions; Š. Šimáčková, Kosta, *Investigations*, 119–35, submits an acoustic analysis of Czech trilled *r*; O. Šefčík, *SPFFBU-A*, 52:99–111, first presents a review of both older and current opinions on the Czech vowel system, then he continues with a theoretical part of an alternation-based analytical phonology, and finally he applies the theory of phoneme alternations on the Czech vowel system; T. Vykypělová, *PLS*, 36:161–68, focuses on substitution and borrowing of the phoneme *f* in Czech (compared to other Slavonic languages).

4. Morphology and Word Formation

J. Siatkowski, Karwatowa, *Procesy*, 211–23, is a study of morphological changes in Czech in the last 10 years; K. Oliva jr., Kosta, *Investigations*, 299–314, is on disambiguation of the reflexive particle *se* and the vocalized conjunction *se* in Czech; V. Petkevič, *ib.*, 315–28, discusses subject-predicate agreement and automatic morphological disambiguation of the Czech National Corpus; J. Obrovská, *SPFFBU-A*,

52:147–59, comments on the transition of feminine nouns belonging to the paradigm *kost* to the paradigm *píseň*; and in Čechová, *Okraj*, 109–15, she analyses variant formants in the genitive plural of feminine nouns with the termination *-yně*; S. Čmejrková, *NŘ*, 86:181–205, analyses the pronoun *svůj* and its use in contemporary texts; and in Hellinger, *Gender*, 27–57, she describes the grammatical and lexical gender in Czech and elucidates nouns of common gender, nouns that do not specify differences of gender, and nouns that lack grammatical gender, then she expounds the feminine derivatives from masculine nouns; the same author, *PLS*, 46:17–31, discusses the relationship between natural and grammatical gender in Czech; J. Šimandl, *NŘ*, 86:23–26, analyses the category of animacy in some legal terms; in another article, *ib.*, 161–64, he follows the development of genitive endings in the Czech names of days of week; H. Konečná, *ib.*, 126–32, explains the origin of dative and instrumental endings in place names (*Prachatice*) occuring in dialects; J. Marvan, *PLS*, 46:109–11, is on aspect in Czech; L. Veselovská, *SPFFBU-A*, 52:161–77, analyses two analytic verbal forms in Czech, the simple past and the periphrastic passive and shows a structural distinction between them. Anna Maria Perissuti, *Determinátory neurčitosti v češtině*, Naples, Univ. degli studi di Napoli, 288 pp., deals with the indefinite determiners in Czech, with their classification, types, etymology, functions, and use in sentences.

WORD FORMATION. Tichá, *Internacionalizmy*, includes several contributions dealing with this topic: P. Kochová (157–65), on formation of international initial abbreviations; Z. Tichá (215–19), on compounds with the component *terapie* and shifts in its meaning in Czech; J. Mravinacová (126–32), on combination of the prefixoids *hyper-*, *giga-*, *maxi-*, *mega-*, *mini-*, *multi-*, *pseudo-*, *super-*, *ultra-*, and *ex-* with Czech expressions; Z. Opavská (35–41), on functions and use of these prefixoids; P. Mitter (126–32), on the component *bio-* and its meaning. Josef Hubáček, *SPFPFSU-D*, 3:196–98, analyses intensifying and attenuating adjectives and their derivation in the work of Jan Amos Komenský; M. Jelínek, *SPFFBU-A*, 52:113–23, is on transpositional active verbal adjectives terminating in *-cí*, *-(v)ší*, *-lý*, *-ný/-tý* and on their formation; P. Mitter, *SaS*, 64:289–97, comments on contemporary hybrid compounds with the first component borrowed; Id., Čechová, *Okraj*, 63–66, on hybrid nouns with the first component *pseudo-*; Z. Opavská, *Varia*, 10:9–12, analyses neologisms in the language of politics (especially the expressions denoting members of political parties, movements, or their opponents); P. Šmídová-Kochová, *ib.*, 179–83, describes juxtaposition and prefiguration from a word-formative point of view; M. Knappová, *NŘ*, 86:113–19, discusses word formation of feminine surnames and their use both from a linguistic and a legal viewpoint; M. Ziková, *SPFFBU-A*, 52:125–32, elucidates the gender value switch as a productive derivational category in Czech.

5. Syntax and Text

Miroslav Vondráček, *Nepredikativnost*, Hradec Králové, Gaudeamus, 249 pp., analyses subject and predicate in Czech from various standpoints: philosophical, semantic, morphological-syntactic, and stylistic, and he also draws attention to interjection in present-day Czech studies. Markus Giger, *Resultativa im modernen Tschechischen: unter Berücksichtigung der Sprachgeschichte in der übrigen slavischen Sprachen*, Berne, Lang, 523 pp., studies syntactic constructions with resultatives in Czech, their forms, meaning, and also resultatives in Czech dialects. Přemysl Hauser, *Základy české skladby*, Brno, Masaryk Univ., 108 pp., describes and expounds the elementary phenomena of Czech syntax.

P. Karlík, *PLS*, 36:56–67, discusses Czech syntactic structures with the infinitive; Id., *SPFFBU-A*, 52:133–45, applies the modified valency theory to deverbative expressions with segments *-n-/-t-* + *-ý/-á/-é* or *-n-/-t-* + *-o/-a/-o* derived both from perfective and imperfective lexemes, and analyses constructions with these expressions (similarly also in *SPFPFSU-D*, 3:154–67); P. Caha, *ib.*, 191–202, investigates Czech accusative + infinitive constructions, especially those governed by verbs of perception; M. Hirschová, Šimková, *Tradícia*, 195–203, points out irregularity in functioning of some adverbials in Czech; Š. Lešnerová and K. Oliva jr., *SaS*, 64:241–52, analyse Czech relative clauses with non-standard structure (based on material from the corpus SYN2000); J. Panevová, *SPFPFSU-D*, 3:145–53, writes on certain shifts in usage occuring in syntax (constructions with two prepositions beside one another, with several attributes not in agreement); L. Uhlířová, *ib.*, 168–76, analyses constructions with the deictic expressions *tento, toto*; L. Zimová, *ib.*, 184–95, refers to conjunctions *když by, i když by* vs. *kdyby, i kdyby* in conditional clauses; P. Kosta, Kosta, *Investigations*, 601–06, discusses the relationship between adverbs and negation in Czech from a syntactic viewpoint; L. Zimová, Čechová, *Okraj*, 126–33, focuses on the representation of the concepts *centrum* and *periferie* in syntactic explanations in contemporary Czech grammars; S. Machová, *ib.*, 134–39, analyses left valency of verbo-nominal predicate with the copulative verb *býti*; I. Kolářová, *ib.*, 140–47, writes on possibilities of substitution of expressions *to, tak* at the beginning and at the end of an utterance; A. Trovesi, *ib.*, 148–55, discusses functions of anaphora in spoken Czech; K. Karhanová, *Varia*, 10:183–90, analyses intertextuality in Czech newspapers from 1994–95.

6. Orthography

R. Adam, '"Bezkopcý úval známý svými hicy předlohou skici mistra Kopanici." Je *c* měkké nebo obojetné?', *NŘ*, 86:169–80, investigates whether the Czech consonant *c* is ambiguous or palatal and gives a survey of treatment of this question in Czech grammars and codifying handbooks; J. Pleskalová, *PLS*, 36:102–11, sums up the development of Czech orthography; B. Lehečka, *ČDS*, 11:136–40, deals with the changes in Czech orthography since the 13th c. and concentrates on the problem of electronic processing of Old Czech spelling.

7. Lexicology and Phraseology

The proceedings Tichá, *Internacionalizmy*, present a number of contributions on lexicon: O. Martincová, on compensating tendencies in the new Czech lexicon (17–22); A. Rangelova, on new means of communication as a naming impulse (229–33); B. Junková, on word borrowings from English in Czech journalistic style in the 1990s (106–14); J. Světlá, on the process of lexicon internationalization in the tourist industry (174–81); I. Bozděchová, on new internationalisms in contemporary special style of medicine (42–47). J. Mravinacová, *Varia*, 10:54–58, draws attention to semantic diversity of borrowed nouns terminating in *-ing/-ink*; M. Vajdlová, *ib.*, 136–47, analyses semantic differentiation of Old Czech lexical units *dívati sě, diviti sě* in the development of Czech until the present day; M. Fryščák, *PLS*, 46:33–39, comments on the system of verbs of motion in Czech, their relationship to the aspect category, and possibilities of prefixation (*jít/chodit, přijít/přicházet*); B. Vykypěl, *ib.*, 36:152–60, discusses the etymology of the expression *král*; E. Lotko, Karwatowa, *Procesy*, 101–15, follows tendencies which are characteristic of the present lexical development (in Czech, Slovak, and Polish); O. Martincová, *ib.*, 117–26, focuses on structural processes in the new Czech lexicon and on the role of neography in the comparative study of contemporary languages; Z. Tichá, *ib.*, 225–30, reports on the main sources of the new Czech lexicon from 1985–95 and on its compilation in the dictionary *Nová slova v češtině* (see *YWMLS*, 60:864); D. Svobodová, Čechová, *Okraj*, 53–59, follows various types of loan words on the periphery and in the centre of the Czech lexicon; A. M. Černá, *NŘ*, 86:133–38, is a semantic analysis of the Old Czech expression *řeřátko*; I. Bozděchová, *ib.*, 71–81, deals with relational adjectives derived from nouns in medical terminology; M. Šulc, *SaS*, 64:253–68, submits a lexicographical description of the conjunction *jestliže*. *ČDS*, 11, includes the following: E. Wehle, with an analysis of metaphorical-metonymical meanings of the expressions *ústa, pusa, huba* in set phrases

(10–14); V. Malínek, on allegorical appelations in sport journalism (44–48); G. Sittová, on names of birds and their connotations (54–57); I. Vaňková, on the motif of the swallow (*vlaštovka*) in Czech metaphors, set phrases, and comparisons (59–64); J. Šlédrová, on the sematics of the expressions *matka, otec, tchyně, tchán* in idioms (64–69); V. Chládková, on the conception of the *Old Czech Dictionary*, the structure of its entries, and methodology of compilation (82–87); M. Vajdlová, expounding the Old Czech expressions *pán, rytieř, panošě* (88–93); M. Jamborová, on the words *padúch* and *kút* (93–94, 114–15); Z. Braunšteinová, on the Old Czech *mistr* (95–98) and *pivo* (108–14); H. Bartošová, on the Old Czech names of the signs of the zodiac (99–104); A. M. Černá, setting right the explanation of the expression *paňbába* in the *Old Czech Dictionary* (105–08), and M. Pytlíková, discussing equivalents of Latin *eunuchus* in four redactions of the Old Czech Bible (125–35).

Vladimír Just, *Slovník floskulí: malá encyklopedie polistopadového newspeaku: klišé, slogany, hantýrky, tiky, partiové metafory, slovní smogy*, Prague, Academia, 216 pp., has compiled a dictionary of empty phrases, clichés, etc. from the 1990s. Eva Mrhačová and Renáta Ponczová, *Zvířata v české a polské frazeologii a idiomatice: česko-polský a polsko-český slovník*, Ostrava, Ostravská Univ., 268 pp., have collected much rich material of idioms, phraseologisms, proverbs, etc., based on the names of animals, and have compiled a Czech-Polish and Polish-Czech phraseological dictionary.

8. Semantics and Pragmatics

J. Hoffmannová, pp. 25–33 of *Vágnost, věda a filosofie: sborník příspěvků*, ed. Jiří Nosek, Prague, Filosofia, 184 pp., analyses oral discourses for how the vagueness of the object and the vagueness of the meta-language are concerned; similarly, S. Dönninghaus, *SaS*, 64:201–18, writes on vagueness in language based on material from *SaS, NŘ*, and *ČMF* in recent years; J. Světlá, *ib.*, 88–106, defines the informative texts, their types and functions, and deals also with the differences between them; J. Kraus, *PLS*, 46:81–89, focuses on the relationship between standard and common Czech in everyday communication, in literature, and in official and scientific discourses; P. Mareš, *ib.*, 99–107, discusses the penetration of substandard and informal features into the public communicative sphere (i.e. into the radio, literature, advertising, etc.); J. Hoffmannová, *ib.*, 57–70, analyses the language and style of present electronic communication; S. Čmejrková, *Prágai Tükör*, no.2:42–48, discusses the impact of this type of communication on Czech; M. Pravdová, *NŘ*, 86:206–17, outlines the specificity of language means in mass media on the lexical and pragmatical level; L. Hašová, *ib.*, 57–70, reports on the types and topics of discussions in an Internet club; Z. Hladká, Šimková, *Tradícia*, 130–33, analyses language usage in a corpus of private correspondence.

Pragmatics in Czech is the main topic of the collection *Jazyk, media, politika*, ed. Světla Čmejrková and Jana Hoffmannová, Prague, Academia, 258 pp.: J. Kraus draws attention to political discourse, to its communicative and language prerequisites, and to the renewed interest in rhetoric, and he also gives a characterization of the present Czech language situation (13–39); J. Hoffmannová contributes on the humour and comic in speeches of Czech MPs, on metalanguage, metacommunication, and on language play in the Czech Parliament (40–79); S. Čmejrková sketches the methodology of media discourse analysis and illustrates it with examples from Czech TV debates (80–115); O. Müllerová, 'Rozhovor s hostem: žánr rozhlasového vysílání na pomezí interview a přátelského popovídání', is an analysis of the radio programme *Presklub* (116–56). J. Alexová, Čechová, *Okraj*, 169–77, analyses monological texts that were primarily oral and then written; the same author, *Ruščákův Vol.*, 191–99, writes on segmentation of a text in informal communication both oral and written, on acoustic and graphic means of the segmentation, and on the function of a paragraph; O. Müllerová, *ib.*, 48–56, defines characteristic features of the language of older people; Z. Hladká, *PLS*, 36:25–34, follows humour in the language of private written correspondence; P. Chleboun, *SaS*, 64:193–200, analyses neutral and confrontational replies in TV and radio debates; K. Karhanová and J. Homoláč, pp. 6–10 of *Očernění*, ed. Filip Pospíšil, Martin Šimáček, and Lenka Vochocová, Prague, Člověk v tísni, 30 pp., report on Czech media discourse and stereotypes used in it.

9. Sociolinguistics and Dialectology

J. Nekvapil and I. Leudar, *SaS*, 64:161–92, analyse Czech media from an ethno-methodological perspective concentrating on Romany identity in dialogical networks; J. Nekvapil, pp. 76–94 of *Mehrsprachigkeit in der erweiterten europäischen Union*, ed. Julianne Besters-Dilger et al., Klagenfurt, Drava, 335 pp., focuses on languages participating on the language situation in the Czech Republic, on languages used in communication, on teaching languages at schools, on the languages of immigrants, etc.; Id., 'Language biographies and the analysis of language situations: on the life of the German community in the Czech Republic', *IJSL*, 162:63–83, analyses the linguistic, social, and political situation in the Czech Republic during the course of the 20th c.; T. Berger, *ib.*, 19–39, deals with the language (cultural and political) contacts of Czechs and Slovaks in history from the sociolinguistic point of view; Jaroslav Hubáček, *SPFPFSU-D*, 3:206–14, is on synonymy in various types of slang (i.e. sport, musical, students', hunters', prisoners', etc.).

DIALECTOLOGY. S. Kloferová, *NŘ*, 86:5–18, comments on the formation of dialectal isoglosses; and in *SPFFBU-A*, 52:203–12, she sketches the development of the Czech national language in the Czech language atlas; Z. Hladká, *ib.*, 231–40, writes on figurative naming in Czech dialects, describes its treatment in the language atlas, and also includes discussion of semantic shifts; L. Čižmárová, *ib.*, 213–21, outlines the development of vowel quantity in Czech and Moravian dialects; Z. Hlubinková, *ib.*, 223–29, refers to the forming of depronominal adverbs in East Moravian dialects; and S. Kloferová, Janyšková, *Studia etymologica*, 365–75, is an essential study on areal linguistics and semantic word formation analysing metaphoric naming and their motivational sources in Czech and Moravian dialects; M. Krčmová, *PLS*, 36:73–81, describes interdialects, their development, use, and specificity; H. Šindlerová, *SPFFBU-A*, 241–48, analyses substandard features in personal correspondence (substandard language, common language, and interdialects). An interesting collection, *Deutsche und tschechische Dialekte im Kontakt*, ed. Albrecht Greule and Marek Nekula, Regensburg, Praesens, 100 pp., includes: S. Kloferová (21–36), on language areals and their characterization (based on material from the *Český jazykový atlas*); L. Čižmárová (37–43), on south Moravian dialects and their contacts with German; M. Muzikant (95–100), on words of Czech origin in German dialects in South Moravia.

Zbyněk Holub, *Lexikon nejjižnějšího úseku českých nářečí*, Dobrá Voda, Čeněk, 711 pp., follows changes in the language in south Bohemian regions and the sources of the dialectal lexicon.

10. STYLISTICS

Marie Čechová et al., *Současná česká stylistika*, Prague, ISV, 342 pp., provide a survey of functional styles, theory of communication, text construction, style norms, and of differentiation of the national language. B. Junková, Čechová, *Okraj*, 193–99, describes expressiveness in journalistic texts of the 1990s; E. Minářová, *ib.*, 178–81, deals with forming factors of regional journalistic style; Z. Hladká, *NŘ*, 86:241–50, discusses foreign-language elements and their function in the correspondence of young people; B. Junková, *Stylistyka*, 12:341–52, focuses on loan words (in particular from English) in Czech journalistic style; and in *Ruščákův Vol.*, 312–22, she writes on the function of quotation marks in present-day Czech journalistic texts; M. Křístek, *SPFPFSU-D*, 3:36–47, compares Czech and English conception of style and stylistics; S. Čmejrková, *ib.*, 48–56, discusses the language and style of Czech electronic communication; A. Macurová, *ib.*, 57–65, deals with epistolary style; J. Hoffmannová, *ib.*, 73–77, analyses the style of women's magazines.

ASPECTS OF THE LANGUAGE OF INDIVIDUAL WRITERS. Petr Mareš, *'Also: Nazdar!': Aspekty textové vícejazyčnosti*, Prague, Karolinum, 233 pp., deals with multilingualism in modern Czech literature, in exile literature, and in literature for children (since the 19th c.). M. Červenka, *SaS*, 64:269–75, comments on the *Prozodies* by Josef Dobrovský (1795 and 1798); J. Konopková, *ib.*, 21–30, deals with the ways in which silence is expressed in a *novella Údolí včel* by Vladimír Körner; G. Balowska, *Lotkův Vol.*, 189–94, follows semantic connotations of the lexeme *zémia* in the language of Óndra Łysohorský, and in Čechová, *Okraj*, 47–52, she analyses the vocabulary of the same poet; J. Jodas, *ib.*, 42–46, discusses the function of a Moravian dialect in several prose works by Karel Matěj Čapek-Chod; J. Hoffmannová, *Ruščákův Vol.*, 39–47, investigates the role of the semi-colon in texts by Karel Čapek; I. Kolářová, *Stylistyka*, 12:225–35, focuses on foreign-language devices in the work of Marie Kubátová.

11. Onomastics

Svatopluk Pastyřík, *Studie o současných hypokoristických podobách rodných jmen v češtině*, Hradec Králové, Gaudeamus, 140 pp., summarizes his research on hypocoristics indicating some possibilities of lexicographic compilation of this type of name and focusing on their word formation and affective meaning. Id., *Lotkův Vol.*, 75–78, follows the correspondences and differences in word formation, conception, and use in Czech and Polish; E. Mrhačová, *ib.*, 153–59, contributes on Czech, Polish, and Slovak surnames with negative prefix *ne-/nie-* (analysed from an etymological and word-formative viewpoint); J. Holeš and T. Typovský, *NŘ*, 86:120–25, is a morphological-semantic analysis of Czech surnames derived from animal names and used in north Moravia; M. Ireinová, *ib.*, 19–22, analyses names of individuals and families in the spoken language of the oldest generation in the city of Jindřichův Hradec; J. Matúšová, *ib.*, 251–56, focuses on the development of German surnames of Czech in the first years after the second world war. S. Paliga, Janyšková, *Studia etymologica*, 433–48, deals with some archaic Czech and Slovak place names (*Praha, Olomouc, Labe, Morava, Tatry*, etc.) and their origin; R. Šrámek, *Lotkův Vol.*, 147–51, analyses plural forms of minor place names in Silesia. P. Štěpán continues his studies of names derived from colours: Čechová, *Okraj*, 97–101, on the centre and periphery of the Czech system of colours (based on toponymic material), and *NŘ*, 86:82–95, on the use and meaning of the adjectives *černý, bílý* in toponyms.

AOn, 44, includes: Z. Hlubinková, on the formation of citizen names in Czech dialects (29–39); J. Malenínská, on the minor place names *Čeří, Čeřina, Čeřinka, Čeřovka* and their etymology (45–47); K. Severin, on toponyms *Voštice* (53–123); P. Štěpán, on the suffix *-ný* in minor place names (131–55); J. Šindelářová, on minor place names in the region of Louny (170–93).

Vlastné meno v komunikácii: 15. slovenská onomastická konferencia Bratislava, 6.–7. septembra 2002: zborník referátov, ed. Pavol Žigo and Milan Majtán, Bratislava, Veda, 339 pp., includes: M. Knappová (87–90), on the use of feminine forms of surnames in official and other communication; J. Malenínská (177–81), on hydronyms; L. Olivová-Nezbedová (183–89), on prepositions *v, na* in Czech minor place names; J. Matúšová (191–97), on the way German anthroponyms and toponyms were turned into Czech forms after 1945. Jiří Zeman, *Výslovnost a skloňování cizích osobních jmen v češtině: francouzská osobní jména*, Hradec Králové, Gaudeamus, 125 pp., is the fourth volume of the series dealing with foreign names and their adaptation in Czech.

12. Language in Contact and Comparative Studies

J. Damborský, *Lotkův Vol.*, 63–67, discusses Czech-Polish bilingualism; I. Bogoczová, *ib.*, 69–74, is on interference occuring in the speech of bilingual speakers (Czech-Polish); J. Jodas, *ib.*, 79–82, glosses tricky words in Polish and Czech; I. Janyšková, Pospíšil, *Česká slavistika*, 83–91, writes on Slavonic names of trees; J. Gazda, Tichá, *Internacionalizmy*, 64–73, throws light on internationalizational tendencies in the development of contemporary West Slavonic languages (Czech, Polish, and Slovak), on the relations of these languages to loan words, and analyses the types of neologisms in them; C. Avramova, *ib.*, 84–93, focuses on *nomina perinentia* derived by means of both home and foreign suffixes in Czech and Bulgarian; H. Sixtová, *ib.*, 99–105, follows the influence of English on Czech and Bulgarian adjectives; J. Rejzek, Janyšková, *Studia etymologica*, 259–65, comments on the etymology and semantic development of four Czech-Slovenian lexical isoglosses (*koprnět/koprnéti, oprat'/oprati, pelichat/peliha, pot'ouchlý, potúhnjen*); I. I. Lučyc-Fedarec, *ib.*, 293–300, follows Czech-Latvian and Czech-Lithuanian lexical parallels; A. Brandner, *SPFFBU-A*, 52:13–24, comments on peculiarities of expressing gender in animate nouns in Czech and Russian; H. Marešová, *Varia*, 10:113–23, describes specific features of the spoken language and the remains of a Czech dialect in the city of Zelov (Poland); P. Krejčí and

N. Staljanova, *OpSl*, 13.4:31–41, submit a semantic characterization of Czech and Bulgarian comparisons in journalistic texts. Hana Gladkova and Iskra Likomanova, *Языковая ситуация: истоки и перспективы (болгарско-чешские параллели)*, Prague, Karolinum, 2002, 452 pp., compare the Czech and Bulgarian language situation, their development, and their present state.

Czech is compared to non-Slavonic languages by Marek Nekula, *'... v jednom poschodí vnitřní babylonské věže ...' Jazyky Franze Kafky*, Prague, Nakladatelství Franze Kafky, 627 pp., who focuses on the correlation between Kafka's Czech and German, analyses both languages in Kafka's work, describes languages used in Kafka's family, and deals with the question of language identity. Inchon Kim, *Fixed Items in Free Word Order Languages: Clitics in Czech and Sentence-Final Markers in Korean*, Dobřichovice, Kava-Pech, 150 pp., studies the word order in both languages. A. Rechzieglová, *SaS*, 64: 107–18, compares assimilation of [*s*] in front of [*j*] at the word-boundary in Dutch and Czech; L. Valehrachová, *LPr*, 13:5–15, writes on Czech and English word order and on the impact of topic focus articulation; L. Dušková, *Firbas Vol.*, 127–45, is on syntactic functions in the same languages; D. Short, *Central Europe*, 1:19–39, deals with words of Czech origin in the English lexicon.

13. Czech Abroad

S. Čmejrková, *IJSL*, 162:103–25, writes on the language situation and language competence of the Czech re-emigrants from the Ukraine; A. Jaklová, *Stylistyka*, 12:327–40, deals with American Czech and analyses the language of Czech periodicals in the USA from a stylistic and pragmatic viewpoint; and in *Ruščákův Vol.*, 323–31, she writes on the specificity of present-day Czech-American journalistic texts; A. Jaklová and V. Smolka, Čechová, *Okraj*, 182–92, also write on the language of contemporary Czech-American periodicals and on the impact of English.

14. Bilingual Dictionaries

Jaroslav Olša, *Česko-indonéský sloník — Kamus Ceko Indonesia*, Voznice, Leda, 271 pp., records the general Czech-Indonesian lexicon with pronunciation rules. Ladislav Hradský, *Maďarsko-český slovník — Magyar Cseh szótár, A-K, L-Z*, 2 vols, Prague, Academia, 1046, 826 pp., is a dictionary focused on standard and spoken language and terminology.

LITERATURE

POSTPONED

II. SLOVAK STUDIES

POSTPONED

III. POLISH STUDIES

LANGUAGE

By Nigel Gotteri, *University of Sheffield*

1. Bibliographies and Surveys

B. Wiemer, 'Grammatische Kategorien und Grammatikalisierung in der Forschung der Sowjetunion und Polens: Beitrag zu einen bislang nicht aufgearbeiteten wissenschaftsgeschichtlichen Kapitel', *ZSl*, 48:55–82. *Najnowsze dzieje języków słowiańskich. Język polski*, ed. S. Gajda, Opole U.P., 2001, 540 pp.

2. Phonetics and Phonology

B. Dunaj, 'Zagadnienia poprawności językowej 1. Wymowa samogłosek nosowych', *JPol*, 83:125–26. G. Holzer, 'Zur Lautgeschichte des baltisch-slavischen Areals', *WSJ*, 47, 2001:33–50. J. Rubach, 'Duke-of-York derivations in Polish', *LI*, 34:601–29, demonstrates how velar palatalization and labial fission require a stage in derivation to be undone subsequently. K. Sykulska, 'Język emocji — foniczne środki ekspresywne', *PJ*, no.5:6–20.

orthography, punctuation. A. Cieślikowa, 'O użyciu łącznika w nazwach miejscowych', *JPol*, 83:239–40; S. Bąba and K. Skibski, 'O pisowni nazw własnych i ich derywatów we frazeologizmach', *ib.*, 288–93.

3. Morphology and Word-Formation

K. Dziwirek, 'A different kind of non-canonical case marking: the Slavic verb "to teach"', *SEEJ*, 46, 2002:319–47. D. Kownacka, 'W sprawie repartycji końcówek w dopełniaczu liczby mnogiej rzeczowników zakończonych na *-arnia*', *PJ*, no.4:36–44, finds *-arń* endings less common than *-arni*.

A. Czesak, 'Jeszcze o papieżówce', *JPol*, 83:79–80. R. Eckert, 'Nominalisierungstendenzen im Slawischen und Baltischen (Nomen actionis und Stelle des Verbum finitum)', *ZSl*, 48:257–66, only mentions Polish briefly. I. Kaproń-Charzyńska, 'Wstępna charakterystyka derywatów złożonych z formantem redukcyjnym', *PJ*, no.6:40–50, examines words beginning with *euro-*, *eko-*, *gim-* and the like. T. Kurdyła, 'Pogranicza słowotwórstwa i leksykologii. Problemy interpretacyjne', *JPol*, 83:187–93. T. Malec, 'Eucharystomobil', *ib.*, 80. R. Marcinkiewicz, 'Lepper, lepperiada, lepperyzmy', *PJ*, no.6:51–61. A. Mizerka, 'Kamp po polsku', *Polonistyka*, 56:603–08, by contrast, is not linguistic, but importantly shows *kamp(-u)*, *kampowy*, *kampowiec* in use. M. Nowosad-Bakalarczyk, 'Płeć a rodzaj gramatyczny we współczesnych ofertach pracy', *PJ*, no.5:21–38. M. Rutkowski, '*Bułęsa z Balceronem.* O deprecjacji denotat za pomocą deformacji nazwy', *ib.*, 50–58.

4. Syntax

M. Derwojedowa and Michał Rudolf, 'Czy Burkina to dziewczyna i co o tym sądzą ich królewskie mości, czyli o jednostkach leksykalnych pewnego typu', *PJ*, no.5:39–49, examines multi-word lexical items with an internal syntactic structure. K. Drożdż-Łuszczyk, 'O klasyfikacji jednostek językowych: wyrażenie *jeden z*', *PJ*, no.6:33–39, wonders whether there should be a 'classifier' word-class (*klasyfikatory*). M. Gawełko, 'Zasady perspektywy funkcjonalnej zdania a tendencja analityczna języków', *PJ*, no.3:22–32. M. Ruszkowski, 'Liczebność próby w statystyczno-składniowych badaniach stylu', *JPol*, 83:174–80. P. Rutkowski, 'Liczebniki jako elementy funkcjonalne w derywacji zdania', *PJ*, no.2:11–32. P. Zbróg, 'O wyrażeniach typu *mili kolega i koleżanka*', *JPol*, 83:181–86.

An issue of *JSL*, 8, 2000[2003], presents 'a cross-section of current research on the syntactic phenomena of Polish', including on clitics: E. Dornisch, 'Pronominal object clitics as the head of transitivity phrase' (29–56), M. L. Rivero, 'Impersonal *się* in Polish: a simple expression anaphor' (199–238), M. McShane, 'Hierarchies of parallelism in elliptical Polish structures' (83–118); on negation: A. Przepiórkowski, 'Long distance genitive of negation in Polish' (119–58); M. Świdziński, 'Negative transmission in Polish constructions with participles and gerunds' (263–94), covering participles (adjectival and adverbial) and verbal nouns; J. Witkoś, 'Nominative-to-genitive shift and the negative copula *nie ma*: implications for checking theory' (295–327); on formal and semantic properties of clauses: B. Citko, 'On the syntax and semantics of Polish adjunct clauses' (5–28), K. Dziwirek, 'Why Polish doesn't like infinitives' (57–82); on formal and semantic properties of nominals: G. C. Rappaport, 'Extractions from nominal phrases in Polish and the theory of determiners' (159–98); B. Rozwadowska, 'Aspectual properties of Polish nominalizations' (239–62).

5. Lexicology and Phraseology

D. Brzozowska, 'Terminy *feminizm*, *seksizm*, *gender* we współczesny języku polskim', *JPol*, 83:273–78. S. Dubisz, 'Historia leksemu *demokracja* w języku polskim (analiza leksykograficzna)', *PJ*, no.3:3–11. J. Kortas, 'O użyciu wyrażenia przysłówkowego *tak naprawdę*', *JPol*, 83:194–98; Id., 'Terminy *argot*, *argotyzm* w polskiej nomenklaturze językoznawczej', *PJ*, no.7:26–35. M. Krzyżanowska, 'Uwagi o definiowaniu i klaryfikowaniu współczesnych skrótowców polskich', *JPol*, 83:281–87. M. Kucała, 'Ukończony został Słownik staropolski', *ib.*, 1–4. J. Kulwicka-Kamińska, 'Historia islamizmów w języku polskim', *ib.*, 96–101. T. Malec, '*Fraktalia*', *ib.*, 153. W. Mańczak, 'Pochodzenia przyimka *ku*', *ib.*, 199–203. M. Pietrucha, 'Wartościowanie w słownikach (na przykładzie hasła *demokracja*)', *PJ*, no.3:12–21. K. Pisarkowa, 'O superlatywie ukrytym w negacji typu *ni ma jak Lwów*', *JPol*, 83:86–89. M. Ruszkowski, '*Homograf* czy *homogram*?', *ib.*, 279–80. E. Sękowska, 'Horyzont polityczny współczesnych Polaków', *PJ*, no.4:3–5. K. Skibski, 'O wyrazach typu: *impra*, *ściema*, *nara*', *JPol*, 83:152–53. W. Twardzik, 'Dodatki do słownika staropolskiego', *ib.*, 5–7. J. Waniakowa, 'Wybrane najstarsze polskie słownictwo astronomiczne', *ib.*, 102–11. M. Wołk, 'Próba ustalenia zakresu odniesienia wyrażeń *ogłoszenie*, *obwieszczenie*, *zawiadomienie* i *komunikat*', *PJ*, no.6:9–24. P. Żmigrodzki, 'Teraźniejszość i przyszłość polskiej leksykografii językoznawczej', *PJ*, no.1:2–33.

Uniwersalny słownik języka polskiego, ed. Stanisław Dubisz, 4 vols, Wa, PWN, xcii + 1313, 1355, 1611, 1141 pp., is intended to come between Doroszewski's and Szymczak's dictionaries. There is a wealth of preliminary material; the dictionary tries to be up to date, and usefully includes place names, often with Anglo-Saxon-looking spelling. The Polish word spelled <pub> is to be pronounced [pab], <shareware> ['ʃarwɛr] and <Shanxi/Shansi> ['ʃanɕi]. *Kompakt* and *zoom* are both included (both with the non-colloquial genitive in *-u*), but not *kamp*. Nothing is said about the stress of *powinienem*. The dictionary is based chiefly on a corpus (see <www.korpus.pwn.pl>) and containing 100,000 informative entries; the whole is extremely well thought out. The use of a variety of fonts in its entries is clear and helpful rather than merely ostentatious. See also *Indeks a tergo do Uniwersalnego słownika języka polskiego*, ed. Mirosław Bańko, Dorota Komosińska, and Anna Stankiewicz, Wa, PWN, 416 pp.

On phraseology: S. Bąba, '*Wiedzieć gdzie stoją konfitury*', *JPol*, 83:151–52; D. Połowniak-Wawrzonek, 'Metafora: DZIAŁANIA EKONOMICZNE TO WALKA ZBROJNA w polskiej frazeologii', *PJ*, no.2:44–57; *Wielki słownik frazeologiczny języka polskiego*, ed. Piotr Müldner-Nieckowski et al., Wa, Świat Książki, 1088 pp.; see also <www.frazeologia.pl>.

6. Semantics and Pragmatics

M. Danielewiczowa and A. Zielińska, 'Mentale Verben in der Polszczyzna północnokresowa: ein Klassifikationsversuch', *ZSL*,

48:481–505. G. Dąbkowski, 'O wieloznaczności w węższym i szerszym kontekście', *PJ*, no.1 : 13–19. A. Karaś, 'Językowa konceptualizacja uczuć z grupy STRACHU na podstawie konstrukcji werbonominalnych', *PJ*, no.4 : 27–35. G. Koniuszaniec and H. Błaszowska, *'Language and gender in Polish', Hellinger, *Gender*, 259–85. M. Kaczor, 'Tabu a estetyka językowa', *JPol*, 83 : 46–49. S. Liesling-Nilsson, 'Stereotyp Polaka w Szwecji (na podstawie badań ankietowych przeprowadzonych wśród studentów)', *ib.*, 38–45. J. Maćkiewicz, 'Jaką częścią jest *część ciała*? Rozważania na temat partytywności', *ib.*, 267–72.

B. Maliszewski, 'Stereotypizacja i profilowanie symbolicznych znaczeń wybranych zwierząt w językowo-potocznym obrazie świata', *PJ*, no.8 : 22–35. M. Mączyński, 'Przysięga dowodowa jako akt mowy (na materiale XVII-wiecznych ksiąg sądowych wiejskich)', *JPol*, 83 : 26–37. R. Przybylska, 'Neosemantyzm *nisza* i przymiotnik *niszowy*', *ib.*, 112–15. M. Wingender, 'Das Wortfeld der Quantität im Polnischen', *ZSl*, 48 : 83–92.

7. Sociolinguistics and Dialectology

M. Bańko, 'Poznaj słownik po okładce. Teksty informacyjno-reklamowe na okładkach słownikowych', *PJ*, no.8 : 3–21. A. Czesak and D. Ochmann, 'O lepszą jakość poradnictwa językowego', *PJ*, no.1 : 68–74, also discuss *Pahonia*, *kornfle(j)ksy*, and *top(-)modelka*. A. Giemza, 'Wartościowanie rzeczywistości w socjolekcie narkomanów', *PJ*, no.2 : 33–43. K. Kozłowska, 'Sposoby rozpoczynania i kończenia wypowiedzi egzaminacyjnej (maturalnej)', *PJ*, no.8 : 36–49. T. Kurdyła, 'Ludowe terminologie rzemieślnicze (na przykładzie słownictwa kowali i kołodziejów jaśliskich)', *JPol*, 83 : 50–54. D. Nowacki, 'Język nas zdradza', *Polonistyka*, 56 : 4–7, looks at language, nationality, and patriotism. M. Nowak and M. Smoleń-Wawrzusiszyn, 'Określanie intensyfikacji i innych cech kolorów w nazewnictwie handlowym', *JPol*, 83 : 267–72. R. Pazuchin, 'Rozkaźnik a metodologia opisu językowego', *ib.*, 169–73. K. Pisarkowa, 'Wytrzępiony język. Przyczynek do roli polityki językowej', *ib.*, 164–68. J. Piwowar, 'O współczesnej polszczyźnie biesiadnej', *PJ*, no.5 : 59–65, looks at language used when getting together over drinks. Rada Języka Polskiego, 'Ulica Fürstenwalde, ulica Wolvegi. Spółka z o.o. Controlling, multiplikacyjny', *PJ*, no.2 : 79–80. S. Spires, 'Polish linguistic purism in Lithuania: the case of Alexander Łętowski', *SEER*, 81 : 601–13. K. Stróżyński, 'Ocenianie jako akt komunikacji', *Polonistyka*, 56 : 225–29, is in part a response to Bolesław Niemierko, **Ocenianie szkolne bez tajemnic*, Wa, WSiP, 2002, 292 pp. I. Szczepankowska, 'Jurydyzacja dyskursu publicznego w środkach masowego przekazu', *PJ*, no.7 : 14–25. B. Walczak, 'Język polski jako nośnik kultury europejskiej', *Polonistyka*, 56 : 324–28. W. Wantuch, 'Język swój czy język . . . obcy', *ib.*, 279–82, argues for closer links between foreign-language and Polish teaching in schools. D. Zielińska, 'Tłumaczenie a redagowanie tekstów użytkowych', *JPol*, 83 : 123–24, advocates short sentences.

Z. Babik, 'Uwagi o gwarowym *gździć (się)*', *JPol*, 83 : 204–08. D. Kopertowska, 'Charakteryczne dla Kielec czyzny zjawiska gwarowe występujące w tekstach folklorystycznychtego regionu', *ib.*, 297–307. W. Mańczak, 'Skąd przybyli Kaszubi?', *ib.*, 23–25. W. Palowska-Kohutek, 'Teksy gwarowe 94. Z Karwiny w Republice Czeskiej', *ib.*, 308–11. H. Popowska-Taborska, 'O domniemanym pochodzeniu Kaszubów', *ib.*, 16–22. *Język kaszubski. Poradnik encyklopedyczny*, ed. Jerzy Treder, Gdańsk, Gdańsk U.P.–Oficyna Czec, 2002, 253 pp.

8. Individuals, Individual Works, Stylistics

BIBLE. D. Bieńkowska, 'Sąd Ostateczny (Mt 25, 31–46) forma literacka i właściwości stylistyczne', *JPol*, 83 : 90–95. A. Płotczyk, 'Analiza leksykalno-semantyczna pierwszego przykazania *Dekalogu*', *PJ*, no.1 : 34–46, examines various Polish translations of the ten commandments. A. Stąsiek, 'Ekwiwalencja słowotwórcza — na przykładzie modernizacji tekstu *Ewangelii św Łukasza* w wydaniach *Biblii* Jakuba Wujka', *PJ*, no.8 : 50–62.

KISIELEWSKI. D. Kownacka, 'O nazwiskach, przezwiskach i wyzwiskach w *Dziennikach* Kisiela', *PJ*, no.1 : 47–57.

LEGEND OF ST ALEXIUS. Z. Wanicowa, 'Gdzie zamierzał dopłynąć św. Aleksy i jakie są tego skutki? Próba nowego rozumienia i odczytania 153. i 154. wersu Legendy o św. Aleksym', *JPol*, 83 : 8–15.

MAŁYSZ. A. Matkowski, 'Małysz a mowa polska', *PJ*, no.3 : 33–42.

PROSE BETWEEN THE WARS. I. Adel'geim, 'Обновление психологического языка в межвоенной польской прозе', *Slavianovedenie*, 46–51, is mainly literary in focus.

STYLISTICS. M. Ruszkowski, 'Długość wystąpienia a stopień jego podrzędności jako wskaźnik stylistycznej charakterystyki tekstu', *PJ*, no.6 : 25–32. W. Śliwiński, 'Somatyzmy jako podstawy poetyckich konstrukcji nominalnych w dawnych i współczesnych utworach wierszowanych', *JPol*, 83 : 251–58.

9. Polish and Other Languages

J. Bańczerowski, 'Некоторые вопросы польско-венгерской контрастивной семантики', *SSH*, 48 : 1–10. A. Bergermayer, 'Zum

Problem der gemeinslavischen Reflexe kw, gw, xw, vs. cw, (d)zw, sw vor Vordervokalen — eine Erklärung auf der Grundlage generativistischer Phonologietheorie', *WSJ*, 48, 2002: 7–20. V. Bianchi, 'The raising analysis of relative clauses: a reply to Borsley', *LI*, 31, 2000: 123–40. K. Bielenin, 'Rytuał zamawiania chorób jako akt mowy', *PJ*, no.7: 36–53, analyses healing charms in Polish and Macedonian folk culture. J. P. Blevins, 'Passives and impersonals', *JL*, 39: 473–520. D. Bunčić, 'Online-Präsentation der Slavistik im deutschsprachigen Raum: Probleme und Chancen', *ASP*, 31: 179–97, deals (187–190) with problems of representing mixtures of Slavonic and other languages in web pages. J. Cieszyńska, 'O dwujęzyczności polskich dzieci w Austrii', *JPol*, 83: 116–22. S. Dubisz, 'Słownictwo pochodzenia ukraińskiego we współczesnej polszczyźnie', *PJ*, no.1: 3–13. J. A. Dziewiątkowski, 'Język polski i świadomość językowa zbiorowości polonijnych w belgijskiej prowincji Flandria Wschodnia', *PJ*, no.3: 43–50. A. Holvoet, 'Modal constructions with "be" and the infinitive in Slavonic and Baltic', *ZSL*, 48: 465–80. I. Hyrnik, 'Podstawowa terminologia z zakresu gimnastyki i jej geneza w polskim i czeskim', *PJ*, no.2: 58–62. A. Krzyżanowski, 'Wyrażania metaforyczne motywowane czynnością spożywania pokarmów (w języku polskim i francuskim)', *PJ*, no.4: 16–26. It should be mentioned that Polish is conspicuous by its absence from B. Kunzmann-Müller, 'Schnittstelle Grammatik-Lexikon am Beispiel nicht persönlicher Konstruktionen im Slavischen', *ZSl*, 48: 365–76, and from P. Kosta, 'Syntaktische und semantische Besonderheiten von Negation und Adverb im Slavischen (unter besonderer Berücksichtigung des Russichen', *ib.*, 377–404. Harry Leeming, **Historical and Comparative Lexicology of the Slavonic Languages* (Prace Komisji Słowianoznawstwa, 52) Kw, PAN, 2001, 422 pp. J. Linde-Usiekniewicz, 'Próba klasyfikacji wybranych pojęć społeczno-politycznych', *PJ*, no.7: 4–13, examines Polish and French. S. M. Newerkla, 'Die Vermittlung deutscher Lehnwörter durch das Tschechische in das Polnische und Slovakische', *WSJ*, 48, 2002: 117–32. Z. Ráduly, 'O kalkach niemieckich w językach słowiańskich', *SSH*, 48: 235–44. M. L. Rivero and M. Milojević Sheppard, 'Indefinite reflexive clitics in Slavic: Polish and Slovenian', *NLLT*, 21: 89–155, deals with constructions like *Tę książkę czytało (mi) się z przyjemnością*, *Marek się bije*, and *Dom szybko się zbudował.* J. Rubach, 'Glide and glottal stop insertion in Slavic languages: a DOT analysis', *LI*, 31, 2000: 271–317. D. Rytel-Kuc, 'Phraseologische Wortpaare in der polnischen Gegenwartssprache im Vergleich zum Tschechischen und Deutschen', *ZSl*, 48: 458–64. J. Siatkowski, 'Językowe wpływy tureckie w Atlasie ogólnosłowiańskim', *SSH*, 48: 379–92, is concerned with East and South Slavonic. B. Wiemer, 'Zur Verbindung dialektologischer, soziolinguistischer und typologischer Methoden in der Sprachkontaktforschung: das Beispiel slavischer und litauischer Varietäten in Nordostpolen, Litauen und Weißrussland', *ZSl*, 48:212–29. À. Zoltan, 'Славяно-венгерские этимологии', *Slavianovedenie*, 2002:48–52.

Collins Polish Dictionary, ed. Jacek Fisiak, Wa, Oficyna Wydawnicza Graf-Punkt, 2002, Polish-English xxiv + 505 pp., English-Polish xvi + 512 pp., aggressively up to date, is disadvantaged by its still limited size; it is therefore a pleasure to welcome its much larger American counterparts, *The New Kosciuszko Foundation Dictionary. Polish-English*, ed. Jacek Fisiak, NY, Kosciuszko Foundation, xxix + 1256 pp., and *Nowy słownik Fundacji Kościuszkowej angielsko-polski*, ed. Jacek Fisiak, NY, Kosciuszko Foundation, xxiii + 1729 pp. A major lexicographical event, naturally the dictionary is still not so large as to have required no exercise of selectivity; for example, though English *hurricane lamp* is glossed as 'latarnia morska' and 'nietoperz', the entry for Polish *nietoperz* gives only the sense 'bat'.

10. Onomastics

E. Breza, 'Imię *Restytut* i podobne', *JPol*, 83:154–55; Id., 'Imiona *Taida*, *Taisa*, *Taisja* i podobne', *ib.*, 294–96. E. Oronowicz-Kida, 'Nazwy własne ptactwa domowego w powiecie jarosławskim', *ib.*, 209–16. R. S., 'Imiona', *PJ*, no.3:71–73, examines *Maciej*, *Mateusz*, *Szczepan*, *Stefan*, *Andrzej*, *Jędrzej*, and *Angelika*.

LITERATURE

By John Bates, *University of Glasgow*

(This survey covers the years 2002–2003)

1. General

Słownik pisarzy polskich, ed. Arkadiusz Latuska, Kw, Zielona Sowa, 720 pp., is a popular work containing the profiles of over 1500 writers. Karen Majewski, *Traitors and True Poles. Narrating a Polish-American Identity 1880–1939*, Athens, US, Ohio U.P., 242 pp., is a highly interesting and innovative approach to the issue of émigré literature. Grossman, *Other*, is an important and innovative interdisciplinary approach to Polish studies, whose individual items relating to literature are dealt with below.

Interpretacje dramatu. Dyskurs, postać, gender, ed. Wojciech Baluch et al., Kw, Księgarnia Akademicka, 2002, 424 pp., contains pieces on leading European dramas, such as T. Stoppard's *Arcadia*, F. Dürrenmatt's *Die Physiker*, W. Gombrowicz's *Iwona*, T. Różewicz's *Akt Przerywany*, and S. Przybyszewski's *Śnieg*. *Ciało Płeć Literatura. Prace ofiarowane Profesorowi Germanowi Ritzowi w pięćdziesiątą rocznicę urodzin*, ed. Magdalena Hornung et al., WP, 2001, xxiv + 727 pp. + 24 illus., collects contributions by leading literary scholars and is not devoted purely to Polish matters. *Wiek kobiet w literaturze*, ed. Jadwiga Zacharska and Marek Kochanowski, Białystok, Trans Humana, 2002, 391 pp., comprises three sections: (i) general issues; (ii) Polish literaure, including the writers E. Orzeszkowa, G. Zapolska, and N. Goerke; (iii) women in other literatures. Inga Iwasiów, *Rewindykacje. Kobieta czytająca dzisiaj*, Kw, Universitas, 2002, 260 pp.

B. Kuczera-Chachulska, *Przemiany form i postaw elegijnych w lyrice polskiej XIX wieku*, Wa, wyd. Uniwersytetu Kardynała Stefana Wyszyńskiego, 2002, 317 pp., deals with the Romantic 'bards' as well as A. Asnyk, M. Konopnicka and A. Feliński. Paweł Majewski, *Odmiany awangardy*, Katowice, Ego, 2001, 177 pp., includes chapters on B. Jasieński's *Palę Paryż*, the New Wave poets, and Różewicz's '*zawsze fragment, recycling*'. B. Pawłowska-Jądrzyk, *Sens i chaos w grotesce literackiej. Od Pałuby do Kosmosu*, Kw, Universitas, 2002, 193 pp. S. Stabro, *Od Emila Zegadłowicza do Andrzeja Bobkowskiego. O prozie polskiej XX wieku*, Kw, Universitas, 2002, 431 pp., deals with the prose of writers such as T. Borowski and J. Kawalec, together with literary critics such as A. Kijowski. *Lyrika polska. Interpretacje*, ed. Jan Prokop and Janusz Sławiński, Gd, Słowo/obraz terytoria, 2001, 614 pp., is a reprint of the second edition of 1970.

Friedrich Nietzsche i pisarze polscy, ed. Wojciech Kunicki and Krzysztof Polechoński, Pń, Poznańskie, 2002, 469 pp., deals with Nietzsche's influence on writers as diverse as S. Brzozowski, J. Kasprowicz, and C. Miłosz, and also contains two highly useful bibliographies on Nietzsche in Polish literature and journalism between 1889 and 1939 (273–440). *Na początku wieku: rozważania o tradycji*, ed. Zofia Trojanowiczowa and Krzysztof Trybuś (Prace Komisji Filologicznej, 44), Pń, Poznańskiego Towarzystwa Przyjaciół Nauk, 2002, 372 pp., includes contributions by leading critics on A. Mickiewicz, C. K. Norwid, Miłosz, F. Chopin, and on American Romanticism.

C. Cavanagh, 'Postkolonialna Polska. Biała plama na mapie współczesnej teorii', *TD*, nos 2–3 : 60–71, suggests that the experience of Communism necessitates a Polish contribution to the debate. M. Czermińska, ' "Punkt widzenia" jako kategoria antropologiczna i narracyjna w prozie niefikcjonalnej', *ib.*, 11–27, examines Miłosz's *Rodzinna Europa*, the diaries of B. Malinowski, and journalistic pieces by R. Kapuściński. A. Dziadek, 'Obraz jako interpretant. Na przykładzie polskiej poezji współczesnej', *PL(W)*, 92.2, 2001 : 127–48, examines compositions inspired by Breughel's painting of Icarus written by leading poets in the years 1956–69. S. Kukorowski, 'Drzewo w literaturze polskiej, czyli o tak zwanej tematologii literackiej', *PrLit*, 40, 2002 : 195–206. A. Łebkowska, 'Narracja biograficzna w fikcji', *TD*, nos 2–3 : 28–40, includes T. Konwicki's *Bohiń* and A. Bolecka's *Biały kamień* in its analysis. M. Michalski, 'Parabola filozoficzna w prozie polskiej XX wieku', *PL(W)*, 93.2, 2002 : 103–24. H. Markiewicz, 'O użyciach i nadużyciach cytatów', *Twórczość*, 58.11–12, 2002 : 152–71. A. Zawadzki, 'Mimika i mimetyka, czyli o naśladowaniu inaczej: mim i pantomima w nowoczesnej świadomości literackiej', *PL(W)*, 92.2, 2001 : 109–26, deals with the question in relation to Norwid and B. Leśmian.

D. A. Goldfarb, 'The Polish poet: traveler, exile, expatriate, world citizen', *Ulbandus*, 7 : 155–73, is an excursion taking in Polish poets' travels from the Renaissance to the present. D. Kozicka, 'Dwudziestowieczne "podróże intelektualne". Między esejem a autobiografią', *TD*, nos 2–3 : 41–59, considers *inter alia* W. Szymborska and Z. Herbert. M. Masłowski, 'Polska tożsamość indywidualna a zbiorowy los od Norwida do Gombrowicza', *Slavia*, 71, 2002 : 9–22. E. Metz and D. Walczak-Delanois, 'L'élément polonais dans la poésie russe — l'élément russe dans la poésie polonaise (1900–1940)', *SlaG*, 29, 2002 : 95–122, is largely devoted to the Polish poets W. Gomulicki, J. Tuwim, W. Broniewski, and the Russians K. D. Bal'mont, F. I. Tiutchev, and V. Maiakovsky.

2. From the Middle Ages up to Romanticism

Janusz K. Goliński, *Peccata capitalia. Pisarze staropolscy o naturze ludzkiej i grzechu*, Bydgoszcz, wyd. Akademii Bydgoskiej im. Kazimierza Wielkiego, 2002, 326 pp., is divided into three parts: the world of man and sin, Old Polish writers on the subject of the seven deadly sins, and the sins themselves within the Sarmatian orbit. Krzysztof Maćkowiak, *Słownik a poezja. Z zagadnień świadomości leksykalnostylistycznej polskiego oświecenia*, Zielona Góra, WSP, 2001, 256 pp., is highly technical. Jan I. J. van der Meer, *Literary Activities in the Stanislavian Age in Poland (1764–1795). A Social System?*, Amsterdam–NY, Rodopi, 2002, 339 pp., is a major work.

RuLit, 43, 2002, contains two essays on Renaissance literary culture: T. Ulewicz, 'Hieronim Spiczyński z Wielunia wśród literatów polskich doby przed-Rejowej' (255–63), and M. Jóźwiak, '*Historyja prawdziwa* [. . .] — literacka wersja dziejów pierwszych lat małżeństwa Katarzyny Jagiellonki i Księcia Jana' (265–75). J. Kiliańczyk-Zięba, 'Cuda Krakowa w najstarszym polskim przewodniku', *RuLit*, 44 : 83–92, examines a medieval guidebook. R. Mazurkiewicz, 'Staroczeskie wzorce i analogie polskich średniowiecznyh pieśni maryjnych', *Slavia*, 70, 2001 : 25–50. Ś. Szpak, 'Obraz szkarady. Wizerunek Śmierci z *Rozmowy mistrza Polikarpa ze Śmiercią* na tle średniowiecznej ikonografii i tradycji literackiej', *PrLit*, 38, 2000 : 5–20. C. K. Święcki, 'Mityczni bogowie natury w literaturze staropolskiej', *PL(W)*, 94.4 : 193–209. W. Wojtowicz, 'Czy Marchołt jest błaznem?', *PrzH*, 45.4, 2001 : 65–75, deals with one of the key figures in an early Renaissance translation of the Latin work *Salomon et Marcolfus*. K. Zimek, 'Miłość cienia. Interpretacja mitu o Narcyzie w erotyku *Do Kasie* z rękopisu Zamoyskich', *PL(W)*, 94.4 : 5–26.

TD, no. 1, contains two general essays: M. Hanuszkiewicz, 'Barokowy komplement' (7–22), which examines such writers as S. Zimorowic, J. A. Morsztyn, and W. Potocki; and E. Lasocińska, 'Postać Diogenesa i motywy diogeniczne w literaturze XVII wieku' (58–73), which exemplifies its theme on the basis of works by S. H. Lubomirski and W. Potocki. J. Kroczak, ' "Sen mi się udał . . ." — o wizjach sennych w epice barokowej', *PrLit*, 38, 2000 : 53–68, examines the theme in relation to K. Twardowski's *Lekcje Kupidynowe* and *Łódź młodzi* as well as works by S. Twardowski and W. Potocki. B. Pfeiffer, 'Galerie i pałace. Kategoria "ekphrasis" w utworach staropolskich', *PL(W)*, 92.2, 2001 : 61–78.

W. Dzwigala, 'Voltaire and the Polish Enlightenment: religious responses', *SEER*, 81 : 70–87, also includes literary responses from I. Krasicki and K. Węgierski. S. Nikołajew, 'Polsko-rosyjskie związki literackie w epoce Stanisława Augusta Poniatowskiego', *RuLit*,

44:1–8. M. Schruba, 'Polnische libertine Dichtungen der Aufklärungszeit im europäischen Kontext', *ZSP*, 62:127–47.

INDIVIDUAL WRITERS

BIELSKI. D. Śnieżko, 'Swojskie i obce w kronice uniwersalnej (przykład Marcina Bielskiego)', *TD*, no. 1:23–40. J. Zagożdżon, 'Rola motywów onirycznych w *Śnie majowym* Marcina Bielskiego', *PL(W)*, 93.3, 2002:59–67.

HAUR. J. Partyka, 'Czarty, gusła i "święta katolicka wiara": *katolicyzm ludowy — katolicyzm sarmacki* na przykładzie *Składu abo skarbca* J.K. Haura', *TD*, no. 1:51–57.

KNIAŹNIN. R. Fieguth, 'Venusdienst und Melancholie. Zur Konstruktion des zyklischen Subjekts in Franciszek Dionizy Kniaźnins *Erotyki* (1779),' *WSl*, 48.1:81–100; Id., 'Du rococo au sentimentalisme: les trois premiers recueils poétiques de Franciszek Dionizy Kniaźnin (1749/1750–1807)', *RSl*, 74:835–60.

KOCHANOWSKI. Jacek Sokolski, *Świat Jana Kochanowskiego*, Ww, Dolnośląskie, 2000, 48 pp., is a very colourful popular introduction intended for children. Tadeusz Ulewicz, *Jan Kochanowski of Czarnolas / Jan Kochanowski z Czarnolasu*, Kw, Kasa im. Józefa Mianowskiego, Collegium Columbinum, 2002, 64/79 pp. + 9 pl., an ingeniously designed bilingual volume, provides a general introduction to K.'s life and work. J. Sokolski, 'Jan Kochanowski i Agostino Steuco. Uwagi na marginesie fraszki *O Łazarzowych księgach*', *PL(W)*, 94.4:225–29. C. Zaremba, 'La disparition d'Ursule. Contribution à l'étude des *Thrènes* de Jan Kochanowski', *RSl*, 74:505–15.

KOCHOWSKI. *Wespazjan Kochowski w kręgu kultury literackiej*, ed. Dariusz Chemperek, UMCS, 189 pp., based on papers from a conference on 13–14 November 2000, provides a comprehensive analysis of K.'s work. L. Ślękowa, 'Quadratum perfectum Wespazjana Kochowskiego. *Niepróżnujące próżnowanie — Liryka polskie, Ogród Panieński, Psalmodia polska*: uwagi o kompozycji', *PL(W)*, 92.2, 2001:149–57.

KRASICKI. Zbigniew Goliński, *Krasicki*, PWN, 2002, 387 pp., is a standard biography. Wacław Walecki, *Wieczny człowiek. 'Historyja' Ignacego Krasickiego i jej konteksty kulturowe i literackie*, Kw, Księgarnia Akademicka, 1999, 175 pp. *W 200. rocznicę śmierci Ignacego Krasickiego*, ed. Stanisław Frycie, Piotrków Trybunalski, Akademickie Naukowe wyd. Piotrkowskie, 2002, 196 pp., is a collection of papers on the major works of K.'s œuvre from a conference on 6 December 2001. *Ignacy Krasicki. Nowe spojrzenia*, ed. Zbigniew Goliński et al., Wa, DiG, 2001, 372 pp., examines K.'s work in terms of his professional life, its relations with music, Plutarch's influence on his writing, its reception in 19th-c. Polish culture, and the attitudes it expresses towards other cultures. Z. Ożóg-Winiarska, 'Florystyczne postacie w bajkach Ignacego Krasickiego,' *PrzH*, 47.2 : 65–74.

KRZYCKI. W. Wojtowicz, 'Korybut Koszyrski i historia literatury nieschludnej. Przyczynek do recepcji obscenów Andrzeja Krzyckiego', *PrLit*, 38, 2000 : 21–31.

LUBOMIRSKI. A. Gurowska, '*Somnus. Fortuna. Invidia. Somni descriptio* — "zakryte przed źrenicą naszą" znaczenie barokowego tekstu', *TD*, no. 1 : 74–88. M. Kunicki-Goldfinger, 'List Stanisława Herakliusza Lubomirskiego do Józefa Zebrzydowskiego', *ib.*, 226–32.

MORSZTYN. *Listy Jana Andrzeja Morstina*, ed. Stefania Ochmann-Staniszewska, Ww, WUW, 2002, 378 pp., is preceded by a largely bibliographical introduction (13–41).

ONOSZKO. D. Samborska-Kukuć, 'Między Bogiem, życiem i śmiercią. Tradycje religijnej poezji baroku w twórczości Jana Onoszki', *PL(W)*, 93.3, 2002 : 131–54.

S. K. POTOCKI. J. I. J. van der Meer, 'Stanisław Kostka Potocki — the first Polish literary critic by profession?', *SEER*, 79, 2001 : 1–14.

W. POTOCKI. *Potocki (1621–1696). Materiały z konferencji naukowej w 300-lecie śmierci poety*, ed. Wacław Walecki, Kw, Uniwersytet Jagielloński, Inst. Filologii Polskiej, 1998, 232 pp., contains major scholarly contributions. D. Dybek, 'Między mitem a historią. Legendy herbowe w *Poczcie herbów* Wacława Potockiego', *PrLit*, 38, 2000 : 69–84, and Id., 'Uwagi o kompozycji *Pocztu Herbów* Wacława Potockiego', *PL(W)*, 93.1, 2002 : 137–53. N. Korniłłowicz, 'Zoologia fantastyczna w *Tygodniu stworzenia świata* Wacława Potockiego', *ib.*, 93.3, 2002 : 105–14.

REJ. A. Kochan has published three articles on R.: 'Kupiec przed polskim sądem. Uwagi i komentarze do *Kupca* Mikołaja Reja', *PL(W)*, 94.4 : 211–23; 'Pojęcie poczciwości w *Źwierciadle* Mikołaja Reja', *PrLit*, 38, 2000 : 33–42; '*Źwierciadło* Mikołaja Reja. Wokół problematyki tytułu dzieła', *PL(W)*, 93.3, 2002 : 155–69.

SĘP SZARZYŃSKI. A. Karpiński, 'Sęp, Kasia i Narcyz', *TD*, no. 1 : 41–50. M. Kay, 'Beauty created through difficulty: dissonance and crisis in the poetry of Mikołaj Sęp Szarzyński', *PolR*, 48.1 : 73–88. G. Tomicki, '"Taki był on mąż." O *Pieśni V. O Fridruszu* Mikołaja Sępa Szarzyńskiego', *Twórczość*, 59.1 : 64–73.

3. ROMANTICISM

Agnieszka Ziołowicz, *Dramat i romantyczne 'Ja'. Studium podmiotowości w dramaturgii polskiej doby romantyzmu*, Kw, Universitas, 2002, 381 pp., analyses works by A. Fredro, J. Słowacki, Norwid, Z. Krasiński, and Part IV of Mickiewicz's *Forefathers' Eve*. *Romantyzm — Poezja — Historia. 'Szkoła ukraińska' w polskim romantyzmie*, ed. Nataliya Tkachova,

Ternopil', Pidruchniki & Posibniki, 2002, 206 pp., focuses (on the Polish side) mainly on S. Goszczyński's work. *Prace ofiarowane Zofii Stefanowskiej*, ed. Maria Prussak and Zofia Trojanowiczowa, IBL, 2002, 395 pp., while focused on the Romantic poets, especially Mickiewicz, covers writers from W. Potocki to K. Wojtyła, and includes a bibliography of Prof. Stefanowska's work (349–80). J. Łyszczyzna, 'Romantycy — nasi współcześni?', *Postscriptum*, no. 4, 2002:6–14. A. Szol, 'Kobieta i małżeństwo w Kole Sprawy Bożej Andrzeja Towiańskiego', *ib.*, 157–65.

INDIVIDUAL WRITERS

FREDRO. Marcin Cieński, *Fredro*, Ww, Dolnośląskie, 209 pp. M. Piechota, 'Kilka uwag o *Zemście* Aleksandra Fredry', *Postscriptum*, no. 4, 2002:74–82. M. Ursel, 'Późne wiersze rodzinne Aleksandra Fredry', *PrLit*, 40, 2002:37–50.

KRASIŃSKI. Maciej Szpargot, *Ziemia rozdziału — niebo połączenia. O lyrice Zygmunta Krasińckiego* (Prace naukowe Uniwersytetu Śląskiego w Katowicach, 1843), Katowice, Uniwersytetu Śląskiego, 2000, 135 pp. *Zygmunt Krasiński — nowe spojrzenia*, ed. Grażyna Halkiewicz-Sojak and Bogdan Burdziej, Toruń, Uniwersytetu Mikołaja Kopernika, 2001, 393 pp., is a major volume consisting of five sections devoted to: (i) K.'s biography and psychology; (ii) his posthumous reception; (iii) interpretations of his prose and drama; (iv) analyses of individual lyrics; (v) literary dialogues with writers such as Słowacki. M. Szargot, 'Motyw coincidentia oppositorum w twórczości Zygmunta Krasińskiego', *Postscriptum*, no. 4, 2002:111–17. R. Wyczliński, '"Bo ja bez pieniędzy nie potrafię żyć." O sylwetce finansowej Zygmunta Krasińskiego', *PrLit*, 38, 2000:127–42.

KRASZEWSKI. B. Szargot, 'Śmierć i dziewczyna. O powieści *Dwie królowe* J. I. Kraszewskiego', *Postscriptum*, no. 4, 2002:137–45.

MALCZEWSKI. P. Śniedziewski, 'W świecie melancholii. O *Marii* A. Malczewskiego i obrazach C. D. Friedricha', *TD*, no. 4:149–59.

MICKIEWICZ. Anita Debska, *Country of the Mind. An Introduction to the Poetry of Adam Mickiewicz*, Wa, Burchard, 2000, 221 pp., is a general overview of M.'s work. Roman Koropeckyj, *The Poetics of Revitalization. Adam Mickiewicz Between Forefathers' Eve, Part 3, and Pan Tadeusz*, Boulder–NY, Columbia U.P., 2001, ix + 263 pp., is an innovative study of M.'s major works from the 1830s. Joanna Salomon, *Cztery godziny albo zegar Dziadów*, Kw, 15 stopni, 1999, 238 pp., is an esoteric but valuable study of *Forefathers' Eve*. Monika Szpiczakowska, *Fonetyczne i fleksyjne cechy języka 'Pana Tadeusza' Adama Mickiewicza na tle normy językowej* XIX *wieku*, Kw, Księgarnia Akademicka, 2001, 176 pp., analyses the two 19th-c. versions of the text — the standard literary printed version and the manuscript's dialect version. *Theatre and Holy Script*, ed. Shimon Levy, Brighton–Portland, Sussex Academic, 1999, vii + 262 pp., has an assessment by E. Wąchocka of 20th-c. performances of *Forefathers' Eve*, '*Dziady*: a mystery play in the modern Polish theatre' (128–39). An important 'forum' presenting innovative new approaches to M.'s work appeared in *SEEJ*, 45, 2001. Its participants were: H. Filipowicz, 'Mickiewicz: "East" and "West"' (606–23); A. Laroux, 'Canonizing the *Wieszcz*: the subjective turn in Polish literary biography in the 1860s' (624–40); I. Kalinowska, 'The sonnet, the sequence, the Qasidah: East-West dialogue in Adam Mickiewicz's *Sonnets*' (641–59); R. Koropeckyj, 'Orientalism in Adam Mickiewicz's *Crimean Sonnets*' (660–78); M. Dixon, 'How the poet sympathizes with exotic lands in Adam Mickiewicz's *Crimean Sonnets* and the *Digression* from *Forefathers' Eve*, Part III' (679–94); S. Goldberg, 'Konrad and Jacob: a hypothetical kabbalistic subtext in Adam Mickiewicz's *Forefathers' Eve*, Part III' (695–715); and K. C. Underhill, '*Aux grands hommes de la parole*: on the verbal messiah in Adam Mickiewicz's *Paris Lectures*' (716–31).

Postscriptum, no. 4, 2002, has six items relevant to M.'s life and work: I. Opacki, 'Romantyczna. Epopeja. Narodowa, Z epilogiem?' (15–25); A. Nawarecki, 'Mickiewicz w Ameryce' (26–34); E. Teodorowicz-Hellman, 'O szwedzkich odczytaniach polskiej epopei narodowej' (35–47); M. Bąk, 'Mickiewicz? Dzisiaj? Szkic do portretu młodego poety' (48–57); L. Zwierzyński, '*Aluszta w nocy* — śmierć i zaślubiny' (146–49); B. Zeler, '*Gdy tu mój trup* . . . Adama Mickiewicza' (150–56). *RuLit*, 43, 2002, contains four essays devoted to M.: J. Borowczyk and R. Okulicz-Kozaryn, 'Obyczaj filomacki w III części *Dziadów*, czyli ponura festyna u bazylianów' (37–46); A. Ziołowicz, 'Przy biesiadnym stole. Z problematyki obrazowania życia zbiorowego w *Panu Tadeuszu*' (47–57); B. Dopart, 'Forma i sens Mickiewiczowskiej *Grażyny*' (135–49); and Z. Wójcicka, 'Spotkania, rozstania i gry pamięci w lyrice Adama Mickiewicza' (151–65). *PrLit*, 38, 2000, contains two essays on M.'s work: B. Zakrzewski, '"Wieść gminna" o II części *Pana Tadeusza*' (85–89); and M. Jonca, '*Bajki* Adama Mickiewicza — dla dzieci?' (91–102). M. Cieśla-Korytowska, 'Szmery i trzaski w *Panu Tadeuszu*', *PL(W)*, 94.4:27–50. A. Litwornia, 'Echo Sannazara w *Dziadach*', *ib.*, 93.1, 2002:163–71. M. Masłowski, 'Le canon de la culture dans l'œuvre d'Adam Mickiewicz', *RSl*, 74:339–52. J. Zieliński, 'Prologomena do wirtualnego muzeum romantycznego poety', *PL(W)*, 92.2, 2001:79–107.

NORWID. P. Chlebowski, 'Epopeja chrześcijańska a epopeja chrześcijańska w twórczości Norwida', *RuLit*, 43, 2002:59–68; Id., '*Modlitwa* Cypriana Norwida', *PL(W)*, 94.4:51–64; Id., 'Romantyczne *silvae rerum*. O Cypriana Norwida notatnikach i albumach',

TD, no. 6, 2002: 167–79. M. Inglot, 'Norwid wobec powieści jako literatury popularnej swoich czasów', *Literatura i Kulturna Popularna*, 10, 2002: 7–22. D. Klimowska, 'Na drodze poszukiwania prawdy o człowieku — *Nieskończony* Norwida', *PrzH*, 45.4, 2001: 11–20. P. Lesińska, 'Intertekstualna lektura *A Dorio ad Phrygium* C. K. Norwida', *Postscriptum*, no. 4, 2002: 118–36. B. Mucha, ' "Obywatel rzymski." Cyprian Norwid i "polski" papież Pius IX', *PrzH*, 45.4, 2001: 1–10. J. Rudnicka, 'Norwida *Sonet do Marcelego Guyskiego*', *RuLit*, 44: 77–82. M. Śliwiński, 'Naród i historia jako kategorie estetyki Norwida. Wokół *Promethidiona*', *PrzH*, 47.2: 45–52. M. Wiater, 'Mojżesz Norwida', *RuLit*, 44: 9–20. B. Wołoszyn, 'Topos śmierci jako rozłączenia duszy z ciałem w twórczości poetyckiej C.K. Norwida', *ib.*, 241–58.

SŁOWACKI. *PrLit*, 39, 2001, contains seven essays on S.'s work: M. Inglot, 'Wanda z gór (Postać Wandy w dramacie polskim I połowy XIX wieku ze szczególnym uwzględnieniem dramatu Juliusza Słowackiego *Beniowski*)' (5–19); K. Biliński, 'Trzy impresje o recepcji *Kordiana*' (21–28); M. Chacko, 'Słowacki na widowni. Rozważania o doświadczeniach teatralnych poety w latach 1814–1842' (29–44); D. Michułka, 'Słowacki jako "prekursor" antypedagogiki. Bajkopowiastka o karierze "Janka, co psom szył buty" ' (45–53); E. Grzęda, 'Motyw czarnoleskiej lipy w twórczości Juliusza Słowackiego' (55–65); R. Wyczliński, 'Juliusza Słowackiego *hossy* i *bessy* nie tylko giełdowe' (67–84); and J. Michalak, 'Strategia i przypadek. Dzieje edycji *Trzech poematów* Juliusza Słowackiego' (85–103). M. Chacko, 'Inscenizacje dramatów Słowackiego: *Kordiana* i *Księcia Niezłomnego* w Teatrze Laboratorium Jerzego Grotowskiego', *PrLit*, 40, 2002: 101–19, and her 'Z paradyzu i z loży. O doświadczeniach teatralnych Juliusza Słowackiego w latach 1814–1842', *ib.*, 38, 2000: 103–26. A. Opacka, 'Z czego Jan psom szył buty w *Kordianie*, czyli pytanie o konteksty', *Postscriptum*, no. 4, 2002: 58–73. A. Pietrzyk, 'Juliusza Słowackiego łódź z żaglem i statek parowy,' *PrzH*, 47.2: 53–63. M. Stanisz, 'Juliusz Słowacki jako krytyk literacki', *TD*, nos 2–3: 270–81.

4. From Realism to Neo-Realism

Sabina Brzozowska, *Klasycyzm i motywy antyczne w poezji Młodej Polski* (Uniwersytet Opolski. Studia i monografie, 289), Opole U.P., 2000, 170 pp., examines Dionysian motifs, the classical hero, and Nietzscheanism. Maria Obrusznik-Partyka, *Literatura i krytyka na łamach 'Biesiady Literackiej' (1876–1906)*, Piotrków Trybunalski, Naukowe Wydawnictwo Piotrkowskie, 2002, 267 pp., covers the period in the Warsaw literary journal's history when W. Maleszewski was editor-in-chief. *Na pozytywistycznej niwie*, ed. Tomasz Lewandowski and

Tomasz Sobieraj (Prace Komisji Filiogicznej, 45), Pń, Poznańskiego Towarzystwa Przyjaciół Nauk, 2002, 319 pp., comprises articles by leading Polish critics in the field. *Pozytywizm. Języki epoki*, ed. Grażyna Borkowska and Janusz Maciejewski, IBL, 2001, 356 pp., examines such issues as the Russian question in post-1863 Polish literature, the writings of A. Świętochowski, and drama and theatre of the latter half of the 19th c. *Prus i inni. Prace ofiarowane Profesorowi Stanisławowi Ficie*, ed. Jakub A. Malik and Ewa Paczoska, KUL, 791 pp., concerns major writers such as B. Prus, Orzeszkowa, S. Żeromski, and includes contemporary critical responses to their works. *Publicystyka okresu pozytywizmu 1860–1900. Antologia*, ed. Stanisław Fita, IBL, 2002, 271 pp., is an extremely useful anthology, presenting key texts on the Romantic tradition and the political, ideological, and social bases of Positivism. *Swedish-Polish Modernism. Literature — Language — Culture*, ed. Małgorzata Anna Packalén and Sven Gustavsson, Stockholm, Motala Grafiska AB, is based on a conference that took place in Cracow on 20–21 April 2001, and includes contributions by major Polish literary scholars. A. Arczyńska, 'Profesje Żydów na przykładzie prozy pozywistycznej (zarys problematyki)', *PrLit*, 39, 2001 : 105–16. W. Bolecki, 'Impresjonizm w prozie modernizmu. Wstęp do modernizmu w literaturze polskiej XX wieku', *TD*, no. 4 : 17–33. W. Gutowski, 'Młodopolskie inicjacje', *RuLit*, 43, 2002 : 122–33. A. Rossa, 'Impresjonistyczne pejzaże w poezji młodopolskiej', *PrzH*, 45.1, 2001 : 33–47. D. Knysz-Tomaszewska, 'Kategoria impresjonizmu w badaniach nad literaturą Młodej Polski (1890–1918)', *ib.*, 1–8.

INDIVIDUAL WRITERS

BEŁCIKOWSKI. H. Filipowicz, 'Othering the Kościuszko uprising: women as problem in Polish insurgent discourse', Grossman, *Other*, 55–83, uses A. Bełcikowski's play *Przekupka warszawska* as its starting point.

DYGASIŃSKI. R. Kupiszewski, 'Pozytywistyczny obraz świata w *Godach życia* A. Dygasińskiego? (Uwagi do krytyki literackiej utworu)', *PrzH*, 45.4, 2001 : 77–82.

DZIEDUSZYCKI. J. Z. Lichański, '*Baśn nad baśniami* Wojciecha Dzieduszyckiego. Epos bohaterski czy prekursorski utwór literatury *fantasy*?', *Literatura i Kultura Popularna*, 10, 2002 : 23–36.

KOMORNICKA. S. Chodorowicz-Glejzer, 'Geniusz i obłąkanie — literacki wizerunek Marii Komornickiej w pięćdziesięciolecie śmierci', *PrLit*, 40, 2002 : 83–90.

ŁUSZCZEWSKA. K. Biliński, 'Z nieopubliowanych wierszy Jadwigi Łuszczewskiej (Deotymy)', *PrLit*, 40, 2002 : 51–52.

MERZBACH. M. Łoboz, 'O matko Polko! O Izraelko! — romantyczny rodowód Henryka Merzbacha', *PrLit*, 38, 2000 : 143–50.

MEYERSONOWA. A. Arczyńska, 'Twórczość Malwiny Meyersonowej', *PrLit*, 40, 2002: 77–82.

ORZESZKOWA. *Twórczość Elizy Orzeszkowej*, ed. Krzysztof Stępnik, UMCS, 2001, 277 pp., deals *inter alia* with language in O.'s works, her concept of Rome, and the relations with Enlightenment traditions in her early novels. *Wokół 'Nad Niemnem'*, ed. Jolanta Sztachelska, Białystok U.P., 2001, 211 pp. L. Pułka, 'Ponad sto lat samotności. O magicznym świecie Elizy Orzeszkowej', *PrLit*, 38, 2000: 181–98.

PRUS. Danuta Wierzchołowska, *Swiat kobiecy w 'Emancypantkach' Bolesława Prusa*, Zielona Góra, WSP im. Tadeusza Kotarbińskiego, 2001, 170 pp. *Bolesław Prus. Pisarz — Publicysta — Myśliciel*, ed. Maria Woźniakiewicz-Dziadosz and Stanisław Fita, UMCS, 438 pp., derives from a conference held from 11 to 13 October 2001 and features contributions from leading critics on a wide variety of issues. E. Lubczyńska-Jeziorna, 'To i owo o humoreskach Bolesława Prusa', *PrLit*, 40, 2002: 53–76. J. Momro, 'Fantazmaty rewolucji i młodości w *Dzieciach* Bolesława Prusa', *RuLit*, 44: 147–61.

PRZERWA-TETMAJER. W. Czernianin, 'Popularność Kazimierza Przerwy-Tetmajera w epoce Młodej Polski', *Literatura i Kultura Popularna*, 11: 189–211.

PRZESMYCKI. Grażyna Legutko, *Zenon Przesmycki (Miriam) — propagator literatury europejskiej*, Kielce, WSP im. Jana Kochanowskiego, 2000, 335 pp.

REYMONT. A. Knapczyk, 'Uwagi o semiotyce kolorów w *Chłopach* Władysława Stanisława Reymonta', *PrLit*, 40, 2002: 91–100.

SIENKIEWICZ. A. Klobucka, '*Desert and Wilderness* revisited: Sienkiewicz's Africa in the Polish national imagination', *SEEJ*, 45, 2001: 243–59.

STAFF. A. Czabanowska-Wróbel, ' "Pamięć dzieciństwa" i "obecność dziecka" w poezji Leopolda Staffa', *RuLit*, 43, 2002: 277–94. A. Wiatr, 'Późna mądrość zapomnianego poety (w czterdziestą piątą rocznicę śmierci Leopolda Staffa)', *Twórczość*, 58.11–12, 2002: 132–45.

WYSPIAŃSKI. M. Popiel, 'Wyspiański i estetyka modernizmu. W kręgu pojęcia konstrukcji artystycznej', *RuLit*, 44: 277–89.

ŻEROMSKI. M. Olędzki, 'Podstawowe kategorie narracyjne i ich statystyczny obraz w *Popiołach* Stefana Żeromskiego', *PrLit*, 39, 2001: 117–50.

5. From 1918 to 1945

Andrzej Karcz, *The Polish Formalist School and Russian Formalism*, Rochester, NY, Rochester U.P., 2002, ix + 263 pp., a well-researched volume, has individual chapters on M. Kridl and K. Wóycicki. Dariusz

Skórczewski, *Spory o krytykę literacką w dwudziestoleciu międzywojennym*, Kw, Universitas, 2002, 404 pp., presents a theoretical attempt to systematize interwar criticism, focusing on the Irzykowski-Boy affair and K. Wyka's early writings. *'Marchołt' (1934–1939). Antologia tekstów*, ed. Jan Musiał, Kw, Arcana, 2002, 473 pp., groups together texts by major interwar critics and thinkers such as J. Stempowski, R. Ingarden, H. Elzenberg, and S. Pigoń, under the three headings of literature, culture, and politics. Part IV (401–41) contains a critical afterword by the editor. Eugenia Prokop-Janiec, *Polish-Jewish Literature in the Interwar* Years, trans. Abe Shenitzer, NY, Syracuse U.P., 314 pp., is a translation of the 1992 Cracow edition. Marzena Sokołowska-Paryż, *The Myth of War in British and Polish Poetry 1939–1945*, Brussels, Lang, 2002, 313 pp. M. Sadlik, 'Skamandryckie zmagania ze spuścizną literacką Wyspiańskiego. Lechoń — Słonimski — Wierzyński', *PL(W)*, 94.4:65–81. D. Skórczewski, '"Sprawa Irzykowskiego i Boya". Wokół głosnego epizodu międzywojennego sporu o krytykę', *TD*, no. 3:223–31.

INDIVIDUAL WRITERS

GAJCY. *RuLit*, 43, 2002, contains three interpretations of the poem *Portret*: M. Michalski, 'Gajcego sztuka portretowa' (169–75); I. Glatzel, 'Niezłomność wymuszona?' (177–88); and T. Mizerkiewicz, 'Szkic do *Portretu* Tadeusza Gajcego' (189–99).

GAŁCZYŃSKI. W. Tomasik, '"Throwing flowers on to the tracks." (New Man and the new community in Socialist Realist literature)', Grossman, *Other*, 205–16, takes G.'s poem *Kwiaty na tor* (1948) as its point of departure.

GOMBROWICZ. *TD*, no. 3, has ten essays dealing with various facets of G.'s creative work, which include: J. Margański, 'Jozio w piekle literatury' (7–21); M. Delaperrière, 'Kościół międzyludzki i absurd totalitarny w teatrze Gombrowicza' (22–35); E. Fiała, 'Transgresje racji moralnych w *Pornografii* Gombrowicza' (35–56); K. A. Grimstad, 'Co zdarzyło się na brygu Banbury? Gombrowicz, erotyka i prowokacja kultury' (57–69); and M. Kacik, 'Lena ocalona' (70–80). There are also three (auto)biographical 'testimonies' (232–56). M. Kacik, 'Mit faustyczny w *Pornografii* Witolda Gombrowicza', *PL(W)*, 94.4:99–115. B. Cocquyt, 'Analiza języka i filozofii rozkoszu Leona w *Kosmosie* Witolda Gombrowicza', *SlaG*, 29, 2002:15–29. M. Kacik, 'Samotność zwycięzcy', *Twórczość*, 58.7–8, 2002:105–20, deals with G.'s last two novels and his *Dziennik*. J.-P. Salgas, 'Erotyzm Gombrowicza', *ib.*, 94–104.

INGARDEN. Zofia Majewska, *Świat Romana Ingardena*, UMCS, 2001, 158 pp. K. Kardyni-Pelikánová, 'Od fenomenów ku pełni znaczeń (Ingardenowskie koncepcje przedmiotowych i podmiotowych badań literackich w świetle ich recepcji', *Slavia*, 71, 2002:179–86.

IRZYKOWSKI. H. Markiewicz, 'Karol Irzykowski a kultura niemiecka', *RuLit*, 43, 2002:1–14; Id., 'Nazywanie "bezimiennego dzieła"', *PL(W)*, 94.1:45–69, concerns *Pałuba*.

IWASZKIEWICZ. R. Romanik, 'Jarosław Iwaszkiewicz, Mieczysław Jastrun — Listy', *Twórczość*, 58.2, 2002:95–128. T. Stefańczyk, 'Pornografia w Skaryszewie, czyli śledztwo w sprawie widzimisię', *ib.*, 58–94, deals with *Kościół w Skaryszewie*, I.'s literary response to Gombrowicz's novel. A. Wiatr, 'Głos z katakumb' *ib.*, 59.5:65–94, concerns I.'s relations with Miłosz.

KONIŃSKI. A. Fitas, 'Wojenna diarystyka Karola Ludwika Konińskiego', *PL(W)*, 93.2, 2002:33–67.

LANDA. W. Tomaszewska, 'Siostry Zofii Teresy Landy spojrzenie na literaturę', *RuLit*, 43, 2002:295–305, deals with L.'s Personalism-influenced critical writings of the 1930s.

LECHOŃ. W. Lewandowski, 'Kłopot z *Herostratesem*', *PL(W)*, 94.4:231–38.

LEŚMIAN. A. Czabanowska-Wróbel, '*Byłem dzieckiem* . . . Elegie dzieciństwa Bolesława Leśmiana', *TD*, nos 2–3:243–59. P. Łopuszański, '"Idący z prawdą u warg i u powiek . . ." Próba nowego spojrzenia na twórczość Bolesława Leśmiana', *TD*, no. 6, 2002:180–95.

PIGOŃ. C. Kłak, 'Wokół "Sprawy o Pigonia"', *RuLit*, 43, 2002:201–14, defends the eminent literary historian against charges of anti-semitism.

PRZYBOŚ. Z. Łapiński, '"Psychopsomatyczne są te moje wiersze". (Impuls motoryczny w poezji Juliana Przybosia)', *TD*, no. 6, 2002:9–17.

SCHULZ. Zbigniew Maszewski, *William Faulkner and Bruno Schulz: A Comparative Study*, Łódz U.P., 191 pp. *TD*, no. 5, contains two essays on S.'s work: J. Jarzębski, 'Schulz i dramat tworzenia' (9–16), and W. Bolecki, '*Principium indivuationis*. Motywy nietzscheańskie w twórczości Brunona Schulza' (17–33). D. de Bruyn, 'Stratégies métafictionnelles dans l'œuvre littéraire de Bruno Schulz', *SlaG*, 26, 1999:39–53. D. V. Powers, 'Fresco fiasco: narratives of national identity and the Bruno Schulz murals of Drogobych', *East European Politics and Society*, 17:622–53.

WITKIEWICZ. *PL(W)*, 93.2, 2002, has ten essays devoted to most aspects of W.'s work: B. Janus, 'Historiozofia Stanisława Ignacego Witkiewicza' (7–32); L. Sokół, 'Zagadnienie nudy w *Szewcach* Witkacego' (33–46); M. Skwara, 'Tytan Witkacego — Witkacy Tytan' (47–69); A. Krajewska, 'Witkacego inscenizacje tekstualne' (71–87);

M. Szpakowska, 'Ciało i seks w *Pożegnaniu jesieni*' (89–97); B. Schultze, 'Temat "z chłopa król" w *Janie Macieju Karolu Wścieklicy* Witkacego' (99–110); W. Tomasik, '*Szalona lokomotywa*, albo: Witkacy kontra Zola' (111–26); M. Dybizbański, 'Nie-Boskość i typowość *Szewców* Stanisława Ignacego Witkiewicza' (127–38); K. Taras, 'Witkacy i film' (139–53); and A. Żakiewicz, 'Język obrazów i rysunków Witkacego' (173–81). It also contains three items presenting new materials: W. Sztaba, 'Skąd się wziął Bungo? Śladami domniemanych witkacjanów' (183–85); 'Witkacy w Nowym Sączu. Listy Stanisława Ignacego Witkiewicza do Heleny i Franciszka Maciaków', ed. J. Degler (187–213); and 'Nieznany traktat filozoficzny Stanisława Ignacego Witkiewicza dedykowany Romanowi Ingardenowi', ed. B. Michalski (215–41). D. Gerould, 'Witkacy's unity in plurality — a world of otherness', Grossman, *Other*, 85–97. W. Skalmowski, 'S. I. Witkiewicz and A. Bely. Parallelism or *Wahlverwandschaft*?', *SlaG*, 27, 2000: 241–45, concludes that there is 'an indirect but strong Russian influence'.

6. 1945 to the Present Day

Literatura polska 1990–2000, ed. Tomasz Cieślak and Krystyna Pietrych, 2 vols, Kw, Zielona Sowa, 2002, 399, 457 pp. *Współcześni polscy pisarze i badacze literatury: słownik encyklopediczny*. Vol. 7: *R-Sta*, ed. Jadwiga Czachowska and Alicja Szałagan, WiSP, 2001, 474 pp. Stanisław Bereś, *Historia literatury polskiej w rozmowach. XX-XXI wiek*, Wa, W.A.B., 2002, 590 pp., apart from classics such as Miłosz, Różewicz, and S. Lem, contains interviews with Kapuściński, W. Terlecki, A. Zagajewski, and writers from the younger generation such as O. Tokarczuk, Bolecka, and M. Gretkowska. Wojciech Browarny, *Opowieści niedyskretne. Formy autorefleksyjne w prozie polskiej lat dziewięćdziesiątych*, Ww, WUW, 2002, 317 pp., comprises three parts: (i) an analysis of the modernist perspective within culture and social reality; (ii) a classification of three types of self-reflexivity (textual, verbal, and authorial subjectivity); (iii) an analysis of works by leading contemporary writers such as A. Stasiuk, K. Varga, Gretkowska, I. Filipiak, Goerke, A. Burzyńska, S. Chwin, and M. Bieńczyk. Maria Janion, *Żyjąc tracimy życie. Niepokojące tematy egzystencji*, Wa, W.A.B., 2001, 431 pp., includes chapters on M. Tulli, H. Krall, G. Grass, and Różewicz. Mieczysław Orski, *Lustratorzy wyobraźni, rewidenci fikcji. O polskiej prozie lat dziewięćdziesiątych*, Wa, OPEN, 119 pp., has chapters on G. Musiał, Tokarczuk, J. Pilch, P. Wojciechowski, Tulli, and Goerke. Krzysztof Uniłowski, *Koloniści i koczownicy. O najnowszej prozie i krytyce literackiej*, Kw, Universitas, 2001, 290 pp., includes essays on the 'Gdańsk School' (Chwin, J. Limon), Pilch, Stasiuk, and leading critics such as J. Jarzębski, W. Bolecki, P. Czapliński, and K. Dunin. *Światy nowej prozy*, ed. Stanisław Jaworski, Kw, Universitas, 2001, 177 pp., contains essays on Tokarczuk, Stasiuk, Gretkowska, and items devoted purely to literary theory.

Joanna Pyszna, *Boje na łamach. Pisarze i literature w praise polskiej lat pięćdziesiątych XX wieku. Szkice*, Ww, WUW, 2002, 129 pp., contains three chapters devoed to self-criticism, the 'Miłosz affair' and the death of J. Lechoń in 1956. *Realizm socjalistyczny w Polsce z perspektywy 50 lat*, ed. Stefan Zabierowski and Małgorzata Krakowiak (Prace naukowe Uniwersytetu Śląskiego w Katowicach, 1993), Katowice, Univ. Śląskiego, 2001, 346 pp., based on papers given at an interdisciplinary conference on 19–20 October 1999, features leading experts on the era. *Życie literackie drugiej emigracji niepodległościowej*, ed. Janusz Kryszak and Rafał Moczkodeen, Toruń, Univ. Mikołaja Kopernika, 2001, 256 pp., deals with S. Vincenz's Hungarian essays, the foundation of Orzeł Biały in the USSR, Gombrowicz, M. Czuchnowski, Lechoń, G. Herling-Grudziński, and J. Mackiewicz.

Slavia, 69, 2000, has several items devoted to contemporary Polish and Czech literary relations: J. Jarzębski, 'Dziesięciolecie prozy' (139–46); K. Kardyni-Pelikánová, 'Zapełnianie "białych plam" w recepcji literatury polskiej w Czechach: Karol Woytyła' (161–70); and L. Štěpán, 'Pociťování postmodernismu w současné polské próze', (177–84), which deals with such writers as P. Huelle, Bieńczyk, Pilch, Tokarczuk, and Tulli. *RSl*, 74, contains two general essays on contemporary Polish literature: M. Delaperrière, 'Modalités de l'histoire dans la littérature polonaise contemporaine' (371–80), and B. Gautier, 'Nier le totalitarisme avant qu'il vous nie . . .: images contemporaines des littératures tchèque et polonaise' (381–87), the latter seeing the moral revolt against totalitarianism as ultimately a literary project involving the Bakhtinian concept of polyphony.

E. Skibińska, 'Zniekształcone odbicie. Proza polska lat 1945–1989 we francuskim przekładzie', *TD*, no. 5:137–51. B. Bodzioch-Bryła, 'Ku ciału post-ludzkiemu. O młodej poezji i nowej rzeczywistości', *TD*, no. 6, 2002:42–57. M. Bujnicka, 'Czy to powieść brukowa? Genologiczne manipulacje', *Literatura i Kultura Popularna*, 10, 2002:51–60, considers K. K. Toeplitz's *Gorący kartofel* and R. M. Groński's *Suche oczy*. E. Chwałko, 'Motyw Don Kichota w wybranych wspólczesnych powieściach (*Auto da fé* Eliasa Canettiego, *Ferdydurke* Witolda Gombrowicza, *Mała apokalipsa* Tadeusza Konwickiego, *Tańcowały dwa Michały* Edwarda Redlińskiego)', *PrLit*, 38, 2000:199–219. U. Glensk, '"W powiększającym szkle marihuany" — narkotyki w prozie lat dziewięćdziesiątych', *ib.*, 40, 2002:121–50. D. Grzybkowska, 'Oswojenie tajemnicy. O aniele zstępującym z nieba dla człowieka. Na przykładzie najnowszych tekstów polskiej literatury fantastycznej', *Literatura i Kultura Popularna*, 11:119–31. L. K. Nagy, 'Czytelniczy sukces polskiej martyrologicznej prozy łagrowej. Reinterpretacja intertekstualna', *Slavica*, 30, 2000:153–70. J. Smulski, 'Class enemy as "the other" in the literature of Socialist Realism', Grossman, *Other*, 217–25. W. Tomasik, 'The railway in communist symbolism (some observations on Soviet and Polish art)', *Blok*, 1, 2002:61–81. D. Tubielewicz Mattsson, 'Mężczyzna w nieludzkim świecie. Wizerunki mężczyzny w poezji i plastyce polskiego socrealizmu', *ib.*, 2:90–116.

INDIVIDUAL WRITERS

BATOR. E. Domańska, 'Autofikcja Joanny Bator', *TD*, nos 2–3:336–45.

BIAŁOSZEWSKI. J. Kunicka, 'Od Genesis do Apokalipsy. Miron Białoszewski wobec wybranych aspektów biblijnej Historii Zbawienia', *RuLit*, 44:163–79.

BOBIŃSKA. K. Obremski, '"Inżynier ludzkich dusz" w museum literatury dawnej. Nad książką Heleny Bobińskiej *Soso*', *PL(W)*, 94.4:133–64.

BOCHEŃSKI. W. Tyszka, 'Między przeszłością a teraźniejszością. Rzeczywistość historyczna w *Boskim Juliuszu* Jacka Bocheńskiego', *PrzH*, 45.4, 2001:55–63.

CZAPSKI. M. A. Jurek, '"Nie wybiegać poza wspomnienie." O funkcjonalności retrospekcji w szkicach Józefa Czapskiego', *PL(W)*, 93.2, 2002:91–102.

FILIPIAK. B. Warnocki, 'Poszukiwanie języka. O twórczości Izabeli Filipiak', *TD*, no. 6, 2002:92–112.

GRYNBERG. O. Orzeł, 'W poszukiwaniu straconego mitu. Obraz dzieciństwa w *Dziejach Syjonu* Henryka Grynberga', *TD*, nos 2–3:260–69.

HARTWIG. D. Walczak-Delanois, 'Błyski zobaczone, okruchy ocalone. O poezji Julii Hartwig', *SlaG*, 28, 2001:235–46.

HERBERT. Joanna Salomon, **Czas Herberta, albo: Na dom w Czarnolesie*, Wa, Oficyna Wydawnicza Volumen, 2002, 378 pp. P. Czapczyk, 'Mitologia na nowo odczytana. Wokół prozy poetyckiej Zbigniewa Herberta', *Twórczość*, 59.4:61–72. E. Filipczuk, 'Tarot Ironiczny Zbigniewa Herberta', *PrLit*, 40, 2002:151–68. D. Kozicka, '"A nade wszystko żebym był pokorny . . ." — Zbigniew Herbert w "ogrodzie" Europy', *RuLit*, 44:33–47. M. Mikołajczuk, 'Czytać *Tren Fortynbrasa* od końca', *ib.*, 315–25; and, by the same author, 'Dialogi martwej natury (o *Kwiatach* Zbigniewa Herberta)', *ib.*, 43, 2002:307–13; and also 'Od Orfeusza do Arijona. Pieśń i muzyka w świecie poetyckim Zbigniewa Herberta', *PL(W)*, 93.2, 2002:137–51.

HERLING-GRUDZIŃSKI. L. Malcew, 'Apokaliptyczny tryptyk Gustawa Herlinga-Grudzińskiego,' *PrzH*, 47.2:75–83, deals with the stories *Drugie Przyjście. Opowieść średniowieczna* (1960), *Pożar w Kaplicy Sykstyńskiej AD 1998* (1984), and *Jubileusz, Rok Święty* (1996). A. Morawiec, 'Pisarze wobec totalitaryzmu (Gustaw Herling-Grudziński o Warłamie Szałamowie)', *Slavia*, 71, 2002:133–46.

HŁASKO. G. Z. Gasyra, 'Life as intertext: distance, deception, and intentionality in Marek Hłasko's *Killing the Second Dog*', *CanSP*, 44.1–2, 2002:19–37.

HOFFMAN. R. Mielhorski, '*Inne tak* Kazimierza Hoffmana', *Twórczość*, 58.10, 2002:87–93.

HUELLE. C. Prunitsch, 'Intertextualität als Vollzug literarischer und geschichtlicher Kontinuität am Beispiel von Günter Grass' *Katz und Maus* und Paweł Huelles *Weiser Dawidek*', *ZSP*, 62:149–74.

KISIELEWSKI. M. Ryszkiewicz, 'Mowa ezopowa w felietonach Kisiela', *PL(W)*, 93.1, 2002:113–35; Id., 'Świadectwo epoki. O koncepcji literatury Stefana Kisielewskiego', *Slavica*, 30, 2000:171–92.

KONWICKI. J. Szachowicz-Sempruch, 'Banality, nostalgia and postmodern aesthetics: reflections on the prose of Tadeusz Konwicki,' *ASEES*, 16, 2002:71–103, discusses the dispersal and fragmentation of Polish identity.

KOSSAK. D. Bawoł, '*Przymierze* Zofii Kossak jako apokryficzne dzieje Abrahama', *PL(W)*, 94.4:83–98.

KRYNICKI. A. Syguła, 'Ryszard Krynicki jako programotwórca', *RuLit*, 44:49–59.

KUNCEWICZOWA. E. Woźnicka, 'Fragment jako forma autobiografii: *Fantomy* i *Natura* Marii Kuncewiczowej', *PL(W)*, 93.2, 2002:69–89.

LEM. Jerzy Jarzębski, *Wszechświat Lema*, WL, 339 pp.

LIPSKA. R. Mielhorski, 'Ewy Lipskiej podróże (w poszukiwaniu wartości)', *TD*, nos 2–3:72–92.

LIPSKI. Jadwiga Kaczyńska, *Jan Józef Lipski. Monografia bibliograficzna*, IBL, 2001, 104 pp.

MIŁOSZ. K. van Heuckelom, 'Między "czarną ziemią" a "błyszczającym punktem". Rzecz o poezji Czesława Miłosza', *SlaG*, 28, 2001:217–33; Id., 'Poezja Czesława Miłosza wobec tradycji okulocentryzmu. Rzecz o późnym wierszu *Oczy*', *ib.*, 30:115–36. M. Heydel, '*Traktat poetycki* Czesława Miłosza po angielsku w kontekście stereotypu (nie)przekładalności', *TD*, no. 5:152–65. M. Zaleski, 'Zamiast', *ib.*, 34–59, deals with M.'s poetry.

MUSIEROWICZ. Stanisław Frycie, *Małgorzata Musierowicz*, Wa, WSP Towarzystwa Wiedzy Powszechnej w Warszawie, 2002, 197 pp., contains an introduction by Frycie (7–51), a select bibliography

(52–57), with the remainder devoted to critical reviews and readers' responses to M.'s work.

NOWAK. Dorota Siwor, *W kręgu mitu, magii i rytuału. O prozie Tadeusza Nowaka*, Kw, Universitas, 2002, 267 pp.

ODOJEWSKI. M. Rembowska-Płuciennik, '"[. . .] w samym środku swego bólu [. . .]." O modelach doznawania cielesności w prozie Włodzimierza Odojewskiego', *TD*, no. 6, 2002 : 58–68.

PANKOWSKI. Krystyna Ruta-Rutkowska, *Dramaturgia Mariana Pankowskiego. Problemy poetyki dramatu współczesnego*, Wa, DiG, 2001, 219 pp., is an important new study of the writer's dramas. K. Kurek, '(Nie)obecność Pankowskiego', *Dialog*, no. 12 : 60–65.

PARNICKI. A. Chomiuk, 'Epistolografia powieściowa jako rodzaj gry z przeszłością. *Słowo i ciało* Teodora Parnickiego', *RuLit*, 44 : 21–32. T. Markiewicz, '"Pamięć, władca [. . .] bezlitosny, wciąż i wciąż wskrzesza to, co minęło . . ." Fragmenty wspomnień Teodora Parnickiego', *PL(W)*, 93.2, 2002 : 153–211.

PILCH. E. Filipczuk, '*Bezzwrotnie utracona leworęczność* Jerzego Pilcha jako przedmiot badań stylistycznych', *PrLit*, 39, 2001 : 151–55; and also by the same critic, 'Dlaczego narratorowi *Bezzwrotnie utraconej leworęczności* Jerzego Pilcha trzęsą się ręce?', *ib.*, 40, 2002 : 169–80.

POŚWIATOWSKA. U. Klatka, 'Wiersze Haliny Poświatowskiej z tomiku *Hymn Bałwochwalczy* (nie publikowane)', *RuLit*, 43, 2002 : 81–92.

PRZYBYLSKI. J. Szurek, 'Zbłądzenia metaforyczne, czyli o nieufności', *PrLit*, 40, 2002 : 207–17, deals with *Pustelnicy i demony* (1994).

PUTRAMENT. Jan Pacławski, *Proza literacka Jerzego Putramenta*, Kielce, Akademii Świętokrzyskiej, 2000 pp., is the first serious monograph devoted to P.

RÓŻEWICZ. Grossman, *Other*, contains two essays on R.'s work: T. Trojanowska, 'Individuality and otherness: reading Różewicz performing Kafka' (115–29), which deals with the play *Pułapka*; and A. Skołasińska, 'Deconstructing the Polish tradition in Tadeusz Różewicz's *Marriage Blanc*' (131–49). T. Drewnowski, 'Trzeci oddech', *Twórczość*, 58.10, 2002 : 57–72, deals with R.'s latest works. A. Girgel, 'Jeszcze raz o dialogu Tadeusza Różewicza z Paulem Celanem', *RuLit*, 44 : 181–95, deals with the works *Todesfuge*, *Der Tod ist ein Meister aus Deutschland*, and *Płaskorzeźby*. A. Krzywania, 'Czym jest poezja?', *Twórczość*, 58.10, 2002 : 73–83. A. Kula, 'Dlaczego Hölderlin', *ib.*, 59.10 : 64–87.

A. RUDNICKI. J. Wróbel, 'Dwie parabole Adolfa Rudnickiego', *RuLit*, 43, 2002 : 69–80, deals with the short stories *Stara ściana* and *Ślad w kolorze*.

SARAMONOWICZ. G. Dragun, 'Czy powieści Małgorzaty Saramonowicz przerażają? Refleksja nad *Siostrą* i *Lustrami* jako przykładami thrillera i kryminału', *Literatura i Kultura Popularna*, 11:87–93, concludes that her novels may be terrifying only to women.

SŁAWIŃSKI. J. Szurek, 'Literalna wierność czy metaforyczna zdrada? O funkcji metafory w tekście literaturoznawczym', *PrLit*, 39, 2001:171–82, focuses on *Próby teoretycznoliterackie* (1992).

STRYJKOWSKI. I. Piekarski, 'Szatan, Bóg i Mesjasz. O *Sarnie* Juliana Stryjkowskiego', *PL(W)*, 93.4:117–32.

SZCZEPAŃSKI. B. Gontarz, 'Historia uwięziona w fikcji. *Kipu* Jana Józefa Szczepańskiego', *RuLit*, 44:197–211.

SZYMBORSKA. M. Czermińska, 'Ekfrazy w poezji Wisławy Szymborskiej', *TD*, nos 2–3:230–42.

ŚWIRSZCZYŃSKA. M. Rudaś-Grodzka, '*Parthenogeneza* w okresie menopauzy', *TD*, no. 6, 2002:69–79.

TERAKOWSKA. E. Filipowicz, 'Kultura magiczna w powieściach *fantasy* Doroty Terakowskiej', *Literatura i Kultura Popularna*, 11:95–118.

TRYZNA. B. Helbig-Mischewski, 'Hexe, Heilige und Hure. Sakralisierung und Dämonisierung von Frauen und Kulturen in Tomek Tryznas *Panna Nikt* (1994)', *ASP*, 27, 1999:109–31.

ZADURA. M. Mikołajczuk, '*Nowa Ostenda* Bohdana Zadury', *Twórczość*, 59.1:74–83.

ZAGAJEWSKI. B. Shallcross, 'The divining moment: Adam Zagajewski's aesthetics of epiphany', *SEEJ*, 44, 2000:234–52.

ŻMIGRODZKA. *Maria Żmigrodzka. Przez wieki idąca powieść. Wybór pism o literaturze XIX i XX wieku*, ed. Maria Kalinowska and Elżbieta Kiślak, IBL, 2002, 523 pp., a collection of essays by the eminent literary scholar, includes a useful bibliography by H. Markiewicz (496–514).

IV. RUSSIAN STUDIES

LANGUAGE

POSTPONED

LITERATURE FROM THE BEGINNING TO 1700

POSTPONED

LITERATURE, 1700–1800

POSTPONED

LITERATURE, 1800–1848

By Boris Lanin, *Professor of Literature, Russian Academy of Education, Moscow*

1. General

Significant studies to appear this year include B. Kramer, *Литературный гнозис: Порядок и отклонение*, StP, Piatyi ugol, 872 pp., and R. Picchio, *Slavia Orthodoxa: Литература и язык*, transl. I. V. Dergacheva and M. I. Kruglova, Mw, Znak, 720 pp. M. Virolainen, *Речь и молчание. Сюжеты и мифы русской словесности*, with foreword by S. G. Bocharov, StP, Amfora, 503 pp., is a major study of silence and speech in Russian literary culture from the time of Ivan the Terrible until the 20th c. See also S. Ekshtut, *Битвы за храм Мнемозины: очерки интеллектуальной истории*, StP, Aleteia, 320 pp.; A. Pen'kovskii, *Нина: Культурный миф золотого века русской литературы в лингвистическом освещении*, Mw, Indrik, 640 pp.; G. M. Gogiberidze, *Диалог культур в системе литературного образования*, Mw, Nauka, 183 pp.; M. N. Kufaev, *История русской книги в 19 веке*, Mw, Pashkov dom, 360 pp.; and *Вожди умов и моды: чужое имя как наследуемая модель жизни*, ed. V. I. Bagno, StP, Nauka, 342 pp.

Several useful reference books have appeared: G. M. Prashkevich, *Самые знаменитые поэты России*, Mw, Veche, 480 pp., and *Русские писатели*, ed. N. M. Voinova, A. I. Zhuravleva, and D. P. Ivinskii, Mw, Rosmen, 352 pp.

The following works discuss various features of Russian 'byt' — everyday life: *Быт пушкинского Петербурга: опыт энциклопедического словаря: А–К*, ed. A. A. Konechnyi, StP, Izdatel'stvo Ivana Limbakha, 304 pp.; M. V. Korotkova, *Путешествие в историю русского быта*, Mw, Drofa, 256 pp.; V. P. Meshcheriakov and M. N. Serbul, *'Дела давно минувших дней ...': историко-бытовой комментарий к произведениям русской классики 18–20 вв*, Mw, Drofa, 384 pp., contains much information that may be useful to literary scholars; *Кулинарный путеводитель по шедеврам мировой литературы*, ed. M. Miloslavskaia, Mw, Tsentrpoligraf, 687 pp.

2. Literary History

There are several excellent works about so called 'local texts' in Russian literature: V. N. Toporov, *Петербургский текст русской литературы: избранные труды*, StP, Iskusstvo–SPB, 616 pp., is a wonderful selection of this scholar's works. *Образ Петербурга в мировой культуре: материалы международной конференции*, ed. V. E. Bagno, StP, Nauka, 607 pp.; O. I. Glazunova, *Петербург в жизни и творчестве русских писателей*, StP, Zlatoust, 456 pp.; A. P. Liusyi, *Крымский текст в русской литературе*, StP, Aleteia, 314 pp.; and *Крымский альбом 2000: Историко-краеведческий и литературно-художественный альманах*, Vol. 5, ed. D. A. Losev, Feodosiia–Mw, Koktebel', 224 pp., contains works on G. Kuznetsova, M. Sabashnikova, and others; *Крымский альбом 2001: Историко-краеведческий и литературно-художественный альманах*, Vol. 6, ed. D. A. Losev, Feodosiia–Mw, Koktebel', 224 pp., contains studies of V. Zhukovskii, A. Grin, and others. See also A. Safonova, 'Сахалинская тетрадь: опыт литературных обобщений', *Znamia*, no.10: 207–11; O. I. Matvienko, *Малая литературная энциклопедия города Сочи*, Sochi, Muzei A. N. Ostrovskogo, 2002, 113 pp.; S. Komarov and O. Lagunova, *На моей земле: О поэтах и прозаиках Западной Сибири последней трети 20 века*, Ekaterinburg, Sredne-Ural'skoe knizhnoe izdatel'stvo, 352 pp.; *Литература Тверского края в контексте древней культуры: Сборник статей и публикаций*, ed. M. V. Stroganov, Tver', Zolotaia bukva, 2002, 226 pp.; M. Gundarin, '"Четвертый Рим" и его обитатели', *Znamia*, no.7: 202–05 is about the town of Barnaul in literature; S. Bocharov, 'Петербургский пейзаж: камень, вода, человек', *NovM*, no.10: 134–41; L. Grigor'eva, 'Прекрасная чужбина', *ib.*, 152–57; L. Pann, 'Аритмия пространства', *ib.*, 142–51; S. N. Povartsov, *Омская стрелка: статьи, очерки, заметки*, Omsk, OmGPU, 202 pp.; *Город как культурное пространство: материалы конференции*, ed. N. P. Dvortsova, Tiumen', IPTs Ekspress, 299 pp. *Сибирь. Литература. Критика. Журналистика: Памяти Ю. С. Постнова*, ed. L. P. Iakimova, Novosibirsk, SO RAN, 2002, 253 pp.; *Псковский край в литературе*, ed. N. L. Vershinina, Pskov, PGPI, 806 pp.; *Псковская энциклопедия: 903–2003*, ed. A. I. Lobachev, Pskov, Pskovskaia entsiklopediia, 912 pp.; E. Pervushina, *Пушкин,*

Павловск, Петродворец, StP, Litera, 224 pp.; *Поэтов свет стихотворений. . . Очерки*, Ufa, Graviton, 49 pp.; M. E. Vasil'ev, *Из истории земли Псковской (исследования, поиски, находки)*, vol. 28, Pushkinskie Gory, Mikhailovskoe, 208 pp.

Several articles illuminate the Russian perception of Homer in the 19th c.: M. Maiofis, '"Рука времен", "божественный Платон" и гомеровская рифма в русской литературе первой половины XIX века: Комментарий к непрочитанной поэме Н. И. Гнедича', *NLO*, no.60:145–70; I. Vinitskii, 'Теодиссея Жуковского: гомеровский эпос и революция 1848–1849 годов', *ib.*, 171–93 ; S. Zav'ialov, 'Гомер в качестве государственного обвинителя на процессе по делу русской поэзии (О книге А. Н. Егунова "Гомер в русских переводах XVIII-XIX веков")' *ib.*, 194–99. See also G. A. Nevelev, *Декабристы и декабристоведы: исследования и материалы*, StP, Tekhnologos, 304 pp.; *Российский консерватизм в литературе и общественной мысли 19 века*, ed. K. A. Koksheneva, Mw, IMLI RAN, 224 pp.; V. Mil'don, 'Недоросли русской литературы (Комедия Фонвизина и взросление литературного героя)', *VL*, no.2:301–13; E. A. Rad', *Трансформация сюжета о блудном сыне в произведениях русской литературы*, Samara, Sterlitamak, 167 pp.; *Театр и литература: сборник статей к 95-летию А. А. Гозенпуда*, ed. V. P. Stark, StP, Nauka, 719 pp.; *Романсы пушкинской поры*, ed. G. V. Larionov, Mw, Eko, 254 pp.; *Русская филология: ученые записки СГПУ*, vol. 7, ed. L. L. Gorelik and M. L. Rogatskina, Smolensk, SGPU, 216 pp.; N. I. Tyapugina, *Русская литература 19–20 вв: статьи и очерки*, Saratov, Saratovskaia gosudarstvennaia akademiia prava, 352 pp.; *Начало*, vol. 6, ed. I. Popova, Mw, IMLI RAN, 304 pp., contains works on Pushkin, Dostoevskii, Bulgakov, and I. S. Lur'e.

V. S. Tomsinov, *Аракчеев: жизнь замечательных людей*, Mw, Molodaia gvardiia, 545 pp.; and V. A. Lopatnikov, *Пьедестал: Время и служение канцлера Горчакова*, Mw, Molodaia gvardiia, 343 pp., are useful historical sources for understanding Pushkin's epoch in Russian history. V. N. Toporov, *Из истории русской литературы: русская литература второй половины 18 века; М. Н. Муравьев: введение в творческое наследие*, vol. 2, Mw, Iazyki slavianskoi kul'tury, 928 pp.; *Russische Aufklärungsrezeption im Kontext offizieller Bildungskonzepte (1700–1825)*, ed. G. Lehmann-Carli et al., Berlin, Spitz, 2001, 679 pp.

3. Theory

general. M. Epshtein, 'Поэтика близости', *Zvezda*, no.1:155–76, is an excellent essay on the poetics of eroticism. See also A. I. Esal'nek, *Основы литературоведения: Анализ художественного произведения: Практикум,* Mw, Flinta–Nauka, 216 pp.; L. P. Krementsov, *Теория литературы: Чтение как творчество,* Mw, Flinta–Nauka, 168 pp.; B. F. Egorov, *От Хомякова до Лотмана,* Mw, Iazyki slavianskoi kul'tury, 368 pp.; I. V. Kuznetsov, *Коммуникативная стратегия притчи в русских повестях 17–19 веков,* Novosibirsk, NIPKiPRO, 166 pp.; P. A. Kropotkin, *Русская литература: идеал и действительность,* transl. V. Baturinskii, Mw, Vek knigi, 320 pp.; I. Kurganov, *Русский литературный анекдот конца 18–начала 19 века,* ed. N. Okhotina, Mw, Materik, 312 pp.; O. G. Egorov, *Русский литературный дневник 19 века: история и теория жанра,* Mw, Flinta–Nauka, 279 pp. *Современные научные концепции в филологии и преподавание словесности,* ed. V. I. Sennikova and G. B. Petrova, Magnitogorsk U.P., 211 pp., contains studies of Tiutchev, Dostoevskii, and Chekhov. Major publications also include B. M. Sarnov, *Занимательное литературоведение, или Новые похождения знакомых героев,* Mw, Tekst, 398 pp., and L. G. Ginzburg and I. B. Kononova, *Занимательное литературоведение,* Mw, Gelios ARV, 382 pp. I. V. Kuznetsov, *Анализ эпического произведения,* Novosibirsk, NIPKiPRO, 81 pp., writes about Nabokov, Bunin, Babel', O. Pavlov, Chekhov, M. Pogodin, Pelevin, and Shukshin. See also *Русская классика: проблемы интерпретации: материалы конференции,* ed. L. G. Satarova and A. S. Kondrat'ev, Lipetsk, LGIUU, 2002, 202 pp.. R. Hodel, *Erlebte Rede in der russischen Literatur: Vom Sentimentalismus zum sozialistischen Realismus* (Slavische Literaturen. Texte und Abhandlungen, 22), Frankfurt, Lang, 2001, 279 pp., explores so called 'free indirect discourse' in Russian literature; A. I. Bol'shakova, 'Образ читателя как литературоведческая категория', *ISLIa,* 62.2:17–26.

ROMANTICISM. U. Persi, '*Не пой, красавица, при мне . . .': Культурная территория русского романтизма,* transl. from Italian by I. Tokareva, Mw, Agraf, 336 pp. *Романтизм: два века осмысления: материалы международной научной конференции,* Kaliningrad U.P., 188 pp.

POETRY. Among recent important studies are L. G. Porter, *Симметрия — владычица стихов: Очерк начал теории поэтических структур,* Mw, Iazyki slavianskoi kul'tury, 256 pp. V. Okeanskii, *Поэтика пространства в русской метафизической лирике XIX века: Е. А. Боратынский, А. С. Хомяков, Ф. И. Тютчев,* Ivanovo U.P., 2002, 203 pp.; S. V. Rudakova, 'Художественные образы "зрительного восприятия" в лирике Е. А. Боратынского', Rassadin, *материалы,* 237–43, A. A. Karpov, 'Батюшков, Гердер, Саади . . .', *ib.,* 206–09.

EPISTOLARY. *Неизвестные письма русских писателей князю Александру Борисовичу Куракину (1752–1818)*, ed. P. A. Druzhinin, Mw, Truten', 2002, 504 pp., is an interesting collection.

COMPARATIVE studies. See *Сравнительное литературоведение: теоретический и исторический аспекты: материалы международной научной конференции 'Сравнительное литературоведение — 5 Поспеловские чтения'*, Moscow U.P., 331 pp. *Славянский мир и литература: материалы международной конференции*, ed. V. I. Greshnykh, Kaliningrad U.P., 212 pp., contains works on Voloshin, Klychkov, Nabokov, Zhitkov, Dovlatov, and Sorokin.

4. Gogol

Among the most interesting work this year are M. Vaiskopf, *Птица-тройка и колесница души: работы 1978–2003 годов*, Mw, NLO, 576 pp., a very interesting and highly acclaimed volume of research; B. Sokolov, *Гоголь: энциклопедия*, Mw, Algoritm, 544 pp.; *Гоголь как явление мировой литературы: сборник статей по материалам международной научной конференции*, Mw, IMLI RAN, 393 pp. V. V. Vinogradov, *Избранные труды: Язык и стиль русских писателей от Гоголя до Ахматовой*, Mw, Nauka, 390 pp., is a classical work, now presented in a revised edition. See also P. A. Kulish, *Николай Васильевич Гоголь: опыт биографии*, Mw, Al'ternativa–Evrolints, 243 pp., and *Gogol: Exploring Absence: Negativity in Nineteenth-Century Russian Literature*, ed. S. Spieker, Bloomington, Indiana U.P., 1999, 216 pp.

Also of interest are G. Ben, 'Был ли Тарас Бульба антисемитом и что думал об этом Гоголь?' *Zvezda*, no.7 : 203–08; L. P. Rassovskaia, *Тема 'лишнего человека' в художественной интерпретации Пушкина и Гоголя*, Samara U.P., 78 pp.

5. Pushkin

Major studies and collections include T. Galushko, *Жизнь. Поэзия. Пушкин*, StP, Zhurnal 'Zvezda', 272 pp.; V. Rak, 'О кризисе академического пушкиноведения и подметках великих пушкинистов', *Neva*, no.1 : 198–201; V. I. Kurbatov, *Перед вечером, или Жизнь на полях*, Pskov, My Pskovskie, 584 pp.; A. A. Latsis, *Верните лошадь! Пушкиноведческий детектив*, Mw, Moskovskie uchebniki i kartolitografiia, 352 pp.; N. M. Lebedev and V. G. Samuilov, *На́ш Пушкин*, Vyshnii Volochek, Irida-pros, 87 pp.; O. G. Zimina, L. A. Kazarskaia, and O. V. Petrov, *А. С. Пушкин в Тверском крае: Тверь — Торжок — Старицкий уезд*, Mw, Gelios ARV, 184 pp.; *А. С. Пушкин и Отечественная война 1812 г.*

Пушкин в Захарове: Материалы 7 научной конференции, Bol'shie Viazemy, Gosudarstvennyi muzei-zapovednik A. S. Pushkina, 222 pp.; *Pro memoria: Памяти академика Г. М. Фридлендера (1915–1995)*, ed. A. V. Arkhipova and N. F. Budanova, StP, Nauka, 352 pp.; N. I. Petrakov, *Последняя игра Александра Пушкина*, Mw, Ekonomika, 126 pp.; *Пушкин и мировая культура: Материалы шестой международной конференции, Крым*, ed. S. A. Fomichev, StP, Simferopol', 192 pp.; *Пушкин и Филарет, митрополит Московский и Коломенский*, ed. N. I. Mikhailova, Mw, Moskovskie uchebniki i kartolitografiia, 240 pp.; *Пушкин: Исследования и материалы*, vols 26–27, ed. R. V. Iezuitov, StP, Nauka, 485 pp.; *Пушкинская энциклопедия 'Михайловское': в 3 т.*, vol. 1, ed. I. T. Budylin, Mw, Mikhailovskoe, 448 pp.; *Пушкинский заповедник и его Хранитель*, ed. O. A. Sandaliuk, Pskov, GUP Pskovskaia oblastnaia tipografiia, 69 pp.; V. Z. Sannikov, *Русская языковая шутка: от Пушкина до наших дней*, Mw, Agraf, 560 pp.; I. Smirnov-Okhtin and D. Shagin, *Правда о Пушкине*, StP, Iuventa, 58 pp.; B. Gasparov, 'История без телеологии. (Заметки о Пушкине и его эпохе)', *NLO*, 59:274–79; M. Maiofis, '"Открытая филология" В. Э. Вацуро', *ib.*, 287–307; V. E. Vatsuro, 'Пушкин и литературное движение его времени', *ib.*, 307–36.

See also *Эткиндовские чтения I: сборник статей по материалам Чтений памяти Е. Г. Эткинда*, ed. B. M. Firsov, StP, Evropeiskii universitet v Sankt-Peterburge, 272 pp.; V. Perel'muter writes about mistakes in controversial works on Pushkin in 'После бала', *Oktiabr'*, no.1 : 176–87. S. Vasil'eva, 'Вернется ли ласточка? Два этюда о литературе и театре', *Oktiabr'*, no.5 : 178–80; D. Baevskii, *Парапушкинистика*, Vologda, Poligrafist — Minneapolis, M.I.P., 400 pp.; S. V. Goriunkov, *Гвидонерия, или Русская история глазами А. С. Пушкина*, StP, Aleteia, 172 pp.; *'Минувшее меня объемлет живо . . .': Мемориальная Пушкиниана Государственного музея А. С. Пушкина*, ed. N. S. Nechaeva and I. V. Pavlova, Mw, Interbuk-biznes, 280 pp. *Михайловская Пушкиниана: К столетию со дня рождения С. С. Гейченко*, vol. 26, ed. N. B. Vasil'evich and V. S. Bozyrev, Pushkinskie Gory, Mikhailovskoe, 312 pp.; *Памятники А. С. Пушкину на пушкинской земле*, vol. 27, ed. A. D. Gdalin and M. R. Ivanova, Pushkinskie Gory, Mikhailovskoe, 350 pp.; K. I. Sharafadina, *'Алфавит Флоры' в образном языке литературы пушкинской эпохи: источники, семантика, формы*, StP, Peterburgskii institut pechati, 309 pp.; I. N. Egorova, *Очарование пушкинских мест*, Mw, Stolichnyi Biznes–Informtsentr, 112 pp.

BIOGRAPHY. Some interesting publications: A. Aleksandrov, *Пушкин: частная жизнь. 1811–1820*, 2nd rev. edn, Mw, Zakharov, 768 pp.; M. Al'tshuller, *Между двух царей. Пушкин, 1824–1836*, StP,

Akademicheskii proekt, 351 pp. D. Bethea, *Воплощение метаморфозы: Пушкин, жизнь поэта*, Mw, OGI, 256 pp., is the translation into Russian of a well-known and highly-acclaimed book. See also *Материалы к летописи жизни и творчества А. С. Пушкина (1830 — 1831): Картотеки М. А. и Т. Г. Цявловских*, vol. 2, part 2, ed. I. V. Garber, Mw, IMLI RAN, 342 pp.; S. S. Belov and V. A. Butorov, *Пушкинское Подмосковье: Памятные места Подмосковья, связанные с жизнью и творчеством А. С. Пушкина*, Mw, Presherne–Glasnost'-AS, 64 pp.; V. I. Belonogova, *Выбранные места из мифов о Пушкине*, Nizhnii Novgorod, Dekom, 120 pp. V. Balan, 'Добрый человек Пушкин', *Lebed', (Boston)*, no. 318, <http://www.lebed.com>; T. I. Galkina, L. B. Mikhailova, and S. V. Pavlova, *Отечество нам Царское село*, Mw, Gelios ARV, 200 pp.; T. M. Rozhnova and V. F. Rozhnov, *Жизнь после Пушкина. Наталья Николаевна и ее потомки*, StP, Vita Nova, 728 pp.; V. Vladmeli (Vladimir Lifson), *Приметы и религия в жизни А. С. Пушкина*, Mw, Bogatykh & Rakitskoi, 160 pp.

See also L. V. Kozmina, *Петровское: Пушкин и Ганнибалы*, Mw, Sovremennyi pisatel', 200 pp.; *Ай да Пушкин! Красный том: картежник, художник, дуэлянт*, ed. K. I. Aksasskii, Obninsk, Institut Munitsipal'nogo upravleniia, 280 pp.; *Мир Пушкина: Семейные предания Пушкиных*, vol. 3, ed. T. I. Krasnoborod'ko, StP, Pushkinskii fond, 328 pp.; V. F. Mironov, *Дуэли в жизни и творчестве А. С. Пушкина*, Mw, Rodina-Folio–Al'fa-Dizain, 104 pp.; I. V. Nemirovskii, *Творчество Пушкина и проблема публичного поведения поэта*, StP, Giperion, 352 pp.; I. M. Nikishov, *Дум высокое стремленье: опыт духовной биографии Пушкина, 1813–1822*, vol. 1, Tver', Zolotaia bukva, 565 pp.; A. P. Liusyi, *Пушкин. Таврида. Киммерия*, Mw, Iazyki russkoi kul'tury, 2000, 234 pp.; M. Romm, 'Известный-неизвестный портрет А. С. Пушкина', *Neva*, no.2:233–34; I. Metter, 'Прадед Пушкина — арап Петра Великого', *ib.*, 228–29.

EVGENII ONEGIN. New studies include D. A. Gaidukov, *Опыт конкорданса к роману А. С. Пушкина 'Евгений Онегин' с приложением текста романа*, Mw, Leks Est, 592 pp., the product of some tremendous work. Also of interest are M. Shapir, 'Отповедь на заданную тему. К спорам по поводу текстологии "Евгения Онегина"', *NovM*, no.4:144–56; V. G. Chikarenko, *Татьяна едет к Пушкину*, Mw, Kompaniia Sputnik, 44 pp.; O. N. Grinbaum, 'Ритмодинамика композиционной структуры романа А. С. Пушкина "Евгений Онегин"', Rassadin, *материалы*, 224–31; A. B. Pen'kovskii, '"Из худших" или "из лучших"? О комментариях к строфе XXXV восьмой главы "Евгения Онегина" и об одной связанной с ними текстологической ошибке', Krasil'nikova, *Поэтика*, 32–39; S. A. Fomichev, 'Десятая глава "Евгения Онегина" (проблемы реконструктивного анализа)', *RusL*, no.3 : 70–87. I. G. Dobrodomov and I. A. Pil'shchikov, 'Из заметок о лексике и фразеологии "Евгения Онегина" ("У ночи много звезд прелестных . . ."), *ISLIa*, 62.1 : 67–70, provide linguistic and literary commentary on P.'s expression *zvezdy prelestnye.* See also N. Korzhavin, 'Ольга и Татьяна', *VL*, no.5 : 152–73.

OTHER WORKS. See L. A. Kogan, 'Опыт драматургического человековедения (о философии "Маленьких трагедий" Пушкина)', *VF*, no.4 : 136–41; O. B. Zaslavskii, '"Нежданная шутка" в "Моцарте и Сальери" А. С. Пушкина', *ISLIa*, 62.6 : 46–53; O. D. Zaslavskii, '"Моцарт и Сальери": гений, злодейство и чаша дружбы', *ib.*, 62.2 : 27–35; M. Eliferova, 'Шекспировские сюжеты, пересказанные Белкиным', *VL*, no.1 : 149–75; V. G. Perel'muter, *Пушкинское эхо: Записки, заметки, эссе*, Mw, Minuvshee — Toronto, Library of Toronto Slavic Quarterly, 512 pp.; M. P'ianykh, '"Медный всадник" Пушкина в восприятии русских писателей и философов трагического XX столетия', *Neva*, no.5 : 199, and *ib.*, no.6 : 164; V. A. Koshelev, 'О замысле Пушкина ("Мстислав")', *RusL*, no.1 : 86–96; V. P. Stark, 'Корсаковы в творчестве Пушкина — реальность и вымысел', *ib.*, 97–109; S. Zhiyn, 'Образ пути и его значение в творчестве Пушкина: "Путешествие в Арзрум во время похода 1829 года", "Стихи, сочиненные во время путешествия"' *ib.*, no.2 : 66–80; I. Shaitanov, 'Две "неудачи": "Мера за меру" и "Анжело"', *VL*, no.1 : 123–48; N. I. Solovei, 'Неосуществленное предисловие А. С. Пушкина к "Борису Годунову" (1825–1830 гг.)', *FilN*, no.5 : 76–86; A. V. Apollonova, 'Мотив "счастья" / "страдания" в лирике А. С. Пушкина 1820-х гг.: иерархическая модель интерпретации поэтического текста', *VMUF*, no.1 : 116–23.

PUSHKIN AND OTHER WRITERS. See A. Skaza, 'Роман "Петербург" Андрея Белого и поэма "Медный всадник" А. С. Пушкина (поэтологический аспект)', *SlavRev*, no.4 : 465–74; F. Raskol'nikov, '"Марфа Посадница" М. Погодина и исторические взгляды Пушкина', *RusL*, no.1 : 3–15; I. I. Pitertseva, 'Мотивы мести и возмездия в "Двойнике, или Моих вечерах в Малороссии" А. Погорельского и "Повестях покойного Ивана Петровича Белкина" А. С. Пушкина (проблема диалога циклов)', Rassadin, *материалы*, 231–37; B. F. Sushkov, *Пророк в своем отечестве: Пушкин. Гоголь. Толстой (о невостребованных идеях и идеалах русских гениев)*, Tula, Grif, 584 pp.; I. Surat, 'Смерть поэта. Мандельштам и Пушкин',

NovM, no.3 : 155–73; D. P. Ivinskii, *Пушкин и Мицкевич: История литературных отношений*, Mw, Iazyki slavianskoi kul'tury, 432 pp.; V. D. Rak, *Пушкин, Достоевский и другие: вопросы текстологии, материалы и комментарии*, StP, Akademicheskii proekt, 256 pp.; N. I. D'iakonova, 'Пушкин и Вордсворт', *FilN*, no.2 : 25–33; A. I. Ivanitskii and A. I. Loskutov, '"Ты знаешь край ..." ("Классическая почва" у Гете и Пушкина)', *ib.*, 34–43; *Пушкин в прижизненной критике: 1831 — 1833*, ed. I. Larionova, StP, Gosudarstvennyi Pushkinskii teatral'nyi tsentr, 544 pp.; I. S. Galimova, 'Три карты ("Пиковая дама" Пушкина и "Король, дама, валет" Набокова)', *RusL*, no.1 : 110–21; S. V. Berezkina, 'Александр Бестужев — адресат эпиграммы Пушкина "Прозаик и поэт"', *ib.*, no.2 : 60–66.

6. Other Individual Authors

Among major publications are *Четвертые Майминские чтения: забытые и 'второстепенные' писатели пушкинской эпохи*, ed. I. V. Moteiunaite, Pskov, 167 pp., contains works on P. Katenin, V. Kiukhel'beker, O. M. Somov, N. A. L'vov, Prince B. V. Golitsyn, A. K. Boshniak, V. L. Pushkin, K. N. Batiushkov, M. N. Zagoskin, O. I. Senkovskii, A. V. Timofeev, V. N. Olin, V. Sollogub, A. Vel'tman. V. Bakhmut and A. Kriazhenkov; *Философ с душой поэта (к 190-летию Н. В. Станкевича)*, Voronezh, IPF Voronezh, 73 pp.

BARATYNSKII. M. Vaiskopf, 'Олива мира (Смерть = художница в поэзии Боратынского)', *ISLIa*, 62.3 : 38–46.

BATIUSHKOV. I. A. Pil'shchikov, *Батюшков и литература Италии: филологические разыскания*, Mw, Iazyki slavianskoi kul'tury, 314 pp.

BOBROV. V. Shubinskii, 'Наше необщее вчера', *Znamia*, no.9 : 192–201.

BELINSKII. N. P. Tokin, *Человеческое достоинство в этике В. Г. Белинского*, Saratov U.P., 163 pp.; I. Nikulichev, 'Вокруг "замечательного десятилетия": от чистых идей к проклятым вопросам', *VL*, no.1 : 209–41.

DERZHAVIN. I. B. Aleksandrova, 'Творчество Г. Р. Державина в литературно-философском контексте эпохи', *FilN*, no.2 : 3–13.

GRIBOEDOV. E. Tsimbaeva, *Грибоедов*, Mw, Molodaia gvardiia, 545 pp.; E. Tsimbaeva, 'Художественный образ в историческом контексте (Анализ биографий персонажей "Горя от ума")', *VL*, no.4 : 98–139; I. I. Khechinov, *Жизнь и смерть Александра Грибоедова*, Mw, Flinta–Nauka, 328 pp.; V. A. Cherkasov, 'К проблеме ума в комедии А. С. Грибоедова "Горе от ума"', *VMUF*, no.5 : 127–32.

IAZYKOV. Rassadin, *материалы*, contains unknown letters by Iazykov, and many interesting articles on Iazykov and other writers of the 19th c. See also N. Bludilina, 'Единый стих, торжественно звучащий (к 200-летию Николая Языкова)', *NSo*, no.3 : 284–88.

KARAMZIN. L. A. Sapchenko, *Н. М. Карамзин: судьба наследия, век 19*, Ul'ianovsk U.P., 379 pp.. M. A. Koropova, 'Жуковский и Карамзин: к проблеме литературной преемственности', *ISLIa*, 62.1 : 60–66, writes about the perception of the allegorical and the emblematic traditions in K.'s and Z.'s poetics. E. Krasnoshchekova, ' "Письма русского путешественника." Проблематика жанра (Н. М. Карамзин и Лоренс Стерн)', *RusL*, no.2 : 3–18.

KHOMIAKOV. I. S. Iunusov, Проблема национального характера в драматургии А. С. Хомякова', *VMUF*, no.2 : 74–83.

KIREEVSKII. I. V. Ludilova, 'Концепция развития поэзии в эстетике раннего И. В. Киреевского', *RL*, no.2 : 19–30.

KIUKHEL'beker. V. I. Kholkin, 'Путник одиночного вдохновения (о двух стихотворениях Кюхельбекера)', *RusL*, no.4 : 121–39.

LERMONTOV. I. Z. Serman, *Михаил Лермонтов. Жизнь в литературе, 1836–1841*, Mw, RGGU, 276 pp.; V. Sakharov, ' "Онегинское" у Лермонтова', *VL*, no.2 : 313–18; I. N. Gusliarov, *Лермонтов в жизни: систематизированный свод подлинных свидетельств современников*, Mw, Olma-Zvezdnyi mir, 413 pp.; A. V. Kuznetsova, *Лирический универсум М. Ю. Лермонтова: семантика и поэтика*, Rostov-na-Donu, RGPU, 211 pp.; S. V. Savinkov, ' "Дурное подражанье... известной книге" (логика самоотрицания в лермонтовском романе', *VMUF*, no.5 : 133–39; V. A. Zakharov, *Летопись жизни и творчества Лермонтова*, Mw, Russkaia Panorama, 703 pp.; G. V. Moskvin, 'Ранняя проза Лермонтова и европейская традиция', *VMUF*, no.1 : 7–23; I. P. Shcheblykin, *Страницы лермонтоведения: интерпретация, анализы, полемика*, Penza U.P., 139 pp.; O. V. Moskovskii, '*Хранится пламень неземной ...*': *мотив тайны в лирике М. Ю. Лермонтова*, Samara U.P., 135 pp.; T. M. Mel'nikova, *Прекрасны вы, поля земли родной... Пейзажи Тархан в поэзии М. Ю. Лермонтова*, Penza, Penzenskaia pravda, 47 pp.; *Тарханский вестник, выпуск 16*, Tarkhany, IPK Penza, 205 pp.; A. Potapov, 'Как погиб Лермонтов?' *Neva*, no.4 : 236–38; O. Miller, 'Неизвестные страницы петербургской жизни М. Ю. Лермонтова', *ib.*, no.2 : 235–37; L. Nazarova, 'Здесь бывали Тургенев и Лермонтов', *ib.*, no.11 : 250–51.

POLEZHAEV. N. L. Vasil'ev, *Словарь языка Полежаева*, Saransk, Mordova U.P., 88 pp.

RADISHCHEV. *А. Н. Радищев: русское и европейское Просвещение: материалы международного симпозиума*, ed. N. D. Kochetkova, StP, Sankt-Peterburgskii nauchnyi tsentr RAN, 158 pp.; among the most interesting articles in this volume are I. Z. Serman, 'Радищев и Ахматова' (9–18), and by the same author, 'Несколько штрихов к портрету Г. А. Гуковского' (152–55); and M. Levitt, 'Диалектика видения в "Путешествии из Петербурга в Москву" Радищева' (36–47).

LITERATURE, 1848–1917

By Boris Lanin, *Professor of Literature, Russian Academy of Education, Moscow*

I. General

Among the major recent publications are the following: *Михаил Тверской: Тексты и материалы*, ed. O. Stroganov and O. Levsha, Tver′, Zolotaia bukva, 2002, 302 pp.; I. I. Karasev, *Русская литература*, Omsk, IPTs OGIS, 135 pp.; and V. Lepakhin, *Икона в русской художественной литературе: Икона и иконопочитание, иконопись и иконописцы*, Mw, Otchii dom, 2002, 736 pp.. I. A. Dinershtein, *Иван Дмитриевич Сытин и его дело,* Mw, Moskovskie uchebniki, 367 pp., contains interesting information about A. Chekhov, L. Tolstoi, L. Andreev, I. Bunin, A. Blok, Vas. Nemirovich-Danchenko, and M. Gor'kii.

Литература: история и современность (проблемы отечественной и зарубежной литературы), ed. G. A. Skleinis, Magadan, Izdatel'stvo Severnogo Mezhdunarodnogo universiteta, 66 pp., contains studies on Derzhavin, Pushkin, Turgenev, Dostoevskii, Tiutchev, Chekhov, Pil'niak, V. Ivanov, and others. Other collections include *Цензура в России в конце 19–начале 20 века: Сборник воспоминаний*, ed. N. G. Patrusheva, StP, Rossiiskaia natsional'naia biblioteka–Dmitrii Bulanin, 366 pp.; L. L. Gerver, *Музыка и музыкальная мифология в творчестве русских поэтов (первые десятилетия XX века)*, Mw, Indrik, 2001, 247 pp.

The Archivio Italo-Russo has published two books: *Русско-итальянский архив*, ed. D. Rizzi and A. Shishkin, Trento, 1997, 625 pp.; and *Русско-итальянский архив,* II, ed. D. Rizzi and A. Shishkin, Salerno, 2001, 471 pp. See also N. I. Ishchuk-Fadeeva, *Жанры русской драмы: традиционные жанры русской драматургии*, Tver′, Liliia-Print, 87 pp.; G. G. Elizavetina, *Писарев-критик: после 'Русского слова'*, Mw, IMLI RAN, 202 pp.; S. I. Dudakov, *Этюды любви и ненависти*, Mw, RGGU, 542 pp.; V. V. Sdobnov, *Русская литературная демонология: этапы развития и творческого осмысления*, Tver′ U.P., 2002, 315 pp.

Useful reference works have been published by V. V. Shadurskii, *Золотое руно: Художественный, литературный и критический журнал (1906–1909): Роспись содержания*, Velikii Novgorod, n.p., 2002, 122 pp. See also *Журнал 'Весы' (1904–1909 гг.): Указатель содержания,* ed. T. V. Igosheva and G. V. Petrova, Velikii Novgorod, n.p., 2002, 117 pp.; *Весы: Ежемесячник литературы и искусства: Аннотированный указатель содержания*, ed. A. L. Sobolev, Mw, Truten', 377 pp.

2. Literary History

I. I. Mineralov, *История русской литературы 19 века (40–60-е годы)*, Mw, Vysshaia Shkola, 300 pp.; *Критика 60-х годов XIX века*, ed. L. I. Sobolev, Mw, AST–Olimp, 443 pp.; A. M. Bulanov, *Художественная феноменология изображения 'сердечной жизни' в русской классике (А. С. Пушкин, М. Ю. Лермонтов, И. А. Гончаров, Ф. М. Достоевский, Л. Н. Толстой)*, Volgograd, Peremena, 190 pp.; I. V. Grechanik, *Религиозно-философские мотивы русской лирики рубежа 19–20 столетий*, Mw, Kompaniia Sputnik +, 170 pp.; R. S. Spivak, *Русская философская лирика, 1910-е годы: И. Бунин. А. Блок. В. Маяковский*, Mw, Flinta–Nauka, 407 pp.; N. N. Starygina, *Русский роман в ситуации философско-религиозной полемики 1860–1870 годов* (Studia philologica), Mw, Iazyki slavianskoi kul'tury, 352 pp.; *В. К. Тредиаковский и русская литература 18–20 веков: материалы Международной научной конференции*, ed. G. G. Isaev, Astrakhan' U.P., 145 pp.; V. G. Shchukin, '"Семейная разладица" или непримиримая распря? Западничество и славянофильство в культурологической перспективе', *VF*, no.5:103–23; O. Lekmanov, 'Русский модернизм и массовая поэзия. Стихи в журнале "Нива", 1890–1917', *VL*, no.4:310–21.

3. Theory

New studies and collections include *Теория литературы в четырех томах: Роды и жанры: Основные проблемы в историческом освещении*, vol. 3, ed. L. I. Sazonova, Mw, IMLI RAN, 592 pp.; L. V. Chernets, 'Виды образа в литературном произведении', *FilN*, no.4:3–14; I. V. Nevzgliadova, 'Звуковая организация и звуковая интерпретация стихотворной речи (Поэтический слух с филологической точки зрения)', *ISLIa*, 62.3:24–37.

Some valuable studies in the theory of literature have been published in Siberia: V. I. Tiupa, L. I. Fukson, and M. N. Darvin, *Литературное произведение:* vol. I: *проблемы теории и анализа*, Kemerovo, Edinstvo, 1997; N. D. Tamarchenko et al., *Литературное произведение:* vol. II: *проблемы теории и анализа*, Kemerovo, Edinstvo, 193 pp.; *Проблемы литературных жанров*, vol. I, ed. O. N. Bakhtina, N. I. Razumova, and N. Z. Vetsheva, Tomsk U.P., 2002, 424 pp.; *Проблемы литературных жанров*, vol. II, ed. O. A. Dashevskaia, T. L. Rybal'chenko, and A. S. Svarovskaia, Tomsk U.P., 2002, 286 pp.; A. A. Faustov, *Язык переживания русской литературы*, Voronezh U.P., 1998, 60 pp.

Also of considerable interest are O. G. Egorov, *Русский литературный дневник XIX века: История и теория жанра: Исследования,*

Mw, Flinta–Nauka, 280 pp.; *Русская литературная классика 19 века*, ed. A. A. Slin'ko and V. A. Svitel'skii, Voronezh, Rodnaia rech', 426 pp.; *Риторическая традиция и русская литература*, ed. P. I. Bukharkin, StP U.P., 250 pp.; L. Berdnikov, '*Счастливый Феникс*': *Очерки о русском сонете и книжной культуре XVIII–начала XIX века*, StP U.P., 1997.

COMPARATIVE STUDIES. O. Ronen, '"Афронтенбург"', *Zvezda*, no.1 : 223–29, discusses Heinrich Heine in Russia. See also A. Vishniakov, 'Невероятные приключения французов в России, или Русские Бальзак, Пруст и Метерлинк', *VL*, no.2 : 329–46; *По страницам русской литературы 19–начала 20 вв.*, ed. I. I. Mel'nikova, Mw, Rudomino, 391 pp.; and A. G. Sheshken, *Русская и югославянские литературы в свете компаративистики*, Mw, Maks, 144 pp.

4. CHEKHOV

Studies include M. B. Mirskii, *Доктор Чехов*, Mw, Nauka, 238 pp.; A. M. Turkov, *Чехов и его время*, 3rd rev. edn, Mw, Geleos, 463 pp.; A. Stepanov, 'Чехов и постмодерн', *Neva*, no.11 : 221; *Проблемы поэтики А. П. Чехова*, ed. G. I. Tamarli, Taganrog, GPI, 151 pp.; A. Izmailov, *Чехов: биография*, Mw, Zakharov, 469 pp.; *А. Н. Островский, А. П. Чехов и литературный процесс 19–20 вв.: сборник статей в память об А. И. Ревякине*, ed. A. A. Reviakina and I. A. Reviakina, Mw, Intrada, 608 pp.

DRAMA. E. A. Polotskaia, '*Вишневый сад*': *Жизнь во времени*, Mw, Nauka, 381 pp. O. Kling, 'Пролет в вечность', *VL*, no.2 : 318–29, writes about Polotskaia's book; see also M. G. Rozovskii, *К Чехову*, Mw, RGGU, 438 pp.

PROSE. N. V. Kapustin, '*Чужое слово*' *в прозе А. П. Чехова: жанровые трансформации*, Ivanovo U.P., 261 pp.; J. J. A. Gatral, 'The paradox of melancholy insight: reading the medical subtext in Chekhov's "A Boring Story"', *SRev*, 62.2 : 258–77, illuminates Nikolai Stepanovich's struggle with the question of whether his newfound pessimism results from his illness or belated insight.

5. DOSTOEVSKII

GENERAL. Some important new books: N. N. Nasedkin, *Достоевский: Энциклопедия*, Mw, Algoritm, 798 pp.; O. N. Kuznetsov and V. I. Lebedev, *Достоевский над бездной безумия*, Mw, Kogito-Tsentr, 227 pp.; *Ф. М. Достоевский и православие*, ed. V. A. Alekseev, Kemerovo, Edinstvo, 447 pp.; Ot. Iustin [Popovich],

Православие и Достоевский, Mw–StP, Sretenskii monastyr', Chasovnia ikony Bozhiei Materi 'Vsekh Skorbiaschikh Radost' s groshikami, 2002, 287 pp.; *Словарь языка Достоевского: Лексический строй идиолекта*, vol. 2, ed. I. N. Karaulov, Mw, Azbukovnik, 510 pp.; V. I. Antysheva, *Творчество Ф. М. Достоевского: лекции, библиография*, Ioshkar-Ola, Mariiskii GPI, 63 pp.; M. Cadot, *Dostoïevski d'un siècle à l'autre, ou la Russie entre Orient et Occident*, Paris, Maisonneuve et Larose, 2001, 350 pp., brings together various studies the author has published in journals or has given as papers at conferences; N. Nasedkin, '"Минус" Достоевского', *NSo*, no.7: 263–73, discusses D. as a convinced anti-Semitic writer; V. Serdiuk, 'Прозрения Достоевского', *ib.*, 274–83; *'Педагогiя' Ф. М. Достоевского*, ed. V. A. Viktorovich, Kolomna, GPI, 218 pp. R. Belknap, *Генезис романа 'Братья Карамазовы': эстетические, идеологические и психологические аспекты создания текста*, trans. L. Vysotskii, StP, Akademichskii proekt, 263 pp., is a translation of *The Genesis of 'The Brothers Karamazov': The Aesthetics, Ideology and Psychology of Text Making*, published by Northwestern University Press in 1990. See also important articles by M. V. Jones, 'Modelling the religious dimension of Dostoevsky's fictional world', *NZSJ*, 37: 41–53, and K. Stepanian, '"Это будет, но будет после достижения цели . . ." ("Жизнь Иисуса" Д. Ф. Штрауса и Э. Ж. Ренана и роман Ф. М. Достоевского "Идиот")', *VL*, no.4: 140–58.

THE IDIOT. S. J. Young, 'Dostoevskii's *Idiot* and the Epistle of James', *SEER*, 81: 401–20, suggests, intriguingly, that Dostoevskii as an artist 'is not as Orthodox as we might have thought'. See also A. I. Kunil'skii, *Опыт истолкования литературного героя (роман Ф. М. Достоевского 'Идиот')*, Petrozavodsk U.P., 94 pp.

DOSTOEVSKII and other writers. V. I. Samokhvalova, 'Достоевский и Мисима (О метафизике красоты)', *VF*, no.11, 2002: 196–211; D. P. Rysakov, *Ф. Кафка и Ф. М. Достоевский: феноменальная рецепция русского реалистического романа ('Процесс' — 'Преступление и наказание')*, Mw, Institut Slavianovedeniia, 2002, 91 pp. K. Dianina, 'Passage to Europe: Dostoevskii in the St. Petersburg Arcade', *SRev*, 62.2: 237–57, writes about the St Petersburg passage and its structural function in D.'s unfinished story 'The Crocodile'; A. I. Sorochan, '"Дети" и "взрослые" в художественном мире А. Ф. Вельтмана и Ф. М. Достоевского', Viktorovich, *Идеи*, 86–91; V. G. Ugrekhelidze, 'Социально-криминальный роман у Диккенса и Достоевского: педагогический потенциал жанра', *ib.*, 192–94; A. P. Vlaskin, 'Заочный диалог Н. С. Лескова и Ф. М. Достоевского по проблемам религиозности и народной культуры', *RusL*, no.1: 16–48; B. N. Tikhomirov, 'Ф. М. Достоевский и другие', *RusL*, no.1: 254–69, is a penetrating analysis of S. V. Belov's book, *'Энциклопедический словарь.' Ф. М. Достоевский и его окружение* StP, Aleteia, 2001; I. N. Sharanova, 'Сюжетообразующая функция скандала в рассказах Ф. М. Достоевского 1860–х гг. ('Дядюшкин сон' и 'Скверный анекдот')', Osovskii, *исследования*, 204–07; O. I. Osovskii, 'Скандал как сюжетообразующая категория у Достоевского: интерпретация М. М. Бахтина', *ib.*, 167–72.

6. Tolstoy

New studies include *Толстой или Достоевский? Философско-эстетические искания в культурах Востока и Запада*, ed. V. I. Bagno, StP, Nauka, 252 pp.; G. V. Chagin, V. B. Remizov, and M. A. Koz'mina, *Два гения (Ф. И. Тютчев и Л. Н. Толстой)*, Mw, Russkoe slovo, 304 pp.; I. I. Luchenetskaia-Burdina, *Парадоксы художника: Особенности индивидуального стиля Л.Н. Толстого в 1870–1890 годы,* Iaroslavl', IaSPU, 2001, 156 pp.

V. A. Kolotaev, 'Концепция искусства Л. Н. Толстого на фоне переходных процессов в художественном мышлении рубежа XIX-XX веков', pp. 282–322 of *Переходные процессы в русской художественной культуре: Новое и Новейшее время*, ed. N. A. Khrenov, Mw, Nauka, 495 pp.; Ot. Ioann [Shakhovskoi], *К истории русской интеллигенции: революция Толстого,* Mw, Lepta, 539 pp.; A. Genis, '"Война и мир" в 21 веке', *Oktiabr'*, no.9: 174–81; V. M. Pereverzin, 'Жанрообразующая роль романизации истории в большой эпической форме (на примере "Войны и мира" Л. Толстого)', *FilN*, no.6: 3–11; T. D. Proskurina, 'О семейной свитости и разъединенности семьи Карениных', *ib.*, no.4: 14–22; A. Ebanoidze, 'Урок самоограничения', *DN*, no.9: 190–93.

7. Turgenev

There are two new monographs on T.: A. G. Kolesnikov, *Соединение природы и искусства: театральная эстетика И. С. Тургенева*, Mw, Teatralis, 150 pp.; N. N. Mostovskaia, *Летопись жизни и творчества И. С. Тургенева (1876–1883)*, StP, Nauka, 621 pp. Also important to varying degrees are: L. Skokova, 'Человек и природа в "Записках охотника" Тургенева', *VL*, no.6: 339–47; A. Truaia, *Иван Тургенев,* transl. L. Serezhkina, Mw, Eksmo, 320 pp.; *И. С. Тургенев и Ф. И. Тютчев в контексте мировой культуры (к 186–летию И. С. Тургенева и 200–летию Ф. И. Тютчева): материалы международной научной конференции,* ed. G. B. Kurliandskaia, Orel U.P., 128 pp.; I. I. Liapushkina, 'Афоризм в художественной структуре романа И. С. Тургенева "Рудин"', *RusL*, no.3 : 114–32; R. I. Danilevskii, 'Научные издания музея-заповедника Спасское-Лутовиново ("Спасский вестник" и сборник исследований Г. Б. Курляндской)', *ib.*, no.2 : 199–203; N. M. Chernov, *Провинциальный Тургенев*, Mw, Tsentrpoligraf, 426 pp., N. A. Kudel'ko, 'Тургенев и импрессионизм', *FilN*, no.6 : 12–19; M. B. Feklin, 'Ф. М. Форд об импрессионизме и восприятие творчества И. С. Тургенева в Англии на рубеже XIX-XX вв.', *ib.*, no.4 : 32–40.

8. Other Individual Authors

S. I. Nadson, *Дневники*, Mw, Zakharov, 272 pp.; N. I. Vrangel', *Воспоминания. От крепостного права до большевиков*, ed. A. Zeide, Mw, NLO, 512 pp.; A. Blium, '"Имя славное Пруткова, имя громкое Козьмы!" К 200–летию со дня рождения великого и незабвенного Козьмы Пруткова', *NG Ex libris*, no. 13 : 3; N. Volodina, *Майковы*, StP, Nauka, 342 pp.; I. I. Merkulova, 'Значение хронотопа дороги в русской исторической прозе 19 века (М. Загоскин и А. Бестужев-Марлинский)', Osovskii, *исследования*, 182–89.

BELYI. D. N. Wells, 'The symbolic structure of Belyi's *Pervoe svidanie*: echoes of Wagner and Steiner', *SEER*, 81 : 201–16, examines the Wagnerian concept of *leitmotiv*, and the anthroposophical ideas of Rudolf Steiner that inform the symbolic structure of Belyi's poems. See also N. A. Nagornaia, '"Второе пространство" и сновидения в романе Андрея Белого "Петербург"', *VMUF*, no.3 : 41–57; I. Shulova, '"Петербург" и "Петербурги" Андрея Белого', *Neva*, no.8 : 237–38.

BUNIN. New studies include I. B. Nichiporov, *Поэзия темна, в словах не выразима. . . Творчество И. А. Бунина и модернизм*, Mw, Metafora, 255 pp.; V. I. Grechnev, 'Рассказ И. Бунина "Далекое"', *RusL*, no.3 : 133–37; *'Ищу я в этом мире сочетания прекрасного и вечного': сборник работ лауреатов и дипломантов Всероссийского литературно-творческого конкурса, посвященного творчеству И. А. Бунина*, Elets U.P., 207 pp.; A. A. Khvan, *Метафизика любви в произведениях А. И. Куприна и И. А. Бунина*, Mw, Institut Khudozhestvennogo tvorchestva, 103 pp. I. A. Bunin, *Письма 1885–1904 гг.*, Mw, IMLI RAN, 767 pp., will be very useful for scholars.

CHERNYSHEVSKII. *Н. Г. Чернышевский: Статьи, исследования и материалы*, vol. 14, ed. A. A. Demchenko, Saratov, Nauchnaia kniga, 213 pp.

FET. *А. А. Фет и русская литература: 17 Фетовские чтения*, ed. V. A. Koshelev, M. V. Stroganova, and N. Z. Kokovina, Kursk U.P., 263 pp., includes unknown stories by F. and articles previously published in 'Moskovskie Vedomosti' (1868–1872); N. M. Myshiakova, *Лирика А. А. Фета: интермедиальные аспекты поэтики*, Orenburg, GPU, 131 pp.; A. Kuz'mina, 'Материалы к биографии А. А. Фета', *RusL*, no.1:122–41; A. V. Achkasov, 'Шекспир в переводах А. А. Фета', *ib.*, no.3:97–113.

GONCHAROV. *И. А. Гончаров: материалы международной научной конференции, посвященной 190-летию со дня рождения И. А. Гончарова*, ed. M. B. Zhdanova and A. V. Lobkareva, Ul'ianovsk, Korporatsiia tekhnologii prodvizheniia, 375 pp.; A. A. Faustov, '"И всяк зевает, да живет ..." (к симптоматике гончаровской "Лихой болести")', *RusL*, no.2:80–93.

GRIGOR'EV. A. A. Iliushin, 'Лихорадочный поэт: к заметкам об Аполлоне Григорьеве', *VMUF*, no.3:7–13.

GUMILEV. O. B. Chernen'kova, 'Прошлое время поэзии Н. С. Гумилева', *VMUF*, no.5:140–47.

KOROLENKO. M. V. Mikhailova, 'Элементы "новейшего реализма" в поэтике рассказа В. Г. Короленко "Не страшное"', *VMUF*, no.4:18–26; M. P. Shustov, 'Сказочная традиция в творчестве В. Г. Короленко', *ib.*, 26–39; M. G. Petrova, '"Идеальный образ русского писателя" (К 150-летию со дня рождения В. Г. Короленко)', *ISLIa*, 62.4:3–9.

LESKOV. A major new study: I. C. Sperrle, *The Organic Worldview of Nikolai Leskov* (Studies in Russian Literature and Theory), Evanston, Northwestern U.P., 2002, xiii + 288 pp. See also A. A. Gorelov, 'Н. С. Лесков и И. С. Аксаков о повести "Захудалый род" (из переписки 1874–1875 годов)', *RusL*, no.2:94–101; A. A. Novikova, 'Основы формирования религиозно-нравственной позиции Н. С. Лескова', *FilN*, no.3: 21–29.

MEREZHKOVSKII. V. N. Bystrov, 'Идея обновления мира у русских символистов (Д. С. Мережковский и А. Белый)', *RusL*, no.3:3–21; no.4:29–51; I. I. Goncharova, '"Религиозная общественность" и террор. Письма Д. Мережковского и З. Гиппиус к Борису Савинкову (1908–1909)', *ib.*, no.4:140–61.

NEKRASOV. V. P. Stakhov, *Поэзия великого духа: читая Некрасова*, StP, n.p., 63 pp., is a very funny book, published 50 years late.

PISEMSKII. There are several important studies on P., all by the same scholar: S. M. Baluev, *Сатирическая публицистика А. Ф. Писемского 1860-х годов*, StP U.P., 2000, 43 pp.; *Очерки А. Ф. Писемского 1850-х годов: Проблематика и стиль*, StP U.P., 2001, 41 pp.; *Писемский — журналист (1850–1860-е годы)*, StP U.P., 170 pp. See also A. A. Shuneiko, 'Некоторые особенности языка романа А. Ф. Писемского "Масоны", Krasil'nikova, *Поэтика*, 334–48.

ROZANOV. There are several new publications on and by R.: V. Fateev, *С русской бездной в душе: жизнеописание Василия Розанова*, StP–Kostroma, GUIPP Kostroma, 2002, 639 pp.; N. Boldyrev, *Семя Озириса, или Василий Розанов как последний ветхозаветный пророк*, Cheliabinsk U.P.–Ural Ltd., 2001, 477 pp.; P. Rudnev, *Театральные взгляды Василия Розанова*, Mw, Agraf, 368 pp.; V. V. Rozanov, *Около народной души: статьи 1906–1908 гг.*, ed. A. N. Nikoliukin, Mw, Respublika, 447 pp. See also I. Prokopchuk, 'Неизвестный псевдоним В. В. Розанова', *VL*, no.3 : 378–82; S. Kuznetsov, 'Предсмертные книги Розанова', *Zvezda*, no.8 : 220–23.

SHEVYREV. K. V. Ratnikov, 'Религиозно-философская концепция позднего творчества С. П. Шевырева (на материале поэмы "Болезнь", 1862)', *VMUF*, no.2 : 84–89; K. V. Ratnikov, *Степан Петрович Шевырев и русские литераторы 19 века*, Cheliabinsk, Okolitsa, 176 pp.

SOLOGUB, F. There are three interesting works on S.: L. M. Kleinbort, '"Встречи. Федор Сологуб"', *RusL*, no.2 : 102–21; T. V. Misnikevich, 'Письма Ю. Н. Верховского к Ф.Сологубу и Ан. Н. Чеботаревской', *ib.*, 121–41; A. I. Gladkii, '"Тяжелые сны" Федора Сологуба на фоне Бахтина. Проблема автора и героя', *Бахтинские чтения — 3*, 75–82.

SOLOV'EV. V. A. Krasnov, 'Художественные образы в произведениях М. И. Махаева и В. С. Соловьева и творчество А. Н. Бенуа', *Neva*, no.3 : 221–22; N. G. Iurina, '*Проза К. К. Случевского в критическом освещении Вл. Соловьева*', Osovskii, *исследования*, 14–20; N. D. Tamarchenko, 'Проблема автора и героя и спор о богочеловечестве (М. М. Бахтина, Е. Н. Трубецкой и Вл. С. Соловьев)', *Бахтинские чтения — 2*, 105–30; A. I. Brodskii, 'Восточный синдром. Философия войны В. С. Соловьева и столкновение цивилизаций', *Zvezda*, no.12 : 205–207.

SUKHOVO-KOBYLIN. New studies and materials include N. D. Starosel'skaia, *Сухово-Кобылин*, Mw, Molodaia Gvardiia, 318 pp. Kham Ion Dzhun, *Поэтика драматургии А. В. Сухово-Кобылина*, StP, Kul't-Inform, 256 pp.; V. Seleznev, '"Всё чистейшее мошенничество и наглость": Неизвестные письма Сухово-Кобылина', *VL*, no.6 : 326–38; V. Seleznev, 'О Сухово-Кобылине', *VL*, no.2 : 377–83.

TIUTCHEV. A very good year for T. studies sees the following major publications: *Ф. И. Тютчев и тютчеведение в начале третьего тысячелетия: материалы конференции,* ed. G. I. Kukatova, Briansk, Brianskaia oblastnaia nauchnaia universal'naia biblioteka, 347 pp., containing V. N. Terekhina, 'Тютчев и Северянин: новые материалы' (178–203); S. I. Vidiushchenko, 'Тютчев и Гумилев: к вопросу о традиции' (204–14); I. N.Shtal', 'Творчество Ф. И. Тютчева и поэма Вен. Ерофеева "Москва — Петушки"' (215–34); S. Ekshtut, *Тютчев. Тайный советник и камергер,* Mw, Progress–Traditsiia, 320 pp.; T. Tret'iakova, *Тютчевы — Мышкинские дворяне: Историко-архивное исследование об ярославских корнях рода Тютчевых, их родственных и владельческих отношениях в Верхневолжье,* Iaroslavl', Aleksandra Rutmana, 112 pp.; T. G. Dinesman, I. A. Koroleva, and B. N. Shchedrinskii, *Летопись жизни и творчества Ф. И. Тютчева: книга 2: 1844–1860,* Mw, Litograf–Muranovo, 407 pp.; A. A. Myrikova, *Ф. И. Тютчев: особенности политического дискурса,* Mw, Vorob'ev, 205 pp.; A. Myrikova and A. Shirin'iants, *Вокруг Тютчева (Полемические заметки),* Mw, Sotsial'no-politicheskaia mysl', 35 pp.; V. F. Pogorel'tsev, 'Проблема религиозности Ф. И. Тютчева', *VF,* no.6:136–41; L. Anninskii, 'Бессильный ясновидец: к 200-летию Ф. И. Тютчева', *DN,* no.6:219–20; V. Pogorel'tsev, 'Как на качелях (О религиозности Ф. И. Тютчева)', *VL,* no.4:301–10; V. S. Baevskii, 'Тютчев: поэзия экзистенциальных переживаний', *ISLIa,* 62.6:3–10; L. F. Katsis and M. P. Odesskii, 'Тютчев и славянский вопрос', *ib.,* 11–24; N. Skatov, 'Погружение во тьму', *NSo,* no.12:260–69; A. Ubogii, 'Россия и Тютчев *(к 200-летию со дня рождения Ф. И. Тютчева)*', *ib.,* no.4:239–59; N. N. Skatov, 'По высям творенья', *RusL,* no.4:3–28.

LITERATURE FROM 1917 TO THE PRESENT DAY

By Boris Lanin, *Professor of Literature, Russian Academy of Education, Moscow*

1. General

Among major new books is L. V. Kamedina, *Обретая смысл заново: опыт прочтения русской литературы в начале третьего тысячелетия*, 2nd rev. edn, Chita, ZabGPU, 165 pp. There are several useful reference guides for scholars in the field of modern Russian literature: O. D. Smilevets, *Второе имя: псевдонимы саратовских писателей и журналистов*, Saratov U.P., 99 pp.; V. V. Ogryzko, *Изборник: материалы к словарю русских писателей конца 20 — начала 21 века*, Mw, Literaturnaia Rossiia, 286 pp.; G. I. Romanova, *Русские писатели 20 века: словарь-справочник*, Mw, Flinta–Nauka, 256 pp.; M. M. Golubkov, *Русская литература 20 века*, Mw, Aspekt, 288 pp. E. Limonov, *Священные монстры*, Mw, Ad Marginem, 320 pp., contains essays on Gumilev, Savinkov, and Akhmatova; see also N. M. Fed', *Литература мятежного века: диалектика российской словесности, 1918–2002*, Mw, Golos, 672 pp. V. Bondarenko, *Пламенные реакционеры: три лика русского патриотизма*, Mw, Algoritm, 752 pp., concerns three branches of the neo-slavophile movement: the 'Red Image' includes Sergei Mikhalkov, Feliks Kuznetsov, and Alexander Zinov'ev; the 'White Image' includes Aleksandr Solzhenitsyn and Dmitrii Galkovskii; and the 'Russian Image' includes Vasilii Shukshin, Vasilii Belov, Lev Gumilev, and Iurii Mamleev. See also A. P. Andriushkin, *Иудеи в русской литературе 20 века*, StP, Svetoch, 319 pp.; I. Vrubel'-Golubkina, *Символ 'Мы': Еврейская хрестоматия новой русской литературы*, Mw, NLO, 464 pp.; *20 век: Проза, поэзия, критика*, Mw, Maks, 199 pp.; N. D. Gorshkova, *Современная поэзия*, Novosibirsk, NGTU, 24 pp.; A. S. Akbasheva and S. Z. Tikeeva, *Сквозь призму быстротечности: монографические очерки по истории литературы 20 века*, Ufa, Gilem, 195 pp.

2. Literary History

There are several interesting theoretical approaches to the history of literature in *NLO*, no.59: T. Venediktova, 'О пользе литературной истории для жизни' (12–21); M. L. Gasparov, 'Как писать историю литературы' (142–47); M. Iampol'skii, 'История культуры как история духа и естественная история' (22–89); D. Bak, 'Литературоведение как провокация чтения: есть ли автор у истории литературы?' (90–92); A. Etkind, 'Русская литература, XIX век: Роман внутренней колонизации' (103–24); A. Shcherbenok, 'История литературы между историей и теорией: история как литература и литература как история' (158–70); A. Stroev, 'История литературы: воспоминание о будущем' (337–40); G. Tihanov, 'Будущее истории литературы: Три вызова XXI века' (341–46).

L. Maksimenkov, 'Очерки номенклатурной истории советской литературы (1932–1946): Сталин, Бухарин, Щербаков и другие', *VL*, no.4 : 212–58, no.5 : 241–97, presents important historical sources. See also V. Lapenkov, 'Ars rossica: литературная Россия и фабула глобализации', *Zvezda*, no.1 : 200–22; E. Kuznetsov, 'Собственное мнение. Сатирические работы Арго 20–30-х годов', *VL*, no.3 : 307–19. *Русское литературоведение в новом тысячелетии: материалы второй международной конференции*, ed. I. G. Kruglov, 2 vols, Mw, Taganka, 448, 416 pp. B. I. Frezinskii, *Судьбы серапионов: портреты и сюжеты*, StP, Akademicheskii proekt, 590 pp., is a valuable work about the Serapion Brothers. Also of interest are M. L. Andreev, *Второе рождение нормативной поэтики*, Mw, GU-VShE, 30 pp.; *Постсимволизм как явление культуры: материалы международной конференции*, ed. I. A. Esaulov, Mw, RGGU, 96 pp.; V. S. Baevskii, *История русской литературы 20 века: компендиум*, 2nd rev. edn, Mw, Iazyki slaviankoi kul'tury, 448 pp.; V. Mil'china, 'Сопоставление контекстов', *NLO*, no.60 : 327–32; D. Rayfield, 'The exquisite inquisitor: Viacheslav Menzhinsky as poet and hangman', *NZSJ*, 37 : 91–109; L. S. Ianitskii, *Архаические структуры в лирической поэзии XX века*, Kemerovo, Kuzbassvuzizdat, 136 pp.; *Философский контекст русской литературы 1920–1930-х годов*, ed. A. G. Gacheva, Mw, IMLI RAN, 399 pp.; V. S. Voronin, *Взаимодействие фантазии и абсурда в русской литературе первой трети XX века*, Volgograd U.P., 292 pp. G. Eikhler, *Для себя лично, или несмотря ни на что: Записки. Отрывки. Дневники. Новеллы. Письма. Воспоминания*, ed. B. S. Vaiberg, Ekaterinburg, Izdanie gazety 'Stern', 137 pp., discusses Chukovskii, Gaidar, Shklovskii, Korolenko, Gor'kii, Pasternak, A. N. Tolstoi.

SILVER AGE. Important studies include the following: A. Hansen-Löwe, *Русский символизм: система поэтических мотивов: мифопоэтический символизм начала века: Космическая символика*, trans. M. I. Nekrasov, StP, Akademicheskii proekt, 814 pp.; *Символизм в авангарде*, 2nd rev. edn, ed. G. F. Kovalenko, Mw, Nauka, 443 pp.; I. I. Ivaniushina, *Русский футуризм: идеология, поэтика, прагматика*, Saratov U.P., 311 pp.; M. N. Zolotonosov, *Братья Мережковские: Отщеpenis Серебряного века*, vol. 1, Mw,

Ladomir, 1030 pp.; N. G. Aref'eva, *Античные традиции в творчестве поэтов серебряного века. Драматургия*, vol. 2, Astrakhan' U.P., 17 pp.; I. G. Mineralova, *Русская литература серебряного века: поэтика символизма*, Mw, Flinta–Nauka, 268 pp.; *Писатели символистского круга: новые материалы*, StP, Dmitrii Bulanin, 509 pp.; V. I. Prokof'eva, *Символизм. Акмеизм. Футуризм. Различные модели поэтического пространства в лексическом представлении*, Orenburg, OGPU, 207 pp.; M. Edel'shtein, 'Серебряный век: женский взгляд (Сестры Герцык. Письма)', *NovM*, no.6 : 193–96; *Проза русских символистов*, Mw, Maks, 52 pp.; *Максимилиан Волошин: из литературного наследия, 3*, ed. A. V. Lavrov, StP, Dmitrii Bulanin, 482 pp.; M. Roubins, 'Экфрасис в раннем творчестве Георгия Иванова', *RusL*, no.1 : 68–85; O. N. Kulishkina, 'Лев Шестов: афоризм как форма "творчества из ничего"', *ib.*, 49–67. L. S. Aleshina and G. I. Sternin, *Образы и люди серебряного века*, Mw, Galart, 2002, 272 pp.

LITERARY CULTURE. An intriguing publication is *Ароматы и запахи в культуре*, ed. O. Vainstein, 2 vols, Mw, NLO, 608, 664 pp. G. Guseinov, *Д. С. П.: Материалы к русскому словарю общественно-политического языка XX века*, Mw, Tri kvadrata, 1022 pp., is a cultural history explored through political vocabulary. See also *Переходные процессы в русской художестенной культуре: Новое и Новейшее время*, ed. A. Khrenov, Mw, Nauka, 495 pp.; M. Zalambani, *Искусство в производстве: Авангард и революция в России 20–х годов*, Mw, IMLI RAN–Nasledie, 240 pp.; N. K. Bonetskaia, 'П. Флоренский: русское гетеанство', *VF*, no.3 : 97–116; G. A. Time, 'Миф о "закате Европы" в мировоззренческой самоиндентификации России начала 1920–х годов', *VF*, no. 6, 2002 : 149–62; V. Kantor, '"Перед лицом русской истории XX столетия" (Сергей Аверинцев и Вячеслав Иванов)', *VL*, no.4 : 331–43.

MODERN LITERATURE. S. Chuprinin, *Новая Россия: мир литературы: Энциклопедический словарь-справочник*, vol. 1 : *А–Л*, vol. 2: *М–Я*, Mw, Vagrius, 832, 928 pp., is an essential reference book that contains biographical data for contemporary Russian writers. Id., *Русская литература сегодня: путеводитель*, Mw, Olma, 445 pp., contains short biographies of 150 of the most popular contemporary Russian writers; see also S. Borovikov, *В русском жанре: из жизни читателя*, Mw, Vagrius, 303 pp.

Other important studies include S. Chuprinin, 'Нулевые годы: ориентация на местности', *Znamia*, no.1 : 180–89; M. Bondarenko, 'Текущий литературный процесс как объект литературоведения: статья первая', *NLO*, 62 : 57–76; E. Ermolin, 'Цена опыта', *DN*, no.2 : 187–90; E. Ivanitskaia and N. Ivanitskaia,

'Masslit', *DN*, no.10: 187–91; M. Zagidullina, '"Новое дело" интеллигенции, или Хождение в народ–2', *Znamia*, no.8: 185–94. E. Ivanitskaia, 'Поджигатели и летописцы', *DN*, no.2: 191–96, discusses O. Pavlov, V. Iskhakov, V. Sharov, R. Senchin, L. Iuzefovich, E. Dolgopiat, M. Vishnevetskaia, and some others.

V. Gubailovskii, 'Место для обгона', *DN*, no.2: 196–99, writes about new works by S. Gandlevskii, A. Gavrilov, D. Shevarov, M. Vishnevetskaia, A. Eppel', D. Bobyshev, M. Butov, I. Ermakova, and S. Stratanovskii. A. Uritskii, 'Не ленитесь читать, господа!' *ib.*, 199–202, mentions works by A. Prokhanov, V. Sorokin, S. Gandlevskii, L. Kostiukov, D. Osokin, G. Ball, A. Gavrilov, and V. Makanin. N. B. Ivanova, *Скрытый сюжет: русская литература на переходе через век*, StP, Blits, 560 pp., is an illuminating study of the ways in which contemporary literature lives and works, including discussion of Russian émigré writers. Those discussed include Marinina, Solzhenitsyn, Astaf'ev, Gorenshtein, Iurii Davydov, Dovlatov, Svetlana Kekova, Limonov, Anatolii Naiman, Prigov, Feliks Svetov, Roman Senchin, Tat'iana Tolstaia, Semen Faibisovich, Oleg Chukhontsev, Vladimir Makanin, and others.

See also *Современная русская литература: проблемы изучения и преподавания: материалы Всероссийской конференции*, ed. M. P. Abasheva, Perm' GPU, 246 pp.; T. N. Markova, *Современная проза: конструкция и смысл (В. Маканин, Л. Петрушевская, В. Пелевин)*, Mw, MGOU, 267 pp.; A. Melikhov, 'Об уроках современной литературы', *Neva*, no.6: 198–99; A. Melikhov, 'Массовая культура: за и против', *ib.*, no.9: 184–85.

THE EMIGRATION. Some important materials: *Россия и российская эмиграция в воспоминаниях и дневниках: аннотированный указатель книг, журналов и газетных публикаций, изданных за рубежом в 1917–1991 гг.*, vol. 1, ed. A. G. Tartakovskii, Mw, Rosspen, 672 pp.; B. Kodzis, *Литературные центры русского зарубежья 1918–1939. Писатели. Творческие объединения. Периодика. Книгопечатание*, Munich, Sagner, 2002, 318 pp. Studies include N. V. Mokina, *Архетипическое и эпохальное в образе лирического героя в творчестве поэтов Серебряного века*, Saratov U.P., 120 pp.; Id., *Проблема смысла жизни и ее образное воплощение в русской поэзии Серебряного века*, Saratov U.P., 238 pp. *Литература русского зарубежья ('Первая волна' эмиграции: 1920–1940 гг.)*, vol. 1, ed. A. I. Smirnova, Volgograd U.P., 242 pp., contains studies of the so-called 'older generation'. Also of interest is A. Adamovich, 'Из записных книжек', ed. V. S. Adamovich and N. A. Shuvagina-Adamovich, *VL*, no.3: 258–87. A. Zverev, *Повседневная жизнь русского литературного Парижа. 1920–1940*, Mw, Molodaia gvardiia, 371 pp., is the swan song of the prominent Russian critic who has recently passed away.

M. Adamovich, 'О времени . . . и о себе', *Znamia*, no.4: 190–98, writes about poets of the second wave of emigration; A. Kurchatkin, 'Убежавший в Россию', *ib.*, no.8: 195–99, writes about Sergei Iur'enen. See also V. G. Makarov, '"Власть ваша, а правда наша" (к 80-летию высылки интеллигенции из Советской России в 1922 г.)', *VF*, no.10, 2002: 108–55; A. Ktorova, *'Минувшее': Москва пятидесятых годов*, Mw, Minuvshee, 336 pp. G. M. Bongard-Levin, *Из 'Русской Мысли'*, StP, Aleteia, 2002, 232 pp., contains studies on Blok, Bal'mont, Shmelev, Zaitsev, Bunin, and Nabokov. *Письма запрещенных людей: Литература и жизнь эмиграции 1950–1980-е годы: по материалам архива И. В. Чиннова*, ed. O. F. Kuznetsova, Mw, IMLI RAN, 832 pp., is an interesting source. See also I. Putilova, 'Моя встреча с Владимиром Максимовым', *Zvezda*, no.12: 187–89; R. Timenchik, 'Петербург в поэзии русской эмиграции', *ib.*, no.10: 194–205; *Центральная Россия и литература русского зарубежья (1917–1939): исследования и публикации*, Orel, Veshnie vody, 283 pp.; *Русское зарубежье — духовный и культурный феномен: материалы международной конференции, в 2 ч.*, 2 vols, Mw, Novyi Gumanitarnyi universitet Natal'i Nesterovoi, 288, 248 pp.

Other studies include L. Spiridonova, '"Правда нужна всякой власти . . ." (К 130-летию со дня рождения И. С. Шмелева)", *NSo*, no. 10: 252–62; A. I. Gorbunova, 'Георгий Адамович — литературный критик', Osovskii, *исследования*, 20–27; *Балтийский архив: русская культура в Прибалтике*. Вып. VII, ed. P. Lavrinets, Vil'nius, Russkie tvorcheskie resursy Baltii–Zvaigzdziu miestas, 2002, 395 pp.

SOCIALIST REALISM. M. Chegodaeva, *Социалистический реализм: Мифы и реальность*, Mw, Zakharov, 224 pp.; S. Povartsov, 'Партийные тайны Георгия Маркова', *VL*, no.3: 371–78; L. Mally, 'Exporting Soviet culture: the case of Agitprop theater', *SRev*, 62.2: 324–42, explores the attempts of the Comintern affiliate MORT (*Mezhdunarodnoe ob"edinenie revoliutsionnykh teatrov*) to export models of Soviet theatrical performance outside the USSR.

CENSORSHIP. A. Rubashkin, 'Александр. Володя, Алик, Геннадий. Вспоминая о цензуре', *Zvezda*, no.3: 208–16; G. Faiman, *Уголовная история советской литературы и театре*, Mw, Agraf, 457 pp., includes material on Fadeev, Zoshchenko, Belinkov, and V. Suvorov from previously (and in several cases — still!) closed KGB and Communist Party archives. Some of them were previously published in *Nezavisimaia gazeta, Obshchaia gazeta, Khranit' vechno,* and *Russkaia mysl'*.

3. Theory

Теоретико-литературные итоги XX века: Художественный текст и контекст культуры, vol. 2, ed. I. Borev, Mw, Nauka, 447 pp.; M. I. Zvegintseva, *Авторские жанровые формы в русской прозе конца 20 века*, Astrakhan', Astrakhanskii gospedinstitut, 2001, 179 pp.; *Основы литературоведения*, ed. V. P. Meshcheriakov, Mw, Drofa, 416 pp.; O. I. Fedotov, *Основы теории литературы*, vol. 1: *Литературное творчество и литературное произведение,* Vol.2: *Стихосложение и литературный процесс*, Mw, Vlados, 272, 240 pp.; B. Lanin, 'О современной русской антиутопии', *Vestnik Instituta Kennana v Rossii,* 3:71–84, discusses O. Divov, Khol'm Van Zaichik, E. Gevorkian, P. Krusanov, and A. Stoliarov.

G. and V. Kuznetsov, 'Сказка — ложь, да в ней намек . . .', *VL,* no.2:295–300, is a postmodern interpretation of Soviet literary tales. See also S. T. Vaiman, *Драматический диалог,* Mw, URSS, 205 pp.; *Русский имажинизм: история, теория, практика: материалы международной конференции,* ed. V. A. Drozdkov, Mw, Linor, 519 pp.; *Творческая индивидуальность писателя: традиции и новаторство,* Elista, Kalmykskii U. P., 184 pp.; *Художественно-историческая интеграция литературного процесса: материалы конференции,* ed. U. M. Panesh, Maikop, Adygeiskii U.P., 180 pp.; *Рукописи не горят* (Scripta manent, 9), ed. E. M. Beregovskaia and M. P. Tikhonov, Smolensk GPU, 208 pp.; H. U. Gumbrekht, 'Начала науки о литературе. . . и ее конец?' *NLO,* no.59:93–102; D. Davydov, 'Меж улицей безъязыкой и Кастальским ключом (наивная словесность как историко-типологическая проблема)', *ib.,* 171–78; L. Gudkov and B. Dubin, '"Эпическое" литературоведение. Стерилизация субъективности и ее цена', *ib.,* 211–31; I. Kalinin, 'Слепота и прозрение: Риторика истории России и "Риторика темпоральности" Поля де Мана', *ib.,* 250–73; A. Piatigorskii, '"Мышление ведь происходит формами . . .". *ib.,* 347–58. I. Kukulin (interviewed by G. Amelin), '"Сумрачный лес" как предмет ажиотажного спроса, или Почему приставка "пост-" потеряла свое значение' *ib.,* 359–91; D. Kuz'min, 'План работ по исследованию внутрисловного переноса', *ib.,* 392–409; E. A. Bal'burov, *Поэтическая философия русского космизма: учение, эстетика, поэтика,* Novosibirsk, SO RAN, 239 pp.; B. G. Bobylev, *Теоретические основы филологического анализа художественного текста,* Orel U.P., 205 pp.

CRITICISM. Of considerable note is S. Chuprinin, *Перемена участи: Статьи последних лет*, Mw, NLO, 400 pp. *Критика 1917–1932 годов*, ed. E. A. Dobrenko, Mw, AST–Astrel', 459 pp., is a valuable anthology of critical texts. A. Nemzer, *Замечательное десятилетие русской литературы*, Mw, Zakharov, 608 pp., is a remarkable event in contemporary criticism, which discusses works by Vladimov, Dmitriev, Makanin, Soloukhin, Solzhenitsyn, Korolev, Kibirov, Losev, Salimon, Vishnevetskaia, Buida, Mamedov, L. Zorin, Vasilenko, M. Uspenskii, Ergali Ger, Kharuzina, Butov, Pelevin, Rozanov, Sorokin, Slapovskii, Egorov, M. Sokolov, Faibisovich, Gasparov, Shklovskii, Gordin, Arkhangel'skii, Naiman, Tolstaia, Pavlova, Proskurin, Chudakov, Dovlatov, Efimov, Cherchesov, M. Kononov, D. Bykov, Slavnikova, Akunin, Pavlov, Annenkov, Ageev, Gandlevskii, Ekushev, E. Popov, Anatolii Kuznetsov, Samoilov, S'ianova, Klimontovich, Bushkov, Pozdniaeva, and Lisnianskaia. See also O. Slavnikova, 'Книга контрабанды (Андрей Немзер. Памятные даты)', *NovM*, no.1:187–90; B. Menzel, 'Перемены в русской литературной критике: взгляд через немецкий телескоп', *Neprikosnovennyi zapas*, no.4:145–53.

On Lotman's theories see Kim Su Kvan, *Основные аспекты творческой эволюции Ю. М. Лотмана*, Mw, NLO, 176 pp.; E. V. Volkova, 'Пространство символа и символ пространства в работах Ю. М. Лотмана', *VF*, 2002, no.11:149–64.

E. Ivanitskaia, 'Интеллектуальные приключения', *Znamia*, no.6:204–13, analyses the study of modern Russian literature by N. Leiderman and M. Lipovetskii; A. Latynina, 'Старшая дочь короля Лира', *NovM*, no.10:158–64, is on the critic Vladimir Bondarenko; see also L. V. Chernets, 'О лекциях С. М. Бонди', *Dialog. Karnaval. Khronotop*, 2001, no.3:183–91. S. Zavialov, 'Мифы литературной эпохи', *DN*, no.4:211–13, writes about Savitskii's work on Russian underground writers; N. Aniko, 'Сны о критике', *Ural*, no.3:229–35, writes about the modern Russian critics M. Remizova, M. Adamovich, A. Ageev, and O. Slavnikova; a response is given by S. Beliakov, 'После снов', *ib.*, 236–43. Other notable studies include V. A. Vozchikov, *Книга — явление культуры: литературоведение, литературная критика, публицистика*, Biisk, NITs BPGU, 311 pp.; I. S. Ovanesian, *Реформаторы и праведники: литературная критика, публицистика*, Mw, Moskovskaia gorodskaia organizatsiia Soiuza pisatelei Rossii, 2002, 203 pp.; A. M. Shteingol'd, *Анатомия литературной критики: природа, структура, поэтика*, StP, Dmitrii Bulanin, 201 pp.; B. Dubin and A. Reitblat, 'Литературные ориентиры современных журнальных рецензентов', *NLO*, no.59:557–70; I. Svitiaeva, '"Критика поэта" или "поэзия критика"? (Павел Белицкий.

Разговоры)', *NovM*, no.10 : 176–80; O. Slavnikova, 'Книга контрабанды (Андрей Немзер. Памятные даты)', *ib.*, no.1 : 187–90.

R. G. Grubel, *Literaturaxiologie: Zur Theorie und Geschichte des ästhetischen Wertes in slavischen Literaturen* (Opera Slavica, n.s. 40), Wiesbaden, Harrassowitz, 2001, 771 pp., is based on theory constructed by the Konstanz school (A. Hansen-Löwe, I. P. Smirnov, R. Lachmann) and includes analysis of works by M. Bakhtin, A. Remizov, A. Pushkin, V. Khlebnikov, and A. Bek. *Критика и ее исследователь: сборник, посвященный памяти профессора В. Н. Коновалова*, Kazan′ U. P., 143 pp.; See also Khe Sin' Khan, 'К истории русского стиховедения последней трети XX века', *RusL*, no.2 : 172–73.

There are interesting works on 'Bakhtinistika': O. I. Osovskii, *В зеркале 'другого': рецепция научного наследия М. М. Бахтина в англо-американском литературоведении 1960-х — середины 1990-х годов*, Saransk, Krasnyi Oktiabr', 147 pp. M. L. Novikova, 'Хронотоп как остраненное единство художественного времени и пространства в языке литературного произведения, *FilN*, no.2 : 60–69; M. I. Asanina, 'Категория смехового слова в научной концепции М. Бахтина', Osovskii, *исследования*, 172–74; L. S. Konkina, 'Проблемы поэтики в работах М. М. Бахтина 1920-х гг.', *ib.*, 215–19; B. F. Egorov, '"М. М. Бахтин и Ю. М. Лотман"', ib., 83–96; K. Sasaki, 'М. М. Бахтин и Тэцуро Вацудзи: вопросы этики и философии языка', *ib.*, 183–86; T. G. Iurchenko, 'Социологическая поэтика М. М. Бахтина и проблема жанра (Опыт интерпретации жанра идиллии)', *ib.*, 2 : 151–59; D. Shepherd, '"Общаясь с мирами иными": Противоположные взгляды на карнавал в недавних российских и западных бахтиноведческих исследованиях', *Dialog. Karnaval. Khronotop*, 2001, no.4 : 151–68; N. D. Tamarchenko, 'Было ли отношение Бахтина к смеху антихристианским?', *ib.*, 92–100; A. A. Kazakov, 'Карнавализация в литературе', *ib.*, 18–34; V. V. Maksimov, 'Проблема речевых жанров. Жанровый мир сплетни', *ib.*, 35–49; L. M. Romanovskaia, 'Бахтин — Руссо: Химера и научность "естественного состояния"', *ib.*, 50–91; Id., 'Карнавал как утопия. Статья вторая: "Рабле" в 60-е годы', *ib.*, no.3 : 160–83; N. D. Tamarchenko, 'Проблема "роман и трагедия" у Ницше, Вяч. Иванова и Бахтина', *ib.*, 116–34; K. Sasami, 'Основы понятия текста у М. М. Бахтина', *ib.*, 99–115.

SOCIOLOGY OF LITERATURE. There is a collection of penetrating studies of current Russian work on the sociology of literature in *NLO*, no.60: A. Dmitriev, '"В свете нашего опыта": социоанализ Пьера Бурдье и российское гуманитарное сознание' (7–16); S. Zenkin, 'Теория писательства и письмо теории, или Филология после Бурдье' (30–37); A. Bikbov, 'Социоанализ культуры: внутренние принципы и внешняя критика' (38–53); M. Magidovich, 'Поле искусства как предмет исследования' (54–69). D. Prigov, 'Где мы живем и где не живем', *Oktiabr'*, no.10 : 172–76; O. Lebedushkina, 'О пользе сравнения собственных понятий с другими', *DN*, no.4 : 214–17; B. Khazanov, 'Поднимайте мосты, закрывайте границы', *Oktiabr'*, no.3 : 178–80. *Популярная литература: Опыт культурного мифотворчества в Америке и в России: Материалы V Фулбрайтовской гуманитарной летней школы*, ed. T. V. Venediktova, Moscow U.P., 199 pp., contains studies by S. Berkovich, M. Hill, S. Zenkin, B. Dubin, A. Dmitriev, A. Reitblat, V. Shnirel'man, M. Levina, G. Zvereva, and M. Litovskaia. See also B. V. Dubin, *Семантика, риторика и социальные функции 'прошлого': к социологии советского и постсоветского исторического романа*, Mw, GU-VShE, 43 pp.; B. Khlebnikov, 'Книжный рынок: немецкий фон для России', *Neprikosnovennyi zapas*, no.4 : 129–35; B. Dubin, 'Между каноном и актуальностью, скандалом и модой: литература и издательское дело в России в изменившемся социальном пространстве', *ib.*, 136–144.

MEMOIRS. Many excellent memoirs were published this year: I. Krelin, *Извивы памяти*, Mw, Zakharov, 286 pp.; L. Sinianskaia, 'Во сне и наяву среди глыб', *Znamia*, no.3 : 142–73 (her memoir of several significant events in the history of Soviet literature); L. Lazarev, 'Записки пожилого человека', *Znamia*, no.7 : 112–36, is a continuation of previously published chapters (in *Znamia*, 1997, no.2; 2001, no.6). *'В начале жизни школу помню я . . .' Л. Зильбер, В. Каверин, А. Летавет, Н. Нейгауз, Ю. Тынянов — о времени и о себе*, Mw, FGUP, 222 pp. N. Serpinskaia, *Флирт с жизнью: мемуары интеллигентки двух эпох*, ed. S. V. Shumikhin, Mw, Molodaia gvardiia, 334 pp., is about K. Bal'mont, V. Maiakovskii, M. Kuzmin, N. Gumilev, S. Esenin, D. Bednyi, and a few other lesser known writers.

E. Rein, *Заметки марафонца: неканонические мемуары*, Ekaterinburg, U-Faktoriia, 528 pp., is on Akhmatova, Saianov, Olesha, Evtushenko, Dovlatov, Shklovskii, Okudzhava, and others; N. Korzhavin, *В защиту банальных истин*, Mw, Moskovskaia shkola politicheskikh issledovanii, 434 pp. I. Burtin, *Исповедь шестидесятника*, Mw, Progress-Traditsiia, 648 pp.; M. P. Lobanov, *В сражении и любви: опыт духовной автобиографии*, Mw, Kovcheg, 624 pp.; L. Borodin, *Без выбора: автобиографическое повествование*, Mw, Molodaia gvardiia, 505 pp.; I. Edlis, 'Ностальгические заметки', *VL*, no.6 : 273–310, and Id., *Четверо в дубленках и другие фигуранты; Записки недотепы*, Mw, AST–KRPA Olimp–Astrel', 348 pp.; B. Vasil'ev, *Век необычайный*, Mw, Vagrius, 240 pp.;

T. Bek, *До свидания, алфавит: эссе, мемуары, беседы, стихи,* Mw, BSG, 639 pp.; I. Dedkov, 'Уже открыт новый счет: Из дневниковых записей 1987-1994 годов', ed. and comm. T. F. Dedkova, *NovM,* no.1 : 139–51; no.2 : 110–23; no.3 : 133–54; no.4 : 124–43. V. Lakshin, 'Последний акт: Дневник 1969—1970 годов', *DN,* no.4 : 146–84; *Юрий и Ольга Трифоновы вспоминают,* ed. O. Trifonova, Mw, Sovershenno sekretno, 256 pp.; T. Iur'eva, *Дневник культурной девушки,* Mw, RGGU, 400 pp., is a unique memoir on literary life in the 1980s; G. Zakhoder, *Заходер и все-все-все . . .,* Mw, Zakharov, 256 pp. L. Timofeev and G. Pospelov, *Устные мемуары,* Mw, Moscow U.P., 224 pp., contains very interesting memoirs, recorded by A. Duvakin and commented upon by N. A. Pan'kov, on the critics Sakulin, Pereverzev, Nusinov, Lifshits, Mikhail Malishevskii, Fokht, and Friche, and the writers Briusov and Shengeli. S. Tikhorzhevskii, 'История и отдельная человеческая жизнь', *Zvezda,* no.9 : 206–209; P. V. Kupriianovskii, *В вечерний час: воспоминания,* Ivanovo, Izdatel'stvo Ivanovo, 173 pp.; I. Milorava, 'Шкловский — тогда', *VL,* no.3 : 287–92; M. Gorbov, 'Война', ed. and comm. M. Gorbova, *Zvezda,* no.11 : 163–95; I. Efimov, 'Шаг вправо, шаг влево', *ib.,* no.9 : 158–66; T. Zolotnitskaia, 'Нью-йоркские встречи', ed. and comm. D. I. Zolotnitskii, *ib.,* no.1 : 188–205; K. Chistov, 'С. Маршак в моей жизни', *ib.,* no.9 : 151–57; *Камил Икрамов и о нем,* ed. O. Sidel'nikova-Ikramova, Mw, Dom-muzei Mariny Tsvetaevoi, 108 pp.; O. A. Rostova, *Алмазный фонд воспоминаний: к 100-летию со дня рождения М. А. Светлова,* Mw, Fair-Press, 207 pp.; G. Andzhaparidze, *Не только о детективе,* Mw, Vagrius, 383 pp.; D. Bobyshev, *Я здесь: человекотекст,* Mw, Vagrius, 399 pp.; T. V. Romanova, *Модальность как текстообразующая в современной мемуарной литературе,* StP U.P., 293 pp.; I. P. Smirnov, 'Три Саши', *Kriticheskaia massa,* no.1 : 147–51, is in memoriam of A. A. Panchenko; S. Zalygin, 'Заметки, не нуждающиеся в сюжете', *Oktiabr',* no.9 : 133–73; no.10 : 139–71; no.11 : 102–120; V. Arro, 'Не смотрите, никто не пришел!', *Znamia,* no.4 : 142–59; L. Timofeev, 'Дневник военных лет', *ib.,* no.12 : 127–59.

COMPARATIVE STUDIES. A number of interesting works include M. Karamitti, 'Моды и перспективы. Сегодняшняя русская литература в Италии и из Италии', *Oktiabr',* no.10 : 177–86; I. V. Sviiasov, *Сафо и русская любовная поэзия 18–начала 20 веков,* StP, Dmitrii Bulanin, 400 pp.; B. Frezinskii, 'Диалог в девятьсот шестьдесят страниц (Диалог писателей. Из истории русско-французских культурных связей XX века. 1920–1970)', *VL,* no.4 : 325–30; V. M. Mul'tatuli, *Расин в русской культуре: пути освоения духовных ценностей иностранной культуры: соотношение национальных форм нравственно-эстетических представлений и средств художественной выразительности*, StP, SPbGUKI, 255 pp.; A. V. Achkasov, *Лирика Гейне в русских переводах 1840–1860-х годов*, Kursk U.P., 198 pp.; *Литература в диалоге культур: материалы международной научной конференции*, Rostov, ITs Kompleks, 159 pp.

PROSE. L. Anninskii, 'За что?' *DN*, no.3:220–21, writes about Valentina Ivanova's prose writings; M. Remizova, '. . . Или нам ждать другого?' *DN*, no.6:183–84, is about N. Konoaev and L. Vaneeva; Id., 'Астенический синдром: Образ интеллигента в современной прозе', *Oktiabr'*, no.3:171–77, writes about V. Kantor, S. Gandlevskii, I. Kaminskii, D. Stakhov, V. Skripkin, V. Sharov, I. Brazhnikov, M. Kucherskaia, and I. Maletskii. See also N. Katerli, 'Почему я больше не пишу фантастику', *Neva,* no.8:194–6. I. Kuz'michev, 'Дом на канале', *Zvezda*, no.4:206–11, writes about O. Bazunov and V. Konetskii; *И в засуху бессмертники цветут. . . К 80-летию писателя Анатолия Знаменского: воспоминания,* ed. V. Rotov, Krasnodar, Periodika Kubani, 238 pp.

POETRY. A special issue of *NLO*, 62, is devoted to modern Russian poetry. Among the most interesting articles are the following: M. L. Gasparov, 'Столетие как мера, или Классика на фоне современности' (13–14); I. Orlitskii, 'Где начинается и где заканчивается современная руская поэзия?' (15–21); S. Zavialov, 'Концепт "современности" и категория времени в "советской" и "несоветской" поэзии' (22–34); A. Dmitriev, 'Скромное величие замысла: вызов теории' (35–46); M. Oklot, 'Современность современной русской поэзии' (47–56); I. Vishnevetskii, 'Изобретение традиции, или Грамматика новой русской поэзии' (174–202); I. Vinitskii, '"Особенная стать": баллады Марии Степановой' (165–73); D. Sukhovei, 'Круги компьютерного рая (Семантика графических приемов в текстах поэтического поколения 1900–2000-х годов)' (212–41); D. Golynko-Vol'fson, 'От пустоты реальности к полноте метафоры ("Метареализм" и картография русской поэзии 1980–1990-х годов)'(286–305); A. Glazova, 'О логосе и голосе в современной поэзии' (314–22); M. Maiofis, '"Не ослабевайте упражняться в мягкосердии": Заметки о политической субъективности в современной русской поэзии' (323–39).

Also of interest are the following: A. Zholkovskii, 'Гандлевский, Бродский, Блок, Твардовский. Из заметок об инфинитивной поэзии', *Zvezda,* no.12:201–204; D. Davydov, 'Мрачный детский взгляд: "переходная" оптика в современной русской поэзии', *NLO,* no.60:279–84; S. G. Chugunnikov, *Превращение фонемы в анаграмму "сублиминальные структуры" в русских формальных и структурных поэтиках*, Magnitogorsk U.P., 2002, 163 pp.; E. Novikov and G. Zhevnova, *Жизнь и смерть Михаила Круга*, Mw, OLma, 254 pp.; L. Anninskii, 'Песни современных лириков', *DN*, no.7 : 216–17, is about Grigorii Vikhrov, Alexander Vasin-Makarov, and Sergei Zolotusskii; V. Britanishskii, 'Похищение Прозерпины Платоном', *Neva*, no.2 : 178–97, is on A. Gorodnitskii, O. Tarutin, and L. Ageev; V. Gandel'sman, 'Поэт и чернь', *Oktiabr'*, no.1 : 188–92. See also E. Iazykova, *О творчестве Сергея Михалкова*, 2nd rev. edn, Mw, Prosveshchenie, 224 pp.; A. Ikonnikov-Galitskii, 'Между невинностью и опытом', *Neva*, no.2 : 167–77 (on D. Golynko-Vol'fson, L. Bakhtinov, and I. Sventsitskaia); I. Kachalkina, 'Смерть поэтического диалога', *Znamia*, no.11 : 205–07. A. Kuznetsova, 'Лукианы двадцатого века', *DN*, no.2 : 203–05, writes on Prigov, Rubinshtein, and Kibirov; A. Kuznetsova, 'Неостановимый авангард', *DN*, no.3 : 194–95, is on Aizenberg, Stratanovskii, Fanailova, Dashevskii, N. Kononov, Filippov, and others. See also V. Lipnevich. 'Единство травы и камня', *DN*, no.12 : 197–200. N. Rabotnov, 'Постный модернизм', *Znamia*, no.7 : 186–95, is on modern poetry; A. Ulanov, 'Ожидающий дар', *DN*, no.2 : 206–07, is on Zhdanov, Eremenko, and Parshchikov; V. Tsyvunin, '"Поэзия — дело седых . . ." (О стихах Леонида Рабичева, Александра Ревича и Наума Басовского)', *VL*, no.6 : 255–65; S. Zavialov, 'Перипетия и трагическая ирония в советской поэзии', *NLO*, no.59 : 244–49; A. Ustinov, 'Нескромное предложение: "малые голландцы" русской поэзии и умозрительность литературной истории', *ib.*, 427–50; N. A. Bogomolov, '"Когда-нибудь дошлый историк . . ." (Обзор изданий второстепенных поэтов XX в.)', *NLO*, no.60 : 333–36; I. Foniakov, 'Поэзия параллельного мира', *Neva*, no.9 : 211–12; O. Ivanova, '"Неоспоримой кровью . . ." (10/30. Стихи тридцатилетних; Дмитрий Воденников. Мужчины тоже могут имитировать оргазм)', *NovM*, no.11 : 174–80; A. Mashevskii, 'Что содержит жизненная форма? (Василий Ковалев. Форма жизни; Денис Датешидзе. другое время)', *ib.*, no.8 : 174–78.

DRAMA. P. Rudnev, 'Страшное и сентиментальное (Репетиция. Пьесы уральских авторов)', *NovM*, no.3 : 182–84; V. P. Grigor'ev, 'Слова в контекстах русской поэзии XX века ("О Словаре избранных экспрессем")', *ISLIa*, 62.3 : 12–23.

ESSAYS. K. Kobrin, 'Из жизни героев', *Oktiabr'*, no.8 : 184–91; L. Kostiukov, 'Дядя с собачкой', *VL*, no.5 : 218–23; S. Gandlevskii, 'Америка на уме', *Zvezda*, no.1 : 206–08; A. Genis, 'Пир во время чумы', *ib.*, no.10 : 206–08; L. Gurevich, 'Всемирная литература, или Дар синтеза', *ib.*, no.8:216–19; A. Kushner, 'Первое впечатление', *ib.*, no.8:202–12; Z. Mirkina, 'Что такое великое одиночество?', *Neva,* no.8:207–09; G. Pomerants, 'Одиноко прочерченный путь', *ib.,* 200–06; B. Roginskii, 'Нечто об еже', *Zvezda,* no.9:219; A. Obraztsov, 'Ночной дозор. Из цикла "Сатана в шкафу"', *NovM,* no.8:132–39; P. Kriuchkov, 'Выпрямление курсивом', *ib.*, no.7:179–81; A. Miroshkin, 'Десять свидетельств о XX веке', VL, no.1:329–35; I. Smirnov, 'О метапозиции. Провинция', *Zvezda,* no.11:216–19.

POSTMODERNISM. N. A. Nagornaia, *Онейросфера в русской прозе 20 века: модернизм, постмодернизм*, Barnaul, GPI, 100 pp.; V. B. Kataev, *Игра в осколки: судьбы русской классики в эпоху постмодернизма*, Moscow U.P., 252 pp.; L. Goralik, 'Как размножаются Малфои. Жанр "фэнфик": потребитель масскультуры в диалоге с медиа-контентом, *NovM,* no.12:131–46; C. Kelly, '"Маленькие граждане большой страны": интернационализм, дети и советская пропаганда' (авторизированный пер. с англ. Я. Токаревой), *NLO,* no.60:218–51; M. Lipovetskii, 'Утопия свободной марионетки, или Как сделан архетип. (Перечитывая "Золотой ключик" А. Н. Толстого)' *ib.*, 252–68; M. A. Alekseenko, 'Текстовая реминисценция как единица интертекстуальности', Sorokin, *культура,* 221–33.

EPISTOLARY. 'С твердой верой в добро ...' (А. Т. Твардовский и Н. Я. Мандельштам), ed. V. A. and O. A. Tvardovskaia, *DN,* no.1:139–44;; K. Chukovskii and L. Chukovskaia, *Переписка. 1912–1969,* pref. S. Lur'e, comm. E. T. Chukovskaia and Z. O. Khavkina, Mw, NLO, 592 pp.; '"Искренне Ваш Юл. Оксман" (письма 1914–1970-х годов)', ed. V. D. Rak and M. D. El'zon, *RusL,* no.3:137–84; no.4:182–219.

RUSSIAN LITERATURE ON THE INTERNET. I. Rakita, '"Кремниевый век" сетевой поэзии', *Oktiabr',* no.4:175–77; K. V. Vigurskii and I. A. Pil'shchikov, 'Филология и современные информационные технологии (К постановке проблемы)', *ISLIa,* 62.2:9–16; O. V. Dedova, 'О гипертекстах: "книжных" и электронных', *VMUF,* no.3:106–20; E. Ermolin, 'Критик в Сети', *Znamia,* no.2:210–14; no.3:195–209, concerns literary criticism in Russian on the Internet.

4. Individual Authors

ABRAMOV. A. Rubashkin, 'Двадцать лет спустя. Уроки Федора Абрамова', *Zvezda,* no.6:192–94.

AKHMATOVA. I. Verblovskaia, *Горькой любовью любимый: Петербург Анны Ахматовой*, 2nd rev. edn, StP, Zhurnal Neva,

352 pp.; 'На этой стороне. Письмо Я. З. Черняка в защиту Анны Ахматовой', ed. I. Efimov, *VL*, no.2 : 287–94; A. L. Babakin, *Словарь рифм Анны Ахматовой,* Tiumen', Mandrika, 205 pp.; M. V. Serova, '"Онегина воздушная громада . . ." (К вопросу о структурных моделях "Поэмы без героя" Анны Ахматовой)', *FilN,* no.3 : 12–20; L. Chukovskaia, 'После конца. Из "ахматовского" дневника', *Znamia,* no.1 : 154–67; V. Shileiko, *Последняя любовь. Переписка с Анной Ахматовой и Верой Андреевой,* ed. A. Shileiko and T. Shileiko, Mw, Vagrius, 320 pp., contains letters from Anna Akhmatova and her ex-husband Vladimir Shileiko (1891–1930) written in the 1920s and 1930s.

AKUNIN. A. Latynina, 'Христос и машина времени', *NovM,* no.8 : 148–53.

ALESHKIN. I. Sheveleva, *Душа нежна: о прозе Петра Алешкина,* Mw, Magistr, 158 pp.

ARBUZOV. L. Kheifets, 'Куда уходят дни?', *Oktiabr',* no.5 : 143–45, is an interesting memoir written by the famous Russian theatrical director.

ASTAF'EV. One of the first monographs on A. has appeared: P. A. Goncharov, *Творчество В. П. Астафьева в контексте русской прозы 1950–1990-х годов,* Mw, Vysshaia shkola, 386 pp. Id., 'О периодизации творчества В. Астафьева', *FilN,* no.6 : 20–27; D. Shevarov, 'У Астафьева', *NovM,* no.8 : 145–47; K. Azadovskii, 'Переписка из двух углов империи', *VL,* no.5 : 3–33, is on Astaf'ev and N. Eidel'man; D. Shevarov, 'Неостывшие письма (Крест бесконечный. В. Астафьев — В. Курбатов: письма из глубины России)', *NovM,* no.6 : 179–84. Two selections of materials by and on Astaf'ev were published in a regional literary journal: 'Остановить бы безумие. Из писательского архива', and A. Bondarenko, 'И стонет мое сердце . . .', *Den' i noch, Krasnoiarsk,* nos. 1–2, <http://www.din.krasline.ru>.

BABEL. A. Pirozhkova, 'Неизвестный рассказ И. Бабеля', *VL,* no.2 : 280–86; I. I. Fuzheron, 'Одесский акцент в "Одесских рассказах" И. Бабеля', Krasil'nikova, *Поэтика,* 325–33.

BAKLANOV. A. Turkov, 'Не покидая передовой: к 80-летию Григория Бакланова', *Znamia,* no.9 : 3–7.

BEK. T. P. Krasnoperov, 'Ветер судьбы', *NovM,* no.1 : 182–87.

BELOV. A. Solzhenitsyn, 'Василий Белов. Из "Литературной коллекции"', *NovM,* no.12 : 154–69.

BLAZHENNYI. K. Ankudinov, 'Стезей избытка', *NovM,* no.1 : 167–74.

BLOK. A. N. Lavrukhin, *А. Блок. Двенадцать. Графический аккомпанемент Александра Лаврухина,* Riazan', Uzoroch'e, 56 pp.

BRODSKII. *Поэтика Иосифа Бродского*, ed. V. P. Polukhina, Tver′ U.P., 468 pp.; *Мир Иосифа Бродского: Путеводитель*, ed. I. A. Gordin, StP, Zhurnal '*Zvezda*', 461 pp.; Li Chzhi Ion, 'О фольклорной свободе и теургизме в поэме И. Бродского "Представление" ', *RusL*, no.4 : 220–31; Z. I. Petrova, 'О способах выражения неопределенности в стихотворениях И. Бродского', Krasil'nikova, *Поэтика*, 155–72; Li Chzhi Ion, 'Романтизм и эсхатологизм в творчестве И. Бродского раннего периода (конец 1950–х–1960–е годы)', *RusL*, no.1 : 220–39.

BULGAKOV. A. Zerkalov, *Евангелие Михаила Булгакова. Опыт исследования ершалаимских глав романа 'Мастер и Маргарита'*, Mw, Tekst, 189 pp.; B. Miagkov, *Родословия Михаила Булгакова*, Mw, Apart, 400 pp.

BYKOV, D. D. K. Ankudinov, 'Превращенный', *NovM*, no.9 : 182–86; M. Edel'shtein, 'Назову себя Клингенмайер', *NovM*, no.12 : 175–78; M. Krongauz, 'Игра в роман и вопросы языкознания (Дмитрий Быков. Орфография. Опера в трех действиях)', *NovM*, no.12 : 170–75.

CHIZHOVA. K. Azadovskii, 'О жертве и милости', *NovM*, no.5 : 167–71; I. Rodnianskaia, 'Оглашенная в Лавре', *ib.*, 171–76; G. Pomerants, 'Перед неподвижным ликом', *Zvezda*, no.11 : 220–26.

DOBYCHIN. I. Sukhikh, 'У прозрачной стены. (1931. "Портрет"; 1935. "Город Эн" Л. Добычина)', *Zvezda*, no.8 : 224–33.

DOVLATOV. L. Ageeva, 'Довлатов: ранние окрестности', *VL*, no.5 : 235–40, contains interesting memoirs about the early years of Dovlatov in St Petersburg; T. A. Kosareva, 'Образ и место рассказчика в прозе Сергея Довлатова', Domanskii, *Парадигмы*, 205–12; A. Mil'chin, 'Довлатов и его герой', *Neva*, no.12 : 251–52; S. Dovlatov, *Сквозь джунгли безумной жизни: Письма к родным и друзьям*, SPb, Zhurnal Zvezda, 384 pp.

ERDMAN. I. Sukhikh, 'Самоубийца (1926–1929. "Самоубийца" Н. Эрдмана)', *Zvezda*, no.12 : 214–29.

ERENBURG. G. Belaia, 'Ложная беременность', *VL*, no.5 : 57–90; B. Frezinskii, 'Какие были надежды! (Илья Эренбург — Николаю Тихонову: 1925–1939; о Николае Тихонове: 1922–1967)', *ib.*, no. 3 : 226–57; A. Rubashkin, 'Письма Ирины Ильиничны Эренбург', *ib.*, no.6 : 372–76.

ERMAKOVA. A. Mamedov, 'Между временем и культурой', *DN*, no. 4 : 197–203, is about the poetry of I. Ermakova and P. Beletskii.

EROFEEV. I. S. Konrad, 'Символика пятничного путешествия героя: "Москва-Петушки" Вен. Ерофеева', Domanskii, *Парадигмы*, 201–04.

ESENIN. *Смерть С. Есенина: документы, факты, версии: материалы комиссии Всероссийского писательского комитета по выяснению обстоятельств смерти поэта*, ed. I. L. Prokushev and M. V. Stakhova, Mw, IMLI RAN, 414 pp.; V. S. Baranov, *Сергей Есенин: Биографическая хроника в воспоминаниях, фотографиях, письмах*, Mw, Raduga, 462 pp.

EVSEEV. A. I. Bol'shakova, *Феноменология литературного письма: о прозе Бориса Евсеева*, Mw, Maks, 126 pp.

EVTUSHENKO. L. Anninskii, 'Без бантиков', *DN*, no.8 : 219–23, is an excellent piece about the controversial Russian poet.

GALICH. *Галич: новые статьи и материалы*, ed. A. I. Krylov, Mw, YuPAPS, 288 pp.

GAMPER. V. Gubailovskii, 'Глубина неподвижности', *NovM*, no.12 : 181–85; I. Nelin, 'Биография души. О поэзии Галины Гампер', *Zvezda*, no.7 : 208–09.

GARROS-EVDOKIMOV. N. Eliseev, 'Трели триллера', *Znamia*, no.3 : 231–34.

GAZDANOV. Two major books: O. Orlova, *Газданов (Жизнь замечательных людей)*, Mw, Molodaia Gvardiia, 275 pp.; O. S. Podust, *Гайто Газданов: у истоков писательской тайны*, Voronezh GPU, 146 pp. See also S. A. Kibal'nik, 'Гайто Газданов и экзистенциальное сознание в литературе русского зарубежья', *RusL*, no.4 : 52–72; S. I. Kibal'nik, 'Газданов и Набоков', *ib.*, no.3 : 22–41; I. Sukhikh, 'Клэр, Машенька, ностальгия (1930. "Вечер у Клэр" Г. Газданова)', *Zvezda*, no.4 : 218–27.

GELASIMOV. M. Remizova, 'Гармонический диссонанс', *NovM*, no.1 : 175–78; D. Bykov, 'Андрей Геласимов похож на писателя', *ib.*, 178–81. A. Karateev, 'Добро перевесит?', *Znamia*, no.3 : 220–22; 'Границы между литературами прозрачны', interview by A. Miroshkin, *Knizhnoe obozrenie,* no.11 : 3.

GENIS. 'Я писал бы тексты даже вниз головой', interview by I. Tolstoi, *Zvezda*, no.2 : 193–203.

GOR'kii. Some interesting new studies: N. N. Primochkina, *Горький и писатели русского зарубежья*, Mw, IMLI RAN, 361 pp.; V. Baranov, '"Надо прекословить!" М. Горький и создание Союза писателей', *VL*, no.5 : 34–56; I. A. Reviakina, *Шаляпин и Горький: двойной портрет в каприйском интерьере*, Mw, Sputnik, 2002, 114 pp.

GRIN. I. Tsar'kova, 'Испытание чуда (Роман А. Грина "Блистающий мир")', *VL*, no.5 : 303–16.

GORLANOVA. M. Abasheva, 'Биография свободы. Свобода биографии', *NovM*, no.11:172–73; '"Без беды нет сюжета"', interview by T. Bek, *VL*, no. 2:255–79.

GROSSMAN. A. Solzhenitsyn, 'Дилогия Василия Гроссмана. Из "Литературной коллекции"', *NovM*, no.8:154–69.

IL'F AND PETROV. N. I. Prokhorova, 'Об источниках психоаналитических мотивов романа И. Ильфа и Е. Петрова "Золотой теленок"', *FilN*, no.3: 86–91. L. Milne, *Zoshchenko and the Ilf-Petrov Partnership: How They Laughed* (Birmingham Slavonic Monographs), Birmingham U.P., xiv + 296 pp., consists of two sections; seven chapters are devoted to Zoshchenko, and nine to Ilf and Petrov. The book compares Zoshchenko to Ilf and Petrov as representative of traditional aspects of the comic muse.

ISAKOVSKII. I. E. Klimenko, *Стол Исаковского*, 2nd rev. edn, Smolensk, Regional'naia organizatsiia zhurnalistov, 135 pp.

IUR'EV. A. Uritskii, 'Переодевания, размышления, приключения ...', *Znamia*, no.3:225–27; D. Bak, 'Исповедь грантососа, или Конец Умберто', *NovM*, no.4:172–75.

IVANOV, VIACH. Vjaceslav Ivanov, *Testi inediti*, Вяч. Иванов, *Новые материалы* (Русско-итальянский архив, Archivio Russo-Italiano, 3), ed. D. Rizzi and A. Shishkin, Salerno, 1997, 574 pp.; S. D. Titarenko, 'Вяч. Иванов в "Зеркале зеркал" русско-итальянского архива', *RusL*, no.3:191–98.

IUZEFOVICH. E. Ivanitskaia, 'Все связано со всем', *DN*, no.7:194–96.

KAMINSKII. I. Nelin, 'Найти просветы', *Zvezda*, no.3:217–21.

KANTOR. A. Liusyi, 'Жертва на Руси: из новейших сведений о русской хирургии', *DN*, no.11:200–03; V. Schukin, 'Тернистый русский путь в Европу', *VL*, no.5:329–38.

KHARMS. D. V. Tokarev, 'Рисунок как слово в творчестве Даниила Хармса', *RusL*, no.3:57–69; V. V. Podkol'skii, 'Два начала поэтики Даниила Хармса', *ib.*, no.4:73–89.

KHLEBNIKOV. N. N. Pertsova, *Словотворчество Велимира Хлебникова*, Moscow U.P., 175 pp.; I. D. Romanenkov, *Творчество Велимира Хлебникова*, Mw, Maks, 389 pp.

KLEKH. G. Efremov, 'Все зеркала расставить по местам: оттиск бессмертия', *DN*, no.3:216–17; A. Ulanov, 'Несладкий пряник', *ib.*, 214–16; A. Uritskii, 'Тексты, окна, двери', *ib.*, 217–18, are all on I. Klekh's essays.

KLIUEV. M. Edel'shtein, 'Олонецкая культура и петербургская стихия (Николай Клюев. Письма к Александру Блоку: 1907–1915)', *NovM*, no.11:187–89.

KONONOV. N. D. Polishchuk, 'Контрольные Кононова (Николай Кононов. Магический бестиарий. В трех разделах)', *NovM*, no.2 : 162–64.

KORNILOV. B. Evseev, 'Закон сохранения веса', *VL*, no.5 : 224–34.

KORNILOVA. A. Latynina, 'Таинственность будничной жизни (Галина Корнилова. Кикимора. Рассказы и пьеса)', *NovM*, no.5 : 177–78.

KORZHAVIN. A. Latynina, 'Андерсеновский мальчик — роль навсегда', *NovM*, no.12 : 147–53.

KRUZHKOV. O. Dmitrieva, 'Театр страстей в монархии ума', *NovM*, no.12 : 185–89.

KRZHIZHANOVSKII. P. Kuznetsov, 'Горе от ума: Сигизмунд Кржижановский и русская литература', *Zvezda*, no.1 : 229–32.

KUSHNER. L. Dubshan, 'Комментарий к кустарнику', *NovM*, no.6 : 187–92.

KUZMIN. L. G. Panova, 'Миф о Софии в поэзии Михаила Кузмина: гностические сюжеты, мотивы, язык', Krasil'nikova, *Поэтика*, 287–301; A. V. Gik, 'Образный ряд: вода — лед — стекло в творчестве М. Кузмина', *ib.*, 301–05.

LEONOV. A. Solzhenitsyn, 'Леонид Леонов — "Вор". Из "Литературной коллекции"', *NovM*, no.12 : 165–71; L. P. Iakimova, *Мотивная структура романа Леонида Леонова 'Пирамида'*, Novosibirsk, SO RAN, 249 pp.

LIMONOV. V. Solov'ev, 'В защиту немолодого подростка. Казус Лимонова', *LitG*, no. 11 : 6; 'Да литература-то. . . Хер с ней', interview by I. Riabinin, *Literaturnaia Rossiia*, no : 11 : 3; L. Pirogov, 'Бедные записки из мертвого дома', *Nezavisimaia gazeta Ex libris*, no.12 : 3; P. Basinskii, 'Тело Эдуарда Лимонова', *LitG*, no. 16 : 6.

LISNIANSKAIA. E. Ermolin, 'Зима и лето Евы', *Znamia*, no.12 : 180–88.

MALETSKII. A. Vial'tsev, 'Физиология любви', *DN*, no.4 : 204–08; E. Ermolin, 'Где ваша улыбка?', *NovM*, no.8 : 170–72.

MAIAKOVSKII. There are two books by Arkadii Vaksberg on Maiakovskii's lover Lilia Brik: *Лиля Брик: жизнь и судьба*, Mw, Olimp — Smolensk, Rusich, 1998, 448 pp., and *Загадка и магия Лили Брик*, Mw, AST–Atrel', 461 pp., see also L. Brik, *Пристрастные рассказы: воспоминания, дневники, письма*, Nizhnii Novgorod, Dekom, 324 pp.; P. J. Johnson (I. V. Maiakovskaia), *Маяковский на Манхэттене: История любви с отрывками из мемуаров Элли Джонс*, Mw, IMLI RAN, 142 pp.

MAMEDOV. M. Remizova, 'Любовь в прозрачном и пористом мире (Афанасий Мамедов. Фрау Шрам. Роман)', *NovM*, no.7: 164–66.

MAMLEEV. M. Zolotonosov, 'Подполье вышло наружу', *MN*, no.10: 12; K. Kostiukov, 'Форма пустоты', *Znamia*, no.3: 214–15.

MANDEL'SHTAM. I. Surat has published two valuable articles: 'Смерть поэта. Мандельштам и Пушкин', *NovM*, no.3: 155; 'Мандельштам и Пушкин. Статья вторая. Лирические сюжеты', *ib.*, no.9: 152. L. G. Panova, *'Мир', 'пространство', 'время' в поэзии Осипа Мандельштама*, Mw, Iazyki slavianskoi kul'tury, 802 pp.; *Актуальные вопросы современного литературоведения и методики преподавания литературы в вузе и школе*, ed. N. I. Erofeeva, Mw, Kompaniia Sputnik + , 47 pp., contains studies on O. Mandel'shtam and E. Chirikov. L. M. Vidgof, 'О. Мандельштам в начале 1930–х годов: выбор позиции', *ISLIa*, 62.5: 21–32; I. L. Tolkach and D. I. Cherashniaia, 'Кто и что играл наизусть в стихоторении О. Мандельштама "Жил Александр Герцевич . . ."?', *ib.*, 2: 33–39; M. A. Gasparov and O. Ronen, 'Похороны солнца в Петербурге. О двух театральных стихотворениях Мандельштама', *Zvezda*, no.5: 207–19; A. N. Murashov, 'Мандельштам 1921–1925 годов: зарисовка на фоне К. Леонтьева', *VMUF*, no.3: 149–52; N. D. Chernykh, 'Языковая картина мира как отражение поэтического сознания акмеистов (на материале лирики О. Мандельштама)', Osovskii, *исследования*, 68–78.

MOZHAEV. V. Bondarenko, 'Живой (к 80–летию Бориса Можаева)', *NSo*, no.6: 278–83.

NABOKOV. V. V. Nabokov, *Энциклопедическое собрание сочинений*, Mw, IDDK, CD-ROM; N. Anastas'ev, 'Не по правилам (*Зверев А.* Набоков. ЖЗЛ)', *VL*, no.4: 351–59, is a discussion of A. Zverev's book on Nabokov. See also B. Averin, *Дар Мнемозины. Романы Набокова в контексте русской автобиографической традиции*, StP, Amfora, 399 pp.; S. Chekalova, ' "То славя прошлое, то запросто ругая . . ." ', *NovM*, no.7: 140–54; N. Mel'nikov, 'Повесть о том, как Алексей Матвеевич поссорился с Владимиром Владимировичем', *ib.*, 155–60; S. Kostyrko, 'Набоков по-американски', *ib.*, 160–63; V. Serdiuchenko, 'Читая Набокова. Чернышевский', *Neva*, no. 8: 211–14; V. Shevchenko, 'Зрячие вещи. Оптические коды Набокова', *Zvezda*, no.6: 209–19; G. Barabtarlo, 'Разрешенный диссонанс', *ib.*, no.4: 190–205. V. A. Cherkasov, 'В. В. Набоков и А. И. Куприн', *FilN*, no.3: 3–11; A. V. Zlochevskaia, 'Творчество В. Набокова в контексте мирового литературного процесса XX века', *ib.*, no.4: 23–31; 'Письма В. В. Набокова к Г. П. Струве. 1925–1931.

Часть первая', ed. I. B. Belodubrovskii and A. A. Dolinin, *Zvezda*, no.11:115–50; I. Filaretova, 'Петербург реальный и "умышленный", созданный Владимиром Набоковым', *Neva*, no.7, 232–33.

NAGIBIN. A. Solzhenitsyn, 'Двоенье Юрия Нагибина. Из "Литературной коллекции"', *NovM*, no.8:164–71.

NAIMAN. V. Kholkin, 'В "кругу" и вне "круга" (Анатолий Найман. Все и каждый. Роман)', *NovM*, no.10:172–76.

NIKOLAEVA. O. L. Gerasimova and N. Gerasimova, 'Глубина свободы', *NovM*, no.1:190–94.

NOSOV. I. L. Konorev, 'С вершины древнего кургана (Из воспоминаний о Евгении Носове), *NSo*, no.6:272–77.

OKUDZHAVA. *Окуджава: проблемы поэтики и текстологии*, ed. A. E. Krylov, Mw, Gosudarstvennyi kul'turnyi tsentr-muzei V. S. Vysotskogo, 2002, 260 pp. V. A. Zaitsev, *Окуджава, Высоцкий, Галич: Поэтика, жанры, традиции*, Mw, Gosudarstvennyi kul'turnyi tsentr-muzei V. S. Vysotskogo, 272 pp.; S. Boiko, 'Булат Окуджава. Ранний автограф песни', *VL*, no.5:298–302; I. B. Nichiporov, '"Московский текст" в русской поэзии XX в.: М. Цветаева и Б. Окуджава', *VMUF*, no.3:58–70; V. A. Zaitsev, 'Жанровое своеобразие стихов-песен Окуджавы, Высоцкого, Галича о войне', *VMUF*, no.4:40–58.

OLESHA. E. R. Men'shikova, 'Редуцированный смех Юрия Олеши', *VF*, 2002, no.10:75–85.

OSTROVSKII. L. I. Lezhneva, *По стопам 'рожденного бурей': Воспоминания. Из дневника учительницы*, Mw, Vagrius, 304 pp.

PASTERNAK. N. A. Fateeva, *Поэт и проза: Книга о Пастернаке*, Mw, NLO, 399 pp.; L. Fleishman, *Борис Пастернак в двадцатые годы*, StP, Akademicheskii proekt, 462 pp. A. K. Zholkovskii, 'У истоков пастернаковской поэтики (О стихотворении "Раскованный голос")', *ISLIa*, 62.4:10–22, discusses P.'s poem as a manifestation of his innovative early style and the roots of his poetic system, using the methods of structural and intertextual analysis, and the techniques of poetry of grammar; B. A. Katz, 'Еще один полифонический опыт Пастернака О музыкальных истоках стихотворения "Раскованный голос")', ib., 23–32, discusses P.'s poem as an example of his early contrapuntal technique, according to the manual on musical composition he studied in his adolescence. R. Salvatore, '"У себя дома" Б. Пастернака: стиль и мировоззрение', ib., 6:54–57; O. I. Kazmirchuk, 'Интерпретация архетипа природного круга в творчестве символистов и в ранней лирике Б. Л. Пастернака', Domanskii, *Парадигмы*, 126–33; I. V. Romanova, '"Существованья ткань сквозная": идея и образ единства в творчестве Пастернака', *FilN*, no.5:3–14; L. Shilov, *Пастернаковское Переделкино*, Mw, YuPAPS, 36 pp. A. Berliant, '"Лягушка в болоте", или воспоминания В. Ливанова "Невыдуманный Борис Пастернак"', *Znamia*, no.11:207–08; 'Новооткрытые письма к Ариадне Эфрон', ed. M. A. Rashkovskaia, comm. E. B. Pasternak, *Znamia*, no.11:156–79; A. Kushner, 'Заболоцкий и Пастернак', *NovM*, no.9:174–81.

PAUSTOVSKII. *Мир Паустовского*, Mw, Zhurnal 'Mir Paustovskogo' — Nizhnii Novgorod, Dekom, 456 pp.

PAVLOV, O. 'Я пишу инстинктом', interview by T. Bek, *VL*, no.5:199–217.

PELEVIN. I. Shaitanov, 'Проект Pelevin', *VL*, no.4:3–4; I. Pronina, 'Фрактальная логика Виктора Пелевина', *ib.*, 5–30; M. Sverdlov, 'Технология писательской власти (О двух последних романах В. Пелевина)' *ib.*, 31–47. See also N. A. Nagornaia, 'Сновидения и реальность в постмодернистской прозе В. Пелевина', *FilN*, no.2:44–51; O. I. Os'mukhina, 'О новых тенденциях в российском романе рубежа 20 — 21 веков (В. Пелевин, В. Сорокин, П. Крусанов)', Osovskii, *исследования*, 189–96.

PEREDREEV. V. Bondarenko, 'Русская душа, зацепившаяся за корягу', *Literaturnaia Rossiia*, no. 12:6.

PETRUSHEVSKAIA. Two monographs on P. have been published in universities: O. A. Kuz'menko, *Проза Л. С. Петрушевской в свете русской повествовательной традиции 19–20 вв.*, Ulan-Ude, Buriatskoe U.P., 128 pp.; N. V. Kablukova, *Поэтика драматургии Людмилы Петрушевской*, Blagoveschensk, GPU, 239 pp.; see also I. Nevzgliadova, 'Три заметки о Петрушевской', *Zvezda*, no.9:210–18.

PIL'NIAK. I. V. Kirillova, 'Тексты Б. Пильняка и их художественное своеобразие', Sorokin, *культура*, 248–53.

PLATONOV. M. Mikheev, *В мир Платонова через его язык: Предположения, факты, истолкования, догадки*, Moscow U.P., 408 pp.; N. V. Kornienko, '*Сказано русским языком ...*': *Андрей Платонов и Михаил Шолохов: встречи в русской литературе*, Mw, IMLI RAN, 536 pp.; S. A. Ipatova, '"Крохотное созданьице" у Достоевского и Платонова, или Прием "ложной этической оценки"', Viktorovich, *Идеи*, 92–100; K. A. Barsht, 'О мотиве любви в творчестве Андрея Платонова', *RusL*, no.2:31–47.

POLIANSKAIA. I. G. Ermoshina, 'Сны времени из малахитовой шкатулки', *DN*, no.3:209–10.

PRISHVIN. A. Varlamov, *Пришвин (Жизнь замечательных людей)*, Mw, Molodaia Gvardiia, 848 pp., is the most complete biography of Prishvin, excellently written by a modern Russian prose-writer. See also L. P. Pautova, *Калужский след Пришвиных*, Kaluga, Fridgel'm, 54 pp.

REMIZOV. There are several interesting studies on R.: A. M. Gracheva, 'Апофеоз "Чужого слова"', *RusL*, no.2: 195–98, is on recent work on Remizov; N. L. Blishch, *Автобиографическая проза А. М. Ремизова (проблема мифотворчества)*, Minsk, Evropeiskii gumanitarnyi universitet, 2002, 115 pp.; I. V. Tyryshkina, *'Крестовые сестры' А. М. Ремизова: Концепция и поэтика*, Novosibirsk U.P., 1997, 234 pp.; S. Dotsenko, *Проблемы поэтики А. М. Ремизова. Автобиографизм как конструктивный принцип творчества*, Tallinn U.P., 2000, 161 pp.; N. A. Nagornaia, *Виртуальная реальность сновидения в творчестве А. М. Ремизова*, Barnaul, Altaiskoe U.P., 2000, 150 pp.; A. M. Gracheva, *Алексей Ремизов и древнерусская литература*, StP, IRLI RAN, 2000, 333 pp.

RODIONOV. D. Davydov, 'Внесистемный элемент среди зеркал и электричек (Творчество Андрея Родионова как культурная инновация)', *NLO*, no.62: 242–52.

RUBTSOV. M. Iupp, 'Коля Рубцов — ранние шестидесятые . . .', *NSo*, no.1: 251–53.

RUSAKOV. V. Tsivunin, 'Горькая дерзость Геннадия Русакова (Геннадий Русаков. Разговоры с богом. Стихи)', *NovM*, no.3: 178–82.

RYZHII. M. Gundarin, 'Борис Рыжий: домой с небес', *Znamia*, no.4: 177–82.

SAMOILOV. A. Solzhenitsyn, 'Давид Самойлов', *NovM*, no.6: 171–78; V. Radzishevskii, 'В кругу себя: труды и дни Давида Самойлова', *DN*, no.4: 185–96; L. Bezymenskii, 'История одного вызова', *VL*, no.6: 317–26; V. Kuznetsov, '". . . Поэт не держит зла"', *ib.*, 310–17; D. Samoilov and L. Chukovskaia, '"Мы живем в эпоху результатов . . .": Переписка', *Znamia*, no.5: 141–76; no.6: 135–77; no.7: 137–77, includes commentary by G. I. Medvedeva-Samoilova, E. T. Chukovskaia, and Z. O. Khavkina.

SALIMON. A. Ermakova, 'Земля, казавшаяся черной', *DN*, no.6: 216–17.

SAPGIR. *Великий Генрих: Сапгир и о Сапгире*, ed. T. G. Mikhailovskaia, Mw, RGGU, 369 pp., contains articles and memoirs about Genrikh Sapgir written by I. Orlitskii, A. Al'chuk, O. Filatova, I. Lemming, V. Nekrasov, O. Dark, G. Ball, V. Pivovarov, O. Rabin, and others, and includes a very useful bibliography that is one of the first on Sapgir.

SHOLOKHOV. *Шолоховские чтения*, ed. I. G. Kruglov, Mw, Taganka, 430 pp.; *Студенческие шолоховские чтения*, ed. I. G.

Kruglov, Mw, Taganka, 272 pp.; *Шолохов и русское зарубежье*, ed. V. V. Vasil'ev, Mw, Algoritm, 446 pp. A. A. Zhuravleva and I. G. Kruglov, *Михаил Шолохов: очерк жизни и творчества*, Mw, Taganka, 171 pp., simply recounts information already known. See also *Новое о Михаиле Шолохове: исследования и материалы*, ed. F. F. Kuznetsov, V. V. Vasil'ev, and N. V. Kornienko, Mw, IMLI RAN, 587 pp.

SKOROBOGATOV. A. Kuznetsova, 'Берега реализма', *DN*, no.5:192–201, writes mostly about S.'s novel *Земля обетованная*.

SLAVUTINSKII. G. Guseinov, 'В подкладке — шелковая нить', *NovM*, no.7:172–75.

SLUTSKII. D. Sukharev, 'Скрытопись Бориса Слуцкого', *VL*, no.1:22–45; I. Plekhanova, 'Игра в императивном сознании. Лирика Бориса Слуцкого в диалоге с временем', *VL*, no.1:46–72; B. Slutskii, 'Семинар Сельвинского', ed. P. Gorelik, *Zvezda*, no.1:122–24.

SOLZHENITSYN. Three new monographs appeared last year: A. V. Urmanov, *Творчество Александра Солженицына*, Mw, Flinta–Nauka, 384 pp.; V. Bushin, *Александр Солженицын*, Mw, Algoritm, 368 pp.; A. N. Semenov, *Картина мира прозы А. И. Солженицына (на примере рассказа* 'Один день Ивана Денисовича'), Khanty-Mansiisk, Iugorskii U.P., 64 pp. P. E. Spivakovskii, 'Символические образы в эпопее А. И. Солженицына "Красное колесо"', *ISLIa*, 62.1:30–40, argues that S.'s symbol is not only an element of the text but also an element of reality, and this double aspect gives it ontological meaning.

STEPUN. G. A. Time, 'Возвращения Федора Степуна', *RusL*, no.3:210–16. Christian Hufen, *Fedor Stepun, ein politischer Intellektueller aus Russland in Europa. Die Jahre 1884–1945*, Berlin, Lucas, 2001, 583 pp.

STRUGATSKII BROTHERS. A. and B. B. Strugatskii, *Комментарий к пройденному*, SPb, Amfora, 311 pp., is the first memoir by the classical writers of Russian science fiction.

SVETOV. I. Kublanovskii, 'Чижик-пыжик и повертон (Феликс Светов. Чижик-пыжик. Роман. Рассказы)', *NovM*, no.8:172–74.

TARLOVSKII. V. Perel'muter, 'Торжественная песнь скворца, ода, ставшая сатирой', *VL*, no.6:27–50, is an interesting article about the forgotten Russian poet Mark Tarlovskii.

TIMOFEEVSKII. V. Gubailovskii, 'Собеседник', *DN*, no.6:206–07; A. Smirnov, 'Дождитесь опоздавшего стрелка (Александр Тимофеевский. Опоздавший стрелок)', *NovM*, no.7:168–70.

TOLSTOI, A. M. A. Lazareva, 'Трагические парадоксы в прозе А. Н. Толстого 20-х годов (К 120-летию со дня рождения писателя)', *VMUF*, no.1 : 70–73. O. Kornienko, 'Сызрань А. Н. Толстого', *NSo*, no.8 : 255–57.

TOLSTAIA, T. S. Borovikov, 'Татьянин день', *Znamia*, no.3 : 227–28.

TRUBETSKOI. S. Averintsev, 'Несколько мыслей о «евразийстве» Н. С. Трубецкого', *NovM*, no.2 : 137–49.

TSVETAEVA. Many excellent studies, including several monographs, have been published during the last year: I. Kudrova, *Просторы Марины Цветаевой: Поэзия, проза, личность*, SPb, Vita Nova, 528 pp.; Marina Tsvetaeva and Nikolai Gronski, *Несколько ударов сердца. Письма 1928–1933 годов*, ed. I. Brodovskaia and I. Korkina, Mw, Vagrius, 320 pp.; I. Aizenstein, *Сны Марины Цветаевой*, StP, Akademicheskii proekt, 464 pp.; L. N. Kozlova, *Сквозь годы: Переписка с А. И. Цветаевой: неизвестные автографы*, Ul'ianovsk, Ul'ianovskoe otdelenie Rossiiskogo soiuza professional'nykh literatorov, 87 pp.; *М. И. Цветаева: судьба и творчество*, ed. N. A. Dvoriashina, Surgut, RIO SurGPI, 114 pp.; G. Brodskaia, *Сонечка Голлидэй. Жизнь и актерская судьба. Документы. Письма. Историко-театральный контекст*, Mw, O.G.I., 464 pp., is devoted to Tsvetaeva's character 'Povest' o Sonechke', actress Sof'ia Evgen'evna Golliday (1894–1934); S. Russova, 'Из уцелевших осколков (Об исследованиях жизни и творчества М. Цветаевой)', *VL*, no.5 : 317–28; O. V. Filippova, 'Ритмико-интонационное своеобразие стихов М. Цветаевой', Osovskii, *исследования*, 65–68; I. A. Romanova, '"А там, вдали, следы оленьи на голубеющем снегу . . ." (Образ Снежной королевы цветаевского цикла "Подруга" и мотив "Полуночного рая" в лирике Софии Парнок)', *RusL*, no.4 : 162–81; I. K. Sobolevskaia, 'Автор и герой как проблема анализа эстетического сознания М. Цветаевой', *ib.*, no.3 : 42–56; V. Maevskaia, '"Стрела с неба" в трагедии М. Цветаевой "Федра"', *VMUF*, no.1 : 134–60; M. Bonfel'd, 'Мощь и невесомость', *VL*, no.5 : 91–99; M. Tsvetkova, 'Английские лики Марины Цветаевой', *ib.*, 100–34; G. Diusembaeva, 'Цветаева и "Габима" ("Гадибук" и "Молодец")', *RusL*, no.2 : 141–48.

TVARDOVSKII. N. Sokolova, 'Перебирая бумаги в старых папках (Тридцатые: А. Бек, Твардовский)', *VL*, no.1 : 291–313; A. Tvardovskii, 'Рабочие тетради 60–х годов' ed. V. A. Tvardovskaia and O. A. Tvardovskaia, *Znamia*, no.8 : 10, 136–70; no.9 : 136–70; no.10 : 137–77.

ULITSKAIA. L. Kuklin, 'Казус Улицкой', *Neva*, no.7 : 177–79.

VASIL'KOVA. O. Postnikova, '"Встречь ветра жгучего . . ." (Ирина Василькова. Поверх лесов и вод. Стихи разных лет; Ирина Василькова. Белым по белому; Ирина Василькова. О первородстве; Ирина Василькова. Темный аквалангист)', *NovM*, no.4 : 175–79.

VEDENIAPIN. G. Efremov, 'Все зеркала расставить по местам: оттиск бессмертия', *DN*, no.3 : 216–17.

VLADIMOV. I. Sukhikh, 'Баллада о добром генерале (1996. "Генерал и его армия" Г. Владимова)', *Zvezda*, no.6 : 220–30.

VYSHNEVETSKAIA. A. Mamedov, 'Еще раз о "Да" и "Нет"', *DN*, no.2 : 209–12.

VYSOTSKI. Y. G. Iazvikova, *В. Высоцкий: взгляд из XXЙ века: Материалы Третьей Международной научной конференции*, Mw, Gosudarstvennyi kul'turnyi tsentr-muzei V.S.Vysotskogo, 480 pp.; I. Sukhikh, 'На разрыв аорты (1960–1980. Песни-баллады В. Высоцкого)', *Zvezda*, no.10 : 225–33.

ZABOLOTSKII. T. Bek, 'Николай Заболоцкий: далее везде', *Znamia*, no.11 : 194–204; S. Kuniaev, 'Победивший косноязычье мира . . . (К 100–летию со дня рождения Николая Заболоцкого)', *NSo*, no.5 : 282–88; S. Beliakov, 'Гностик из Уржума. Заметки о натурфилософских взглядах Н. А. Заболоцкого', *Ural*, no. 5 : 233–50; *Николай Заболоцкий и его литературное окружение: Материалы юбилейной научной конференции, 9–10 апреля 2003 г.*, ed. V. P. Muromskii and A. I. Mikhailov, StP, Nauka, 182 pp.; N. Zabolotskaia, 'Воспоминания об отце', *VL*, no.6 : 265–73; S. I. Kormilov, 'Творчество Н. А. Заболоцкого в литературоведении рубежа 20–21 вв. (к 100–летию со дня рождения поэта)', *VMUF*, no.3 : 135–48.

ZAITSEV. New and revised books include M. B. Balandina, *Художественный мир Б. Зайцева*, Magnitogorsk U.P., 34 pp.; T. M. Stepanova, *Поэзия и правда: структура и поэтика публицистической прозы Бориса Зайцева*, 2nd rev. edn, Mw, MGOU, 287 pp.; A. M. Liubomudrov, *Духовный реализм в литературе русского зарубежья: Б. К. Зайцев, И. С. Шмелев*, StP, Dmitrii Bulanin, 272 pp.

ZALYGIN. S. Kostyrko, '" . . .Не надо бояться себя" о Сергее Залыгине', *NovM*, no.12 : 114–30.

ZAMIATIN. New books include *Творческое наследие Евгения Замятина: взгляд из сегодня: статьи, очерки, заметки, библиография*, vol. 11, ed. A. Gildner, Tambov U.P., 265 pp.; V. N. Evseev, *Художественная проза Евгения Замятина: проблемы метода, жанровые процессы, стилевое своеобразие*, Mw, Prometei, 223 pp.; N. V. Frolova, *Поэтика романа Е. Замятина 'Мы'*, Samara U.P., 16 pp.; V. A. Tunimanov, 'Новое о Замятине', *RusL*, no.4 : 241–48.

V. UKRAINIAN STUDIES

POSTPONED

VI. BELARUSSIAN STUDIES

POSTPONED

VII. SERBO-CROAT STUDIES

POSTPONED

VIII. BULGARIAN STUDIES

POSTPONED

ABBREVIATIONS

I. ACTA, FESTSCHRIFTEN AND OTHER COLLECTIVE AND GENERAL WORKS

Adams, *Bilingualism: Bilingualism in Ancient Society. Language Contact and the Written Text*, ed. J. N. Adams, Mark Janse, and Simon Swain, Oxford, OUP, 2002, x + 483 pp.

AILLC 12: Actes del dotzè col·loqui internacional de llengua i literatura catalanes (Universitat de París IV–Sorbonne, 2000), ed. Marie-Clarie Zimmermann and Anne Charlon, PAM–AILLC, 2 vols, 466, 312 pp.

AISC 7: Momenti di Cultura Catalana in un Millennio. Atti del VII Convegno dell'Associazione Italiana di Studi Catalani (Napoli, 2000), ed. Anna Maria Compagna, Alfonsina De Benedetto, and Núria Puigdevall, Naples, Liguori, 2 vols, 581, 500 pp.

Akselberg, *Dialektologi: Nordisk dialektologi*, ed. Gunnstein Akselberg, Anne Marit Bødal, and Helge Sandøy, Oslo, Novus, 575 pp.

Álvarez Barrientos, *Espacios: Espacios de la comunicación literaria*, ed. Joaquin Álvarez Barrientos, Madrid, CSIC, 2002.

Akten (Wien), VI: *Akten des X. Internationalen Germanistenkongresses Wien 2000. VI*, ed. Peter Wiesinger (Jahrbuch für internationale Germanistik. Reihe A, 58), Berne–Berlin, Lang, 2002, 524 pp.

Akten (Wien), VIII: *Akten des X. Internationalen Germanistenkongresses Wien 2000. VIII*, ed. Peter Wiesinger (Jahrbuch für internationale Germanistik. Reihe A, 53), Berne–Berlin, Lang, 361 pp.

Akten (Wien), IX: *Akten des X. Internationalen Germanistenkongresses Wien 2000. IX*, ed. Peter Wiesinger (Jahrbuch für internationale Germanistik. Reihe A, 61), Berne–Berlin, Lang, 390 pp.

Akten (Wien), X: *Akten des X. Internationalen Germanistenkongresses Wien 2000. X*, ed. Peter Wiesinger (Jahrbuch für internationale Germanistik. Reihe A, 62), Berne–Berlin, Lang, 425 pp.

Akten (Wien), XII: *Akten des X. Internationalen Germanistenkongresses Wien 2000. XII*, ed. Peter Wiesinger (Jahrbuch für internationale Germanistik. Reihe A, 54), Berne–Berlin, Lang, 2002, 213 pp.

Alarcos Vol.: Indagaciones sobre la lengua, estudios de filología y lingüística españolas en memoria de Emilio Alarcos, ed. E. Méndez, J. Mendoza, and Y. Congosta, Seville, Universidad de Sevilla, 2002, 508 pp.

Allières Vol.: Hommage a Jacques Allières, ed. Michel Aurnague and Michel Roché, 2 vols, I: *Domaines basque et pyrénéen*, II: *Romania sans frontières*, Anglet, Atlantica, 2002, 1–324, 325–656 pp.

Andersen, *Language Contacts: Language Contacts in Prehistory. Studies in Stratigraphy. Papers from the Workshop on Linguistic Stratigraphy and Prehistory at the Fifteenth International Conference on Historical Linguistics, Melbourne, 17 August 2001*, ed. Henning Andersen (Current Issues in Linguistic Theory, 239), Amsterdam, Benjamins, viii + 292 pp.

Arnold, *Kanonbildung: Literarische Kanonbildung*, ed. Heinz Ludwig Arnold, Munich, Text + Kritik, 2002, 372 pp.

Atti (Lecce): *I capricci di Proteo: percorsi e linguaggi del Barocco. Atti del Convegno internazionale di Lecce, 23–26 ottobre 2000*, Rome, Salerno, 2002, 979 pp.

Aub-Buscher, *Francophone Caribbean: The Francophone Caribbean Today. Language, Literature, Culture*, ed. Gertrud Aub-Buscher and Beverley Ormerod Noakes, Univ. of the West Indies Press, xxiv + 191 pp.

Aurnhammer, *Antike: 'Mehr Dionysus als Apoll.' Antiklassizistische Antike-Rezeption um 1900*, ed. Achim Aurnhammer and Thomas Pittrof, Frankfurt, Klostermann, 2002, viii + 520 pp.

Baccar Bournaz, *Afrique: L'Afrique au XVIIe siècle: mythes et réalités*, ed. Alia Baccar Bournaz (Biblio 17, 149), Tübingen, Narr, 422 pp.

Baena 2: Cancioneros en Baena: Actas del II Congreso Internacional Cancionero de Baena, in memoriam Manuel Alvar, ed. Jesús L. Serrano Reyes, Baena, Ayuntamiento, 2 vols, 634, 478 pp.

Barolini, *Dante: Dante for the New Millennium*, ed. Teodolinda Barolini and H. Wayne Storey, New York, Fordham Press, xxii + 498 pp.

Battaglia, *Dante: Leggere Dante*, ed. Lucia Battaglia Ricci, Ravenna, Longo, 389 pp.

Baumgartner, *Progrès: Progrès, réaction, décadence dans l'occident médiéval*, ed. Emmanuèle Baumgartner and Laurence Harf-Lancner, Geneva, Droz, 274 pp.

Bertelsmeier-Kierst, *Umbruch: Eine Epoche im Umbruch. Volkssprachliche Literalität 1200–1300. Cambridger Symposium 2001*, ed. Christa Bertelsmeier-Kierst and Christopher Young, Tübingen, Niemeyer, xi + 348 pp.

Betten, *Judentum: Judentum und Antisemitismus. Studien zur Literatur und Germanistik in Österreich*, ed. Anne Betten and Konstanze Fliedl (Philologische Studien und Quellen, 176), Berlin, Schmidt, 360 pp.

Bianciotto, *L'Epopée romane: L'Épopée romane: actes du XVe Congrès international Rencesvals tenu à Poitiers du 21 au 27 août 2000*, ed. Gabriel Bianciotto and Claudio Galderisi, 2 vols, Université de Poitiers, Centre d'Etudes Supérieures de Civilisation Médiévale, 2002, 1068 pp.

Bertrand, *Penser la nuit: Penser la nuit (XVe–XVIIe siècle)*, ed. Dominique Bertrand (Colloques, congrès et conférences, 35), Paris, Champion, 549 pp.

Biller, *Religion: Religion and Medicine in the Middle Ages*, ed. Peter Biller and Joseph Ziegler, York, York Medieval Press, 2001, xvi + 253 pp.

Blank, *Kognitive Onomasiologie: Kognitive romanische Onomasiologie und Semasiologie*, ed. Andreas Blank and Peter Koch (LA, 467), Tübingen: Niemeyer, viii + 233 pp.

Braet, *Laughter: Risus Medievalis: Laughter in Medieval Literature and Art*, ed. Herman Braet, Guido Latré, and Werner Verbeke, Louvain University Press, vi + 233 pp.

Bray, *Filosofia: Filosofia in volgare nel Medioevo. Atti del convegno della Società Italiana per lo studio del pensiero medievale (S.I.S.P.M.), Lecce, 27–29 settembre 2003*, ed. Nadia Bray and Loris Sturlese (Textes et études du Moyen Âge, 21), Louvain-la-Neuve, Fédération International des Instituts d'Etudes Médiévales, 527 pp.

Brinson, *Broadcasting: 'Stimme der Wahrheit': German Language Broadcasting by the BBC*, ed. Charmian Brinson and Richard Dove (Yearbook of the Research Centre for German and Austrian Exile Studies, 5), Amsterdam, Rodopi, xv + 250 pp.

Britnell, *Female Saints: Female Saints and Sinners/ Saintes et mondaines (France 1450–1650)*, ed. Jennifer Britnell and Ann Moss (Durham Modern Language Series), University of Durham, 2002, xiii + 298 pp.

Brouard-Arends, *Lectrices: Lectrices d'Ancien Régime*, ed. Isabelle Brouard-Arends (Interférences), Presses universitaires de Rennes, 722 pp.

Brummack Vol.: Ironische Propheten. Sprachbewußtsein und Humanität in der Literatur von Herder bis Heine. Studien für Jürgen Brummack zum 65. Geburtstag, ed. Markus Heilmann and Birgit Wägenbaur in Verbindung mit dem Deutschen Seminar der Universität Tübingen, Narr, 2001, 295 pp.

Buschinger, *Aliénor d'Aquitaine: Autour d'Aliénor d'Aquitaine: Actes du colloque de Saint Riquier (Décembre 2001)*, ed. Danielle Buschinger and Marie-Sophie Masse, Amiens, Centre d'Études médiévales de l'Université de Picardie, 2002, 65 pp.

Bustos, *Textualización: Textualización y oralidad*, ed. José Jesús de Bustos, Madrid, Visor, 207 pp.

Bustos Vol.: Estudios ofrecidos al Profesor José Jesús de Bustos Tovar, ed. José Luis Girón Alconchel et al., Madrid, Editorial Complutense, 2 vols, 1576 pp.

Büttner, *Sammeln: Sammeln, Ordnen, Veranschaulichen. Zur Wissenkompilatorik in der Frühen Neuzeit*, ed. Frank Büttner, Markus Friedrich, and Helmut Zedelmaier, Münster, LIT, 364 pp.

Casas, *Iberia cantat: Iberia cantat: estudios sobre poesía hispánica medieval*, ed. Juan Casas Rigall and Eva Maria Díaz Martínez, Santiago de Compostela U.P., 2002, 589 pp.

Caubet, *Codification: Codification des langues de France. Actes du Colloque de l'Inalco 'Les Langues de France et leur codification. Ecrits divers — Ecrits ouverts', 29–31 mai 2000*, ed. Dominique Caubet, Salem Chaker, and Jean Sibille, Paris, L'Harmattan, 2002, 459 pp.

Cazauran Vol.: *Devis d'amitié: Mélanges en l'honneur de Nicole Cazauran*, ed. Jean Lecointe, Catherine Magnien, Isabelle Pantin, and Marie Claire Thomine, Paris, Champion, 2002, 976 pp.

Čechová, *Okraj*: *Okraj a střed v jazyce a literatuře: sborník z mezinárodní konference*, ed. Marie Čechová and Dobrava Moldanová, Ústí nad Labem, Univ. J. E. Purkyně, 504 pp.

Cercignani, *Wieland*: *Christoph Martin Wieland, Heinrich Heine, Georg Büchner, Thomas Bernhard, Joseph Roth, Heimito von Doderer*, ed. Fausto Cercignani (Studia Theodisca, 8), Milan, CUEM, 2001, 189 pp.

CHLM 3: *Actas [del] III Congreso Hispánico de Latín Medieval (León, 26–29 de septiembre de 2001)*, ed. Maurilio Pérez González, León, Universidad de León, 2002, 2 vols, 446 + 447–856 pp.

CILPR 23: *Actas del XXIII Congreso Internacional de Lingüística y Filología Románica, Salamanca 2001*, ed. Fernando Sánchez Miret, I: *Discursos inaugurales. Conferencias plenaras. Sección 1, Fonética y fonología; Sección 2, Morfología. Índices: Índice de autores, Índice general*; II/1: *Sección 3, Sintaxis, semántica y pragmática (primera parte)*; II/2: *Sección 3, Sintaxis, semántica y pragmática (segunda parte)*; III: *Sección 4, Semántica léxica, lexicología y onomástica*; IV: *Sección 5, Edición y crítica textual; Sección 6, Retórica, poética y teoría literaria*; V: *Sección 7, Lingüística aplicada; Sección 8, Historia de la lingüística; Mesas redondas*, Tübingen, Niemeyer. xii + 508, x + 490, x + 502, x + 502, x + 429, x + 396 pp.

Claramunt, *Món*: *El món urbà a la Corona d'Aragó del 1137 als decrets de Nova Planta: XVII Congrés d'Història de la Corona d'Aragó (Barcelona — Lleida, 2000)*, ed. Salvador Claramunt, 3 vols., Barcelona U.P., xxii + 632, xii + 910, xiii + 1101 pp.

Cotteri, *Alfieri*: *XXIII Simposio Internazionale di Studi Italo-Tedeschi: 'Vittorio Alfieri. Il poeta del mito' / XXIII. Internationales Symposium deutsch-italienischer Studien: 'Vittorio Alfieri. Der Dichter des Mythos'*, ed. Roberto Cotteri, Accademia di Studi Italo-tedeschi, Merano, 2002, 256 pp.

Csáky, *Ambivalenz*: *Ambivalenz des kulturellen Erbes. Vielfachcodierung des historischen Gedächtnisses. Paradigma: Österreich*, ed. Moritz Csáky and Klaus Zeyringer, Innsbruck, Studien–Verlag, 2000, 295 pp.

Czapla, *Lyrik*: *Lateinische Lyrik der frühen Neuzeit. Poetische Kleinformen und ihre Funktionen zwischen Renaissance und Aufklärung*, ed. Beate Czapla, Ralf Georg Czapla, and Robert Seidel (Frühe Neuzeit, 77), Tübingen, Niemeyer, ix + 457 pp.

D'Agostino, *Corona*: *XVI Congresso Internazionale di Storia della Corona d'Aragona: La Corona d'Aragona ai tempi di Alfonso il Magnanimo (Napoli 1997)*, ed. Guido D'Agostino and Giulia Buffardi, 2 vols, Naples, Paparo, 2000, xxx + 1910 pp.

Dell'Aquila, *Nominanza*: Michele Dell'Aquila, *L'onrata nominanza. Studi su Dante, Manzoni e altra letteratura*, Pisa, Giardini, 2001, 169 pp.

Décultot, *Lire*: *Lire, copier, écrire. Les bibliothèques manuscrites et leurs usages au XVIIIe siècle*, ed. Elisabeth Décultot, Paris, CNRS Editions, 246 pp.

Detering, *Autorschaft*: *Autorschaft. Positionen und Revisionen*, ed. Heinrich Detering, Stuttgart, Metzler, 2002, xvi + 608 pp.

Dethloff, *Realismen*: *Europäische Realismen. Facetten — Konvergenzen — Differenzen. Diversités des réalismes européens: convergences et différences. Internationales Symposium der Fachrichtung Romanistik an der Universität des Saarlandes, 21.–23. Oktober 1999*, ed. Uwe Dethloff, St. Ingbert, Röhrig, 2001, 423 pp.

Díez de Revenga, *Cernuda y Alberti*: *Aire del sur buscado. Estudios sobre Luis Cernuda y Rafael Alberti*, ed. Francisco Javier Díez de Revenga y Mariano de Paco, Murcia, Fundación CajaMurcia, 450 pp.

Dilg, *Natur*: *Natur im Mittelalter. Konzeptionen — Erfahrungen — Wirkungen. Akten des 9. Symposiums des Mediävistenverbandes, Marburg, 14.–17. März 2001*, ed. Peter Dilg, Berlin, Akademie, x + 498 pp.

Dinshaw, *Companion*: *The Cambridge Companion to Medieval Women's Writing*, ed. Carolyn Dinshaw and David Wallace, CUP, 289 pp.

Doll, *Écrivains*: *Les Écrivains juifs autrichiens (du 'Vormärz' à nos jours). Judentum und österreichische Literatur (vom Vormärz bis zur Gegenwart)*, ed. Jürgen Doll, Poitiers, La Licorns, 2000, 318 pp.

Dover, *Companion: A Companion to the Lancelot-Grail Cycle*, ed. Carol Dover (Arthurian Studies, 54), Cambridge, Brewer, xiii + 267 pp.

Dürhammer, *Witz: Raimund, Nestroy, Grillparzer — Witz und Lebensangst*, ed. Ilija Dürhammer and Pia Janke, Vienna, Praesens, 2001, 223 pp.

Eibl, *Kritiker: Goethes Kritiker*, ed. Karl Eibl and Bernd Scheffer, Paderborn, Mentis, 2001, 208 pp.

Elx 6: Actes del Seminari celebrat del 29 al 31 d'octubre de 2000 amb motiu del del VI Festival del Teatre i Música Medieval d'Elx (2000), Elx, Institut Municipal de Cultura – Ajuntament d'Elx, 2002.

Erler, *Gendering: Gendering the Master Narrative: Women and Power in the Middle Ages*, ed. Mary C. Erler and Maryanne Kowaleski, Ithaca–London, Cornell U.P., 269 pp.

Ernst, *RS*, 1: *Romanische Sprachgeschichte/Histoire linguistique de la Romania. Ein internationales Handbuch zur Geschichte der romanischen Sprachen/Manuel international d'histoire linguistique de la Romania*, vol. 1, ed. Gerhard Ernst,Martin-Dietrich Glessgen,Christian Schmitt, Wolfgang Schweikard, Berlin–New York, de Gruyter, 1152 pp.

Esselborn, *Utopie: Utopie, Antiutopie und Science Fiction im deutschsprachigen Roman des 20. Jahrhunderts. Vorträge des deutsch-französischen Kolloquiums*, ed. Hans Esselborn, Würzburg, Königshausen & Neumann, 230 pp.

Ertzdorff, *Erkundung: Erkundung und Beschreibung der Welt. Zur Poetik der Reise- und Länderberichte. Vorträge eines interdisziplinären Symposiums vom 19. bis 24. Juni 2000 an der Justus-Liebig-Universität Gießen*, ed. Xenja von Ertzdorff and Gerhard Giesemann (Chloe, 34), Amsterdam, Rodopi, x + 662 pp.

Fanlo, *Millénarisme: Formes du millénarisme en Europe à l'aube des temps modernes. Actes du colloque de Marseille (10–12 septembre 1998)*, ed. Jean-Raymond Fanlo and André Tournon, Paris, Champion, 2001, 480 pp.

Fest. Bender: 'Das Schöne soll sein.' 'Aisthesis' in der deutschen Literatur. Festschrift für Wolfgang F. Bender, ed. Peter Hesselmann, Michael Huesmann, and Hans-Joachim Jakob, Bielefeld, Aisthesis, 2001, 494 pp.

Fest. Bormann: Poesie als Auftrag. Festschrift für Alexander von Bormann, ed. Dagmar Ottmann and Markus Symannk, Würzburg, Königshausen & Neumann, 2002, 375 pp.

Fest. Brandt: Schönheit, welche nach Wahrheit dürstet. Beiträge zur deutschen Literatur von der Aufklärung bis zur Gegenwart. Festschrift für Helmut Brandt, ed. Gerhard R. Kaiser and Heinrich Macher (Jenaer Germanistische Forschungen, n.F., 16), Heidelberg, Winter, x + 350 pp.

Fest. Butler: Writers' Morality / Die Moral der Schriftsteller. Festschrift for / für Michael Butler, ed. Ronald Spiers, Oxford, Lang, 2000, 222 pp.

Fest. Ernst : Roma et Romania. Festschrift für Gerhard Ernst zum 65. Geburtstag, ed. Sabine Heinemann, Gerald Bernhard and Dieter Kattenbusch, Tübingen, Niemeyer, 2002, viii + 427 pp.

Fest. Fiedler: Überschreitungen. Dialoge zwischen Literatur- und Theaterwissenschaft, Architektur und Bildender Kunst. Festschrift für Leonhard M. Fiedler, ed. Jörg Sader and Anette Wörner, Würzburg, Königshausen & Neumann, 2002, 352 pp.

Fest. Gärtner: Magister et amicus. Festschrift für Kurt Gärtner zum 65. Geburtstag, ed. Václav Bok and Frank Shaw, Vienna, Praesens, 991 pp.

Fest. Gebhard: Das Gedichtete behauptet sein Recht. Festschrift für Walter Gebhard zum 65. Geburtstag, ed. Klaus H. Kiefer, Frankfurt–Berlin, Lang, 2001, xvi + 592 pp.

Fest. Hirao: Zwischenzeiten, Zwischenwelten. Festschrift für Kozo Hirao, ed. Josef Fürnkäs, Frankfurt–Berlin, Lang, 2001, 551 pp.

Fest. Honemann: Literatur — Geschichte — Literaturgeschichte. Beiträge zur mediävistischen Literaturwissenschaft. Festschrift für Volker Honemann zum 60. Geburtstag, ed. Nine Miedema and Rudolf Suntrup, Frankfurt, Lang, xvi + 949 pp.

Fest. Jacobs: Der europäische Roman zwischen Aufklärung und Postmoderne. Festschrift zum 65. Geburtstag von Jürgen C. Jacobs, ed. Friedhelm Marx and Andreas Meier, Weimar, Verlag und Datenbank für Geisteswissenschaften, 2001, vi + 273 pp.

Fest. Janota: Forschungen zur deutschen Literatur des Spätmittelalters. Festschrift für Johannes Janota, ed. Horst Brunner and Werner Williams-Krapp, Tübingen, Niemeyer, viii + 316 pp.

Fest. Kirsch: Wenn Ränder Mitte werden: Zivilisation, Literatur und Sprache im interkulturellen Kontext, Festschrift für Fritz Peter Kirsch zum 60. Geburtstag, ed. Chantal Adobati et al., Vienna, WUV, 2001, 728 pp.

Fest. Knobloch: Grenzgänge. Studien zur Literatur der Moderne. Festschrift für Hans-Jörg Knobloch, ed. Helmut Koopmann and Manfred Misch, Paderborn, Mentis, 2002, 469 pp.

Fest Müller: Aufklärungen: Zur Literaturgeschichte der Moderne. Festschrift für Klaus Detlef Müller zum 65. Geburtstag, ed. Werner Finck, Susanne Komfort-Hein, Marion Schmaus, and Michael Voges, Tübingen, Niemeyer, xi + 463 pp.

Fest. Nay: Recht, Ethik, Religion: Der Spannungsbogen für Aktuelle Fragen, historische Vorgaben und bleibende Probleme, Festgabe für Bundesrichter Dr. Giusep Nay zum 60. Geburtstag, ed. Dietmar Mieth et al., Lucerne, Exodus, 2002, 262 pp.

Fest. Paufler: Romanische Sprachen in Amerika. Festschrift für Hans-Dieter Paufler zum 65. Geburtstag, ed. Kerstin Störl and Johannes Klare, Frankfurt, Lang, 2002, photo + 642 pp.

Fest. Perels: Goethezeit — Zeit für Goethe. Auf den Spuren deutscher Lyriküberlieferung in die Moderne. Festschrift für Christoph Perels zum 65. Geburtstag, ed. Konrad Feilchenfeldt et al., Tübingen, Niemeyer, vii + 432 pp. + 12 pls.

Fest. Ruberg: Vox sermo res. Beiträge zur Sprachreflexion, Literatur- und Sprachgeschichte vom Mittelalter bis zur Neuzeit. Festschrift für Uwe Ruberg, ed. Wolfgang Haubrichs, Stuttgart–Leipzig, Hirzel, 2001, 291 pp.

Fest. Scheible: Dona Melanchthoniana. Festgabe für Heinz Scheible zum 70. Geburtstag, ed. Johanna Loehr, Stuttgart–Bad Cannstatt, Frommann-Holzboog, 2001, 590 pp.

Fest. Schings: Prägnanter Moment. Studien zur deustchen Literatur der Aufklärung und Klassik. Festschrift für Hans-Jürgen Schings, ed. Peter-André Alt, Alexander Košenina, Hartmut Reinhart, and Wolfgang Riedel, Würzburg, Königshausen & Neumann, 2002, xi + 522 pp.

Fest. Stotz: Strenarum lanx. Beiträge zur Philologie und Geschichte des Mittelalters und der Frühen Neuzeit. Festgabe für Peter Stotz zum 40-jährigen Jubiläum des Mittellateinischen Seminars der Universität Zürich, ed. Martin H. Graf and Christian Moser, Zug, Achius, 374 pp.

Fest. Vizkelety: 'swer sînen vriunt behaltet, daz ist lobelîch.' Festschrift für András Vizkelety zum 70. Geburtstag, ed. Márta Nagy, Lázló Jónácsik, and Edit Madas, Piliscsaba, Kath. Péter-Pázmány-Univ., Philos. Fak., 2001, 608 pp.

Fest Windfuhr: Literarische Fundstücke. Wiederentdeckungen und Neuentdeckungen. Festschrift für Manfred Windfuhr, ed. Ariane Neuhaus-Koch and Gertrude Cepl-Kaufmann (Beiträge zur neueren Literaturgeschichte, 188), Heidelberg, Winter, 2002, 527 pp.

Fest. Wünsch: Weltentwürfe in Literatur und Medien. Phantastische Wirklichkeiten — realistische Imaginationen. Festschrift für Marianne Wünsch, ed. Hans Krah and Claus-Michael Ort, Kiel, Ludwig, 2002, 448 pp.

Fiorentino, *Romance Objects: Romance Objects. Transitivity in Romance Languages*, ed. Giuliana Fiorentino (Empirical Approaches to Language Typology), Berlin–New York, Mouton de Gruyter, xxii + 330 pp.

Firbas Vol.: Language and Function: To the memory of Jan Firbas, ed. Josef Hladký, Amsterdam, Benjamins, 336 pp.

Flood Vol.: 'Vir ingenio mirandus.' Studies Presented to John L. Flood, ed. William J. Jones, William A. Kelly, and Frank Shaw (Göppinger Arbeiten zur Germanistik, 710), 2 vols, Göppingen, Kümmerle, xxxix + 1–517, 518–1090 pp.

Floris, *Il segreto: Il segreto. Atti del Convegno di Studi Cagliari 1–4 aprile 1998*, ed. U. Floris and M. Virdis, Rome, Bulzoni, 2000, 570 pp.

Foehr-Janssens, *Fortune: La Fortune: Thèmes, représentations, discours*, ed. Yasmina Foehr-Janssens and Emmanuelle Métry, Geneva, Droz, 220 pp.

Fossat Vol.: Mélanges offerts à Jean-Louis Fossat, ed. Lídia Rabassa (*Cahiers d'Etudes Romanes*, n.s., 11–12), Toulouse, Université de Toulouse Le Mirail, Centre de Linguistique et de Dialectologie, vi + 362 pp.

Gabler Vol.: Schrift — Text — Edition. Hans Werner Gabler zum 65. Geburtstag, ed. Christiane Henkes et al. (Beihefte zu *Editio*, 19), Tübingen, Niemeyer, viii + 360 pp.

Gallagher, *Ici-Là: Ici-là. Place and Displacement in Caribbean Writing in French*, ed. Mary Gallagher, Amsterdam-NY, Rodopi, xxix + 308 pp.

Giles, *Counter-Cultures: Counter-Cultures in Germany and Central Europe. From Sturm und Drang to Baader-Meinhof*, ed. Steve Giles and Maike Oerkel, Oxford, Lang, 397 pp.

Godsall-Myers, *Speaking: Speaking in the Medieval World*, ed. Jean E. Godsall-Myers (Cultures, Beliefs, and Traditions: Medieval and Early Modern Peoples, 16), Leiden, Brill, xii + 194 pp.

Going Romance 2001: Romance Languages and Linguistic Theory 2001. Selected Papers from 'Going Romance', Amsterdam, 6–8 December 2001, ed. Josep Quer, Jan Schroten, Mauro Scorretti, Petra Sleeman, and Els Verheugd (Current Issues in Linguistic Theory, 245), Amsterdam, Benjamins, viii + 353 pp.

Goyens, *Vernacular: The Dawn of the Written Vernacular in Western Europe*, ed. Michèle Goyens and Werner Verbeke, Leuven University Press, 498 pp.

Grossman, *Other: Studies in Language, Literature, and Cultural Mythology in Poland. Investigating the 'Other'*, ed. Elwira M. Grossman (Slavic Studies, 7), Lewiston–Queenston–Lampeter, Mellen, 2002, xiii + 327 pp.

Grucza, *Beziehungen: Tausend Jahre polnisch-deutsche Beziehungen. Sprache, Literatur, Kultur, Politik. Materialien des Millenium-Kongresses 5.–8. April 2000, Warszawa*, ed. Franciszek Grucza, Warsaw, Graf-Punkt, 2001, 1008 pp.

Gutenberg, *Fähigkeit: Zitier-Fähigkeit. Findungen und Erfindungen des Anderen*, ed. Andrea Gutenberg and Ralph J. Poole, Berlin, Schmidt, 2001, 328 pp.

Haensch Vol.: Lexicografía y lexicología en Europa y América. Homenaje a Günther Haensch en su 80 aniversario, ed. María Teresa Echenique Elizondo and Juan Sánchez Méndez, Madrid, Gredos, 695 pp.

Harms, *Ordnung: Ordnung und Unordnung in der Literatur des Mittelalters*, ed. Wolfgang Harms et al., Stuttgart, Hirzel, 230 pp.

Haslinger, *Textgenese: Textgenese und Interpretation. Vorträge und Aufsätze des Salzburger Symposions 1997*, ed. Adolf Haslinger, Stuttgart, Heinz, 2000, 172 pp.

Hassauer Vol. : The Querelle des Femmes in the Romania: Studies in Honour of Friederike Hassauer, Vienna, Turia und Kant, 2002, 233 pp.

Haywood, *Dante: Dante Metamorphoses: Episodes in a Literary Afterlife*, ed. Eric G. Haywood, Dublin, Four Courts Press, 252 pp.

Hellinger, *Gender: Gender Across Languages: The Linguistic Representation of Women and Men*, Vol. 3, ed. Marlis Hellinger and Hadumod Bussmann, Amsterdam, Benjamins, 390 pp.

Henkel, *Dialoge: Dialoge. Sprachliche Kommunikation in und zwischen Texten im deutschen Mittelalter. Hamburger Colloquium 1999*, ed. Nikolaus Henkel et al., Tübingen, Niemeyer, x + 391 pp.

Hillgarth Vol.: Religion, Text, and Society in Medieval Spain and Northern Europe: Essays in honor of J. N. Hillgarth, ed. Thomas E. Burman, Mark D. Meyerson, and Leah Shopkow, Toronto, Pontifical Institute of Mediaeval Studies, 2002, 374 pp.

HLS 6: Theory, Practice and Acquisition. Papers from the 6th Hispanic Linguistics Symposium and the 5th Conference on the Acquisition of Spanish and Portuguese, ed. Paula Kempchinsky and Carlos-Eduardo Piñeros, Somerville, Mass., Cascadilla Press, 423 pp.

Holtz Vol.: La Tradition vive. Mélanges d'histoire des textes en l'honneur de Louis Holtz, ed. Pierre Lardet, Paris, Turnhout, xxviii + 466 pp.

Horn, *Possessions: Possessions: Essays in French Literature, Cinema and Theory*, ed. Julia Horn and Lynsey Russell-Watts, Berne, Lang, 223 pp.

Hutchinson, *Landmarks: Landmarks in German Short Prose*, ed. Peter Hutchinson (British and Irish Studies in German Language and Literature, 33), Oxford–New York–Berne, Lang, 208 pp.

Ichim, *Limba: Limba si literatura româna în spatiul etnocultural dacoromânesc si în diaspora*, ed. Ofelia Ichim and Florin-Teodor Olariu, pref. Dan Manuca, Iasi, Trinitas, 542 pp.

ICHL 15: Historical Linguistics 2001. Selected Papers from the 15th International Conference on Historical Linguistics, Melbourne, 13–17 August 2001, ed. Barry J. Blake and Kate Burridge, with the assistance of Jo Taylor (Current Issues in Linguistic Theory, 237), Amsterdam, Benjamins, vi + 442 pp.

ICLS 9: The Court Reconvenes: Courtly Literature Across the Disciplines (Selected Papers from the Ninth Triennial Congress of the International Courtly Literature Society, University of British

Columbia, 25–31 July 1998), ed. Barbara K. Altman and Carleton W. Carroll, Woodbridge, Brewer, x + 370 pp.

Ingen, *Beer: Johann Beer. Schriftsteller, Komponist und Hofbeamter, 1655–1700. Beiträge zum Internationalen Beer-Symposion in Weißenfels, Oktober 2000*, ed. Ferdinand van Ingen and Hans-Gert Roloff (JIG, Reihe A, 70), Berne, Lang, 642 pp.

Janyšková, *Studia etymologica: Studia etymologica Brunensia 2: sborník příspěvkù z mezinárodní vědecké konference Etymologické symposion Brno 2002, pořádané etymologickým oddělením Ústavu pro jazyk český AV ČR v Brně ve dnech 10.–12. září 2002*, ed. Ilona Janyšková and Helena Karlíková,Prague, Nakl. Lidové noviny, 453 pp.

Jordan, *Lyrik: Niederländische Lyrik und ihre deutsche Rezeption in der Frühen Neuzeit*, ed. Lothar Jordan (Wolfenbütteler Forschungen, 99), Wiesbaden, Harrassowitz, 2002, 272 pp.

Karwatowa, *Procesy: Procesy innowacyjne w jezykach slowianskich*, ed. Zofia Ewa Rudnik-Karwatowa. Warsaw, Slawistyczny Osrodek Wydawniczy, 257 pp.

Kessler, *Res: Res et Verba in der Renaissance*, ed. Eckhard Kessler and Ian Maclean (Wolfenbütteler Abhandlungen zur Renaissanceforschung, 21), Wiesbaden, Harrassowitz, 2002, 400 pp.

Kosta, *Investigations: Investigations into Formal Slavic Linguistics: Contributions of the Fourth European Conference on Formal Description of Slavic Languages —FDSL IV held at Potsdam University, November 28–30, 2001. Part 1*, ed. Peter Kosta, Joanna Blaszczak et al., Frankfurt, Lang, 433 pp.

Krobb, *Project: Poetry Project. Irish Germanists Interpret German Verse*, ed. Florian Krobb and Jeff Morrison (British and Irish Studies in German Language and Literature, 25), Oxford–New York, Lang, 276 pp.

Le Disez, *Seuils: Seuils et traverses: enjeux de l'écriture du voyage. Vol I*, ed. Jean-Yves Le Disez, Brest, Université de Bretagne occidentale, 2002, 325 pp.

Lehmann-Benz, *Schnittpunkte: Schnittpunkte. Deutsch-Niederländische Literaturbeziehungen im späten Mittelalter*, ed. Angelika Lehmann-Benz et al. (Studien zur Geschichte und Kultur Nordeuropas, 5), Münster, Waxmann, 352 pp.

López Vol.: Lengua, variación y contexto: Estudios dedicados a Humberto López Morales, ed. F. Fernández Moreno et al., Madrid, Arco/Libros, 2 vols, 1098 pp.

Lotkův Vol.: České, polské a slovenské jazykové a literární souvislosti: sborník referátů z mezinárodního odborného semináře uspořádaného u příležitosti sedmdesátin prof. PhDr. Edvarda Lotka, CSc., na Filozofické fakultě Univerzity Palackého v Olomouci dne 20, února 2002, ed. Ingeborg Fialová, Olomouc, Palackého Univ., 248 pp.

LSRL 31: A Romance Perspective on Language Knowledge and Use. Selected Papers from the 31st Linguistic Symposium on Romance Languages (LSRL), Chicago, 19–22 April 2001, ed. Rafael Núñez-Cedeño, Luis López, and Richard Cameron (Current Issues in Linguistic Theory, 238), Amsterdam, Benjamins, xvi + 384 pp.

LSRL 32: Romance Linguistics: Theory and Acquisition. Selected Papers from the 32nd Linguistic Symposium on Romance Languages (LSRL), Toronto, April 2002, ed. Ana Teresa Pérez-Leroux and Yves Roberge (Current Issues in Linguistic Theory, 244), Amsterdam, Benjamins, viii + 388 pp.

Luserke, *Goethe: Goethe nach 1999. Positionen und Perspektiven*, ed. Matthias Luserke, Göttingen, Vandenhoeck & Ruprecht, 2001, 175 pp.

Luserke, *Rokoko: Literatur und Kultur des Rokoko*, ed. Matthias Luserke, Reiner Marx, and Reiner Wild, Göttingen, Vandenhoeck & Ruprecht, 2001, 328 pp.

Lyons, *Savoir: Le Savoir au XVIIe siècle*, ed. John D. Lyons and Cara Welch (Biblio 17, 147), Tübingen, Narr, 404 pp.

Martin, *Racine: Jean Racine et l'Orient*, ed. Isabelle Martin and Robert Elbaz (Biblio 17, 148), Tübingen, Narr, 229 pp.

Massoure, *Langues: Langues et parlers pyrénéens*, ed. Jean-Louis Massoure (*Pyrénées*, 454), Lourdes, 2002, 452 pp.

Mazouer, *Animal: L'Animal au XVIIe siècle*, ed. Charles Mazouer (Biblio 17, 146), Tübingen, Narr, 198 pp.

McKenna, *Résurgence: La Résurgence des philosophes antiques*, ed. Antony McKenna and Pierre-François Moreau (Libertinage et philosophie au XVIIe siècle, 7), Université de Saint-Étienne, 339 pp.
Meier, *Lenz: Jakob Michael Reinhold Lenz. Vom Sturm und Drang zur Moderne*, ed. Andreas Meier, Heidelberg, Winter, 2001, 145 pp.
Ménager Vol.: *Cité des hommes, Cité de Dieu. Travaux sur la littérature de la Renaissance en l'honneur de Daniel Ménager* (THR, 375), 624 pp.
Messner Vol.: *Vocabula et vocabularia: études de lexicologie et de (méta-) lexicographie romanes en l'honneur du 60e anniversaire de Dieter Messner*, ed. Bernard Pöll and Franz Rainer, Frankfurt, Lang, 2002, 361 pp.
MHRS 11: *Papers of the Medieval Hispanic Research Seminar: Proceedings of the Eleventh Colloquium*, ed. Alan Deyermond and Jane Whetnall (PMHRS, 34), 2002, 86 pp.
Molas Vol.: *Professor Joaquim Molas: Memòria, Escriptura, Història*, Barcelona U.P., 2 vols, 1245 pp.
Mühlethaler, *Parodie: Formes de la critique: parodie et satire dans la France et l'Italie médiévales*, ed. Jean-Claude Mühlethaler, Alain Corbellari, and Barbara Wahlen, Paris, Champion, 270 pp.
Müller, *Alterungsprozesse: Alterungsprozesse: Reifen — Veralten — Erneuern*, ed. Eva Katrin Müller, Holger Siever, and Nicole Magnus, Bonn, Romanistischer Vlg, 328 pp.
Nauroy, *Désert: Le Désert, un espace paradoxal. Actes du colloque de Metz (13–15 septembre 2001)*, ed. Gérard Nauroy, Pierre Halen and Anne Spica, Berne, Lang, x + 592 pp.
Nérardeau Vol.: *Lectures d'Ovide publiées à la mémoire de Jean-Pierre Néraudeau*, ed. Emmanuel Bury, Paris, Les Belles Lettres, 562 pp.
Nivelle, *Écrivains: Colloque Littéraire international: Les écrivains de Marseille*, ed. N. Nivelle and J.-C. Latil, Marseilles, Académie Europe XXI, 2001, 311 pp.
Niven, *Politics: Politics and Culture in Twentieth Century German*, ed. William Niven and James Jordan (Studies in German Literature, Linguistics, and Culture), Woodbridge, Camden House, 288 pp.
Ó Baoill, *Rannsachadh: Rannsachadh na Gàidhlig 2000*, ed. Colm Ó Baoill and Nancy R. McGuire, Aberdeen, An Clò Gaidhealach, 2002, 312 pp.
Olsen, *Essays*: Per Olsen, *Ekbátana tur/retur. Essays om liv og lyst især i dansk litteratur*, ed. Aage Jørgensen, Aarhus, AKA-PRINT, 160 pp.
PatRom 5: *Miscelânea Patromiana. Actas do V Colóquio (Lisboa) seguidas das Comunicações do VII Colóquio (Neuchâtel) e de duas Comunicações do VIII Colóquio (Bucurećti)*, ed. Dieter Kremer, Ivo Castro, and Wulf Müller, Tübingen, Niemeyer, x + 298 pp.
Paul, *Schriften*: Fritz Paul, *Kleine Schriften zur Nordischen Philologie*, ed. Joachim Grage et al., Vienna, Praesens, 350 pp.,
Perdiguero, *Lengua romance: Lengua romance en textos latinos de la Edad Media. Sobre los orígenes del castellano escrito*, ed. Hermógenes Perdiguero Villarreal, Burgos, Univ. de Burgos – Instituto de la lengua castellano y leonés, 277 pp.
Plachta, *Zusammenarbeit: Literarische Zusammenarbeit*, ed. Bodo Plachta, Tübingen, Niemeyer, 2001, ix + 316 pp.
PLS 36: *Přednášky a besedy z 36. běhu Letní školy slovanských studií*, ed. Eva Rusinová, Brno, Masaryk Univ., 182 pp.
PLS 46: *Přednášky z 46. běhu Letní školy slovanských studií*, ed. Jan Kuklík and Jiří Hasil, Prague, Charles Univ., 309 pp.
Pospíšil, *Česká slavistika: Česká slavistika 2003: české přednášky pro XIII. mezinárodní kongres slavistů, Ljubljana 15.–21. 8. 2003*, ed. Ivo Pospíšil and Miloš Zelenka, Prague, Academia, 386 pp.
Ravier Vol.: *'Sempre los camps auràn segadas resurgantas'. Mélanges offerts au professeur Xavier Ravier par ses collègues, disciples et amis*, ed. Jean-Claude Bouvier, Jacques Gourc, and François Pic (Coll. Méridiennes), Toulouse, CNRS — Université de Toulouse-Le Mirail, 662 pp.
Rickard Vol.: *Interpreting the History of French: A Festschrift for Peter Rickard on the Occasion of his Eightieth Birthday*, ed. Rodney Sampson and Wendy Ayres-Bennett, Amsterdam–NY, Rodopi, 2002, xix + 373 pp.

Ridley Vol.: *Sentimente, Gefühle, Empfindungen. Zur Geschichte und Literatur des Affektiven von 1770 bis heute. Tagung zum 60. Geburtstag von Hugh Ridley im Juli 2001*, ed. Anne Fuchs and Sabine Strümper-Krobb, Würzburg, Königshausen & Neumann, 267 pp.

Rizzo, *Identità*: *L'identità nazionale nella cultura letteraria italiana. Atti del 3° Congresso nazionale dell'ADI, Lecce–Otranto 20–22 settembre 1999*, ed. Gino Rizzo, 2 vols, Galatina, Congedo, 2001, ix + 563, 374 pp.

RK 13: *Schreiben in einer anderen Sprache. Zur Internationalität romanischer Sprachen und Literaturen. Romanistisches Kolloquium XIII*, ed. Wolfgang Dahmen, Günter Holtus, Johannes Kramer, Michael Metzeltin, Wolfgang Schweickard and Otto Winkelmann (Tübinger Beiträge zur Linguistik, 448), Tübingen, Narr, 2000, xvi + 321 pp.

RK 14: *Kanonbildung in der Romanistik und in den Nachbardisziplinen. Romanistisches Kolloquium XIV*, ed. Wolfgang Dahmen, Günter Holtus, Johannes Kramer, Michael Metzeltin, Wolfgang Schweickard, and Otto Winkelmann, Tübingen, Narr, 2000, xii + 496 pp.

Roloff, *Editionsverfahren*: *Geschichte der Editionsverfahren vom Altertum bis zur Gegenwart im Überblick. Ringvorlesung*, ed. Hans-Gert Roloff (Berliner Beiträge zur Editionswissenschaft, 5), Berlin, Weidler, 358 pp.

Rudolph, *Polenbilder*: *Ein weiter Mantel. Polenbilder in Gesellschaft, Politik und Dichtung*, ed. Andrea Rudolph and Ute Stolz, Dettelbach, Röll, 2002, 416 pp.

Ruščákův Vol.: *Komunikácia a text: zborník materiálov z vedeckej konferencie s medzinárodnou účast'ou organizovanej pri príležitosti životného jubilea doc. PhDr. Františka Ruščáka, CSc., v dnoch 15.–16. novembra 2001 v Prešove*, ed. Zuzana Stanislavová, Prešov, Náuka, 284 pp.

Schiewer, *Forschungsberichte*: *Forschungsberichte zur internationalen Germanistik. Germanistische Mediävistik, Teil 2*, ed. Hans-Jochen Schiewer and Jochen Conzelmann (*Jahrbuch für Internationale Germanistik*, Reihe C, Forschungsberichte, 6), Berne, Lang, 273 pp.

Schmitz, *Wissen*: *Wissen und neue Medien. Bilder und Zeichen von 800 bis 2000*, ed. Ulrich Schmitz and Horst Wenzel (Philologische Studien und Quellen, 177), Berlin, Schmidt, 289 pp.

Sellier, *Essais*: Philippe Sellier, *Essais sur l'imaginaire classique: Pascal, Racine, Précieuses et Moralistes, Fénelon* (Lumière classique, 50), Paris, Champion, 394 pp.

Sharpe, *Goethe*: *The Cambridge Companion to Goethe*, ed. Lesley Sharpe, Cambridge University Press, 2002, xvi + 277 pp.

Simion Vol.: *Manual de trudire a cuvântului. Omagiu lui Eugen Simion cu ocazia împlinirii a 70 de ani*, Bucharest, Univers enciclopedic, 423 pp.

Šimková, *Tradícia*: *Tradícia a perspektívy gramatického výskumu na Slovensku*, ed. Mária Šimková, Bratislava, Veda, 243 pp.

Singh, *Explorations*: *Explorations in Seamless Morphology*, ed. Rajendra Singh and Stanley Starosta, New Delhi–London, Sage, 348 pp.

Smedts, *Taalkunde*: *De Nederlandse taalkunde in kaart*, ed. W. Smedts and P. C. Paardekooper, Leuven–Amersfoort, Acco, 1999, 288 pp.

Spalding Vol.: *Experiencing Tradition: Essays of Discovery. In Memory of Keith Spalding (1913–2002)*, ed. Hinrich Siefken and Anthony Bushell, York, Ebor, 268 pp.

Tato Vol.: *Homenaxe a Fernando R. Tato*, ed. Ramón Lorenzo Vázquez, Universidade de Santiago de Compostela, 2002, 726 pp.

Tervooren, *Literaturgeschichtsschreibung*: *Regionale Literaturgeschichtsschreibung. Aufgaben, Analysen und Perspektiven*, ed. Helmut Tervooren and Jens Haustein (ZDP, 122, Sonderheft), Berlin, Schmidt, 312 pp.

Thompson Vol.: *Essays in Italian Literature in honour of Doug Thompson*, ed. George Talbot and Pamela Williams, Dublin, Four Courts Press, 2002, 249 pp.

Tichá, *Internacionalizmy*: *Internacionalizmy v nové slovní zásobě: sborník příspěvků z konference Praha, 16.–18. června 2003*, ed. Zdeňka Tichá and Albena Rangelova, Prague, ÚJC AV ČR, 239 pp.

Tschuggnall, *Dialog*: *Religion — Literatur — Künste*, Vol. 2: *Ein Dialog. Mit einem Grußwort von Bischof Alois Kothgasser*, ed. Peter Tschuggnall, Anif-Salzburg, Müller Speiser, 2002, xiv + 593 pp.

Tschuggnall, *Perspektiven*: *Religion — Literatur — Künste*, Vol. 3: *Perspektiven einer Begegnung am Beginn eines neuen Milleniums. Mit einem Vorwort von Paul Kardinal Poupard und dem Brief an die Künstler von Johannes Paul*, ed. Peter Tschuggnall, Anif-Salzburg, Müller Speiser, 2001, 558 pp.

Tobin Vol.: *Theatrum Mundi: Studies in honor of Ronald W. Tobin*, ed. Claire L. Carlin and Kathleen Wine (EMF Critiques), Charlottesville, VA, Rookwood Press, 280 pp.

Wetsel, *Femmes*: *Les Femmes au Grand Siècle. Le Baroque: musique et littérature. Musique et liturgie*, ed. David Wetsel and Frédéric Canovas (Biblio 17, 144), Tübingen, Narr, 269 pp.

Wetsel, *Pascal*: *Pascal — New Trends in Port-Royal Studies*, ed. David Wetsel and Frédéric Canovas (Biblio 17, 143), Tübingen, Narr, 2002, 276 pp.

Wetsel, *Spiritualité*: *La Spiritualité / l'épistolaire / le merveilleux au Grand Siècle*, ed. David Wetsel and Frédéric Canovas (Biblio 17, 145), Tübingen, Narr, 302 pp.

Wild, *Bücher*: *Dennoch leben sie. Verfemte Bücher, verfolgte Autorinnen und Autoren. Zu den Auswirkungen nationalsozialistischer Literaturpolitik*, ed. Rainer Wild et al., Munich, edition text + kritik, 454 pp.

Winter Vol.: *Language in Time and Space. A Festschrift for Werner Winter on the Occasion of his 80th Birthday*, ed. Brigitte L. M. Bauer and Georges-Jean Pinault (Trends in Linguistics, Studies and Monographs, 144), Berlin–New York, Mouton de Gruyter, plate + xxvi + 443 pp.

Wolfzettel, *Das Wunderbare*: *Das Wunderbare in der arthurischen Literatur. Probleme und Perspektiven*, ed. Friedrich Wolfzettel, Tübingen, Niemeyer, xii + 379 pp.

Žigo, *Vlastné meno*: *Vlastné meno v komunikácii: 15. slovenská onomastická konferencia Bratislava 6.–7. septembra 2002: zborník referátov*, ed. Pavol Žigo and Milan Majtán, Bratislava, Veda, 339 pp.

II. GENERAL

abbrev.	abbreviation, abbreviated to
Acad., Akad.	Academy, Academia, etc.
acc.	accusative
AN	Anglo-Norman
ann.	annotated (by)
anon.	anonymous
appx	appendix
Arg.	Argentinian (and foreign equivalents)
AS	Anglo-Saxon
Assoc.	Association (and foreign equivalents)
Auv.	Auvergnat
Bel.	Belarusian
BL	British Library
BM	British Museum
BN	Bibliothèque Nationale, Biblioteka Narodowa, etc.
BPtg.	Brazilian Portuguese
bull.	bulletin
c.	century
c.	circa
Cat.	Catalan
ch.	chapter
col.	column
comm.	commentary (by)
comp.	compiler, compiled (by)
Cz.	Czech
diss.	dissertation
ed.	edited (by), editor (and foreign equivalents)
edn	edition
EPtg.	European Portuguese
fac.	facsimile
fasc.	fascicle
Fest.	Festschrift, Festskrift
Fin.	Finnish
Fr.	France, French, Français
Gal.-Ptg.	Galician-Portuguese (and equivalents)
Gasc.	Gascon
Ger.	German(y)
Gk	Greek
Gmc	Germanic
IE	Indo-European
illus.	illustrated, illustration(s)
impr.	impression
incl.	including, include(s)
Inst.	Institute (and foreign equivalents)
introd.	introduction, introduced by, introductory
It.	Italian
izd.	издание
izd-vo	издательство
Jb.	Jahrbuch
Jg	Jahrgang
Jh.	Jahrhundert
Lang.	Languedocien

Lat.	Latin
Lim.	Limousin
lit.	literature
med.	medieval
MHG	Middle High German
Mid. Ir.	Middle Irish
Mil.	Milanese
MS	manuscript
n.d.	no date
n.F.	neue Folge
no.	number (and foreign equivalents)
nom.	nominative
n.p.	no place
n.s.	new series
O Auv.	Old Auvergnat
O Cat.	Old Catalan
Occ.	Occitan
OE	Old English
OF	Old French
O Gasc.	Old Gascon
OHG	Old High German
O Ir.	Old Irish
O Lim.	Old Limousin
O Occ.	Old Occitan
O Pr.	Old Provençal
O Ptg.	Old Portuguese
OS	Old Saxon
OW	Old Welsh
part.	participle
ped.	педагогический, etc.
PIE	Proto-Indo-European
Pied.	Piedmontese
PGmc	Primitive Germanic
pl.	plate
plur.	plural
Pol.	Polish
p.p.	privately published
Pr.	Provençal
pref.	preface (by)
Procs	Proceedings
Ptg.	Portuguese
publ.	publication, published (by)
Ren.	Renaissance
repr.	reprint(ed)
Rev.	Review, Revista, Revue
rev.	revised (by)
Russ.	Russian
s.	siècle
ser.	series
sg.	singular
Slg	Sammlung
Soc.	Society (and foreign equivalents)
Sp.	Spanish
supp.	supplement

Sw.	Swedish
Trans.	Transactions
trans.	translated (by), translation
Ukr.	Ukrainian
Univ.	University (and foreign equivalents)
unpubl.	unpublished
U.P.	University Press (and foreign equivalents)
Vlg	Verlag
vol.	volume
vs	versus
W.	Welsh
wyd.	wydawnictwo

* before a publication signifies that it has not been seen by the contributor.

III. PLACE NAMES

B	Barcelona
BA	Buenos Aires
Be	Belgrade
Bo	Bologna
C	Coimbra
F	Florence
Gd	Gdańsk
Kw	Kraków, Cracow
L	Lisbon
M	Madrid
Mi	Milan
Mw	Moscow
Na	Naples
NY	New York
O	Oporto
Pń	Poznań
R	Rio de Janeiro
Ro	Rome
SC	Santiago de Compostela
SPo	São Paulo
SPb	St Petersburg
T	Turin
V	Valencia
Wa	Warsaw
Ww	Wrocław
Z	Zagreb

IV. PERIODICALS, INSTITUTIONS, PUBLISHERS

AA, Antike und Abendland
AAA, Ardis Publishers, Ann Arbor, Michigan
AAA, Archivio per l'Alto Adige
AAASS, American Association for the Advancement of Slavic Studies
AABC, Anuari de l'Agrupació Borrianenca de Cultura
AAC, Atti dell'Accademia Clementina
AAL, Atti dell'Accademia dei Lincei
AALP, L'Arvista dl'Academia dla Lenga Piemontèisa
AAM, Association des Amis de Maynard
AAPH, Anais da Academia Portuguesa da História
AAPN, Atti dell'Accademia Pontaniana di Napoli
AAPP, Atti Accademia Peloritana dei Pericolanti. Classe di Lettere Filosofia e Belle Arti
AARA, Atti della Accademia Roveretana degli Agiati
AASB, Atti dell'Accademia delle Scienze dell'Istituto di Bologna
AASF, Annales Academiae Scientiarum Fennicae
AASLAP, Atti dell'Accademia di Scienze, Lettere ed Arti di Palermo

AASLAU, Atti dell'Accademia di Scienze, Lettere e Arti di Udine
AASN, Atti dell'Accademia di Scienze Morali e Politiche di Napoli
AAST, Atti dell'Accademia delle Scienze di Torino
AAVM, Atti e Memorie dell'Accademia Virgiliana di Mantova
AAWG, Abhandlungen der Akademie der Wissenschaften in Göttingen, phil.-hist. Kl., 3rd ser., Göttingen, Vandenhoeck & Ruprecht
AB, Analecta Bollandiana
ABa, L'Année Balzacienne
ABÄG, Amsterdamer Beiträge zur älteren Germanistik
ABB, Archives et Bibliothèques de Belgique — Archief- en Bibliotheekswezen in België
ABC, Annales Benjamin Constant
ABDB, Aus dem Antiquariat. Beiträge zum Börsenblatt für den deutschen Buchhandel
ABDO, Association Bourguignonne de Dialectologie et d'Onomastique, Fontaine lès Dijon
ABHL, Annual Bulletin of Historical Literature
ABI, Accademie e Biblioteche d'Italia
ABN, Anais da Biblioteca Nacional, Rio de Janeiro
ABNG, Amsterdamer Beiträge zur neueren Germanistik, Amsterdam, Rodopi
ABNG, Amsterdamer Beiträge zur neueren Germanistik
ABor, Acta Borussica
ABP, Arquivo de Bibliografia Portuguesa
ABR, American Benedictine Review
ABr, Annales de Bretagne et des Pays de l'Ouest
ABS, Acta Baltico-Slavica
ABSJ, Annual Bulletin of the Société Jersiaise
AC, Analecta Cisterciensa, Rome
ACCT, Agence de Coopération Culturelle et Technique
ACer, Anales Cervantinos, Madrid
ACIS, Association for Contemporary Iberian Studies
ACo, Acta Comeniana, Prague
AColl, Actes et Colloques
Acme, Annali della Facoltà di Filosofia e Lettere dell'Università Statale di Milano
ACP, L'Amitié Charles Péguy
ACUA, Anales del Colegio Universitario de Almería
AD, Analysen und Dokumente. Beiträge zur Neueren Literatur, Berne, Lang
ADEVA, Akademische Druck- und Verlagsanstalt, Graz
AE, Artemis Einführungen, Munich, Artemis
AE, L'Autre Europe
AEA, Anuario de Estudios Atlánticos, Las Palmas
AECI, Agencia Española de Cooperación Internacional
AEd, Arbeiten zur Editionswissenschaft, Frankfurt, Lang
AEF, Anuario de Estudios Filológicos, Cáceres
AEL, Anuario de la Escuela de Letras, Mérida, Venezuela
AELG, Anuario de Literarios Galegos
AEM, Anuario de Estudios Medievales
AF, Anuario de Filología, Barcelona
AFA, Archivo de Filología Aragonesa
AfAf, African Affairs
AfC, Afrique Contemporaine
AFe, L'Armana di Felibre
AFF, Anali Filološkog fakulteta, Belgrade
AFH, Archivum Franciscanum Historicum
AFHis, Anales de Filología Hispánica
AfHR, Afro-Hispanic Review
AfL, L'Afrique Littéraire
AFLE, Annali della Fondazione Luigi Einaudi
AFLFUB, Annali della Facoltà di Lettere e Filosofia dell'Università di Bari

AFLFUC, Annali della Facoltà di Lettere e Filosofia dell'Università di Cagliari
AFLFUG, Annali della Facoltà di Lettere e Filosofia dell'Università degli Studi di Genova
AFLFUM, Annali della Facoltà di Lettere e Filosofia dell'Università di Macerata
AFLFUN, Annali della Facoltà di Lettere e Filosofia dell'Università di Napoli
AFLFUP(SF), Annali dellà Facoltà di Lettere e Filosofia dell'Università di Perugia. 1. Studi Filosofici
AFLFUP(SLL), Annali della Facoltà di Lettere e Filosofia dell'Università di Perugia. 3. Studi Linguistici-Letterari
AFLFUS, Annali della Facoltà di Lettere e Filosofia dell'Università di Siena
AFLLS, Annali della Facoltà di Lingua e Letterature Straniere di Ca' Foscari, Venice
AFLLSB, Annali della Facoltà di Lingue e Letterature Straniere dell'Università di Bari
AFLN, Annales de la Faculté des Lettres et Sciences Humaines de Nice
AFLS, Association for French Language Studies
AFP, Archivum Fratrum Praedicatorum
AFrP, Athlone French Poets, London, The Athlone Press
AG, Anales Galdosianos
AGB, Archiv für Geschichte des Buchwesens
AGF, Anuario Galego de Filoloxia
AGGSA, Acta Germanica. German Studies in Africa
AGI, Archivio Glottologico Italiano
AGP, Archiv für Geschichte der Philosophie
AH, Archivo Hispalense
AHAM, Acta Historica et Archaeologica Mediaevalia
AHCP, Arquivos de História de Cultura Portuguesa
AHDLMA, Archives d'Histoire Doctrinale et Littéraire du Moyen Âge
AHF, Archiwum Historii Filozofii i Myśli Społecznej
AHP, Archivum Historiae Pontificae
AHPr, Annales de Haute-Provence, Digne-les-Bains
AHR, American Historical Review
AHRF, Annales Historiques de la Révolution Française
AHRou, Archives historiques du Rouergue
AHSA, Archives historiques de la Saintonge et de l'Aunis, Saintes
AHSJ, Archivum Historicum Societatis Jesu
AHSS, Annales: Histoire — Science Sociales
AI, Almanacco Italiano
AIB, Annali dell'Istituto Banfi
AIBL, Académie des Inscriptions et Belles-Lettres, Comptes Rendus
AIEM, Anales del Instituto de Estudios Madrileños
AIEO, Association Internationale d'Études Occitanes
AIFMUR, Annali dell'Istituto di Filologia Moderna dell'Università di Roma
AIFUF, Annali dell'Istituto di Filosofia dell'Università di Firenze
AIHI, Archives Internationales d'Histoire des Idées, The Hague, Nijhoff
AIHS, Archives Internationales d'Histoire des Sciences
AIL, Associação Internacional de Lusitanistas
AILLC, Associació Internacional de Llengua i Literatura Catalanes
AION(FG), Annali dell'Istituto Universitario Orientale, Naples: Sezione Germanica. Filologia Germanica
AION(FL), Annali dell'Istituto Universitario Orientale, Naples: Sezione Filologico-letteraria
AION(SF), Annali dell'Istituto Universitario Orientale, Naples: Studi Filosofici
AION(SL), Annali dell'Istituto Universitario Orientale, Naples: Sezione Linguistica

AION(SR), Annali dell'Istituto Universitario Orientale, Naples: Sezione Romanza
AION(SS), Annali dell'Istituto Universitario Orientale, Naples: Sezione Slava
AION(ST), Annali dell'Istituto Universitario Orientale, Naples: Sezione Germanica. Studi Tedeschi
AIPHS, Annuaire de l'Institut de Philologie et de l'Histoire Orientales et Slaves
AIPS, Annales Instituti Philologiae Slavica Universitatis Debreceniensis de Ludovico Kossuth Nominatae — Slavica
AISIGT, Annali dell'Istituto Storico Italo-Germanico di Trento
AITCA, Arxiu informatizat de textos catalans antics
AIV, Atti dell'Istituto Veneto
AJ, Alemannisches Jahrbuch
AJCAI, Actas de las Jornadas de Cultura Arabe e Islámica
AJFS, Australian Journal of French Studies
AJGLL, American Journal of Germanic Linguistics and Literatures
AJL, Australian Journal of Linguistics
AJP, American Journal of Philology
AKG, Archiv für Kulturgeschichte
AKML, Abhandlungen zur Kunst-, Musik- und Literaturwissenschaft, Bonn, Bouvier
AL, Anuario de Letras, Mexico
AlAm, Alba de América
ALB, Annales de la Faculté des Lettres de Besançon
ALC, African Languages and Cultures
ALE, Anales de Literatura Española, Alicante
ALEC, Anales de Literatura Española Contemporánea
ALet, Armas y Letras, Universidad de Nuevo León
ALEUA, Anales de Literatura Española de la Universidad de Alicante
ALFL, Actes de Langue Française et de Linguistique
ALG, Atlas Linguistique de la Gascogne
ALH, Acta Linguistica Hungaricae
ALHA, Anales de la Literatura Hispanoamericana
ALHa, Acta Linguistica Hafniensia
ALHisp, Anuario de Lingüística Hispánica
ALHist, Annales: Littérature et Histoire
ALit, Acta Literaria, Chile
ALitH, Acta Litteraria Hungarica
ALLI, Atlante Linguistico dei Laghi Italiani
ALM, Archives des Lettres Modernes
ALMA, Archivum Latinitatis Medii Aevi (Bulletin du Cange)
ALo, Armanac de Louzero
ALP, Atlas linguistique et ethnographique de Provence, CNRS, 1975–86
AlS, Almanac Setòri
ALT, African Literature Today
ALu, Alpes de Lumière, Fourcalquier
ALUB, Annales Littéraires de l'Université de Besançon
AM, Analecta Musicologica
AMAA, Atti e Memorie dell'Accademia d'Arcadia
AMAASLV, Atti e Memorie dell'Accademia di Agricultura, Scienze e Lettere di Verona
Amades, Amades. Arbeitspapiere und Materialien zur deutschen Sprache
AMAGP, Atti e Memorie dell'Accademia Galileiana di Scienze, Lettere ed Arti in Padova
AMal, Analecta Malacitana
AMAPet, Atti e Memorie dell'Accademia Petrarca di Lettere, Arti e Scienze, Arezzo
AMAT, Atti e Memorie dell'Accademia Toscana di Scienze e Lettere, La Colombaria
AMDLS, Arbeiten zur Mittleren Deutschen Literatur und Sprache, Berne, Lang

AMDSPAPM, Atti e Memorie della Deputazione di Storia Patria per le Antiche Province Modenesi
AMGG, Abhandlungen der Marburger Gelehrten Gesellschaft, Munich, Fink
AmH, American Hispanist
AMid, Annales du Midi
AmIn, América Indígena, Mexico
AML, Main Monographien Literaturwissenschaft, Frankfurt, Main
AMSSSP, Atti e Memorie della Società Savonese di Storia Patria
AN, Академия наук
AN, Americana Norvegica
ANABA, Asociación Nacional de Bibliotecarios, Arquiveros y Arqueólogos
AnAlf, Annali Alfieriani
AnEA, Anaquel de Estudios Arabes
ANeo, Acta Neophilologica, Ljubljana
ANF, Arkiv för nordisk filologi
AnI, Annali d'Italianistica
AnL, Anthropological Linguistics
AnM, Anuario Medieval
AnN, Annales de Normandie
AnnM, Annuale Medievale
ANPOLL, Associação Nacional de Pós-graduação e Pesquisa em Letras e Lingüística, São Paulo
ANQ, American Notes and Queries
ANS, Anglo-Norman Studies
AnS, L'Année Stendhalienne
ANTS, Anglo-Norman Text Society
AnVi, Antologia Vieusseux
ANZSGLL, Australian and New Zealand Studies in German Language and Literature, Berne, Lang
AO, Almanac occitan, Foix
AÖAW, Anzeiger der Österreichischen Akademie der Wissenschaften
AOn, Acta Onomastica
AP, Aurea Parma
APIFN, Актуальные проблемы истории философии народов СССР.
APIL, Antwerp Papers in Linguistics
APK, Aufsätze zur portugiesischen Kulturgeschichte, Görres-Gesellschaft, Münster
ApL, Applied Linguistics
APL, Associação Portuguesa de Linguística
APPP, Abhandlungen zur Philosophie, Psychologie und Pädagogik, Bonn, Bouvier
APr, Analecta Praemonstratensia
AProu, Armana Prouvençau, Marseilles
APS, Acta Philologica Scandinavica
APSL, Amsterdamer Publikationen zur Sprache und Literatur, Amsterdam, Rodopi
APSR, American Political Science Review
APUCF, Association des Publications de la Faculté des Lettres et Sciences Humaines de l'Université de Clermont-Ferrand II, Nouvelle Série
AQ, Arizona Quarterly
AqAq, Aquò d'aquí, Gap
AR, Archiv für Reformationsgeschichte
ARAJ, American Romanian Academy Journal
ARAL, Australian Review of Applied Linguistics
ARCA, ARCA: Papers of the Liverpool Latin Seminar
ArCCP, Arquivos do Centro Cultural Português, Paris
ArEM, Aragón en la Edad Media
ArFil, Archivio di Filosofia
ArI, Arthurian Interpretations
ARI, Архив русской истории
ARL, Athlone Renaissance Library
ArL, Archivum Linguisticum
ArLit, Arthurian Literature
ArP, Археографски прилози
ArSP, Archivio Storico Pugliese
ArSPr, Archivio Storico Pratese
ArSt, Archivi per la Storia
ART, Atelier Reproduction des Thèses, Univ. de Lille III, Paris, Champion
AS, The American Scholar
ASAHM, Annales de la Société d'Art et d'Histoire du Mentonnais, Menton
ASAvS, Annuaire de la Société des Amis du vieux-Strasbourg
ASB, Archivio Storico Bergamasco

ASc, Auteurs en scène, Montpellier, Les Presses du Languedoc
ASCALF, Association for the Study of Caribbean and African Literature in French
ASCALFB, ASCALF Bulletin
ASCALFY, ASCALF Yearbook
ASE, Annali di Storia dell'Esegesi
ASEES, Australian Slavonic and East European Studies
ASELGC, 1616. Anuario de la Sociedad Española de Literatura General y Comparada
ASGM, Atti del Sodalizio Glottologico Milanese
ASI, Archivio Storico Italiano
ASJ, Acta Slavonica Japonica
ASL, Archivio Storico Lombardo
ASLSP, Atti della Società Ligure di Storia Patria
ASMC, Annali di Storia Moderna e Contemporanea
ASNP, Annali della Scuola Normale Superiore di Pisa
ASNS, Archiv für das Studium der Neueren Sprachen und Literaturen
ASocRous, Annales de la Société J.-J. Rousseau
ASolP, A Sol Post, Editorial Marfil, Alcoi
ASP, Anzeiger für slavische Philologie
AsP, L'Astrado prouvençalo. Revisto Bilengo de Prouvenco/Revue Bilingue de Provence, Berre L'Etang.
ASPN, Archivio Storico per le Province Napoletane
ASPP, Archivio Storico per le Province Parmensi
ASR, Annalas da la Societad Retorumantscha
ASRSP, Archivio della Società Romana di Storia Patria
ASSO, Archivio Storico per la Sicilia Orientale
ASSUL, Annali del Dipartimento di Scienze Storiche e Sociali dell'Università di Lecce
AST, Analecta Sacra Tarraconensia
ASt, Austrian Studies
ASTic, Archivio Storico Ticinese
AŞUI, (e), (f), Analele Ştiinţifice ale Universităţii 'Al. I. Cuza' din Iaşi, secţ. e, Lingvistică, secţ. f, Literatură
AT, Athenäums Taschenbücher, Frankfurt, Athenäum
ATB, Altdeutsche Textbibliothek, Tübingen, Niemeyer
ATCA, Arxiu de Textos Catalans Antics, IEC, Barcelona
Ate, Nueva Atenea, Universidad de Concepción, Chile
ATO, A Trabe de Ouro
ATS, Arbeiten und Texte zur Slavistik, Munich, Sagner
ATV, Aufbau Taschenbuch Verlag, Berlin, Aufbau
AtV, Ateneo Veneto
AUBLLR, Analele Universităţii Bucureşti, Limba şi literatura română
AUBLLS, Analele Universităţii Bucureşti, Limbi şi literaturi străine
AUC, Anales de la Universidad de Cuenca
AUCP, Acta Universitatis Carolinae Pragensis
AuE, Arbeiten und Editionen zur Mittleren Deutschen Literatur, Stuttgart–Bad Cannstatt, Frommann-Holzboog
AUL, Acta Universitatis Lodziensis
AUL, Annali della Facoltà di Lettere e Filosofia dell'Università di Lecce
AUMCS, Annales Uniwersytetu Marii Curie-Skłodowskiej, Lublin
AUML, Anales de la Universidad de Murcia: Letras
AUMLA, Journal of the Australasian Universities Modern Language Association
AUN, Annali della Facoltà di Lettere e Filosofia dell'Università di Napoli
AUNCFP, Acta Universitatis Nicolai Copernici. Filologia Polska, Toruń
AUPO, Acta Universitatis Palackianae Olomucensis
AUS, American University Studies, Berne — New York, Lang

AUSP, Annali dell'Università per Stranieri di Perugia
AUSt, Acta Universitatis Stockholmiensis
AUTŞF, Analele Universităţii din Timişoara, Ştiinţe Filologice
AUU, Acta Universitatis Upsaliensis
AUW, Acta Universitatis Wratislaviensis
AVen, Archivio Veneto
AVEP, Assouciacien vareso pèr l'ensignamen dòu prouvençou, La Farlède
AVEPB, *Bulletin AVEP*, La Farlède
AvT, L'Avant-Scène Théâtre
AWR, Anglo-Welsh Review

BA, Bollettino d'Arte
BAAA, Bulletin de l'Association des Amis d'Alain
BAAG, Bulletin des Amis d'André Gide
BAAJG, Bulletin de l'Association des Amis de Jean Giono
BAAL, Boletín de la Academia Argentina de Letras
BaB, Bargfelder Bote
BAC, Biblioteca de Autores Cristianos
BACol, Boletín de la Academia Colombiana
BÄDL, Beiträge zur Älteren Deutschen Literaturgeschichte, Berne, Lang
BADLit, Bonner Arbeiten zur deutschen Literatur, Bonn, Bouvier
BAE, Biblioteca de Autores Españoles
BAEO, Boletín de la Asociación Española de Orientalistas
BAFJ, Bulletin de l'Association Francis Jammes
BAG, Boletín de la Academia Gallega
BAIEO, Bulletins de l'Association Internationale d'Études Occitanes
BAJR, Bulletin des Amis de Jules Romains
BAJRAF, Bulletin des Amis de Jacques Rivière et d'Alain-Fournier
BALI, Bollettino dell'Atlante Linguistico Italiano
BALM, Bollettino dell'Atlante Linguistico Mediterraneo
BalS, Balkan Studies, Institute for Balkan Studies, Thessaloniki
BAN, Българска Академия на Науките, София
BAO, Biblioteca Abat Oliva, Publicacions de l'Abadia de Montserrat, Barcelona
BAPC, Bulletin de l'Association Paul Claudel
BAPRLE, Boletín de la Academia Puertorrigueña de la Lengua Española
BAR, Biblioteca dell'Archivum Romanicum
BARLLF, Bulletin de l'Académie Royale de Langues et de Littératures Françaises de Bruxelles
BAWA, Bayerische Akademie der Wissenschaften. Phil.-hist. Kl. Abhandlungen, n.F.
BB, Biblioteca Breve, Lisbon
BB, Bulletin of Bibliography
BBAHLM, Boletín Bibliografico de la Asociación Hispánica de Literatura Medieval
BBaud, Bulletin Baudelairien
BBB, Berner Beiträge zur Barockgermanistik, Berne, Lang
BBGN, Brünner Beiträge zur Germanistik und Nordistik
BBib, Bulletin du Bibliophile
BBL, Bayreuther Beiträge zur Literaturwissenschaft, Frankfurt, Lang
BBLI, Bremer Beiträge zur Literatur- und Ideengeschichte, Frankfurt, Lang
BBMP, Boletín de la Biblioteca de Menéndez Pelayo
BBN, Bibliotheca Bibliographica Neerlandica, Nieuwkoop, De Graaf
BBNDL, Berliner Beiträge zur neueren deutschen Literaturgeschichte, Berne, Lang
BBSANZ, Bulletin of the Bibliographical Society of Australia and New Zealand

BBSIA, Bulletin Bibliographique de la Société Internationale Arthurienne
BBSMES, Bulletin of the British Society for Middle Eastern Studies
BBUC, Boletim da Biblioteca da Universidade de Coimbra
BC, Bulletin of the 'Comediantes', University of Wisconsin
BCB, Boletín Cultural y Bibliográfico, Bogatá
BCEC, Bwletin Cymdeithas Emynwyr Cymru
BCél, Bulletin Célinien
BCh, Болдинские чтения
BCLSMP, Académie Royale de Belgique: Bulletin de la Classe des Lettres et des Sciences Morales et Politiques
BCMV, Bollettino Civici Musei Veneziani
BCRLT, Bulletin du Centre de Romanistique et de Latinité Tardive
BCS, Bulletin of Canadian Studies
BCSM, Bulletin of the Cantigueiros de Santa Maria
BCSS, Bollettino del Centro di Studi Filologici e Linguistici Siciliani
BCSV, Bollettino del Centro di Studi Vichiani
BCZG, Blätter der Carl Zuckmayer Gesellschaft
BD, Беларуская думка
BDADA, Bulletin de documentation des Archives départementales de l'Aveyron, Rodez
BDB, Börsenblatt für den deutschen Buchhandel
BDBA, Bien Dire et Bien Aprandre
BDL, Beiträge zur Deutschen Literatur, Frankfurt, Lang
BDP, Beiträge zur Deutschen Philologie, Giessen, Schmitz
BEA, Bulletin des Études Africaines
BEC, Bibliothèque de l'École des Chartes
BelE, Беларуская энцыклапедыя
BelL, Беларуская лінгвістыка
BelS, Беларускі сьвет
BEP, Bulletin des Études Portugaises
BEPar, Bulletin des Études Parnassiennes et Symbolistes
BEzLit, Български език и литература
BF, Boletim de Filologia
BFA, Bulletin of Francophone Africa
BFC, Boletín de Filología, Univ. de Chile
BFE, Boletín de Filología Española
BFF, Bulletin Francophone de Finlande
BFFGL, Boletín de la Fundación Federico García Lorca
BFi, Bollettino Filosofico
BFLS, Bulletin de la Faculté des Lettres de Strasbourg
BFo, Biuletyn Fonograficzny
BFPLUL, Bibliothèque de la Faculté de Philosophie et Lettres de l'Université de Liège
BFR, Bibliothèque Française et Romane, Paris, Klincksieck
BFR, Bulletin of the Fondation C.F. Ramuz
BFr, Börsenblatt Frankfurt
BG, Bibliotheca Germanica, Tübingen, Francke
BGB, Bulletin de l'Association Guillaume Budé
BGDSL, Beiträge zur Geschichte der deutschen Sprache und Literatur, Tübingen
BGKT, Беларускае грамадска-культуральнае таварыства
BGL, Boletin Galego de Literatura
BGLKAJ, Beiträge zur Geschichte der Literatur und Kunst des 18. Jahrhunderts, Heidelberg, Winter
BGP, Bristol German Publications, Bristol U.P
BGREC, Bulletin du Groupe de Recherches et d'Études du Clermontais, Clermont-l'Hérault
BGS, Beiträge zur germanistischen Sprachwissenschaft, Hamburg, Buske
BGS, Beiträge zur Geschichte der Sprachwissenschaft
BGT, Blackwell German Texts, Oxford, Blackwell
BH, Bulletin Hispanique
BHGLL, Berliner Hefte zur Geschichte des literarischen Lebens

BHR, Bibliothèque d'Humanisme et Renaissance
BHS, Bulletin of Hispanic Studies, Liverpool
BHS(G), Bulletin of Hispanic Studies, Glasgow (1995–2001)
BHS(L), Bulletin of Hispanic Studies, Liverpool (1995–2001)
BI, Bibliographisches Institut, Leipzig
BIABF, Bulletin d'informations-Association des bibliothécaires français
BibAN, Библиотека Академии наук СССР
BIDS, Bulletin of the International Dostoevsky Society, Klagenfurt
BIEA, Boletín del Instituto de Estudios Asturianos
BIHBR, Bulletin de l'Institut Historique Belge de Rome
BIHR, Bulletin of the Institute of Historical Research
BIO, Bulletin de l'Institut Occitan, Pau
BJA, British Journal of Aesthetics
BJCS, British Journal for Canadian Studies
BJECS, The British Journal for Eighteenth-Century Studies
BJHP, British Journal of the History of Philosophy
BJHS, British Journal of the History of Science
BJL, Belgian Journal of Linguistics
BJR, Bulletin of the John Rylands University Library of Manchester
BKF, Beiträge zur Kleist-Forschung
BL, Brain and Language
BLAR, Bulletin of Latin American Research
BLBI, Bulletin des Leo Baeck Instituts
BLe, Börsenblatt Leipzig
BLFCUP, Bibliothèque de Littérature Française Contemporaine de l'Université Paris 7
BLI, Beiträge zur Linguistik und Informationsverarbeitung
BLi, Беларуская літаратура. Міжвузаўскі зборнік.
BLJ, British Library Journal
BLL, Beiträge zur Literatur und Literaturwissenschaft des 20. Jahrhunderts, Berne, Lang
BLR, Bibliothèque Littéraire de la Renaissance, Geneva, Slatkine–Paris, Champion
BLR, Bodleian Library Record
BLVS, Bibliothek des Literarischen Vereins, Stuttgart, Hiersemann
BM, Bibliothek Metzier, Stuttgart
BMBP, Bollettino del Museo Bodoniano di Parma
BMCP, Bollettino del Museo Civico di Padova
BML, Беларуская мова і літаратура ў школе
BMo, Беларуская мова. Міжвузаўскі зборнік
BNE, Beiträge zur neueren Epochenforschung, Berne, Lang
BNF, Beiträge zur Namenforschung
BNL, Beiträge zur neueren Literaturgeschichte, 3rd ser., Heidelberg, Winter
BNP, Beiträge zur nordischen Philologie, Basel, Helbing & Lichtenhahn
BNTL, Bibliografie van de Nederlandse Taal- en Letterkunde
BO, Biblioteca Orientalis
BOCES, Boletín del Centro de Estudios del Siglo XVIII, Oviedo
BOP, Bradford Occasional Papers
BP, Български писател
BP, Lo Bornat dau Perigòrd
BPTJ, Biuletyn Polskiego Towarzystwa Językoznawczego
BR, Болгарская русистика.
BRA, Bonner Romanistische Arbeiten, Berne, Lang
BRABLB, Boletín de la Real Academia de Buenas Letras de Barcelona
BRAC, Boletín de la Real Academia de Córdoba de Ciencias, Bellas Letras, y Nobles Artes
BRAE, Boletín de la Real Academia Española
BRAG, Boletín de la Real Academia Gallega
BRAH, Boletín de la Real Academia de la Historia
BrC, Bruniana & Campanelliana

BRIES, Bibliothèque Russe de l'Institut d'Études Slaves, Paris, Institut d'Études Slaves
BRJL, Bulletin ruského jazyka a literatury
BrL, La Bretagne Linguistique
BRP, Beiträge zur romanischen Philologie
BS, Biuletyn slawistyczny, Łódź
BSAHH, Bulletin de la Société archéologique et historique des hauts cantons de l'Hérault, Bédarieux
BSAHL, Bulletin de la Société archéologique et historique du Limousin, Limoges
BSAHLSG, Bulletin de la Société Archéologique, Historique, Littéraire et Scientifique du Gers
BSAM, Bulletin de la Société des Amis de Montaigne
BSAMPAC, Bulletin de la Société des Amis de Marcel Proust et des Amis de Combray
BSASLB, Bulletin de la Société Archéologique, Scientifique et Littéraire de Béziers
BSATG, Bulletin de la Société Archéologique de Tarn-et-Garonne
BSBS, Bollettino Storico–Bibliografico Subalpino
BSCC, Boletín de la Sociedad Castellonense de Cultura
BSD, Bithell Series of Dissertations — MHRA Texts and Dissertations, London, Modern Humanities Research Association
BSD, Bulletin de la Société de Borda, Dax
BSDL, Bochumer Schriften zur deutschen Literatur, Berne, Lang
BSDSL, Basler Studien zur deutschen Sprache und Literatur, Tübingen, Francke
BSE, Галоўная рэдакцыя Беларускай савеюкай энцыклапедыі
BSEHA, Bulletin de la Société d'Études des Hautes-Alpes, Gap
BSEHTD, Bulletin de la Société d'Études Historiques du texte dialectal
BSELSAL, Bulletin de la Société des Études Littéraires, Scientifiques et Artistiques du Lot
BSF, Bollettino di Storia della Filosofia
BSG, Berliner Studien zur Germanistik, Frankfurt, Lang
BSHAP, Bulletin de la Société Historique et Archéologique du Périgord, Périgueux
BSHPF, Bulletin de la Société de l'Histoire du Protestantisme Français
BSIH, Brill's Studies in Intellectual History, Leiden, Brill
BSIS, Bulletin of the Society for Italian Studies
BSL, Bollettino di Studi Latini
BSLA, Bulletin Suisse de Linguistique Appliquée
BSLLW, Bulletin de la Société de Langue et Littérature Wallonnes
BSLP, Bulletin de la Société de Linguistique de Paris
BSLSAC, Bulletin de la Société des lettres sciences et arts de la Corrèze
BSLV, Bollettino della Società Letteraria di Verona
BSM, Birmingham Slavonic Monographs, University of Birmingham
BSOAS, Bulletin of the School of Oriental and African Studies
BSP, Bollettino Storico Pisano
BSPC, Bulletin de la Société Paul Claudel
BSPia, Bollettino Storico Piacentino
BSPN, Bollettino Storico per le Province di Novara
BSPSP, Bollettino della Società Pavese di Storia Patria
BSR, Bulletin de la Société Ramond. Bagneres-de-Bigorre
BsR, Beck'sche Reihe, Munich, Beck
BSRS, Bulletin of the Society for Renaissance Studies
BSS, Bulletin of Spanish Studies, Glasgow
BSSAAPC, Bollettino della Società per gli Studi Storici, Archeologici ed Artistici della Provincia di Cuneo

BSSCLE, Bulletin of the Society for the Study of the Crusades and the Latin East
BSSP, Bullettino Senese di Storia Patria
BSSPHS, Bulletin of the Society for Spanish and Portuguese Historical Studies
BSSPin, Bollettino della Società Storica Pinerolese, Pinerolo, Piemonte, Italy.
BSSV, Bollettino della Società Storica Valtellinese
BSZJPS, Bałtosłowiańskie związki językowe. Prace Slawistyczne
BT, Богословские труды, Moscow
BTe, Biblioteca Teatrale
BTH, Boletim de Trabalhos Historicos
BulEz, Български език
BW, Bibliothek und Wissenschaft
BySt, Byzantine Studies

CA, Cuadernos Americanos
CAAM, Cahiers de l'Association Les Amis de Milosz
CAB, Commentari dell'Ateneo di Brescia
CAC, Les Cahiers de l'Abbaye de Créteil
CadL, Cadernos da Lingua
CAFLS, Cahiers AFLS
CAG, Cahiers André Gide
CAH, Les Cahiers Anne Hébert
CaH, Les Cahiers de l'Humanisme
CAIEF, Cahiers de l'Association Internationale des Études Françaises
CalLet, Calabria Letteraria
CAm, Casa de las Américas, Havana
CAm, Casa de las Américas, Havana
CanJL, Canadian Journal of Linguistics
CanJP, Canadian Journal of Philosophy
CanL, Canadian Literature
CanSP, Canadian Slavonic Papers
CanSS, Canadian–American Slavic Studies
CarA, Carmarthenshire Antiquary
CARB, Cahiers des Amis de Robert Brasillach
CarQ, Caribbean Quarterly
CAT, Cahiers d'Analyse Textuelle, Liège, Les Belles Lettres
CatR, Catalan Review
CAVL, Cahiers des Amis de Valery Larbaud
CB, Cuadernos Bibliográficos
CC, Comparative Criticism
CCe, Cahiers du Cerf XX
CCend, Continent Cendrars
CCF, Cuadernos de la Cátedra Feijoo
CCMA, Champion Classiques Moyen Age, Paris, Champion
CCMe, Cahiers de Civilisation Médiévale
CCol, Cahiers Colette
CCU, Cuadernos de la Cátedra M. de Unamuno
CD, Cuadernos para el Diálogo
CDA, Christliche deutsche Autoren des 20. Jahrhunderts, Berne, Lang
CdA, Camp de l'Arpa
CDB, Coleção Documentos Brasileiros
CDi, Cuadernos dieciochistas
CDr, Comparative Drama
ČDS, Čeština doma a ve světě
CDs, Cahiers du Dix-septième, Athens, Georgia
CDU, Centre de Documentation Universitaire
CduC, Cahiers de CERES. Série littéraire, Tunis
CE, Cahiers Élisabéthains
CEA, Cahiers d'Études Africaines
CEAL, Centro Editor de América Latina
CEB, Cahiers Ethier-Blais
CEC, Conselho Estadual de Cultura, Comissão de Literatura, São Paulo
CEC, Cahiers d'Études Cathares, Narbonne
CECAES, Centre d'Études des Cultures d'Aquitaine et d'Europe du Sud, Université de Bordeaux III
CEcr, Corps Écrit
CEDAM, Casa Editrice Dott. A. Milani
CEG, Cuadernos de Estudios Gallegos

CEL, Cadernos de Estudos Lingüísticos, Campinas, Brazil
CELO, Centre d'Etude de la Littérature Occitane, Bordes.
CEM, Cahiers d'Études Médiévales, Univ. of Montreal
CEMa, Cahiers d'Études Maghrebines, Cologne
CEMed, Cuadernos de Estudios Medievales
CEPL, Centre d'Étude et de Promotion de la Lecture, Paris
CEPON, Centre per l'estudi e la promocion de l'Occitan normat.
CEPONB, CEPON Bulletin d'échange.
CER, Cahiers d'Études Romanes
CERCLiD, Cahiers d'Études Romanes, Centre de Linguistique et de Dialectologie, Toulouse
CEROC, Centre d'Enseignement et de Recherche d'Oc, Paris
CERoum, Cahiers d'Études Roumaines
CeS, Cultura e Scuola
CESCM, Centre d'Études Supérieures de Civilisation Médiévale, Poitiers
CET, Centro Editoriale Toscano
CEtGer, Cahiers d'Études Germaniques
CF, Les Cahiers de Fontenay
CFC, Contemporary French Civilization
CFI, Cuadernos de Filologia Italiana
CFLA, Cuadernos de Filología. Literaturas: Análisis, Valencia
CFM, Cahiers François Mauriac
CFMA, Collection des Classiques Français du Moyen Âge
CFol, Classical Folia
CFS, Cahiers Ferdinand de Saussure
CFSLH, Cuadernos de Filología: Studia Linguistica Hispanica
CFTM, Classiques Français des Temps Modernes, Paris, Champion
CG, Cahiers de Grammaire
CGD, Cahiers Georges Duhamel
CGFT, Critical Guides to French Texts, London, Grant & Cutler
CGGT, Critical Guides to German Texts, London, Grant & Cutler
CGP, Carleton Germanic Papers
CGS, Colloquia Germanica Stetinensia
CGST, Critical Guides to Spanish Texts, London, Támesis, Grant & Cutler
CH, Crítica Hispánica
CHA, Cuadernos Hispano-Americanos
CHAC, Cuadernos Hispano-Americanos. Los complementarios
CHB, Cahiers Henri Bosco
ChC, Chemins Critiques
CHCHMC, Cylchgrawn Hanes Cymdeithas Hanes y Methodistiaid Calfinaidd
CHLR, Cahiers d'Histoire des Littératures Romanes
CHP, Cahiers Henri Pourrat
CHR, Catholic Historical Review
ChR, The Chesterton Review
ChRev, Chaucer Review
ChrA, Chroniques Allemandes
ChrI, Chroniques Italiennes
ChrL, Christianity and Literature
ChrN, Chronica Nova
ChS, Champs du Signe
CHST, Caernarvonshire Historical Society Transactions
CHum, Computers and the Humanities
CI, Critical Inquiry
CiD, La Ciudad de Dios
CIDO, Centre International de Documentation Occitane, Béziers
CIEDS, Centre International d'Etudes du dix-huitième siècle, Ferney-Voltaire
CIEL, Centre International de l'Écrit en Langue d'Òc, Berre
CIEM, Comité International d'Études Morisques
CIF, Cuadernos de Investigación Filológica
CIH, Cuadernos de Investigación Historica
CILF, Conseil International de la Langue Française
CILH, Cuadernos para Investigación de la Literatura Hispanica

CILL, Cahiers de l'Institut de Linguistique de l'Université de Louvain
CILT, Centre for Information on Language Teaching, London
CIMAGL, Cahiers de l'Institut du Moyen Âge Grec et Latin, Copenhagen
CIn, Cahiers Intersignes
CIRDOC, Centre Inter-Régional de Développement de l'Occitan, Béziers
CIRVI, Centro Interuniversitario di Ricerche sul 'Viaggio in Italia', Moncalieri
CISAM, Centro Italiano di Studi sull'Alto Medioevo
CIt, Carte Italiane
CIUS, Canadian Institute of Ukrainian Studies Edmonton
CivC, Civiltà Cattolica
CJ, Conditio Judaica, Tübingen, Niemeyer
CJb, Celan-Jahrbuch
CJC, Cahiers Jacques Chardonne
CJG, Cahiers Jean Giraudoux
CJIS, Canadian Journal of Italian Studies
ČJL, Český jazyk a literatura
CJNS, Canadian Journal of Netherlandic Studies
CJP, Cahiers Jean Paulhan
CJR, Cahiers Jules Romains
CL, Cuadernos de Leiden
CL, Comparative Literature
ČL, Česká literatura
CLA, Cahiers du LACITO
CLAJ, College Language Association Journal
CLCC, Cahiers de Littérature Canadienne Comparée
CLCHM, Cahiers de Linguistique et Civilisation Hispaniques Médiévales
CLCWeb, Comparative Literature and Culture, A WWWeb Journal, <http://www.arts.ualberta.ca/clcwebjournal/>
CLE, Comunicaciones de Literatura Española, Buenos Aires
CLe, Cahiers de Lexicologie
CLEAM, Coleción de Literatura Española Aljamiado–Morisca, Madrid, Gredos
CLESP, Cooperativa Libraria Editrice degli Studenti dell'Università di Padova, Padua
CLett, Critica Letteraria
CLEUP, Cooperativa Libraria Editrice, Università di Padova
CLF, Cahiers de Linguistique Française
CLHM, Cahiers de Linguistique Hispanique Médiévale
CLin, Cercetări de Lingvistica
CLit, Cadernos de Literatura, Coimbra
ClL, La Clau lemosina
CLO, Cahiers Linguistiques d'Ottawa
ClP, Classical Philology
CLS, Comparative Literature Studies
CLSl, Cahiers de Linguistique Slave
CLTA, Cahiers de Linguistique Théorique et Appliquée
CLTL, Cadernos de Lingüística e Teoria da Literatura
CLUEB, Cooperativa Libraria Universitaria Editrice Bologna
CLus, Convergência Lusíada, Rio de Janeiro
CM, Cahiers Montesquieu, Naples, Liguori — Paris, Universitas — Oxford, Voltaire Foundation
CM, Classica et Mediaevalia
CMA, Cahier Marcel Aymé
CMar, Cuadernos de Marcha
CMCS, Cambrian Medieval Celtic Studies
CMERSA, Center for Medieval and Early Renaissance Studies, State University of New York at Binghamton. Acta
ČMF (PhP), Časopis pro moderni filologii: Philologica Pragensia
CMHLB, Cahiers du Monde Hispanique et Luso-Brésilien
CMi, Cultura Milano
CML, Classical and Modern Literature
ČMM, Časopis Matice Moravské
CMon, Communication Monographs
CMP, Cahiers Marcel Proust
CMRS, Cahiers du Monde Russe et Soviétique
CN, Cultura Neolatina
CNat, Les Cahiers Naturalistes

CNCDP, Comissão Nacional para a Comemoração dos Descobrimentos Portugueses, Lisbon
CNor, Los Cuadernos del Norte
CNR, Consiglio Nazionale delle Ricerche
CNRS, Centre National de la Recherche Scientifique
CNSL, Centro Nazionale di Studi Leopardiani
CNSM, Centro Nazionale di Studi Manzoniani
CO, Camera Obscura
CoF, Collectanea Franciscana
CogL, Cognitive Linguistics
COJ, Cambridge Opera Journal
COK, Centralny Ośrodek Kultury, Warsaw
CoL, Compás de Letras
ColA, Colóquio Artes
ColGer, Colloquia Germanica
ColH, Colloquium Helveticum
ColL, Colóquio Letras
ComB, Communications of the International Brecht Society
ComGer, Comunicaciones Germánicas
CompL, Computational Linguistics
ConL, Contrastive Linguistics
ConLet, Il Confronto Letterario
ConLit, Contemporary Literature
ConS, Condorcet Studies
CORDAE, Centre Occitan de Recèrca, de Documentacion e d'Animacion Etnografica, Cordes
CorWPL, Cornell Working Papers in Linguistics
CP, Castrum Peregrini
CPE, Cahiers Prévost d'Exiles, Grenoble
CPL, Cahiers Paul Léautand
CPr, Cahiers de Praxématique
CPR, Chroniques de Port-Royal
CPUC, Cadernos PUC, São Paulo
CQ, Critical Quarterly
CR, Contemporary Review
CRAC, Cahiers Roucher — André Chénier
CRCL, Canadian Review of Comparative Literature
CREL, Cahiers Roumains d'Études Littéraires
CREO, Centre régional d'études occitanes
CRev, Centennial Review
CRI, Cuadernos de Ruedo Ibérico
CRIAR, Cahiers du Centre de Recherches Ibériques et Ibéro-Américains de l'Université de Rouen
CRIN, Cahiers de Recherches des Instituts Néerlandais de Langue et Littérature Françaises
CRITM, Cahiers RITM, Centre de Recherches Interdisciplinaires sur les Textes Modernes, Université de Paris X-Nanterre
CRLN, Comparative Romance Linguistics Newsletter
CRM, Cahiers de Recherches Médiévales (XIIIe–XVe siècles), Paris, Champion
CRQ, Cahiers Raymond Queneau
CRR, Cincinnati Romance Review
CRRI, Centre de Recherche sur la Renaissance Italienne, Paris
CRRR, Centre de Recherches Révolutionnaires et Romantiques, Université Blaise-Pascal, Clermont-Ferrand.
CrT, Critica del Testo
CS, Cornish Studies
CSAM, Centro di Studi sull'Alto Medioevo, Spoleto
ČSAV, Československá akademie věd
CSDI, Centro di Studio per la Dialettologia Italiana
CSem, Caiete de Semiotică
CSFLS, Centro di Studi Filologici e Linguistici Siciliani, Palermo
CSG, Cambridge Studies in German, Cambridge U.P.
CSGLL, Canadian Studies in German Language and Literature, Berne — New York — Frankfurt, Lang
CSH, Cahiers des Sciences Humaines
CSIC, Consejo Superior de Investigaciones Científicas, Madrid
CSJP, Cahiers Saint-John Perse
CSl, Critica Slovia, Florence

CSLAIL, Cambridge Studies in Latin American Iberian Literature, CUP
CSLI, Center for the Study of Language and Information, Stanford University
CSM, Les Cahiers de Saint-Martin
ČSp, Československý spisovatel
CSS, California Slavic Studies
CSSH, Comparative Studies in Society and History
CST, Cahiers de Sémiotique Textuelle
CSt, Critica Storica
CT, Christianity Today
CTC, Cuadernos de Teatro Clásico
CTE, Cuadernos de Traducción e Interpretación
CTe, Cuadernos de Teología
CTed, Cultura Tedesca
CTex, Cahiers Textuels
CTH, Cahiers Tristan l'Hermite
CTh, Ciencia Tomista
CTHS, Comité des Travaux Historiques et Scientifiques, Paris
CTJ, Cahiers de Théâtre. Jeu
CTL, Current Trends in Linguistics
CTLin, Commissione per i Testi di Lingua, Bologna
CUECM, Cooperativa Universitaria Editrice Catanese Magistero
CUER MA, Centre Universitaire d'Études et de Recherches Médiévales d'Aix, Université de Provence, Aix-en-Provence
CUP, Cambridge University Press
CUUCV, Cultura Universitaria de la Universidad Central de Venezuela
CV, Città di Vita
CWPL, Catalan Working Papers in Linguistics
CWPWL, Cardiff Working Papers in Welsh Linguistics

DAEM, Deutsches Archiv für Erforschung des Mittelalters
DaF, Deutsch als Fremdsprache
DAG, Dictionnaire onomasiologique de l'ancien gascon, Tübingen, Niemeyer
DalR, Dalhousie Review
DanU, Dansk Udsyn
DAO, Dictionnaire onomasiologique de l'ancien occitan, Tübingen, Niemeyer
DaSt, Dante Studies
DB, Дзяржаўная бібліятэка БССР
DB, Doitsu Bungaku
DBl, Driemaandelijkse Bladen
DBO, Deutsche Bibliothek des Ostens, Berlin, Nicolai
DBR, Les Dialectes Belgo-Romans
DBr, Doitsu Bungakoranko
DCFH, Dicenda. Cuadernos de Filología Hispánica
DD, Diskussion Deutsch
DDG, Deutsche Dialektgeographie, Marburg, Elwert
DDJ, Deutsches Dante-Jahrbuch
DegSec, Degré Second
DELTA, Revista de Documentação de Estudos em Lingüística Teórica e Aplicada, São Paulo
DESB, Delta Epsilon Sigma Bulletin, Dubuque, Iowa
DeutB, Deutsche Bücher
DeutUB, Deutschungarische Beiträge
DFC, Durham French Colloquies
DFS, Dalhousie French Studies
DGF, Dokumentation germanistischer Forschung, Frankfurt, Lang
DgF, Danmarks gamle Folkeviser
DHA, Diálogos Hispánicos de Amsterdam, Rodopi
DHR, Duquesne Hispanic Review
DhS, Dix-huitième Siècle
DI, Deutscher Idealismus, Stuttgart, Klett-Cotta Verlag
DI, Декоративное искусство
DIAS, Dublin Institute for Advanced Studies
DiL, Dictionnairique et Lexicographie
DiS, Dickinson Studies
DisA, Dissertation Abstracts
DisSlSHL, Dissertationes Slavicae: Sectio Historiae Litterarum
DisSlSL, Dissertationes Slavicae: Sectio Linguistica
DisSoc, Discourse and Society
DisSt, Discourse Studies
DK, Duitse Kroniek

DkJb, Deutschkanadisches Jahrbuch
DKV, Deutscher Klassiker Verlag, Frankfurt
DL, Детская литература
DLA, Deutsche Literatur von den Anfängen bis 1700, Berne — Frankfurt — Paris — New York, Lang
DLit, Discurso Literario
DLM, Deutsche Literatur des Mittelalters (Wissenschaftliche Beiträge der Ernst-Moritz-Arndt-Universität Greifswald)
DLR, Deutsche Literatur in Reprints, Munich, Fink
DLRECL, Diálogo de la Lengua. Revista de Estudio y Creación Literaria, Cuenca
DM, Dirassat Masrahiyyat
DMRPH, De Montfort Research Papers in the Humanities, De Montfort University, Leicester
DMTS, Davis Medieval Texts and Studies, Leiden, Brill
DN, Дружба народов
DNT, De Nieuwe Taalgids
DOLMA, Documenta Onomastica Litteralia Medii Aevi, Hildesheim, Olms
DOM, Dictionnaire de l'occitan médiéval, Tübingen, Niemeyer, 1996–
DosS, Dostoevsky Studies
DoV, Дошкольное воспитание
DPA, Documents pour servir à l'histoire du département des Pyrénées-Atlantiques, Pau
DPL, De Proprietatibus Litterarum, The Hague, Mouton
DpL, День поэзии, Leningrad
DpM, День поэзии, Moscow
DR, Drama Review
DRev, Downside Review
DRLAV, DRLAV, Revue de Linguistique
DS, Diderot Studies
DSEÜ, Deutsche Sprache in Europa und Übersee, Stuttgart, Steiner
DSL, Det danske Sprog- og Litteraturselskab
DSp, Deutsche Sprache
DSRPD, Documenta et Scripta. Rubrica Paleographica et Diplomatica, Barcelona
DSS, XVIIe Siècle
DSt, Deutsche Studien, Meisenheim, Hain
DSt, Danske Studier
DT, Deutsche Texte, Tübingen, Niemeyer
DteolT, Dansk teologisk Tidsskrift
DtL, Die deutsche Literatur
DTM, Deutsche Texte des Mittelalters, Berlin, Akademie
DTV, Deutscher Taschenbuch Verlag, Munich
DUB, Deutschunterricht, East Berlin
DUJ, Durham University Journal (New Series)
DUS, Der Deutschunterricht, Stuttgart
DUSA, Deutschunterricht in Südafrika
DV, Дальний Восток
DVA, Deutsche Verlags-Anstalt, Stuttgart
DVLG, Deutsche Vierteljahresschrift für Literaturwissenschaft und Geistesgeschichte

E, Verlag Enzyklopädie, Leipzig
EAL, Early American Literature
EALS, Europäische Aufklärung in Literatur und Sprache, Frankfurt, Lang
EAS, Europe-Asia Studies
EB, Estudos Brasileiros
EBal, Etudes Balkaniques
EBLUL, European Bureau for Lesser Used Languages
EBM, Era Bouts dera mountanho, Aurignac
EBTch, Études Balkaniques Tchécoslovaques
EC, El Escritor y la Crítica, Colección Persiles, Madrid, Taurus
EC, Études Celtiques
ECan, Études Canadiennes
ECar, Espace Caraïbe
ECent, The Eighteenth Century, Lubbock, Texas
ECentF, Eighteenth-Century Fiction

ECF, Écrits du Canada Français
ECI, Eighteenth-Century Ireland
ECIG, Edizioni Culturali Internazionali Genova
ECL, Eighteenth-Century Life
ECla, Les Études Classiques
ECon, España Contemporánea
EconH, Économie et Humanisme
EcR, Echo de Rabastens. Les Veillées Rabastinoises, Rabastens (Tarn)
ECr, Essays in Criticism
ECre, Études Créoles
ECS, Eighteenth Century Studies
EdCat, Ediciones Cátedra, Madrid
EDESA, Ediciones Españolas S.A.
EDHS, Études sur le XVIIIe Siècle
EDIPUCRS, Editora da Pontífica Universidade Católica de Rio Grande do Sul, Porto Alegre
EDL, Études de Lettres
EDT, Edizioni di Torino
EDUSC, Editora da Universidade de Santa Catarina
EE, Erasmus in English
EEM, East European Monographs
EEQ, East European Quarterly
EF, Erträge der Forschung, Darmstadt, Wissenschaftliche Buchgesellschaft
EF, Études Françaises
EFAA, Échanges Franco-Allemands sur l'Afrique
EFE, Estudios de Fonética Experimental
EFF, Ergebnisse der Frauenforschung, Stuttgart, Metzler
EFil, Estudios Filológicos, Valdivia, Chile
EFL, Essays in French Literature, Univ. of Western Australia
EFR, Éditeurs Français Réunis
EG, Études Germaniques
EH, Europäische Hochschulschriften, Berne–Frankfurt, Lang
EH, Estudios Humanísticos
EHer, Etudes Héraultaises, Montpellier
EHESS, École des Hautes Études en Sciences Sociales, Paris
EHF, Estudios Humanísticos. Filología
EHN, Estudios de Historia Novohispana
EHQ, European History Quarterly
EHR, English Historical Review
EHRC, European Humanities Research Centre, University of Oxford
EHS, Estudios de Historia Social
EHT, Exeter Hispanic Texts, Exeter
EIA, Estudos Ibero-Americanos
EIP, Estudos Italianos em Portugal
EJJR, Études Jean-Jacques Rousseau
EJWS, European Journal of Women's Studies
EL, Esperienze Letterarie
El, Elementa, Würzburg, Königshausen & Neumann –Amsterdam, Rodopi
ELA, Études de Linguistique Appliquée
ELF, Études Littéraires Françaises, Paris, J.-M. Place — Tübingen, Narr
ELH, English Literary History
ELin, Estudos Lingüísticos, São Paulo
ELit, Essays in Literature
ELL, Estudos Lingüísticos e Literários, Bahia
ELLC, Estudis de Llengua i Literatura Catalanes
ELLF, Études de Langue et Littérature Françaises, Tokyo
ELLUG, Éditions littéraires et linguistiques de l'université de Grenoble
ELM, Études littéraires maghrebines
ELR, English Literary Renaissance
EMarg, Els Marges
EMH, Early Music History
EMS, Essays in Medieval Studies
EMus, Early Music
ENC, Els Nostres Clàssics, Barcelona, Barcino
ENSJF, École Nationale Supérieure de Jeunes Filles
EO, Edition Orpheus, Tübingen, Francke
EO, Europa Orientalis
EOc, Estudis Occitans
EP, Études Philosophiques

Ep, Epistemata, Würzburg, Königshausen & Neumann
EPESA, Ediciones y Publicaciones Españolas S.A.
EPoet, Essays in Poetics
ER, Estudis Romànics
ERab, Études Rabelaisiennes
ERB, Études Romanes de Brno
ER(BSRLR), Études Romanes (Bulletin de la Société Roumaine de Linguistique Romane)
ERL, Études Romanes de Lund
ErlF, Erlanger Forschungen
ERLIMA, Équipe de recherche sur la littérature d'imagination du moyen âge, Centre d'Études Supérieures de Civilisation Médiévale/Faculté des Lettres et des Langues, Université de Poitiers.
EROPD, Ежегодник рукописного отдела Пушкинского дома
ERR, European Romantic Review
ES, Erlanger Studien, Erlangen, Palm & Enke
ES, Estudios Segovianos
EsC, L'Esprit Créateur
ESGP, Early Studies in Germanic Philology, Amsterdam, Rodopi
ESI, Edizioni Scientifiche Italiane
ESJ, European Studies Journal
ESk, Edition Suhrkamp, Frankfurt, Suhrkamp
ESoc, Estudios de Sociolinguística
ESor, Études sorguaises
EspA, Español Actual
ESt, English Studies
EstE, Estudios Escénicos
EstG, Estudi General
EstH, Estudios Hispánicos
EstL, Estudios de Lingüística, Alicante
EstLA, Estudios de Linguística Aplicada
EstR, Estudios Románticos
EStud, Essays and Studies
ET, L'Écrit du Temps
ETF, Espacio, Tiempo y Forma, Revista de la Facultad de Geografía e Historia, UNED
EtF, Etudes francophones
EtH, Études sur l'Hérault, Pézenas
EthS, Ethnologia Slavica
ETJ, Educational Theatre Journal
ETL, Explicación de Textos Literarios
EtLitt, Études Littéraires, Quebec
EUDEBA, Editorial Universitaria de Buenos Aires
EUNSA, Ediciones Universidad de Navarra, Pamplona
EUS, European University Studies, Berne, Lang
ExP, Excerpta Philologica
EzLit, Език и литература

FAL, Forum Academicum Literaturwissenschaft, Königstein, Hain
FAM, Filologia Antica e Moderna
FAPESP, Fundação de Amparo à Pesquisa do Estado de São Paulo
FAR, French-American Review
FAS, Frankfurter Abhandlungen zur Slavistik, Giessen, Schmitz
FBAN, Фундаментальная бiблiятэка Акадэмii навук БССР
FBG, Frankfurter Beiträge zur Germanistik, Heidelberg, Winter
FBS, Franco-British Studies
FC, Filologia e Critica
FCE, Fondo de Cultura Económica, Mexico
FCG — CCP, Fondation Calouste Gulbenkian — Centre Culturel Portugais, Paris
FCS, Fifteenth Century Studies
FD, Fonetică şi Dialectologie
FDL, Facetten deutscher Literatur, Berne, Haupt
FEI, Faites entrer l'infini. Journal de la Société des Amis de Louis Aragon et Elsa Triolet
FEK, Forschungen zur europäischen Kultur, Berne, Lang
FemSt, Feministische Studien
FF, Forum für Fachsprachenforschung, Tübingen, Narr
FF, Forma y Función
FFM, French Forum Monographs, Lexington, Kentucky
FGÄDL, Forschungen zur Geschichte der älteren deutschen Literatur, Munich, Fink

FH, Fundamenta Historica, Stuttgart-Bad Cannstatt, Frommann-Holzboog
FH, Frankfurter Hefte
FHL, Forum Homosexualität und Literatur
FHS, French Historical Studies
FIDS, Forschungsberichte des Instituts für Deutsche Sprache, Tübingen, Narr
FHSJ, Flintshire Historical Society Journal
FilM, Filologia Mediolatina
FilMod, Filologia Moderna, Udine –Pisa
FilN, Филологические науки
FilR, Filologia Romanza
FilS, Filologické studie
FilZ, Filologija, Zagreb
FiM, Filologia Moderna, Facultad de Filosofía y Letras, Madrid
FinS, Fin de Siglo
FIRL, Forum at Iowa on Russian Literature
FL, La France Latine
FLa, Faits de Langues
FLang, Functions of Language
FLG, Freiburger literaturpsychologische Gespräche
FLin, Folia Linguistica
FLinHist, Folia Linguistica Historica
FLK, Forschungen zur Literatur- und Kulturgeschichte. Beiträge zur Sprach- und Literaturwissenschaft, Berne, Lang
FLP, Filologia e linguística portuguesa
FLS, French Literature Series
FLV, Fontes Linguae Vasconum
FM, Le Français Moderne
FMADIUR, FM: Annali del Dipartimento di Italianistica, Università di Roma 'La Sapienza'
FMDA, Forschungen und Materialen zur deutschen Aufklärung, Stuttgart — Bad Cannstatt, Frommann-Holzboog
FMI, Fonti Musicali Italiane
FMLS, Forum for Modern Language Studies
FMon, Le Français dans le Monde
FmSt, Frühmittelalterliche Studien
FMT, Forum Modernes Theater
FN, Frühe Neuzeit, Tübingen, Niemeyer
FNDIR, Fédération nationale des déportés et internés résistants
FNS, Frühneuzeit-Studien, Frankfurt, Lang
FoH, Foro Hispánico, Amsterdam
FNT, Foilseacháin Náisiúnta Tta
FoI, Forum Italicum
FoS, Le Forme e la Storia
FP, Folia Phonetica
FPub, First Publications
FR, French Review
FrA, Le Français Aujourd'hui
FranS, Franciscan Studies
FrCS, French Cultural Studies
FrF, French Forum
FrH, Französisch Heute
FrP Le Français Préclassique
FrSoc, Français et Société
FS, Forum Slavicum, Munich, Fink
FS, French Studies
FSB, French Studies Bulletin
FSlav, Folia Slavica
FSSA, French Studies in Southern Africa
FT, Fischer Taschenbuch, Frankfurt, Fischer
FT, Finsk Tidskrift
FTCG, 'La Talanquere': Folklore, Tradition, Culture Gasconne, Nogano
FUE, Fundación Universitaria Española
FV, Fortuna Vitrea, Tübingen, Niemeyer
FZPT, Freiburger Zeitschrift für Philosophie und Theologie

GA, Germanistische Arbeitshefte, Tübingen, Niemeyer
GAB, Göppinger Akademische Beiträge, Lauterburg, Kümmerle
GAG, Göppinger Arbeiten zur Germanistik, Lauterburg, Kümmerle
GAKS, Gesammelte Aufsätze zur Kulturgeschichte Spaniens
GalR, Galician Review, Birmingham
GANDLL, Giessener Arbeiten zur neueren deutschen Literatur und

Literaturwissenschaft, Berne, Lang
Garona, Garona. Cahiers du Centre d'Etudes des Cultures d'Aquitaine et d'Europe du Sud, Talence
GAS, German-Australian Studies, Berne, Lang
GASK, Germanistische Arbeiten zu Sprache und Kulturgeschichte, Frankfurt, Lang
GB, Germanistische Bibliothek, Heidelberg, Winter
GBA, Gazette des Beaux-Arts
GBE, Germanistik in der Blauen Eule
GC, Generalitat de Catalunya
GCFI, Giornale Critico della Filosofia Italiana
GEMP, Groupement d'Ethnomusicologie en Midi-Pyrénées, La Talvèra
GerAb, Germanistische Abhandlungen, Stuttgart, Metzler
GerLux, Germanistik Luxembourg
GermL, Germanistische Linguistik
GeW, Germanica Wratislaviensia
GF, Giornale di Fisica
GFFNS, Godišnjak Filozofskog fakulteta u Novom Sadu
GG, Geschichte und Gesellschaft
GGF, Göteborger Germanistische Forschungen, University of Gothenburg
GGF, Greifswalder Germanistische Forschungen
GGVD, Grundlagen und Gedanken zum Verständnis des Dramas, Frankfurt, Diesterweg
GGVEL, Grundlagen und Gedanken zum Verständnis erzählender Literatur, Frankfurt, Diesterweg
GIDILOc, Grop d'Iniciativa per un Diccionari Informatizat de la Lenga Occitana, Montpellier
GIF, Giornale Italiano di Filologia
GIGFL, Glasgow Introductory Guides to French Literature
GIGGL, Glasgow Introductory Guides to German Literature
GIP, Giornale Italiano di Psicologia
GJ, Gutenberg-Jahrbuch
GJb, Goethe Jahrbuch
GJLL, The Georgetown Journal of Language and Linguistics
GK, Goldmann Klassiker, Munich, Goldmann
GL, Germanistische Lehrbuchsammlung, Berlin, Weidler
GL, General Linguistics
GLC, German Life and Civilisation, Berne, Lang
GLCS, German Linguistic and Cultural Studies, Frankfurt, Lang
GLL, German Life and Letters
GLM, Gazette du Livre Médiéval
GLML, The Garland Library of Medieval Literature, New York –London, Garland
GLR, García Lorca Review
GLS, Grazer Linguistische Studien
Glyph, Glyph: Johns Hopkins Textual Studies, Baltimore
GM, Germanistische Mitteilungen
GML, Gothenburg Monographs in Linguistics
GMon, German Monitor
GN, Germanic Notes and Reviews
GoSt, Gothic Studies
GPB, Гос. публичная библиотека им. М. Е. Салтыкова-Щедрина
GPI, Государственный педагогический институт
GPSR, Glossaire des Patois de la Suisse Romande
GQ, German Quarterly
GR, Germanic Review
GREC, Groupe de Recherches et d'Études du Clermontais, Clermont-l'Hérault
GRECF, Groupe de Recherches et d'Études sur le Canada français, Edinburgh
GREHAM, Groupe de REcherche d'Histoire de l'Anthroponymie Médiévale, Tours, Université François-Rabelais
GRELCA, Groupe de Recherche sur les Littératures de la Caraïbe, Université Laval
GRLH, Garland Reference Library of the Humanities, New York — London, Garland
GRLM, Grundriss der romanischen Literaturen des Mittelalters

GRM, Germanisch-Romanische Monatsschrift
GrSt, Grundtvig Studier
GS, Lo Gai Saber, Toulouse
GSA, Germanic Studies in America, Berne–Frankfurt, Lang
GSC, German Studies in Canada, Frankfurt, Lang
GSI, German Studies in India
GSl, Germano-Slavica, Ontario
GSLI, Giornale Storico della Letteratura Italiana
GSR, German Studies Review
GSSL, Göttinger Schriften zur Sprach- und Literaturwissenschaft, Göttingen, Herodot
GTN, Gdańskie Towarzystwo Naukowe
GTS, Germanistische Texte und Studien, Hildesheim, Olms
GV, Generalitat Valenciana
GY, Goethe Yearbook

H, Hochschulschriften, Cologne, Pahl-Rugenstein
HAHR, Hispanic American Historical Review
HB, Horváth Blätter
HBA, Historiografía y Bibliografía Americanistas, Seville
HBG, Hamburger Beiträge zur Germanistik, Frankfurt, Lang
HDG, Huis aan de Drie Grachten, Amsterdam
HEI, History of European Ideas
HEL, Histoire, Epistémologie, Language
Her(A), Hermes, Århus
HES, Histoire, Économie et Société
HeyJ, Heythrop Journal
HF, Heidelberger Forschungen, Heidelberg, Winter
HHS, History of the Human Sciences
HI, Historica Ibérica
HIAR, Hamburger Ibero-Amerikanische Reihe
HICL, Histoire des Idées et Critique Littéraire, Geneva, Droz
HIGL, Holland Institute for Generative Linguistics, Leiden
HisJ, Hispanic Journal, Indiana–Pennsylvania
HisL, Hispanic Linguistics
HistL, Historiographia Linguistica
HistS, History of Science
His(US), Hispania, Ann Arbor
HJ, Historical Journal
HJb, Heidelberger Jahrbücher
HJBS, Hispanic Journal of Behavioural Sciences
HKADL, Historisch-kritische Arbeiten zur deutschen Literatur, Frankfurt, Lang
HKZMTLG, Handelingen van de Koninklijke Zuidnederlandse Maatschappij voor Taalen, Letterkunde en Geschiedenis
HL, Hochschulschriften Literaturwissenschaft, Königstein, Hain
HL, Humanistica Lovaniensia
HLB, Harvard Library Bulletin
HLitt, Histoires Littéraires
HLQ, Huntington Library Quarterly
HLS, Historiska och litteraturhistoriska studier
HM, Hommes et Migrations
HMJb, Heinrich Mann Jahrbuch
HP, History of Psychiatry
HPh, Historical Philology
HPos, Hispanica Posnaniensia
HPR, Hispanic Poetry Review
HPS, Hamburger Philologische Studien, Hamburg, Buske
HPSl, Heidelberger Publikationen zur Slavistik, Frankfurt, Lang
HPT, History of Political Thought
HR, Hispanic Review
HRef, Historical reflections / Reflexions historiques
HRel, History of Religions
HRev, Hrvatska revija
HRJ, Hispanic Research Journal
HRSHM, Heresis, revue semestrielle d'hérésiologie médiévale
HS, Helfant Studien, Stuttgart, Helfant
HS, Hispania Sacra
HSLA, Hebrew University Studies in Literature and the Arts
HSlav, Hungaro-Slavica
HSMS, Hispanic Seminary of Medieval Studies, Madison

HSp, Historische Sprachforschung (Historical Linguistics)
HSR, Histoire et Sociétés Rurales
HSSL, Harvard Studies in Slavic Linguistics
HSt, Hispanische Studien
HSWSL, Hallesche Studien zur Wirkung von Sprache und Literatur
HT, Helfant Texte, Stuttgart, Helfant
HT, History Today
HTe, Hecho Teatral (Revista de teoría y práctica del teatro hispánico)
HTh, History and Theory
HTR, Harvard Theological Review
HUS, Harvard Ukrainian Studies
HY, Herder Yearbook
HZ, Historische Zeitschrift

IÅ, Ibsen-Årbok, Oslo
IAP, Ibero-Americana Pragensia
IAr, Iberoamerikanisches Archiv
IARB, Inter-American Review of Bibliography
IASL, Internationales Archiv für Sozialgeschichte der deutschen Literatur
IASLS, Internationales Archiv für Sozialgeschichte der deutschen Literatur: Sonderheft
IB, Insel-Bücherei, Frankfurt, Insel
IBKG, Innsbrucker Beiträge zur Kulturwissenschaft. Germanistische Reihe
IBL, Instytut Badań Literackich PAN, Warsaw
IBLA, Institut des Belles Lettres Arabes
IBLe, Insel-Bücherei, Leipzig, Insel
IBS, Innsbrücker Beiträge zur Sprachwissenschaft
IC, Index on Censorship
ICALP, Instituto de Cultura e Língua Portuguesa, Lisbon
ICALPR, Instituto de Cultura e Língua Portuguesa. Revista
ICC, Instituto Caro y Cuervo, Bogotà
ICLMF, Istitut Cultural Ladin 'Majon de Fasegn'
ICLMR, Istitut Cultural Ladin 'Micurà de Rü'
ICMA, Instituto de Cooperación con el Mundo Árabe
ID, Italia Dialettale
IDF, Informationen Deutsch als Fremdsprache
IDL, Indices zur deutschen Literatur, Tübingen, Niemeyer
IdLit, Ideologies and Literature
IEC, Institut d'Estudis Catalans
IEI, Istituto dell'Enciclopedia Italiana
IEO, Institut d'Estudis Occitans
IEPI, Istituti Editoriali e Poligrafici Internazionali
IES, Institut d'Études Slaves, Paris
IF, Impulse der Forschung, Darmstadt, Wissenschaftliche Buchgesellschaft
IF, Indogermanische Forschungen
IFAVL, Internationale Forschungen zur Allgemeinen und Vergleichenden Literaturwissenschaft, Amsterdam–Atlanta, Rodopi
IFC, Institutión Fernando el Católico
IFEE, Investigación Franco-Española. Estudios
IFiS, Instytut Filozofii i Socjologii PAN, Warsaw
IFOTT, Institut voor Functioneel Onderzoek naar Taal en Taalgebruik, Amsterdam
IFR, International Fiction Review
IG, Information grammaticale
IHC, Italian History and Culture
IHE, Índice Histórico Español
IHS, Irish Historical Studies
II, Information und Interpretation, Frankfurt, Lang
IIa, Институт языкознания
IIFV, Institut Interuniversitari de Filologia Valenciana, Valencia
III, Институт истории искусств
IJ, Italian Journal
IJAL, International Journal of American Linguistics
IJBAG, Internationales Jahrbuch der Bettina-von-Arnim Gesellschaft
IJCS, International Journal of Canadian Studies

IJFS, International Journal of Francophone Studies, Leeds
IJHL, Indiana Journal of Hispanic Literatures
IJL, International Journal of Lexicography
IJP, International Journal of Psycholinguistics
IJSL, International Journal for the Sociology of Language
IJSLP, International Journal of Slavic Linguistics and Poetics
IK, Искусство кино
IKU, Institut za književnost i umetnost, Belgrade
IL, L'Information Littéraire
ILAS, Institute of Latin American Studies, University of London
ILASLR, Istituto Lombardo. Accademia di Scienze e Lettere. Rendiconti
ILen, Искусство Ленинграда
ILG, Instituto da Lingua Galega
ILing, Incontri Linguistici
ILTEC, Instituto de Linguistica Teórica e Computacional, Lisbon
IMA, Imagines Medii Aevi, Wiesbaden, Reichert
IMN, Irisleabhar Mhá Nuad
IMR, International Migration Review
IMU, Italia Medioevale e Umanistica
INCM, Imprensa Nacional, Casa da Moeda, Lisbon
InfD, Informationen und Didaktik
INLF, Institut National de la Langue Française
INIC, Instituto Nacional de Investigação Científica
InL, Иностранная литература
INLE, Instituto Nacional del Libro Español
InstEB, Inst. de Estudos Brasileiros
InstNL, Inst. Nacional do Livro, Brasilia
IO, Italiano e Oltre
IPL, Istituto di Propaganda Libraria
IPZS, Istituto Poligrafico e Zecca dello Stato, Rome
IR, L'Immagine Riflessa
IRAL, International Review of Applied Linguistics
IRIa, Институт русского языка Российской Академии Наук
IrR, The Irish Review
IRSH, International Review of Social History
IRSL, International Review of Slavic Linguistics
ISC, Institut de Sociolingüística Catalana
ISI, Institute for Scientific Information, U.S.A.
ISIEMC, Istituto Storico Italiano per l'Età Moderna e Contemporanea, Rome
ISIM, Istituto Storico Italiano per il Medio Evo
ISLIa, Известия Академии наук СССР. Серия литературы и языка
ISOAN, Известия сибирского отделения АН СССР, Novosibirsk
ISP, International Studies in Philosophy
IsPL, Istitut pedagogich Ladin
ISPS, International Studies in the Philosophy of Science
ISS, Irish Slavonic Studies
IsS, Islamic Studies, Islamabad
ISSA, Studi d'Italianistica nell'Africa Australe: Italian Studies in Southern Africa
ISt, Italian Studies
ISV, Informazioni e Studi Vivaldiani
IT, Insel Taschenbuch, Frankfurt, Insel
ItC, Italian Culture
ItJL, Italian Journal of Linguistics
ITL, ITL. Review of Applied Linguistics, Instituut voor Toegepaste Linguistiek, Leuven
ItQ, Italian Quarterly
ItStudien, Italienische Studien
IUJF, Internationales Uwe-Johnson-Forum
IULA, Institut Universitari de Lingüística Aplicada, Universitat Pompeu Fabra, Barcelona
IUP, Irish University Press
IUR, Irish University Review
IV, Istituto Veneto di Scienze, Lettere ed Arti

IVAS, Indices Verborum zum altdeutschen Schrifttum, Amsterdam, Rodopi
IVN, Internationale Vereniging voor Nederlandistiek

JAAC, Journal of Aesthetics and Art Criticism
JACIS, Journal of the Association for Contemporary Iberian Studies
JAE, Journal of Aesthetic Education
JAIS, Journal of Anglo-Italian Studies, Malta
JAMS, Journal of the American Musicological Society
JanL, Janua Linguarum, The Hague, Mouton
JAOS, Journal of the American Oriental Society
JAPLA, Journal of the Atlantic Provinces Linguistic Association
JARA, Journal of the American Romanian Academy of Arts and Sciences
JAS, The Journal of Algerian Studies
JASI, Jahrbuch des Adalbert-Stifter-Instituts
JATI, Association of Teachers of Italian Journal
JazA, Jazykovědné aktuality
JazLin, Jazykověda: Linguistica, Ostravska University
JazŠ, Jazykovedné štúdie
JAZU, Jugoslavenska akademija znanosti i umjetnosti
JBSP, Journal of the British Society for Phenomenology
JČ, Jazykovedný časopis, Bratislava
JCanS, Journal of Canadian Studies
JCHAS, Journal of the Cork Historical and Archaeological Society
JCL, Journal of Child Language
JCLin, Journal of Celtic Linguistics
JCS, Journal of Celtic Studies
JDASD, Deutsche Akademie für Sprache und Dichtung: Jahrbuch
JDF, Jahrbuch Deutsch als Fremdsprache
JDSG, Jahrbuch der Deutschen Schiller-Gesellschaft
JEA, Lou Journalet de l'Escandihado Aubagnenco
JEGP, Journal of English and Germanic Philology
JEH, Journal of Ecclesiastical History
JEL, Journal of English Linguistics
JES, Journal of European Studies
JF, Južnoslovenski filolog
JFA, Jahrbuch Felder-Archiv
JFDH, Jahrbuch des Freien Deutschen Hochstifts
JFG, Jahrbuch der Fouqué Gesellschaft
JFinL, Jahrbuch für finnisch-deutsche Literaturbeziehungen
JFL, Jahrbuch für fränkische Landesforschung
JFLS, Journal of French Language Studies
JFR, Journal of Folklore Research
JG, Jahrbuch für Geschichte, Berlin, Akademie
JGO, Jahrbücher für die Geschichte Osteuropas
JHA, Journal for the History of Astronomy
JHI, Journal of the History of Ideas
JHispP, Journal of Hispanic Philology
JHP, Journal of the History of Philosophy
JHR, Journal of Hispanic Research
JHS, Journal of the History of Sexuality
JIAS, Journal of Inter-American Studies
JIES, Journal of Indo-European Studies
JIG, Jahrbuch für Internationale Germanistik
JIL, Journal of Italian Linguistics
JILAS, Journal of Iberian and Latin American Studies (formerly *Tesserae*)
JILS, Journal of Interdisciplinary Literary Studies
JIPA, Journal of the International Phonetic Association
JIRS, Journal of the Institute of Romance Studies
JJQ, James Joyce Quarterly
JJS, Journal of Jewish Studies

JKLWR, Jahrbuch zur Kultur und Literatur der Weimarer Republik
JL, Journal of Linguistics
JLACS, Journal of Latin American Cultural Studies
JLAL, Journal of Latin American Lore
JLAS, Journal of Latin American Studies
JLH, Journal of Library History
JLS, Journal of Literary Semantics
JLSP, Journal of Language and Social Psychology
JMemL, Journal of Memory and Language
JMEMS, Journal of Medieval and Early Modern Studies
JMH, Journal of Medieval History
JMHRS, Journal of the Merioneth Historical and Record Society
JML, Journal of Modern Literature
JMLat, Journal of Medieval Latin
JMMD, Journal of Multilingual and Multicultural Development
JMMLA, Journal of the Midwest Modern Language Association
JModH, Journal of Modern History
JMP, Journal of Medicine and Philosophy
JMRS, Journal of Medieval and Renaissance Studies
JMS, Journal of Maghrebi Studies
JNT, Journal of Narrative Technique
JONVL, Een Jaarboek: Overzicht van de Nederlandse en Vlaamse Literatuur
JOWG, Jahrbuch der Oswald von Wolkenstein Gesellschaft
JP, Journal of Pragmatics
JPC, Journal of Popular Culture
JPCL, Journal of Pidgin and Creole Languages
JPh, Journal of Phonetics
JPHS, The Journal of the Pembrokeshire Historical Society
JPol, Język Polski
JPR, Journal of Psycholinguistic Research
JQ, Jacques e i suoi Quaderni
JRA, Journal of Religion in Africa
JRG, Jahrbücher der Reineke-Gesellschaft
JRH, Journal of Religious History
JRIC, Journal of the Royal Institution of Cornwall
JŘJR, Jazyk a řeč jihočeského regionu. České Budějovice, Pedagogická fakulta Jihočeské univerzity
JRMA, Journal of the Royal Musical Association
JRMMRA, Journal of the Rocky Mountain Medieval and Renaissance Association
JRS, Journal of Romance Studies
JRUL, Journal of the Rutgers University Libraries
JS, Journal des Savants
JSCS, Journal of Spanish Cultural Studies
JSEES, Japanese Slavic and East European Studies
JSem, Journal of Semantics
JSFG, Jahrbuch für schwäbisch-fränkische Geschichte
JSFWUB, Jahrbuch der Schlesischen Friedrich-Wilhelms-Universität zu Breslau
JSH, Jihočeský sborník historický
JSHR, Journal of Speech and Hearing Research
JSL, Journal of Slavic Linguistics
JSoc, Journal of Sociolinguistics
JSS, Journal of Spanish Studies: Twentieth Century
JTS, Journal of Theological Studies
JU, Judentum und Umwelt, Berne, Lang
JUG, Jahrbuch der ungarischen Germanistik
JUS, Journal of Ukrainian Studies
JV, Jahrbuch für Volkskunde
JVF, Jahrbuch für Volksliedforschung
JVLVB, Journal of Verbal Learning and Verbal Behavior
JWCI, Journal of the Warburg and Courtauld Institutes
JWGV, Jahrbuch des Wiener Goethe-Vereins, Neue Folge
JWH, Journal of World History
JWIL, Journal of West Indian Literature
JWRH, Journal of Welsh Religious History
JZ, Jazykovedný zborník

KANTL, Koninklijke Akademie voor Nederlandse Taal- en Letterkunde
KASL, Kasseler Arbeiten zur Sprache und Literatur, Frankfurt, Lang
KAW, Krajowa Agencja Wydawnicza
KAWLSK, Koninklijke Academie voor Wetenschappen, Letteren en Schone Kunsten van België, Brussels
KB, Književni barok
KBGL, Kopenhagener Beiträge zur germanistischen Linguistik
Kbl, Korrespondenzblatt des Vereins für niederdeutsche Sprachforschung
KDC, Katholiek Documentatiecentrum
KDPM, Kleine deutsche Prosadenkmäler des Mittelalters, Munich, Fink
KGOS, Kultur- und geistesgeschichtliche Ostmitteleuropa-Studien, Marburg, Elwert
KGS, Kölner germanistische Studien, Cologne, Böhlau
KGS, Kairoer germanistische Studien
KH, Komparatistische Hefte
KhL, Художественная литература
KI, Književna istorija
KiW, Książka i Wiedza
KJ, Književnost i jezik
KK, Kirke og Kultur
KKKK, Kultur og Klasse. Kritik og Kulturanalyse
KlJb, Kleist-Jahrbuch
KLWL, Krieg und Literatur: War and Literature
Klage, Klage: Kölner linguistische Arbeiten. Germanistik, Hürth-Efferen, Gabel
KN, Kwartalnik Neofilologiczny
KnK, Kniževna kritika
KO, Университетско издателство 'Климент Охридски'
KO, Книжное обозрение
KP, Книжная палата
KRA, Kölner Romanistische Arbeiten, Geneva, Droz
KS, Kúltura slova
KSDL, Kieler Studien zur deutschen Literaturgeschichte, Neumünster, Wachholtz
KSL, Kölner Studien zur Literaturwissenschaft, Frankfurt, Lang
KSt, Kant Studien
KTA, Kröners Taschenausgabe, Stuttgart, Kröner
KTRM, Klassische Texte des romanischen Mittelalters, Munich, Fink
KU, Konstanzer Universitätsreden
KUL, Katolicki Uniwersytet Lubelski, Lublin
KuSDL, Kulturwissenschaftliche Studien zur deutschen Literatur, Opladen, Westdeutscher Verlag
KZG, Koreanische Zeitschrift für Germanistik
KZMTLG, Koninklijke Zuidnederlandse Maatschappij voor Taal- en Letterkunde en Geschiedenis, Brussels
KZMTLGH, Koninklijke Zuidnederlandse Maatschaapij voor Taal- en Letterkunde en Geschiedenis. Handelingen

LA, Linguistische Arbeiten, Tübingen, Niemeyer
LA, Linguistic Analysis
LaA, Language Acquisition
LAbs, Linguistics Abstracts
LaF, Langue Française
LAILJ, Latin American Indian Literatures Journal
LaLi, Langues et Linguistique
LALIES, LALIES. Actes des sessions de linguistique et de littérature. Institut d'Etudes linguistiques et phonétiques. Sessions de linguistique. Ecole Normale Supérieure Paris, Sorbonne nouvelle
LALR, Latin-American Literary Review
LaM, Les Langues Modernes
LangH, Le Langage et l'Homme

LangLit, Language and Literature, Journal of the Poetics and Linguistics Association
LArb, Linguistische Arbeitsberichte
LARR, Latin-American Research Review
LaS, Langage et Société
LATR, Latin-American Theatre Review
LatT, Latin Teaching, Shrewsbury
LB, Leuvense Bijdragen
LBer, Linguistische Berichte
LBIYB, Leo Baeck Institute Year Book
LBR, Luso-Brazilian Review
LC, Letture Classensi
LCC, Léachtaí Cholm Cille
LCh, Literatura Chilena
LCP, Language and Cognitive Processes
LCrit, Lavoro Critico
LCUTA, Library Chronicle of the University of Texas at Austin
LD, Libri e Documenti
LdA, Linha d'Agua
LDan, Lectura Dantis
LDanN, Lectura Dantis Newberryana
LDGM, Ligam-DiGaM. Quadèrn de lingüística e lexicografía gasconas, Fontenay aux Roses
LE, Language and Education
LEA, Lingüística Española Actual
LebS, Lebende Sprachen
LEMIR, Literatura Española Medieval y del Renacimiento, Valencia U.P.; http://www.uv.es/~lemir/Revista.html
Leng(M), Lengas, Montpellier
Leng(T), Lengas, Toulouse
LenP, Ленинградская панорама
LetA, Letterature d'America
LetC, La Lettre Clandestine
LetD, Letras de Deusto
LETHB, Laboratoires d'Études Théâtrales de l'Université de Haute-Bretagne. Études et Documents, Rennes
LetL, Letras e Letras, Departmento de Línguas Estrangeiras Modernas, Universidade Federal de Uberlândia, Brazil
LetLi, Letras Libres, Mexico D.F.
LetMS, Letopis Matice srpske, Novi Sad
LetP, Il Lettore di Provincia
LetS, Letras Soltas
LevT, Levende Talen
Lex(L), Lexique, Lille
LF, Letras Femeninas
LFil, Listy filologické
LFQ, Literature and Film Quarterly
LGF, Lunder Germanistische Forschungen, Stockholm, Almqvist & Wiksell
LGGL, Literatur in der Geschichte, Geschichte in der Literatur, Cologne–Vienna, Böhlau
LGL, Langs Germanistische Lehrbuchsammlung, Berne, Lang
LGP, Leicester German Poets, Leicester U.P.
LGW, Literaturwissenschaft — Gesellschaftswissenschaft, Stuttgart, Klett
LH, Lingüística Hispánica
LHum, Litteraria Humanitas, Brno
LI, Linguistic Inquiry
LIA, Letteratura italiana antica
LIÅA, Litteraturvetenskapliga institutionen vid Åbo Akademi, Åbo Akademi U.P.
LiB, Literatur in Bayern
LIC, Letteratura Italiana Contemporanea
LiCC, Lien des chercheurs cévenols
LIE, Lessico Intellettuale Europeo, Rome, Ateneo
LiL, Limbă şi Literatură
LiLi, Zeitschrift für Literaturwissenschaft und Linguistik
LingAk, Linguistik Aktuell, Amsterdam, Benjamins
LingBal, Балканско езикознание – Linguistique Balkanique
LingCon, Lingua e Contesto
LingFil, Linguistica e Filologia, Dipartimento di Linguistica e Letterature Comparate, Bergamo
LingLett, Linguistica e Letteratura
LíngLit, Língua e Literatura, São Paulo
LinLit, Lingüística y Literatura
LINQ, Linq [Literature in North Queensland]
LInv, Linguisticae Investigationes

LiR, Limba Română
LiR(M), Limba Română (Revist ă de ştiinţ ă şi culturą), Casa limbii române, Moldova
LIT, Literature Interpretation Theory
LIt, Lettera dall'Italia
LitAP, Literární archív Památníku národního pisemnictví
LItal, Lettere Italiane
LitB, Literatura, Budapest
LitC, Littératures Classiques
LitG, Литературная газета, Moscow
LitH, Literature and History
LItL, Letteratura Italiana Laterza, Bari, Laterza
LitL, Literatur für Leser
LitLing, Literatura y Lingüística
LitM, Literární měsícník
LitMis, Литературна мисъл
LitP, Literature and Psychology
LitR, The Literary Review
LittB, Litteraria, Bratislava
LittK, Litterae, Lauterburg, Kümmerle
LittS, Litteratur og Samfund
LittW, Litteraria, Wrocław
LitU, Literaturnaia Ucheba
LiU, Літературна Україна
LivOS, Liverpool Online Series. Critical Editions of French Texts. Department of Modern Languages. University of Liverpool <http://www.liv.ac.uk/www/french/LOS/>
LJb, Literaturwissenschaftliches Jahrbuch der Görres–Gesellschaft
LK, Literatur-Kommentare, Munich, Hanser
LK, Literatur und Kritik
LKol, Loccumer Kolloquium
LL, Langues et Littératures, Rabat
LlA, Lletres Asturianes
LLC, Literary and Linguistic Computing
LlC, Llên Cymru
LlLi, Llengua i Literatura
LLS, Lenguas, Literaturas, Sociedades. Cuadernos Hispánicos
LLSEE, Linguistic and Literary Studies in Eastern Europe, Amsterdam, Benjamins
LM, Le Lingue del Mondo
LN, Lingua Nostra
LNB, Leipziger namenkundliche Beiträge
LNL, Les Langues Néo-Latines
LNouv, Les Lettres Nouvelles
LoP, Loccumer Protokolle
LOS, Literary Onomastic Studies
LP, Le Livre de Poche, Librairie Générale Française
LP, Lingua Posnaniensis
LPen, Letras Peninsulares
LPh, Linguistics and Philosophy
LPLP, Language Problems and Language Planning
LPO, Lenga e Païs d'Oc, Montpellier
LPr, Linguistica Pragensia
LQ, Language Quarterly, University of S. Florida
LQu, Lettres québécoises
LR, Linguistische Reihe, Munich, Hueber
LR, Les Lettres Romanes
LRev, Linguistic Review
LRI, Libri e Riviste d'Italia
LS, Literatur als Sprache, Münster, Aschendorff
LS, Lingua e Stile
LSa, Lusitania Sacra
LSc, Language Sciences
LSil, Linguistica Silesiana
LSNS, Lundastudier i Nordisk Språkvetenskap
LSo, Language in Society
LSp, Language and Speech
LSPS, Lou Sourgentin/La Petite Source. Revue culturelle bilingue nissart-français, Nice
LSty, Language and Style
LSW, Ludowa Spółdzielnia Wydawnicza
LTG, Literaturwissenschaft, Theorie und Geschichte, Frankfurt, Lang
ŁTN, Łódzkie Towarzystwo Naukowe
LTP, Laval Théologique et Philosophique
LU, Literarhistorische Untersuchungen, Berne, Lang

LU, Literatur im Unterricht
LVC, Language Variation and Change
LW, Literatur und Wirklichkeit, Bonn, Bouvier
LWU, Literatur in Wissenschaft und Unterricht
LY, Lessing Yearbook

MA, Moyen Âge
MAASC, Mémoires de l'Académie des Arts et des Sciences de Carcassonne
MACL, Memórias da Academia de Ciências de Lisboa, Classe de Letras
MAe, Medium Aevum
MAKDDR, Mitteilungen der Akademie der Künste der DDR
MAL, Modern Austrian Literature
MaL, Le Maghreb Littéraire – Revue Canadienne des Littératures Maghrébines, Toronto
MaM, Marbacher Magazin
MAPS, Medium Aevum. Philologische Studien, Munich, Fink
MARPOC, Maison d'animation et de recherche populaire occitane, Nimes
MAST, Memorie dell'Accademia delle Scienze di Torino
MatSl, Matica Slovenská
MBA, Mitteilungen aus dem Brenner-Archiv
MBAV, Miscellanea Bibliothecae Apostolicae Vaticanae
MBMRF, Münchener Beiträge zur Mediävistik und Renaissance-Forschung, Bachenhausen, Arbeo
MBRP, Münstersche Beiträge zur romanischen Philologie, Münster, Kleinheinrich
MBSL, Mannheimer Beiträge zur Sprach- und Literaturwissenschaft, Tübingen, Narr
MC, Misure Critiche
MCV, Mélanges de la Casa de Velázquez
MD, Musica Disciplina
MDan, Meddelser fra Dansklærerforeningen.
MDG, Mitteilungen des deutschen Germanistenverbandes
MDL, Mittlere Deutsche Literatur in Neu- und Nachdrucken, Berne, Lang
MDLK, Monatshefte für deutschsprachige Literatur und Kultur
MDr, Momentum Dramaticum
MEC, Ministerio de Educação e Cultura, Rio de Janeiro
MedC, La Méditerranée et ses Cultures
MedH, Medioevo e Umanesimo
MedLR, Mediterranean Language Review
MedP, Medieval Perspectives
MedRom, Medioevo Romanzo
MedS, Medieval Studies
MEFR, Mélanges de l'École Française de Rome, Moyen Age
MerH, Merthyr Historian
MerP, Mercurio Peruano
MF, Mercure de France
MFDT, Mainzer Forschungen zu Drama und Theater, Tübingen, Francke
MFS, Modern Fiction Studies
MG, Молодая гвардия
MG, Молодая гвардия
MGB, Münchner Germanistische Beiträge, Munich, Fink
MGG, Mystik in Geschichte und Gegenwart, Stuttgart-Bad Cannstatt, Frommann-Holzboog
MGS, Marburger Germanistische Studien, Frankfurt, Lang
MGS, Michigan Germanic Studies
MGSL, Minas Gerais, Suplemento Literário
MGTBE, Medieval German Texts in Bilingual Editions, Kalamazoo, MI, Medieval Institute
MH, Medievalia et Humanistica
MHJ, Medieval History Journal
MHLS, Mid-Hudson Language Studies
MHRA, Modern Humanities Research Association
MichRS, Michigan Romance Studies

MILUS, Meddelanden från Institutionen i Lingvistik vid Universitetet i Stockholm
MINS, Meddelanden från institutionen för nordiska språk vid Stockholms universiteit, Stockholm U.P.
MiscBarc, Miscellanea Barcinonensia
MiscEB, Miscel·lània d'Estudis Bagencs
MiscP, Miscel·lània Penedesenca
MITWPL, MIT Working Papers in Linguistics
MJ, Mittellateinisches Jahrbuch
MK, Maske und Kothurn
MKH, Deutsche Forschungsgemeinschaft: Mitteilung der Kommission für Humanismusforschung, Weinheim, Acta Humaniora
MKNAWL, Mededelingen der Koninklijke Nederlandse Akademie van Wetenschappen, Afd. Letterkunde, Amsterdam
ML, Mediaevalia Lovaniensia, Leuven U.P.
ML, Modern Languages
MLAIntBibl, Modern Language Association International Bibliography
MLIÅA, Meddelanden utgivna av Litteraturvetenskapliga institutionen vid Åbo Akademi, Åbo Akademi U.P.
MLIGU, Meddelanden utgivna av Litteraturvetenskapliga institutionen vid Göteborgs universitet, Gothenburg U.P.
MLit, Мастацкая літаратура
MLit, Miesięcznik Literacki
MLIUU, Meddelanden utgivna av Litteraturvetenskapliga institutionen vid Uppsala universitet, Uppsala U.P.
MLJ, Modern Language Journal
MLN, Modern Language Notes
MLQ, Modern Language Quarterly
MLR, Modern Language Review
MLS, Modern Language Studies
MM, Maal og Minne
MMS, Münstersche Mittelalter-Schriften, Munich, Fink
MN, Man and Nature. L'Homme et la Nature
MNGT, Manchester New German Texts, Manchester U.P.
MO, Monde en Oc. Aurillac (IEO)
ModD, Modern Drama
ModS, Modern Schoolman
MoL, Modellanalysen: Literatur, Paderborn, Schöningh–Munich, Fink
MON, Ministerstwo Obrony Narodowej, Warsaw
MonS, Montaigne Studies
MosR, Московский рабочий
MoyFr, Le Moyen Français
MP, Modern Philology
MQ, Mississippi Quarterly
MQR, Michigan Quarterly Review
MR, Die Mainzer Reihe, Mainz, Hase & Koehler
MR, Medioevo e Rinascimento
MRev, Maghreb Review
MRo, Marche Romane
MRS, Medieval and Renaissance Studies
MRTS, Medieval and Renaissance Texts and Studies, Tempe, Arizona, Arizona State University
MS, Marbacher Schriften, Stuttgart, Cotta
MS, Moderna Språk
MSB, Middeleeuwse Studies en Bronnen, Hilversum, Verloren
MSC, Medjunarodni slavistički centar, Belgrade
MSG, Marburger Studien zur Germanistik, Marburg, Hitzeroth
MSHA, Maison des sciences de l'homme d'Aquitaine
MSISS, Materiali della Socièta Italiana di Studi sul Secolo XVIII
MSL, Marburger Studien zur Literatur, Marburg, Hitzeroth
MSLKD, Münchener Studien zur literarischen Kultur in Deutschland, Frankfurt, Lang
MSLP, Mémoires de la Société de Linguistique de Paris
MSMS, Middeleeuse Studies — Medieval Studies, Johannesburg
MSNH, Mémoires de la Société Néophilologique de Helsinki

MSp, Moderne Sprachen (Zeitschrift des Verbandes der österreichischen Neuphilologen)
MSR, Mot so razo
MSS, Medieval Sermon Studies
MSSp, Münchener Studien zur Sprachwissenschaft, Munich
MSUB, Moscow State University Bulletin, series 9, philology
MTCGT, Methuen's Twentieth-Century German Texts, London, Methuen
MTG, Mitteilungen zur Theatergeschichte der Goethezeit, Bonn, Bouvier
MTNF, Monographien und Texte zur Nietzsche-Forschung, Berlin — New York, de Gruyter
MTU, Münchener Texte und Untersuchungen zur deutschen Literatur des Mittelalters, Tübingen, Niemeyer
MTUB, Mitteilungen der T. U. Braunschweig
MUP, Manchester University Press
MusL, Music and Letters
MusP, Museum Patavinum
MyQ, Mystics Quarterly

NA, Nuova Antologia
NAFMUM, Nuovi Annali della Facoltà di Magistero dell'Università di Messina
NAJWS, North American Journal of Welsh Studies
NArg, Nuovi Argomenti
NAS, Nouveaux Actes Sémiotiques, PULIM, Université de Limoges
NASNCGL, North American Studies in Nineteenth-Century German Literature, Berne, Lang
NASSAB, Nuovi Annali della Scuola Speciale per Archivisti e Bibliotecari
NAWG, Nachrichten der Akademie der Wissenschaften zu Göttingen, phil.-hist. Kl., Göttingen, Vandenhoeck & Ruprecht
NBG, Neue Beiträge zur Germanistik
NBGF, Neue Beiträge zur George-Forschung
NC, New Criterion
NCA, Nouveaux Cahiers d'Allemand
NCEFRW, Nouvelles du Centre d'études francoprovençales 'René Willien'
NCF, Nineteenth-Century Fiction
NCFS, Nineteenth-Century French Studies
NCL, Notes on Contemporary Literature
NCo, New Comparison
NCSRLL, North Carolina Studies in the Romance Languages and Literatures, Chapel Hill
ND, Наукова думка
NDH, Neue deutsche Hefte
NdJb, Niederdeutsches Jahrbuch
NDL, Nachdrucke deutscher Literatur des 17. Jahrhunderts, Berne, Lang
NDL, Neue deutsche Literatur
NdS, Niederdeutsche Studien, Cologne, Böhlau
NDSK, Nydanske Studier og almen kommunikationsteori
NdW, Niederdeutsches Wort
NE, Nueva Estafeta
NEL, Nouvelles Éditions Latines, Paris
NFF, Novel: A Forum in Fiction
NFS, Nottingham French Studies
NFT, Német Filológiai Tanulmányok. Arbeiten zur deutschen Philologie
NG, Nevasimaia Gazeta
NG, Nordistica Gothoburgensia
NGC, New German Critique
NGFH, Die Neue Gesellschaft/ Frankfurter Hefte
NGR, New German Review
NGS, New German Studies, Hull
NH, Nuevo Hispanismo
NHi, Nice Historique
NHLS, North Holland Linguistic Series, Amsterdam
NHVKSG, Neujahrsblatt des Historischen Vereins des Kantons St Gallen
NI, Наука и изкуство
NIJRS, New International Journal of Romanian Studies
NIMLA, NIMLA. Journal of the Modern Language Association of Northern Ireland

NJ, Naš jezik
NJb, Neulateinisches Jahrbuch
NJL, Nordic Journal of Linguistics
NKT, Norske klassiker-tekster, Bergen, Eide
NL, Nouvelles Littéraires
NLÅ, Norsk Litterær Årbok
NLD, Nuove Letture Dantesche
NLe, Nuove Lettere
NLH, New Literary History
NLi, Notre Librairie
NLLT, Natural Language and Linguistic Theory
NLN, Neo-Latin News
NLO, Novoe Literaturnoe obozrenie
NLO, Novoe Literaturnoe obozrenie
NLT, Norsk Lingvistisk Tidsskrift
NLWJ, National Library of Wales Journal
NM, Народна младеж
NMi, Neuphilologische Mitteilungen
NMS, Nottingham Medieval Studies
NN, Наше наследие
NNH, Nueva Narrativa Hispanoamericana
NNR, New Novel Review
NOR, New Orleans Review
NORNA, Nordiska samarbetskommittén för namnforskning, Uppsala
NovE, Novos Estudos (CEBRAP)
NovM, Новый мир
NovR, Nova Renascenza
NOWELE, North-Western European Language Evolution. Nowele
NP, Народна просвета
NP, Nouvello de Prouvènço (Li), Avignon, Parlaren Païs d'Avignoun
NQ, Notes and Queries
NR, New Review
NŘ, Naše řeč
NRE, Nuova Rivista Europea
NRe, New Readings, School of European Studies, University of Wales, College of Cardiff
NRF, Nouvelle Revue Française
NRFH, Nueva Revista de Filología Hispánica
NRL, Neue russische Literatur. Almanach, Salzburg
NRLett, Nouvelles de la République des Lettres
NRLI, Nuova Rivista di Letteratura Italiana
NRMI, Nuova Rivista Musicale Italiana
NRO, Nouvelle Revue d'Onomastique
NRP, Nouvelle Revue de Psychanalyse
NRS, Nuova Rivista Storica
NRSS, Nouvelle Revue du Seizième Siècle
NRu, Die Neue Rundschau
NS, Die Neueren Sprachen
NSc, New Scholar
NSh, Начальная школа
NSL, Det Norske Språk- og Litteraturselskap
NSlg, Neue Sammlung
NSo, Наш современник . . . Альманах
NSP, Nuovi Studi Politici
NSS, Nysvenska Studier
NSt, Naše stvaranje
NT, Навука і тэхніка
NT, Nordisk Tidskrift
NTBB, Nordisk Tidskrift för Bok- och Biblioteksväsen
NTC, Nuevo Texto Crítico
NTE, Народна творчість та етнографія
NTg, Nieuwe Taalgids
NTk, Nederlandse Taalkunde
NTQ, New Theatre Quarterly
NTSh, Наукове товариство ім. Шевченка
NTW, News from the Top of the World: Norwegian Literature Today
NU, Narodna umjetnost
NV, Новое время
NVS, New Vico Studies
NWIG, Niewe West-Indische Gids
NyS, Nydanske Studier/Almen Kommunikationsteori
NYSNDL, New Yorker Studien zur neueren deutschen Literaturgeschichte, Berne, Lang
NYUOS, New York University Ottendorfer Series, Berne, Lang
NZh, Новый журнал

NZh (StP), Новый журнал, St Petersburg
NZJFS, New Zealand Journal of French Studies
NZSJ, New Zealand Slavonic Journal

OA, Отечественные архивы
OB, Ord och Bild
OBS, Osnabrücker Beiträge zur Sprachtheorie, Oldenbourg, OBST
OBTUP, Universitetsforlaget Oslo–Bergen–Tromsø
ÖBV, Österreichischer Bundesverlag, Vienna
OC, Œuvres et Critiques
OCan, Onomastica Canadiana, Winnipeg
OcL, Oceanic Linguistics
Oc(N), Oc, Nice
OCP, Orientalia Christiana Periodica, Rome
OCS, Occitan/Catalan Studies
ÖGL, Österreich in Geschichte und Literatur
OGS, Oxford German Studies
OH, Ottawa Hispánica
OIU, Oldenbourg Interpretationen mit Unterrichtshilfen, Munich, Oldenbourg
OL, Orbis Litterarum
OLR, Oxford Literary Review
OLSI, Osservatorio Linguistico della Svizzera italiana
OM, L'Oc Médiéval
ON, Otto/Novecento
ONS, Obshchestvennye Nauki i Sovremennost'
OPBS, Occasional Papers in Belarusian Studies
OPEN, Oficyna Polska Encyklopedia Nezależna
OPI, Overseas Publications Interchange, London
OPL, Osservatore Politico Letterario
OPM, 'Ou Païs Mentounasc': Bulletin de la Société d'Art et d'Histoire du Mentonnais, Menton
OPRPNZ, Общество по распространению политических и научных знаний
OpSl, Opera Slavica
OPSLL, Occasional Papers in Slavic Languages and Literatures
OR, Odrodzenie i Reformacja w Polsce
ORP, Oriental Research Partners, Cambridge
OS, 'Oc Sulpic': Bulletin de l'Association Occitane du Québec, Montreal
OSP, Oxford Slavonic Papers
OSUWPL, Ohio State University Working Papers in Linguistics
OT, Oral Tradition
OTS, Onderzoeksinstituut voor Taal en Spraak, Utrecht
OUP, Oxford University Press
OUSL, Odense University Studies in Literature
OUSSLL, Odense University Studies in Scandinavian Languages and Literatures, Odense U.P.
OWPLC, Odense Working Papers in Language and Communication

PA, Présence Africaine
PAc, Primer Acto
PAf, Politique Africaine
PAGS, Proceedings of the Australian Goethe Society
Pal, Palaeobulgarica — Старобългаристика
PAM, Publicacions de l'Abadia de Montserrat, Barcelona
PAN, Polska Akademia Nauk, Warsaw
PaP, Past and Present
PapBSA, Papers of the Bibliographical Society of America
PAPhS, Proceedings of the American Philosophical Society
PapL, Papiere zur Linguistik
ParL, Paragone Letteratura
Parlem!, Parlem! Vai-i, qu'as paur! (IEO-Auvergne)
PartR, Partisan Review
PaS, Pamiętnik Słowiański
PASJ, Pictish Arts Society Journal
PaT, La Parola del Testo
PAX, Instytut Wydawniczy PAX, Warsaw

PB, Д-р Петър Берон
PBA, Proceedings of the British Academy
PBib, Philosophische Bibliothek, Hamburg, Meiner
PBLS, Proceedings of the Annual Meeting of the Berkeley Linguistic Society
PBML, Prague Bulletin of Mathematical Linguistics
PBSA, Publications of the Bibliographical Society of America
PC, Problems of Communism
PCLS, Proceedings of the Chicago Linguistic Society
PCP, Pacific Coast Philology
PD, Probleme der Dichtung, Heidelberg, Winter
PDA, Pagine della Dante
PdO, Paraula d'oc, Centre International de Recerca i Documentació d'Oc, Valencia
PE, Poesía Española
PEGS, Publications of the English Goethe Society
PenP, Il Pensiero Politico
PENS, Presses de l'École Normale Supérieure, Paris
PerM, Perspectives Médiévales
PEs, Lou Prouvençau à l'Escolo
PF, Présences Francophones
PFil, Prace Filologiczne
PFPS, Z problemów frazeologii polskiej i słowiańskiej, ZNiO
PFSCL, Papers on French Seventeenth Century Literature
PG, Païs gascons
PGA, Lo pais gascon/Lou pais gascoun, Anglet
PGIG, Publikationen der Gesellschaft für interkulturelle Germanistik, Munich, Iudicium
PH, La Palabra y El Hombre
PhilosQ, Philosophical Quarterly
PhilP, Philological Papers, West Virginia University
PhilR, Philosophy and Rhetoric
PhilRev, Philosophical Review
PhLC, Phréatique, Langage et Création
PHol, Le Pauvre Holterling
PhonPr, Phonetica Pragensia
PhP, Philologica Pragensia
PhR, Phoenix Review
PHSL, Proceedings of the Huguenot Society of London
PI, педагогический институт
PId, Le Parole e le Idee
PIGS, Publications of the Institute of Germanic Studies, University of London
PiH, Il Piccolo Hans
PIMA, Proceedings of the Illinois Medieval Association
PIMS, Publications of the Institute for Medieval Studies, Toronto
PIW, Państwowy Instytut Wydawniczy, Warsaw
PJ, Poradnik Językowy
PLing, Papers in Linguistics
PLit, Philosophy and Literature
PLL, Papers on Language and Literature
PL(L), Pamiętnik Literacki, London
PLRL, Patio de Letras/La Rosa als Llavis
PLS, Přednášky z běhu Letní školy slovanských studií
PL(W), Pamiętnik Literacki, Warsaw
PM, Pleine Marge
PMH, Portugaliae Monumenta Historica
PMHRS, Papers of the Medieval Hispanic Research Seminar, London, Department of Hispanic Studies, Queen Mary and Westfield College
PMLA, Publications of the Modern Language Association of America
PMPA, Publications of the Missouri Philological Association
PN, Paraulas de novelum, Périgueux
PNCIP, Plurilinguismo. Notizario del Centro Internazionale sul Plurilinguismo
PNR, Poetry and Nation Review
PNUS, Prace Naukowe Uniwersytetu Śląskiego, Katowice
PoetT, Poetics Today
PolR, Polish Review
PortSt, Portuguese Studies
PP, Prace Polonistyczne
PPNCFL, Proceedings of the Pacific Northwest Conference on Foreign Languages

PPr, Papers in Pragmatics
PPU, Promociones y Publicaciones Universitarias, S.A., Barcelona
PQ, The Philological Quarterly
PR, Podravska Revija
PrA, Prouvenço aro, Marseilles
PraRu, Prace Rusycystyczne
PRev, Poetry Review
PRF, Publications Romanes et Françaises, Geneva, Droz
PRH, Pahl-Rugenstein Hochschulschriften, Cologne, Pahl–Rugenstein
PrH, Provence Historique
PrHlit, Prace Historycznoliterackie
PrHum, Prace Humanistyczne
PRIA, Proceedings of the Royal Irish Academy
PrIJP, Prace Instytutu Języka Polskiego
Prilozi, Prilozi za književnost, jezik, istoriju i folklor, Belgrade
PrilPJ, Prilozi proučavanju jezika
PRIS-MA, Bulletin de liaison de l'ERLIMA, Université de Poitiers
PrLit, Prace Literackie
PRom, Papers in Romance
PrRu, Przegląd Rusycystyczny
PrzH, Przegląd Humanistyczny
PrzW, Przegląd Wschodni
PS, Проблеми слов'янознавства
PSCL, Papers and Studies in Contrastive Linguistics
PSE, Prague Studies in English
PSGAS, Politics and Society in Germany, Austria and Switzerland
PSLu, Pagine Storiche Luganesi
PSML, Prague Studies in Mathematical Linguistics
PSQ, Philologische Studien und Quellen, Berlin, Schmidt
PSR, Portuguese Studies Review
PSRL, Полное собрание русских летописей
PSS, Z polskich studiów slawistycznych, Warsaw, PWN
PSSLSAA, Procès-verbaux des séances de la Société des Lettres, Sciences et Arts de l'Aveyron
PSV, Polono-Slavica Varsoviensia
PT, Pamiętnik Teatralny
PUC, Pontifícia Universidade Católica, São Paulo
PUCRS, Pontífica Universidade Católica de Rio Grande do Sul, Porto Alegre
PUE, Publications Universitaires, Européennes, NY–Berne–Frankfurt, Lang
PUF, Presses Universitaires de France, Paris
PUG Pontificia Università Gregoriana
PUMRL, Purdue University Monographs in Romance Languages, Amsterdam — Philadelphia, Benjamins
PUStE, Publications de l'Université de St Étienne
PW, Poetry Wales
PWN, Państwowe Wydawnictwo Naukowe, Warsaw, etc

QA, Quaderni de Archivio
QALT, Quaderni dell'Atlante Lessicale Toscano
QASIS, Quaderni di lavoro dell'ASIS (Atlante Sintattico dell'Italia Settentrionale), Centro di Studio per la Dialettologia Italiana 'O. Parlangèli', Università degli Studi di Padova
QCFLP, Quaderni del Circolo Filologico Linguistico Padovano
QDLC, Quaderni del Dipartimento di Linguistica, Università della Calabria
QDLF, Quaderni del Dipartimento di Linguistica, Università degli Studi, Firenze
QDLLSMG, Quaderni del Dipartimento di Lingue e Letterature Straniere Moderne, Università di Genova
QDSL, Quellen zur deutschen Sprach- und Literaturgeschichte, Heidelberg, Winter
QFCC, Quaderni della Fondazione Camillo Caetani, Rome
QFESM, Quellen und Forschungen zur Erbauungsliteratur des späten Mittelalters und der frühen Neuzeit, Amsterdam, Rodopi
QFGB, Quaderni di Filologia Germanica della Facoltà di

Lettere e Filosofia dell'Università di Bologna
QFIAB, Quellen und Forschungen aus italienischen Archiven und Bibliotheken
QFLK, Quellen und Forschungen zur Literatur- und Kulturgeschichte, Berlin, de Gruyter
QFLR, Quaderni di Filologia e Lingua Romanze, Università di Macerata
QFRB, Quaderni di Filologia Romanza della Facoltà di Lettere e Filosofia dell'Università di Bologna
QFSK, Quellen und Forschungen zur Sprach- und Kulturgeschichte der germanischen Völker, Berlin, de Gruyter
QI, Quaderni d'Italianistica
QIA, Quaderni Ibero-Americani
QIGC, Quaderni dell'Istituto di Glottologia, Università degli Studi 'G. D'Annunzio' di Chieti, Facoltà di Lettere e Filosofia
QIICM, Quaderni dell'Istituto Italiano de Cultura, Melbourne
QILLSB, Quaderni dell'Istituto di Lingue e Letterature Straniere della Facoltà di Magistero dell'Università degli Studi di Bari
QILUU, Quaderni dell'Istituto di Linguistica dell'Università di Urbino
QINSRM, Quaderni dell'Istituto Nazionale di Studi sul Rinascimento Meridionale
QJMFL, A Quarterly Journal in Modern Foreign Literatures
QJS, Quarterly Journal of Speech, Speech Association of America
QLII, Quaderni di Letterature Iberiche e Iberoamericane
QLL, Quaderni di Lingue e Letterature, Verona
QLLP, Quaderni del Laboratorio di Linguistica, Scuola Normale Superiore, Pisa
QLLSP, Quaderni di Lingua e Letteratura Straniere, Facoltà di Magistero, Università degli Studi di Palermo
QLO, Quasèrns de Lingüistica Occitana
QM, Quaderni Milanesi
QMed, Quaderni Medievali
QP, Quaderns de Ponent
QPet, Quaderni Petrarcheschi
QPL, Quaderni Patavini di Linguistica
QQ, Queen's Quarterly, Kingston, Ontario
QR, Quercy Recherche, Cahors
QRCDLIM, Quaderni di Ricerca, Centro di Dialettologia e Linguistica Italiana di Manchester
QRP, Quaderni di Retorica e Poetica
QS, Quaderni di Semantica
QSF, Quaderni del Seicento Francese
QSGLL, Queensland Studies in German Language and Literature, Berne, Francke
QSt, Quaderni Storici
QStef, Quaderni Stefaniani
QSUP, Quaderni per la Storia dell'Università di Padova
QT, Quaderni di Teatro
QuF, Québec français
QuS, Quebec Studies
QV, Quaderni del Vittoriale
QVen, Quaderni Veneti
QVer, Quaderni Veronesi di Filologia, Lingua e Letteratura Italiana
QVR, Quo vadis Romania?, Vienna

RA, Romanistische Arbeitshefte, Tübingen, Niemeyer
RA, Revista Agustiniana
RAA, Rendiconti dell'Accademia di Archeologia, Lettere e Belle Arti
RABM, Revista de Archivos, Bibliotecas y Museos
RAct, Regards sur l'Actualité
Rad, Rad Jugoslavenske akademije znanosti i umjetnosti
RAE, Real Academia Española
RAfL, Research in African Literatures
RAG, Real Academia Galega
RAL, Revista Argentina de Lingüística

RAN, Regards sur l'Afrique du Nord
RANL, Rendiconti dell'Accademia Nazionale dei Lincei, Classe di scienze morali, storiche e filologiche, serie IX
RANPOLL, Revista ANPOLL, Faculdade de Filosofia, Letras e Ciências Humanas, Univ. de São Paulo.
RAPL, Revista da Academia Paulista de Letras, São Paulo
RAR, Renaissance and Reformation
RAS, Rassegna degli Archivi di Stato
RASoc, Revista de Antropología Social
RB, Revue Bénédictine
RBC, Research Bibliographies and Checklists, London, Grant & Cutler
RBDSL, Regensburger Beiträge zur deutschen Sprach- und Literaturwissenschaft, Frankfurt–Berne, Lang
RBG, Reclams de Bearn et Gasconha
RBGd, Rocznik Biblioteki Gdańskiej PAN (Libri Gedanenses)
RBKr, Rocznik Biblioteki PAN w Krakowie
RBL, Revista Brasileira de Lingüística
RBLL, Revista Brasileira de Lingua e Literatura
RBN, Revista da Biblioteca Nacional
RBPH, Revue Belge de Philologie et d'Histoire
RBS, Rostocker Beiträge zur Sprachwissenschaft
RC, Le Ragioni Critiche
RCat, Revista de Catalunya
RČAV, Rozpravy Československé akademie věd, Prague, ČSAV
RCB, Revista de Cultura Brasileña
RCCM, Rivista di Cultura Classica e Medioevale
RCEH, Revista Canadiense de Estudios Hispánicos
RCEN, Revue Canadienne d'Études Néerlandaises
RCF, Review of Contemporary Fiction
RCL, Revista Chilena de Literatura
RCLL, Revista de Crítica Literaria Latino-Americana
RCo, Revue de Comminges
RCSF, Rivista Critica di Storia della Filosofia
RCVS, Rassegna di Cultura e Vita Scolastica
RD, Revue drômoise: archéologie, histoire, géographie
RDE, Recherches sur Diderot et sur l''Encyclopédie'
RDi, Res diachronicae. Anuario de la Asociación de Jóvenes Investigadores de Historiografía e Historia de la Lengua Española
RDM, Revue des Deux Mondes
RDsS, Recherches sur le XVIIe Siècle
RDTP, Revista de Dialectología y Tradiciones Populares
RE, Revista de Espiritualidad
REC, Revista de Estudios del Caribe
RECat, Revue d'Études Catalanes
RedLet, Red Letters
REE, Revista de Estudios Extremeños
REEI, Revista del Instituto Egipcio de Estudios Islámicos, Madrid
REH, Revista de Estudios Hispánicos, Washington University, St Louis
REHisp, Revista de Estudios Hispánicos, Puerto Rico
REI, Revue des Études Italiennes
REJ, Revista de Estudios de Juventud
REJui, Revue des Études Juives, Paris
REL, Revue des Études Latines
RELA, Revista Española de Lingüística Aplicada
RelCL, Religion in Communist Lands
RELI, Rassegna Europea di Letteratura Italiana
RELing, Revista Española de Lingüística, Madrid
RelLit, Religious Literature
ReMS, Renaissance and Modern Studies
RenD, Renaissance Drama
RenP, Renaissance Papers
RenR, Renaissance and Reformation
RenS, Renaissance Studies

RER, Revista de Estudios Rosalianos
RES, Review of English Studies
RESEE, Revue des Études Sud-Est Européennes
RESS, Revue Européenne des Sciences Sociales et Cahiers Vilfredo Pareto
RevA, Revue d'Allemagne
RevAl, Revista de l'Alguer
RevAR, Revue des Amis de Ronsard
RevAuv, Revue d'Auvergne, Clermont-Ferrand
RevEL, Revista de Estudos da Linguagem, Faculdade de Letras, Universidade Federal de Minas Gerais
RevF, Revista de Filología
RevHA, Revue de la Haute-Auvergne
RevG, Revista de Girona
RevIb, Revista Iberoamericana
RevL, Revista Lusitana
RevLex, Revista de Lexicografía
RevLM, Revista de Literatura Medieval
RevLR, Revista do Livro
RevO, La Revista occitana, Montpellier
RevP, Revue Parole, Université de Mons-Hainault
RevPF, Revista Portuguesa de Filosofia
RevR, Revue Romane
RF, Romanische Forschungen
RFE, Revista de Filología Española
RFe, Razón y Fe
RFHL, Revue Française d'Histoire du Livre
RFLI, Rivista de Filologia e Letterature Ispaniche
RFLSJ, Revista de Filosofía y Lingüística de San José, Costa Rica
RFLUL, Revista da Faculdade de Letras da Universidade de Lisboa
RFLUP, Línguas e Literaturas, Revista da Faculdade de Letras, Univ. do Porto
RFN, Rivisti di Filosofia Neoscolastica
RFo, Ricerca Folklorica
RFP, Recherches sur le Français Parlé
RFR, Revista de Filología Románica
RFr, Revue Frontenac
RFULL, Revista de Filologia de la Universidad de La Laguna
RG, Recherches Germaniques
RGand, Romanica Gandensia
RGCC, Revue du Gévaudan, des Causses et des Cévennes
RGG, Rivista di Grammatica Generativa
RGI, Revue Germanique Internationale
RGL, Reihe Germanistische Linguistik, Tübingen, Niemeyer
RGo, Romanica Gothoburgensia
RGT, Revista Galega de Teatro
RH, Reihe Hanser, Munich, Hanser
RH, Revue Hebdomadaire
RHA, Revista de Historia de America
RHAM, Revue Historique et Archéologique du Maine
RHCS, Rocznik Historii Czasopiśmiennictwa Polskiego
RHDFE, Revue Historique de Droit Français et Étranger
RHE, Revue d'Histoire Ecclésiastique
RHEF, Revue d'Histoire de l'Église de France
RHel, Romanica Helvetica, Tübingen and Basle, Francke
RHFB, Rapports — Het Franse Boek
RHI, Revista da Historia das Ideias
RHis, Revue Historique
RHL, Reihe Hanser Literaturkommentare, Munich, Hanser
RHLF, Revue d'Histoire Littéraire de la France
RHLP, Revista de História Literária de Portugal
RHM, Revista Hispánica Moderna
RHMag, Revue d'Histoire Maghrébine
RHMC, Revue d'Histoire Moderne et Contemporaine
RHPR, Revue d'Histoire et de Philosophie Religieuses
RHR, Réforme, Humanisme, Renaissance

RHRel, Revue de l'Histoire des Religions
RHS, Revue Historique de la Spiritualité
RHSc, Revue d'Histoire des Sciences
RHSt, Ricarda Huch. Studien zu ihrem Leben und Werk
RHT, Revue d'Histoire du Théâtre
RHTe, Revue d'Histoire des Textes
RI, Rassegna Iberistica
RIA, Rivista Italiana di Acustica
RIa, Русский язык
RIAB, Revista Interamericana de Bibliografía
RIaR, Русский язык за рубежом
RICC, Revue Itinéraires et Contacts de Culture
RICP, Revista del Instituto de Cultura Puertorriqueña
RicSl, Ricerche Slavistiche
RID, Rivista Italiana di Dialettologia
RIE, Revista de Ideas Estéticas
RIEB, Revista do Instituto de Estudos Brasileiros
RIL, Rendiconti dell'Istituto Lombardo
RILA, Rassegna Italiana di Linguistica Applicata
RILCE, Revista del Instituto de Lengua y Cultura Españoles
RILI, Revista Internacional de Lingüística Iberoamericana
RILP, Revista Internacional da Língua Portuguesa
RIM, Rivista Italiana di Musicologia
RIndM, Revista de Indias
RInv, Revista de Investigación
RIO, Revue Internationale d'Onomastique
RIOn, Rivista Italiana di Onomastica
RIP, Revue Internationale de Philosophie
RIS, Revue de l'Institute de Sociologie, Université Libre, Brussels
RiS, Ricerche Storiche
RITL, Revista de Istorie şi Teorie Literară, Bucharest
RivF, Rivista di Filosofia
RivL, Rivista di Linguistica
RJ, Romanistisches Jahrbuch
RKHlit, Rocznik Komisji Historycznoliterackiej PAN
RKJŁ, Rozprawy Komisji Językowej Łódzkiego Towarzystwa Naukowego
RKJW, Rozprawy Komisji Językowej Wrocławskiego Towarzystwa Naukowego
RLA, Romance Languages Annual
RLaR, Revue des Langues Romanes
RLB, Recueil Linguistique de Bratislava
RLC, Revue de Littérature Comparée
RLD, Revista de Llengua i Dret
RLet, Revista de Letras
RLettI, Rivista di Letteratura Italiana
RLex, Revista de Lexicologia
RLF, Revista de Literatura Fantástica
RLFRU, Recherches de Linguistique Française et Romane d'Utrecht
RLH, Revista de Literatura Hispanoamericana
RLI, Rassegna della Letteratura Italiana
RLib, Rivista dei Libri
RLing, Russian Linguistics
RLiR, Revue de Linguistique Romane
RLit, Revista de Literatura
RLJ, Russian Language Journal
RLLCGV, Revista de Lengua y Literatura Catalana, Gallega y Vasca, Madrid
RLLR, Romance Literature and Linguistics Review
RLM, Revista de Literaturas Modernas, Cuyo
RLMC, Rivista di Letterature Moderne e Comparate
RLMed, Revista de Literatura Medieval
RLMexC, Revista de Literatura Mexicana Contemporánea
RLMod, Revue des Lettres Modernes
RLModCB, Revue des Lettres Modernes. Carnets Bibliographiques
RLSer, Revista de Literatura Ser, Puerto Rico

RLSL, Revista de Lingvisticä şi Ştiinţä Literarä
RLT, Russian Literature Triquarterly
RLTA, Revista de Lingüística Teórica y Aplicada
RLV, Revue des Langues Vivantes
RLVin, Recherches Linguistiques de Vincennes
RM, Romance Monograph Series, University, Mississippi
RM, Remate de Males
RMAL, Revue du Moyen Âge Latin
RMar, Revue Marivaux
RMC, Roma Moderna e Contemporanea
RMEH, Revista Marroquí de Estudios Hispánicos
RMH, Recherches sur le Monde Hispanique au XIXe Siècle
RMI, Rivista Musicale Italiana
RMM, Revue de Métaphysique et de Morale
RMon, Revue Montesquieu
RMRLL, Rocky Mountain Review of Language and Literature
RMS, Reading Medieval Studies
RMus, Revue de Musicologie
RNC, Revista Nacional de Cultura, Carácas
RNDWSPK, Rocznik Naukowo-Dydaktyczny WSP w Krakowie
RO, Revista de Occidente
RoczH, Roczniki Humanistyczne Katolickiego Uniw. Lubelskiego
RoczSl, Rocznik Slawistyczny
ROl, Rossica Olomucensia
RoM, Rowohlts Monographien, Reinbek, Rowohlt
RomGG, Romanistik in Geschichte und Gegenwart
ROMM, Revue de L'Occident Musulman et de la Méditerranée
RoN, Romance Notes
RoQ, Romance Quarterly
RORD, Research Opportunities in Renaissance Drama
RoS, Romance Studies
RoSl, Роднае слова
RP, Радянський письменник
RP, Revista de Portugal
RPA, Revue de Phonétique Appliquée
RPac, Revue du Pacifique
RPC, Revue Pédagogique et Culturelle de l'AVEP
RPF, Revista Portuguesa de Filologia
RPFE, Revue Philosophique de la France et de l'Étranger
RPh, Romance Philology
RPL, Revue Philosophique de Louvain
RPl, Río de la Plata
RPLit, Res Publica Litterarum
RPM, Revista de Poética Medieval
RPN, Res Publica nowa, Warsaw
RPol, Review of Politics
RPP, Romanticism Past and Present
RPr, Raison Présente
RPS, Revista Paraguaya de Sociologia
RPyr, Recherches pyrénéennes, Toulouse
RQ, Renaissance Quarterly
RQL, Revue Québécoise de Linguistique
RR, Romanic Review
RRe, Русская речь
RRL, Revue Roumaine de Linguistique
RRou, Revue du Rouergue
RRR, Reformation and Renaissance Review
RS, Reihe Siegen, Heidelberg, Winter
RS, Revue de Synthèse
RSBA, Revista de studii britanice şi americane
RSC, Rivista di Studi Canadesi
RSCI, Rivista di Storia della Chiesa in Italia
RSD, Rivista di studi danteschi
RSEAV, Revue de la Société des enfants et amis de Villeneuve-de-Berg
RSF, Rivista di Storia della Filosofia
RSH, Revue des Sciences Humaines
RSh, Радянська школа
RSI, Rivista Storica Italiana
RSJb, Reinhold Schneider Jahrbuch
RSL, Rusycystyczne Studia Literaturoznawcze
RSl, Revue des Études Slaves
RSLR, Rivista di Storia e Letteratura Religiose
RSPT, Revue des Sciences Philosophiques et Théologiques

RSR, Rassegna Storica del Risorgimento
RSSR, Rivista di Storia Sociale e Religiosa
RST, Rassegna Storica Toscana
RSt, Research Studies
RSTe, Rivista di Studi Testuali
RStI, Rivista di Studi Italiani
RT, Revue du Tarn
RTAM, Recherches de Théologie Ancienne et Médiévale
RTLiM, Rocznik Towarzystwa Literackiego im. Adama Mickiewicza
RTr, Recherches et Travaux, Université de Grenoble
RTUG, Recherches et Travaux de l'Université de Grenoble III
RUB, Revue de l'Université de Bruxelles
RUC, Revista de la Universidad Complutense
RuLit, Ruch Literacki
RUM, Revista de la Universidad de Madrid
RUMex, Revista de la Universidad de México
RUOt, Revue de l'Université d'Ottawa
RUS, Rice University Studies
RusH, Russian History
RusL, Русская литература, ПД, Leningrad
RusM, Русская мысль
RusMed, Russia Medievalis
RusR, Russian Review
RUW, Rozprawy Uniwersytetu Warsawskiego, Warsaw
RV, Revue Voltaire
RVB, Rheinische Vierteljahrsblätter
RVF, Revista Valenciana de Filología
RVi, Revue du Vivarais
RVQ, Romanica Vulgaria Quaderni
RVV, Romanische Versuche und Vorarbeiten, Bonn U.P.
RVVig, Reihe der Villa Vigoni, Tübingen, Niemeyer
RZLG, Romanistische Zeitschrift für Literaturgeschichte
RZSF, Radovi Zavoda za slavensku filologiju
SA, Studien zum Althochdeutschen, Göttingen, Vandenhoeck & Ruprecht
SAB, South Atlantic Bulletin
Sac, Sacris Erudiri
SAG, Stuttgarter Arbeiten zur Germanistik, Stuttgart, Heinz
SAH, Studies in American Humour
SANU, Srpska akademija nauka i umetnosti
SAOB, Svenska Akademiens Ordbok
SAQ, South Atlantic Quarterly
SAR, South Atlantic Review
SAS, Studia Academica Slovaca
SaS, Slovo a slovesnost
SASc, Studia Anthroponymica Scandinavica
SATF, Société des Anciens Textes Français
SAV, Slovenská akadémia vied
SAVL, Studien zur allgemeinen und vergleichenden Literaturwissenschaft, Stuttgart, Metzler
SB, Slavistische Beiträge, Munich, Sagner
SB, Studies in Bibliography
SBAW, Sitzungsberichte der Bayerischen Akad. der Wissenschaften, phil-hist. Kl., Munich, Beck
SBL, Saarbrücker Beiträge zur Literaturwissenschaft, St. Ingbert, Röhrig
SBL, Старобългарска литература
SBR, Swedish Book Review
SBVS, Saga-Book of the Viking Society
SC, Studia Celtica, The Bulletin of the Board of Celtic Studies
SCB, Skrifter utgivna av Centrum för barnkulturforskning, Stockholm U.P.
SCC, Studies in Comparative Communism
SCen, The Seventeenth Century
SCES, Sixteenth Century Essays and Studies, Kirksville, Missouri, Sixteenth Century Journal
SCFS, Seventeenth-Century French Studies
SchG, Schriftsteller der Gegenwart, Berlin, Volk & Wissen

SchSch, Schlern-Schriften, Innsbruck, Wagner
SchwM, Schweizer Monatshefte
SCJ, Sixteenth Century Journal
SCL, Studii şi Cercetări Lingvistice
SCl, Stendhal Club
ScL, Scottish Language
ScM, Scripta Mediterranea
SCN, Seventeenth Century News
SCO, Studii şi Cercetări de Onomastică
ScO, Scriptoralia, Tübingen, Narr
ScPo, Scientia Poetica
SCR, Studies in Comparative Religion
ScRev, Scandinavian Review
ScSl, Scando-Slavica
ScSt, Scandinavian Studies
SD, Sprache und Dichtung, n.F., Berne, Haupt
SD, Современная драматургия.
SdA, Storia dell'Arte
SDFU, Skrifter utgivna genom Dialekt- och folkminnesarkivet i Uppsala
SDG, Studien zur deutschen Grammatik, Tübingen, Stauffenburg
SDL, Studien zur deutschen Literatur, Tübingen, Niemeyer
SDLNZ, Studien zur deutschen Literatur des 19. und 20. Jahrhunderts, Berne, Lang
SdO, Serra d'Or
SDOFU, Skrifter utgivna av Dialekt-, ortnamns- och folkminnesarkivet i Umeå
SDS, Studien zur Dialektologie in Südwestdeutschland, Marburg, Elwert
SDSp, Studien zur deutschen Sprache, Tübingen, Narr
SDv, Sprache und Datenverarbeitung
SE, Série Esludos Uberaba
SeC, Scrittura e Civiltà
SECC, Studies in Eighteenth-Century Culture
SECCFC, Sociedad Estatal para la Conmemoración de los Centenarios de Felipe II y Carlos V
SEDES, Société d'Éditions d'Enseignement Supérieur
SEEA, Slavic and East European Arts
SEEJ, The Slavic and East European Journal
SEER, Slavonic and East European Review
SEES, Slavic and East European Studies
SEI, Società Editrice Internazionale, Turin
SELA, South Eastern Latin Americanist
SemL, Seminarios de Linguística, Universidade do Algarve, Faro
SEN, Società Editrice Napoletana, Naples
SEP, Secretaría de Educación Pública, Mexico
SeS, Serbian Studies
SEz, Съпоставително езикознание
SF, Slavistische Forschungen, Cologne — Vienna, Böhlau
SFAIEO, Section Française de l'Association Internationale d'Études Occitanes, Montpellier
SFI, Studi di Filologia Italiana
SFIS, Stanford French and Italian Studies
SFKG, Schriftenreihe der Franz–Kafka–Gesellschaft, Vienna, Braumüller
SFL, Studies in French Literature, London, Arnold
SFL, Studi di Filologia e Letteratura
SFPS, Studia z Filologii Polskiej i Słowiańskiej PAN
SFR, Stanford French Review
SFr, Studi Francesi
SFRS, Studia z Filologii Rosyjskiej i Slowiańskiej, Warsaw
SFS, Swiss-French Studies
SFUŠ, Sborník Filozofickej Fakulty Univerzity P. J. Šafárika, Prešov
SG, Sprache der Gegenwart, Düsseldorf, Schwann
SGAK, Studien zu Germanistik, Anglistik und Komparatistik, Bonn, Bouvier
SGECRN, Study Group on Eighteenth-Century Russia Newsletter
SGEL, Sociedad General Española de Librería

SGesch, Sprache und Geschichte, Stuttgart, Klett-Cotta
SGF, Stockholmer Germanistische Forschungen, Stockholm, Almqvist & Wiksell
SGG, Studia Germanica Gandensia
SGGed, Studia Germanica Gedanensia
SGI, Studi di Grammatica Italiana
SGLL, Studies in German Language and Literature, Lewiston-Queenston-Lampeter
SGLLC, Studies in German Literature, Linguistics, and Culture, Columbia, S.C., Camden House, Woodbridge, Boydell & Brewer
SGP, Studia Germanica Posnaniensia
SGS, Stanford German Studies, Berne, Lang
SGS, Scottish Gaelic Studies
SGU, Studia Germanistica Upsaliensia, Stockholm, Almqvist & Wiksell
SGUV, Studia Germanica Universitatis Vesprimiensis
SH, Slavica Helvetica, Berne, Lang
SH, Studia Hibernica
ShAn, Sharq al-Andalus
SHCT, Studies in the History of Christian Thought, Leiden, Brill
SHPF, Société de l'Histoire du Protestantisme Français
SHPS, Studies in History and Philosophy of Science
SHR, The Scottish Historical Review
SI, Sprache und Information, Tübingen, Niemeyer
SIAA, Studi di Italianistica nell'Africa Australe
SiCh, Слово і час
SIDES, Société Internationale de Diffusion et d'Édition Scientifiques, Antony
SIDS, Schriften des Instituts für deutsche Sprache, Berlin, de Gruyter
Siglo XX, Siglo XX/20th Century
SILTA, Studi Italiani di Linguistica Teorica ed Applicata
SiN, Sin Nombre
SINSU, Skrifter utgivna av institutionen för nordiska språk vid Uppsala universitet, Uppsala U.P.
SIR, Stanford Italian Review
SISMEL, Società Internazionale per lo Studio del Medioevo Latino, Edizioni del Galluzzo, Florence
SIsp, Studi Ispanici
SISSD, Società Italiana di Studi sul Secolo XVIII
SJLŠ, Slovenský jazyk a literatúra v škole
SKHAW, Schriften der phil.-hist. Klasse der Heidelberger Akademie der Wissenschaften, Heidelberg, Winter
SkSt, Skandinavistische Studien
SKZ, Srpska Književna Zadruga, Belgrade
SL, Sammlung Luchterhand, Darmstadt, Luchterhand
SL, Studia Linguistica
SLÅ, Svensk Lärarföreningens Årsskrift
SlaG, Slavica Gandensia
SlaH, Slavica Helsingensia
SlaL, Slavica Lundensia
SlavFil, Славянска филология, Sofia
SlavH, Slavica Hierosolymitana
SlavLit, Славянските литератури в България
SlavRev, Slavistična revija
SlaW, Slavica Wratislaviensia
SLeg, Studium Legionense
SLeI, Studi di Lessicografia Italiana
SLESPO, Suplemento Literário do Estado de São Paulo
SLF, Studi di Letteratura Francese
SLG, Studia Linguistica Germanica, Berlin, de Gruyter
SLI, Società di Linguistica Italiana
SLI, Studi Linguistici Italiani
SLIGU, Skrifter utgivna av Litteraturvetenskapliga institutionen vid Göteborgs universitet, Gothenburg U.P.
SLILU, Skrifter utgivna av Litteraturvetenskapliga institutionen vid Lunds universitet, Lund U.P.
SLinI, Studi di Lingua Italiana

SLit, Schriften zur Literaturwissenschaft, Berlin, Dunckler & Humblot
SLit, Slovenská literatúra
SLitR, Stanford Literature Review
SLIUU, Skrifter utgivna av Litteraturvetenskapliga institutionen vid Uppsala universitet, Uppsala U.P.
SLK, Schwerpunkte Linguistik und Kommunikationswissenschaft
SLL, Skrifter utg. genom Landsmålsarkivet i Lund
SLM, Studien zur Literatur der Moderne, Bonn, Bouvier
SlN, Slovenský národopis
SLO, Slavica Lublinensia et Olomucensia
SlO, Slavia Orientalis
SlOc, Slavia Occidentalis
SlOth, Slavica Othinensia
SlPN, Slovenské pedagogické nakladateľstvo
SlPoh, Slovenské pohľady
SlPr, Slavica Pragensia
SLPS, Studia Linguistica Polono-Slovaca
SLR, Société de Linguistique Romane
SLR, Second Language Research
SLRev, Southern Literary Review
SLS, Studies in the Linguistic Sciences
SlSb, Slezský sborník
SlSl, Slavica Slovaca
SlSp, Slovenský spisovateľ
SLu, Studia Lulliana
SLWU, Sprach und Literatur in Wissenschaft und Unterricht
SM, Sammlung Metzler, Stuttgart, Metzler
SM, Studi Medievali
SMC, Studies in Medieval Culture
SME, Schöninghs mediävistische Editionen, Paderborn, Schöningh
SMer, Студенческий меридиан
SMGL, Studies in Modern German Literature, Berne – Frankfurt – New York, Lang
SMHC, Studies in Medieval History and Culture, New York, Routledge
SMI, Stilistica e metrica italiana
SMLS, Strathclyde Modern Language Studies
SMRT, Studies in Medieval and Reformation Thought, Leiden, Brill
SMS, Sewanee Medieval Studies
SMu, Советский музей
SMV, Studi Mediolatini e Volgari
SN, Studia Neophilologica
SNL, Sveučilišna naklada Liber, Zagreb
SNM, Sborník Národního muzea
SNov, Seara Nova
SNTL, Státní nakladatelství technické literatury
SÖAW, Sitzungsberichte der Österreichischen Akademie der Wissenschaften, phil.-hist. Klasse
SOBI, Societat d'Onomastica, Butlleti Interior, Barcelona
SoCR, South Central Review
SOH, Studia Onomastica Helvetica, Arbon, Eurotext: Historisch-Archäologischer Verlag
SoK, Sprog og Kultur
SopL, Sophia Linguistica, Tokyo
SoRA, Southern Review, Adelaide
SoRL, Southern Review, Louisiana
SOU, Skrifter utgivna genom Ortnamnsarkivet i Uppsala
SP, Sammlung Profile, Bonn, Bouvier
SP, Studies in Philology
SPat, Studi Patavini
SpC, Speech Communication
SPCT, Studi e Problemi di Critica Testuale
SPES, Studio per Edizioni Scelte, Florence
SPFB, Sborník Pedagogické fakulty v Brně
SPFFBU, Sborník prací Filosofické fakulty Brněnské Univerzity
SPFFBU-A, Sborník prací Filosofické fakulty Brněnské Univerzity, A - řada jazykovědná
SPGS, Scottish Papers in Germanic Studies, Glasgow
SPFPFSU-D, Sborník prací filozoficko-přírodovědecké fakulty Slezské univerzity v Opavě, řada jazykovědná D
SPh, Studia philologica, Olomouc

SPi, Serie Piper, Munich, Piper
SPIEL, Siegener Periodicum zur Internationalen Empirischen Literaturwissenschaft
SPIL, Stellenbosch Papers in Linguistics
SPK, Studia nad polszczyzną kresową, Wrocław
SpLit, Sprache und Literatur
SpMod, Spicilegio Moderno, Pisa
SPN, Státní pedagogické nakladatelství
SPol, Studia Polonistyczne
SPR, Slavistic Printings and Reprintings, The Hague, Mouton
SpR, Spunti e Ricerche
SPRF, Société de Publications Romanes et Françaises, Geneva, Droz
SPS, Specimina Philologiae Slavicae, Munich, Otto Sagner
SPS, Studia Philologica Salmanticensia
SPSO, Studia Polono–Slavica–Orientalia. Acta Litteraria
SpSt, Spanish Studies
SPUAM, Studia Polonistyczna Uniwersytetu Adama Mickiewicza, Poznań
SR, Slovenská reč
SRAZ, Studia Romanica et Anglica Zagrabiensia
SRev, Slavic Review
SRF, Studi e Ricerche Francescane
SRL, Studia Romanica et Linguistica, Frankfurt, Lang
SRLF, Saggi e Ricerche di Letteratura Francese
SRo, Studi Romanzi
SRom, Studi Romeni
SRoP, Studia Romanica Posnaniensia
SRP, Studia Rossica Posnaniensia
SRU, Studia Romanica Upsaliensia
SS, Symbolae Slavicae, Frankfurt–Berne–Cirencester, Lang
SS, Syn og Segn
SSBI, Skrifter utgivna av Svenska barnboksinstitutet
SSB, Strenna Storica Bolognese
SSCJ, Southern Speech Communication Journal
SSDSP, Società Savonese di Storia Patria
SSE, Studi di Storia dell'Educazione
SSF, Studies in Short Fiction
SSFin, Studia Slavica Finlandensia
SSGL, Studies in Slavic and General Linguistics, Amsterdam, Rodopi
SSH, Studia Slavica Academiae Scientiarum Hungaricae
SSL, Studi e Saggi Linguistici
SSLF, Skrifter utgivna av Svenska Litteratursällskapet i Finland
SSLP, Studies in Slavic Literature and Poetics, Amsterdam, Rodopi
SSLS, Studi Storici Luigi Simeoni
SSMP, Stockholm Studies in Modern Philology
SSPHS, Society for Spanish and Portuguese Historical Studies, Millersville
SSR, Scottish Studies Review
SSS, Stanford Slavic Studies
SSSAS, Society of Spanish and Spanish-American Studies, Boulder, Colorado
SSSlg, Sagners Slavistische Sammlung, Munich, Sagner
SSSN, Skrifter utgivna av Svenska språknämnden
SSSP, Stockholm Studies in Scandinavian Philology
SST, Sprache — System und Tätigkeit, Frankfurt, Lang
SSt, Slavic Studies, Hokkaido
ST, Suhrkamp Taschenbuch, Frankfurt, Suhrkamp
ST, Studi Testuali, Alessandria, Edizioni dell'Orso
StB, Studi sul Boccaccio
StBo, Studia Bohemica
STC, Studies in the Twentieth Century
StCJ, Studia Celtica Japonica
STCL, Studies in Twentieth Century Literature
StCL, Studies in Canadian Literature
STCM, Sciences, techniques et civilisations du moyen âge à l'aube des temps modernes. Paris, Champion
StComH, Studia Comeniana et historica

StCrit, Strumenti Critici
StD, Studi Danteschi
StF, Studie Francescani
StFil, Studia Filozoficzne
STFM, Société des Textes Français Modernes
StG, Studi Germanici
StGol, Studi Goldoniani
StH, Studies in the Humanities
StI, Studi Italici, Kyoto
StIt, Studi Italiani
StL, Studium Linguistik
StLa, Studies in Language, Amsterdam
StLI, Studi di Letteratura Ispano-Americana
StLi, Stauffenburg Linguistik, Tübingen, Stauffenburg
StLIt, Studi Latini e Italiani
StLM, Studies in the Literary Imagination
StLo, Studia Logica
STM, Suhrkamp Taschenbuch Materialien, Frankfurt, Suhrkamp
StM, Studies in Medievalism
STMFN, Studien und Texte zum Mittelalter und zur frühen Neuzeit, Münster, Waxmann
STML, Studies on Themes and Motifs in Literature, New York, Lang
StMon, Studia Monastica
StMus, Studi Musicali
StMy, Studia Mystica
StN, Studi Novecenteschi
StNF, Studier i Nordisk Filologi
StO, Studium Ovetense
StP, Studi Piemontesi
StPet, Studi Petrarcheschi
StR, Studie o rukopisech
StRLLF, Studi e Ricerche di Letteratura e Linguistica Francese
StRmgn, Studi Romagnoli
StRo, Studi Romani
StRom, Studies in Romanticism
StRu, Studia Russica, Budapest
StS, Studi Storici
StSec, Studi Secenteschi
StSem, Studia Semiotyczne
StSen, Studi Senesi
StSet, Studi Settecenteschi
STSG, Schriften der Theodor-Storm-Gesellschaft, Heide in Holstein, Boyens
StSk, Studia Skandinavica
STSL, Studien und Texte zur Sozialgeschichte der Literatur, Tübingen, Niemeyer
StSp, Studies in Spirituality
StT, Studi Tassiani
STUF, Sprachtypologie und Universalienforschung
StV, Studies on Voltaire and the 18th Century
STW, Suhrkamp Taschenbücher Wissenschaft, Frankfurt, Suhrkamp
STW, Studies in Travel Writing
StZ, Sprache im technischen Zeitalter
SU, Studi Urbinati
SUBBP, Studia Universitatis Babeş-Bolyai, Philologia, Cluj
SUDAM, Editorial Sudamericana, Buenos Aires
SuF, Sinn und Form
SUm, Schede Umanistiche
SUP, Spisy University J. E. Purkyně, Brno
SupEz, Съпоставително езикознание, Sofia
SV, Studi Veneziani
SVEC, Studies in Voltaire and the Eighteenth Century, Oxford, Voltaire Foundation (formerly *StV*)
SZ, Studia Zamorensia

TAL, Travaux d'Archéologie Limousine, Limoges
TAm, The Americas, Bethesda
TAPS, Transactions of the American Philosophical Society
TB, Tempo Brasileiro
TBL, Tübinger Beiträge zur Linguistik, Tübingen, Narr
TC, Texto Critico
TCBS, Transactions of the Cambridge Bibliographical Society
TCERFM, Travaux du Centre d'Études et de Recherches sur François Mauriac, Bordeaux

TCHS, Transactions of the Caernarvonshire Historical Society
TCL, Twentieth-Century Literature
TCLN, Travaux du Cercle Linguistique de Nice
TCMA, Traductions des Classiques du Moyen Age, Paris, Champion
TCWAAS, Transactions of the Cumberland and Westmorland Antiquarian and Archaeological Society
TD, Teksty Drugie
TDC, Textes et Documents pour la Classe
TEC, Teresiunum Ephemerides Carmeliticae
TECC, Textos i Estudis de Cultura Catalana, Curial — Publicacions de l'Abadia de Montserrat, Barcelona
TeK, Text und Kontext
TELK, Trouvaillen — Editionen zur Literatur- und Kulturgeschichte, Berne, Lang
TeN, Terminologies Nouvelles
TeSt, Teatro e Storia
TE(XVIII), Textos y Estudios del Siglo XVIII
TF, Texte zur Forschung, Darmstadt, Wissenschaftliche Buchgesellschaft
TFN, Texte der Frühen Neuzeit, Frankfurt, Keip
TGLSK, Theorie und Geschichte der Literatur und der Schönen Künste, Munich, Fink
TGSI, Transactions of the Gaelic Society of Inverness
THESOC, Thesaurus Occitan
THL, Theory and History of Literature, Manchester U.P.
THM, Textos Hispánicos Modernos, Barcelona, Labor
THR, Travaux d'Humanisme et Renaissance, Geneva, Droz
THSC, Transactions of the Honourable Society of Cymmrodorion
TI, Le Texte et l'Idée
TidLit, Tidskrift för Litteraturvetenskap
TILAS, Travaux de l'Institut d'Études Latino-Américaines de l'Université de Strasbourg
TILL, Travaux de l'Institut de Linguistique de Lund
TJ, Theatre Journal
TK, Text und Kritik, Munich
TK, Text und Kritik
TKS, Търновска книжевна школа, Sofia
TL, Theoretical Linguistics
TLF, Textes Littéraires Français, Geneva, Droz
TLFI, Trésor de la langue française informatisé, <http://atilf.inalf.fr/tlfv3.htm>
TLit, Travaux de Littérature
TLP, Travaux de Linguistique et de Philologie
TLQ, Travaux de Linguistique Québécoise
TLTL, Teaching Language Through Literature
TM, Les Temps Modernes
TMJb, Thomas Mann-Jahrbuch
TMo, O Tempo e o Modo
TMS, Thomas-Mann Studien, Frankfurt, Klostermann
TN, Theatre Notebook
TNA, Tijdschrift voor Nederlands en Afrikaans
TNT, Towarzystwo Naukowe w Toruniu
TOc, Tèxtes Occitans, Bordeaux
TODL, Труды Отдела древнерусской литературы Института русской литературы АН СССР
TP, Textual Practice
TPa, Torre de Papel
TPS, Transactions of the Philological Society
TQ, Theatre Quarterly
TR, Телевидение и радиовещание
TravL, Travaux de Linguistique, Luxembourg
TRCTL, Texte-Revue de Critique et de Théorie Littéraire
TRI, Theatre Research International
TRISMM, Tradition — Reform — Innovation. Studien zur

Modernität des Mittelalters, Frankfurt, Lang
TrK, Трезвость и культура
TrL, Travaux de Linguistique
TrLit, Translation and Literature
TRS, The Transactions of the Radnorshire Society
TS, Theatre Survey
TSC, Treballs de Sociolingüística Catalana
TSDL, Tübinger Studien zur deutschen Literatur, Frankfurt, Lang
TSJ, Tolstoy Studies Journal
TSL, Trierer Studien zur Literatur, Frankfurt, Lang
TSLL, Texas Studies in Literature and Language
TSM, Texte des späten Mittelalters und der frühen Neuzeit, Berlin, Schmidt
TsNTL, Tijdschrift voor Nederlandse Taal- en Letterkunde
TSRLL, Tulane Studies in Romance Languages and Literature
TsSk, Tijdschrift voor Skandinavistiek
TsSV, Tijdschrift voor de Studie van de Verlichting
TSWL, Tulsa Studies in Women's Literature
TT, Tekst en Tijd, Nijmegen, Alfa
TT, Travail Théâtral
TTAS, Twayne Theatrical Arts Series, Boston–New York
TTG, Texte und Textgeschichte, Tübingen, Niemeyer
TTr, Terminologie et Traduction
TUGS, Texte und Untersuchungen zur Germanistik und Skandinavistik, Frankfurt, Lang
TVS, Theorie und Vermittlung der Sprache, Frankfurt, Lang
TWAS, Twayne's World Authors Series, Boston–New York
TWQ, Third World Quarterly

UAB, Universitat Autònoma de Barcelona
UAC, Universidad de Antioquia, Colombia
UAM, Uniwersytet Adama Mickiewicza, Poznań
UB, Universal-Bibliothek, Stuttgart, Reclam
UBL, Universal-Bibliothek, Leipzig, Reclam
UCLWPL, UCL Working Papers in Linguistics
UCPL, University of California Publications in Linguistics
UCPMP, University of California Publications in Modern Philology
UDL, Untersuchungen zur deutschen Literaturgeschichte, Tübingen, Niemeyer
UDR, University of Dayton Review
UERJ, Universidade Estadual do Rio de Janeiro
UFPB, Universidade Federal da Paraiba
UFRGS, Univ. Federal do Rio Grande do Sul (Brazil)
UFRJ, Universidade Federal do Rio de Janeiro
UFSC, Universidade Federal de Santa Catarina
UFSM, Universidade Federal de Santa Maria
UGE, Union Générale d'Éditions
UGFGP, University of Glasgow French and German Publications
UGLD, Union generala de Ladins dles Dolomites
UL, Українське літературознавство, Lvov U.P.
UM, Українська мова і література в школі
UMCS, Uniwersytet Marii Curie-Skłodowskiej, Lublin
UMov, Українське мовазнавство
UNAM, Universidad Nacional Autónoma de Mexico
UNC, Univ. of North Carolina
UNCSGL, University of North Carolina Studies in Germanic Languages and Literatures, Chapel Hill
UNED, Universidad Nacional de Enseñanza a Distancia
UNESP, Universidade Estadual de São Paulo
UNMH, University of Nottingham Monographs in the Humanities

UPP, University of Pennsylvania Press, Philadelphia
UQ, Ukrainian Quarterly
UR, Umjetnost riječi
USCFLS, University of South Carolina French Literature Series
USFLQ, University of South Florida Language Quarterly
USH, Umeå Studies in the Humanities, Stockholm, Almqvist & Wiksell International
USLL, Utah Studies in Literature and Linguistics, Berne, Lang
USP, Universidade de São Paulo
UTB, Uni-Taschenbücher
UTET, Unione Tipografico-Editrice Torinese
UTPLF, Università di Torino, Pubblicazioni della Facoltà di Lettere e Filosofia
UTQ, University of Toronto Quarterly
UVAN, Українська Вільна Академія Наук, Winnipeg
UVK, Universitätsverlag Konstanz
UVWPL, University of Venice Working Papers in Linguistics
UWCASWC, The University of Wales Centre for Advanced Studies in Welsh and Celtic
UZLU, Ученые записки Ленинградского университета

VAM, Vergessene Autoren der Moderne, Siegen U.P.
VAS, Vorträge und Abhandlungen zur Slavistik, Giessen, Schmitz
VASSLOI, Veröffentlichungen der Abteilung für Slavische Sprachen und Literaturen des Osteuropa–Instituts (Slavistiches Seminar) an der Freien Universität Berlin
VB, Vestigia Bibliae
VBDU, Веснік Беларускага дзяржаўнага ўніверсітэта імя У. І. Леніна. Серыя IV
VCT, Les Voies de la Création Théâtrale
VDASD, Veröffentlichungen der Deutschen Akademie für Sprache und Dichtung, Darmstadt, Luchterhand
VDG, Verlag und Datenbank für Geisteswissenschaften, Weimar
VF, Вопросы философии
VGBIL, Всесоюзная государственная библиотека иностранной литературы
VH, Vida Hispánica, Wolverhampton
VHis, Verba Hispanica
VI, Военно издателство
VI, Voix et Images
VIa, Вопросы языкознания
VIN, Veröffentlichungen des Instituts für niederländische Philologie, Erftstadt, Lukassen
ViSH, Вища школа
VIst, Вопросы истории
Vit, Вітчизна
VKP, Всесоюзная книжная палата
VL, Вопросы литературы
VLet, Voz y Letras
VM, Время и мы, New York — Paris — Jerusalem
VMKA, Verslagen en Mededelingen, Koninklijke Academie voor Nederlandse Taal- en Letterkunde
VMUF, Вестник Московского университета. Серия IX, филология
VMUFil, Вестник Московского университета. Серия VII, философия
VÖAW, Verlag der Österreichischen Akademie der Wissenschaften, Vienna
Voz, Возрождение
VP, Встречи с прошлым, Moscow
VPen, Vita e Pensiero
VR, Vox Romanica
VRKhD, Вестник Русского христианского движения
VRL, Вопросы русской литературы
VRM, Volkskultur am Rhein und Maas
VS, Вопросы семантики
VSAV, Vydavateľstvo Slovenskej akadémie vied
VSh, Вышэйшая школа
VSh, Визвольний шлях
VSPU, Вестник Санкт-Петербургского университета

VSSH, Вечерняя средняя школа
VV, Византийский временник
VVM, Vlastivědný věstník moravský
VVSh, Вестник высшей школы
VWGÖ, Verband der wissenschaftlichen Gesellschaften Österreichs
VySh, Вища школа
VysSh, Высшая школа
VyV, Verdad y Vida
VZ, Vukova zadužbina, Belgrade

WAB, Wolfenbütteler Arbeiten zur Barockforschung, Wiesbaden, Harrassowitz
WADL, Wiener Arbeiten zur deutschen Literatur, Vienna, Braumüller
WAGAPH, Wiener Arbeiten zur germanischen Altertumskunde und Philologie, Berne, Lang
WAiF, Wydawnictwa Artystyczne i Filmowe, Warsaw
WAR, Wolfenbütteler Abhandlungen zur Renaissanceforschung, Wiesbaden, Harrassowitz
WaT, Wagenbachs Taschenbücherei, Berlin, Wagenbach
WB, Weimarer Beiträge
WBDP, Würzburger Beiträge zur deutschen Philologie, Würzburg, Königshausen & Neumann
WBG, Wissenschaftliche Buchgesellschaft, Darmstadt
WBN, Wolfenbütteler Barock-Nachrichten
WBS, Welsh Book Studies
WF, Wege der Forschung, Darmstadt, Wissenschaftliche Buchgesellschaft
WGCR, West Georgia College Review
WGY, Women in German Yearbook
WHNDL, Würzburger Hochschulschriften zur neueren Deutschen Literaturgeschichte, Frankfurt, Lang
WHR, The Welsh History Review
WI, Word and Image
WIFS, Women in French Studies
WJMLL, Web Journal in Modern Language Linguistics
WKJb, Wissenschaftskolleg. Institute for Advanced Study, Berlin. Jahrbuch
WL, Wydawnictwo Literackie, Cracow
WŁ, Wydawnictwo Łódzkie
WLub, Wydawnictwo Lubelskie
WLT, World Literature Today
WM, Wissensliteratur im Mittelalter, Wiesbaden, Reichert
WNB, Wolfenbütteler Notizen zur Buchgeschichte
WNT, Wydawnictwa Naukowo-Techniczne
WoB, Wolfenbütteler Beiträge
WoF, Wolfenbütteler Forschungen, Wiesbaden, Harrassowitz
WP, Wiedza Powszechna, Warsaw
WPEL, Working Papers in Educational Linguistics
WPFG, Working Papers in Functional Grammar, Amsterdam U.P.
WRM, Wolfenbütteler Renaissance Mitteilungen
WS, Wort und Sinn
WSA, Wolfenbütteler Studien zur Aufklärung, Tübingen, Niemeyer
WSiP, Wydawnictwa Szkolne i Pedagogiczne, Warsaw
WSJ, Wiener Slavistisches Jahrbuch
WSl, Die Welt der Slaven
WSlA, Wiener Slawistischer Almanach
WSP, Wyższa Szkoła Pedagogiczna
WSp, Word and Spirit
WSPRRNDFP, Wyższa Szkoła Pedagogiczna w Rzeszowie. Rocznik Naukowo-Dydaktyczny. Filologia Polska
WSS, Wiener Studien zur Skandinavistik
WUW, Wydawnictwo Uniwersytetu Wrocławskiego
WuW, Welt und Wort
WVUPS, West Virginia University Philological Papers
WW, Wirkendes Wort
WWAG, Woman Writers in the Age of Goethe
WWE, Welsh Writing in English. A Yearbook of Critical Essays

WZHUB, Wissenschaftliche Zeitschrift der Humboldt-Universität, Berlin: gesellschafts- und sprachwissenschaftliche Reihe
WZPHP, Wissenschaftliche Zeitschrift der pädagogischen Hochschule Potsdam. Gesellschafts- und sprachwissenschaftliche Reihe
WZUG, Wissenschaftliche Zeitschrift der Ernst-Moritz-Arndt- Universität Greifswald
WZUH, Wissenschaftliche Zeitschrift der Martin-Luther-Universität Halle-Wittenberg: gesellschafts- und sprachwissenschaftliche Reihe
WZUJ, Wissenschaftliche Zeitschrift der Friedrich-Schiller-Universität Jena/Thüringen: gesellschafts-und sprachwissenschaftliche Reihe
WZUL, Wissenschaftliche Zeitschrift der Karl Marx Universität Leipzig: gesellschafts- und sprachwissenschaftliche Reihe
WZUR, Wissenschaftliche Zeitschrift der Universität Rostock: gesellschafts- und sprachwissenschaftliche Reihe

YaIS, Yale Italian Studies
YB, Ysgrifau Beirniadol
YCC, Yearbook of Comparative Criticism
YCGL, Yearbook of Comparative and General Literature
YDAMEIS, Yearbook of the Dutch Association for Middle Eastern and Islamic Studies
YEEP, Yale Russian and East European Publications, New Haven, Yale Center for International and Area Studies
YES, Yearbook of English Studies
YFS, Yale French Studies
YIP, Yale Italian Poetry
YIS, Yearbook of Italian Studies
YJC, Yale Journal of Criticism
YM, Yearbook of Morphology
YPL, York Papers in Linguistics
YR, Yale Review
YSGP, Yearbook. Seminar for Germanic Philology
YSPS, The Yearbook of the Society of Pirandello Studies
YWMLS, The Year's Work in Modern Language Studies

ZÄAK, Zeitschrift für Ästhetik und allgemeine Kunstwissenschaft
ZB, Zeitschrift für Balkanologie
ZBL, Zeitschrift für bayerische Landesgeschichte
ZbS, Zbornik za slavistiku
ZCP, Zeitschrift für celtische Philologie
ZD, Zielsprache Deutsch
ZDA, Zeitschrift für deutsches Altertum und deutsche Literatur
ZDL, Zeitschrift für Dialektologie und Linguistik
ZDNÖL, Zirkular. Dokumentationsstelle für neuere österreichische Literatur
ZDP, Zeitschrift für deutsche Philologie
ZFKPhil, Zborník Filozofickej fakulty Univerzity Komenského. Philologica
ZFL, Zbornik za filologiju i lingvistiku
ZFSL, Zeitschrift für französische Sprache und Literatur
ZGB, Zagreber germanistische Beiträge
ZGer, Zeitschrift für Germanistik
ZGKS, Zeitschrift der Gesellschaft für Kanada-Studien
ZGL, Zeitschrift für germanistische Linguistik
ZGS, Zürcher germanistische Studien, Berne, Lang
ZK, Zeitschrift für Katalanistik
ZKB, Zeitschrift für Kultur und Bildungswissenschaften
ZL, Zeszyty Literackie, Paris
ZMS(FL), Zbornik Matice srpske za filologiju i lingvistiku
ZMS(KJ), Zbornik Matice srpske za književnost i jezik

ZMS(Sl), Zbornik Matice srpske za slavistiku
ZNiO, Zakład Narodowy im. Ossolińskich, Wrocław
ZnS, Знание — сила
ZNTSh, Записки Наукового товариства ім. Шевченка
ZNUG, Zeszyty Naukowe Uniw. Gdańskiego, Gdańsk
ZNUJ, Zeszyty Naukowe Uniw. Jagiellońskiego, Cracow
ZNWHFR, Zeszyty Naukowe Wydziału Humanistycznego. Filologia Rosyjska
ZNWSPO, Zeszyty Naukowe Wyższej Szkoly Pedagogicznej w Opolu
ZO, Zeitschrift für Ostforschung
ZPŠSlav, Zborník Pedagogickej fakulty v Prešove Univerzity Pavla Jozefa Šafárika v Košiciach-Slavistika, Bratislava
ZR, Zadarska revija
ZRAG, Записки русской академической группы в США
ZRBI, Зборник радова бизантолошког института, Belgrade
ZRL, Zagadnienia Rodzajów Literackich
ZRP, Zeitschrift für romanische Philologie
ZS, Zeitschrift für Sprachwissenschaft
ZSJ, Zápisnik slovenského jazykovedca
ZSK, Ze Skarbca Kultury
ZSL, Zeitschrift für siebenbürgische Landeskunde
ZSl, Zeitschrift für Slawistik
ZSP, Zeitschrift für slavische Philologie
ZSVS, Zborník Spolku vojvodinských slovakistov, Novi Sad
ZT, Здесь и теперь
ZV, Zeitschrift für Volkskunde
ZvV, Звезда востока
ZWL, Zeitschrift für württembergische Landesgeschichte

INDEX